MANAGEMENT

THIRD EDITION

MANAGEMENT

KATHRYN M. BARTOL
University of Maryland
College Park

DAVID C. MARTIN
American University

 **Irwin**
McGraw-Hill

Boston, Massachusetts   Burr Ridge, Illinois   Dubuque, Iowa   Madison, Wisconsin
New York, New York   San Francisco, California   St. Louis, Missouri

Irwin/McGraw-Hill

A Division of The McGraw·Hill Companies

MANAGEMENT

Copyright © 1998, 1994, 1991 by The McGraw-Hill Companies, Inc. All rights reserved. Printed in the United States of America. Except as permitted under the United States Copyright Act of 1976, no part of this publication may be reproduced or distributed in any form or by any means or stored in a data base or retrieval system, without the prior written permission of the publisher.

This book is printed on acid-free paper.

ISBN 0-07-005722-2

USE   3 4 5 6 7 8 9 0 VNH VNH 9 0 9 8
IE   2 3 4 5 6 7 8 9 0 VNH VNH 9 0 9 8

This book was set in New Baskerville by GTS Graphics. The editors were Adam Knepper, Karen Mellon, Rhona Robbin, and Peggy Rehberger; the designer was Joan E. O'Connor; the production supervisor was Kathryn Porzio. The cover was illustrated by Roy Weimann. The photo editor was Inge King. The permissions editor was Elsa Peterson. Von Hoffmann Press, Inc., was printer and binder.

Acknowledgments and Photo Credits appear on pages 751–000 and on this page by reference.

Library of Congress Cataloging-in-Publication
Bartol, Kathryn M.
    Management / Kathryn M. Bartol, David C. Martin— 3d ed.
        p.   cm.
    Includes bibliographical references and indexes.
    ISBN 0-07-005722-2 (alk. paper)
    1. Management.   I.   Martin, David C.
II. Title.
    HD31.B36942   1998
    658—dc21   96-46735

INTERNATIONAL EDITION
Copyright © 1998, 1994. Exclusive rights by The McGraw-Hill Companies, Inc. for manufacture and export. This book cannot be re-exported from the country to which it is consigned by McGraw-Hill. The International Edition is not available in North America.

When ordering this title, use ISBN 0-07-115206-7

http://www.mhcollege.com

Kathryn M. Bartol is Professor of Organizational Behavior and Human Resource Management in the College of Business and Management at the University of Maryland, College Park. She is a past president of the Academy of Management and is a Fellow of the Academy of Management, the American Psychological Association, and the American Psychological Society. She holds a Ph.D. in Management from Michigan State University, has published articles in numerous scholarly journals and professional publications, and was Associate Editor of the *Academy of Management Executive*. She has twice received the Allen Krowe Award for Excellence in Teaching from the College of Business and Management and also has been named a University of Maryland Distinguished Scholar-Teacher for excellence in both research and teaching.

David C. Martin is Professor of Management and Human Resource Management at Kogod College of Business Administration at the American University. He received his Ph.D. degree in Management from the University of Maryland. He is the author of many publications in both academic and professional journals. Professor Martin has been recognized as the Kogod College of Business Administration Teacher of the Year, Faculty Administrator of the Year, Teacher-Scholar of the Year, and the Scholarship/Researcher of the Year.

To my husband, Bob, and my father,
Walter Ottinger. Thank you again
for your constant love and support.

KMB

To Jan and Kathy, whose continued
love, support, understanding, and
willingness to wait made this
book possible.

DCM

CONTENTS IN BRIEF

CONTENTS

PART FIVE CONTROLLING

PREFACE

■ INTRODUCING *MANAGEMENT,* THIRD EDITION

Individuals working in organizations in the twenty-first century will have a greater need than ever for effective management skills. Fierce global competition is expected to continue its acceleration. Domestic competition is increasing as well. Gaining a competitive advantage will be more critical to survival and success in the new millennium than ever before. How then will tomorrow's managers innovate fast enough to achieve and maintain market leadership? How will they make the best use of diverse viewpoints to achieve optimal results? How will they promote crucial world class quality? How will they acquire the global perspective that is so necessary to understanding the business environment of the future? Such are the exciting challenges that you and other readers of this book face in tomorrow's increasingly competitive world.

To help you meet such challenges, we introduce you to the third edition of *Management.* We hasten to point out that this third edition has benefited greatly from many useful suggestions from others. For example, in preparing this edition, we have been careful to retain the many features that adopters and student users of our earlier editions applaud. At the same time, we have worked hard to incorporate suggestions that would make this third edition even better than our earlier two. Many of these suggestions have come from adopters of our earlier editions at more than 200 colleges and universities.

Special Features

These features are discussed in greater detail at later points in this preface:

- Numerous company cases
- Many integrated examples
- Contemporary themes

- Skill-building focus
- Revised, but flexible chapter sequencing
- Strong organizational behavior coverage
- Reflects current research and major trends
- Integrated international coverage

Major Themes

The four major themes highlighted in this edition are presented in a variety of ways:

MANAGING DIVERSITY Special sections on "Managing Diversity" can be found throughout the book. These sections give explicit recognition to the increasing diversity of the work force in the United States and in many other parts of the world. They provide information regarding how diversity can be used to advantage in enhancing organizational effectiveness. In addition, "Managing Diversity" boxes highlight companies, such as the Bank of Montreal, that illustrate effective approaches to the management of diversity.

MANAGING CHANGE AND INNOVATION Given the requirement that organizations must continuously improve their performance, the text highlights means of managing change and promoting innovation in today's organizations. Many chapters incorporate a special section that explains methods of "Promoting Innovation" that mesh appropriately with the relevant subject matter. At the same time, a separate chapter on change management and innovation highlights major approaches to effectively managing change in an era in which innovating quickly to stay ahead of the competition has become more important than ever. All of the Gaining the Edge cases at the beginning of chapters illustrate companies that are innovators.

GLOBAL PERSPECTIVE As mentioned earlier, we provide integrated and extensive coverage of international topics in this third edition. These materials combine to help students begin to acquire a global perspective in thinking about management issues.

VALUING QUALITY This edition also contains special boxes on "Valuing Quality," that reinforce the importance of total quality management and demonstrate how the quality message is being put into action in several exemplary organizations, such as Federal Express. Moreover, we also feature increased coverage of total quality management concepts in the chapter on TQM and managerial control methods.

Organizational Changes

Based on feedback from adopters and potential adopters, we have positioned the chapter on managerial decision making at the beginning rather than at the end of the section on planning. This gives the reader a firm grasp of approaches to effective decision making before moving on to issues of establishing goals, plans, and strategies. Because of the increasing importance of change management to the function of leadership, we have located the chapter on change management and innovation at the beginning of the section addressing the leading function. This placement emphasizes the importance of the role of the leadership function in influencing and managing change.

New Coverage Highlights

This edition brings extensive updating of cases, examples, and materials throughout. Moreover, a number of sections have undergone extensive revision. In the process, we have made judicious cuts to bring new important information to the reader. Some of the new coverage highlights in this edition include:

- Labor supply trends and diversity
- Strategic alliances
- Macroculture concept
- Computer-assisted group decision making
- Scenario analysis
- Resource-based view of strategic management
- Strategic hypercompetition
- Downsizing trends
- Process structure
- Networked structure
- Broadbanding
- 360-degree feedback
- Eight-step process for change management and innovation
- Attribution theory
- Cultural context and communication
- Electronic means to facilitate communication
- Organizational citizenship behaviors
- Levers of control
- Outsourcing
- TQM philosophy and intervention techniques
- The service delivery system
- Knowledge work information systems
- Sustaining competitive information technology advantage
- Group decision support systems
- Regiocentric orientation toward international management
- Repatriation
- Entrepreneurs working from home
- And much more!

Excellent Case Examples

The text includes numerous carefully *integrated examples* of practices in real organizations that clearly illustrate the concepts being explained. The examples include a wide variety of organizations ranging from California-based Asian Business Co-op, a start-up telemarketing firm, to France-based Groupe Michelin, the world's largest tire maker.

Each chapter opens with an introductory *Gaining the Edge* case, which illustrates successful innovative practices in a real organization and other aspects of theory and research subsequently discussed in the chapter. See, for example, new Gaining the Edge cases featuring Warnaco, the New York maker of women's intimate apparel and menswear; Microsoft, the Redmond, Washington–based giant software purveyor, and Mattel, the El Segundo, California–based creator of the celebrity doll, Barbie.

Moreover, each chapter contains two or three *Case in Point*, or *minicase*, discussions. These cases are fully integrated into the text presentation. They provide students with extended examples of how the concepts in the text apply to real organizations. The organizations featured in these minicases range from Filofax, the London-based creator of the well-known, notebooklike personal organizer, to not-for-profit Carnegie Hall, the famous cultural center located in New York City, to USF&G, a Baltimore-based insurance company undergoing transformation. For the most part, at least one Case in Point in each chapter depicts managerial practices in an international organization.

Each chapter also features *two concluding cases* that further illustrate the major points made. At least one of these concluding cases focuses on an international company and/or situation. For example, concluding cases include Zurich-based ABB (Asea Brown Boveri), a global conglomerate, Denmark-based LEGO, maker of the plastic bricks found in children's toy chests throughout the world, and Kodak, the Rochester, New York–based photography giant fighting to become a global digital imaging leader. The concluding cases and accompanying questions provide students with an opportunity to relate the concepts discussed to practical situations found literally around the world.

Strong Pedagogy

A number of features of this third edition are aimed particularly at facilitating the learning process:

SKILL-BUILDING AND SELF-ASSESSMENT EXERCISES At the end of each chapter, the reader will find either a skill-building or a self-assessment exercise that is geared to help extend and reinforce the learning from the chapter. The skill-building exercises allow the reader to check comprehension and/or practice applying the chapter concepts. The self-assessment exercises help the reader gain insight into his/her own orientation in relationship to effective principles of management.

MANAGEMENT SKILLS FOR THE TWENTY-FIRST CENTURY DISCUSSIONS Special sections in many chapters focus on management skills for the twenty-first century. Such discussions provide readers with practical advice on how to implement certain concepts discussed in the text that will be particularly useful for managing effectively in the new millennium. For example, Management Skills for the Twenty-First Century discussions offer guidance on how to conduct an interview, how to run a meeting, and how to set goals.

MANAGEMENT EXERCISES Each chapter contains a management exercise that incorporates the need to use major concepts that were covered within the chapter. The exercises give students an opportunity to apply the concepts in the chapter in an experiential way.

DISCUSSION QUESTIONS FOR CHAPTER OPENING CASES Discussion questions for the chapter opening case appear at the end of each chapter to facilitate further discussion if an instructor so desires.

EXCEPTIONALLY READABLE WRITING STYLE One consistent and exceptionally readable writing style is used throughout the book to capture and hold the interests of readers.

CHAPTER OUTLINES AND OBJECTIVES Each chapter begins with a topical outline and related objectives that highlight the major points to be covered. The outline and objectives help orient the reader to the chapter content.

GLOSSARIES A marginal running glossary highlights and defines significant terms in the margin near their first appearance in the book. The extensive Glossary at the back of the text repeats the marginal definitions of key terms in order to provide a ready reference source for the reader.

CHAPTER SUMMARIES OF KEY POINTS At the end of each chapter, there is a summary of the main points covered within the chapter.

STATE-OF-THE-ART ILLUSTRATIONS Since an illustration is often worth a thousand words, many of the points in the text are underscored visually through carefully selected drawings, graphs, and photographs. Frameworks that are frequently used to delineate interrelationships among concepts are typically depicted in illustrations that help the reader visualize these interrelationships. The extensive use of color further serves to enhance the impact of the illustrations. Moreover, the captions accompanying the photographs clearly tie the subject matter to concepts in the text, making the photographs a particularly effective learning tool.

INDEXES Several indexes located at the back of the text facilitate easy access to various types of information. These are separate name, subject, organization, and international organization indexes.

Instructor Supplements

INTEGRATED INSTRUCTOR'S RESOURCE MANUAL, PREPARED BY AMIT SHAH (FROSTBURG STATE UNIVERSITY) This manual includes a number of features designed to facilitate effective teaching. A course planning guide is included to help instructors develop an overall plan for teaching the course. Lecture outlines, with real-life examples, are provided for each chapter. Each lecture outline is followed by an enrichment module that provides a supplementary minilecture on a topic of current interest. This manual also includes detailed teaching notes for all of the cases and exercises in the text as well as a part-ending case for each of the six main sections of the book.

TEST BANK, PREPARED BY THOMAS K. PRITCHETT AND BETTY M. PRITCHETT (BOTH OF KENNESAW STATE COLLEGE) The *Test Bank* features over 2500 high-quality multiple-choice, true-false, fill-in-the-blank, and short-answer questions. Each question is coded to show the correct solution, text page reference, and question type: definition, fact, application, concept, and mathematical.

COMPUTERIZED TEST BANK A computerized version of the printed *Test Bank* is available for use in Windows 3.1. This powerful system, which has on-line testing capabilities, allows tests to be prepared quickly and easily. Instructors can view questions as they are selected for a test; scramble questions; add, delete, and edit questions; select questions by type, objective, and difficulty level; and view and save tests.

OVERHEAD TRANSPARENCIES The overhead transparency program includes 150 full-color overheads. It is comprised of both figures from the text and new illustrations intended to augment the text presentation.

POWERPOINT PRESENTATIONS The overhead transparency program will also be available as PowerPoint electronic presentation slides. Many of the slides will build upon one another.

VIDEO PROGRAM Videos, selected from NBC News Archives, are available to help instructors enhance their lectures.

Student Supplements

STUDY GUIDE, PREPARED BY E. LEROY PLUMLEE (WESTERN WASHINGTON UNIVERSITY) The *Study Guide* assists students in gaining a firm grasp of text materials. It is written with the common question raised by students in mind: "How should I be studying for this course?" Each chapter of the *Study Guide* is divided into three major parts: (1) an overview of the chapter called Notes for the Student; (2) a detailed chapter outline; and (3) an extensive set of exercises identified and grouped by the major headings in the text. Exercises consist of fill-in-the-blank, true/false, and multiple-choice questions.

PC CASE SECOND EDITION, DEVELOPED BY DAN BAUGHER AND ANDREW VARANELLI (BOTH OF PACE UNIVERSITY) This unique user-friendly software program provides a comprehensive, experiential learning exercise that allows beginning management students to take on the role of decision-maker in a variety of business settings. This edition is rewritten to exploit color and graphics, enhancing its attractiveness to students. It includes a new behaviorally oriented case and updated versions of the three popular cases in the first edition.

Acknowledgments

In developing *Management*, we have been greatly aided by many individuals to whom we owe a debt of gratitude. We appreciate the ongoing support of Acting Dean Judy D. Olian, College of Business and Management, University of Maryland, College Park, and Acting Dean Stevan R. Holmberg, Kogod College of Business Administration, American University, as well as our colleagues in management at both of these institutions.

We also thank the members of a focus group that helped us originally launch this project, as well as the many reviewers, listed below, who have commented on the various stages of its development. This text is a much better product as a result of their candor and many helpful contributions: Colonel Rita A. Campbell, U.S. Air Force Academy; Richard L. Clarke, Clemson University; Satishe P. Deshpande, Western Michigan University; Gary M. Izumo, Moorpark College; Martin Kilduff, Pennsylvania State University; Thomas Kuffel, University of Wisconsin—La Crosse; Thomas W. Lloyd, Westmoreland County Community College; Patrick Rogers, North Carolina Agricultural and Technical State University; Amit Shah, Frostburg State University; Kenneth R. Tillery, Middle Tennessee State University; George White, Insurance Institute of America.

We deeply appreciate the wonderful support that we have received from many individuals associated with our publisher, Irwin/McGraw-Hill. Gary Burke, publisher, maintained continual interest in the project and provided the necessary resources. Sponsoring editor Adam Knepper took over and improved upon a vision for the third edition and has been a true champion of the project. We are grateful for his enthusiastic and continuing support. Dan Loch, senior marketing manager, ably provided guidance and assistance concerning making this book more "student friendly."

Rhona Robbin, senior developmental editor, has been a constant colleague, friend, and advocate through all three editions. She has provided continuity of direction, offered invaluable feedback, and raised the penetrating questions on behalf of our future readers that caused us to continually improve our presentations. Her high professional standards have continued to mesh well with our own. Her valuable ideas and insights are reflected throughout this text. We remain grateful for her countless contributions to this and previous editions. Our supplements editor, Terry Varveris, ably brought together a team of unusually qualified professionals who helped us produce what is arguably the best set of supplemental materials ever prepared for a management text.

We have been fortunate that editing manager Peggy C. Rehberger once again painstakingly oversaw the editing and production of this third edition, as she did with both the first and second editions. As always, she has contributed many helpful ideas and produced a book of outstanding production quality. We continue to be grateful for her smooth and very able coordination of the entire process. Joan O'Connor, the designer since the first edition, has again created a striking book design that provides a wonderful showcase for our material. Leslie Anne Weber, with her skillful and consistent editing, aided our presentations while preserving our ideas. Kathryn Porzio, production supervisor, coordinated the production process so that all the production elements were of high quality and handled in a timely manner.

We welcome our newest partners from the Irwin editorial, marketing, advertising, and sales teams. Karen Mellon, sponsoring editor, and Michael Campbell, marketing manager, have become this book's advocates and stewards. We appreciate their commitment to making the third edition a great success. We also acknowledge the advertising effort, headed by Dempsey Carter, which has kept this book in the forefront of our colleagues' minds. And to our Irwin/McGraw-Hill sales force of exceptional professionals, our best wishes and continuing offers of support through the life of this edition.

Our photo editor, Inge King, has also been with us since the first edition. We thank her for once again assembling a collection of captivating photographs that provide a valuable additional learning dimension. Elsa Peterson obtained the many necessary permissions.

This list certainly would not be complete without acknowledging the valuable clipping service provided by Walter R. Ottinger, the father of Kathryn Bartol. We also want to highlight the continuing encouragement of our spouses, Bob Bartol and Jan Martin. In deference to our deadlines, they once again postponed activities they wanted to pursue and took on tasks that needed to be done. As was true with earlier editions, they listened to our frustrations and continued to express faith in our efforts. Throughout, they were there when we needed them, and this third edition is certainly better as a result.

Thank you, to all who have helped us. We truly could not have produced this third edition without you!

Kathryn M. Bartol
David C. Martin

MANAGEMENT

As we move into the twenty-first century, management is at one of its most significant stages in history. Global competition has become a way of life. Changes in technology, international affairs, business practices, and organizational social responsibility are causing managers to reexamine their methods and goals, as well as place increased emphasis on innovation. In this section we will consider how some of the basic principles of management apply in today's rapidly changing environment.

Chapter 1 provides an overview of the management process. It focuses on what managers actually do and on the skills and knowledge they need to be effective and innovative. Yet innovative practices do not emerge in a vacuum; they build on the best ideas about management that have been developed over a period of time. **Chapter 2** analyzes the roots of current approaches: the scientific, behavioral, quantitative, and contemporary management perspectives.

As **Chapter 3** makes clear, effective management requires a knowledge of both the organization's outside environment and its internal culture. Successful managers are able to deal with external and internal factors in ways that support the achievement of organizational goals. A broad perspective also encompasses the ongoing debate concerning how much social responsibility an organization should assume relative to shareholders, employees, customers, the community, and society at large. **Chapter 4** explores the nature and extent of organizational social responsibility and examines managerial ethics.

CHAPTER ONE

THE CHALLENGE OF MANAGEMENT

LEARNING OBJECTIVES

After studying this chapter, you should be able to:

- Explain the four functions of management and identify the other major elements in the management process.

- Describe three common work methods that managers use and ten major roles that managers play.

- Identify the main factors influencing work agendas and explain how managers use such agendas to channel their efforts.

- Delineate the three major types of skills needed by managers.

- Distinguish between effectiveness and efficiency as they relate to organizational performance.

- Describe how managerial jobs differ according to hierarchical level and responsibility area.

- Explain how managers at different hierarchical levels can use the entrepreneurial role to foster innovation.

- Describe the role of management education and experience in preparing managers.

- Identify four major trends that will particularly influence managing in the twenty-first century.

GAINING THE EDGE

OVER THE LONG HAUL, HEWLETT-PACKARD CONTINUES TO EXCEL

 Hewlett-Packard Company (HP) has long had an enviable reputation for innovation and solid performance. The Palo Alto company was founded in 1939 by engineers William Hewlett and David Packard. Today, HP is a $32 billion electronics company making more than 24,000 products sold in over 120 countries.

From the start, HP has actively sought to be an egalitarian work setting where individuals can develop their capabilities, stretch themselves, and encourage each other to develop cutting-edge technology. Current CEO Lewis Platt says he doesn't see his job as "running" the company. Instead, the founders and their successors have set up largely autonomous divisions, which are bound together by shared values and high performance goals. Divisions map out their own strategies and take responsibility for their own bottom lines. Decision making is decentralized. Platt says, "I spend a lot of time talking about values rather than trying to figure out the business strategies." He adds, "The most important aspect of the management of this company is cultural control," meaning that a critical part of Platt's job is working to preserve the company culture that has served HP so well.

The Laser Jet Solutions Group, based in Boise, Idaho, illustrates the decentralized way HP operates. The group went ahead largely on its own to develop a popular line of laser printers that quickly captured about 60 percent of the U.S. laser printer market despite formidable competition from Apple, IBM, and many Japanese companies. Part of the printer group's success was its ability to translate economies of scale into lower prices, which made it more difficult for competitors to mount serious challenges. The group also introduced a well-timed series of technological advances calculated to stay ahead of the competition. Carolyn Ticknor, HP vice president and general manager of the Laser Jet Solutions Group, says that the group is now working on a plan called Digital Workplace aimed at streamlining office processes by integrating printing and scanning into information distribution.

In addition to decentralization of decision making, another important HP

Hewlett-Packard Company (HP) has gained a competitive edge by letting its employees develop products and make decisions in largely autonomous divisions. These HP employees are part of the team that helped introduce a new class of servers, which manage data flow on computer networks, to business consumers. HP is also committed to egalitarian work settings, openness, quality, employment continuity, and diversity in the work force.

value is openness. Early on, the founders encouraged engineers to leave their work out on their desks so that others would know what they were doing, could make suggestions, and would be able to stay informed about technological developments. According to one observer, "At HP, they are very demanding of one another. It's the respect of their colleagues they're striving for."

Another major asset of HP is its dedication to and reputation for quality. Unlike many of its competitors, HP has been willing to take back from retailers products that have been returned by unhappy customers. This policy has allowed HP to gain early information on problems with its products and take quick steps to rectify them. Recently HP has gained market share in workstations and has moved from number 17 to the top 6 in personal computers.

One particularly notable characteristic of HP has been its ability to grow and maintain top performance without the painful layoffs and disruptive restructurings that have characterized many other companies of similar size. During the particularly difficult 1970 recession, employees were asked to take a 10 percent pay cut, but no one lost a job due to the downturn. Some observers suggest the employment continuity is indicative of a management that has been effective at allocating resources, rather than allowing the work-force size to become bloated. The company currently employs about 98,000 people, 59,000 of whom work in the United States.

Not surprisingly, HP also has been a strong supporter of work-force diversity. Platt says diversity is one of the company's top three priorities, along with customer satisfaction and order fulfillment. The company recently was honored by the Council of Economic Priorities, a nonprofit public interest research group, for its commitment to avoiding layoffs and its support of progressive employment practices like flextime, job sharing, and work-at-home arrangements.[1]

■■■

Hewlett-Packard is an innovative organization making great strides toward gaining the competitive edge in the twenty-first century. This book will examine many such organizations as we consider the management approaches that will be critical to organizational success in the new millennium.

In the process, we will highlight several themes of particular importance to future managers. For one thing, we will examine techniques that are especially effective for managing change and promoting innovation. Such techniques help to explain how a company like Hewlett-Packard has been able to develop many new products, like its new scanner that hooks into a computer network and scans pages of documents into many personal computers. For another, we will explore why forward-looking companies like HP have placed so much emphasis on developing quality and initiating total quality management systems. Yet another theme is the importance of building and successfully managing a diverse work force. Statistics show that due to the changing profile of the U.S. population, women and minorities will constitute a growing proportion of the work force in the twenty-first century. Finally, we will be highlighting the importance of adopting a global perspective. Increasingly managers must operate in an international marketplace. Almost 70 percent of HP's business comes from sources outside the United States, and HP is one of the top 10 U.S. exporters.[2] We will be returning to these themes in various places throughout the book as we explore the exciting horizons of management.

We begin the current chapter with an overview of the nature of management and the basic processes involved. We then consider what managers actually do by describing the work methods that they use, the different roles that they play, and the work agendas that guide their actions. We also examine the knowledge base and skills that managers need in order to achieve high performance. We explore two major dimensions along which managerial jobs differ, and we consider how the entrepreneurial role at different levels of management can foster innovation. Finally, we investigate what it takes to become an effective manager, taking into account education, experience, and a suitable understanding of future trends and issues.

■ MANAGEMENT: AN OVERVIEW

For most of us, organizations are an important part of our daily lives. By **organization,** we mean two or more persons engaged in a systematic effort to produce goods or services. We all deal with organizations when we attend classes, deposit money at the bank, buy clothing, and attend a movie. Our lives are indirectly affected by organizations through the products we use. For example, if you have opened a refrigerator or used a washing machine lately, there is a good chance that it was made by Whirlpool, the company based in Benton Harbor, Michigan, that is the world's largest major appliance maker. Whirlpool took over the number one spot in the appliance business when it paid $1 billion for N. V. Philip's faltering European appliance business in 1989. Since then, Whirlpool has transformed itself from a primarily North American company into a $7 billion global giant with manufacturing facilities in 11 countries and marketing efforts in more than 120 locations, ranging from Thailand to Hungary to Argentina.[3]

> **Organization** Two or more persons engaged in a systematic effort to produce goods or services

Whirlpool began to experience enhanced success after a new chief executive officer (CEO), David R. Whitwam, took over in 1987. Within a few years, the company was beginning to outpace its industry rivals and revenues had increased by several billion dollars. In contrast, over an 11-year period, CEO William H. Bricker transformed Diamond Shamrock from a profitable chemical company with modest oil holdings into a debt-ridden energy company and was forced to resign. Since then the firm has been working to recuperate and operate as a successful energy company.[4] To understand how management can make such a major difference in an organization, we need to explore the nature of management.

What Is Management?

Management is the process of achieving organizational goals by engaging in the four major functions of planning, organizing, leading, and controlling. This definition recognizes that management is an ongoing activity, entails reaching important goals, and involves knowing how to perform the major functions of management. Since these functions are crucial to effective management, we use them as the basic framework for this book.[5] Accordingly, Parts Two through Five of the text are devoted, respectively, to planning, organizing, leading, and controlling. In this section, we provide a brief overview of the four functions (see Figure 1-1). Then we consider how they relate to other major aspects of managerial work.

> **Management** The process of achieving organizational goals by engaging in the four major functions of planning, organizing, leading, and controlling

PLANNING Planning is the management function that involves setting goals and deciding how best to achieve them. For example, Whirlpool's overall objective is to achieve world-class performance in delivering shareholder value, which the company defines as being in the top 25 percent of publicly held companies in total returns during a given economic cycle. To achieve that goal, Whirlpool is making an intensive effort to understand the customer so that it is possible to respond to genuine needs through breakthrough products and

> **Planning** The process of setting goals and deciding how best to achieve them

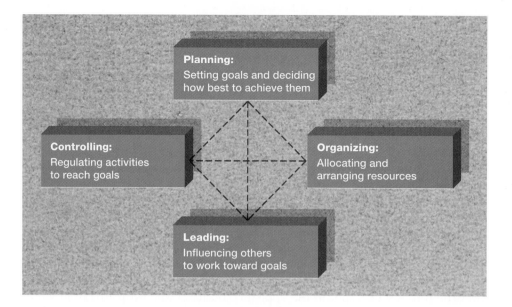

Figure 1-1 *The functions of management.*

services. Part of the strategy is to be one company worldwide. Whirlpool wants to drastically change the previous strategy followed by Philips, whereby the company made a completely different product for each national market. Now Whirlpool is working toward developing innovative common "platforms" that allow various models to be built using the same basic internal chassis. If Whirlpool is successful, the company can save substantially on development and manufacturing costs and can incorporate the latest advances in technology more easily across brands.[6]

At Diamond Shamrock under Bricker, the major goal was to change the chemical company into a major energy company; this was based on Bricker's view in the late 1970s (later proven to be faulty) that energy prices would continue their upward trend. Even so, progress toward the goal was somewhat erratic and reflected poor planning. Diamond Shamrock sold its gas stations to Sigmor Corporation and then bought them back 5 years later. It overpaid by $600 million when purchasing San Francisco–based Natomas, an oil and gas producer, for $1.3 billion. At one point, the company even purchased a stake in a prize bull (partially owned by the CEO).[7]

Organizing The process of allocating and arranging human and nonhuman resources so that plans can be carried out successfully

ORGANIZING Organizing is the management function that focuses on allocating and arranging human and nonhuman resources so that plans can be carried out successfully. Through the organizing function managers determine which tasks are to be done, how tasks can best be combined into specific jobs, and how jobs can be grouped into various units that make up the structure of the organization. Staffing jobs with individuals who can successfully carry out plans is also part of the organizing function.

For example, in the quest to be a truly global company Whirlpool wants to be able to take advantage of the best expertise in the company regardless of where it is in the world. At first engineers and manufacturers from the United States who went to look at the new European plants purchased from Philips took the attitude that things were done much better in the United States. Similarly, the Europeans who toured U.S. facilities took the same parochial attitude. Gradually, though, the groups began to work together. Recently, Whirlpool won a contest sponsored by 24 U.S. utilities for the design of a refrigerator that would best reduce energy consumption and damage to the environment. Whirlpool's award-winning, super-energy-efficient refrigerator, which cools without the use of harmful chlorofluorocarbons, was developed using insulation technology from the European group, compressor technology from Brazilian affiliates, and manufacturing and design inputs from U.S. personnel. The refrigerator will be marketed under the Whirlpool, KitchenAid, and Kenmore brand names.[8]

In contrast, at Diamond Shamrock under Bricker considerable organizing effort was channeled toward developing luxurious facilities for use by top management and the board of directors. Despite the company's difficulties, resources were allocated for such amenities as a 12,000-acre Texas ranch worth $9 million that was used for corporate meetings and entertainment, a $1 million box at the Dallas Cowboys' home stadium, and a fleet of corporate airplanes.[9]

LEADING Leading is the management function that involves influencing others to engage in the work behaviors necessary to reach organizational goals. Leading includes communicating with others, helping to outline a vision of what can be accomplished, providing direction, and motivating organization members to put forth the substantial effort required. This function also includes encouraging the necessary levels of change and innovation.

At Whirlpool, the vision is clearly articulated to everyone: Be one company worldwide and provide world-class performance in terms of shareholder value. Still, it was important to explain throughout the organization that creating shareholder value would also make it possible to create value for the other stakeholders in the company—employees, local communities, suppliers, and so on. Previously, there was a tendency in the company for the high-level managers to tell employees what to do. Whitwam argues that a contemporary CEO must convince employees why a transformation is required so that they will enthusiastically support the new direction and be motivated to develop innovative new ideas as well. He had to build a shared understanding across a diverse group of multilingual, multinational employees.[10]

At Diamond Shamrock, Bricker had been chosen partially for his support of the company's tradition of participatory management. After becoming CEO, however, he assumed an autocratic style. Many executives concluded that it was useless to fight with Bricker over his high-risk ideas.[11]

CONTROLLING Controlling is the management function aimed at regulating organizational activities so that actual performance conforms to expected organizational standards and goals.[12] To do the necessary regulating, managers need to monitor ongoing activities, compare the results with expected standards or progress toward goals, and take corrective action as needed. For example, to aid the globalization thrust, Whirlpool created 15 projects, which they called One Company Challenges. One of the projects was aimed at creating a companywide total quality management system that incorporates the best features of the European and U.S. parts of the company to ensure that activities meet targeted quality standards and are aimed at continuous improvement. Whitwam argues that it is not enough to create a vision and a great plan; it is also critical to engage in "relentless follow-through" and establish accountability throughout the organization in order to "protect good intentions from the distractions of the moment" and ensure the vision is realized. Indeed, Whirlpool faces formidable challenges. A reorganization of the sales force in Europe from a country focus to a type-of-customer focus (e.g., large discounters, small retailers) led to a drop in European sales as the sales force struggled to build new contacts. Start-up costs in Asia have been high and the

The dynamic leadership of Ana Patricia Botin, chief executive of Spain's Santander Investment, has helped her company take advantage of its capital base in Latin America to build a large market share in Mexico. Because of its prominence in the region, her company won a major role in bringing Mexico back to the capital markets.

Leading The process of influencing others to engage in the work behaviors necessary to reach organizational goals

Controlling The process of regulating organizational activities so that actual performance conforms to expected organizational standards and goals

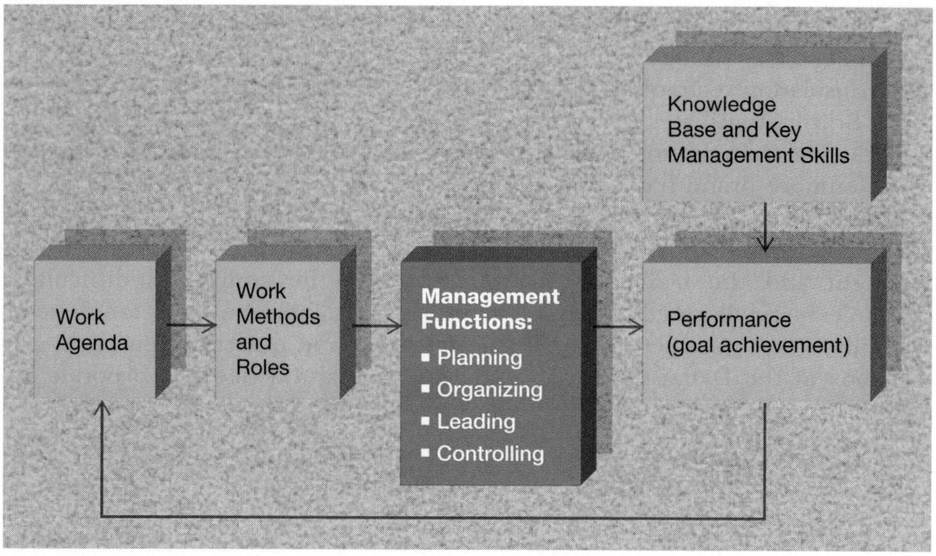

Figure 1-2 *An extended model of the management process. (Adapted from Stephen J. Caroll and Dennis J. Gillen, "Are the Classical Management Functions Useful in Describing Managerial Work?"* Academy of Management Review, *vol. 12, 1987, pp. 38–51.)*

company continues to face formidable competition at home, particularly from GE and Maytag.[13]

On the other hand, as oil prices and earnings began to drop, Diamond Shamrock started to sell assets and cut expenses. Still, the $9 million ranch was retained. Although the original fleet of five company planes was cut back to three, the company leased extra planes for various trips. News of potential conflicts of interest involving company dealings with Bricker's friends began to emerge.[14] As the contrast between Whirlpool and Diamond Shamrock illustrates, the degree to which managers effectively execute the four functions of management can vary greatly.

The Management Process

While the four major functions of management form the basis of the managerial process, there are several additional key elements in the process. These elements were identified by management scholars Steven J. Carroll and Dennis J. Gillen on the basis of their review of major studies on managerial work.[15] As Figure 1-2 shows, work methods and managerial roles, as well as work agendas, feed into the core management functions. A manager's knowledge base and key management skills are other important factors that contribute to high performance (goal achievement). We consider each of these elements in greater detail in the next two sections of this chapter. Throughout this discussion, keep in mind that the management process applies not only to profit-making organizations, such as Hewlett-Packard and Whirlpool, but also to not-for-profit organizations.[16] A **not-for-profit organization** (sometimes called a *nonprofit organization*) is an organization whose main purposes center on issues other than making profits. Common examples are government organizations (e.g., the federal government), educational institutions (your college or university), cultural institutions (New York's Carnegie Hall), charitable institutions (United Way), and many health-care facilities (Mayo Clinic).

Not-for-profit organization
An organization whose main purposes center on issues other than making profits

■ WHAT MANAGERS ACTUALLY DO

One of the most famous studies of managers was conducted by management scholar Henry Mintzberg, who followed several top managers around for one week each and recorded everything that they did.[17] In documenting their activities, Mintzberg reached some interesting conclusions about the manager's work methods and about several major roles that managers play.

Work Methods

Mintzberg found that in their actual work methods, the managers differed drastically from their popular image as reflective, systematic planners who spend considerable quiet time in their offices poring over formal reports. Three of his findings provide particularly intriguing glimpses into the world of high-level managers.

UNRELENTING PACE The managers in Mintzberg's study began working the moment they arrived at the office in the morning and kept working until they left at night. Rather than taking coffee breaks, the managers usually drank their coffee while they attended meetings, which averaged eight each day. Similarly, lunches were almost always eaten in the course of formal or informal meetings. When not in meetings, the managers handled an average of 36 pieces of mail per day, as well as other written and verbal communications. If they happened to have a free minute or two, the time was usually quickly usurped by subordinates anxious to have a word with the boss. Donald Schuenke, head of Northwestern Mutual Life Insurance, estimates that he would have to work no less than 24 hours per day if he were to honor all the requests for just a small amount of his time.[18]

BREVITY, VARIETY, AND FRAGMENTATION Mintzberg found that the managers handled a wide variety of issues throughout the day, ranging from awarding a retirement plaque to discussing the bidding on a multi-million-dollar contract. Many of their activities were surprisingly brief: About half the activities that Mintzberg recorded were completed in less than 9 minutes, and only 10 percent took more than 1 hour. Telephone calls tended to be short, lasting an average of 6 minutes. Work sessions at the manager's desk and informal meetings averaged 15 and 10 minutes, respectively. The managers experienced continual interruptions from telephone calls and subordinates. They often stopped their own desk work to place calls or request that subordinates drop in. Leaving meetings before the end was common. Because of the fragmentation and interruptions, a number of top managers save their major brainwork for times outside the normal workday. For example, Mary Kay Ash, founder of the Mary Kay Cosmetics firm, typically gets up at 5 a.m. six days a week in order to have some peaceful, uninterrupted time in which to work.[19]

VERBAL CONTACTS AND NETWORKS The managers in Mintzberg's study showed a strong preference for verbal communication, through either phone conversations or meetings, rather than written communication, such as memos and formal reports. For obtaining and transmitting information, they relied heavily on networks. A **network** is a set of cooperative relationships with individuals whose help is needed in order for a manager to function effectively. The network of contacts in Mintzberg's study included superiors, subordinates, peers, and other individuals inside the organization, as well as numerous outside individuals. Some of the contacts were personal, such as friends and peers. Others were professional, such as consultants, lawyers, and insurance underwriters. Still others were trade association contacts, customers, and suppliers.

Network A set of cooperative relationships with individuals whose help is needed in order for a manager to function effectively

IMPLICATIONS OF MINTZBERG'S FINDINGS Although Mintzberg's study focused on top-level managers, his findings apply to a wide variety of managers.[20] For example, one study of factory supervisors found that they engaged in between 237 and 1073 activities within a given workday—or more than one activity every 2 minutes.[21] Such research strongly supports the notion that managers need to develop a major network of contacts in order to have influence and to operate effectively.[22] For some ideas on how you might be able to develop such contacts as a manager, see the Management Skills for the Twenty-First Century discussion, "How to Build Networks."

MANAGEMENT SKILLS FOR THE TWENTY-FIRST CENTURY

How to Build Networks

Experts agree that building networks of influence with others involves the principle of reciprocity. *Reciprocity* means that people generally feel that they should be paid back for the various things they do and that one good (or bad) turn deserves another. For the most part, individuals do not expect to be paid back right away or in specific amounts; approximations will usually do. Because individuals anticipate that their actions will be reimbursed in one way or another, influence and networking are possible.

One way to think about using the reciprocity principle in networking is to view oneself as a "trader" and to use the metaphor of "currencies" as a means of approaching the process of exchange. Just as there are many types of currencies used in the world, there are many different kinds of currencies that are used in organizational life. Too often individuals think only in terms of money, promotions, and status, but there are actually many possibilities.

SOME POSSIBLE CURRENCIES
Some possible currencies that you might be able to trade include the following:

Resources: giving budget increases, personnel, space, etc.

Assistance: helping with projects or taking on unwanted tasks

Information: furnishing organizational and/or technical knowledge

Recognition: acknowledging effort, accomplishment, or abilities

Visibility: providing the chance to be known by higher-ups

Advancement: giving tasks that can aid in promotion

Personal support: providing personal and emotional backing

Understanding: listening to others' concerns

HOW TO USE CURRENCIES
In using currencies, it helps to consider these four steps:

1 *Think of each individual whom you need to deal with as a potential ally or network member.* If you want to have influence within an organization and get the job done, you will need to create internal network members or allies. Assume that even a difficult person is a potential network member.

2 *Get to know the world of the potential network member, including the pressures that the person is under, as well as the person's needs and goals.* An important factor influencing behavior is how performance is measured and rewarded. If you ask an individual to do things that will be perceived as poor performance within that individual's work unit, you are likely to encounter resistance.

3 *Be aware of your own strengths and potential weaknesses as a networker.* Sometimes networkers underesti-mate the range of currencies that they have available to exchange. Make a list of potential currencies and resources that you have to offer. Then think about your own preferred style of interaction with others. Would-be networkers often fail to understand how their preferred style of interaction fits or doesn't fit with the potential ally's preferred style. For instance, does the potential ally like to socialize first and work later? If so, that person may find it difficult to deal with someone who likes to solve the problem first and only then talk about the weather, the family, or office politics. Skilled networkers learn to adapt their own style to that of others in dealing with potential allies.

4 *Gear your exchange transactions so that both parties can come out winners.* For the most part, transactions in organizations are not one-time occurrences. Usually the parties will need to deal with one another again, perhaps frequently. In fact, that is the idea of networks—to have contacts to call on as needed. The implication here is that in most exchange relationships there are two outcomes that ultimately make a difference. One is success in achieving the task goals at hand. The other is maintaining and improving the relationship so that the contact remains a viable one. With networking, it is better to lose the battle than to lose the war.[23]

Managerial Roles

To make sense of the reams of data he collected, Mintzberg attempted to categorize the managers' various activities into roles. A **role** is an organized set of behaviors associated with a particular office or position.[24] Positions usually entail multiple roles. For example, roles for a salesperson position in a retail store might include information giver, stock handler, and cashier.

Role An organized set of behaviors associated with a particular office or position

The three general types of roles that Mintzberg observed were interpersonal, informational, and decisional roles. *Interpersonal* roles grow directly out of the authority of a manager's position and involve developing and maintaining positive relationships with significant others. *Informational* roles pertain to receiving and transmitting information so that managers can serve as the nerve centers of their organizational units. *Decisional* roles involve making significant decisions that affect the organization. Within these role types, Mintzberg outlined 10 more specific roles that managers play (see Table 1-1).

Mintzberg's categorization of managerial activities into roles provides some insight into what managers actually do during their workday. The roles also give us clues about the kinds of skills that managers are likely to need to carry out their work effectively.

Mintzberg's role approach provides a somewhat different perspective on management than do the four management functions. At first glance, it might seem that Mintzberg's findings are incompatible with the view that planning, organizing, leading, and controlling are an important part of the management process. However, Mintzberg's study did not consider *why* managers were engaging in the different roles that he described. When the *why* is taken into consideration, it becomes clear that the functions of management provide an important blueprint that helps managers channel their role behaviors in ways

TABLE 1-1 MINTZBERG'S 10 MANAGERIAL ROLES	
ROLE	**DESCRIPTION**
INTERPERSONAL	
Figurehead	Performs symbolic duties of a legal or social nature
Leader	Builds relationships with subordinates and communicates with, motivates, and coaches them
Liaison	Maintains networks of contacts outside work unit who provide help and information
INFORMATIONAL	
Monitor	Seeks internal and external information about issues that can affect organization
Disseminator	Transmits information internally that is obtained from either internal or external sources
Spokesperson	Transmits information about the organization to outsiders
DECISIONAL	
Entrepreneur	Acts as initiator, designer, and encourager of change and innovation
Disturbance handler	Takes corrective action when organization faces important, unexpected difficulties
Resource allocator	Distributes resources of all types including time, funding, equipment, and human resources
Negotiator	Represents the organization in major negotiations affecting the manager's areas of responsibility

Source: Based on Henry Mintzberg, *The Nature of Managerial Work,* Harper & Row, New York, 1980.

that will ultimately lead to goal achievement.[25] For example, transmitting information through the disseminator role or representing the organization through the negotiator role has little meaning unless it is linked to a purpose such as a management function. But how do managers tie their various activities and roles into the planning, organizing, leading, and controlling that are necessary to achieve goals? Part of the answer is suggested by another well-known study, conducted by management researcher John Kotter.

Managerial Work Agendas

Kotter's study focused on 15 general managers in 9 different corporations representing a broad range of industries.[26] General managers typically have responsibility for a major business sector of the corporation. On the basis of his findings, Kotter suggested that managers focus their various efforts productively through the use of work agendas.

Work agenda A loosely connected set of tentative goals and tasks that a manager is attempting to accomplish

NATURE OF WORK AGENDAS A **work agenda** is a loosely connected set of tentative goals and tasks that a manager is attempting to accomplish. Managers usually develop work agendas during their first 6 months on a new job, although the agendas are continually subject to reassessment in the face of changing circumstances and emerging opportunities. Typically, such agendas address immediate, as well as more long-run, job responsibilities and are used in addition to more formal organizational plans. Kotter found that to put their work agendas into practice, general managers work hard to establish the extensive networks of relationships identified by Mintzberg.

By making use of work agendas and networking strategies, the managers in Kotter's study were able to engage in short, seemingly disjointed conversations and still accomplish their missions. To illustrate the typical way in which the managers worked, Kotter documented a set of short discussions held by John Thompson, a division manager in a financial services corporation.[27] The conversation began one morning in Thompson's office when two of his subordinates, Anne Dodge and Jud Smith, were present:

Thompson: "What about Potter?"
Dodge: "He's OK."
Smith: "Don't forget about Chicago."
Dodge: "Oh yeah." *(Makes a note to herself)*
Thompson: "OK. Then what about next week?"
Dodge: "We're set."
Thompson: "Good. By the way, how is Ted doing?"
Smith: "Better. He got back from the hospital on Tuesday. Phyllis says he looks good."
Thompson: "That's good to hear. I hope he doesn't have a relapse."
Dodge: "I'll see you this afternoon." *(Leaves the room)*
Thompson: "OK. *(To Smith)* Are we all set for now?"
Smith: "Yeah." *(Gets up and starts to leave)*
Lawrence: *(Steps into the doorway from the hall and speaks to Thompson)* "Have you seen the April numbers yet?"
Thompson: "No, have you?"
Lawrence: "Yes, 5 minutes ago. They're good except for CD, which is off by 5 percent."
Thompson: "That's better than I expected."
Smith: "I bet George is happy."
Thompson: *(Laughing)* "If he is, he won't be after I talk to him." *(Turner, Thompson's secretary, sticks her head through the doorway and tells him Bill Larson is on the phone)*

Thompson: "I'll take it. Will you ask George to stop by later? *(Others leave and Thompson picks up the phone)* Bill, good morning, how are you? . . . Yeah. . . . Is that right? . . . No, don't worry about it. . . . I think about a million and a half. . . . Yeah. . . . OK. . . . Yeah, Sally enjoyed the other night, too. Thanks again. . . . OK. . . . Bye."

Lawrence: *(Steps back into the office)* "What do you think of the Gerald proposal?"

Thompson: "I don't like it. It doesn't fit with what we've promised Corporate or Hines."

Lawrence: "Yeah, that's what I thought, too. What is Stacy going to do about it?"

Thompson: "I haven't talked to her yet. *(Turns to the phone and dials)* Let's see if she's in."

Although the dialogue was clear to the participants, it would probably seem somewhat chaotic to outsiders. This is because outsiders lack the specific business and organizational knowledge shared by the managers. For example, an outsider would not be able to readily identify Potter, Ted, Phyllis, Bill Larson, Sally, Hines, or Stacy. Nor would an outside observer understand the full meaning of the references to "Chicago," "April numbers," "CD," or the "Gerald proposal" or, more importantly, know Thompson's agenda and where these various pieces fit in that agenda.

Yet these conversations actually accomplished a great deal. Among other things, Thompson learned the following facts:

■ Mike Potter agreed to help with a problem loan that could otherwise thwart Thompson's business expansion plans in a certain area.

■ Plans for the loan for the following week were moving along as intended.

■ Ted Jenkins, one of Thompson's subordinates and a central figure in his plans for the division over the next 2 years, is feeling better after an operation.

■ Division income for April met budget except for one area, saving Thompson from having to divert attention from other plans to take remedial action.

In addition, Thompson initiated several actions:

■ He set up a meeting with George Masolia about the one off-target area in the April budget report to see what can be done to get things on target again.

■ He passed on some useful information to Bill Larson, a peer who has done him favors in the past and who could help him in the future.

■ He placed a call to Stacy Wilkins, one of his subordinates, to find out her reaction to a proposal that could impact Thompson's division, especially its 5-year revenue goals.

Thompson's discourse shows the fast pace, brevity, variety, and fragmentation that are characteristic of a manager's workday, and it illustrates the use of the verbal contacts and networks that were identified in Mintzberg's study. Many of Thompson's remarks (until he began to speak about the Gerald proposal) reflect mainly the controlling function—checking to be sure that various important activities are moving along as expected. The discussion about the Gerald proposal reflects the planning function. When he talks with George about the budget problem, Thompson will engage in leading and planning.

Without a work agenda (the manager's own working plan), similar discussions could actually be fairly random and far from efficient. Even with an agenda, managers need to make sure that they work within its guidelines. Within a year after he became chief executive officer at First Chicago, a major bank holding company, Barry Sullivan had a solid idea about his priorities. Still, he had a vague sense that in the course of relentless day-to-day activity, he was not spending his time in ways that adequately matched his priorities. With the help of consultants, he learned the cause of his problem: "I was responding to demands on my time in more of an ad hoc manner rather than against some broad idea of how much time I really wanted to allocate to different things." As a result, he began deciding how much time he wanted to assign to certain activities and would tentatively block out parts of his calendar up to a year in advance to help him match his time with his priorities.[28]

Work agendas provide rough guidelines within which managers operate in determining how to orient their various activities and roles. But what factors influence the content of work agendas?

FACTORS INFLUENCING WORK AGENDAS According to Rosemary Stewart, a British expert on managerial work, there are three main factors that are likely to have an impact on a manager's work agenda: demands, constraints, and choices.[29]

Job demands are the activities a manager *must* do in a job. For example, managers usually have responsibilities related to the major goals and plans of the organization (such as achieving a 10 percent increase in sales) that are difficult to ignore.

Job constraints are the factors, both inside and outside the organization, that limit what a manager can do. Constraints include such variables as resource limitations, legal restrictions, union contract provisions, technological limitations, and the degree to which the work of a manager's unit is defined.

Job choices are work activities that the manager can do but does not have to do. For example, without a directive to do so, a manager might initiate a proposal to develop a computerized customer service tracking system. Thus work agendas tend to reflect, at least to some extent, the personal preferences and career objectives of individual managers.

■ MANAGERIAL KNOWLEDGE, SKILLS, AND PERFORMANCE

For managers to develop work agendas, act out roles, and engage in planning, organizing, leading, and controlling, they need a sound knowledge base and key management skills. In this section, we discuss these essential elements in the management process and explain how they relate to the issue of performance.

Knowledge Base

Although managers often switch companies and work in different industries, they are apt to run into difficulties if they don't have a reasonably extensive knowledge base relevant to their particular managerial job. A *knowledge base* can include information about an industry and its technology, company policies and practices, company goals and plans, company culture, the personalities of key organization members, and important suppliers and customers. For exam-

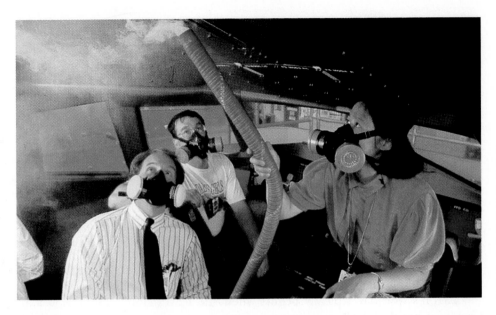

Managers at Boeing displayed a keen knowledge of their clientele as well as their competitors by coming up with the innovative idea of letting customers put their own engineers on the Boeing design team. This plan allows Boeing to get a jump on the competition and enables the customers to purchase planes tailored to their needs.

ple, Kotter found that one reason why the general managers in his study were able to accomplish so much within short periods of time was that they could take action with only small bits of information at their disposal. Their extensive knowledge base enabled them to attach the appropriate meaning to the information fragments they obtained.[30]

Key Management Skills

In addition to having a knowledge base, managers need certain skills to carry out the various functions of management. A *skill* is the ability to engage in a set of behaviors that are functionally related to one another and that lead to a desired performance level in a given area.[31] For managers, three types of skills are necessary: technical, human, and conceptual.

TECHNICAL SKILLS Technical skills are skills that reflect both an understanding of and a proficiency in a specialized field. For example, a manager may have technical skills in accounting, finance, engineering, manufacturing, or computer science.

HUMAN SKILLS Human skills are skills associated with a manager's ability to work well with others, both as a member of a group and as a leader who gets things done through others. Managers with effective human skills are typically adept at communicating with others and motivating them to develop themselves and perform well in pursuit of organizational goals.

CONCEPTUAL SKILLS Conceptual skills are skills related to the ability to visualize the organization as a whole, discern interrelationships among organizational parts, and understand how the organization fits into the wider context of the industry, community, and world. Conceptual skills, coupled with technical skills, human skills, and a knowledge base, are important ingredients in organizational performance, as can be seen in the example of Carnegie Hall, a not-for-profit organization (see the Case in Point discussion).

Technical skills Skills that reflect both an understanding of and a proficiency in a specialized field

Human skills Skills associated with a manager's ability to work well with others, both as a member of a group and as a leader who gets things done through others

Conceptual skills Skills related to the ability to visualize the organization as a whole, discern interrelationships among organizational parts, and understand how the organization fits into the wider context of the industry, community, and world

CASE IN POINT

BEHIND-THE-SCENES SKILLS AT CARNEGIE HALL

As they enjoy performances at New York's Carnegie Hall, few members of the audience probably give any thought to the management knowledge and skills at work behind the scenes of the nation's most celebrated cultural center. Since 1986, Carnegie Hall has been run by Judith Arron, executive and artistic director of the concert landmark. Although she has a university degree in cello and piano, she decided to make concert management her career. Among her previous managerial positions, she served for 10 years as orchestra manager of the Cincinnati Symphony Orchestra before winning the Carnegie Hall position.

She arrived at Carnegie Hall in the midst of a $50 million renovation project, the most extensive in the concert center's history. When concerts resumed, Arron's responsibilities included the overseeing of season planning, artist procurement, marketing and promotion, overall supervision of hall operations, and development of community outreach programs. In the latter, Carnegie sponsors musical events in local communities, shelters, and, particularly, elementary schools or brings various special groups to Carnegie Hall for concerts.

Arron's workday typically begins when she leaves home about 7:30 a.m. Usually at her desk by 9, a major part of her day is consumed by meetings with such groups as senior staff members, department heads, the board of directors, orchestra representatives, artists, conductors, and staff members. Although her workday tends to end about 6:30 p.m., she may stay for a weeknight concert, and she frequently comes in for concerts or special events on weekends. "We may have an established superstar or a newcomer I want to hear, or a new orchestra that needs special care." She generally plans to "work 6 days a week and go to two or three concerts."

She is known for being particularly skilled at handling people, including some of the temperamental, but talented, artists who play on Carnegie's stage. Indeed, the cast of artists has been stellar, including such luminaries as Leonard Bernstein, Itzhak Perlman, Mstislav Rostropovich, Alicia de Larrocha, Dame Joan Sutherland, and Marilyn Horne.[32] ■ ■ ■

A major concert, such as this one at New York City's Carnegie Hall, involves far more than just the collective musical talents on stage. Behind the scenes are stagehands, electricians, light operators, sound technicians, piano tuners, guards, ticket sellers, public relations personnel, and many others. Conducting the performance of all these individuals is Judith Arron, general manager and artistic director of Carnegie Hall. Arron also oversees program planning, artist procurement, and marketing of events. She must call on her technical skills in music, her human skills in handling artists and employees, and her conceptual skills in planning seasons.

Arron came to her job at Carnegie Hall with an extensive knowledge base about the concert field, gleaned from her years as orchestra manager of the Cincinnati Symphony and several previous jobs. In addition, her strong technical skills in music, human skills in handling people, and conceptual skills in seeing the big picture have been important factors in her high performance and that of Carnegie Hall.

Performance

What constitutes high performance in an organization? Peter Drucker, the noted management writer and consultant, points out that performance achieved through management is actually made up of two important dimensions: effectiveness and efficiency.[33]

EFFECTIVENESS Effectiveness is the ability to choose appropriate goals and achieve them. For example, Dallas-based Southwest Airlines has become a major player in the airline industry by focusing on offering friendly, no-frills service (no meals) between a variety of high-traffic cities for a relatively low cost. In the process, the company has been rare among airlines in remaining consistently profitable and in building an exceptionally loyal customer base.[34] Thus Southwest Airlines illustrates what Drucker means when he points out that effectiveness is essentially doing (accomplishing) *the right things.*

Effectiveness The ability to choose appropriate goals and achieve them

EFFICIENCY Efficiency is the ability to make the best use of available resources in the process of achieving goals. Part of the success of Southwest Airlines is attributable to its notable efficiency. For example, in one recent survey, the company's turnaround time, the average time on the ground after landing before taking off again, was 39 minutes compared with 70 to 90 minutes for most other major airlines. Its passengers per employee ratio, the number of passengers the airline carries per employee, was more than double the figure for other major airlines. Part of the reason behind such efficiencies is the company's heavy emphasis on teamwork. Employees work together to use resources well in providing excellent low-cost service. For example, pilots might help out at the boarding gate when things are backed up or a ticket agent might pitch in with baggage loading when necessary.[35] Through such unusual means, Southwest Airlines illustrates what Drucker has in mind when he speaks of efficiency as doing *things right.*

Efficiency The ability to make the best use of available resources in the process of achieving goals

In essence, organizations need to exhibit both effectiveness (doing the right things) and efficiency (doing things right) in order to be good performers. Because these dimensions are so closely linked, we will generally use the term "effectiveness" in reference to both effectiveness and efficiency. We do this for the sake of simplicity and readability.

■ MANAGERIAL JOB TYPES

Although we have been discussing the nature of managerial work in general, managerial jobs vary somewhat on the basis of two important dimensions. One is a vertical dimension, focusing on different hierarchical levels in the organization. The other is a horizontal dimension, addressing variations in managers' responsibility areas. We explore these dimensions and their implications in this section. Because of its importance in fostering innovation, we give special attention to the entrepreneurial role at various hierarchical levels (refer back to Table 1-1).

Vertical Dimension: Hierarchical Levels

Along the vertical dimension, managerial jobs in organizations fall into three categories: first-line, middle, and top management. These categories represent vertical differentiation among managers because they involve three different levels of the organization, as shown in Figure 1-3.

First-line managers/ supervisors Managers at the lowest level of the hierarchy who are directly responsible for the work of operating (nonmanagerial) employees

FIRST-LINE MANAGERS First-line managers (or **first-line supervisors**) are managers at the lowest level of the hierarchy who are directly responsible for the work of operating (nonmanagerial) employees. They often have titles that include the word "supervisor." First-line managers are extremely important to the success of an organization because they have the responsibility of seeing that day-to-day operations run smoothly in pursuit of organizational goals.

Because they operate at the interface between management and the rest of the work force, first-line supervisors can easily find themselves in the middle of conflicting demands. At the same time, the power of first-line supervisors has been gradually eroding because of such factors as union influence, the increasing educational level of workers, the trend toward work teams, and the growing use of computers to track many activities formerly regulated by first-line managers. Consequently, the job of the first-line supervisor in the future is likely to involve greater emphasis on dealing with internal human relations and on representing the unit externally.

Middle managers Managers beneath the top levels of the hierarchy who are directly responsible for the work of managers at lower levels

MIDDLE MANAGERS Middle managers are managers located beneath the top levels of the hierarchy who are directly responsible for the work of managers at lower levels. The managers for whom they have direct responsibility may be other middle managers or first-line managers. Sometimes middle managers also

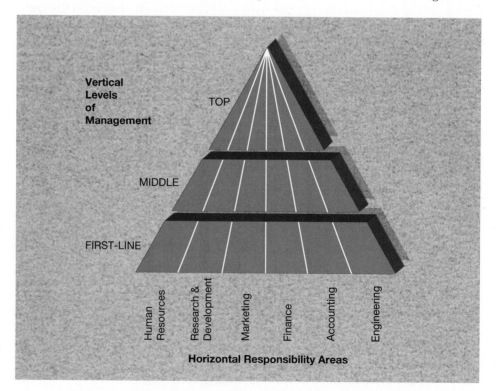

Figure 1-3 *Types of managers by hierarchical level and responsibility area.*

Roy S. Roberts, top executive at General Motors Corporation (GMC), had the tricky task of merging GMC divisions with Pontiac recently. It required cutting some 600 overlapping middle management positions as well as eliminating stand-alone Pontiac and GMC dealerships. While sensitive to what he calls "the people side of the business," Roberts believes that streamlining the system makes good business sense.

supervise operating personnel, such as administrative assistants and specialists (e.g., engineers or financial analysts). Many different titles are used for middle managers, including "manager," "director of," "chief," "department head," and "division head." Middle managers are mainly responsible for implementing overall organizational plans so that organizational goals are achieved as expected.

Organizations, particularly very large ones, traditionally have tended to have several layers of middle managers. For example, at one point, General Motors (GM) had 14 or 15 management levels. That number reflects a post-World War II trend aimed at adding layers of middle management to help coordinate expanding activities. By the early 1980s, however, the trend began to reverse. Many companies cut the number of managerial levels in an attempt to lower costs, reduce the layers involved in decision making, and facilitate communication. During the 1990s, for example, GM has struggled to streamline still further in the face of relatively high costs and cutthroat international competition.[36] AT&T announced it would cut 40,000 positions, many of them in middle management.[37]

Reducing layers of middle management has brought with it both challenges and opportunities. One common result of having fewer layers is that the remaining middle-management levels gain greater autonomy and responsibility. Not surprisingly, pressure on middle managers appears to be increasing in the face of these changes. In one survey, more than half the respondents reported that the middle managers in their organizations are working longer hours than they had previously, and one-fourth said that they are spending more weekends in the office.[38] For those individuals who lose their positions through downsizing, the dislocation can be painful until other suitable jobs are found.[39]

Although there may be fewer middle managers in the future, management researcher Rosabeth Moss Kanter argues that the distinction between managers and those managed is also declining. She predicts that there will be less emphasis on hierarchical level and, instead, more weight on horizontal influence, increased reliance on peer networks, greater access to information, and more control over assignments at lower levels.[40] Thus it appears that as middle managers assume additional responsibilities, many of their current duties will be distributed to lower levels in the organization, thereby raising the importance of positions at those levels.

Top managers Managers at the very top levels of the hierarchy who are ultimately responsible for the entire organization

TOP MANAGERS Top managers are managers at the very top levels of the hierarchy who are ultimately responsible for the entire organization. They are few in number, and their typical titles include "chief executive officer" (CEO), "president," "executive vice president," "executive director," "senior vice president," and, sometimes, "vice president." Top-level managers are often referred to as executives, although the term "executive" is also sometimes used to include the upper layers of middle managers as well. Top managers have direct responsibility for the upper layer of middle managers. They typically oversee the overall planning for the organization, work to some degree with middle managers in implementing that planning, and maintain overall control over the progress of the organization.

In public corporations, whose stock is sold to the public, top management ultimately reports to the board of directors. The board is composed of a group of individuals elected by the shareholders for the purpose of guiding corporate affairs and selecting officers. A board typically has from 15 to 25 members, depending on company size. In some companies, boards may essentially "rubber-stamp" management initiatives, particularly when the majority of the board is made up of top managers and outside individuals with close ties to management. In others, boards include more outsiders, operate more independently, and are more proactive—factors that often lead to better corporate performance.[41] Typically, the board appoints the CEO, who then selects other top managers, including most vice presidents, subject to board approval. Often the CEO also serves as chairperson of the board. A recent study, however, suggests that companies perform better when the CEO does not also hold the position of board chairperson, as this arrangement allows the board to more adequately monitor the performance of top management.[42]

Differences among Hierarchical Levels

Although the same basic managerial process applies to all three hierarchical levels of management, there are some differences in emphasis. Major differences stem mainly from the importance of the four functions of management, the skills necessary to perform effectively, the emphasis on managerial roles at each level, and the use of the entrepreneurial role.

FUNCTIONS OF MANAGEMENT The relative importance of planning, organizing, leading, and controlling varies somewhat depending on managerial level.[43] As indicated in Figure 1-4, planning tends to be more important for top managers than for middle or first-line managers. This is primarily because top managers are responsible for determining the overall direction of the organization, a charge that requires extensive planning.

At the same time, organizing is somewhat more important for both top and middle managers than for first-line managers. This stems from the fact that it is the top and middle levels of management that are mainly responsible for allocating and arranging resources, even though this function is also performed to some extent by first-line supervisors.

In contrast, leading is substantially more important for first-line supervisors than for managers at higher levels. Since first-line supervisors are charged with the ongoing production of goods or services, they must engage in sub-

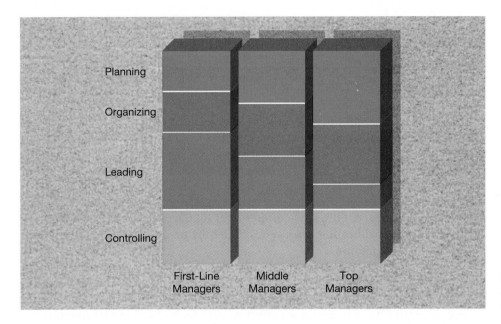

Figure 1-4 *Use of management functions at different hierarchical levels.*

stantially higher amounts of communicating, motivating, directing, and supporting—all of which are associated with leading.

Finally, the management function that is most similar at all three hierarchical levels is controlling. This similarity reflects a common degree of emphasis at all levels on monitoring activities and taking corrective action as needed.

MANAGEMENT SKILLS The three levels of management also differ in the importance attached to the key skills discussed earlier: technical, human, and conceptual (see Figure 1-5).[44] Generally, conceptual skills are most important at the top management level. Top managers have the greatest need to see the organization as a whole, understand how its various parts relate to one another, and associate the organization with the world outside. Whirlpool's David Whitwam points out that looking at an organization as a whole can be difficult, par-

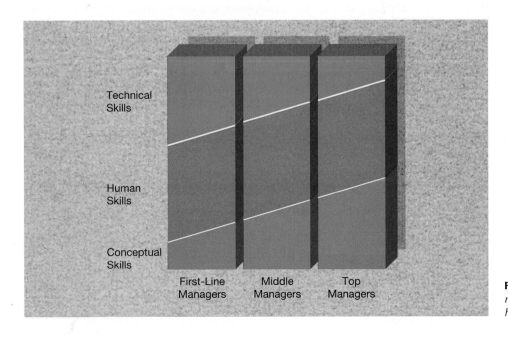

Figure 1-5 *Use of key management skills at different hierarchical levels.*

ticularly when a company is doing well and there is no imminent crisis on the horizon. He said that Whirlpool was doing well domestically; but, nevertheless, top management faced up to the challenge of looking at the big picture because they could envision their future growing more difficult and complicated. When they took a more holistic view, they realized that they had to globalize to survive and prosper.[45]

In contrast, first-line managers have the greatest need for technical skills, since they directly supervise most of the technical and professional employees who are not managers. Yet middle managers, too, often need sufficient technical skills so that they can communicate with subordinates and recognize major problems.[46] Even top managers must have some technical skills, particularly when technology is an important part of the products or services their organizations produce. Otherwise, upper-level managers will have difficulty fostering innovation, allocating resources efficiently, or devising strategies to stay ahead of the competition.

Not surprisingly, all three levels of management require strong human skills because they all must get things done through people.[47] Ironically, promotions to first-level management are often based on individuals' good technical skills, with little consideration given to the adequacy of their human skills. Managers who lack sufficient human skills usually run into serious difficulties when they attempt to deal with individuals inside and outside their work units. In fact, a series of studies focusing on the primary reasons why executives derail suggests that human skills are particularly important factors (see Table 1-2). Derailed executives are those who reach relatively high levels but then find there is little chance of further upward movement because their personal skills do not match job requirements.[48]

MANAGERIAL ROLES Although Mintzberg argued that the 10 managerial roles he identified apply to all levels of management (see Table 1-1), he did note that there may be some differences in emphasis at various levels.[49] Subsequent research by others suggests that the figurehead role and several others such as liaison and spokesperson may become more important as a manager moves up the hierarchy. On the other hand, the leader role appears to be more critical at the lower levels, a finding that supports the idea that the leading function itself has greater importance for lower-level managers than for those higher up.[50]

In a study of the importance of the various roles, managers at all levels gave particularly high ratings to the entrepreneurial role.[51] Several experts on innovation, however, argue that the entrepreneurial role varies in some important ways depending on a manager's level in the hierarchy.[52] Because of the particular importance of innovation to the success of organizations, we explore the differences below.

TABLE 1-2 REASONS FOR EXECUTIVE DERAILMENT
1. Problems with interpersonal relationships
2. Failure to meet business objectives
3. Inability to build and lead a team
4. Inability to develop or adapt

Source: Adapted from Ellen Van Velsor and Jean Brittain Leslie, "Why Executives Derail: Perspectives across Time and Cultures," *Academy of Management Executive,* vol. 9, 1995, p. 64.

Promoting Innovation: The Entrepreneurial Role

An **innovation** is a new idea applied to initiating or improving a process, product, or service.[53] The process of innovation is closely allied with the entrepreneurial role in organizations, particularly since that role relates to discovering and exploiting new opportunities. In fact, innovative activities in organizations, especially major ones, have frequently been referred to as entrepreneurship within organizations. More recently, individuals who engage in entrepreneurial roles inside organizations are often called **intrapreneurs.** The term is used to differentiate innovators working inside existing organizations from individuals who innovate by creating new organizations (the latter are often called *entrepreneurs;* see Chapter 21). Similarly, the process of innovating within an existing organization is sometimes referred to as **intrapreneurship.**

Encouraging innovation in organizations takes special effort. Furthermore, successful innovations are rarely the product of only one person's work. Rather, the innovative process usually involves individuals at various levels who fulfill three different types of entrepreneurial roles: idea generator or champion, sponsor, and orchestrator.[54]

IDEA CHAMPION An **idea champion** is an individual who generates a new idea or believes in the value of a new idea and supports it in the face of numerous potential obstacles. We often think of such individuals as entrepreneurs, inventors, creative individuals, or risk takers. They are usually individuals at lower levels in the organization who recognize a problem and help develop a solution. First-line supervisors act as idea champions when they come up with innovative ideas, nurture ideas in others, and fight tenaciously to help make the ideas a reality. However, because idea champions are relatively far down in the hierarchy, they often do not have the power and status to get their innovations accepted by the organization. This situation creates the need for the next type of role.

SPONSOR A **sponsor** is an individual, usually a middle manager, who recognizes the organizational significance of an idea, helps obtain the necessary funding for development of the innovation, and facilitates its actual implementation. Sponsors tend to be middle managers because their higher-level position in the organization makes it more feasible for them to provide the strong backing necessary for the survival of innovations. While innovations in organizations are not likely to occur without a sponsor, their occurrence also depends on an individual who fills a third role.

ORCHESTRATOR An **orchestrator** is a high-level manager who articulates the need for innovation, provides funding for innovating activities, creates incentives for middle managers to sponsor new ideas, and protects idea people. Because innovations often constitute a challenge to the current ways of doing things, they are frequently resisted by those who are comfortable with or have a particular stake in the status quo. (For example, an expert in a process may resist a change that will cause it to be outmoded.) An orchestrator maintains the balance of power so that new ideas have a chance to be tested in the face of possible negative reactions. By filling the role of orchestrator, top managers encourage innovation.

Without all three roles, major innovations are much less likely to occur. The development of the VHS videocassette recorder at JVC illustrates the importance of entrepreneurial, or innovative, roles at the various levels of the organization (see the Case in Point discussion).

Innovation A new idea applied to initiating or improving a process, product, or service

Intrapreneurs Individuals who engage in entrepreneurial roles inside organizations

Intrapreneurship The process of innovating within an existing organization

Idea champion An individual who generates a new idea or believes in the value of a new idea and supports it in the face of numerous potential obstacles

Sponsor A middle manager who recognizes the organizational significance of an idea, helps obtain the necessary funding for development of the innovation, and facilitates its actual implementation

Orchestrator A high-level manager who articulates the need for innovation, provides funding for innovating activities, creates incentives for middle managers to sponsor new ideas, and protects idea people

CASE IN POINT

JVC PERSISTS WITH THE VIDEOCASSETTE RECORDER

Engineers at JVC (Victor Company of Japan, Ltd.), an independent subsidiary of the giant Matsushita Electric Industrial Company, Ltd., were intrigued when, in 1964, six American engineers at Ampex Corporation built the first magnetic tape recorder that captured pictures as well as sound. The Ampex machine was very large (about the size of an old-fashioned jukebox), used 2-inch-wide reel-to-reel tape, and was extremely expensive. Nevertheless, it was readily adopted by TV networks and affiliates, since it enabled them to broadcast prerecorded shows at times that best fit audience schedules rather than having to broadcast live. At that point, engineers Yuma Shiraishi and Shizuo Takano set out to develop a JVC magnetic tape recorder.

By 1970, Sony produced a prototype ¾-inch tape in a cassette. Sony shared the prototype with Matsushita and JVC in return for help on perfecting the tape technology. The resulting improved ¾-inch-tape cassette was a major breakthrough in technology. Although each of the companies then went on independently to produce its own videocassette recorder (VCR), the machines they developed were still too big, bulky, complex, and expensive for home use. Sony, with inroads into major businesses and schools, made a modest profit, while Matsushita and JVC lost money on their ventures. At this point, JVC's top management canceled most of its backing for the project, leaving only a small team headed by Shiraishi and supported by Takano, both of whom continued to be obsessed with the idea of a VCR for home use.

Frustrated, Shiraishi and three other engineers decided to start over from scratch. In thinking about what should go into a home-use machine, they compiled a new list of specifications. For example, they decided that the minimum recording time should be *2 hours* so that consumers would be able to videotape movies for later viewing. By now, Takano was senior managing director of JVC's video products division. He continued to ignore suggestions from upper management that he drop work on the home VCR. Keeping the work at a low profile, Takano and his team developed a fairly advanced ½-inch VCR prototype. Using a format that they called VHS (video home system), the machine would run for 2 hours.

When Konosuke Matsushita, the chairman of JVC's parent company, visited the video products division, he happened upon the prototype. Matsushita had already seen a competing Sony prototype VCR based on a ¾-inch-tape format called Betamax. After the technical aspects of the JVC prototype were explained to him, he smiled, leaned over, pressed his cheek to the recorder, and said, "It's marvelous. You have made something very nice." Although Matsushita made no official statement of support and issued no directives, the story quickly ran through the grapevine. From then on, the development team found it much easier to operate internally.

Even though Sony brought its VCR to market first, the company was not able to persuade Matsushita or JVC to adopt its Betamax standards because its tape would run for only 1 hour. Several months later, the JVC project group completed its work on the VCR with the VHS format. JVC was then able to get several other manufacturers, including Matsushita, to use its format. The VHS videocassette pioneered by JVC was formally introduced in September 1976 and has become the industry standard.[55] ■■■

In the JVC situation, the company would never have been successful with the VHS videocassette recorder without Shiraishi and Takano as original idea champions. Top managers at JVC operated as orchestrators early on, but they withdrew much of their support later. Still, Takano was able to act as a sponsor and allow the project to continue despite some negative pressure from above. Ultimately, the indirect intervention of Matsushita as an orchestrator became crucial. These three types of entrepreneurial roles constitute another vertical difference among managers.

Horizontal Dimension: Responsibility Areas

In addition to their vertical differences, managerial jobs differ on a horizontal dimension that relates to the nature of the responsibility area involved (see Figure 1-3). In horizontal differentiation, there are three major types of managerial jobs: functional, general, and project.

FUNCTIONAL MANAGERS Functional managers are managers who have responsibility for a specific, specialized area (often called a *functional area*) of the organization and supervise mainly individuals with expertise and training in that area. Common specialized, or functional, areas include finance, manufacturing or operations, marketing, human resource management, accounting, quality assurance, and engineering.

Functional managers Managers who have responsibility for a specific, specialized area of the organization and supervise mainly individuals with expertise and training in that area

GENERAL MANAGERS General managers are managers who have responsibility for a whole organization or a substantial subunit that includes most of the common specialized areas. In other words, a general manager presides over a number of functional areas (hence the term "general"). General managers have a variety of titles, such as "division manager" and "president," depending on the circumstances. A small company will usually have only one general manager, who is the head of the entire organization. Depending on how it is organized, a large company may have several general managers (in addition to the chief executive officer), each of whom usually presides over a major division. For example, when Susan King was president of Corning Inc.'s Steuben Division, which produces fine crystal, she was considered a general manager because she presided over a major division that includes most of its own main functions, such as production, marketing, and human resources. When she later became senior vice president of corporate affairs, she was considered a functional manager because she presided over a specialized area. At the same time, Corning's CEO would be considered a general manager because the CEO is responsible for the entire corporation. Sometimes plant managers with major responsibilities who have some accounting, human resource, and other staff members reporting to them are also called general managers.[56]

General managers Managers who have responsibility for a whole organization or a substantial subunit that includes most of the common specialized areas

PROJECT MANAGERS Project managers are managers who have responsibility for coordinating efforts involving individuals in several different organizational units who are all working on a particular project. Because the individuals report not only to the managers in their specific work units but also to their project manager, project managers usually must have extremely strong interpersonal skills to keep things moving smoothly (we discuss this issue further in Chapter 9). Project managers are frequently used in aerospace and other high-technology firms to coordinate projects, such as airplane or computer project development. They are also used in some consumer-oriented companies to launch or stay on top of market development for specific products, such as cookies or margarine.[57]

Project managers Managers who have responsibility for coordinating efforts involving individuals in several different organizational units who are all working on a particular project

These M.B.A. students at Boston College's Carroll School of Management learn about the social responsibilities of business and gain practical experience by acting as mentors for 8-to-14-year olds from Boston's South End. As one M.B.A. student put it: "Society's changing. It's not me, me, me anymore. There are bigger issues we need to address. This is our way of doing our part." (Fortune, Oct. 5, 1992, p. 16)

■ LEARNING TO BE AN EFFECTIVE MANAGER

How can one learn to be an effective manager? Most observers agree that becoming effective takes a combination of education and experience.

Managerial Education

Recent surveys of CEOs indicate the growing importance of formal education in preparing managers. One survey cataloged responses from almost 250 CEOs representing 800 of the largest industrial and service firms in the United States.[58] Among the CEOs, 99 percent had attended college and 91 percent were college graduates.

Business was by far the most popular major, followed by engineering and liberal arts. Furthermore, almost half the CEOs held advanced degrees, with an M.B.A. being the most common and a law degree the next most common. Results from an international study of CEOs support the trend toward college graduates as company leaders. The study also found that graduate degrees are growing in prevalence.[59]

For most managers, education does not end with college and graduate school degrees. Instead, managers usually take additional management-related courses as part of special programs on college campuses, organizational training programs offered in-house, or commercial programs offered by a variety of trade associations and vendors. In essence, effective managers think of management education as a process that continues throughout their careers.

Management Experience

Not surprisingly, experience is also a major factor in learning to be an effective manager. For the CEO respondents in the survey of 800 large U.S. companies, work experience started in high school (79 percent had jobs) and largely continued in college (56 percent had jobs). Another early source of management experience was holding office in college clubs. Approximately 70 percent of the respondent CEOs held at least one office in a club, fraternity, or other campus organization while in college.[60]

The age at which managers tend to be promoted to the CEO position also supports the notion that experience plays an important role. One study showed that 75 percent of CEOs were at least 45 years old before they were promoted to the position, with more than half being 50 or over at the time of promotion.[61]

■ MANAGING IN THE TWENTY-FIRST CENTURY

Successful managers learn to keep an eye on future trends that are likely to impact actions they must take to keep their organizations moving forward. As we mentioned at the beginning of this chapter, several important themes are emerging as researchers study trends relevant to managing in the twenty-first century. Here, we expand upon these four themes briefly and explain how they will be addressed throughout this book to help you become a successful twenty-first-century manager.

Managing Change and Innovation

As we move into the twenty-first century, effectively managing change and innovation is becoming more critical than ever. *Change* is any alteration of the status quo to which a company must respond. *Innovation* is a new idea applied to initiating or improving a process, product, or service. Most companies confront serious competitive challenges due to the rapid rate and unpredictability of technological change. Changes related to information technology will be a particular hallmark of the twenty-first century. Firms also face many other types of pressures, such as alterations in strategies by competitors, shifts in economic conditions, or modifications in customer preferences. Companies that will survive and prosper are those whose managers can guide the process of change so that the organization makes the necessary adaptations in the face of altering conditions. But they also must do more. Increasingly, successful companies are those that place considerable emphasis on the opportunities available through innovation.[62]

For example, Rubbermaid, the company based in Wooster, Ohio, that makes plastic household and commercial items, has built a solid reputation for innovation through a constant stream of sturdy new plastic products ranging from backyard gym sets to "litterless lunch boxes" to computer furniture. The company has organized its employees into teams to generate new ideas. They are so innovative that the $2 billion company launches a new product almost every day. Currently the company is aggressively working to penetrate foreign markets and is now number two in European housewares.[63]

We discuss issues relating to managing change and innovation further in an entire chapter (see Chapter 11) and also in special Promoting Innovation sections that appear in several chapters. In addition, throughout the book we frequently refer to examples of organizations that have been successful in managing change and innovation.

Managing Diversity: Workforce 2000 *and Beyond*

Ever since the Hudson Institute published its influential report entitled *Workforce 2000*, which highlighted the growing diversity of the labor pool, many organizations have been reassessing their ability to manage a more diverse work force.[64] **Managing diversity** is the planning and implementing of organizational systems and practices that maximize the potential of employees to contribute to organizational goals and develop their capabilities unhindered by group

Managing diversity The planning and implementing of organizational systems and practices that maximize the potential of employees to contribute to organizational goals and develop their capabilities unhindered by group identities such as race, gender, age, or ethnic group

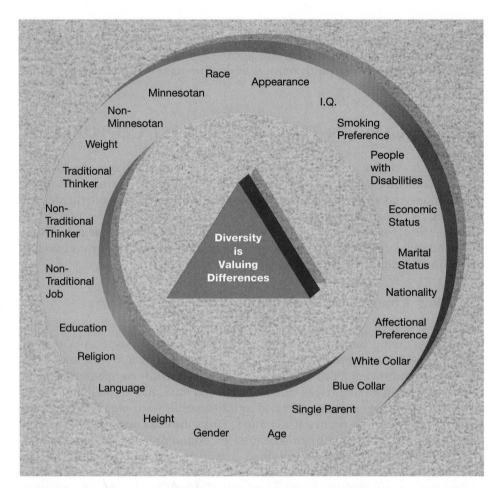

Figure 1-6 *Northern States Power diversity study diagram. (Reprinted from Mary J. Winterle,* Work Force Diversity: Corporate Challenges, Corporate Responses, *Report Number 1013, The Conference Board, New York, 1992.)*

identities such as race, gender, age, or ethnic group.[65] According to estimates by the U.S. Bureau of Labor Statistics, for example, women will constitute about 47 percent of the work force and minorities about 27 percent by the year 2000 (we assess the specifics in greater detail in Chapter 3). In many organizations, discussions of such demographic trends have ultimately highlighted many ways in which organizational members may differ from one another. A listing of such differences compiled in the spirit of valuing diversity at Minneapolis-based Northern States Power Company, a utility serving Minnesota and surrounding states, is shown in Figure 1-6.

A recent survey indicates that more than 70 percent of the Fortune top 50 have diversity management programs in place. Another 16 percent are developing programs or have various initiatives at division levels.[66] Why are so many organizations setting up diversity programs? The motivations behind such efforts are several. For one thing, companies are concerned about being able to attract and retain the best available talent. Companies with the most positive reputations for managing diversity will likely be at a competitive advantage in assembling the most talented individuals domestically and abroad. For another thing, the customer base of most companies also is growing more diverse. Such changes induced CIGNA, a major insurance company, to develop corporatewide initiatives aimed at changing its internal culture and the composition of its senior management.[67] Finally, as will be discussed below, as organizations operate more globally, diverse employees are an advantage in dealing not only with customers but also with vendors, suppliers, and governments.[68]

Essentially in the coming millennium, managers themselves will reflect the emerging diversity and, at the same time, will need to be able to effectively utilize an increasingly diverse work force. We discuss the diversity issue further in Managing Diversity sections in several chapters and periodically spotlight important organizational efforts in this area through the use of Managing Diversity boxes in various appropriate places.

Developing a Global Perspective

Along with diversity initiatives, organizations must increasingly assume a global perspective in conducting their business for three major reasons. First, businesses are facing more and more global competition. As Louis Gerstner, CEO of IBM, points out, "The world is going to become more competitive in an industrial, commercial sense. More competitive perhaps than we've seen in the history of modern economic society."[69] Second, more and more companies are likely to be doing business in other countries. Hewlett-Packard, for example, conducts a large part of its business in Europe, but also has principal markets in Japan, Canada, Australia, the Far East, and Latin America.[70] As a look at Table 1-3 will indicate, many familiar U.S. firms derive significant revenues from foreign operations.

Third, businesses are increasingly becoming globalized in the sense of operating as one company, despite far-flung operations. Tadahiro Sekimoto, chairman of the board of NEC Corp., the giant Japan-based electronics company, notes that "the world is becoming borderless, thanks to sophisticated information and transport infrastructure."[71] Whirlpool CEO Whitwam argues that Asia will soon be the largest appliance market in the world. "It will remain so forever," he says.[72] As these trends imply, managers will need to have greater knowledge of international business in the twenty-first century. Accordingly, we

TABLE 1-3 U.S. FIRMS WITH THE LARGEST FOREIGN REVENUES			
RANK	FIRM	FOREIGN REVENUES (IN MILLIONS OF U.S. $)	FOREIGN SALES AS % OF TOTAL SALES
1.	Exxon	77,125	77.4
2.	General Motors	44,041	28.4
3.	Mobil	40,318*	67.6
4.	IBM	39,934	62.3
5.	Ford Motor	39,075	29.6
6.	Texaco†	24,760	55.9
7.	Citicorp	19,703	62.3
8.	Chevron†	16,533	42.9
9.	Philip Morris Cos.	16,329	30.4
10.	Procter & Gamble	15,650E	51.7
11.	E.I. du Pont de Nemours	14,322	42.1
12.	Hewlett-Packard	13,522	54.1
13.	General Electric	11,872	19.8
14.	American Intl. Group	11,636	51.8
15.	Coca-Cola	11,048	68.3
16.	Dow Chemical	10,073	50.3
17.	Motorola	9,770E	43.9
18.	Xerox†	9,678	47.8
19.	United Technologies	8,300*	39.2
20.	Digital Equipment	8,274	61.5

*Includes other income.

†Includes proportionate interest in unconsolidated subsidiaries or affiliates.

E: Estimate.

Source: Data taken from Forbes, July 17, 1995, pp. 274–275.

Whirlpool Corp., under CEO David Whitwam, is undertaking a worldwide integrated quality program known as the Whirlpool Excellence System. This program, which combines the best of U.S. and European approaches, represents a commitment to total quality management.

devote an entire chapter to international management (see Chapter 20) and include international material in a number of other chapters. In addition, we frequently use international companies as examples so that you can learn more about such organizations and the way they do business.

The Quest for Total Quality and Continuous Improvement

Due to increasing global competition, particularly from Japanese companies, many organizations throughout the world have been placing greater emphasis on quality and embracing concepts of continuous improvement. Such programs often are referred to as total quality management (TQM). *Total quality management* is a management system that is an integral part of an organization's strategy and is aimed at continually improving product and service quality so as to achieve high levels of customer satisfaction and build strong customer loyalty.[73] Whirlpool is trying to combine the best of the U.S. and European approaches into one integrated quality program called the Whirlpool Excellence System.

Many companies have benefited from an emphasis on TQM; however, it does require a considerable amount of companywide commitment to be successful. We, therefore, refer to quality issues in several chapters and provide extended coverage of this topic in Chapter 17 on quality and other managerial control methods. We also highlight major organizational quality efforts in Valuing Quality boxes, which appear in a number of chapters.

In this chapter, we have provided an overview of the basic challenge of management, including a forward glance at trends that are likely to influence the way managers work in the future. In the next chapter, we take a look back at the pioneering ideas that helped shape our knowledge of management today.

■ CHAPTER SUMMARY

Management is the process of achieving organizational goals by engaging in the four major functions of planning, organizing, leading, and controlling. While these functions form the basis of the managerial process, several other elements contribute to an understanding of how managers actually operate. For instance, work methods and managerial roles, as well as work agendas, feed into the management functions aimed at performance. A manager's knowledge base and management skills are also important factors in reaching targeted performance.

Mintzberg's famous study of top managers found that their work methods were characterized by an unrelenting pace, brevity, variety, fragmentation, and heavy use of verbal contacts and networks. In order to make sense of the voluminous data that he collected while observing the managers, Mintzberg isolated three major categories of roles: interpersonal, informational, and decisional. Within these categories, he identified 10 specific roles: figurehead, leader, liaison, monitor, disseminator, spokesperson, entrepreneur, disturbance handler, resource allocator, and negotiator. To a large extent, these work methods and roles are also characteristic of managers at other levels of organizations.

On the basis of his research on general managers, Kotter found that managers channel their various efforts through the use of work agendas, which are loosely connected sets of tentative goals and tasks that a manager is attempting to accomplish. Work agendas usually develop from the demands, constraints, and choices associated with a manager's job.

For managers to develop work agendas, act out roles, and engage in planning, organizing, leading, and controlling, they also need a knowledge base and key management skills. The key skills fit into three categories: technical, human, and conceptual. These skills, as well as the other elements in the management process, impact performance. Performance is made up of two important dimensions: effectiveness and efficiency. Effectiveness is the ability to choose appropriate goals and achieve them, while efficiency is the ability to make the best use of available resources in the process of achieving goals.

Managerial jobs differ according to hierarchical level (a vertical dimension) and responsibility areas (a horizontal dimension). They are generally divided into three hierarchical levels: first-line, middle, and top. Managers at these levels vary in the emphasis they place on planning, organizing, leading, and controlling. They also differ in the importance that they place on the key management skills and in the degree to which they use the different types of managerial roles. Although managers at all levels rate the entrepreneurial role as highly important, the way that they use this role to encourage innovation depends on their hierarchical level, as follows: idea champion (first-line), sponsor (middle), and orchestrator (top). In contrast, horizontal managerial job differences focus on responsibility area and involve three major types of managers: functional, general, and project.

The consensus is that it takes a combination of education and experience to be an effective manager. According to several recent informal surveys, managerial work in the future is particularly likely to be affected by an increasing need to manage change and innovation, the growing diversity of the work force, the burgeoning globalization of business, and the expanding concern with issues of quality and continuous improvement.

■ QUESTIONS FOR DISCUSSION AND REVIEW

1 Describe each of the major functions of management: planning, organizing, leading, and controlling. For a campus or other organization to which you belong, give an example of a manager engaging in each of these functions. If one or more of the functions are lacking, what are the implications?

2 List three common managerial work methods identified by Mintzberg. How could a manager misuse these work methods, to the extent that they would lead to poor performance?

3 Explain the three general types of roles and the ten specific roles that managers play. Suppose that you opened a ski-and-surf shop near campus that carries clothing, skis, and other accessories for recreation at ski resorts and beaches. Assume that you have six employees. How might you use the ten roles in managing your shop?

4 Outline three major sources of managerial work agendas. How do work agendas help managers channel their efforts toward the appropriate level of performance?

5 Contrast effectiveness and efficiency as they apply to organizational performance. What happens when you have one without the other?

6 Describe how managerial jobs vary according to hierarchical level. What are the implications for managers?

7 Outline how managers at different hierarchical levels use the entrepreneurial role. What do you think is likely to happen if the entrepreneurial role is missing from the middle or top levels of the organization?

8 Indicate how managerial jobs vary according to responsibility area. What are the implications for managers?

9 Summarize what major studies have revealed about

the management education and experience of CEOs. How can this information be helpful to beginning manager?

10 Identify the four themes mentioned in the chapter as important trends likely to influence managing in the twenty-first century. How can learning more about these trends help you become a more effective manager?

■ DISCUSSION QUESTIONS FOR CHAPTER OPENING CASE

1 What evidence of planning, organizing, leading, and controlling can you find at Hewlett-Packard?

2 Assess the degree to which technical, human, and conceptual skills are important in Platt's position. What evidence exists that he uses these skills?

3 What entrepreneurial role does Platt play? What has been the impact? What entrepreneurial role does Carolyn Ticknor play?

■ EXERCISES FOR MANAGING IN THE TWENTY-FIRST CENTURY

EXERCISE 1
SKILL BUILDING: IDENTIFYING MANAGEMENT FUNCTIONS

 You have just accepted a position as a manager of a local pizzeria. You are reviewing the management activities you will be expected to perform. You are aware that they will be part of one of the four major management functions. Indicate which function would normally include each of the activities listed in the chart at right.

EXERCISE 2
MANAGEMENT EXERCISE: PRODUCING THE NEW BINDING MACHINE

 You are a first-line supervisor in the production department of a local concern that manufactures a variety of office products, such as staplers, binders, and cellophane-tape holders. Recently, the research department developed an innovative small machine that binds reports in one easy operation. According to market research and early sales figures, the demand for the new machine (on which the company holds the patent) is expected to be strong because the machine produces good-looking reports at a very reasonable price. Because sales of the machine are already brisk, the company has decided to add a new production unit. A new first-line supervisor will be hired to head the unit.

You, your boss (who heads the production department), and a few other first-line supervisors who also report to your boss are having a working lunch in a small room off the company cafeteria. The purpose of the meeting is to discuss the basic requirements of the new job and the details that should be explained to job candidates. It is likely that many of the candidates will not have management experience and, hence, may be somewhat unfamiliar with the nature of managerial jobs.

Using your knowledge of the management process and managerial job types, list the kinds of information that the group might provide to candidates.

ACTIVITY	PLANNING	ORGANIZING	LEADING	CONTROLLING
1. Decide whether to open a second pizzeria				
2. Assign job duties				
3. Check register slips to ensure proper prices are being charged				
4. Provide incentives for employees				
5. Check that pizzas are prepared on time				
6. Decide what new menu items to offer				
7. Hire experienced cooks				
8. Determine profit margins to be achieved for the year				
9. Institute employee suggestion program				
10. Monitor that pizzeria opens, closes as scheduled				

CONCLUDING CASE 1

A DAY IN THE LIFE OF A BANK MANAGER

It is 7:15 a.m. in Hayward, California, and Marjorie Wong-Gillmore, a 32-year-old bank manager and mother of two, is driving down Highway 17. She usually arrives at the Milpitas branch of Bank of America by 8 a.m. To help plan her typically hectic day, Wong-Gillmore already has a three-page list of things to do that she prepared last night.

Deregulation of banks has increased competitive pressures and made it much more necessary for bank managers to be proactive in attracting new business. As a result, Wong-Gillmore's number-one priority is customer service—keeping current customers satisfied and signing up new ones. To bring in new customers, she tries to make visits each day to potential business clients. Unless she finds the time for such visits, she is unlikely to meet her goal of expanding the branch's business-customer base. She has already scheduled several appointments for this afternoon. One visit will be to a Chinese restaurant whose proprietor is installing a new credit card imprinter that will deposit credit slips into a Bank of America acceptance account.

Near the top of her list is a new-customer campaign that has most recently been aimed at certified public accountants. She has already sent letters to local CPAs, trying to interest them in a special type of account that lets the account holder write himself or herself a loan as needed. Now, as she fights the traffic moving toward the heart of Silicon Valley, Wong-Gillmore is thinking about follow-up phone calls.

Wong-Gillmore is also thinking about a personnel problem. One of her assistant managers, Yvonne Frechette, was recently promoted to a better job at a larger branch in nearby Sunnyvale. While she is happy for Frechette, the promotion has left the Milpitas branch with only one assistant manager instead of the usual two. The situation makes Wong-Gillmore's job much more difficult because she must absorb some of the extra work load. Hopefully, she will have a replacement soon.

As Wong-Gillmore arrives at her office, she is quickly immersed in a flurry of activities. First, she reviews her circulation file. The file contains new procedures she is to initiate at the branch, as well as information about new promotions (such as discounts on traveler's checks or incentives to open checking accounts) that must be implemented.

Next, she reviews reports from the previous day's activities. One report shows rejected debits, indicating insufficient funds. On the basis of a customer's account history, Wong-Gillmore must decide whether to cover a check or let it bounce—a task that would usually be handled by an assistant manager if the branch were not shorthanded because of Frechette's promotion.

The remaining assistant manager is busy coordinating the counting of cash deposits from the night depository. Since this is a Monday, a large number of deposits were made by business owners over the weekend. As a result, Mondays are especially busy. On other days, Wong-Gillmore holds staff meetings at 9 a.m., often to review the bank's various products, such as the seven types of checking accounts that staff members must be able to explain to customers.

At 10 a.m. the branch opens, and customers begin pouring in. During the peak time in the middle of the day, Wong-Gillmore becomes what she calls a "utility player," pitching in wherever needed. She might review loan applications, talk with customers, or handle special problems, such as the breakdown of an automated teller machine. If customer lines get particularly long, she works at a teller window. She must also sometimes deal with irate customers, who may be upset because lines are long or a mistake has been made.

Still, as much as possible, she likes to leave the operations of the branch to her assistant managers. Otherwise, she might get caught up in day-to-day problems and lose sight of her main task—getting more customers for the bank.

An added pressure is the fact that the teller lines close at 3 p.m. each day. All paper records of the day's transactions must be ready to be picked up by courier at 3:30 for transfer to the regional office.

Wong-Gillmore likes working with her staff. She says that when people do well, as Frechette did in getting promoted, "that's not only a reflection of their achievement, but a reflection of my achievement as well." Conversely, she states that when an employee does not do well, "you feel like you're failing, too." She explains, "This year we've had to let go of two or three people. That's not easy, especially when you know they're good people, and they were trying their best, but they just weren't careful enough."[74]

Note: Since this case was written, Wong-Gillmore has become vice president and commercial lending officer for Plaza Bank in San Jose.

QUESTIONS FOR CONCLUDING CASE 1

1 To what extent does Wong-Gillmore's day coincide with the managerial work methods identified by Mintzberg? What roles are evident in her activities?

2 Identify the planning, organizing, leading, and controlling functions performed by Wong-Gillmore.

3 What work agendas does she seem to have? How do technical, human, and conceptual skills come into play in her job?

CONCLUDING CASE 2

GEORGE FISHER WORKS TO TURNAROUND KODAK

George Fisher is the first outsider ever to become CEO of Rochester-based Eastman Kodak Co. Fisher was recruited in 1993 from Motorola, where he was CEO, to take the helm of the troubled photography giant. Kodak has been suffering from declining earnings, slow growth, heavy debt, and a demoralized work force.

A big part of Fisher's job is to plan a strategy for troubled Kodak. Over the years, the company had envisioned that its photographic technology might some day become outmoded and had done some preliminary work on digital images. However, many in the company were concerned that going in the digital direction would destroy Kodak's core photography business, which relies on selling film and development processes. Indeed, at this point in time, the photographic business accounts for about 90 percent of Kodak's $14 billion in revenues. Fisher, though, has painted a vision of the company as a global digital imaging leader. With digital imaging technology it will eventually be possible for consumers to take pictures, crop them, print them, and send them electronically. Fisher, who has a Ph.D. in applied mathematics, believes the photographic business will be important for years to come, but unless Kodak assumes leadership in the area of digital images, the company will eventually become technologically obsolete.

Since coming to Kodak, Fisher has been putting in 18-hour days studying every part of Kodak's business, even to the point of learning how to operate a photo finishing minilab and comparing Kodak photographic paper with the competition. Many observers say that Kodak's culture tends to support emphasis on hierarchical authority and long deliberation before taking action, a culture ill-suited to the stiff competition the company faces. Fisher is trying to change the dysfunctional culture by setting tough goals and then letting his managers decide how best to achieve them. He also sold Kodak's health- and home-products divisions and used the money to pay off a big part of Kodak's burdensome debt.

Despite his view that digital imaging technology will be an important part of Kodak's future, Fisher believes that Kodak's photographic business also has significant growth potential. He considers expansion in international markets to be particularly important. For example, he wants the company to do better in the fast-growing economies of Asia, where Kodak trails its archrival Fuji Photo. There are also major markets in Russia, India, and Brazil that offer vast potential, but have barely been tapped by Kodak. Within the United States, Kodak has been quietly growing its share of the wholesale photofinishing market through its Qualex subsidiary, which handles most of the photofinishing for large retailers, such as Wal-Mart and Kmart. This approach will likely be expanded internationally as well.

Now that Kodak has made a commitment to building strength in digital imaging, Fisher has set up a new digital division composed of various digital resources that had been spread throughout the company. He has also hired an executive from Digital Equipment Corporation to lead it. The company has also announced several product and service alliances with companies like IBM, Microsoft, and Sprint. By Kodak's own count, the company faces no fewer than 599 global competitors who are also trying to make their mark with the emerging technology.

To help break through the rigid bureaucracy and convey his message throughout the organization, Fisher has made himself more accessible than Kodak's CEOs of the recent past. He frequently visits the offices of researchers to obtain information and talks with employees in the cafeteria where he has breakfast every morning. He invites employees to send him e-mail messages and usually answers them within a day with handwritten notes on the messages his secretary prints out.

At meetings, Fisher often puts up a slide with a single word: accountability. In the past, goals would be set, but managers often missed them by a wide margin with no consequences. Now Fisher works with managers to set realistic goals, but he makes it clear that he expects them to track their progress and meet the goals. Compensation systems are being adjusted to reward managers who meet their performance goals. Fisher is particularly concerned about cycle time, the time it takes to do things like introduce new products. There still are tough times ahead. Kodak's costs are high. According to one estimate, Fuji brings in $358,000 per employee versus $144,000 for Kodak. No one knows how quickly the digital technology will overtake photographic technology. And changing the culture of a large company takes time.[75]

QUESTIONS FOR CONCLUDING CASE 2

1 Categorize each of Fisher's activities according to the four functions of management: planning, organizing, leading, and controlling.
2 Which of Mintzberg's roles are apparent in Fisher's activities?
3 Point to evidence that Fisher possesses technical, human, and conceptual skills. To what extent do you believe Fisher's efforts at Kodak will be successful? Give your reasoning.

CHAPTER TWO

PIONEERING IDEAS IN MANAGEMENT

CHAPTER OUTLINE

The Birth of Management Ideas
The Evolution of Management Theories
Preclassical Contributors

Classical Viewpoint
Scientific Management
Bureaucratic Management
Administrative Management

Behavioral Viewpoint
Early Behaviorists
Hawthorne Studies
Human Relations Movement
Behavioral Science Approach

Quantitative Management Viewpoint
Management Science
Operations Management
Management Information Systems

Contemporary Viewpoints
Systems Theory
Contingency Theory
Emerging Views

Promoting Innovation: Contributions of the Major Viewpoints

LEARNING OBJECTIVES

After studying this chapter, you should be able to:

■ Identify several early innovative management practices and explain the basic evolution of management theories.

■ Trace the preclassical contributions to the field of management.

■ Explain the major approaches within the classical viewpoint of management.

■ Describe the major developments contributing to the establishment of the behavioral viewpoint.

■ Explain the major approaches within the quantitative management viewpoint.

■ Discuss the relevance of systems theory and contingency theory to the field of management.

■ Explain how management in Japan has influenced the emerging Theory Z viewpoint of management.

■ Explain how current knowledge about management is the result of innovative processes involving many management pioneers.

GAINING THE EDGE

HENRY FORD PUTS PIONEERING IDEAS TO WORK

Henry Ford, founder of the Ford Motor Company, was born to successful Michigan farmers, Mary and William Ford, on July 30, 1863. The young Ford showed an early interest in mechanical things and was repairing watches by the age of 7. At age 16, Henry left the farm to complete an apprenticeship as a mechanic. After several jobs, in 1891, Henry accepted a position as a mechanic with the Detroit Illuminating Company and soon became head engineer. This job gave him some time to think about building an automobile.

When not working at his job, Henry was building his first car, which was completed in 1896. It was called a Quadricycle and looked like two bicycles held together by an engine. The car demonstrated that his gasoline engine could be used successfully to power a multipurpose vehicle. An improved Quadricycle, produced 3 years later, brought financial backers. His first company, the Detroit Automobile Company, was formed in 1899. Unfortunately, it was dissolved a year and a half later after disputes between Henry, who wanted to perfect his car, and the backers, who were interested in mass production.

During the next year, Henry produced another improved car, which won a major U.S. auto race. A new group of backers provided money for a new company, the Henry Ford Company, in November 1901. Within 4 months, Henry was ousted, again because he preferred working on his racing cars to producing automobiles for public consumption. As his part of the settlement, he received $900, the blueprints for his next racing car, and the agreement that the firm could no longer use his name. However, unlike his first company, this organization remained in business, taking a new name, Cadillac. Eight years later, the Cadillac Company joined with the Buick and Olds companies to become the fledgling General Motors Corporation.

Henry's next racing car won another major race in October 1902. A new wave of investors came forth with money to found the Ford Motor Company. This time, Henry was more attentive to the business of producing automobiles and, within 3 years, would buy out the other stockholders. In 1903, the company introduced the Model A Ford into a receptive market. Several other mod-

Henry Ford is standing between his first car, the Quadricycle, and the 10 millionth Model T car off the production line. Ford Motor Company was able to produce cars in such great numbers because Henry Ford had made a thorough study of scientific management techniques and used these ideas to develop the mechanized assembly line at his plant.

els soon followed, perhaps the most famous being the Model T Ford, introduced in 1908. Priced at $825, the Model T generated a demand in the thousands, but the manufacturing process was not geared to producing such large numbers of cars.

New manufacturing methods were needed, and Henry became a student of the modern management methods that were emerging at the time. For example, he was familiar with the work of Frederick Taylor, the driving force behind the new principles of scientific management and the use of time-and-motion studies to increase job efficiency. Legend has it that Henry Ford also visited the Sears mail-order plant in Chicago, where he witnessed a mass-production facility with an assembly line, a conveyor belt, standardized and interchangeable parts, and plantwide production scheduling. Henry believed that production efficiency could be increased through both the use of scientific management methods and the judicious use of machines.

By combining these pioneering ideas, Henry Ford established his famous mechanized assembly line in the Highland Park plant in 1913. The average time for assembling a motor and chassis dropped from 12½ hours to 93 minutes. The number of workers required to assemble a car also dropped dramatically. Although Ford was a mechanical wizard and an insightful entrepreneur, he did have his darker side. While at first Ford treated his workers well, he later installed Harry Bennett as head of the infamous Ford Service Department. Gradually Bennett resorted to intimidation and even violence against workers in the quest to maintain control over production. Nevertheless, because of Henry Ford's inventiveness, world transportation, manufacturing, and management were never the same. Henry's innovative use of the latest management ideas of his time set the stage for the Ford Motor Company to become one of America's largest corporations.[1]   ■■■

Imagine inventing a highly desirable product but having difficulty producing it in the quantities required. In devising a solution to this problem, Ford made use of scientific management, the most advanced management approach of his day. Throughout this book, we discuss leading-edge approaches to management. Still, as the case of Henry Ford illustrates, new ideas do not typically arise in a vacuum. More frequently, they emerge from a foundation of the best available ideas that have been developed over a period of time, as well as recognition of the shortcomings of those ideas.

Thus, in this chapter, we explore the birth of management ideas. We briefly examine the pioneering approaches of several preclassical contributors, individuals who predated modern management thinking but helped lay some initial groundwork. We consider the tenets of scientific management, the approach that heavily influenced Henry Ford, and also take a look at other important perspectives that fit under the umbrella of the classical management viewpoint. Next, we analyze each of the three other major management viewpoints: the behavioral, quantitative, and contemporary perspectives. Finally, we summarize the innovative contributions of the major viewpoints as they relate to modern management.

■ THE BIRTH OF MANAGEMENT IDEAS

The Evolution of Management Theories

Although examples of management practice go back several thousand years, the development of management as a field of knowledge is much more recent.

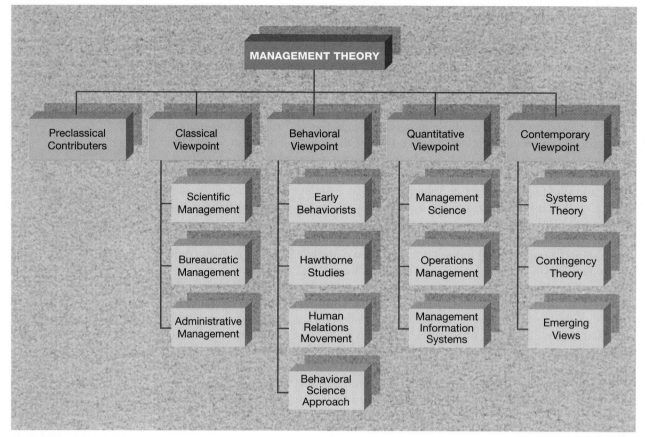

Figure 2-1 *Major viewpoints in the development of modern management.*

Much of the impetus for developing management theories and principles stemmed from the industrial revolution, which spawned the growth of factories in the early 1800s. With the proliferation of factories came the widespread need to coordinate the efforts of large numbers of people in the continual production of goods.

This challenge brought forth a number of individuals who began to think about innovative ways to run factories more effectively. This group, known as the preclassical contributors to management (see Figure 2-1), focused largely on particular techniques that might be applied to solve specific problems. They were followed by individuals who began to develop broader principles and theories that became the bases of major viewpoints, or schools, of management: classical, behavioral, quantitative, and contemporary. Several approaches have contributed to the development of each of these viewpoints (see Figure 2-1). We examine them in later sections of this chapter after we first focus briefly on the preclassical contributors.

Preclassical Contributors

A number of individuals in the preclassical period of the middle and late 1800s offered ideas that laid the groundwork for subsequent, broader inquiries into the nature of management. Among the principal preclassical contributors are Robert Owen, Charles Babbage, and Henry R. Towne (see Table 2-1).

ROBERT OWEN A successful British entrepreneur, Robert Owen (1771–1858) was well ahead of his time in recognizing the importance of human resources.

He became particularly interested in the working and living conditions of his employees while running a cotton mill in New Lanark, Scotland. As was common, the mill employed 400 to 500 young children, who worked 13-hour days that included 1½ hours off for meals. Although his business partners resisted some of his ideas, Owen tried to improve the living conditions of the employees by upgrading streets, houses, sanitation, and the educational system in New Lanark. At the time, Owen was considered to be a radical, but today his views are widely accepted. His ideas laid the groundwork for the human relations movement, which is discussed later in this chapter.[2]

CHARLES BABBAGE English mathematician Charles Babbage (1792–1871) is widely known as "the father of modern computing." His projects produced the world's first practical mechanical calculator and an "analytical engine" that had the basic elements of a modern-day computer.[3] Difficulties in directing his various projects, however, led him to explore new ways of doing things. In the process, he made direct contributions to management theory.

Charles Babbage, a 19th century English mathematician, pioneered not only in the field of computing but also in management. He saw that work specialization could apply to mental tasks as well as physical ones, and he devised ways to motivate workers through bonuses and profit sharing.

Babbage was enthralled with the idea of *work specialization,* the degree to which work is divided into various jobs. (Work specialization is discussed further in Chapter 8.) He recognized that not only physical work but mental work as well could be specialized.[4] In this sense, he foresaw the prospect of specialists, such as accountants who limit their practice to either personal or corporate taxes.

Babbage also devised a profit-sharing plan that had two parts, a bonus that was awarded for useful suggestions and a portion of wages that was dependent on factory profits. His ideas foreshadowed some modern-day group incentive plans, such as the Scanlon Plan, in which workers offer suggestions to improve productivity and then share in the resulting profits.

HENRY R. TOWNE President of the Yale and Towne Manufacturing Company and a mechanical engineer, Henry R. Towne (1844–1924) articulated the need to consider management as a separate field of *systematic* inquiry on a par with engineering. He outlined his views in a landmark paper titled "The Engineer as an Economist," which was delivered in 1886 to the American Society of Mechanical Engineers in Chicago. He observed that although good engineering skills and good business skills were rarely combined in the same individual, both skills were needed to run an organization effectively. Accordingly, the paper called for the establishment of a science of management and the development of principles that could be applied across management situations. Although the engineering society itself did not become a major force in developing knowledge about management, one of the people who attended Towne's presentation, Frederick Taylor, was subsequently instrumental in building the management field.[5]

Henry Towne realized the importance of both good business skills and good engineering skills in running a company. He called for studying management as a science and developing systematic principles that could be used in all types of management situations.

TABLE 2-1 THE PRECLASSICAL CONTRIBUTORS AND THEIR PIONEERING IDEAS

CONTRIBUTOR	PIONEERING IDEAS
Robert Owen	Advocated concern for the working and living conditions of workers
Charles Babbage	Built the first practical mechanical calculator and a prototype of modern computers; predicted the specialization of mental work; suggested profit sharing
Henry R. Towne	Outlined the importance of management as a science and called for the development of management principles

ASSESSING THE PRECLASSICAL CONTRIBUTORS Although the early pioneers explored several different avenues relating to management, their efforts were somewhat fragmentary. They were largely oriented toward developing specific techniques, often to solve visible problems. For example, to prevent meetings from becoming disorderly, Henry Robert produced *Robert's Rules of Order,* a publication of the preclassical era that is still used today to run many large, formal meetings (see the Case in Point discussion).

CASE IN POINT **ROBERT'S RULES BRING ORDER**

During the late 1800s, when Henry Martyn Robert, a brigadier general in the U.S. Army, was pursuing his military career as a civil engineer, he frequently attended meetings with people from many backgrounds. Often he had to preside at these meetings.

He quickly learned about the challenge of running meetings when the first meeting over which he presided, involving a group of Baptist ministers, ended in total chaos. Robert was perplexed because nothing was settled or resolved. He had prepared his subject well and had even gathered advice on how to conduct a meeting. He decided that he would never again participate in such a disastrous encounter.

For the next 7 years, he collected information concerning how to conduct a meeting, and he subsequently produced a 176-page book titled *Pocket Manual of Rules of Order for Deliberative Assemblies.* The book provided a set of parliamentary rules for conducting meetings.

He promoted the book, which he had published on his own, by sending 1000 copies to the best parliamentarians in the United States, including governors, legislators, the vice president, and a few attorneys, and he asked the recipients for their comments. After receiving many enthusiastic responses and several very good suggestions, he modified the original text, changing the title to *Robert's Rules of Order.* The book has become a classic source of guidance for running large, formal meetings and is used by many legislative bodies, government councils, associations, and other organizations in which decisions are made by member vote. First published in 1876, the book has not been out of print since. More than 4 million copies have been sold throughout the English-speaking world. It has also been published in Braille.[6] ■■■

Since they generally came from technical backgrounds, the early pioneers did not tend to think in terms of management as a separate field—that is, until Towne presented his influential paper. Still, they were important innovators who laid the groundwork for other major management thinkers who came after them. Their forward-looking ideas have endured the test of time.

■ CLASSICAL VIEWPOINT

Classical viewpoint A perspective on management that emphasizes finding ways to manage work and organizations more efficiently

Henry Towne's call for establishing management as a separate field of inquiry helped usher in a major new approach called the classical viewpoint. The **classical viewpoint** is a perspective on management that emphasizes finding ways to manage work and organizations more efficiently. It is made up of three different approaches: scientific management, administrative management, and bureaucratic management. This viewpoint is labeled "classical" because it encompasses early works and related contributions that have formed the main roots of the field of management.[7]

Scientific Management

Scientific management is an approach within classical management theory that emphasizes the scientific study of work methods in order to improve worker efficiency. Major representatives of this approach include Frederick Winslow Taylor, Frank and Lillian Gilbreth, and Henry Gantt.

FREDERICK WINSLOW TAYLOR Frederick Winslow Taylor (1856–1915) is known as "the father of scientific management." Born into a relatively wealthy Philadelphia family, Taylor became an apprentice pattern maker and machinist for a local firm before moving on to Midvale Steel. At Midvale, his meteoric rise from laborer to chief engineer in 6 years gave him an opportunity to tackle a serious problem that he had observed—soldiering by workers.[8] **Soldiering** is deliberately working at less than full capacity. Taylor believed that workers engaged in soldiering for three main reasons. First, they feared that increasing their productivity would cause them or other workers to lose their jobs. Second, faulty wage systems set up by management encouraged workers to operate at a slow pace. For example, some companies cut incentive pay when workers began to exceed standards, thus making workers reluctant to excel. Third, general methods of working and rules of thumb handed down from generation to generation were often very inefficient.

Taylor believed that managers could resolve the soldiering problem by developing a *science* of management based on the four principles summarized in Table 2-2. Central to the approach was the concept of using scientific means to determine how tasks should be done rather than relying on the past experience of each individual worker. Specifically, Taylor pioneered a method now known as the *time-and-motion study* (Taylor called it a time study). This type of study involves breaking down the work task into its various elements, or motions, eliminating unnecessary motions, determining the best way to do the job, and then timing each motion to determine the amount of production that could be expected per day (with allowances for delays and rest periods).[9]

In order to solve the problem of wage systems that encouraged soldiering, Taylor advocated the use of wage incentive plans. He argued that workers should be paid from 30 to 100 percent higher wages for using the scientifically developed work methods and for attaining daily standards.[10]

A famous study by Taylor at Bethlehem Steel focused on shoveling. Until Taylor introduced scientific management, workers typically brought their own tools to the job. Taylor noted that a worker might use the same shovel for both iron ore and ashes, even though the relative weights of the materials were very different. On the basis of his studies, Taylor determined that the optimum weight for shoveling was 21 pounds. Therefore, he argued that it made sense

Frederick Taylor took up Henry Towne's challenge to develop specific principles of scientific management. His ideas included time and motion studies and wage incentives. While his methods did achieve greater productivity and work efficiency, some observers criticized Taylor for "exploiting" workers to get them to produce more.

Scientific management An approach that emphasizes the scientific study of work methods in order to improve worker efficiency

Soldiering Deliberately working at less than full capacity

TABLE 2-2 TAYLOR'S FOUR PRINCIPLES OF SCIENTIFIC MANAGEMENT

1. Scientifically study each part of a task and develop the best method for performing the task.
2. Carefully select workers and train them to perform the task by using the scientifically developed method.
3. Cooperate fully with workers to ensure that they use the proper method.
4. Divide work and responsibility so that management is responsible for planning work methods using scientific principles and workers are responsible for executing the work accordingly.

to have shovels of different sizes for different classes of materials so that the weight of what was being shoveled would be about 21 pounds. Results of implementing his plan with company-owned shovels demonstrated that the average number of tons shoveled per worker per day increased from 16 to 59. At the same time the average earnings per worker per day increased from $1.15 to $1.88, and the average cost of handling a long ton (2240 pounds) decreased from $0.072 to $0.033. Taylor's plan included additional incentive pay for workers and was beneficial for the company.[11] Taylor ran into opposition from some members of management, citizens of Bethlehem, and others who argued that he was exploiting workers by getting them to produce more and causing large reductions in the work force of Bethlehem Steel.

A strike at the Watertown (Massachusetts) Army Arsenal (1911–1912), where some of Taylor's ideas were being tested, led to a congressional investigation. The results of the investigation concluded that there was not any concrete evidence that workers were being abused in any way by "Taylorism." Still, the negative publicity slowed the momentum of scientific management to some degree.[12] Nonetheless, by the end of World War I scientific management, aided by several French management experts, was spreading throughout Europe and was being used in such diverse places as English chocolate factories, Icelandic fisheries, German paper mills, and Swedish typewriter factories.[13]

There is little doubt that the innovative ideas that Taylor popularized remain in use today. As we will see in Chapter 8, the use of scientific management can sometimes make jobs overspecialized, often resulting in worker resentment, monotony, poor quality, absenteeism, and turnover.

THE GILBRETHS Other major advocates of scientific management were the husband and wife team of Frank (1868–1924) and Lillian (1878–1972) Gilbreth. Although Frank had qualified for admission to the Massachusetts Institute of Technology, he decided to become a bricklayer because of the importance of the profession at the time. As Frank became involved in training young bricklayers, he noticed the inefficiencies that were handed down from experienced workers.

To remedy the situation, he proposed using motion studies to streamline the bricklaying process. Frank also designed special scaffolding for different types of jobs and devised precise directions for mortar consistency. On the basis of these and other ideas, Frank was able to reduce the motions involved in bricklaying from 18½ to 4. Using his approach, workers increased the number of bricks laid per day from 1000 to 2700 with no increase in physical exertion.[14]

Meanwhile, Frank married Lillian Moller, who began working with him on projects while she completed her doctorate in psychology. The two continued their studies aimed at eliminating unnecessary motions and expanded their interests to exploring ways of reducing task fatigue. Part of their work involved the isolation of 17 basic motions, each called a *therblig* ("Gilbreth" spelled backward, with the "t" and "h" reversed). Therbligs included such motions as select, position, and hold—motions that the Gilbreths used to study tasks in a number of industries. The Gilbreths also pioneered the use of motion picture technology in studying jobs.[15]

Lillian's doctoral thesis, published as the book *The Psychology of Management,* was one of the early works applying the findings of psychology to the workplace.[16] At the insistence of the publisher, the author was listed as L. M. Gilbreth to disguise the fact that the book was written by a woman. She also had a particular interest in the human implications of scientific management, arguing that the purpose of scientific management is to help people reach their maximum potential by developing their skills and abilities.[17]

In 1924, Frank died suddenly of a heart attack, leaving Lillian with their

Frank and Lillian Gilbreth are shown with 11 of their dozen children. Two of the children wrote a book, Cheaper by the Dozen, *that describes life with their efficiency-minded parents. For example, their father would use two shaving brushes at once to put shaving cream on his face, thereby saving 17 seconds. He found that shaving with two razors took 44 seconds less time than it did with one razor. Unfortunately, it took 2 minutes to apply bandages to the resulting cuts. His children reported that the loss of 2 minutes, not the cuts, made him abandon the two-razor approach.*

dozen children, ranging in age from 2 to 19. She then continued the couple's innovative studies and consulting work, finally becoming a professor of management at Purdue University.[18] Lillian Gilbreth ranks as the first woman to gain prominence as a major contributor to the development of management as a science.

HENRY L. GANTT One of Taylor's closest associates was Henry Gantt (1861–1919), who worked with Taylor in several companies, including Midvale Steel and Bethlehem Steel.[19] Gantt later became an independent consultant and made several contributions of his own. The most well known is the *Gantt chart,* a graphic aid to planning, scheduling, and control that is still in use today. (An example of a Gantt chart is given in the Supplement to Chapter 5.) He also devised a unique pay incentive system that not only paid workers extra for reaching standard in the allotted time but also awarded bonuses to supervisors when workers reached standard. Thus the system encouraged supervisors to coach workers who were having difficulties.

Bureaucratic Management

Another branch of the classical viewpoint is **bureaucratic management,** an approach that emphasizes the need for organizations to operate in a rational manner rather than relying on the arbitrary whims of owners and managers. The bureaucratic management approach is based mainly on the work of prominent German sociologist Max Weber.

Weber (1864–1920) was born into an affluent family with strong political and social connections.[20] He pursued a career as a consultant, professor, and author. Among his most important contributions to the discipline of management are his ideas on the need for organizations to operate on a more rational basis.

In formulating his ideas, Weber was reacting to the prevailing norms of class consciousness and nepotism. For example, it was customary practice to allow only individuals of aristocratic birth to become officers in the Prussian Army or to attain high-level positions in government and industry. Weber felt that the situation not only was unfair but also led to a significant waste of

Bureaucratic management
An approach that emphasizes the need for organizations to operate in a rational manner rather than relying on the arbitrary whims of owners and managers

This time-exposure photograph taken by Frank Gilbreth shows the motions necessary to move and file 16 boxes full of glass. Such time-and-motion studies were used to increase efficiency in the workplace.

TABLE 2-3 MAJOR CHARACTERISTICS OF WEBER'S IDEAL BUREAUCRACY

CHARACTERISTIC	DESCRIPTION
Specialization of labor	Jobs are broken down into routine, well-defined tasks so that members know what is expected of them and can become extremely competent at their particular subset of tasks.
Formal rules and procedures	Written rules and procedures specifying the behaviors desired from members facilitate coordination and ensure uniformity.
Impersonality	Rules, procedures, and sanctions are applied uniformly regardless of individual personalities and personal considerations.
Well-defined hierarchy	Multiple levels of positions, with carefully determined reporting relationships among levels, provide supervision of lower offices by higher ones, a means of handling exceptions, and the ability to establish accountability of actions.
Career advancement based on merit	Selection and promotion is based on the qualifications and performance of members.

human resources. He also believed that running organizations on the basis of *whom* one knows rather than *what* one knows and engaging in nepotism (the hiring of relatives regardless of their competence) tended to interfere with organizational effectiveness.

In an effort to visualize how the large organizations evolving out of the industrial revolution might ideally operate, Weber formulated characteristics of the "ideal bureaucracy" (see Table 2-3). He coined the term "bureaucracy" (based on the German *büro*, meaning "office") to identify large organizations that operated on a rational basis. Weber understood clearly that his ideal bureaucracy did not actually exist. In fact, he never intended that his ideas be used as guidelines for managers. Rather, his purpose was to develop ideas that could be used as a starting point in understanding such organizations.[21] However, when his work was translated into English in the late 1940s, many U.S. management scholars used his ideas as a guide to how organizations could be more effectively managed.

Because of the possibility of carrying Weber's ideas to excess, the term "bureaucracy" is sometimes used in a pejorative sense to denote red tape and excessive rules. Yet there clearly are advantages to the bureaucratic characteristics outlined by Weber. For example, recent troubles at family-owned U-Haul can be traced to confusion over roles, secret meetings of the board of directors, hidden rule changes, and advancement determined by family ties—all violations of Weber's ideal. The resulting feuds and court battles among family members are seriously threatening the viability of the national renter of trucks, trailers, and other equipment.[22]

Administrative Management

Administrative management
An approach that focuses on principles that can be used by managers to coordinate the internal activities of organizations

While the advocates of scientific management concentrated on developing principles that could be used to help organize individual worker tasks more effectively and Weber struggled with the concept of bureaucracy, another branch within the classical viewpoint was also developing. The **administrative management** approach focuses on principles that can be used by managers to coordinate the internal activities of organizations. Major contributors include Henri Fayol and Chester Barnard, both of whom were executives of large enterprises.

HENRI FAYOL French industrialist Henri Fayol (1841–1925) was born into a middle-class family near Lyon, France.[23] Trained as a mining engineer, he joined a coal-and-iron combine as an apprentice and rose to the top position of managing director in 1888. He accomplished the arduous task of moving the company out of severe financial difficulties and into a strong position by the time of his retirement at age 77. The company survives today as part of LeCreusot-Loire, a large mining and metallurgical group in central France.

On the basis of his experiences as a top-level manager, Fayol was convinced that it should be possible to develop theories about management that could then be taught to individuals with administrative responsibilities. His efforts toward developing such theories were published in a monograph titled *General and Industrial Management.*

Fayol attempted to isolate the main types of activities involved in industry or business. Within the category of "managerial activities," he delineated five major functions: planning, organizing, commanding, coordinating, and controlling. Thinking of management as encompassing these functions is known as the *functional* approach to management. You have probably noticed the similarity between Fayol's functions and the four functions of management (planning, organizing, leading, and controlling) used as the framework for this book. Many contemporary books on management use a form of the functional approach that has roots in Fayol's work.

Fayol also outlined a number of principles (see Table 2-4) that he found useful in running his large coal-and-iron concern. Although contemporary research has found exceptions to his principles under some conditions (which

The functional approach to management—focusing on major managerial activities— owes much to the pioneering work of Henri Fayol, a French industrialist.

TABLE 2-4 FAYOL'S GENERAL PRINCIPLES OF MANAGEMENT

1. *Division of work.* Work specialization can result in efficiencies and is applicable to both managerial and technical functions. Yet there are limitations to how much that work should be divided.

2. *Authority.* Authority is the right to give orders and the power to exact obedience. It derives from the formal authority of the office and from personal authority based on factors like intelligence and experience. With authority comes responsibility.

3. *Discipline.* Discipline is absolutely necessary for the smooth running of an organization, but the state of discipline depends essentially on the worthiness of its leaders.

4. *Unity of command.* An employee should receive orders from one superior only.

5. *Unity of direction.* Activities aimed at the same objective should be organized so that there is one plan and one person in charge.

6. *Subordination of individual interest to general interest.* The interests of one employee or group should not prevail over the interests and goals of the organization.

7. *Remuneration.* Compensation should be fair to both the employee and the employer.

8. *Centralization.* The proper amount of centralization or decentralization depends on the situation. The objective is the optimum use of the capabilities of personnel.

9. *Scalar chain.* A scalar (hierarchical) chain of authority extends from the top to the bottom of an organization and defines the communication path. However, horizontal communication is also encouraged as long as the managers in the chain are kept informed.

10. *Order.* Materials should be kept in well-chosen places that facilitate activities. Similarly, due to good organization and selection, the right person should be in the right place.

11. *Equity.* Employees should be treated with kindness and justice.

12. *Stability of personnel tenure.* Because time is required to become effective in new jobs, high turnover should be prevented.

13. *Initiative.* Managers should encourage and develop subordinate initiative to the fullest.

14. *Esprit de corps.* Since union is strength, harmony and teamwork are essential.

Source: Adapted from Henri Fayol, *General and Industrial Management,* Constance Storrs (trans.), Pitman & Sons, Ltd., London, 1949, pp. 19–42.

Chester Barnard's acceptance theory of authority holds that authority flows from the bottom to the top. How much authority managers wield depends to a large extent on the willingness of employees to accept the directives of managers. Thus, managers should communicate their requirements in a way that takes the feelings and capabilities of employees into account.

Acceptance theory of authority A theory that argues that authority does not depend as much on "persons of authority" who *give* orders as on the willingness to comply of those who *receive* the orders

Behavioral viewpoint A perspective on management that emphasizes the importance of attempting to understand the various factors that affect human behavior in organizations

will be discussed in later chapters), the principles are generally in widespread use today.

CHESTER BARNARD Another major contributor to administrative management was Chester Barnard (1886–1961). Born in Massachusetts, he attended Harvard but did not complete his degree work.[24] After joining AT&T as a statistician, he rose rapidly and was named president of the New Jersey Bell Telephone Company in 1927. Barnard recorded his observations about effective administration in a single classic book, *The Functions of the Executive,* published in 1938.

One of Barnard's best-known contributions is his **acceptance theory of authority.** This theory argues that authority does not depend as much on "persons of authority" who *give* orders as on the willingness to comply of those who *receive* the orders. Thus, in Barnard's view, it is really the employees who decide whether or not to accept orders and directions from above. From a practical point of view, Barnard felt that managers are generally able to exert authority on a day-to-day basis because each individual possesses a "zone of indifference" within which the individual is willing to accept orders and directions without much question.

On the basis of his view that authority flows from the bottom to the top, Barnard argued that employees are more willing to accept directions from a manager if they (1) understand the communication, (2) see the communication as consistent with the purposes of the organization, (3) feel that the actions indicated are in line with their needs and those of other employees, and (4) view themselves as mentally and physically able to comply.

Barnard helped integrate concern with authority, which was growing out of the administrative and bureaucratic approaches, with emphasis on worker needs, which was simultaneously developing within the behavioral viewpoint. He also knew of the early behaviorists and the Hawthorne studies, which were a primary force in the development of the behavioral viewpoint, to which we turn next.[25]

■ BEHAVIORAL VIEWPOINT

The classical theorists generally viewed individuals as mechanisms of production. As a result, they were primarily interested in finding ways for organizations to use these productive mechanisms more efficiently. Barnard's views notwithstanding, the idea that an employee's behavior might be influenced by internal reactions to various aspects of the job situation was generally not seen as particularly relevant to the quest for greater efficiency. In contrast, the **behavioral viewpoint** is a perspective that emphasizes the importance of attempting to understand the various factors that affect human behavior in organizations. In exploring this viewpoint, we examine four aspects of its development: the contributions of the early behaviorists, the Hawthorne studies, the human relations movement, and the more contemporary behavioral science approach.

Early Behaviorists

With the growing interest in the subject of management, individuals from other backgrounds began to offer alternatives to the emphasis on engineering that characterized the scientific management approach. Two early behaviorists, psychologist Hugo Münsterberg and political scientist Mary Parker Follett, contributed pioneering ideas that helped make the behavioral perspective a major viewpoint.

HUGO MÜNSTERBERG Born and educated in Germany, Hugo Münsterberg (1863–1916) earned both a Ph.D. in psychology and a medical degree. In 1892, he set up a psychological laboratory at Harvard and began seeking practical applications of psychology. Before long, his attention turned to industrial applications, leading him to publish an important book, *Psychology and Industrial Efficiency*, which appeared in 1913. The book argued that psychologists could help industry in three major ways. The first was closely allied to scientific management: psychologists could study jobs and find ways of identifying the individuals who are best suited to particular jobs. According to Münsterberg, the second way that psychologists could help industry was by identifying the psychological conditions under which individuals are likely to do their best work. The third was by developing strategies that would influence employees to behave in ways that are compatible with management interests. The ideas and examples he provided ignited the imagination of others and led to the establishment of the field of *industrial psychology*, the study of human behavior in a work setting. Thus, Münsterberg is considered to be "the father of industrial psychology."[26]

Hugo Münsterberg, a German psychologist, pioneered in the field of industrial psychology. He was especially interested in identifying the conditions that would promote an individual's best work and in finding ways to influence workers to act in accord with management interests.

MARY PARKER FOLLETT Another well-known early behaviorist was Mary Parker Follett (1868–1933). Born in Boston and educated in political science at what is now Radcliffe College, Follett was a social worker who became interested in employment and workplace issues.

Follett attributed much greater significance to the functioning of groups in organizations than proponents of the classical view of management. She argued that members of organizations are continually influenced by the groups within which they operate. In fact, she held that groups have the capacity to exercise control over themselves and their own activities, a concept that is compatible with the recent interest in self-managing teams in American business (see Chapter 15). For example, at General Motors' Saturn plant, most of the work is done by teams that have no traditional boss.[27]

Another of Follett's forward-looking ideas was her belief that organizations should operate on the principle of "power with" rather than "power over." Power, to her, was the general ability to influence and bring about change. She argued that power should be a jointly developed, cooperative concept, involving employees and managers working together, rather than a coercive concept based on hierarchical pressure. Although her views probably influenced Barnard's acceptance theory of authority, Follett advocated sharing power whereas Barnard emphasized encouraging the appropriate response from below.[28]

Follett suggested that one way to foster the "power with" concept was by resolving conflict through integration. By *integration* she meant the process of finding a solution that would satisfy both parties. She cited an example involving a dairy cooperative that almost disbanded because of a controversy over the pecking order in unloading milk cans. The creamery was located on the downgrade of a hill, and members who came downhill and those who came uphill both thought they should be given precedence in unloading. The situation was at an impasse until an outsider pointed out that the position of the loading dock could be changed so that both groups could unload their cans at the same time. Follett noted, "Integration involves invention, and the clever thing is to

Mary Parker Follett, an early behaviorist, focused on group dynamics in her work and writings. Her ideas on power sharing, conflict resolution, and the integration of organizational systems were far in advance of their time.

recognize this, and not to let one's thinking stay within the boundaries of two alternatives that are mutually exclusive."[29] Her ideas on integration heralded modern methods of conflict resolution (see Chapter 15).

Follett placed great importance on achieving what she called *integrative unity*, whereby the organization would operate as a functional whole, with the various interrelated parts working together effectively to achieve organizational goals. Yet she saw the process of working together as a dynamic process because environmental factors would necessitate change. As we will see, her ideas anticipated the systems viewpoint of management.[30] One contemporary reviewer of her work has argued that its overall significance "rivals the long-standing influence of such giants as Taylor and Fayol."[31] A new book of her writings was recently published by Harvard Business School Press.[32]

Hawthorne Studies

Hawthorne studies A group of studies conducted at the Hawthorne plant of the Western Electric Company during the late 1920s and early 1930s whose results ultimately led to the human relations view of management

While Follett was doing her speaking and writing, a number of researchers were involved in the Hawthorne studies. The **Hawthorne studies** are a group of studies conducted at the Hawthorne plant of the Western Electric Company during the late 1920s and early 1930s whose results ultimately led to the human relations view of management, a behavioral approach that emphasized concern for the worker. To understand their significance, we need to trace the studies from their beginning.

When they started, the Hawthorne studies reflected the scientific management tradition of seeking greater efficiency by improving the tools and methods of work—in this case, lighting. The General Electric Company wanted to sell more lightbulbs, so, along with other electric companies, it supported studies on the relationship between lighting and productivity that were to be conducted by the National Research Council. The tests were to be held at the Hawthorne Works (Chicago) of the Western Electric Company, an equipment-producing subsidiary of AT&T.[33] Ultimately, three sets of studies were done.

FIRST SET OF STUDIES The first set of studies, called the Illumination Studies, took place between 1924 and 1927 under the direction of several engineers. In one of these studies, light was decreased over successive periods for the experimental group (the group for whom the lighting was altered), while light was held at a constant level for the control group (a comparison group working in a separate area). In both groups, performance rose steadily, even though the lighting for the experimental group became so dim that the workers complained that they could hardly see. At that point, performance in the experimental group finally began to decline (see Figure 2-2). The researchers concluded that factors other than lighting were at work (since performance rose in both groups), and the project was discontinued.[34] In retrospect, one possibility based on the records of the studies is that the experimental and control groups were in contact and may have begun competing with each other.

SECOND SET OF STUDIES Intrigued with the positive changes in productivity, some of the engineers and company officials decided to attempt to determine the causes through further studies. Accordingly, a second set of experiments took place between 1927 and 1933. The most famous study involved five women who assembled electrical relays in the Relay Assembly Test Room, where they were away from other workers and the researchers could alter work conditions and evaluate the results. Before the study began, the researchers were apparently concerned about possible negative reactions from the workers who would

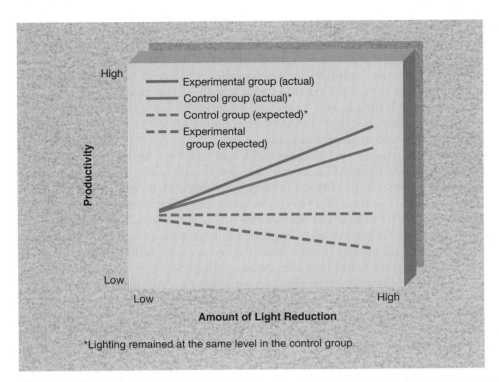

*Lighting remained at the same level in the control group.

Figure 2-2 *Actual versus expected results for the experimental and control groups in one of the Hawthorne Illumination Studies.*

be included in the experiment. To lessen potential resistance, the researchers changed the usual supervisory arrangement so that there would be no official supervisor. Instead, the workers would operate under the general direction of the experimenters. The workers were also given special privileges, such as being able to leave their workstation without permission, and they received considerable attention from the experimenters and company officials.[35] The study was aimed at exploring the best combination of work and rest periods, but a number of other factors were also varied (sometimes simultaneously), such as pay, length of workday, and provisions for free lunches. Generally, productivity increased over the period of the study, regardless of how the factors under consideration were manipulated.[36]

One of the Hawthorne studies monitored for several years the productivity of five women (shown here) who assembled electrical relays. Researchers found that regardless of what working conditions they manipulated, the women still increased their productivity over the period. Later researchers concluded that the major reason for the rise in productivity was a change in supervisory arrangements that had been made to facilitate the experiments and that was not part of the experimental manipulations.

A Harvard University research group (involved in assessing the results) ultimately concluded that the change in the supervisory arrangement was the major reason for the increase in productivity in the Relay Assembly Test Room study and in two related studies involving different work groups. The researchers felt that the physical changes, such as rest periods, free lunches, and shortened hours, as well as the group incentive pay plans, were factors of lesser importance (largely because adverse changes in some of these factors did not seem to decrease performance).

Since the supervisory arrangement had been set up by the researchers before the study began, this change was not actually part of the study manipulations and was not intended to affect the results. One outcome of the studies was the identification of a famous concept that ultimately came to be known as the Hawthorne effect. The **Hawthorne effect** is the possibility that individuals singled out for a study may improve their performance simply because of the added attention they receive from the researchers, rather than because of any specific factors being tested in the study.[37]

Hawthorne effect The possibility that individuals singled out for a study may improve their performance simply because of the added attention they receive from the researchers, rather than because of any specific factors being tested

More contemporary investigations now suggest that the Hawthorne-effect concept is too simplistic to explain what happened during the Hawthorne studies and that the concept itself is defective. It now appears likely that the results obtained at the Hawthorne plant stemmed from the fact that the workers interpreted what was going on around them differently from the researchers (rather than from the idea that the workers reacted positively simply because of attention from the researchers). The workers most likely viewed the altered supervision as an important positive change in their work environment, even though that was not what the researchers intended.[38]

THIRD SET OF STUDIES The third set of Hawthorne studies built on the emerging findings of the second set. It included the famous Bank Wiring Observation Room study (1931–1932), which involved a group of male workers. Studying the group provided knowledge about informal social relations within groups and about the use of group norms to restrict output when doing so seems advantageous to the group.[39]

IMPACT OF THE HAWTHORNE STUDIES As a result of the Hawthorne studies, the focus of the field of management was drastically altered. In strong contrast to the impersonality that characterized the classical approach, the Hawthorne studies pointed to the impact that social aspects of the job had on productivity, particularly the effects of personal attention from supervisors and relationships among group members. As one writer has pointed out, "No other theory or set of experiments has stimulated more research and controversy nor contributed more to a change in management thinking than the Hawthorne studies and the human relations movement they spawned."[40]

Human Relations Movement

However flawed the studies, the Hawthorne research set the stage for intense interest in the social dimension of human behavior in organizations. The key to productivity from a managerial point of view appeared to lie in showing greater concern for workers so that they would feel more satisfied with their jobs and be willing to produce more. Emphasis was placed on building more collaborative and cooperative relationships between supervisors and workers. Consequently, managers now needed social skills in addition to technical skills. They also required a better understanding of how to make workers feel more satisfied with their jobs. While the Hawthorne studies provided some clues, managers needed more definitive guidance. Two major theorists, Abraham Maslow and Douglas McGregor, were among those who came forward with ideas that managers found helpful.

ABRAHAM MASLOW Abraham Maslow (1908–1970) received his doctorate in psychology from the University of Wisconsin and eventually became chairman of the psychology department at Brandeis University. He developed a theory of motivation that was based on three assumptions about human nature. First, human beings have needs that are never completely satisfied. Second, human action is aimed at fulfilling the needs that are unsatisfied at a given point in time. Third, needs fit into a somewhat predictable hierarchy, ranging from basic, lower-level needs at the bottom to higher-level needs at the top.[41] The hierarchy outlined by Maslow has five levels of needs: physiological (lowest), safety, belongingness, esteem, and self-actualization (highest). Self-actualization needs refer to the requirement to develop our capabilities and reach our full potential.[42]

Maslow's work dramatized to managers that workers have needs beyond the basic requirement of earning money to put a roof over their heads. This concept conflicted with the views of scientific management, which emphasized the importance of pay. Of all the management-related theories, Maslow's hierarchy of needs theory is probably the best known among managers today.

DOUGLAS MCGREGOR The movement toward having managers think of workers in a new light was also given impetus by the work of Douglas McGregor (1906–1964). McGregor earned a doctorate at Harvard and spent most of his career as a professor of industrial management at the Massachusetts Institute of Technology. A 6-year stint as president of Antioch College led him to realize that the notion of trying to have everyone like the boss (i.e., maintaining good human relations) offered inadequate guidance to managers.

To fill the void, he developed the concept of Theory X versus Theory Y, a dichotomy dealing with the possible assumptions that managers make about workers. McGregor felt that such assumptions exert a heavy influence on how managers operate. Theory X managers (see Table 2-5) tend to assume that workers are lazy, need to be coerced, have little ambition, and are focused mainly on security needs. In contrast, Theory Y managers (see Table 2-5) assume that workers do not inherently dislike work, are capable of self-control, have the capacity to be creative and innovative, and generally have higher-level needs that are often unmet on the job.

McGregor believed that managers who hold Theory X assumptions are likely to treat workers accordingly. Hence, such a manager sets up elaborate controls and attempts to motivate strictly through economic incentives. As a result, workers are likely to respond in a manner that reinforces the manager's original assumptions.

In contrast, managers with Theory Y assumptions have the potential for integrating individual goals with organizational goals. McGregor believed this integration could occur if managers give workers latitude in performing their tasks, encourage creativity and innovation, minimize the use of controls, and attempt to make the work more interesting and satisfying in regard to higher-level needs. Under such conditions, workers are likely to exhibit greater commitment to organizational goals, because the goals coincide more closely with their own. McGregor understood, however, that some relatively immature and dependent workers might require greater controls at first in order to develop the maturity needed for the Theory Y approach.[43]

Abraham Maslow contributed to the human relations movement with his theory of motivation. Maslow concluded that human needs go beyond the most basic ones for food and shelter. The discovery of the need for self-actualization (developing one's own potential) has provided managers with new insights on how to motivate workers.

Douglas McGregor influenced how managers think about and deal with their employees. He maintained that managers who expect the worst of their employees and treat them accordingly often find that the employees respond in ways that reinforce these assumptions. But managers who assume the best about their employees and give them wide latitude to perform are generally rewarded with committed and satisfied workers.

TABLE 2-5 THEORY X AND THEORY Y MANAGERIAL ASSUMPTIONS

THEORY X ASSUMPTIONS

1. The average person dislikes work and will try to avoid it.

2. Most people need to be coerced, controlled, directed, and threatened with punishment to get them to work toward organizational goals.

3. The average person wants to be directed, shuns responsibility, has little ambition, and seeks security above all.

THEORY Y ASSUMPTIONS

1. Most people do not inherently dislike work; the physical and mental effort involved is as natural as play or rest.

2. People will exercise self-direction and self-control to reach goals to which they are committed; external control and threat of punishment are not the only means for ensuring effort toward goals.

3. Commitment to goals is a function of the rewards available, particularly rewards that satisfy esteem and self-actualization needs.

4. When conditions are favorable, the average person learns not only to accept but also to seek responsibility.

5. Many people have the capacity to exercise a high degree of creativity and innovation in solving organizational problems.

6. The intellectual potential of most individuals is only partially utilized in most organizations.

Like Maslow's hierarchy, McGregor's Theory X and Theory Y approach helped managers develop a broader perspective on the nature of workers and new alternatives for interacting with them. The innovative ideas of both men had an intuitive appeal to managers searching for ways of operating more effectively. Their theories became extremely popular and are still widely applied today.

Behavioral Science Approach

Maslow, McGregor, and others who helped develop the human relations viewpoint tried to show that there was an alternative to the classical school's rational economic perspective of workers. They depicted workers as social creatures, who had a variety of needs to be met on the job. Still, the picture that they drew was fairly general and somewhat simplistic. It often left managers uncertain about the specific actions that they should take and the implications of such actions. The need for a more complex view of the work situation led to the rise of the behavioral science perspective.

Behavioral science An approach that emphasizes *scientific research* as the basis for developing theories about human behavior in organizations that can be used to establish practical guidelines for managers

The **behavioral science** approach emphasizes *scientific research* as the basis for developing theories about human behavior in organizations that can be used to establish practical guidelines for managers. It draws on findings from a variety of disciplines, including management, psychology, sociology, anthropology, and economics. Concepts are thoroughly tested in business organizations, and sometimes also in laboratory settings, before they are announced as viable approaches for managers. The ultimate aim of the behavioral science approach is to develop theories that managers can use as guides in assessing various situations and deciding on appropriate actions. Since humans themselves are complex and their interactions with others are even more so, the quest for an understanding of organizations and their members is an ongoing activity of considerable challenge.

An example of the useful outcomes of behavioral science research is the idea that individuals perform better with challenging, but attainable, goals than they do without goals. Of course, the goals must be specific and measurable ("I want to get an A in my management course this semester"), rather than vague ("I want to do well in my courses this semester"). The idea that goal setting leads to better performance was the result of extensive research by management researcher Edwin A. Locke and others.[44] We consider the motivational aspects of goal setting more extensively in Chapter 6.

■ QUANTITATIVE MANAGEMENT VIEWPOINT

The quantitative management viewpoint emerged as a major force during World War II. The sheer magnitude of the war effort caused the British and then the U.S. military services to turn to quantitative methods for help in determining the most effective use of resources. For example, one set of quantitative studies by the U.S. Navy led to eliminating the "catch-as-catch-can" method that airplanes had used in searches for enemy vessels. Instead, quantitative analysis produced a pattern for such airplane searches that not only reduced the number of search planes needed for a given area but also increased the coverage. Aside from conserving scarce resources, the new search pattern in the South Atlantic led to the seizure of enemy ships carrying valuable cargo that significantly aided the Allied effort.[45] This and other important applications of quantitative methods gained the attention of business organizations, particularly as quantitative specialists found jobs in non-military-related organizations after the war.

The quantitative management viewpoint focuses on the use of mathematics, statistics, and information aids to support managerial decision making and organizational effectiveness.[46] Three main branches have evolved: management science, operations management, and management information systems.

Management Science

Management science is an approach aimed at increasing decision effectiveness through the use of sophisticated mathematical models and statistical methods. (*Caution:* This term is *not* used synonymously with the term "scientific management," discussed earlier.) Another name commonly used for management science is **operations research.** The increasing power of computers has greatly expanded the possibilities for using the mathematical and statistical tools of management science in organizations. Management science was applied, for example, at Avon, the well-known maker of beauty, health-care, and fashion jewelry products. Group Vice President for Planning and Development Robert W. Pratt used statistical methods to analyze the implications of changing the company's common practice of offering heavy product discounts to generate larger orders. His results indicated that the ailing company could improve profits significantly by lowering the discounts, even if doing so meant smaller average orders per salesperson.[47] In the Supplement to Chapter 5, we take a closer look at some operations research tools, such as linear programming; queuing, or waiting-line, models; and routing, or distribution, models.

Operations Management

Operations management is the function, or field of expertise, that is primarily responsible for managing the production and delivery of an organization's products and services.[48] It includes such areas as inventory management, work

Management science An approach aimed at increasing decision effectiveness through the use of sophisticated mathematical models and statistical methods

Operations research Another name commonly used for management science

Operations management The function, or field of expertise, that is primarily responsible for managing the production and delivery of an organization's products and services

scheduling, production planning, facilities location and design, and quality assurance. Operations management is often applied to manufacturing settings in which various aspects of production need to be managed, including designing the production process, purchasing raw materials, scheduling employees to work, and storing and shipping the final products. For example, Seeq Technology, a Silicon Valley maker of microchips, relied heavily on operations management when a sudden market glut of its main 128K EPROM chip caused the price to plummet from $15 to $2 in a period of a few months. Since the per-chip costs at that point were $5, the company had to rethink its production process, improve inventory management, and lower machine maintenance costs in order to stay in business while it completed proprietary new technology.[49] Operations management applies to delivering services as well. We consider some of these techniques in the Supplement to Chapter 5 and explore the area of operations management at considerable length in Chapter 18.

Management Information Systems

Management information systems   The field of management that focuses on designing and implementing computer-based information systems for use by management

The term **management information systems** refers to the field of management that focuses on designing and implementing computer-based information systems for use by management. Such systems turn raw data into information that is useful to various levels of management. In many industries, computer-based information systems are becoming a powerful competitive weapon because organizations are able to handle large amounts of information in new and better ways. For example, the creation of *USA Today*, the national newspaper, was made feasible by advances in computer-based telecommunication systems. We discuss computer-based information systems more thoroughly in Chapter 19, on information systems for management.

■ CONTEMPORARY VIEWPOINTS

While the classical, behavioral, and quantitative approaches continue to make contributions to management, other viewpoints have also emerged. These are contemporary in the sense that they represent major innovations in ways of thinking about management. Two of the most important contemporary viewpoints are the systems and contingency theories. In addition, at any given point in time, there are emerging views that influence the development of the management field even though they have not reached the status of enduring viewpoints.

Systems Theory

Systems theory   An approach based on the notion that organizations can be visualized as systems

System   A set of interrelated parts that operate as a whole in pursuit of common goals

Inputs   The various human, material, financial, equipment, and informational resources required to produce goods and services

Transformation processes   The organization's managerial and technological abilities that are applied to convert inputs into outputs

The **systems theory** approach is based on the notion that organizations can be visualized as systems.[50] A **system** is a set of interrelated parts that operate as a whole in pursuit of common goals. The systems approach as applied to organizations is based largely on work in biology and the physical sciences.[51] In this section, we consider major systems components, open versus closed systems, and the characteristics of open systems.

MAJOR COMPONENTS According to the systems approach, an organizational system has four major components (see Figure 2-3). **Inputs** are the various human, material, financial, equipment, and informational resources required to produce goods and services. **Transformation processes** are the organization's managerial and technological abilities that are applied to convert inputs into out-

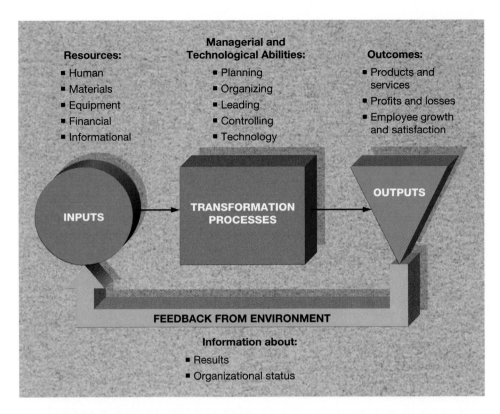

Figure 2-3 *A systems view of organizations.*

puts. **Outputs** are the products, services, and other outcomes produced by the organization. **Feedback** is information about results and organizational status relative to the environment.[52]

The systems approach has a number of advantages. First, it can analyze systems at different levels.[53] For example, systems expert J. Miller has outlined a typology of hierarchical levels of living systems, ranging from an individual human cell, including atoms and molecules, up to a supranational system consisting of two or more societies.[54] For the most part, managers consider the organism (individual), group, organization, and society levels, although the growing global emphasis is bringing the supranational level increasingly into play. Second, the systems view provides a framework for assessing how well the various parts of an organization interact to achieve a common purpose. Third, it emphasizes that a change in one part of the system may affect other parts. In thinking about the interrelationships among parts in an organization, you might visualize that the parts are interconnected by rubber bands. A pull on one part may well affect the position of other parts. Fourth, the systems approach considers how an organization interacts with its environment—the factors outside the organization that can affect its operations. In order to consider the environment adequately, an organization needs to operate as an open system.

OPEN VERSUS CLOSED SYSTEMS Systems can be open or closed. An **open system** is one that operates in continual interaction with its environment. Through such interaction the system takes in new inputs and learns about how its outputs are received by various important outside elements. In contrast, a **closed system** does little or no interacting with its environment and receives little feedback. From a practical point of view, all organizations are open systems to some extent, since it is virtually impossible for an organization to operate for a significant period of time without some interaction with the environment. Still,

Outputs The products, services, and other outcomes produced by the organization

Feedback Information about results and organizational status relative to the environment

Open system A system that operates in continual interaction with its environment

Closed system A system that does little or no interacting with its environment and receives little feedback

organizations can vary tremendously in the degree to which they operate along the open–closed continuum. If an organization operates too closely to the closed end, it might not find out about important environmental factors that can affect it until problems are major.[55] Consider what happened when the Ford Motor Company attempted to launch a new automobile called the Edsel (see the Case in Point discussion).

CASE IN POINT

FORD'S EDSEL FLOPS

During the late 1940s, managers at Ford realized that they had a problem. According to studies, 1 out of 5 car buyers each year was moving from a low-priced to a medium-priced car. Furthermore, among the owners of General Motors (GM) cars, about 87 percent of those trading up stayed with GM, choosing either a Pontiac, Oldsmobile, or Buick. Almost 47 percent of the Plymouth owners moving to a medium-priced car picked a Dodge or DeSoto—which, like the Plymouth, was within the Chrysler family. Ford, however, had only one medium-priced car, the Mercury, and only 26 percent of the Ford owners trading up selected a Mercury. Accordingly, the company began a decade of elaborate planning and preparation aimed at creating a successful new midpriced car geared to young executives and professionals.

The endeavor proved to be quite a challenge. For one thing, finding the right name turned out to be difficult. After extensive marketing research, 10 names were sent to the executive committee. Even so, the committee chose a name that was not on the list—Edsel, the name of Henry Ford's only son. The name "Edsel" was picked despite the fact that market research had shown that it provoked mixed customer reactions.

Another major issue was styling. The search for a distinctive, yet discreet, design involved 800 stylists, all of whom finally agreed on a vertical front grille shaped like a horse collar. Other features of the car included a body that was 2 inches longer than the largest Oldsmobile, numerous push buttons (e.g., for the transmission), and an extremely powerful engine—all characteristics determined by market research in the early 1950s to appeal to midrange car buyers.

To build and distribute the car, Ford set up a separate division at headquarters and separate Edsel dealers, rather than selling the car through one of its established divisions and chains of experienced dealerships. While it was felt that this would allow the new division and dealers to concentrate totally on the Edsel, the system also added greatly to the overhead associated with the car. To make a profit, Ford would have to sell a large number of Edsels. The executives felt that they were being conservative in estimating that 200,000 cars (or about 650 per day) would be sold the first year.

Although advertising was launched on July 22, 1957, the actual style of the car was kept a closely guarded secret until its introduction day, September 4 (about a month before competitors would be introducing their 1958 models). Sales of the Edsel on the first day were somewhat promising, but they quickly dwindled. In 1958, only about 35,000 Edsels were sold, far short of the conservative target. The 1959 Edsel models were shorter, lighter, less powerful, and less costly, and they were handled through a merged Lincoln-Mercury-Edsel division. Sales that year were about double those of the first year. When the 1960 models failed to generate additional excitement, production of the Edsel was scrapped. Losses reached about $200 million.

What went wrong? First, there was a stock market collapse in August 1957

the EDSEL

"Mile by mile, your   satisfaction grows"

The Edsel car, introduced by the Ford Motor Company with great fanfare in 1957, was a dud. Production shut down two years later. Ford managers had perceived the need for a midpriced car but paid insufficient attention to negative feedback and events outside the company that combined to make sales sluggish.

that had a severe negative impact on purchases of medium-size cars that year. Second, Ford relied heavily on initial marketing data in planning the car. It failed to alter the plans in the face of the growing impact of smaller, more fuel-efficient foreign cars, which were beginning to capture portions of the U.S. market. Third, the first Edsels were prone to oil leaks, mysterious rattles, faulty brakes, and starting difficulties—problems that should have been detected before they reached the newspapers and national visibility. Because of these maladies, the car was quickly labeled a "lemon" and became the source of jokes. Fourth, Ford relied on a network of inexperienced new dealers to woo prospective customers. Fifth, the car was introduced while other car makers were offering discounts on their previous year's models, making the new Edsel seem expensive. Finally, top management ignored negative marketing information from potential customers when it selected the name "Edsel."

Perhaps the Edsel could have survived one of these difficulties, but in combination, the problems were lethal. The situation illustrates the need to pay close attention to things going on outside that can affect system functioning and success. ■■■

CHARACTERISTICS OF OPEN SYSTEMS Organizations that operate closer to the open end of the continuum share certain characteristics that help them survive and prosper. Two major characteristics of open systems are negative entropy and synergy.[56]

Entropy refers to the tendency of systems to decay over time. In contrast, **negative entropy** is the ability of open systems to bring in new energy, in the form of inputs and feedback from the environment, in order to delay or arrest entropy. One reason the Edsel ran into trouble was that Ford relied on market research conducted in the early 1950s and ignored the newer signs indicating that consumers were turning to more fuel-efficient foreign cars.

A second major characteristic of open systems is **synergy,** the ability of the whole to equal more than the sum of its parts. This means that an organization ought to be able to achieve its goals more effectively and efficiently than would be possible if the parts operated separately. At Ford, the organization's

Negative entropy The ability of open systems to bring in new energy, in the form of inputs and feedback from the environment, in order to delay or arrest entropy

Synergy The ability of the whole to equal more than the sum of its parts

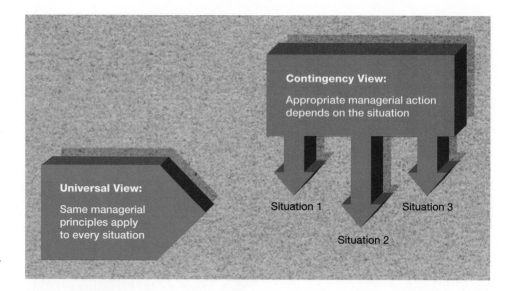

Figure 2-4 *The contingency managerial viewpoint.*

parts were not operating in synchronization when the top management committee ignored market research and chose the ill-fated "Edsel" tag.

According to the systems viewpoint, managers are likely to be more successful if they attempt to operate their units and organizations as open systems that are carefully attuned to the factors in the environment that could significantly affect them. We discuss environmental factors more specifically in Chapter 3.

Contingency Theory

The classical theorists, such as Taylor and Fayol, were attempting to identify "the one best way" for managers to operate in a variety of situations. If universal principles could be found, then becoming a good manager would essentially involve learning the principles and how to apply them. Unfortunately, things were not to be that simple. Researchers soon found that some classical principles, such as Fayol's unity of command (each person should report to only one boss), could sometimes be violated with positive results. Consequently, contingency theory began to develop. **Contingency theory** is a viewpoint that argues that appropriate managerial action depends on the particular parameters of the situation. Hence, rather than seeking *universal* principles that apply to every situation, contingency theory attempts to identify *contingency* principles that prescribe actions to take depending on the characteristics of the situation (see Figure 2-4).[57]

Contingency theory A viewpoint that argues that appropriate managerial action depends on the particular parameters of the situation

To be fair, Fayol and most of the other classical theorists recognized that some judgment was needed in applying their various principles. Still, they emphasized universal principles and were rather vague about when the principles might *not* apply.[58]

Throughout this book you will encounter theories and concepts related to the contingency viewpoint—that is, areas in which applications of management ideas depend on situational factors. The contingency approach applies particularly well in such areas as environmental factors, strategy, organizational design, technology, and leadership.

Emerging Views

Given that management is a complex endeavor, innovative approaches are constantly needed to help advance the knowledge base. Some new approaches

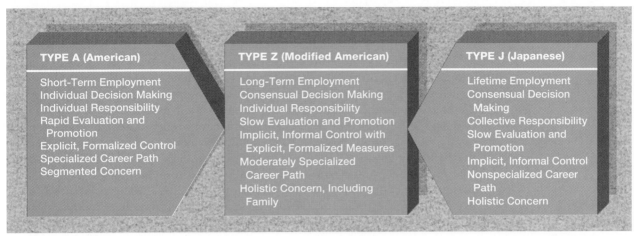

TYPE A (American)	TYPE Z (Modified American)	TYPE J (Japanese)
Short-Term Employment Individual Decision Making Individual Responsibility Rapid Evaluation and Promotion Explicit, Formalized Control Specialized Career Path Segmented Concern	Long-Term Employment Consensual Decision Making Individual Responsibility Slow Evaluation and Promotion Implicit, Informal Control with Explicit, Formalized Measures Moderately Specialized Career Path Holistic Concern, Including Family	Lifetime Employment Consensual Decision Making Collective Responsibility Slow Evaluation and Promotion Implicit, Informal Control Nonspecialized Career Path Holistic Concern

Figure 2-5 *Characteristics of Theory Z management. (Adapted from William G. Ouchi and Alfred M. Jaeger, "Theory Z Organizations: Stability in the Midst of Mobility," Academy of Management Review, vol. 3, 1978, pp. 308, 311.)*

develop into major viewpoints when research and managerial practice show that they are effective. Other new ideas wither after investigations indicate that they are not living up to their promise.

One recent perspective that has gained attention can best be termed the **Japanese management** approach, since it focuses on aspects of management in Japan that may be appropriate for adoption in the United States. The interest in Japanese management has arisen because of the recent admirable success of Japanese companies, particularly in manufacturing such items as televisions, videocassette recorders, and computer printers.[59]

On the basis of his research of both American and Japanese management approaches, management expert William Ouchi has outlined Theory Z. **Theory Z** combines positive aspects of American and Japanese management into a modified approach aimed at increasing U.S. managerial effectiveness while remaining compatible with the norms and values of American society and culture (see Figure 2-5). The Theory Z approach involves giving workers job security; including them in some decision making; emphasizing group responsibil-

Japanese management An approach that focuses on aspects of management in Japan that may be appropriate for adoption in the United States

Theory Z A concept that combines positive aspects of American and Japanese management into a modified approach aimed at increasing U.S. managerial effectiveness while remaining compatible with the norms and values of American society and culture

Honda's Civic, a new subcompact introduced in the early 1990s, found itself getting outpriced in the U.S. market. That's when Honda's Japanese management learned a lesson in Civics: they implemented the numerous money-saving suggestions generated by engineering teams in Japan and at the company's Ohio plant (shown). The result? A more competitively priced model four years later. Involving workers in decision making and encouraging group responsibility are key elements in Theory Z, which combines the best of American and Japanese management practices.

ity; increasing quality; establishing gradual-advancement policies, more informal controls, and broader career paths; and showing greater concern for employees' work and nonwork well-being. A number of U.S. companies, such as General Motors, the Ford Motor Company, Hewlett-Packard, and Intel, have adopted aspects of Theory Z, particularly the concepts of involving workers in decision making, instituting more informal controls, and encouraging group members to accept responsibility for work in their unit.

Another perspective that has become important in recent years is total quality management (TQM). *Total quality management* is a management system that is an integral part of an organization's strategy and is aimed at continually improving product and service quality so as to achieve high levels of customer satisfaction and build strong customer loyalty.[60] Many companies, such as Whirlpool, Corning, Inc., Ford Motor, and Xerox, have instituted total quality management systems as part of their efforts to increase global competitiveness. We discuss total quality management more extensively in Chapter 17.

■ PROMOTING INNOVATION: CONTRIBUTIONS OF THE MAJOR VIEWPOINTS

TABLE 2-6 MAIN INNOVATIVE CONTRIBUTIONS OF MAJOR VIEWPOINTS	
VIEWPOINT	**INNOVATIVE CONTRIBUTIONS**
Classical	Highlights the need for a scientific approach to management
	Points out that work methods often can be improved through study
	Identifies a number of important principles that are useful in running organizations efficiently
	Emphasizes the potential importance of pay as a motivator
Behavioral	Spotlights the managerial importance of such factors as communication, group dynamics, motivation, and leadership
	Articulates practical applications of behavioral studies
	Draws on the findings of a number of disciplines such as management, psychology, sociology, anthropology, and economics
	Highlights the importance of organization members as active human resources rather than as passive tools
Quantitative	Provides quantitative aids to decision making
	Develops quantitative tools to assist in providing products and services
	Pioneers new computer-based information systems for management
Contemporary (systems and contingency)	Emphasizes that organizations can be visualized as systems of interrelated parts
	Points out the potential importance of the environment and feedback to organizational success
	Argues that there is no one best way to manage and identifies the circumstances or contingencies that influence which particular approach will be effective in a given situation

Each major viewpoint has added important ideas to current knowledge about management and, in the process, has changed the way that managers think about and behave in organizations. The main contributions of the major viewpoints are summarized in Table 2-6.

■ CHAPTER SUMMARY

Although management practices can be traced back to ancient times, much of the impetus for developing management theories and principles grew out of the industrial revolution and the need for better ways to run the resulting factory systems. Preclassical contributors such as Robert Owen, Charles Babbage, and Henry R. Towne provided some initial ideas that led to the identification of management as an important field of inquiry. From this base, four major viewpoints have developed: classical, behavioral, quantitative, and contemporary.

The classical viewpoint emphasizes finding ways to manage work and organizations more efficiently. It includes three different approaches. The scientific management approach, represented by the work of Frederick Winslow Taylor, Frank and Lillian Gilbreth, and Henry Gantt, emphasizes the scientific study of work methods in order to improve worker efficiency. The bureaucratic approach, pioneered by Max Weber, focuses on the need for organizations to operate in a rational manner rather than relying on the arbitrary whims of owners and managers. The administrative management approach, supported by Henri Fayol and Chester Barnard, explores principles that can be used by managers to coordinate the internal activities of organizations.

The behavioral viewpoint is a perspective that seeks to understand the various factors that affect human behavior in organizations. Hugo Münsterberg and Mary Parker Follett were early behaviorists. It was the Hawthorne studies, though, that dramatically demonstrated that workers were more than mere tools of production. Although flawed, the studies produced insights that led to the establishment of the human relations movement, with its emphasis on concern for the worker. Abraham Maslow's hierarchy of needs theory and Douglas McGregor's Theory X and Theory Y provided some guidance for managers but were still fairly general. The

behavioral science approach, with its emphasis on scientific research, emerged to build more specific theories about behavior in organizations that can be used to provide practical guidelines for managers.

The quantitative viewpoint focuses on the use of mathematics, statistics, and information aids to support managerial decision making and effectiveness. It has three main branches. Operations research is an approach aimed at increasing decision effectiveness through the use of sophisticated mathematical models and statistical methods. Operations management is the field of expertise that is primarily responsible for managing the production and delivery of an organization's products and services. The management information systems field focuses on designing and implementing computer-based information systems for use by management.

The contemporary viewpoints represent recent major innovations in ways of thinking about management. They include the systems and contingency theories, as well as emerging views. The systems theory approach is based on the notion that organizations can be visualized as systems, including inputs, transformation processes, outputs, and feedback. Contingency theory argues that appropriate managerial action depends on the particular parameters of a given situation. Emerging viewpoints include new, promising approaches that may develop into major viewpoints if research supports their relevance. One important emerging view is Japanese management, represented by Theory Z. This theory combines the positive aspects of American and Japanese management into a modified approach appropriate to business in the United States. Another important emerging view is total quality management.

All the major viewpoints contribute significantly to innovation in the field of management. Other viewpoints will likely develop as the field progresses.

■ QUESTIONS FOR DISCUSSION AND REVIEW

1 Explain how the preclassical contributors helped set the stage for the development of management as a science. Identify a situation in which you have used the guidelines in *Robert's Rules of Order* or seen them used. Why have the rules been so popular over a considerable period of time?

2 Contrast the three major approaches within the classical viewpoint: scientific management, bureaucratic management, and administrative management. Give

some examples of how these approaches are reflected in an organization with which you are familiar.

3 Review the scientific management principles advocated by Frederick Taylor. How effective do you think these principles would be in eliminating soldiering? What might be some disadvantages of his approach? What did Frank and Lillian Gilbreth add to Taylor's approach?

4 Summarize the contributions of Mary Parker Follett. For each contribution, give an example illustrating the relevance of her ideas today.

5 Explain the development of the behavioral viewpoint. How is it possible that a flawed set of studies—the Hawthorne studies—helped bring about the behavioral viewpoint of management?

6 Differentiate among the three major approaches within the quantitative management viewpoint. How have computers aided the development of this viewpoint?

7 Explain the major ideas underlying the systems viewpoint. Use this viewpoint to analyze your college or university. To what extent would you consider it to be an open system? Give reasons for your view.

8 Describe the reasoning behind the contingency viewpoint. Why did it emerge? What are the implications for managerial education?

9 Explain the Theory Z approach to management. Under which system would you prefer to work: American (Type A), Japanese (Type J), or modified American (Type Z)? Why? Which system do you think would work best in the following work environments: research, production, mining, agriculture, service?

10 Show how current management knowledge is the result of innovative processes involving many management pioneers. What can we learn about the process of innovation from studying these people's ideas?

■ DISCUSSION QUESTIONS FOR CHAPTER OPENING CASE

1 How did scientific management help Henry Ford build the Ford Motor Company?

2 Use the systems view to analyze the reasons for the failure of Ford's first two companies and the success of his third, the Ford Motor Company.

3 If the Hawthorne studies had been conducted in the early 1890s and the human relations movement had been emerging at that time, how might they have influenced Henry Ford's approach?

■ EXERCISES FOR MANAGING IN THE TWENTY-FIRST CENTURY

EXERCISE 1
SELF-ASSESSMENT EXERCISE: WHAT KIND OF A MANAGER AM I?

Select the response that best describes how you would manage a group of employees.

1 = Strongly disagree
2 = Somewhat disagree
3 = Neither agree nor disagree
4 = Somewhat agree
5 = Strongly agree

_____ 1 I would normally give explicit instructions concerning both what is to be accomplished and how it is to be done.

_____ 2 I would make sure that subordinates know they could lose their jobs if they do not produce well.

_____ 3 I would motivate mainly through an incentive awards program based on individual output.

_____ 4 I would measure individual contribution based strictly on economic efficiencies.

_____ 5 I would make an effort to recognize and develop individual skills.

_____ 6 I would install a detailed monitoring system to ensure that everyone is following proper procedures.

_____ 7 I would attempt to arrange organizational and personal goals so that both could be accomplished simultaneously.

_____ 8 I would intervene immediately, at will, to modify an employee's behavior to reach the organization's goals.

_____ 9 If I had to choose between using an employee for something today or having that employee gain experience for the future, I would emphasize output for today.

_____ 10 I would rely on my subordinates' imagination and creativity to solve organizational challenges.

EXERCISE 2
MANAGEMENT EXERCISE: PROBLEMS AT THE ICE CREAM PLANT

 You are the manager of a plant that produces a special type of extra-creamy ice cream. Sales had been increasing every quarter for the past 4 years, until last quarter. During that quarter sales slipped 17 percent, production was about 15 percent short of projections, absenteeism was about 20 percent higher than it was in the previous quarter, and tardiness increased steadily. You believe that the problems are probably management-related, but you are not sure about their causes or the steps you should take to correct them. You decide to call in a consultant to help you determine what to do next. The consultant tells you that she wholeheartedly supports scientific management and usually looks at problems from that point of view. She mentions that there are other consultants in the area who tend to take other views. In order to get the most complete idea of what should be done at your plant, you call in five other consultants, each of whom supports one of the following approaches: administrative management, bureaucracy, human relations, quantitative management, and systems theory.

Form a group with two of your classmates. Have each member of the group select two of the six management approaches mentioned above. Be sure that all six approaches are included. Each member will play the role of a consultant for one of the approaches that he or she has selected and then repeat the process for his or her second consultant role. The person should analyze the likely problems at the ice cream plant and offer solutions from the point of view of the particular management approach that he or she is representing. The other two group members will critique the explanations presented by the consultant.

CONCLUDING CASE 1

FORD MOTOR CHARGES AHEAD AND INTO GLOBALIZATION

Amidst the auto industry downturn of the early 1980s, Henry Ford's motor company was hemorrhaging. Henry Ford II had just retired from his position as chairman of the company that his grandfather had built. Between 1979 and 1982, the company lost $3 billion. It was plagued by a reputation for producing cars designed for yesterday's consumers, and—worse—quality was poor.

Cutting costs and raising quality were clear priorities. By the mid-1980s, the company had reduced its hourly work force, cut back on white-collar workers, and shut down eight U.S. plants. The remaining 81 plants were revamped and upgraded technologically to make the work as efficient as possible. Computerized robots and upgraded inventory control were part of the massive changes. At the same time, Ford tied its efficiency and cost-cutting efforts to its quality quest. It adopted the Japanese management view that higher quality ultimately means lower costs. Such changes reduced costs by $5 billion by the mid-1980s, with another $5 billion in savings by the early 1990s.

The company also redirected the design of its cars. Whereas in the past the tendency had been to follow the competition, top management now told designers to "design the kind of cars *you* would like to drive." With the new approach, Ford has produced a number of automobiles that have sold well, most notably the Taurus and the Sable.

Some of the less visible changes at Ford relate to its new approach to internal management. Once considered to have the most autocratic managers in the U.S. auto industry, the company launched a program called Employee Involvement that has pushed decision making to lower levels, including the assembly line. For example, assembly-line workers are now authorized to stop the line if they see a problem. Ford emphasizes teamwork and uses the team concept to involve individuals from various areas, such as design, engineering, and manufacturing, in the development of new models. Ideas come from the bottom of the company as well as from the top.

Ford would like to capture 30 percent of the North American car and truck market, compared with its present 26 percent market share. The company would also like to increase its 12 percent of the European market to 15 percent.

Lately, the company is attempting to further dismantle the old corporate pyramid and place more emphasis on a matrix-type organization structure in which many parts of the organization work together, but retain their autonomy. As one part of the change, Ford eliminated separate North American and European engineering operations in favor of moving 15,000 employees into five worldwide product-development centers—four in Dearborn and one in Europe. Under this arrangement, instead of developing separate Escort-size cars for sale in Europe, the United States, and Australia, the European center would develop a basic design that could be modified for use in various markets. The other centers would be responsible for basic designs for other types of vehicles—for example, large cars and minivans or trucks. Through such an approach Ford had hoped to create excellent products within a shorter time period with increased efficiency so that vehicles can be sold at an affordable price. Within a year, though, the company was paring the number of centers back to three, an arrangement somewhat similar to the original one. Ford found that having so many centers was leading to confusion, duplicate work, and turf bat-tles. Purchasing was also to be globally integrated, but Ford is still struggling to make the approach work. Meanwhile, Ford has encountered price resistance to its cars, which are loaded with desirable new features but have hefty price tags. The company is quickly shifting gears to turn out low-priced, stripped-down models.

A major challenge facing Ford is to sell its products in more markets. Ford has targeted China and India as high priority countries for expansion. Indonesia, Thailand, and Vietnam also are important. In addition, the company is expending major efforts to build a greater presence in Latin America, particularly in Argentina, Brazil, and Venezuela.

At the turn of the century Ford hopes to be much more efficient. The company wants to be able to generate more products with a smaller group of engineers and manufacturing personnel. The company also aims to improve its record of customer service and, in essence, be a much more effective competitor in global markets. Bringing about such changes is a formidable task.[61]

QUESTIONS FOR CONCLUDING CASE 1

1 Identify influences from the classical, behavioral, and quantitative viewpoints in the way the Ford Motor Company is managed today.

2 Use systems theory to contrast the way the Ford Motor Company operated at the time the Edsel was introduced with the way the company is currently operating, including its worldwide emphasis.

3 Explain the influence of Japanese management (Theory Z) on current management at the Ford Motor Company.

CONCLUDING CASE 2

SIEMENS IS GROOMING A NEW GENERATION OF MANAGERS

When German electronics giant Siemens decided to reorganize itself for the 1990s, top management identified a primary need for managers who are oriented to change. Even though the company's sales are in the $60 billion range, Siemens is under intense competitive pressure, particularly from the Japanese. Historically, "European companies take longer to react," says board member Hermann Franz. To stay ahead of competitors in the future, Siemens wants managers who can cut the reaction time and jump ahead of competitors.

To develop and encourage such managers, Siemens is breaking up the massive structure that required talented managers to labor for years at lower levels before attaining promotions. Instead, the company is creating smaller business units and seeking entrepreneurial candidates to head them. In the process, Siemens has identified 500 managers who seem to have the appropriate entrepreneurial bent. Most of them are in their twenties and thirties, although a few are in their forties. These managers are expected to assume senior posts by ages 35 to 45, instead of the more usual 50 to 60 range. The 500 have been placed on the fast track and have been given challenging assignments. If they perform at the extraordinary levels expected, they will be moved up quickly. Instead of relying solely on the advanced technology that has been a major strength of Siemens, this group is also expected to emphasize marketing and sales.

To become one of the "chosen 500," candidates must be recommended by their immediate superior. They then spend a full week taking a battery of tests, engaging in role playing, and handling case situations at Siemens' management training center, south of Munich. In one exercise, teams of four participants are given a management crisis and limited time to solve it. The team must determine, for example, how to handle the press and demonstrators who are gathering around a factory after a mercury spill. Top managers and a psychologist assess each participant's product knowledge, creativity, and leadership ability. In addition, each participant criticizes his or her colleagues' performance and rates them on such attributes as risk-taking propensity and information gathering. Candidates who perform exceptionally well are placed in the chosen group.

Selected candidates can expect a fast-paced career, in which they transfer from one challenging job to another, moving across divisions and into foreign countries. The new managers will have a global focus, which will facilitate acquiring and managing companies in faraway lands. Salary is very competitive for excellent performers, with raises that can reach 30 percent of base pay. To remain in the chosen group, however, one's performance must continue to be stellar. Siemens needs exceptional performance from this new cadre of managers to stay competitive against major global rivals like ABB and GE.

Leading the fast-trackers is chief executive officer Heinrich von Pierer. When he was head of Siemens' $3.2 billion energy unit, von Pierer established a solid reputation for recognizing the need for change and taking appropriate action. He foresaw that the nuclear-power-plant business would encounter difficulties in the late 1980s, and he switched emphasis to conventional gas-and-steam turbine production early enough to take full advantage of the market shift.

The changes are all part of what von Pierer calls a "cultural revolution," which puts new emphasis on innovation within the company. Von Pierer, known as a careful listener and a consensus builder, takes the initiative and breaks through dysfunctional bureaucracies. For example, he typically calls lower-level managers to his office to obtain information firsthand instead of going through a long chain of command. For von Pierer, the most critical challenge has been to get managers to abandon long-entrenched practices and take on a new mindset. In place of endless meetings, requirements for many levels of approvals, and deemphasis on risks, Siemens needs managers who can be more aggressive in developing new products and markets. So far, there are signs that the revolution is working in the form of new product innovations, increased levels of cooperation within the company, and increased business. Still, von Pierer realizes that he needs to keep leading the revolution. "We have to keep asking ourselves: 'Are we flexible enough? Are we changing enough?'" Von Pierer recently gave the heads of the company's 17 divisions more autonomy in making investment decisions after a company survey in which the CEO was criticized for becoming too deeply involved in day-to-day matters at the expense of concentrating on strategic issues. Siemens' long-term strategy is to dominate the global market for electronic systems.[62]

QUESTIONS FOR CONCLUDING CASE 2

1 Explain how Siemens is changing to an open system.
2 To what extent are the Theory X and Theory Y concepts relevant to the changes being made at Siemens?
3 How could Siemens effectively use contingency theory to help train its new group of managers?

CHAPTER THREE

UNDERSTANDING COMPETITIVE ENVIRONMENTS AND ORGANIZATIONAL CULTURES

CHAPTER OUTLINE

Types of External Environments
Mega-Environment
Task Environment

Analyzing Environmental Conditions
Views of the Organization-Environment Interface
Characteristics of the Environment

Managing Environmental Elements
Adaptation
Favorability Influence
Domain Shifts

The Internal Environment: Organizational Culture
Nature of Organizational Culture
Manifestations of Organizational Culture
Promoting Innovation: An Adaptive, Entrepreneurial
    Culture
Changing Organizational Culture
How Leaders Influence Cultural Change

LEARNING OBJECTIVES

After studying this chapter, you should be able to:

- Explain the concept of mega-environment and outline its major elements.

- Distinguish between the concepts of task environment and mega-environment and describe the major elements of the task environment.

- Contrast the population ecology and resource dependence views of the organization-environment interface.

- Explain how environmental uncertainty and munificence impact organizations.

- Describe the major methods that organizations use to manage their environments.

- Explain the nature of organizational culture and its major manifestations.

- Contrast entrepreneurial and administrative cultures as means of promoting innovation.

- Explain how organizational cultures can be changed.

GAINING THE EDGE

WACHNER BUILDS WARNACO INTO AN EMPIRE

 In Linda Wachner's glassed-in conference room 26 stories above street level in New York City, a model is posing in lacy underwear. Several male and female executives run in and out of the room carrying other samples of the company's main products—intimate apparel and menswear, including such well-know brand names as Olga, Warner, Fruit of the Loom, Christian Dior, Hathaway, Chaps by Ralph Lauren, and Jack Nicklaus. Linda Wachner, CEO, has a multiline telephone close by which she picks up periodically to ask questions or give instructions. The stitch shop where samples of new designs are made is in the same building, allowing Wachner to comment on new products such as the items being modeled. Wachner owns about 13 percent of Warnaco, which at recent stock prices is worth over $100 million.

One reason for the company's success is its devotion to staying close to the customer. Wachner and other Warnaco executives spend a great deal of time studying selling reports that come in from various retail accounts. Wachner herself roams store aisles throughout the country, talking with salespeople, watching what people are buying, and learning firsthand why certain products appeal to them. "Linda's strength is that she is constantly in touch with customers in the stores and her retailers," says Leslie Wexner, chairman of The Limited. On one occasion, Wachner was in Hong Kong, but took the time to meet with a group of Limited executives who were there on a buying trip. Notes Wexner, "Linda is always willing to go the extra mile. I can't get some of my vendors to fly from Pittsburgh to Columbus" (headquarters for The Limited). One result is that Warnaco now produces many of the private-label goods for Victoria's Secret, which is owned by The Limited and has begun producing shirts and blouses for The Limited. Says William Dillard II, president of Dillard Department Stores headquartered in Little Rock, Arkansas, "I probably talk to Linda more than any other CEO I do business with." One result is that Warnaco is usually a leader in developing new styles, such as the nude look or animal prints like zebra and leopard, for women's lingerie. Warnaco must be diligent about keeping close tabs on customers because the company faces formidable competition from three other major intimate apparel firms—Sara Lee Intimates, Vanity Fair Mills, and Maidenform Worldwide.

As a boss, Wachner has a reputation for being tough. She and the other executives at Warnaco all carry spiral notebooks embossed on the cover with Wachner's favorite motto: "Do It Now." They use the notebooks to keep track of the many things that need to be done. Everyone has clear goals to achieve. Wachner says that the biggest obstacle to change that she encounters is keeping people's energy up. She typically works 16-hour days and will stay up 2 or 3 days in a row if necessary to get something critical accomplished. Sometimes individuals say they can't do any more, but Wachner tells them, "Yes, you can, and here's why." She tries to get them to dream the dream. Many of the Warnaco managers also have equity positions in the company. Being successful is a major positive reinforcement, says Wachner. Some, however, have found the pressure to reach goals too great and have left the company.

Recently Warnaco has acquired the Calvin Klein underwear businesses for men and women. Warnaco is expanding the Calvin Klein businesses internationally and is making a globalization push for many of the company's other brands. Wachner is particularly eyeing Asia and the Middle East, but other com-

Linda Wachner, CEO of Warnaco, lives by the motto "Do it
now." She expects the same of
her employees. Her can-do
attitude and her strong efforts
to understand and meet customer needs contribute to an
organizational culture that has
made the clothing company a
global success.

External environment The
major forces outside the
organization that have the
potential to significantly
influence the likely success of
products or services

Internal environment The
general conditions that exist
within an organization

Organizational culture A
system of shared values,
assumptions, beliefs, and
norms that unite the members
of an organization

petitors, such as Vanity Fair, Arrow shirts, Italy's Benetton, and Britain's Van Heusen, also are establishing outlets there. Warnaco has more than 13,000 employees and 40 factories around the world.[1]   ■■■

A major factor in the success of Warnaco, has been Wachner's recognition of the importance of understanding the needs of retailers and the customers who ultimately buy the company's products. As this situation illustrates, an organization's effectiveness is influenced by its **external environment,** the major forces outside the organization that have the potential to significantly influence the likely success of products or services. At the same time, Warnaco might not have achieved its major success without a compatible **internal environment,** the general conditions that exist within an organization. The internal environment encompasses such factors as organization members, the nature of their inter-actions, and the physical setting within which they operate. Nevertheless, the notion of organizational culture is often used as an overall description of the general conditions, or internal environment, of an organization. **Organizational culture** is a system of shared values, assumptions, beliefs, and norms that unite the members of an organization.[2] For example, at Warnaco, the organizational culture includes emphasizing the motto "Do It Now," striving for difficult goals, and working many hours if necessary to achieve them.

In this chapter, we examine the external environment of organizations. We consider both the general environment, or mega-environment, within which an organization functions and the more specific, immediate elements that make up an organization's task environment. We also explore differing views about the relationship between an organization and its environment and consider important environmental characteristics. Next, we investigate the possibilities for managing environmental elements. Finally, we examine the internal envi-ronment by looking at how an organization's culture can influence its prospects for success. Our discussion also considers the relationship between innovation and an entrepreneurial culture.

■ TYPES OF EXTERNAL ENVIRONMENTS

While Warnaco has been successful in capitalizing on new trends, the Warren Featherbone Company had the opposite problem—recognizing the ebbing of a lucrative market. The Warren Featherbone Company built a thriving business about 100 years ago around its patented product, the featherbone. Made of finely split turkey quills combined to form a cord, the product was used to stiffen corsets, collars, bustles, and gowns. Although the company made it through the Great Depression in fairly good shape, technological advances such as plastic were emerging. The company recognized the trend and, in 1938, started making plastic baby pants to go over diapers, just as the demand for featherbone was sinking badly. It also made a rocky expansion into baby clothing. Fortunately, its baby clothing developed into a solid business in the mid-1960s, just about the time that the emergence of the disposable diaper destroyed much of the demand for the plastic pants.[3] As the history of the Warren Featherbone Company makes clear, organizations can be drastically affected by the environment within which they operate. Therefore, they need to be prepared to continually change and innovate.

Systems theory helps highlight the importance of the environment to organizations. According to the systems view, an organization is likely to be more successful if it operates as an open system that continually interacts with and receives feedback from its external environment (see Chapter 2). Consequently, organizations need to have managers who expend considerable effort understanding the nature of the external environment that their organizations face. The external environment of an organization can be divided into two major segments: the general environment, or mega-environment, and the task environment. These segments and their elements are depicted in Figure 3-1. (The internal environment, as reflected in the notion of organizational culture, is also shown. Organizational culture is discussed later in this chapter.)

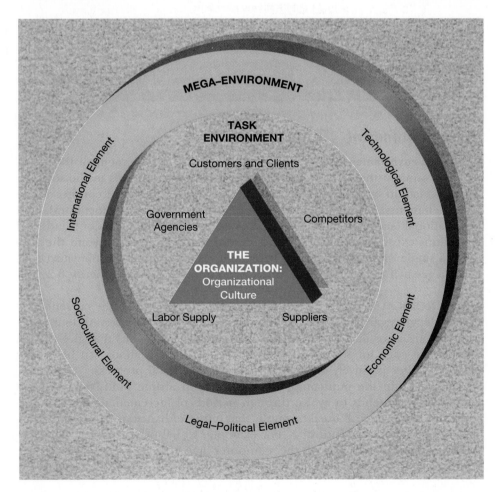

Figure 3-1 *The internal and external environments of the organization.*

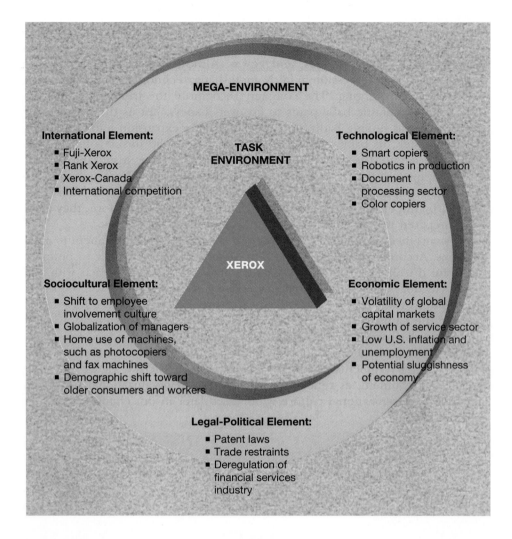

MEGA-ENVIRONMENT

International Element:
- Fuji-Xerox
- Rank Xerox
- Xerox-Canada
- International competition

TASK ENVIRONMENT

Technological Element:
- Smart copiers
- Robotics in production
- Document processing sector
- Color copiers

XEROX

Sociocultural Element:
- Shift to employee involvement culture
- Globalization of managers
- Home use of machines, such as photocopiers and fax machines
- Demographic shift toward older consumers and workers

Economic Element:
- Volatility of global capital markets
- Growth of service sector
- Low U.S. inflation and unemployment
- Potential sluggishness of economy

Legal-Political Element:
- Patent laws
- Trade restraints
- Deregulation of financial services industry

Figure 3-2 *Elements of the mega-environment of the Xerox Corporation.*

Mega-Environment

Mega-environment The broad conditions and trends in the societies in which an organization operates

The **mega-environment,** or general environment, is the segment of the external environment that reflects the broad conditions and trends in the societies within which an organization operates. The mega-environment consists of five major elements: technological, economic, legal-political, sociocultural, and international (see Figure 3-1).[4] Because these elements reflect major trends and conditions existing outside the organization, they tend to be beyond the ability of a single organization to affect or alter directly, at least in the short run. The mega-environment of the Xerox Corporation is shown in Figure 3-2.

Technological element The current state of knowledge regarding the production of products and services

TECHNOLOGICAL ELEMENT The **technological element** reflects the current state of knowledge regarding the production of products and services. Although specific organizations may have technical knowledge and patents that give them a competitive edge for some period of time, most organizations can be greatly affected, either positively or negatively, by technological progress.

Research in the minicomputer, cement, and airline industries indicates that technology tends to evolve through periods of incremental change punctuated by technological breakthroughs that either enhance or destroy the competence of firms in an industry.[5] For example, Nobel prize–winning Bell Laboratory physicists pioneered the computer age with the invention of the transistor in 1947. Subsequent developments with microchips have affected businesses and their products in a wide range of industries, from automobile and small-appliance manufacturing to home building.

In order to remain competitive, organizations must stay abreast of current technological developments that may affect their ability to offer desirable products and services. A number of sources provide information regarding technological and other environmental elements. Among them are major business periodicals (such as *Business Week, Forbes,* and *Fortune*), various trade journals targeted to specific industries, government publications (such as the *Statistical Abstract of the United States,* which contains social, demographic, political, and economic information), business services (such as various indexes from Dun & Bradstreet), and on-line services (such as LEXIS/NEXIS, a service that provides access to many publications and information sources of interest to business).

ECONOMIC ELEMENT The **economic element** encompasses the systems of producing, distributing, and consuming wealth. Companies based in the United States function primarily within a capitalist economy, although they may do business with and/or operate in countries that have socialist economies. In a **capitalist economy,** economic activity is governed by market forces and the means of production are privately owned by individuals, either directly or through corporations. In a **socialist economy,** the means of production are owned by the state and economic activity is coordinated by plan.

In practice, countries tend to have hybrid economies. Although the United States operates close to the capitalist end of the continuum, there is considerable government regulation in such areas as utilities and communications. Today, the socialist end can be represented by the People's Republic of China. The economies of most countries, such as Sweden, France, and Hungary, fall somewhere between the capitalist and socialist extremes. Third world countries (mainly poor countries of the world with very low per capita income, little industry, and high birthrates) also provide many variations in patterns as they struggle to decide whether to emulate the capitalist or socialist economic model.

Because of these differences, organizations that do business in a variety of countries typically confront strikingly diverse sets of economic ground rules within which they must operate. Within any given economic system, of course, organizations are influenced by a variety of economic factors over which they have little independent control, such as inflation, interest rates, and recessions.

LEGAL-POLITICAL ELEMENT The **legal-political element** includes the legal and governmental systems within which an organization must function. Trends in legislation, court decisions, politics, and government regulation are particularly important aspects of the legal-political environment.

For example, organizations must operate within the general legal framework of each country in which they do business. They are also governed by a variety of laws that specifically address the manner in which they function. Such laws in the United States include the Clean Air and Clean Water acts, which are aimed at controlling pollution, and the Occupational Safety and Health Act, which specifies safety regulations. At the same time, organizations are subject to an increasing number of lawsuits filed by a growing variety of interest groups, ranging from employees to clients. The increase has been spurred in part by the large sums of money awarded by juries, particularly in cases related to product liability.[6]

Various political processes also influence the legal system. For example, the political party of the incumbent President, as well as the relative numbers of

Economic element The systems of producing, distributing, and consuming wealth

Capitalist economy An economy in which economic activity is governed by market forces and the means of production are privately owned by individuals

Socialist economy An economy in which the means of production are owned by the state and economic activity is coordinated by plan

Legal-political element The legal and governmental systems within which an organization must function

Democrats and Republicans in the Senate and House of Representatives, often has a bearing on the types of laws passed. Political issues may also influence the extent of government regulation of various laws. For instance, recent Wall Street scandals have increased political pressure on the Securities and Exchange Commission (SEC) to step up computerized tracking and criminal prosecutions of illegal stock trading by "insiders." Insider trading involves stock transactions by individuals, such as company officers or investment bankers for a company, who have access to company information that is likely to affect stock prices when it becomes public.

Sociocultural element The attitudes, values, norms, beliefs, behaviors, and associated demographic trends that are characteristic of a given geographic area

SOCIOCULTURAL ELEMENT The **sociocultural element** includes the attitudes, values, norms, beliefs, behaviors, and associated demographic trends that are characteristic of a given geographic area. Sociocultural variables are often discussed in comparisons of different countries, such as the United States and Japan or Great Britain and Germany. Multinational companies face the challenge of understanding various sociocultural differences among countries that may influence competitive success. In recognition of such differences, McDonald's requires that its foreign franchisees stick closely to operating procedures, but it allows room for different marketing methods and even a few menu modifications. For example, in Brazil McDonald's sells a soft drink made from an Amazonian berry, and in Malaysia the menu features milk shakes flavored with durian, a southeast Asian fruit considered locally to be an aphrodisiac.[7]

Because sociocultural aspects are subject to change, it is important for managers to monitor trends that might offer new opportunities or pose significant threats. Sociocultural trends can result in important shifts in the demands for certain types of products. Among the current changes affecting Americans are the tendency to delay marriage until a later age, the emergence of the single head of household as an expanding consumer element, the aging of the large baby-boomer group, the growing diversity of the work force, expanding longevity creating needs for elder care, recent trends toward downsizing in many organizations, and the increasing influence of minorities in business, politics, and community life.[8]

International element The developments in countries outside an organization's home country that have the potential to influence the organization

INTERNATIONAL ELEMENT The **international element** includes the developments in countries outside an organization's home country that have the potential to influence the organization. Although we have discussed international aspects of the other mega-environment elements, we consider international developments as a separate element because of their growing importance. The international element can have a major impact on organizations.

For one thing, international developments can greatly affect the ability of an organization to conduct business abroad. For example, fluctuations of the dollar against foreign currencies influence an organization's ability to compete in the world market. When the value of the dollar is high against foreign currencies, U.S. companies find that their opportunities to compete internationally are limited. Conversely, when the dollar falls against foreign currencies, new business opportunities open up.

Free-trade agreements, such as the North American Free Trade Agreement (NAFTA) involving Canada, Mexico, and the United States, offer vast possibilities for long-term market growth within the free-trade region. They typically allow goods, services, and funds to move more easily between the countries involved, as tariffs and other trade barriers are gradually eliminated. Such agreements, however, can also cause major changes in the ability of individual businesses to compete. Thus international factors largely beyond the direct manipulation of a particular organization can have profound effects on managers' efforts to operate successfully.

A major Swedish furniture retailer, which conducts business in 21 countries, considered many potential environmental factors in selecting its first business site in the United States (see the Case in Point discussion).

IKEA CHOOSES U.S. BEACHHEAD

CASE IN POINT

IKEA (pronounced "eye-KEY-ah"), a privately owned Swedish home-furnishings company, has been successful internationally by orienting itself toward providing well-designed furniture at an affordable price. The ready-to-assemble furniture comes packaged in cartons, is easily put together at home, and sells for 30 to 50 percent less than competing, fully assembled furniture. Another factor in the company's success is its showrooms. Usually two-story buildings, the IKEA stores are typically situated on inexpensive, undeveloped suburban land near major highways.

When IKEA decided to enter the U.S. market, its first choice for a store site was California. The retailer was already operating stores in 18 countries, including 9 in Canada, and had annual revenues approaching $2 billion. A closer look at California, though, revealed problems. California had a number of exceptionally stringent fire and safety laws governing such things as the standard for flammability in upholstered furniture. As a result, the company would have been forced either to perform a battery of time-consuming tests before opening a store in California or to produce special goods for the California market. Another obstacle was California's location. Since most of IKEA's products are made in Europe, they would need to be shipped a long distance. As a result, company executives began to explore possibilities on the east coast.

In looking for an east coast site, IKEA first went to Boston, where economic development officials gave the company representatives the usual briefing and supplied them with maps. "We drove around Boston for 2 or 3 days and really didn't get a feel for the place," says Bjorn Bayley, the president of the North American operations of IKEA. The reception around Washington, D.C., the second east coast site of interest, was similarly cool.

IKEA, a Swedish-based home furnishings company, won over its American market with well-designed, moderately priced furniture as well as such in-store facilities as a supervised "ballroom" for children to play in while their parents shop. In locating its stores, IKEA considers environmental factors, including availability of inexpensive land near highways, the right demographics, and state regulations on furniture standards.

In Philadelphia, the third choice, IKEA received substantial help from the enthusiastic Greater Philadelphia International Network, Inc., a small, business-backed group that helps attract foreign companies to the area. Furthermore, the Philadelphia area (including Delaware and southern New Jersey) provided other advantages, including plenty of young, middle-income families and relatively inexpensive commercial real estate. With the network's help, the company found suitable space in a mall, located next to a turnpike exit, in the suburb of Plymouth Meeting.

The store opened in 1985 and attracted close to 130,000 shoppers within its first few weeks. Since then, IKEA has opened stores along the east coast in such places as Washington, D.C. (Virginia suburbs); Baltimore; Pittsburgh; Elizabeth, New Jersey; and Long Island. IKEA also now has several stores in California. Several factors made the recent move to California feasible. First, the establishment of markets in the United States and Canada made it possible for IKEA to adjust many of its products to meet California fire and safety specifications. Second, over 50 percent of the items sold in North America are now manufactured in North America, further facilitating the specification changes and reducing shipping costs. Third, the company opened a distribution center in California to provide a local means of keeping stock in the stores there. IKEA is now in the process of invading the midwest.[9] ■ ■ ■

IKEA's success was greatly aided by the company's careful attention to broad environmental factors that would boost the odds in its favor. Although many aspects of the environment could not be directly altered, the managers recognized clearly that they did have some choices in regard to the environmental conditions within which they would subsequently function. They considered particularly the economic and sociocultural aspects of the Philadelphia location. The legal environment nixed the California location initially.

Task Environment

Task environment The specific outside elements with which an organization interfaces in the course of conducting its business

In the case of IKEA, attention to the broad environmental conditions that make for success was coupled with more specific concerns about the task environment. The **task environment** is the segment of the external environment made up of the specific outside elements with which an organization interfaces in the course of conducting its business. The task environment depends largely on the precise products and services that an organization decides to offer and on the locations where it chooses to conduct its business. While a single organization usually has difficulty exerting a direct influence on the mega-environment, it may be more successful in affecting its task environment. Major elements in an organization's task environment typically include customers and clients, competitors, suppliers, labor supply, and government agencies. Each organization must assess its own situation to determine its specific task environment. Elements of the task environment of the Xerox Corporation are shown in Figure 3-3.

Customers and clients Those individuals and organizations that purchase an organization's products and/or services

CUSTOMERS AND CLIENTS An organization's **customers and clients** are those individuals and organizations that purchase its products and/or services. A number of organizations have recently been making greater efforts to stay close to the customer. They are paying particular attention to service and quality, looking for niches where they can serve customers better than any other firm, and listening to customers about their needs. For example, IKEA provides baby-sitting and a cafeteria to make customers feel at home and want to stay and shop. Finding it difficult to tap the New York City area because of the lack of

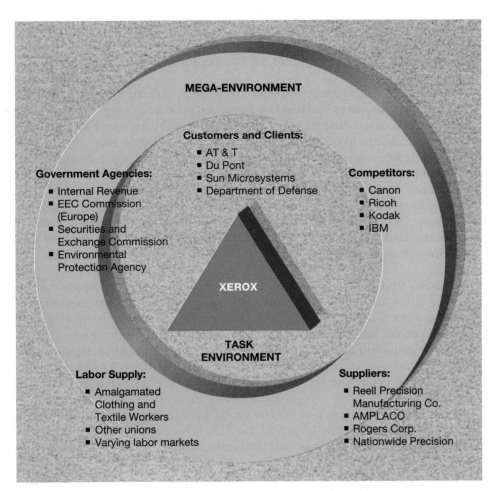

Figure 3-3 *Elements of the task environment of the Xerox Corporation.*

two major ingredients, easy access by automobile and inexpensive real estate, IKEA is testing an innovative solution. The company has opened a relatively small nontraditional store (7400 square feet compared to the 230,000-square-foot store in Elizabeth, New Jersey) on Manhattan's East 57th Street. The shop is redesigned every 2 to 3 months around a particular merchandise theme, such as "IKEA Cooks," "IKEA Rests," or "IKEA Dines," featuring items related only to the theme. Buses run hourly on the weekend to the Elizabeth store.[10]

COMPETITORS An organization's **competitors** are other organizations that either offer or have a high potential of offering rival products or services. Organizations not only need to be concerned with known competitors but also need to monitor the competitive scene for potential newcomers. For example, the office-supply-store market is currently being invaded by at least two major discount merchants—Staples and OfficeMax. These merchants operate warehouse-type stores that offer discounts ranging from 20 to 75 percent off retail prices on a huge selection of office supplies.[11]

While organizations need to concern themselves with who their competitors are, they also need to keep abreast of what their competitors are doing. For example, Xerox uses a technique called benchmarking to estimate what a competitor does and how much it costs. To get a fix on Kodak's distribution and handling costs, for instance, Xerox managers ordered some Kodak copiers and then noted where they were shipped from, how they were shipped, and

Competitors Other organizations that either offer or have a high potential of offering rival products or services

even how they were packed.[12] For some ideas about how organizations obtain information about competitors, see the Management Skills for the Twenty-First Century discussion, "Keeping Tabs on Competitors."

Suppliers Those organizations and individuals that supply the resources an organization needs to conduct its operations

SUPPLIERS An organization's **suppliers** are those organizations and individuals that supply the resources (such as raw materials, products, or services) the organization needs to conduct its operations. Traditionally, the conventional belief in the United States has been that it is best to have multiple suppliers in order to reduce dependence on any one source. World competition is changing that view. Companies are finding that they are better able to cut costs by reducing the number of suppliers they deal with and negotiating contracts with them. In 1980, Xerox ordered parts and components from 5000 vendors worldwide. Since then, by using fewer vendors, Xerox has been able to enforce tougher quality standards, get better prices, and build more cooperative working relationships with its suppliers.[13]

Labor supply Those individuals who are potentially employable by an organization

MANAGING DIVERSITY: LABOR SUPPLY An organization's **labor supply** consists of those individuals who are potentially employable by the organization. The ability to attract, motivate, and retain the human resources necessary to provide competitive products and services is a crucial variable for most organizations. The Automobile Association of America (AAA) moved its headquarters from a Washington, D.C., suburb to Orlando, Florida, primarily because of consultant reports projecting severe labor shortages in the D.C. area over the next several decades.[14]

Employers can expect to recruit from a labor supply that is becoming increasingly diverse. A breakdown of the U.S. labor force by gender and non-Hispanic and Hispanic groups for 1990, with projections for 2005, is shown in Table 3-1.

TABLE 3-1 SHARE OF U.S. LABOR FORCE, NON-HISPANIC AND HISPANIC GROUPS, 1990 AND PROJECTIONS FOR 2005 (NUMBERS IN THOUSANDS)

GROUP	LABOR FORCE 1990 NUMBER	PERCENT OF TOTAL	LABOR FORCE 2005 NUMBER	PERCENT OF TOTAL
White, non-Hispanic	98,013	78.5	110,015	73.0
Men	53,784	43.1	57,545	38.2
Women	44,229	35.4	52,470	34.8
African American, non-Hispanic	13,340	10.7	17,447	11.6
Men	6,628	5.3	8,537	5.7
Women	6,712	5.4	8,910	5.9
Hispanic	9,577	7.7	16,789	11.1
Men	5,756	4.6	9,902	6.6
Women	3,822	3.1	6,888	4.6
Asian and other, non-Hispanic*	3,855	3.1	6,482	4.3
Men	2,064	1.6	3,356	2.2
Women	1,791	1.4	3,126	2.1

*Includes Asians, Pacific Islanders, American Indians, and Alaskan natives.

Source: Compiled by Janice Hamilton Outtz, using *Outlook 1990–2005*, BLS Bulletin 2402, p. 39. Reprinted from Anthony Patrick Carnevale and Susan Carol Stone, *The American Mosaic: An In-Depth Report on the Future of Diversity at Work,* McGraw-Hill, New York, 1995.

MANAGEMENT SKILLS FOR THE TWENTY-FIRST CENTURY

Keeping Tabs On Competitors

Here are 10 legal ways to track what your competitors are doing:

1. Commercial data bases are an easy and fast means of obtaining information. Data bases contain published articles from newspapers, magazines, and trade publications, as well as reports from stock analysts, patent filings, biographical information, and so on. This information can be accessed by computer. Information about various data bases is contained in the *Directory of Online Data Bases,* published by Cuandra/Elsevier (New York). Also many companies now have web sites on the World Wide Web that contain useful information about new products, special promotions, and other activities.

2. Specialty trade publications that deal with industries and product areas provide very current information about major personnel changes, product advertising, new product announcements, trade show notices, and the like. The *Standard Periodical Directory* and the *Oxbridge Directory of Newsletters,* both published by Oxbridge Communications (New York), may help you locate trade publications applicable to your area of interest.

3. News clippings from local newspapers often provide specific information not available in national publications. You can either subscribe to the newspapers themselves or hire a clipping service. Clipping services charge a basic fee, as well as a fee for each clipping. Check your telephone directory for clipping services.

4. Help-wanted advertisements give clues about expansion plans, new technologies competitors are pursuing, and even financial status information that may be embedded in ads, especially those for high-level managers. Since clipping services will usually clip ads for certain types of jobs but will generally not clip ads for only a particular company, you may want to subscribe to your competitor's hometown papers and check the Sunday edition, in particular.

5. Published market research reports can often be helpful. To learn about these reports, consult *Findex,* published by the National Standards Association (Gaithersburg, Maryland). *Findex* appears annually, with midyear supplements, and is also available in a computerized data base that is updated on a more frequent basis.

6. Wall Street reports give information about public companies (stock is publicly traded) and their various subsidiaries through analysis by securities analysts at brokerage firms. These reports are often available through a data base called Investext, which is offered by several data-base services. Another source of information is the *Wall Street Transcript,* a weekly newsletter that covers round table discussions about particular industries, including private as well as public companies.

7. Trade shows and the product literature that can be obtained at such shows are good sources of information about new product innovations, price changes, and marketing methods. Speeches and presentations given at trade shows are often helpful as well.

8. Public filings (federal, state, and local) often provide information about financial data and future plans. The filings include reports that public companies must submit to the SEC, records of bankruptcy cases and other court cases, state-required annual reports, Uniform Commercial Code (UCC) filings (required by most states when a company obtains a commercial loan from a bank), and franchise filings (often required by states when a franchise is sold).

9. Advertisements give clues about competitors' marketing strategies. Advertising or clipping services can often obtain copies of advertisements for you. Information about competitors' advertising expenditures by product in various media (TV, magazine, etc.) can be obtained from services like Leading National Advertisers in New York.

10. Personal contacts can provide many tidbits of useful information about competitors' movements. A contact base may include university professors who have knowledge about technological advances, suppliers, customers, purchasing agents, service technicians, and Wall Street analysts. Trade shows and professional conferences are particularly good places to develop contacts.[15]

In combination, diversity and the baby boomers will have the major impact on changes in the character of the work force by 2005. However, the diversity influence will be growing more pronounced, while the baby-boomer impact will be lessening. Researchers have identified several trends based on U.S. Bureau of Labor Statistics data. Although their share of the total will decrease, white non-Hispanic workers will still be the dominant force in 2005, constituting 73 percent of the total work force. Half of the new workers entering the labor force between 1990 and 2005 will be women, although the rate of increase in the proportion of women in the labor force is slowing down. By 2005, more than 6 out of every 10 women who are working age will be in the labor force, a rate that is close to the labor participation of men. Minorities will continue to increase their share of the work force by 2005. The increase will be partially due to higher minority immigration rates and increases in labor participation by minority women. African-American workers will represent almost 12 percent of the total, while Hispanic workers will number about 11 percent of the work force. Workers in the "Asian and other" category will number just over 4 percent. If the shifts shown in Table 3-1 do not look dramatic at first, keep in mind that a 1 percent change between 1990 and 2005 will involve about 1.25 million persons. The labor force will continue to grow, but at a slower pace than it did during the 1970s and 1980s, when baby boomers entered the labor force in swelling numbers. Overall, by 2005, the work force is expected to number about 151 million, compared with 125 million in 1990.

Baby boomers, who have been a dominant element in the work force for the last couple of decades, will have a gradually lessening impact in the workplace. They will constitute less than half of the labor force by 2005, down from about 55 percent in the mid-1980s. By 2005, some baby boomers will have moved into the older-worker category of 55 years of age and older, because the first group of baby boomers turns 55 years of age in 2001. Older workers will constitute about 14.7 percent of the work force by 2005, compared with 12.3 percent in 1990.

As a result of the increasing diversity, many companies have instituted programs aimed at helping organization members value and effectively utilize a more diverse work force. Kentucky Fried Chicken is one such company (see the Managing Diversity box).

Given the increasing globalization of business, at least one observer speaks of a global work force in the twenty-first century. According to this view, workers (especially the better educated) will tend to migrate to countries in need of their skills, despite immigration laws that often discourage such movements.[16] Labor supply issues are discussed further in Chapter 10.

Government agencies
Agencies that provide services and monitor compliance with laws and regulations at local, state or regional, and national levels

GOVERNMENT AGENCIES Various **government agencies** provide services and monitor compliance with laws and regulations at local, state or regional, and national levels. For the most part, the task environment of a particular organization involves interactions with representatives of specific government agencies. At the local level, interactions may involve representatives from such organizations as zoning commissions, local tax agencies, consumer affairs offices, and police departments. Agencies at the state level may include health departments, state tax agencies, and worker's compensation commissions. At the national level, interfaces may be necessary with such diverse agencies as the Equal Employment Opportunities Commission, Department of Labor, Internal Revenue Service, U.S. Customs Service, and Federal Communications Commission.

MANAGING DIVERSITY

Kentucky Fried Chicken Seeks "Designates"

When Larry Drake was mixing mashed potatoes, breading onion rings, or scrubbing floors at Kentucky Fried Chicken (KFC) outlets around Pittsburgh, it probably was not obvious to onlookers that he had already been "designated" for much bigger things. Within 9 months, though, Drake became KFC's most senior black executive when he was promoted to vice president and general manager for the midwest region. Drake's promotion was part of KFC's Designate program, a special approach by which the fast-food chain recruits seasoned managers from other companies. In the course of recruiting individuals with fresh ideas, KFC uses the program to increase the number of female and minority executives.

Under the Designate program, KFC typically retains a variety of search firms owned by women, minorities, and white males. Often, different search firms will be given the same criteria, but each will be asked to prepare a slate of candidates with a given demographic characteristic—for example, all women, all minority men, or all white men. Then KFC might hire one person from each list, ensuring a diversity of executives for the company.

For instance, the first 13 individuals hired under the program included 2 white women, 2 black women, 3 black men, and 6 white men.

Drake, for example, was recruited from Coca-Cola, where he had managed $100 million worth of bottler accounts, to join KFC, which is owned by Coke's arch rival, PepsiCo. In Drake's case, part of his training under the Designate program was learning the business from the bottom up—first working in stores, then managing a cluster of restaurants, and then managing

Bill Armstrong, a KFC market manager in Chicago, was hired under the Designate program, a program aimed at recruiting managers from other companies and at adding to the ranks of female and minority executives. Armstrong was recruited from a pool of junior military officers.

entire markets. His subsequent promotion to vice president and general manager in the midwest included responsibility for several hundred company and franchise restaurants with combined revenues of about $800 million. KFC has also been working to ensure diversity in the middle management ranks.[17]

■ ANALYZING ENVIRONMENTAL CONDITIONS

Although most organizational researchers view the environment as an important element affecting organizations, perspectives differ on the exact nature of the relationship between organizations and their environments. In this section, we examine two major views of the organization-environment interface, and we explore major characteristics of the environment.

Views of the Organization-Environment Interface

Among the most prominent approaches to explaining the nature of the interface are the population ecology and resource dependence models.[18]

Population ecology model A model that focuses on populations or groups of organizations and argues that environmental factors cause organizations with appropriate characteristics to survive and others to fail

Natural selection model A term sometimes used for the *population ecology model*

POPULATION ECOLOGY MODEL The **population ecology model** is a view that focuses on populations or groups of organizations and argues that environmental factors cause organizations with appropriate characteristics to survive and others to fail. The model is sometimes referred to as the **natural selection model.** In the population ecology view, organizational survival is largely due to fortuitous circumstances in which particular organizational forms happen to fit particular environmental conditions. Since organizations generally do not change rapidly, according to this view, managers have limited capacity to affect the fates of their organizations.[19]

The potential ramifications of the environment are illustrated by a study conducted by *Forbes* magazine on its seventieth anniversary in 1987. *Forbes* wanted to determine how many of the 100 largest companies (in terms of assets) in 1917 were still among the 100 largest 70 years later. Only 22 of the original companies appeared on the list in 1987. Of these, 11 had the same company name as they had in 1917 (American Telephone & Telegraph; Eastman Kodak; E. I. Du Pont de Nemours; Ford Motor; General Electric; General Motors; Pacific Gas & Electric; Procter & Gamble; Sears, Roebuck; Southern California Edison; and Westinghouse Electric). The other 11 had changed their names. The 78 companies that were no longer on the list had met a variety of fates. Some had grown, but too slowly to retain their top position; others had been acquired; still others had faltered badly and faded from sight. At now-defunct Baldwin Locomotive, for example, executives had insisted that new technology could never replace the steam locomotive. On the other hand, Atlantic Gulf & West Indies Steam Ship Lines presumably ran into a string of bad luck associated with the loss of ships on high seas.[20] Could something have been done to keep these major companies prospering? Proponents of the population ecology model do not think so. The resource dependence model, however, presents a different perspective on the situation.

Resource dependence model A model that highlights organizational dependence on the environment for resources and argues that organizations attempt to manipulate the environment to reduce that dependence

RESOURCE DEPENDENCE MODEL The **resource dependence model** is a view that highlights organizational dependence on the environment for resources and argues that organizations attempt to manipulate the environment to reduce that dependence.[21] In the resource dependence view, no organization can generate internally all the various resources (such as financing, materials, and services) it needs to operate effectively. For example, even giant General Motors purchases many of its parts from outside, rather than making them internally. By forming relationships with other organizations, an organization can solve many of its own resource problems. However, such interorganizational relationships create dependence on the other organizations and reduce the flexibility that a given organization has in making its own decisions and taking its own actions. Hence, organizations attempt to be as independent as possible by controlling as many of their critical resources as they can or developing alternative sources.

For example, when IBM was developing its PS/2 personal computer, the company contracted with the Microsoft Corporation of Redmond, Washington, for preparation of a new software operating system called OS/2. By contracting the software preparation, IBM could speed up the introduction of its new computer. Unfortunately, Microsoft developed not only the specified system for IBM but also a competing, superior product called Windows. Moreover, the Windows program would run on older IBM computers, making them easier to use. One reason why Microsoft developed the competing program was that the company did not want to be overly dependent on sales of the new PS/2, which were far from ensured. Ironically, the availability of the Windows program caused slower sales of IBM's new PS/2 computer. IBM reacted by developing its own competing software, but the move came too late to gain a substantial market share over Windows.[22] This situation illustrates how resource needs and dependence intertwine as organizations seek to deal with their environments.

In contrast to the population ecology approach, which holds that managerial actions are of limited consequence in dealing with the environment, the resource dependence model argues that managers do have strategic choices, or options, and that these choices influence organizational success. Managers not only have choices in their reactions to environmental change but also have options in their attempts to influence the nature of the environment itself.[23] Hence, in regard to the *Forbes* study mentioned previously, perhaps Baldwin Locomotive would have fared better had its managers paid closer attention to the changing environment. Even in the case of Atlantic Gulf & West Indies Steam Ship Lines, the company could perhaps have oriented some part of the business to less risky ventures.

RECONCILING THE DIFFERING MODELS Both the population ecology and the resource dependence models offer perspectives that are useful to managers. The population ecology model helps highlight the fact that organizations have little control over a number of environmental factors that may influence them and that luck may play some role in an organization's success.

On the other hand, the resource dependence approach points out that managers often do have options in influencing many aspects of the environment, including relationships with other organizations. Hence, managers should attempt to monitor, understand, and potentially influence environmental elements, recognizing that unforeseen environmental factors can have major impacts on organizations.

Characteristics of the Environment

Accurately assessing the environment is a difficult, if not impossible, task. From one point of view, an organization's environment is an *objective* reality—a set of concrete conditions that theoretically could be measured perfectly to give managers complete information. Yet, from a practical point of view, managers are more likely to take action on the environment as they see it. Thus, the environment may be more realistically thought of as a *subjective* reality, existing in the minds of managers.[24] Since managers are likely to act on their own perceptions, they need to verify those perceptions, if possible, through alternative sources of information (perhaps the opinions of others, as well as objective data).[25]

In analyzing the environmental situation faced by an organization, it is useful to consider two key concepts: environmental uncertainty and environmental munificence, or capacity. Although the main focus is on the task environment, relevant trends in the mega-environment should also be considered.

ENVIRONMENTAL UNCERTAINTY Environmental uncertainty is a condition in which future environmental circumstances affecting an organization cannot be accurately assessed and predicted.[26] The more uncertain an organization's environment, the more time and effort managers must expend monitoring it, assessing the implications for the organization and deciding what present and future actions to take. The degree of environmental uncertainty is a function of two major factors, complexity and dynamism.[27]

Complexity The term **environmental complexity** refers to the number of elements in an organization's environment and their degree of similarity. Envi-

Environmental uncertainty A condition in which future environmental circumstances affecting an organization cannot be accurately assessed and predicted

Environmental complexity The number of elements in an organization's environment and their degree of similarity

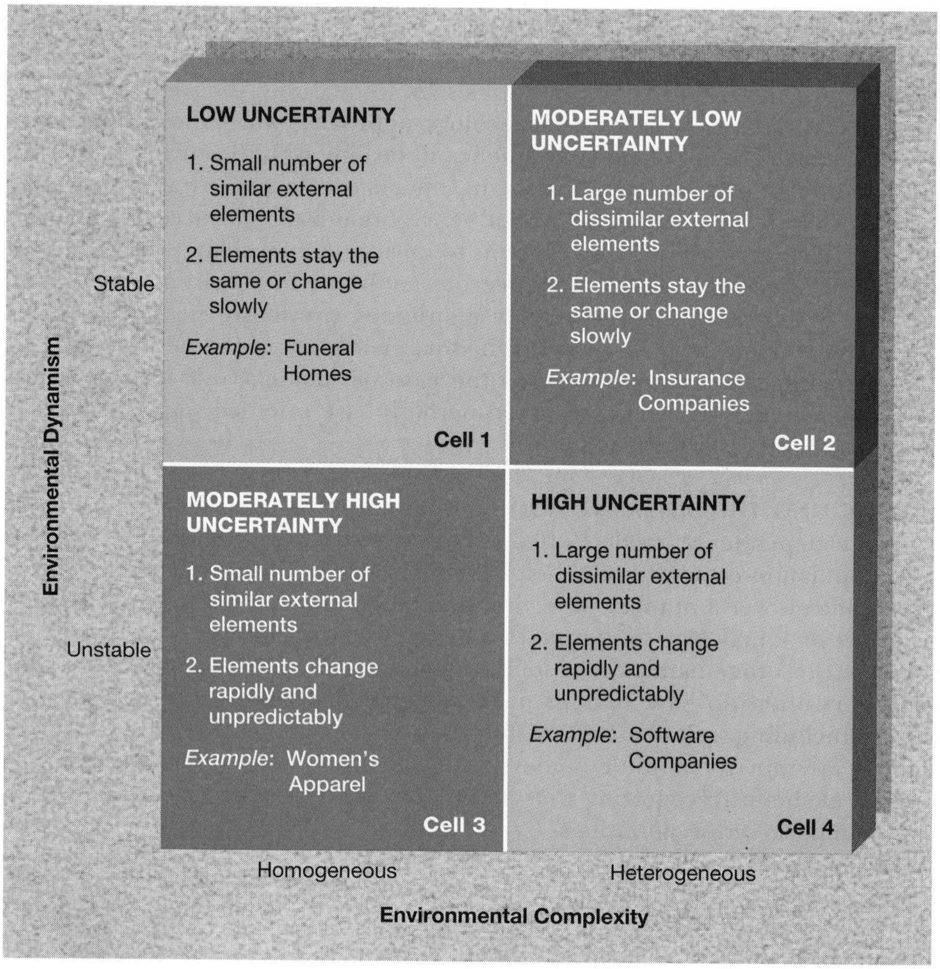

Figure 3-4 *Assessing the degree of environmental uncertainty. (Adapted from Robert Duncan, "What Is the Right Organization Structure? Decision Tree Analysis Provides the Answer," Organizational Dynamics, Winter 1979, p. 63.)*

ronments in which there are a relatively small number of similar items are said to be *homogeneous*. In contrast, environments in which there are a large number of dissimilar items are considered to be *heterogeneous*. As the elements in the environment become more heterogeneous, managers have more variables with which they must contend.

Environmental dynamism
The rate and predictability of change in the elements of an organization's environment

Dynamism The term **environmental dynamism** refers to the rate and predictability of change in the elements of an organization's environment. Environments in which the rate of change is slow and relatively predictable are considered to be *stable*. Conversely, environments in which the rate of change is fast and relatively unpredictable are said to be *unstable*. As elements in the environment become more unstable, they present greater challenges to managers.

Assessing Environmental Uncertainty The concepts of complexity and dynamism can be used to make an overall assessment of the degree of environmental uncertainty. Such an assessment can be done by analyzing the important elements in the task environment and the major potential influences in the mega-environment (see Figure 3-4). As cell 1 in Figure 3-4 suggests, uncertainty is relatively low when both dynamism and complexity are low. Such a situation is likely to prevail in the case of the funeral industry, in which there is slow change and a relatively steady stream of customers with similar needs. In cell 2, dynamism is low but complexity is high, creating a situation of moderately low uncertainty. An example of this type of situation is the insurance industry, in which companies serve a diverse set of customer needs but competitive elements change fairly slowly. In cell 3, dynamism is high but complexity is low, leading to moderately high uncertainty. This situation is characteristic of the women's apparel industry, in which the customers and retailers constitute fairly homogeneous market segments but fashion trends change rapidly. Finally, cell 4 represents both high dynamism and high complexity, resulting in a condition of high uncertainty. High environmental uncertainty is currently found in the computer software industry, in which conditions change rapidly and a large number of environmental factors (such as technological change, vast numbers of diverse customers, and strenuous competition) exert strong heterogeneous pressures.

Conditions of uncertainty may change over a period of time. For example, an environment that is relatively homogeneous and stable at one point can change (perhaps gradually) to a condition of greater uncertainty. As a result, managers need to make periodic reassessments of their situations.

ENVIRONMENTAL MUNIFICENCE Another important characteristic of the environment is **environmental munificence,** the extent to which the environment can support sustained growth and stability.[28] Environmental munificence can range from relatively rich to relatively lean, depending on the level of resources that are available to the organization within the environment.[29] When organizations operate in rich environments, they are able to build up a cushion of internal resources, such as capital, equipment, and experience. A high level of internal resources can subsequently fund the innovations and expansions that may help an organization sustain its position, as well as weather leaner times. Unfortunately, rich environments eventually tend to attract other organizations. At the Champion Spark Plug Company, managers did not perceive the impact of some of the major changes taking place in their environment, including the declining munificence (see the Case in Point discussion).

Environmental munificence
The extent to which the environment can support sustained growth and stability

---

CHAMPION LOSES ITS SPARK

CASE IN POINT

Almost since 1910, when it was founded by the Stranahan brothers in Toledo, Ohio, the Champion Spark Plug Company has been the leading U.S. maker of spark plugs. In the mid-1980s, the company had a 38 percent share of the market for spark plugs.

Unfortunately, market share was not the only issue. Since the early 1970s, when the oil shortage spurred efforts to make cars more fuel-efficient, there has been a steady decline in the proportion of eight-cylinder cars. By the mid-1980s, at least 45 percent of the new cars built in North America had four-cylinder engines, compared with about 3 percent in the mid-1970s. The fewer the cylinders, the fewer the spark plugs that are needed. In addition, the introduction of electronic ignitions and unleaded fuel has meant that a spark plug can now last for 30,000 miles, rather than 10,000 miles, as in the past. Another development affecting the demand for spark plugs is the fact that most Japanese cars sold in the United States have spark plugs made by Japanese companies. As a result of these factors, Champion's profit levels began to decline.

Although the downward trend in spark plug use had been apparent for some time, Champion, led by a son of one of the founders, was slow to respond.

While competitors began expanding their product lines and setting up motor tune-up franchises, Champion kept its brand name attached to a single product. "If you're a gardener of roses and grow championship roses, you don't introduce new strains," says Duane Stranahan, Jr., grandson of one of the company's founders and a member of the board.

Finally, the Stranahan clan brought in a new chief executive, O. Lee Henry, who began to bring about needed major changes. For example, the Champion name was put on a new line of products that included air filters, ignition cables, and fuel additives. Progress was slow, however, because the limited shelf space in auto-supply stores meant that many retailers were reluctant to stock the new Champion products. Despite efforts by the Stranahan family, which controlled 31 percent of the stock, to keep the company independent, Champion was acquired by Cooper Industries, a Houston-based industrial-products maker, in 1989. Under Cooper, Champion has closed plants in Detroit and Toledo (leaving 15 plants worldwide), consolidated operations, and saved $50 million. Cooper, which had run mainly domestic enterprises before buying Champion, is using the spark plug company's operations in other countries to learn how to operate internationally.[30]   ■■■

■ MANAGING ENVIRONMENTAL ELEMENTS

Perhaps the problems at the Champion Spark Plug Company could have been avoided. While recognizing that there are limitations in managing environmental factors, a number of organizational theorists (e.g., those advocating the resource dependence model) view environmental elements as somewhat responsive to action by managers and advocate proactive measures. For example, Carnival Cruise Lines, the world's largest cruise operator, has been successful in attracting new passengers by shifting to an approach aimed more at the mass market. Carnival's new Las Vegas–type cruises include the amenities of a resort at a reasonable price.[31] Managers essentially have three major options: adapt to the existing environmental elements, attempt to influence environmental favorability, and/or shift the domain of operations away from threatening environmental elements and toward more beneficial ones.[32] The major methods of implementing these approaches are presented in Table 3-2. The feasibility of any or all of these approaches depends on the situation, but prospects are enhanced if the environment offers high munificence or if the organization has built a cushion of resources.

Adaptation

The adaptation approach involves changing internal operations and activities to make the organization more compatible with its environment. This strategy

TABLE 3-2 APPROACHES TO MANAGING ENVIRONMENTAL IMPACTS	
APPROACH	**METHODS**
Adaptation	Buffering, smoothing, forecasting, and rationing
Favorability influence	Advertising and engaging in public relations, boundary spanning, recruiting, negotiating contracts, co-opting, establishing strategic alliances, joining trade associations, and engaging in political activity
Domain shifts	Changing domain completely or diversifying into some new areas

Carnival Cruise Lines' Ecstasy *sails for the Bahamas with 2500 passengers pampered with such amenities as a saltwater pool and adjoining jacuzzi, a neon-lit casino, state-of-the-art fitness rooms, and sumptuous midnight buffets. Carnival has successfully shifted its appeal from an older market to a younger crowd representing a broader income base. With cabins 100 percent full, Carnival is breaking sales records.*

essentially accepts the existing environment as a given and seeks to develop some rational process for adjusting to it. Four common methods used by organizations to adapt to environmental fluctuations are buffering, smoothing, forecasting, and rationing.[33]

BUFFERING The use of **buffering** involves stockpiling either inputs into or outputs from a production or service process in order to cope with environmental fluctuations. Buffering by stockpiling inputs is used when it is difficult to line up reliable sources of inputs, such as supplies. Conversely, buffering by maintaining inventories of finished products is used when wide fluctuations in market demand make it difficult to produce outputs efficiently as they are ordered. Buffering is not always feasible because of high expense, perishability of materials, or the difficulty of stockpiling services, such as customer service in a restaurant. Furthermore, substantial buffering of inputs and finished products can lead to obsolescence before the items are used or sold.

Buffering Stockpiling either inputs into or outputs from a production or service process in order to cope with environmental fluctuations

SMOOTHING While buffering seeks to accommodate market fluctuations, **smoothing** involves taking actions aimed at reducing the impact of fluctuations, given the market. For example, utilities often discount their rates during certain time periods to encourage use of energy in designated slow-demand periods. Department stores may run sales during slow months. Restaurants often offer coupons that can be used only on certain weekday nights when business is typically slow. Such actions may avoid the inefficiencies that occur when expansion to meet peak demands results in underutilized resources during nonpeak times.

Smoothing Taking actions aimed at reducing the impact of fluctuations, given the market

FORECASTING Another method for dealing with environmental fluctuations is *forecasting,* the process of making predictions about changing conditions and future events that may significantly affect the business of an organization. To the extent that it is possible to predict future conditions with a reasonable level of accuracy, it may be possible to prepare in advance to meet the fluctuations. For example, on the basis of customers' shopping habits, grocery stores frequently hire part-time cashiers to supplement regular staff during expected busy periods. For situations such as this, forecasts based on experience with patterns may be reasonably accurate. When environmental fluctuations are related to more complex and dynamic factors, such as trends in the economy, more sophisticated forecasting techniques may be required. Many companies have staff economists and/or subscribe to services that provide economic forecasts based on elaborate econometric models.

RATIONING Environmental fluctuations are sometimes also handled by **rationing,** providing limited access to a product or service that is in high demand. For example, many colleges and universities ration slots for popular majors by establishing program prerequisites, such as the achievement of a certain grade point average by the end of the sophomore year. By rationing, the organization can avoid having to expand capacity to meet a temporary upward swing in demand. This is advantageous, since many costs associated with capacity expansion (e.g., extra plants, equipment, or classroom buildings) continue during downward demand swings. Rationing is also used when demand exceeds forecasts or when new production expands slowly (e.g., because of heavy costs and considerable risk if forecasted demand does not materialize). Rationing does have a disadvantage, however. In denying a consumer a product or service, the organization is turning away potential business. For example, after IKEA, the Swedish furniture retailer, first opened stores in the United States, shortages of the most popular items cost the company an estimated $500 million in annual sales.[34]

Rationing Providing limited access to a product or service that is in high demand

Favorability Influence

In contrast to adaptation strategies, the favorability influence approach involves attempting to alter environmental elements in order to make them more compatible with the needs of the organization. Rather than accepting environmental elements as givens, this approach holds that at least some aspects of the environment can be changed by the organization in advantageous ways.

There are a number of major methods that organizations can use in attempting to influence significant environmental elements. These include advertising and engaging in public relations, boundary spanning, recruiting, negotiating contracts, co-opting, establishing strategic alliances, joining trade associations, and engaging in political activities.[35]

ADVERTISING AND PUBLIC RELATIONS One means of influencing the environment is *advertising,* the use of communications media to gain favorable publicity for particular products and services. Closely aligned to advertising is *public relations,* the use of communications media and related activities to create a favorable overall impression of the organization among the public. In combination, advertising and public relations can help promote a positive feeling toward an organization among environmental elements. For example, in addition to regular advertising, many major companies sponsor such events as U.S. participation in the Olympics, take part in charitable endeavors such as the United Way, and donate time and money to a variety of groups including colleges and universities.

Boundary spanning Creating roles within the organization that interface with important elements in the environment

BOUNDARY SPANNING Another means of influence is **boundary spanning,** creating roles within the organization that interface with important elements in the environment. Boundary spanners, the people in these roles, can fulfill two different functions.[36] First, they can serve an information-processing function by collecting information from the environment, filtering out what is important, and transmitting it to those inside the organization who can act on the information. Second, they can perform an external representation function by

NYNEX has formed a joint venture with the Charoen Pokphand (CP) Group, head-quartered in Bangkok, to increase the number of telephone lines per person in Thailand from 3 to 10 per 100 by the turn of the century. Joint ventures like this one, called Telecom Asia, allow companies to pool their resources to achieve greater effectiveness.

presenting information about the organization to those outside. Boundary spanners include salespersons, purchasing specialists, personnel recruiters, admissions officers, shipping and receiving agents, receptionists, lawyers, and scientists who maintain close ties with developments in their fields.

RECRUITING A further means of environmental influence is *recruiting,* the process of finding and attempting to attract job candidates who are capable of effectively filling job vacancies. This tool can be used for environmental influence when organizations seek job candidates who have a knowledge of and close ties to a significant element of the environment. For example, organizations often hire executives from specific companies or in particular industries because of their environmental knowledge and connections. Many executives in rival computer firms began their careers at IBM.

NEGOTIATING CONTRACTS In some cases, influence attempts are made by *negotiating contracts,* which means seeking favorable agreements on matters of importance to the organization. Specific agreements with customers and suppliers are one common means of creating environmental favorability.

CO-OPTING Another means of influence is **co-opting,** the process of absorbing key members of important environmental elements into the leadership or policy-making structure of an organization. A common example of co-optation is the addition of key members of the environment to boards of directors. For instance, most universities have prominent individuals on their boards of directors or regents. These individuals often help the universities deal more effectively with environmental elements, particularly in the area of raising funds from business and/or legislatures. Powerful and influential outside individuals, however, may raise serious questions about the organization's practices and, thereby, constitute a threat to current management.[37]

Co-opting Absorbing key members of important environmental elements into the leadership or policy-making structure of an organization

STRATEGIC ALLIANCES An increasing phenomenon, a **strategic alliance** is an arrangement whereby two or more independent organizations form a cooper-

Strategic alliance An arrangement whereby two or more independent organizations form a cooperative partnership to gain some mutual strategic advantage

Joint venture An agreement involving two or more organizations that arrange to produce a product or service jointly

ative partnership to gain some mutual strategic advantage.[38] Often strategic alliances involve joint ventures. A **joint venture** is an agreement involving two or more organizations that arrange to produce a product or service through a jointly owned enterprise. Strategic alliances usually occur because there is some mutual advantage for the organizations involved that would be difficult to duplicate if each acted alone. Such alliances are becoming more common largely because cost, market, and technological factors often encourage the pooling of resources for greater effectiveness.[39] For example, Toys 'R' Us and McDonald's (which owns a 20 percent stake) have formed a joint venture to establish a chain of toy stores in Japan, sometimes with McDonald's food outlets on the premises. So far, the venture has captured 6 percent of the toy market in Japan, making it number one.[40] Unfortunately, some 7 out of 10 joint ventures fall short of expectations or are disbanded. This is primarily because the technology or market doesn't materialize, a partner's objectives change, or managers in the allied organizations find it difficult to work together.[41]

Trade associations Organizations composed of individuals or firms with common business concerns

TRADE ASSOCIATIONS Trade associations are organizations composed of individuals or firms with common business concerns. Members of trade associations include manufacturers, distributors, importers, brokers, and retailers of a product or group of products. They may also be individuals or organizations concerned with supplying, transporting, or using the goods or services of a particular industry. Examples of trade associations are the National Coffee Service Association, a group of 700 companies that supply coffee, snacks, and vending equipment to America's offices; the National Tire Dealers and Retreaders Association, consisting of 5000 tire dealers and retreaders; and the Third Class Mail Association, representing 500 companies that depend on the less costly third-class postal rate.[42] Because they represent the pooled resources of many individuals or organizations, trade associations can be highly effective in conducting public relations campaigns, influencing legislation through lobbying efforts, and otherwise positively affecting the favorability of the environment within which their members operate.

POLITICAL ACTIVITY The environment can also be affected by *political activity*, in which organizations attempt to enhance their competitive situations by influencing legislation and/or the behavior of government regulatory agencies. Political activities may be carried out by a single organization in its own behalf or by several organizations or associations for the collective well-being of the group. When the Dayton Hudson Corporation, a Minneapolis-based retailer, was threatened by a takeover attempt from Washington's Haft family, the company swung into political action. Although it had a good reputation in Minnesota, the company hired the top five lobbying firms in the state, got its employees to engage in a massive letter-writing campaign, and called in favors from Minnesota charities that it had supported for years. As a result, emergency legislation was passed that gave Minnesota one of the toughest antitakeover laws in the country. It was signed by the governor just 7 days after the company asked the state to tighten its takeover laws.[43]

Domain Shifts

Domain shifts Changes in the mix of products and services offered so that an organization will interface with more favorable environmental elements

Another approach to managing environmental elements is to make **domain shifts,** changes in the mix of products and services offered so that an organization will interface with more favorable environmental elements. One way of doing this is to move entirely out of a current product, service, or geographic area and into a more favorable domain. Another way is to expand current domains through diversification, the expansion of products and services offered. For example, when the Acmat Corporation, a leading asbestos removal company, ran into severe difficulties renewing its liability insurance, the company invested in the insurance business. The result was United Coastal Insurance, which specializes in writing asbestos liability policies.[44] One well-known company that has used both domain shifts and favorability influence methods to deal with environmental threats is Harley-Davidson (see the Case in Point discussion).

HARLEY-DAVIDSON ON THE ROAD AGAIN

Harley-Davidson, Inc., the Milwaukee-based maker of large, heavy motorcycles called "hogs" by owners, has staged a major comeback after almost being driven out of business by imports. Harley's troubles began in the mid-1970s, when the company was owned by AMF, Inc., and had a reputation for uneven quality and a slow rate of innovation. The engine used on the Harley cycles was known for leaking oil and vibrating excessively. Moreover, Japanese cycles of much better quality were invading the market.

To solve these problems, AMF hired Vaughn Beals to run Harley. Beals quickly set up a quality control program and began to develop new product lines. As the onslaught of competition from Japanese bikes continued, AMF lost interest in the company and sold it to Beals and 12 other Harley executives in 1980.

Over the next 18 months, Harley lost close to $30 million as the executives struggled to cut costs, install a new inventory system, and encourage worker involvement in making improvements. A major break came when Harley convinced President Reagan and the U.S. International Trade Commission that Japanese competitors were selling excess inventory in the United States at below-cost prices. The commission set a 5-year tariff on heavy motor-

Workers at Harley-Davidson plants have to double production to meet the demands of its "HOG"-wild customers. It was not always this sweet for the motorcycle company. In the late 1970s the popularity of Japanese imports almost ran Harley-Davidson out of business. The turnaround came when new management improved the quality of its products, expanded the product line, influenced the government to set tariffs on imports, and launched a catchy advertising campaign.

cycles that would gradually decline from 45 percent to 10 percent within 5 years.

Quality began to improve significantly, and Harley launched a major advertising campaign to get the word to potential customers. A series of television ads invited bikers to visit any of more than 600 dealers for a free ride on a new Harley. Within 3 weeks, dealers had given 90,000 rides to 40,000 people (about 50 percent owned bikes made by other manufacturers). So many of the riders eventually bought Harley bikes that Harley now has fleets of demonstration cycles that it sends to various motorcycle rallies. The company also created the Harley Owners Group (HOG), which currently has approximately 100,000 members and produces a bimonthly newsletter.

Within a couple of years, Harley was making enough profits to sell stock to the public. The company used the funds to help accelerate new product development and to purchase a motor-home maker, Holiday Rambler. At the same time, the company asked to have the Japanese tariffs removed one year early.

Today Harley enjoys a 58 percent share of the U.S. market for heavy-weight bikes. The company has sold the Holiday Rambler division, which had been only marginally profitable. Demand for Harley-Davidson motorcycles is so great that bikers must wait 18 months for a new bike to be delivered. Harley holds only 10 percent of the even larger European market because of a promise to American dealers that the company will not ship more than 30 percent of its motorcycles abroad while a shortage persists in the United States. Even so, Harley holds 16 percent of the Japanese market for heavy-weight bikes. Harley does face the danger that continuing major shortages will cause potential customers to purchase bikes from Japanese competitors. Through Plan 2003, Harley is making a concerted effort to double production and will be increasing its international focus. Meanwhile here in the United States, an estimated 200,000 Harley fans continue to bike to Sturgis, South Dakota, each year for the annual Sturgis Rally and Race. During the celebration, bikers from all walks of life can enjoy admiring each other's Harley-Davidson motorcyles. While Harley is sometimes known as the only product individuals have tattooed to their bodies, current CEO Rich Teerlink says it is more than that. "They've got it tattooed to their heart and soul," he says.[45] ■■■

Thus Harley-Davidson is dealing with environmental difficulties partially by expanding its domain to areas in which prospects look promising to company officials. At the same time, the company's survival and success is partially due to its efforts to influence the favorability of the environment by engaging in political activity. Advertising and public relations were other means of influencing the environment that the company used. The survival of Harley-Davidson highlights the fact that organizations can be proactive in managing parts of their environment through adaptation, favorability influence, and domain shifts.

■ THE INTERNAL ENVIRONMENT: ORGANIZATIONAL CULTURE

Harley-Davidson both influenced the favorability of and adapted to its environment. Part of the transformation of the company involved changes in its organizational culture, a major aspect of the internal environment of an organization. For example, in the process of making various changes, the company involved workers in suggesting improvements and in supporting the needed emphasis on quality. This stance was a major departure from the policy of the past, in which engineers figured out what to do and then managers told the employees what should be done.[46] In this section, we examine the concept of culture more closely, considering the nature and manifestations of culture, as well as how culture can be used as a means of promoting innovation.

Nature of Organizational Culture

As mentioned earlier in this chapter, organizational culture is a system of shared values, assumptions, beliefs, and norms that unite the members of an organization.[47] Culture reflects common views about "the way things are done around here." Organizational culture is sometimes referred to as **corporate culture** because the concept is frequently used to describe the internal environment of major corporations. Yet culture can also be used to describe internal conditions in not-for-profit organizations, such as government agencies, charitable organizations, and museums. Culture is important to organizations because as individuals act on shared values and other aspects of organizational culture, their behaviors can have a significant impact on organizational effectiveness.

Corporate culture The term sometimes used for *organizational culture*

Organizational cultures develop from a variety of sources.[48] As new organizations are formed, cultures often develop that reflect the drive and imagination of the individuals involved. Strong founders, too, may have a major impact on the culture that forms. For example, Ray Kroc, the founder of McDonald's, espoused "quality, service, cleanliness, and value," still the corporate creed. As reward systems, policies, and procedures are instituted, they influence culture by further specifying notions of appropriate behavior. Moreover, critical incidents, such as an employee's being rewarded or fired for pushing a major innovation, may add to individuals' perceptions of internal norms over time. Changes in the environment, such as the rise of new competitors, may force organizations to reassess acceptable norms in areas like quality.

Three aspects of organizational culture are particularly important in analyzing the likely impact of culture on a given organization: direction, pervasiveness, and strength.[49] *Direction* refers to the degree to which a culture supports, rather than interferes with, reaching organizational goals. *Pervasiveness* addresses the extent to which a culture is widespread among members, as opposed to being unevenly distributed. *Strength* refers to the degree to which members accept the values and other aspects of a culture.

A culture can have a *positive* impact on organizational effectiveness when it supports organizational goals, is widely shared, and is deeply internalized by organization members.[50] For example, a consistent and shared emphasis on innovation has helped 3M produce a steady stream of new products, as well as make continual improvements in existing ones. In contrast, a culture can have a *negative* impact when the culture is widely shared and well internalized but influences behaviors in directions that do not further (and possibly interfere with) organizational goals. More mixed situations tend to have less impact. For example, a culture that is unevenly distributed and weakly held is unlikely to have much impact (either positive or negative), regardless of its direction.

Manifestations of Organizational Culture

An interesting feature of organizational culture is that the values, assumptions, beliefs, and norms that constitute a particular culture are generally not directly observable. Rather, we often infer the nature of a particular culture through the organization's use of concrete manifestations, such as symbols, stories, rites, and ceremonials.[51]

Symbol An object, act, event, or quality that serves as a vehicle for conveying meaning

SYMBOLS A **symbol** is an object, act, event, or quality that serves as a vehicle for conveying meaning. For example, a very explicit symbol used to support an organizational value is Corning, Inc.'s use of a "quapple," a pin shaped like a combination of the letter "Q" and an apple. Organization members receive the quapple after successfully completing their initial training course in quality improvement, and they wear it to signify their own commitment to quality.[52]

Story A narrative based on true events, which sometimes may be embellished to highlight the intended value

STORIES A **story** is a narrative based on true events, which sometimes (but not always) may be embellished to highlight the intended value. According to one story told at 3M, a worker was fired because he continued to work on a new product idea even after his boss had told him to stop. Despite being fired and taken off the payroll, the individual continued to come to work, pursuing his idea in an unused office. Eventually, he was rehired, developed the idea into a huge success, and was made a vice president. In this case, the story conveys an important value in the innovative 3M culture—persisting when you believe in an idea.[53]

Rite A relatively elaborate, dramatic, planned set of activities intended to convey cultural values to participants and, usually, an audience

Ceremonial A system of rites performed in conjunction with a single occasion or event

RITES AND CEREMONIALS A **rite** is a relatively elaborate, dramatic, planned set of activities intended to convey cultural values to participants and, usually, an audience. A **ceremonial** is a system of rites performed in conjunction with a single occasion or event. One company that is well known for its ceremonial activities is Mary Kay Cosmetics, which holds "seminars" that involve extravagant events presented at the Dallas Convention Center. Hundreds of Mary Kay salespeople attend training sessions during the day. At night they participate in lavish activities that company founder Mary Kay Ash describes as "a combination of the Academy Awards, the Miss America Pageant, and a Broadway opening!" The highlight is a 5-hour extravaganza at which Mary Kay crowns the best salespersons in various categories. The crowned individuals receive expensive gifts as they are surrounded by a court of other outstanding salespeople. The message: Sales are critical to company and personal success.[54]

Promoting Innovation: An Adaptive, Entrepreneurial Culture

Mounting evidence indicates that successful organizations foster an adaptive, entrepreneurial culture. The organization opportunity matrix (see Figure 3-5) classifies organizations according to the extent to which a firm's culture supports both a desire for change and a belief in its capacity to influence the competitive environment.[55]

As the matrix indicates, adaptive, entrepreneurial organizations tend to have cultures in which members view growth and change as desirable and also believe that they can affect the competitive environment to their advantage. Hewlett-Packard, the Silicon Valley electronics firm, has a reputation for being an adaptive organization. For example, the firm recently altered its competitive environment by halving the time it takes to design and produce many products. The speed enabled the company to produce a matchbox-size disk drive called the Kittyhawk well ahead of the competition.[56] In the opposite vein, bureaucratic and lethargic organizations are more likely to have members who prefer the status quo and have little faith in their ability to influence the competitive environment.

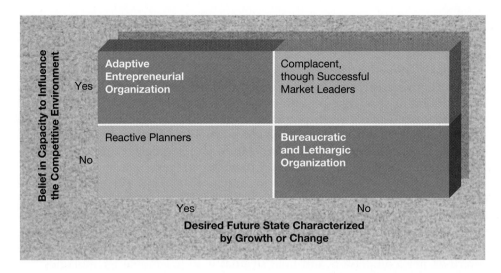

Figure 3-5 *Organization opportunity matrix. (Adapted from Howard H. Stevenson and David E. Gumpert, "The Heart of Entrepreneurship," Harvard Business Review, March–April 1985, p. 93.)*

In more mixed situations, cultures may support a desire for change but foster little belief in the ability to influence competitive situations. These types of cultures are likely to exist in reactive planner organizations, in which managers try to plan for environmental change yet are not proactive in attempting to influence the environment. Finally, cultures oriented to very slow change, coupled with a belief in their ability to affect the competitive environment, are likely to produce organizations that are complacent. Such organizations may actually be successful market leaders, but only as long as environmental changes occur very slowly. For example, Baldwin Locomotive, mentioned earlier, was extremely successful until major technological change made its main product, the steam engine, obsolete.

The organizational culture continuum (see Table 3-3) differentiates cultures on the basis of several dimensions. At one end of the continuum are a number of characteristics associated with adaptive, entrepreneurial cultures. With such a culture, an organization is better equipped to anticipate and

| | ENTREPRENEURIAL | | ADMINISTRATIVE |
DIMENSION	CHARACTERISTICS	↔	CHARACTERISTICS
Strategic orientation	Driven by perceptions of opportunity		Driven by controlled resources
Commitment to seize opportunities	Revolutionary change within short period		Evolutionary change over long period
Commitment of resources	Many stages, with minimal exposure at each stage		A single stage, with complete commitment based on one decision
Control of resources	Use of freelance help and rental of required resources		Employment or ownership of required resources
Management structure	Few levels, with emphasis on informal communication patterns		Many levels, with emphasis on communication through formal hierarchy

TABLE 3-3 CHARACTERISTICS OF ENTREPRENEURIAL VERSUS ADMINISTRATIVE CULTURES

Source: Adapted from Howard H. Stevenson and David E. Gumpert, "The Heart of Entrepreneurship," *Harvard Business Review,* March–April 1985, p. 89.

respond to changes in the environment. At the other end of the continuum are characteristics of organizations with administrative cultures. These organizations are less likely than their adaptive counterparts to make necessary modifications as the environment changes.

Recently, researchers have suggested that culture can even be common to an entire industry, such as the automobile industry. Such an interorganizational *macroculture* can occur when particular organization-related beliefs are shared among managers across organizations in a whole or particular segment of an industry.[57] If an industry has a macroculture and it reflects more the administrative culture end of the continuum than the adaptive, entrepreneurial end, the entire industry may be slow to innovate and change. For example, some observers believe that the auto industry was slow to respond to competitive threats from Japanese automakers, not only because of the relative inertia among individual U.S. automakers but because a macroculture among the "Big Three" automakers (General Motors, Ford, and Chrysler) encouraged them to overlook new competitors and hold steadfastly to traditional technologies.

Changing Organizational Culture

Because they involve fairly stable values, assumptions, beliefs, and norms, organizational cultures can be difficult to change.[58] One procedure for changing organizational culture involves five main steps:[59]

1 **Surfacing actual norms.** This step entails having organization members list the actual norms (expected behaviors in the organization) that they believe currently influence their attitudes and actions. This process typically takes place in a workshop setting and may involve a representative group of employees or many groups of employees, depending on how many the location can accommodate. For organizations in which the impact of culture on effectiveness is negative, such sessions often reveal norms such as "Don't rock the boat," "Don't enjoy your work," and "Don't share information with other groups."
2 **Articulating new directions.** In this step, group members discuss the current direction of the organization and the behaviors that are necessary for organizational success.
3 **Establishing new norms.** In this step, group members develop a list of new norms that would have a positive impact on organizational effectiveness.
4 **Identifying culture gaps.** This step involves identifying the areas in which there is a major difference (culture gap) between actual norms and those that would positively influence organizational effectiveness.
5 **Closing culture gaps.** This step entails agreeing on new norms and designing means of reinforcing them, such as developing reward systems that encourage members to follow the new cultural norms.

While this process is useful as a general approach to changing organizational culture, top leaders often have specific cultural changes in mind that they wish to implement.

How Leaders Influence Cultural Change

Despite the inherent difficulties, a number of top managers have been successful in encouraging specific cultural changes that they believe are critical to organizational success.[60] In doing so, they typically convince organization members that a crisis has occurred or is likely to occur. Next, they communicate a vision that outlines a new direction or strategy for the organization. Finally, they motivate others to take leadership in implementing the vision and its corresponding strategy, including the required cultural changes.

For example, when Barry Sullivan took over as CEO of the ailing First Chicago Bank, he made sure that multiple levels of bank employees understood there was a profitability crisis. Then, to rectify the situation, Sullivan worked with top managers to articulate a vision that emphasized commitment to customers, a well-conceived credit process (because of previous bad loans), teamwork, and a domestic and regional focus (rather than the ill-fated international one the company had been pursuing). Among other things, the bank instituted daily meetings to discuss customers and their problems, bought several smaller regional banks, and redesigned the compensation system to reward efforts reflecting the new direction. The cultural change took more than nine years, but it was a major factor in First Chicago's emergence as a leading midwestern bank.

Additional approaches for bringing about change in organizations are discussed in Chapter 11. Meanwhile, the issue of values, beliefs, and norms in organizations is also important to the topic of the next chapter, organizational social responsibility and managerial ethics.

■ CHAPTER SUMMARY

Organizations are affected by the external environment, the major outside forces that have the potential of significantly influencing the success of products or services. Broad conditions and trends in the societies within which an organization operates constitute an organization's mega-environment. The mega-environment consists of five major elements: technological, economic, legal-political, sociocultural, and international. Generally, elements of the mega-environment tend to be beyond the ability of a single organization to alter directly, at least in the short run.

The task, or operational, environment consists of the specific outside elements with which an organization interfaces in the course of conducting its business. The task environment depends largely on the specific products and services that an organization decides to offer and on the locations where it chooses to conduct its business. A single organization may be more successful in affecting its task environment than the mega-environment. Major elements in the task environment of an organization typically include customers and clients, competitors, suppliers, labor supply, and government agencies.

Two important, but differing, perspectives on the nature of the relationship between organizations and their environments are the population ecology model and the resource dependence model. Managers can analyze their organization's environmental situation in terms of two key concepts: environmental uncertainty and environmental munificence, or capacity. Environmental uncertainty refers to the extent to which future conditions affecting an organization cannot be accurately assessed and predicted. Environmental munificence refers to the extent to which the environment can support sustained growth and stability. The degree of environmental uncer-

tainty is a function of two factors, complexity and dynamism.

Three major approaches to managing environmental elements are adaptation, favorability influence, and domain shifts. Adaptation involves changing internal operations and activities to make the organization more compatible with its environment. Methods of adaptation include buffering, smoothing, forecasting, and rationing. Favorability influence focuses on attempting to alter environmental elements in order to make them more compatible with the needs of the organization. The resource dependence perspective argues that the environmental areas that organizations are most likely to attempt to influence are those on which they are most dependent. Major methods of favorability influence include advertising and engaging in public relations, boundary spanning, recruiting, negotiating contracts, co-opting, establishing strategic alliances, joining trade associations, and engaging in political activities. Domain shifts are changes in the mix of products and services offered so that an organization will interface with more favorable environmental elements. One domain-shift method involves moving entirely out of a current product, service, or geographic area and into a more favorable domain. Another method is diversification through the expansion of products and services offered.

Organizational culture is a system of shared values, assumptions, beliefs, and norms that unite members of an organization. The nature of a particular organization's culture is typically inferred through the organization's use of concrete manifestations, such as symbols, stories, rites, and ceremonials. In entrepreneurial cultures that encourage innovation, members tend to view growth and change as desirable and also believe that they can affect the competitive environment. Changing organizational culture can be difficult and is likely to involve a multistep process. Top managers often attempt to influence cultural changes that will enhance organizational prospects for success.

■ QUESTIONS FOR DISCUSSION AND REVIEW

1   Outline the major elements that make up the megaenvironment. Identify an important trend in each of these elements that could influence the organization in which you or some member of your family works.

2   Identify the major elements that typically make up the task environment of an organization. Use these major elements to develop an outline of the task environment of an organization in which you or some member of your family works.

3   Contrast the population ecology and resource dependence views of the organization-environment interface. Identify a situation in which environmental change caused an organization to go out of existence. What possible actions, if any, might management have taken to avoid the organization's demise?

4   Explain how environmental uncertainty affects organizations. How would you assess environmental uncertainty for Harley-Davidson, the maker of heavy motorcycles?

5   Describe how environmental munificence influences organizations. How would you assess environmental munificence for Harley-Davidson?

6   Outline the major methods that can be used to help organizations adapt to their environmental elements. For each method, give an example based on an organization with which you are familiar.

7   Enumerate the major methods that can be used to help organizations favorably influence their environments. For five of these methods, give an example based on an organization with which you are familiar.

8   Explain how domain shifts can help organizations cope with their environments. Give an example of an organization that made a major domain shift. Was the shift beneficial to the organization? Why, or why not?

9   Explain the nature of organizational culture, and list its principal manifestations. Give an example of each manifestation that indicates the culture at your college or university. Briefly describe your perception of the culture at your college or university.

10   Explain the difference between an entrepreneurial and an administrative culture. Contrast the organizational culture of IKEA with that of Champion Spark Plug. How would you bring about cultural change at Champion Spark Plug if you were placed in charge?

■ DISCUSSION QUESTIONS FOR CHAPTER OPENING CASE

1   Identify the major elements of the task environment at Warnaco. Assess the company's handling of these elements.

2   What avenues exist for Warnaco to further manage environmental elements that have the potential of affecting the company?

3   How effective would you say Linda Wachner has been in establishing a viable corporate culture at Warnaco? What changes would you recommend Wachner make (including what steps she should take), if any?

■ EXERCISES FOR MANAGING IN THE TWENTY-FIRST CENTURY

EXERCISE 1
SELF-ASSESSMENT EXERCISE: THE KIND OF ORGANIZATION I WOULD MANAGE

 Select the response which best reflects the culture you would work to instill in an organization you would manage.

1 = Strongly disagree
2 = Somewhat disagree
3 = Neither agree nor disagree
4 = Somewhat agree
5 = Strongly agree

_____ 1. For many projects, I would prefer to obtain needed additional professional human resources on a part-time or contract basis.

_____ 2. I would prefer to indicate my support for a program/project by committing all the required resources when I approve it.

_____ 3. I believe change is often best accomplished by making major changes within a short time frame.

_____ 4. Programs/projects usually are improved by many reviews through the chain of command.

_____ 5. Current resource availability should dictate the size and type of long-term programs and projects attempted.

_____ 6. I would be inclined to have very few levels of management.

_____ 7. I would base resource commitments on successes at several points in a program/project.

_____ 8. I would prefer owning all the resources needed for a project/program so that they would be immediately available when required.

_____ 9. Normally it is relatively easy to recognize opportunities that will arise and to plan for them well in advance.

_____ 10. Most of the communication regarding programs/projects under development is best handled through the formal hierarchy.

EXERCISE 2
MANAGEMENT EXERCISE: ASSESSING A SKI SHOP ENVIRONMENT

 Your best friend's sister and brother-in-law run the local ski shop near campus in your college town, but they have recently bought another type of business in another town. They want you and your friend to take over managing the ski shop. If you run it successfully, you and your friend will gradually be given substantial equity in the shop and eventually would own the whole business.

So far, the shop has been only marginally profitable. Although the shop carries ski equipment and ski clothing, it has habitually run out of both during the peak skiing season. Extra merchandise hastily ordered to meet the demand has often arrived so late that it could not be sold until the next season, if at all. In addition, the shop does very little business from March through August.

Due to a dispute over the size and prominence of the outside sign displaying the shop's name, the relationship with local government officials is extremely poor. Tact and diplomacy are not major strengths of your friend's brother-in-law. As a result, the shop gets more than its share of inspections by the fire marshal, and a recent effort to gain permission to expand the parking lot was turned down by the zoning board.

So far, other than some minimal advertising, nothing has been done to make inroads on campus. Yet it would seem that the campus, with its 12,000 students, would be a lucrative market. The town's population of 120,000 also includes a large number of avid skiers, since good skiing is only about 1½ hours away by car. Unfortunately, many of these skiers purchase their ski equipment and clothing at the ski lodges that they frequent. This is partly because the lodges tend to have good arrangements for repairing and maintaining ski equipment.

Your initial assessment is that, so far, the ski shop has not attempted to deal adequately with its environment. There have been persistent rumors that another ski shop may open in the next year, creating a local competitor. You and your friend (and possibly some of your other friends who are willing to give you advice) plan to get together soon to try to develop approaches that will help the ski shop manage its environment better. This analysis is crucial to your ultimate decision about whether to take on managing the shop. Also, your friend's sister and brother-in-law want to hear your ideas.

First, outline the major elements in the ski shop's task environment. Then prepare a proposal indicating how you would attempt to better manage the environmental impacts on the shop.

CONCLUDING CASE 1

XEROX WORKS TO MEET ENVIRONMENTAL CHALLENGES

After once holding a near monopoly in the photocopier business, the Xerox Corporation has been making significant changes to retain its position as a major player. Xerox's saga begins with founder and entrepreneur Joseph C. Wilson, who turned his tiny company, originally called Haloid, into a giant by purchasing exclusive world rights to inventor Chester F. Carlson's xerographic process in 1947. The company launched the first commercial plain-paper copier in 1959, and by 1972, Xerox's annual sales reached $2.4 billion.

Meanwhile, Wilson had named a successor, C. Peter McColough, who took over as CEO in 1968. In order to cope with the rapid growth, McColough began instituting a variety of controls and procedures, coupled with increasing layers of management. Unfortunately, these efforts were somewhat excessive and turned the company into a slow-moving bureaucracy, in which product development was subject to long delays. Nevertheless, the company continued its massive growth. Its sales and service groups were among the best.

Under McColough, the company decided in 1972 not to import a low-volume copy machine from Fuji Xerox, a Japanese affiliate. Instead, McColough wanted to develop a similar machine in the United States. Seven years later, after several product development failures, Xerox finally imported the machine from Fuji. By then, Japanese competitors, such as Canon, had gained strong footholds that enabled them to capture most of the low-end market. McColough emphasized development of mid- and high-volume copiers, focusing on potential threats from IBM and Kodak. Efforts in this direction have helped Xerox retain close to 40 percent of the market at the mid- and high-volume ends.

Meanwhile, McColough began to acquire a variety of high-technology companies, particularly in the computer industry. Although most of them were not especially successful, they did produce a number of innovations. Xerox's Palo Alto research center developed much of the basic technology used in personal computers, yet Xerox did not capitalize on such advances. Instead, a "cold war" developed between the east coast copier faction at Xerox headquarters in Rochester, New York, and the west coast computer specialists. The cultures of these two groups were quite different: the headquarters culture was very bureaucratic, while the west coast group was more entrepreneurial.

By the time David T. Kearns came in as CEO in 1982, Xerox had discovered that its Japanese competitors' costs per machine were 40 to 50 percent less than its own, making it easy for competitors to undercut Xerox prices. Furthermore, Xerox's net income had declined almost 50 percent as the company gave up market share and lowered prices in order to compete. Kearns quickly began emphasizing cost cutting, a renewed dedication to customer service, and high quality.

Kearns attempted to restore the entrepreneurial culture that had existed under founder Wilson. Management layers were cut, greater authority was delegated to lower levels, and employees became more involved in major decisions and activities. Under the Leadership Through Quality program, begun in 1980, more than 100,000 employees learned the importance of emphasizing quality and meeting customers' requirements. In recognition of its great strides in quality, Xerox received the prestigious Malcolm Baldrige National Quality award in 1989. Moreover, Xerox's market share in copiers began to rise.

When Paul Allaire took over as CEO in 1990, Xerox was unveiling its first entry in the digital-imaging market—an expensive DocuTech machine that could produce large-quantity copies of documents sent electronically from personal computers. Four years later, the company introduced new software, called DocuSP, that can tie its digital printers to a wide array of personal computers, scanners, and data storage devices anywhere in the world. Since then the company has unveiled a new corporate logo: "THE DOCUMENT COMPANY—Xerox." The upper right-hand corner of the X was broken into a number of little black and white boxes to appear digitized. Some observers report conflict within Xerox between the "tone heads," a name given to individuals from the copier side of Xerox, and the "computer nerds," who represent the newer software-oriented side, over future product development directions. Allaire is positioning the company to become oriented to handling electronic documents on the belief that data in the future will be largely stored electronically and be printed directly to printers. Due to intense outside competition, Allaire has been reorganizing parts of the company and pushing product development decisions down to lower levels, where the day-to-day knowledge of technical issues and market developments resides.[61]

QUESTIONS FOR CONCLUDING CASE 1

1 How have major elements of the mega-environment and task environment impacted Xerox?

2 What major methods has Xerox used in attempting to manage environmental influences?

3 Compare and contrast the organizational cultures at Xerox during the McColough and Kearns eras. What direction does Allaire seem to be encouraging?

CONCLUDING CASE 2

SOFTWARE AG: A TALE OF TWO CULTURES

Software AG is one of the 10 largest software companies in the world. Its ADABAS program, one of its most famous products, enables organizations to easily retrieve specific information from massive amounts of computerized data (such as airline reservations, inventories, or bank transactions). In one *Computerworld* survey of data-base management systems, ADABAS received the highest user-satisfaction ratings.

The company was founded by six engineers in the 1960s as a private "trust." Under the plan, long-time employees own the company's stock, thereby shielding the company from hostile takeover. The employees receive no dividends and must return the stock to the trust when they leave the company. Under provisions of the trust, 70 percent of the profits are devoted to research and development, 20 percent are earmarked for pensions and bonuses, and 10 percent are set aside for social causes. Software AG is run by a five-person management team and has over 4000 employees.

At Software AG's headquarters, 15 miles from Frankfurt, employees set their own work hours, dress as they please, occasionally take breaks for tennis, and typically work 10-hour days. The company tries to give its technical staff the responsibility and freedom needed to develop software that remains on the cutting edge. While many of the software developers are German, there are also Americans, Czechs, Slovaks, and other nationalities; English is spoken by many employees.

The U.S. subsidiary of Software AG is located in Reston, Virginia. This subsidiary is important to the company because the United States is not only the world's largest market for software but also the home of most of Software AG's major competitors. Although the parent company is privately held (under the trust), the U.S. subsidiary was a public company until 1988. At that time, the parent bought out the stock of the subsidiary and subsequently asked the U.S. head to leave. Peter Pagé, who joined the company in 1971 and was, until recently, the most prominent member of the corporate management team, says the subsidiary was "too quarterly-results-driven." Pagé took over as chairman of the U.S. subsidiary in addition to serving as Software AG's chief executive and a member of the corporate management team.

Serious cultural conflicts have been common between the U.S. subsidiary and corporate headquarters. Subsidiary managers have urged the company to be more aggressive in marketing its products and pursuing the latest trends in computing. In contrast, managers at the company's German headquarters have opted for more cautious moves. According to Pagé, the company is "more trusting of evolutionary systems that will get our customers from today into tomorrow without having to throw everything away everytime they need new things." He argues that American customers are often attracted by "fancy technology" but in the end opt for what can truly help them solve their computing problems.

A founder and prominent management team member, Peter Schnell, says that in the United States "they design products with marketing in mind. The appearance of software is key. Instead of high performance, it is shiny appearance that is important—color screens, whether there is voice input, the touch screen." In one famous story, Software AG was asked by customers to make one of its products compatible with a software program provided by IBM. Schnell reportedly responded, "We could do it, but it would be like putting whipped cream on fish." Former employees cite the story as an example of corporate headquarters' unwillingness to respond to U.S. marketing considerations. Software AG did eventually address the compatibility issue, but U.S. employees say the delay cost the company significant sales in the United States.

One industry analyst argues that product decisions are made by developers in Germany who tend to ignore U.S. market considerations. Even Pagé has acknowledged that the company needs to pay more attention to market considerations, and he recently gave the U.S. subsidiary responsibility for worldwide marketing for Software AG. He said that the arrangement would allow Software AG to benefit from the "tension" between the "revolutionary" orientation of the U.S. group and the "evolutionary" bent of the German group. Pagé noted that, in the past, there have been problems between the two parts of the company, but he said, "The U.S. company has been brought into the family." Two months later Pagé abruptly resigned from Software AG, allegedly over a dispute with one of the founders.[62]

QUESTIONS FOR CONCLUDING CASE 2

1　What elements of the mega-environment and task environment appear to be important to the success of Software AG at the present time?

2　Compare and contrast the organizational cultures in the German and U.S. parts of Software AG. Where would you place them on the entrepreneurial versus administrative continuum?

3　What advice would you give Pagé's successor regarding the handling of the two cultures?

CHAPTER FOUR

SOCIAL RESPONSIBILITY AND ETHICS IN MANAGEMENT

LEARNING OBJECTIVES

After studying this chapter, you should be able to:

■ Explain three major perspectives on corporate social responsibility and identify the six major stakeholder groups frequently mentioned in conjunction with social responsibility.

■ Assess the extent to which organizational social responsibility pays.

■ Explain the characteristics of vanguard companies.

■ Outline approaches that can be used to monitor social demands and expectations.

■ Describe internal social response mechanisms available to organizations.

■ Contrast the three major types of managerial ethics.

■ Outline ethical guidelines for managers and explain actions managers can take to handle ethical situations and avoid ethical conflicts.

■ Describe situational factors that influence ethical behavior and outline mechanisms for ethical management.

GAINING THE EDGE

JOHNSON & JOHNSON TURNS TO CREDO IN CRISIS

A crisis confronted Johnson & Johnson (J&J) managers when seven Chicago-area residents died after taking Extra-Strength Tylenol capsules contaminated with cyanide in the fall of 1982. Not only was $400-million-per-year Tylenol the best-selling U.S. drug, but it was a product that symbolized the Johnson & Johnson reputation for quality, gentleness, and fine health care.

Despite the pressures of dealing with national media coverage, J&J executives immediately opened their doors to the press and took great pains to keep the public informed about the situation. It soon became apparent that the cyanide had been put into the capsules after they had left J&J's factories, and the problem seemed to be confined to the Chicago area. Nevertheless, Tylenol sales sank to 20 percent of their previous level, and an opinion poll showed that 61 percent of Tylenol users intended to stop using the product.

A major question that arose was what to do about the 31 million bottles of Extra-Strength Tylenol on drugstore shelves throughout the country. The FBI and the Food and Drug Administration advised J&J managers not to take any drastic action. Even so, the managers promptly took the unprecedented step of recalling the unsold bottles, at a cost to the firm of $100 million. A few weeks later they decided to reintroduce Tylenol capsules in a triple-sealed, tamper-resistant package. In the months following the tragedy, the company established a consumer hot line and continued extensive cooperation with the media. It also made a widely advertised refund offer to consumers for any precrisis capsules they still had, and its chairman, James E. Burke, appeared on the *Donahue* show. In an opinion poll taken 3 months after the tragedy, 93 percent of the public felt that Johnson & Johnson had done a good job of handling its responsibilities.

In considering these events, David R. Claire, J&J's president, said, "Crisis planning did not see us through this tragedy nearly as much as the sound business management philosophy that is embodied in our Credo." The J&J Credo was originally drafted by General Robert Wood Johnson in the 1940s. In the late 1970s, it was revised through a series of credo challenge sessions held with the management of all J&J companies and is updated periodically. The Credo's opening sentence is: "We believe our first responsibility is to the doctors, nurses and patients, to mothers and fathers and all others who use our products and services." A copy of the document (see Figure 4-5) is given to every new employee, and copies adorn walls throughout the company.

Unfortunately, the importance of relying on the Credo was soon demonstrated again by another crisis. In early 1986, a 23-year-old woman died after taking a cyanide-laced Tylenol capsule. The company quickly offered to replace all capsules with caplets, tablets in the shape of capsules. The replacement effort cost J&J $150 million. In addition, J&J announced that it would no longer offer Tylenol in capsules—another bold and costly move in keeping with its Credo. The actions of J&J in the two Tylenol incidents earned the company widespread praise.[1] Among *Fortune*'s 300 most admired U.S. corporations, J&J was rated number one the following year on community and environmental responsibility, and it continues to be on the magazine's list of most admired companies.[2]

■■■

"The public comes first" is the essence of the Johnson & Johnson Credo, a set of principles that governs the company's actions. It was this Credo that led Johnson & Johnson to remove all boxes of Extra-Strength Tylenol from retail shelves across the country after cyanide-laced Tylenol capsules caused seven deaths in the Chicago area. The overwhelmingly favorable response from the public proved that this socially responsible action was also a sound business decision.

Johnson & Johnson's actions in the Tylenol situation were unusually swift, decisive, and costly. The company's handling of the crisis is considered to be a classic example of corporate social responsibility.[3] A contrasting approach was taken by the managers of the A. H. Robins Company, manufacturer of the Dalkon Shield, an intrauterine contraceptive device. The company faced close to 9000 claims involving serious injury and, in a few cases, death from infections related to the shield's use. When approving one $4.6 million liability suit against Robins, Judge Miles Lord of the federal district court chided top management for failing to withdraw the product from the market when difficulties began to appear. The judge noted that, instead, the managers had concentrated their efforts on legal maneuvers and congressional lobbying to absolve the company of any responsibility.[4] Eventually, Robins filed for bankruptcy protection in an attempt to limit its mounting liabilities, and it set up a court-ordered trust to help compensate victims. The company was acquired by American Home Products Corp.

As the Johnson & Johnson and A. H. Robins cases illustrate, managers can take very different stances on their responsibilities to others. Furthermore, while the J&J and Robins situations involved specific products, such problems constitute only one type of organizational social issue. Many of the situations confronting managers are less clear-cut, often falling into murky, gray areas. The variety of events that involve issues of organizational social responsibility can be seen in the following list of news items:

■ A president of the United Way of America was forced to retire amid charges that he had developed a "lavish lifestyle." Among other things, an outside report commissioned by the not-for-profit organization showed that he had made frequent trips to Las Vegas, had incurred $92,000 in limousine-service bills over 4 years, and had made 49 trips through Gainesville, Florida, the home of a close female friend. He was later sentenced to 7 years in federal prison.[5]

■ Aydin Corp. of San Jose was fined $2 million for faking test results on expensive battlefield radios to indicate they operated adequately under high-temperature conditions. The radios, which cost the Pentagon $23,000 each, were used during Operation Desert Storm and frequently failed. Two top Aydin officials were convicted of felony counts.[6]

■ Defects identified during the manufacture of artificial heart valves at Pfizer, Inc., a drug company, were marked as repaired, although they had not been. Deaths of 300 patients have been attributed to the subsequent failure of the defective implanted valves.[7]

■ The chief executive officer of Cascade International, a women's clothing and cosmetics retailer, disappeared after the discovery of wrongdoing. The company actually had far fewer than the 255 cosmetic counters it had claimed to have in operation. In addition, the company was secretly selling 6 million shares of unauthorized stock.[8]

■ The chief executive officer of Astra USA, a unit of Swedish drugmaker Astra AB, was fired after a headquarters probe of alleged sexual harassment and financial improprieties. The probe was triggered by inquiries about sexual misconduct at the company by *Business Week* magazine.[9]

Issues like these focus attention on the social responsibility of organizations and the ethics of their managers. For example, in one national poll, 58 percent of the respondents rated the ethical standards of business executives as only fair or poor.[10] *Ethics* are standards of conduct and moral judgment that differentiate right from wrong.[11] **Managerial ethics,** then, are standards of conduct and moral judgment used by managers of organizations in carrying out their business. In this chapter, we explore the nature and extent of the social

Managerial ethics Standards of conduct and moral judgment used by managers of organizations in carrying out their business

responsibilities of organizations, including those that are both socially responsible and innovative. We consider various methods by which organizations can fulfill their social responsibilities. We also look at the issue of managers' ethics. Finally, we examine the challenge of managing an ethical organization.

■ ORGANIZATIONAL SOCIAL RESPONSIBILITY

Organizational social responsibility refers to the obligation of an organization to seek actions that protect and improve the welfare of society along with its own interests. Organizational social responsibility is often called **corporate social responsibility** because the concept is typically applied to business firms. Views differ on the degree to which businesses and other organizations should consider social responsibilities in conducting their affairs.

Major Perspectives

Major concerns about organizational social responsibility are a relatively recent phenomenon. Social responsibilities began to emerge as an issue during the late 1800s when large organizations arose, commanded by such captains of industry as Cornelius Vanderbilt, John D. Rockefeller, and Andrew Carnegie. Anticompetitive practices (e.g., kickbacks and price-fixing) eventually led to government regulations and labor movement pressures for reform. A few important figures, such as Andrew Carnegie, became major donors to various social causes. The movement toward greater concern for social responsibilities gained momentum during the Great Depression, when the stock market crash served as a backdrop for the creation of the Securities and Exchange Commission and the enactment of additional laws regulating business. By 1936, General Robert E. Wood, CEO of Sears, had become one of the first top managers to argue for managerial, rather than just governmental, actions in behalf of social concerns. The various social movements of the 1960s (e.g., civil rights, women's liberation, and environmentalism) highlighted still further the public notion that organizations have social responsibilities.[12]

These historical developments have led to three major contrasting perspectives on corporate social responsibility: the invisible hand, the hand of government, and the hand of management.[13]

THE INVISIBLE HAND The chief spokesperson for the invisible-hand, or classical, perspective of corporate social responsibility is economist Milton Friedman, but its roots can be traced back to eighteenth-century economist Adam Smith. The **invisible-hand** view holds that the entire social responsibility of a corporation can be summed up as "make profits and obey the law." According to this view, each corporation should actively attempt to increase profits through legal means. In this way, corporate responsibility will be guided by the invisible hand of free market forces, which ultimately ensure that resources are allocated efficiently for the betterment of society. Otherwise, business executives will take on the right to allocate resources, thereby gaining excessive power while having little accountability to society for their allocation decisions. Further, Friedman argues that charitable activities by corporations are not socially responsible because, in making such contributions, the corporation prevents individual stockholders from making their own decisions about how to dispose of their funds.[14]

Organizational social responsibility The obligation of an organization to seek actions that protect and improve the welfare of society along with its own interests

Corporate social responsibility A term often used in reference to the concept of organizational social responsibility as applied to business organizations

Invisible hand A view that holds that the entire social responsibility of a corporation can be summed up as "make profits and obey the law"

These tobacco company executives testified in Washington in 1994 at a House committee hearing looking into the need for regulation of cigarettes. The "hand of government" comes into play when society's interests call for legal regulation of an industry or product.

Hand of government A view that argues that the interests of society are best served by having the regulatory hands of the law and the political process, rather than the invisible hand, guide the results of corporations' endeavors

Hand of management A view that states that corporations and their managers are expected to act in ways that protect and improve the welfare of society as a whole as well as advance corporate economic interests

Antifreeloader argument An argument that holds that since businesses benefit from a better society, they should bear part of the costs by actively working to bring about solutions to social problems

Capacity argument An argument that states that the private sector, because of its considerable economic and human resources, must make up for recent government cutbacks in social programs

Enlightened self-interest argument An argument that holds that businesses exist at society's pleasure and that, for their own legitimacy and survival, businesses should meet the expectations of the public regarding social responsibility

Iron law of responsibility A law that states that "in the long run, those who do not use power in a manner that society considers responsible will tend to lose it"

THE HAND OF GOVERNMENT Under the hand-of-government perspective of corporate responsibility, the role of corporations is also to seek profits within existing laws. However, the **hand-of-government** view argues that the interests of society are best served by having the regulatory hands of the law and the political process, rather than the invisible hand, guide the results of corporations' endeavors.[15] Thus, undesirable side effects of business functioning can be overcome by passing laws such as the Equal Pay Act of 1963, the Toxic Substances Control Act of 1976, the Plant Closing Act of 1988, and the Americans with Disabilities Act of 1990 and by expanding the authority of regulatory agencies as necessary. Neither the invisible-hand nor the hand-of-government approach is willing to give corporate leaders latitude in the area of social issues.

THE HAND OF MANAGEMENT The **hand-of-management** perspective states that corporations and their managers are expected to act in ways that protect and improve the welfare of society as a whole as well as advance corporate economic interests.[16] Three major arguments are typically advanced in favor of organizational social responsibility.[17] The **antifreeloader argument** holds that since businesses benefit from a better society, they should bear part of the costs of improving it by actively working to bring about solutions to social problems. The **capacity argument** states that the private sector, because of its considerable economic and human resources, must make up for recent government cutbacks in social programs. The **enlightened self-interest argument** holds that businesses exist at society's pleasure and that, for their own legitimacy and survival, businesses should meet the expectations of the public regarding social responsibility. Otherwise, they are likely to eventually suffer financially and go out of business. This argument is related to the **iron law of responsibility,** which states that "in the long run, those who do not use power in a manner that society considers responsible will tend to lose it."[18] Generally, society's expectations appear to be expanding regarding the social responsibilities of business firms. For example, one recent *Business Week*/Harris poll indicated most Americans believe that businesses have social responsibilities beyond concentrating exclusively on profit-making for shareholders (See Table 4-1).[19] Thus, the hand-of-

TABLE 4-1 *BUSINESS WEEK*/HARRIS POLL RESULTS REGARDING CORPORATE SOCIAL RESPONSIBILITY	
Question: Which of the following statements do you agree with more strongly?	**% RESPONDING**
U.S. corporations should have only one purpose—to make the most profit for their shareholders—and their pursuit of that goal will be best for America in the long term.	5
or	
U.S. corporations should have more than one purpose. They also owe something to their workers and the communities in which they operate, and they should sometimes sacrifice some profit for the sake of making things better for their workers and communities.	95

Source: Business Week, Mar. 11, 1996, p. 65.

management approach has increasing relevance as the basis for corporate action.

Social Responsibilities of Management

The idea that managers have social responsibilities stems, in large part, from the growing interdependencies of present times. Such interdependencies have woven an intricate web of common interests between corporations and the communities in which they exist. This broad view of the social responsibilities of management encompasses economic, legal, ethical, and discretionary responsibilities, as depicted in Figure 4-1.[20] The proportions shown in the figure suggest the magnitude of each responsibility for corporate leaders.

ECONOMIC AND LEGAL RESPONSIBILITIES The economic and legal responsibilities of management are recognized by all three perspectives on corporate responsibility—the invisible hand, the hand of government, and the hand of management. These responsibilities involve making a profit and obeying the law.

ETHICAL AND DISCRETIONARY RESPONSIBILITIES The hand-of-management perspective recognizes ethical and possible discretionary responsibilities in addition to the economic and legal responsibilities dictated by the invisible-hand and hand-of-government views. *Ethical responsibilities* include behaviors and activ-

Figure 4-1 *Social responsibilities of management. (Adapted from Archie B. Carroll, "A Three-Dimensional Conceptual Model of Corporate Performance," Academy of Management Review, vol. 4, 1979, p. 499.)*

The bite of a fly that breeds along rivers in tropical climates transmits a parasite that causes a progressive disease resulting in blindness. In many African villages, children act as guides for their blind elders. The Merck company offered free supplies of a drug that prevents the disease to medically qualified programs in the affected areas, a discretionary action that has won widespread praise for the company. When Merck learned there was no effective mechanism to distribute the drug, it even organized a committee to oversee distribution.

ities that are expected of business by society's members. For example, during the 1980s, mounting public pressure, as well as managerial concerns about apartheid, led many organizations to discontinue doing business in South Africa even though they were not legally obligated to take such action.[21] Ethical responsibilities tend to be somewhat ill-defined, frequently controversial, and subject to change over time. As a result, it is often difficult for business leaders to clearly identify such responsibilities.

On the other hand, *discretionary responsibilities* include voluntary beneficial activities that are not strongly expected of business by society's members. While an organization would not generally be viewed as unethical per se if it declined to participate in them, elements of society may view such activities as highly desirable. Examples of discretionary activities are making philanthropic contributions, sponsoring a clinic for AIDS victims, and training the economically disadvantaged. For instance, Merck decided to provide free supplies of its new drug, Ivermectin, to millions of individuals in Africa, South America, and the Middle East to protect them from a serious parasitic disease called "river blindness." The program is costing the drug company millions of dollars in forgone profits.[22]

Social Stakeholders

If corporations and their managers are to be socially responsible, then one important issue is: To whom are they to be responsible? Six major, somewhat overlapping groups are frequently mentioned: shareholders, employees, customers, the local community, general society (regional and national), and the international community.[23] These groups are considered social stakeholders because they can be affected for better or worse by the business activities of corporations.

SHAREHOLDERS Despite increasing social perceptions that business has obligations to a number of constituencies, there is still general agreement that the primary role of management in publicly held corporations is to earn profits and dividends for shareholders.[24] The shareholders have fulfilled a crucial role by providing the capital that allows the corporation to survive and grow.

At the same time, managers tend to view themselves as also being responsible for the survival of the firm, perpetuating the firm through development and expansion, and balancing the demands of all stakeholders so that multiple demands do not jeopardize the achievement of company objectives. The somewhat different perspectives held by shareholders and management can sometimes lead to conflict, particularly over such matters as the amount of dividends (versus reinvestment allocations) or the size of expenditures for executive perquisites such as stock options, country club memberships, and other fringe benefits.

Shareholders sometimes use their position to pressure for change in the social stance of management. Currently, shareholders are concerned that many CEOs are being paid millions of dollars annually even though their companies' performance has been less than stellar. Moreover, top managers are often reluctant to disclose the full extent of their compensation. AT&T CEO Robert E. Allen recently was criticized by politicians, the press, and others for pocketing a supplementary stock option grant worth nearly $11 million even as he announced plans to lay off 40,000 employees—other important stakeholders.[25]

MANAGING DIVERSITY: EMPLOYEES At a minimum, business firms and other organizations need to honor specific agreements made with employees and to obey laws relating to employee-employer relationships. Laws and government regulations now specify employer responsibilities in such areas as equal employment, pensions and benefits, and health and safety. The increasing number of such regulatory measures reflects growing recognition of a diverse work force as well as public displeasure regarding abuses on the part of some employers.

Although it has become fashionable for top managers to speak of their organization's employees as "family," actual treatment of employees can vary considerably. An extreme lack of social concern for employees is illustrated by a case involving Film Recovery Systems, Inc. Officials from the company's suburban Chicago plant were found guilty of murder in the death of an employee from cyanide poisoning. The death occurred because the workers, mostly non-English-speaking immigrants, had not been warned that cyanide was being used to extract silver from film scraps and had been provided with only minimal safety equipment.[26]

At the other end of the continuum of social concern for employees, Du Pont Co. has made major efforts to help employees balance family and work pressures. For example, the company spent $1.5 million over a 3-year period to build and renovate child-care centers near various company work sites. Du Pont also has a relatively generous leave policy for birth, adoption, or a relative's illness. Employees receive 6 weeks off with full pay and may take up to 6 months of unpaid leave with full benefits.[27]

The Du Pont actions reflect efforts to effectively manage diversity. *Managing diversity* is the planning and implementing of organizational systems and practices that maximize the potential of employees to contribute to organizational goals and develop their capabilities unhindered by group identities (such as gender, race, or ethnic group).[28] It is possible to argue that managers should manage diversity effectively simply because it is the socially responsible thing to do. However, as is often the case, socially responsible actions in this instance make good business sense as well. As Table 4-2 illustrates, social responsibility is only one of several arguments that can be made for building competitive advantage by effectively managing diversity.

CUSTOMERS Although *caveat emptor* ("let the buyer beware") was once the motto of many businesses, consumers have come to expect more. Two areas of cur-

TABLE 4-2 ARGUMENTS IN FAVOR OF MANAGING DIVERSITY FOR COMPETITIVE ADVANTAGE	
Socially responsible	Managing diversity can protect and improve the welfare of society while advancing corporate economic interests.
Cost effective	Attracting workers is costly; firms that effectively manage diversity will be able to attract and retain good workers.
Enhances prospects for customer satisfaction	A work force that mirrors the diversity of the customer base provides unique insight into the needs of customers, thereby enhancing prospects for customer satisfaction.
Encourages innovation	Innovations are more likely to emerge when diversity of thinking is applied to business problems.
Facilitates globalization	Openness to other cultures and ways of doing things is helpful in successfully doing business around the globe.

rent social concern regarding consumers are health and safety matters and quality issues.

In the area of health and safety, product liability suits are becoming everyday occurrences and can drastically affect business prospects. For example, at one point the value of Bic Corporation stock dropped when the company revealed a number of suits claiming that Bic lighters had exploded, causing severe injuries and even death.[29] Due to the growing number of product liability cases, many organizations are experiencing difficulties in obtaining liability insurance. As a result, questions have been raised about the social responsibilities of businesses, and some observers wonder whether the pendulum has swung too far in favor of the consumer. One argument is that a manufacturer should be held liable for a product's safety only if the manufacturer "knew, or should have known, about its dangers." However, even this approach has perils, since it is difficult to determine how much research a manufacturer should do to ensure that every safety contingency is considered. A stringent 100 percent requirement may mean that most products would take years to get to market—if they make it at all—and would be extremely expensive. Consequently, some businesses that care about consumers are compromising: attempting to be 99 percent certain that the product is safe, taking out large insurance policies, and hoping for the best.

Quality has also been gaining increased prominence as a consumer stakeholder issue. Keeping up with the competition is, of course, important. At the same time, a number of companies are also recognizing that quality is an issue related to social responsibility. For example, when Harley-Davidson produced motorcycles of poor quality during the 1970s, customers became upset and the reputation of the entire company suffered. Great efforts were required to turn the situation around (see the Case in Point in Chapter 3). Richard Teerlink, CEO of Harley-Davidson, notes: "We are living proof that you can win your reputation back. But it's not easy."[30] France-based Source Perrier S.A. learned about the hazards of quality issues and social responsibility when it removed its Perrier mineral water from retail shelves in 1990 because of benzene contamination. Even though the Food and Drug Administration ruled that the amount of benzene in the mineral water was harmless, the company wanted to protect its reputation with consumers. Unfortunately, during the 4 months that the company took to correct the problem, many consumers switched to competing brands. The company was recently acquired by Nestlé, and the brand is still struggling to regain its former prominence.[31]

LOCAL COMMUNITY In reference to social responsibility, an organization's com-

When a fire destroyed Malden Mills, a textile manufacturing company in Methuen, Massachusetts, the first thought of its owner was for his employees. Within three days of the disaster, Aaron Feuerstein (shown here) met with his employees to assure them that he would continue to pay full salaries and that he would put them back to work within 90 days. He was true to his word, winning the gratitude and the loyalty of the mill workers. According to Feuerstein, "I don't deserve credit. Corporate America has made it so that when you behave the way I did it's abnormal." (Time, Jan. 8, 1996, p. 49)

munity is its area of local business influence.[32] Most communities have social needs that extend beyond the available resources. As a result, businesses are likely to receive more requests for assistance than it is reasonable to honor, necessitating priorities in giving. During a single year, a large manufacturer in the midwest received major funding requests pertaining to such diverse interests as air and water pollution control, artistic and cultural activities, urban planning and development, local health-care programs, the local school system, and the local United Way drive.[33]

While communities often desire business aid, businesses in turn need various forms of support from communities. Such support includes an adequate

U.S. West, a telephone company that covers 16 western states, has funded a $6 million program to revitalize the rural economy in its area of business influence. This craft shop in Nogales, Arizona, has benefited from counseling on marketing and business and financial planning.

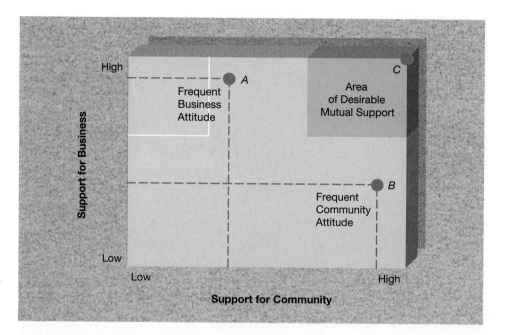

Figure 4-2 *Possible levels of business and community mutual support.*

transportation system, equitable taxes, adequate school and recreational facilities, and complete public services, such as police and fire protection and sewage, water, gas, and electric services. Because of these complementary needs, businesses and the communities in which they operate are somewhat interdependent, and both can often function more effectively with a high level of mutual support (see Figure 4-2). For example, when the H. B. Fuller Company, based in St. Paul, Minnesota, decided to build a glue factory in Minneapolis, company managers invited nearby homeowners and city officials to offer their suggestions about how the company could be a good neighbor. As a result, Fuller agreed to pay for expensive street lighting in the neighborhood, build a jogging track, and preserve a wooded area.[34]

SOCIETY Social responsibility at the societal level encompasses issues that are regional and national in scope. For example, many business leaders are involving themselves in educational reform so that future members of the labor pool will be adequately prepared. In one case, RJR Nabisco, Inc., is awarding $30 million in grants to 45 schools with innovative reform proposals. A number of employers are also providing training in basic skills to help workers meet the requirements of available jobs. For instance, Aetna Life & Casualty Co. trains up to 700 employees annually in basic skills such as reading, writing, and math.[35] The weaker the connection between corporate social expenditures and concrete business-related results, the more proponents of the invisible-hand view of social responsibility are likely to object. Conversely, the hand-of-government view would favor government regulation of social expenditures, possibly through higher taxes on corporations to allow governmental allocation of funding.

INTERNATIONAL COMMUNITY Increasingly, social responsibilities encompass international issues. Recently, the Union of International Associations in Brussels developed a list of 10,000 world problems and grouped them into several major categories, including international tensions, disappearing resources, and growing pollution.[36] Some companies are responding to these global concerns by altering their business practices. For example, to help save disappearing resources, Herman Miller, the office-furniture maker in Zeeland, Michigan, has recently stopped using tropical woods, such as rosewood, in its furniture, despite the possibility the change would hurt sales. So far, the move has not had a detrimental impact on sales and has further enhanced the company's reputation for social responsibility. In fact, the Business and Institutional Furniture Manufacturers Association now advocates that all its members take a similar step.[37] Bristol-Myers-Squibb has developed a companywide pollution prevention program labeled Environment 2000. The program is based on assessing the environmental impact of its products through the entire product life cycle beginning with product development and ending when the consumer ultimately disposes of the product (see Figure 4-3).

Does Social Responsibility Pay?

One intriguing question is whether companies that are socially responsible are more successful financially. Studying this issue is problematic because it is difficult to accurately measure the social responsibility of one firm against that of another. While this makes a definitive answer impossible, the cumulative research indicates that no clear relationship exists between a corporation's degree of social responsibility and its financial success—at least in the short run.[38]

Some research suggests that a firm's financial performance may predict, rather than result from, social responsibility. For example, organizations that are doing well financially may feel they are in a better position to undertake socially responsible activities. There are also indications that firms may engage in social responsibility to bring about more stable relationships with major stakeholders and to help reduce the risk of lawsuits and governmental fines that could threaten organizational well-being.[39]

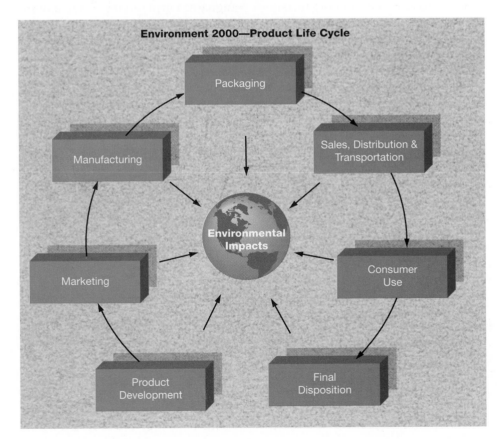

Figure 4-3 *Bristol-Myers-Squibb (Reprinted from Marc J. Epstein,* Measuring Corporate Environmental Performance: Best Practices for Costing and Managing an Effective Environmental Strategy, *Irwin Professional Publishing, Chicago, 1996, p. 37.)*

While research has found that the announcement of corporate illegal actions tends to have an adverse effect on a firm's stock price when the story is released, the long-term impact is unclear.[40] Ironically, research suggests that generous charitable donations may contribute to perceptions of companies as socially responsible even if they behave illegally.[41] Corporate giving of contributions for charitable and social responsibility purposes is called **corporate philanthropy**.

Corporate philanthropy
Corporate contributions for charitable and social responsibility purposes

To help balance conflicting expectations from stakeholders who favor socially responsible behavior and those who favor a concentration on profit making, many corporations are focusing on socially responsible activities that can affect their bottom line. For example, Dayton Hudson, a Minneapolis-based department store chain that contributes 5 percent of its taxable income to social causes, has recently been concentrating the funds in two areas, social action and the arts. Social action is considered important because by helping the poor become more prosperous, the company is increasing the potential pool of shoppers. The arts foster an appreciation for creativity and beauty that may ultimately encourage the purchase of fashionable clothing and household items. Amoco Corp., a Chicago-based oil company, is concentrating its giving on education because of the need for well-trained workers and the company's large market share in the inner city.[42]

Promoting Innovation: Vanguard Companies

Although there might not be a direct relationship between social responsibility and financial performance (at least in the short run), a number of firms score highly on *both* social responsibility and success. In his book *Vanguard Management: Redesigning the Corporate Future,* social responsibility scholar James O'Toole has termed such organizations "vanguard" corporations.[43] Some of his examples are Atlantic Richfield, Dayton Hudson, John Deere, Honeywell, Levi Strauss, Motorola, and Weyerhaeuser. Vanguard organizations have the following four characteristics in common:

1 **They try to satisfy all their stakeholders.** The basic idea is that the interests of the shareholders are best served in the long run when corporations

Honeywell is an example of a vanguard company that scores high on both social responsibility and success. Hundreds of Honeywell volunteers participate in Habitat for Humanity projects in their communities, helping to provide housing for those in need. The company also donates products for use in Habitat homes.

attempt to satisfy the legitimate concerns of all stakeholders. Such organizations work particularly hard at resolving conflicts and finding ways to simultaneously serve all their constituencies.

2 **They are committed to a higher purpose.** These corporations see their role as providing society with necessary goods and services, furnishing employment, and creating surplus wealth in the form of profits that can ultimately increase the general standard of living and quality of life. In this sense, profit is the means, rather than the end, of corporate efforts.

3 **They value continuous learning.** These companies recognize that flexibility, change, and responsiveness are vital to organizational survival. As a result, they monitor changes in the environment and assess the applicability of their own strategies and practices.

4 **They aim high.** They are dedicated to being the best at everything they do. As a result, they place a heavy emphasis on innovation as a vehicle that will help them reach high goals. Through their commitment to these principles, vanguard companies have achieved a fairly high level of social responsibility and have been very successful financially as well.

■ ORGANIZATIONAL SOCIAL RESPONSIVENESS

While managers may have a particular concept of their organization's social responsibilities, the concept takes on practical meaning only when managers actually *respond* to those social responsibilities. **Organizational social responsiveness** refers to the development of organizational decision processes whereby managers anticipate, respond to, and manage areas of social responsibility. Organizational social responsiveness is often called **corporate social responsiveness** because the idea is most frequently applied to business organizations. Keep in mind, though, that social responsiveness is also important for other types of organizations. For example, not-for-profit schools and hospitals are also expected to monitor the changing expectations of their various stakeholders and to be responsive to them.

Two processes are usually essential in developing organizational social responsiveness. First, it is necessary to establish methods of monitoring social demands and expectations in the external environment. Second, it is important to develop internal social response mechanisms.

Monitoring Social Demands and Expectations

Major means of assessing social demands and expectations relative to organizations include social forecasting, opinion surveys, social audits, issues management, and social scanning. Each of these is discussed in turn.

SOCIAL FORECASTING **Social forecasting** is the systematic process of identifying social trends, evaluating the organizational importance of those trends, and integrating these assessments into the organization's forecasting program. One approach to social forecasting is the use of **futurists,** individuals who track significant trends in the environment and attempt to predict their impact on the organization, usually 10 or more years into the future. Many organizations also use consultants and research institutes that specialize in social forecasting.

OPINION SURVEYS Associations and major business publications often conduct surveys of public opinion on various issues of social concern. These surveys frequently provide useful feedback to businesses regarding the perceptions of

Organizational social responsiveness A term that refers to the development of organizational decision processes whereby managers anticipate, respond to, and manage areas of social responsibility

Corporate social responsiveness A term used in reference to the concept of organizational social responsiveness as applied to business organizations

Social forecasting The systematic process of identifying social trends, evaluating the organizational importance of those trends, and integrating these assessments into the organization's forecasting program

Futurists Individuals who track significant trends in the environment and attempt to predict their impact on the organization

social responsibility among various groups. For example, one Harris poll showed that only 31 percent of the public rate business executives as having good moral and ethical standards (also see Table 4-1).[44]

Social audit A systematic study and evaluation of the social, rather than the economic, performance of an organization

SOCIAL AUDITS A **social audit** is a systematic study and evaluation of the social, rather than the economic, performance of an organization. It includes an assessment of the social impact of a firm's activities, an evaluation of programs specifically aimed at achieving social goals, and a determination of areas in need of organizational action. Social audits are difficult to carry out because disagreements can arise regarding what should be included, results can be somewhat intangible and/or difficult to measure, and interpretations of what is adequate or good social performance are likely to vary. Nevertheless, companies are increasingly assessing their social performance through social audits.[45] Some companies, such as Atlantic Richfield, prepare special reports on social performance for release to the public. Ben & Jerry's Homemade, Inc., the ice cream maker, includes results of social audits in its annual reports.[46]

Issues management The process of identifying a relatively small number of emerging social issues of particular relevance to the organization, analyzing their potential impact, and preparing an effective response

ISSUES MANAGEMENT As it applies to social responsiveness, **issues management** is the process of identifying a relatively small number of emerging social issues of particular relevance to the organization, analyzing their potential impact, and preparing an effective response. Typically, 10 to 15 issues are identified, but the number can vary somewhat depending on organizational circumstances. Issues management attempts to minimize "surprises" resulting from environmental forces and to facilitate a proactive stance toward environmental change.[47] At the Monsanto Company, for example, the top-level Executive Management Committee, chaired by the company president, worked with various parts of the organization to identify 170 different relevant social issues. Ultimately, the list was narrowed to five issues of critical importance related to the Monsanto business environment: fair trade, biotechnology regulation, intellectual property rights, agricultural policy, and hazardous waste and public compensation. Through issues management, the company has become a leader in the increasing cooperation between industry and environmental groups. Among other things, Monsanto has been instrumental in the creation of Clean Sites, Inc., a partnership formed between environmental groups and industry to help accelerate the cleanup of hazardous waste sites.[48]

Social scanning The general surveillance of various elements in the task environment to detect evidence of impending changes that will affect the organization's social responsibilities

SOCIAL SCANNING **Social scanning** is the general surveillance of various elements in the task environment to detect evidence of impending changes that will affect the organization's social responsibilities. Unlike issues management, social scanning is usually done on an informal and somewhat unsystematic basis. Executives frequently draw upon their own experiences of factors that are likely to have important organizational implications. They may also rely on data from more systematic assessments, such as those discussed above.[49]

On the basis of his assessment of social expectations in the United States, at one point the president and CEO of Minolta, Sadahei Kusumoto, urged U.S. subsidiaries of Japanese companies to pay greater attention to U.S. standards of corporate social responsibility. The subsidiaries were not engaging in corporate philanthropy in the United States, partially because tax incentives for such activities were much lower in Japan and because such corporate giving was not the norm in Japan. Kusumoto argued that the United States subsidiaries of Japanese companies must play a more active role in the community in the United States or risk being branded as "irresponsible outsiders" and thereby "dim their prospects for the future." Kusumoto was fulfilling an important role in scanning the environment and noting important trends that could affect Japanese companies operating in the United States. Recently, Japan doubled the corporate tax deduction for foreign charitable giving, causing Japanese corporate giving globally to more than double.[50] While monitoring social demands and expectations is important, organizations must also develop social response mechanisms.

Internal Social Response Mechanisms

The internal social response mechanisms of an organization include the departments, committees, and human resources that affect its responsiveness to changes in the social environment.[51] Common means used by organizations to facilitate effective social responses include individual executives, temporary task forces, permanent committees, permanent departments, or combinations of these elements.[52]

INDIVIDUAL EXECUTIVES Individuals can be used as a social response mechanism by either appointing or allowing certain executives to handle critical social issues as they occur. This type of approach is used more often in relatively small organizations than in large ones.

TEMPORARY TASK FORCES For this mechanism, several persons are appointed to serve on a committee for a limited period of time to deal with a critical social issue. When the necessary action is taken, the committee or task force is disbanded. Temporary task forces can be particularly effective when an important social issue arises suddenly and requires input from various parts of the organization.

PERMANENT COMMITTEES There are many variations in the use of permanent committees. Almost 100 of the Fortune 500 companies have special committees on the board of directors that deal with social issues. These committees are often called public policy, public issues, social responsibility, and corporate responsibility committees.[53] Other arrangements include permanent committees made up of individuals at the executive level, committees composed of members from all layers of management, and division-level committees that channel critical issues to higher-level committees.

PERMANENT DEPARTMENTS Many companies have a permanent department that coordinates various ongoing social responsibilities and identifies and recommends policies for new social issues. Although there are many alternative names, this department is often referred to as the **public affairs department.** It may be responsible for coordinating government relations, community relations, and other external activities. In one study of large and medium-size U.S. business firms, 361 of the 400 respondents had some type of public affairs unit, with one-third of them established since 1975. A recent update of the study shows the trend toward establishing such departments continuing into the 1990s.[54]

Public affairs department
A permanent department that coordinates various ongoing social responsibilities and identifies and recommends policies for new social issues

COMBINATION APPROACHES In practice, organizations may use a combination of mechanisms to enhance social performance.[55] For example, division-level committees may make recommendations to an executive-level committee, or a public affairs department may make recommendations to an executive-level committee, or a public affairs department may make recommendations to certain key executives. One unique use of permanent committees has been pioneered by Levi Strauss, a company with a strong positive reputation in the area of social responsiveness. Involving employees from throughout the organization, the program is coordinated through regional and corporate community affairs departments (see the Case in Point discussion).

CASE IN POINT

LEVI STRAUSS'S COMMUNITY INVOLVEMENT TEAMS

An important element in the success of Levi Strauss's philanthropic programs is the idea that merely giving *money* is not enough—time and effort are the greatest gifts one can give. To encourage employee involvement in volunteer projects that would help their communities, the company established community involvement teams (CITs) at each company site in the United States. The program went international in 1977, when it was introduced at plants in Canada, Asia, Europe, Brazil, and Mexico. Today, there are CITs in 15 countries.

As a company brochure explains, "The CITs are comprised of employees who elect their own officers, identify the needs of their communities, and develop a variety of projects to meet those needs. The projects are directed by the employees themselves through volunteer time." When a local team has decided where it wants to expend its energy and time, the members meet with the staff person at the regional community affairs office. The staff person in turn reports to a division of the Levi Strauss corporate community affairs department. If the projects suggested by the local team are approved by the regional and national offices, the Levi Strauss Foundation donates some of the required funds. The community affairs staff helps arrange other funding sources, such as government grants, and is available to advise CIT members as they work on their projects.

The CIT projects are as varied as the communities they serve. The teams establish volunteer fire departments in small U.S. towns. They dig wells or build water treatment plants in Pacific Basin villages. They take senior citizens on holiday outings and hold Special Olympics for handicapped youngsters. They have founded and furnished a shelter for abused women and children, and they have donated equipment to local schools as well.[56] The company estimates that about one-quarter of all employees volunteer their time to participate in the CITs. ■■■

■ BEING AN ETHICAL MANAGER

Ultimately, questions of organizational social responsibility and responsiveness depend on the ethical standards of managers. Lately, newspaper and magazine articles about ethical problems in business have been common. In one recent study involving simulated business situations, 47 percent of the top executives, 41 percent of the controllers, and 76 percent of the graduate-level business students surveyed were willing to commit fraud by understating write-offs associated with a reduction in the value of certain assets. Taking the write-offs would have lowered the level of the company's profits, which were about to be reported.[57] Faced with these potential difficulties, many companies are taking steps to clarify ethical standards. In one clever approach to helping employees understand company standards, Citicorp and Lockheed Martin Corp. have developed games that include cards depicting situations and issues that their employees are likely to confront. Game participants progress on the game board by choosing correctly from among several alternatives for handling the depicted situation. They gain or lose points depending on how closely their choices fit company standards. Try your hand at answering some of the questions from the Lockheed Martin game in the "Gray Matters" exercise at the end of this chapter.[58]

A particular issue is the rising rate of *white-collar crime* (crime, such as fraud or embezzlement, committed by an individual in business, government, or not-for-profit organizations, or by a professional engaged in occupational activities).[59] According to one estimate, common street crime costs the nation approximately $4 billion a year, while white-collar crime drains at least $40 billion from corporations and governments—and ultimately from consumers and taxpayers. Major reasons given for the rise are the current heavy emphasis on materialism and competitive pressures to perform. Women, long a stronghold against business crime, are increasingly appearing in the white-collar criminal ranks.[60]

The current difficulties and public concerns with business ethics raise three particularly important issues in regard to being an ethical manager: the types of managerial ethics existing in organizations, the kinds of ethical guidelines a manager might consider adopting, and the ethical career issues that one is likely to face.

Types of Managerial Ethics

Managerial ethics, as explained earlier in this chapter, are standards of conduct or moral judgment used by managers in carrying out their business. Such standards arise from the general norms and values of society; from an individual's experiences within family, religious, educational, and other types of institutions; and from interpersonal interactions with others. Therefore, managerial ethics may differ among individuals.[61] An eminent researcher in the area of social responsibility, Archie B. Carroll, notes that three major levels of moral, or ethical, judgment characterize managers: immoral management, amoral management, and moral management (see Figure 4-4).[62]

IMMORAL MANAGEMENT "Immoral" and "unethical" can be considered synonymous in business. Thus **immoral management** not only lacks ethical principles but is actively opposed to engaging in ethical behavior. This perspective is characterized by principal or exclusive concern for company profits and company success at virtually any price, a willingness to treat others unfairly, a view of laws as obstacles to be overcome, and a propensity to "cut corners." The key operating principle of immoral management is: "Can we make money with this action, decision, or behavior?" Implied in this approach is the view that other considerations matter little, if at all.

One example of immoral management cited by Carroll involved three plant managers at a GM Chevrolet truck plant in Flint, Michigan. In a flagrant violation of the company contract with the United Auto Workers, they used a

Immoral management An approach that not only lacks ethical principles but is actively opposed to ethical behavior

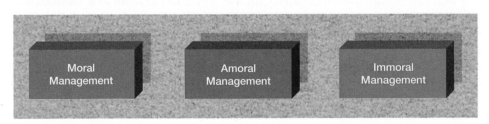

Figure 4-4 *Types of managerial ethics. (Reprinted from Archie B. Carroll, "In Search of the Moral Manager," Business Horizons, March–April 1987, p. 8.)*

Was he immoral or amoral? William Aramony, former chief of the charitable organization United Way, was forced to retire when it was discovered that he used funds from the national charity to pay for an illicit romance and extravagant vacations. In 1995 a federal court sentenced him to seven years imprisonment for federal mail, wire, and tax fraud and conspiracy charges.

Amoral management An approach that is neither immoral nor moral but, rather, ignores or is oblivious to ethical considerations

Moral management An approach that strives to follow ethical principles and precepts

secret control box to override a control panel that normally set the speed of the assembly line. The managers, under heavy pressure from higher-level executives because of missed deadlines, soon began meeting production goals and receiving praise from their bosses. When the scheme was discovered, workers won a $1 million settlement because of the extra work they had been forced to do.

AMORAL MANAGEMENT The **amoral management** approach is neither immoral nor moral but, rather, ignores or is oblivious to ethical considerations. There are two types of amoral management: intentional and unintentional. *Intentional* amoral managers do not include ethical concerns in their decisions and actions because they think that general ethical standards are more appropriate to non-business areas of life. *Unintentional* amoral managers do not think about ethical issues in their business dealings because they are inattentive or insensitive to the moral implications of their decisions and actions. Overall, amoral managers are generally well-meaning, but they pursue profitability as a goal while paying little attention to the impact of their behavior on others. They generally leave other managers free to behave as they wish unless their behavior leads to outside notoriety or pressure. The basic principle governing amoral management is: "Within the letter of the law, can we make money with this action, decision, or behavior?"

One example of amoral management is Nestlé's decision to market baby formula in third world countries. The Switzerland-based company did not anticipate the negative effects on mothers and babies of marketing formula in areas with impure water, poverty, and illiteracy. Its indifference eventually led to a worldwide consumer boycott of all Nestlé products. Similarly, when PepsiCo used the "Frito-Bandito" theme to promote its corn chips, it did not foresee the concept's offensiveness to a group of Mexican-Americans who ultimately pressured the company into withdrawing the advertising.

MORAL MANAGEMENT In contrast to both immoral and amoral management, **moral management** strives to follow ethical principles and precepts. While moral managers also desire to succeed, they seek to do so only within the parameters of ethical standards and the ideals of fairness, justice, and due process. As a result, moral managers pursue business objectives that involve simultaneously making a profit and engaging in legal and ethical behaviors. They follow not only the letter but also the spirit of the law, recognizing that moral management generally requires operating well above what the law mandates. The central guiding principle is: "Is this action, decision, or behavior fair to us and all parties involved?"

One example of moral management in which an organization assumed ethical leadership involved the McCulloch Corporation, a manufacturer of chain saws. The acute dangers of chain saws were highlighted in Consumer Product Safety Commission statistics showing that chain saws were involved in 123,000 medically attended injuries annually. Despite this alarming data, the Chain Saw Manufacturers Association fought mandatory safety standards, arguing that the statistics were inflated and did not provide sufficient justification for mandatory standards. Displaying moral leadership, McCulloch decided to use chain brakes on all its saws. Later, the company withdrew from the association after its repeated attempts to persuade the group to adopt higher safety standards failed.

Carroll believes that the amoral management style predominates in organizations today. He argues, however, that a moral management stance is in the long-run more likely to be in the best interests of organizations.

Ethical Guidelines for Managers

Not everyone has the same ethical standards. For example, in a survey by *INC.* magazine, 43 percent of respondents believed it was acceptable to pay suppliers within 60 days, while expecting your accounts receivables to be paid in 30 days. Sixteen percent of respondents agreed it was acceptable to persuade dealers to buy more product than they are likely to really need.[63] Unfortunately, it is difficult to write hard-and-fast rules for every possible condition, because situations differ from one another. Furthermore, some situations seem ambiguous and fall into gray areas. For example, at what point does a "token gift" from a supplier constitute a bribe?[64] To help employees grapple with this sticky issue, General Motors recently issued a new policy on "gifts, entertainment, and other gratuities," which was outlined in a 12-page document including instructional scenarios involving fictional characters. One such scenario, along with an explanation of the proper application of General Motors policy, is shown in Table 4-3.

Despite the difficulty of outlining specific ethical standards, there are a few commonsense guidelines that can be helpful in thinking about the ethical implications of managerial decisions and behaviors. The guidelines discussed below are basically consistent with the principle of enlightened self-interest.[65]

- **Obey the law.** A basic tenet of social responsibility and managerial ethics is obedience to the law, preferably both the letter and the spirit of the law. Frank Williams was executive director of the American Parkinson Disease Association before resigning under charges that he embezzled about $80,000 per year from the association over a 10-year period. Williams is credited with great success in expanding the association and involving celebrities like Muhammad Ali and Madonna. Williams says he took the money because he resented certain members of the board of directors who he believed were unwilling to approve a salary and benefits commensurate with his accomplishments on behalf of the association. He faces 5 years in prison and a $250,000 fine, if convicted.[66]
- **Tell the truth.** Telling the truth is important in building trust with relevant stakeholders. When a group of employees asked the Digital Equipment Corporation (DEC) to look into an apparent high rate of miscarriages among women working on the semiconductor assembly lines, DEC swiftly commis-

TABLE 4-3 GENERAL MOTORS' REVISED GRATUITIES POLICY
Guidelines for a specific scenario as set out in the GM Revised Policy on Gifts, Entertainment, and Other Gratuities:
SCENARIO:
A distinguished investment banking firm has successfully concluded a major acquisition for GM and invites, at the firm's expense, all the GM employees who worked with it to a dinner in New York at which each will be given a nice mantle clock, appropriately inscribed, as a memento of the successful venture.
POLICY:
The dinner and clock should be politely declined. While 'thank you' gestures are a nice custom socially, they can create wrong appearances if they are lavish or extravagant. Firms that provide high value services should be rewarded by being considered for future work. There is no need or expectation that they 'thank' individual GM employees with gifts, entertainment, or other gratuities. Consistent with business custom and management approval, items of no or nominal commercial value commemorating significant accomplishments or expressing appreciation for past GM support, such as a Lucite block, certificate, or baseball cap, may be accepted from suppliers on an infrequent basis.

Source: Reprinted from *The Wall Street Journal,* June 5, 1996, p. B1.

sioned a study. The study, which cost several hundred thousand dollars, revealed that the miscarriage rate was 39 percent in the semiconductor area in comparison to only 18 percent in other parts of the company and in the general population. DEC quickly informed employees of the results and shared them with the Semiconductor Industry Association.[67]

■ **Show respect for people.** The notion of treating people with respect has deep roots in the study of ethics. Respect for the individual is an important aspect of the recent emphasis on valuing diversity. In California, for example, ethnic and racial minorities, as an aggregate, are expected to be in the majority by the end of this decade. In an effort to ensure that its increasingly diverse customers are treated with appropriate respect and consideration, Pacific Bell now has service representatives who can speak English, Spanish, Vietnamese, Korean, Cantonese, or Mandarin.[68]

■ **Stick to the Golden Rule.** The Golden Rule, "Do unto others as you would have others do unto you," provides a benchmark for evaluating the ethical dimensions of business decisions. Translated into business terms, it means treating individuals fairly, just as the managers would want the business treated if it were an individual.[69] When Cummins Engine announced the closure of a components plant in Darlington, England, British trade union leaders went to company headquarters in Columbus, Indiana, to try to get the company to reverse its position. Although Cummins felt it had to stand by its decision, it did offer funding for a program to help the 500 displaced workers find new jobs. The union leaders praised the company for its sympathetic concern.[70]

■ **Above all, do no harm.** (*Primum non nocere*). This principle—the first rule of medical ethics— is considered by some writers to be the bottom-line ethical consideration and one easily adaptable to business. H. J. Heinz told growers supplying fruit and vegetables for its baby foods that products could not be treated with chemicals that were being studied by federal agencies as possible threats to health. This unprecedented step was taken even though the chemicals are legal to use.[71]

■ **Practice participation, not paternalism.** This principle is aimed at learning about the needs of stakeholders, rather than deciding what is best for them. Weyerhaeuser, a forest-products company, has built a good reputation among environmentalists by eliciting their views before finalizing any plans for land or facility development.

■ **Always act when you have responsibility.** Managers have the responsibility of taking action whenever they have the capacity or resources to do so. Managerial action is particularly important if those nearby are in need and a manager is the only one who can help. For example, when Merck pledged to provide free supplies of the Invermectin drug to combat river blindness in third world countries, the company found there was no effective distribution system available. Therefore, Merck went a step further and organized a committee to oversee distribution of the drug.

For a guide that can help you, as a manager, utilize these principles, see the Management Skills for the Twenty-First Century discussion, "Questions to Facilitate Ethical Business Decisions."

Ethical Career Issues

Like most managers, you are likely to experience some ethical dilemmas during the course of your career. Typically, such dilemmas arise from gray areas, where different interpretations of a situation are possible. In addition to con-

MANAGEMENT SKILLS FOR THE TWENTY-FIRST CENTURY

Questions to Facilitate Ethical Business Decisions

When you face an ethical dilemma, you may find it useful to work through the following list of questions. These questions will help you clarify your thinking and decide what to do.

1 Have you defined the problem accurately?
2 How would you define the problem if you stood on the other side of the fence?
3 How did this situation occur in the first place?

4 To whom and to what do you give your loyalty as a person and as a member of the corporation?
5 What is your intention in making this decision?
6 How does this intention compare with the probable results?
7 Whom could your decision or action injure?
8 Can you discuss the problem with the affected parties before you make your decision?
9 Are you confident that your position will be as valid over a long period of time as it seems now?

10 Could you disclose without qualm your decision or action to your boss, your CEO, the board of directors, your family, or society in general?
11 What is the symbolic potential of your action if understood? If misunderstood?
12 Under what conditions would you allow exceptions to your stand?[72]

Reprinted by permission of *Harvard Business Review.* See references at back of book.

sidering the social responsibilities involved, managers need to think carefully about personal values and self-protection in determining how they will handle such situations. They also need to consider what actions they can take to anticipate and avoid ethical conflicts.[73]

ASSESSING VALUES AND PROTECTING YOURSELF When you are faced with an ethical dilemma, three steps are important in career terms. First, seek expertise and support from a wide network of people whom you trust. There may be times when others in the workplace accept a practice as ethical but you see it as questionable. In such cases, you should check with trusted friends, former schoolmates, peers, and/or experts. This will help you clarify your own values on the issue and decide whether further action is needed. Second, if necessary, take internal actions to bring about change. As a manager, you must make sure that you have your facts straight before suggesting that the behaviors of others may be inappropriate or illegal. Then you need to bring the matter to the attention of superiors and attempt to persuade them to take corrective action. If the ethical dilemma persists, it may be necessary to move to the third step, which is to take internal actions to protect yourself. As a manager in the chain of command, you may be in danger of becoming the scapegoat for actions that were implicitly or explicitly condoned by those above. Attempting to argue that you were only following orders will not get you off the hook in an illegal action. Instead, it is often a good idea to write a memo for the file, outlining your objections and conversations with others. Talk with other employees about your concerns. Actively seeking another job is a further step that you should seriously consider. Above all, *do not engage in illegal activities.* Together, these actions build a strong case supporting the fact that you have attempted to halt the ethical difficulty.

ANTICIPATING ETHICAL CONFLICTS Although it is often difficult to accurately predict the likelihood of ethical conflicts, there are some steps that you can take to do so. First, when seeking employment, look for signals that indicate conflicts are likely. Ask your family, friends, and teachers about the organization. Check the library for recent articles and background information. Use job interviews to learn about how the organization operates. If possible, it is often helpful to meet with some of the people whom you would be working with. Try to detect signs of serious dissatisfaction and dissension in the ranks that may signal ethical conflicts. Second, check on industry practices. Industries that have been stable for a long period of time may have developed informal networks that encourage collusion among competitors. Industries at the other end of the spectrum, where there is easy entry and a highly competitive environment, may also be particularly susceptible to ethical difficulties because of severe market pressures. Third, avoid making even small ethical compromises: they have a way of escalating out of control. Managers can avoid such compromises, according to some experts, by setting aside backup money in a bank account so that they can walk out of an unbearable situation. Otherwise, managers could find themselves caught up in a trap like the one José L. Gomez fashioned for himself (see the Case in Point discussion).

CASE IN POINT   ## CAUGHT IN A TRAP OF HIS OWN MAKING

José L. Gomez, a former managing partner of the Grant Thornton accounting firm, found himself in prison serving a 12-year term for his part in a fraud that made front-page news.

Gomez was 39 years old when he pleaded guilty to charges involving his role in the fraud at E.S.M. Government Securities, Inc. The once-obscure Fort Lauderdale, Florida, firm collapsed in the mid-1980s, triggering one of the biggest financial scandals of the century. As E.S.M's auditor, Gomez had knowingly approved the firm's false financial statements for 5 years, thus allowing the massive fraud to continue.

In these days of growing white-collar crime, Gomez's story is a particularly telling one. In some regards, he was almost a cliché: an ambitious young man who rose too fast and wound up in the worst sort of trouble. He says he crossed the line into criminality without even realizing it.

When Gomez's activities came to light, many people were stunned, for he had seemed to be the model of success. He was one of the youngest people ever to be made a partner at his Chicago-based firm, which then was called Alexander Grant & Company. He was active in community affairs.

But he was also a fraud. Investors initially lost some $320 million in the scheme Gomez helped perpetrate, and the scandal was even blamed for a brief decline in the dollar on international markets.

In an interview, Gomez talked of his rise and fall. He said he never intended to do anything wrong. However, just days after being told of his promotion to the position of partner at Grant, two officers of E.S.M. told him of a crude accounting ruse that was hiding millions of dollars in losses. They had to bring Gomez in on the scheme to keep it from unraveling.

Gomez said he had missed the ruse in two previous annual audits, signing bogus financial statements that showed E.S.M. to be in robust condition. According to Gomez, one of the E.S.M. officers used that error to draw him into the fraud.

Gomez explained that he decided to go along with the scheme at E.S.M. because he was convinced that the firm's managers could make up the losses. E.S.M.'s losses continued to mount, and Gomez continued to approve phony financial statements. E.S.M. officers even began arranging loans for Gomez, who was having personal financial problems. The loans, which weren't repaid, totaled $200,000.[74]

The aftershocks of the E.S.M. collapse led to the Ohio savings and loan crisis and related problems in other states. The crisis began when it became clear that the Cincinnati-based Home State Savings Bank, whose loans were secured by a deposit insurance fund that was considered to be inadequate, was likely to suffer severe losses from the E.S.M. troubles. Ultimately, the Grant Thornton accounting firm paid more than $80 million to settle charges filed against it.[75] ■■■

■ MANAGING AN ETHICAL ORGANIZATION

In an interview with *The Wall Street Journal,* Gomez argued that in hindsight he thinks he was too inexperienced to be handling an audit and there was too much emphasis on the ability to produce new clients—charges that the Grant Thornton accounting firm vigorously denies. Although it is easy in retrospect to blame everyone else, and although individuals are ultimately responsible for their own actions, Gomez's allegations do have some relevance for managers. An important management challenge is operating an organization so that members conduct their business in an ethical manner. To do so, managers need to be knowledgeable about environmental and organizational conditions that increase the likelihood of unethical behavior. They should also use mechanisms that facilitate ethical behaviors.

Situational Factors That Influence Ethical Behavior

Much of the research on ethical versus unethical behavior in organizations has focused on actually breaking the law. These studies suggest that several factors in the environment of an organization can be conducive to illegal and unethical behavior (see Table 4-4).[76] Of course, the values of managers themselves also have a bearing on whether individual managers actually engage in unethical behavior, even though some types of situations make it more likely.

For example, *environmental competitiveness* tends to encourage unethical behavior. Some industries in which price-fixing has been common, such as those producing automobiles, paper cartons, plumbing fixtures, and heavy electrical equipment, tend to have strong competition, products that are fairly similar, and frequent price changes and negotiations. Competition can foster unethical behavior in not-for-profit organizations as well. Such behavior is manifested in illegal payments to college athletes, illegal campaign contributions to political candidates, and misrepresentations of the amount of charitable contributions actually going to those being helped.

TABLE 4-4 SITUATIONAL FACTORS INFLUENCING ETHICAL BEHAVIOR	
EXTERNAL FACTORS	**INTERNAL FACTORS**
Environmental competitiveness	Pressure for high performance
Environmental munificence	Labor dissatisfaction
Extreme dependency	Delegation
	Encouragement of innovation

Both low and high *environmental munificence* may also be conducive to unethical behavior. When munificence is very low, the opportunities for success are limited. The struggle for financial performance in such an environment may cause some organizations to behave unethically. This was the case at the Beech-Nut Nutrition Corporation, the second-largest U.S. baby food manufacturer. Beech-Nut executives ignored chemists' warnings that the apple concentrate the company was buying at below-market prices was probably extensively altered. Ultimately, two top executives each received prison terms and fines for their role in selling the completely synthetic juice, which had been labeled "100 percent fruit juice." The scandal also adversely affected sales of the company's baby food products. The executives had ignored the warnings because the company was bordering on insolvency.[77]

On the other hand, very high munificence may also lead to unethical behavior as organizations attempt to grow quickly and take advantage of a favorable situation. For example, an executive of Halsey Drug Co., a Brooklyn, New York, maker of generic drugs, was sentenced to 18 months in prison for conspiring to add ingredients that did not have the approval of the Food and Drug Administration (FDA) to generic drugs for irregular heartbeats, meningitis, and hyperthyroidism.[78] The official was apparently attempting to boost the effectiveness of the drugs in order to take advantage of the burgeoning markets for generics that cost less but are supposed to be therapeutically equivalent to brand-name drugs.

A third important external factor that can influence unethical behavior is *extreme dependency* of one organization on another. Such dependencies can create pressures for bribes and payoffs. For example, before various drugs can be offered to the public, they must be approved by the FDA. Efforts by some generic drugmakers to expedite approvals led to a scandal in which three FDA employees pleaded guilty to taking illegal gratuities from the drugmakers and two drugmakers admitted submitting false data to the agency.[79]

Internal organizational factors can also increase the likelihood of unethical behavior. Heavy *pressure for higher performance* and output may induce individuals to take "shortcuts," such as fixing prices, secretly speeding up the assembly line, or releasing unsafe products. For example, Salomon Brothers, a Wall Street investment firm, was fined $290 million by the Securities and Exchange Commission after the firm admitted that two of its traders had submitted false bids in government Treasury auctions. The bids allowed the firm to exert excessive control over the multi-trillion-dollar Treasury market used to finance the public debt. The traders and several high-level executives who learned of the false bids, but did not report them to the government, were forced to resign.[80]

Labor dissatisfaction may also result in unethical behavior as anger replaces more constrained and rational behavior. Ironically, *delegation* of authority and encouragement of *innovation* may increase the likelihood of unethical behavior because of the greater latitude and creativity involved. For example, at Adam Opel AG, the German automaking subsidiary of General Motors, three senior board members and a number of employees resigned amidst allegations that they had either accepted gratuities, such as free work on their homes, or engaged in a kickback scheme involving the awarding of contracts. Opel Chairman David Herman said that in making cutbacks to become "leaner" the company may have eliminated too many of the checks and balances on the company's financial operations. He warned, "This is a word to the wise in other companies."[81]

Since external factors and internal pressures may increase the likelihood of unethical acts, managers need to monitor such conditions. When the conditions exist, managers must expend even greater effort in conveying the importance of ethical behavior on the part of organization members.

One study suggests that upper-level managers may not feel as much ethical pressure as managers at the middle and lower levels.[82] This might imply that upper-level managers are not sufficiently aware of the pressures on middle and lower levels and, as a result, do not take sufficient action to counter such pressures.

Mechanisms for Ethical Management

An important issue, then, is: What can managers do to foster ethical behavior in others in the organizations? While there are no easy ways to influence behavior, there are a number of mechanisms that can help managers create an ethical climate. These mechanisms include the following:[83]

TOP MANAGEMENT COMMITMENT Managers can demonstrate their commitment by instituting a variety of the mechanisms discussed below and by setting positive examples through their own behaviors. Vernon R. Loucks, Jr., president and CEO of Baxter Travenol Laboratories, Inc., argues that subordinates are likely to pay more attention to what you do than to what you say.

CODES OF ETHICS It is estimated that 90 percent of the major U.S. corporations have written codes of ethics. A **code of ethics** is a document prepared for the purpose of guiding organization members when they encounter an ethical dilemma. While almost all the companies that have codes say that the code is helpful in maintaining ethical behavior among employees, one study showed that only 36 percent distribute the code to all employees and only 20 percent display it throughout the organization.[84] One code that is given to every new employee and displayed throughout the organization is the Johnson & Johnson Credo, shown in Figure 4-5. A comparative study of business firms in Britain, France, and what was then West Germany showed that only about 40 percent had codes of ethics and that the content varied considerably from country to country due to political, legal, and sociocultural differences.[85]

> **Code of ethics** A document prepared for the purpose of guiding organization members when they encounter an ethical dilemma

ETHICS COMMITTEES According to a survey by the Ethics Resource Center, about one-third of the Fortune 1000 companies have ethics committees. An **ethics committee** is a group charged with helping to establish policies and resolve major questions involving ethical issues confronting organization members in the course of their work. The committee may also oversee training programs on ethics. Often the committee consists of several individuals from top management and/or the board of directors.

> **Ethics committee** A group charged with helping to establish policies and resolve major questions involving ethical issues confronting organization members in the course of their work

ETHICS AUDITS Some organizations conduct **ethics audits,** systematic efforts to assess conformance to organizational ethical policies, aid understanding of those policies, and identify serious breaches requiring remedial action. Even with such efforts, ethical problems can be difficult to identify. For example,

> **Ethics audits** Systematic efforts to assess conformance to organizational ethical policies, aid understanding of those policies, and identify serious breaches requiring remedial action

Our Credo

We believe our first responsibility is to the doctors, nurses and patients,
to mothers and fathers and all others who use our products and services.
In meeting their needs everything we do must be of high quality.
We must constantly strive to reduce our costs
in order to maintain reasonable prices.
Customers' orders must be serviced promptly and accurately.
Our suppliers and distributors must have an opportunity
to make a fair profit.

We are responsible to our employees,
the men and women who work with us throughout the world.
Everyone must be considered as an individual.
We must be considered as an individual.
We must respect their dignity and recognize their merit.
They must have a sense of security in their jobs.
Compensation must be fair and adequate,
and working conditions clean, orderly and safe.
We must be mindful of ways to help our employees fulfill
their family responsibilities.
Employees must feel free to make suggestions and complaints.
There must be equal opportunity for employment, development
and advancement for those qualified.
We must provide competent management,
and their actions must be just and ethical.

We are responsible to the communities in which we live and work
and to the world community as well.
We must be good citizens – support good works and charities
and bear our fair share of taxes.
We must encourage civic improvements and better health education.
We must maintain in good order
the property we are privileged to use,
protecting the environment and natural resources.

Our final responsibility is to our stockholders.
Business must make a sound profit.
We must experiment with new ideas.
Research must be carried on, innovative programs developed
and mistakes paid for.
New equipment must be purchased, new facilities provided
and new products launched.
Reserves must be created to provide for adverse times.
When we operate according to these principles,
the stockholders should realize a fair return.

Johnson & Johnson

Figure 4-5 *The Johnson & Johnson Credo.*

Dow Corning had a seemingly model ethics program encompassing ethics audits, yet the company became embroiled in a serious ethical situation (see the Case in Point discussion).

DOW CORNING CONFRONTS ETHICAL ISSUE

CASE IN POINT

Dow Corning Corp., a specialty chemical company based in Midland, Michigan, was a pioneer in corporate ethics. Yet the company suddenly found itself facing an ethical nightmare when the U.S. Food and Drug Administration announced a moratorium on breast implants. Strong concerns had surfaced that the implants could rupture or leak, potentially allowing the silicone to seep inside patients' bodies, where serious harm could result. As the major maker of the silicone-gel implants, Dow Corning quickly came under fire for selling a product that might be unsafe.

The company at first denied that there were any problems with the product. As criticism mounted, the CEO was replaced and the company released 800 pages of internal documents indicating that it had been aware of the problems for 25 years. Evidence that surfaced included a 1977 memo from a Dow Corning engineer who left the company in protest after questioning the safety of implants to no avail.

Many observers were surprised at the situation, since the company had made numerous efforts as far back as 1976 to include ethics in its corporate culture. For example, members of its Business Conduct Committee, which reported directly to the board of directors, audited every business operation once every 3 years. The audits monitored company compliance with ethical policies and provided an opportunity for dialogue about ethical problems that organization members might be facing. Two company training programs, as well as the company's semiannual employee opinion survey, included the topic of ethics. Yet four separate audit meetings since 1983, held at the Dow Corn-

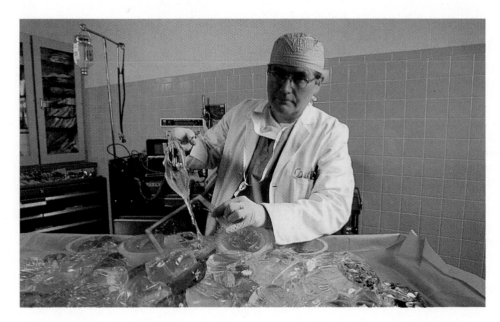

Despite its traditionally strong commitment to corporate ethics, Dow Corning Corp. inexplicably ignored mounting in-company and external evidence of the dangers of silicone breast implants and continued to market its 25-year-old product line. Finally, in 1992 the company announced it would no longer sell the implants. Soaring legal costs of class action suits have since forced the company into federal bankruptcy protection.

ing facility where the silicone implants were made, failed to reveal any concerns with the product's safety.

Ultimately, the company announced that it would no longer sell the implants, which accounted for about 1 percent of Dow Corning's sales. In addition, it would help pay for removal of implants, and it would continue research on the safety of the product. Ensuing litigation and controversies over the terms of a potential class action settlement with women who had received breast implants made by Dow Corning finally caused the company to file for federal bankruptcy protection. Mixed results from medical studies attempting to link the implants with immune-system diseases have fueled the debate. Litigation and settlement efforts continue as more suits are filed against Dow Chemical, which owned one-half of Dow Corning.[86] ■■■

Ethics hot line A special telephone line established to enable employees to bypass the normal chain of command in reporting grievances and serious ethical problems

Whistle-blower An employee who reports a real or perceived wrongdoing under the control of his or her employer to those who may be able to take appropriate action

ETHICS HOT LINES An **ethics hot line** is a special telephone line established to enable employees to bypass the normal chain of command in reporting grievances and serious ethical problems. The line is usually handled by an executive designated to investigate and help resolve issues that are reported. A hot line facilitates the internal handling of problems and thus reduces the likelihood that employees will become external whistle-blowers. A **whistle-blower** is an employee who reports a real or perceived wrongdoing under the control of his or her employer to those who may be able to take appropriate action. When a whistle-blower goes to an outside person or organization, unfavorable publicity, legal investigations, and lawsuits often result.[87]

ETHICS TRAINING Many organizations use ethics training to encourage ethical behavior. Such training may focus exclusively on ethical concerns or may be integrated into training programs that cover a variety of organizational issues. By clarifying expectations and ethical standards, such training can help reduce unethical behavior.[88] An enhanced understanding of organizational standards can help managers and other employees engage in appropriate decision making, the subject of the next chapter.

■ CHAPTER SUMMARY

Organizational, or corporate, social responsibility refers to the obligation of a business firm to seek actions that protect and improve the welfare of society along with its own interests. Three major contrasting perspectives on the nature of corporate social responsibility are the invisible hand, the hand of government, and the hand of management. Due to expanding societal expectations regarding the social responsibility of businesses and other organizations, the hand-of-management view is increasingly relevant to managers. The iron law of responsibility suggests that socially responsible behavior may have a positive long-run effect on organizational success.

The social responsibilities of management focus mainly on six major stakeholder groups: shareholders, employees, customers, the local community, society, and

the international community. Studies to date indicate that there is no clear relationship between a corporation's degree of social responsibility and its short-run financial success. Nevertheless, it is possible to be both socially responsible and financially successful. Increasingly, organizations are attempting to orient their socially responsible activities toward areas that also can affect their bottom line and ultimately give them a competitive edge.

Corporate social responsiveness refers to the development of organization decision processes whereby managers anticipate, respond to, and manage areas of social responsibility. Two processes usually are essential. First, it is necessary to establish methods of monitoring social demands and expectations. Major means are social forecasting, opinion surveys, social audits, and issues management. Second, it is important to develop internal social response mechanisms. These include individual executives, temporary task forces, permanent committees, permanent departments, or combinations of these elements.

Ultimately, questions of corporate social responsibility and social responsiveness depend on the ethical standards of managers. Three types of managerial ethics are immoral, amoral, and moral. While amoral behavior tends to prevail, moral management is likely to be in the long-run best interests of organizations. Ethical guidelines for managers include obey the law; tell the truth; show respect for people; stick to the Golden Rule; above all, do no harm; practice participation, not paternalism;

and always act when you have responsibility. Ethical career issues for managers may involve assessing their own values and protecting themselves, as well as considering what actions they can take to anticipate and avoid ethical conflicts.

An important management challenge is operating an organization so that members conduct their business in an ethical manner. To do so, managers need to be knowledgeable about environmental and organizational conditions that increase the likelihood of unethical behavior. They should also use mechanisms that facilitate ethical behavior, such as top management commitment, codes of ethics, ethics committees, ethics audits, ethics training, and ethics hot lines.

■ QUESTIONS FOR DISCUSSION AND REVIEW

1 Explain the three major perspectives on corporate social responsibility. What criteria might you use to determine whether an organization's management subscribes most closely to the invisible-hand, hand-of-government, or hand-of-management view?

2 Identify the six stakeholder groups often mentioned in conjunction with social responsibility. To what extent do these groups apply to your college or university? What other stakeholders might you add?

3 Evaluate the extent to which organizational social responsibility is likely to pay off financially. Colleges and universities are often the recipients of corporate philanthropy. Identify two ways in which such philanthropy has helped your college or university. How might contributors benefit from such donations?

4 Identify major approaches that can be used to monitor social demands and expectations. Choose an organization with which you are familiar and suggest how it might use these methods to monitor relevant social issues.

5 Explain several internal social response mechanisms available to organizations. Identify two mechanisms that are used by your college or university.

6 Distinguish among the three major types of managerial ethics. Use *Business Week* or *The Wall Street Journal* to identify an example of one of these types.

7 Enumerate the ethical guidelines for managers that were discussed in the chapter. How might these guidelines have helped José Gomez, the former managing partner of the Grant Thornton accounting firm, avoid his ethical problems?

8 Suggest some steps you could take when seeking employment that might help you detect potential ethical problems. To what extent do your friends consider these issues when seeking jobs?

9 Describe situational factors that are likely to influence ethical behavior. Analyze José Gomez's situation in terms of these factors.

10 Outline the basic mechanisms for ethical management. Suppose that you have just been appointed to a top-level executive position with a major defense contractor. How would you use these mechanisms to help prevent some of the ethical difficulties, such as misrepresenting costs on defense contracts, that have plagued other major contractors?

■ DISCUSSION QUESTIONS FOR CHAPTER OPENING CASE

1 Identify the major stakeholders in the two Tylenol crises. To what extent were the interests of the various stakeholders satisfied by J&J's actions?

2 What evidence of corporate social responsiveness is apparent from the information given about J&J?

3 Would you characterize the type of managerial ethics evidenced at J&J during the Tylenol crises as immoral, amoral, or moral? Explain the reasoning behind your assessment.

■ EXERCISES FOR MANAGING IN THE TWENTY-FIRST CENTURY

EXERCISE 1
SKILL BUILDING: BUSINESS ETHICAL DILEMMAS FROM LOCKHEED MARTIN'S "GRAY MATTERS: THE ETHICS GAME"[89]

 Use the questions in the Management Skills for the Twenty-First Century discussion ("Questions to Facilitate Ethical Business Decisions") in this chapter to help you choose what to do in each of the following situations taken from Lockheed Martin's ethics game.

Situation 1
Since program funds are short, you have been directed by your supervisor to charge your time to an account you know to be improper. What do you do?

Potential Answers to Situation 1 (Choose One)
A Explain to your supervisor that mischarging on a government contract is fraud.
B Refuse to mischarge.
C Mischarge as directed by your supervisor.
D Ask finance for an overhead number to charge your time to.

Situation 2
A company-sponsored training course in your field is being held in Orlando, Florida. You have no interest in the training, but you are ready for a vacation and have never been to Disney World. What do you do?

Potential Answers to Situation 2 (Choose One)
A Even though you have no interest in the training, ask your supervisor if he thinks it will benefit you.
B Obviously, or maybe not so obviously, it will be of some benefit to you, so you sign up.
C Reluctantly decline to go.
D Suggest that someone else go who has both a need and the interest.

Situation 3
On the bus going home at night, the woman sitting next to you mentions that she is being sexually harassed by one of her fellow employees. Although she does not work for you, you both work for the same company. You are a manager in the company. What do you do?

Potential Answers to Situation 3 (Choose One)
A Listen politely, but since she doesn't work for you, stay out of it.
B Suggest she speak to her supervisor about it.
C Suggest she speak to either your company equal opportunity office or ethics office.
D You contact your company's equal opportunity office or ethics office.

EXERCISE 2
MANAGEMENT EXERCISE: A QUESTION OF ETHICS

 After earning an undergraduate degree in history and an M.B.A. in finance, Roberta was offered a position with a medium-sized real estate development firm in her hometown. Much to her liking, the job involved working in the firm's "community projects" area, where she would oversee the books for the company's construction of low-cost housing projects.

The opportunity to work in finance while also aiding the public good appealed to Roberta. She had interviewed for other jobs in finance and real estate, but she didn't like the competitive atmosphere at the larger firms, where the size of salaries and bonuses seemed to be the overriding concern of most new hires.

After a few weeks in her position, Roberta discovered a discrepancy in the books of one of her firm's housing projects. Six separate checks for $10,000 each had been written by Roberta's boss over the past year, and each was made payable to cash with no further explanation. When Roberta approached her boss, she was told that they were just another cost of doing business and that she should inflate the cost of other items to cover the payments.

Through further investigation, Roberta learned that the checks were being paid to building inspectors so that they would overlook the use of certain substandard materials. Roberta again protested to her boss, who responded with obvious irritation. He said such payments were common and the use of substandard materials wouldn't affect safety.

The boss implied that significant cost savings on materials were necessary if the firm was to build low-income housing on a profitable basis. He noted that the cost of each unit would increase by only $2000 to cover the payments and that the eventual owners probably expect that they'll have to upgrade their units from time to time anyway.

Roberta knows that, at the least, replacement or repairs would be needed after only 2 or 3 years because of the substandard materials. Concerned that a wrong was committed and fearful that she might personally become entangled in the mess, Roberta protested to her boss's supervisor. The supervisor told Roberta that he "would look into it." Roberta hasn't heard anything in 3 weeks and has just discovered that a seventh $10,000 check payable to cash has come through. What should Roberta do now?[90]

CONCLUDING CASE 1

TONY SANTINO'S DILEMMA

Tony Santino was a 39-year-old manager facing an ethical dilemma. Three years earlier he had received his M.B.A. from a leading business school, but he had not yet established a stable work history. He lost his first job after graduate school when he, along with a small band of fellow M.B.A. "hotshots," got caught in the cross fire between two warring executives in an aerospace firm. Tony's mentor left the company as a result of the battle, and shortly after, Tony did too. He had hoped to find a job with another large firm in the same industry, but at 37 his lack of a private-sector track record seemed to be a liability.

After a prolonged and disappointing job search, Tony was appointed director of marketing for a small firm that manufactured undifferentiated, inexpensive—but critical—parts for industrial equipment. Once again Tony discovered he was trapped between two warring executives. The company was displeased with the performance of the current vice president of marketing. During Tony's job interview, the president said Tony could hope to replace that vice president, who meanwhile was Tony's direct boss.

One of Tony's first assignments from the vice president was to acquire information about a competitor by pretending to be an executive recruiter. Tony at first protested, but remembering his recent job search and the fact that the assignment came after only one month on the job, he reluctantly performed the task.

Next, the president and the marketing vice president, who were both strong-willed individuals and frequently did not see eye to eye, joined forces when Tony expressed reluctance to sign and distribute what he believed was an illegal and unethical price list. Tony's employer, as it turned out, had been illegally setting prices in collusion with its major competitor for years, yielding a handsome profit.

One of the competing firms had invested this monopoly profit back into R&D and developed a process for manufacturing the same product line at 40 percent of the current cost. The competitor was passing on the savings to customers and devouring the market, especially for new customers. Tony's firm, anxious to maintain its market share with less competitive goods, developed a fictitious product line that would sell at the competitor's price.

The lower-priced items were exactly the same as the higher-priced products, but they were labeled differently and were made available only to new customers. The purchasing engineers of old customers were too loyal and lazy to run the certification tests necessary to switch to a new product line or supplies. The deception in Tony's company would involve lab technicians, phone-order clerks, and the company sales force.

Tony believed this practice was a violation of the Robinson-Patman, Clayton, and Sherman antitrust laws, which generally prohibit price-fixing and price discrimination—an opinion he conveyed to his superiors. He suggested that the only way to compete effectively in an industry with an undifferentiated product was by being a cost leader. Tony's bosses, however, defended their proposed action as common industry practice and asked Tony not to be so "negative."

Tony consulted with a local lawyer, a friend, who confirmed the illegality of the proposed pricing scheme but also emphasized that "small companies were known for this kind of stuff." The probability of apprehension and any kind of legal action was negligible, the lawyer said.

In addition, Tony hired an outside marketing consultant to advise the company on broad strategic issues. In a meeting attended by the consultant, Tony, and his superiors, Tony asked about the Robinson-Patman violation. His bosses looked on in horror as he described the pricing decision, but they were relieved as the consultant said, "The jails are not big enough to hold all the people who do this sort of thing."

Tony had to obtain forged lab test results from the company's R&D engineers to implement the pricing scheme. Although they complied promptly, one of the engineers commented, "Tony, I know you're just caught in the middle, but I've been around here 39 years and have never been able to like these things any better."

The dilemma was exacerbated when Tony's bosses asked him to sign the cover sheet of the new price list. He confided to a friend: "I still think I know what's right, but with all these other voices telling me to sign the price list, maybe I'm just making a mountain out of a molehill. Then again, maybe I compromised myself through the executive headhunter intrigue. I already feel like a bit of a prostitute. And if I leave, how do I explain my short job tenure to any potential employer?"[91]

QUESTIONS FOR CONCLUDING CASE 1

1 What ethical guidelines for managers are relevant to this situation?
2 What steps would you recommend that Tony take to clarify his own values and protect himself in this situation?
3 How might Tony try to avoid getting into a similar situation if he seeks a new job?

CONCLUDING CASE 2

THE ROCHESTER CORPORATION: BURIED TREASURE

Al Canales stared at the visitor and felt his heart sink. "What are you telling me? That lovely hill, covered with flowers and trees, is really a waste dump?"

"Exactly. Kinda funny, isn't it? In the old days, no one really worried about all this stuff. It's mostly lead from the wire cooling process, I imagine. Yeah. Well, we had to take better care of our waste products by the late seventies, but before then, we just piled it up. Probably nobody here at the plant even remembers those days. Yeah, times have changed. Anyway, it's sure nice of you to have these 'open houses' for the community. Gives us 'old-timers' a chance to reminisce."

"Oh, it is our pleasure," Canales said, with a rueful smile. As president of the Rochester Corporation, he was not really feeling pleasure. His first thought was, "Why did I have to hear that?" He sighed and decided to gather more information before taking action.

A BRIEF HISTORY OF THE CORPORATION

The Rochester Corporation was founded in the 1700s to produce rope used by sailors as they navigated the oceans. Originally located in Hagerstown, Maryland, the firm was moved to its current site in Culpeper, Virginia, in 1940. In 1983, BTR, Ltd., a huge international conglomerate headquartered in London, purchased the firm. The BTR empire is extremely decentralized. As long as the over 1300 subsidiaries and operating units met their profit goals, they were left alone.

Over the past 200 years Rochester has evolved. From its hemp-rope days in the 1700s, the company went on to produce wire rope in the 1920s and then used the wire rope to encase cables for the oil and gas industries in the 1950s. By the 1960s the company was producing signal-carrying cables for oceanographic exploration. In the 1990s it was manufacturing state-of-the-art fiber-optic cables. Rochester's continuous success is evidenced by the awards for excellence its products earned in World War II and by its acceptance as a qualified supplier on technically sophisticated U.S. defense contracts.

A PRESENT-DAY MEETING

Less than a month after hearing about the possibility of a toxic waste problem on Rochester's property, Al Canales called two of his top executives to his office to discuss a strategy for dealing with the problem.

Al Canales: "Well, I just had a call from the environmental engineering firm that we had inspect our hill. As we had feared, that hill is really a pile of lead and other chemicals. What is our exposure here, Dennis?"

Dennis Ehrhart (controller): "I talked to the corporate attorneys in Stamford [Connecticut]. We cannot go back against the previous owners because of the releases we signed when we bought the company in 1983."

Canales: "How about 'Superfund'? We really didn't cause this problem, you know."

Ehrhart: "Well, 'Superfund' is a federal program for severe problems when there is no one around to foot the bill."

Canales: "That sounds exactly like what we've got here!"

Ehrhart: "No. *We* are around, Al."

Canales: "Well, that's great! . . . So, what next?"

Earnie Fascett (V.P. of manufacturing): "While the federal government establishes the regulations, the state monitors hazardous waste cleanups. Maybe we ought to call the office in Richmond and let them know what we've got here."

Ehrhart: "Is there any chance we could hold off for a few months? That dirt is not going anywhere, we haven't had any complaints, and this could be a real budget buster. A cleanup would probably cost us a million dollars or so."

Canales: "A million bucks! You've got to be kidding! It's just a pile of dirt!"

Fascett: "Yeah. But getting rid of it is going to be tricky."[92]

QUESTIONS FOR CONCLUDING CASE 2

1   Who are the major stakeholders in this situation?

2   What are the options available to Al Canales and the Rochester Corporation?

3   What do you think Al Canales should do next?

PART TWO

PLANNING AND DECISION MAKING

PLANNING AND DECISION MAKING

An organization without planning is like a sailboat minus its rudder. Without planning, organizations are subject to the winds of environmental change, yet have little means to take advantage of the prevailing currents in determining their own direction. Planning is the management function that involves setting goals and deciding how best to achieve them. The function also includes considering what must be done to encourage necessary levels of change and innovation. Planning provides a basis for the other major functions of management—organizing, leading, and controlling—by charting the course and providing the steering mechanism. This section, then, is geared to helping you acquire a basic knowledge of the planning function.

The kinds of problems that managers attempt to resolve through decision making, as well as the appropriate steps to take in the decision process, are the focus of **Chapter 5.** The chapter also addresses creativity, an important ingredient in innovation.

As the **Supplement to Chapter 5** shows, managers have recourse to many aids in their planning and related decision making, such as forecasting techniques, various planning models, quantitative analysis, and computer-based expert systems.

Chapter 6 examines the overall planning process and explores how setting goals can facilitate organizational performance. As you will learn, goals and the related plans necessary to carry them out vary in important ways according to organizational level.

One of the most important aspects of planning is strategic management. **Chapter 7** explores how managers formulate and implement large-scale action plans called strategies that help the organization attain a competitive edge.

CHAPTER FIVE

MANAGERIAL DECISION MAKING

CHAPTER OUTLINE

The Nature of Managerial Decision Making
Types of Problems Decision Makers Face
Differences in Decision-Making Situations

Managers as Decision Makers
The Rational Model
Nonrational Models

Steps in an Effective Decision-Making Process
Identifying the Problem
Generating Alternative Solutions
Evaluating and Choosing an Alternative
Implementing and Monitoring the Chosen Solution

Overcoming Barriers to Effective Decision Making
Accepting the Problem Challenge
Searching for Sufficient Alternatives
Recognizing Common Decision-Making Biases
Avoiding the Decision Escalation Phenomenon

Managing Diversity: Group Decision Making
Advantages and Disadvantages of Group Decision
   Making
Enhancing Group Decision-Making Processes
Computer-Assisted Group Decision Making

**Promoting Innovation: The Creativity Factor in
Decision Making**
Basic Ingredients
Stages of Creativity
Techniques for Enhancing Group Creativity

LEARNING OBJECTIVES

After studying this chapter, you should be able to:

■ Explain the major types of problems facing decision makers and describe the difference between programmed and nonprogrammed decisions.

■ Contrast the rational and nonrational models of managers as decision makers.

■ Describe each of the steps in an effective decision-making process.

■ Explain how to overcome the barriers associated with accepting the problem challenge and searching for sufficient alternatives.

■ Describe how to recognize common decision-making biases and avoid the decision escalation phenomenon.

■ Assess the advantages and disadvantages of group decision making.

■ Explain the three basic ingredients and four stages of creativity.

■ Describe the major techniques for enhancing group creativity.

GAINING THE EDGE

COKE GETS BACK ITS KICK

 Several times per day, Roberto C. Goizueta (pronounced "Goy-SWET-ah"), the chief executive officer of the Coca-Cola Company, walks from his oak-floored office in Atlanta down the hall to a Quotron machine in order to check Coke's stock price. Since he was awarded the top slot at Coca-Cola in 1981, the news from the Quotron has usually been good.

Goizueta, a chemical engineer from Havana, Cuba, who fled the Castro regime, has made major changes in the once-sleepy company and its southern traditions. For one thing, he began emphasizing that management's chief job is maximizing shareholder value so that shareholders receive good returns on their investments in the company's stock. Boosting returns has meant greater risk taking. To encourage such risk taking, Goizueta has worked hard to create an atmosphere in which new ideas can flourish. Yet, to encourage teamwork, he insists that he and his three top officers agree before any major corporate decision is made. Goizueta once vetoed a major acquisition because one member of the team opposed the move.

Perhaps his biggest gamble was putting Coke's name on a diet coke. Although the decision seems simple in retrospect, Goizueta says it was the most difficult one top management has made. They saw horrendous risk in putting the venerable Coke name on a product that could fail. Up until that time, the name "Coca-Cola" was attached to only one product. Nevertheless, they took the gamble. Within 5 years, Diet Coke became the third-largest-selling soft drink in the United States. Since then, the world's most valuable trademark has been attached successfully to several other soft-drink variations.

Then there is the issue of New Coke. Goizueta continues to argue strongly that Coke was correct in offering the new, sweeter-tasting formula back in 1985 because of Pepsi's increasing popularity, particularly with children. Looking back, though, he wishes that he had brought old Coke back in 1 month, rather than waiting 3 months before announcing that the old formula would be reintroduced as Coca-Cola Classic. He says he will never forget having to appear

Coca-Cola is a leading soft drink in China—and 159 other countries. Coca-Cola management decided to step up its efforts in international markets after soft drink consumption began leveling off at home.

on television to tell the American people that he had made a mistake. Coca-Cola Classic continues to be the top-selling cola in the United States. The New Coke situation is particularly famous because, before introducing the new soft drink, the company conducted extensive market tests in over 30 U.S. cities. In obtaining the opinions of more than 40,000 people, Coke sampled eight times the usual number of consumers. Tests, with the brand name hidden, indicated a consumer preference for the New Coke formula when compared with the old formula and with Pepsi. The general consensus is that the company did everything right in terms of following the best market research procedures. Nevertheless, no one predicted the vehemence of customer reactions.

Thus, even though Coke did extensive market research, the efforts did not lead to the best final decision. Still, the managers did follow an appropriate decision-making process, which included generating alternative formulas and evaluating them carefully. Fortunately, in this case, the decision was reversible. By following effective decision-making procedures, managers at Coke do increase the likelihood of making good decisions. Moreover, since recovering from the New Coke problem, the company is more willing to take risks with the Coke name and new products, such as Mountain Blast Powerade sports drink and Strawberry Passion Awareness Fruitopia fruit drink.

Taking risks—though well considered ones—is becoming even more important as the company steps up its efforts in the international arena. Soft-drink consumption is leveling off in mature markets like the United States, Western Europe, Mexico, and Japan. For example, on average, every American annually consumes about 19 gallons of soft-drink products made by Coke. The company must look to emerging areas like Russia and China for its future growth. Recently Coke has opened plants in Romania, Norway, Fiji, and India and is in the process of establishing plants in China, Hungary, Lithuania, Central Asia, and Thailand. Coca-Cola was the first U.S. company to enter a joint venture in Vietnam after the embargo was lifted in 1995. Already a leading soft-drink company in 160 countries, Coca-Cola has between 50 and 60 percent of the market in most of the countries in which it does business. So far, Coke's track record for decision making has been very good. The price of Coke stock has increased a whopping average annual compounded rate of 24 percent per year since Goizueta took the helm.[1] ■■■

Decision making The process through which managers identify organizational problems and attempt to resolve them

As the Coca-Cola situation graphically illustrates, gaining and maintaining a competitive edge requires extensive managerial decision making. **Decision making** is the process through which managers identify organizational problems and attempt to resolve them. In Goizueta's situation, he recognized that Coke was in danger of losing its preeminence in the soft-drink industry. He also saw that the company was not using its tremendous assets to their full capacity. Hence he took steps to solve these problems. Managers may not always make the right decision, but they can use their knowledge of appropriate decision-making processes to increase the odds.

In this chapter we explore the nature of managerial decision making, including the types of problems and decision-making situations that managers are likely to face. We also evaluate managers as decision makers and consider the steps in an effective decision-making process. We examine how barriers to effective decision making can be overcome, and we weigh the advantages and disadvantages of group decision making. Finally, we show how managers can promote innovation through the use of creativity in the decision-making process.

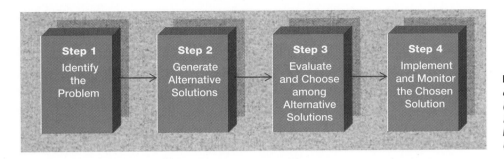

Figure 5-1 *Steps in the decision-making process. (Adapted from George P. Huber,* Managerial Decision Making, *Scott, Foresman, Glenview, Ill., 1980, p. 8.)*

■ THE NATURE OF MANAGERIAL DECISION MAKING

Like Goizueta, managers make many different decisions in the course of their work. While managers at lower levels in organizations might not make such monumental decisions as changing the formula for a revered product, many smaller decisions at lower levels have a cumulative effect on organizational effectiveness. For example, Motorola has built its reputation for high quality and innovation (particularly in semiconductors, electronic pagers, and cellular telephones) partially by encouraging individuals from design, manufacturing, and marketing departments to involve themselves early in decision making for new projects.[2] Good decision-making processes are important at all levels.

An effective decision-making process generally includes the four steps shown in Figure 5-1.[3] Some authors refer to these four steps as "problem solving" and reserve the term "decision making" for the first three steps—the process up to, but not including, implementation and follow-up.[4] Here we use "decision making" and "problem solving" interchangeably to refer to the broad process depicted in Figure 5-1. We do this because "decision making" is the term more commonly used in business, and we believe that it will be clear when we are using this term in its more narrow sense. We analyze the four steps in the decision-making process in greater detail in a later section of this chapter. First, though, it is useful to examine the major types of problems that managers usually encounter and to consider the important differences in managerial decision-making situations.

Types of Problems Decision Makers Face

Managerial decision making typically centers on three types of problems: crisis, noncrisis, and opportunity problems.[5]

CRISIS A **crisis problem** is a serious difficulty requiring immediate action. An example of a crisis is the discovery of a severe cash-flow deficiency that has a high potential of quickly evolving into serious losses. Coca-Cola faced a crisis when loyal customers protested the demise of the classic Coke formula. New Coke still exists as Coke II in some markets, but accounts for just one-tenth of 1 percent of all carbonated beverage volume.[6]

Crisis problem A serious difficulty requiring immediate action

NONCRISIS A **noncrisis problem** is an issue that requires resolution but does not simultaneously have the importance and immediacy characteristics of a crisis. Many of the decisions that managers make center on noncrisis problems. Examples of such problems are a factory that needs to be brought into con-

Noncrisis problem An issue that requires resolution but does not simultaneously have the importance and immediacy characteristics of a crisis

formity with new state antipollution standards during the next 3 years and an employee who is frequently late for work. At one point, flat earnings in Coke's troubled food division, which mainly produced Minute Maid juices, represented a noncrisis problem. After Goizueta appointed a new president and CEO of the division, the situation began to improve significantly.[7]

Opportunity problem A situation that offers a strong potential for significant organizational gain if appropriate actions are taken

OPPORTUNITY An **opportunity problem** is a situation that offers strong potential for significant organizational gain if appropriate actions are taken. Opportunities typically involve new ideas and novel directions and, therefore, are major vehicles for innovation. Top management at Coca-Cola saw opportunity in the possibility of placing the Coke name on a more extensive line of soft drinks. More recently, the company has been making adjustments to the Japanese market where consumers like a steady flow of new products. After building a sophisticated new product development center in Japan, which is Coke's most profitable market, Coke is releasing as many as 50 new beverages a year there.[8] Opportunities involve ideas that *could* be used, rather than difficulties that *must* be resolved. Noninnovative managers sometimes fall prey to focusing on various crisis and noncrisis problems, and in the process, they may neglect opportunities. In one study of 78 managerial decision-making situations, 13 percent of the situations were crisis problems, 62 percent were noncrisis problems, and 25 percent involved taking advantage of opportunities.[9] In addition to facing three types of decision problems, managers also typically deal with different types of decision-making situations.

Differences in Decision-Making Situations

Managers would be overwhelmed with decision making if they had to handle each and every problem as if it were a completely new situation. Fortunately, that is not the case. Generally, managerial decision situations fall into two categories: programmed and nonprogrammed. Examples of decisions in each category are shown in Table 5-1.

Programmed decisions Decisions made in routine, repetitive, well-structured situations through the use of predetermined decision rules

PROGRAMMED DECISIONS Programmed decisions are those made in routine, repetitive, well-structured situations through the use of predetermined decision rules. The decision rules may be based on habit, computational techniques, or established policies and procedures. Such rules usually stem from prior experience or technical knowledge about what works in a particular type of situation. For example, most organizations have established policies and procedures for handling basic employee disciplinary problems.

Although programmed decisions are applicable to routine, well-structured situations, they can be quite complex. Computers have enhanced the possibil-

TABLE 5-1 EXAMPLES OF MANAGERIAL DECISION-MAKING SITUATIONS

TYPE OF ORGANIZATION	PROGRAMMED DECISION	NONPROGRAMMED DECISION
Fast-food restaurant	Determine supplies to be reordered.	Identify location for new franchise.
University	Decide if students meet graduation requirements.	Choose new academic programs.
Automaker	Determine union employee pay rates.	Select new car design.

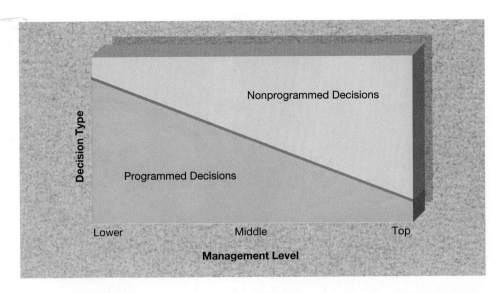

Figure 5-2 *Relationship of decision-making situation to management level in organizations.*

ities for making sophisticated programmed decisions, because they can collect and analyze vast amounts of information that can facilitate programmed managerial decision making. For example, managers at San Diego Gas & Electric switch gas and oil suppliers on the basis of decisions made hourly in the utility's vast computerized "mission control" room.[10] When a person shops with a credit card, a programmed decision is often made by computer regarding the authorization of the purchase. However, if the person wishes to charge an unusually large dollar amount or one that exceeds the ceiling for her or his account, a supervisor may have to engage in further programmed decision making based on policies and procedures governing such situations.

Most of the decisions made by first-line managers and many of those made by middle managers are the programmed type. In contrast, top-level managers make comparatively few programmed decisions (see Figure 5-2).

NONPROGRAMMED DECISIONS Nonprogrammed decisions are those for which predetermined decision rules are impractical because the situations are novel and/or relatively unstructured.[11] Most of the significant decisions that managers make fall into the nonprogrammed category. Because of their nature, nonprogrammed decisions usually involve considerable amounts of **uncertainty,** a condition in which the decision maker must choose a course of action without complete knowledge of the consequences that will follow implementation.

Decisions made under uncertainty involve **risk,** the possibility that a chosen action could lead to losses rather than the intended results.[12] Uncertainty can stem from a variety of sources. For example, elements in the environment that are difficult to predict or control can affect the success of a decision. Cost and time constraints can limit the information that can realistically be collected. Social and political factors in the organization, such as poor communication across units, can make relevant information gathering difficult. Finally, situations can change rapidly, causing current information to quickly become obsolete.[13] Partially to cope with rapid change and the declining U.S. dollar, Annette Roux, head of France-based Chantiers Bénéteau, decided to open a U.S. manufacturing plant in South Carolina to manufacture the company's line of pleasure craft, including sailboats.[14]

The proportion of nonprogrammed decisions that managers must make increases at each level of the hierarchy (see Figure 5-2). Because such decisions

Nonprogrammed decisions Decisions for which predetermined decision rules are impractical because the situations are novel and/or ill-structured

Uncertainty A condition in which the decision maker must choose a course of action without complete knowledge of the consequences that will follow implementation

Risk The possibility that a chosen action could lead to losses rather than the intended results

Changes in the environment can force nonprogrammed decisions on managers. Tecnol started making surgical masks 8 years ago, when it became apparent that rising epidemics of AIDS, hepatitis, and TB would require far more use of masks to protect doctors, nurses, dentists, other health care providers, and rescue workers. Tecnol uses a patented process to make a soft seamless mask that resists the intake of fluids (like blood). Today Tecnol leads the market, edging out such bigger companies as Johnson & Johnson.

require effective decision-making skills—and, frequently, creativity—they provide the biggest decision-making challenges to managers. This chapter focuses mainly on issues related to nonprogrammed decisions.

■ MANAGERS AS DECISION MAKERS

Because the decisions that managers make have a profound impact on the success of the organization, managerial approaches to decision making have been the subject of considerable curiosity and research. In this section, we describe two major types of models regarding how managers make decisions: rational and nonrational.

The Rational Model

The rational model of managerial decision making, a view that was in vogue during the first half of this century, has roots in the economic theory of the firm. In developing theories about the economic behavior of business firms, economists tended to make the simplifying assumption that managers would always make decisions that were in the best economic interests of their firms. This assumption was initially accepted by many management theorists. According to the **rational model,** managers engage in completely rational decision processes, ultimately make optimal decisions, and possess and understand all information relevant to their decisions at the time they make them (including all possible alternatives and all potential outcomes and ramifications). If you recently purchased a major competitive item such as a personal computer or an automobile, you most likely experienced the difficulties of obtaining perfect information and making "optimal" decisions in complex situations. As a result, you will probably not be surprised to find that there are serious flaws in the rational view of how managers make decisions.[15] Nevertheless, the rational view is useful in providing a benchmark against which to compare actual managerial decision-making patterns.

Rational model A model that suggests that managers engage in completely rational decision processes, ultimately make optimal decisions, and possess and understand all information relevant to their decisions at the time they make them

Nonrational Models

In contrast to the rational view, several **nonrational models** of managerial decision making suggest that information-gathering and processing limitations make it difficult for managers to make optimal decisions. Within the nonrational framework, researchers have identified three major models of decision making: satisficing, incremental, and garbage can.

SATISFICING MODEL During the 1950s economist Herbert Simon (who later won a Nobel prize for his work in this area) began to study the actual behaviors of managerial decision makers. On the basis of his studies, Simon offered the concept of bounded rationality as a framework through which actual managerial decision making can be better understood.[16] **Bounded rationality** means that the ability of managers to be perfectly rational in making decisions is limited by such factors as cognitive capacity and time constraints. The concept suggests that the following factors commonly limit the degree to which managers are perfectly rational in making decisions:

- Decision makers may have inadequate information, not only about the nature of the issue to be decided but also about possible alternatives and their strengths and limitations.
- Time and cost factors often constrain the amount of information that can be gathered in regard to a particular decision.
- Decision makers' perceptions about the relative importance of various pieces of data may cause them to overlook or ignore critical information.
- The part of human memory that is used in making decisions can retain only a relatively small amount of information at one time.
- The calculating capacities associated with intelligence limit the degree to which decision makers can determine optimal decisions, even assuming that perfect information has been gathered.[17]

Rather than optimizing their decisions, Simon argued, managers follow the **satisficing model,** which holds that managers seek alternatives only until they find one that looks *satisfactory.* Satisficing can be an appropriate decision-making approach when the cost of delaying a decision or searching for a better alternative outweighs the likely payoff from such a course. For example, if one is driving on an unfamiliar highway with only a little bit of gas left, it might be better to choose a gas station within sight than to hold out for one's favorite brand. On the other hand, managers sometimes make a habit of using the simplistic satisficing approach even in situations in which the cost of searching for further alternatives is justified given the potential gain.[18]

For instance, Sant Singh Chatwal, founder of Bombay Palace Restaurants, Inc., a New York–based chain, wanted to expand in Manhattan but found that leasing property there was extremely expensive. To solve his problem, he quickly merged with another chain, Lifestyle Restaurants, Inc., which owned a number of cheap leases, particularly in very expensive parts of Manhattan. Chatwal says that he had heard about the Lifestyle chairman's "reputation for rough business practices" but still went ahead with the merger. Within 4 months Chatwal was in court attempting to break the contract because of allegedly undisclosed Lifestyle tax liabilities and other problems.[19] Thus Chatwal's haste in selecting what seemed to be a quick solution to his leasing problems illustrates the potential pitfalls of satisficing.

INCREMENTAL MODEL Another approach to decision making is the **incremental model,** which holds that managers make the smallest response possible that

Nonrational models Models that suggest that information-gathering and processing limitations make it difficult for managers to make optimal decisions

Bounded rationality A concept that suggests that the ability of managers to be perfectly rational in making decisions is limited by such factors as cognitive capacity and time constraints

Satisficing model A model stating that managers seek alternatives only until they find one that looks *satisfactory,* rather than seeking the optimal decision

Incremental model A model stating that managers make the smallest response possible that will reduce the problem to at least a tolerable level

The satisficing model backfired for Sant Singh Chatwal, founder of a chain of Indian restaurants. He made a quick decision to merge with another chain in New York City in order to gain access to cheap leases in expensive parts of the city. Within months, however, he was trying to get out of the contract because of bad business practices and undisclosed tax liabilities in his partner company.

Garbage-can model A model stating that managers behave in virtually a random pattern in making nonprogrammed decisions

Descriptive decision-making models Models of decision making that attempt to document how managers actually do make decisions

Normative decision-making models Models of decision making that attempt to prescribe how managers *should* make decisions

will reduce the problem to at least a tolerable level.[20] This approach is geared more toward achieving short-run alleviation of a problem than toward making decisions that will facilitate long-term goal attainment. Like the satisficing model, the incremental model does not require that managers process a great deal of information in order to take action. One researcher likened incrementalizing to the actions of a homeowner who deals with the problem of insufficient electric outlets by using various multioutlet adapters, such as extension cords. In the long run, the homeowner's incremental decisions may prove to be unworkable, since additional pieces of electrical equipment (e.g., VCRs and personal computers) may cause fuses to blow.[21]

GARBAGE-CAN MODEL The **garbage-can model** of decision making holds that managers behave in virtually a random pattern in making nonprogrammed decisions. In other words, decision outcomes occur by chance, depending on such factors as the participants who happen to be involved, the problems about which they happen to be concerned at the moment, the opportunities that they happen to stumble upon, and the pet solutions that happen to be looking for a problem to solve. The garbage-can strategy is most likely to be used when managers have no goal preferences, the means of achieving goals are unclear, and/or decision-making participants change rapidly.[22] Desirable outcomes can sometimes be achieved with a garbage-can strategy, but this approach can also lead to serious difficulties. For example, Gould, Inc., was once a $2 billion maker of computers, silicon chips, automation systems, and other electronic gear. However, the company ran into problems when its "iron-willed" CEO, William Ylvisaker, decided to remake the company by investing in Florida real estate (including a polo club; Ylvisaker was a polo buff) and other endeavors that did not fit a reasonably defined strategy. Finally, the company was taken over by Japan-based Nippon Mining after Nippon made a $1.1 billion offer for what was left of Gould.[23]

Thus, while the garbage-can approach can sometimes lead managers to take advantage of unforeseen opportunities, it can also lead to severe problems from which it may be difficult to recover. The garbage-can approach is often used in the absence of strategic management. (See Chapter 7 for a discussion of strategic management.)

■ STEPS IN AN EFFECTIVE DECISION-MAKING PROCESS

The models of managerial decision making just outlined are sometimes referred to as **descriptive decision-making models** because they attempt to document how managers actually *do* make decisions. In contrast, models such as the one outlined in Table 5-2 are sometimes referred to as **normative decision-making models** because they attempt to prescribe how managers *should* make decisions. According to decision-making experts, managers are more likely to be effective decision makers if they follow the general approach outlined in Table 5-2. Although following such steps does not guarantee that all decisions will have the desired outcomes, it does increase the likelihood of success.[24] While managers frequently do not have control over many factors affecting the success of their decisions, they do have substantial control over the process that they use to make decisions. In this section, we discuss the four-step decision-making process in greater detail.

TABLE 5-2 STEPS IN AN EFFECTIVE DECISION-MAKING PROCESS

STEP	ACTIVITIES
Identify the problem.	Scan the environment for changing circumstances. Categorize the situation as a problem (or nonproblem). Diagnose the problem's nature and causes.
Generate alternative solutions.	Restrict criticism of alternatives. Freewheel to stimulate thinking. Offer as many ideas as possible. Combine and improve on ideas.
Evaluate and choose an alternative.	Evaluate feasibility. Evaluate quality. Evaluate acceptability. Evaluate costs. Evaluate reversibility. Evaluate ethics.
Implement and monitor the chosen solution.	Plan the implementation of the solution. Be sensitive to the decision's effects on others. Develop follow-up mechanisms.

Identifying the Problem

The first step in the decision-making process is identifying the problem. Part of identifying the problem, of course, is recognizing that a problem even exists. **Organizational problems** are discrepancies between a current state or condition and what is desired. This step has three general stages: scanning, categorization, and diagnosis.[25]

Organizational problems
Discrepancies between a current state or condition and what is desired

SCANNING STAGE The *scanning stage* involves monitoring the work situation for changing circumstances that may signal the emergence of a problem. At this point, a manager may be only vaguely aware that an environmental change could lead to a problem or that an existing situation is constituting a problem. For example, during the 1970s, Swiss watchmakers began to notice the appearance of relatively inexpensive watches being produced in Japan and Hong Kong.[26]

CATEGORIZATION STAGE The *categorization stage* entails attempting to understand and verify signs that there is some type of discrepancy between a current state and what is desired. At this point, the manager attempts to categorize the situation as a problem or a nonproblem, even though it may be difficult to specify the exact nature of the situation. For example, sales of the Swiss watches, which were relatively expensive, began to decline rather precipitously.

DIAGNOSIS STAGE The *diagnosis stage* involves gathering additional information and specifying both the nature and the causes of the problem. Without appropriate diagnosis, it is difficult to experience success in the rest of the decision process. At this stage, the problem should be stated in terms of the discrepancy between current conditions and what is desired, and causes of the discrepancy should be specified. At first, the watchmakers thought that the cheaper watches would be a fad that would soon disappear. By 1983, however, the situation had not reversed, and Switzerland's two largest watchmakers, SSIH and Asuag, were deeply in debt. The two firms represented several of the world's best-known watch brands—Omega, Longines, Tissot, and Rado. It was becoming apparent that the new, cheaper watches from Japan and Hong Kong posed a serious long-term threat to the Swiss watchmakers. The banks holding the debt for SSIH and Asuag called in Zurich-based management consultant Nicolas G. Hayek to help generate alternatives.

Generating Alternative Solutions

The second step in the decision-making process is developing alternatives. This practice usually leads to higher-quality solutions,[27] particularly when the situation calls for creative and innovative ones. The development of alternatives can often be facilitated through **brainstorming,** a technique for enhancing creativity that encourages group members to generate as many novel ideas as possible on a given topic without evaluating them. There are four principles involved:

Brainstorming A technique that encourages group members to generate as many novel ideas as possible on a given topic without evaluating them

1 **Don't criticize ideas while generating possible solutions.** Criticism during the idea-generation stage inhibits thinking. Also, because discussion tends to get bogged down when early ideas are criticized, only a few ideas are generated.
2 **Freewheel.** Offer even seemingly wild and outrageous ideas. Although they may never be used, they may trigger some usable ideas from others.
3 **Offer as many ideas as possible.** Pushing for a high volume of ideas increases the probability that some of them will be effective solutions.
4 **Combine and improve on ideas that have been offered.** Often the best ideas come from combinations of the ideas of others.[28]

Although brainstorming is typically done in a group, the principles can also be used by individuals. The manager jots down a number of possible solutions, including farfetched ideas, tries to generate a high idea volume, and combines or builds on ideas as he or she proceeds. Brainstorming and other methods of generating ideas will be considered further when we discuss creativity in a later section of this chapter.

At this point, it is important to note that a number of alternatives should be generated during this phase of the decision-making process. For example, Hayek, the bankers, and the heads of the watch companies developed several alternatives, such as liquidating the companies, diversifying into other products, and merging the two companies and mounting an offensive against the overseas threat.

Evaluating and Choosing an Alternative

This step involves carefully considering the advantages and disadvantages of each alternative before choosing one of them. Each alternative should be evaluated systematically according to six general criteria: feasibility, quality, acceptability, costs, reversibility, and ethics.

FEASIBILITY The feasibility criterion refers to the extent to which an alternative can be accomplished within related organizational constraints, such as time, budgets, technology, and policies. Alternatives that do not meet the criterion of feasibility should be eliminated from further consideration. In the case of the watch companies, at first they did not recognize the feasibility of fighting the overseas threat.

QUALITY The quality criterion refers to how effectively an alternative solves the problem under consideration. Alternatives that only partially solve the problem or represent a questionable solution are eliminated at this stage.

ACCEPTABILITY This criterion refers to the degree to which the decision makers and others who will be affected by the implementation of the alternative are willing to support it. Acceptability has long been recognized as an important criterion against which to judge decisions.[29]

COSTS The costs criterion refers to both the resource levels required and the extent to which the alternative is likely to have undesirable side effects. Thus the term "costs" is used here in the broad sense to include not only direct monetary expenditures but also more intangible issues such as possible vigorous competitor retaliation.

REVERSIBILITY This criterion refers to the extent to which the alternative can be reversed, if at all. When the Coca-Cola Company ran into difficulties in introducing its new formula for Coke, it was able to reverse the decision by reintroducing its old formula as Coke Classic. Other types of decisions may be much more difficult to reverse.[30] In such cases, the alternative should be reconsidered very carefully before it is selected. For example, liquidating the watchmakers would have been difficult to reverse. Instead, the group decided to merge the two companies, creating the Swiss Corporation for Microelectronics and Watchmaking (known as SMH), with Hayek as chairman. SMH then launched an inexpensive, technologically innovative plastic Swatch watch, which can be assembled at low cost on a fully automated assembly line. By 1995, the company had sold more than 150 million of the Swatch timepieces and was competing with Hattori Seiko of Japan to be the world's number-one watchmaker. Unlike its Japanese competitors, SMH also continues to produce both medium-priced and luxury watches.[31]

ETHICS The ethics criterion refers to the extent to which an alternative is compatible with the social responsibilities of the organization and the ethical standards of its managers. For instance, Hayek is considered to be somewhat of a hero in Switzerland for saving the Swiss watchmaking industry and many jobs. Some forward-thinking companies, like Aluminum Company of America, expend considerable effort to ensure that managers consider the ethical implications of their decisions (see the Case in Point discussion).

ALCOA SETS "CORE VALUES"

CASE IN POINT

Shortly after Paul H. O'Neill became chairman of the Aluminum Company of America, he learned that one of the perquisites of his position was a membership in a local, but nationally known, golf resort. When his inquiry determined that women and blacks were not allowed as members, he declined to become a member. He further decreed that no company money should be spent on memberships or activities in such clubs. The action was the first step in what has become a reshaping of the corporate conscience at Alcoa.

At the heart of the reshaping are six "core values" that top management spent 100 hours hammering out. The values are integrity, safety and health, quality of work, treatment of people, accountability, and profitability. The com-

Alcoa's chairman Paul H. O'Neill spearheaded a reshaping of the aluminum company's conscience. All employees are expected to use six core values—integrity, safety and health, quality of work, treatment of people, accountability, and profitability—to guide their decisions and actions. This approach has garnered awards and respect in the industry.

pany has spent millions of dollars and thousands of work hours training Alcoa's more than 60,000 employees to use the values as principles to guide their decision making and actions.

For example, Ken Blevins, president of Alcoa Electronic Packaging, Inc., decided not to release initial shipments of a new Alcoa packaging material for microchips because he was not satisfied with the quality. The new material was ultimately not released for almost 18 months, while company members sought and found solutions to the quality problems. The delay cost Alcoa "a considerable amount of money" and resulted in negative publicity in which the packaging enterprise was described as "floundering" by a business publication. Blevins says that his decision was aided by the core-values training. The training helped him recognize more clearly that producing a product that measures up to promises made to customers is, in fact, a moral decision. In his view, to do less is a compromise of integrity.

"We are systematically taking our vision and our values and trying to make them a reality in how we run the place," says O'Neill. Company officials willingly acknowledge, though, that living up to the core values is challenging. Alcoa recently was awarded the Gold Medal for International Corporate Environment Achievement from the World Environmental Center, a well-regarded, not-for-profit environmental group, in recognition of Alcoa's outstanding and well-implemented worldwide environmental policies.[32] ■■■

Implementing and Monitoring the Chosen Solution

For the decision-making process to be successful, managers must give considerable thought to *implementing* and *monitoring* the chosen solution. It is possible to make a "good" decision in terms of the first three steps and still have the process fail because of difficulties at this final step.

IMPLEMENTING THE SOLUTION Successful implementation usually depends on two main factors: careful planning and sensitivity to those involved in the implementation and/or affected by it.

In regard to planning, minor changes may require only a small amount of planning, while major changes may call for extensive planning efforts, such as written plans, coordination with units inside and outside the organization, and special funding arrangements. In general, the more difficult it is to reverse a solution, the more important it is to plan for effective implementation.

Implementation also tends to occur more smoothly when decision makers show sensitivity in considering the possible reactions of those the decision will affect. For instance, when Pacific Southwest Cable in San Diego, California, decided to place heavy emphasis on service, both to internal (individuals inside the company) and external customers, the company spent considerable time orienting and training workers. Part of the change involved giving employees more latitude in taking service actions, such as allowing service representatives to make billing adjustments without prior management approval. As a result of the careful orientation and training, workers were able to implement the change smoothly. This led, in turn, to considerable increases in market penetration and profits.[33]

MONITORING THE SOLUTION Managers need to monitor decision implementation to be sure that things are progressing as planned and that the problem that triggered the decision-making process has been resolved. The more important the problem, the greater the effort that needs to be expended on appropriate follow-up mechanisms.

■ OVERCOMING BARRIERS TO EFFECTIVE DECISION MAKING

Unfortunately, as the nonrational models of managerial decision making suggest, managers often do not follow the four-step process just outlined. Despite the fact that this general approach is endorsed by a number of decision experts, managers may not be aware of the experts' recommendations. In addition, managers face several barriers to effective decision making. In this section, we discuss means of overcoming four key decision-making barriers: accepting the problem challenge in the first place, searching for sufficient alternatives, recognizing common decision-making biases, and avoiding the decision escalation phenomenon.

Accepting the Problem Challenge

Decision researchers have identified four basic reaction patterns that characterize the behavior of individuals when they are faced with a legitimate problem in the form of a difficulty or an opportunity. The first three, complacency, defensive avoidance, and panic, represent barriers to effective decision making. The fourth, deciding to decide, constitutes a more viable approach for decision makers to follow.[34]

COMPLACENCY The **complacency** reaction occurs when individuals either do not see the signs of danger or opportunity or ignore them. With complacency, the failure to detect the signs usually stems from inadequate scanning of the environment. Ignoring the signs altogether is more akin to the "ostrich" effect—putting one's head in the sand and hoping that the danger or opportunity will resolve itself. Complacency can be present even when an individual

Complacency A condition in which individuals either do not see the signs of danger or opportunity or ignore them

appears to be responding to the situation. For example, it occurs when an individual immediately accepts a job offer that looks like a good opportunity without devoting any time or effort to assessing the situation thoroughly.

Defensive avoidance A condition in which individuals either deny the importance of a danger or an opportunity or deny any responsibility for taking action

DEFENSIVE AVOIDANCE With **defensive avoidance,** individuals either deny the importance of a danger or an opportunity or deny any responsibility for taking action. Defensive avoidance can take three different forms: rationalization ("It can't happen to me"), procrastination ("It can be taken care of later"), or buck-passing ("It's someone else's problem"). All three forms apparently came into play when officials at Barings Bank in London ignored warning signs that their Singapore-based derivatives trader, 28-year-old Nicholas Leeson, was taking unwarranted risks that led to the loss of more than $1 billion and the collapse of the bank. An investigation of the situation indicated that bank officials had "failed to follow up on a number of warning signals over a prolonged period." Among the warning signals were unrealistically high levels of profitability; unusually high amounts of funding required to finance the Singapore office's trades; and earlier auditing reports, which were never acted upon because of warring factions within the bank, indicating controls were lax. Leeson was sentenced to 6½ years in prison on two charges of fraud.[35]

Panic A reaction in which individuals become so upset that they frantically seek a way to solve a problem

PANIC With **panic** or paniclike reactions, individuals become so upset that they frantically seek a way to solve a problem. In their haste, they often seize upon a quickly formulated alternative without noticing its severe disadvantages and without considering other, potentially better, alternatives. Panic is particularly likely to occur with crisis problems.[36]

Deciding to decide A response in which decision makers accept the challenge of deciding what to do about a problem and follow an effective decision-making process

DECIDING TO DECIDE With the **deciding-to-decide** response, decision makers accept the challenge of deciding what to do about a problem and follow an effective decision-making process. Deciding to decide is an important reaction to a legitimate problem situation. Of course, managers cannot attend to every potential problem, no matter how minor and remote, that appears on the horizon. Some guidelines for deciding to decide are presented in Table 5-3.

Searching for Sufficient Alternatives

For many decision situations, particularly nonprogrammed decisions, it is unrealistic for decision makers to collect enough information to identify *all* poten-

TABLE 5-3 GUIDELINES FOR DECIDING TO DECIDE
APPRAISE CREDIBILITY OF INFORMATION Is the source in a position to know the truth? If so, is the source likely to be honest? Is there any evidence, and how good is it?
ASCERTAIN IMPORTANCE OF THREAT OR OPPORTUNITY How likely is a real danger or opportunity? If a threat, how severe might the losses be? If an opportunity, how great might the gains be?
DETERMINE THE NEED FOR URGENCY Is the threat or opportunity likely to occur soon? Will it develop gradually, or is sudden change likely? If some action is urgent, can part be done now and the rest later?

Source: Adapted from Daniel D. Wheeler and Irving L. Janis, *A Practical Guide for Making Decisions,* Macmillan, New York, 1980, pp. 34–35.

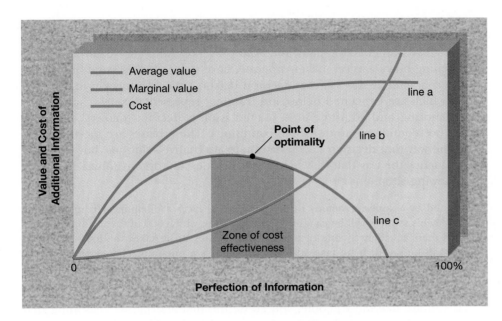

Figure 5-3 *The cost of additional information. (Adapted from E. Frank Harrison,* The Managerial Decision-Making Process, *3d ed., Houghton Mifflin, Boston, 1987, p. 47.)*

tial alternatives and assess *all* possible pluses and minuses. Information acquisition is limited, in large part, because it typically requires time and money. Such costs accrue even when information gathering is confined to checking with knowledgeable organization members or holding a meeting. As a result, decision makers must evaluate how much time, effort, and money should be spent gathering information that will help in making a particular decision.

This information-gathering dilemma is depicted in Figure 5-3. The horizontal axis indicates potential information about the decision, spanning from 0 to 100 percent. The vertical axis depicts the value and cost of additional information. As indicated by line *a*, as the decision maker collects more and more information, the value of the additional information in many situations begins to level off. At the same time, as shown by line *b*, the cost of additional information during the initial search is usually not very high but tends to get much higher as one moves toward obtaining perfect information. As a result, the marginal, or incremental, value of additional pieces of information (line *c*) rises at first to a point of optimality and then starts to decline as cost begins to exceed the value of additional pieces of information. The area of optimal information gathering is also shown.

Decision makers' efforts tend to fall seriously *below* the zone of cost effectiveness in the process of identifying a sufficient number of potential alternatives. For example, one study of 78 decision-making situations found that in 85 percent of the cases, there was little or no search for viable alternatives. Instead, decision makers tended to quickly copy a solution used by others, accept an off-the-shelf solution offered by a consultant, or seize upon an idea of unknown or debatable value and try to find support for it. Even in the 15 percent of the cases in which a deliberate effort was made to develop viable alternatives, the search process tended to be cut off after only a few possibilities had been identified.[37] Unless countered, the tendency to skip or cut short the search for alternatives is likely to have a stifling effect on innovation. Some approaches that may be helpful in generating decision alternatives will be discussed later in this chapter in the section on creativity. Of course, for rather trivial decisions, managers may correctly feel that the time and effort involved in identifying multiple alternatives are not warranted.

Save on gas. Pay with cash.

Prospect theory at work: oil companies are betting that those who use credit cards instead of cash to pay for gasoline will think of themselves as simply giving up a discount rather than paying a surcharge (an actual loss).

Recognizing Common Decision-Making Biases

Psychologists Daniel Kahneman and Amos Tversky, who for years have been investigating how decision makers operate, have pointed out several biases that tend to characterize the way that decision makers process information.[38] These biases, which are explained below, are framing, representativeness, availability, and anchoring and adjustment. A related issue is decision makers' tendency toward overconfidence under some conditions. These biases are most likely to affect the way that decision makers evaluate alternative solutions, but they may also influence the way that they identify difficulties and opportunities. Consider the following situation:

Threatened by a superior enemy force, the general faces a dilemma. His intelligence officers say his soldiers will be caught in an ambush in which 600 of them will die unless he leads them to safety by one of two available routes. If he takes the first route, 200 soldiers will be saved. If he takes the second, there's a one-third chance that 600 soldiers will be saved and a two-thirds chance that none will be saved. Which route should he take?

If you are like most people, you chose the first alternative, reasoning that the general should save the 200 rather than risk even higher losses. Suppose, however, that the situation is as follows:

The general again has to choose between two escape routes. But this time his aides tell him that if he takes the first, 400 soldiers will die. If he takes the second, there's a one-third chance that no soldiers will die and a two-thirds chance that 600 soldiers will die. Which route should he take?

In this situation, most people argue that the general should take the second route. Their rationale is that with the first route 400 will certainly be dead. With the second route there is at least a one-third chance that no one will die, and casualties will only be 50 percent higher if the scheme fails.

Interestingly, most people draw the opposite conclusion from these two problems. In the first problem, people favor the first alternative 3 to 1; in the second problem, they choose the second alternative 4 to 1. Yet a close look will reveal that the problems in both cases are exactly the same: they are just stated differently. The first problem is stated in terms of lives saved, the second in terms of lives lost. The tendency to make different decisions depending on how a problem is presented is called **framing.**

Framing The tendency to make different decisions depending on how a problem is presented

Prospect theory A theory positing that decision makers find the prospect of an actual loss more painful than giving up the possibility of a gain

To explain the paradoxical decision pattern exhibited in the general's dilemmas, Kahneman and Tversky have developed the prospect theory. Based on the belief that decision makers tend to be "loss averse," the **prospect theory** posits that they find the prospect of an actual loss more painful than giving up the possibility of a gain.[39] The oil industry seems to have an intuitive understanding of prospect theory. By a common arrangement, customers receive "discounts for cash" at gas stations rather than being charged "credit surcharges" for using their credit cards. Prospect theory suggests that customers may be less willing to pay an *extra* charge for using credit cards (an actual loss) than they are to forgo a discount for paying cash (a potential gain). Even so, the system is drawing increasing complaints from credit customers.[40]

Linda is 31, single, outspoken, and very bright. She majored in philosophy in college. As a student, she was deeply concerned with discrimination and other social issues and participated in antinuclear demonstrations. Which of the following statements is more likely?

a Linda is a bank teller.
b Linda is a bank teller and active in the feminist movement.

Most people choose the alternative that says that Linda is both a bank teller and a feminist. Actually, however, the laws of probability suggest that an occurrence (bank teller) is more likely to happen on its own than in conjunction with another occurrence (bank teller *and* feminist). The Linda problem illustrates a common decision shortcut called **representativeness,** the tendency to be overly influenced by stereotypes in making judgments about the likelihood of occurrences. We increase the odds of decision-making difficulties when our judgments run counter to the laws of probability.

Representativeness The tendency to be overly influenced by stereotypes in making judgments about the likelihood of occurrences

In a typical English text, does the letter "K" appear more often as the first letter in a word or as the third letter?

People generally judge that the letter "K" is more likely to be the first letter in a word even though the letter is almost twice as likely to appear in the third position. We do this because of a bias called **availability,** the tendency to judge the likelihood of an occurrence on the basis of the extent to which other like instances or occurrences can easily be recalled. In this case, it is usually easier to recall words beginning with the letter "K" than words in which "K" is the third letter. Availability also shows up in tendencies to overestimate the likelihood of deaths due to vividly imaginable causes such as airplane accidents, fires, and murder and to underestimate more common, but less spectacular, causes such as emphysema and stroke.[41] Managers may fall victim to the availability bias in a number of ways. For example, they may base annual performance appraisals on the most recent and easily recalled performance of subordinates, judge how well competitors' products are doing by the extent to which the managers have seen them in use, or gauge employee morale by relying on the views of immediate subordinates.

Availability The tendency to judge the likelihood of an occurrence on the basis of the extent to which other like instances or occurrences can easily be recalled

A newly hired engineer for a computer firm in the Boston metropolitan area has 4 years' experience and good all-around qualifications. When asked to estimate the starting salary for this employee, a chemist who had very little knowledge about the profession or industry guessed an annual salary of $17,000. What is your estimate?[42]

Most people do not think that the chemist's guess influenced their own estimate. Yet people tend to give higher salary estimates when the chemist's estimate is stated as $60,000 than when it is $17,000. This tendency to be influenced by an initial figure, even when the information is largely irrelevant, is known as **anchoring and adjustment.** For example, employers often ask a job candidate about her or his current salary and then use the figure as a basis for extending an offer, even though the candidate may currently be underpaid or overpaid.

Anchoring and adjustment The tendency to be influenced by an initial figure, even when the information is largely irrelevant

These information-processing biases suggest that decision makers should be cautious about the accuracy of their estimates regarding the likelihood of events. Evidence suggests, however, that decision makers often exhibit **overconfidence,** the tendency to be more certain of judgments regarding the likelihood of a future event than one's actual predictive accuracy warrants.[43] Ironically, overconfidence appears most likely to occur when decision makers are working in unfamiliar areas.[44] The overconfidence stems from a failure to fully understand the potential pitfalls involved. Thus managers may be particularly susceptible to overconfidence when they are planning moves into new, unfamiliar areas of business. For example, Louisiana-Pacific Corp., a Portland, Oregon–based lumber company, ran into difficulty when it marketed a version of its cheap plywood substitute known as oriented strand board (OSB) for outside use. The OSB product, made from paper-thin slices of small trees glued together, seemed to function well for floor and roof sheeting, but using the innovative new product outside was another matter. A growing volume of class

Overconfidence The tendency to be more certain of judgments regarding the likelihood of a future event than one's actual predictive accuracy warrants

action suits and government investigators claim the outside version begins to deteriorate in just a few years, leading to rotting, cracking, and even mushroom sprouts. As warranty claims mounted, the now-ousted CEO continued to claim that new production techniques would solve the problem. The company was finally indicted by a Colorado grand jury as legal difficulties continue.[45]

Managers can avoid some of the ill effects of information-processing biases by being aware of how such biases are likely to affect their judgments. Gathering enough information to be fairly well versed about the issues associated with important decisions is also helpful. In addition, decision makers should think about why their judgments might be wrong or far off the target. Such thinking may help reveal contradictions and inaccuracies.[46] Increasing evidence suggests that our decision making also is influenced by a variety of other factors, such as emotions, habits, and motivation regarding the subject at hand.[47] Some quantitative methods that can help decision makers make more accurate judgments are covered in the Supplement to this chapter.

Avoiding the Decision Escalation Phenomenon

When a manager makes a decision, it is often only one decision in a series of decisions about a particular issue. Further decisions may be necessary, depending on the results of a previous decision. For example, suppose that you decide to hire a new employee because you expect that the person will be an excellent performer. However, after several months on the job it is apparent that the person is not performing at an acceptable level. Should you take steps to terminate the worker? Of course, at this point you have invested considerable time and money in training the new employee, and it is possible that the individual is still learning the job. So you decide to spend more time helping the worker, and you line up some further training. Even with these additional inputs, 2 months later the worker is still not performing at the necessary level. What do you decide now? Although you have more reason to "cut your losses," you also have even more invested in making the individual productive. When do you discontinue your "investment"?[48]

Decision situations like this one present difficult dilemmas for managers. Substantial costs have already been incurred because of an earlier decision. On the other hand, future actions have the potential of either reversing the situation or compounding the initial losses. Such situations are sometimes referred to as **escalation situations,** because they signal the strong possibility of escalating commitment and accelerating losses.[49]

Research studies indicate that when managers incur costs associated with an initial decision, they often react by allocating more resources to the situation even when the prospects for turning the situation around are dim. Such situations can develop into nonrational escalation. **Nonrational escalation,** or the escalation phenomenon, is the tendency to increase commitment to a previously selected course of action beyond the level that would be expected if the manager followed an effective decision-making process.[50] As experts in the fields of economics and accounting have pointed out, costs that have already been incurred (e.g., time and money) should be considered **sunk costs.** Such costs, once incurred, are not recoverable and should not enter into considerations of future courses of action. Yet decision makers are often heavily influenced by prior costs when they themselves have made the initial decisions.

Part of the reason for the escalation phenomenon is that decision makers tend to be loss-averse when it comes to writing off prior costs. Thus the tendency may be related to prospect theory, discussed earlier. In addition, the decision maker may be concerned that a change in the course of action may cause

Escalation situations Situations that signal the strong possibility of escalating commitment and accelerating losses

Nonrational escalation The tendency to increase commitment to a previously selected course of action beyond the level that would be expected if the manager followed an effective decision-making process; also called *escalation phenomenon*

Sunk costs Costs that, once incurred, are not recoverable and should not enter into considerations of future courses of action

An escalation decision breathed life into Expo 86, the world's fair held in Vancouver, British Columbia. The government proceeded with the fair as planned despite a growing realization of overestimated revenues and underestimated costs. To have called a halt to the fair would have entailed a loss of $80 million, not to mention a loss of pride and prestige.

others to regard the original decision as a mistake or failure. Methods of avoiding nonrational escalation include setting advance limits on how far to extend the commitment, asking tough questions about why the commitment is being continued, reviewing the costs involved, and watching for escalation situations that may constitute commitment traps.[51] Otherwise, decision makers may find themselves in a situation similar to that which led to the $2 billion loss for Orange County in California. When interest rates began to rise unexpectedly, County Treasurer Robert L. Citron, who was in charge of a $7.4 billion investment portfolio for the county and some surrounding areas, made extremely risky investments in an apparent effort to make up for some losses. Instead, the even riskier investments led to losses that ballooned to the $2 billion figure before he was forced to resign.[52]

■ MANAGING DIVERSITY: GROUP DECISION MAKING

Major decisions in organizations are most often made by more than one person in order to take advantage of a diversity of outlooks. For example, at Coca-Cola, Goizueta and several other top executives must agree on any major decision. Even at nonsupervisory levels, groups are increasingly involved in making operational decisions. For instance, Gencorp Automotive has geared its new reinforced plastics plant near Indianapolis to run with just three levels: plant manager, team leaders, and 25 teams of 5 to 15 production workers. Each team makes most of the decisions involving its work area.[53] In this section, we consider the advantages and disadvantages of group decision making, as well as means of enhancing group decision-making processes.[54]

Advantages and Disadvantages of Group Decision Making

Group decision making has several advantages over individual decision making. These advantages are summarized in Table 5-4. According to a study of more than 200 project teams, who were involved in educational courses related to

TABLE 5-4 ADVANTAGES AND DISADVANTAGES OF GROUP DECISION MAKING	
ADVANTAGES	**DISADVANTAGES**
1. More information and knowledge is focused on the issue. 2. An increased number and diversity of alternatives can be developed. 3. Greater understanding and acceptance of the final decision are likely. 4. Members develop knowledge and skills for future use.	1. It is usually more time-consuming. 2. Disagreements may delay decisions and cause hard feelings. 3. The discussion may be dominated by one or a few group members. 4. Groupthink may cause members to overemphasize achieving agreement.

management, the groups outperformed their most proficient group member 97 percent of the time. Part of the advantage of groups stems from the diversity of ideas that can be brought to bear on a problem.[55]

Despite its advantages, group decision making also has several potential disadvantages when contrasted with individual decision making. These disadvantages are summarized in Table 5-4. One of these, the possibility of groupthink, requires further elaboration.

Groupthink The tendency in cohesive groups to seek agreement about an issue at the expense of realistically appraising the situation

Groupthink is the tendency in cohesive groups to seek agreement about an issue at the expense of realistically appraising the situation.[56] According to the theory underlying groupthink, group members are so concerned about preserving the cohesion of the group that they are reluctant to bring up issues that may cause disagreements or to provide information that may prove unsettling to the discussion. Some National Aeronautics and Space Administration (NASA) officials and other observers have attributed the *Challenger* tragedy to groupthink. Despite receiving some contrary information, upper-level officials at NASA and at Morton Thiokol, the company that manufactured the solid rocket boosters, decided to go ahead with the mission. These officials tended to ignore information from engineers at Morton Thiokol and from others about possible malfunctions due to unusually cold weather conditions. Unfortunately, all seven crew members, including teacher Christa McAuliffe, were killed in the explosion at takeoff.[57] Recent research suggests that groupthink may occur even when groups are not highly cohesive if the group leader states a particular preference early in the discussion.[58] Other researchers recently have criticized the groupthink concept, arguing among other things that decision making in groups is actually more complex than suggested by groupthink.[59] Still, the groupthink idea may be useful in highlighting the need to follow a more effective decision-making process, as outlined earlier in the chapter, when operating in groups.

Enhancing Group Decision-Making Processes

Managers can take a number of steps that will help them not only avoid the major pitfalls of group decision making but also reap the advantages of the process. One step is involving the group in decisions when the information and knowledge of the group are important to decision quality. That way, the time consumed by group decision making can probably be justified.

Another step in using diversity to advantage is configuring groups. For example, there is growing evidence that diversity of membership can enhance group performance. In one important study, culturally homogeneous groups (all members from the same nationality and ethnic background) initially performed more effectively than culturally heterogeneous groups (members from different nationality and ethnic backgrounds). Over the course of time, however, the heterogeneous groups caught up with and then surpassed the performance of the homogeneous groups. Data showed that the heterogeneous groups had more difficulty interacting effectively at first, but gradually learned how to capitalize on the diversity of perspectives in the group.[60] With increasing work-force diversity and the growing globalization of business, managers of the future will need to be particularly adept at effectively handling group dynamics to reap the benefits of the available diversity (we discuss this issue further in Chapter 15).[61]

An additional step is carefully considering other important aspects involving group composition. For example, including individuals who are likely to concentrate on major organizational goals helps overcome any tendency toward self-interest. Problems caused by dominating individuals can often be minimized by including someone who is skilled at encouraging the ideas of others.

Yet another step that can be taken to facilitate group decision making is setting up specific mechanisms that help avoid a groupthink-type phenomenon. For instance, managers can designate one or more **devil's advocates,** individuals who are assigned the role of making sure that the negative aspects of any attractive decision alternatives are considered. Managers can also encourage the group to engage in **dialectical inquiry,** a procedure in which a decision situation is approached from two opposite points of view.[62]

Computer-Assisted Group Decision Making

Advances in information technology also offer the potential of enhancing group decision making through the assistance of computers. One means is through *teleconferencing,* the simultaneous communication among groups of individuals by telephone or via computer using specially designed software.[63] Such software is often referred to as **groupware,** software designed to support collaborative efforts among group members, such as scheduling meetings, holding meetings, collaborating on projects, and sharing documents. Group decision making sometimes is also aided by relatively new specialized computer-based information systems called *group decision-support systems,* which support decision makers working together to solve problems that are not well structured. (See also Chapters 14 and 19.) Groupware is heavily oriented toward facilitating communication among group members, whereas group decision-support systems focus more on helping the group actually make a decision.

Because the use of computers to assist decision making is relatively new, applicable research is just beginning to accumulate.[64] Preliminary results to date suggest that computer-assisted groups tend to interact and exchange to a lesser degree than face-to-face groups and take longer to complete their work. The impact on performance appears to depend on the nature of the task. Computer assistance seems to help groups generate better ideas. On the other hand, face-to-face groups appear to perform better when there are difficult problems to solve and particularly when major conflicts must be resolved. One analysis of 13 studies of computer-assisted group decision making suggested that there were decreases in consensus regarding the decision, as well as satisfaction with the decision and the decision-making process itself. It appears that, for now, face-to-face meetings may be advisable when there are likely to be major differences of opinion among group members and the commitment of group members is critical to successfully implementing the resulting decision. This

Lotus Notes, a type of software, enables group members to communicate with one another and share documents without engaging in face-to-face meetings. Such computer-assisted group decision making works best when there are few major differences of opinion among the group members. To resolve major conflicts or to ensure the commitment of individual members, face-to-face encounters are still preferable.

Devil's advocates Individuals who are assigned the role of making sure that the negative aspects of any attractive decision alternatives are considered

Dialectical inquiry A procedure in which a decision situation is approached from two opposite points of view

Groupware Software designed to support collaborative efforts among group members, such as scheduling meetings, holding meetings, collaborating on projects, and sharing documents

conclusion could change as groupware and group decision-support systems improve and as studies are able to better assess the circumstances under which computer assistance is helpful.[65]

Computer assistance does seem to aid the generation of more creative ideas and, hence, may be useful during those phases of decision making in which creativity is particularly important. Creativity is an essential part of the decision-making process because it helps generate novel alternatives that lead to innovation and also fosters the development of unique perspectives on the nature of problems. In the next section, we discuss several approaches for encouraging greater creativity in individuals and groups.

■ PROMOTING INNOVATION: THE CREATIVITY FACTOR IN DECISION MAKING

Creativity The cognitive process of developing an idea, concept, commodity, or discovery that is viewed as novel by its creator or a target audience

Creativity is the cognitive process of developing an idea, concept, commodity, or discovery that is viewed as novel by its creator or a target audience.[66] Hence creativity is usually identified by assessing outcomes.[67] In fact, creativity researcher Teresa M. Amabile argues, "Creativity is not a quality of a person; it is a quality of ideas, of behaviors, or products."[68] Creativity is crucial to solving problems in ways that result in important organizational innovations. As worldwide competition heats up, greater emphasis is being placed on creativity. Japan, in particular, is trying to overcome its reputation as a copycat of the technology of other countries through increased efforts at creativity. For example, at the Matsushita Electronics Corporation, semiconductor executives wear badges stating "Create." At the Nippon Electric Company (NEC), posters and placards encourage workers to "invent the new VCR" and offer $100 awards for creative ideas.[69]

Convergent thinking The effort to solve problems by beginning with a problem and attempting to move logically to a solution

Divergent thinking The effort to solve problems by generating new ways of viewing a problem and seeking novel alternatives

Try your hand at the classic creativity problem shown in Figure 5-4. Then look at Figure 5-5, which presents some possible solutions to the problem. Many individuals are unable to solve the nine-dot problem because they make the assumption that the lines cannot go outside the nine dots. As this problem illustrates, creativity requires both convergent and divergent thinking. **Convergent thinking** is the effort to solve problems by beginning with a problem and attempting to move logically to a solution. One might liken convergent thinking to searching for oil by digging an ever bigger and deeper hole.[70] **Divergent**

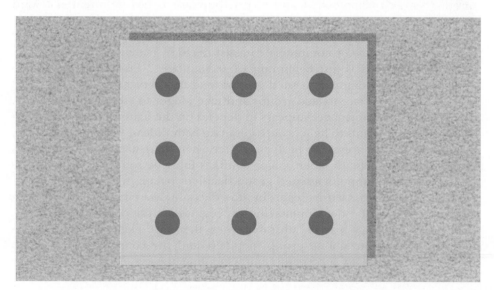

Figure 5-4 *The nine-dot problem. Without lifting your pencil from the paper, draw no more than four straight lines that will cross through all nine dots.*

This puzzle is difficult to solve if the imaginary boundary (limit) enclosing the nine dots is not exceeded. A surprising number of people will not exceed the imaginary boundary, for often this constraint is unconsciously in the mind of the problem-solver, even though it is not in the definition of the problem at all. The overly strict limits are a block in the mind of the solver. The widespread nature of this block is what makes this puzzle classic. (Adams, 1980, p. 24)

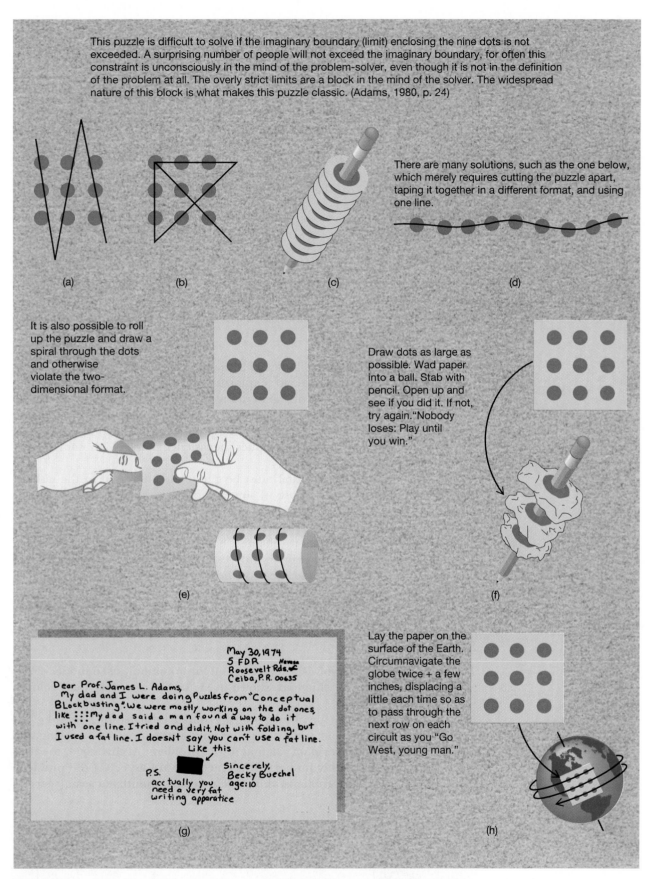

There are many solutions, such as the one below, which merely requires cutting the puzzle apart, taping it together in a different format, and using one line.

(a)   (b)   (c)   (d)

It is also possible to roll up the puzzle and draw a spiral through the dots and otherwise violate the two-dimensional format.

Draw dots as large as possible. Wad paper into a ball. Stab with pencil. Open up and see if you did it. If not, try again. "Nobody loses: Play until you win."

(e)   (f)

May 30, 1974
5 FDR
Roosevelt Rds. Naval
Ceiba, P.R. 00635

Dear Prof. James L. Adams,
My dad and I were doing Puzzles from "Conceptual Blockbusting". We were mostly working on the dot ones, like :::: My dad said a man found a way to do it with one line. I tried and did it. Not with folding, but I used a fat line. I doesn't say you can't use a fat line. Like this

P.S.
acctually you need a very fat writing apparatice

Sincerely,
Becky Buechel
age:10

Lay the paper on the surface of the Earth. Circumnavigate the globe twice + a few inches, displacing a little each time so as to pass through the next row on each circuit as you "Go West, young man."

(g)   (h)

Figure 5-5 *Some possible solutions to the nine-dot problem. (Based on J. L. Adams,* Conceptual Blockbusting: A Guide to Better Ideas, *2d ed., Norton, New York, pp. 25–30; reprinted from Diane E. Papalia and Sally Wendkos Olds,* Psychology, *McGraw-Hill, New York, 1985, p. 297.)*

thinking, on the other hand, is the effort to solve problems by generating new ways of viewing a problem and seeking novel alternatives. Rather than digging in the same hole, a divergent thinker digs in many different places to generate new perspectives. In the creative process, convergent thinking helps define a problem and evaluate proposed solutions. Divergent thinking helps develop alternative views of problems, as well as seek novel ways of dealing with them. In this section, we examine the basic ingredients of creativity, describe the stages of the creative process, and offer some major techniques for enhancing group creativity that can be used by managers.

Basic Ingredients

According to creativity expert Amabile, the following three basic ingredients are necessary for creativity.

DOMAIN-RELEVANT SKILLS These skills are associated with expertise in the relevant field. They include related technical skills or artistic ability, talent in the area, and factual knowledge.

CREATIVITY-RELEVANT SKILLS These skills include a cognitive style, or method, of thinking that is oriented to exploring new directions, knowledge of approaches that can be used for generating novel ideas, and a work style that is conducive to developing creative ideas. A creative work style is characterized by the ability to concentrate effort and attention for long periods of time, the ability to abandon unproductive avenues, persistence, and a high energy level.

TASK MOTIVATION The individual must be genuinely interested in the task for its own sake, rather than because of some external reward possibility, such as money. Recent evidence suggests that primary concern with external rewards tends to inhibit the creative process. For example, a scientist attempting to develop a new drug in order to obtain a bonus or prize is not likely to be as creative as a scientist whose primary interest is learning more about a promising new direction.[71] For some ideas on how to boost your creativity, see the Management Skills for the Twenty-First Century discussion, "How to Be More Creative."

Stages of Creativity

The creativity process involves several stages. One commonly used model of creativity has four stages,[72] which are shown in Figure 5-6 and described below.

PREPARATION This stage involves gathering initial information, defining the problem or task requiring creativity, generating alternatives, and seeking and carefully analyzing further data relating to the problem. At this stage, the individual becomes thoroughly immersed in every relevant aspect of the problem. For complex technical problems, this stage may take months or even years.

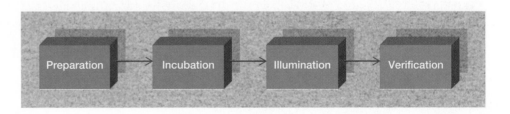

Figure 5-6 *Stages of creativity.*

MANAGEMENT SKILLS FOR THE TWENTY-FIRST CENTURY

HOW TO BE MORE CREATIVE

Some of the following suggestions, which are based on research and thinking on creativity, may help you be more creative in your work and your daily life.

WHAT DO YOU WANT TO DO?
- Take time to understand a problem before you begin trying to solve it.
- Get all the facts clearly in mind.
- Identify the facts that seem to be the most important before you try to work out a detailed solution.

HOW CAN YOU DO IT?
- Set aside a sizable block of time to focus on a particular problem, rather than attending to it in scattered sessions.
- Work out a plan for attacking the problem.
- Establish subgoals. Solve part of the problem and go on from there. You don't have to do everything at once. Write out your thoughts. This allows you to capture important points and to come back to them later. It also allows you to look for patterns.
- Imagine yourself acting out the problem. *Actually* act out the problem.
- Think of a similar problem you've solved in the past and build on the strategy you used then.
- Use analogies whenever possible. See whether you can generalize from a similar situation to your current problem.
- Use several different problem-solving strategies—verbal, visual, mathematical, acting. Draw a diagram to help you visualize the problem, or talk to yourself out loud, or "walk through" a situation.
- Look for relationships among various facts.
- Trust your intuition. Take a guess and see whether you can back it up.
- Play with ideas and possible approaches. Try looking at the same situation in a number of different ways.

HOW CAN YOU DO IT BETTER?
- Try consciously to be original, to come up with new ideas.
- Don't worry about looking foolish if you say or suggest something unusual or if you come up with the wrong answer.
- Eliminate cultural taboos in your thinking (such as gender stereotyping) that might interfere with your ability to come up with a novel solution.
- Try to be right the first time, but if you're not, explore as many alternatives as you need to.
- Keep an open mind. If your initial approach doesn't work, ask whether you made assumptions that might not be true.
- If you get stuck on one approach, try to get to the solution by another route.
- Be alert to odd or puzzling facts. If you can explain them, your solution may be at hand.
- Think of unconventional ways to use objects and the environment. Look at familiar things as if you've never seen them before.
- Consider taking a detour that delays your goal but eventually leads to it.
- Discard habitual ways of doing things, and force yourself to figure out new ways.
- Do some brainstorming with one or more other people. This involves trying to produce as many new and original ideas as possible, without evaluating any of them until the end of the session.
- Strive for objectivity. Evaluate your own ideas as you would those of a stranger.

INCUBATION This stage of the creativity process involves mainly subconscious mental activity and divergent thinking to explore unusual alternatives. During this stage, the individual generally does not consciously focus on the problem; this allows the subconscious to work on a solution.

ILLUMINATION At this stage, a new level of insight is achieved, often through a sudden breakthrough in "eureka" fashion.

VERIFICATION This stage involves testing the ideas to determine the validity of the insight. At this point, convergent, logical thinking is needed to evaluate the solution. If the solution does not prove feasible, it may be necessary to cycle back through all or some of the previous stages.

The invention of the computerized axial tomography scanner (often referred to as the CAT scanner) illustrates the creativity process. This revolutionary device allows radiologists to take three-dimensional pictures of the inside of the body with much greater clarity than conventional X rays. Inventor Godfrey Hounsfield received a Nobel prize for his work (see the Case in Point discussion).

CASE IN POINT

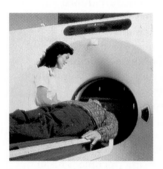

The CAT scanner, which gives a 3-D look into the human body, allows doctors to make diagnoses without the need for exploratory surgery. This technological miracle was the brainstorm of an electrical engineer with an extensive computer background.

THE CAT SCANNER GREETS AN ASTONISHED WORLD

CAT scanner inventor Godfrey Hounsfield worked as an electrical engineer for EMI, Ltd., a British pioneer in entertainment and electronic technologies, which is located in Hayes, England. Although Hounsfield made some major breakthroughs in computer memory storage in the 1960s, EMI elected not to pursue the technology because the company did not want to take on IBM. So Hounsfield's boss told him to find another idea to work on. Armed with computer knowledge from his previous work, Hounsfield was comparing notes with a colleague when they made an interesting observation. If one were able to take readings that could detect the presence of materials from all angles through a box, in three dimensions, it would be possible to determine what was in the box without opening it. The notion was related to pattern recognition, a highly theoretical field that was gaining attention from scientists in engineering and mathematics. Scientists were trying to find ways by which computers could recognize images as swiftly as the eye and brain and take appropriate action.

For some reason, Hounsfield's mind leaped to a different vision—a mathematical puzzle so vast that solving it by conventional means would be impossible. He also kept thinking about the box. He speculated that if the object was reduced to "picture points," like the tiny dots that make the picture on a TV screen, then all the picture points could be assigned a mathematical value. The picture points could be recorded through the use of X rays, and each point could be viewed as the result of a mathematical equation. Then, if one assembled all the relevant mathematical equations outside the box and had a computer reassemble them, one could show the object inside the box on a computer screen.

Hounsfield mulled over his notion for some time. Then, suddenly, his thoughts joined two unrelated planes, linking his knowledge of computerized pattern recognition with that of medical radiology. What if one could make pictures of what is inside the human body? As he thought about it, he realized that the pictures could be three-dimensional, giving the medical profession vastly improved information about a patient's condition. Formidable obstacles still lay ahead in developing a practical means of implementing his ideas. Hounsfield worked with an enormous dedication, often until midnight each night, to develop a practical prototype. Finally, in 1972, a demonstration of the first head scanner was made in Chicago to an enraptured audience at a meeting of the Radiological Society of North America. Since then, the device has eliminated much exploratory surgery and greatly enhanced effective treatment prospects for many patients throughout the world.[73] ■■■

Techniques for Enhancing Group Creativity

Whereas the preceding discussion focused on an individual's creative efforts, this section examines techniques for enhancing creativity in group settings. Two major techniques are brainstorming and the nominal group technique. (We discuss two other methods that can be used to enhance group creativity, the Delphi method and scenario analysis, in the Supplement to this chapter.)

BRAINSTORMING The brainstorming technique is a means of enhancing creativity that encourages group members to generate as many novel ideas as possible on a given topic without evaluating them. The four basic rules—do not criticize during idea generation, freewheel, offer many ideas, and improve on already offered ideas—were discussed earlier in the chapter. Recent research suggests that computer-assisted brainstorming is superior to face-to-face brainstorming in the generation of ideas. At least part of the reason seems to be that there is more time for idea production because members can offer their ideas simultaneously rather than having to listen to others or wait for them to stop speaking before offering an idea.[74]

NOMINAL GROUP TECHNIQUE The **nominal group technique (NGT)** is a means of enhancing creativity and decision making that integrates both individual work and group interaction within certain ground rules. The technique was developed to foster individual, as well as group, creativity and to overcome the tendency of group members to criticize ideas when they are offered. The ground rules, or steps, involved in NGT are as follows:

> **Nominal group technique (NGT)** A technique that integrates both individual work and group interaction within certain ground rules

1 The individual members independently prepare lists of their ideas on a problem.
2 Each group member presents his or her ideas in a round-robin session (one idea at a time from each group member in turn) without discussion. The ideas are recorded on a blackboard or flip chart so that everyone can see them. If a presented idea triggers a new idea for someone else, that member adds the new idea to her or his list for presentation on a future round-robin turn.
3 When all the individual ideas are recorded on the group list, the members discuss the ideas for clarification and evaluation purposes.
4 The members silently and independently vote on the ideas, using a rank-ordering or rating procedure. The final outcome is determined by pooling the individual votes.[75]

Evidence generally supports the effectiveness of NGT in developing large numbers of creative alternatives while maintaining group satisfaction. There is evidence that NGT may be more effective than brainstorming at generating ideas when groups are operating face-to-face, but is less effective than computer-assisted brainstorming.[76]

Thus there are a number of means that managers can use to encourage creativity and innovation in work settings. While this chapter has focused on understanding various aspects of decision processes in organizations, the Supplement to this chapter highlights a variety of specific tools that can assist organization members in both planning and decision making.

■ CHAPTER SUMMARY

Decision making is the process through which managers identify organizational problems and attempt to resolve them. Managers deal with three types of problems: crisis, noncrisis, and opportunity. Opportunity problems are major vehicles for organizational innovation. Because op-

portunities involve ideas that could be used, rather than difficulties that must be resolved, they sometimes receive insufficient attention.

Generally, managerial decision situations fall into two categories: programmed and nonprogrammed. Because of their nature, nonprogrammed decisions usually involve significant amounts of uncertainty and risk.

Two types of models have been developed to better understand the way in which managers make decisions. The rational model suggests that managers are almost perfect information handlers and, therefore, make optimal decisions. In contrast, several nonrational models of managerial decision making, including the satisficing, incremental, and garbage-can models, suggest that information-gathering and processing limitations make it difficult for managers to make optimal decisions.

An effective decision-making process includes four major steps: (1) Identifying the problem involves the scanning, categorization, and diagnosis stages. (2) Generating alternative solutions emphasizes the importance of alternatives in achieving a high-quality solution. (3) Evaluating and choosing an alternative requires consideration of feasibility, quality, acceptability, costs, reversibility, and ethics. (4) Implementing and monitoring the solution focuses on careful planning, sensitivity to those involved in the implementation and/or affected by it, and the design of follow-up mechanisms.

As the nonrational models of managerial decision making suggest, managers sometimes do not follow an effective decision-making process. This is largely because they face four major decision barriers. Managers must be familiar with the means of overcoming each one. The first entails accepting the problem challenge. This requires deciding to decide, rather than reacting with complacency, defensive avoidance, or panic. The second involves searching for sufficient alternatives. The third

focuses on recognizing common decision-making biases, such as framing, representativeness, availability, anchoring and adjustment, and overconfidence. The fourth centers on avoiding the escalation phenomenon, or nonrational escalation. This phenomenon is the tendency to increase commitment to a previously selected course of action beyond the level that would be expected if the manager followed an effective decision-making process.

Group decision making has several advantages and disadvantages. The advantages are that more information and knowledge is focused on the issue, an increased number and diversity of alternatives can be developed, greater understanding and acceptance of the final decision are likely, and members develop knowledge and skills for future use. The disadvantages are that group decisions are usually more time-consuming, disagreements may delay decision making and cause hard feelings, the discussion may be dominated by one or a few group members, and groupthink may cause members to overemphasize gaining agreement. Managers can take a number of steps to help minimize the disadvantages including taking advantage of diversity in configuring groups.

A major aspect of promoting innovation is the creativity factor. Creativity involves both convergent and divergent thinking. Basic ingredients of the creative process are domain-relevant skills, creativity-relevant skills, and task motivation. The creativity process comprises four stages: preparation, incubation, illumination, and verification. Techniques for enhancing creativity include brainstorming and the nominal group technique.

■ QUESTIONS FOR DISCUSSION AND REVIEW

1 Outline the major types of problems that managers are likely to confront. Give an example of each type that has occurred or could occur at your college or university.

2 Explain the difference between programmed and nonprogrammed decision situations. Choose an organization with which you are familiar and identify two programmed and two nonprogrammed decision situations.

3 Contrast the rational and nonrational models of managers as decision makers. Think of a recent nonprogrammed decision situation that you have seen handled in an organization (perhaps a student group or association to which you belong). Which of the following models best describes the decision process involved: rational, satisficing, incremental, or garbage can? Explain why.

4 Describe each of the steps in an effective decision-making process. We sometimes witness serious organizational problems, such as poor quality products or services, that go unresolved. What are some po-

tential managerial reactions to problem situations that might account for why such problems persist?

5 Explain the main decision barriers involved with accepting the problem challenge and searching for sufficient alternatives. How can these barriers be overcome?

6 Give an example of each of the common decision-making biases. Explain how these biases might influence evaluations of alternative solutions.

7 Explain the conditions under which the escalation phenomenon is most likely to occur. What steps can a manager take to minimize the possibilities of falling prey to nonrational escalation?

8 Assess the advantages and disadvantages of group decision making. Give an example of (a) a situation in which you felt the advantages outweighed the disadvantages and (b) one in which you felt the opposite was true. In the latter case, what could have been done to prevent the decision-making difficulty? Could effectively managing diversity have helped?

9 Explain the main ingredients necessary for creativ-

ity. Identify evidence indicating that these ingredients were present in Godfrey Hounsfield's inventing of the CAT scanner.

10 Suppose that you are the chairperson of a bank task force charged with coming up with new ideas for enhancing customer service. What approaches might be used to facilitate the flow of creative ideas? Which one would you pick, and why?

■ DISCUSSION QUESTIONS FOR CHAPTER OPENING CASE

1 Would you characterize the various decisions made in the case as programmed or nonprogrammed? Why?

2 To what extent does it appear that Goizueta and the top management at Coca-Cola generally follow an effective decision-making process?

3 Assess the manner in which Goizueta and Coke's top management react to problem challenges.

■ EXERCISES FOR MANAGING IN THE TWENTY-FIRST CENTURY

EXERCISE 1
SKILL BUILDING EXERCISE: EFFECTIVE DECISION MAKING

 You are the owner of the Happy Hamburger chain of 10 restaurants in your local area. You were informed 2 weeks ago that the competitor in your town has introduced "funny" hamburgers that come in different shapes and sizes. These have reportedly been very popular with the teenage set. You are noticing a drop in sales at several of your restaurants, and your managers tell you that they are serving fewer teenage customers. Yesterday you became aware of a device that can be used to cut ground meat into hamburgers of specific weights and a variety of shapes (e.g., round, automobiles, sailboats, and bicycles). You recognize that this could give you the capability to compete with the other restaurant. Further, your employees are currently making hamburgers by hand. These are round in shape and weigh about ⅓ of a pound. The hamburger cutter can be rented or purchased. Refer to Table 5-2 to determine which of the following considerations would be included in each step of the decision-making process.

CONSIDERATION	IDENTIFY THE PROBLEM/ OPPORTUNITY	GENERATE ALTERNATIVE SOLUTIONS	EVALUATE/ CHOOSE ALTERNATIVE	IMPLEMENT/ MONITOR SOLUTION
1. Could rent device				
2. Provides variety; competitor has device				
3. Device would save some money by precise weighing				
4. Could continue making present round shapes by hand				
5. If device is rented, could opt out				
6. Evaluate sales, costs, satisfaction monthly				
7. Could purchase device				
8. New shapes would appeal to younger buyers				
9. Costs $300 each per month to rent and $1750 each to buy				
10. Schedule an electrician to install the necessary wiring				

EXERCISE 2
MANAGEMENT EXERCISE: BRAINSTORMING

Objectives

■ To learn how the brainstorming technique for stimulating creativity operates

■ To gain experience in generating ideas in a brainstorming session

Instructions

1 Select a problem of common interest to the members of the group. If the group has difficulty selecting a problem, try one of these:

   a. How can students be more involved in developing the policies of your college or university (e.g., new programs, admissions and transfers, and electives)?

   b. What kind of game could be developed to help learn how to make better decisions?

   c. What features would you like cars to have 10 years from now?

   d. What new approaches could seniors use in developing job leads?

2 Spend 30 minutes brainstorming alternative solutions. Someone in the group should record all the ideas. Even if the group runs out of steam after 15 minutes or so, keep brainstorming. Usually, the best ideas occur later in the brainstorming session. Freewheel. Offer ideas even if they seem wild and impractical. Remember, no criticizing is allowed during the brainstorming phase.

3 Go over the list and select the 10 best ideas. Evaluation is allowed in this phase of the process.

4 Narrow the list to the 5 best ideas, and then select the best idea.

5 Be prepared to discuss your top 5 ideas with the class as a whole.

CONCLUDING CASE 1

PROFITS FINALLY COME TO *USA TODAY*

Allen H. Neuharth, Gannett Company's chairman, threw a little champagne party in June 1987 at company headquarters in Arlington, Virginia, to celebrate the first profitable month for Gannett's national newspaper, *USA Today*. Buoyed by advertising and circulation gains, Neuharth savored the triumph. He told his staff to expect a long and successful future for the venture they had launched in the fall of 1982.

But as glasses clicked and trays of oysters and pâté made the rounds, many people in the room knew that *USA Today*'s success had come at a high price. The project, which had become Neuharth's obsession, had made and broken careers at Gannett. Meanwhile, 5 years of heavy operating losses had severely pinched the media chain's 90 other newspapers and disheartened their staffs.

The publication of *The Making of McPaper* stirred up fresh discord. A Neuharth-authorized book, it described the obstacles and sacrifices involved in creating and expanding *USA Today*. Reactions within the Gannett organization were strong, renewing the clash between Neuharth's backers and the financial and production executives who had early doubts.

The book airs plenty of dirty linen. It describes the bitter infighting at Gannett and reveals tales of those who suffered breakdowns in the anxious, early days of *USA Today*'s publication. Even the book's title causes resentment among staffers, dredging up the derogatory nickname assigned to the paper by critics who viewed it as "fast-food" journalism.

Some Gannett executives believe that the book unfairly casts as villains people who Neuharth apparently felt had plotted to thwart his project. Douglas H. McCorkindale, the company's chief financial officer at the time, for instance, is described by Neuharth as one of the "enemies within" who "planned for failure" instead of success. According to Peter Prichard, the book's author, questions McCorkindale raised about the project cost him the chief executive's job, now held by John J. Curley, who is also chairman.

Though a supporter of the venture, McCorkindale says he did oppose the way the *USA Today* project was carried out. Neuharth and Curley abandoned Gannett's usually careful procedures for planning major capital expenditures, such as new printing plants, McCorkindale says. In addition, the management and staff of *USA Today* in Arlington were allowed to spend large sums of money, while Gannett's other daily newspapers were forced to pinch pennies.

"There's a lackadaisical attitude toward a lot of things now because of what many in the company saw as the inordinate waste involved in the project," states McCorkindale in the book. "They say, 'Why should we kill ourselves in Gitchagumee, Idaho (to make money), when they'll just waste it over there (at *USA Today*) anyway.'"

"*USA Today* should have been playing by the same rules" as Gannett's other papers, McCorkindale says. "The planning wasn't complete. It was full of holes. They didn't want questions raised because it would raise more questions, and people don't like that."

Indeed, *USA Today*'s financial cost to Gannett exceeded even McCorkindale's forecasts. Excluding capital expenditures and the costs of employees that *USA Today* borrowed from other newspapers, the publication amassed operating losses of more than $230 million in the 5 years after its launch. Both those who left and those who are still with Gannett cite the organization's disarray during the start-up, the new rules that were made up daily, and the intense pressure that resulted from Neuharth's direct involvement in the project. Neuharth made it clear that everyone's future with Gannett was on the line.[77]

After becoming marginally profitable for a brief period, the paper slipped back into the red ink, amassing losses by 1992 estimated to be about $800 million. Within the last year or two, the paper has been making a small profit. Even though circulation continues to grow and is now in the 2 million range, *USA Today* has continued to experience serious difficulties in attracting enough advertising to make consistent profits. McCorkindale has since become vice chairman.[78]

QUESTIONS FOR CONCLUDING CASE 1

1　Which model of decision making best matches the situation involving the birth of *USA Today*?

2　Evaluate the extent to which Gannett top executives used an effective decision-making approach in deciding to launch *USA Today* and in dealing with subsequent problems. What was the impact?

3　Evaluate the extent to which the *USA Today* situation represented an escalation situation (between the time the paper was launched and the time it began to make money).

CONCLUDING CASE 2

ROYAL DUTCH/SHELL VIGOROUSLY PURSUES OPPORTUNITIES

Risks are enormous in the petroleum business. The price of raw materials can swing from $4 to $40 per unit, dictators can affect the business climate at will, and human error resulting in an oil spill can cost $3 billion or more. Royal Dutch/Shell, an Anglo-Dutch multinational corporation, has a reputation for handling such risks well. Despite soft prices in the oil industry, mounting costs for development of new oil fields, and greater environmental requirements, Royal Dutch/Shell has adopted a growth strategy.

At Royal Dutch/Shell, pursuing growth amid uncertainty has led to significant rewards. In 1990, the company passed Exxon to become the world's largest oil company. The company has annual revenues exceeding $100 billion and is able to handle most of its capital spending through cash flow.

Still, weak oil and gas prices have made Shell's operating profits somewhat flat over the past decade. Because the company has continued to invest in exploration and new facilities that cannot yield large immediate returns, Shell has been under pressure to cut costs in order to boost profit levels and return on equity. Recently oil prices have improved somewhat, and the cost-cutting efforts are beginning to have a positive effect on profit levels.

Royal Dutch/Shell has developed several approaches to help handle the uncertainties of the industry. Within a culture that encourages individual initiative, the approximately 260 operating units until recently were generally free to make their own decisions, with the help of service units that offer research and technical support. The relative autonomy allowed managers of operating units, such as Shell Oil Company, a U.S. subsidiary, to consider local conditions, monitor regulatory requirements, and shift quickly to handle customer needs or crises. Both to help with the cost cutting and to achieve better coordination, Shell has recently instituted a more centralized approach whereby teams of senior executives oversee global divisions such as exploration and production.

Strategic directions for Royal Dutch/Shell are determined by the committee of managing directors. The six members are chosen from the top ranks of Royal Dutch Petroleum and Shell Transport & Trading, the Dutch and British holding companies that own Royal Dutch/Shell. The committee operates on the basis of consensus, key strategic and personnel decisions must be unanimous, and the focus is long-term.

Shell uses three major mechanisms to deal with uncertainty: geographic diversification, concentric product diversification, and speedy adaptation to change. For example, Shell explores for oil and gas in about 50 countries, has refineries in 34, and sells its products in 100. As a result, political or economic upheaval in a particular country cannot severely damage the company. Shell expects particularly high returns in high-risk countries; otherwise, it does not do business there. In the area of product diversification, Shell stays close to the energy and chemical businesses that it knows best (i.e., a concentric product diversification). Speed is also a key factor. When Spain discontinued the state monopoly over service stations, Shell quickly began developing a network of stations there.

Shell's managing directors try to identify changes in the industry by studying and debating scenarios prepared by their planning department. The scenarios attempt to depict reasonable, but alternative, pictures of conditions in the world 10 years in the future. Each of the geographic regions and operating companies then uses the scenarios to formulate its own strategies within the overall strategic plan.

Supplementing the scenario process, war gaming helps Shell handle the unexpected. For example, local operating companies are expected to simulate supply disruptions and prepare alternatives. As a result, when the Gulf war disrupted supplies from the Middle East, Shell was able to quickly redirect alternative supplies. Shell is currently being severely criticized by some shareholders and activists for polluting the environment around the Niger delta in Nigeria and for supporting Nigeria's military dictatorship by continuing to work in some parts of the country. Shell has admitted that its environmental standards in the country were not as high as elsewhere and has offered to clean up the area, but does not want to abandon all of its operations in Nigeria. Cor Herkstroter, Shell's Dutch president, says: "We want a constructive solution. Leaving Nigeria doesn't get you that. It is much more constructive to stay there and do the right things, such as reconciliation."[79]

QUESTIONS FOR CONCLUDING CASE 2

1 To what extent does Shell appear to emphasize the handling of crisis, noncrisis, and opportunity problems?

2 What evidence exists that Shell uses an effective decision-making process in making various decisions? What evidence exists regarding problems with decision making?

3 How do scenarios help Shell's managing directors engage in divergent thinking (see the Supplement to this chapter for more information on scenario analysis)? What might be some limitations of such an approach?

PLANNING AND DECISION AIDS

Faced with increased rivalry among its major competitors, including American, Delta, and Northwest, United Airlines decided to significantly expand its flight schedules. During a single month, for example, United added 67 departures to its operations at Chicago's O'Hare Airport. It soon became the first airline with service to cities in all 50 states. While the expansion brought the desired increase in passenger volume, it also began to strain the work-force scheduling and planning systems. Because of airline-ticket price pressures and heavy discounting by competitors, it was imperative that United control its labor costs and, at the same time, maintain desired customer service levels. The schedules and plans that the managers prepared by hand were no longer adequate.

To meet the challenge of providing good reservation and airport service while controlling costs, the airline turned to management science. *Management science* (also often called *operations research*) is a management perspective aimed at increasing decision effectiveness through the use of sophisticated mathematical models and statistical methods. (Background information about management science is provided in Chapter 2.) Management science offers a variety of quantitative techniques that can greatly help managers in planning for and making decisions about complex situations such as those facing United. By combining management science techniques and computers, United was able to develop a very successful scheduling and work planning system called the Station Manpower Planning System (SMPS). The SMPS, which continues to be changed to meet expanding needs, has helped United realize significant labor cost savings, improve customer service, and increase employee satisfaction.

The success of the SMPS at United is the result of a growing number of aids available to help managers gain the competitive edge through innovations in the areas of planning and decision making. Many, but not all, of these aids rely heavily on quantitative techniques associated with the field of management science.[1]

At United Airlines, computers are not just tools that these reservation representatives use to book flights. A sophisticated computer system also devises the employees' work schedules. This planning aid has yielded United many benefits: more flexible work force scheduling, improved customer service, labor cost savings, and greater employee satisfaction.

Forecasting The process of making predictions about changing conditions and future events that may significantly affect the business of an organization

Quantitative forecasting A type of forecasting that relies on numerical data and mathematical models to predict future conditions

Time-series methods Methods that use historical data to develop forecasts of the future

Generally, managers do not require in-depth knowledge of mathematics and computers to utilize management science tools. Rather, they need to have a basic understanding of the major tools available so that they can visualize possible applications of such tools. Under some circumstances, managers will need to obtain advice and help from management science experts. However, with the growing availability of packaged software that can be adapted to a variety of work settings, several of the techniques in this Supplement are more accessible and much less costly than they were in the past. As a result, the importance of these planning and decision-making aids is likely to increase in the future.

In this Supplement, we describe a number of the major aids to planning and decision making. In doing so, we consider several forecasting methods, including one that is useful for promoting innovation. We also examine tools that are widely used for planning and controlling projects and explore a variety of useful quantitative planning techniques. Finally, we investigate several quantitative aids for decision making.

■ FORECASTING

Forecasting is the process of making predictions about changing conditions and future events that may significantly affect the business of an organization. The forecasting process is important to both planning and decision making because each depends heavily on assessments of future conditions. Forecasting is used in a variety of areas, such as production planning, budgeting, strategic planning, sales analysis, inventory control, marketing planning, logistics planning, purchasing, material requirements planning, and product planning.[2] Forecasting methods fall into three major categories: quantitative; technological, or qualitative; and judgmental.[3]

Quantitative Forecasting

Quantitative forecasting relies on numerical data and mathematical models to predict future conditions. The two main types of quantitative forecasting methods are time-series and explanatory methods.

TIME-SERIES METHODS Time-series methods use historical data to develop fore-

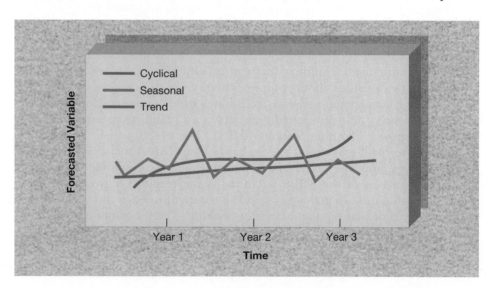

Figure 5s-1 *Examples of patterns that may be identified through time-series methods. (Adapted from Charles A. Gallagher and Hugh J. Watson,* Quantitative Methods for Business Decisions, *McGraw-Hill, New York, 1980, p. 116.)*

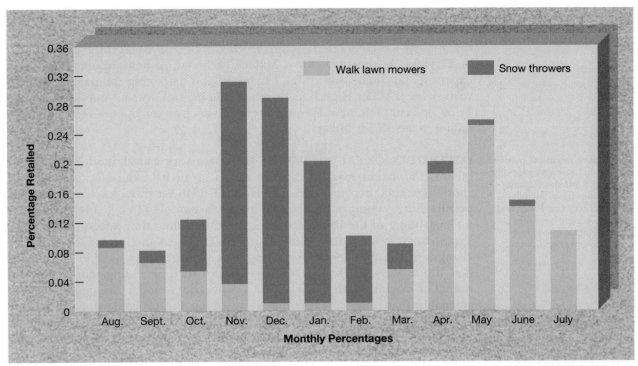

Figure 5s-2 *Toro consumer division's retail sales percentages for two major product lines. (Courtesy of The Toro Company.)*

casts of the future. The assumption underlying time-series models is that there are patterns or combinations of patterns that repeat over time. Time-series models use extensive amounts of historical data, such as weekly sales figures, to identify such patterns and then base future projections on those patterns.

Examples of the types of patterns that may be identified by time-series methods are shown in Figure 5s-1. A *trend* reflects a long-range general movement in either an upward or a downward direction. For example, even though coffeehouse chains like Starbucks Coffee Co. are expanding rapidly, the market could become saturated quickly because coffee consumption in the United States has been declining over the past three decades, particularly among individuals in their twenties, who average less than one cup per day.[4] A *seasonal* pattern indicates upward or downward changes that coincide with particular points in a given year, such as particular seasons. The Toro Company sells both lawn mowers and snow throwers as a means of handling seasonal differences in customer demand patterns (see Figure 5s-2). A *cyclical* pattern involves changes at particular points in time that span longer than a year. For example, sunspot intensity varies over an 11-year cycle and has an effect on the agriculture industry.[5]

Because time-series methods rely strictly on historical data, they are not very useful in predicting the impact of present or future actions that managers might take to bring about change. Instead, they are more suited to predicting broad environmental factors, such as general economic prospects, employment levels, general sales levels, or cost trends, that may be heavily influenced by past events. There are a variety of methods for analyzing time series, many of them quite sophisticated and requiring the use of computers. Although time-series methods attempt to predict the future by identifying patterns, they do not concern themselves with the causes of such patterns.

While time-series approaches can be useful, there are dangers in relying too heavily on past trends. Miller Brewing learned about such dangers the hard way. On the basis of a 10-year pattern in which the company grew at a hefty

640 percent, while the beer industry as a whole grew at only about 40 percent, Miller decided to build a huge new brewery in Trenton, Ohio. In 1982, just as the brewery was completed, American sales of beer leveled off for the first time in 25 years. At the same time, Miller's archrival, Anheuser-Busch, began an expensive, but highly successful, expansion and marketing campaign. Within 5 years, sales of Miller High Life, once the number-two beer in America, declined by 50 percent. The new Trenton brewery, which never opened, led to a $280 million write-off for Miller.[6]

Explanatory, or causal, models Models that attempt to identify the major variables that are related to or have caused particular past conditions and then use current measures of those variables (predictors) to predict future conditions

EXPLANATORY, OR CAUSAL, MODELS Explanatory, or **causal, models** attempt to identify the major variables that are related to or have caused particular past conditions and then use current measures of those variables (predictors) to predict future conditions. Developing such models often leads to a better understanding of the situations being forecasted than time-series models offer. Explanatory models also allow managers to assess the probable impact of changes in the predictors. For example, a manager may be able to estimate how future sales will be affected by changes such as adding more sales personnel or expanding shelf space. Thus explanatory models are generally more amenable than time-series models to assessing the probable impact of managerial actions relative to the variables.

Regression models Equations that express the fluctuations in the variable being forecasted in terms of fluctuations in one or more other variables (predictors)

Three major categories of explanatory models are regression models, econometric models, and leading indicators. **Regression models** are equations that express the fluctuations in the variable being forecasted in terms of fluctuations in one or more other variables. An example of simple regression, in which one variable (a predictor) is used to predict the future level of another (forecasted) variable, is shown in Figure 5s-3. Here, a company that sells burglar alarm systems for homes is attempting to predict the demand for alarm systems (forecasted variable) on the basis of the number of information leaflets (predictor variable) requested by the public. The leaflets are offered in an advertisement run in newspapers in a major metropolitan area. The various data points plotted in Figure 5s-3 represent leaflets requested and sales within 1 month of the leaflet request. In a simple regression, the relationship between the predictor and the forecasted variables is stated in mathematical form. The form is $y = a + bx$, where y is the forecasted variable, x is the predictor variable, a is a constant representing the point where the regression line crosses

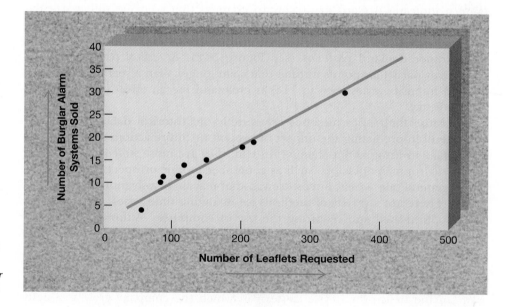

Figure 5s-3 *Data points and regression line for number of leaflets requested and number of burglar alarm systems sold.*

the vertical axis, and *b* indicates how much the value of *y* changes when the value of *x* changes 1 unit. A statistical technique is used to develop the straight line that best fits the data points and to provide the values for *a* and *b*. Then future projections can be made by substituting different values for *x* in the equation and determining the impact on *y*. For example, if our equation came out to be $y = 1.5 + .07x$, then substituting 350 leaflets for *x* would predict sales of 26 alarm systems.

More complex multiple regression models incorporating multiple predictor variables are also used for forecasting. Relying on such a model, Elaine Garzarelli, then executive vice president for research at Shearson Lehman Brothers, was one of the rare Wall Street figures who predicted "black Monday." In forecasting the market crash that occurred on October 19, 1987, she used quantitative analysis of thirteen pieces of data, three relating to economic cycles, several pertaining to monetary issues, and three concerning market valuation. Garzarelli continues to use the indicators in her efforts to build a successful forecasting track record on Wall Street with her own firm, Garzarelli Investment Management.[7]

The second major category of explanatory models is **econometric models.** The term most often refers to systems of simultaneous multiple regression equations involving several predictor variables that are used to identify and measure relationships or interrelationships that exist in the economy. Such models attempt to predict the likely future directions of the economy and, often, the impact of changes such as proposed tax legislation on various segments of the economy. The development of econometric models is complex and expensive. As a result, these models are beyond the scope of most managerial jobs and all but very large organizations. However, companies can subscribe to a number of econometric forecasting services, such as the Wharton School, Chase Econometric Associates, and Mapcast (GE). By doing so, a company obtains many of the benefits of econometric forecasting at a cost that is substantially less than the cost of developing its own econometric model.

The third major category of explanatory models is **leading indicators,** variables that tend to be correlated with the phenomenon of major interest but also tend to occur in advance of that phenomenon. In general, the use of leading indicators is a fairly simple method of forecasting, although the methods of analysis involved can be quite sophisticated. For example, the semiconductor industry uses a book-to-bill ratio as a key leading indicator. The book-to-bill ratio is based on a comparison of orders against shipments. Therefore, a ratio of .78 would signify that for every $100 worth of products shipped, only $78 were already ordered. Compared with a ratio of .79 the previous month, the new figure would signal declining sales. However, it usually takes several months to establish a trend.[8] PLY GEM Industries, Inc., a New York–based maker of exterior building products used extensively for home improvements, uses consumer confidence indexes and existing home sales rates as leading indicators of future home improvement expenditures.[9] Unfortunately, it often can be difficult to identify a leading indicator that provides reasonably accurate predictions.

When Elaine Garzarelli was an executive at Shearson Lehman Brothers, she predicted the stock market crash of October 1987. Her crystal ball was a complicated multiple regression model that looked at 13 indicators relating to economic cycles, monetary issues, and market evaluation.

Econometric models   Systems of simultaneous multiple regression equations involving several predictor variables that are used to identify and measure relationships or interrelationships that exist in the economy

Leading indicators   Variables that tend to be correlated with the phenomenon of major interest but also tend to occur in advance of that phenomenon

Technological, or **qualitative, forecasting**   A type of forecasting aimed primarily at predicting long-term trends in technology and other important aspects of the environment

Promoting Innovation: Technological, or Qualitative, Forecasting

Technological, or **qualitative, forecasting** is aimed primarily at predicting long-term trends in technology and other important aspects of the environment. Particular emphasis is placed on technology, since the ability of organizations to innovate and remain competitive is often related to being able to take advantage of opportunities evolving from technological change. Technological, or qualitative, forecasting differs from quantitative approaches in that it focuses more heavily on longer-term issues that are less amenable to numerical analysis. Therefore, rather than relying on quantitative methods, technological forecasting depends on such qualitative factors as expert knowledge, creativity, and judgment. This type of forecasting provides an excellent opportunity to generate innovative thinking among participants because the emphasis is on future possibilities. The difficulties of accurately predicting the future are obvious, and predictors have often missed major shifts, such as the magnitude and speed of the increase in global competition. Although a number of approaches have been developed to facilitate technological, or qualitative, forecasting, two of the most prominent are the Delphi method and scenario analysis.

Delphi method A structured approach to gaining the judgments of a number of experts on a specific issue relating to the future

THE DELPHI METHOD The **Delphi method** is a structured approach to gaining the judgments of a number of experts on a specific issue relating to the future. One unique aspect of the Delphi method is that the experts are not brought together to discuss their views. On the contrary, they are intentionally kept apart so that each one's initial judgments will not be influenced by those of other participants in the process.[10] The Delphi method has been used in a variety of organizations, including TRW, IBM, AT&T, Corning Glass Works, Goodyear, ICL in Britain, and NEC in Japan. Although experts participating in the Delphi method can come from inside or outside the organization, many organizations prefer to use internal experts in order to retain better control over the results.[11] The Delphi method can be used to seek creative solutions to problems; however, its most frequent function is forecasting, particularly predicting technological change.

There are three basic steps in the Delphi method:

1 A panel of experts is asked to anonymously identify likely scientific breakthroughs in a given area within a specific long-term period (e.g., over the next 50 years). The experts are also asked to estimate when, within the specified period, they expect the breakthroughs to occur. On the basis of the information received, a list of potential breakthroughs is compiled, including information regarding the estimated time frame within which each is likely to occur.
2 The list is sent back to the experts, who are asked to estimate (often on the basis of a 50-50 probability) whether each breakthrough is likely to occur earlier or later than the average estimated time frame. They may also be permitted to specify that they do not believe the breakthrough will occur during the time period (e.g., the 50 years) under consideration.
3 The experts are provided with a new list that represents the information gathered in step 2. If there is consensus, those who disagree with the majority are asked to explain why they do. If there are major differences among the experts, the participants may be asked to furnish reasons for their views. Experts can, and often do, alter their estimates at this point. If there continues to be a wide divergence of opinion, step 3 may be repeated and may include a reassessment of the explanations previously given.

Although these steps outline the basic approach used in the Delphi method, organizations frequently make minor alterations to suit their particular needs. The Delphi method was used by the Alaska Department of Commerce and Economic Development to assess Alaska's energy, economy, and resource development future.[12] It was also used in technological forecasting for power generation by Bharat Heavy Electricals, Ltd. (BHEL), a billion-dollar company in India (see the Case in Point discussion).[13]

THE DELPHI METHOD AT BHEL

Bharat Heavy Electricals, Ltd., the largest heavy-electrical-equipment company in India, has used the Delphi process to explore the future direction of power development, especially in the areas of electric energy and electric transportation. The company's products form systems for the generation of electric power through thermal, nuclear, and hydro sources, as well as for the transmission of power to the industrial and transportation sectors. The Delphi process involved 286 company members from a variety of engineering disciplines.

In the first step, or round, an open-ended questionnaire was sent to prospective respondents. The purpose of this round was to gather as many ideas as possible regarding major technological breakthroughs that could conceivably be developed within the next 30 to 40 years. Participants also estimated when they expected the technological breakthroughs to occur.

In the second round, the list of technological breakthroughs and the estimated timings of the breakthroughs were fed back to the participants. The participants were then asked to reconsider their earlier timing estimates and give fresh ones, provide reasons if their estimates were outside the general range of timings projected in the first round, and supply a priority ranking for each technological development in terms of the urgency of each requirement. The replies from the second round led to an emerging trend toward consensus on most issues.

In the third round, participants were given the collated comments and the new information about estimated timings that had been collected in round 2. In this round, participants were asked for their final estimates as well as their rationale for their forecasts.

Not only did the process identify the likely development of 19 different forms of energy sources, but it also provided "refined guesstimates" regarding when such new energy sources would appear. Bharat felt that these and other estimates would be useful in corporate planning. In addition, the results were extremely useful in formulating R&D projects related to corporate plans.[14]

■■■

SCENARIO ANALYSIS Developed in France and used widely in Europe, scenario analysis (sometimes also called *scenario planning* or the *La Prospective* approach) argues that there are many different possible futures depending on such factors as confrontations among actors, the continuation of current trends, regulatory and other constraints, and the relative power of the actors involved.[15] As a result, organizations need to consider a number of futures and attempt to make decisions and take actions that do not greatly inhibit further freedom of choice. Otherwise, taking inflexible and irreversible actions may lead to severe difficulties if forecasts turn out to be grossly off the mark. **Scenario analysis** addresses a variety of possible futures by evaluating major environmental variables, assessing the likely strategies of other significant actors (e.g., other organizations), devising possible counterstrategies, developing ranked hypotheses about the variables, and formulating alternative scenarios. Scenarios are outlines of possible future conditions, including paths the organization could take that would likely lead to these conditions. Scenario analysis has been used extensively by Royal Dutch/Shell (see Concluding Case 2 in Chapter 5) and by Southern California Edison. Scenario analysis is increasingly being used in the United States.[16]

Scenario analysis An approach that addresses a variety of possible futures by evaluating major environmental variables, assessing the likely strategies of other significant actors, devising possible counterstrategies, developing ranked hypotheses about the variables, and formulating alternative scenarios

Judgmental Forecasting

Judgmental forecasting A type of forecasting that relies mainly on individual judgments or committee agreements regarding future conditions

Judgmental forecasting relies mainly on individual judgments or committee agreements regarding future conditions. Although judgmental forecasting is the most widely used forecasting method in industry, this approach typically relies on informal opinion gathering and is the least systematic of the forecasting methods. As a result, judgmental forecasting methods are highly susceptible to the common decision-making biases discussed in Chapter 5.[17] Two major means of judgmental forecasting are the jury of executive opinion and sales-force composites.

Jury of executive opinion A means of forecasting in which organization executives hold a meeting and estimate, as a group, a forecast for a particular item

THE JURY OF EXECUTIVE OPINION The **jury of executive opinion** is a means of forecasting in which organization executives hold a meeting and estimate, as a group, a forecast for a particular item. However, since the estimators are in direct contact with one another, the outcome may be heavily weighted by power and personality factors within the group. The process can be improved by providing relevant background information to the executives before the meeting.

Sales-force composite A means of forecasting that is used mainly to predict future sales and typically involves obtaining the views of various salespeople, sales managers, and/or distributors regarding the sales outlook

SALES-FORCE COMPOSITES The **sales-force composite** is a means of forecasting that is used mainly to predict future sales and typically involves obtaining the views of various salespeople, sales managers, and/or distributors regarding the sales outlook. While salespeople and distributors tend to be relatively close to the customer, they often do not have information about broad economic factors that may affect future sales. On the other hand, when sales management makes the forecasts, the process may be subject to the difficulties encountered in a jury of executive opinion. Some companies have improved the process by providing salespeople and distributors with economic trend information before having them make their estimates.

Choosing a Forecasting Method

Various criteria that can be used in selecting a forecasting method are summarized in Table 5s-1, which also presents the general characteristics of the forecasting methods. As the information in this table suggests, managers need to consider such factors as the desired time horizon for the forecast, type of accuracy needed, ease of understanding, and development costs. Each method has advantages and disadvantages, depending on the needs of the particular forecasting situation.

TABLE 5S-1 CRITERIA FOR CHOOSING A FORECASTING METHOD			
	QUANTITATIVE	**TECHNOLOGICAL**	**JUDGMENTAL**
CRITERIA			
Time horizon*	Short to medium	Medium to long	Short to long
Time required	Short if method developed; long otherwise	Medium to long	Short
Development costs	Often high	Medium	Low
Accuracy in identifying patterns	High	Medium	Medium to high
Accuracy in predicting turning points	Low for time series; medium for other methods	Medium	Low
Ease of understanding	Low to medium	High	High

*Short term = 1 to 3 months; medium term = 3 months to 2 years; long term = 2 years or more.

Source: Adapted from Spyros Makridakis and Steven C. Wheelwright, "Forecasting an Organization's Futures," in Paul C. Nystrom and William H. Starbuck (eds.), *Handbook of Organizational Design,* Oxford University Press, New York, 1981, p. 132.

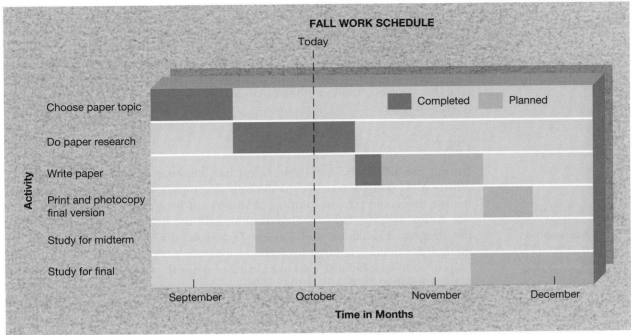

Figure 5s-4 *Partial Gantt chart for completing a management course.*

■ PROJECT PLANNING AND CONTROL MODELS

Managers are frequently responsible for *projects,* one-time sets of activities that have a clear beginning and ending. For example, a manager may be responsible for such projects as designing and implementing a new computer system, building a new manufacturing plant, or developing a new product. Each project is unique, although the manager may have been responsible for similar types of projects in the past. When projects are large and complex, the manager may need to utilize a planning and control model to help manage the project effectively. Two well-known planning and control models are the Gantt chart and PERT.

Gantt Charts

One of the earliest and most flexible project planning tools is the **Gantt chart,** a specialized bar chart developed by Henry L. Gantt (a prominent member of the scientific management school; see Chapter 2) that shows the current progress on each major project activity relative to necessary completion dates. A simple Gantt chart is shown in Figure 5s-4.

A project, in this case completing a management course, is broken down into separate major activities that are then listed on the left side of the chart. The time frame for the entire project is indicated at the top or on the bottom of the chart. The duration and scheduling of each activity is then shown by a bar, with each bar shaded to indicate the degree of the activity's completion. Thus it is possible to determine at a glance the current status of each activity in terms of project deadlines. You could construct a Gantt chart to help you plan and control the major activities necessary for successfully completing a course or even a whole semester or quarter. A status check of the chart in Figure 5s-4 for "Today" shows that the individual has chosen a topic for a paper, has completed the research, and is ahead of schedule on writing the paper. However, the individual is a bit behind schedule on studying for the midterm and needs to make a special effort to catch up.

Gantt chart A specialized bar chart developed by Henry L. Gantt that shows the current progress on each major project activity relative to necessary completion dates

Because of the popularity of Gantt charts, they are increasingly available in software packages designed to help managers plan and control projects.[18] While Gantt charts are extremely useful in a variety of situations, they do have one major weakness. They do not show how various activities are interrelated. For relatively small projects, interrelationships are fairly obvious. For large, complex projects, more sophisticated means of planning and control are frequently needed.

PERT

Program Evaluation and Review Technique (PERT)   A network planning method for managing large projects

During the 1950s, the U.S. Navy faced the immense task of coordinating the efforts of 11,000 contractors involved in developing the Polaris, the first submarine that could remain submerged while launching a long-range ballistic missile. As a result, the Defense Department, with the help of Lockheed, invented the **Program Evaluation and Review Technique (PERT),** a network planning method for managing large projects. Around the same time, Du Pont, with the help of Remington-Rand, created a similar network planning approach called the Critical Path Method (CPM).[19] Network planning methods involve breaking projects down into activities and determining the required length of time for each, but they go beyond Gantt charts by explicitly considering the interrelationships among activities.

Setting up PERT to help manage a major project involves six main steps:

1   All activities in the project must be clearly specified.
2   The sequencing requirements among activities must be identified (i.e., which activities need to precede others).
3   A diagram reflecting the sequence relationships must be developed.
4   Time estimates for each activity must be determined.
5   The network must be evaluated by calculating the critical path. The various activities can then be scheduled.
6   As the project progresses, actual activity times must be recorded so that any necessary schedule revisions and adjustments can be made.[20]

In order to understand how PERT works, we will walk through a relatively simple example. Suppose an organization that furnishes nursing-home care, Good Care, Inc., decides to expand and upgrade its services to include skilled-level care. Because of federal regulations for skilled care, the organization needs to build a new facility. The administrator of Good Care, Inc., must first develop a list of the major activities that are involved in the project and then determine which activities must precede others (see Table 5s-2).

The next step is constructing a **network diagram,** which is a graphic depiction of the interrelationships among activities. A network diagram for the Good Care project is shown in Figure 5s-5.

Network diagram   A graphic depiction of the interrelationships among activities

Activity   A work component to be accomplished

Node, or **event**   An indication of the beginning and/or ending of activities in the network

On the diagram, an **activity,** or work component to be accomplished, is represented by an arrow. Activities take a period of time to accomplish. A **node,** or **event,** is an indication of the beginning and/or ending of activities in the network. It represents a single point in time. The nodes are numbered for easy identification, usually by tens (e.g., 10, 20, 30) so that additions can be made to the network without requiring renumbering. The diagram depicts the interrelationships among the various activities. In Figure 5s-5, for example, building the facility (A) must precede the safety inspection (B), and recruiting staff (E) must precede training staff (F). However, as the diagram indicates, the building and safety inspection processes (A, B) can be accomplished at the same time as the staff recruiting and training processes (E, F).

Developing the diagram may also include providing initial time estimates for the duration of each activity. Unless the times are well established, an esti-

TABLE 5S-2 MAJOR ACTIVITIES, PREDECESSOR ACTIVITIES, AND TIME ESTIMATES FOR GOOD CARE, INC.

ACTIVITY	PREDECESSOR ACTIVITY	TIME ESTIMATES (WEEKS) t_o	t_m	t_p	EXPECTED TIME, T_e
A. Build facility	None	20	24	30	24.3
B. Conduct safety inspection	A	2	3	4	3.0
C. Install equipment	A	8	10	20	11.0
D. Decorate interior	B	3	5	9	5.3
E. Recruit staff	None	2	2	3	2.1
F. Train staff	E	4	5	6	5.0
G. Perform pilot	C, D, F	4	5	9	5.5

Source: Adapted from Everett E. Adam, Jr., and Ronald J. Ebert, *Production and Operations Management: Concepts, Models, and Behavior,* 5th ed., copyright © 1992, p. 342. Adapted by permission of Prentice-Hall, Englewood Cliffs, N.J.

mate is usually made of the optimistic (t_o), pessimistic (t_p), and most likely (t_m) times necessary to complete each activity (see Table 5s-2). The *expected,* or *average, time* for each activity is then calculated using the following formula, which gives heavy weight to the most likely time for activity completion:

$$t = (t_o + 4t_m + t_p)/6$$

The expected time (in weeks) for each activity is shown next to its respective arrow on the network diagram.

The next step is identifying the **critical path,** the path in the network that will take the longest to complete. This network has three different paths: 10-20-40-50-60, 10-20-50-60, and 10-30-50-60. By adding up the expected times on each path, we can determine that the path 10-20-50-60 will take the longest (40.8 weeks) and is, therefore, the critical path. This means that a delay in any of the activities on this path will also delay project completion. Therefore, the manager needs to pay particular attention to this path. In addition, by allocating further resources to this path, it may be possible to shorten the project com-

Critical path The path in the network that will take the longest to complete

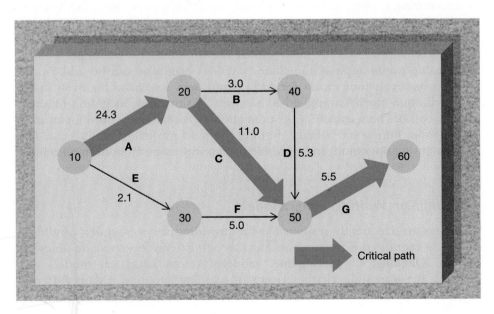

Figure 5s-5 *Network diagram, critical path, and expected time for each activity in the Good Care, Inc., project. (Adapted from Everett E. Adam, Jr., and Ronald J. Ebert,* Production and Operations Management: Concepts, Models, and Behavior, *5th ed., copyright © 1992, p. 343. Adapted by permission of Prentice-Hall, Englewood Cliffs, N.J.)*

pletion time. For example, if the amount of time required to install equipment could be shortened by 2 weeks, project completion time could be reduced to 38.8. When activity times on the critical path are significantly shortened, another path sometimes becomes critical. This could happen if activity C (20-50) was shortened to 8 weeks. Then the path 10-20-40-50-60 would become the critical path. On the noncritical paths, there is some latitude about when various activities can be started without endangering the completion date of the entire project. This latitude is commonly referred to as **slack.**

Slack   Latitude about when various activities on the noncritical paths can be started without endangering the completion date of the entire project

Once the critical path is developed, it is important to periodically record the actual time it takes to complete the various activities and then to review the implications. For example, when activities on the critical path take longer than estimated, action must be taken to rectify the situation. Otherwise, the entire project will be delayed. Similarly, if an activity on a noncritical path takes substantially longer than expected, the critical path could change. Thus PERT helps managers not only plan but also control projects. (Issues of control are discussed more extensively in Chapters 16 through 19.) The ability of individual managers to use PERT to plan and control both small and large projects has vastly increased with the widespread availability of software packages that are relatively easy to use.

■ OTHER PLANNING TECHNIQUES

A number of other quantitatively oriented planning techniques exist that can greatly assist managers. Some of the most prominent include the use of linear programming; queuing, or waiting-line, models; routing, or distribution, models; and simulation models. We discuss each of these techniques very briefly. Typically, the development of effective applications of these techniques requires the help of a management science expert.

Linear Programming

Linear programming (LP)   A quantitative tool for planning how to allocate limited or scarce resources so that a single criterion or goal (often profits) is optimized

Linear programming (LP) is a quantitative tool for planning how to allocate limited or scarce resources so that a single criterion or goal (often profits) is optimized. It is the most widely used quantitative planning tool in business. Linear programming is most likely to be applicable when a single objective (such as maximizing profits) must be achieved, constraints exist that must be satisfied, and variables are linearly related to the objective.[21] A variable is linearly related to an objective when an increase (or decrease) in the variable leads to a proportional increase (or decrease) in the objective. For example, a linear relationship would apply if one chair (variable) produced can be sold for $30 profit (objective), four chairs for $120 profit, and six chairs for $180 profit. The technique has been applied to a variety of situations, including minimizing the cost of "hen scratch" (a combination of cereal grains) while maintaining a proper nutritional balance, finding the most profitable product mix in a manufacturing operation, and maximizing capacity usage at modern oil refineries.[22]

Queuing, or Waiting-Line, Models

Queuing, or waiting-line, models   Mathematical models that describe the operating characteristics of queuing situations, in which service is provided to persons or units waiting in line

Managers are frequently responsible for providing services under conditions that may require the persons or units needing service to wait in lines, or queues. **Queuing,** or **waiting-line, models** are mathematical models that describe the operating characteristics of queuing situations. Many different

How do the more than one thousand Gap stores keep stocked with fresh merchandise? It's easy with the Gap's high-tech automated distribution center in Baltimore. Routing, or distribution, models help the company ensure that its merchandise reaches its many outlets on time.

queuing models exist because of the need to describe a variety of different queuing situations (such as a single service window at a small post office versus multiple service points that one must pass through in getting a driver's license). Unlike linear programming, queuing, or waiting-line, models do not provide an optimal solution. Rather, the models allow managers to vary the parameters of the situation and determine the probable effects. Queuing models were an important part of the Station Manpower Planning System developed by United. The airline needed models of situations in which customers would be waiting in lines so that it could determine how to schedule its staff effectively.

Routing, or Distribution, Models

Many organizations distribute a product or service to multiple customers. **Routing,** or **distribution, models** are quantitative tools designed to assist managers in planning the most effective and economical approaches to distribution problems. The development and use of these models is sometimes referred to as *network optimization analysis.* Among the companies that use routing models is Joyce Beverages, a bottler that delivers a variety of soft-drink products to approximately 5000 customers in Maryland, Virginia, and Washington, D.C. Delivery personnel visit between 500 and 600 customers daily, about 65 percent of them need the deliveries within a specified time frame, and vehicle routes must be changed from day to day. Adopting a computerized vehicle-routing model helped the company both improve customer service and save money.[23]

Routing, or **distribution, models** Quantitative models that can assist managers in planning the most effective and economical approaches to distribution problems

Simulation Models

Simulation is a mathematical imitation of reality. The technique is used when the situation of interest is too complex for more narrow techniques such as linear programming or queuing theory. Rather than constituting a standardized set of formulas that can be applied to a broad set of problems, simulations are usually custom-made to fit a situation.[24] As a result, they can be very expensive to develop. Simulations allow managers to change parameters so that different

Simulation A mathematical imitation of reality

In the 1970s, forecasters at Canadian National Railway predicted the need for significant expansion in the mountain region of western Canada, including laying a double track in place of a single track. But how could this be done in stretches of mountainous terrain and through tunnels, such as shown here? The use of simulation models allowed the company's planners to determine where to lay the double track most advantageously and economically.

assumptions and/or approaches can be evaluated. Canadian National Railway (CN) developed a simulation model to help managers determine the most advantageous areas for laying more than $1 billion of double track that would handle expanding rail traffic through rugged mountain terrain.[25] Simulation has been utilized in production, inventory control, transportation systems, market strategy analysis, industrial and urban growth patterns, environmental control, and a variety of other areas.[26]

■ QUANTITATIVE AIDS FOR DECISION MAKING

Although the aids that we have discussed so far are mainly considered planning tools, they often also assist managers in making the decisions that are part of the planning process. In addition, there are a number of aids that are aimed specifically at helping managers make certain types of decisions. Two particularly well known quantitative aids for decision making are payoff tables and decision trees.

Payoff Tables

Payoff table or **decision matrix** A two-dimensional matrix that allows a decision maker to compare how different future conditions are likely to affect the respective outcomes of two or more decision alternatives

Payoff The amount of decision-maker value associated with a particular decision alternative and future condition

One helpful method of framing managerial decision situations is the use of the payoff table. A **payoff table** is a two-dimensional matrix that allows a decision maker to compare how different future conditions are likely to affect the respective outcomes of two or more decision alternatives. The payoff table is often referred to as a **decision matrix**.[27] Typically, in a payoff table, the decision alternatives are shown as row headings in the matrix, and the possible future conditions are shown as column headings. The number at the intersection of a row and a column represents the **payoff**, the amount of decision-maker value associated with a particular decision alternative and future condition. An example will be helpful in clarifying these concepts.[28]

Put yourself in the place of a decision maker at a college where there is a good possibility that enrollments may increase but existing classroom space is being used to capacity. Investigation of the situation reveals that there are three viable alternatives for increasing space: Construct a new building, expand an old building, or rent or lease another building. These alternatives are shown as row headings in Table 5s-3. There are also three possible future conditions. Student enrollments may go up, go down, or remain unchanged. These conditions are shown as column headings in the table. The potential payoff for each combination of alternative and possible future condition is listed at the appropriate intersection in the table. If it were clear which future condition would occur, then it would be a simple matter to select the alternative that has the highest payoff for that condition. Unfortunately, it is not possible to know exactly which condition will occur. However, on the basis of past experience, current enrollment trends, and personal judgment, the decision maker is able to assign probabilities to the possible future conditions. A *probability* is a decision maker's best estimate regarding the likelihood that a future condition will occur. Such estimates are usually made in the form of a percentage ranging from 0 to 100. For example, as shown in the table, the decision maker estimates that there is a 50 percent probability that student enrollments will go up, while probabilities that enrollments will go down or remain unchanged are each estimated at 25 percent. Which alternative should the decision maker choose?

Decision-making experts recommend choosing the alternative with the highest expected value. The **expected value** for a given alternative is the sum of the payoffs times the respective probabilities for that alternative. For example, the expected value (EV) for expanding an old building is determined as follows:

Expected value The sum of the payoffs times the respective probabilities for a given alternative

$$EV = .50(400,000) + .25(100,000) + .25(100,000) = \$250,000$$

Likewise, the expected value for constructing a new building is (notice that when the payoff is a loss, a minus sign is used)

$$EV = .50(500,000) - .25(200,000) - .25(100,000) = \$175,000$$

Similar computations show an expected value of $225,000 for renting or leasing another building. Therefore, the alternative with the highest expected value in this case is expand an old building.

The value of payoff tables is that they help decision makers evaluate situations in which the outcomes of various alternatives depend on the likelihood of future conditions. As such, payoff tables are most useful when the decision maker is able to determine the major relevant alternatives, the payoffs can be quantified, and reasonably accurate judgments can be made regarding future

TABLE 5S-3 PAYOFF TABLE FOR CLASSROOM SPACE PROBLEM

	POSSIBLE FUTURE CONDITIONS			
ALTERNATIVES	STUDENT ENROLLMENTS UP [.50]*	STUDENT ENROLLMENTS DOWN [.25]	STUDENT ENROLLMENTS UNCHANGED [.25]	EXPECTED VALUE
Construct new building	$500,000	($200,000)†	($100,000)	$175,000
Expand old building	$400,000	$100,000	$100,000	$250,000
Rent or lease another building	$400,000	($100,000)	$200,000	$225,000

*Numbers in brackets are probability estimates for possible future conditions.
†Numbers in parentheses represent losses.
Source: Adapted from E. Frank Harrison, *The Managerial Decision-Making Process*, Houghton Mifflin, Boston, 1987, p. 375.

probabilities.[29] For example, payoff tables have been used to decide which new products to introduce, real estate investments to select, crops to plant, and restaurant staffing levels to implement.[30] Managers at Hallmark, the greeting-card company, use payoff matrixes to help determine the production quantities of unique products, such as a special Muppet promotion that includes albums, plaques, gift wrap, stickers, party patterns, and other items.[31]

Decision Trees

Decision tree A graphic model that displays the structure of a sequence of alternative courses of action and usually shows the payoffs associated with various paths and the probabilities associated with potential future conditions

A **decision tree** is a graphic model that displays the structure of a sequence of alternative courses of action. It usually also shows the payoffs associated with various paths and the probabilities associated with potential future conditions.

A simple decision tree is shown in Figure 5s-6. Here, the manager is faced with an initial decision about whether to build a large or a small manufacturing plant, given some uncertainty regarding future demand for the product. If a large plant is built and demand is high, the company will make a $12 million profit. However, if demand is low, it will make only a $2 million profit (the profit is low because of the overhead on the large plant). The latter amount is

Figure 5s-6 *Decision tree and expected values for building a large or a small manufacturing plant.*

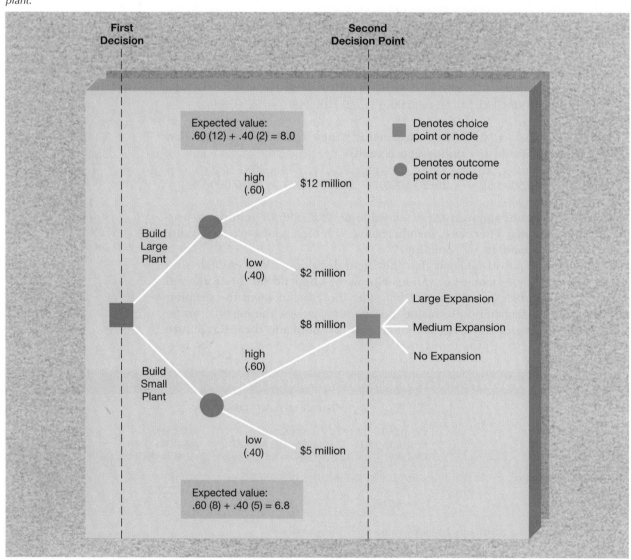

less than the profit that will be made with a small plant under conditions of either high or low demand ($8 million and $5 million, respectively). To help make the decision, we compute the expected value for each alternative. The expected value for the large-plant alternative is $8 million [(.60 × $12 million) + (.40 × $2 million)]. The expected value for the small-plant alternative is $6.8 million [(.60 × $8 million) + (.40 × $5 million)]. This analysis suggests that the manager should seriously consider building the large plant.

So far, the decision tree operates as a graphic alternative to the payoff table. However, a major advantage of a decision tree is that it allows decision makers to consider more complex alternatives. For example, a manager may want to consider the implications of initially building a small plant and then possibly expanding it when the nature of the demand becomes more obvious. In our example in Figure 5s-6, building a small plant and then facing high demand for the product would raise the possibility of a second, later decision point, at which time a manager could take further action ranging from a large plant expansion to no expansion. These later decision possibilities can be considered and their expected values computed by using complex decision trees involving multiple decision points. A decision tree can help managers identify different options, as well as consider the potential impact of various alternative branches of the tree. The device was used to assist the U.S. Postal Service in its decision to continue the nine-digit zip code (zip + 4) for first-class business mailers and to purchase additional capital equipment in conjunction with its postal automation efforts.[32]

Break-Even Analysis

Break-even analysis is a technique that helps decision makers understand the relationships among sales volume, costs, and revenues in an organization.[33] Although break-even analysis is often conducted graphically, as shown in Figure 5s-7, it also can be done mathematically.[34] The technique allows managers to determine the break-even point, which is the level of sales volume at which total revenues equal total costs. At the break-even point the organization neither loses nor makes money; that is, it just breaks even. The break-even point is important because only with a sales volume beyond that point does the organization begin to make a profit.

Several major elements are included in the break-even analysis shown in Figure 5s-7. *Fixed costs* are costs that remain the same regardless of volume of output (e.g., the costs of heating, lighting, administration, mortgage on building, and insurance). Fixed costs in Figure 5s-7 are illustrated by the horizontal line at $600,000. *Variable costs* are costs that vary depending on the level of output (e.g., the costs of raw materials, labor, packaging, and freight). In this particular situation, variable costs are $40 per unit for a unit that sells for $60. These data can be used to draw the lines on the graph for total costs (fixed costs plus variable costs) and total revenues, respectively. The break-even point, shown graphically, is at 30,000 units. At this point, fixed costs of $600,000 plus variable costs of $1,200,000 [30,000 × $40 (variable costs per unit)] equal $1,800,000. Revenues also equal $1,800,000 [30,000 × $60 (sale price per unit)] at this point. Hence the organization would break even at 30,000 units.

Break-even analysis is useful because it is a rough means of determining how many units of a product or service the organization must sell before it begins to make a profit. The analysis also provides a means of assessing the impact of cutting costs when profits begin. For example, if the organization lowered its fixed and/or variable costs, the total cost line in Figure 5s-7 would drop, lowering the break-even point.

Break-even analysis A graphic model that helps decision makers understand the relationships among sales volume, costs, and revenues in an organization

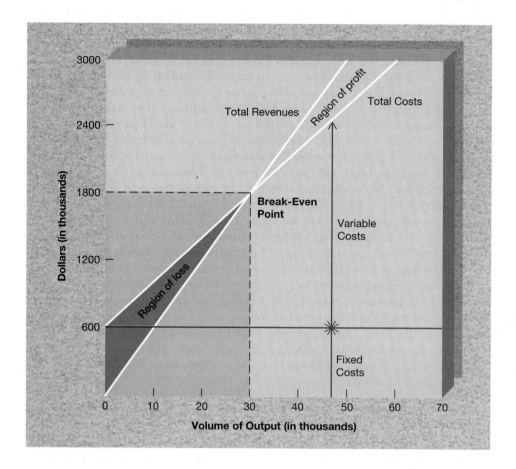

Figure 5s-7 *Break-even analysis.*

Korean Air has been setting fares for its domestic flights at the break-even point to avoid a fare war with a competing Korean airline, Asiana Air, and also to build passenger loyalty for the more lucrative international flights. International travel by Korean citizens has been growing rapidly since the government lifted tight restrictions on international travel in 1988.[35] Recently Microsoft CEO Bill Gates estimated that to reach its break-even point the company must sell $15 million worth of products per day.[36]

Break-even analysis makes some simplifying assumptions. For instance, it assumes that a given price will be charged for all units (yet, some customers may get discounts) and that the fixed costs will remain the same across a wide range of outputs. Such assumptions suggest that the technique is valuable for doing rough analyses, rather than for precisely fine-tuning volumes, costs, and revenues. More complex types of break-even analyses, particularly those involving computers, are available for more precise needs.[37]

CHAPTER SIX

ESTABLISHING ORGANIZATIONAL GOALS AND PLANS

LEARNING OBJECTIVES

After studying this chapter, you should be able to:

■ Describe the major components in the overall planning process.

■ Explain the concept of organizational mission and the purposes of a mission statement.

■ Outline the major benefits of goals and explain how goals differ according to organizational level.

■ Describe the various components that help explain how goals facilitate performance.

■ Explain how plans differ by organizational level and extent of recurring use.

■ Assess the role of goals and plans in promoting innovation.

■ Outline the major steps in management by objectives and assess the strengths and weaknesses of the approach.

GAINING THE EDGE

CYPRESS SEMICONDUCTOR THRIVES ON "TURBO MBO"

When the Cypress Semiconductor Corporation was founded in 1983, the president and CEO, Dr. Thurman John Rodgers (more commonly known as "T. J."), instituted a management by objectives (MBO) program that obtains positive results. Starting from scratch; the organization now has an annual income in excess of $300 million and more than 1000 employees.

Cypress's basic mission is to be a profitable $1 billion semiconductor company that ships quickly, operates efficiently, and is a technological leader. A major portion of the company's business is producing speedy static random-access memory chips, known as SRAMS, used in personal computers, networking, and telecommunications. Intel, AT&T, and Motorola are customers.

The management by objectives system, which Rodgers likes to call "Turbo MBO," helps the company manage its intricate operations by having employees set goals each week that are then tracked by computer. "Producing a semiconductor is a very unforgiving entity," says Rodgers. "If it takes 1000 tasks to make one and you do 999 right but then you forget one or do one wrong, the semiconductor will not work. The [MBO] system forces management to stick its nose in a big book every single week and find out what is going on. We can't afford surprises."

Under the MBO system, senior management and the board of directors develop broad corporate goals for a 5-year period and engage in strategic planning to determine the best way to reach the goals. In the process, they review the projected sales, marketing, and manufacturing plans and consider other important variables such as the number of employees and the amount of capital involved relative to expected outcomes. The 5-year plan is updated annually. The results are then forwarded to middle managers, who develop goals and related plans (often called tactical goals and plans) at their level that are to be accomplished during the coming year. The tactical goals and plans are given, in turn, to project and program leaders at the next lower level. These leaders develop goals and plans (often called operational goals and plans) that are oriented to the current year and frequently to an even shorter period, such as the immediate quarter. Within the goals and plans developed at the strategic, tactical, and operational levels, the Turbo MBO system operates on a weekly basis.

The weekly goal cycle starts on Monday, when every project leader holds a meeting with the project group to review the status of goals that are due and to map out what each group member will do that week. All the new goals for the week are put into the computer system so that more than 40 managers have access to the data through their personal computers. The system is designed to report goals that are delinquent (past due) and identify individuals who are behind on three or more goals.

On Tuesdays, managers review the goals put into the computer the previous day. They consider such issues as priorities, timeliness, equity of workloads, and appropriate progress on projects. On Wednesday afternoons, Rodgers and his seven vice presidents review the status of goals for significant projects. They also consider critical management ratios, such as revenue per employee, revenue to gross capital, performance to original schedule, sales and administration as a percent of revenue, and other measures for which goals have been set for the company as a whole. By the end of this weekly meeting, goals have been reviewed and revised where appropriate. At this point, a printout of every-

An engineer by training, Cypress Semiconductor's CEO T. J. Rodgers runs his company with precision and attention to detail. Employees set goals each Monday, which are tracked by computer and reviewed by Rodgers and his seven vice presidents (shown here) at midweek meetings. Managers who are behind on their goals are likely to get a handwritten memo inscribed at the top with "From the Desk of God." Although he drives his employees hard, he drives himself the hardest, spending 13-hour days at the office and then taking work home.

one's weekly goals is distributed to each employee. It takes employees about 30 minutes to review and update their goals each week.

A permanent record of each employee's goal accomplishments is made monthly. These records are accumulated and used as input for each employee's annual performance evaluation, which is the basis for annual merit increases.

Employees tend to favor the system because it is "bottom-up." That is, they are able to set their own goals within the overall-goals framework. Managers are enthusiastic because the system provides a high level of communication between themselves and the employees who have goals in their areas. Cypress's financial backers praise it because it keeps the company performing according to plan. Thus using its MBO system for goal setting and planning has generally paid off handsomely for Cypress.[1]   ■ ■ ■

Rodgers learned the value of goals and planning while a project manager at American Microsystems (another high-technology firm). There he filled blackboards with lists of "several hundred things to get done, who would do it, and when." Turbo MBO at Cypress is essentially a computerized refinement of that system, an innovation that has helped Cypress succeed in a very competitive industry. While few organizations set goals as often as weekly, there is strong support in the management literature for the importance of goals and related planning, which jointly form the heart of the planning function. In this chapter, we examine the overall planning process, including the development of the mission of the organization. We also consider the nature of organizational goals and examine a model that helps explain how goals facilitate performance. We next probe the link between goals and plans, considering how plans differ according to level, extent of recurring use, and time horizon and examining the role of goals and plans in promoting innovation. Finally, we explore the steps in the management by objectives process and review the major strengths and weaknesses of MBO.

■ THE OVERALL PLANNING PROCESS

How was Steve Bostic, head of the American Photo Group, able to increase annual sales from $149,000 to $78 million before selling the high-technology company to Eastman Kodak for a reported $45 million? Bostic attributes his success to having a vision, being able to put specifics down on paper, and having things "well planned and well thought out."[2] As Bostic's experience suggests, having a good idea of the organization's overall mission, as well as more specific, written goals and carefully configured plans, can be important to an organization's success. In this section, we introduce these major components of the planning process.

Major Components of Planning

Goal A future target or end result that an organization wishes to achieve

One could argue that it is virtually impossible for organizations to function without at least some goals and plans. A **goal** is a future target or end result that an organization wishes to achieve. Many managers and researchers use the term "goal" interchangeably with "objective." Others consider "goal" to be a broader term, encompassing a longer time horizon, and use "objective" to refer to more narrow targets and shorter time frames.[3] We use both terms interchangeably in this text for the sake of simplicity. When distinction between the two is important to the concepts being examined, it will be clear from the context whether a broad or narrow scope or a long or short time frame is involved.

Plan The means devised for attempting to reach a goal

Whereas a goal is a future end result that an organization wants to achieve, a **plan** is the means devised for attempting to reach a goal. *Planning*, then, is the management function that involves setting goals and deciding how best to achieve them. Managers make extensive use of their decision-making skills, as well as various planning and decision aids (see Chapter 5 and the Supplement to Chapter 5), in the course of carrying out the planning function. An overall view of the planning process is shown in Figure 6-1. Hopefully, setting goals and developing plans will lead to goal attainment and, ultimately, to organizational efficiency and effectiveness. As the diagram indicates, the planning process also involves the mission of the organization.

Organizational Mission

Mission The organization's purpose or fundamental reason for existence

Mission statement A broad declaration of the basic, unique purpose and scope of operations that distinguish the organization from others of its type

Essentially, the planning process builds on the **mission** of the organization, the organization's purpose or fundamental reason for existence. A **mission statement** is a broad declaration of the basic, unique purpose and scope of operations that distinguish the organization from others of its type.[4] A mission statement serves several purposes. For managers, it can be a benchmark against which to evaluate success. For employees, a mission statement defines a common purpose, nurtures organizational loyalty, and fosters a sense of community among workers. For external parties, such as investors, governmental agencies, and the public at large, the statement helps provide unique insight into the organization's values and future directions.[5] In some organizations, the mission statement is explicitly presented as a formal written document. In others, the statement is implicitly understood. Of course, in the latter case, there is the danger that various organization members may have different perceptions of the organization's mission, perhaps without realizing it.[6]

One study estimates that about 60 percent of the Fortune 500 companies have written mission statements.[7] According to a related study, which examined the statements of 75 firms from the Business Week 1000, mission statements tend to be made up of some or all of the following nine components:[8]

1 **Customers.** Who are the organization's customers?
2 **Products or services.** What are the organization's major products or services?
3 **Location.** Where does the organization compete?

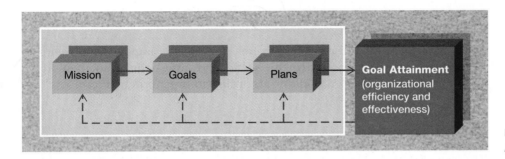

Figure 6-1 *The overall planning process.*

4 **Technology.** What is the firm's basic technology?

5 **Concern for survival.** What is the organization's commitment to economic objectives?

6 **Philosophy.** What are the basic beliefs, values, aspirations, and philosophical priorities of the organization?

7 **Self-concept.** What are the organization's major strengths and competitive advantages?

8 **Concern for public image.** What are the organization's public responsibilities, and what image is desired?

9 **Concern for employees.** What is the organization's attitude toward its employees?

Excerpts from mission statements that match each of these components are shown in Table 6-1. Laura Nash, a management researcher who has studied mission statements, reports that her favorite statement hangs, yellow with age, on the wall of a Boston shoe repair shop. It reads: "We are dedicated to the saving of soles, heeling, and administering to the dyeing."[9]

TABLE 6-1 MAJOR COMPONENTS OF MISSION STATEMENTS AND SAMPLE EXCERPTS

MAJOR COMPONENT	SAMPLE EXCERPT
Customers	The purpose of Motorola is to honorably serve the needs of the community by providing products and services of superior quality at a fair price to our customers. (Motorola)
Products or services	We provide our customers with retail banking, real estate finance, and corporate banking products which will meet their credit, investment, security, and liquidity needs. (Carteret Savings and Loan Association)
Location	Sara Lee Corporation's mission is to be a leading consumer marketing company in the United States and internationally. (Sara Lee Corporation)
Technology	Du Pont is a diversified chemical, energy, and specialty products company with a strong tradition of discovery. Our global businesses are constantly evolving and continually searching for new and better ways to use our human, technological, and financial resources to improve the quality of life of people around the world. (Du Pont)
Concern for survival	To serve the worldwide need for knowledge at a fair profit by gathering, evaluating, producing, and distributing valuable information in a way that benefits our customers, employees, authors, investors, and our society. (McGraw-Hill)
Philosophy	It's all part of the Mary Kay philosophy—a philosophy based on the golden rule. A spirit of sharing and caring where people give cheerfully of their time, knowledge, and experience. (Mary Kay Cosmetics)
Self-concept	Crown Zellerbach is committed to leapfrogging competition within 1000 days by unleashing the constructive and creative abilities and energies of each of its employees. (Crown Zellerbach)
Concern for public image	The company feels an obligation to be a good corporate citizen wherever it operates. (Eli Lilly and Company)
Concern for employees	To compensate its employees with remuneration and fringe benefits competitive with other employment opportunities in its geographical area and commensurate with their contributions toward efficient corporate operations. (Public Service Electric and Gas Company)

Source: Adapted from Fred David, "How Companies Define Their Mission," *Long Range Planning,* February 1989, pp. 92–93.

■ THE NATURE OF ORGANIZATIONAL GOALS

As we have seen, organizational goals form one of the important elements in the overall planning process. In this section, we assess the major benefits of goals and examine how goals differ according to organizational level.

Benefits of Goals

The use of goals has several major benefits.[10] For one thing, goals can *increase performance*. When challenging goals are set, increases in performance frequently range from 10 to 25 percent, and they are sometimes even higher. Furthermore, such increases have occurred among a variety of employee groups, including clerical personnel, maintenance workers, production workers, salespeople, managers, engineers, and scientists.[11]

Another benefit of goals is that they help *clarify expectations*. With goals, organization members usually have a clear idea of the major outcomes that they are expected to achieve. Without goals, the members lack direction. Thus, even when they are all working very hard, they may collectively accomplish very little—as if they were rowers independently rowing the same boat in different directions and together making little progress.

Goals also *facilitate the controlling function*, because they provide benchmarks against which progress can be assessed so that corrective action can be taken as needed. Thus goals not only help individuals gauge their progress but also assist managers in maintaining control over organizational activities. The situation at W. W. Grainger, Inc., based in Skokie, Illinois, serves as an example. The company sells equipment such as sump pumps, industrial staplers, warehouse fans, and commercial air conditioners to contractors, small manufacturers, and distributors. During the 1970s, Grainger charged premium prices but also provided premium service. Unfortunately, the emphasis on service gradually took a backseat to other priorities, and by the early 1980s, earnings began to slow. The company reacted by placing major displays within reach of its customers in its retail outlets, which now number more than 300, and renewing its emphasis on service. With half its sales stemming from its 24,000-item catalog, Grainger has put considerable effort into training its rows of phone-order clerks. A board at the front of their room keeps a tally on progress. The goal is 0 percent customer waiting. On one day in fall 1989, for example, 1.6 percent of the 367 callers had to wait before placing their orders. Three years earlier, 25 percent had been the norm. The goal of 0 percent customer waiting was reached in 1992.[12]

Yet another benefit of goals is that they *increase motivation*. Meeting goals, feeling a sense of accomplishment, and receiving recognition and other rewards for reaching targeted outcomes all serve to enhance motivation.

An intriguing study conducted by goal-setting researchers Gary P. Latham and Edwin A. Locke demonstrates the benefits of goal setting. The situation involved truck drivers of a forest-products company in the western United States. The unionized drivers were concerned that if their log-hauling trucks were overloaded, they could be fined by the highway department and subsequently lose their jobs. For this reason, they seldom loaded their trucks to more than 63 percent of capacity. Interestingly, the company had not provided any goals concerning the load level it expected.

In an experiment aimed at improving the situation, the company coordinated a plan with the union that specified the goal of loading to 94 percent of each truck's legal capacity. Under the terms of the agreement, no driver would

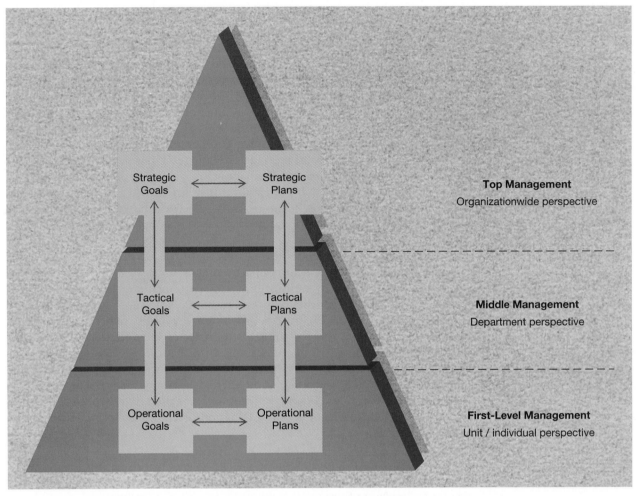

Figure 6-2   *Levels of goals and plans.*

be reprimanded if the goal was not met. No monetary rewards or fringe benefits were offered as incentives. However, verbal praise was given when drivers loaded their trucks to greater levels than they had previously. During the first month of the experiment, the trucks were hauling 80 percent of their capacity, more than they ever had before. In the second month, however, performance decreased to 70 percent of capacity. Interviews with the drivers revealed that they were testing management to determine whether action would be taken against drivers who did not reach the goal. When the drivers realized that no action was going to be taken, they increased their performance. Loading capacity reached over 90 percent in the third month and remained at that level for more than 7 years. The company saved more than $250,000 in the 9-month period during which the study was conducted.[13] Thus the goal clarified expectations, helped increase motivation, provided a standard against which progress could be gauged, and led to improved performance. This experiment is one of many studies that support the importance of goal setting throughout the organization.[14]

Levels of Goals

Organizations typically have three levels of goals: strategic, tactical, and operational, as shown in Figure 6-2. (Also shown are three parallel levels of plans, which will be discussed later in this chapter.)

Strategic goals Broadly defined targets or future end results set by top management

STRATEGIC GOALS Strategic goals are broadly defined targets or future end results set by top management. Such goals typically address issues relating to the organization as a whole and may sometimes be stated in fairly general terms. Strategic goals are sometimes called *official goals* because they are formally stated by top management.[15] At Cypress Semiconductor, for example, one official goal related to productivity is to provide the very highest quality product as well as on-time delivery. Because of efforts to meet this goal, the company was recognized by Hughes (a subsidiary of General Motors) as one of only three suppliers to achieve a zero-defect, 100 percent on-time delivery record.[16]

Management consultant Peter Drucker suggests that organizations need to set goals in at least eight major areas (shown in Table 6-2). These areas encompass a number of aspects that are important to the health and survival of most profit-making organizations.[17] For example, US West has set a goal of pluralism in the area of human resources (see the Managing Diversity box).

Tactical goals Targets or future end results usually set by middle management for specific departments or units

TACTICAL GOALS Tactical goals are targets or future end results usually set by middle management for specific departments or units. Goals at this level spell out what must be done by various departments to achieve the results outlined in the strategic goals. Tactical goals tend to be stated in more measurable terms than is sometimes true of strategic goals. For example, at Cypress Semiconductor, a tactical goal for the static random-access memories (SRAM) group, the largest of Cypress's product divisions, is to achieve preferred supplier status with specified customers. Cypress recently received preferred SRAM supplier status from AT&T, a designation earned by only four other semiconductor suppliers (Motorola, Hitachi, Fujitsu, and Toshiba).[18] The preferred status makes it easier to do business with a firm and usually leads to increased future orders.

Operational goals Targets or future end results set by lower management that address specific measurable outcomes required from the lower levels

OPERATIONAL GOALS Operational goals are targets or future end results set by lower management that address specific measurable outcomes required from the lower levels. At Cypress, for example, in order to achieve the tactical and strategic goals related to product quality and on-time delivery, manufacturing

TABLE 6-2 EIGHT MAJOR AREAS FOR STRATEGIC GOALS

MAJOR AREA	DESCRIPTION
Market standing	Desired share of present and new markets, including areas in which new products are needed, and service goals aimed at building customer loyalty
Innovation	Innovations in products or services, as well as innovations in skills and activities required to supply them
Human resources	Supply, development, and performance of managers and other organization members; employee attitudes and development of skills; relations with labor unions, if any
Financial resources	Sources of capital supply and how it will be utilized
Physical resources	Physical facilities and how they will be used in the production of goods and services
Productivity	Efficient use of resources relative to outcomes
Social responsibility	Responsibilities in such areas as concern for the community and maintenance of ethical behavior
Profit requirements	Level of profitability and other indicators of financial well-being

Source: Based on Peter F. Drucker, *Management: Tasks, Responsibilities, Practices,* Harper & Row, New York, 1974, pp. 103–117.

MANAGING DIVERSITY

US West Makes Pluralism a Goal

At Denver-based US West achieving "pluralism" in its work force is a major goal. The company has become well known as a pioneer in recruiting women and minority workers and moving them into positions of significant responsibility. The company is composed of two main groups, the Communications Group that provides telephone and other telecommunications services to customers in 14 western states and the Media Group that is involved in cable and other media-related endeavors.

Among US West's 61,000 employees, about 15 percent are "people of color," the terminology the company uses to describe minority members of the organization. Hispanics are the largest minority group, with blacks accounting for a slightly smaller number. Native Americans and Asian-Pacific Islanders constitute only small percentages of the work force. Women make up just over 50 percent of the employees.

The company compiles "pluralistic slates" of exceptionally qualified candidates for positions to ensure that women and minorities receive appropriate consideration for hiring and promotions. In addition, company officials have developed a special management track to encourage talented "women of color" to pursue managerial careers. To aid

the effort, US West sets various goals and timetables based on surveys of the experienced labor force in the 14 states it serves and managers' raises and bonuses are partially tied to the color and sex of the employees whom they hire and promote. In addition to increasing diversity in the management ranks, pluralism at US West involves diversity training to help company members accept and appreciate the various ethnic and cultural differences. Even with these efforts, however, progress toward pluralism is gradual. Few minorities are found in top management ranks. One top-level minority is Solomon Trujillo, president and CEO of the Communications Group who has been honored by the Hispanic Association on Corporate Responsibility

US West is committed to expanding the representation of minorities and women in management, as shown here at a management retreat with the CEO in Tucson. The company sees advantages in filling leadership positions with people who care about and understand the concerns of its growing segments of minority customers as well as its minority work force.

as an outstanding Hispanic business leader.

In pursuing its diversity efforts, $11 billion US West says that it is attempting to be responsive to shifts in both the customer population and the general work force. US West's territory includes a number of states with large and expanding ethnic populations.[19]

units within divisions such as the SRAM group must set stringent operational goals aimed at zero defects and 100 percent on-time delivery. Reflecting such operational goals, the company's computerized MBO system keeps close track of unscheduled orders (orders on backlog whose production scheduling will require more than 3 days) and performance on the quality dimension.[20]

HIERARCHY OF GOALS The three levels of goals can be thought of as forming a *hierarchy of goals*. With a hierarchy, goals at each level need to be synchronized so that efforts at all levels are ultimately channeled toward achieving the major goals of the organization. In this way, the various levels of goals form a *means-*

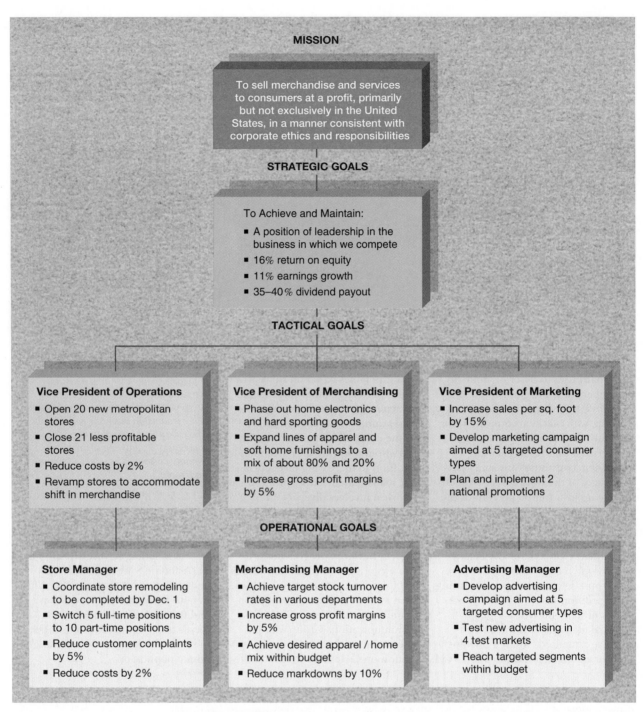

MISSION

To sell merchandise and services to consumers at a profit, primarily but not exclusively in the United States, in a manner consistent with corporate ethics and responsibilities

STRATEGIC GOALS

To Achieve and Maintain:
- A position of leadership in the business in which we compete
- 16% return on equity
- 11% earnings growth
- 35–40% dividend payout

TACTICAL GOALS

Vice President of Operations
- Open 20 new metropolitan stores
- Close 21 less profitable stores
- Reduce costs by 2%
- Revamp stores to accommodate shift in merchandise

Vice President of Merchandising
- Phase out home electronics and hard sporting goods
- Expand lines of apparel and soft home furnishings to a mix of about 80% and 20%
- Increase gross profit margins by 5%

Vice President of Marketing
- Increase sales per sq. foot by 15%
- Develop marketing campaign aimed at 5 targeted consumer types
- Plan and implement 2 national promotions

OPERATIONAL GOALS

Store Manager
- Coordinate store remodeling to be completed by Dec. 1
- Switch 5 full-time positions to 10 part-time positions
- Reduce customer complaints by 5%
- Reduce costs by 2%

Merchandising Manager
- Achieve target stock turnover rates in various departments
- Increase gross profit margins by 5%
- Achieve desired apparel / home mix within budget
- Reduce markdowns by 10%

Advertising Manager
- Develop advertising campaign aimed at 5 targeted consumer types
- Test new advertising in 4 test markets
- Reach targeted segments within budget

Figure 6-3 *Hierarchy of goals for a hypothetical department store chain.*

end chain. The goals at the operational level (means) must be achieved in order to reach the goals at the tactical level (end). Likewise, the goals at the tactical level (means) must be reached in order to achieve the goals at the strategic level (end). In the case of Cypress Semiconductor, the company cannot meet its strategic goal of high quality and on-time delivery without reaching related goals at the tactical and operational levels. Similarly, in Figure 6-3, the partial hierarchy of annual goals, based on the mission and several strategic objectives for a hypothetical department store chain, illustrates how the coordination of goals at various levels creates a united effort toward accomplishing the organization's overall goals.

■ HOW GOALS FACILITATE PERFORMANCE

To make effective use of goals, managers must understand just how goals can facilitate performance. The major components involved in enhancing performance are shown in Figure 6-4.

In this section, we consider these components, highlighting particularly the goal content, goal commitment, work behavior, and feedback aspects.

Goal Content

Goals that are effective in channeling effort toward achievement at the strategic, tactical, and operational levels have a content that reflects five major characteristics. Goals should be challenging, attainable, specific and measurable, time-limited, and relevant.

CHALLENGING Extensive research indicates that, within reasonable limits, challenging, difficult goals lead to higher performance. Assuming that the goals are accepted, people tend to try harder when faced with a challenge. This was the case at Kronus, Inc., maker of innovative electronic time clocks with software that ties into computerized company payroll systems. The Waltham, Massachusetts, company was losing money with founder and inventor Mark Ain at the helm. One of the first actions taken by an outsider brought in to manage the company was raising sales quotas by 60 percent, a goal that was easily met by the 94 sales and service offices. Back to developing new products, Ain mused, "I'm a bad manager."[21] Interestingly, when individuals are asked to do their "best," they typically do not perform nearly as well as they do when they have specific, challenging goals.

Figure 6-4 *How goals facilitate performance. (Adapted from Thomas W. Lee, Edwin A. Locke, and Gary P. Latham, "Goal Setting Theory and Job Performance," in Lawrence A. Pervin, ed.,* Goal Concepts in Personality and Social Psychology, *Lawrence Erlbaum, Hillsdale, N.J., 1989.)*

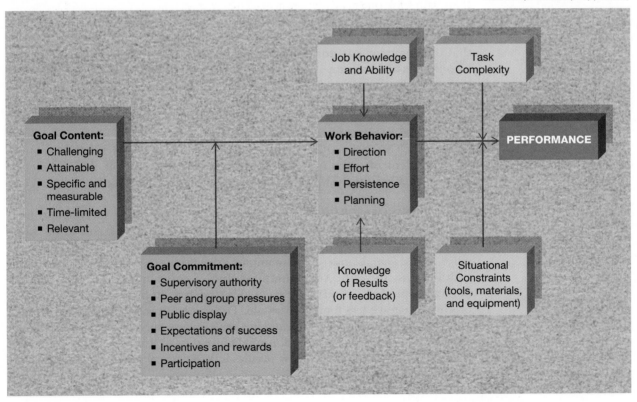

Idle trains that were eating into corporate profits goaded the chief of CSX, a railroad and shipping company, into action. He challenged his employees to earn the full cost of capital and then exceed it by making better use of the railway equipment. Once the CSX workers were convinced that the goal was not impossible, they actually felt spurred on by the stretch target. They reduced the fleet and began to run trains with fewer cars instead of holding locomotives idle while waiting to assemble a long train. Within 3 years they had lowered capital expenditures enough to reach the cost of capital.

ATTAINABLE Although goals need to be challenging, they usually work best when they are attainable. If individuals are making maximum use of their skills and abilities, they cannot achieve higher performance levels. Asking workers to meet difficult, but attainable, goals is more likely to promote sustained performance over a period of time than continually asking them to do the impossible.[22] Still, research shows that individuals perform better with difficult goals than with easy ones.

When CEO John Snow of CSX, the $9.5 billion railroad and shipping company, conducted financial analyses relating to return on capital, he concluded that the company was not doing well on that criterion. The problem was that locomotives and railcars worth multiple billions of dollars sat idle much of the time at loading docks and seaport terminals. Snow set goals aimed at reaching the cost of capital and then exceeding it by making better use of the locomotives and railcars. At first, subordinates thought the goal was impossible, but the logic of needing to earn more than the cost of capital hit home. Within three years, CSX deleted 20,000 railcars from its inventory of 125,000—cutting the equivalent of a train stretching from Chicago to Detroit. Having met its goal of equaling the cost of capital, the company now has goals to exceed it.[23]

SPECIFIC AND MEASURABLE To be effective, goals need to be specific and measurable so that workers clearly understand what is expected and know when the goal has been achieved. When possible, goals should be stated in quantitative terms. *Quantitative goals* encompass objective numerical standards that are relatively easy to verify. At Rubbermaid, Inc., a company with a reputation for innovative products, a quantitative goal is to derive 30 percent of its sales from products that are less than 5 years old. For some purposes, though, qualitative goals are more appropriate. *Qualitative goals* involve subjective judgment about whether or not a goal is reached. A qualitative goal at Rubbermaid is to develop an idea and prototype for a new plastic desk accessory that is useful, long-lasting, and inexpensive.[24]

TIME-LIMITED Goals also need to be time-limited; that is, there should be a defined period of time within which a goal must be accomplished. Otherwise, goals have little meaning, since individuals can keep putting off achieving them. At Cypress Semiconductor, the weekly goals keep attention focused on meeting goals within the desired time frame. In many organizations, goals are set annually but may be reviewed more often, such as quarterly.[25]

RELEVANT Goals are more likely to elicit support when they are clearly *relevant* to the major work of the organization and the particular department or work unit. Jack Stack, head of the Springfield Remanufacturing Corporation in Springfield, Missouri, learned an important lesson about goals and relevancy after he took the helm of the ailing equipment manufacturing plant. The company had contracted to ship 800 tractors to Russia, but it lacked some parts needed to complete the machines and the shipping date was less than a month away. In desperation, Stack put up a huge sign that read, "Our Goal: 800 Tractors." The workers responded by coming in at night to figure out what parts were missing from which tractors. They then got the parts through every means they could think of. As a result, the very difficult goal was met.[26]

For guidelines on how to go about actually setting goals, see the Management Skills for the Twenty-First Century discussion, "How to Set Goals."

Goal Commitment

A critical element in using goals effectively is getting individuals and/or work groups to be committed to the goals they must carry out. **Goal commitment** is one's attachment to, or determination to reach, a goal.[27] Without commitment, setting specific, challenging goals will have little impact on performance. How, then, can managers foster commitment to important organizational goals? They can draw on five major factors that positively influence goal commitment: supervisory authority, peer and group pressure, public display of commitment, expectations of success, and incentives and rewards. A sixth factor, participation, is also sometimes helpful.

Goal commitment One's attachment to, or determination to reach, a goal

SUPERVISORY AUTHORITY Individuals and groups are often willing to commit themselves to a goal when the goal and reasons for it are explained by a person with supervisory authority, usually one's boss. With this approach, goals are essentially assigned by the supervisor, who explains the reason for the goals to his or her employees and provides them with any necessary instructions. The explanation and instructions are likely to be more effective when the supervisor is supportive rather than authoritative. Instead of bluntly telling subordinates to meet the goals, the supervisor should provide encouragement and offer opportunities for individuals to ask questions.

PEER AND GROUP PRESSURE Pressure from peers and work group members can enhance goal commitment when everyone's efforts are channeled in the same direction. This is because enthusiasm about potential accomplishments becomes infectious. In addition, successful individuals can serve as role models to others who observe their efforts. On the other hand, peer and group pressure can sometimes detract from goal commitment, particularly if the goals are perceived as unfair.

PUBLIC DISPLAY Recent evidence suggests that commitment to difficult goals is higher when the commitment is public (made in front of others) than when

How to Set Goals

There are six main steps in setting goals to obtain optimal results:

1 *Specify the goal to be reached or tasks to be done.* What do you want to accomplish? Do you want to increase sales? Reduce costs? Improve quality? Boost customer service? Maybe, at the moment, you are thinking that you would like to obtain an A in a particular course this semester (perhaps the one involving this textbook).

2 *Specify how the performance will be measured.* Some outcomes can be measured more easily than others. (e.g., number of units sold and dollar volume of sales). Work outcomes (the results achieved) are typically measured according to one of three parameters:

   Physical units: For example, quantity of production, market share, number of errors, number of rejects (quality control)

   Time: For example, meeting deadlines, servicing customers, completing a project, coming to work each day, being punctual

   Money: For example, profits, sales, costs, budgets, debts, income

   Similarly, many course-of-study outcomes can be measured in terms of physical units (such as the number of questions answered correctly on examinations and grades received on papers and assignments) and in terms of time (such as meeting deadlines for assignments and attending classes).

   Sometimes, outcomes are difficult to measure, perhaps because the measurement process would be too costly or because the outcomes are affected by factors beyond an individual's control. In such cases, it may be necessary to measure behaviors or actions rather than outcomes. For example, if a manager's goal of overcoming worker resistance to certain impending changes is likely to be significantly affected by the actions of others, it may be possible to measure crucial activities instead of outcomes. Such activities might include whether the manager clearly explains why the change is needed, outlines how the change will affect others, and listens to employee's concerns. When possible, though, the goal-setting process should focus on outcomes.

3 *Specify the standard or target to be reached.* This step builds on the type of measure chosen in step 2 by spelling out the *degree* of performance to be included in the goal. For example, the target might be producing 40 units per hour, reducing errors by 2 percent, completing a project by December 15, answering the telephone within three rings, or increasing sales by 10 percent.

   In pursuing the objective of attaining an A in a particular course, you might set targets such as correctly answering at least 90 percent of the questions on the midterm and final exams, offering one knowledgeable point during the discussion part of each class, and fulfilling written assignments well enough to earn high grades. Setting subgoals, such as the number of textbook pages to be read and outlined each day, can also help goal achievement.

4 *Specify the time span involved.* To have a positive impact on performance, goals need to have a time span within which they are to be completed. In a production situation, the goal may be stated in terms of production per hour or day. In a service situation, the goal may involve the time it takes to deliver the service. For example, a photocopier repair service may have the goal of responding to customer calls within 2 hours. Other goals, such as major projects, may have time spans involving several months or even years. For instance, your goals for the semester may involve a few months, while goals associated with obtaining your degree and developing your career may span several years.

5 *Prioritize the goals.* When multiple goals are present, as is likely with most jobs, they need to be prioritized so that effort and action can be directed in proportion to the importance of each goal. Otherwise, individual effort can be focused improperly.

   For example, suppose that in the course in which you want to obtain an A, examinations count 70 percent, a paper counts 20 percent, and discussion in class counts 10 percent toward the grade. In this case, a goal related to the examinations should be given first priority, while goals related to the paper and the class discussion should receive second and third priority, respectively.

6 *Determine coordination requirements.* Before a set of goals is finalized, it is important to investigate whether achieving the goals depends on the cooperation and contributions of other individuals. If so, coordination with those individuals may be necessary. In organizations, coordinating vertically is usually relatively easy. It may be more difficult, but nevertheless important, to achieve coordination horizontally, particularly if some of the individuals report to other managers outside your work unit.

   In the case of the course in which you are attempting to excel, your efforts may require coordination with your boss (if you are employed) so that your work schedule allows you sufficient study time before exams. If you plan ahead, you may also be able to get parents, a spouse, or friends to help you out with other duties at crucial times during the semester, such as right before exams, so that you have plenty of time to review.[28]

it is private. At Nordstrom's, the Seattle-based apparel, shoe, and soft-goods retailer known for excellent customer service, store managers must publicly state their sales goals at regional meetings. Once a manager has declared his or her store sales goals, a top executive shows goals for the same store developed by a "secret committee." Managers whose goals fall below those of the secret committee are booed by the group, while those whose goals are above the secret-committee level are cheered.[29]

EXPECTATIONS OF SUCCESS Goal commitment is more likely when individuals or groups perceive that they have high expectations of success. That is, individuals tend to become committed when they believe that they have a good chance of performing well on the tasks involved in reaching the goal. If individuals believe they cannot accomplish the tasks involved, they are unlikely to be committed to the goal.

INCENTIVES AND REWARDS Goal commitment is also enhanced by incentives and rewards. Incentives are offered during the goal-setting process, while rewards occur upon goal achievement. Some incentives may be tangible, such as money, while others may be intangible, such as challenge of the job, anticipation of or positive feelings about accomplishment, feedback, competition (as long as it is constructive), and recognition for goal attainment. At Nordstrom's, salespeople with especially good results are honored monthly as "All-Stars" and receive $100 and large discounts on store merchandise. The highest achievers are inducted annually into the Pace Setters Club, which also makes them eligible for major discounts. The names of managers who excel at reaching their goals are engraved on a plaque in the company's executive headquarters.[30]

While positive outcomes foster commitment, negative outcomes inhibit it. For example, if workers fear that producing more will lead to layoffs, their commitment to high production goals will be low. It is important to ensure that the achievement of goals is not associated with unfavorable consequences.

PARTICIPATION Although research indicates that participation is not usually needed to gain goal commitment, having individuals participate in the goal-setting process can be an effective means of fostering commitment. Participation can be particularly helpful in developing plans for implementing goals. For these reasons, managers often include subordinates in goal setting and in the subsequent planning of how to achieve the goals.[31]

Work Behavior

Given goals and commitment, how does the goal-setting process ultimately influence behavior? Goal content and goal commitment appear to affect an individual's actual work behavior by influencing four factors: direction, effort, persistence, and planning.

DIRECTION Goals provide direction by channeling attention and action toward activities related to the goals, rather than toward other activities. Thus, when individuals are committed to specific goals, those goals can help them make better choices about the activities that they will undertake.

EFFORT In addition to channeling activities, goals to which individuals are committed boost effort by mobilizing energy. Individuals are likely to put forth more effort when goals are difficult than when they are easy.

PERSISTENCE Persistence involves maintaining direction and effort in behalf of a goal until it is reached. Thus for some goals persistence may be required over an extended period of time. Commitment to goals makes it more likely that individuals will persist in attempting to reach them.

PLANNING In addition to their relatively direct effects on work behavior in terms of direction, effort, and persistence, goals have an important indirect effect through their influence on planning. Individuals who have committed themselves to achieving difficult goals are likely to develop plans or methods that can be used to attain those goals. With easy goals, however, little planning may be necessary. By setting high goals and engaging in careful planning, Pasquale Natuzzi has transformed his Industrie Natuzzi SpA into a global leather furniture empire within a relatively short period of time (see the Case in Point discussion).

CASE IN POINT

NATUZZI IS ON TARGET IN LEATHER

Natuzzi leather furniture, such as black, white, and canary-colored sofas, can be found in more than 10,000 stores throughout the world, including Bloomingdale's, IKEA, Macy's, and Sears Canada. By offering a variety of price categories and pursuing high goals for growth, Industrie Natuzzi SpA, based in Santerano (Bari), Italy, has transformed itself into the world's largest manufacturer of contemporary leather furniture in little more than a decade. There is often an 8-week order backlog for its popular leather furniture.

When company president Pasquale Natuzzi started his enterprise, U.S. retail prices for a leather sofa began in the $3000 range and accounted for only about 1 percent of total furniture sales. By taking a lower profit margin, but still pursuing a goal of making at least a 12 percent profit, Natuzzi was able to introduce leather sofas starting at $999. Mr. Natuzzi's approach has helped expand the U.S. market for leather furniture to about 15 percent of total upholstery sales.

One of Mr. Natuzzi's goals is maintaining a 30 to 40 percent annual growth rate. The company has been able to achieve that goal through high-volume production of made-to-order leather furniture in an industry largely populated by small, inefficient manufacturers. Natuzzi offers over 400 models of 8 furniture pieces in 230 colors and 28 varieties of leather. By offering a broad range of price levels, the company is able to sell to a wide variety of outlets. Natuzzi ships to more than 200 stores in the New York City area alone. The United States and other countries in North and South America account for 43 percent of the company's sales; Europe, for 48 percent.

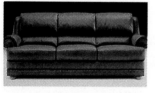

No one sits down on the job at Industrie Natuzzi SpA, an Italian furniture company that combined high goals with aggressive planning to take control of the worldwide leather furniture market. In order to boost sales to over $1 billion by the turn of the century, the company has recently moved into the manufacture of fabric furniture as well.

Another of Mr. Natuzzi's goals is to build a $1.3 billion company by the turn of the century, compared with sales of $432 million in 1994. Natuzzi and his two daughters hold 54 percent of the company stock. In order to reach this revenue goal, Natuzzi is branching into fabric, which accounts for 80 percent of the world furniture market (compared with 20 percent for leather). The company introduced its first fabric furniture in 1994 and is pursuing a goal of obtaining 22 percent of its sales from fabric furniture within 6 years. To increase sales in Europe, Natuzzi is establishing several furniture store chains in areas where distribution tends to be fragmented, such as Italy, Portugal, Greece, Turkey, and Spain. There are goals and timetables associated with setting up the chains. The company also is building a new showroom in High Point, North Carolina, to better serve the U.S. market. Mr. Natuzzi is optimistic about his company's future: "We always reach our targets," he says.[32] ■■■

Other Process Components

Several other components influence the impact of goals on job performance. For one thing, *job knowledge* and *ability* are likely to affect an individual's work behavior and prospects for reaching goals, even when there is strong commitment. For another, the *complexity of the task* may affect the degree to which goal-directed work behaviors influence job performance. According to related studies, the impact of goals on performance is greater with relatively simple tasks (such as basic arithmetic, toy assembly tasks, or basic typing) than with more complex ones (such as supervision or engineering projects).[33] Apparently, the effect of goals on the direction, effort, and persistence of work behavior, as well as on planning, is dissipated somewhat into the different aspects of a complex task.

Situational constraints constitute another element that influences the impact of goals on performance. Having the proper tools, materials, and equipment is important for achieving difficult goals. Finally, *knowledge of results* or feedback about progress toward goals is a particularly influential factor in the effectiveness of goals. While goals set the target, knowledge of results influences goal achievement by enabling individuals to measure their progress.[34] Thus, goal setting is an important tool in increasing productivity and quality. Still, care must be taken to use goal setting properly, lest problems arise.

Potential Problems with Goals

Although there are many positive features associated with using goals in organizations, there are also some potential pitfalls to be avoided.[35] These problems and possible solutions to each one are summarized in Table 6-3.

■ LINKING GOALS AND PLANS

Goals and plans are closely related. Even though an organization may establish goals at the strategic, tactical, and operating levels, these goals will have little meaning unless careful consideration is given to how the goals will actually be

TABLE 6-3 POTENTIAL GOAL-SETTING PROBLEMS AND POSSIBLE SOLUTIONS

POTENTIAL PROBLEM	POSSIBLE REMEDIES
Excessive risk taking	Analyze risk; avoid careless or foolish risks.
Increased stress	Eliminate unnecessary stress by adjusting goal difficulty, adding staff, and offering training in necessary skills.
Undermined self-confidence (due to failure)	Treat failure as a problem to be solved rather than a signal to punish.
Ignored nongoal areas	Make sure goals encompass key areas.
Excessive short-run thinking	Include some long-term goals.
Dishonesty and cheating	Set example of honesty, avoid using goals punitively, offer help in overcoming difficulties, give frequent feedback, and be open to information indicating goals are inappropriate.

Source: Based on Edwin A. Locke and Gary P. Latham, *Goal Setting: A Motivational Technique That Works,* Prentice-Hall, Englewood Cliffs, N.J., 1984, pp. 171–172.

Ready-to-assemble kits of airplane parts now allow Boeing plant workers to speed production of the aircraft. The kits were developed through tactical and operational planning in response to strategic goals aimed at cutting the cost of manufacture and reducing the time needed to build the planes.

Strategic plans Detailed action steps mapped out to reach strategic goals

Tactical plans The means charted to support implementation of the strategic plan and achievement of tactical goals

Operational plans The means devised to support implementation of tactical plans and achievement of operational goals

achieved. While goals are the desired ends, plans are the means used to bring about those ends. The importance of developing plans becomes apparent when one considers that there may be more than one means of reaching a particular goal. Plans differ by level in the organization and also by extent of recurring use.

Levels of Plans

In much the same way that there are levels of goals, plans also differ according to level in the organization (see Figure 6-2). Thus there are strategic, tactical, and operational plans.[36]

STRATEGIC PLANS Strategic plans are detailed action steps mapped out to reach strategic goals. These plans address such issues as how to respond to changing conditions, how to allocate resources, and what actions should be taken to create a unified and powerful organizationwide effort ultimately aimed at strategic goals.[37] Strategic plans are generally developed by top management in consultation with the board of directors and with middle management. They typically cover a relatively long time horizon, often extending 3 to 5 years or more into the future. At Cypress Semiconductor, for example, strategic planning considers the next 5 years. Comprehensive statements of strategic plans in organizations often include the mission and goals because these form the basis for strategic action steps. We discuss issues related to strategic planning in more detail in the next chapter.

TACTICAL PLANS Tactical plans are the means charted to support implementation of the strategic plan and achievement of tactical goals. These plans tend to focus on intermediate time frames, usually encompassing 1 to 3 years. Generally, tactical plans are more specific and concrete than strategic plans. Tactical plans outline the major steps that particular departments will take to reach their tactical goals. For the most part, these plans are developed by middle managers, who may consult lower-level managers before making commitments to top-level management. In developing tactical plans, managers may consider a number of possibilities before settling on a final plan (the plan is, of course, subject to change, should things not progress as expected). Tactical plans are important to the success of strategic plans. For example, middle-level managers at Cypress Semiconductor develop tactical plans that support top-level strategic plans.

OPERATIONAL PLANS Operational plans are the means devised to support implementation of tactical plans and achievement of operational goals. These plans generally consider time frames of less than 1 year, such as a few months, weeks, or even days. For example, at Cypress Semiconductor, considerable emphasis is placed on operational plans covering 1 week. Plans at the operational level are usually developed by lower-level managers in consultation with middle managers. Such plans spell out specifically what must be accomplished over short time periods in order to achieve operational goals. Unless operational goals are achieved in organizations, tactical and strategic plans will not be successful and goals at those levels will not be achieved.

Plans According to Extent of Recurring Use

Plans can also be categorized on the basis of how frequently they will be used. There are two types of plans: single-use plans and standing plans (see Figure 6-5).

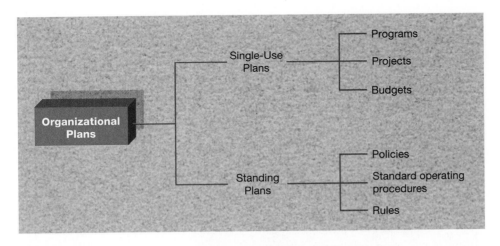

Figure 6-5 *Plans according to extent of recurring use.*

SINGLE-USE PLANS Single-use plans are aimed at achieving a specific goal that, once reached, will most likely not recur in the future. There are two major types of single-use plans: programs and projects.

A **program** is a comprehensive plan that coordinates a complex set of activities related to a major nonrecurring goal. Programs typically involve several different departments or units of the organization, are composed of several different projects, and may take more than 1 year to complete. Programs usually include six basic steps: (1) dividing what is to be done into major parts, or projects, (2) determining the relationships among the parts and developing a sequence, (3) deciding who will take responsibility for each part, (4) determining how each part will be completed and what resources will be necessary, (5) estimating the time required for completion of each part, and (6) developing a schedule for implementing each step.[38] Programs frequently have their own budgets. A *budget* is a statement that outlines the financial resources needed to support the various activities included in the program. An example of a program is the plan that coordinated U.S. Sprint's construction of a 20,000-mile optical-fiber network at a cost of several billion dollars. Stretching from coast to coast, each pair of fiber strands within the cable can handle 16,000 simultaneous conversations.[39] Installing the Sprint network was a nonrecurring goal, because once the network has been completed, there is no need to be concerned with redoing it for a considerable period of time.

A **project** is a plan that coordinates a set of limited-scope activities that do not need to be divided into several major components in order to reach an important nonrecurring goal. Like programs, projects often have their own budgets. A project may be one of several related to a particular program. For example, the fiber-optic program of Sprint consisted of many smaller projects that involved laying the fiber-optic cable in various locations. Conversely, a project may be a separate, self-contained set of activities sufficient to reach a particular goal. For instance, at U.S. Sprint, work continues on a project to develop a voice card that would allow a caller to speak into a phone and have a Sprint computer recognize the voice and automatically bill the call.[40] The voice-card project is a self-contained activity that will not need to be repeated once it is completed.

STANDING PLANS Standing plans provide ongoing guidance for performing recurring activities. The three main types of standing plans are policies, procedures, and rules.[41]

A **policy** is a general guide that specifies the broad parameters within which organization members are expected to operate in pursuit of organizational goals. Policies do not normally dictate exactly what actions should be taken.

Single-use plans Plans aimed at achieving a specific goal that, once reached, will most likely not recur in the future

Program A comprehensive plan that coordinates a complex set of activities related to a major nonrecurring goal

Project A plan that coordinates a set of limited-scope activities that do not need to be divided into several major projects in order to reach a major nonrecurring goal

Standing plans Plans that provide ongoing guidance for performing recurring activities

Policy A general guide that specifies the broad parameters within which organization members are expected to operate in pursuit of organizational goals

"Service" is a general policy governing employees of the Ritz-Carlton Hotel. At the Ritz-Carlton, all employees are taught to operate according to "The Ritz-Carlton Basics," a document specifying the behaviors that will maintain the gold standard of service. For instance, employees are urged to maintain positive eye contact and use the proper vocabulary with guests (e.g., "Good Morning," "Certainly," "I'll be happy to," and "My pleasure").

Procedure A prescribed series of related steps to be taken under certain recurring circumstances

Figure 6-6 *Time horizons for goals and plans.*

Rather, they provide general boundaries for action. For example, policies frequently spell out important constraints. Many retail stores have a policy requiring that returned merchandise be accompanied by a sales receipt. Similarly, policies often outline desirable actions. At the Hechinger Company, a Maryland-based retailer of hardware and home and garden products, returns are accepted even when the customer has obviously abused the item. In fact, Hechinger managers can have a dozen roses sent to customers who are particularly upset.[42]

A **procedure** is a prescribed series of related steps to be taken under certain recurring circumstances. Well-established and formalized procedures are often called *standard operating procedures* (SOPs). Unlike policies, which tend to be fairly general, procedures provide detailed, step-by-step instructions as to

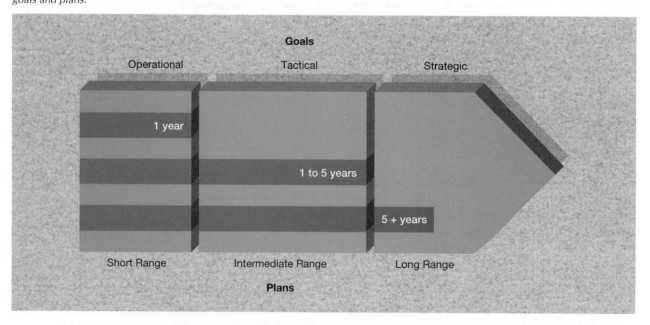

what should be done. Thus they do not allow much flexibility or deviation. For example, banks typically have SOPs that govern how tellers handle deposits. Because they specify detailed desired actions in recurring circumstances, SOPs are frequently good tools for training new employees.

A **rule** is a statement that spells out specific actions to be taken or not taken in a given situation. Unlike procedures, rules do not normally specify a series of steps. Instead, they dictate exactly what must be or must not be done, leaving little flexibility or room for deviation.

Rule A statement that spells out specific actions to be taken or not taken in a given situation

Time Horizons of Goals and Plans

The different levels of goals and plans are related to different time horizons (see Figure 6-6). Strategic goals and plans usually address long-range issues involving time periods of 5 years or more. The period varies somewhat depending on the industry. When the environment changes rapidly, long-range planning may focus on periods of less than 5 years. When the environment is relatively stable (such as that of the utility industry), long-range planning may extend to periods of 10 to 20 years. Tactical goals and plans typically address intermediate-range issues involving periods that vary from 1 year to 5 years. Operational goals and plans are mainly oriented toward short-range issues spanning periods of 1 year or less.

Promoting Innovation: The Role of the Planning Process

The overall planning process can play a vital role in innovation in organizations through the mission, goals, and plans components. Creativity expert Teresa M. Amabile argues that an organization's basic orientation toward innovation must stem primarily from the highest levels.[43] Ideally, the CEO envisions a future for the organization that is based on innovation and then attempts to communicate that vision to organization members. One primary means of signaling the importance of innovation is the organizational mission statement, which can also address the general areas in which innovation is to be emphasized. For example, the Cypress Semiconductor mission statement designates the major types of "leading-edge process technologies" that will be emphasized, and it specifies that "Cypress's products are strategic components for next-generation computation, instrumentation, telecommunication, military, and aerospace systems." Thus, in its statement, Cypress has clearly committed itself to innovation in order to provide "next-generation" components, and it offers general information about the major areas of innovation.[44] The vision incorporated in such mission statements helps highlight the importance of innovation and motivate organization members to innovate.

The goals component of the planning process can also support innovation. For example, translating a mission into strategic goals might lead to the following specification: "Within 5 years, the organization will be the number-one provider of state-of-the-art semiconductor chips in a [specified broad] area." The "state-of-the-art" designation signals the need for product innovation. A corresponding goal at the tactical level might be: "Within 2 years, the programmable logic devices division will introduce 20 new products." Finally, at the operational level, a goal for a particular work unit might be: "Within 1 year, the unit will have a working prototype that meets the following general specifications. . . ." Thus goals at each level can be used to encourage innovation.

The plans component of the planning process also plays a role in innovation. While goals calling for innovative outcomes can be stated in at least general terms, actual plans for achieving such outcomes (e.g., new products) are often somewhat looser than plans involving relatively predictable situations. This greater flexibility reflects the difficulty of specifying exactly what should be done when seeking innovative breakthroughs and nurturing new ideas, particularly in product or service development. Of course, the likelihood of achieving innovative goals can be increased if managers make sure that organizational conditions foster innovation. We discuss several of these conditions, such as organizational structure, resource levels, communication patterns, and leadership, in subsequent chapters. One company that is well known for using goals to effectively promote the development of innovative products is 3M (see the Case in Point discussion).

CASE IN POINT   3M MINES THE WORK FORCE FOR IDEAS

A company with a strong reputation for innovative products, 3M has a vast catalog of 60,000 items ranging from Scotch brand transparent tape to reflecting road signs. During the late 1980s, the company began to experience heavy global competition from rivals that developed their own new products, often at prices less than those charged by 3M. In response, 3M had to expend a considerable amount of its innovative efforts to reduce unit manufacturing costs by 10 percent.

Although successful at the cost cutting, it seemed that 3M had lost its innovative product edge by the time Livio DeSimone ascended to the chairman and CEO position in 1992. Sales rose less than 1 percent and profits grew only about 2.4 percent in 1993. DeSimone wanted 10 percent annual increases in profits, and he was particularly concerned about the relative dearth of major new products. Up to this point, 3M had had a goal of generating 25 percent of its annual sales from products that had been introduced within the past 5 years. To emphasize the critical need for innovation, DeSimone unveiled a new, more difficult target: 30 percent of annual sales from products introduced within the past 4 years. Moreover, by the late 1990s he wanted 10 percent of annual sales to come from products less than 1 year old. To ensure that efficiency is considered simultaneously, DeSimone also promulgated tough financial goals. 3M's return on equity was targeted at between 20 and 25 percent, return on capital was set at 27 percent, and sales per employee were fixed to rise by 8 percent per year.

To help the innovation process, the company launched a "Pacing Program" aimed at identifying a small number of products and technologies that look like they will produce substantial profits within 2 years or less. There are usually about 200 Pacing Programs going on at any one time, at least one per business. In the past, a laboratory with 100 individuals might be working on 20 or more formal programs. Under the pacing process, the same number of individuals are likely to be focused on 5 or 6 programs. A considerable amount of 3M research is still allocated to longer term projects, but the pacing system seems to be helping. It is aided by data banks that help share information among 3M scientists, technical forums, and even "Talks with Desi (DeSimone's nickname)" to get experts in diverse technologies talking with one another.

One of the successes of the pacing approach is Scotch-Brite Never Rust soap pads, which represent a major new technology applied to the function of scrubbing. Traditional scouring pads, like Brillo or SOS, are made of steel wool that can leave rust spots and metal splinters. In contrast, Never Rust is manufactured from recycled plastic beverage bottles. Within a year, Never Rust was launched and quickly captured an amazing 22 percent of the $100 million market in the United States from Brillo and SOS.

The goal of 30 percent of sales on products that are 4 years old or less is already being consistently met. The news has not been as positive regarding the financial goals. As a result, DeSimone has presided over some restructuring. 3M has withdrawn from its computer diskette, videotape, and audiotape businesses because the projected returns were too low, given the future investments that would have been required. The company also spun off its data storage, imaging, and publishing products units into a new company called Imation. As a separate entity, the new company can concentrate on building business processes that are better suited to the lower margin markets in which these businesses must compete. Says DeSimone, "Managers must set goals, then get out of the way." When goals are not being met though, further managerial actions may be required.[45]   ■■■

As illustrated in the 3M situation, plans can also be used to help achieve goals that do not represent innovative outcomes but, rather, rely on innovative means. Even if a goal focuses on a traditional end result, such as cost cutting or quality improvement, the development of plans can encourage finding innovative means of reaching the target. In this way, the emphasis is on developing innovative ways to reach goals that are not themselves stated in terms of innovative outcomes.

Potential Obstacles to Planning

Several potential obstacles threaten the ability of organizations to develop effective plans. One barrier is a rapidly changing environment, which makes planning more difficult because plans must be altered frequently. Another obstacle is the view among some managers that planning is unnecessary. This stance may arise when managers have a general idea in their heads about future directions and means of reaching organizational goals. Steve Bostic, whose American Photo Group tallied a 52,244 percent increase in sales over the 5-year period before he sold the company to Kodak, argues that plans must be put on paper: "I want people to buy into the plan, so it isn't just my plan anymore. It becomes theirs as well. That way, I know everybody is following the same road map when we go out into the real world." Bostic believes that unless the plan is specific enough to be put on paper, communications with others about the plan will be vague, and they will not be able to give it their full support.[46] Another potential barrier to planning is the day-to-day work pressures on managers. Even when managers believe that planning is beneficial, daily burdens may channel their attention away from planning.[47] Yet another obstacle is poor preparation of line managers in terms of their planning knowledge and skills. Finally, effective planning is sometimes thwarted if staff specialists are allowed to dominate the planning process. This can lead to low involvement by managers, who must ultimately implement the plans.[48]

Organizations can take several steps to reduce the obstacles to planning. One step is conveying strong top-management support for the planning process. Top-level managers can signal their commitment by being personally involved in the planning process and by maintaining interest in how the plans are being implemented. Such commitment encourages managers at lower levels to engage in and support planning. Another step is ensuring that planning staffs, often known as corporate planners, maintain a helping role, rather than do the actual planning. A **planning staff** is a small group of individuals who

Planning staff A small group of individuals who assist top-level managers in developing the various components of the planning process assist top-level managers in developing the various components of the planning process. Such staffs typically help monitor both internal and external environments in order to generate data for strategic decisions by top management. They also suggest possible changes in organizational missions, goals, and plans. From the 1960s through the early 1980s, the influence of corporate planners grew to the point where they often dominated the planning process, leaving line managers with minor roles. Since then, many organizations reacted by reducing the role of planning staffs.[49] For instance, when John F. Welch, Jr., took over as chairman at General Electric, he cut the corporate planning group from 58 to 33. Other corporate planners were eliminated in various divisions and units throughout the company.[50]

The moves at GE reflect another step that organizations can take to reduce the obstacles to planning. Top management can actively involve the managers who will be primarily responsible for carrying out the plans. In part, this entails providing such managers with training in the planning process. Managers should be encouraged to review plans frequently, particularly when the environment tends to change rapidly. To cope with a rapidly changing environment, managers can also engage in contingency planning. **Contingency planning** is the development of alternative plans for use in the event that environmental conditions evolve differently than anticipated, rendering original plans unwise or unfeasible.

Contingency planning The development of alternative plans for use in the event that environmental conditions evolve differently than anticipated, rendering original plans unwise or unfeasible

■ MANAGEMENT BY OBJECTIVES

One method used by a number of organizations to facilitate the linking of goals and plans is management by objectives, an approach used successfully by the Cypress Semiconductor Corporation as described in the chapter opening case. **Management by objectives (MBO)** is a process through which specific goals are set collaboratively for the organization as a whole and every unit and individual within it. The goals are then used as a basis for planning, managing organizational activities, and assessing and rewarding contributions. MBO usually incorporates considerable participation among managers and subordinates in setting goals at various levels.

Management by objectives (MBO) A process through which specific goals are set collaboratively for the organization as a whole and every unit and individual within it; the goals are then used as a basis for planning, managing organizational activities, and assessing and rewarding contributions

Although the origins of MBO are not completely clear, General Electric appears to be the first organization that implemented the process, and noted management consultant Peter Drucker is generally credited with being the first individual who wrote about it.[51] Over the years, MBO has been used by a variety of organizations to help coordinate the goal-setting and planning processes at various levels so that the collective efforts of organization members ultimately support organizational goals. Organizations that have used MBO include Purex, Black and Decker, Tenneco, Texas Instruments, Wells Fargo Bank, Boeing, and Westinghouse.[52]

Steps in the MBO Process

There can be considerable variation in the way that MBO is practiced in different organizations. Yet most viable MBO processes include the following six steps (see Figure 6-7):[53]

1 **Develop overall organizational goals.** Goals at this stage are based on the mission of the organization and address targets to be achieved by the organization as a whole (e.g., a certain rate of return for a given period or a specific increase in market share). These goals are essentially strategic goals set by top management.

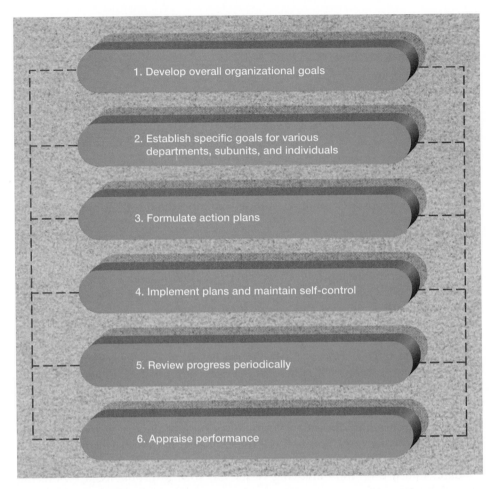

1. Develop overall organizational goals

2. Establish specific goals for various departments, subunits, and individuals

3. Formulate action plans

4. Implement plans and maintain self-control

5. Review progress periodically

6. Appraise performance

Figure 6-7 *Steps in the MBO process.*

2 **Establish specific goals (or objectives) for various departments, subunits, and individuals.** In this step, coordinating goals are set for various organizational levels so that each goal contributes to reaching the overall goals set in step 1. This stage of the process begins when upper-level managers formulate specific objectives that they plan to accomplish, usually related to their own departments or areas of responsibility (such as marketing or production). These goals are usually developed in collaboration with managers at the next lower level. For example, the head of the marketing department, together with the regional sales managers, may set the goal of increasing a certain product's sales volume to 100,000 during the coming year. Then the regional sales managers confer with their district managers in setting goals at the regional levels. In the eastern region, for instance, the sales manager and district managers may decide on the goal of increasing sales volume to 25,000 for the particular product, thus contributing toward the 100,000 goal at the national level. The process, which is sometimes referred to as the cascading of goals, continues until all units at various levels have specific goals for the coming year. At each level, goals are typically set in key areas, where results are critical to the success of the organization.

Although many organizations follow the top-down process just described, some use a bottom-up approach, in which goal setting begins at the lower levels. These levels propose their goals on the basis of what they believe they can achieve. Goals are then developed at the tactical level that are based on the proposed goals provided by the operational level. The tactical goals are then proposed to the strategic level. Even with a bottom-up approach, however, goal setting usually follows at least some general guide-lines developed at the strategic level. In any event, with MBO, there is typically some give-and-take among levels before goals at the various levels are finalized.

3 **Formulate action plans.** Once goals are set, action plans must be developed that focus on the methods or activities necessary to reach particular goals. In essence, an *action plan* is a description of what is to be done, how, when, where, and by whom in order to achieve a goal. Action plans contribute to the feasibility of reaching goals, aid in identifying problem areas, assist in spelling out areas in which resources and assistance will be needed, and facilitate the search for more efficient and effective ways to achieve objectives. Such plans are usually developed by subordinates in conjunction with their supervisors.

4 **Implement and maintain self-control.** A basic notion underlying MBO is that once goals are set and action plans determined, individuals should be given considerable latitude in carrying out their activities. The rationale is that, with MBO, individuals know what they are supposed to achieve, have mapped out plans, and can gauge their progress against set goals. There-fore, it should not be necessary for the supervisor to become as involved in the individual's day-to-day activities as might be the case without goals and action plans. The notion of self-control is particularly true with respect to managerial positions. Of course, supervisors still need to be kept informed about progress and any unanticipated difficulties that arise. They may need to provide coaching and support if subordinates are having difficulties.

5 **Review progress periodically.** Periodic reviews are important to ensure that plans are being implemented as expected and that goals will ultimately be met. Such reviews provide a good opportunity for checking performance to date, identifying and removing obstacles, solving problems, and altering action plans that are not achieving the expected results. Reviews also make it possible to assess the continuing appropriateness of the goals and to change them or add new ones as necessary. How frequently progress reviews are held will depend on how quickly situations change, but quarterly reviews are common.

6 **Appraise performance.** At the end of the goal-setting cycle, which usually runs for a period of 1 year, managers meet with each of their subordinates to conduct an appraisal of performance over the cycle. The appraisal typically focuses on the extent to which goals were met, as well as on shortfalls, the reasons for them, and actions that can be taken to prevent the same difficulties in the future. The appraisal session includes praise and recognition for areas in which the subordinate has performed effectively, as well as discussion of areas in which he or she could benefit from future development of knowledge and skills. Goals and plans for the next cycle may also be discussed at this point.

As Figure 6-7 indicates, feedback from each step may lead to the revision of prior goals or the setting of future ones. While constant revision of prior goals tends to defeat the purpose of MBO, some revisions may be necessary to accommodate major changes in circumstances. The purpose of the goal-setting and planning processes is essentially to coordinate efforts toward important organizational goals. If those goals need changing, then efforts probably require redirecting as well; hence, corresponding goals at various levels should also be changed.

TABLE 6-4 STRENGTHS AND WEAKNESSES OF MBO

STRENGTHS	WEAKNESSES
1. Aids coordination of goals and plans	1. Tends to falter without strong, continual commitment from top management
2. Helps clarify priorities and expectations	2. Necessitates considerable training of managers
3. Facilitates vertical and horizontal communication	3. Can be misused as a punitive device
4. Fosters employee motivation	4. May cause overemphasis of quantitative goals

Strengths and Weaknesses of MBO

As suggested by the successful use of MBO at Cypress Semiconductor, management by objectives has a number of major strengths. On the other hand, MBO also has several weaknesses. The main strengths and weaknesses of MBO are summarized in Table 6-4.[54]

The possible implications of two of the potential weaknesses—using MBO as a punitive device and overemphasizing quantitative goals—can be seen in the case of MiniScribe, a computer disk-drive company. The Colorado-based firm had been doing poorly before Q. T. Wiles, who had a reputation for resuscitating ill companies, took over the helm. Under Wiles, the value of Mini-Scribe's stock quintupled within 2 years on the basis of strong financial reports before it was finally revealed that the data were bogus. Interviews with current and former executives, employees, competitors, suppliers, and others familiar with the company revealed major internal difficulties. Wiles had set unrealistic sales goals and used an abusive management style that created intense pressure. In an effort to keep up, managers began to falsify data by booking shipments as sales and simply fabricating figures. MiniScribe ultimately filed for bankruptcy and sold its assets.[55] At Nordstrom's, the Seattle-based retailer, some present and former employees have complained of extreme pressure to meet sales goals. A recent investigation by the Washington State Department of Labor and Industries found that the company systematically violated state law by failing to pay employees for the time spent delivering merchandise to customers or working on inventory.[56]

Assessing MBO

Because of the possible weaknesses, MBO has not always reached its potential. According to one estimate, MBO has been used in almost half the Fortune 500 companies, yet it has been successful only about 20 to 25 percent of the time.[57] Failures of MBO systems seem to stem from a lack of adequate support from top management and poor goal-setting and communication skills among managers who must implement the system. According to a recent study, however, when top management commitment to the MBO program and processes was high, the average gain in productivity was 56 percent.[58] Hence, the way in which managers implement MBO may undermine its effectiveness. While overall organizational or strategic goals are important to the MBO process, they are also a critical element in strategic management, a subject that we explore in the next chapter.

■ CHAPTER SUMMARY

Major components of the overall planning process are the mission, goals, and plans of the organization. The mission is the organization's purpose or fundamental reason for existence. The mission statement, a broad declaration of the basic, unique purpose and scope of operation that distinguish the organization from others of its type, has several purposes. The statement can be a benchmark against which to evaluate success; a means of defining a common purpose, nurturing loyalty, and fostering a sense of community among members; and a signal about values and future directions. A goal is a future target or end result that an organization wishes to achieve. A plan is a means devised for attempting to reach the goal.

Goals have several potential benefits. They can increase performance, clarify expectations, facilitate the controlling function, and help increase motivation. Organizations typically have three levels of goals: strategic, tactical, and operational. These levels of goals can be conceptualized as a hierarchy of goals.

A number of key components help explain how goals facilitate performance. Goal content is one component. Goals should be challenging, attainable, specific and measurable, time-limited, and relevant. Goal commitment is another key component. Commitment can usually be positively influenced through supervisory authority, peer and group pressure, public display of commitment, expectations of success, and incentives and rewards. Participation also may engender goal commitment. Work behavior is also a major component. Goal content and goal commitment influence the direction, effort, persistence, and planning aspects of work behavior. Other major components are job knowledge and ability, complexity of task, and situational constraints. Care must be taken to avoid a number of potential problems with goal setting.

In much the same way that there are levels of goals, plans also differ according to level in the organization. Thus there are strategic, tactical, and operational plans. Plans can also be categorized on the basis of how frequently they will be used. Single-use plans are usually not needed again in the future and include programs and projects. Standing plans are used on a recurring basis and include policies, procedures, and rules. The different levels of goals and plans are related to different time horizons. Strategic goals and plans are usually focused on long-range issues 5 years or more in the future, tactical goals and plans are aimed at intermediate-range issues 1 to 5 years in the future, and operational goals and plans are oriented toward 1 year or less. Research suggests that the planning process can be used to promote innovation in several ways. These include wording the mission statement so that it signals the importance of innovation, setting goals aimed at innovative outcomes, and developing loose plans that allow latitude in the innovation process or focus on innovative means of reaching goals. Managers must take steps to reduce or avoid several potential obstacles to developing plans.

Management by objectives includes the following steps: develop overall organizational goals; establish specific goals for various departments, subunits, and individuals; formulate action plans; implement and maintain self-control; review progress periodically; and appraise performance. MBO has several strengths and weaknesses. Failures of MBO systems seem to stem from a lack of adequate support from top management and poor goal-setting and communication skills among managers who must implement the system.

■ QUESTIONS FOR DISCUSSION AND REVIEW

1 Outline the major components in the overall planning process. Give examples of these components in an organization with which you are familiar.

2 Define the concept of organizational mission, and explain the purposes of a mission statement. Think of an organization that you would like to establish. What type of mission would you develop?

3 Outline the major benefits of goals. Describe a situation in which you have observed these benefits.

4 Explain how goals and plans differ according to organizational level. Describe how goals and plans may be different at the various levels of management at your college or university.

5 Discuss the major components in the diagram indicating how goals facilitate performance (Fig. 5-4). Describe a situation in which you have seen goals work well and one in which goals did not seem to work. Use the diagram to explain each situation.

6 Explain how to set goals. List four goals that you might set for yourself during the coming semester.

7 Delineate several potential problems with goal setting. Discuss how two of these problems might apply in an organization with which you are familiar (perhaps an organization on campus). What steps might you take to avoid such problems?

8 Explain the various types of single-use and standing plans. Give an example of each type of plan at your college or university.

9 Assess the role of goals and plans in promoting innovation. Explain how goals and plans helped 3M increase innovation.

10 Explain the steps in the management by objectives process, and assess the strengths and weaknesses of MBO.

■ DISCUSSION QUESTIONS FOR CHAPTER OPENING CASE

1 Trace the overall planning process at Cypress Semiconductor.

2 Assess the benefits of the use of goals at Cypress, and explain how the goal-setting process works.

3 Evaluate the strengths and weaknesses of MBO as practiced by Cypress.

■ EXERCISES FOR MANAGING IN THE TWENTY-FIRST CENTURY

EXERCISE 1
SKILL BUILDING: WHAT TYPE OF GOAL IS IT?

 You are reviewing goals for the chain of ice cream stores your family operates in a local five-state area. You are aware of the levels of goals used by organizations. Today you want to classify these goals according to the normal hierarchy. Classify the following:

1. Strategic
2. Tactical
3. Operational

_____ **1** Increase sales at least 18% each year for the next 2 years

_____ **2** Reduce turnover to 10% in all stores during the next fiscal year

_____ **3** 40% of revenues will come from our brand of products during the next 5 years

_____ **4** Improve customer service 15% in all stores in the region

_____ **5** Increase visibility of stores in the region

_____ **6** Decrease shrinkage to 5% in store X

_____ **7** Achieve minimum stock turnover ratio of once each month at all stores within 2 years

_____ **8** Remodel Johnston store by April

_____ **9** Be the ice cream/frozen yogurt industry leader in this five-state region in 5 years

_____ **10** Achieve profits equal to $2000 monthly per employee in all stores this fiscal year

EXERCISE 2
MANAGEMENT EXERCISE: WORKING WITH MBO

 You recently received your degree and accepted a position as a department head at a local hardware store that is part of a small, but growing, chain. The chain uses an MBO system. Some of the strategic goals are reaching $400 million in annual sales within 5 years, building a reputation for excellent customer service, and having a double-digit return on investment throughout the period. Some of the tactical goals include opening six new stores each year for the next 3 years, opening one new large experimental store in your district next year, reaching annual sales of $8 million, earning a return on investment of 14 percent, increasing customer satisfaction by 5 percentage points on the annual survey, and having sales of $99,000 for each employee in the department.

On the basis of these strategic and tactical goals, draft some goals for the operational level of your own department.

CONCLUDING CASE 1

WAL-MART LEAPFROGS THE COMPETITION

Wal-Mart is the world's largest retailing company. Achieving this position was the result of a great deal of hard work by the company's more than 525,000 employees, who are called "associates."

The initial success of the company can be traced directly to founder Samuel Moore Walton. Soon after returning from military duty in World War II, he opened the first Walton's Ben Franklin store (a five-and-dime type of store) in Versailles, Missouri, in the late 1940s. After losing his lease in 1950, Walton moved his business to Bentonville, Arkansas, where he opened a Walton 5 & 10. He also established Ben Franklin franchises and had 15 by 1962, when he opened the first Wal-Mart Discount City. By 1969, when the company became Wal-Mart Stores, Inc., there were 18 Wal-Mart and 15 Ben Franklin stores operating throughout Arkansas, Missouri, Kansas, and Oklahoma. Today there are approximately 2200 Wal-Marts, 260 supercenters, and 430 Sam's Wholesale Clubs, and the company operates in all 50 states. Wal-Mart also has stores in Argentina, Puerto Rico, and Canada and operates in Hong Kong, Brazil, and Mexico under joint venture agreements. They have combined revenues of more than $100 billion.

Wal-Mart has followed a strategy of building and expanding in areas where the local population is under 50,000. At first, only one or two stores are built. Next, a distribution center is constructed nearby that will support further expansion in the area. Other stores are then built within a day's drive of the distribution center. Wal-Mart currently has more than 25 distribution centers, which are widely considered to be major factors in the company's spectacular success.

The Wal-Mart organization stresses its relationship with associates, which is based on the premise that they are partners. Associates have access to information about their stores, such as costs, freight charges, and profit margins, that many other organizations show only to general managers. Associates play a major role in achieving overall Wal-Mart and individual store goals.

Goals play an important part in the way that Wal-Mart is managed. They are developed using MBO as part of the planning process. At Wal-Mart, the top level of management provides some guidelines in areas such as profits and growth. These are used as a basis for setting goals at the division and store levels. Most of the more specific tactical goals are developed at the division level. They are then forwarded to the corporate or top level, where they are reviewed and are used to formulate the final goals at the strategic level. Stores also have some input into the goals that are ultimately set, and they have annual operational goals of their own to achieve. Some of the specific goals set at Wal-Mart during a recent annual goal-setting effort included the following:

- Adding 75 new Wal-Mart stores in the United States
- Opening 12 new Sam's Wholesale Clubs
- Opening 100 supercenters
- Opening 30 to 35 stores in Canada, China, Argentina, Brazil, Mexico, and Puerto Rico
- Reducing inventory by $300 million

Individual stores are generally expected to achieve at least a 10 percent increase in sales over the previous year. Stores also have profit goals. Associates receive a share of the profits above the goals set for each store. Once goals are set, the various levels engage in action planning to determine the specific means that will be used to achieve the goals.

Goals are monitored throughout the fiscal year to ensure that they are being achieved as intended. For the most part, goals have been met. Recently, however, after 99 straight quarters of reporting increasing earnings, Wal-Mart reported a dip in earnings for the first time. Still, Wal-Mart has been extremely successful. A $1000 investment in Wal-Mart's initial stock offering in 1970 would be worth more than half a million dollars today. Wal-Mart is frequently among the leaders in *Fortune*'s survey of the most admired corporations in America. Sam Walton died on April 5, 1992. He had already chosen David D. Glass, a longtime Wal-Mart executive, to take over as CEO.

Since then, the company has been concentrating its expansion in the west, northwest, and northeast parts of the United States, with increasing focus on international growth. So far, though, its international operations are only marginally profitable. Prospects for further growth of the Sam's Club division are hampered by a general maturing of the merchandise club industry. Regular Wal-Mart discount stores are now in all 50 states, although there is still some room for expansion. Glass believes "our biggest growth opportunity is supercenters." The supercenters combine a supermarket and general-merchandise store under one roof.[59]

QUESTIONS FOR CONCLUDING CASE 1

1 Trace the overall planning process at Wal-Mart.
2 Use the goal-setting process to explain why the use of goals at Wal-Mart enhances performance.
3 Describe the MBO process at Wal-Mart.

CONCLUDING CASE 2

PLANNING AT CANON: THE KEY TO SUCCESS

When the Precision Optics Laboratory (the original name for Japan-based Canon) was founded in 1933, there was little advance planning. The company had a single production facility that manufactured cameras for local sale on the basis of rough assessments of likely demand. Today $80 billion Canon produces an array of image, information, and communication products. Production in its numerous worldwide facilities is based on carefully developed plans that include specific goals. Currently, about 75 percent of sales are in business machines, 20 percent in cameras, and 6 percent in optical products.

The Canon planning process began in 1962 with the company's first long-range plan, covering 5 years. At that point, 95 percent of Canon's sales came from cameras, but the company was concerned that market growth for cameras was leveling off. Therefore, its initial plan focused on diversification into other products, mainly business machines. The specific goal was to achieve 20 percent of its sales from products other than cameras in 5 years. The next two 5-year plans included other critical goals, such as furthering diversification, boosting production capacity to meet anticipated demand, establishing a worldwide distribution system for Canon products, and expanding into the image information industry.

In 1975, the company experienced serious difficulties. It had expanded into producing handheld electronic calculators. Unfortunately, more than 10 major competitors emerged who aggressively marketed new technologies and/or lowered prices. Moreover, a serious defect in a critical calculator part Canon had purchased from an outside supplier led to massive returns. Overly optimistic estimations of market demand also led to an excessive inventory of products that soon became obsolete. An oil crisis, fluctuations in foreign exchange, and a recession added to the company's woes, causing major losses. Canon was determined never to get in a situation like that again.

From then on, Canon launched a campaign to become a leading global company that would be better able to deal effectively with environmental forces. The company reorganized to provide separate divisions for each major product area, stressed the development of innovative products, and greatly expanded the planning process.

Today the planning system consists of long-range (strategic), medium-range (tactical), and short-range (operational) plans. A central planning staff helps with the planning process.

The long-range (strategic) plan (with a horizon of up to 10 years) outlines broad major directions and goals for the company within the context of the rapidly changing environment. Goals are normally set for the final year of the plan and may include such factors as sales volumes, pretax income, and capital investment. Other parts of the plan are revised annually as necessary. These parts focus mainly on the orientation of the company, changes of structure, and employee motivation and revitalization.

The medium-range (tactical) plans address shorter-term issues that amplify long-range plans and goals. They are normally 3-year plans that are revised annually on the basis of current business considerations. Tactical plans guide the allocation of resources, such as human resources, facilities, equipment, and funding, to achieve tactical goals. They also center on what must be done by the various product divisions to meet overall strategic directives. Contingency plans are also developed to deal with potential serious threats, even when the probabilities of such circumstances are relatively low.

Canon's short-range (operational) goals and plans are oriented to the maximum use of all resources to obtain planned results during the current fiscal year. Operational reports are compared with previously established goals to determine the effectiveness of individual units and the overall company.[60]

QUESTIONS FOR CONCLUDING CASE 2

1   Discuss how Canon has used its planning process to position itself as a global business.

2   How would you envision tactical goals and plans flowing from the strategic plans at Canon?

3   Explain how you would implement goal setting and planning in an international organization.

CHAPTER SEVEN

STRATEGIC MANAGEMENT

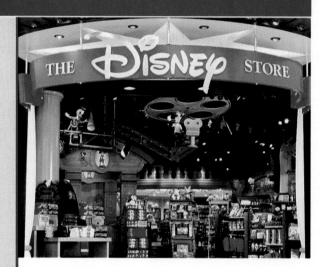

CHAPTER OUTLINE

The Concept of Strategic Management
The Strategic Management Process
Importance of Strategic Management
Levels of Strategy

The Role of Competitive Analysis in Strategy Formulation
Environmental Assessment
Organizational Assessment

Formulating Corporate-Level Strategy
Grand Strategies
Portfolio Strategy Approaches

Formulating Business-Level Strategy
Porter's Competitive Strategies

Formulating Functional-Level Strategy

Strategy Implementation
Carrying Out Strategic Plans
Maintaining Strategic Control

LEARNING OBJECTIVES

After studying this chapter, you should be able to:

- Explain the concept of strategic management and identify the three main levels of strategy.

- Outline the major components of the strategic management process.

- Describe the role of competitive analysis in strategy formulation and explain the major approaches to such analysis.

- Enumerate the main generic strategies available at the corporate level.

- Explain the three major portfolio strategy approaches for use at the corporate level.

- Describe Porter's competitive strategies for the business level.

- Explain the role of strategies at the functional level.

- Outline the process of strategy implementation.

GAINING THE EDGE

THE MAGIC RETURNS TO DISNEY

 By the early 1980s, the magical kingdom of Walt Disney Productions had lost its sparkle. It seemed that the creative juices in the company had slowly ebbed after the death in 1966 of Walt Disney, creator of such well-known characters as Mickey Mouse, Minnie Mouse, and Donald Duck. Walt Disney's immediate successors were wary of tampering with what had been a successful formula and, thus, made changes only slowly. As a result, attendance at the Disney theme parks in California and Florida began to level off, Tomorrowland began to lose its forward look, and, for the first time in almost three decades, no Disney-produced show was on network television. With few exceptions, Disney movies were dismal failures at the box office.

The dire situation reversed dramatically after the board brought in Michael D. Eisner as chairman and chief executive officer. Eisner, who has a creative bent, had been an extremely successful president of Paramount Pictures. When he took charge at Disney in 1984, he quickly began to infuse the company with a renewed entrepreneurial spirit. Eisner concluded that the company's major assets were the Disney name, the Disney culture, its movies, and its library. Therefore, he planned to revitalize these assets and, at the same time, to embellish them with new assets. In doing so, Disney introduced new movies, new ideas, new theme parks, and new executives.

The company, now called The Walt Disney Company, has three main operating divisions: filmed entertainment, consumer products, and theme parks and resorts. In the filmed entertainment division, the new management team has converted Walt Disney Studios from a lackluster performer to a leader of the pack with such hits as *The Hunchback of Notre Dame, The Lion King, Pocahontas,* and *Toy Story,* the first completely computer animated feature film. Many of Disney's films are adult fare, released under such labels as Touchstone and Hollywood Pictures.

In addition, there are more than 525 Disney Store locations around the globe. Many products sold by The Disney Store are exclusive and are not found at other retailers.

The theme parks and resorts division is also moving forward at a rapid pace. Under Eisner, the company has revamped Walt Disney World and Disneyland to such an extent that the number of visitors to the parks has increased dramatically. For example, Tomorrowland at Walt Disney World has been completely reconfigured, and a new high-technology version of the Main Street Electrical Parade is being prepared at Disneyland. Disney's Disneyland Resort opened near Paris in 1992, but was a money loser until recently. Disney has reduced its stake from 49 percent to 39 percent. The company has been building a number of new resort hotels, including an All-Star Music Resort and a Boardwalk Resort that re-creates the charm of Atlantic City in the 1900s—both at Disney World. Disney Cruise Lines is now operating in Florida.

Some of the ideas for films, consumer products, and park attractions originate with Eisner himself, who counts on others to squelch his more impractical suggestions, such as his vision of a 43-story hotel in the shape of Mickey Mouse. Many ideas begin with the famous Disney Imagineering division, an innovative group that is mainly responsible for dreaming up new ideas and figuring out how they can become realities. One of its concepts is an American

For a time in the early 1980s, it appeared as if Mickey Mouse and the rest of the Disney crew were losing their appeal. But with a shift in Disney management in 1984 came an infusion of new life for the company. As a result of innovative and energetic strategic planning, Disney's three main divisions—filmed entertainment, consumer products, and theme parks and resorts—are now flourishing. The Disney Store pictured here is one of 525 spread over the globe. (Photos © Disney Enterprises, Inc.)

history theme park. Disney wanted to develop the park in a rural area about 30 miles from Washington, D.C., but is looking for a new site after encountering opposition from some local groups who were concerned about the impact. Disney is refurbishing the landmark New Amsterdam Theater on 42nd Street in New York City, which was closed and had fallen into major disrepair. The renovated theater will be the centerpiece of a massive $1.8 billion entertainment complex being planned to rejuvenate the area around Times Square. Disney will also have a Disney store in the area, but is not running the entire complex.

One of Eisner's most spectacular recent moves is Disney's $19 billion merger with Capital Cities/ABC, which adds 60 percent to the size of the Walt Disney Company. With the merger, Disney can now market its movies, prime-time shows, and cartoons over the ABC network and Capital Cities' global ESPN sports channel, both of which distribute, rather than create, entertainment. In Eisner's view, his chief duty at Disney is leading creatively and being an orchestrator, thinker, inventor, and cheerleader for new ideas.[1]   ■ ■ ■

How was Eisner able to take a languishing company and make it so visibly prosperous again? His success stems in part from his strong commitment to Disney's growth and his ability to map out important strategic directions for the company. In Chapter 6, we considered various levels of goals and plans, including those at the strategic level. Strategic goals and plans are a particularly important part of the managerial planning function because they ultimately determine the overall direction of the organization. Accordingly, in this chapter, we take a more thorough look at strategic-level planning issues, exploring how companies like Disney are managed strategically. We begin by examining the concept of strategic management. We then consider how competitive analysis can form the basis for developing effective strategies aimed at gaining an edge over competitors. We next analyze policy formulation at the corporate, business, and functional levels. Finally, we probe the process of strategy implementation.

■ THE CONCEPT OF STRATEGIC MANAGEMENT

Strategies Large-scale action plans for interacting with the environment in order to achieve long-term goals

Strategic management A process through which managers formulate and implement strategies geared toward optimizing strategic goal achievement, given available environmental and internal conditions

Most well-run organizations attempt to develop and follow **strategies,** large-scale action plans for interacting with the environment in order to achieve long-term goals.[2] A comprehensive statement of an organization's strategies, along with its mission and goals, constitutes an organization's strategic plan.[3] To learn where such strategies originate and how they are put into action, we need to examine carefully an aspect of the planning function called strategic management. **Strategic management** is a process through which managers formulate and implement strategies geared toward optimizing strategic goal achievement, given available environmental and internal conditions.[4] This definition recognizes that strategic management is oriented toward reaching long-term goals, weighs important environmental elements, considers major internal characteristics of the organization, and involves developing specific strategies. Thus the strategic management process encompasses a major part of the planning process introduced in Chapter 5.

The Strategic Management Process

The strategic management process is made up of several major components, as shown in Figure 7-1. The process begins with identifying the organization's mis-

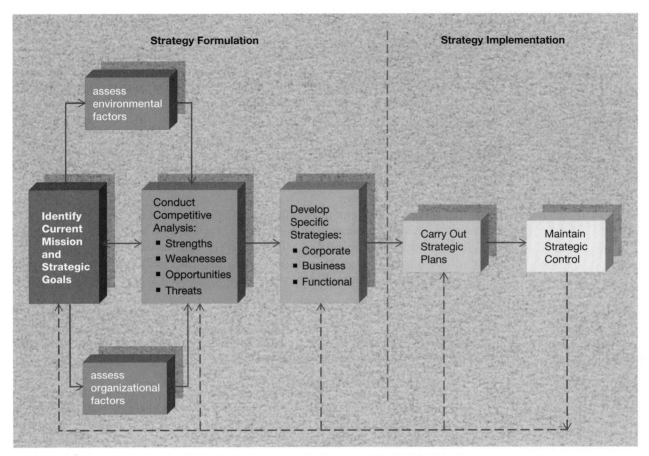

Figure 7-1 *The strategic management process.*

sion and strategic goals (see Chapter 6). Next, it involves analyzing the competitive situation, taking into consideration both the external environment and relevant organizational factors. After such an analysis, managers can begin to develop, or formulate, various strategies that can be used to reach strategic goals. The part of the strategic management process that includes identifying the mission and strategic goals, conducting competitive analysis, and developing specific strategies is often referred to as **strategy formulation.** In contrast, the part of the process that focuses on carrying out strategic plans and maintaining control over how those plans are carried out is known as **strategy implementation.**[5] Strategy implementation is increasingly highlighted as a distinct part of the strategic management process because even the most brilliantly formulated strategies will achieve nothing if they are not implemented effectively.

Importance of Strategic Management

Strategic management is important for several reasons.[6] For one thing, the process helps organizations identify and develop a **competitive advantage,** which is a significant edge over the competition in dealing with competitive forces.[7] For example, Disney has been able to gain a competitive advantage in the family entertainment industry by creating amusement parks, movies, and products based on the renowned Disney characters.

Strategic management is also important because it provides a sense of direction so that organization members know where to expend their efforts. Without a strategic plan, managers may concentrate on day-to-day activities only

Strategy formulation The process of identifying the mission and strategic goals, conducting competitive analysis, and developing specific strategies

Strategy implementation The process of carrying out strategic plans and maintaining control over how those plans are carried out

Competitive advantage A significant edge over the competition in dealing with competitive forces

to find that a competitor has maneuvered itself into a favorable position by taking a more comprehensive, long-term view of strategic directions. This was the case at the Rayovac Corporation, a battery and flashlight maker based in Madison, Wisconsin. Rayovac had fallen behind competitors in the early 1980s because of its aging product line, outdated packaging, and slowness in entering the market for alkaline batteries (which became the industry standard). Since that time, a new chairman and vice-chairman, the husband-and-wife team of Thomas and Judith Pyle, have rejuvenated the company, partially through a variety of innovative products. For instance, the Luma 2 is a sleek flashlight with an extremely bright krypton light and a lithium-powered, long-lasting backup bulb. Rayovac says that with the backup system, the flashlight should work for about 10 years.[8]

Strategic management can also help highlight the need for innovation and provide an organized approach for encouraging new ideas related to strategies.[9] In addition, the process can be used to involve managers at various levels in planning, thus making it more likely that they will understand the resulting plans and be committed to their implementation.

Levels of Strategy

Corporate-level strategy A type of strategy that addresses what businesses the organization will operate, how the strategies of those businesses will be coordinated to strengthen the organization's competitive position, and how resources will be allocated among the businesses

Many organizations develop strategies at three different levels: corporate, business, and functional. The three levels are shown in Figure 7-2.[10]

CORPORATE-LEVEL STRATEGY Corporate-level strategy addresses what businesses the organization will operate, how the strategies of those businesses will be coordinated to strengthen the organization's competitive position, and how resources will be allocated among the businesses. Strategy at this level is typically developed by top management, often with the assistance of strategic planning personnel, at least in large organizations.

The board of directors is also involved in developing corporate-level strategy, although the degree of board participation varies. Within the strategic management process, a board of directors can typically be most helpful by advising on new directions for growth, suggesting when major changes in strategy are needed, and providing input on the timing of major investments.[11]

Figure 7-2 *Levels of strategy. (Adapted from John A. Pearce II and Richard B. Robinson, Jr.,* Strategic Management: Strategy Formulation and Implementation, *3d ed., Irwin, Homewood, Ill., 1988, p. 9.)*

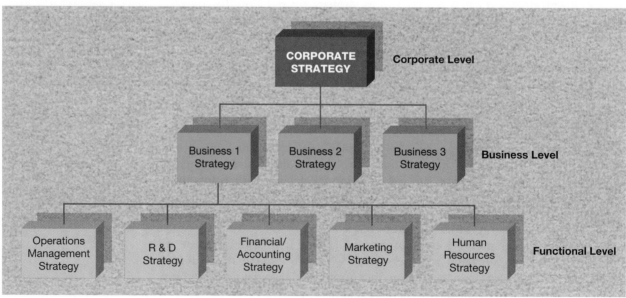

BUSINESS-LEVEL STRATEGY Many organizations include a number of strategic business units. A **strategic business unit (SBU)** is a distinct business, with its own set of competitors, that can be managed relatively independently of other businesses within the organization.[12] **Business-level strategy** concentrates on the best means of competing within a particular business while also supporting the corporate-level strategy. Strategies at this level are aimed at deciding the type of competitive advantage to build, determining responses to changing environmental and competitive conditions, allocating resources within the business unit, and coordinating functional-level strategies. Most often, the heads of the respective business units develop business strategies, although such strategies are typically subject to the approval of top management. When an organization comprises only a single business, corporate-level and business-level strategies are essentially the same. Thus the corporate-level and business-level distinction applies only to organizations with separate divisions that compete in different industries.

Strategic business unit (SBU) A distinct business, with its own set of competitors, that can be managed relatively independently of other businesses within the organization

Business-level strategy A type of strategy that concentrates on the best means of competing within a particular business while also supporting the corporate-level strategy

FUNCTIONAL-LEVEL STRATEGY **Functional-level strategy** focuses on action plans for managing a particular functional area within a business in a way that supports the business-level strategy. Strategies at this level address main directions for each of the major functional areas within a business, such as manufacturing or operations, marketing, finance, human resource management, accounting, research and development, and engineering. Functional-level strategies are important because they often reflect strong functional competencies that can be used to competitive advantage.

Functional-level strategy A type of strategy that focuses on action plans for managing a particular functional area within a business in a way that supports the business-level strategy

COORDINATING LEVELS OF STRATEGY Coordinating strategies across the three levels is critical in maximizing strategic impact. The business-level strategy is enhanced when functional-level strategies support its basic thrust. Similarly, the corporate-level strategy is likely to have greater impact when it is bolstered by business-level strategies that complement one another.[13] Thus the three levels must be closely coordinated as part of the strategic management process.

■ THE ROLE OF COMPETITIVE ANALYSIS IN STRATEGY FORMULATION

Before managers can devise an effective strategy for gaining a competitive edge, they need to carefully analyze the organization's competitive situation. This involves assessing both the environmental and the organizational factors that influence an organization's ability to compete effectively. Such an assessment can be made with SWOT analysis. **SWOT analysis** is a method of analyzing an organization's competitive situation that involves assessing organizational strengths (S) and weaknesses (W), as well as environmental opportunities (O) and threats (T). Identifying strengths and weaknesses requires assessing internal characteristics, while detecting opportunities and threats involves evaluating relevant environmental factors.

SWOT analysis A method of analyzing an organization's competitive situation that involves assessing organizational strengths (S) and weaknesses (W), as well as environmental opportunities (O) and threats (T)

For SWOT analysis purposes, a *strength* is an internal characteristic that has the potential of improving the organization's competitive situation. In contrast, a *weakness* is an internal characteristic that leaves the organization potentially vulnerable to strategic moves by competitors. An *opportunity* is an environmental condition that offers significant prospects for improving an organization's situation relative to competitors. Conversely, a *threat* is an environmental condition that offers significant prospects for undermining an organization's competitive situation.

Environmental Assessment

In analyzing opportunities and threats, managers need to consider elements in the general environment, or mega-environment, that can positively or adversely influence an organization's ability to reach its strategic goals. Such elements are broad factors, including technological, economic, legal-political, sociocultural, and international influences. Managers also need to assess major elements in the organization's task environment, which includes the more specific outside elements with which the organization interfaces in conducting its business. Such elements include customers, competitors, and suppliers. Elements of the general, as well as the task, environment are discussed in detail in Chapter 3.

Five competitive forces model Porter's approach to analyzing the nature and intensity of competition in a given industry in terms of five major forces

PORTER'S FIVE COMPETITIVE FORCES MODEL Strategy expert Michael E. Porter developed the **five competitive forces model** to analyze the nature and intensity of competition in a given industry in terms of five major forces. The forces are rivalry, bargaining power of customers, bargaining power of suppliers, threat of new entrants, and threat of substitute products and services. The collective strength of these forces directly affects the profit potential, or long-term return on investment, available to businesses operating in the particular industry. The major reasons for lower profit potential are summarized in Table 7-1.

Rivalry is the extent to which competitors continually jockey for position by using such tactics as price competition, advertising battles, product introductions, and increased customer service or warranties. All these tactics have the ability to lower profits for the various competitors in the industry either by lowering the prices that can be charged or by raising the costs of doing business. For example, when Post Cereal Co., a division of Philip Morris Cos. and the third largest cereal maker in the United States, announced a 20 percent price cut on all its cereals, competitor Kellogg Co. responded with a price cut of its own 2 months later. Kellogg, the nation's largest cereal maker, was forced to make the price cuts after its market share dropped by 4 percent. Both companies issued statements warning investors to expect reduced earnings per share as a result. Industry observers said that, up to this point, price cuts by cereal makers had been rare. Other cereal manufacturers also were obliged to review their pricing.[14] Thus this situation illustrates Porter's premise that the greater the rivalry, the lower the profit potential for businesses operating in the industry.

The *bargaining power of customers* is the extent to which customers are able

TABLE 7-1 FIVE COMPETITIVE FORCES MODEL	
COMPETITIVE FORCES	**REASONS FOR LOWER PROFIT POTENTIAL**
Rivalry	Various competitive tactics among rivals lower prices that can be charged or raise costs of doing business.
Bargaining power of customers	Customers force price reductions or negotiate increases in product quality and service at the same price.
Bargaining power of suppliers	Suppliers threaten price increases and/or reductions in the quality of goods or services.
Threat of new entrants	New entrants bid prices down or cause incumbents to increase costs in order to maintain market position.
Threat of substitute products or services	Availability of substitutes limits the prices that can be charged.

Source: Based on Michael E. Porter, *Competitive Strategy,* Free Press, New York, 1980, pp. 3–28.

Strong rivalry among competitors poses a threat to a company's plans and goals (and sometimes its existence). Federal Express used to be the acknowledged king of the express mail business. Lately, however, FedEx management has had to cut back on its expansionist goals because of streetfighting with such price-cutting competitors as Airborne Express and DHL. Instead FedEx has been pioneering use of the Internet to provide shipping capability to on-line customers.

to force prices down, bargain for higher quality or more service at the same price, and play competitors against each other. Customers tend to be powerful when the quantities they purchase are large in proportion to a seller's total sales, when the products or services represent a significant portion of a customer's costs, or when the items needed are standard in the supplier industry. For instance, U.S. suppliers in the auto-parts industry have found that they must offer better quality at lower prices than they did in the past to gain orders from Japanese automakers operating plants in the United States. Such measures are necessary particularly because many Japan-based auto-parts suppliers have built U.S. plants, providing alternative sources of supplies.[15] The greater the bargaining power of customers, the lower the profit potential in the industry.

The *bargaining power of suppliers* is the extent to which suppliers can exert power over businesses in an industry by threatening to raise their prices or reduce the quality of their goods and services. Suppliers tend to be powerful when there are only a few of them selling to many businesses in an industry, when there are no substitutes for their products or services, or when their products or services are critical to the buyer's business. The greater the bargaining power of suppliers, the lower the profit potential for businesses operating in the industry.

For example, French makers of champagne are running into difficulties because of a shortage of grape-growing land in the Champagne region of France. The region is famous for producing ideal grapes that have made the sparkling wine increasingly popular throughout the world. Thus suppliers of grapes in that area can command premium prices. To remedy the supply shortage, Moët and other French champagne makers, such as Pommery et Greno and Laurent-Perrier, are purchasing wineries and land suitable for growing grapes in the United States (mainly in California and Oregon), as well as in Australia, Spain, Latin America, and elsewhere. Still, a debate rages over the comparative virtues of grapes grown in France versus those grown in other locations. Some champagne producers argue that top-quality champagne requires grapes from France's Champagne region, affording area growers considerable power as suppliers.[16]

The *threat of new entrants* is the extent to which new competitors can enter the same product or service markets. New entrants bring added capacity and

French vineyard owners in the champagne region of France (shown here) can ask top prices for their grapes because their product is in short supply. French champagne makers have responded by purchasing land for vineyards in other parts of the world. Purists insist, however, that there is no substitute for French grapes in making top-quality champagne.

possibly substantial resources. The results are price wars and/or increases in costs for existing businesses, which frequently must increase expenditures (for additional advertising, a larger sales force, better service, etc.) in order to just maintain market position. The threat of entry depends on how hard it is to break into the market. High barriers to entry exist when large capital investments are required to start a business (as is the case in the steel industry) or when economies of scale make it difficult for a new entrant to start small and gradually build up volume (as with television manufacturing). High barriers also exist when established competitors have products or services that are perceived as unique by loyal customers (e.g., a brand-name perfume).

When barriers to entry are high and new entrants can expect vigorous reaction from existing competitors, the threat of new entrants is low. For example, Anheuser-Busch, the nation's largest brewer, at one point announced that it would start matching the steep discounts that smaller competitors were offering in their attempt to invade some of the brewer's markets. Because of economies of scale, Anheuser-Busch's costs per barrel of beer are substantially lower than those of competitors, giving it heavy ammunition in a price war. With the handwriting on the wall, the smaller brewers quickly discontinued much of their heavy price-cutting.[17] In contrast, when barriers are low and new entrants can expect mild reactions from incumbent competitors, the threat of new entrants is high and, consequently, the profit potential in the industry is low.

The *threat of substitute products or services* is the extent to which businesses in other industries offer substitute products for an established product line. For example, artificial sweeteners can be substituted for sugar, electricity can often be substituted for gas in producing energy, and paint can be substituted for wallpaper. The availability of substitutes constrains the prices that firms in an industry (such as the coffee industry) can charge, since price increases might encourage customers to switch to a substitute (such as Coca-Cola). Already Americans now drink an average of 1.87 cups of coffee a day compared with a peak of 3.12 cups a day in 1962.[18] Thus, the availability of substitute products or services tends to reduce the profit potential in the industry.

HYPERCOMPETITION Conditions in some industries appear to be shifting to hypercompetition.[19] **Hypercompetition** is a state of rapidly escalating competition in which competitors make frequent, daring, and aggressive moves that have the cumulative effect of creating conditions of continual disequilibrium and change in the industry. With hypercompetition, environments spiral to increasingly high levels of uncertainty, dynamism, and heterogeneity of players. Companies attempt to develop sources of competitive advantage more quickly and to undermine competitors' advantages, often in a series of temporary moves aimed at disrupting the status quo and making superior profits at least for a short period.

Hypercompetition makes it more difficult for organizations to sustain competitive advantage. Therefore, companies facing such competitive conditions typically need to disrupt their own competitive advantage by continually innovating. They also need to work aggressively to undermine the competitive advantages enjoyed by their competitors. Methods include continually finding new ways to satisfy customers and then using speed and/or surprise to implement the new ways ahead of the competition. For example, Intel, the Santa Ana, California–based maker of microchips, has greatly increased the speed with which it incorporates new functions in the microprocessors it manufactures for use in personal computers, even though it has more than 80 percent of the market for PC microprocessors. In one instance, Intel has been retooling its microprocessors to include several multimedia and communications functions. These functions were previously performed by products from other manufacturers who made specialized chips to surround the microprocessors on the main circuit board used in PCs. For example, Intel's new microprocessors enable stereo sound and include modems, making it unnecessary to add special auxiliary cards made by other manufacturers to handle these functions.[20]

Hypercompetition A state of rapidly escalating competition in which competitors make frequent, daring, and aggressive moves that have the cumulative effect of creating conditions of continual disequilibrium and change in the industry

Organizational Assessment

While SWOT analysis includes an in-depth assessment of environmental opportunities and threats, it also must involve an evaluation of internal strengths and weaknesses. One useful approach to internal assessment is sometimes referred to as the *resource-based strategic view* of the firm because it focuses on an evalu-

Intel, the microchip maker, controls more than 80 percent of the market for preinstalled microprocessors in personal computers. One of Intel's competitors, Cyrix, planted this tombstone in its headquarters atrium, as a sign it expects to eventually bury its archrival. Meanwhile, Cyrix has run up a legal bill of $20 million in a series of suits and countersuits against Intel.

ation of the competitive implications of an organization's internal resources and capabilities.[21]

An organization's *resources and capabilities* encompass the financial, physical, human, and organizational assets used in producing goods and services. Financial resources include debt, equity, retained earnings, and other money-related matters. Physical resources include buildings, machinery, vehicles, and other material items used to operate. Human resources include the skills, abilities, experience, and other work-related characteristics of the individuals associated with the organization. Organizational resources include the history, relationships, levels of trust, and organizational culture dimensions that are associated with groups within the organization, as well as the organization's formal reporting structure, control systems, and compensation systems.

In the process of assessing the competitive implications of their resources and capabilities relative to their environments, organizations must ask questions related to four major factors of particular importance (see Table 7-2). The four factors are critical to the ability of organizations to build competitive advantage using their internal resources and capabilities.

The first critical factor is *value*. A resource or capability adds value to the extent that it enables the organization to capitalize on opportunities and/or nullify threats. For example, Sony Corp. possesses specialized expertise in designing, manufacturing, and marketing miniaturized electronic technology. Sony has been able to use this expertise to produce a variety of successful products, including portable tape players, portable disc players, and easy-to-handle video cameras, ahead of competitors.

The second significant factor is *rareness*. A resource or capability is rare to the extent that it is uncommon among competing firms. A valuable resource or capability that is commonly possessed by other competing firms is typically a source of competitive parity—that is, necessary to equal competitors on a given dimension. Partially because Sony maintains and builds the expertise through relatively large expenditures for research and development, the depth of expertise has remained uncommon among competing firms.

The third pivotal factor is *degree of imitability*. A resource or capability has a low degree of imitability when it is difficult for competing firms to duplicate it or find a substitution for it. Duplication occurs when a competing firm builds the same type of resources or capabilities as the organization it is imitating. Substitution arises when a competing firm is able to create an equivalent resource or capability that is no more costly to develop. Although competitors have been able to relatively quickly reverse-engineer new Sony products and develop competing offerings, Sony's ability to achieve initially high profits by

TABLE 7-2 RESOURCE-BASED STRATEGIC FACTORS AND QUESTIONS

FACTORS	RELATED QUESTIONS
Value	Do a firm's resources and capabilities add value by enabling it to exploit opportunities and/or neutralize threats?
Rareness	How many competing firms already possess these valuable resources and capabilities?
Imitability	Do firms without a resource or capability face a cost disadvantage in obtaining it compared to firms that already possess it?
Organization	Is a firm organized to exploit the full competitive potential of its resources and capabilities?

Source: Based on Jay B. Barney, "Looking Inside for Competitive Advantage," *Academy of Management Executive,* vol. 9, no. 4, 1995, pp. 49–61.

being first with a stream of innovative new products has afforded the company sustained competitive advantage.

The fourth important factor is *organization*. An organization's competitive advantage depends on the value, rareness, and imitability of its resources and capabilities. To implement this competitive advantage, however, requires that a firm be organized to maximize the usefulness of its resources and capabilities. Organizational components, such as formal reporting structures, control systems, and reward systems, are considered to be complementary resources because they have limited ability to create competitive advantage by themselves. However, they can work effectively in combination with other resources and capabilities to maximize competitive advantage. For example, Sony's encouragement of collaboration across various units with expertise in miniaturized electronic technology (such as tape recorders and earphones) helped leverage Sony's collective expertise in miniaturized electronics to produce innovative new products. As Sony attempts to move into the digital era, the company has been experiencing more difficulty with organizational issues. It is struggling to achieve competitive advantage by effectively combining its hardware expertise with its growing software-related entertainment empire including its Sony Music Entertainment (formerly CBS Records) and its Sony Pictures Entertainment (formerly Columbia Pictures).[22]

Sustained competitive advantage cannot be attained solely by analyzing environmental factors and attempting to develop businesses in industries in which the competitive forces are favorable. Instead, achieving sustained competitive advantage also depends on developing resources and capabilities that are valuable, rare, and difficult to imitate. A resource or capability that is valuable, rare, and difficult to imitate is sometimes called a **distinctive competence.** Organization factors that facilitate effective exploitation of distinctive competencies also are critical to building competitive advantage. (Note that the resource-based strategic view discussed here has some conceptual connections with the resource dependence model addressed in Chapter 3. The resource dependence model, though, focuses on reducing dependence on the environment by attempting to control as many critically needed resources as possible. On the other hand, the resource-based strategic view emphasizes the need to develop internal resources and capabilities that can provide sustained competitive advantage. Thus the two perspectives are somewhat complementary in helping managers focus on important issues involving organization resources and effectiveness.) Carefully conducted organizational and environmental assessments set the stage for developing corporate-level strategies.

Distinctive competence A strength that is unique and that competitors cannot easily match or imitate

■ FORMULATING CORPORATE-LEVEL STRATEGY

Corporate-level strategy comprises the overall strategy that an organization will follow. Its development generally involves selecting a grand strategy and using portfolio strategy approaches to determine the various businesses that will make up the organization.

Grand Strategies

A **grand strategy** (sometimes called a *master strategy*) provides the basic strategic direction at the corporate level.[23] There are several generic types, which can be grouped into three basic categories: growth, stability, and defensive grand strategies.[24] These strategies and their major subcategories are shown in Figure 7-3.

Grand strategy A master strategy that provides the basic strategic direction at the corporate level

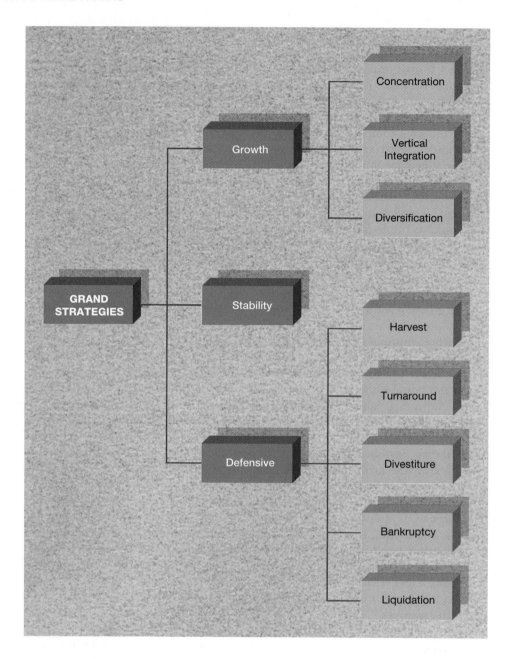

Figure 7-3 *Types of grand strategies.*

Growth strategies Grand strategies that involve organizational expansion along some major dimension

Concentration An approach that focuses on effecting the growth of a single product or service or a small number of closely related products or services

GROWTH Growth strategies are grand strategies that involve organizational expansion along some major dimension. In business organizations, growth typically means increasing sales and earnings, although other criteria (such as number of geographic locations) are possible. Not-for-profit organizations can grow in terms of revenue, clients served, or other criteria. Three major growth strategies are concentration, vertical integration, and diversification.

Concentration focuses on effecting the growth of a single product or service or a small number of closely related products or services. Concentration usually takes place through *market development* (gaining a larger share of a current market or expanding into new ones), *product development* (improving a basic product or service or expanding into closely related products or services), or *horizontal integration* (adding one or more businesses that are similar, usually by purchasing such businesses). For example, France-based Groupe Michelin engaged in horizontal integration when it took over the Uniroyal Goodrich Tire Company, making Michelin the world's largest tire manufacturer. Indicative of its strategy of high concentration, more than 90 percent of Michelin's annual sales are based on tires.[25]

Vertical integration involves effecting growth through the production of inputs previously provided by suppliers or through the replacement of a customer role (such as that of a distributor) by disposing of one's own outputs. When a business grows by becoming its own supplier, the process is known as *backward integration*.[26] One interesting organization that is prospering partially through backward integration is PGA Tour, Inc., the professional golf association. In the early 1970s, its annual revenues from professional golfing events were $3.1 million. Today, annual revenues top $100 million. This is partly because the Tour now owns, operates, or licenses more than 13 courses and clubs used each year for Tour events. The remainder of the time, the courses and clubs are available to members, who pay dues. Thus the Tour not only has become its own supplier of sites for tournaments but also receives revenues. In addition, it often receives close to 20 percent of the gains from residential development on certain properties next to courses.[27]

When organizational growth encompasses a role previously fulfilled by a customer, the process is known as *forward integration*. Authentic Fitness Corp., a swimsuit and sports apparel company that is a subsidiary of Warnaco, recently engaged in forward integration by opening Speedo Authentic Fitness stores.[28] This move has enabled the company to sell directly to consumers, rather than selling exclusively through department stores and outlets owned by others. According to one study, organizations are more likely to use a vertical integration strategy when product or service demand is reasonably certain, rather than highly uncertain.[29]

Diversification entails effecting growth through the development of new areas that are clearly distinct from current businesses. In addition to diversifying for growth reasons, organizations often diversify to reduce the risk that can be associated with single-product or single-industry operations.[30] There are two types of diversification: conglomerate and concentric. *Conglomerate diversification* takes place when an organization diversifies into areas that are unrelated to its current business. Organizations that adopt a conglomerate diversification strategy are often referred to as *conglomerates*. For example, Rockwell International Corp., an $11 billion conglomerate, receives about 48 percent of its revenues from electronics and industrial automation, 26 percent from automotive components, 20 percent from aerospace, and 6 percent from printing presses. Some of the businesses are metal fabrication companies that bend, weld, and fuse metals into components for cars, trucks, and aircraft fuselages. Others are high-technology companies involved in telecommunications and industrial automation. The company hopes to gain synergy among the different businesses by using the high technology from some of the companies to keep the metal fabrication companies at the forefront of their industries.[31] Because of the variety of businesses involved, conglomerates can be difficult for top management to administrate effectively. *Concentric diversification* occurs when an organization diversifies into a related, but distinct, business. With concentric diversification, businesses can be related through products, markets, or technology. In the case of The Limited, Inc., the concentric diversification involved related products, mainly women's clothing (see the Case in Point discussion).

Vertical integration An approach that involves effecting growth through the production of inputs previously provided by suppliers or through the replacement of a customer role by disposing of one's own outputs

Diversification An approach that entails effecting growth through the development of new areas that are clearly distinct from current businesses

CASE IN POINT   **THE UNLIMITED LIMITED**

When Leslie Wexner opened his first women's clothing store in Columbus, Ohio, in 1963 with a $5000 stake, few would have predicted that the shop was the beginning of a major women's clothing empire. Wexner called his first shop "The Limited" because it offered only women's sportswear. He got the idea of specializing after working in his parents' clothing store and noticing that office garments and fancy dresses did not sell nearly as fast as sportswear. When he attempted to persuade his parents to concentrate on sportswear and eliminate the other merchandise, they insisted that the shop needed a wide variety of clothing to attract customers. In fact, his father told him: "You'll never be a merchant." Within a year, the son's new shop proved to be so successful that the parents closed their store and joined forces with their "merchant" son. By 1969, when The Limited, Inc., made a public stock offering, Wexner had opened six stores. By the end of the 1980s there were more than 700 stores under The Limited umbrella; today there are several thousand.

Along with the growth of The Limited stores, there have been shifts in emphasis. Since The Limited originally targeted women between 15 and 25, Wexner found that he was losing his customers as they grew older. Accordingly, he repositioned The Limited to appeal to women in the 20-to-35 age bracket, and he started a new chain, the Express, to appeal to teenagers and women in their early twenties.

In order to keep the company growing at a fast pace, Wexner has expanded into other areas related to women's clothing. For example, he bought a small chain of lingerie stores, called Victoria's Secret, with annual sales of $7 million and has expanded it into a fast-growing chain. He purchased the Lane Bryant stores and eliminated the tall and largest sizes because of the relatively small market. Instead, he expanded offerings in sizes 14 through 20, noting that 40 percent of women are size 14 or larger.

Next, Wexner bought the huge Lerner chain. It was close to bankruptcy, owing largely to poor management, including abysmal inventory control. Lerner now carries the same type of merchandise found in The Limited stores, but the items are geared to a lower-priced market. Wexner also bought Abercrombie & Fitch, a chain that sells men's and women's sportswear and gift items. In 1990 he opened the Structure, a men's apparel chain, created as part of The Limited's strategy of having several stores colocated in shopping centers. Wexner then opened four more new chains: Cacique, a more conservative women's lingerie chain than Victoria's Secret; Penhaligon's, based in London and a specialty retailer of English luxury personal care and related gift products; Limited Too, aimed at girls; and Bath & Body Works, a women's cosmetics chain. Recently purchased Henri Bendel, an upscale New York boutique known for its exclusive and less widely available labels from newer designer, cosmetics, and accessory firms, is slated to expand from 4 stores to 50 by the turn of the century.

Lately though, Wexner's $7 billion empire has had to scramble to keep profits up in the face of fierce competition and a general slowdown in women's apparel sales. Wexner says he has discovered that he is better at spotting trends and starting new businesses than dealing with the operation details of running them. As a result, he is going to delegate more and is also breaking the company into clusters to facilitate better management. Wexner has spun off some units as Intimate Brands, a separate lingerie and personal care company 83 percent owned by The Limited. Intimate Brands contains Bath & Body Works, Victoria's Secret stores, Victoria's Secret catalog, Penhaligon's, and Cacique. Intimate Brands has been making efforts to distribute its personal care items through other retailers and is running tests at Sears, Roebuck & Co. and Walt Disney's specialty stores. Meanwhile he has clustered The Limited, Express, Lerner, Henri Bendel, and Lane Bryant stores into one group. Abercrombie & Fitch, Structure, and Limited Too operate as a second group.[32]   ■■■

All three growth strategies, including the diversification approach used by The Limited, can be implemented through internal growth or through acquisition, merger, or joint venture. With internal growth the organization expands by building on its own internal resources. The organization's core characteristics can be coupled with changes in technology and marketing, resulting in increased profit and growth.[33] An **acquisition** is the purchase of all or part of one organization by another, while a **merger** is the combining of two or more companies into one organization (see Chapter 11). Finally, a joint venture occurs when two or more organizations provide resources to support a given project or product offering (see Chapter 3). Thus there are several alternative routes to implementing particular growth strategies.

Acquisition The purchase of all or part of one organization by another

Merger The combining of two or more companies into one organization

STABILITY A **stability strategy** involves maintaining the status quo or growing in a methodical, but slow, manner. Organizations might choose a stability strategy for a number of reasons. For instance, if a company is doing reasonably well, managers may not want the risks or hassles associated with more aggressive growth. This is often the case in small, privately owned businesses, which constitute the largest group likely to adopt a strategy of stability. For example, Bob Sidell started California Cosmetics after formulating special cosmetics to cope with the skin problems of teenage actors appearing in the TV show *The Waltons*. Within 3 years, Sidell and his partner, Paula Levey, had developed their mail-order operation into a company with annual sales of $10 million. Such fast growth, though, brought botched orders, rising complaints, and returns and nondeliveries in the 17 percent range. After some initial cutbacks to gain stability, the company plans to grow much more slowly. "We'll probably never be the richest folks on the block," says Levey. "But we're going to be around years from now."[34] Another reason for choosing stability is that it provides a chance to recover. An organization that stretched its resources during a period of accelerated growth may need to attain stability before it attempts further accelerated growth. On the other hand, if managers believe that growth prospects are low, they may choose a stability strategy in an attempt to hold on to current market share. (Worsening situations, however, may call for defensive strategies.) Finally, a stability strategy may even occur through default if managers are unconcerned with their strategic direction.

Stability strategy A strategy that involves maintaining the status quo or growing in a methodical, but slow, manner

DEFENSIVE **Defensive strategies** (sometimes called *retrenchment strategies*) focus on the desire or need to reduce organizational operations, usually through cost reductions (such as cutting back on nonessential expenditures and instituting hiring freezes) and/or asset reductions (such as selling land, equipment, and businesses).[35] Defensive strategies include harvest, turnaround, divestiture, bankruptcy, and liquidation.

Harvest entails minimizing investments while attempting to maximize short-run profits and cash flow, with the long-run intention of exiting the market.[36] A harvest strategy is often used when future growth in the market is doubtful or will require investments that do not appear to be cost-effective. For example, the vacuum-tube market collapsed because of the late 1940s' invention of the transistor and subsequent advanced solid-state circuitry. Consequently, many large producers of vacuum tubes (e.g., Western Electric, General

Defensive strategies Strategies that focus on the desire or need to reduce organizational operations, usually through cost and/or asset reductions

Harvest A strategy that entails minimizing investments while attempting to maximize short-run profits and cash flow, with the long-run intention of exiting the market

In the early 1990s, Sears, which was experiencing slow growth due to some lackluster merchandise and a failed multibrand, low price strategy, underwent a spectacular turnaround. Its new CEO, Arthur Martinez (shown here inspecting a Sears store), took drastic action: he closed a number of stores, got rid of the Sears catalog, and focused the company's sights on the working woman.

Electric, and Westinghouse) gradually phased out their production.[37] With a harvest strategy, the resulting short-run profits are often used to build other businesses with better future prospects.

Turnaround A strategy designed to reverse a negative trend and restore the organization to appropriate levels of profitability

A **turnaround** is designed to reverse a negative trend and restore the organization to appropriate levels of profitability. Such efforts often require at least temporary reductions in order to conserve funds. (The term "turnaround" is sometimes used more loosely to denote a major shift from a negative direction to a positive one.) A **divestiture** involves an organization's selling or divesting of a business or part of a business. According to one study, when divestitures are congruent with the corporate or business strategies outlined in company publications, they have a positive effect on the price of the firm's stock. Conversely, when divestitures are conducted in the absence of clear strategic goals, they generally have a negative market effect.[38]

Divestiture A strategy that involves an organization's selling or divesting of a business or part of a business

Bankruptcy A strategy in which an organization that is unable to pay its debts can seek court protection from creditors and from certain contract obligations while it attempts to regain financial stability

Under Chapter 11 of the Federal Bankruptcy Act, **bankruptcy** is a means whereby an organization that is unable to pay its debts can seek court protection from creditors and from certain contract obligations while it attempts to regain financial stability. For example, Federated Department Stores, which operated several department store chains, including Bloomingdale's, Abraham & Straus in New York, and Rich's in Atlanta, filed for bankruptcy when its parent company, Canada-based Campeau Corporation, ran into a cash-flow problem in 1990. Federated emerged from the largest bankruptcy in retail history and went on to acquire two other high profile chains in financial trouble: Macy's and Los Angeles–based Broadway Stores.[39] **Liquidation** entails dissolving an organization by disposing of all its assets and settling its remaining debts. Liquidation usually occurs when serious difficulties, such as bankruptcy, cannot be resolved.

Liquidation A strategy that entails selling or dissolving an entire organization

Portfolio Strategy Approaches

Portfolio strategy approach A method of analyzing an organization's mix of businesses in terms of both individual and collective contributions to strategic goals

While grand strategies address an organization's overall direction, portfolio strategy approaches help managers determine the types of businesses in which the organization should be engaged. More specifically, a **portfolio strategy approach** is a method of analyzing an organization's mix of businesses in terms of both individual and collective contributions to strategic goals. The concept is similar to the approach an individual takes when attempting to assemble a group, or portfolio, of stocks that will provide balance in terms of risk, long-term growth, and other important factors. Two of the most frequently used portfolio approaches are the BCG growth-share matrix and the product/market evolution matrix. Each uses a two-dimensional matrix, which measures one variable along one dimension and another along a second dimension to form four or more cells. Portfolio approaches apply to analyzing existing or potential strategic business units.

BCG GROWTH-SHARE MATRIX One of the earliest portfolio approaches to gain extensive use is the four-cell matrix developed by the Boston Consulting Group (BCG), a prominent management consulting firm. The **BCG growth-share matrix,** shown in Figure 7-4, compares various businesses in an organization's portfolio on the basis of relative market share and market growth rate. Relative market share is the ratio of a business's market share (in terms of unit volume) compared with the market share of its largest rival. Market growth rate is the growth in the market during the previous year relative to growth in the economy as a whole.[40] In the BCG matrix shown in Figure 7-4, each business, represented by a circle, is plotted on the matrix according to its position along both dimensions. The size of the circle indicates the business's percent revenue relative to the revenues generated by other businesses in the portfolio. The resulting matrix divides the businesses into four categories.

The *star* has a high market share in a rapidly growing market. Because of their high growth potential, stars often initially require substantial investment capital beyond what they are able to earn themselves. For example, General Electric spent $2.3 billion to acquire a chemical business that was part of the Borg-Warner Corporation. Combined with GE's other chemical operations, this acquisition gave GE a larger presence and a star in the fast-growing plastics business.[41]

BCG growth-share matrix A four-cell matrix (developed by the Boston Consulting Group) that compares various businesses in an organization's portfolio on the basis of relative market share and market growth rate

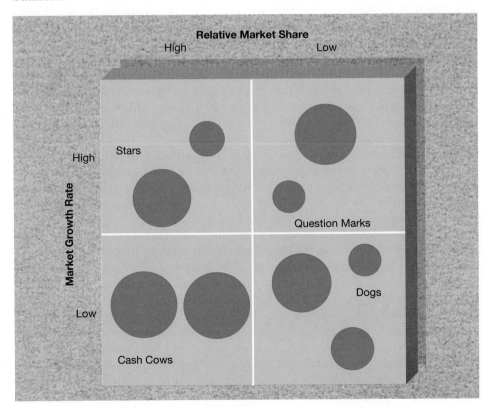

Figure 7-4 *BCG growth-share matrix.*

A *question mark* (often also called a *problem child*) has a low market share in a rapidly growing market. Question marks present somewhat of a dilemma for their organizations. Like stars, they require substantial investment to take advantage of the rapidly growing market, yet their low market share usually means that they have limited ability to generate large amounts of cash themselves. Thus, they are "cash hogs." For example, Cincinnati-headquartered Roto-Rooter, Inc., is best known as a service that uses a motor-driven auger to unclog drains and sewer lines. Since the early 1980s, the company has been attempting to expand into residential plumbing repair work and industrial pipe cleaning. So far, the company has captured more than 1 percent of the plumbing market, but it will take considerable further funding to build up what might be the first large national plumbing company.[42] With question marks, managers must usually either provide substantial cash to fuel growth or divest the business.

The *cash cow* has a high market share in a slowly growing market. As a result, it tends to generate more cash than is necessary to maintain its market position. Cash cows, often former stars, can be valuable in a portfolio because they can be "milked" to provide cash for stars and question marks. For instance, the drain-cleaning business of Roto-Rooter provides excess cash that has been used to open new company outlets and buy back old franchises to facilitate the buildup of the plumbing business.[43]

A *dog* has a low market share in an area of low growth. Thus it typically generates only a modest cash flow or may even have a small negative cash flow. Usually, dogs are harvested, divested, or liquidated. For example, General Electric sold a consumer electronics division that was only marginally profitable to the French electronics giant Thomson S.A. Thomson was interested in the acquisition as a means of acquiring operations in the United States.[44]

Overall, the BCG matrix suggests using revenues from cash cows to fund the growth of stars, as well as to build the market share of the question marks with the best prospects. Dogs and the remaining question marks are usually divested unless they provide sufficient positive cash flow to justify retaining them, at least in the short run. One recent study suggests that dogs may generate more cash than they are generally given credit for and that managers, therefore, should evaluate them carefully before taking the divestiture step.[45]

The BCG matrix has a number of shortcomings.[46] Among the most important is that it does not directly pertain to the majority of businesses that have average market shares in markets of average growth (note that the matrix has only two categories, high and low, for each dimension). In addition, generalizations based on the matrix may be misleading, since organizations with low market shares are not necessarily question marks. For example, at Germany-based Daimler-Benz, managers raise car production only after careful debate, lest the Mercedes lose its exclusive image.[47] Similarly, businesses with large market shares in slow growth markets are not necessarily cash cows. Some may actually need substantial investments to retain their market position. For example, Nabisco Brands (a division of RJR Nabisco) has about 45 percent of the U.S. cookie (e.g., Oreos) and cracker (e.g., Ritz) markets, with both markets growing relatively slowly. Still, RJR Nabisco had planned to spend $4 billion in capital investments to retain the division's position as a low-cost producer. The expenditures were placed on hold in 1989 because Nabisco had to pay off massive debts associated with its takeover by the investment firm of Kohlberg, Kravis, Roberts & Company. When Nabisco's popular SnackWell line of low-fat cookies, especially its Devil's Food Cake cookie, was first introduced, the company did not have sufficient manufacturing capacity to keep up with consumer demand.[48] Another shortcoming of the matrix is that it provides little guidance regarding which question marks to support and which dogs to salvage. Finally, one survey suggests that executives dislike the BCG terminology. According to one executive, "We try to avoid the use of words such as 'cash cow' or 'dog' like the plague. If you call a business a dog, it'll respond like one. It's one thing to know that you are an ugly duckling; much worse to be told explicitly that you are."[49] Despite these shortcomings, the BCG matrix does have research support in regard to its ability to differentiate among businesses for purposes of thinking about strategy.[50] Still, the matrix does not specify the strategies that should be followed by various businesses, nor does it provide a means for identifying businesses that are just about to move into a period of high growth.[51]

PRODUCT/MARKET EVOLUTION MATRIX To facilitate identifying companies, particularly new businesses, that are about to accelerate their growth, strategy researcher Charles W. Hofer has suggested a matrix refinement.[52] The **product/market evolution matrix** (sometimes called the *life-cycle portfolio matrix*) is a 15-cell matrix in which businesses are plotted according to the business unit's strength, or competitive position, and the industry's stage in the evolutionary product/market life cycle (see Figure 7-5). The first dimension, the business unit's competitive position, is similar to the relative market share of the BCG matrix, but includes an average category. On the second dimension, however, the two approaches differ. Whereas the BCG matrix measures market growth rate, the product/market evolution matrix shows the industry's stage in the evo-

Product/market evolution matrix A 15-cell matrix (developed by Hofer) in which businesses are plotted according to the business unit's business strength, or competitive position, and the industry's stage in the evolutionary product/market life cycle

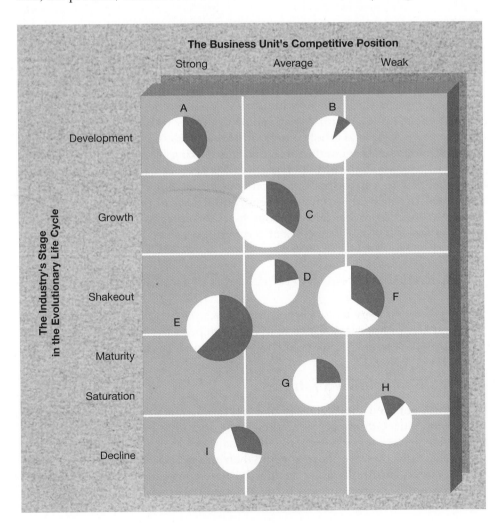

Figure 7-5 *Product/market evolution matrix.*

lutionary life cycle. This starts with initial development and proceeds through the growth, competitive shakeout, maturity and saturation, and decline stages. The maturity and saturation stage is particularly important because it often lasts for an extended period of time. An industry is said to have reached *maturity* when growth slows and the market moves toward the saturation point, where demand is limited to replacement of the product or service.[53] The challenge in the maturity and saturation stage is preserving or slowly expanding market share while avoiding the decline stage.[54]

On the grid, each business is represented by a circle, with the size of the circle proportional to the size of the industry (measured by total industry sales) in which the business competes. (Note that the meaning of the circle differs from that in the BCG matrix, in which the circle represents the business's percent revenue relative to the revenues generated by other portfolio businesses.) The pie slice within the circle shows the business's market share within the industry.

The data shown in Figure 7-5 suggest that business A has good prospects for growth and should be developed. Business B is in a rather weak competitive position and likely would be considered a question mark in BCG matrix terminology. Business E is well established and would be considered a star, although it is moving toward maturity. Business F is gradually losing its competitive position but is a probable cash cow. Business H is most likely a candidate for divesting or liquidating and would be considered a dog.

ASSESSING THE PORTFOLIO MATRIXES Each portfolio matrix offers a somewhat different perspective that is likely to be useful in the strategy formulation process. Therefore, it is possible to use one or both to enhance thinking about the mix of businesses in an organization's portfolio. For example, South Korea–based Samsung Group has recently been using the portfolio approach to diversify into a variety of new industries. Among other things, the company has signed agreements with Nissan Motor Company to build cars and France's Eurocopter S.A. to make helicopters. It acquired Union Optical Co., a Japan-based semiconductor manufacturer, and was looking for microchip fabrication plants, which cost about $1 billion each, in Europe, Asia, and the United States. The plan was to expand its operations outside of South Korea using money generated largely by the company's semiconductor group.[55] Portfolio matrixes, however, do not provide advice about specific strategies for businesses. Such specifics are covered by strategies at the business level.

■ FORMULATING BUSINESS-LEVEL STRATEGY

Business-level strategy is concerned with how a particular business competes. The best-known approach for developing strategy at the SBU level is based on the research of strategy expert Michael E. Porter.

Porter's Competitive Strategies

Porter has outlined three generic business-level strategies that can be used to gain competitive advantage over other firms operating in the same industry.[56] The strategies are termed "generic" because they are applicable to a variety of situations. Still, they are more specific than the generic corporate-level strategies discussed in the previous section. Porter's competitive strategies are cost leadership, differentiation, and focus. Common requirements for successfully pursuing these strategies are summarized in Table 7-3.

TABLE 7-3 COMMON REQUIREMENTS FOR SUCCESSFULLY PURSUING PORTER'S COMPETITIVE STRATEGIES

GENERIC STRATEGY	COMMONLY REQUIRED SKILLS AND RESOURCES	COMMON ORGANIZATIONAL REQUIREMENTS
Overall cost leadership	Sustained capital investment and access to capital Process engineering skills Intense supervision of labor Products designed for ease in manufacture Low-cost distribution system	Tight cost control Frequent, detailed control reports Structured organization and responsibilities Incentives based on meeting strict quantitative targets
Differentiation	Strong marketing abilities Product engineering Creative flair Strong capability in basic research Corporate reputation for quality or technological leadership Long tradition in the industry or unique combination of skills drawn from other businesses Strong cooperation from channels	Strong coordination among functions in R&D, product development, and marketing Subjective measurement and incentives instead of quantitative measures Amenities to attract highly skilled labor, scientists, or creative people
Focus	Combination of the above policies directed at the particular strategic target	Combination of the above policies directed at the particular strategic target

Source: Reprinted from Michael E. Porter, *Competitive Strategy,* Free Press, New York, 1980, pp. 40–41.

COST LEADERSHIP A **cost leadership strategy** involves emphasizing organizational efficiency so that the overall costs of providing products and services are lower than those of competitors. With this low-cost approach, careful attention must be paid to minimizing necessary costs in every aspect of the business. This entails developing efficient production methods, keeping tight controls on overhead and administrative costs, seeking savings by procuring supplies at low prices, and monitoring costs in other areas (such as promotion, distribution, and service). Lower costs enable an organization to offer lower prices and thus gain an edge over competitors. They can also lead to above-average profits because of higher profit margins or large sales volumes. For instance, Union Carbide has positioned itself as the low-cost producer of polyethylene and ethylene glycol—ingredients used in a wide variety of products ranging from garbage bags to polyester to antifreeze. Prices of the two commodities have been rising. According to one estimate, each time polyethylene prices rise 1 cent per pound, Union Carbide adds 15 cents profit per share.[57]

For a cost leadership strategy to be effective, lower costs cannot come at the expense of necessary quality. The H. J. Heinz Company learned this lesson when its low-cost strategy led to difficulties at its Ore-Ida division. Cost-cutting efforts related to the strategy caused changes in manufacturing methods for popular Tater Tots frozen spuds. As a result, the Tater Tot insides were mushy and the outsides had lost their light and crispy coating. Ultimately, sales began to decline. With the changes reversed, Tater Tots captured more than 55 percent of the market for frozen fried potatoes.[58]

A low-cost strategy is not without risks. To be effective, the strategy usually requires that a business be *the* cost leader, not just one of several. Two or more businesses vying for cost leadership can engage in a rivalry that drives profits down to extremely low levels. Therefore, the business must have a cost advantage that is not easily or inexpensively imitated, and it must stay abreast of new technologies that can alter the cost curve. In addition, managers must still consider making some product or service innovations, at least the ones that are

Cost leadership strategy A strategy outlined by Porter that involves emphasizing organizational efficiency so that the overall costs of providing products and services are lower than those of competitors

Fewer babies are being born these days, which means that diaper makers are facing a maturing market: growth is slow and the saturation point is near. Kimberly-Clark's Wayne R. Sanders came up with a unique product—Huggies Pull-Ups—to help preserve its position as industry leader. The Pull-Ups use a stretchy fabric in a diaper that a child can easily pull up and down, making the toilet-training process easier.

very important to customers. Otherwise, competitors using a differentiation strategy may lure customers away with significant product or service improvements.

Differentiation strategy A strategy outlined by Porter that involves attempting to develop products and services that are viewed as unique in the industry

DIFFERENTIATION A **differentiation strategy** involves attempting to develop products and services that are viewed as unique in the industry. Successful differentiation allows the business to charge premium prices, leading to above-average profits. Differentiation can take many forms; for example, design or brand image (Coach in handbags, Ralph Lauren in menswear), technology (Hewlett-Packard in laser printers, Coleman in camping equipment), customer service (IBM in computers, Nordstrom in apparel retailing), features (Jenn-Air in ranges), quality (Xerox in copiers, Swarovski in rhinestones), and selection (Echlin in auto parts). The businesses making up the Walt Disney Company (see the chapter opening case) generally follow a differentiation strategy, mainly associated with the Disney characters, culture, and name. With differentiation, perceptions of product or service uniqueness are more important than costs. However, a company still cannot afford to ignore costs.

There are a few vulnerabilities associated with a differentiation strategy. If prices are too high, customers may choose less costly alternatives, even though they forgo some desirable features. Also, customer tastes and needs can change, so businesses following a differentiation strategy must carefully assess customers' shifting requirements. Differentiation, of course, works best when the differentiating factor is both important to customers and difficult for competitors to imitate. While differentiation is usually aimed at a fairly broad market, a focus strategy concentrates on a narrow niche.

Focus strategy A strategy outlined by Porter that entails specializing by establishing a position of overall cost leadership, differentiation, or both, but only within a particular portion, or segment, of an entire market

FOCUS A **focus strategy** entails specializing by establishing a position of overall cost leadership, differentiation, or both, but only within a particular portion, or segment, of an entire market. The segment may be a group of customers, a geographic area, or a part of the product or service line. The rationale is that a market segment can be served more effectively by an organization that specializes than by competitors that attempt to cover the entire market. The focus strategy still relies on a low-cost or a differentiation approach, or perhaps both, to establish a strong position within the particular market segment, or niche. Differentiation within a focus strategy can occur by tailoring products to the specialized needs of the market segment. This may simultaneously produce a cost advantage, since a firm that specializes may be able to offer better prices on custom orders than a firm that has the cost of leadership in serving the larger-volume needs of the broader market. A company that has successfully used a focus strategy is Baxters of Speyside (see the Case in Point discussion).

BAXTERS OF SPEYSIDE FOCUSES ON SPECIALTY FOODS

CASE IN POINT

"We take the produce of the hills and glens of Bonnie Scotland and make beautiful things," says Gordon Baxter, president, summing up the basic approach that has made Scotland's specialty food producer, Baxters of Speyside, a major success. Baxters of Speyside has become a popular brand name in Britain and is increasingly well known elsewhere for its premium soups, jams, and other specialties. For example, the company offers soups with such intriguing names as Cream of Pheasant, Cream of Scampi, Cock-a-Leekie, and Royal Game. These innovative products have helped establish the company's reputation in Britain's premium-food market, where overseas customers are willing to pay as much as twice the price of competing brands for Baxters specialties. Baxter's wife, Ena, developed most of the exotic recipes. Now, a team of chefs and food technologists help her.

The family-run company, with annual sales topping $70 million, has evolved from a grocery store founded in 1868 by Baxter's grandfather. Baxter's father added a jam factory and began selling items to two of Britain's best-known department stores, Harrods and Fortnum & Mason, during the 1920s and 1930s. After the company nearly went out of business during World War II, Baxter and his brother rebuilt and expanded it. Recently the three children of Gordon and Ena Baxter—Audrey, Andrew, and Michael—have taken over

It started in 1868 as a grocery store in a tiny town in the Scottish highlands; today Baxters of Speyside sells about $40 million worth of soups, jams, and specialty foods worldwide each year. Baxters has been so successful because the firm never lost sight of its special segment of the market—premium foods. Baxters' family proprietorship and exotic recipes help to differentiate the firm and are an important part of the company's focus strategy.

managing most of the day-to-day operations of the company, adding a fourth generation of involvement.

Capitalizing on its unusual products and location, Gordon Baxter and his entourage often wear kilts and even bring along bagpipes on sales trips to the United States. "Scotland is very projectable," he says. According to one salesperson at Harrods in London, Baxters of Speyside products sell partly because customers visualize the product being carefully stirred by hand in a pot, even though the foods are made in a modern factory.

Sales began to grow significantly when Baxter was able to persuade some of Britain's chain retailers to carry the premium brand. As a result, the company has about 77 percent of Britain's premium soup market.

With only about 4 percent of its total sales in the United States, the potential for growth is great. Not surprisingly, Baxter's files contain letters from many U.S. companies, such as General Foods, General Mills, Campbell, and Heinz, expressing interest in purchasing Baxters of Speyside. Baxters operates within its cash flow; the company has no debt. The Baxter family owns 96.5 percent of the shares. Profit margins are above the industry average.[59]　　■ ■ ■

Despite the success of Baxters of Speyside, adopting a focus strategy involves several risks that a business needs to guard against. For one thing, costs for the focused firm may become too great relative to those of less focused competitors. As time goes on, differentiation can become less of an advantage, since competitors serving broader markets may embellish their products. In addition, competitors may begin focusing on a group *within* the customer population being served by the focused firm. For example, Roadway Package Systems (RPS) is attempting to invade the market for door-to-door ground delivery of packages, currently dominated by United Parcel Service (UPS). RPS signs contracts with individuals, who lease or buy distinctive white RPS delivery trucks. Each individual picks up and delivers packages in a particular territory for RPS. These independents are paid only for work performed, whereas UPS employees typically receive higher unionized wages and generous benefits. While UPS limits packages to 70 pounds and delivers to residents as well as businesses, RPS has set a 100-pound limit and restricts delivery to businesses. The company began in 1985 as a small operation with 36 package terminals; today it is a $1 billion company with 339 facilities that serve virtually all the United States and parts of Canada.[60]

There is growing evidence that it may be possible to combine two strategies at once, although such combinations are difficult to achieve.[61] At Euclid, Ohio–based Lincoln Electric Co. worker productivity is so high that the company is able to offer high-quality arc-welding equipment and motors at relatively low prices. Part of the reason is the company's piece-rate pay system whereby workers are paid based on what they produce.[62] Regardless of which generic strategy is used, the ability to carry it out successfully depends on distinctive competencies. Such competencies typically develop at the functional level.

■ FORMULATING FUNCTIONAL-LEVEL STRATEGY

Functional-level strategies spell out the specific ways that functional areas can be used to bolster the business-level strategy. For example, under a product differentiation strategy, the R&D department might be called upon to accelerate the innovation process in order to provide new products in advance of the competition. Similarly, to support the new product lines, marketing might develop a plan that calls for premium prices, distribution through prestigious locations, and a special promotion scheme aimed at targeted market segments. Operations, the function that is responsible for actually producing the product, might devise a functional strategy based on using excellent raw materials, incorporating the latest technology, and subcontracting some components in order to produce a premium product.

In essence, strategies at the functional level can be extremely important in supporting a business-level strategy. Typically, the functional areas develop the distinctive competencies that lead to potential competitive advantages. Such competencies do not usually occur by chance. Instead, they need to be carefully conceived and may take several years to develop. For example, the talent that Disney has accumulated in its Imagineering group provides a distinctive competence that helps the company continually innovate.

■ STRATEGY IMPLEMENTATION

While strategy formulation is an important part of the strategic management process, strategies are unlikely to have the intended impact unless they are implemented effectively. Strategy implementation involves any management activities that are needed to put the strategy in motion, institute strategic controls for monitoring progress, and ultimately achieve organizational goals (see Figure 7-6).

Carrying Out Strategic Plans

Strategy implementation experts Jay R. Galbraith and Robert K. Kazanjian suggest that several major internal aspects of the organization may need to be synchronized in order to put a chosen strategy into action. Principal factors (shown in Figure 7-6) are technology, human resources, reward systems, decision processes, and structure.[63] The factors tend to be interconnected, so a change in one may necessitate changes in one or more others.

TECHNOLOGY Technology comprises the knowledge, tools, equipment, and work techniques used by an organization in delivering its product or service. Technology is often an important factor in strategy implementation because the technological emphasis must fit the strategic thrust. Organizational strategy, at all levels, must consider the technical functions of the business. For example, if an organization pursues a low-cost strategy, changes in technology

Figure 7-6 *The strategy implementation phase of the strategic management process.*

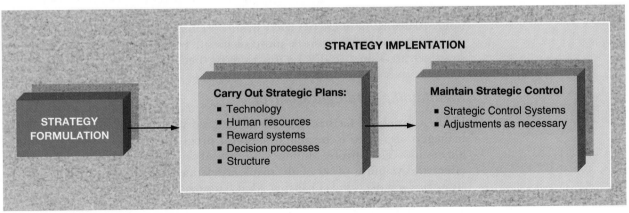

may be necessary to reduce costs. Following a differentiation strategy may also entail technological change in order to develop and/or produce the enhanced products or services.

HUMAN RESOURCES Human resources are the individuals who are members of the organization. Having the individuals with the necessary skills in the appropriate positions is a prerequisite for effective strategy implementation. This is accomplished by conducting strategic human resource planning, which links the human resource needs with the strategies to be pursued. Furthermore, the skills and experience of an organization's human resources are often a source of competitive advantage. For example, the Metropolitan Life Insurance Company developed "focus circles" to enhance both the diversity and the skills of the work force for competitive advantage (see the Managing Diversity box).

A skilled work force usually has a greater ability to find ways to reduce costs or produce new products or services than a less experienced staff. We discuss human resources more thoroughly in Chapter 10.

REWARD SYSTEMS Reward systems include bonuses, awards, or promotions provided by others, as well as intangible rewards such as personal feelings of achievement and challenge. Carefully considered reward systems are likely to constitute an important source of motivation to support a given strategy. For example, at Albertson's, Inc., a major food and drug retail chain with stores in 17 sunbelt and western states, employee bonuses are based on profits in order to encourage productivity and better service.[64] Specific rewards may be matched to the type of strategy being pursued. Thus a manager in an organization following a stability strategy might receive a bonus for a job well done, whereas a manager following a growth strategy may be given stock in the expanded venture as a reward for meeting organizational goals. We discuss motivational issues further in Chapter 12.

DECISION PROCESSES Decision processes include the means of resolving questions and problems that occur in organizations. Issues of resource allocation are particularly important to strategy implementation because strategic plans are more likely to be successful when the resources they call for are readily available. Decision-making processes can also help resolve specific problems and issues that arise during the course of implementing the plan. We discussed managerial decision making at greater length in Chapter 5.

STRUCTURE Organization structure is the formal pattern of interactions and coordination designed by management to link the tasks of individuals and groups in achieving organizational goals. Such patterns help various parts of the organization coordinate their efforts. The broad outline of an organization's structure is often depicted in an organization chart. Current research suggests that strategies may be more successful when the structure supports the strategic direction. We discuss this issue further in Chapter 9.

Maintaining Strategic Control

While a variety of factors must be considered in carrying out strategic plans, managers also need to be able to monitor progress. They do so through strategic control. This involves monitoring critical environmental factors that could affect the viability of strategic plans, assessing the effects of organizational strategic actions, and ensuring that strategic plans are implemented as intended. Instituting strategic control includes designing information systems

MANAGING DIVERSITY

MetLife Finds Competitive Advantage in "Focus Circles"

As part of its strategic planning process, top management of Metropolitan Life Insurance Company made an analysis of how its marketplace was changing with respect to gender, age, ethnicity, demographics, and product needs. An extension of that analysis led the company to conduct an assessment of its staffing profile. According to Edward McDonnel, assistant vice president and diversity director, "It was clear that to remain competitive and on the cutting edge of the industry, we had to reinforce and expand our diverse markets. To do so, our sales representatives and management had to reflect that diverse consumer base."

In assessing how such a goal could be accomplished, McDonnel found that associates were very interested in having a mentor. In order to make the idea of a mentor inclusive and allow many individuals to have development opportunities, the company developed a creative approach called "focus circles" and implemented it in its largest business segment. The segment has a sales force of nearly 10,000 persons in almost 50 regions in the United States and manages a portfolio of Life Insurance in Force equal to $1.3 billion.

With the focus circles, six or seven individuals from a variety of backgrounds, genders, lifestyles, and ethnicities work together with a leader who guides and coaches circle members in the development of their careers. The purpose is to provide broader opportunities for accelerated development of high-performing individuals and also to help individuals learn to interact and collaborate in diverse groups that reflect the business marketplace within which MetLife increasingly will operate. As part of the process, circle members each go through a personalized assessment program and work as a team on a visible project of importance to the company. Individuals receive feedback through the assessment program, as well as from peers and others associated with the project. Circle members are learning more about themselves, acquiring advanced skills, and working more effectively with each other. Morale and productivity both have risen as a result of the focus circle approach.[65]

that provide feedback on the way strategic plans are being carried out, as well as on their apparent effects. Such systems enable managers to make adjustments in the implementation of strategic plans, as necessary. Issues related to strategic control are considered in Chapters 16 and 17. Chapter 19 investigates various management information systems that can be used for strategic control purposes.

The strategy implementation process, of which strategic control is a part, essentially entails bringing about change and innovation. In the next chapter, we give special attention to the basic elements of organization structure.

■ CHAPTER SUMMARY

Strategic management is a process through which managers formulate and implement strategies geared toward optimizing strategic goal achievement. The part of the strategic management process that includes identifying the mission and strategic goals, conducting competitive analysis, and developing specific strategies is often referred to as strategy formulation. The part of the process that focuses on carrying out strategic plans and maintaining control over how those plans are carried out is known as strategy implementation. The overall process helps organizations identify and develop a competitive advantage, a significant edge over the competition in dealing with competitive forces.

Many organizations develop strategies at three different levels: corporate, business, and functional. Corporate-level strategy addresses what businesses the organization will operate, how the strategies of those businesses will be coordinated to strengthen the organization's competitive position, and how resources will be allocated among the businesses. Business-level strategy concentrates on the best means of competing within a particular business while also supporting the corporate-level strategy. Functional-level strategy focuses on action plans for managing a particular functional area within a business in a way that supports the business-level strategy.

Before attempting to devise an effective strategy,

managers need to assess both the environmental and the organizational factors that influence an organization's ability to compete effectively. One general method is SWOT analysis, which involves assessing organizational strengths (S) and weaknesses (W), as well as environmental opportunities (O) and threats (T). Porter's five competitive forces model helps analyze the nature and intensity of competition in a given industry in terms of five major forces: rivalry, bargaining power of customers, bargaining power of suppliers, threat of new entrants, and threat of substitute products or services. The resource-based strategic view helps organizations assess their internal resources and capabilities in terms of value, rareness, imitability, and organization.

Corporate strategy development generally involves selecting a grand strategy and using portfolio strategy approaches to determine the various businesses that will make up the organization. The three basic types of grand strategies are growth (including concentration, vertical integration, and diversification), stability, and defensive

(including harvest, turnaround, divestiture, bankruptcy, and liquidation). Two of the most frequently used portfolio approaches are the BCG growth-share matrix and the product/market evolution matrix.

At the business level, use of Porter's competitive strategies, which include cost leadership, differentiation, and focus strategies, constitutes the best-known approach. Functional-level strategies specify major ways that functional areas can be used to bolster the business-level strategy.

In carrying out strategic plans, managers need to consider major internal aspects of the organization that may need to be synchronized. Such aspects include technology, human resources, reward systems, decision processes, and structure. Strategy implementation also includes maintaining strategic control. This involves monitoring critical environmental factors that could affect the viability of strategic plans, assessing the effects of organizational strategic actions, and ensuring that strategic plans are implemented as intended.

■ QUESTIONS FOR DISCUSSION AND REVIEW

1 Explain the concept of strategic management and the notion of competitive advantage. Identify an organization that you think has a competitive advantage in its industry, and describe the nature of its advantage.

2 Outline the major components of the strategic management process. Explain why engaging in strategic management is likely to be beneficial for an organization.

3 Distinguish among the three levels of strategy. Explain the role of each in an organization that has separate divisions competing in different industries.

4 Explain SWOT analysis. Conduct a brief SWOT analysis of your college or university by developing two items for each of the four SWOT categories.

5 Outline Porter's five competitive forces model. Use the model to assess the nature and intensity of competition in an industry with which you are familiar.

6 Explain how the resource-based strategic view can be used to aid organizational assessment. Use the view to assess the resources and capabilities of an organization in the industry you analyzed in the previous question.

7 Describe the three major generic strategies available at the corporate level, and explain the subcategories within each. For each generic strategy, identify an organization that appears to be pursuing that particular strategy.

8 Contrast the two major approaches to portfolio strategy at the corporate level. If you were on the strategic planning staff of a major company with 35 different businesses, which approach would you recommend and why?

9 Describe Porter's competitive strategies for the business level. Assess the competitive strategy of an organization with which you are familiar, and explain its usefulness in dealing with Porter's five competitive forces.

10 Outline the process of strategy implementation. Which corporate-level generic strategy do you believe is being pursued by your college or university? Evaluate the effectiveness of strategy implementation at your college or university.

■ DISCUSSION QUESTIONS FOR CHAPTER OPENING CASE

1 What type of grand strategy does the Walt Disney Company appear to be pursuing? Cite evidence to support your conclusion.

2 Use Porter's five competitive forces model to analyze the competitive situation facing the Walt Disney Company.

3 Which of Porter's competitive strategies best characterizes the strategy being used by the various Disney businesses, such as the theme parks and resorts, consumer products, and filmed entertainment divisions? Assess the appropriateness of the strategy. To what extent would each of Porter's competitive strategies be appropriate for each of the divisions?

■ EXERCISES FOR MANAGING IN THE TWENTY-FIRST CENTURY

EXERCISE 1
SKILL BUILDING: WHAT STRATEGY IS THIS?

 Porter has proposed three generic strategies that could be used to gain a competitive advantage. Select the strategy that the following characteristics could be expected to support.

CHARACTERISTIC	COST LEADERSHIP	DIFFERENTIATION	FOCUS
1. Innovative products (Rubbermaid)			
2. High quality and reasonable price (Craftsman tools from Sears)			
3. Niche selling (Tiffany)			
4. Buy resources in quantity (Wal-Mart)			
5. Strong customer orientation; insurance sold primarily to active and retired military officers and families (USAA Insurance)			
6. Culture supporting leading-edge software development (Microsoft)			
7. Hamburgers sold for an average of less than 40 cents (White Castle)			
8. Homeowners insurance sold primarily to wealthy people with expensive possessions (Chubb Corporation)			
9. Designer jeans (Calvin Klein)			
10. Will not be undersold (Circuit City)			

EXERCISE 2
MANAGEMENT EXERCISE: DEVELOPING A STRATEGY FOR PMB

 You have been an extremely successful entrepreneur. Your Pedal More Bicycle (PMB) Company has more than doubled its sales each year for the past 10 years. PMB manufactures various types of bicycles, including racing and mountain bikes. PMB also makes accessories, such as seat covers, travel packs, and reflectors, and does a brisk business in bicycle parts. Your company has been successful by offering better quality and more innovative designs and features than can be obtained from competitors. Last year, your firm went public and was an instant hit on the market, making the controlling interest that you retained worth a great deal of money. PMB still has considerable growth potential. Nevertheless, you are now ready to take on new challenges. PMB has a sound reputation, which will be an asset if you want to borrow money to expand your business. You are aware of several current business opportunities:

1 The Winston Roller Bearing Company, a manufacturer of fabricated steel products and roller bearings, can be purchased for a fair price. The company is currently family-owned.

2 The Roxborough Leather Company, which produces leather goods for automobiles and shoes, can be acquired or leased on a long-term basis.

3 A Harley-Davidson motorcycle sales franchise is available in your area.

4 A very good location for an auto-parts outlet is going to be available within the next year. The information you have at this time indicates that such an outlet would be received very well in the area.

5 A small chain of three retail bicycle outlets will soon be offered for sale because the owners want to move back to their hometown, about 800 miles away. The outlets have done reasonably well, but improvements could be made that would probably increase sales dramatically.

6 The XYZ computer outlet, a retailer of home computers and software, is looking for a buyer. The current owners, who have been very successful, want to retire and move to the family farm in southern California.

You believe that sufficient funds could be raised to acquire two of these businesses. However, there are probably other considerations. Assume that PMB has strong manufacturing and marketing capabilities and no glaring internal weaknesses relative to competitors in the bicycle business. Develop a grand strategy for PMB, and use a portfolio strategy approach to analyze the various business alternatives. Choose one of Porter's generic strategies for each business that you select. Be prepared to explain the reasoning behind your choices.

CONCLUDING CASE 1

CRAY RESEARCH FINDS A RESCUER IN SILICON GRAPHICS

In the field of supercomputers during the past 25 years or so, one name has stood out: Cray. Eagan, Minnesota–based Cray Research, Inc., was founded by Seymour Cray in 1972, with the goal of building the world's fastest computers.

Originally, the Cray staff estimated that there was a world market for about 80 to 100 of the ultraspeed computers, which currently can cost more than $30 million each. As defense agencies, government agencies, and large firms grew interested in speedy computing, the market grew to well over $1 billion. Cray captured about 75 percent of the market for computers capable of exceptionally high speed data analysis.

In 1989, Cray Research concluded that it could not continue to fund Seymour Cray's efforts to build a new high-speed computer based on a difficult-to-use semiconductor material called gallium arsenide. Undaunted, Seymour Cray set up a new company called Cray Computer Corp. with $100 million in funds, but his company was forced to file for bankruptcy in 1995.

While Cray Research worked to make its machines faster, several competitors developed cheaper alternatives for some applications of high-speed computers by tying together hundreds of thousands of cheap microprocessors in massively parallel processing (MPP) computers sold at about one-fifth the price of traditional Cray machines. Cray responded by developing its own MPP computers.

Meanwhile, the end of the cold war and shrinking government budgets began to erode the market for expensive, high-end supercomputers. In the face of the changing market, Cray altered its strategy to focus on two broad thrusts: (1) build supercomputers that dominate the high end, middle range, and low end of the supercomputer market; and (2) develop and provide the software to be used with Cray machines. Cray soon released a low-end minisupercomputer, the J90, which starts at $250,000. Cray had 100 orders on hand even before the J90 was released. Cray hoped to snare new customers with the J90, who would then later trade up to its more powerful machines.

For all its efforts, Cray Research was only breaking even in the mid-1990s. At that point the company brought in a new chairman and CEO, J. Phillip Samper. Samper had been president of Sun Microsystem's largest unit, Sun Microsystems Computer Corp., and was credited with turning the unit around within a 12-month period. He was the first outsider ever to head Cray Research. Samper's initial assessment was that Cray Research had been doing a very good job of penetrating each of its target markets but that it needed to work on increasing productivity and lowering costs. Cray next reported a loss of $225 million, primarily due to expenses associated with attempts to cut costs and shrink its payroll. Some of Cray's large corporate and government customers began to exhibit reluctance to continue buying proprietary machines from a company that was not strong financially. Thus, Cray began to experience difficulties with its traditional high-end computer customers, even though it had a backlog of orders worth $437 million and still dominated the market for supercomputers.

As a result, Samper approached $2.2 billion Silicon Graphics, Inc. (SGI), based in Mountain View, California, about acquiring Cray. SGI is best known for producing workstations with sophisticated three-dimensional graphics capabilities. For example, SGI machines were used to create the special effects for the dinosaurs in the movie *Jurassic Park* and are used extensively in Hollywood productions. Before acquiring Cray, SGI had been expanding into the low end of supercomputers (costing up to $1 million). The acquisition of Cray gives SGI a presence at the high end. So far, SGI has maintained its lead in visual computing through vertical integration and continual innovation. The company's machines are based on its own proprietary MIPS microprocessor chips, which require huge development costs but so far have allowed SGI to produce differentiated products for which premium prices can be charged. Cray will begin using the MIPS chips in its new machines. Both SGI and its Cray subsidiary face considerable pressure to innovate significantly ahead of lower-end machines from competitors who are continually upgrading their offerings. They face particular threats from Hewlett-Packard and from so-called Wintel standard machines built with powerful new Intel chips and using Microsoft Windows' NT operating system.[66]

QUESTIONS FOR CONCLUDING CASE 1

1. Analyze the current situation facing SGI and Cray using Porter's five competitive forces model.

2. How would you assess the current status at SGI and Cray in terms of the degree to which their internal resources and capabilities provide the basis for competitive advantage? To what extent do you believe that acquiring Cray was a positive step for SGI?

3. Which of Porter's competitive strategies best matches the original strategy used by Cray? How would you characterize the current competitive strategies being used by Cray and SGI?

CONCLUDING CASE 2

STAR TV: THE FIRST PAN-ASIAN TV NETWORK

Most of the 2.7 billion people living in the 38 countries extending from Egypt through India to Japan and from the Russian Far East to Indonesia do not have television sets and satellite dishes. Yet, in 1991, Star TV debuted a 24-hour all-sports television program, beaming the U.S. Open tennis tournament via satellite to this vast potential audience in Asia.

Star TV, which is an acronym for Satellite Television Asian Region, was owned by the Hong Kong–based HutchVision Group and was launched at an initial cost of $300 million. Originally offering only one channel, Star TV soon added four more to its menu.

Star TV was initially targeted to a select 5 percent of the population in major markets in Hong Kong, Taiwan, South Korea, Indonesia, and India. This segment of the potential audience is made up of English-speaking, well-educated, well-traveled, wealthy Asians. Japan was not initially a major target for Star TV because that country already has a well-developed satellite TV network of its own.

Some observers predicted that Star TV would lose massive amounts of money attempting to build an audience. However, when the Star TV sports channel offered the World Cup cricket championships in 1992, sales of satellite dishes skyrocketed, particularly in areas that had once been British colonies. Initially, Star TV was making its money solely from advertising. The plan was to introduce pay channels in the near future. Estimates were that the network was reaching 3.75 million households in eight countries a year after it began operating.

In 1993, News Corp., headed by media mogul Rupert Murdoch, purchased 64 percent of Star TV and later bought the remaining shares for a total cost of $825 mil-

lion. In less than a year, Murdoch reversed the mainly English strategy aimed at a select audience in favor of supplying regionally oriented programs in the main regional languages, including Chinese and Hindi.

Murdoch first began to customize the satellite network's music programs. The company found that in Taiwan, the audience prefers saccharine Chinese love ballads, while Indian viewers are more drawn to dynamic music videos. Therefore, the northern beam of Star's satellite, which broadcasts to Taiwan, Hong Kong, and an estimated 30 million viewers in mainland China, carries mainly Chinese pop music. The southern beam, aimed at India and Southeast Asia, focuses on Hindi and English music. The customization has carried over to other types of programming as well. For example, Star has split the signal on its sports channel to provide more cricket to Indians and more soccer, gymnastics, and track to the Chinese. Movie channels are being geared up to broadcast in seven languages—Mandarin, Hindi, English, Bahasa Indonesian, Tagalog, Cantonese, and Japanese. Murdoch says his plan is to dominate four key program categories: sports, music, movies, and general entertainment. By the mid-1990s, Star TV was reaching an estimated 54 million households. Even with this coverage the satellite network is experiencing major losses.

Murdoch has determined that Star TV cannot bring in sufficient revenues from advertising alone to make a significant profit. Instead it will be necessary to have viewers pay to watch some programs on the network. News Corp. is attempting to develop systems that will allow the company to collect viewer payments at a reasonable cost.

Star TV now has access to the sophisticated AsiaSat-2 satellite, which is positioned to cover two-thirds of the world's population.

The satellite provides Star TV with 30 or more new channels of digital television. Moreover the digitalization process allows Star TV to simultaneously offer the same program in several different languages, thus supporting the network's regional focus. With the increased technology, Star has entered the Japanese market, offering a 24-hour Japanese-language channel, and the company plans to offer six more channels in the near future.

Star TV faces growing competition from others attempting to launch various satellite networks in the area, such as NBC, ABN (Dow Jones), CNN, and Nine Network Australia. As Star TV attempts to target its programs more regionally, it will be competing with regional broadcasters. Murdoch views the situation as an investment. So far, Star TV has the highest market penetration of any satellite network. To be successful in the long run, though, it will need to gain additional share in various markets.[67]

QUESTIONS FOR CONCLUDING CASE 2

1 Which generic grand strategy and which of its subcategories best describe the strategy Star TV was initially pursuing? Which of Porter's competitive strategies did the network appear to be following?

2 Which generic grand strategy and which of its subcategories best describe the strategy Star TV is currently pursuing? Which of Porter's competitive strategies does the network appear to be following?

3 What factors should Murdoch and his senior management of Star TV consider in making an environmental assessment at this point? What types of strategies should they be reviewing for use at the beginning of the twenty-first century?

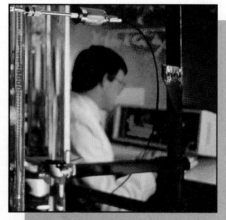

PART THREE

ORGANIZING

Planning, as we saw in the previous part, is a crucial management function that charts major organizational directions. Nevertheless, even the most carefully devised plans at the strategic, tactical, and operational levels mean little if an organization does not have effective means for carrying them out. That is where organizing comes into play. In fulfilling the organizing function, managers allocate and arrange both human and nonhuman resources in ways that enable plans to be achieved successfully. In the process, the organizing function provides a valuable tool for fostering innovation and facilitating needed changes.

Chapter 8 presents the basic elements of organization structure. Organization charts, job design, types of departmentalization, and methods of vertical and horizontal coordination are important parts of a well-structured organization.

Yet the manner in which one successful organization is structured may not necessarily suit the needs of another equally successful organization. As **Chapter 9** explains, managers need to take a strategic approach to designing organizations, assessing alternative structures, and considering contingency factors that have an influence on the effectiveness of structural choices.

Organizing, though, is not just a matter of developing charts and means of coordination: people form the heart of any organization structure. **Chapter 10** examines the strategic use of human resource management to enhance the effectiveness of an organization's work force through such means as human resource planning, staffing, development, evaluation, and compensation.

CHAPTER EIGHT

BASIC ELEMENTS OF ORGANIZATION STRUCTURE

CHAPTER OUTLINE

The Nature of Organization Structure
Organization Structure Defined
The Organization Chart

Job Design
Approaches to Job Design
Managing Diversity: Alternative Work Schedules

Types of Departmentalization

Methods of Vertical Coordination
The Role of Formalization
Span of Management: The Trend toward Downsizing
Centralization versus Decentralization
Delegation
Line and Staff Positions

Promoting Innovation: Methods of Horizontal Coordination
Slack Resources
Information Systems
Lateral Relations

LEARNING OBJECTIVES

After studying this chapter, you should be able to:

■ Describe the four elements that make up organization structure.

■ Explain the importance of organization charts and the chain-of-command concept.

■ Outline the main approaches to job design, including the principal alternatives to traditional work schedules.

■ Explain five major methods of vertical coordination, including formalization, span of management, centralization versus decentralization, delegation, and line and staff positions.

■ Explain how slack resources and information systems can be used as means of horizontal coordination.

■ Describe the major types of lateral relations and explain their usefulness in facilitating horizontal coordination.

GAINING THE EDGE

1-800-FLOWERS BECOMES THE WORLD'S LARGEST FLORIST

Jim McCann, president of Long Island–based 1-800-FLOWERS, was a social worker looking for a means of making some extra money when a friend told him about a local floral shop that was for sale. Within 10 years, he owned 14 of the Flora Plenty shops in the New York City area and was thinking about developing them into a national chain.

As a member of the florist industry, though, he watched a Dallas group launch 1-800-FLOWERS, which made ordering flowers very easy through a 24-hour telephone service. When the Dallas group ran into financial troubles in 1987, McCann went into debt to buy them out. He closed the Dallas facility, which was losing $400,000 per week, and moved the operation to Queens, New York, where he and his brother Chris built 25 phone cubicles in a flower shop. They kept costs low, used family members to help, and sold several of their floral shops to fund the operation. McCann knew he had to market the brand name and get customers accustomed to ordering flowers by phone. He also had to provide good, reliable service so that customers would keep coming back. At the end of the first year, the company had sales of $500,000.

Today the company headquarters contains a huge room with many rows of workstations from which phone representatives service customer orders, which amount to more than $250 million annually. At one end is a raised platform, called "The Bridge," where technicians watch over the banks of phones and the computer terminals that control thousands of calls per day. Calls are transferred among telecenters in seven cities to ensure quick service. A sophisticated computer system tracks orders from start to finish so that the company can determine at any time the status of an order and when and to whom it has been delivered. Currently 1-800-FLOWERS has more than 150 company and franchised stores. About 25 percent of the company's orders come from its retail stores, about two-thirds from the 800 number, and another 10 percent via the Internet and the company's web site. Orders are then relayed to florist members of its BloomNet netware, who prepare and deliver the orders.

Some of McCann's approaches to organizing have been influenced by the excessive amounts of formalization he witnessed while a social worker. He says that if he had done all the things the bureaucracy required for accountability, he would not have had time to do his job effectively. At 1-800-FLOWERS he tries to balance things so that staff members are encouraged to be entrepreneurial and yet still follow an overall direction for the common good. McCann views his role as a "cultural engineer" who is continually "tossing hand grenades and asking questions." He says he likes to "keep mixing this pot of stew to make sure it's a fun place."

The phone representatives who answer calls on the 1-800-FLOWERS number have the authority to do what they think is right in handling customer situations. McCann notes that the company has evolved from attempting to determine who is right or wrong to taking the philosophy that "whether the customer is right or wrong, we have to make it right." In fact, the company calls the unit in which the phone representatives work the "customer satisfaction department." To provide recognition when a phone representative takes a particularly noteworthy action in behalf of customer service, the story goes in the Legend Book and in the company newsletter (for one such legend as heard from one of the

Dial a number, send some flowers. It sounds easy, but Jim McCann, president of 1-800-Flowers, can tell you that it takes a significant amount of organization. A sophisticated computer system, overseen by technicians, allocates customer order calls to phone representatives located in seven different cities. The system also tracks orders to help ensure proper, on-time delivery. One secret of McCann's organizing success: He encourages his employees to be entrepreneurial and to use their own initiative in handling customers, which adds to both worker and customer satisfaction.

associates at 1-800-FLOWERS, see Figure 8-1). Making the legend stories available to everyone helps staff members understand what can be done and what the parameters are. McCann tells phone representatives, "We don't want you to wait to ask your supervisor. Whatever you think is the right thing to do on the phone—you make the decision."[1] ■ ■ ■

One reason for the success of 1-800-FLOWERS is that Jim McCann put considerable effort into the managerial function of *organizing*, the process of allocating and arranging human and nonhuman resources so that planned goals can be achieved. Organizing is important to managers because it is the means they use to align work with resources so that organizational plans and decisions (discussed in Part Two) can be made and carried out effectively.

Often, means of organizing that work under one set of circumstances become inappropriate as the situation changes. For instance, McCann says he keeps trying new approaches and changing things, because what worked last year won't necessarily work this year.[2] As a result, organizing is an ongoing management function. Managers need to give frequent consideration to organizing issues in order to keep the company moving on target. As we begin this first chapter of Part Three, we initially probe the nature of organization structure. We also explore major considerations in dividing work in ways that are meaningful to individuals and that are likely to energize their efforts to put forth their best performance. We then review major ways of grouping jobs and units in developing an overall organization structure. We next investigate several important methods of coordinating efforts up and down the hierarchy. Finally, we examine methods of horizontal coordination that not only help various departments and units synchronize their efforts but also encourage innovation.

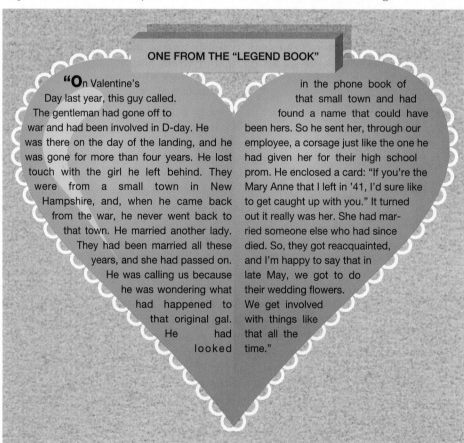

ONE FROM THE "LEGEND BOOK"

"**O**n Valentine's Day last year, this guy called. The gentleman had gone off to war and had been involved in D-day. He was there on the day of the landing, and he was gone for more than four years. He lost touch with the girl he left behind. They were from a small town in New Hampshire, and, when he came back from the war, he never went back to that town. He married another lady. They had been married all these years, and she had passed on. He was calling us because he was wondering what had happened to that original gal. He had looked in the phone book of that small town and had found a name that could have been hers. So he sent her, through our employee, a corsage just like the one he had given her for their high school prom. He enclosed a card: "If you're the Mary Anne that I left in '41, I'd sure like to get caught up with you." It turned out it really was her. She had married someone else who had since died. So, they got reacquainted, and I'm happy to say that in late May, we got to do their wedding flowers. We get involved with things like that all the time."

Figure 8-1 *One from the "Legend Book."*

■ THE NATURE OF ORGANIZATION STRUCTURE

If you are like most people, you have probably had the experience of running into a problem that made you want to speak to the supervisor or next in command in an organization. Under such conditions, you would probably respond with disbelief if you were told that no one knew who the supervisor was or whose job it was to handle a complaint like yours. We expect such matters to be worked out—at least by organizations that have some hope of long-run survival. In essence, we expect organizations to have developed reasonably effective organization structures.

Organization Structure Defined

Organization structure is the formal pattern of interactions and coordination designed by management to link the tasks of individuals and groups in achieving organizational goals. The word "formal" in this context refers to the fact that organization structures are typically created by management for specific purposes and, hence, are official, or formal, outcomes of the organizing function. Organizations also have informal structures, or patterns of interaction, which are not designed by management but usually emerge because of common interests or friendship. We discuss informal patterns of interaction further when we consider groups in Chapter 15.

Organization structure consists mainly of four elements:[3]

1. The assignment of tasks and responsibilities that define the jobs of individuals and units
2. The clustering of individual positions into units and of units into departments and larger units to form an organization's hierarchy
3. The various mechanisms required to facilitate vertical (top-to-bottom) coordination, such as the number of individuals reporting to any given managerial position and the degree of delegation of authority
4. The various mechanisms needed to foster horizontal (across departments) coordination, such as task forces and interdepartmental teams

The process of developing an organization structure is sometimes referred to as **organization design.** One aid to visualizing structure is the organization chart. Therefore, we briefly describe this type of chart before analyzing the four main elements of organization structure in greater detail.

The Organization Chart

The **organization chart** is a line diagram that depicts the broad outlines of an organization's structure. Organization charts vary in detail, but they typically show the major positions or departments in the organization. They also indicate the way the positions are grouped into specific units, the reporting relationships from lower to higher levels, and the official channels for communicating information. Some charts show titles associated with the positions, as well as the current position holders. An overall organization chart indicating the major managerial positions and departments in the Acacia Mutual Life Insurance Company, based in Washington, D.C., is shown in Figure 8-2.

Such charts are particularly helpful in providing a visual map of the chain of command. The **chain of command** is the unbroken line of authority that ultimately links each individual with the top organizational position through a managerial position at each successive layer in between.[4] The basic idea is that

Organization structure The formal pattern of interactions and coordination designed by management to link the tasks of individuals and groups in achieving organizational goals

Organization design The process of developing an organization structure

Organization chart A line diagram that depicts the broad outlines of an organization's structure

Chain of command The unbroken line of authority that ultimately links each individual with the top organizational position through a managerial position at each successive layer in between

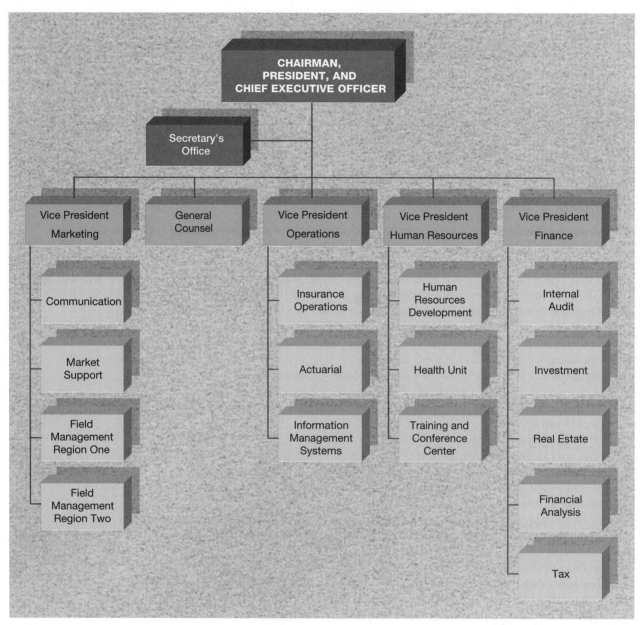

Figure 8-2 *Organization chart for the Acacia Mutual Life Insurance Company.*

each individual in an organization should be able to identify his or her boss and trace the line of authority through the organization all the way to the top position.

Today, most organizations that include more than a few individuals are likely to have organization charts showing the chain of command and the basic structure of the organization. Although such charts provide a broad view, they do not include all aspects of the structure picture. For example, organization charts do not normally include detailed information about how work is divided into specific jobs. Yet, as noted earlier in the definition of organization structure, the design of jobs is an important aspect of structure. Therefore, it is the subject to which we now turn.

■ JOB DESIGN

Different types of jobs can involve very different activities. A job as a buyer for Macy's, the New York–based department store chain, may involve keeping in contact with various suppliers in a certain specialty area (such as shoes), previewing new offerings, developing sources for in-house brands, and studying trends in consumer tastes. In contrast, the job of a salesperson may include learning about new items in certain departments, keeping merchandise neatly arranged, helping customers, and ringing up sales at the register. The differing activities of the buyer and the salesperson reflect **work specialization,** the degree to which the work necessary to achieve organizational goals is broken down into various jobs. Without some specialization, it would be difficult for most organizations to function. This is because it is usually impossible for every organization member to have the entire range of skills necessary to run an effective organization.

On the other hand, even jobs with similar titles can differ substantially in the activities performed. For example, a job as an administrative assistant may include typing, filing, and photocopying, or it could involve such activities as coordinating meetings and travel, investigating trouble spots, and making decisions about a certain range of issues. What is included in a given job depends on **job design,** the specification of task activities associated with a particular job.

Job design is important to the organizing function for two major reasons. For one thing, task activities need to be grouped in reasonably logical ways. Otherwise, it may be very difficult for organization members to function efficiently. For another, the way that jobs are configured, or designed, has an important influence on employee motivation to perform well. (We discuss specific concepts of motivation in Chapter 12.) Thus managers need to consider both efficiency and motivational issues in designing jobs that will facilitate effective performance.

Work specialization The degree to which the work necessary to achieve organizational goals is broken down into various jobs

Job design The specification of task activities associated with a particular job

Approaches to Job Design

There are four major approaches to job design: job simplification, job rotation, job enlargement, and job enrichment.[5]

JOB SIMPLIFICATION **Job simplification** is the process of designing jobs so that jobholders have only a small number of narrow activities to perform (see Figure 8-3a). Economist Adam Smith was one of the first to highlight the advantages of work specialization and simplification. Using his now-famous example involving pins, Smith pointed out that an individual working alone could make 20 pins per day, while 10 people working on specialized tasks could make 48,000 pins per day.[6] The simplification idea was further popularized by Frederick Taylor through his scientific management viewpoint, which emphasizes reducing jobs to narrow tasks and training workers in the best way to do them (see Chapter 2).

Because the jobs involved in job simplification are simple and repetitive, workers are almost interchangeable, making training new workers relatively easy. Perhaps the most obvious example of job simplification is the assembly-line approach commonly used to make automobiles. Unfortunately, job simplification can be carried too far, creating narrow, repetitive jobs that are not conducive to motivating employees. Instead, such jobs often result in negative

Job simplification The process of configuring jobs so that jobholders have only a small number of narrow activities to perform

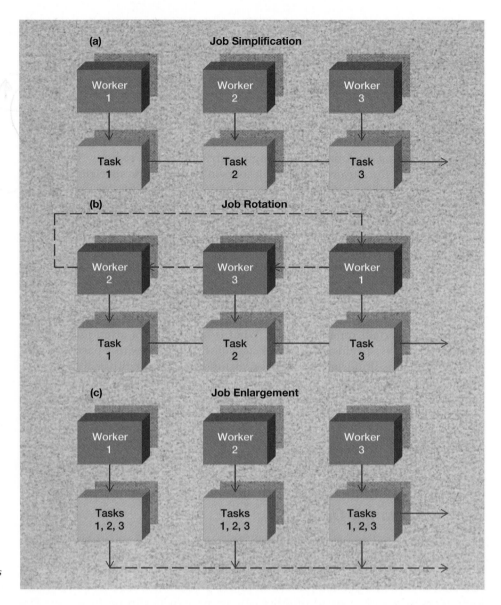

Figure 8-3 *Major approaches to job design.*

side effects, such as worker boredom, low job satisfaction, absenteeism, turnover, sabotage, and inflexibility in serving customers with different needs.[7]

Job rotation The practice of periodically shifting workers through a set of jobs in a planned sequence

JOB ROTATION Job rotation is the practice of periodically shifting workers through a set of jobs in a planned sequence (see Figure 8-3*b*). The approach is often aimed at reducing the boredom associated with job simplification by providing some task variety. Job rotation also has the advantage of *cross-training* workers (training them to do the tasks involved in several jobs) so that there is greater flexibility in job assignments. Although job rotation can be useful in alleviating monotony and boredom, its advantage with simple jobs may be short-lived. With such jobs, employees are likely to learn the new jobs quickly and become relatively bored again.

Job rotation is generally more successful as an employee development tool. In this approach, employees are rotated through a series of more challenging jobs in order to increase their capabilities, expand job assignment flexibility, and enhance their understanding of various aspects of the organization. At

This worker at National Steel can fix a hydraulic leak, weld an iron frame, and cut a hose section. By mixing job tasks and broadening responsibilities, instead of restricting workers to narrow, routine tasks, the company has been able to increase job satisfaction as well as improve the speed and quality of production.

Morgan Guaranty, for example, the bank makes a regular practice of rotating managers through various departments. As a result, the managers tend to be more cooperative with one another because they either have been or will be in the other person's job at some point.[8] Job rotation across different units or geographic locations may also help stimulate innovation, since it promotes the exchange of ideas. One recent study suggests it may be useful to seek out job rotation opportunities because they tend to lead to promotions, increased pay, and other career benefits.[9] Potential problems with job rotation are that departments may view the rotating individuals as temporary help (and give them only trivial things to do) and may also question their departmental loyalty.

JOB ENLARGEMENT Job enlargement is the allocation of a wider variety of similar tasks to a job in order to make it more challenging (see Figure 8-3*c*). For example, Maytag changed the assembly process for washing-machine pumps so that each worker could assemble a complete pump rather than apply only one part on an assembly line.[10] Job enlargement broadens **job scope,** the number of different tasks an employee performs in a particular job. Although it is an improvement over narrow job specialization, job enlargement has generally had somewhat limited success in motivating employees. This is primarily because a few more similar tasks often do not provide sufficient challenge and stimulation. In fact, if it is overdone, job enlargement may lead to reduced job satisfaction, lower efficiency, mental overload, increased errors, and reduced customer satisfaction.[11]

JOB ENRICHMENT Job enrichment is the process of upgrading the job-task mix in order to increase significantly the potential for growth, achievement, responsibility, and recognition. The concept of job enrichment was pioneered by Frederick Herzberg, whose work during the late 1960s highlighted the importance of job content as a significant force in motivation.[12] Job enrichment increases **job depth,** the degree to which individuals can plan and control the work involved in their jobs.

To guide job enrichment efforts, job design researchers Richard Hackman and Greg Oldham developed the **job characteristics model.**[13] The model, shown in Figure 8-4, involves three main elements: core job characteristics, critical psychological states, and outcomes. There are five *core job characteristics:*

1 **Skill variety** is the extent to which the job entails a number of activities that require different skills.
2 **Task identity** is the degree to which the job allows the completion of a major identifiable piece of work, rather than just a fragment.

Job enlargement The allocation of a wider variety of similar tasks to a job in order to make it more challenging

Job scope The number of different tasks an employee performs in a particular job

Job enrichment The process of upgrading the job-task mix in order to increase significantly the potential for growth, achievement, responsibility, and recognition

Job depth The degree to which individuals can plan and control the work involved in their jobs

Job characteristics model A model developed to guide job enrichment efforts that include consideration of core job characteristics, critical psychological states, and outcomes

Skill variety The extent to which the job entails a number of activities that require different skills

Task identity The degree to which the job allows the completion of a major identifiable piece of work, rather than just a fragment

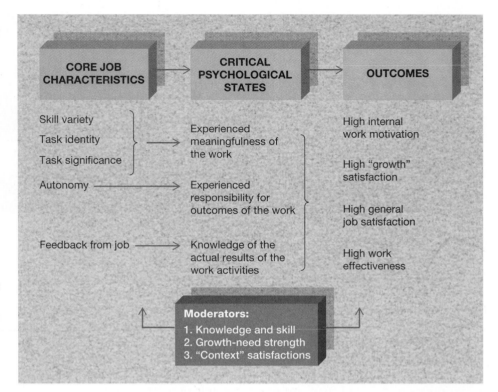

Figure 8-4 *Job characteristics model. (Reprinted from J. Richard Hackman and Greg R. Oldham,* Work Redesign, *Addison-Wesley, Reading, Mass., 1980, p. 90; used by permission of J. Richard Hackman.)*

Task significance The extent to which the worker sees the job output as having an important impact on others

Autonomy The amount of discretion allowed in determining schedules and work methods for achieving the required output

Feedback The degree to which the job provides for clear, timely information about performance results

3 **Task significance** is the extent to which the worker sees the job output as having an important impact on others.

4 **Autonomy** is the amount of discretion allowed in determining schedules and work methods for achieving the required output.

5 **Feedback** is the degree to which the job provides for clear, timely information about performance results.

The more that these core characteristics are reflected in jobs, the more motivating the jobs are likely to be.

The motivational value of these characteristics stems from workers' experiencing three *critical psychological states:* feeling the work is meaningful, knowing that they are responsible for the outcomes, and actually finding out about results. According to the model, these critical states then lead to the major outcomes (listed in Figure 8-4), including higher internal work motivation, greater satisfaction of growth needs, higher general job satisfaction, and increased work effectiveness. The increased work effectiveness usually stems from higher work quality, although greater quantity may sometimes result, depending largely on the improvements made in the flow of work.

Research indicates that workers may differ in their reactions to increases in the core job characteristics (see the moderators listed in Figure 8-4). Not surprisingly, individuals are more likely to feel motivated by job changes if they have the knowledge and skills necessary to perform well in the redesigned job, if they have high **growth-need strength** (the degree to which an individual needs personal growth and development on the job), and if they feel satisfied with other aspects of the job context (such as supervision, pay, coworkers, and job security).[14] One organization that has successfully used the job characteristics model to implement job enrichment is First National Bank of Chicago (see the Case in Point discussion).

Growth-need strength The degree to which an individual needs personal growth and development on the job

---

JOB ENRICHMENT AT FIRST NATIONAL BANK OF CHICAGO   CASE IN POINT

First National Bank of Chicago has used the job characteristics model to redesign jobs in its unit that prepares letters of credit for businesses. Before the redesign, preparation of the letters, which let businesses know how much credit the bank is willing to extend, was fragmented into a "paperwork assembly." The jobs involved narrow skills, little sense of the overall product and its impact on client businesses, limited autonomy, and virtually no feedback from clients. For example, one person's whole job was feeding tape into a Telex machine.

Although the unit was notorious for poor service, managers had little success in their attempts to improve the quality and speed of the process. One survey of employees in the line-of-credit department showed that 80 percent of the staff members were dissatisfied with their jobs. The 20 percent who were satisfied were managers and technical professionals. Even the managerial jobs were limited. There was one manager for about every five workers. On the basis of the survey, a group of workers were asked to help with the redesign of their jobs. The aim was to involve the entire staff in bringing about change.

The redesign ultimately eliminated a layer of management and changed the nature of the jobs. Each employee now performs customer contact work (resulting in higher task identity, task significance, and feedback) as well as research, writing, costing, and other letter-preparation tasks (resulting in increased skill variety, autonomy, and task identity) associated with a specific client group. The changes also led to staff reductions (mainly through attrition and transfers) of about 40 percent, extensive staff training, and pay increases of $7000 to $8000 per year for the individuals remaining (because they now had higher-skilled jobs). Within a year, profits related to the department rose by $2 million, employee morale rose dramatically, and customer satisfaction increased significantly.[15] ■■■

Considering the job content is one method of organizing work to meet organizational and worker needs; another is devising alternative work schedules.

Managing Diversity: Alternative Work Schedules

A related aspect of designing jobs is creating **alternative work schedules,** schedules based on adjustments in the normal work schedule rather than in the job content or activities. The basic objective of this approach is to increase workers' job satisfaction and motivation by arranging work schedules that allow a diverse work force greater flexibility in balancing both work life and personal life. Alternative work schedules tend to be particularly helpful to workers who are attempting to juggle work and family responsibilities, such as caring for small children or elderly relatives; but they are useful in a variety of other situations as well. Three major types of alternative work schedules are flextime, the compressed workweek, and job sharing.

FLEXTIME Flextime is a work schedule that specifies certain core hours when individuals are expected to be on the job and then allows flexibility in starting and quitting times as long as individuals work the total number of required

Alternative work schedules Schedules based on adjustments in the normal work schedule rather than in the job content or activities

Flextime A work schedule that specifies certain core hours when individuals are expected to be on the job and then allows flexibility in starting and quitting times as long as individuals work the total number of required hours per day

hours per day. For example, a company may have core hours between 10 a.m. and 3 p.m. (with an hour for lunch). Workers may then choose various schedules, such as 7 a.m. to 4 p.m. or 10 a.m. to 7 p.m., that comprise 8 hours of work per day and include the core hours. One recent study showed that the most popular core period is 9 a.m. to 3 p.m.

Major advantages of flextime are improvements in employee morale, accommodation of the needs of working parents, decreased tardiness, and reductions in traffic problems because workers can avoid the peak congestion times. Flextime often also results in lower absenteeism and lower turnover. Major disadvantages include lack of supervision during some hours of work, unavailability of key people during certain periods, understaffing during some periods, and coordination difficulties if the outputs of some employees are inputs for other workers. Also, keeping track of the various schedules may increase administrative work. Overall, however, flextime has been a successful innovation, and its use appears to be growing.[16]

Compressed workweek A work schedule whereby employees work four 10-hour days or some similar combination, rather than the usual five 8-hour days

COMPRESSED WORKWEEK The **compressed workweek** is a work schedule whereby employees work four 10-hour days or some similar combination, rather than the usual five 8-hour days. Some companies close for 3 days each week. This often provides operating economies, such as reductions in energy use that result from cutting down on heating and cooling for the 3 days off. For example, at the Alabama-based Birmingham Steel Corporation, workers put in 12-hour days, working 3 days one week and 4 days the following week. The schedule has had a major positive effect on productivity by cutting the number of shifts and time-consuming changeovers from three to two.[17]

Other organizations coordinate employee schedules to remain open for 5 days each week. The basic idea behind the compressed workweek, sometimes called the 4/40 workweek, is to make the job attractive to employees by providing 3 (usually consecutive) days off per week. Another impetus is the federal Clear Air Act, requiring employers to reduce commuter auto emissions. Potential disadvantages include possible fatigue, loss of productivity, and accidents, as well as difficulties interfacing with other organizations that operate on traditional workweek schedules. More research is needed on the effects of the compressed workweek. According to one study, the compressed schedule initially led to greater job satisfaction and higher performance, but the positive effects disappeared within 2 years.[18] A 9/80 schedule is gaining popularity at a number of companies, such as Dow Chemical and Shell Oil Co. With a 9/80 arrangement, employees work a 9-hour day on Mondays through Thursdays and an 8-hour day on alternating Fridays, so that they can have the other Fridays off. Thus employees have one free Friday during each 2-week period.[19]

Job sharing A work practice in which two or more people share a single full-time job

JOB SHARING Job sharing is a work practice in which two or more people share a single full-time job. With job sharing, one person can work in the morning and the other in the afternoon, or they can alternate days or develop some other sharing schedule. Individuals who share jobs may be parents who are sharing work and family responsibilities or mothers attempting to juggle both home and work activities. One survey of 348 U.S. and Canadian firms found that 11 percent had job sharing, and the practice appears to be increasing.[20]

■ TYPES OF DEPARTMENTALIZATION

While the way in which individual jobs are arranged is one important dimension of organization structure, another important aspect is departmentalization.

Departmentalization is the clustering of individuals into units and of units into departments and larger units to facilitate achieving organizational goals. Differing overall patterns of departmentalization are often referred to as *organization designs*.

Four of the most commonly used patterns of departmentalization are functional, divisional, hybrid, and matrix.[21] Briefly, the *functional structure* groups positions into units on the basis of similarity of expertise, skills, and work activities (e.g., marketing, accounting, production or operations, and human resources). In contrast, the *divisional structure* groups positions into units according to the similarity of products or markets (e.g., a separate division for each of several products). The *hybrid structure* combines aspects of both the functional and divisional forms, with some jobs grouped into departments by function and others grouped by products or markets. Finally, the *matrix structure* superimposes, or overlays, a horizontal set of divisional reporting relationships onto a hierarchical functional structure. We discuss these methods of departmentalization, or organization design, in greater detail in Chapter 9.

Regardless of the organization design, however, managers typically need to take further steps to achieve the vertical and horizontal coordination that makes a structure effective. In the next section, we discuss methods of vertical coordination.

Departmentalization The clustering of individuals into units and of units into departments and larger units in order to facilitate achieving organizational goals

■ METHODS OF VERTICAL COORDINATION

Although the various types of departmentalization provide basic structures within which individuals carry out organizational work activities, a number of additional mechanisms are important to effective vertical coordination. **Vertical coordination** is the linking of activities at the top of the organization with those at the middle and lower levels in order to achieve organizational goals. Without such coordination, the various parts of the organization have difficulty working effectively together. Five particularly important means of achieving effective vertical coordination are formalization, span of management, centralization versus decentralization, delegation, and line and staff positions.[22]

Vertical coordination The linking of activities at the top of the organization with those at the middle and lower levels in order to achieve organizational goals

The Role of Formalization

One common method of achieving vertical coordination is formalization. **Formalization** is the degree to which written policies, rules, procedures, job descriptions, and other documents specify what actions are (or are not) to be taken under a given set of circumstances.[23] Formalization helps bring about vertical coordination by specifying expected behaviors in advance. For example, policies provide general guidelines within which organization members are expected to operate; procedures spell out actions to be taken under certain recurring circumstances; and rules specify what should or should not be done in a given situation (see Chapter 6). Job descriptions detail the tasks and activities associated with particular jobs (see Chapter 10).

Most organizations rely on at least some means of formalization. For example, major student organizations are likely to have written policies about basic qualifications for office, as well as procedures governing how elections should be conducted. Without such means of formalization, it would be necessary to decide these issues every year, a situation that could be time-consuming and might lead to significant inequities. On the other hand, extensive rules and procedures can be stifling and discourage necessary amounts of change and innovation.[24]

Formalization The degree to which written policies, rules, procedures, job descriptions, and other documents specify what actions are (or are not) to be taken under a given set of circumstances

This occurred at J. Bildner & Sons, Inc., a Boston-based upscale grocery store. When it began an ill-fated expansion attempt, the company developed formal policies and rules that unwittingly sometimes thwarted its intended emphasis on service. In one instance, a customer at a recently opened New York store inquired about the cost of buying a roasted turkey for Christmas. Rather than quoting a price based on the cost of the turkey and a reasonable markup for profit, the manager followed the rules and multiplied the price per slice by the number of slices in a turkey. Naturally, the price was absurd and the customer walked out.[25]

When organizations are small, they can usually run very informally, with few written documents specifying policies and procedures. As they grow, however, organizations tend to require additional degrees of formalization to coordinate the efforts of increasing numbers of individuals. The challenge is to avoid becoming overly formalized. Consider the experience of Celestial Seasonings as it grew larger, became part of a giant company, and then became an independent company again (see the Case in Point discussion).

CASE IN POINT

CELESTIAL SEASONINGS RETAINS ITS INNOVATIVE FLAIR

The origins of Celestial Seasonings, makers of herbal tea, are legendary. In 1970, Mo Siegel and his friend Wyck Hay gathered herbs in the mountains of Colorado, mixed their first blend of herb tea, loaded the mixture in muslin bags sewn by their wives, and began selling the tea to local health food stores.

The company took the name "Celestial Seasonings," which was the nickname of an early investor's girlfriend. Tea names, chosen by Mo's friends and company members, were equally whimsical, beginning with Mo's 24 Herb Tea, Red Zinger Herb Tea, and Morning Thunder Tea. The tea was packaged in colorful recyclable boxes that featured such idyllic scenes as roaming buffalo and picnicking couples. Up to that time, herb teas had largely been somewhat bitter-tasting brews used for medicinal purposes. The fledgling company changed all that with its flavorful new creations, which soon found themselves on supermarket shelves, and virtually created the herb tea industry.

From the start, the company operated relatively informally, encouraged employee participation in decision making, and was dedicated to all-natural ingredients. In the early days, major decisions were made in all-company meetings lasting as long as 8 hours, volleyball games were played every lunch hour,

Celestial Seasonings' colorful boxes and tea names are a familiar sight on supermarket shelves. Beginning as a very informal home-based venture among friends, the company grew into a multimillion dollar business entailing various formalized procedures. Too much formalization can be stifling for a small company, however. When the company's founder recently returned as chairman and CEO, he brought back much of the original unconventional spirit as well.

and toddling children could be found playing in Mo's office. As Celestial grew, the company brought in managers from such major corporations as Pepsi, Coca-Cola, Smuckers, and Lipton to help. Automation became a necessity as the amount of tea blended per day approached 8 tons. Still, the company managed to retain its informality. Employees were asked to contribute ideas in such areas as new ways to automate, possible new teas, and names for new flavors (often chosen through employee contests).

The success of the innovative company attracted the attention of Kraft, Inc., which bought Celestial from Mo Siegel in 1984 for approximately $40 million, with assurances that the company would be left alone to continue its solid growth. "Although Kraft let us operate as an independent business," says Barnet Feinblum, who was promoted to president when Siegel left, "little by little we were having to comply with Kraft's policies, whether it was employee benefit plans or decisions on purchasing equipment. If we had continued that way, Celestial Seasonings would have gradually and inexorably become just like Kraft." By 1989, Kraft had decided to leave the beverage business, and it attempted to sell Celestial to the tea company's archrival, Thomas J. Lipton, Inc. However, an antitrust suit filed by R. C. Bigelow, Inc., a small competitor in the herb tea market, blocked the sale. Kraft then agreed to sell Celestial Seasonings to its management and a venture capital firm. Kraft had doubled Celestial Seasonings' advertising budget, and sales were approaching $50 million when Celestial became independent again.

Unfortunately, sales began to level off. The company then offered founder Mo Siegel an opportunity to acquire 25 percent equity if he would return as chairman and CEO. By this time, Mo, who had been working with a variety of nonprofit organizations, missed the corporate environment and agreed to return. Mo has brought a renewed sense of excitement to Celestial. He combines a flair for selecting winning tea flavors with strong philosophical views about such things as health, the environment, and recycling. The company makes Sleepytime, the best-selling herbal tea in the United States, and more than 40 other blends. Distribution is expanding into Asia, Australia, Europe, and the Middle East. Optimism once again pervades Celestial.[26]   ■ ■ ■

As the Celestial Seasonings situation under Kraft illustrates, too much formalization can begin to stifle an organization, particularly when it is relatively small. On the other hand, even Celestial Seasonings has had to develop policies, such as using only natural ingredients, and rules, such as procedures for cleaning various spice ingredients imported from all over the world. In addition to formalization, span of management is an important means of vertical coordination.

Span of Management: The Trend toward Downsizing

Span of management, or **span of control,** is the number of subordinates who report directly to a specific manager. Span of management is important to vertical coordination because it has a direct bearing on the degree to which managers can interact with and supervise subordinates. With too many subordinates, managers can become overloaded, experience difficulty coordinating activities, and lose control of what is occurring in their work units. On the other hand, with too few subordinates, managers are underutilized and tend to engage in excessive supervision, leaving subordinates little discretion in doing their work.[27]

Span of management or span of control The number of subordinates who report directly to a specific manager

Downsizing has an upside as well. When corporate giants such as Burroughs Wellcome cut jobs in North Carolina's Research Triangle Park, they unleashed dozens of budding entrepreneurs. These entrepreneurs, such as those shown here who formed Triangle Pharmaceuticals, are responsible for starting up about 160 high-tech companies in the area.

FACTORS INFLUENCING SPAN OF MANAGEMENT In general, spans of management can be wider under the following conditions:[28]

■ **Low interaction requirements.** When the work is such that subordinates are able to operate without frequent interaction with each other and/or with their superiors, managers can supervise more individuals.

■ **High competence levels.** High job-related skills and abilities of managers and/or subordinates make it possible for managers to handle more subordinates.

■ **Work similarity.** When employees in a given unit do similar work, it is easier for a manager to maintain adequate supervision than when tasks vary widely.

■ **Low problem frequency and seriousness.** When problems, particularly serious ones, are infrequent, there is less need for managerial attention.

■ **Physical proximity.** When subordinates are located within close physical proximity of one another, managers can coordinate activities more easily.

■ **Few nonsupervisory duties of manager.** Managers can handle more subordinates when they have few nonsupervisory duties to perform, such as doing part of the subordinates' work themselves.

■ **Considerable available assistance.** Managers can supervise more subordinates when they have considerable additional help, such as assistant and secretarial support.

■ **High motivational possibilities of work.** When the work itself offers a high challenge, subordinates are more likely to increase their performance levels because of opportunities to exercise discretion, making it less necessary for continual managerial involvement.

LEVELS IN THE HIERARCHY Although it is not always obvious to the casual observer, spans of management for various managerial positions directly influence the number of hierarchical levels in an organization. A **tall structure** is one that has many hierarchical levels and narrow spans of control. In contrast, a **flat structure** is one that has few hierarchical levels and wide spans of control.

Tall structure A structure that has many hierarchical levels and narrow spans of control

Flat structure A structure that has few hierarchical levels and wide spans of control

To understand how span of control is related to the number of levels, it is helpful to contrast the two hypothetical organizations depicted in Figure 8-5. Organization A, the taller structure on the left, has seven levels; while organization B, the flatter organization on the right, has five levels. If we assume a span of control of 4 in organization A, then the number of managers (beginning with the top level) would be 1, 4, 16, 64, 256, and 1024, respectively, for a total of 1396 managers (levels 1 through 6). At the seventh (bottom) level, there would be 4096 nonmanagerial employees. In contrast, if we assume that organization B has a span of control of 8, then the number of managers (beginning with the top level) would be 1, 8, 64, and 512, respectively, for a total of 585 managers (levels 1 through 4). Organization B also has 4096 nonmanagerial employees in its bottom level, which is level 5. Hence, organization A requires 811 *more* managers than organization B.[29]

If one wanted to reduce the number of hierarchical levels in organization A, the only way to do so without reducing the number of employees at the bottom would be to increase spans of control. Of course, in a real organization, spans of control are not the same throughout the whole organization, as they are in Figure 8-5. Still, the principle is the same. When average spans of control in an organization are narrow, the organization most likely has a tall structure. Very tall organizations raise administrative overhead (because there are more managers to be paid, given office space, etc.), slow communication and decision making (because of the many levels), make it more difficult to pinpoint responsibility for various tasks, and encourage the formation of dull, routine jobs.

Because of such problems with tall structures, many companies have recently been downsizing. **Downsizing** is the process of significantly reducing the layers of middle management, increasing the spans of control, and shrinking the size of the work force for purposes of improving organizational efficiency and effectiveness.[30] A closely related term that is often used synonymously with "downsizing" is "restructuring." **Restructuring** is the process of making a major change in organization structure that often involves reducing management levels and possibly changing some major components of the organization through divestiture and/or acquisition.[31] Again, the purpose is to boost efficiency and effectiveness. Restructuring frequently, but not always, involves reducing the size of an organization's work force.

Downsizing   The process of significantly reducing the layers of middle management, increasing the spans of control, and shrinking the size of the work force

Restructuring   The process of making a major change in organization structure that often involves reducing management levels and possibly changing components of the organization through divestiture and/or acquisition, as well as shrinking the size of the work force

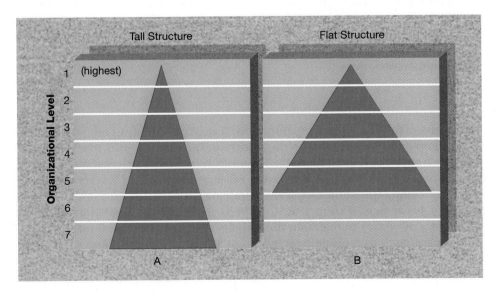

Figure 8-5   *Tall versus flat structure.*

In one example of downsizing, the Ford Motor Company reduced its number of management levels after finding that it was laboring under 12 layers of management, compared with 7 layers at Toyota.[32] The additional levels at Ford represented expensive overhead not borne by a significant competitor, causing a competitive disadvantage for Ford. In addition, having many levels made it more difficult for the company to move quickly in its increasingly competitive situation. Soon after Ford made its reductions, Toyota was back cutting management levels of its own (see the Case in Point discussion).

CASE IN POINT

TOYOTA SHEDS MANAGEMENT LEVELS

Faced with increasing global competition, management at the Toyota Motor Corporation undertook a restructuring aimed at eliminating two management levels. In keeping with the Japanese tradition of attempting to avoid layoffs, the company shifted a number of middle managers to "hands-on work," rather than cutting their jobs.

Toyota's primary aim in restructuring was to streamline decision making by reducing the number of layers through which decisions must travel. The changes affected about 25,000 of the approximately 65,000 Toyota employees, including about 1000 managers. Cost cutting did not seem to be a major factor for the Toyota move because the company has been making admirable profits in recent years.

Instead, the restructuring appeared to stem from the fact that the company was often slower to take competitive action than its smaller Japanese rivals. For instance, Toyota opened its own U.S. assembly plant only after Honda, Nissan, and Mazda were already manufacturing in the United States. The company also trailed behind Honda in making its entry in the luxury-car market.

At Toyota, there were "so many, many steps to reach top management that it [took] time to make a decision," noted a Toyota spokesperson. Furthermore, there were significant numbers of middle managers whose main activities could be summarized as "sit quietly without doing anything," the spokesperson added. Now the displaced managers will need to "become involved in the process of creating and doing hands-on work." Recently appointed Hiroshi Okuda, the first nonfamily president of Toyota since 1967, has reduced management levels still further and continues to cut the size of the work force through mandatory retirements and attrition. The company also is aiming to hire 30 percent of its new workers as contract employees so that it can reduce its commitments to lifetime employment.[33] ■ ■ ■

While many Japanese companies have restructured during the past decade, they generally have been able to do so without the major layoffs that have characterized many U.S. companies.[34] In contrast many large companies in the United States have downsized by laying off large numbers of workers. A listing of the 15 companies announcing the elimination of the largest number of jobs during a 4-year period from 1992 to 1996 is shown in Table 8-1. Downsizing is sometimes necessary to maintain the viability of business under threatening circumstances, such as economic recessions or strong competitive pressures. Done well, it can significantly reduce costs, speed up decision making, energize employees through more challenging jobs, reduce redundancies, and increase

TABLE 8-1 COMPANIES DOWNSIZING THE MOST* EMPLOYEES

COMPANY	JOBS CUT
AT&T	123,000
IBM	122,000
General Motors	99,400
Boeing	61,000
Sears, Roebuck	50,000
Digital Equipment	29,800
Lockheed Martin	29,100
BellSouth	21,200
McDonnell Douglas	21,000
Pacific Telesis	19,000
Delta Airlines	18,800
GTE	18,400
Nynex	17,400
Eastman Kodak	16,800
Baxter International	16,000

*Based on layoff announcements reported in major newspapers. Some announced cuts may not have taken place as of press time.

Source: People Trends; Challenger, Gray & Christmas. Adapted from *HRMagazine,* May 1996, p. 56.

innovation. Done poorly, it can cause the loss of valuable employees (either because they are laid off or because they decide to leave), demoralize survivors, and result in at least short-run productivity declines as employees attempt to pick up additional responsibilities.[35] An American Management Association study indicates that profits rose at only 51 percent of the companies that downsized between 1989 and 1994, while productivity increased only 34 percent of the time. Employee morale, though, decreased in 86 percent of the cases. Critics argue that the continual downsizing is eroding employee loyalty and commitment, with potentially dire long-term consequences (we discuss this issue further in Chapter 10). Others point to the possibility of *corporate anorexia,* a condition in which an organization focuses so heavily on downsizing that it no longer has the resources or will to grow. Petro-Canada, a Calgary-based oil and gas giant, has experienced downsizing and restructuring in the past few years. Recently, the firm's president, Jim Stanford, has announced the firm will put much more emphasis on revenue growth. "You can't shrink to greatness," he says.[36]

Centralization versus Decentralization

To foster vertical coordination, managers also need to consider the appropriate level of **centralization,** the extent to which power and authority are retained at the top organizational levels. The opposite of centralization is **decentralization,** the extent to which power and authority are delegated to lower levels. Centralization and decentralization form a continuum, with many possible degrees of delegation of power and authority in between. The extent of centralization affects vertical coordination by influencing the amount of decision making at the upper and lower levels.[37]

Centralization has several positive aspects.[38] If all major decisions are made at the top levels, it can be easier to coordinate the activities of various units and individuals. Coordination from the top can help reduce duplication of effort and resources by ensuring that similar activities are not carried on by different organizational units. In addition, top managers usually have the most experience and may make better decisions than individuals at lower levels. Sim-

Centralization The extent to which power and authority are retained at the top organizational levels

Decentralization The extent to which power and authority are delegated to lower levels

Nordstrom's, a Seattle-based fashion retailer, has a highly decentralized structure. Individual store buyers and regional managers are encouraged to make decisions on the spot. Within the headquarters, four co-presidents (shown here) oversee day-to-day operations; each is responsible for a different merchandising area, and each enjoys a great deal of autonomy. Nordstrom's three co-chairmen concern themselves mainly with strategic decisions, such as site selection and expansion areas.

ilarly, top-level managers usually have a broader perspective and can better balance the needs of various parts of the organization. Finally, centralization promotes strong leadership in an organization because much of the power remains at the top.

Decentralization also has a number of major advantages.[39] Encouraging decision making at lower levels tends to ease the heavy workloads of executives, leaving them more time to focus on major issues. Decentralization also enriches the jobs of lower-level employees by offering workers the challenge associated with making significant decisions that affect their work. In addition, it leads to faster decision making at the lower levels, because most decisions do not have to be referred up the hierarchy. Individuals at lower levels may be closer to the problem and, therefore, in a better position to make good decisions. Finally, decentralization often leads to the establishment of relatively independent units, such as divisions, whose output is easier to measure than that of units in a functional design. It is worth noting, though, that a divisional structure is not synonymous with decentralization. In some divisional structures, much of the power and authority is still held at the top, and most decisions of significance must be referred to the executive levels.

Given that both approaches have advantages, how does top management decide on the degree of centralization versus decentralization? There are four main factors that begin to tilt the scale away from the centralization side of the continuum and toward the decentralization side:[40]

Large size: It is more difficult for top-level managers in large organizations to have either the time or the knowledge to make all the major decisions.

Geographic dispersion: Top executives frequently find it impossible to keep abreast of the details of operations at various locations.

Technological complexity: It is typically difficult for upper management to keep up technologically.

Environmental uncertainty: The fast pace of change interferes with top management's ability to assess situations with the speed required for timely decisions.

In one recent move toward decentralization, Paul H. O'Neill, chairman of the Aluminum Company of America (Alcoa), stunned a meeting of worldwide Alcoa executives by announcing that he planned to eliminate 2 layers of upper management and give Alcoa's 25 business-unit managers much greater latitude in managing their businesses. "We felt liberated," said Australian business-unit manager Robert F. Slagle.[41]

Delegation

Another means of vertical coordination that is closely related to the central-ization-decentralization issue is delegation. Suppose that you have just become the manager of a restaurant that is part of a chain. Let's assume that you are one of ten restaurant managers who report to a district manager. When you take over as restaurant manager, you probably expect to be assigned **responsibility,** the obligation to carry out duties and achieve goals related to a position. For example, you might have the responsibility of keeping the restaurant open during certain hours, seeing that food is served, making sure the customers are satisfied, and achieving a certain profit margin. You probably also expect to be given **authority,** the right to make decisions, carry out actions, and direct others in matters related to the duties and goals of a position. For example, as the restaurant manager, you might expect to have the authority to hire employees, assign work, and order the food and supplies necessary to keep things running smoothly. You would also expect the position to involve **accountability,** the requirement to provide satisfactory reasons for significant deviations from duties or expected results.

Carrying our story a step further, suppose you soon found that when you attempted to make decisions, such as hiring a new worker, the district manager tended to interfere and even frequently reversed your decisions. Yet, when the end of the month came and you had not achieved your expected profit margin (largely because of interference from the district manager), the district manager still held you accountable for the shortfall in results. Under this set of circumstances, you might correctly conclude that you had been given the responsibility but not the authority needed to do your job.

In this situation, the district manager failed to engage in adequate **delegation,** the assignment of part of a manager's work to others, along with both the responsibility and the authority necessary to achieve expected results. Delegation involves moving decision-making authority and responsibility from one level of the organization to the next lower level. The delegating managers, though, are still ultimately responsible for achieving the results and will be held accountable by their own bosses. Delegation is important to vertical coordination because it allows the hierarchy to be both more efficient and more effective by enabling work to be done at the lowest level possible.[42] In addition, delegation facilitates developing subordinates to fill future managerial positions, thus strengthening prospects for adequate vertical coordination in the future. Generally, more delegating is done in a decentralized structure than in a centralized one. Even within a centralized structure, though, top managers must do some delegating. They cannot do everything themselves.

Although even classical theorists placed considerable emphasis on the need to delegate, many managers still find delegation difficult. Some managers are reluctant to delegate because they fear blame if subordinates fail, believe they lack the time to train subordinates, or wish to hold on to their authority and power. Others avoid delegating because they enjoy doing tasks that subordinates could perform, feel threatened that competent subordinates may perform too well and possibly make the manager look poor by comparison, or simply are concerned about ensuring that the work is completed properly.[43] Jim McCann, CEO of 1-800-FLOWERS, says his biggest challenge has been learning to delegate. For various periods of time he was the best designer, the best telephone representative, and the best delivery person because he was the only

Responsibility The obligation to carry out duties and achieve goals related to a position

Authority The right to make decisions, carry out actions, and direct others in matters related to the duties and goals of a person

Accountability The requirement to provide satisfactory reasons for significant deviations from duties or expected results

Delegation The assignment of part of a manager's work to others, along with both the responsibility and the authority necessary to achieve expected results

MANAGEMENT SKILLS FOR THE TWENTY-FIRST CENTURY

Guidelines for Effective Delegating

These guidelines will help you be an effective delegator:

- The secret of delegating is determining what each member of a work unit can do. Carefully choose the subordinate who should take on the project. Usually it is someone immediately below you in the corporate hierarchy. If you want to skip down two ranks, work through that person's supervisor.
- Next, decide whether you want the subordinate to pinpoint the problem or propose a solution. If the latter, should he or she take action or just present you with alternatives? And do you choose the solution jointly or by yourself?
- Once you define your goals, consider whether the person you have chosen can handle the responsibility. Will the task be a challenge, but not so difficult that the subordinate gets frustrated? "The art of managing is to figure out what each person is capable of, and create assignments that are within their reach, or slightly above, so they can learn," according to one expert.
- Do not make the mistake of spelling out in detail how the subordinate should approach the task. Be clear in your objectives, though, because some people fear that they will appear ignorant if they ask questions. Encourage questions. To give a sense of purpose, explain why the task is important. If it is something that seems menial or insignificant, note that it is a prelude to more meaningful assignments later on.
- Make sure that the subordinate has the time, budget, and data or equipment needed to get the job done—on a deadline. If someone needs training to accomplish the task, be prepared to make the investment. Yes, you could do the job yourself in the time it takes to train someone else, but the hours spent training the individual will be recouped many times over in the future.
- Unless the project is relatively simple, set up specific checkpoints to review progress so that both you and your subordinate can be sure that work is progressing as planned. That way you can provide additional help, if needed, before the project is in serious trouble. If things are going well, you can let the subordinate know that you appreciate good work.
- Be prepared, too, to live with a less than perfect result. Let subordinates know you will support the outcome of their efforts, good or bad. Take responsibility for an occasional blooper, says an expert, and you will have loyal followers for life.[44]

one doing these jobs. As the business began to grow, he realized it would be advantageous to hire people because there were things he could do that they couldn't. Now he says he has people doing every job who are "probably doing it 10 times better than I ever could have done. You have to make the transition to bring other people on board," he notes.[45]

The failure to delegate can hurt managerial careers. A study by the Center for Creative Leadership showed that overmanaging, or the inability to delegate and build a team, was one of the "fatal flaws" that caused executives on the fast track to become derailed.[46] For some guidelines on how to delegate, see the Management Skills for the Twenty-First Century discussion, "Guidelines for Effective Delegating."

Line and Staff Positions

Line position A position that has authority and responsibility for achieving the major goals of the organization

Staff position A position whose primary purpose is providing specialized expertise and assistance to line positions

Another issue related to vertical coordination is the configuration of line and staff positions. A **line position** is a position that has authority and responsibility for achieving the major goals of the organization. A **staff position** is a position whose primary purpose is providing specialized expertise and assistance to line positions. Sometimes the term "staff" is also used to refer to personal staff, individuals who provide assistance to a particular position as required (e.g., an administrative assistant to a division head).

The positions and related departments that are considered either line or staff vary with the type of organization. For example, in a grocery chain, line departments might be store operations, pharmacy operations, and food operations (directly related to major organizational goals), while staff departments might be human resources and consumer affairs (more indirectly related to major goals). In a manufacturing organization, production and sales are typically considered line departments, while purchasing and accounting are normally staff departments. Among the departments that are considered staff in many organizations are human resources, legal, research and development, and purchasing. However, each organization must be evaluated in terms of its own major goals in designating line and staff.[47] For instance, in a major law firm, the legal function would be a line department, despite the fact that it often is a staff department in other types of organizations.

The usefulness of the distinction between line and staff departments becomes more clear when one considers the differences between line authority and staff authority. Line departments have **line authority,** which is authority that follows the chain of command established by the formal hierarchy. On the other hand, staff departments have **functional authority,** which is authority over others in the organization in matters related directly to their respective functions. For example, in the structure for a bank, shown in Figure 8-6, the line departments receive their authority through the chain of command connected to the president. The bank's staff departments have functional authority in relation to other departments, that is, authority only in their area of staff expertise. Staff departments facilitate vertical coordination by making their considerable expertise available where it is needed, rather than following the strict chain of command.

Still, conflicts frequently arise. For example, staff departments sometimes grow very large and begin to oversee the departments they are supposed to assist. Before they were cut back, burgeoning staffs at Xerox second-guessed managers to such a point that new-product development steps which should have taken 2 to 4 weeks took 2 years because of continual reviews by staff units.[48] Nevertheless, such conflicts are not inevitable, particularly if areas of responsibility are clarified and line and staff personnel are encouraged to operate as a team with joint accountability for final results.

Recently, there has been a trend toward reducing the number of corporate-level staff personnel, as companies attempt to cut costs and speed up decision making. This can be seen, for example, at Nucor, a South Carolina–based company that runs steel minimills. Although it has annual revenues that exceed $2.25 billion, Nucor operates with a corporate staff of less than 25. The small central office mainly monitors budgets, cash flow, and overall operations.[49] Enhancing vertical coordination is one structural issue in organizations; promoting horizontal coordination is another.

Line authority The authority that follows the chain of command established by the formal hierarchy

Functional authority The authority of staff departments over others in the organization in matters related directly to their respective functions

■ PROMOTING INNOVATION: METHODS OF HORIZONTAL COORDINATION

Suppose that you purchased a television set at a large local department store with the understanding that the TV would be delivered within 3 days but the set failed to arrive on time. Imagine that when you called to inquire about the delay, your call was passed up the hierarchy until you were talking with a vice president of the department store. You would probably begin to wonder about an organization in which a vice president is drawn into what should have been a routine transaction between sales and shipping. If all such problems had to be handled vertically, organizations would quickly become paralyzed.

Instead, most organizations take steps to facilitate **horizontal coordination,**

Horizontal coordination The linking of activities across departments at similar levels

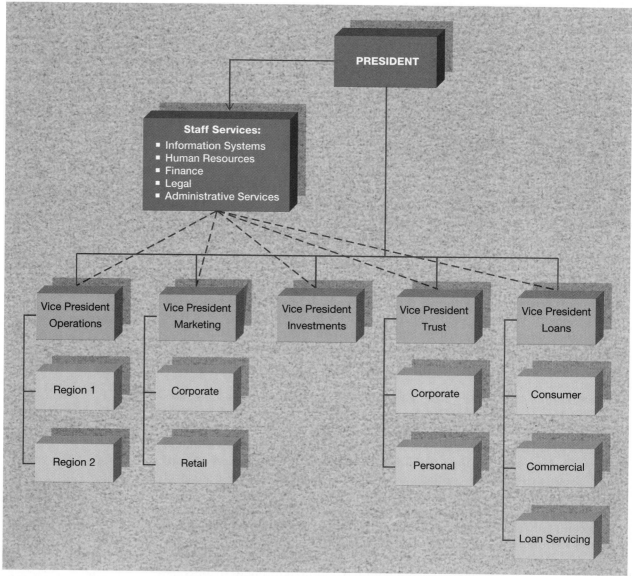

Figure 8-6 *Line and staff departments of a bank.*

the linking of activities across departments at similar levels. Horizontal coordination provides an additional means of processing information in organizations. Organization structure specialist Jay R. Galbraith argues that the more organizations need to process information in the course of producing their products or services, the more methods of horizontal coordination they will need to use.[50] Organizations typically need to process more information when they face complex and/or changing technology, environmental uncertainty, and growing size. (We discuss these issues further in Chapter 9.) For example, when William H. Wilson founded the Pioneer/Eclipse Corporation, a small company that specializes in a floor-cleaning system, he was able to provide most of the necessary coordination himself within a traditional functional structure. As the company grew larger and more complex, it began to lose money because of insufficient horizontal coordination. In one situation, the sales department launched a promotion only to find that manufacturing and purchasing knew nothing about it and had insufficient materials and stock on hand to fill orders. In another instance, the credit department denied credit to a major account before the sales department could resolve the conflict more amicably. "The left hand," says one observer, "did not know what the right hand was doing."[51]

Because horizontal coordination facilitates processing information across the organization, it also helps promote innovation.[52] There are three reasons for this: First, new ideas are more likely to emerge when a diversity of views are shared. Second, awareness of problems and opportunities across areas can spark creative ideas. Third, involving others in the development of ideas often positively influences their willingness to help implement new ideas (see Chapter 11).

By facilitating the exchange of information across units at similar levels, horizontal coordination mechanisms, in essence, supplement the basic hierarchy and related methods of vertical coordination. Three major means that are particularly useful in promoting horizontal coordination are slack resources, information systems, and lateral relations (see Figure 8-7).[53]

Slack Resources

One interesting means of supporting horizontal coordination is the use of **slack resources,** a cushion of resources that facilitates adaptation to internal and external pressures, as well as initiation of changes.[54] You have probably benefited from the availability of slack resources in your personal life. For example, in your family, a slack resource might be an extra car, an extra television set, or your own telephone line. Through coordination and tighter programming of mutual schedules, your family might be able to get by with less, but doing so would take more effort and might hinder quick changes in plans. Because organizations face similar choices, they, too, often use slack resources, such as extra people, time, equipment, and inventory, to reduce the need for constant coordination among units and to provide some latitude in how resources are used.

Slack resources can also help foster creativity and innovation.[55] For example, 3M encourages researchers to spend 15 percent of their time on projects of their own choice that have potential for long-term payoff (a practice the

Slack resources A cushion of resources that facilitates adaptation to internal and external pressures, as well as initiation of changes

Figure 8-7 *Horizontal coordination methods for increasing information-processing capacity as needed.*

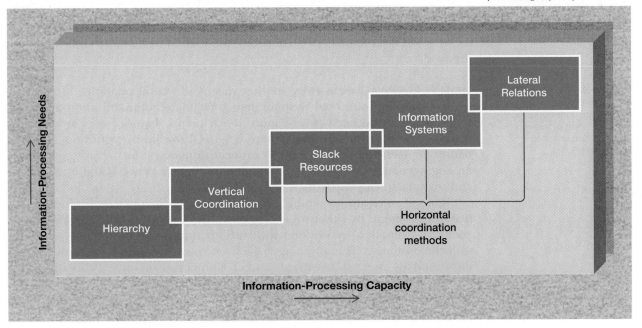

company calls "bootlegging"). In essence, this practice promotes the use of slack resources (time, equipment, and materials) to enhance the prospects for innovation.

Information Systems

Another important and growing means of horizontal coordination is the use of information systems, particularly computerized ones, to coordinate various parts of organizations. For example, because of its far-flung international operations and its use of divisional structures, Citicorp experienced horizontal coordination difficulties. The company was frequently embarrassed when a client of one Citicorp unit would use the services of other units, perhaps even in other parts of the world, and receive conflicting advice. Even when the advice did not actually conflict, the fragmented guidance offered to clients did not maximize Citicorp's capacity to provide good service. The solution? Citicorp greatly enhanced the ability of various departments to exchange information by instituting a new computerized conferencing system. Called PARTICIPATE, the system allows offices around the world to communicate and coordinate their efforts quickly.[56] (We consider computerized information systems further in Chapter 19.)

Lateral Relations

Another approach to horizontal coordination that is increasingly being used is lateral relations. **Lateral relations** is the coordination of efforts through communicating and problem solving with peers in other departments or units, rather than referring most issues up the hierarchy for consideration. Such collaboration promotes innovative solutions to difficulties and fosters creative responses to opportunities. Major means of lateral relations are direct contact, liaison roles, task forces, teams, and managerial integrators.[57]

Lateral relations The coordination of efforts through communicating and problem solving with peers in other departments or units, rather than referring most issues up the hierarchy for resolution

DIRECT CONTACT One means of lateral relations is **direct contact,** communication between two or more persons at similar levels in different work units for purposes of coordinating work and solving problems. Direct contact allows many managers at middle and lower levels to resolve issues without having to involve upper-level managers. In fact, problems can frequently be handled better by lower-level managers because they may be more familiar with the issues involved.

Direct contact Communication between two or more persons at similar levels in different work units for purposes of coordinating work and solving problems

LIAISON ROLES A **liaison role,** another means of lateral relations, is a role to which a specific individual is appointed to facilitate communication and resolution of issues between two or more departments. Liaison roles are typically reserved for situations in which there is a need for almost continuous coordination between the departments in order to function effectively. For example, an engineer may be appointed to maintain contact between the engineering and manufacturing departments.[58]

Liaison roles are becoming more common between private businesses and major customers. In this type of situation, the liaison person enhances horizontal coordination by working with various internal departments, as well as with the customer. The advantage of liaison roles in dealing with customers is illustrated by the comments of a steel company executive (who wished to remain anonymous). The executive maintains a full-time liaison person on site at Honda's plant in Marysville, Ohio. He explained that if there is a problem with stamping steel to make fenders and other car-body parts and if there were

Liaison role A role to which a specific individual is appointed to facilitate communication and resolution of issues between two or more departments

Teamwork can take time, patience, and cajoling. The manager of a product-development team at Textron found that she had to act as parent, teacher, and referee in the course of getting team members to work effectively together. Her patience paid off: the team created a new coating that makes plastic automobile grilles shine like chrome.

no liaison person, the scenario would go like this: The Honda people affected by the problem would go to their purchasing department. The purchasing department would contact the steel company salesperson. The salesperson would complain to the steel company product office. The product office would pass the issue on to the steel company department that made the steel for Honda. At that point, said the executive, the offending department is likely to deny responsibility for the problem and argue that "it's a Honda stamping problem" (i.e., the problem is not caused by the way in which the steel is made but, rather, by the way in which the steel is being stamped at the Honda plant).[59] A liaison person helps cut through such red tape by dealing directly with the departments closely associated with the problem.

TASK FORCES AND TEAMS A *task force* is a temporary interdepartmental group usually formed to make recommendations on a specific issue. Task-force recommendations typically constitute advice. The person or group that appointed the task force can then decide whether or not to implement the recommendations. Task forces promote horizontal coordination by providing a vehicle through which individuals from different organizational units can share their ideas on specific issues and plan viable courses of action.

Teams, on the other hand, are either temporary or ongoing groups that are expected to solve problems and implement solutions related to a particular issue or area. Teams are often composed of individuals from different departments, but they may also be made up of members from the same organizational unit. At its nylon fiber plant in Pensacola, Florida, Monsanto uses an interesting combination of liaison roles and teams in its new Adopt A Customer program, aimed at offering outstanding customer service. Under the program, Monsanto matches top customers with key employees who act as liaison persons. When problems arise, the liaison employees become "resource team leaders" who help bring about quick resolution of problems. For example, if a customer notifies the liaison employee that yarn is breaking during processing, the liaison person then becomes an internal resource team leader. He or she notifies the technical salespeople and quickly puts together a team with the necessary expertise and resources to resolve the difficulty promptly and offer innovative solutions if necessary. "The whole idea of Adopt A Customer is to give top priority to that problem not in three days, but on day one, with the first phone call from our customer," says Monsanto's manager of technical sales for carpet fibers.[60] We discuss teams and task forces further in Chapter 15.

Managerial integrator   A separate manager who is given the task of coordinating related work that involves several functional departments

MANAGERIAL INTEGRATORS A **managerial integrator,** another means of lateral relations, is a separate manager who is given the task of coordinating related work that involves several functional departments. Such managers typically have titles like "project manager," "product manager," or "brand manager" and are not members of any of the departments whose activities they help coordinate. *Project managers* are usually responsible for coordinating the work associated with a particular project until its completion. They are used extensively in the aerospace, defense, and construction industries, in which large, technically complex projects must be completed within specified time limits and at contracted costs. *Product managers* orchestrate the launching of new products and services and may then continue coordinating interdepartmental work related to those products and services. *Brand managers* coordinate organizational efforts involving particular name-brand products, most often within the soap, food, and toiletries industries. Brand managers help devise and implement brand strategies and plans, monitor results, and correct problems as they occur. In essence, managerial integrators act as horizontal coordinating agents. For example, Ralcorp Holdings, Inc., which uses brand managers to oversee its major brands, has a brand manager for its well-known Wheat, Rice, and Corn Chex.[61] The use of managerial integrators allows fast reaction to environmental change and efficient use of resources because functional resources can be switched among various projects relatively easily. In addition, managerial integrators are in a good position to act as sponsors of innovative ideas.

They typically do not have line authority over the individuals and functional departments that they are attempting to coordinate. Rather, they must obtain the cooperation of the functional managers who control the major resources. In doing so, they must compete with others (e.g., managerial integrators for other projects) who also want the help of various functional departments in making their projects, products, or brands a success. As a result, managerial integrators must use their knowledge, competence, personality, group management skills, and persuasion abilities in working with functional managers and individuals who work within the functional departments and are assigned to their project.[62]

In this chapter, we have considered several of the major elements of organization structure, including methods of vertical and horizontal coordination. In the next chapter, we explore the link between strategy and organization structure in enhancing organizational effectiveness.

■ CHAPTER SUMMARY

Organizing is the process of arranging work and resources so that planned goals can be achieved. One important part of the organizing function is determining organization structure. Organization structure consists of four main elements: job design, departmentalization of positions and units, methods of vertical coordination, and methods of horizontal coordination. Organization charts provide a graphic depiction of the broad outlines of an organization's structure and help employees trace the chain of command.

There are four main approaches to job design: job simplification, job rotation, job enlargement, and job enrichment. The job characteristics model helps guide job enrichment efforts by explaining the importance of core job characteristics, critical psychological states, and high growth-need strength to job outcomes. A related aspect of designing jobs is providing alternative work schedules, which are often helpful in meeting the needs of a diverse work force. Major types of alternative work schedules include flextime, the compressed workweek, and job sharing.

Among the most commonly used forms of departmentalization are functional, divisional, hybrid, and matrix. There are five major means of achieving vertical coordination, which is the linking of activities at the top of the organization with those at the middle and lower levels: formalization, span of management, centralization versus decentralization, delegation, and line and staff positions.

Three major means that are particularly useful in facilitating horizontal coordination are slack resources, information systems, and lateral relations. Slack resources provide a cushion of resources that allows adaptation to change, while information systems enhance information exchange. Lateral relations, which involves coordinating efforts with peers in other departments and units, has several main forms: direct contact, liaison roles, task forces, teams, and managerial integrators. Methods of horizontal coordination are particularly useful in promoting innovation because they facilitate the exchange of ideas across organizational units.

■ QUESTIONS FOR DISCUSSION AND REVIEW

1 Explain the four elements that make up organization structure. What evidence can you see of these elements at your college or university?

2 Describe the relationship between an organization chart and an organization's chain of command. If you were new to an organization, how could an organization chart help you become oriented?

3 Contrast the various major approaches to job design. Use the job characteristics model to explain how you might go about enriching a particular job.

4 Distinguish among the three main types of alternative work schedules. What adjustments might be required to accommodate nontraditional work schedules?

5 Explain the role that formalization plays in vertical coordination. Give an example of a policy or rule that is likely to have a dysfunctional impact on organizational effectiveness. In what way should the policy or rule be changed to have a positive influence?

6 Explain the relationship between span of management and the extent to which an organization is flat or tall. Why are a number of major organizations attempting to make their structures more flat? What are some potential pitfalls associated with downsizing?

7 Contrast the advantages of centralization and those of decentralization, and explain when each approach is likely to be most appropriate. Why is delegation important to both?

8 Explain the differences between a line position and a staff position. Which type of position would you prefer to hold? Why?

9 Explain the concepts of slack resources and computer-based information systems as they apply to horizontal coordination. Cite examples showing how each one has been used to facilitate horizontal coordination in organizations?

10 Distinguish among the various types of lateral relations. How could they be used effectively in your college or university?

■ DISCUSSION QUESTIONS FOR CHAPTER OPENING CASE

1 What methods of vertical coordination are evident at 1-800-FLOWERS? What other vertical coordination approaches might you suggest?

2 What methods of horizontal coordination are apparent at 1-800-FLOWERS? What changes might be necessary?

3 What types of structural issues is 1-800-FLOWERS likely to face if the company develops a national chain of retail florists?

■ EXERCISES FOR MANAGING IN THE TWENTY-FIRST CENTURY

EXERCISE 1
SKILL BUILDING: UNDERSTANDING ORGANIZATION STRUCTURE

 Managers who carry out the organizing function effectively need to have a firm grasp of the organizational structure concept. The significant issues pertaining to how an organization is structured are indicated in the left column. Match these with the examples indicated in the right column.

Organizational Issues

1. _____ Chain of command
2. _____ Organization chart
3. _____ Job simplification
4. _____ Job rotation
5. _____ Job enlargement
6. _____ Job enrichment
7. _____ Flextime
8. _____ Compressed workweek
9. _____ Job sharing
10. _____ Departmentalization
11. _____ Vertical coordination
12. _____ Formalization
13. _____ Span of control
14. _____ Centralization
15. _____ Authority
16. _____ Accountability
17. _____ Line authority
18. _____ Functional authority
19. _____ Slack resources
20. _____ Lateral relations

Definition/Example

a. Written policies, procedures (rules for purchasing equipment)
b. Provide reasons for significant deviations (explain change in production from 40 to 90)
c. First, second, third, and fourth levels working together (four levels of managers in manufacturing meet to discuss possible new technology)
d. A cushion of resources used to meet unprogrammed requirements (additional trucks to deliver unusual number of orders)
e. Work four 10-hour days (6 a.m. to 4 p.m., Monday through Thursday)
f. Authority related to specific function (pay policy enforced by vice president of human resources)
g. Authority follows chain of command (president decides which three plants will be closed following reorganization)
h. Line of authority (John reports to Sue)
i. Number of reporting units (seven divisions reporting to vice president of operations)
j. Adding variety of similar tasks (assume the functions of peer in addition to current job)
k. Assigned only a few specific activities (make new files; file papers)
l. Line diagram that reflects structure (organization has nine SBUs)
m. Elastic work hours; core hours (9 a.m. to 5 p.m.; 6 a.m. to 2 p.m.; 10 a.m. to 2 p.m.)
n. Power and authority retained (need permission from headquarters)
o. Upgrading the job-task mix (taking on budgeting, planning, and other functions)
p. Coordination with other units/departments (engineering, sales, and manufacturing working out a problem)
q. Two employees/one job (John works mornings; Joe works afternoons)
r. Right to make decisions (can spend up to $75,000 per purchase)
s. Clustering into work groups, units, divisions (assembly team, motors division)
t. Shifting workers through functions (sales, then human resources, then finance)

EXERCISE 2
MANAGEMENT EXERCISE: DESIGNING AN INNOVATING ORGANIZATION

 You have just landed a job as the administrative assistant to the CEO of Chameleon Technology, a fast-growing high-technology firm. You took the job because you want to learn more about how to manage high-technology firms. Also, you figure that because the company is growing rapidly, some very good career opportunities will open up quickly.

Chameleon has had tremendous success with its initial product, a small hard-disk drive for personal computers that holds considerably more data and costs less than offerings from competitors. Recently, the company introduced a new high-resolution video screen for use with personal computers that is also selling better than anticipated. Because the company is growing so quickly, the CEO is experiencing acute difficulties trying to handle long-range planning as well as the day-to-day developments in a rapidly changing competitive environment. For example, in a number of recent instances, sales were made but products were not shipped in a timely manner. In another case, although production was expanded to meet the rising demand, the human resource area was not notified of the need for additional workers. In both situations, the bottleneck occurred because the CEO's office did not coordinate these activities as well as it had in the past.

In addition, the CEO is concerned with fostering the kind of innovative thinking that will lead not only to improvements in existing products but also to new offerings. The CEO feels that Chameleon is too dependent on its two products and that the company is not moving fast enough in improving the disk drive and developing new products.

Because of your recent management studies, the CEO asks you to develop some ideas about how to achieve better coordination of the company's activities and also foster innovation. Chameleon is currently organized in a functional structure, with major departments in the following areas: manufacturing, sales, human resources, finance and accounting, and engineering. The company currently has about 600 employees.

Prepare a proposal to present to the CEO outlining the steps that could be taken to achieve better vertical and horizontal coordination, as well as to encourage more innovation.

CONCLUDING CASE 1

TEACHING AN ELEPHANT TO DANCE—GM REORGANIZES

When Roger B. Smith became chairman of General Motors in 1981, the automobile giant's share of the U.S. car market was crumbling and the company had just reported its first loss since 1921. Smith quickly appointed a task force of 10 select executives to consider a massive reorganization of a structure that had been in existence for decades. At that point, the major skeleton of the company consisted of two huge fiefdoms, Fisher Body and the General Motors Assembly Division (GMAD), as well as the five famous car divisions: Chevrolet, Pontiac, Oldsmobile, Buick, and Cadillac. With centralized design, engineering, and manufacturing, all GM's cars had begun to look remarkably similar, regardless of the nameplate and price tag. The situation had become so bad that Ford's Lincoln-Mercury division scored big with ads that poked fun at owners of GM luxury cars who were trying to pick their cars out from a sea of moderately priced, moderately altered clones.

At the same time, GM was criticized because it responded to the popular smaller cars of its Japanese competitors merely by making shrunken versions of its larger cars, a strategy that was essentially a failure. In addition, the company's structure made responsibility difficult to pinpoint, even though multiple organizational units had to sign their agreement for most decisions. Smith wanted a structure that would enable GM to respond more quickly to the market and to measure more easily the performance of its major organizational units.

After 15 months of planning, the world's largest corporation (the first to top $100 billion in sales) began a major structural overhaul in 1984 that was destined to take several years because of GM's monstrous size. The main reorganization created two new-car groups: Buick, Oldsmobile, Cadillac (BOC) and Chevrolet, Pontiac, GM of Canada (CPC). The BOC group concentrated on large cars, while CPC was in charge of smaller cars. Each group had its own design, engineering, and manufacturing resources, while Fisher Body and GMAD were dissolved.

Smith's bold moves were aimed at giving GM "the key to the twenty-first century." Unfortunately, the reorganization took longer than planned, and critics argue that Smith did not move quickly enough to cut costs. GM's share of the U.S. auto market, which was about 45 percent when Smith took over, dropped to around 35 percent by the time he retired in 1990. His successor, Robert C. Stempel, faced a formidable competitive situation.

After GM posted a record loss of $4.45 billion in 1991, Stempel announced that the company would cut 74,000 employees and 21 production facilities by the mid-1990s. Because losses in GM's core North American automobile operations had been as much as $7 billion, GM's board of directors became impatient with the pace of change and, in an unusual move, forced a reshuffling of the company's top management. The board named John F. Smith, former head of GM's highly profitable European operations, as CEO and ousted Stempel.

John Smith soon announced a management reorganization. The car design and manufacturing activities of the two major car groups, BOC and CPC, were merged into one group, North American Passenger Car Platforms. In addition, all vehicle sales and marketing operations were combined into one group, North American Vehicles Sales and Marketing. The heads of these two groups reported directly to Smith, eliminating a layer of management and enabling the company to more readily make fundamental changes and cut costs. Within a few months, GM announced plans to cut 74 percent of its corporate headquarters, which would reduce the size of the corporate staff from 13,500 to 3500. Later Smith subdivided the platforms group into three segments: trucks, midsize and luxury cars, and small cars.

Within a couple of years, Smith initiated a further major reorganization, aimed at speeding new-model development and better managing the GM brand names. The reorganization created 16 to 18 product managers who are responsible for coordinating various personnel, such as designers, engineers, manufacturing managers, and marketing executives, to produce new cars more quickly and effectively. The reorganization also established more than 30 brand managers, one for each of its major vehicle brands, such as the Oldsmobile Bravada. Some divisions were merged, such as Pontiac and GMC. The move to brand managers was aimed at more clearly targeting products to specific customer need segments and building the long-term image and equity of the GM brands.[63]

QUESTIONS FOR CONCLUDING CASE 1

1 How would you characterize the new changes in organization structure at GM? What difficulties might they create?
2 What can John Smith do to enhance vertical coordination?
3 What can John Smith do to boost horizontal coordination?

CONCLUDING CASE 2

VOLKSWAGEN GEARS UP FOR GLOBAL COMPETITION

During most of the 1980s and into the 1990s, Volkswagen AG has pursued a daring expansion strategy. The company acquired two major carmakers, Seat in Spain and Skoda in Czechoslovakia. The strategy was aimed at creating a "federated" European company: a true multinational emerging from the European theater, gaining the capacities to compete across the board worldwide. As part of the federated notion, there are separate divisions for each of the company's two existing *marques,* or brands, Volkswagen and Audi, and separate divisions for both Seat and Skoda. Each division has been given a great deal of operating autonomy.

The rationale behind the structure is to allow the different brands to customize their products to meet the requirements of their particular groups of customers. At the same time, each division is to emphasize Volkswagen's traditional strengths— namely, solid engineering and drivability. For this reason, a major research and development center is maintained in Germany for the use of all the divisions. Even with their autonomy, the divisions are still expected to cooperate and share when it is in the best interest of the company.

In Germany, the principle of "codetermination" applies, whereby publicly traded companies have both a board of management and a supervisory board. The board of management usually has about six members, who are top executives in the company. This board is responsible for the day-to-day management and operation of the company and helps coordinate the activities of the four divisions when necessary. In contrast, the supervisory board exercises oversight. Half of its 12 to 20 members are employee representatives, and half represent owners

and are elected in a manner similar to the election of board directors in the United States. The supervisory board has the exclusive power to appoint members of the management board, and it awards each executive a contract for from 1 to 5 years (renewable if the executive is performing satisfactorily). The supervisory board also participates in matters that can significantly affect employment. Hence its approval is necessary for foreign acquisitions (such as those of Seat and Skoda) and plans to establish factories abroad.

A major problem for Volkswagen is that it operates less efficiently than most other car manufacturers in the world. Finding ways to cut costs is a major priority. One planned approach is to reduce the number of platforms on which cars are built from a relatively high 16 down to 4. Similar-sized cars in the four divisions would share thousands of common parts, from steel floor pans to windshield-wiper motors. Current company chairman Ferdinand Piëch explains that with only four platforms "we will be able to offer a much greater number of models than before while keeping their designs highly distinctive." Estimates are that sharing common platforms could produce savings as high as $150 per car. Critics argue that going to so few platforms could undermine the sporty image of the Audi, while adding higher costs to lower-priced brands.

One of Volkswagen's major cost factors is its large and expensive work force in Germany. The town of Wolfsburg, Germany, site of Volkswagen headquarters, contains the world's largest automotive plant under one roof. Partially because labor costs are exceptionally high, Volkswagen has expended considerable effort to automate the plant. The move has enabled the company to focus workers on more complex tasks, such as customization. At the same time, Piëch estimates the com-

pany has an excess of about 30,000 workers. The firm's employees working in Germany constitute 42 percent of the worldwide work force of 242,000, but account for 58 percent of total wage costs. The supervisory board does not want to allow any type of major downsizing or restructuring because of its negative impact on the work force. About 57 percent of Volkswagen's automobiles are made in the company's German plants. Attrition is expected to reduce the work force by 20,000, but it will take several years.

Meanwhile, Volkswagen has been building or retooling plants in various parts of the world, such as former East Germany, China, and Mexico. This expansion has enabled the company to serve national markets more effectively, as well as to reduce labor costs. Although the expansion has led to greater market share, it has been extremely expensive. The profit picture has improved for now, but margins are low. The company faces increased competition from Japanese cars that are made at significantly less cost and from U.S. car manufacturers with operations in Europe.[64]

QUESTIONS FOR CONCLUDING CASE 2

1 Identify the type of departmentalization used by Volkswagen. To what extent does Volkswagen appear to use decentralization as a means of vertical coordination?

2 What other methods of vertical coordination are apparent at the company? What dilemmas does Volkswagen face with regard to downsizing and restructuring?

3 What mechanisms for promoting horizontal coordination and innovation can be identified? What could Volkswagen do to increase horizontal coordination and innovation?

CHAPTER NINE

STRATEGIC ORGANIZATION DESIGN

CHAPTER OUTLINE

Designing Organization Structures: An Overview
Which Comes First—Strategy or Structure?
Factors Influencing Organization Design

Assessing Structural Alternatives
Functional Structure
Divisional Structure
Hybrid Structure
Matrix Structure
Emerging Structures

Weighing Contingency Factors
Technology
Size
Environment

Matching Strategy and Structure

Promoting Innovation: Using Structural Means to Enhance Prospects
Vital Roles
Reservations
Differentiation Paradox
Transfer Process

LEARNING OBJECTIVES

After studying this chapter, you should be able to:

■ Summarize current views about the link between strategy and organization structure.

■ Explain the functional, divisional, hybrid, and matrix types of departmentalization.

■ List the major advantages and disadvantages of each type of departmentalization, as well as discuss the basic circumstances under which each is likely to be effective.

■ Explain the stages of matrix departmentalization.

■ Identify emerging types of structures.

■ Assess how contingency factors, such as technology, size, and environment, impact organization structure.

■ Delineate how strategy and structure can be matched.

■ Indicate how structure can be used to enhance prospects for innovation.

GAINING THE EDGE

Post-it note pads are one of 3M's most successful products, but they might never have made it to the production line without 3M's strong emphasis on encouraging innovation and supporting research and development. 3M makes strategic use of organization design to promote the development of unique products that give the company an edge on the market.

POST-IT NOTES WIN OUT AT 3M

One company that has earned a solid reputation for innovation is 3M. A look at the development of the famous Post-it note pads illustrates the challenge of the innovation process.

The path to success was long and arduous, beginning when chemist Spence Silver accidentally discovered an adhesive with odd properties. Although it would stick to something, it would not bond tightly. You could pull it off without damaging the item to which it had been attached. Yet no one could think of a practical application. Only after a ferocious battle with management was Silver able to get the $10,000 necessary to have the substance patented.

After several years, Silver finally persuaded a new venture team, a group formed to explore innovative product ideas, to take another look at the substance. Fortunately, one of the people on the team was Arthur Fry, a chemical engineer who also happened to sing in his church choir. He would use little slips of paper to mark the hymns that were to be sung, but the slips had a habit of falling out of the hymn book, leaving him fumbling furiously in church. He considered putting a little bit of Silver's adhesive on the paper. From that original insight, he envisioned the possibility of creating note pads with many uses and took over the spearheading of the project.

There were further obstacles ahead. Two other members of the new venture team found it necessary to develop a special coating for the paper in order to make the product work properly. Then engineering told Fry that there was no reasonable way to manufacture the pads. As a result, Fry constructed a prototype of a machine that is now a closely guarded secret. In the end the note pads became one of the most successful products in 3M history.

Even with its bumpy history, the Post-it note pad story would probably never have occurred without 3M's well-known efforts at fostering innovation. The company has more than 90 product divisions. Each division has its own R&D group that concentrates on projects that can be brought to market in the near future. At 3M, each division is expected to generate at least 25 percent of its revenue each year from products that were not in existence 5 years earlier. In pursuing that aim, one can obtain funding from multiple places, such as one's own division, other divisions, and new venture teams. In addition, scientists are expected to use up to 15 percent of their time pursuing avenues of discovery of their own choosing.

The company makes ample use of teams to explore new product ideas, and it holds special technical symposia at which researchers present the results of current projects and marketers discuss present strategies and marketplace needs. 3M is lenient about mistakes, believing that when individuals venture into new areas, errors are inevitable. Research and development groups that report to upper-level management concentrate on long-term projects and leading-edge technology.[1]   ■■■

3M has become famous for its ability to foster innovation and produce a steady stream of successful new products. Because so many of its businesses pursue a differentiation strategy based on unique products, innovation is critical to the company's strategic effectiveness. In part, 3M's success is due to its managers' ability to use structural means to support differentiation strategies and encourage innovation.

In the previous chapter, we considered a number of basic organizing elements, such as job design, type of departmentalization, and methods of vertical and horizontal coordination, that can be used to design organization structures. In this chapter, we examine how organizations like 3M use various tools to design structures that support critical strategic directions. Accordingly, we begin by presenting a brief overview of the strategy-structure relationship and then outline the factors that influence organization design. We next assess the advantages and disadvantages of major structural alternatives. We also examine important contingency factors that are likely to influence the success of different organization structures. We then probe the issue of matching strategy with structure. Finally, we investigate structural devices that help boost the likelihood of significant innovations.

■ DESIGNING ORGANIZATION STRUCTURES: AN OVERVIEW

As mentioned in Chapter 8, the process of developing an organization structure is sometimes referred to as organization design. In designing organization structures, what factors do managers need to consider? According to a famous study, one important issue is an organization's strategy.

Which Comes First—Strategy or Structure?

In a landmark book called *Strategy and Structure,* noted business historian Alfred D. Chandler studied the origins of the largest U.S. firms.[2] He was particularly interested in whether strategy development preceded or followed the design of organization structures. On the basis of his studies, Chandler concluded that major companies (such as Du Pont; General Motors; Sears, Roebuck; and Standard Oil) generally follow a pattern of strategy development and then structural change, rather than the reverse.

In Chandler's view, organizations often change their strategies in order to better utilize their resources to fuel growth. The changes in strategy then lead to management difficulties because the current structures do not fit the new strategies. Unless organizations subsequently make adjustments in structure, the new strategies cannot realize their potential and serious inefficiencies will result.

Other researchers have questioned the structure-follows-strategy thesis, claiming that it is too simplistic. It appears that particular structures are likely to influence the strategies that organizations are apt to adopt.[3] For example, former CEO Colby Chandler (no relation to Alfred Chandler) estimates that Eastman Kodak lost about $3.5 billion in sales between 1981 and 1985 to competitors such as Fuji Photo film. The reason was that Kodak's functional structure did not allow for the kinds of specific strategies needed in its multiple businesses, and hence, specific strategies were not developed. Accordingly, Colby Chandler reorganized the $17-billion-per-year company into 34 divisions, ranging from color film to copiers, so that they could operate as strategic business units. Within 2 years, all business units had developed specific strategies, almost all had gained market share, and Kodak's exports increased by 23 percent.[4] Thus it is possible that there are causal linkages each way between structure and strategy. Structure may follow strategy at one point; then the new structures may influence the development of new strategies. In any event, Alfred Chandler's work suggests that a mismatch between strategy and structure can lead to organizational difficulties.

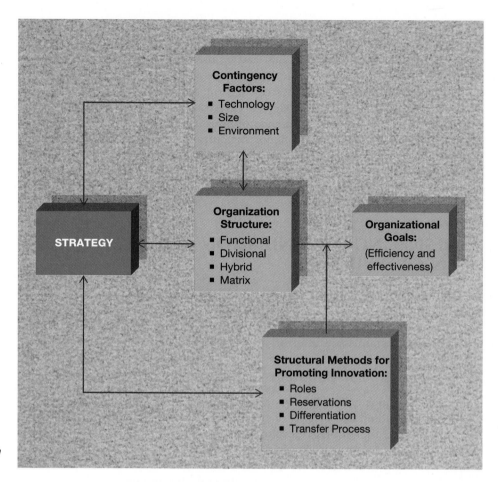

Figure 9-1 *Major components influencing the design of effective organization structures.*

Factors Influencing Organization Design

While there is an important connection between strategy and organization structure, the effectiveness of a particular type of structure is also influenced by certain contingency factors, such as the dominant type of technology used or the organization's size.[5] In addition, structural methods for promoting innovation can facilitate strategic implementation and the attainment of organizational goals. These components and their relationships to organization structure are shown in Figure 9-1. We explore these relationships in the remainder of this chapter. We begin by examining in greater detail the major types of organization structure, or departmentalization, that were introduced in Chapter 8, since they represent the principal structural alternatives available.

■ ASSESSING STRUCTURAL ALTERNATIVES

As discussed briefly in the previous chapter, the four most common types of departmentalization are functional, divisional, hybrid, and matrix. They are often referred to as organization structures or organization designs. Each type has major advantages and disadvantages.[6]

Functional Structure

Functional structure is a type of departmentalization in which positions are grouped according to their main functional (or specialized) area. In other

Functional structure A structure in which positions are grouped according to their main functional (or specialized) area

words, positions are combined into units on the basis of similarity of expertise, skills, and work activities.

COMMON FUNCTIONS Several specialties are commonly associated with functional structures in business organizations.[7] For example, the *production,* or *operations,* function combines activities directly related to manufacturing a product or delivering a service. *Marketing* focuses on the promotion and sale of products and services. *Human resources* is responsible for attracting and retaining organization members and enhancing their effectiveness. *Finance* is concerned with obtaining and managing financial resources. *Research and development* is responsible for producing unique ideas and methods that will lead to new and/or improved products and services. *Accounting* deals with financial reporting to meet the needs of both internal and external sources. Finally, the *legal* function handles legal matters affecting the organization. Notice that when we are speaking of organization structure, the term "function" (or specialized area of expertise) has a different meaning than it does when we are discussing the major functions of management, that is, planning, organizing, leading, and controlling. The functional organization structure for Celestial Seasonings, the Denver-based herbal tea company, is shown in Figure 9-2. The structure includes many of the common functional areas discussed above.

An organization developing a functional structure must consider the specialized areas that are relevant to its own needs. For example, a large utility company with a functional design might have an energy department that is equivalent to the production, or operations, department often found in other organizations, since the company is geared to producing energy. It might also have a distribution department as a major function because of the importance of energy distribution to a utility. However, a major bank with a functional organization structure might have a functional department for investments and another for loans.

ADVANTAGES OF FUNCTIONAL STRUCTURE The functional form of organization has several major advantages, which are summarized in Table 9-1. For one thing, it encourages the development of expertise because employees can concentrate on fostering specialties within a single function. For example, if you were the vice president for human resources in a functional structure, you might be able to develop specialists in such areas as recruiting, compensation, and training. Another advantage is that employees have clear career paths within their particular function, giving them further encouragement to develop

Figure 9-2 *Celestial Seasonings' functional structure.*

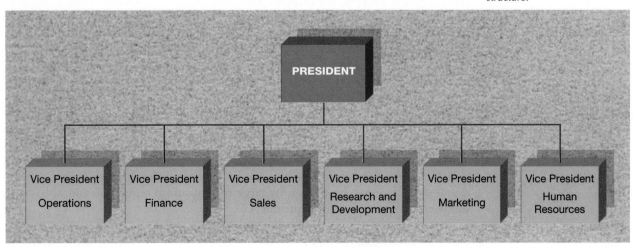

TABLE 9-1 MAJOR ADVANTAGES AND DISADVANTAGES OF A FUNCTIONAL STRUCTURE	
ADVANTAGES	**DISADVANTAGES**
In-depth development of expertise	Slow response time on multifunctional problems
Clear career path within function	Backlog of decisions at top of hierarchy
Efficient use of resources	Bottlenecks due to sequential tasks
Possible economies of scale	Restricted view of organization among employees
Ease of coordination within function	Inexact measurement of performance
Potential technical advantage over competitors	Narrow training for potential managers

their expertise. In addition, a functional structure usually facilitates efficient use of resources because it is fairly easy to shift individuals from one project to another as needed when they work in the same department. Economies of scale may also be possible, either because large amounts of work can be handled efficiently when individuals specialize or because major equipment can be justified by work volume. An additional advantage is that a functional structure may facilitate ease of coordination within departments, since the activities are all related in one way or another to the same specialized area. Finally, grouping by functions increases the potential for developing specialized technical competencies that can constitute an advantage over competitors.

DISADVANTAGES OF FUNCTIONAL STRUCTURE Functional designs also have several disadvantages, as summarized in Table 9-1. For one thing, the coordination across functions that is necessary in handling complex problems may seriously delay responses because major issues and conflicts must be passed up the chain for resolution. Also, bottlenecks may develop as one function waits for another to complete its work. In addition, specialists sometimes become so narrow in orientation that they cannot relate to the needs of other functions or to the overall goals of the organization. At the same time, performance of a particular unit may be difficult to measure because various functions have a hand in the organizational results. Finally, a functional structure provides a fairly narrow training ground for managers because they tend to move up within one function and, hence, have only limited knowledge of other functions.

USES OF FUNCTIONAL STRUCTURE The functional form of departmentalization is most often used in small and medium-size organizations that are too large to coordinate their activities without some type of formal structure but are not so large as to make coordination across functions difficult. Such organizations frequently have a limited number of related products or services or deal with a relatively homogeneous set of customers or clients. For example, Domino's Pizza, Inc., which deals mainly in pizza and related items, has a functional structure, with operations, distribution, and finance and administration as the major functional departments. A functional design may also be useful in large or more diverse organizations, such as insurance companies, that normally operate in relatively stable environments in which change occurs at a slow enough rate for the various functions to coordinate their efforts. In addition, a functional structure may be chosen by large organizations when considerable coordination is required among products.[8]

Divisional Structure

Divisional structure is a type of departmentalization in which positions are grouped according to similarity of products, services, or markets. Figure 9-3 shows the difference between functional and divisional structures. With a divisional structure, each division contains the major functional resources it needs to pursue its own goals with little or no reliance on other divisions. For example, Figure 9-4 shows the divisional structure for the seven telephone divisions of the Bell Atlantic Corporation, a regional Bell operating company that provides local telephone service to customers in several mid-Atlantic states and the District of Columbia. If the seven divisions were organized in a functional structure, all the telephone operators would be grouped in a central operations department and all the field repair personnel would be grouped in a central repair services department. Instead, with the divisional structure shown, telephone operators and repair personnel are allocated to the various divisions so that each division can operate fairly independently. In this case, the divisions

Divisional structure A structure in which positions are grouped according to similarity of products, services, or markets

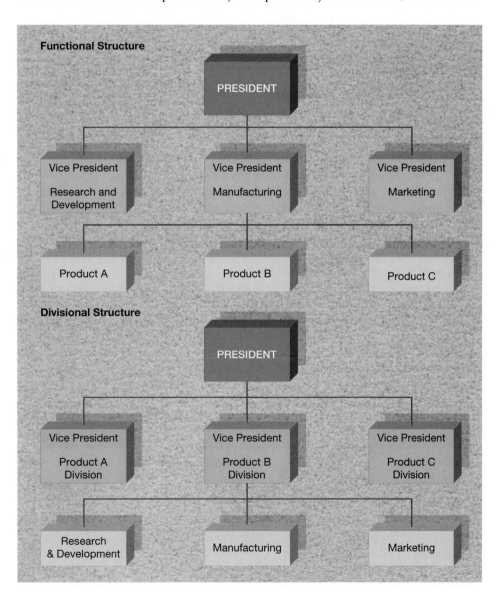

Figure 9-3 *Functional versus divisional structure.*

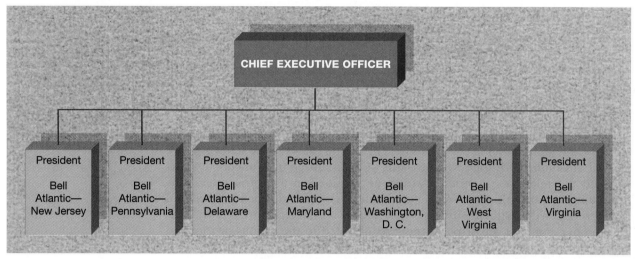

CHIEF EXECUTIVE OFFICER

President Bell Atlantic— New Jersey

President Bell Atlantic— Pennsylvania

President Bell Atlantic— Delaware

President Bell Atlantic— Maryland

President Bell Atlantic— Washington, D. C.

President Bell Atlantic— West Virginia

President Bell Atlantic— Virginia

Figure 9-4 *Seven divisions of the Bell Atlantic Corporation.*

are operated as separate companies. Divisional structures are sometimes referred to as *self-contained structures* because the major functions are generally contained within each division.

FORMS OF DIVISIONAL STRUCTURE There are three major forms of divisional structure: product, geographic, and customer. A simplified example of each one is shown in Figure 9-5. Which form an organization uses depends on the rationale for forming the divisions.

> **Product divisions** Divisions created to concentrate on a single product or service or at least a relatively homogeneous set of products or services

Product divisions are divisions created to concentrate on a single product or service or at least a relatively homogeneous set of products or services. When this type of organization structure is chosen, there are usually large differences in the product or service lines that would make coordination within a functional design extremely slow and inefficient. With a divisional structure, each product department has its own functional specialists, in areas such as marketing, manufacturing, and personnel, who perform work associated with the product of their specific division only.

> **Geographic divisions** Divisions designed to serve different geographic areas

Geographic divisions are divisions designed to serve different geographic areas. This type of departmentalization is often adopted when it is important to provide products and services that are tailored to the needs of different regions. For example, the U.S. Agency for International Development is structured by geography because of the differing needs it serves in various parts of the world. Similarly, the Bell Atlantic telephone divisions referred to earlier and shown in Figure 9-4 also represent divisions organized by geography.

TABLE 9-2 MAJOR ADVANTAGES AND DISADVANTAGES OF A DIVISIONAL STRUCTURE	
ADVANTAGES	**DISADVANTAGES**
Fast response to environmental change	Duplication of resources in each division
Simplified coordination across functions	Reduction of in-depth expertise
Simultaneous emphasis on division goals	Heightened competition among divisions
Strong orientation to customer requirements	Limited sharing of expertise across divisions
Accurate measurement of division performance	Restriction of innovation to divisions
Broad training in general management skills	Neglect of overall goals

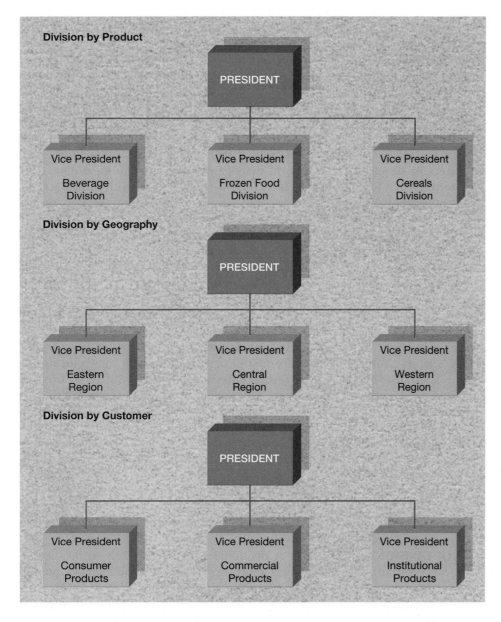

Figure 9-5 *Major forms of divisional structure.*

Customer divisions are divisions set up to service particular types of clients or customers. This organization design is used mainly when there are major differences among types of customers that preclude adequate coordination of the customers' various needs within a standard functional structure. With customer divisions, each department contains individuals who perform the necessary functions for a specific type of customer. For example, Citicorp Investment Management, Inc., reorganized its institutional-asset management unit from a product structure, the industry's traditional method of organizing, to a customer structure. The new structure included four major divisions: national corporate and public funds group, regional companies group, specialized domestic institutions group, and international institutions group.[9]

Customer divisions Divisions set up to service particular types of clients or customers

ADVANTAGES OF DIVISIONAL STRUCTURE Divisional structure has several major advantages (see Table 9-2). With this design, divisions can react quickly when necessary because they normally do not need to coordinate with other divisions before taking action. Furthermore, necessary coordination across functions is greatly simplified because the various functions are contained within the division itself. Moreover, the functions can simultaneously emphasize division goals. The divisional structure also tends to encourage a strong orientation toward serving the customer. This is because the focus is either on a limited number of products or services (product divisions) or on a limited audience (geographic or customer divisions). In addition, accountability for performance is possible with a divisional structure, since results can be tied to a particular product, service, geographic area, or type of customer, depending on the form of divisional structure. Finally, the divisional structure provides opportunities for managers to develop more general management skills because, unlike their counterparts in a functional structure, they are likely to deal with multiple functions within their divisions.

DISADVANTAGES OF DIVISIONAL STRUCTURE Divisional structure also has several disadvantages (see Table 9-2). Organizing by divisions often leads to a duplication of resources. For example, each division may need to have its own major computer system (whereas such a system can be shared by the departments in a functional structure), even though in each case the system may be somewhat underutilized. Moreover, individuals in a divisional structure are not able to develop in-depth areas of specialization to the degree that they could if they were in a functional structure. For example, when an organization changes from a functional to a product design, management may allocate the various specialists in the human resource department to the different product groups. Consequently, an individual who specialized in recruiting may also have to handle compensation and other issues in a product department, since each product department cannot afford to duplicate the entire human resource department that existed under the functional arrangement. Another disadvantage is that divisions may become preoccupied with their own concerns and engage in destructive rivalries for resources.[10] Often there is a limited sharing of expertise and innovations across divisions. Finally, with a divisional structure, employees sometimes focus on immediate divisional goals to the detriment of longer-term organizational goals.

USES OF DIVISIONAL STRUCTURE A divisional structure is likely to be used in fairly large organizations in which there are substantial differences among either the products or services, geographic areas, or customers served. It sometimes is not feasible to organize into self-contained units if the nature of the organization makes it necessary to share common resources, such as expensive manufacturing equipment.

Hybrid Structure

Hybrid structure A structure that adopts parts of both functional and divisional structures at the same level of management

Hybrid structure is a form of departmentalization that adopts parts of both functional and divisional structures at the same level of management.[11] It attempts to incorporate advantages of both structures. Many organizations, especially large ones, have some combination of functional and divisional departments. Functional departments are usually created to take advantage of resource utilization efficiencies, economies of scale, or in-depth expertise. At the same time, divisional departments are used when there are potential benefits from a stronger focus on products, services, or markets. IBM's hybrid structure is shown in Figure 9-6. At IBM, functional departments handle such areas as communications, finance, human resources, research—areas in which in-depth expertise is important and resources can be utilized more effectively through a functional arrangement. Then there are four major product divi-

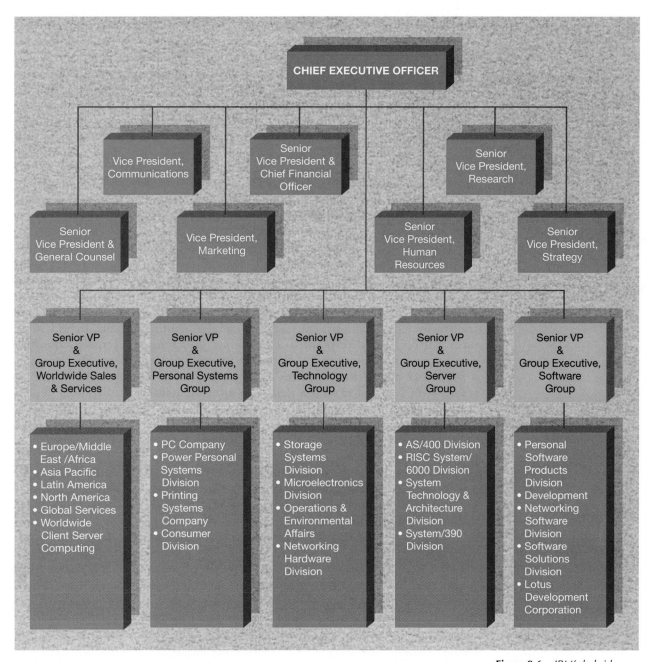

Figure 9-6 *IBM's hybrid structure.*

sions to concentrate on product development in areas that require somewhat different expertise and must deal with rapidly changing technology. IBM chose not to give each product division its own sales and service group. Instead, IBM has centralized the sales and service function in a separate division organized by geography. The functional departments within a hybrid design are sometimes referred to as *corporate departments* because they typically have staff authority relative to the divisional departments, and that authority emanates from the top, or corporate, level of the organization.

ADVANTAGES OF HYBRID STRUCTURE In general, hybrid structure has several advantages (see Table 9-3). With a hybrid design, an organization can often achieve specialized expertise and economies of scale in major functional areas. At the same time, adaptability and flexibility in handling diverse product or ser-

TABLE 9-3 MAJOR ADVANTAGES AND DISADVANTAGES OF A HYBRID STRUCTURE	
ADVANTAGES	**DISADVANTAGES**
Alignment of corporate and divisional goals	Conflicts between corporate departments and divisions
Functional expertise and/or efficiency	Excessive administrative overhead
Adaptability and flexibility in divisions	Slow response to exceptional situations

vice lines, geographic areas, or customers are possible through a partial divisional structure. Finally, the mix of functional and divisional departmentalization helps align divisional and corporate goals.

DISADVANTAGES OF HYBRID STRUCTURE Managers need to be alert to the disadvantages of the hybrid structure in order to minimize potential weaknesses (see Table 9-3). Hybrid organizations gradually tend to develop excessively large staffs in the corporate-level functional departments. As the corporate departments grow larger, they may attempt to exercise increasing amounts of control over the divisions, causing considerable conflict. Finally, hybrid structures can be slow to respond to exceptional situations that require coordination between a division and a corporate functional department. For example, a personnel matter that requires an exception to policy may take longer to resolve with a hybrid structure than with either functional or divisional departmentalization.

USES OF HYBRID STRUCTURE A hybrid structure tends to be used in organizations that not only face considerable environmental uncertainty that can best be met through a divisional structure but also require functional expertise and/or efficiency. Typically, the hybrid approach is reserved for medium-size or large organizations that have sufficient resources to justify divisions as well as some functional departmentalization.

Matrix Structure

Matrix structure A structure that superimposes a horizontal set of divisional reporting relationships onto a hierarchical functional structure

A **matrix structure** is a type of departmentalization that superimposes a horizontal set of divisional reporting relationships onto a hierarchical functional structure. Thus the structure is both a functional and a divisional organization at the same time. There are two chains of command, one vertical and one horizontal. A basic matrix structure is shown in Figure 9-7. In this case, the vice presidents of operations, marketing, finance, engineering, and research and development represent the functional departments that make up the vertical hierarchy. Simultaneously, the managers of businesses A, B, and C represent the divisional units that operate horizontally across the structure. The heads of the functional and divisional departments that make up the matrix (e.g., the vice presidents and business managers in Figure 9-7) are sometimes referred to as *matrix bosses.*

One major characteristic of a matrix structure is that employees who work within the matrix report to two matrix bosses. For example, as Figure 9-7 shows, a marketing researcher might report up the vertical chain to the vice president of marketing and across the horizontal chain to the manager of business A. This system of dual authority violates the classical principle of unity of command (an individual should have only one boss at any given point in time), making a matrix structure somewhat complex to operate.

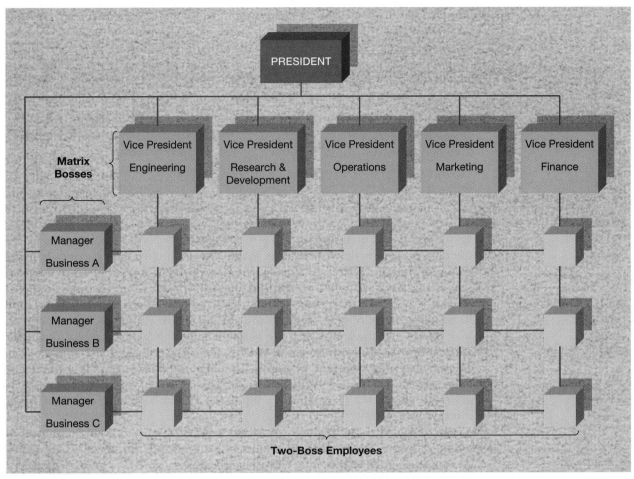

Figure 9-7 *Matrix organization structure.*

MATRIX STAGES Organizations that ultimately adopt a matrix structure usually go through several identifiable structural stages:[12]

Stage 1 is a *traditional structure,* usually a functional structure, which follows the unity-of-command principle.

Stage 2 is a *temporary overlay,* in which managerial integrator positions are created to take charge of particular projects (e.g., project managers), oversee product launches (e.g., product managers), or handle some other issue of finite duration that involves coordination across functional departments. These managers often lead or work with temporary interdepartmental teams created to address the issue.

Stage 3 is a *permanent overlay,* in which the managerial integrators operate on a permanent basis (e.g., a brand manager coordinates issues related to a brand on an ongoing basis), often through permanent interdepartmental teams.

Stage 4 is a *mature matrix,* in which matrix bosses have *equal* power.

Even though a true matrix incorporates equal power for functional and divisional managers, stages 2 and 3, which involve managerial integrators (see Chapter 8), are often referred to as matrix structures.

Each matrix stage offers increasing amounts of horizontal integration, but at the cost of greater administrative complexity.[13] Even with managerial inte-

TABLE 9-4 MAJOR ADVANTAGES AND DISADVANTAGES OF A MATRIX STRUCTURE	
ADVANTAGES	**DISADVANTAGES**
Decentralized decision making	High administrative costs
Strong project or product coordination	Potential confusion over authority and responsibility
Improved environmental monitoring	Heightened prospects for interpersonal conflicts
Fast response to change	Excessive focus on internal relations
Flexible use of human resources	Overemphasis on group decision making
Efficient use of support systems	Possible slow response to change

grators, there is dual authority to some extent because the integrators frequently work directly with various members of functional departments (e.g., engineers or marketing specialists) assigned to help with their project. In their capacity as coordinators, managerial integrators informally supervise the work of individuals assigned to their projects, even though they usually do not have direct line authority over these individuals. Typically, teamwork is emphasized.

With the mature matrix, there is true dual authority.[14] All major decisions must have the approval of both the functional manager and the divisional manager. The mature matrix is used when the functional and divisional dimensions of an organization are of prime and equal importance. Dow Corning has experimented with such a design, even adding a third dimension for a simultaneous international focus.[15]

Matrix structures, particularly in the forms of temporary and permanent overlays, operate successfully in a variety of organizations. However, the advantages and disadvantages must be carefully weighed before a matrix design is adopted (see Table 9-4).[16]

ADVANTAGES OF MATRIX STRUCTURE With a matrix design, decisions can be decentralized so that they are made at the level of the divisional project manager and the functional manager. This allows upper-level management to concentrate on longer-term strategic issues. Moreover, use of the matrix adds strong horizontal coordination to projects (or products or brands) beyond what is normally possible in the functional design alone, increasing the probability of success. The matrix arrangement also facilitates monitoring environmental conditions with respect to both the projects and the functional areas. Often, the matrix structure can react quickly to change because many decisions are made at lower levels. Still another advantage is that functional specialists can be added to or reassigned from projects as needed, allowing effective use of human resources. Finally, support systems, such as computers, special equipment, and software, can be allocated among many projects on an as-needed basis, thereby reducing the costs of such systems.

DISADVANTAGES OF MATRIX STRUCTURE Because the matrix arrangement adds a layer of project managers and their immediate support staff to a functional hierarchy, the structure increases administrative costs. Moreover, since there are two bosses, individuals working within the matrix may have difficulty determining who has authority and responsibility for various decisions. The increased communication required and the dual-authority arrangements heighten possibilities of conflicts, particularly between project managers and functional managers. The individuals in the structure can become preoccupied with internal relations at the expense of clients and project goals. In addition, matrix designs can encourage group decision making to the point where even relatively minor decisions are made in groups, causing a serious erosion of productivity. Finally, while the matrix can be particularly adaptable to change, it can also be extremely slow to respond if the interpersonal skills of participants are poor or upper management attempts to retain centralized control. For a time, the latter problem began to cripple the brand management structure at Procter & Gamble (see the Case in Point discussion).

BRAND MANAGEMENT AT PROCTER & GAMBLE   CASE IN POINT

Since Procter & Gamble (P&G) first used the concept way back in 1927 to manage Camay soap, brand management has been almost synonymous with the Cincinnati-based company. Because of its great success, Procter & Gamble has been viewed as practically a textbook case on how to run a consumer-oriented company. Following its lead, even major competitors, such as General Mills, began to adopt the brand management approach, often hiring talent from P&G. By the early 1980s, however, P&G's share in a number of important markets had begun to slip.

Despite its emphasis on brand management, P&G had maintained a fairly centralized approach to decision making. In the beginning, the approach worked well. Over the years, however, excessive centralization began to bog down the company. Gradually, almost every decision was pushed to the top. A former P&G brand manager laughingly relates that the decision about whether the company's new decaffeinated instant Folgers coffee should have a green or a gold cap was elevated all the way to the CEO (he chose gold).

The chief medium in the decision-making process, and the symbol of the growing centralization, was the one-page memo. Managers had to carefully summarize any proposal in a single page, which was rewritten almost endless times as it made its way up the hierarchy.

Brand managers were particularly frustrated because they lacked authority and had to answer to layers of management as well as staff areas such as the legal department. These conditions effectively canceled the horizontal coordination that the brand managers could provide.

Spurred by the company's difficulties, P&G executives took steps to dismantle the overly bureaucratic practices that had become an anchor on the product management structure. For one thing, they substituted use of a "talk sheet" for strict adherence to the one-page memo. The talk sheet is an informal outline that allows managers on several levels to develop and refine a proposal through discussions, rather than through paper only.

Management also began to decentralize decision making. Under the new approach, teams are often put together that include representatives from functional areas who help develop the proposal itself. This system has helped P&G cut costs, get new products on shelves more quickly, and greatly increase sales. The company emphasizes explicit missions for teams and clear goals for team members to ensure that the groups and their participants stay focused on the competition. Procter & Gamble continues to have a reputation as a premier exploiter of brand management for competitive advantage.[17]   ■■■

WHEN TO CONSIDER A MATRIX STRUCTURE Matrix designs are not suited for many organizations. For example, Texas Instruments abandoned its much-touted matrix structure after blaming it for the company's failure to keep up with the competition.[18] The need for horizontal coordination must be sufficient to justify the additional administrative complexity at the lower levels. Matrix designs are usually appropriate when the following three conditions exist:[19]

1   There is considerable pressure from the environment that necessitates a simultaneous and strong focus on *both* functional and divisional dimensions. For example, the existence of diverse products may call for a product orientation, but increasing sophistication in engineering technology may argue for a functional orientation.
2   The demands placed on the organization are changing and unpredictable, making it important to have a large capacity for processing information and coordinating activities quickly. For example, in the microchip industry, foreign competitors frequently make technological improvements and lower prices simultaneously.
3   There is pressure for shared resources. For example, in competitive markets, organizations may need to attain flexibility in the use of functional resources across projects or products.

There is growing evidence that matrix designs require a corresponding change in an organization's culture to support the increased need for collaborative decision making.[20] In addition, managers and other employees may require special training, particularly in interpersonal skills, in order to function effectively within the structure.[21] While many organizations do not need a mature matrix structure, the temporary and permanent overlay stages are increasingly being used, particularly in the form of temporary and permanent cross-functional teams.

Emerging Structures

Although many different types of organizational structures are possible as organizations experiment with new ways of doing things, two emerging types of structures are of particular interest: the process structure and the networked structure, or the virtual corporation.[22]

Process structure A type of departmentalization in which positions are grouped according to a complete flow of work

PROCESS STRUCTURE A **process structure** is a type of departmentalization in which positions are grouped according to a complete flow of work. The basic idea is that individuals from each function who work on a process are grouped into process teams and given beginning-to-end responsibility for that process or identifiable work flow. Under this type of structure, divisions might have names like new product development, order fulfillment, or customer acquisition and maintenance—signifying the processes for which they are responsible. The process structure is sometimes referred to as the *horizontal organization*, because the structures tend to be relatively flat. Functional specialties work together in a team environment making it possible for most operating decisions to be made at relatively low levels in the organization by the teams. Recently General Motors Acceptance Corporation (GMAC), which offers financing for consumer purchases of GM automobiles and trucks and also for dealer inventories, reorganized by process. Before the reorganization, GMAC had a geographical structure with 220 all-purpose offices handling all aspects of financing. To fight aggressive lending competition from banks, GMAC organized into four types of offices focused on specialized processes: sales purchase, which serves only dealer needs; customer service, which answers questions from car buyers; field support, which handles accounting, administration, and collection processes once loans are made; and salvage collection, which takes over bad accounts and repossessions.[23]

NETWORKED STRUCTURE The **networked structure** is a form of organizing in which many functions are contracted out to other independent firms and coordinated through the use of information technology networks to operate as if they were within a single corporation. This type of structure often is called the *virtual corporation* because it performs as if it were virtually one corporation. For example, Benetton, the Italian clothing maker, contracts its manufacturing to about 350 small firms, but achieves economies of scale by buying materials for all of them. By having many small firms do the labor-intensive sewing and packing, Benetton has a great deal of flexibility in making changes in response to rapidly shifting fashions. One major disadvantage of the virtual corporation is that proprietary information may need to be exchanged, possibly creating potential competitors.[24]

While managers need to weigh the advantages and disadvantages of various structural alternatives in developing an appropriate organization design—including emerging structures—they must also consider major contingency factors that can affect structural requirements. We review these factors next.

Computer microchips are manufactured on an assembly line using the large-batch and mass production methods. This type of technology, with its standardized procedures and large numbers of workers, calls for a centralized and formalized organizational structure.

Networked structure A form of organizing in which many functions are contracted out to other independent firms and coordinated through the use of information technology networks to operate as if they were within a single corporation

■ WEIGHING CONTINGENCY FACTORS

Early in the study of management, classical theorists (see Chapter 2) attempted to develop the ideal organization structure. Instead, they found that a structural configuration that seemed to work for one organization was a deterrent to effectiveness in another. Gradually, contingency theory began to emerge. This management viewpoint argues that appropriate managerial action depends on the particular parameters of the situation (see Chapter 2). Researchers came to recognize that the best structure for a given organization depends on such contingency factors as technology, size, and environment.

Technology

Different organizations require different structures partly because of **technology,** the knowledge, tools, equipment, and work techniques used by an organization in delivering its product or service. Two critical aspects of technology are technological complexity and technological interdependence.[25]

TECHNOLOGICAL COMPLEXITY Famous research that highlighted the importance of technology was conducted during the 1950s by a team led by British sociologist Joan Woodward.[26] The team wanted to determine the extent to which the management principles espoused by the classical theorists were actually practiced by a group of 100 British manufacturing firms.

The researchers were surprised to find that there did not seem to be any connection between the use of the classical principles in structuring organizations and the success of a firm. In fact, practices varied widely. After careful study, Woodward determined that three different types of *technology* were reasonably predictive of the structural practices of the firms in the study:

1 In **unit and small-batch production,** products are custom-produced to meet customer specifications or they are made in small quantities primarily by craft specialists. Examples are diamond cutting in New York's diamond center and the production of stretch limousines.

Technology The knowledge, tools, equipment, and work techniques used by an organization in delivering its product or service

Unit and small-batch production A type of technology in which products are custom-produced to meet customer specifications or they are made in small quantities primarily by craft specialists

Large-batch and mass production A type of technology in which products are manufactured in large quantities, frequently on an assembly line

Continuous-process production A type of technology in which products are liquids, solids, or gases that are made through a continuous process

2 In **large-batch and mass production,** products are manufactured in large quantities, frequently on an assembly line. Examples are the production of most automobiles and the manufacture of microchips used in computers and related products.

3 In **continuous-process production,** products are liquids, solids, or gases that are made through a continuous process. Examples are petroleum products, such as gasoline, and chemical products.

The research team noted that the technologies are increasingly complex to manage, with small-batch and unit production being the least complex and continuous-process production being the most complex. The increasing complexity stems mainly from the use of more elaborate machinery and its greater role in the work process. This technological complexity, in turn, appeared to help explain the differences in the structural practices used by the firms in the study (see Table 9-5).

For example, the researchers found that increasing complexity was associated with more levels of management (a taller structure), more staff personnel per line worker, and larger spans of control at upper management levels. Woodward's results also indicated that formalization and centralization both tended to be high in organizations engaged in large-batch and mass-production technology, in which the efforts of large numbers of workers need to be standardized. In contrast, formalization and centralization were low in organizations using unit and small-batch, as well as continuous-process, technologies, in which appropriate work decisions must be made at the lower levels.

At the level of the first-line supervisor, the span was greatest with large-batch and mass-production technology because one supervisor could handle a relatively large number of workers doing the fairly routine work. It was smallest for continuous-process where very serious problems can result if there are process difficulties.[27]

Overall, Woodward's research indicated that the more successful firms had structural characteristics that were close to the median for their particular technology. Research since Woodward's groundbreaking study has supported the importance of technological complexity in influencing organization structure.[28]

Technological interdependence The degree to which different parts of the organization must exchange information and materials in order to perform the required activities

TECHNOLOGICAL INTERDEPENDENCE Another aspect of technology that affects organizing considerations is **technological interdependence,** the degree to which different parts of the organization must exchange information and materials in order to perform their required activities.[29] There are three major types of technological interdependence: pooled, sequential, and reciprocal.[30]

TABLE 9-5 WOODWARD'S FINDINGS ON STRUCTURAL CHARACTERISTICS AND TECHNOLOGY			
STRUCTURAL CHARACTERISTICS	**SMALL BATCH**	**MASS PRODUCTION**	**CONTINUOUS PROCESS**
Levels of management	3	4	6
Executive span of control	4	7	10
Supervisory span of control	23	48	15
Industrial workers vs. staff (ratio)	8:1	5.5:1	2:1
Formalization	Low	High	Low
Centralization	Low	High	Low

Data are medians for the organizations within each technological category.

Source: Joan Woodward, *Industrial Organization: Theory and Practice,* Oxford University Press, London, 1965, pp. 52–82.

The type that involves the least interdependence is known as **pooled interdependence,** in which units operate independently but their individual efforts are important to the success of the organization as a whole (hence the term "pooled"). For example, when you go to the local branch of your bank, there is rarely a need for that branch to contact another branch in order to complete your transaction. If, however, the branch performs poorly and loses you and other customers, its problems will ultimately have a negative effect on the health of the bank as a whole.

In contrast, with **sequential interdependence,** one unit must complete its work before the next unit in the sequence can begin work. For example, a strike over a local issue at one General Motors plant frequently causes workers at other plants to be laid off temporarily. The layoffs occur when parts manufactured by the striking plant are needed for the sequentially interdependent assembly process at the nonstriking plants.

Finally, the most complex situation is **reciprocal interdependence,** in which one unit's outputs become inputs to the other unit and vice versa. When an airplane lands, the flight crew turns the plane over to the maintenance crew. After refueling the plane, replenishing supplies, and performing other necessary activities, the maintenance crew releases the plane back to the flight crew so that the plane can continue its journey. Thus the flight crew's output becomes the maintenance crew's input, and then the process is reversed. As you might expect, reciprocal interdependence is likely to require greater efforts at horizontal coordination than the other two types. As a result, managers need to give some thought to technological interdependence, as well as complexity, when developing organization structure. In addition, organization size is sometimes a relevant factor.

Pooled interdependence A relationship in which units operate independently but their individual efforts are important to the success of the organization as a whole

Sequential interdependence A relationship in which one unit must complete its work before the next unit in the sequence can begin work

Reciprocal interdependence A relationship in which one unit's outputs become inputs to the other unit and vice versa

Size

Woodward's research team also investigated the possibility of a clear relationship between size and various structural characteristics but found nothing definitive. Since that time a number of other studies have attempted to untangle the relationship between size and structure, with only modest success. Part of the problem appears to be that size is just one element in the equation. There are several other important factors, such as environment and technology, that also affect organization structure. In addition, organization size can be measured in various ways, such as by gross sales or profits or by number of employees (the measure most typically used), sometimes making it difficult to compare studies.

Four trends have been identified by studies of size effects on structure:

1 As organizations grow, they are likely to add more departments and levels, making their structures increasingly complex. With functional structures, such growth creates pressure for a change to divisional structure.[31]
2 Growing organizations tend to take on an increasing number of staff positions in order to help top management cope with the expanding size. This tendency levels off when a critical mass of staff has been achieved,[32] but it helps lead to the third trend.
3 Additional rules and regulations seem to accompany organizational growth. While such guidelines can be useful in achieving vertical coordination, the unchecked proliferation of additional rules and regulations may lead to excessive formalization and lower efficiency.[33]
4 As organizations grow larger, they tend to become more decentralized. This is probably due in part to the additional rules and regulations that set guidelines for decision making at lower levels.[34]

VALUING QUALITY

Saturn Produces a Winning Automobile

When the Saturn project was conceived by General Motors in the early 1980s, its mission was to build cars that could beat foreign imports in the small-car market. It was also to be a laboratory for innovative methods that could ultimately transform General Motors itself. Since then, Saturn, located in Spring Hill, Tennessee, has operated on a relatively independent basis from the rest of the corporation. Heavily funded by GM, the unit has been free to adopt the best technology and managerial methods available to achieve high quality and productivity.

A critical element at Saturn is a unique labor-management agreement whereby the company's union, the United Auto Workers, is heavily involved in every facet of the business. For example, many of the initial ideas for developing Saturn came from the Group of 99, a team of Saturn workers who collectively traveled 2 million miles seeking innovative approaches. A major result of their efforts has been the extensive use of work teams throughout the Saturn plant. The teams, which average about 10 workers, have unusual latitude. Each team interviews and approves new hires for its group, handles its own

budget, stops the assembly line when it perceives a problem, and participates in work decisions that affect its area (such as the purchase of new equipment). All workers are paid a salary, rather than wages on an hourly basis, and a percentage of their salaries depends on meeting targets for quality.

The cars have earned a reputation for high quality, contemporary styling, and nimble handling. Customers have also appreciated the revolutionary approach of setting a basic price and eliminating the haggling, an innovation that has been copied by others in the automotive industry. In a recent industry

Workers at the Saturn unit of General Motors proudly unveil a new sports car. GM involves teams of union workers in the unit in every aspect of the business, from gathering ideas for the design to budgeting and making assembly-line work decisions. The use of teams and smaller work units encourages innovation and employee commitment.

survey by the J. D. Powers organization, Saturn finished third in customer satisfaction and first in sales satisfaction.[35]

Because of potential size effects, many successful divisionalized companies try to ensure that subunits do not become too large by creating new divisions when existing ones become unwieldy. For example, in an effort to reap the advantages of smaller size and encourage innovation, Johnson & Johnson operates with more than 150 autonomous divisions.[36] At General Motors, the separate Saturn unit is a pacesetter in quality (see the Valuing Quality box). The approach taken by these companies is compatible with recent research indicating that larger organizational subunits are often less efficient than their smaller counterparts. While size has a bearing on structural requirements, environment is also a major factor.

Environment

One of the most famous studies on the effects of environment on organization structure was conducted by British scholars Tom Burns and G. M. Stalker.[37] In studying 20 British industrial firms, they discovered that the firms had different structural characteristics, depending on whether they operated in a stable environment with relatively little change over time or an unstable environment with rapid change and uncertainty.

MECHANISTIC AND ORGANIC CHARACTERISTICS The firms that operated in a stable environment tended to have relatively **mechanistic characteristics,** such as highly centralized decision making, many rules and regulations, and mainly hierarchical communication channels. Much of the emphasis was on vertical coordination, but with very limited delegation from one level of management to the next. The firms were able to operate with these characteristics and still be reasonably successful because changes in their environments usually occurred gradually, making it possible for upper levels of management to stay on top of the changes.

In contrast, the firms that operated in a highly unstable and uncertain environment were far more likely to have relatively **organic characteristics,** such as decentralized decision making, few rules and regulations, and both hierarchical and lateral communication channels. Much of the emphasis was on horizontal coordination, with considerable delegation from one level to the next. The firms required these characteristics because their rapidly changing environments made it necessary for individuals at many levels to monitor the environment and help decide how to respond. The characteristics of mechanistic and organic organizations are summarized in Table 9-6.

DIFFERENTIATION AND INTEGRATION Two management professors working in the United States, Paul R. Lawrence and Jay W. Lorsch, went a step further with the notion that environment influences organization structure. They reasoned that organizational environments might have different effects on various units within the same organization. To test this possibility, they investigated three

Mechanistic characteristics
Characteristics such as highly centralized decision making, many rules and regulations, and mainly hierarchical communication channels

Organic characteristics
Characteristics such as decentralized decision making, few rules and regulations, and both hierarchical and lateral communication channels

TABLE 9-6 CHARACTERISTICS OF MECHANISTIC AND ORGANIC ORGANIZATIONS

MECHANISTIC	ORGANIC
Work is divided into narrow, specialized tasks.	Work is defined in terms of general tasks.
Tasks are performed as specified unless changed by managers in the hierarchy.	Tasks are continually adjusted as needed through interaction with others involved in the task.
Structure of control, authority, and communication is hierarchical.	Structure of control, authority and communication is a network.
Decisions are made by the specified hierarchical level.	Decisions are made by individuals with relevant knowledge and technical expertise.
Communication is mainly vertical, between superior and subordinate.	Communication is vertical and horizontal, among superiors, subordinates, and peers.
Communication content is largely instructions and decisions issued by superiors.	Communication content is largely information and advice.
Emphasis is on loyalty to the organization and obedience to superiors.	Emphasis is on commitment to organizational goals and possession of needed expertise.

Source: Adapted from T. Burns and G. M. Stalker, *The Management of Innovation,* Tavistock, London, 1961, pp. 119–122.

Differentiation The extent to which organizational units differ from one another in terms of the behaviors and orientations of their members and their formal structures

Integration The extent to which there is collaboration among departments that need to coordinate their efforts

departments, manufacturing, sales, and research and development, in three industries with very different environments—plastics, food processing, and containers. Their focus was on **differentiation,** the extent to which organizational units differ from one another in terms of the behaviors and orientations of their members and their formal structures.[38] As expected, Lawrence and Lorsch found significant differentiation among the three types of units studied. The R&D departments tended to concentrate on new developments, operate fairly informally, and be concerned with long-term success. In contrast, the sales departments were mainly oriented toward immediate customer satisfaction, operated more formally, and were interested largely in short-term sales results. Somewhat in between were the manufacturing departments, which concerned themselves primarily with efficiency, operated less formally than the sales departments but more formally than the R&D departments, and were oriented toward an intermediate-term time frame. Interestingly, the differentiation among departments was greatest in the plastics industry, which had the most unstable environment, and was least in the container industry, which operated in the most stable environment.

But differentiation was only half the story. When they considered firm effectiveness, the researchers found that the most effective firms attempted to balance differentiation with efforts toward **integration,** the extent to which there is collaboration among departments that need to coordinate their efforts. The greater the differentiation among departments because of environmental instability, the greater the efforts toward integration in the most successful companies. For example, the successful container companies relied on a functional hierarchy and rules and regulations to achieve the necessary degree of integration. The successful plastics companies, however, used a variety of vertical and horizontal coordinating mechanisms to attain effective integration in the face of high differentiation.[39] Methods of horizontal coordination, such as those discussed in Chapter 8 (e.g., teams and managerial integrators) were particularly important.

■ MATCHING STRATEGY AND STRUCTURE

In addition to considering contingency issues, managers need to think about how they can match strategy and structure to achieve optimum effectiveness. Strategy specialist Danny Miller has attempted to match strategies similar to Porter's competitive strategies (see Chapter 7) with appropriate structures.[40] Miller considered four main strategies:

■ **Niche differentiation.** This strategy is aimed at distinguishing one's products and services from those of competitors for a narrow target market. (It is equivalent to Porter's focus strategy using differentiation.)
■ **Cost leadership.** This strategy emphasizes organizational efficiency so that products and services can be offered at prices lower than those of competitors. (It is equivalent to Porter's cost leadership strategy.)
■ **Innovative differentiation.** This strategy is aimed at distinguishing one's products and services from those of competitors by leading in complex product or service innovations. (It is similar to Porter's differentiation strategy but more narrowly oriented, specifically to sophisticated innovations.)
■ **Market differentiation.** This is a strategy aimed at distinguishing one's products and services from those of competitors through advertising, prestige pricing, and market segmentation. (It is similar to Porter's differentiation strategy but more narrowly oriented, specifically to market approaches.) The

TABLE 9-7 MAJOR MATCHES OF STRUCTURE AND STRATEGY

TYPE OF DEPARTMENTALIZATION	STRATEGY
Functional	Niche differentiation, or focus
Functional	Cost leadership; possibly market differentiation
Divisional or hybrid	Market differentiation or cost leadership at division level
Matrix, integrators	Innovative differentiation

product and service designs themselves may not necessarily be better than those of competitors, but the firm may offer attractive packaging, good service, convenient locations, and good product or service reliability.

Miller's matches of structure and strategy are shown in Table 9-7. In making these matches, Miller also considered the appropriateness of the environment for the strategy-structure combinations, following much of the logic involved in the contingency approaches.

With a niche differentiation or focus strategy, the organization is typically small or medium in size and deals with a relatively homogeneous set of customers and clients, making the functional structure appropriate. A functional structure can also support a cost leadership strategy, even in a large organization, when a limited number of related products or services are involved. Similarly, a market differentiation strategy may be feasible with a functional structure as long as the products and services offered span a relatively narrow range and thus can be coordinated effectively across functional units.

The divisional or the hybrid structure is generally well matched with market differentiation. A cost leadership strategy can also work with these structures as long as the strategy is carried out at the division level.

The matrix structure is generally compatible with a strategy of innovative differentiation. Matrix structures emphasize flexibility and collaboration among specialists, conditions conducive to developing new products.

■ PROMOTING INNOVATION: USING STRUCTURAL MEANS TO ENHANCE PROSPECTS

The ability of structure to support strategy can be further enhanced by using structural means to encourage innovation. Innovation is particularly critical to the various differentiation strategies (especially the innovative differentiation strategy). In this section, we consider four major aspects of structuring organizations to facilitate innovation: the vital roles necessary for innovation, the need for innovative units called reservations, the differentiation paradox, and the transfer process.[41]

Vital Roles

Successful innovations are rarely the product of only one person's work. The innovative process is much more likely to occur when individuals fulfill three vital entrepreneurial roles: idea champion, sponsor, and orchestrator. We discussed these roles in Chapter 1 and review them briefly here.

An *idea champion* is an individual who generates a new idea or believes in the value of a new idea and supports it in the face of numerous potential obsta-

Toshi T. Doi, jazz enthusiast and head of research and development at Sony Corp., knows how to champion an idea. He came up with a promising prototype for a new product, but the production people told him it would take 2 years to implement. Realizing that this time frame would open the door to competitors, he took his case directly to Sony's president, who gave him the money to speed up production. The result was a low-priced computer workstation (called News, for network station) that left Sony's rivals in the dust and launched the company in the desktop publishing boom.

cles. Such individuals are often entrepreneurs, inventors, creative individuals, or risk takers. Since they are typically far down in the hierarchy, they often have difficulty gaining acceptance of their innovations without the help of a sponsor. A *sponsor* is usually a middle manager who recognizes the organizational significance of an idea, helps obtain the necessary funding to continue development of the innovation, and facilitates actual implementation of the new idea. Still, innovations also need the help of an orchestrator. An *orchestrator* is a high-level manager who articulates the need for innovation, provides funding for innovating activities, creates incentives for middle managers to sponsor innovating ideas, and protects idea people. Orchestrators are vital because innovations usually disturb the status quo and may, therefore, be resisted by individuals who will need to make adjustments to accommodate the new ideas. Although these roles are very important, their effectiveness can be greatly aided by the creation of special units called reservations.

Reservations

Major-breakthrough ideas are more likely to occur if the early efforts at development are differentiated, or separated, from the operating units of the organization.[42] The reason is that most operating units are aimed at performing similar tasks efficiently on a recurring basis (e.g., producing the millionth automobile, processing the millionth check, or serving the millionth hamburger). Because they focus on performing assigned tasks well, operating units are not particularly adept at developing major new ways of doing things. Therefore, many organizations seeking to encourage innovation set up **reservations**, that is, organizational units that devote full time to the generation of innovative ideas for future business. The aim is to create "garagelike" atmospheres in which people can try new approaches. Steven Jobs and Steven Wozniak literally created the first Apple computer in a garage, which became, in effect, a reservation for their work.

Reservations are often ongoing, relatively permanent units, such as research and development departments. Sometimes, organizations set up **new venture units,** which are typically either separate divisions or specially incorporated companies created for the specific purpose of developing new products or business ideas and initiatives.[43] For example, Xerox Corp. has long had a famous research and development unit in Palo Alto, California, known as the Palo Alto Research Center (PARC).

Reservations can also be temporary task forces or teams made up of individuals who have been relieved of their normal duties for a period in order to

Reservations Organizational units that devote full time to the generation of innovative ideas for future business

New venture units Either separate divisions or specially incorporated companies created for the specific purpose of developing new products or business ideas and initiatives

develop a new process, product, or program. Such teams are sometimes called **new venture teams.** Although differentiation, particularly the setting up of reservations, is effective in encouraging innovation, there is an important paradox associated with it.

Differentiation Paradox

The **differentiation paradox** poses the idea that although separating innovation efforts from the rest of the organization increases the likelihood of developing radical ideas, such differentiation also decreases the likelihood that the radical ideas will ever be implemented. The reason is that the new ideas often are perceived as so different that they are considered threatening or are rejected as nonapplicable. The differentiation paradox is strongest when the innovation is radical and must be implemented by operating units of the organization. Under such circumstances, the operating units may be inclined to reject the ideas. For example, during the 1970s scientists at Xerox's Palo Alto Research Center invented the first computer for personal use, along with the mouse, the picture-oriented layout based on icons, and word processing software that displayed the fonts as they would appear on the page. Unfortunately, the rest of the organization was unable to appreciate the value of these inventions and Xerox never followed through to capitalize on them.[44] Instead, Apple, Microsoft, and many other computer-related companies have benefited greatly from commercializing these innovations. Thus the PARC situation at Xerox illustrates the differentiation paradox and the need for concern about technological transfer.

Transfer Process

As suggested by the differentiation paradox concept, the more that innovators are separated from the rest of the organization, the more difficulty an organization may encounter in ultimately turning innovations into marketable products or services. For example, world-renowned Bell Labs has averaged almost a patent a day since it was founded in 1925 to provide cutting-edge research support to AT&T. Yet AT&T has experienced acute difficulty in translating Bell's research into products and services that will fuel company growth.[45]

It is probably best to think of an effective transfer, or transition, process as a series of stages. In the first stage, the idea generator, or champion, works on an idea in a reservation. If the initial tests are positive but the idea needs more work, it may be possible to involve people with relevant expertise from other parts of the organization to help hone the idea. Then, if the results are still positive, the next stage may involve testing the idea in one of the operating divisions. In the final stage, the new innovation can be fully implemented. Of course, the process may not always work so smoothly and may be easier when the innovations represent only incremental changes. However, to develop and implement significant innovations on a consistent basis, organizations need to foster innovative efforts and provide for the transfer of new ideas from the innovating units to the rest of the organization.

Sometimes, organizations set up separate new venture units and then, when they are large enough, transfer them to the main organization as separate divisions, thus lessening the transfer difficulties. One company that has been successful with this method, as well as with other approaches to innovation, is Perstorp, a Swedish specialty chemical maker (see the Case in Point discussion).

New venture teams
Temporary task forces or teams made up of individuals who have been relieved of their normal duties in order to develop a new process, product, or program

Differentiation paradox The idea that although separating efforts to innovate from the rest of the organization increases the likelihood of developing radical ideas, such differentiation also decreases the likelihood that the radical ideas will ever be implemented

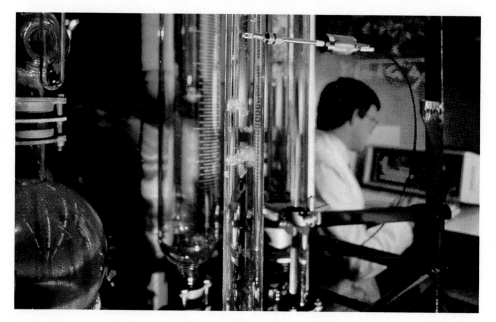

Perstorp AB, a Swedish chemical manufacturer, encourages innovation and long-term product research by funding special cooperative projects at university research centers around the world. The IDEON research center at Sweden's University of Lund, shown here, is developing instruments that use fiber optics to control sequences of chemical processes.

CASE IN POINT

PERSTORP EXCELS AT INNOVATION

Perstorp AB, a large Swedish specialty chemical maker with major businesses in polymers, laminates, and biotechnology, is well known for the variety of methods it uses to encourage innovation. About 25 percent of the products that Perstorp sells did not exist a decade ago. The new products include additives, noise abatement products, carbohydrate-based pharmaceuticals, analysis systems, laminate flooring, and copper foil. Most of the company's other products have been changed radically over the years. Perstorp places major emphasis on innovation because most of its profits come from relatively mature products that need constant rejuvenation. The company's strategy is to have its various businesses hold first, second, or third position in their markets. Five years ago, about half of Perstorp's businesses were in these top categories. Today, almost 70 percent are.

In its drive to increase innovation, Perstorp discontinued its corporate research laboratory in favor of having its divisions conduct more of their own R&D work. The company reasoned that by placing the research efforts closer to the customer base (i.e., in the operating divisions), R&D would be oriented toward products for which there is a market. One negative aspect of the reorganization, though, was that the divisions experienced conflict between short-run profits and longer-term research for future products.

To encourage a longer-term view, Perstorp has two mechanisms for funding in-house research: the President's Fund and the Research Foundation. The President's Fund supports product development and focuses on long-term projects that divisions would normally not want to undertake because expenditures would affect current profit levels. The Research Foundation provides funding for special projects conducted externally in conjunction with universities and other R&D institutions. Furthermore, Perstorp's general manager of corporate development can offer grants of up to $15,000 without formalities. Higher funding requests are considered frequently by Perstorp's executive management committee. For very large projects, Perstorp obtains advice from a council of six university professors with expertise in physics, chemistry, and marketing.

Another means of encouraging innovation is Perstorp's new business development company, Pernovo AB. This subsidiary, acting like a venture-capital company, purchases equity in small, promising high-technology firms in Europe and the United States. Pernovo invests only in firms that have the potential of involving Perstorp in new technologies with niche products for international markets. Companies that prove to be successful become divisions of Perstorp.[46]

■■■

This chapter has focused on designing structure to support an organization's strategy. In the next chapter, we consider another important aspect of the organizing function, human resource management.

■ CHAPTER SUMMARY

Alfred Chandler's study of the origins of the largest U.S. firms helped establish the notion that managers should design organization structures to support the organization's strategy. At the same time, structures that are needed to reach organizational goals effectively and efficiently are also likely to be influenced by major contingency factors and structural methods for promoting innovation.

Four of the most commonly used forms of departmentalization are functional, divisional, hybrid, and matrix. Functional structure combines positions into units on the basis of similarity of expertise, skills, and work activities. Divisional structure groups positions according to similarity of products, services, or markets. The three major forms of divisional structure are product divisions, geographic divisions, and customer divisions. Hybrid structure adopts parts of both functional and divisional structures at the same level of management. A mature matrix is a structure that is simultaneously both a functional and a divisional organization, with two chains of command (one vertical and one horizontal). Matrix structures may progress through several stages, beginning with the traditional structure and then moving to a temporary overlay, a permanent overlay, and, perhaps, the mature matrix stage.

Matrix structures are appropriate when pressure from the environment necessitates a strong focus on both functional and divisional dimensions; changing, unpredictable demands call for rapid processing of large amounts of information; and there is pressure for shared resources. Functional, divisional, hybrid, and matrix structures all have advantages and disadvantages. There are differences in the circumstances under which each is likely to be effective. Emerging structures include the process structure and the networked structure.

The best structure for a given organization depends on such contingency factors as technology, size, and environment. Higher levels of both technological complexity and technological interdependence require greater efforts at horizontal coordination. Increasing size tends to lead to more departments and levels, a greater number of specialists, more staff positions, and an eventual tendency toward decentralization. Organizations operating in more stable environments tend to have relatively mechanistic characteristics, while those operating in more unstable environments tend to have relatively organic characteristics. Unstable environments are also associated with greater differentiation among internal units, which increases the need for efforts at integration. Effective integration is achieved largely through methods of horizontal coordination.

Some matches of structure and strategy are more likely than others to be successful: functional structure and niche differentiation, cost leadership, and market differentiation; divisional or hybrid structure and market differentiation or cost leadership at the division levels; and matrix structure and innovative differentiation.

Enhancement of the prospects for organizational innovation is possible through several structural mechanisms. The vital roles of idea champion, sponsor, and orchestrator are important ingredients for innovation. Organizations also need to designate reservations, or units that devote full time to innovation. However, the differentiation paradox must also be taken into account. On one hand, innovation is more likely if the innovating units are separated from the rest of the organization physically, financially, and/or organizationally. On the other hand, the separation makes it more difficult to transfer innovations to other parts of the organization.

■ QUESTIONS FOR DISCUSSION AND REVIEW

1 Summarize current views about the link between strategy and organization structure. To what extent can these differing views be reconciled?

2 Contrast the functional and divisional types of departmentalization, including their respective advantages and disadvantages. Given your particular career interests, develop a list of pros and cons for (*a*) working in a company organized by function and (*b*) working in a company organized by product.

3 Describe hybrid, or mixed, departmentalization. How does this type of structure help incorporate some of the advantages of both the functional and divisional types?

4 Outline the advantages and disadvantages of matrix departmentalization. How do they relate to the conditions under which it is appropriate to use matrix structures?

5 Contrast the critical aspects of technological complexity and technological interdependence. Give examples of small-batch, mass-production, and continuous-process technologies. Alternatively, provide examples of the three types of technological interdependence.

6 Explain the four trends identified by studies of size effects on structure. Can you present any evidence of these trends in organizations with which you are familiar?

7 Contrast the mechanistic and organic characteristics of organizations. To what extent do you view your college or university as having relatively mechanistic or relatively organic characteristics? Cite examples to support your view. Why might organizations with organic characteristics require greater managerial efforts at integration?

8 Outline how strategy and structure could be matched to help enhance organizational success. What implications would this have for subsequent changes in strategy or structure?

9 Explain the notion of a reservation as it applies to encouraging organizational innovation. How does the differentiation paradox help explain the difficulties that AT&T has had in utilizing Bell Labs' innovative ideas in marketable products?

10 Describe the typical stages in an effective innovation transfer process. What steps has Perstorp taken to encourage innovation transfer?

■ DISCUSSION QUESTIONS FOR CHAPTER OPENING CASE

1 Classify the type of departmentalization, or structure, used by 3M.

2 Identify the presence of the orchestrator, sponsor, and idea champion roles in the Post-it note pad situation at 3M. What other evidence indicates that 3M expends considerable effort on encouraging innovation?

3 How does the Post-it note pad situation illustrate the differentiation paradox?

■ EXERCISES FOR MANAGING IN THE TWENTY-FIRST CENTURY

EXERCISE 1
SKILL BUILDING: RECOGNIZING STRUCTURAL STRENGTHS AND WEAKNESSES

 The four basic alternative types of structure for an organization are functional, divisional, hybrid, and matrix. Each has certain characteristics, advantages, and disadvantages. Indicate the type of structure the following statements best fit by placing the first letter of that type of structure in the blank.

Functional   **D**ivisional   **H**ybrid   **M**atrix

1 _____ Corporate and divisional goals can be aligned.
2 _____ These organizations can react quickly to changes in the environment.
3 _____ Employees generally have clear career paths.
4 _____ Functional specialists can be added or removed from projects as needed, allowing effective use of human resources.
5 _____ These organizations tend to develop excessively large staffs in the corporate functional departments.
6 _____ Goals may conflict with overall organizational goals.
7 _____ These organizations focus on development of in-depth expertise.
8 _____ Response time on multifunctional problems may be slow because of coordination problems.
9 _____ Line of authority and responsibility may not be clear to individual employees.
10 _____ Specialized expertise and economies of scale can be achieved in major functional areas.
11 _____ Employees work for two bosses.
12 _____ Department performance is easily measured.

EXERCISE 2
MANAGEMENT EXERCISE: DEVELOPING AN ORGANIZATION STRUCTURE

 The Sun Petroleum Products Company, a subsidiary of Sun Company, Inc., is a successful refining company. Its six refineries manufacture three main business products: fuels, petrochemicals, and lubricants. The products are sold to Sunmark Industries (another Sun subsidiary), chemical manufacturers, industrial plants, the auto industry, and a variety of other customers. The $7 billion company has a work force of about 5400.

Sun Petroleum currently has a functional organization structure, with the following major positions reporting directly to the president: chief counsel; vice president, financial services; vice president, technology; director, planning and administration (includes the human resource function); and vice president, operations (to whom a vice president of marketing and a vice president of manufacturing and supply distribution report).

Because of changing conditions in the markets for the company's main products, Sun Petroleum is thinking about changing its organization structure to a hybrid design. In the process, the president is considering adding a senior vice president of resources and strategy to oversee the company's strategic planning.

First, draw an organization chart depicting Sun Petroleum's current organization structure.

Second, draw a chart showing the proposed change from Sun Petroleum's current structure to a hybrid organization structure.

Third, be prepared to discuss the pros and cons of the proposed new structure and some possible ways of promoting innovation.[47]

CONCLUDING CASE 1

THE METAMORPHOSIS AT APPLE

Steven P. Jobs, charismatic cofounder and chairman of Apple Computer, Inc., recruited John Sculley, the young, dynamic president of Pepsi-Cola USA, to be president of Apple in the early 1980s. While Jobs oversaw technical innovation, Sculley was to boost Apple's marketing expertise and help penetrate the business market for personal computers.

One of Sculley's first moves was reorganizing the company's nine product-oriented and highly decentralized divisions into two major divisions, one for the existing Apple II and one, headed by Jobs himself, for the forthcoming Macintosh. The reorganization allowed the company to focus resources on its two major product lines.

Troubles arose when the Mac did not sell as well as anticipated, partially because the Mac division chronically missed deadlines for the development of crucial Mac-system parts. Pushed by the board of directors to take greater control, Sculley finally proposed a new functional organization structure aimed in part at reducing the duplication of positions in such areas as marketing, human resources, and manufacturing. The new structure included product operations (R&D, manufacturing, service, and distribution), marketing and sales, finance and management information systems, legal services, and human resources. With the Mac division dissolved, Jobs resigned his position as chairman and left the company.

Within 18 months, sales of the Mac, with its technologically advanced desktop-publishing capability and its relative ease of use for computer novices, started to take off. But other companies, including IBM, quickly began to develop products to match the Mac capabilities.

Meanwhile, Apple sales had grown tenfold and the number of employees almost doubled to more than 10,000 worldwide. This massive growth led Sculley to reorganize once again, this time into major geographic divisions (Apple USA, Apple Pacific, and Apple Europe), with a separate division for Apple products. The Apple products division was responsible for all aspects of product development, from basic research and product definition to manufacturing, introduction, and coordination of marketing. Popular new products began to appear, such as the low-cost Macintosh Classic computers and the PowerBook laptop computers.

Still, Apple was facing acute competition from other computer hardware manufacturers emphasizing low cost. At the same time, software from independent developers (e.g., Windows from Microsoft) was enabling IBM PCs and their clones to have graphics capabilities similar to those of the Macintosh. Sculley began to believe that Apple could not continue its differentiation strategy if it remained strictly a maker of personal computers. Instead he envisioned Apple as a global electronics and information-technology conglomerate. Therefore, he broke the Apple products division into five new divisions focusing on hardware, software, networking and communications, portable information tools, and longer-term research and development.

In reaction to cost cutting by competitors, Apple cut prices. Profits declined. Market share also was declining, causing major software development firms to be reluctant to write versions of their software to run on Macintosh machines. Many observers faulted Sculley for not having licensed Macintosh software to other computer makers and for not allowing other companies to clone its machines so there would be more Mac-compatible computers in the marketplace. Under pressure from the board of directors, Sculley resigned in 1993.

He was succeeded by his chief operating officer, Michael Spindler, who began licensing clone makers, but by now there were only a few takers. Apple introduced a new, more powerful line of Power Macs that were far more popular than anticipated. Backorders mushroomed to $1 billion. As the shortage eased, Apple's market share began to rise, but the company was reporting losses. Spindler was fired in early 1996 and was replaced by Gilbert Amelio, former chairman and chief executive of National Semiconductor. He refocused Apple on a differentiation strategy and initiated a reorganization. The redesigned structure contained four new product divisions: Power Macintosh products, imaging (printers, scanners, etc.), information appliance products (low-cost, special-purpose products like Newton, the electronic personal assistant), and servers and alternate platform products (servers and non-Macintosh based products). Software was consolidated into a single functional department called Apple-Soft. Other functional departments include AppleNet (Internet technologies), reliability and quality assurance, segment marketing, worldwide sales, human resources, and legal.[48]

QUESTIONS FOR CONCLUDING CASE 1

1. Trace the various reorganizing efforts by Apple, and explain the apparent reasons for each.
2. Use your knowledge of organization design to assess the probable effectiveness of Apple's new organization structure.
3. How has the growth in size at Apple affected its organization structure options? What possibilities currently exist?

CONCLUDING CASE 2

THE ORGANIZING LOGIC OF ABB

Asea Brown Boveri (ABB), a $33 billion conglomerate headquartered in Zurich, is a global organization of staggering business diversity. Yet its organizing principles are stark in their simplicity. Along one dimension, the company is a distributed global network. Executives around the world make decisions on product strategy and performance without regard for national borders. Along a second dimension, it is a collection of traditionally organized national companies, each serving its home market as effectively as possible. ABB's global matrix holds the two dimensions together.

At the top of the company sit CEO Göran Lindahl and 12 colleagues on the executive committee. The group, which meets every 3 weeks, is responsible for ABB's global strategy and performance. The executive committee consists of Swedes, Swiss, Germans, and Americans. Several members of the executive committee are based outside of Zurich, and their meetings are held around the world.

Reporting to the executive committee are leaders of the 50 or so business areas (BAs), located worldwide, into which the company's products and services are divided. The BAs are grouped into eight business segments, for which different members of the executive committee are responsible. For example, the "industry" segment, which sells components, systems, and software to automate industrial

processes, has five BAs, including metallurgy, drives, and process engineering. The BA leaders report to Gerhard Schulmeyer, a German member of the executive committee who works out of Stamford, Connecticut.

Each BA has a leader responsible for optimizing the business on a global basis. The BA leader devises and champions a global strategy, holds factories around the world to cost and quality standards, allocates export markets to each factory, and shares expertise by rotating people across borders, creating mixed-nationality teams to solve problems, and building a culture of trust and communication. The BA leader for power transformers, who is responsible for 25 factories in 16 countries, is a Swede who works out of Mannheim, Germany. The BA leader for instrumentation is British. The BA leader for electric metering is an American based in North Carolina.

Alongside the BA structure sits a country structure. ABB's operations in the developed world are organized as national enterprises with presidents, balance sheets, income statements, and career ladders. In Germany, for example, Asea Brown Boveri Aktiengesellschaft, ABB's national company, employs 36,000 people and generates annual revenues of more than $4 billion. The managing director of ABB Germany, Eberhard von Koerber, plays a role comparable with that of a traditional German CEO. He reports to a supervisory board whose members include German

bank representatives and trade union officials. His company produces financial statements comparable with those from any other German company and participates fully in the German apprenticeship program.

The BA structure meets the national structure at the level of ABB's member companies. CEO Göran Lindahl advocates strict decentralization. Whenever possible, ABB creates separate companies to do the work of the 50 business areas in different countries. For example, ABB does not merely sell industrial robots in Norway. Norway has an ABB robotics company charged with manufacturing robots, selling to and servicing domestic customers, and exporting to markets allocated by the BA leader.

There are 1300 such local companies around the world. Their presidents report to two bosses—the BA leader, who is usually located outside the country, and the president of the national company of which the local company is a subsidiary. At this intersection, ABB's "multidomestic" structure becomes a reality.[49]

QUESTIONS FOR CONCLUDING CASE 2

1 Evaluate the extent to which ABB is a mature matrix. Give reasons for your assessment.
2 What are the advantages of the matrix structure for ABB?
3 What are some disadvantages of the matrix structure for ABB?

CHAPTER TEN

MANAGING DIVERSE HUMAN RESOURCES

CHAPTER OUTLINE

Strategic Human Resource Management
The HRM Process: An Overview
The Strategic Importance of HRM

Human Resource Planning
Job Analysis
Demand for Human Resources
Supply of Human Resources
Reconciling Demand and Supply

Staffing
Recruitment
Selection

Development and Evaluation
Training and Development
Performance Appraisal

Compensation
Types of Equity
Designing the Pay Structure
Employee Benefits

Maintaining Effective Work-Force Relationships
Labor-Management Relations
Current Employee Issues

LEARNING OBJECTIVES

After studying this chapter, you should be able to:

■ Outline the human resource management process and trace the development of its strategic importance.

■ Explain how human resource planning is conducted.

■ Differentiate between internal and external recruiting.

■ Assess the usefulness of the major selection methods.

■ Explain the main phases in the training process, as well as the most common types of training programs.

■ Delineate the major methods for rating performance, common rating errors, and the roles that supervisors play in the performance appraisal interview.

■ Explain how pay structures are developed and how benefits figure in compensation.

■ Explain the process through which unions are certified and decertified, as well as the growing importance of employee-rights issues.

GAINING THE EDGE

CHANGES IN HUMAN RESOURCE MANAGEMENT BOOST CARE

 CARE, one of the world's largest not-for-profit, nonsectarian relief and development organizations based in Atlanta, Georgia, was founded after World War II to provide a means by which Americans would send packages of food and clothing to European victims of the war. CARE, which stands for Cooperative for Assistance and Relief Everywhere, reaches some 48 million people in 66 countries in Africa, Asia, Eastern Europe, and Latin America. Since its founding in 1945, CARE has touched the lives of more than 1 billion people in 125 countries. CARE allocates 93 percent of its expenditures to emergency assistance and planning, girls' education, agriculture, and the environment.

In 1990, CARE began to experience major challenges in the human resource management of approximately 275 domestic employees and 300 expatriates (individuals from CARE on assignment in other countries). At that point, human resource planning was not viewed as an organizational or strategic priority, and the department concentrated almost exclusively on domestic human resource issues. However, the growing needs of international employees and the benefits to be derived from greater concentration on international human resources caused CARE to reevaluate the situation.

In 1993, a new team was brought in to revamp CARE's human resource management. The new vice president of human resources, who brings an overseas CARE perspective and firsthand field experience, now reports directly to the chief executive officer and is an active member of the executive management team. In support of CARE's overall strategy and to take greater advantage of its global presence, the human resource function has set four strategic objectives: (1) launch a global staffing plan, (2) enhance people management strategies through such means as training and development programs, (3) reengineer total pay and information processes and systems to maximize time and cost efficiencies, and (4) provide better global service to internal and external clients.

As its first major task, the new team completed a job evaluation project (over 3 years in the works) and corrected inaccuracies found in the pay system for employees. Job descriptions were revamped for every CARE job. CARE also created an improved compensation system and a job hierarchy for all domestic positions, allowing for greater mobility and consistency between international and domestic jobs. It recently adopted a more cost-effective, flexible health insurance plan that includes preventive care. The benefit package offers a number of other features, such as an employee assistance plan and optional long-term disability insurance. CARE also updated its human resource information system, which incorporates data on payroll, performance appraisals, and skill inventories, and includes an upgraded report-writing capability.

CARE has also created two new programs to recognize extraordinary service. One, the CARE Best Employee Recognition Program, honors 10 employees each quarter and chooses 3 for a special annual award. The other, a Sabbatical Program, allows a selected employee to spend a year pursuing work or study external to CARE.

Such continuing efforts have helped CARE maintain and enhance its reputation as one of America's best-run charities. Human resource management improvement is moving to the strategic forefront at CARE.[1] ■■■

In the early 1990s CARE was struggling, but the organization is now considered one of America's best-run charities. Major changes in the management of the agency's human resources contributed significantly to the turnaround. Employees, such as this manager of a women's development project in Bangladesh, have been given boosts in salaries, job training, standards for performance, greater mobility within the organization, a flexible health plan, employee recognition programs, and sabbaticals.

While there were multiple causes for the problems that beset CARE by 1990, many of the difficulties can be traced to shortcomings in acquiring, developing, and utilizing human resources. In the previous two chapters, we considered the organizing function as it relates to various means of structuring organizations so that planned goals can be achieved efficiently and effectively. In this chapter, we continue our discussion of the organizing function by examining how organizations, like CARE, can acquire and develop the diverse human resources needed to effectively activate structural elements. Without employees who can perform the various necessary tasks, organizations have little hope of achieving their goals.

Human resource management (HRM) is the management of various activities designed to enhance the effectiveness of an organization's work force in achieving organizational goals.[2] In exploring this topic, we look first at the human resource management process and consider its strategic importance. We next investigate human resource planning and various aspects of staffing the organization. We also examine methods of developing organization members and evaluating their performance. Finally, we consider important issues in the areas of compensating organization members and maintaining effective work-force relationships.

Human resource management (HRM) The management of various activities designed to enhance the effectiveness of an organization's work force in achieving organizational goals

■ STRATEGIC HUMAN RESOURCE MANAGEMENT

Forward-looking organizations, like CARE and 3M, are at the forefront of a trend toward recognizing human resources as a crucial element in the strategic success of organizations.[3] In this section, we introduce the major aspects of the human resource management process before exploring further the strategic importance of human resource management.

The HRM Process: An Overview

As indicated in Figure 10-1, human resource management encompasses a number of important activities. One critical aspect of the process is human resource planning. This involves assessing the human resource needs associated with an organization's strategic plan and developing plans to meet those needs. The staffing component includes attracting and selecting individuals for appropriate positions. Once individuals become part of the organization, their ability to contribute effectively is usually enhanced by various development and evaluation efforts, such as training and periodic performance evaluations. Compensating employees is another important factor in the HRM process, because adequate rewards are critical not only to attracting but also to motivating and retaining valuable employees. Finally, managers must respond to various issues that influence work-force perceptions of the organization and its treatment of employees.

Human resource professionals operating within human resource departments typically play a major role in designing the elements in the HRM process and in supporting their use by line managers. Nevertheless, line managers are ultimately responsible for the effective utilization of human resources within their units. Thus line managers carry out many aspects of the HRM process.

The Strategic Importance of HRM

Understanding the strategic potential of human resource management in organizations is a relatively recent phenomenon, one that has evolved through three

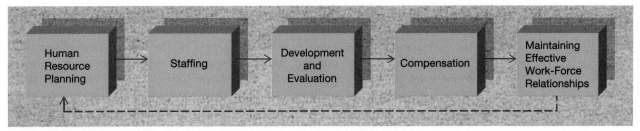

Figure 10-1 *The human resource management process.*

main stages.[4] From early in this century until the mid-1960s, HRM activities were in the *file maintenance* stage, with emphasis on processing personnel-related paperwork and planning company social functions (such as the company picnic). The second stage, *government accountability,* began when the mid-1960s ushered in an era of accelerated governmental regulation of employment issues, which continues to a large degree today. Major federal legislation governing employment is outlined and briefly summarized in Table 10-1. Some laws, particularly those governing relations with unions, were passed earlier than the mid-1960s.

The third stage, which began in the late 1970s and early 1980s, is the *competitive advantage* stage. In this stage, human resource management is increas-

---

TABLE 10-1 MAJOR FEDERAL LAWS GOVERNING EMPLOYMENT

EQUAL EMPLOYMENT OPPORTUNITY

Title VII of the Civil Rights Act of 1964 (amended by the Equal Employment Opportunity Act of 1972) prohibits discrimination based on race, color, religion, sex, or national origin.

Age Discrimination in Employment Act of 1967 (amended in 1978 and 1986) prohibits discriminating against employees over 40 years old.

Rehabilitation Act of 1973, Executive Order 11491 (1973) prohibits federal contractors and the federal government from discriminating against individuals based on physical or mental handicap.

Vietnam Era Readjustment Act of 1974, Executive Order 11701 (1973) prohibits the federal government and federal contractors from discriminating against disabled veterans and Vietnam era veterans, and requires affirmative action.

Pregnancy Discrimination Act (1978) requires that employer-sponsored medical insurance must provide the same level of coverage for pregnancy as for other medical conditions.

Immigration Reform and Control Act of 1986 requires employers to check identities and work authorization papers of all employees, while providing amnesty procedures for those living in the United States since before 1982.

Americans With Disabilities Act (1990) prohibits discrimination against disabled persons and dictates that organizations make reasonable accommodation for disabled persons to perform their job duties.

Older Workers Benefit Protection Act (1990) prohibits age discrimination in employee benefits.

Civil Rights Act of 1991 strengthens Title VII of the 1964 Civil Rights Act, granting the opportunity for compensatory damages and clarifying obligations of employers and employees in unintentional discrimination cases.

LABOR RELATIONS

National Labor Relations Act of 1935 provides the guidance for establishing unions and includes the requirement for collectively bargaining with unions.

Taft Hartley Act (1947) permits states to pass right-to-work laws, promotes free choice in accepting or rejecting union membership.

Labor Management Reporting and Disclosure Act (1959) gives employees more rights against union leaders, eliminates sweetheart contracts, requires disclosure of union financial affairs.

Worker Adjustment and Retraining Notification Act (1988) requires employers with 100 or more employees to give 60 days notice in plant closings or mass layoffs.

COMPENSATION AND BENEFITS

Fair Labor Standards Act (1938) sets minimum wage and overtime rates, child labor laws, and reporting requirements.

Equal Pay Act (1963) requires same pay for women as for men doing similar work under similar working conditions.

Employee Retirement Income Security Act (1974) specifies how pension plans are managed.

The Comprehensive Omnibus Budget Reconciliation Act (1986) requires an extension of insurance benefits after specified changes in employment or dependency status.

Family and Medical Leave Act of 1993 requires employers to provide up to 12 months unpaid leave for family or medical purposes, to include pregnancy.

ingly viewed as an important means to build internal capabilities that constitute a competitive advantage (see Chapter 7). For example, as Mirage Resorts, Inc., prepared to open two new casino hotels in Las Vegas, The Mirage and Treasure Island, the company explored how to compete effectively with the more than 80 other properties in close proximity along the Las Vegas strip. Mirage management concluded that the best source of competitive advantage would be to have employees who could and would deliver excellent service. Therefore, with the help of the human resource function, managers expended a great deal of effort to recruit, select, and train the individuals who would work at the two new properties. Management candidates were required to have hotel-management majors, grade point averages of at least 3.0, experience as interns, and high recommendations. More than 22,000 applicants were screened for various jobs through such methods as application blanks and behavioral interviews. About $3.5 million was spent on training employees before The Mirage opened, while $3 million was spent on training for the opening of Treasure Island. One result is a turnover rate of 13.5 percent, compared with the 40 percent average in Las Vegas. Moreover, the two hotels are consistently full at a rate of 98.6 percent compared with an average occupancy of 90 percent at other Las Vegas hotels.[5] The process of staffing and training, of course, began with human resource planning.

■ HUMAN RESOURCE PLANNING

Human resource planning
The process of determining future human resource needs relative to an organization's strategic plan and devising the steps necessary to meet those needs

Human resource planning is the process of determining future human resource needs relative to an organization's strategic plan and devising the steps necessary to meet those needs.[6] Human resource professionals and line managers consider both demand and supply issues, as well as potential steps for addressing any imbalances. Such planning often relies on job analysis as a means of understanding the nature of jobs under consideration.

Job Analysis

Job analysis The systematic collection and recording of information concerning the purpose of a job, its major duties, the conditions under which it is performed, the contacts with others that job performance requires, and the knowledge, skills, and abilities needed to perform the job effectively

Job analysis is the systematic collection and recording of information concerning the purpose of a job, its major duties, the conditions under which it is performed, the contacts with others that job performance requires, and the knowledge, skills, and abilities needed to perform the job effectively. Job analysis information can be collected in a variety of ways. These include observing individuals as they do their jobs, conducting interviews with individuals and their superiors, having individuals keep diaries of job-related activities, and distributing questionnaires to be completed by job incumbents and their supervisors.[7]

Job description A statement of the duties, working conditions, and other significant requirements associated with a particular job

Job specification A statement of the skills, abilities, education, and previous work experience that are required to perform a particular job

The results of job analysis are often used to develop job descriptions. A **job description** is a statement of the duties, working conditions, and other significant requirements associated with a particular job. Job descriptions are frequently combined with job specifications (see Table 10-2). A **job specification** is a statement of the skills, abilities, education, and previous work experience that are required to perform a particular job. Formats for job descriptions and job specifications tend to vary among organizations, but the information is typically used for activities that require a solid understanding of the job and the qualifications necessary for performing it. Such activities include human resource planning, recruitment, selection, performance appraisal, and compensation.[8]

TABLE 10-2 SAMPLE JOB DESCRIPTION AND JOB SPECIFICATION

THE PORT AUTHORITY OF NEW YORK AND NEW JERSEY

DATA CONTROL CLERK (1127)

Under immediate supervision receives and reviews input and output data for recurring computer reports and records. Receives detailed instructions on assignments which are not routine. Work is checked through standard controls.

DUTIES

JOB DESCRIPTION

Operates data-processing equipment such as Sorters (IBM 083), Bursters (Std Register and Moore), decollators (Std Register), Communications Terminal (IBM 3775), and interactive operation of IBM 327X family of terminals to process accounting, personnel, and other statistical reports.

Feeds and tends machine according to standard instructions.

Makes minor operating adjustments to equipment.

Submits data with necessary documentation for computer processing.

Reviews output data and corrects problems causing incorrect output.

Revises and maintains lists, control records, and source data necessary to produce reports.

Distributes output reports by predetermined instructions.

Operates magnetic-tape cleaning and testing equipment.

Corrects and/or adjusts files via use of time-sharing terminals.

QUALIFICATIONS

JOB SPECIFICATION

Six months experience in operating data-processing equipment.

Ability to reconcile differences and errors in computer data.

Source: Reprinted from David J. Rachman, Michael H. Mescon, Courtland L. Bovée, and John V. Thill, *Business Today,* 6th ed., McGraw-Hill, New York, 1990, p. 244.

Demand for Human Resources

A significant aspect of human resource planning is assessing the demand for human resources. Such an assessment involves considering the major forces that affect the demand and using basic forecasting aids to predict it (see the Supplement to Chapter 5).

Human resource demand is affected by an organization's *environment,* including factors in both the general environment, or mega-environment, and the task environment (see Chapter 3). For example, during the past decade a number of organizations have downsized or restructured, largely because of economic downturns and heightened competitive pressures. On the other hand, sometimes those same employers were adding workers in business areas facing more favorable environmental conditions. For example, at one point Allied Signal announced the elimination of 3100 jobs in its auto parts division; but simultaneously the company was hiring new employees with different skills in its chemicals, plastics, and fibers businesses. Socially responsible employers use transfer, retraining, and other means to retain workers whenever possible.

In addition to environmental factors, *changing organizational requirements,* such as alterations in the strategic plan, can also influence the demand for human resources. According to a 1993 American Management Association survey of manufacturing companies with more than $10 million in annual revenues, only 45 percent of the downsizing companies experienced an increase in operating profits as a result. Not surprisingly, many companies are now focusing on efforts to grow—a strategy that could increase the demand for workers.[9]

Contingent workers Those workers hired on a temporary or sporadic basis to handle areas of fluctuating demand or changing needs that cannot be met by the organization's traditional, full-time workers

Similarly, internal *work-force changes,* such as retirements, resignations, terminations, deaths, and leaves of absence, frequently cause major shifts in the need for human resources. To retain greater flexibility, many employers are increasing their use of contingent workers. **Contingent workers** are those hired on a temporary or sporadic basis to handle areas of fluctuating demand or changing needs that cannot be met by the organization's traditional, full-time workers. They include temporary workers, part-time workers, and workers hired on an independent contractor basis.

Supply of Human Resources

Demand is only one side of the equation governing whether an organization will have sufficient human resources to operate effectively. In assessing the other side, supply, human resource professionals and managers consider both internal and external labor supplies.

Skills inventory A data bank (usually computerized) containing basic information about each employee that can be used to assess the likely availability of individuals for meeting current and future human resource needs

INTERNAL LABOR SUPPLY One prime supply source is the pool of current employees who can be transferred or promoted to help meet demands for human resources. Major means of assessing the internal labor supply include skills inventories, replacement planning, and succession planning.[10]

A **skills inventory** is a data bank (usually computerized) containing basic information about each employee that can be used to assess the likely availability of individuals for meeting current and future human resource needs. A skills inventory typically contains information regarding each employee's performance, knowledge, skills, experience, interests, and relevant personal characteristics.

Replacement chart A partial organization chart showing the major managerial positions in an organization, current incumbents, potential replacements for each position, and the age of each person on the chart

Replacement planning is a means of identifying potential candidates to fill specific managerial positions. This is done through the use of replacement charts. A **replacement chart** is a partial organization chart showing major managerial positions, current incumbents, potential replacements for each position (usually including, for each individual, a current performance rating and an assessment of preparedness to assume the position), and the age of each person on the chart (see Figure 10-2). With replacement charts, age is used to track possible retirements, but it is not considered in determining promotions. On the contrary, managers must be careful not to discriminate against older workers in making such choices (note, as indicated in Table 10-1, that it also is against the law to do so).

Replacement planning focuses on specific candidates who could fill designated managerial positions. In contrast, *succession planning* is a means of identifying individuals with high potential and ensuring that they receive appropriate training and job assignments aimed at their long-run growth and development. Thus succession planning provides the organization with a well-qualified pool of individuals from which middle and top managers can be drawn in the future.

EXTERNAL LABOR SUPPLY Some reliance on the external labor supply is usually necessary because of organizational expansion and/or employee attrition. Periodic estimates of labor supplies in a variety of categories are made by government agencies, including the Bureau of Labor Statistics of the U.S. Department of Labor, and by industry and human resource associations. In addition, human resource professionals, particularly those heavily engaged in recruitment and selection, are often knowledgeable about supply trends in given areas and can supplement the knowledge of line managers.

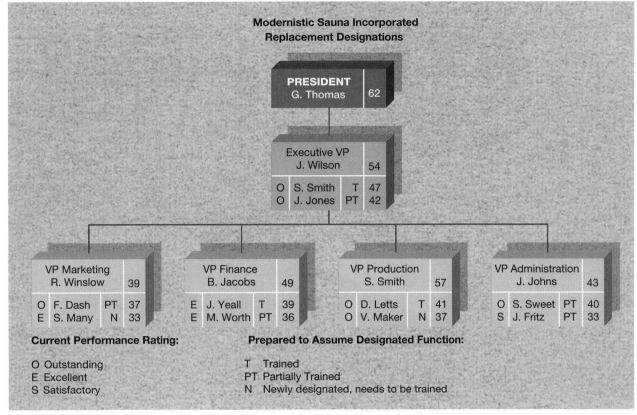

Modernistic Sauna Incorporated
Replacement Designations

PRESIDENT
G. Thomas | 62

Executive VP
J. Wilson | 54

| O | S. Smith | T | 47 |
| O | J. Jones | PT | 42 |

VP Marketing
R. Winslow | 39

| O | F. Dash | PT | 37 |
| E | S. Many | N | 33 |

VP Finance
B. Jacobs | 49

| E | J. Yeall | T | 39 |
| E | M. Worth | PT | 36 |

VP Production
S. Smith | 57

| O | D. Letts | T | 41 |
| O | V. Maker | N | 37 |

VP Administration
J. Johns | 43

| O | S. Sweet | PT | 40 |
| S | J. Fritz | PT | 33 |

Current Performance Rating:

O Outstanding
E Excellent
S Satisfactory

Prepared to Assume Designated Function:

T Trained
PT Partially Trained
N Newly designated, needs to be trained

Figure 10-2 *Replacement chart for Modernistic Sauna, Inc.*

Reconciling Demand and Supply

After estimating the demand and supply of human resources, managers must often take steps to balance the two. If estimates show that the internal supply of labor is too large, then managers need to make plans to reduce the number of employees through such measures as resignations and retirements, early retirement programs, or, possibly, layoffs. On the other hand, if additional employees are necessary, then plans must be made for promoting and transferring current organization members, if desirable, as well as for hiring new workers.

AFFIRMATIVE ACTION ISSUES One important aspect of reconciling supply and demand is considering the affirmative action implications. **Affirmative action** is any special activity undertaken by employers to increase equal employment opportunities for groups protected by federal equal employment opportunity laws and related regulations. As shown in Table 10-1, Title VII of the Civil Rights Act of 1964 (as amended by the Equal Employment Opportunity Act of 1972) forbids employment discrimination on the basis of race, color, religion, sex, or national origin.[11] Groups covered by Title VII and related laws and regulations are often referred to as "protected groups."

Organizations often have patterns of employment in which protected groups are underrepresented in certain areas, such as management, relative to the number of group members who have appropriate credentials in the marketplace. To remedy this, an organization may adopt an **affirmative action plan,** a written, systematic plan that specifies goals and timetables for hiring, training, promoting, and retaining groups protected by federal equal employment

Affirmative action Any special activity undertaken by employers to increase equal employment opportunities for groups protected by federal equal employment opportunity laws and related regulations

Affirmative action plan A written, systematic plan that specifies goals and timetables for hiring, training, promoting, and retaining groups protected by federal equal employment laws and related regulations

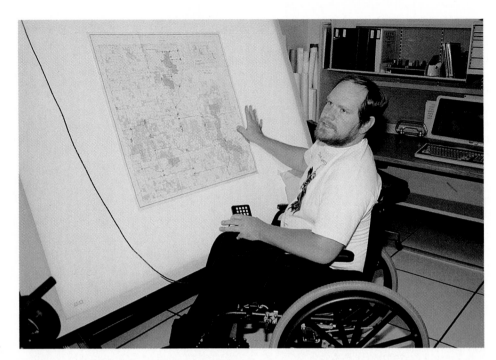

A disabled employee of the U.S. Forest Service is shown here digitizing a map for computers. The Americans with Disabilities Act passed in 1990 helps protect him and other disabled workers from discrimination in employment.

laws and related regulations.[12] Such plans are required, by federal regulations (Executive Order 11246 issued in 1965), in organizations with federal contracts greater than $50,000 and with 50 or more employees. The plans, which must be filed with the Department of Labor, have to include provisions for hiring members of the three protected groups covered by Title VII and also the disabled (as later stipulated by the Rehabilitation Act of 1973). Courts sometimes require that organizations formulate affirmative action plans because of evidence of past discriminatory practices. Many organizations, though, establish affirmative action programs on a voluntary basis.[13]

Such programs must balance efforts to assist women and minorities against the rights of others who may be competing for the same jobs. For example, courts have generally been unwilling to approve plans that cause individuals to lose their jobs in order to make room for members of protected groups, but they have allowed more limited burdens, such as postponements of promotions.[14] One recent Supreme Court ruling suggests that affirmative action programs must be narrowly aimed at redressing past discrimination.[15] Affirmative action programs continue to be challenged in the courts by individuals and groups who do not fit into the protected category and, therefore, charge reverse discrimination.

POPULATION TRENDS Demographic shifts are also causing organizations to place emphasis on hiring women and minorities. Bureau of Labor Statistics' projections indicate that annual work-force growth has slowed since 1988 and will not increase until at least the year 2000. This is partly because most of the baby boomers wishing to work have already been absorbed into the work force and there is no similar bulge of workers behind them. It is estimated that, out of necessity, women will constitute about 47 percent of the work force and minorities and immigrants about 27 percent by the year 2000 (see Chapter 3). As a result, organizations are taking steps to more effectively manage the increasing diversity. *Managing diversity* is the planning and implementing of organizational systems and practices that maximize the potential of employees to contribute to organizational goals and develop their capabilities unhindered by group identities such as race, gender, age, or ethnic group.[16] One such company is the Digital Equipment Corporation. At its factory in Boston, which makes computer keyboards, the 350 employees represent 44 countries. Because of the 19 different languages spoken, written plant announcements are printed in English, Chinese, French, Spanish, Portuguese, Vietnamese, and Haitian Creole.[17] McGraw-Hill publishes an internal newsletter for employees called *Diversity Management*. The newsletter helps to explain the company's philosophy regarding diversity management and provides useful information in support of the company's diversity theme, "We are many . . . we are one."

Some organizations are filling vacancies with part-time workers, many of whom are senior citizens who have retired from full-time jobs. For instance, the Travelers Corporation, an insurance company based in Hartford, Connecticut, runs a job bank for area retirees in order to have workers available for part-time and temporary clerical and administrative jobs.[18] Affirmative action issues, population trends, and other considerations that grow out of human resource planning then become the basis for staffing efforts.

■ STAFFING

Staffing is the set of activities aimed at attracting and selecting individuals for positions in a way that will facilitate the achievement of organizational goals. Increasingly, companies are recognizing that having committed employees with superior competencies can represent an important source of competitive advantage. A critical element in building competitive advantage through people is attracting and hiring the right people through the recruitment and selection processes associated with staffing.[19]

Staffing The set of activities aimed at attracting and selecting individuals for positions in a way that will facilitate the achievement of organizational goals

Recruitment

Recruitment is the process of finding and attempting to attract job candidates who are capable of effectively filling job vacancies.[20] Job descriptions and job

Recruitment The process of finding and attempting to attract job candidates who are capable of effectively filling job vacancies

Soaring immigration rates, combined with a slowing in the numbers of native-born Americans entering the work force, means that more and more jobs will be claimed by immigrants. This demographic shift in the workplace puts more pressure on organizations to manage diversity. American Megatrends Inc., a Georgia-based manufacturer of computer motherboards and software, makes a point of mixing immigrant and American-born workers; the company itself was founded by an immigrant from India.

TABLE 10-3 ADVANTAGES AND DISADVANTAGES OF INTERNAL AND EXTERNAL RECRUITMENT

ADVANTAGES	DISADVANTAGES
INTERNAL RECRUITMENT	
1. Candidates are already oriented to the organization.	1. There may be fewer new ideas.
2. Reliable information is available about candidates.	2. Unsuccessful contenders may become upset.
3. Recruitment costs are lower.	3. Selection is more susceptible to office politics.
4. Internal morale is increased as a result of upward-mobility opportunities.	4. Expensive training may be necessary.
5. Good performance is rewarded.	5. Candidates' current work may be disrupted.
EXTERNAL RECRUITMENT	
1. Candidates are a potential source of new ideas.	1. The probability of mistake is higher because of less reliable information.
2. Candidates may have broader experience.	2. Potential internal candidates may be resentful.
3. Candidates may be familiar with competitors.	3. The new employee may have a slower start because of the need for orientation to the organization.
4. Candidates may have new specialties.	4. The recruitment process may be expensive.

specifications, both mentioned earlier, are important in the recruiting process because they specify the nature of the job and the qualifications required of job candidates. Recruiting can be conducted both internally and externally.

INTERNAL RECRUITMENT Most vacant positions in organizations are filled through internal recruitment, the process of finding potential *internal* candidates and encouraging them to apply for and/or be willing to accept organizational jobs that are open.[21] CARE, for example, has a policy of filling job vacancies from within and conducts recruiting through external sources only when a job cannot be filled internally. The advantages and disadvantages of internal recruitment are summarized in Table 10-3.[22]

Job posting A practice whereby information about job vacancies is placed in conspicuous places in an organization, such as on bulletin boards or in organizational newsletters

One major method of recruiting internally is **job posting,** a practice whereby information about job vacancies is placed in conspicuous places in an organization, such as on bulletin boards or in organizational newsletters. At CARE, for instance, all nonunion jobs are posted for at least 15 working days, while union jobs are posted for at least 3 working days, in conformance with union contracts. Skills inventories and replacement charts, mentioned earlier, are also used to locate potential candidates for internal recruiting.

EXTERNAL RECRUITMENT External recruitment is the process of finding potential *external* candidates and encouraging them to apply for and/or be willing to accept organizational jobs that are open. The advantages and disadvantages of external recruitment are listed in Table 10-3.

A variety of sources exist for obtaining external job candidates. Advertising is generally the most heavily used recruiting source. Other sources include college recruiting programs, employment agencies, and referrals by employees. Rather than focusing on a particular recruitment source per se, recruiters should usually concentrate first on the types of qualifications that are required and then think of the best way to locate individuals who have those qualifications.[23]

One major issue related to external recruiting is the tendency of recruiters and managers to provide candidates with an overly positive view of the organization in order to attract new employees. Unfortunately, this strategy can backfire: an individual who accepts a position on such terms may become dissatisfied and leave when the position fails to meet his or her inflated expectations. An alternative approach is the **realistic job preview,** a technique used during the recruiting process in which the job candidate is presented with a balanced view of both the positive and the negative aspects of the job and the organization.[24] Even though realistic job previews may reduce the number of candidates interested in a position, such previews are likely to have a positive effect on job satisfaction, performance, and the length of employment of those ultimately hired.[25] Recruiting, though, is only one part of the staffing process. Decisions must also be made about the candidates to whom job offers will be extended.

Selection

Selection is the process of determining which job candidates best suit organizational needs.[26] During this process, managers must determine the extent to which job candidates have the skills, abilities, and knowledge required to perform effectively in the positions for which they are being considered. Before discussing more specifically the most commonly used selection methods, we examine an important concept underlying their use: validity.

VALIDITY In order to make adequate assessments of candidates, selection methods must have validity. **Validity** is the degree to which a measure actually assesses the attribute that it is designed to measure. As applied to selection, validity addresses how well a selection device (such as a test) actually predicts a candidate's future job performance.[27]

Organizations often conduct studies to determine the validity of selection methods, particularly if the methods have an adverse impact on groups protected by equal employment opportunity laws and regulations. A selection method is generally considered to have an **adverse impact** when the job selection rate for a protected group is less than 80 percent of the rate for the majority group. For example, requiring a high school diploma for entry-level positions might have an adverse impact because the percentage of minority-group members with high school diplomas tends to be smaller than that of majority-group members. Under such conditions, an organization can continue to use the selection method only if it can demonstrate that the method is a valid predictor of job performance and that there is no other approach that would have similar validity without the adverse impact.

Organizations are permitted to discriminate against certain groups in employment when a **bona fide occupational qualification (BFOQ)** exists. A BFOQ is a legitimate job qualification that necessitates an employer's selecting an individual in a certain sex, religion, national-origin, or age group.[28] For example, in hiring models to display men's clothing, a mail-order firm can limit the job to males. Generally, there are few circumstances under which employers can use a BFOQ as a justification for employment discrimination.

MAJOR SELECTION METHODS More than one selection method is typically used in assessing job candidates. The most prevalent methods include the use of application blanks, selection interviews, tests, assessment centers, and reference checks.[29]

An **application blank** is a form containing a series of inquiries about an applicant's educational background, previous job experience, physical health,

Realistic job preview A technique used during the recruiting process in which the job candidate is presented with a balanced view of both the positive and the negative aspects of the job and the organization

Selection The process of determining which job candidates best suit organizational needs

Validity The degree to which a measure actually assesses the attribute that it is designed to measure

Adverse impact The effect produced when a job selection rate for a protected group is less than 80 percent of the rate for the majority group

Bona fide occupational qualification (BFOQ) A legitimate job qualification that necessitates an employer's selecting an individual in a certain sex, religion, national-origin, or age group

Application blank A form containing a series of inquiries about such issues as an applicant's educational background, previous job experience, physical health, and other information that may be useful in assessing an individual's ability to perform a job

A large majority of companies favor the personal interview as a means for selecting employees. Unstructured interviews are spontaneous and convey warmth, but they make it difficult to compare applicants; structured interviews yield more valid data, but can seem cold and mechanical to the applicant. A mixture of the two—a semistructured interview—seems to work best: it allows the interviewer to ask a set of standardized questions and to explore issues that are unique to the applicant.

Selection interview A relatively formal, in-depth conversation conducted for the purpose of assessing a candidate's knowledge, skills, and abilities, as well as providing information to the candidate about the organization and potential jobs

and other information that may be useful in assessing an individual's ability to perform a job. It serves as a prescreening device to help determine whether an applicant meets the minimum requirements of a position, and it allows preliminary comparisons with the credentials of other candidates.[30] Résumés furnished by job applicants often also provide useful background information.

Another selection method, the **selection interview,** is a relatively formal, in-depth conversation conducted for the purpose of assessing a candidate's knowledge, skills, and abilities, as well as providing information to the candidate about the organization and potential jobs.[31] As an indication of the perceived importance of the interview, 90 percent of the responding companies in one large survey reported that they placed more confidence in the selection interview than in any other selection method.[32] Ironically, despite their popularity, interviews, as they are widely conducted, have relatively low validity as a selection device. A major reason for this is that many interviewers follow a format that constitutes an *unstructured interview*. With this type of interview, little planning is done regarding the information to be collected, and the interviewer asks whatever questions happen to come to mind.[33] Because of the lack of structure, data about candidates are collected in a nonsystematic way that yields insufficient information for evaluating or comparing candidates adequately.

One potential remedy is the *structured interview*, in which the interviewer has a predetermined set of questions that are asked in sequence, with virtually no deviations. This type of interview is sometimes used to advantage if a large number of candidates are to be prescreened or if interviewers are relatively untrained. While a structured interview yields more valid data than an unstructured one, a structured interview is almost mechanical and may convey disinterest to the candidate. It also does not allow the interviewer to probe interesting or unusual issues that may arise.

To overcome these disadvantages and still acquire reasonably valid data for making a selection decision, interviewers can use a *semistructured interview*.[34] With this format, the interviewer relies on a number of predetermined questions but also asks spontaneous questions to explore any unique issues that arise in regard to a particular candidate (such as an unexplained break in work history, unusual work experience, or the individual's particular strengths and

MANAGEMENT SKILLS FOR THE TWENTY-FIRST CENTURY

How to Conduct an Effective Interview

You have a job vacancy in your unit and need to interview several job candidates. What should you do? There are a number of steps you can take before, during, and after the interview to increase the likelihood of obtaining information that will be useful in making your selection decision.

BEFORE THE INTERVIEW
Much of the secret of conducting an effective interview is in the preparation. The following guidelines will enhance your preparatory skills:

Determine the Job Requirements
Using the job description and job specification, prepare a list of characteristics that the person will need to possess in order to perform the job. For example, suppose that you are a bank manager and have a job opening for a teller. Important characteristics would include oral communication skills, a willingness to check for errors, the ability to get along with others, and a service orientation in handling customers. Once the major characteristics are identified, you can develop an interview guide.

Prepare a Written Interview Guide
A written guide of what you wish to cover during the interview will ensure that major points are addressed with each interviewee. You need to plan questions that assess the degree to which job candidates possess the characteristics necessary for the job.

Past performance is often a good predictor of future performance. Therefore, it is useful to ask questions about what a person has actually done, rather than focusing on generalities or speculations about what the person will do in the future. For example, in assessing how well the individual interacts with customers, a relatively *poor*

question would be: "How well do you handle problem customers?" For the most part, a candidate is unlikely to answer that he or she has difficulty handling problem customers, even if that is the case.

A *good* question would be framed in terms of how the individual has dealt with customers in the past. For example, you might say, "Please describe a time when a customer paid you an especially nice compliment because of something you did. What were the circumstances?" You might follow up by asking, "Tell me about a time when you had to deal with a particularly irritating customer. How did you handle the situation?" Answers to these types of specific questions can provide insight into how an individual is likely to treat customers and handle trying situations in the future. (If the individual has no job experience, questions can be adjusted accordingly—for example, ". . . a time when you had to deal with a particularly irritating *person*.")

Next, prepare a step-by-step plan outlining how you will present the position to the job candidate. Develop a similar plan for the points you wish to make about the work unit and the organization. Such plans will help you present the information in an organized fashion and will ensure that you cover all the important points you wish to make.

Review the Candidate's Application and/or Résumé
By reviewing the candidate's background materials, you will be familiar with the particular experiences and accomplishments that are most relevant to the requirements of the job. Read the application and/or résumé before the interview; otherwise, you may appear (correctly so) unprepared. In addition, it is easy to miss gaps, discrepancies, and relevant experience when the materials are reviewed quickly in front of the candidate.

DURING THE INTERVIEW
Your carefully prepared questions will help you maintain control of the dialogue during the interview. Here are some additional guidelines for actually conducting the interview:

Establish Rapport
Small talk at the beginning of the interview will often help put the candidate at ease. You may be able to comment about some item on the résumé, such as a hobby that you and the candidate have in common or a place where you both have lived. Be careful, though, not to let the interview get too far off track with an extended discussion of, say, your respective golf games.

Avoid Conveying the Response You Seek
Suppose that you are attempting to determine the candidate's ability to work with other tellers, all of whom must work within a relatively small area. You ask, "Do you think that you will be able to work well with the other tellers, especially given our space constraints?" The candidate easily replies, "Of course, no problem." A bright interviewee can quickly realize, from your question, the answer that you are seeking. A better approach would be to say something like this: "We all sometimes have unpleasant experiences with coworkers. Tell me about the most difficult time that you have ever had working with a coworker."

Listen and Take Notes
Be sure to do a great deal of listening. Some experts recommend that the interviewer should talk 20 to 30 percent of the time and allow the interviewee to talk (the interviewer listens) 70 to 80 percent of the time. You want to learn as much as possible about the job candidate in the relatively limited time that you have available. Take a few notes to help you remember important points.

(continued)

MANAGEMENT SKILLS FOR THE TWENTY-FIRST CENTURY

Ask Only Job-Relevant Questions
Interviewers sometimes stray into asking questions that are discriminatory. One example is asking a female applicant what kind of work her spouse does. Such a question is discriminatory since it is seldom directed at a male candidate and is irrelevant to job requirements or the

person's qualifications. The best policy is to ask only questions that are clearly and directly related to job requirements.

AFTER THE INTERVIEW
Write a short report right after the interview, scoring the candidate on the characteristics required for

functioning effectively in the job. Briefly indicate your rationale, perhaps using examples or summaries of responses. By documenting your ratings immediately after the interview, you will have good data to help you with your selection decision.[35]

weaknesses). Aetna Life and Casualty recently developed an "Interview and Selection Guide" to help managers formulate questions regarding the most important competencies for managerial positions. Managers also received training in interviewing to help further enhance the effectiveness of selection decisions.[36] For some hints on conducting a semistructured interview, see the Management Skills for the Twenty-First Century discussion, "How to Conduct an Effective Interview."

Employment test A means of assessing a job applicant's characteristics through paper-and-pencil responses or simulated exercises

Another selection device is an **employment test,** a means of assessing a job applicant's characteristics through paper-and-pencil responses or simulated exercises. Three major types of tests used in the selection process are ability, personality, and performance tests.[37]

Ability tests measure mainly mental (such as intelligence), mechanical, and clerical abilities or sensory capacities (such as vision and hearing). Except for measures of sensory capacities, the tests are usually the paper-and-pencil type.

Personality tests are means of measuring characteristics, such as patterns of thoughts, feelings, and behaviors, that are distinctly combined in a particular individual and influence that individual's interactions in various situations. Paper-and-pencil personality tests measure such characteristics as sociability, independence, and need for achievement. The use of personality tests for selection purposes is subject to considerable debate because of both the difficulty of accurately measuring personality characteristics and the problems associated with matching them appropriately to job requirements. They should be used with caution in selection processes.[38]

Performance, or *work sample, tests* are means of measuring practical ability on a specific job. In this type of test, the applicant completes some job activity under structured conditions. For example, a word-processing applicant might be asked to prepare materials on equipment that would be used on the job. These tests tend to be less susceptible to the adverse-impact problems that plague many paper-and-pencil tests.

Assessment center A controlled environment used to predict the probable managerial success of individuals mainly on the basis of evaluations of their behaviors in a variety of simulated situations

An **assessment center** is a controlled environment used to predict the probable managerial success of individuals mainly on the basis of evaluations of their behaviors in a variety of simulated situations. The situations (or exercises) are essentially performance tests that reflect the type of work done in managerial positions. According to one estimate, assessment center programs are in operation in more than 2000 organizations, including AT&T, where the technique was originally pioneered.[39]

Reference checks Attempts to obtain job-related information about job applicants from individuals who are knowledgeable about the applicant's qualifications

Reference checks are attempts to obtain job-related information about job applicants from individuals who are knowledgeable about the applicants' qualifications. Such checks are conducted to verify information on application blanks and résumés and, sometimes, to collect additional data that will facilitate the selection decision. One reason for the widespread use of reference checks is that, according to one estimate, between 20 and 25 percent of all candidate application blanks and résumés contain at least one major fabrication.[40]

■ DEVELOPMENT AND EVALUATION

After individuals are hired, both they and their employing organizations will ultimately gain from efforts aimed at enhancing their knowledge, skills, and abilities. Major approaches to increasing the effectiveness of organization members include training and development, as well as performance appraisal.

Training and Development

Training and development is a planned effort to facilitate employee learning of job-related behaviors in order to improve employee performance.[41] Experts sometimes distinguish between the terms "training" and "development": "training" denotes efforts to increase employee skills on present jobs, while "development" refers to efforts oriented toward improvements relevant to future jobs.[42] In practice, though, the distinction is often blurred (mainly because upgrading skills in present jobs usually improves performance in future jobs). We adopt the increasingly common practice of using both terms interchangeably. According to one estimate, U.S. businesses spend close to $60 billion annually on internally run training and education programs.[43]

Training and development A planned effort to facilitate employee learning of job-related behaviors in order to improve employee performance

PHASES OF THE TRAINING PROCESS Training efforts generally encompass three main phases.[44] The training process begins with the *assessment phase*. This phase involves identifying training needs, setting training objectives, and developing criteria against which to evaluate the results of the training program. Training requirements are determined by conducting a needs analysis. A **needs analysis** is an assessment of an organization's training needs that is developed by considering overall organizational requirements, tasks (identified through job analysis) associated with jobs for which training is needed, and the degree to which individuals are able to perform those tasks effectively.[45]

Need analysis An assessment of an organization's training needs that is developed by considering overall organizational requirements, tasks associated with jobs for which training is needed, and the degree to which individuals are able to perform those tasks effectively

The next part of the process is the *training design and implementation phase*. This involves determining training methods, developing training materials, and actually conducting the training. Although formal classroom training is common, a considerable amount of training is conducted using *on-the-job training (OJT) methods*. With such methods, the trainee learns while actually performing a job, usually with the help of a knowledgeable trainer.

The final part of the training process is the *evaluation phase*. This entails evaluating the results of the training in terms of the criteria developed during the assessment phase. Major ways to evaluate training include measuring participants' reactions to the training to determine how useful they thought it was, assessing actual learning (perhaps through tests before and after training), determining the extent of behavioral change (possibly by having the supervisor or subordinates of a trainee assess changes in the individual's behavior), and measuring actual results on the job (such as increased output).

TYPES OF TRAINING PROGRAMS The most common types of training programs are orientation training, technical skill training, and management development training.[46] *Orientation training* is usually a formal program designed to provide new employees with information about the company and their jobs. *Technical skill training* is oriented toward providing specialized knowledge and developing facility in the use of methods, processes, and techniques associated with a particular discipline or trade. Training that helps individuals learn various aspects of their jobs falls into the category of technical skill training. *Management development programs* focus on developing managerial skills for use at the supervisory, managerial, and executive levels (see Chapter 1). Training can have a positive impact on both productivity and employee morale (see the Case in Point discussion).

CASE IN POINT   **TRAINING MAKES A DIFFERENCE AT FIRST SERVICE BANK**

Service is an important factor in the success of First Service Bank, a small thrift institution headquartered in Leominster, Massachusetts. Yet the bank found its competitive position threatened by high turnover of competent bank tellers. In assessing the situation, bank managers and human resource professionals decided that raising pay was not the only answer, although the pay scale was adjusted upward somewhat. They believed that growth opportunities were also likely to be important to the type of employee that the bank hoped to attract and retain. Thus an extensive training program was devised.

Job analysis revealed that the teller position involved a broader range of skills and abilities than it had in the past. The employees' duties now included such tasks as entering information into the data base and retrieving it when necessary for customers, explaining numerous products and services to customers, recognizing opportunities to sell additional products and services, and handling diverse transactions such as commercial checking accounts and credit card payments. To reflect the expanded scope of the position, the bank changed the title of the teller job to "bank service representative" (BSR).

On the basis of needs analysis, a trilevel training and certification program—BSR I, BSR II, and BSR III—was developed. BSR I includes an overview of various bank policies, as well as training in specific procedures. BSR II focuses on product knowledge, sales referral, security, and telephone etiquette, as well as a stress reduction session led by a psychologist. BSR III covers more advanced topics and offers train-the-trainer seminars in which participants learn to train new hires. Training methods include the use of workbooks, videotapes, and participatory exercises, such as role playing. Seminars for each level average 2 to 4 hours per week and extend over a 3- to 6-month period. Proficiency skills tests must be passed before receiving a certificate for each level.

In support of the program, raises are tied to BSR certifications, as well as to on-the-job standards for quality (such as degree of overages and shortages), absenteeism, and punctuality. Through a sales commission and bonus system, the BSRs receive cash, trips, and tickets to cultural events for meeting certain sales goals. Individuals who aspire to be managers can enroll in additional courses aimed at management development. Within 1 year of the training program's institution, productivity rose by more than 25 percent, turnover declined by 50 percent, and the bank's assets increased by more than 70 percent.[47] ■■■

At First Service Bank, the BSR training system, with its built-in potential career progression, was also tied to the performance appraisal system.

Rating Factors	LEVEL OF PERFORMANCE				
	Unsatisfactory	Conditional	Satisfactory	Above Satisfactory	Outstanding
ATTENDANCE					
APPEARANCE					
DEPENDABILITY					
QUALITY OF WORK					
QUANTITY OF WORK					
RELATIONSHIP WITH PEOPLE					
JOB KNOWLEDGE					

Figure 10-3 *A portion of a graphic rating scale. (Reprinted from Wayne F. Cascio,* Managing Human Resources, *4th ed., McGraw-Hill, New York, 1995, p. 287.)*

Performance Appraisal

Performance appraisal is the process of defining expectations for employee performance; measuring, evaluating, and recording employee performance relative to those expectations; and providing feedback to the employee.[48] A major purpose of performance appraisal is to influence, in a positive way, employee performance and development. In addition, the process is used for a variety of other organizational purposes, such as determining merit pay increases, planning future performance goals, determining training and development needs, and assessing the promotional potential of employees.[49]

MAJOR METHODS FOR RATING PERFORMANCE Because performance is multidimensional, performance appraisal methods must consider various aspects of a job. The most widely used approaches focus on employee behavior (behavior-oriented) or performance results (results-oriented).[50]

Within the behavior-oriented category, two important assessment means are graphic rating scales and behaviorally anchored rating scales. **Graphic rating scales** list a number of factors, including general behaviors and characteristics (such as attendance, appearance, dependability, quality of work, quantity of work, and relationships with people), on which an employee is rated by the supervisor. (See Figure 10-3 for an example of a graphic rating scale.) Supervisors rate individuals on each factor, using a scale that typically has about five gradations (e.g., unsatisfactory, conditional, satisfactory, above satisfactory, and outstanding). Because the rating factors tend to be fairly general, they are relatively flexible and can be used to evaluate individuals in a number of different jobs. However, the general nature of graphic rating scales makes them somewhat susceptible to inconsistent and inaccurate ratings of employees. This is mainly because considerable interpretation is needed to apply the factors to specific jobs (e.g., what does "quality" mean in different jobs?).[51]

In an effort to reduce the subjective interpretation inherent in graphic rating scales, performance appraisal experts have developed **behaviorally**

Performance appraisal The process of defining expectations for employee performance; measuring, evaluating, and recording employee performance relative to those expectations, and providing feedback to the employee

Graphic rating scales Scales that list a number of factors, including general behaviors and characteristics, on which an employee is rated by the supervisor

Behaviorally anchored rating scales (BARS) Scales that contain sets of specific behaviors that represent gradations of performance used as common reference points (or anchors) for rating employees on various job dimensions

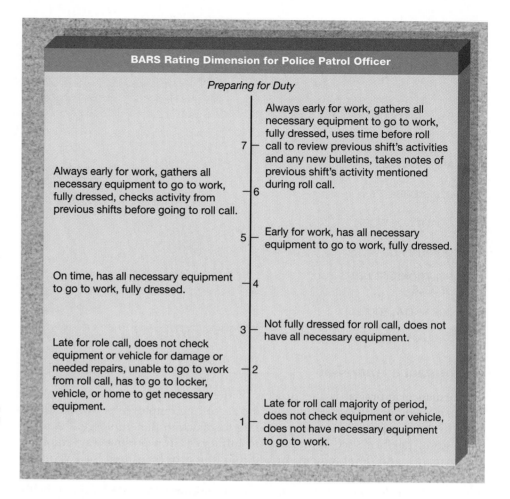

BARS Rating Dimension for Police Patrol Officer

Preparing for Duty

7 — Always early for work, gathers all necessary equipment to go to work, fully dressed, uses time before roll call to review previous shift's activities and any new bulletins, takes notes of previous shift's activity mentioned during roll call.

Always early for work, gathers all necessary equipment to go to work, fully dressed, checks activity from previous shifts before going to roll call.
6 —

5 — Early for work, has all necessary equipment to go to work, fully dressed.

On time, has all necessary equipment to go to work, fully dressed.
4 —

3 — Not fully dressed for roll call, does not have all necessary equipment.

Late for role call, does not check equipment or vehicle for damage or needed repairs, unable to go to work from roll call, has to go to locker, vehicle, or home to get necessary equipment.
2 —

Late for roll call majority of period, does not check equipment or vehicle, does not have necessary equipment to go to work.
1 —

Figure 10-4 *A behaviorally anchored rating scale for assessing the preparation for duty of police patrol officers. (Adapted from R. Harvey, "Job Analysis," in M. Dunnette and L. Hough, eds.,* Handbook of Industrial and Organizational Psychology, *2d ed. vol. 2, 1991, p. 138.)*

anchored rating scales (BARS). BARS contain sets of specific behaviors that represent gradations of performance used as common reference points (or anchors) for rating employees on various job dimensions. Figure 10-4 shows one scale, or set of specific behaviors, from a BARS series developed to assess various aspects of police patrol officer performance. An officer being rated on this scale can be allocated points ranging from 1 through 7 for duty preparation, depending upon where the supervisor places the individual relative to the anchors. Of course, the officer would be rated on other BARS dimensions as well, such as judgment, use of equipment, relations with the public, oral and written communication, and dependability.[52] Developing a BARS series involves extensive job analysis and the collection of critical incidents (examples of very good and very bad performance). Therefore, creating the scales for a particular job is expensive and time-consuming. As a result, BARS tend to be used mainly in situations in which relatively large numbers of individuals perform similar jobs. For example, a BARS approach was used successfully to develop a performance appraisal system for reporters, copy editors, and supervising editors at the *Times-Union* and the *Democrat and Chronicle,* two metropolitan newspapers in Rochester, New York, that are owned by the Gannett Company, Inc.[53]

An alternative and widely used results-oriented rating method is *management by objectives* (MBO), a process through which specific goals are set collaboratively for the organization as a whole, various subunits, and each individual member (see Chapter 6). With MBO, individuals are evaluated, usually annually (although more frequent discussions of progress are often held), on the basis of how well they have achieved the results specified by the goals. MBO, or goal setting, is particularly applicable to nonroutine jobs, such as those of managers. For example, the various projects undertaken by CARE lend themselves to the MBO approach, which is used extensively by the agency.

COMMON RATING ERRORS The performance appraisal process is complicated by the fact that raters' memories are somewhat fallible and raters are susceptible to biases that produce rating errors.[54] One such bias is the *halo effect,* the tendency to use a general impression based on one or a few characteristics of an individual in order to judge other characteristics of that individual (see Chapter 14). Another bias is the *contrast error,* the tendency to compare subordinates with one another rather than against a performance standard. Thus, when compared with two unsatisfactory workers, an average worker may end up being rated "outstanding." In the *recency error,* supervisors assign ratings on the basis of the employee's more recent performance. In the *leniency error,* raters tend to be unjustifiably easy in evaluating employee performance, while in the *severity error,* they tend to be unjustifiably harsh. Finally, the *self-serving bias* is the tendency to perceive oneself as responsible for successes and to see others as responsible for failures (see Chapter 14). Efforts to use rater training as a means of overcoming these biases have met with mixed success. One review of a number of studies involving rater training suggested that results may be better with simulation training methods that actively involve participants in the training process.[55]

THE PERFORMANCE APPRAISAL INTERVIEW In a performance appraisal interview, the self-serving bias is not limited to raters only. According to numerous studies, about 80 percent of the interviewees in performance appraisal interviews initially believe that they have been performing at an above-average level.[56] The statistical reality, however, at least in large organizations, is that no more than 50 percent of a company's employees can be above-average performers. Hence the performance appraisal interview is a challenging situation for supervisors to handle.

To perform effectively as raters, supervisors must essentially play three different, and somewhat incompatible, roles during the interview: leader, coach, and judge.[57] As leader, the rater must assign work duties; work with the subordinate to establish standards, or expectations, about the level of performance required; and furnish resources, such as additional personnel, equipment, time, materials, and space, that are required to do the job. As coach, the rater is responsible for ensuring that the individual is trained adequately to reach the required level of performance and must provide support and encouragement for the subordinate's efforts. Yet, as judge, the rater must evaluate the accomplishments of the employee as objectively as possible. The rater's judge role makes it somewhat difficult to simultaneously build the trust and openness that are necessary, in particular, for the coaching role.

Given this context, it is not surprising that interviews with 60 managers indicate that they are generally more concerned with using the appraisal process to motivate and retain subordinates than with using it to assess performance accurately.[58] Yet the general tendency to inflate ratings gives subordinates false feedback. It can also lead to serious lawsuits should the managers subsequently need to terminate employees who have received unjustified positive performance appraisals.[59]

To solve some of these problems and provide broader sources of feedback, companies are increasingly adopting an approach called **360-degree feedback.** This evaluation approach provides an individual with ratings of performance

360-degree feedback An approach that provides an individual with ratings of performance from a variety of relevant sources, such as peers, subordinates, superiors, and often external customers or clients, which can then be compared with the individual's own self-assessment

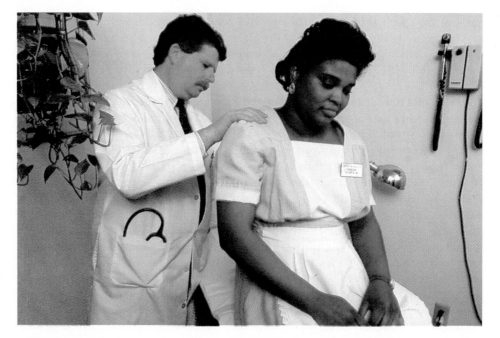

Benefits are a form of compensation for employees. For instance, workers at Marriott Corp. can obtain immediate medical attention from on-site nurses at many of its facilities. The nurses can then refer more serious problems to company-run clinics, like the one shown here. The clinics, which Marriott operates in many cities, don't just benefit the employees; they also reduce the work time lost to injuries.

from a variety of relevant sources, such as peers, subordinates, superiors, and often external customers or clients, which can then be compared with the individual's own self-assessment. Often a human resource professional or an outside consultant helps the individual interpret the feedback for the purpose of identifying areas for both organizational and individual improvement. Companies using 360-degree feedback include General Electric, AT&T, and Digital Equipment Corporation. Some companies use 360-degree feedback for developmental purposes only, while others incorporate it into the formal performance appraisal process.[60]

The results of formal performance appraisal processes often influence pay raises allocated through the organization's compensation system.

■ COMPENSATION

Compensation Wages paid directly for time worked, as well as more indirect benefits that employees receive as part of their employment relationship with an organization

Benefits Forms of compensation beyond wages for time worked, including various protection plans, services, pay for time not worked, and income supplements

Compensation consists of wages paid directly for time worked, as well as more indirect benefits that employees receive as part of their employment relationship with an organization.[61] Wages paid for time worked are typically payments made in cashable form that reflect direct work-related remuneration such as base pay, merit increases, or bonuses. **Benefits,** on the other hand, are forms of compensation beyond wages for time worked, including various protection plans (such as health insurance or life insurance), services (such as an organizational cafeteria or drug counseling), pay for time not worked (such as vacations or sick leave), and income supplements (such as stock ownership plans). Benefits are considered a more indirect form of compensation because they are generally not as closely tied to job and performance issues as other forms of remuneration.

Types of Equity

Most organizations attempt to develop compensation systems that carefully consider issues of equity, or fairness. Equity issues are important because, as equity theory points out (see Chapter 12), individuals tend to compare their own relative inputs and outcomes with those of others in assessing the degree of equitable treatment that they receive. In practice, though, developing fair compensation systems is quite challenging, primarily because three major types of equity are involved.[62] *External equity* is the extent to which the organization's pay rates for particular jobs correspond to rates paid for similar jobs in the external job market. *Internal equity* is the degree to which pay rates for various jobs inside the organization reflect the relative worth of those jobs. *Individual equity* is the extent to which pay rates allocated to specific individuals within the organization reflect variations in individual merit. How, then, are these three types of equity incorporated into compensation systems?

Designing the Pay Structure

Because of the complexity involved, many organizations, particularly large ones, have compensation specialists in the human resource department who oversee the compensation system development process. At the foundation of most major compensation systems is evaluation. **Job evaluation** is a systematic process of establishing the relative worth of jobs within a single organization in order to determine equitable pay differentials among jobs. Such evaluations typically rely on job analysis and resulting job descriptions for the specific information used to compare jobs.

Job evaluation A systematic process of establishing the relative worth of jobs within a single organization in order to determine equitable pay differentials among jobs

Although there are a number of different approaches to job evaluation, the most popular approach is the point factor method, which was used by CARE in designing its new compensation system. The **point factor method** is a job evaluation approach in which points are assigned to jobs on the basis of the degree to which the jobs contain selected compensable factors. *Compensable factors* are any characteristics that jobs have in common that can be used for comparing job content.

Point factor method A job evaluation approach in which points are assigned to jobs on the basis of the degree to which the jobs contain selected compensable factors

The first step of job evaluation with the point factor method is selecting the compensable factors that will be used to rate each job. The most commonly used factors are responsibility, skill required, effort required, and working conditions, although others, such as education required and experience required, are also frequently used.

The second step is developing a set of levels, or scale, for each compensable factor and assigning weighted points to each level. The total points allocated to each factor differ, depending on how much weight top management (advised by a compensation specialist) wants to give a specific factor in evaluating all jobs. For example, Table 10-4 shows a point factor scale for assessing the contribution of education to the relative worth of jobs in an organization.

TABLE 10-4 POINT FACTOR SCALE FOR EDUCATION

EDUCATION—300 POINTS

This factor measures the amount of formal education required to satisfactorily perform the job. Experience or knowledge received through experience is not to be considered in evaluating jobs on this scale.

POINTS

20	Level 1	Eighth-grade education
90	Level 2	High school diploma or eighth-grade education and four years of formal apprenticeship
160	Level 3	Two-year college degree or high school diploma and three years of formal apprenticeship
230	Level 4	Four-year college degree
300	Level 5	Graduate degree

Source: Reprinted from Marc J. Wallace, Jr., and Charles H. Fay, *Compensation Theory and Practice,* 2d ed., PWS-Kent, Boston, 1988, p. 214.

Note that education is divided into five different levels, ranging from eighth-grade education to graduate degree. Each level has been assigned points that constitute the level's weighting within the total of 300 points allocated to the education factor. Of course, the job would be rated on other compensable factors as well. Other scales being used in this situation might be experience, worth a maximum of 300 points; responsibility, worth up to 200 points; and physical demands and working conditions, each worth a possible 100 points.

The third step in the point factor method is measuring each job on each compensable factor and adding the points to obtain a total score reflecting the worth of each job. Thus, in the above situation, a job could receive a maximum of 1000 points if it rated the highest number of points on each compensable factor. The total scores are used to establish a wage rate for each job. As is probably obvious from the description so far, job evaluation helps establish internal equity by grading the worth of each job relative to that of others in the organization. How, then, does external equity figure into the pay scheme?

Pay survey   A survey of the labor market to determine the current rates of pay for benchmark, or key, jobs

In order to address the external-equity issue, most organizations utilize information from pay surveys. A **pay survey** (often called a *wage-and-salary survey*) is a survey of the labor market to determine the current rates of pay for benchmark, or key, jobs. *Benchmark*, or *key, jobs* represent a cross section of the jobs in an organization, usually reflecting a mix of scores on the compensable factors, various levels in the organization, and a sizable proportion of the organization's work force. At least 25 to 30 percent of an organization's jobs are typically designated as benchmark jobs.

Most pay surveys are conducted by mailing questionnaires or using the telephone (for relatively short surveys). Organizations may conduct their own surveys and/or use surveys from other sources, such as other organizations (which often share their surveys with companies that participate in them), the Bureau of Labor Statistics and other government agencies, professional groups (such as industry associations), and private companies that specialize in compensation issues (such as Sibson and Company). One of the key considerations in evaluating survey data is which organizations should be used for comparisons.

Pay-survey information for benchmark jobs is matched to job evaluation points in order to develop a pay policy line (see Figure 10-5). The pay policy line is the basis for developing the pay grades and the associated minimum and maximum pay rates for each grade that make up the organization's pay structure. Other jobs are then allocated to the pay grades on the basis of their job evaluation points. Thus organizations do not typically have a wage rate for each job. Instead, jobs are usually grouped into grades, or classifications, within some type of pay structure.

Individual equity becomes an issue when specific pay raises are allocated to individuals. The main determinants of pay increases within the specified pay range for a given grade are typically seniority and/or performance. Many organizations have recently placed renewed emphasis on the notion of pay for performance by awarding pay on the basis of merit and/or offering various incentive pay programs tied to performance.

Broadbanding   A compensation approach whereby as many as four or five traditional grades are collapsed into a single grade or band, thus providing managers with more flexibility in setting salaries

Skill-based pay   A compensation system in which employees' rates of pay are based on the number of predetermined skills the employees have mastered

Efforts are also being made in a number of organizations to foster innovation through nontraditional forms of compensation. One approach is **broadbanding**, a compensation approach whereby as many as four or five traditional grades are collapsed into a single grade or band, thus providing managers with more flexibility in setting salaries.[63] One attraction of broadbanding is that it facilitates lateral movements across functions and is compatible with contemporary flatter organizational structures with fewer levels of hierarchy. Another nontraditional approach is **skill-based pay,** a compensation system in which employees' rates of pay are based on the number of predetermined skills the

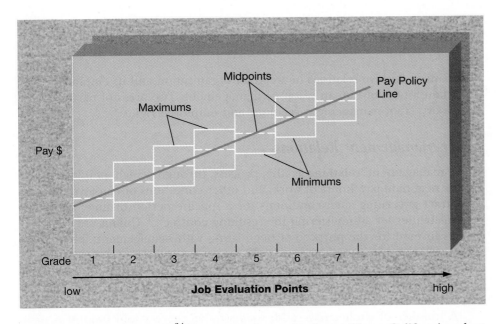

Figure 10-5 *Pay structure.*

employees have mastered.[64] For example, at the Santa Clara, California, plant of Northern Telecom, a leading supplier of digital-communication switching systems, workers receive a pay increase for each new skill that they master. Workers who once performed narrow tasks now move freely among several different tasks, allowing the company to cut the number of job grades from 25 to 5 and to capitalize on the innovative ideas that result.[65] Yet another approach that is attracting increased attention is **gainsharing,** in which employees throughout an organization are encouraged to become involved in solving problems and are then given bonuses tied to organizationwide performance improvements.[66]

Gainsharing A compensation system in which employees throughout an organization are encouraged to become involved in solving problems and are then given bonuses tied to organizationwide performance improvements

Employee Benefits

Benefits account for a growing portion of total compensation. According to the U.S. Chamber of Commerce, which annually surveys a national cross section of private-sector firms, benefits rose, on average, from 18.7 percent of direct payroll costs in 1951 to 40.7 percent by 1994.[67] Thus an employee who earns an annual salary of $20,000 is likely to receive another $8140 in benefits. The rise in benefits is attributable to several factors.[68] Among the most important are the rise in employer costs for social security, federal tax policies that provide tax advantages to employers and allow employees to receive the benefits on a tax-free or tax-deferred basis, pressure from labor unions for generous benefit packages, employer concern for employee needs, and attempts to encourage productivity improvements through rewards provided by benefits.

Employers are legally required to make payments so that employees are covered by social security, unemployment compensation, and workers' compensation (in case of injury on the job). However, most benefits provided by employers are not required by law (even though some may be governed by law if they are offered). One organization that has a reputation for being particularly generous with benefits is privately owned Hallmark Cards, Inc. Employee benefits at Hallmark include low-interest, $2500-per-year college loans for employees' children, interest-free loans of up to $1000 for emergencies, adoption assistance of up to $3000, paternity or maternity leave of up to 6 months for the parent of a newborn or newly adopted baby, and a physical fitness facility combined with an extensive wellness program.[69]

■ MAINTAINING EFFECTIVE WORK-FORCE RELATIONSHIPS

Maintaining positive relations between an organization and its employees is an important aspect of human resource management. Two areas of particular relevance are labor-management relations and employee rights.

Labor-Management Relations

Labor-management relations The process through which employers and unions negotiate pay, hours of work, and other conditions of employment; sign a contract governing such conditions for a specific period of time; and share responsibilities for administering the resulting contract

Unions Employee groups formed for the purpose of negotiating with management about conditions relating to their work

Labor-management relations is the process through which employers and unions negotiate pay, hours of work, and other conditions of employment; sign a contract governing such conditions for a specific period of time; and share responsibilities for administering the resulting contract.[70] **Unions** are employee groups formed for the purpose of negotiating with management about conditions relating to their work. Some employee groups call themselves associations rather than unions (e.g., the American Nurses Association). When recognized by the National Labor Relations Board (NLRB), unions have the legal right to negotiate with employers and help administer the resulting contract.

A number of studies have addressed why employees join unions. A main factor is dissatisfaction with various working conditions, such as wages, job security, benefits, treatment by supervisors, and prospects for promotion. Still, even dissatisfied workers will typically not join a union unless they believe that it will be effective in remedying the situation.[71]

The number of employees who are dues-paying union members has been declining, from a peak of 22,618,000 in 1979 to 16,360,000 in 1995.[72] Although the causes of the decline are not completely clear, some reasons given are more effective human resource management in organizations, a decrease in union organizing attempts, a decline in the economic well-being of companies (making it more difficult for unions to pressure for better wages and benefits), and increasingly effective management opposition to unions.[73]

CERTIFICATION PROCESS Unions are normally established in organizations through an *organizing drive*.[74] The drive begins when employees sign authorization cards designating the union as their exclusive bargaining representative. At least 30 percent of employees within the group to be represented must sign cards before the union can petition the National Labor Relations Board to conduct an election. Once the NLRB verifies that the required percentage of employees seek union representation, the board notifies management of that fact. At this point, management and the union can attempt to agree on union representation and the group of employees that will be considered the bargaining unit. Usually, though, the two parties do not agree, and the NLRB must determine the unit. Next, an election is held. The union must receive a majority of the votes cast in order to be certified as the exclusive representative for the bargaining unit. Regardless of the outcome, no further union elections associated with the bargaining unit can take place for 1 year. Recent trends indicate that although unions are experiencing considerable success in obtaining authorization cards from the necessary 30 percent of affected workers, they are subsequently winning certification elections less than half the time.

UNION DECERTIFICATION If a union does win an election, it can be decertified in the future, but not earlier than 1 year after the certification election. If there is evidence that at least 30 percent of the employees want to decertify the union, the NLRB can be asked to hold a decertification election. Recent trends indicate that unions have been losing such elections about three-fourths of the time, although about six times more certification than decertification elections are held each year (e.g., 3623 certified versus 587 decertified in 1990).[75]

Current Employee Issues

Maintaining effective work-force relationships requires that both human resource professionals and line managers stay abreast of and make appropriate responses to issues affecting employees. Several areas of current concern are the shifting nature of the psychological contract of employment, sexual harassment, drug and alcohol abuse, privacy rights, and family issues.

SHIFTING PSYCHOLOGICAL CONTRACT OF EMPLOYMENT Recent restructurings and downsizings appear to be changing the nature of the *psychological contract* of employment, the largely unwritten expectations that exist between an employer and employees about what each will give and what each expects to receive from the employment relationship. Until the late 1980s, many workers, particularly in the managerial and professional levels of large corporations, had the expectation that if they performed well in behalf of their organization and fit within the organization's culture, they could be assured of a job until they retired or decided to leave. In return, employers expected dedication to reaching organizational goals, good performance, and loyalty.[76]

Some observers believe that economic necessities related to increasing competitive pressures and technological change have made the traditional arrangement unworkable. They argue that, since employers can no longer offer lifetime employment, workers should consider themselves a portfolio of skills to be enhanced through employment relationships. One implication would seem to be that workers would then choose and change jobs based on their development potential rather than being concerned about loyalty to a particular employer. For their part, employers would need to provide appropriate inducements (stimulating assignments, training, pay, etc.) to attract workers with the skill sets they need at a given point in time.[77]

Critics argue that, while some renegotiation of the psychological contract may be necessary, organizations could do more to avoid downsizings through such means as improved human resource planning and retraining.[78] To help avoid downsizing, some organizations are developing a cadre of *core employees,* whose capabilities constitute sources of competitive advantage. They then supplement this core with contingent workers. One worry, though, is that this strategy may be creating a large group of workers who typically receive no benefits (such as health insurance) and may have difficulty earning a living wage.[79]

SEXUAL HARASSMENT Sexual harassment is another issue of growing concern in organizations. The two types of sexual harassment defined by the Equal Employment Opportunity Commission are outlined in Table 10-5. To a large extent, employers are legally responsible for sexual harassment, particularly by managers and others with authority to make employment-related decisions. However, as indicated in Table 10-5, employees also have responsibility for the type of environment that exists. In fact, a recent study of large corporations by the American Management Association indicated that of the 1366 sexual harassment complaints brought to the attention of officials, about half involved peers or coworkers. In contrast, 26 percent of the complaints involved the victims' direct supervisors.[80] An alleged hostile environment and alleged problems with coworkers appear to figure heavily in the recent sexual-harassment suit filed against Mitsubishi Motor Manufacturing of America (see the Case in Point discussion).

TABLE 10-5 TWO TYPES OF SEXUAL HARASSMENT DEFINED BY THE EEOC

QUID PRO QUO
- Making the submission to unwelcome sexual advances or other verbal or physical conduct of a sexual nature a term or condition, implicitly or explicitly, of an individual's employment.
- Basing employment decisions affecting the individual on his or her submission to or rejection of such conduct.

HOSTILE ENVIRONMENT
- Making unwelcome sexual advances or other verbal or physical conduct of a sexual nature with the purpose of, or that creates the effect of, unreasonably interfering with an individual's work performance or creating an intimidating, hostile or offensive working environment.

Source: Equal Employment Opportunity Commission.

CASE IN POINT

EEOC SUES MITSUBISHI SUBSIDIARY FOR SEXUAL HARASSMENT

The Equal Employment Opportunity Commission filed suit against Mitsubishi Motor Manufacturing of America, Inc., in April 1996. The class-action suit alleged that the unit of Japan's Mitsubishi Motors Corp. tolerated the sexual harassment of as many as 500 women who work at its assembly plant in Normal, Illinois. Among the allegations of the women who filed complaints were that they had their breasts and genitals grabbed, were routinely called bitches and whores, and were the subjects of drawings of female worker body parts taped to car fenders coming down the assembly line. Most of the complaints were associated with the plant's production and maintenance units and involved line workers, their immediate supervisors, and lower-level management. After a number of complaints were filed with the EEOC, the agency conducted a 15-month investigation, interviewing more than 100 female employees and also alleged harassers and third-party witnesses. The commission filed the suit after negotiations with company officials did not lead to a settlement. The director of the EEOC Chicago district office said it appears that company officials knew about the problem but did not take sufficient action to solve it. A company spokesperson denied the charges.[81] ■■■

To discourage sexual harassment, employers should widely disseminate written policies against such behavior, have written complaint procedures, guarantee safety against retaliation for sexual harassment complaints, investigate complaints immediately, and take prompt action to redress claims that are found to be justified.[82]

DRUG AND ALCOHOL ABUSE Another important issue affecting employees and their employers is drug and alcohol abuse. Such abuse typically leads to increases in absenteeism, workplace accidents, and use of medical benefits, and causes declines in productivity. A recent report indicates that productivity losses related to alcohol problems amount to about $86 billion per year and drug-related losses cost more than $54 billion.[83]

In a constructive response to substance abuse problems, more than 10,000 employers have established employee assistance programs.[84] An **employee assistance program (EAP)** is a program through which employers help employees overcome personal problems that are adversely affecting their job performance.

Employee assistance program (EAP) A program through which employers help employees overcome personal problems that are adversely affecting their job performance

Under such programs, supervisors may refer workers to EAP counselors or out-side counselors who help identify problems and arrange for appropriate assis-tance. Workers can usually also contact EAP counselors themselves. Although drug and alcohol abuse are the major problems covered, such programs increasingly provide assistance for a broader range of issues, including stress, smoking cessation, weight control, financial matters, legal difficulties, and other personal issues that cause difficulties for employees.

PRIVACY RIGHTS The employee's right to privacy is another human resource issue of current importance. One privacy concern related to the drug abuse problem just discussed is *drug testing*, the attempt to detect drug usage through analysis of blood, urine, or other body substances. According to one estimate, at least 30 percent of the employers of recent college graduates engage in drug testing of new employees, and the number is growing.[85] Although the legal issues are far from resolved, courts have generally been willing to allow employ-ers to test job applicants, on the premise that applicants choose to submit to the tests in order to obtain a job. On the other hand, courts are generally much less tolerant of mandatory drug and alcohol testing of employees. This type of testing is more likely to survive legal challenge under the following conditions: The employees have jobs that involve public safety (e.g., airline pilots) or that are dangerous (e.g., electricians); testing is limited to situations in which there is reasonable suspicion of on-the-job impairment; there is a written and publi-cized substance abuse policy; there are procedural protections (such as careful labeling and secondary tests to confirm positive results); and employers offer voluntary rehabilitation programs rather than firing employees for first offenses.

A related privacy issue is *genetic screening*, the attempt to detect, through tests, genetic factors that may contribute to certain occupational diseases. So far, only a few companies, mainly in the chemical industry, are using genetic screening as a means of identifying those workers who are more likely to con-tract diseases after exposure to certain chemicals or toxins. While the screen-ing has the potential to protect workers from hazardous working conditions, it could also possibly be used to deny employment to individuals on the basis of

No one loses in this corporate day-care facility at Corning Inc. in Painted Post, New York. Parents appreciate having their children well cared-for and nearby, the children reap the benefits of a learning environ-ment at an early age, and the company enjoys a positive working relationship with its employees. Family issues have increased in importance with the growing numbers of dual-career couples and single working parents.

their genetic makeup.[86] As a result, genetic screening appears likely to generate considerable controversy in the future.

The rapid spread of information technology is creating privacy issues related to new workplace communication media like voice mail and e-mail. We discuss this issue in Chapter 19.

FAMILY ISSUES Given the rising proportion of women in the workplace, the growing number of dual-career couples, and the frequency of single parenting, family issues as they affect workers are increasing in importance. To help employees more effectively handle the often conflicting responsibilities of work and family, several major companies, such as Du Pont, now have family issues specialists on their human resource staffs. The specialists help develop policies and also assist employees in regard to such issues as leaves from work, child care, and elder care.[87] This type of approach is likely to promote positive working relationships with employees and facilitate the management function of leading. We begin exploring the leading function in the next chapter, which focuses on change management and innovation.

■ CHAPTER SUMMARY

Human resource management is the management of various activities designed to enhance the effectiveness of an organization's work force. Major activities include human resource planning, staffing, development and evaluation, compensation, and maintenance of effective work-force relationships. The strategic importance of HRM has been increasing, particularly since the late 1970s and early 1980s.

Human resource planning considers both demand for and supply of human resources relative to an organization's strategic plan. Such planning relies on job analysis and resulting job descriptions and job specifications. Assessing demand involves considering the major forces that can influence demand and using basic forecasting techniques to predict future demand. Assessing supply entails determining internal and external labor supplies. In reconciling demand and supply, organizations need to consider affirmative action implications.

Staffing is the set of activities aimed at attracting and selecting individuals for positions in a way that will facilitate the achievement of organizational goals. Most organizations engage in extensive internal recruitment in order to offer job opportunities to current employees. For the most part, organizations engage in external recruiting only when there are no suitable internal candidates for particular positions. An important issue in selection is validity, which addresses how well a selection device or method actually predicts a candidate's future job performance. The most prevalent selection methods include the use of application blanks, selection interviews, tests, assessment centers, and reference checks.

Training and development is a planned effort to facilitate employee learning of job-related behaviors in order to improve employee performance. Training typically includes three main phases: assessment, training design and implementation, and evaluation. The major types of training programs are orientation training, technical skill training, and management development programs.

Performance appraisal is the process of defining expectations for employee performance; measuring, evaluating, and recording employee performance relative to those expectations; and providing feedback to the employee. Major methods of performance appraisal include behavior-oriented approaches, such as the use of graphic rating scales and behaviorally anchored rating scales, and results-oriented approaches, such as management by objectives. Because performance raters tend to be susceptible to biases that produce rating errors, they must engage in three somewhat incompatible roles (leader, coach, and judge) in carrying out an effective performance appraisal interview. Some companies are introducing 360-degree feedback as a means of improving performance evaluation information conveyed to employees.

Compensation systems need to consider internal, external, and individual equity in developing pay structures and allocating individual pay. The most common approach to devising pay structures is the point factor method of job evaluation. Organizations are attempting to encourage work-force flexibility and innovation through specialized pay approaches such as broadbanding, skill-based pay, and gainsharing.

Maintaining positive work-force relationships involves engaging in effective labor-management relations and making appropriate responses to current employee issues. Organizations become unionized through a certification process regulated by the National Labor Relations Board. Unions can become decertified through a similar process. Among the employee issues of current concern are the shifting nature of the psychological contract of employment, sexual harassment, drug and alcohol abuse, privacy rights, and family matters as they affect workers.

■ QUESTIONS FOR DISCUSSION AND REVIEW

1 Briefly describe the major elements in the human resource management process, and explain why HRM has gradually increased in strategic importance in organizations. To what extent do you believe that effective human resource management is strategically important for your college or university? Explain your reasoning.

2 Discuss the role of job analysis in human resource planning. Why would job descriptions (and job specifications) based on job analysis be useful in a variety of human resource activities, such as recruitment, selection, and performance appraisal?

3 Identify the major factors that managers need to consider in attempting to predict future demand for human resources. How can forecasting methods help? What factors do managers need to examine in assessing the future supply of human resources? What options do managers have in reconciling demand and supply imbalances?

4 Distinguish between internal and external recruiting. What are the major advantages and disadvantages of each?

5 Explain the role of validity in selection. Identify the most widely used selection methods, and assess their usefulness as valid means of making selection decisions. Evaluate the validity of a selection device used in an organization with which you are familiar.

6 Identify the main phases of training, the major categories of training methods, and the most common types of training programs. Give an example of each type of training method from your own experience either as an individual being trained or as a trainer.

7 Explain the major methods for rating employee performance, the common biases that affect ratings, and the roles that supervisors must play during the performance appraisal interview. Think of a time when your performance was appraised by someone. How well did the individual balance the roles of leader, coach, and judge? Explain your view. Would 360-degree feedback have been helpful?

8 Describe how pay structures are developed using the point factor method. Why might nontraditional compensation systems, such as the ones described in the chapter, be better at encouraging innovation than more traditional approaches?

9 Explain the nature of benefits. Why are they growing as a portion of total compensation? List several benefits that either you or someone in your family receives as part of job compensation.

10 Describe the processes through which unions are certified and decertified. Describe the role that employee-rights issues potentially play in unionization efforts?

■ DISCUSSION QUESTIONS FOR CHAPTER OPENING CASE

1 Explain the strategic importance of human resource management at CARE.

2 Present evidence of various elements of the HRM process at CARE.

3 Identify and evaluate the organization's recent changes in HRM.

■ EXERCISES FOR MANAGING IN THE TWENTY-FIRST CENTURY

EXERCISE 1
SKILL BUILDING: LINKING HRM COMPONENTS WITH SPECIFIC ACTIVITIES

Several important components of the human resource management process are listed below. Please match these components with the 15 specific activities/issues shown. Indicate the appropriate human resource management component by putting the first letter of that component in the appropriate blank.

Human Resource Management Process Components

Selection

Training and development

Compensation

Recruitment

Human resource planning

Performance appraisal

Labor relations

1 _____ Employees plan to organize
2 _____ Management by objectives
3 _____ Orientation, technical skill, management development
4 _____ Assessment center
5 _____ Halo, contrast, leniency, severity, self-serving bias
6 _____ Job descriptions
7 _____ Job posting
8 _____ Skills inventory
9 _____ Replacement planning
10 _____ Interview
11 _____ Needs analysis
12 _____ Internal equity
13 _____ Realistic job preview
14 _____ Decertification
15 _____ Point factor method

EXERCISE 2
MANAGEMENT EXERCISE: MANAGING HUMAN RESOURCES IN RETAIL HARDWARE

 You have just accepted a position as a department head in a large hardware store. The owner, who is the store manager, likes to involve others in decisions. During your interviews for the job, the store manager mentioned that if you became department head, he would ask for your views on ways to improve human resource management in the store. He is particularly interested in your input because he is thinking about opening up several other stores in the region. (In fact, you are taking the job partially because you believe that such expansion can only help your career.)

The manager said that he, the assistant manager, and all 10 department heads will soon be holding some strategic planning meetings at which they will consider the impact of human resources in regard to the expansion plans. Also, he anticipates holding subsequent meetings that focus on various aspects of human resource management. He further stated that he wants to maintain a working environment that is stimulating, challenging, and exciting. At the same time, he would prefer to avoid having the store become unionized, since he feels that opening up new stores in the area would be more complicated if a union were involved.

From what you have been able to learn, the 18 percent annual growth of the store and the 15 percent return on investment could definitely be improved. In addition, human resource management seems to be almost nonexistent at this point.

To prepare for the upcoming meeting, outline the suggestions you will offer on the following topics:

1 What issues should be considered as part of human resource planning?

2 What approaches can be taken in regard to recruiting and selecting human resources?

3 What are the store's options for training, performance appraisal, and compensation?

CONCLUDING CASE 1

NUCOR PROSPERS IN TOUGH STEEL INDUSTRY

The Nucor Corporation has pioneered so-called minimills, which melt scrap iron to produce basic products such as joists, decking, and steel bars. Through this method, Nucor has been making steel very efficiently—at about one-third of its competitors' costs. This has resulted in an annual compounded growth rate of more than 20 percent during the past decade or so.

Despite Nucor's almost $3.5 billion in annual sales, company headquarters (located in suburban Charlotte, North Carolina) operates with a small staff of 24 or so. There are only four management levels. The chairman, F. Kenneth Iverson, and John Correnti, who has succeeded Iverson as CEO, make up the first level. The second level consists of vice presidents, each of whom is also a general manager of a steel mill, a joist plant, or a division. At the third level are the department heads, who might be managers of melting and casting, sales managers, or division controllers. The fourth level comprises the first-line supervisors. The company tries hard to eliminate distinctions between management and workers. For example, there are no assigned parking spaces, no executive dining rooms, and no hunting lodges. Management and workers have the same benefits, such as vacation time and insurance.

A particularly unique aspect of Nucor within the steel industry is the company's incentive pay system. A significant portion of most organization members' pay depends on worker productivity or on company success. For example, in the steel mills, the company identifies groups of 25 to 35 people doing a complete task and puts them on a bonus program. There are typically nine bonus groups. In each case, a standard is set for production. The group then receives extra pay based on the amount it produces above the standard. There is no maximum, and the bonuses are paid weekly so that workers can see the fruits of their efforts quickly. Standards about punctuality and attendance also apply. "If you're late even 5 minutes, you lose your bonus for the day," says Iverson. Lateness of more than 30 minutes or absenteeism for any reason results in a bonus loss for the week (there are four "forgiveness days" available to each worker per year). The bonuses received by groups are normally more than 100 percent above base pay, giving the steelworkers an average annual pay of more than $30,000, with some making more than $40,000. Also, the company has a profit sharing plan, whereby 10 percent of earnings before taxes are distributed to employee accounts within the plan.

Although pay is higher at Nucor than at its competitors' facilities, productivity in terms of tons per employee has been running more than double. This is partly because workers have suggested many innovative ideas. The Nucor system is not for everyone. When the company starts up a new mill, turnover is usually in the range of 200 percent the first year. After that, turnover is extremely low. Iverson says that the system appeals best to goal-oriented individuals who are willing to work hard.

Nucor has a no-layoff policy. When 3½- or 4-day workweeks are necessary to avoid layoffs, a worker's pay may be cut by as much as 25 percent. The pay of department heads and officers is cut even more, perhaps as much as 40 and 70 percent, respectively.

Nucor limits the work force at each of its plants to 500 employees. "We don't feel that a general manager can communicate effectively with employees when you have a group larger than that," says Iverson. Company policy requires that the general manager have dinner with every employee in his or her plant at least once a year, in groups no larger than 50. Most general managers have dinner with employees twice a year. After the first dinner, employees learn that they can speak up. Iverson remembers one incident in particular: "A fellow got up and said, 'You guys are really rotten. You haven't done anything about the parking lot, and they're stealing us blind out there.' Another one stood up and said, 'They stole so much gas out of my car I couldn't even start it when I came off my shift.' A third had a $400 car stereo stolen. We didn't know about any of this, of course. It took us exactly 3 days to fence the parking lot and put up lights. That's the way we work."

Nucor faces fierce competition as competing new minimills start up. The company is gambling on staying ahead with an experimental $100 million iron carbide plant in Trinidad based on a new technology that can produce a substitute for scrap iron—the raw material used in its minimills. It's the first plant of its kind, and despite a number of difficulties, it is finally operating at about 60 percent capacity. Correnti says Nucor's most immediate challenges include maintaining the pace of technological innovation; expanding into related, steel-product businesses; and moving into higher margin steels.[88]

QUESTIONS FOR CONCLUDING CASE 1

1. Explain the components of the HRM process evident at Nucor.
2. To what extent does human resource management appear to be part of strategic management at Nucor? Cite evidence to support your view.
3. Assess the handling of external, internal, and individual equity in the compensation system at Nucor.

CONCLUDING CASE 2

STRATEGIC HUMAN RESOURCE PLANNING AT ABB

Asea Brown Boveri (ABB) is a $33 billion "multidomestic" organization operating in such diverse areas as power generation, transportation, and financial services. ABB headquarters is in Zurich, and subordinate companies are located in more than 130 countries. Although the organization has about 215,000 employees, only 170 of them make up the corporate staff. There are about 50 major business areas (BAs) into which the company's various businesses are divided. The BAs, in turn, are grouped into the eight global business segments.

Strategic human resource planning is oriented toward providing the leadership for the major parts of the organization. Most human resources are host-country nationals, giving rise to ABB's preferred designation as a "multidomestic" company. Potential managers are recruited in their home countries. The organization requires that within 24 hours of identifying the need for a new manager, a list of five internal candidates must be on the appropriate business head's desk. Thus the human resource managers need to know their potential leaders well.

Management talent begins to be identified very early in a person's career. A typical job path for individuals identified early in their careers as having the potential to hold the most senior management positions are shown below:

Position	Age
Company president	40
Division manager	37
Production manager	34
Production planning manager	31
Project manager	29
Entry-level position	26

Individuals being prepared for senior management positions are trained in general management tasks by being exposed to multifunctional experiences. As high-potential managers, they can expect transfers across organizational border lines and work assignments on mixed-nationality teams helping to solve problems. Göran Lindahl, the company's CEO, believes that the "global managers" needed for senior management are made, rather than born, and argues that they can best be developed through line experience in several countries. Lindahl estimates that the company needs 500 people who can manage global businesses, understand and respect different cultures, create new personal alliances, and build mixed-nationality teams. He says that "international job rotation for young managers is the cornerstone in creating that breed of global manager." Since the company is doing business in all major markets throughout the world, there is a wide recruitment base.

A job posted internally at ABB typically brings applications from employees representing 15 to 20 nationalities. English has been chosen as the corporate language so that individuals throughout ABB can converse with one another. ABB insists that all individuals who move to senior management be able to speak fluent English. Courses in English are offered for all employees whose first language is not English, a group consisting of 89 percent of all individuals working for ABB. The courses are taught at five different starting levels. Arne Olsson, ABB's head of human resources, recently told attendees at a company conference in Germany: "English is the global business language. Learn to speak and write it. You can survive everywhere with it."

ABB also encourages employees to add an additional area of specialization to their area of expertise. For example, an engineer might acquire banking or financial experience. "Broad-based people" are particularly valued within the company. Such preparation better equips individual managers to work within the empowerment philosophy of the company. Managers are expected to solve problems at their level whenever possible, rather than attempting to pass them up to higher levels. ABB's "Mission, Values, and Policies," a booklet of operating guidelines says, "Taking action and doing the right thing is obviously best." "Taking action, doing the wrong thing, and quickly correcting it is second best," it adds. "Creating delays or losing opportunities is the worst course of action."

When ABB dispatches high-potential managers from various countries to foreign assignments, the immediate purpose is to open their minds "to other ways of solving problems," says Lindahl. The corporate human resource function is responsible for ensuring that individuals with the potential to assume senior management positions are both identified and trained. Still, according to one country manager, Eric Drewery, CEO of ABB-United Kingdom, London, "Young managers knock on my door and want to know what I have in mind for their future. They don't just wait to be told."[89]

QUESTIONS FOR CONCLUDING CASE 2

1. How might human resource planning be conducted in a multidomestic company like ABB?
2. Discuss the role of the corporate HRM office in identifying and developing senior managers for the organization.
3. How would you proceed if you wanted to be one of the high-potential managers at ABB?

PART FOUR

LEADING

LEADING

While planning provides direction and organizing arranges the resources, the leading function adds the action ingredient. Leading involves influencing the work behavior of others toward achieving organizational goals. In the process of leading, effective managers can become catalysts in encouraging organizational innovation. Leaders kindle the dynamic spirit that underlies successful organizations.

To be able to kindle that spirit, managers need to have an in-depth understanding of the processes involved in bringing about change and innovation. **Chapter 11** probes ways that managers can effectively facilitate needed change and innovation to achieve competitive advantage. The energy of an organization comes from the motivation of its workers. As **Chapter 12** notes, managers can utilize several motivational approaches that focus on individual needs, the thought processes involved in deciding whether or not to expend effort, and the reinforcements and rewards available.

Does leadership depend on inherent traits, or are there effective leader behaviors that anyone can learn and apply to various situations? **Chapter 13** considers both these possibilities in exploring the essence of leadership. In order to have influence, leaders must have effective ways of communicating their ideas and visions, as well as workable methods of learning about the thoughts of others. **Chapter 14** discusses the nature of managerial communication, including an exploration of the different types of communication and the various channels involved. At the same time, many managers have come to realize that groups or teams can be a powerful means of accomplishing organizational goals. As **Chapter 15** explains, understanding group dynamics and being able to encourage the productive power inherent in group activities is an important part of the leading function.

CHAPTER ELEVEN

CHANGE MANAGEMENT AND INNOVATION

LEARNING OBJECTIVES

After studying this chapter, you should be able to:

■ Distinguish change from innovation and identify the major forces for change and innovation.

■ Enumerate the four life-cycle stages of organizations and discuss organizational revitalization and termination.

■ Explain the eight-step model of the change and innovation process.

■ Explain the meaning of organizational development and the techniques used in interventions.

■ Indicate why employees resist change.

■ Explain how to overcome resistance to change, including the use of force-field analysis.

■ Specify the four factors necessary to link innovation and competitive advantage.

■ Describe the common characteristics of intrapreneurs and the factors that induce them to pursue new ideas within existing organizations.

■ Outline the key organizational components that usually must be altered in the process of implementing major changes and innovations.

GAINING THE EDGE

MERCK PRODUCES BIOTECH STARS

 Merck & Company, the world's largest drug firm, is famous for a string of best-selling drugs produced over the past two decades. Much of the company's success took place under the guidance of P. Roy Vagelos, a physician and biochemist who took over leadership of Merck's research labs in 1976 and later became CEO.

When Vagelos arrived at Merck, he outlined a bold new approach to developing innovative drugs. He argued that the best path to drug innovations was studying how diseases affect the body's chemistry. On the basis of his vision, he persuaded researchers to study the biochemical reactions that a disease triggers and then to develop a chemical that could arrest those reactions.

As researchers adopted the new approach, Merck supported them by annually pouring hundreds of millions of dollars into research. The company also spent heavily to build plant capacity for drugs under development. Meanwhile, Merck worked harder than ever to recruit and retain research scientists working at the leading edge in such areas as biochemistry, neurology, immunology, and molecular biology. They were attracted not only by the high pay but also by the lavishly equipped facilities, which some likened to "a college campus in heaven." Such efforts not only led to successful new drugs but also resulted in 17 research centers and more than 4500 research and development employees located in several European countries, Japan, and North America.

At one point, the company worried about whether it was making a sufficient return on its investment, given the high costs and risks associated with attempting to discover new drugs. Using a sophisticated simulation model, chief financial officer Judy Lewent demonstrated that the company portfolio of drugs was extremely profitable. In fact, her analysis showed the importance of having a large pipeline of drugs under development because any one of them could fail clinical trials, register a moderate success, or become a blockbuster drug. As a result, Merck raised it annual research budget from several hundred million dollars per year to $1.2 billion.

Despite its successes, Merck faces a changing environment. Managed health care plans through companies, unions, and health maintenance organizations are increasingly interested in lowering the cost of prescription drugs used by their patients. As a result, managers of these plans have great influence over which drugs are prescribed. If a doctor in one of these health plans prescribes an expensive drug for which there is a cheaper alternative, a pharmacist working for the plan will likely urge the doctor to prescribe the cheaper alternative or a generic drug, if available. For example, when the price of Mevacor, Merck's well-known cholesterol-lowering drug, was higher than an effective but less costly alternative, a large mail-order prescription company working with many of the managed health care plans began to recommend the less costly alternative. The mail-order company was Medco Containment Services, which had grown to the point that it was shipping $2 billion in prescription drugs for health plans. Because of its size, Medco was becoming increasingly able to negotiate lower prices for various drugs from drug companies.

In the face of changing markets for its drugs, Merck took the bold step of buying Medco for $6 billion. The acquisition gives Merck access to information on 33 million patients and some influence over prescription patterns. For example, Merck studies show that after 18 months, 50 percent of patients who should continue taking medications for chronic conditions stop taking the drugs. Medco

Merck & Company outpaces its drug company competitors by staying on the cutting edge of research. Lavishly equipped laboratories and a yearly budget of over $1 billion enable researchers to develop innovative drugs. Biologist Paulette Midgette, shown here, is working on creating a DNA-based flu vaccine that doesn't rely on using the whole virus as a vaccine. Such a vaccine could lead to ways to inoculate against HIV and herpes.

is in a position to monitor such situations and contact the patients' doctors, an action that would benefit not only patients but also Merck when the patients are taking Merck drugs. Of course, Medco will need to also work effectively with other drug companies to maintain its contracts with various medical plans. Merck will also need to strongly consider the best interests of patients in working with its Medco unit. Vagelos, who has retired since the Medco acquisition, noted that the purchase of Medco was a chance to change the "paradigm" under which Merck had been operating, given its changing environment. To punctuate the need for change, the Merck board chose an outsider as Vagelos's successor—Raymond V. Gilmartin, CEO of Becton Dickinson & Co., a manufacturer of medical equipment.[1]   ■■■

When Vagelos joined Merck, the company was not doing well. Fortunately, he recognized the importance of managing the process of change and innovation. But innovation does not occur automatically. Instead, requirements for innovation and change must be an integral part of the planning process. Only then will there be a common understanding throughout the organization that innovation and change are necessary both for organizational survival and for individual job security and success. Vagelos's ability to incorporate the need for innovation and change into Merck's strategic management process was a key factor in his success as senior vice president in charge of research and his later selection as chief executive officer.[2]

In this chapter, we consider the nature of change and innovation, including major forces that pressure organizations to alter their ways. We examine how organizational life cycles affect the need for the management of change and innovation. We also consider the process that is involved in the management of change and innovation, examine why people resist change and how to overcome that resistance, and consider how innovation can be used to build competitive advantage. We then outline the key organizational components that can be used to help implement change.

■ THE NATURE OF CHANGE AND INNOVATION

The fierce domestic and foreign competition during the past decade has brought about a new emphasis on innovation and change in organizations. General Electric's Major Appliance Business Group discovered the hazards of failing to innovate when Whirlpool quietly introduced a number of new features that virtually wiped out GE's lead in side-by-side refrigerator-freezers. The GE appliance had remained essentially unchanged for almost 15 years.[3] Similarly, although the videocassette recorder was an American invention, originally conceived by Ampex and RCA in the 1960s, U.S. manufacturers failed to persist in developing the technology into a successful product. As a result, Japanese manufacturers succeeded in monopolizing the entire U.S. market for VCRs.[4] Events like these have caused managers to become increasingly interested in issues of change and innovation. In this section, we provide a closer look at these concepts, and we briefly consider the major forces that exert pressure on organizations to change and innovate.

Distinguishing between Change and Innovation

Change Any alteration of the status quo

In considering more closely the concepts of change and innovation, it is useful to distinguish between the two terms. **Change** is any alteration of the status quo, whereas innovation is a more specialized kind of change. **Innovation** is a new idea applied to initiating or improving a process, product, or service.[5] As long as an idea for bringing about an improvement is perceived as new by the individuals involved, it is generally considered to be an innovation even though outside observers may view it as an imitation of something already existing elsewhere.[6] All innovations imply change; but not all changes are innovations, since some types of changes may not involve new ideas or lead to significant improvements—and could even cause difficulties (for example, a tornado damaging a factory).

Innovations in organizations can range from radical new breakthroughs (such as laser technology) to small, incremental improvements (such as an improved paper tray on a computer printer). Both types of innovations can be advantageous.[7] Japanese companies, in particular, have become known for their ability to enhance products and services through a variety of small, incremental improvements. For example, at the Japan-based Matsushita Electric Industrial Company, a team of 100 technicians, Ph.D. scientists, and factory engineers persisted for 8 years before developing an improved glass lens for use in projection televisions and several laser-based products, such as videodisc systems and compact disc players. Furthermore, the new lenses can be made for 90 percent less than the cost of existing lenses. Thus a relatively modest goal—improving a component in successful products—led to a rapidly expanding market share for Matsushita lenses, particularly for those used in compact disc players.[8]

As management researcher Rosabeth Moss Kanter points out, the innovation process encompasses a distinctive combination of characteristics. For one thing, innovation involves considerable *uncertainty,* since progress and successful outcomes may be difficult to predict. For another, the process tends to be *knowledge-intensive* in the sense that those close to the development of the innovation may possess most of the knowledge about the situation, at least during the development stages. Still another characteristic is that the innovation process is often *controversial,* because resources aimed at a particular innovation effort could presumably be used to pursue alternative courses of action. Finally, the innovation process often *crosses organizational boundaries,* because development and implementation frequently involve more than one business unit, increasing the complexity of the effort. Therefore, there is a need for managers not only to understand the major aspects of change but also to plan for the special needs of the innovation process.

Increasingly, greater pressure from both global and domestic competitors is forcing organizations to become more nimble and innovative. As a result, many organizations are engaging in what is sometimes referred to as change management—efforts by managers to make their organizations more proactive in changing and innovating for competitive advantage. Throughout this chapter, we use the term "change" to connote any type of alteration in the status quo, including an innovation, in an organization. We use the term "innovation" in the more narrow sense of a new idea associated with an improvement. At times, we may use both terms, or the term "change management," to highlight the particular importance of the discussion for both change and innovation.

Forces for Change and Innovation

A variety of forces influence change and innovation in organizations. Some of these forces stem from external factors, while others arise from factors that are mainly internal to organizations.

EXTERNAL FORCES External forces on organizations frequently create a need for

Innovation A new idea applied to initiating or improving a process, product, or service

How does a restaurant adapt to changes in eating habits that keep more and more people at home? By offering take-out and take-home specialties. Marty's Food and Wine Emporium in Dallas, Texas, caters to the singles and working couples who find it convenient to pick up microwavable dinners on the way home from the office. While forced to adapt to changes in the mega-environment (such as the microwave, the VCR, and dual-career families), Marty's was able to shape the behavior of one aspect of its task environment—its customers.

change and innovation (see the discussion of environment in Chapter 3). For example, environmental forces ranging from earthquakes and hurricanes to increased government regulatory pressures and escalating competition are forcing many insurance companies to consolidate and innovate at a faster pace. When executives at Baltimore-based Fidelity & Deposit Co. (F&D) discovered that their expense ratios were 6 to 8 percent higher than those of their competitors, they began to search for new ways to cut costs. One successful approach was to have some of their field representatives, particularly those selling insurance to financial services groups, work out of their homes using company-furnished laptop computers, fax machines, and cellular phones.[9] Thus, while some external forces may pressure organizations to change in ways that are less than desirable, such forces often open up opportunities for applications of innovative ideas.[10]

INTERNAL FORCES Internal forces for change and innovation develop from a variety of sources. Some of these forces include alterations of strategies and plans, ethical difficulties that arise because of employee behaviors, decisions that entail changes and innovations, organizational culture shifts, reorganizations, technological advances, and leadership changes. For instance, a new emphasis on quality led to internal changes at the Hach Company, a Loveland, Colorado, maker of water-analysis equipment. Kathryn Hach, the company's chairperson and chief executive, found that workers had insufficient knowledge of basic reading and math to handle the company's new approach. Some quality techniques involved keeping statistical charts and understanding basic algebra, while operating some of the company's new computer-controlled machinery required a knowledge of trigonometry. After offering several basic courses that led to major productivity gains, Hach now spends 9 percent of its payroll costs on employee training.[11] Quality was also an issue in the internal changes at Intermountain Health Care, Inc. (see the Valuing Quality box).

Of course, as in the Hach and Intermountain situations, many internal changes ultimately can be traced to factors in the environment. Some of the needs for internal change that confront organizations are predictable to some extent because organizations tend to follow certain life cycles.

■ ORGANIZATIONAL LIFE CYCLES

Life cycles Predictable stages of development that organizations typically follow

Organizational termination The process of ceasing to exist as an identifiable organization

Life cycles are predictable stages of development that organizations typically follow. The evolution through each stage requires certain changes in order for organizations to survive and grow. Otherwise, **organizational termination,** the process of ceasing to exist as an identifiable organization, may occur. Organizational terminations are common events. Many new businesses fail within their first 5 years. If you think about your local shopping center or business district, you can probably name several businesses that started up but did not survive.

Four Life-Cycle Stages

Organizations tend to evolve through four major stages of development.[12] These stages and their common characteristics are presented in Table 11-1. Each stage requires that changes be made in the methods of operating if the organization is to survive and prosper. Paradoxically, unless managers take steps to plan for and encourage innovation, some of the changes required at each step may eventually inhibit the organization's ability to make further innova-

VALUING QUALITY

Intermountain Improves Medical Care

Intermountain Health Care (IHC), Inc., is using quality principles to make innovative improvements in its health services. The nonprofit chain of hospitals in Idaho, Utah, and Wyoming has targeted a tough challenge: finding and eliminating inappropriate variations in medical care.

In one experiment, Intermountain's LDS Hospital in Salt Lake City set out to lower the rate of postoperative wound infections. Before the effort began, the hospital's infection rate was slightly below the national average. By using a bedside computer system to make sure that antibiotics were given to patients 2 hours before surgery, the hospital decreased the infection rate in 4484 cases by half, to .9 percent. Since that effort, the hospital's postop infection rate has dropped even further, to .4 percent. This represents 4 cases per 1000, compared with the national average of 20 cases per 1000. Since the average postop infection adds $14,000 to the hospital bill, the change results in major savings.

Even more important is the medical benefit to the patient. An infection causes a fever and an inflamed incision line. Treatment entails cleaning the sutures over the abscess and packing the wound with gauze—a painful procedure. "It's not what a patient would call a high-quality event," says Dr. Brent C.

James, Intermountain's quality chief. "At the very least, it requires a few more days in the hospital with antibiotics," he says. At worst, it can result in death.

The postop study was just one of many in which IHC has compared the results and costs of the performance of physicians. At first, the medical staff felt threatened by the quality program, says James. To allay their fears, James fed back the survey information using codes so that doctors could compare themselves with the norm without being concerned that other physicians would see their scores. Some physicians said the report was a "piece of trash" and threw it in the wastebasket. In the end, however, the doctors recog-

Intermountain Health Care Inc. wanted to improve the quality of its health care by eliminating inappropriate variations in care. One target was to cut down on the number of postoperative wound infections. At Intermountain's LDS Hospital in Salt Lake City (shown here) a computer tracking system for the administration of antibiotics resulted in a dramatic drop in postoperative infections, decreasing health care costs and hospital stays and increasing patient comfort.

nized that there were wide variations in treatment success and costs. Now physicians use the data to consult with one another about which treatments constitute the best care. Then, they offer it.[13]

---

tions. The potential effects of the four life-cycle stages on innovation are shown in Figure 11-1.

ENTREPRENEURIAL STAGE At the *entrepreneurial stage,* a new organization is created, usually to support an invention or a major innovation. Frequently, the organization is formed through the initiative of a single individual and is a one-person show, although a few others may be involved initially. Since the organization is still in its infancy, there is little planning and coordination. The prime inventor, or entrepreneur, makes the decisions.

TABLE 11-1 CHARACTERISTICS ASSOCIATED WITH THE FOUR LIFE-CYCLE STAGES

CHARACTERISTIC	ENTREPRENEURIAL STAGE	COLLECTIVITY STAGE	FORMALIZATION AND CONTROL STAGE	ELABORATION OF STRUCTURE STAGE
Structure	Little or none	Informal	Functional; centralization	Self-contained; decentralization
Focus	Survival; seeking resources	Growth	Efficiency; coordination	Restructuring
Innovation	Invention	Enhancement	Implementation	Renewal
Planning	Little or none	Short range	Long range	Long range; opportunistic
Commitment	Individual sense	Group sense	Complacency	Recommitment
Managers	Entrepreneurs	Entrepreneurs and early joiners	Professional managers	Professional managers and orchestrators

Source: Based on Larry E. Greiner, "Evolution and Revolution as Organizations Grow," *Harvard Business Review,* July–August 1972, pp. 37–46; and Robert E. Quinn and Kim S. Cameron, "Organizational Life Cycles and Shifting Criteria of Effectiveness: Some Preliminary Evidence," *Management Science,* vol. 29, 1983, pp. 33–51.

The continuing need for resources eventually causes a crisis. At this point, the entrepreneurial enterprise usually either fails or moves to the next stage. For example, Howard Head, a metals expert, ski enthusiast, and inventor of the famous Head skis, persisted for more than 3 years in his efforts to develop a metal ski to replace wooden ones. His various attempts met with acute skepticism from ski pros, and he frequently returned from the ski slopes with broken and twisted skis. When his fledgling company began to run out of money, he faced a resource crisis. The company was saved by an influx of funds from investors in return for 40 percent ownership of the firm. When Head finally perfected his design several years later, the resulting product was so good that the skis were called "cheaters."[14] The need to involve others as investors and helpers, however, had taken the Head company to the next stage of development.

Figure 11-1 *Potential effects of the four life-cycle stages on innovation.*

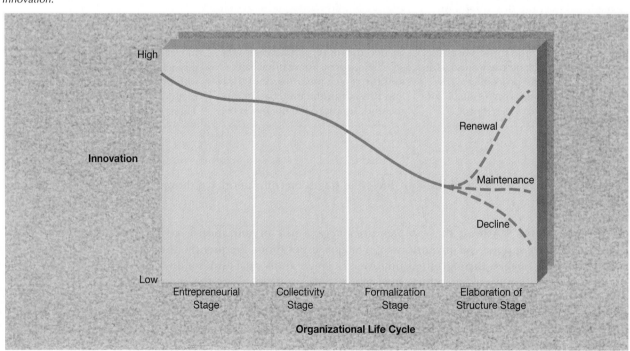

COLLECTIVITY STAGE At the *collectivity stage,* the entrepreneur is joined by a few dedicated others who believe in the idea. The organization is in its youth. There are strong feelings of group identification and a real sense of mission. Members of the organization put in many long hours, demonstrate a high level of commitment, and receive much of their pay in stock that is relatively worthless at that point. The vision is of grander days to come. The structure and communication patterns are informal; major decisions may involve the group. Innovation continues to be relatively high.

A crisis usually occurs when growth accelerates and the informal management systems characteristic of this stage provide inadequate leadership direction and control. Often the entrepreneurs who began the organization are not particularly well suited in either temperament or ability for managing a larger organization, so they bring in a professional manager. This was the case at Apple when cofounder Steven Jobs lured John Sculley from Pepsi-Cola USA to serve as president of the computer maker. Apple was experiencing serious coordination difficulties that Jobs believed could be handled more effectively by a seasoned manager such as Sculley. Within 2 years, though, Jobs resigned after Sculley stripped him of his job as executive vice president of the Macintosh division because of schedule delays and development problems.[15]

FORMALIZATION AND CONTROL STAGE At the *formalization and control stage,* the organization is characterized by a more formalized structure. Departments are usually organized according to major specialized areas, such as finance, manufacturing, or marketing. Emphasis at this stage tends to shift toward efficiency and maintenance of market share. To help provide coordination, rules and procedures become more commonplace and there is greater centralization of control. With the organization reaching adulthood, this stage helps it consolidate its position, achieve better direction, and continue to grow. Frequently, innovation is replaced by a more conservative stance that may unwittingly discourage risk taking and future innovation. Eventually, as growth continues, the organization becomes larger and more difficult to coordinate.

During this stage, competitive challenges, technological change, and other factors may increase the information-processing needs of the hierarchy, making it slow to respond. A crisis occurs when members of the organization are hampered by the detrimental effects of red tape and centralized control. At one point, Levi Strauss, for example, had operated for years in a market so favorable that the company could not keep up with the demand. However, the procedures established during this growth period left the jeans giant unable to react quickly to a subsequent slowdown in the jeans market and the move to more fashionable apparel. One former employee observed that the company had "enough staff and organization to run General Motors."[16] At this point in the life cycle, an organization is ready for the next stage.

ELABORATION-OF-STRUCTURE STAGE At the *elaboration-of-structure stage,* managers begin to seek ways to streamline the excess bureaucratization that cropped up during the formalization and control stage. Decision making is decentralized, often by organizing departments around specific products or services. Considerable emphasis is frequently placed on coordinating individuals who are at similar levels in different work units. This often involves forming temporary or ongoing groups to address interdepartmental issues. (We discuss these groups further in Chapters 8 and 15.) In addition to making changes in organizational structure, which are commonplace at this stage, managers often engage in considerable cost cutting and reemphasize promising strategic directions.

Essentially, the chief aim of efforts at the elaboration-of-structure stage is

TABLE 11-2 DYSFUNCTIONAL CONSEQUENCES OF ORGANIZATIONAL STABILIZATION AND DECLINE

CONSEQUENCE	EXPLANATION
Curtailed innovation	No experimentation is conducted; risk aversion is prevalent, and skepticism exists about activities that are not related specifically to current major directions.
Scapegoating	Leaders are blamed for the pain and uncertainty.
Resistance to change	Conservatism and turf protection lead to rejection of new alternatives.
Turnover	The most competent leaders tend to leave first, causing leadership anemia.
Conflict	Competition and infighting for control predominates when resources are scarce.

Source: Adapted from Kim S. Cameron, David A. Whetten, and Myung U. Kim, "Organizational Dysfunctions of Decline," *Academy of Management Journal,* vol. 30, 1987, p. 128.

Revitalization The renewal of the innovative vigor of organizations

revitalization, the renewal of the innovative vigor of organizations.[17] Not all organizations attempt or are successful at revitalization. Some organizations stabilize and manage to maintain themselves at least for a period of time. Others decline, despite revitalization efforts, and may eventually fail.[18] Unfortunately, stabilized and declining organizations are particularly susceptible to several major dysfunctions that make them more difficult to manage.[19] These dysfunctions, which are explained in Table 11-2, also make renewal and revitalization all the more difficult. The experience of Wang Laboratories illustrates the organizational life cycle and the particular difficulties inherent in making the transition from the formalization and control stage to revitalization in the elaboration-of-structure stage (see the Case in Point discussion).

CASE IN POINT

WANG FIGHTS TO REVITALIZE

Wang Laboratories, once a leader in word-processing and data-processing equipment, was founded by Dr. An Wang. Wang, a native of Shanghai, received his doctorate from Harvard in 1948 and started Wang Laboratories in 1951 above a store in Boston's South End.

The company's first success came in 1964, with the introduction of an electronic desktop calculator. In the early 1970s, when competitors started to use semiconductors to make small, inexpensive calculators, the Wang versions became obsolete. By that time, however, the company had already begun producing word processors and small computers. Wang competed successfully against companies such as IBM and the Digital Equipment Corporation by offering relatively low prices on word-processing machines with a wide array of peripheral equipment and programs tailored to customers' needs. Within a decade, the small group of early employees had expanded dramatically as Wang became a $2 billion company.

In the early 1980s, with the future looking bright, An Wang withdrew somewhat from active management of the company. But serious problems began to emerge with the increasing popularity of personal computers. Because they could be used for both word processing and computing, the PCs were more flexible than the Wang products. Wang announced 14 new products and promised delivery in 8 months. Unfortunately, the company was a year late in producing the products, which ultimately fell far short of customer needs. The situation made some customers wary of further Wang purchases.

Fred Wang, An Wang's son, took over as president in 1987. Two years later, Wang Laboratories began to report major losses, prompting Fred Wang's resignation. Although recuperating from cancer surgery, An Wang took over as chief executive officer. He hired an outsider, Richard W. Miller, as president and chief operating officer. Miller, a veteran of the RCA Corporation and General Electric, had little experience in the computer field. Unfortunately, he could not turn the company around fast enough, and 2 years later Wang was forced to file for protection under Chapter 11 of the U.S. Bankruptcy Code.

Wang emerged from bankruptcy with Joseph Tucci, a computer-industry veteran, at the helm. Most of Wang's current $950 million in annual revenue comes from consulting and maintenance related to its 30,000 VS minicomputer systems. Yet, as customers move to more powerful and versatile personal computer networks, this business is expected to erode. Therefore, Tucci is using the money Wang earns to move as quickly as possible into the workflow and imaging field. The software enables workers to scan documents into a computer and pass the image from one worker to another electronically.

As part of a settlement of a patent-infringement dispute with Microsoft, Wang was allowed to install a component of its imaging software on Windows 95. Wang will not make any royalties from its Windows 95 element, but expects to obtain orders for its workflow and imaging systems as a result of the exposure. Wang now has about 7000 workers, down from its peak of about 33,000 employees. But it is growing again. In imaging software, Wang faces formidable competition from companies such as FileNet, IBM, Xerox, and Kodak.[20] ■■■

Organizational Termination

Although the problems at Wang may not put the company completely out of business, recent years have witnessed many organizational terminations. Such terminations occur when organizations run into difficulties and cease to exist as known entities. An organization may be terminated for several reasons (see Table 11-3).

Most frequently, organizations face termination because they have not been able to innovate and change fast enough to compete. Termination can occur at any stage in the life cycle. Therefore, managers need to think about where their organization currently fits in the life cycle. This analysis helps them determine the types of changes that may be necessary to move the organization to the next stage of development.

TABLE 11-3 METHODS OF ORGANIZATIONAL TERMINATION	
Bankruptcy	Under Chapter 11 of the Federal Bankruptcy Code, an organization that is unable to pay its debts can seek court protection from creditors and from certain contract obligations while it attempts to regain financial stability. If the organization continues to experience problems, its assets will be sold in order to settle debts with creditors.
Liquidation	The sale or dissolution of an entire organization for reasons usually associated with serious business difficulties and seemingly insurmountable obstacles.
Merger	The combining of two or more organizations into one.
Acquisition	The purchase of all or part of one organization by another.
Takeover	The purchase of a controlling share of voting stock in a publicly traded company.

■ THE CHANGE MANAGEMENT AND INNOVATION PROCESS

Reactive change Change that occurs when one takes action in response to perceived problems, threats, or opportunities

Planned change Change that involves actions based on a carefully thought-out process that anticipates future difficulties, threats, and opportunities

The processes of change management and innovation tend to be difficult because they involve incorporating significant new ideas. Managers are typically involved with two types of change. **Reactive change** occurs when one takes action in response to perceived problems, threats, or opportunities. Since one is reacting to events, there is often insufficient time to analyze the situation carefully and prepare a well-conceived response. In one famous example, Johnson & Johnson faced a crisis in the early 1980s when seven people died after taking Extra-Strength Tylenol capsules laced with cyanide (see Chapter 4). The company moved quickly to recall 31 million bottles of the pain reliever at a cost of $100 million. Then, when its market share plummeted, J&J boosted advertising by more than 30 percent. The company's subsequent regaining of all but a fraction of its former market share was termed "one of the greatest marketing feats in our industry" by one drugstore executive.[21] The Tylenol situation illustrates that it is not possible for managers to anticipate every problem that will arise and that sometimes managers are forced by events to react.

However, there are many situations in which it is possible to engage in **planned change,** which involves actions based on a carefully thought-out process that anticipates future difficulties, threats, and opportunities. For example, although everyone hoped that the Tylenol crisis was an isolated incident, J&J repackaged the product in a tamper-resistant container. Furthermore, 4 years later, when another woman died after taking a cyanide-laced Tylenol capsule, J&J's reaction indicated that the company had prepared for a possible crisis. Chairman James E. Burke appeared on television almost immediately and announced that J&J was eliminating the use of the capsule in favor of a capsule-shaped tablet that he called a "caplet." He had with him an enlarged model of the caplet. The company offered to replace all outstanding capsules with the caplets, a move that cost $150 million. Furthermore, the decision to stop using the capsule cost the company millions of dollars. It was clear from the speed and forthrightness of these major steps that J&J's managers had done considerable planning for a potential threat and were ready with a carefully conceived course of action, including a plan for implementation.[22]

When managers habitually operate in a reactive mode, they dramatically increase their chances of making serious mistakes because they are continually making changes without proper planning. As a result, most effective managers engage in planned, or managed, change and innovation whenever possible.

An Eight-Step Model

Managers are likely to be more effective in bringing about change and innovation when they follow the process outlined in Figure 11-2.[23] There are eight basic steps in the process.

1 **Gain recognition of an opportunity or a problem.** Most major changes and innovations begin when some individuals or groups identify a problem situation or an opportunity. It is usually easier to recognize problems when things clearly are going poorly. For example, when IBM spun off its Lexington, Kentucky, maker of printers, everyone in the new company (called Lexmark) realized that the business had not been doing well and change would be critical.[24] On the other hand, when Roberto Goizueta took over as CEO at Coca-Cola, the company seemed to be doing well. Goizueta, however, discovered that its fountains business (sales to retail outlets, like

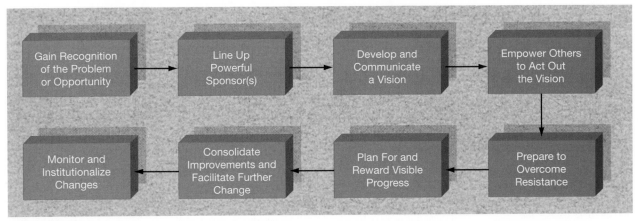

Figure 11-2 *The change management and innovation process.*

McDonald's, that use systems called fountains to dispense Coca-Cola into cups or glasses for immediate consumption) was actually earning less than its cost of capital. He mobilized managers to analyze the returns from various other parts of the company. They, too, were actually losing money. Moreover, Goizueta says an erroneous belief within the company that the soft-drink industry was maturing led managers to ignore a multitude of opportunities for growth.[25] Opportunities are all too easy to overlook.

Noted management consultant Peter Drucker argues convincingly that one reason managers are not more innovative is that there is a tendency to focus on immediate problems and to ignore opportunities. Drucker offers several suggestions for increasing the focus on opportunities. He notes that management in most companies requires a report on operating performance each month. Typically, the first page lists areas in which performance is not going as well as expected. Drucker suggests the addition of a second "first page" that would list things that are going better than expected, calling attention to possible unexploited opportunities. Another of Drucker's ideas is holding meetings every 6 months or so in which three or four executives report on entrepreneurial activities that have gone exceptionally well and that others might adopt.[26]

2 **Line up powerful sponsor(s).** Change and innovation do not usually occur without the support of individuals who are powerful enough to marshal the necessary resources and influence others to support the new approach. Major organizational renewals typically require a coalition of several sponsors. At one point, General Electric's Appliance Park in Louisville, Kentucky, was in danger of losing its role as the primary manufacturer of GE washing machines because it appeared that the manufacturing could be done more cheaply by outside vendors. The Park had been losing $45 million annually. Dick Burke, who was then head of manufacturing, engineering, and purchasing for the Park, involved a number of senior GE executives, the president of the local union, and even the governor of Kentucky in dramatizing the need for change and in successfully persuading General Electric's CEO, Jack Welch, to give the Park a chance to come up with new solutions.

3 **Develop and communicate a vision.** To bring about change and innovation, it is important to be able to develop a picture of the future that is fairly easy to communicate and has appeal to those who must change or support change and innovation. General Electric's appliance executives determined that the Appliance Park would have to develop a dramatically new washing machine—one that would greatly surpass the offerings of competitors. On

General Electric executives gave its design team a vision for a new washing machine: it was to be quiet, reliable, attractive, affordable, and have a large capacity. The result was GE's first dramatically different washer in 42 years—the Profile Maxus super capacity washing machine. The redesign is paying off: appliance dealers can't keep the washers in the store.

the basis of consumer research, a viable new washer would have to have bigger capacity, have no vibration, clean clothes better, be more attractive, be less noisy, be even more reliable, and retail for $399. Executives gave a design team 20 days to come up with a washing machine that would cost 30 percent less to make and lead in major critical areas such as capacity and aesthetics by a factor of two over offerings by competitors.[27]

4 **Empower others to act out the vision.** Managers need to embolden employees to take actions in behalf of the vision. Managers also need to remove obstacles that preclude employees from doing so. At the new printer manufacturer, Lexmark, teams were formed to make production lines more efficient and to raise quality. One team of assembly workers completely redesigned the laser printer production process.

5 **Prepare to overcome resistance.** The fact that one group, even top management, decides to adopt a change does not mean that others will readily go along with it. At Lexmark, when members of the assembly worker team presented their redesigned laser printer production process to their boss for approval, he said that each member of the team would have to sign the plans before he would sign them. The team was hesitant to take the responsibility that went with the empowerment. The team spent another month before they presented a redesign they were all willing to sign. Later in the chapter, we describe the reasons why employees resist change and the means of overcoming such resistance.

6 **Plan for and reward visible progress.** Major changes and innovations can take time, risking that individuals involved will lose focus or give up. One means of maintaining the momentum is to include some projects or phases that are likely to be successful within 12 to 24 months. Then providing celebrations, recognitions, and other rewards sends the message that the changes are important and keeps attention focused on the vision. When Amoco, a Chicago-based oil company, needed to cut costs because they were higher than those of competitors, one idea was to have workers on offshore platforms in the Gulf of Mexico not only increase productivity in their regular jobs but also take on the job of cleaning, sandblasting, and painting the rigs. These latter jobs had been done by contractors. When workers on one platform finally took on the new duties and did an excellent job, Amoco

was quick to provide merit awards. The company realized that taking on these additional duties was not particularly popular, but the firm greatly appreciated the workers' endeavors. In addition, the field manager went out, took pictures, and gave the project widespread visibility within the company. Such actions helped everyone see that changes in behalf of the new vision were possible.[28]

7 **Consolidate improvements and facilitate further change.** With change processes and quests for innovation, it is all too easy to achieve clear improvements and then stop. At Lexmark, the first goal was to reach profitability. Given the tough competition the company faces, though, it needs to continue lowering costs and rolling out product improvements. To do that, Lexmark management is proceeding with its emphasis on empowering the work force. Teams of workers are seeking further improvement in such areas as production, inventory, and shipping.

8 **Monitor and institutionalize the changes.** Unfortunately, renewal progress and strides toward innovation can reverse themselves very quickly unless they become part of the corporate culture. Therefore, it is important to keep pointing out the need for the new behaviors and their connection to company success until they become an integral part of the way in which things are done. The washing machine developed by the GE design team was ultimately a success. The new assembly line and many other related changes involved an unprecedented amount of employee input, teamwork, and management-union cooperation—approaches that have changed the way things are done at Appliance Park. Other parts of GE have been asking for help in bringing about similar types of renewal.[29] Companies particularly known for innovation, such as 3M and Hewlett-Packard, have spent years cultivating cultures that support innovation and consider their cultures to be part of their competitive advantage.

Organizational Development

A specialized approach to change that can help organizations improve their effectiveness through enhancing the way individuals and groups interact is called organizational development. More specifically, **organizational development (OD)** is a change effort aimed at enhancing interpersonal working relationships and organizational effectiveness through planned interventions made with the help of a change agent who is well versed in the behavioral sciences.[30] The **change agent,** or consultant, is an individual with a fresh perspective and a knowledge of the behavioral sciences who acts as a catalyst in helping the individuals and groups approach old problems in new or innovative ways. The change agent role can be filled by an outside consultant, an OD specialist who is an employee of the organization, a new manager, or an enlightened manager who is able to look beyond traditional approaches.

OD was originally envisioned as a method of handling large-scale organizational change; however, much of its actual focus has been on improving working relationships among individuals and groups. As such, OD efforts are compatible with the change management and innovation process just discussed. OD efforts typically involve three major steps: diagnosis, intervention, and evaluation (see Figure 11-3).[31]

DIAGNOSIS The first step, diagnosis, often focuses particular attention on the shared beliefs, values, and norms of organization members that may be interfering with maximum effectiveness. The change agent and others who are helping with the process typically use multiple means of gathering data, such as

Organizational development (OD) A change effort that is planned, focused on an entire organization or a large subsystem, managed from the top, aimed at enhancing organizational health and effectiveness, and based on planned interventions

Change agent An individual with a fresh perspective and a knowledge of the behavioral sciences who acts as a catalyst in helping the organization approach old problems in new or innovative ways

Change can be painful, as Amoco workers discovered when they were asked to take on maintenance tasks in addition to learning new ways of doing their regular jobs on off-shore drilling platforms. Amoco executives, such as off-shore drilling boss Clive Fowler, made the effort more palatable by handing out merit awards, publicizing the progress made, and demonstrating concern for worker safety.

Figure 11-3 *The organizational development process.*

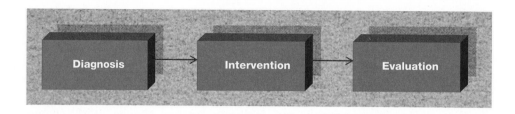

interviews, questionnaires, observations of employee behaviors, and various internal documents and reports. When the Hartmarx Corporation, a Chicago-based clothing maker and retailer, initiated a questionnaire survey of its 25,000 employees, the data were compiled and then fed back to employees in small groups to elicit additional information for use in diagnosis.[32]

INTERVENTION Once the situation has been properly diagnosed, the next step is intervention. Usually OD interventions, or change strategies, are designed and implemented with the help of the change agent. There are numerous OD change strategies. Four of the major techniques used by OD specialists are described briefly below.[33]

Process consultation A technique concerned with the interpersonal relations and dynamics operating in work groups

Process consultation is concerned with the interpersonal relations and dynamics operating in work groups. The OD change agent, or consultant, observes the group and provides feedback regarding dysfunctions in such areas as communication patterns, handling of conflicts, and decision making. The goal is to help group members gain the skills they need to identify and resolve group dynamics issues on their own.

Team building A technique aimed at helping work groups become effective at task accomplishment

Team building is aimed at helping work groups become effective at task accomplishment. Like process consultation, it typically includes OD consultant feedback in such areas as communication and conflict resolution. However, it also includes OD consultant help in assessing group tasks, member roles, and strategies for accomplishing work tasks.

Third-party intervention A technique concerned with helping individuals, groups, or departments resolve serious conflicts that may relate to specific work issues or may be caused by suboptimal interpersonal relations

Third-party intervention is concerned with helping individuals, groups, or departments resolve serious conflicts that may be related to specific work issues or may be caused by suboptimal interpersonal relations. The OD consultant helps the parties resolve their differences through such techniques as problem solving, bargaining, and conciliation.

Technostructural activities Activities intended to improve work technology and/or organization structure

Technostructural activities are intended to improve work technology and/or organizational structure. Through this approach, the OD consultant helps organization members enhance their own work effectiveness by showing them how to evaluate and make appropriate changes in work methods, task design, and organization structure.

EVALUATION Step three is evaluation. As with any change effort, it is important to monitor the effectiveness of OD efforts. The ability to evaluate the effects of OD interventions depends heavily on how well the diagnosis stage pinpointed the areas in need of change and specified the desired results. Both organizational development and the change management and innovation process must take into consideration issues of resistance to change.

Managing Resistance to Change

One of the reasons it takes concerted managerial planning and skill to bring about innovation and change is that people are often resistant. Sometimes they oppose a change even when it appears to others that the change is in the best interests of those affected. In this section, we consider why individuals resist change, and we examine ways of overcoming such resistance.

WHY INDIVIDUALS RESIST CHANGE Why are people—including ourselves—sometimes against change? Although there are many reasons for resistance, several major ones stand out.[34]

One reason is *self-interest*. When people hear about a change, they have a natural tendency to ask, "How will this change affect me?" If an individual perceives the answer to be "adversely," some effort may be made to resist the change. How much resistance is mounted will usually depend on how strongly the individual feels his or her self-interests are affected. Citicorp lost a number of its top investment banking experts in Europe when it took steps to integrate its international commercial and investment banking businesses. The departing investment experts perceived the change as an undesirable intrusion on their turf.[35]

Another common reason for resisting change is *misunderstanding and lack of trust*. People are frequently against change when they don't understand it. In addition, low levels of trust between managers and employees, which are common in many organizations, contribute to the possibility that misunderstandings will occur. As you may have discovered in your own work experience, it is not always the employees who resist change. Managers who mistrust employees and fear loss of power often oppose efforts to involve employees in decisions about their work.[36]

Resistance also often results from *different assessments* of the virtues of the change. Differential assessment is a prime reason for lack of support for innovations. Because innovations involve new concepts, their value is not always obvious to others. Hence individuals may not see a change as useful and may even view it as detrimental to the organization.

Finally, individuals differ in their ability to adjust to new situations, with some individuals having a *low tolerance for change*. As a result, they sometimes resist a change because they fear that they will not be able to learn the new skills and behaviors it entails.

Managers should diagnose the potential reasons why individuals who must be involved in a change might resist it. This assessment helps managers choose a means of overcoming resistance. Otherwise, their efforts to foster innovation and change may be unexpectedly broadsided.

OVERCOMING RESISTANCE TO CHANGE One well-known approach to overcoming resistance has been offered by organizational researcher Kurt Lewin, who divides the change process into three steps.[37] The first step, *unfreezing*, involves developing an initial awareness of the need for change. The second step, *changing*, focuses on learning the new required behaviors. The third step, *refreezing*, centers on reinforcing the new behaviors, usually through positive results, feelings of accomplishment, and/or rewards from others. Lewin's approach helps managers recognize that an unfreezing period is usually necessary before individuals are willing to change. Furthermore, the refreezing element is important for reinforcing and maintaining desired changes.

There are several methods that managers can adopt to help overcome initial resistance to change and facilitate unfreezing.[38] These alternatives, the situations in which they are commonly used, and the advantages and disadvantages of each method are summarized in Table 11-4.

One strategy for overcoming resistance to change is *education and communication*. This involves providing adequate information and making sure that

TABLE 11-4 METHODS OF OVERCOMING RESISTANCE TO CHANGE

APPROACH	COMMONLY USED IN SITUATIONS	ADVANTAGES	DRAWBACKS
Education + communication	Where there is a lack of information or inaccurate information and analysis	Once persuaded, people will often help with the implementation of the change	Can be very time-consuming if lots of people are involved
Participation + involvement	Where the initiators do not have all the information they need to design the change, and where others have considerable power to resist	People who participate will be committed to implementing change, and any relevant information they have will be integrated into the change plan	Can be very time-consuming if participators design an inappropriate change
Facilitation + support	Where people are resisting because of adjustment problems	No other approach works as well with adjustment problems	Can be time-consuming and expensive and still fail
Negotiation + agreement	Where someone or some group will clearly lose out in a change, and where that group has considerable power to resist	Sometimes it is a relatively easy way to avoid major resistance	Can be too expensive in many cases if it alerts others to negotiate for compliance
Manipulation + co-optation	Where other tactics will not work or are too expensive	It can be a relatively quick and inexpensive solution to resistance problems	Can lead to future problems if people feel manipulated
Explicit + implicit coercion	Where speed is essential and the change initiators possess considerable power	It is speedy and can overcome any kind of resistance	Can be risky if it leaves people mad at the initiators

Source: Reprinted from John P. Kotter and Leonard A. Schlesinger, "Choosing Strategies for Change," *Harvard Business Review,* March–April 1979, p. 111.

the change is clearly communicated to those it will affect. At Zebco, a unit of the Brunswick Corporation that makes fishing reels, the union work force resisted efforts by management to increase productivity, so management took a busload of employees to a trade show in Dallas. The show was dominated by Japanese and Korean competitors that had doubled their exports over the previous 5 years. The growing competition had forced Zebco to limit price increases over that time period to a meager 4 percent. Subsequent worker efforts and pressure on suppliers to provide better parts resulted in a doubling of productivity over a 4-year period. As one worker sagely commented, "They got to keep the company, and we got to keep our jobs."[39]

Another means of overcoming resistance to change is *participation and involvement.* Resistance tends to be less pronounced when the individuals who will be affected by a change are allowed to participate in planning and implementing it. At Corning, worker involvement has been a key factor in the success of a cost-saving effort. For instance, a maintenance employee recommended substituting one flexible tin mold for a number of different fixed molds that were used to shape wet ceramic material so that it could be baked into catalytic converters for automobiles. This suggestion produced savings of $99,000 per year.[40] There is evidence, however, that managers tend to underutilize participation as a means of overcoming resistance to change.[41]

The use of *facilitation and support* is another way to overcome resistance. When individuals react to impending changes with fear and anxiety, encouragement and help from the manager often reduce their resistance. Other means of facilitation and support include training and providing the proper equipment and materials.

Another approach to lessening resistance to change is *negotiation and agreement.* Negotiation can be a particularly important strategy when one group perceives that it will be hurt by the change and is in a position to cause the change effort to fail. If other strategies, such as education and participation, falter, it may be necessary to negotiate in order to gain cooperation with the change effort. After a 12-day strike at the Chrysler Corporation, the company agreed to return to annual guaranteed wage increases for union members. The following year, Chrysler was able to negotiate "modern operating agreements" at 5 of its 31 factories. The changes, aimed at improving flexibility in job assignments and making operations more efficient, increased net income by about $32 million.[42]

Another means of overcoming resistance is *manipulation and co-optation.* Manipulation usually involves selectively providing information about a change so that it appears more attractive or necessary to potential resisters. Ethical questions arise when the selective use of information misrepresents the potential negative aspects of the change. In co-optation, a leader or an influential person among the potential resisters is given a seemingly desirable role in the change process in order to gain cooperation. Usually, the role is somewhat symbolic, in the sense that the individual has very little say in the change process. However, the role may be advantageous enough to the influential person to obtain his or her support. The danger with manipulation and co-optation is that this strategy can backfire if the person recognizes what is being done and feels manipulated.

Finally, *explicit and implicit coercion* can also be used to overcome resistance to change. This strategy involves the direct or indirect use of power to pressure change resisters to conform. Tactics usually focus on direct or veiled threats regarding loss of jobs, promotions, pay, recommendations, and the like. Individuals may be fired or transferred. With coercion, there is a strong probability that the recipients of the pressure will be resentful even if they succumb. Furthermore, the coercion may escalate the resistance. When Kaiser Cement imposed its final contract offer on the work force at one of its plants in California, the offer included a sizable cut in seniority rights, a loosening of work rules, a loss of 5 paid sick days, and a lower pay tier for new employees. As a result, the union filed 4000 grievances over a 3-month period, and the company began to experience serious sabotage problems, such as having metal tools end up in cement-grinding mills.[43] If a change is relatively unpopular but must be implemented quickly, managers may be forced to use this strategy. Evidence indicates, however, that managers resort to coercion more often than necessary, thereby fostering negative feelings among subordinates that may impede future changes.[44]

Of course, it is not always employees who resist change. For example, B. Thomas Golisano was sales manager for Electronic Account Systems, Inc., a small computerized payroll-processing organization in Rochester, New York. Electronic catered to larger companies, but Golisano recognized that there might be a market in going after business from smaller companies. He presented the idea to his bosses, but no one would listen. So he started his own company, Paychex, which is now the second largest payroll-processing company in the United States. Says his former employer, "He was right and we were wrong."[45]

FORCE-FIELD ANALYSIS In overcoming resistance to change, managers sometimes find it helpful to use **force-field analysis.** Developed by psychologist Kurt Lewin, the method involves analyzing the two types of forces, driving forces and restraining forces, that influence any proposed change and then assessing how best to overcome resistance. **Driving forces** are those factors that pressure *for* a particular change, whereas **restraining forces** are those factors that pressure *against* a change. At any given point in time, the two types of forces push in opposite directions, leading to an equilibrium that defines current conditions,

Force-field analysis A method that involves analyzing the two types of forces, driving forces and restraining forces, that influence any proposed change and then assessing how best to overcome resistance

Driving forces Factors that pressure *for* a particular change

Restraining forces Factors that pressure *against* a change

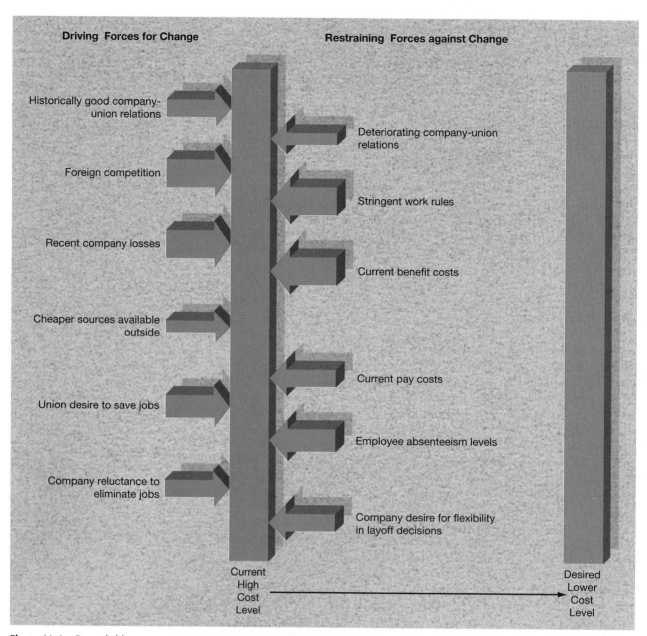

Figure 11-4 *Force-field analysis of the forces maintaining high cost level at Xerox plant.*

or the status quo. To change the status quo to the desired condition, it is therefore necessary to increase the driving forces, to decrease the restraining forces, or to do both. Although managers tend to think in terms of increasing the driving forces, such increases, according to Lewin, are highly likely to provoke a corresponding increase in the resistant forces. Hence managers have a better chance of bringing about a successful change if they work on reducing the restraining forces.[46]

Faced with serious competition from abroad, Xerox set a goal of halving the manufacturing costs at its copier manufacturing operation near Rochester, New York. The effort included plans to have wiring harnesses made by a subcontractor, a move that would lower costs but would also eliminate about 150 jobs. Because there was a high desire among union leaders to save jobs and because company-union relations had been historically good, union leaders asked to meet with managers to consider ways to keep the wiring harness work in the plant.

Figure 11-4 shows a force-field analysis of the major driving and restraining forces maintaining the status quo—costs that were too high for Xerox to compete effectively. The wider the arrow, the stronger the force. In discussing possible solutions, the union leaders suggested relaxing some work rules so that workers could do such things as make minor repairs on machines instead of having to wait for machine maintenance workers to fix the equipment. Union leaders and management also studied other ways to save money that finally led to eliminating 6 paid days off, cutting medical insurance, and developing better ways to control absenteeism. In return, the company promised no layoffs for the next 3 years. By working mainly on some of the restraining forces, the company and the union were able to come to an agreement that resulted in lower cost levels in the plant without contracting out the wiring harness work.[47]

Innovation for Competitive Advantage

It is possible to be innovative and still not achieve business success. To gain a sustainable competitive advantage from innovative activities, four factors are important.[48] First, innovations should be *difficult to imitate* so that competitors cannot easily duplicate the activity. Second, innovations should *reflect market realities* in terms of meeting significant customer needs. For example, researchers at Salinas, California–based Fresh International Corp. experimented for years before coming up with a patented bag that keeps ready-to-eat salads fresh on grocery shelves. The new product was an immediate success.[49] Third, innovations should enable an organization to *exploit timing characteristics* of the particular industry. For example, in some situations, it may be advantageous to be the first to offer an innovation. This may be true, for instance, in brand name situations in which customers can become committed to a particular product or service before competitors can react. In other situations, early followers may be able to gain cost advantages. For example, Los Angeles–based a.b.s. USA produces relatively inexpensive knockoffs of designer clothing soon after they are introduced on fashion runways or chic boutiques in Milan, Paris, and New York. In some cases, the knockoffs appear even before the originals are available in stores. Fourth, innovations should *rely on capabilities and technologies that are readily accessible* to the organization, but not readily available to competitors.

One company that has been able to incorporate the four factors for competitive advantage through innovation is the recently merged Avery Dennison Corp. (see the Case in Point discussion).

AVERY DENNISON BECOMES AN INNOVATOR

CASE IN POINT

The new self-stick postage stamps recently introduced by the U.S. Postal Service are a product of Avery Dennison Corp., a company created by the merger of Avery International Corp. and Dennison Manufacturing Corp. in 1990. Avery was well known for pressure-sensitive materials, particularly removable stick-on labels invented by founder Stan Avery in the 1930s. Over the years the company prospered by expanding into new markets for adhesives and labels, like the peel-off address labels used on 1040 tax forms from the IRS. Dennison was making stationery, notebooks, and markers. Each company came to believe a larger global entity would be a more powerful competitor as well as a supplier to the growing number of office superstores. Dennison's commodity types of items were particularly vulnerable to competition on price. The two companies faced bigger rivals, such as American Brands, Inc., and Esselte AB of Sweden. The merger created a larger company under the leadership of Charles D.

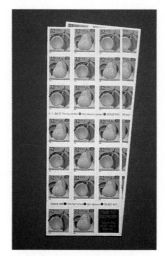

Self-adhesive postage stamps were a product whose time had come. Avery Dennison Corp. is the manufacturing company that made it happen. A unique product, a market niche, good timing, and the requisite technology all combined to make the innovation a success for the company.

Miller, who had been running Avery. Miller's vision was to concentrate on offering innovative products that would not be as subject to price squeezes.

Miller soon discovered that Dennison managers were accustomed to a hierarchical approach in which orders were passed down from the top. In contrast, Avery's structure gave heavy responsibility to division managers. Miller met over coffee and doughnuts with groups of Dennison managers and was very frank about which operations were underperforming and which products were unprofitable. Interestingly, such information, particularly about profitability of products, had not been shared with some of the managers previously. Miller told the managers that he wanted to empower them to make more decisions and take more responsibility for developing new, innovative products. Moreover, he instituted an incentive plan that gave managers bonuses if certain return-on-capital goals were met.

Managers responded by working with employees to develop a variety of new products, including labels for laser printers and ink-jet printers. A real coup occurred when Stephanie Streeter, an assistant product manager, persuaded Microsoft, Lotus, and other major computer software companies to adopt the Avery label dimensions and product stock numbers as their printing standards. She has since been promoted to group vice president of worldwide office products. Other recent products include the new self-stick stamps and products for children, such as Glitter Glue Stics and markers with glow-in-the-dark ink and ink that changes color with the heat of your hand. The company continually obtains feedback from customers about the new products and ways to make them even better. Nearly 30 percent of sales come from products introduced within the past 5 years.[50] ■■■

Intrapreneurship

In order to actively foster innovation, a number of organizations have been encouraging individuals to take on entrepreneurial roles, such as idea generator or champion, sponsor, and orchestrator (see Chapter 1). These roles are sometimes referred to as *intrapreneurial roles* when they are carried out by individuals inside existing organizations. (We consider the entrepreneurial role as it relates to creating new organizations in Chapter 21.)

Although individuals fulfilling any of the three roles fit into the intrapreneurial category, the idea champion is most often referred to as an intrapreneur. This is because he or she has the actual hands-on responsibility of turning the idea into a reality.[51] The *idea champion* is the individual who either generates a new idea or recognizes its value and then supports it despite numerous obstacles.

According to one expert, intrapreneurs tend to have certain characteristics that can be learned, at least to some extent, if one wishes to become more intrapreneurial. For one thing, intrapreneurs tend to visualize what they wish to create. Their vision comes from spending a great deal of time thinking about an idea. Intrapreneurs also tend to be action-oriented, extremely dedicated, and willing to do mundane tasks in order to avoid project delays. They are also likely to set goals for themselves beyond those asked of them, maintain high internal standards about their work, and rebound from mistakes and failures. For example, intrapreneur Phil Palmquist continued to work on reflective coatings at 3M even though his bosses told him to stop because it was not his job. Working four nights a week from 7 to 10 p.m., he finally produced the reflective coating now used on most highways. It is 100 times brighter than white paint.[52] Of course, part of the secret of being a good intrapreneur is choosing a good idea to pursue. For some guidelines on how to recognize a good intrapreneurial idea and what to do if it is rejected, see the Management Skills for the Twenty-First Century discussion, "Checklist for Choosing Intrapreneurial Ideas."

Why would individuals want to pursue an entrepreneurial idea within a company (i.e., be intrapreneurs) rather than start their own company? Existing companies, particularly large ones, can often offer a strong technological base (such as proprietary knowledge and scientific resources), marketing resources (such as a known name, sales staff, and advertising funds), a network of individuals who can help, established production facilities, and in-house financing. Intrapreneur Art Fry, who championed the development of 3M's famous Post-it note pads (see the opening case in Chapter 9), views it this way: "I have only so much time in my life and I want to do as much as I can. I can do things faster here as part of 3M and so I get to do more things."[53] In the process of helping to turn ideas into realities, intrapreneurs typically take on official or unofficial management duties and, like managers, must have a good understanding of how to bring about change in organizations.

■ KEY ORGANIZATIONAL CHANGE COMPONENTS

Significant changes or innovations usually involve alterations in one or more of these key components: structure, technology, human resources, and culture (see Figure 11-5).[54] Since these elements are somewhat interrelated, a change in one may create the need for adjustments in others.

Structural Components

Organization structure is the pattern of interactions and coordination designed by management to link the tasks of individuals and groups in achieving organizational goals. Structure includes such factors as the way jobs are defined and

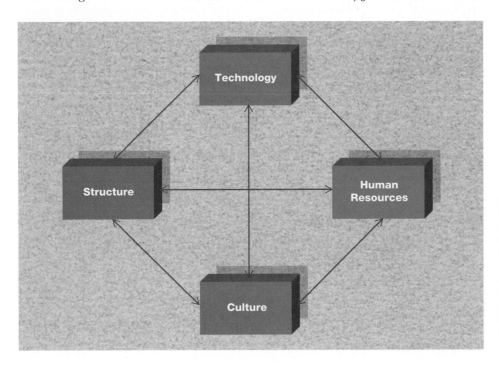

Figure 11-5 *Key components for implementing change. (Adapted from Harold J. Leavitt, "Applied Organization Change in Industry: Structural, Technical, and Human Approaches," in W. W. Cooper, H. J. Leavitt, M. W. Shelly II, eds.,* New Perspectives in Organization Research, *Wiley, New York, 1964, p. 56.)*

Changes in technology can affect the way whole nations do business. By flooding the Chinese market with cellular phones, Motorola is helping the People's Republic of China to bypass a very costly stage in communications evolution: the need to tie every home and business together with copper wire.

clustered into work units and the various mechanisms used to facilitate vertical and horizontal communication (e.g., delegation and the use of interdepartmental teams).[55] Because structures must be adapted as circumstances change, reorganizations are common. Reorganizations influence change by altering the pattern of interactions and coordination. (Specific structural alternatives are discussed in Chapters 8 and 9.) According to one estimate, well over half the companies on *Fortune*'s list of the 1000 largest U.S. corporations underwent a major reorganization during the 1980s, and the reorganizations have continued into the 1990s.[56] Minor structural changes also occur frequently in most large organizations, although many of these changes are made to "fine-tune" a previous reorganization. Research suggests that reorganizations representing a *quantum* change—a change that is both concerted and dramatic—tend to be more frequently associated with subsequent high performance than piecemeal and incremental reorganizations.[57]

Technological Components

Technology involves the knowledge, tools, equipment, and work techniques used by an organization in delivering its products or services. Changes in technology are reflected both in major new products and services (such as computer scanners and Internet connections) and in frequent improvements in current products and services. Technological change is an important factor in international competition. At one point, when two Japanese companies, Yamaha Motor and Honda Motor, were competing for the Japanese motorcycle market, Yamaha declared that it would surpass Honda. Unfortunately for Yamaha, Honda reacted by flooding the Japanese market with new models, sometimes at a rate of one per week. Continually forced to discount obsolete models, Yamaha Motor lost $300 million in 2 years.[58]

Technological innovations are also altering the work methods in organizations. For example, the advent of word-processing equipment and personal

MANAGEMENT SKILLS FOR THE TWENTY-FIRST CENTURY

Checklist for Choosing Intrapreneurial Ideas

Good intrapreneurial ideas must meet three kinds of needs: yours, the customer's, and the company's. Otherwise, the intrapreneurial endeavor is unlikely to be successful. To help test an idea, you can use the following checklist.

FIT WITH YOUR SKILLS AND EXPERIENCE
■ Do you believe in the product or service?
■ Does the need it fills mean something to you personally?
■ Do you like and understand the potential customers?
■ Do you have experience in this type of business?
■ Do the basic success factors of this business fit your skills?
■ Are the tasks of the intrapreneurial project ones you could enjoy doing yourself?
■ Are the people who would work on the project ones you will enjoy working with and supervising?

■ Has the idea begun to take over your imagination and spare time?

FIT WITH CUSTOMERS AND THE MARKET
■ Is there a real customer need?
■ Can you get a price that gives you good margins?
■ Would customers believe in the product coming from your company?
■ Does the product or service you propose produce a clearly perceivable customer benefit that is significantly better than that provided by competing means of satisfying the same basic need?
■ Is there a cost-effective way to get the message and the product to the customer?

FIT WITH THE COMPANY
■ Is there a reason to believe that your company could be very good at the business?
■ Does it fit the company culture?
■ Can you imagine who might sponsor it?
■ Does it look profitable (high margin, low investment)?

■ Will it lead to larger markets and growth?

WHAT TO DO IF YOUR IDEA IS REJECTED
Frequently, as an intrapreneur, you will find that your idea has been rejected. There are a few things you can do:

1 Give up and select a new idea.
2 Listen carefully, understand what is wrong, improve your idea and your presentation, and try again.
3 Find someone else to whom you can present your idea by considering:
   a. Who will benefit most if it works, and can that person be a sponsor?
   b. Who are the potential customers, and will they demand the product?
   c. How can you get to the people who really care about intrapreneurial ideas?[59]

---

computers has eliminated the necessity of retyping whole documents when corrections are needed. Access to computerized data banks is providing more and better information to various specialists, such as doctors, engineers, educators, and research scientists. In the field of biotechnology, robot apprentices are helping scientists study deoxyribonucleic acid (DNA), the raw material of genes, by performing in hours tests that it used to take a trained chemist weeks or months to do.[60] Technological changes often affect the number of employees required and the types of skills they need.

Human Resource Components

Bringing about change in individuals in the workplace is typically aimed at altering the knowledge, skills, perceptions, and behaviors needed to do the job. Changing individuals generally relies on training and development activities, supplemented by performance appraisal and reward systems that reinforce the needed behaviors. Frequently, recruitment and selection systems must be adjusted to reflect the need for individuals with differing skills. Having individuals who possess the knowledge and skills required to handle changing circumstances takes careful planning. For example, Motorola is well known for the extensive training programs it provides employees. One program, the Vice President Institute (VPI), helps vice presidents learn and practice essential innovation and leadership skills. The vice presidents need such skills to sustain Motorola's enviable growth rate. The program also assists Motorola in managing diversity, since vice presidents from different countries and cultures have opportunities to build networks with one another.[61] Characteristics of effective human resource systems are discussed more extensively in Chapter 10. Changes in such systems are necessary to enhance the effectiveness of alterations made in other organizational components, such as structure and technology.

Cultural Components

Organizational culture is a system of shared values, assumptions, beliefs, and norms that unite the organization's members.[62] A number of organizations, such as McDonald's, J. C. Penney, Hewlett-Packard, and Wal-Mart, attribute their success partly to distinctive cultures that are rooted in values articulated by strong founders and reinforced by subsequent top executives.[63] Others have made culture changes based on such factors as visions of their leaders or threats to survival. For example, at one point British Airways was a money-losing, state-owned entity that showed little concern for customers, costs, or productivity. Since then, strong leadership has helped change the culture to one that emphasizes customer focus, productivity, and initiative. In the process, the carrier became a private company and is currently vying to become a major global airline. Thus, the change in culture was part of other major changes that helped transform the airline.[64] Major organizational changes often require alterations in organizational culture (see Chapter 3).

Interrelationship among Components

Although minor changes may pertain to only one of these components of change, major changes are likely to encompass all four of them. This is largely because a major change in one component tends to have implications for the others. You might think of the components as being connected by rubber bands. As you move one component, it creates tensions on the others until they are adjusted accordingly. This interrelationship is illustrated by a large-scale change effort initiated by one of Europe's largest companies, N. V. Philips (see the Case in Point discussion).

CASE IN POINT

CULTURAL REVOLUTION AT EUROPE'S PHILIPS

N. V. Philips, an electronics company headquartered in Eindhoven, Netherlands, and one of *Fortune*'s 50 largest industrial corporations in the world, has undergone massive changes during the past two decades or so. After a quarter of a century of dynamic growth both in volume and in profits, Philips found itself facing new challenges in the 1970s. Sales growth had slowed. Furthermore, international Japanese companies such as Hitachi and Sony represented a serious threat to Philips's aspirations in the United States and the rest of the world.

In studying its Japanese competitors, Philips found several major differences between its operating methods and those of the Japanese. Historically, Philips had based its industrial structure on countries, not continents, and had concentrated on products that catered to local needs. As a result, Philips had small factories in a variety of countries and produced many different products

Organizational changes, technology, use of human resources, and corporate culture have breathed new life into N. V. Philips, a global electronics company based in the Netherlands. Philips has been a leader in developing technology that brings the Internet to the living room TV screen in a consumer-friendly fashion.

geared to local markets. For example, radios sold in Italy differed from those sold in France. The Japanese strategy of producing relatively few products in large factories at low cost was a serious threat to the way that Philips did business. Moreover, higher European labor cost added significantly to the challenge.

At first, little was done. Then, between 1985 and 1990, under Cornelis J. Van der Klugt, chairman and CEO, management took major steps to revamp the company. After reorganizing the structure and centralizing product decision making, the Philips executives began to study the current level of technology in their products. New emphasis was placed on encouraging innovation, improving research and development, and focusing research efforts on areas likely to yield product breakthroughs. Efforts were also made to upgrade methods of production, and plants whose costs could not be lowered significantly were closed.

Training for managers was increased, and developmental assignments were geared to moving managers into responsible positions at a much faster pace. Recruiting was widened to attract the best scientific talent available, and human resource systems were designed to reinforce the need for innovations that could be turned into marketable products.

At the same time, Philips took steps to abandon its paternalistic culture, which in 1970 had included such benefits as delivery of employees' babies by company midwives, use of company nursery schools, and visits from company doctors if employees or their parents became sick. In place of complacency and self-satisfaction, the top executives tried to instill a new corporate culture based on the belief that the organization must strive continuously to improve quality throughout the company if it is to compete effectively. Despite the changes, Van der Klugt was forced to resign in 1990 after profits fell substantially below his optimistic forecasts.

The new chairman, Jan D. Timmer, previously earned the nickname "Hurricane Gilbert" from Dutch newspapers because of his vigorous efforts in leading Philips's consumer electronics division to high performance. Under his leadership, top managers instituted a 20 percent cut of Philips's worldwide work force, eliminating close to 55,000 jobs. Timmer initiated a major reeducation program, Operation Centurion, aimed at focusing managers on profits. The company sold money-losing divisions, increased its focus on new technologies, and returned to profitability. Timmer's steadfast refusal to sell the semiconductor division paid off when it made a spectacular turnaround. Now, though, the division faces a possible slowdown in the chip market, and a current slump in consumer electronics is pressuring company earnings. To increase prospects for long-term growth, Timmer placed greater emphasis on microchip-related areas, such as multimedia, software, and telecommunications. The risks were high as Timmer retired. His successor, Cor Boonstra, head of Asia/Pacific operations, has experience in an area of targeted growth for Philips.[65]   ■ ■ ■

In the Philips situation, when the managers began to make major changes in the company, they found it necessary to alter all four components of change: structure, technology, human resources, and culture. At first, the Philips managers were reacting largely to external forces, rather than using planned change and an effective change management and innovation process.

Of course, major efforts involving innovation and change also require an in-depth understanding about how to motivate people. In the next chapter, we explore the motivational processes and examine how managers can become effective motivators of others.

■ CHAPTER SUMMARY

Largely because of increasing competition, the management of change and innovation is becoming more and more important to the survival and prosperity of organizations. Change is any alteration in the status quo, while innovation is a new idea applied to initiating or improving a process, product, or service. Forces for change can be external or internal. As they grow, organizations tend to go through four life cycles, or predictable stages of development: entrepreneurial, collectivity, formalization and control, and elaboration of structure. Movement through these stages requires changes in methods of operating, but these changes may inhibit innovation unless managers plan and encourage it. Failure to adapt to changing conditions may lead to organizational termination through bankruptcy, voluntary liquidation, and merger, acquisition, or takeover.

Although managers may sometimes be forced to react to unpredictable situations, effective managers attempt to plan for major changes and innovations whenever possible. They typically follow an eight-step process: (1) gain recognition of the problem or opportunity, (2) line up powerful sponsor(s), (3) develop and communicate a vision, (4) empower others to act out the vision, (5) prepare to overcome resistance, (6) plan for and reward visible progress, (7) consolidate improvements and facilitate further change, and (8) monitor and institutionalize changes.

Organizational development (OD) is a change effort aimed at enhancing interpersonal working relationships and organizational effectiveness through planned interventions made with the help of a change agent who is well versed in the behavioral sciences. Organizational development involves three major stages: diagnosis, intervention, and evaluation. Four intervention techniques used by OD specialists include process consultation, team building, third-party intervention, and technostructural activities.

In planning to overcome resistance to change, managers must understand why people are resistant. Major reasons are self-interest, misunderstanding and lack of trust, different assessments, and low tolerance for change. Managers must also have a knowledge of methods for overcoming resistance to change. These include education and communication, participation and involvement, facilitation and support, negotiation and agreement, manipulation and co-optation, and explicit and implicit coercion. Force-field analysis is helpful in understanding the driving forces and restraining forces that account for the status quo. It is frequently more effective to try to reduce the restraining forces than to attempt to increase the driving forces for change. To gain a competitive advantage through innovation, four factors are important. Innovations should be difficult to imitate, reflect market realities, exploit timing characteristics of the industry, and rely on capabilities and technologies that are readily accessible to the organization. Intrapreneurship is growing in importance in organizations, and intrapreneurs have certain characteristics that are somewhat learnable, such as being visionary, action-oriented, and willing to set goals associated with new ideas.

Major changes usually involve adjustments to one or more of the key organizational change components: structure, technology, human resources, and culture. Since the components are somewhat interrelated, a change in one frequently calls for adjustments in others to carry out successful change and innovation efforts.

■ QUESTIONS FOR DISCUSSION AND REVIEW

1 Explain the difference between change and innovation. Think of some changes that you have noticed on campus in the past year. In each case, explain the extent to which the forces for change were external or internal. Which changes would you classify as innovations? Why?

2 Describe the four life-cycle stages of organizations. Choose an organization with which you are familiar and determine its stage in the organizational life cycle. On the basis of your analysis, what changes are likely to be needed in the future?

3 Explain the eight-step model of the change and innovation process. Use this model to develop a plan for getting a student group to take advantage of an unexploited opportunity.

4 Explain the concept of organizational development. Suppose that you are helping with an OD project at your college or university. What major steps will be involved? What data-collection methods would you suggest for the diagnosis step?

5 Delineate the major intervention techniques used by OD specialists. On the basis of the information that you have regarding the cultural revolution at Philips, what types of OD interventions might have helped the company make appropriate changes?

6 Explain the major approaches for overcoming resistance to change. Suppose you are a manager in a small manufacturing plant that is facing increased competition from foreign-made products and needs to increase productivity. Design a plan for overcoming employee resistance to the changes and innovations that are necessary to increase productivity. What is your most preferred strategy? What is your least preferred strategy?

7 Explain force-field analysis. Suggest three change situations that it might help you analyze.

8 Specify how an organization can use innovation to bring about competitive advantage. What possibilities for using innovation as a competitive advantage tool appear to exist at your college or university?

9 Describe some common characteristics of intrapreneurs. Assuming that these characteristics are learnable, how might you go about acquiring them?

10 Enumerate the key organizational components that must usually be adjusted in implementing major changes and innovations. Identify a recent change at your college or university that was aimed mainly at one of these components. To what extent did the change in that component alter the others?

■ DISCUSSION QUESTIONS FOR CHAPTER OPENING CASE

1 Would you characterize the approach to change and innovation at Merck as reactive or planned? What evidence exists to support your view?

2 At what stage in the organizational life cycle would you place Merck? Why? What changes are likely to be needed in the future?

3 To what extent does Merck appear to use innovation as a source of competitive advantage? What advice would you give to Merck about how the company should handle this issue in the future?

■ EXERCISES FOR MANAGING IN THE TWENTY-FIRST CENTURY

EXERCISE 1
SKILL BUILDING: DIAGNOSING RESISTANCE TO CHANGE

 Understanding why people resist change is key to implementing new structures, procedures, methods, and technologies. Five of the major reasons people resist change are indicated below. The typical comments associated with these reasons are listed. Indicate the reason that would normally be associated with each of the comments.

Self-interest   Different assessments
Misunderstanding   Lack of trust
Tolerance (low) for change

1 _____ I don't want to take the job because my family will have to move again.

2 _____ We've done it that way for years.

3 _____ I still have trouble following the explanation about why we need this new complicated machine.

4 _____ Management thinks it's an improvement; I have a different view.

5 _____ Upper management won't admit it, but this merger will cost us jobs.

6 _____ Their explanation wasn't very clear regarding how working with them is going to help our unit.

7 _____ The last time they asked to make a change like this, our benefits ended up being reduced.

8 _____ It appears that producing buggy whips is not what our organization should be doing in 2 years.

9 _____ I just perfected using this method, and now there's another change to cope with.

10 _____ I can't see where that job will help my career.

11 _____ I'm not sure my manager has been candid about the likely impact of the new procedure.

12 _____ Marketing believes we need field representatives, engineering doesn't believe they are required, and production wants to control costs. Are they really necessary?

EXERCISE 2
MANAGEMENT EXERCISE: FORCE-FIELD ANALYSIS

Specification

Think about a situation in which you would like to make a change or institute an innovation, but you face resistance. (The situation might involve getting a better grade in a course, instituting an innovative project in a student organization, overcoming a challenge at work, or improving a relationship with a peer or friend.) Write a sentence or two describing the status quo. Then write a brief description of the situation as you would like it to be if you could change it.

Analysis

List the major driving forces, the factors that pressure *for* change, and then list the major restraining forces, the factors that pressure *against* change. Draw a force-field analysis diagram like the one shown in Figure 11-4. Remember, the wider the arrow, the stronger the force.

Solution

Select two or three restraining forces in your diagram and develop means for reducing the degree of resistance. Be prepared to explain your diagram and solutions to another class member, who will act as your consultant.[66]

CONCLUDING CASE 1

BANKAMERICA WIDENS ITS HORIZONS

The BankAmerica Corporation's roots are unusual for a major bank. Shortly after the turn of the century, its founder, a successful young executive named A. P. Giannini, became a member of the board of directors of a savings and loan in the North Beach area of San Francisco. A. P. soon ran into difficulty when he tried to convince the other directors to extend banking services to everyone, not just the relatively rich. Rebuffed, he left the board and started his own bank, the Bank of America, which Giannini referred to as the "Bank of the Little People."

Giannini's idea of banking included many innovations, such as advertising, having bank officers sit in the lobby to help customers, and pioneering time-plan loans. By 1940, 1 out of every 3 Californians was a Bank of America customer. When Giannini died in 1949, he left behind a legacy of visionary leadership and human concern.

The next few decades were characterized by heavy regulation in the banking industry, and the organizational culture at the Bank of America gradually changed. During the 1970s the Bank of America emerged as the BankAmerica Corporation. Under A. W. Clausen, a CEO whose authoritarian ways earned him the title "the dictator," BankAmerica became the most profitable banking company in the country. When Clausen left in 1981 to head the World Bank, BankAmerica looked great on paper. Yet critics argued that Clausen had made too many high-risk loans, spent virtually nothing on new technology such as automated teller machines, and allowed BankAmerica to become the most undercapitalized major bank in the country.

Samuel H. Armacost, Clausen's handpicked successor, was a 42-year-old banking wonder whose rise at BankAmerica had been meteoric. As Armacost took over, however, the banking industry was becoming increasingly deregulated. Troubles stemming from the previous regime began to show up in the form of earnings declines. Faced with these difficulties, management hired consultants to assess the corporate culture. They found that many employees believed a job with BankAmerica was a job for life, that they didn't have to be particularly concerned with performance, and that it was not smart to try new approaches and risk failure.

With Armacost at the helm, earnings declined steadily, largely because of the actions of his predecessor. Armacost did build a major automated teller network that helped the bank catch up technologically. Still, critics argue that he was hesitant about firing anyone, including incompetent executives, and was unable to influence the large BankAmerica bureaucracy to support the necessary strategic directions. When the bank experienced an unexpected $640 million loss, the board reluctantly asked for Armacost's resignation and took the unusual move of bringing back the former CEO, Clausen.

Clausen immediately brought in several top managers from the bank's aggressive archrival, Wells Fargo & Company. The bank became extremely proactive in pushing retail banking through a variety of new services, massive advertising, and promotions. Costs were cut by trimming 33,000 employees from the payroll. Branches were given quotas for selling new bank products and services. Branch managers who did not meet targets were fired. Profitability quickly returned, and Clausen announced his retirement in 1990.

Under his successor, Richard M. Rosenberg, a marketing specialist who joined the firm in 1987, BankAmerica paid $4.7 billion to merge with Security Pacific Corporation. Because of culture differences and sheer size, the merger of the two large banks proved more difficult than anticipated. The situation was compounded by the discovery that many bad real estate loans had been made by Security Pacific. Next Rosenberg acquired Chicago-based Continental Bank Corp. For a period Rosenberg was criticized as profits lagged; but then BankAmerica began logging impressive profits, and its assets surpassed the $230 billion mark. As Rosenberg announced his impending retirement, his successor, David A. Coulter, took over. Coulter was credited with overseeing a very smooth integration of BankAmerica's and Continental Bank's wholesale operations. He had a reputation for being fair and having excellent people skills. Coulter began by calling for an end to the notorious turf wars and office politics that had long distracted senior executives at the bank; instead he emphasized the need for teamwork. One industry analyst noted that "it's his style to make changes in an evolutionary, not a revolutionary, way." Meanwhile, BankAmerica received federal permission to operate federal savings banks in all 50 states and was operating retail commercial banks in 10 states. Abroad, BankAmerica continued to maintain a strong presence in Asia.[67]

QUESTIONS FOR CONCLUDING CASE 1

1 Where would you place BankAmerica in the organizational life cycle? What changes does your analysis suggest?

2 How would you characterize top management's approach to change and innovation? How might the bank improve the change and innovation process?

3 How useful would organizational development be in this situation? How might one proceed with such a program?

CONCLUDING CASE 2

GE LIGHTING TUNGSRAM VENTURE STRUGGLES "FOR A BRIGHTER WORLD"

In an effort to obtain a foothold in the European market for lightbulbs, General Electric bought a controlling interest in Hungary's lightbulb maker, Tungsram, in 1990 and assumed full ownership in 1993. Even though the company had previously operated under a Communist regime, it held a respectable 9 to 10 percent of the western European lightbulb market.

GE has faced a formidable challenge in transforming Tungsram into an integral part of GE. Under communism, virtually all decision making had been centralized at the top. Workers were expected to do what they were told and to avoid taking initiative. In contrast, GE encourages employees to be innovative and take charge of solving problems. Hence a major culture change was needed at Tungsram.

The first issue, however, was paring the excessive number of workers. Hungarian newspapers had made dire predictions regarding layoffs when GE bought its controlling interest. Although the 17,600-member work force was trimmed by more than 5000 during the first 18 months, most of the cuts were made through early retirements, attrition, and retraining. Unfortunately, eastern European markets, which accounted for 30 percent of Tungsram's sales, collapsed suddenly in 1992 due to economic problems related to a shift to capitalism. Meanwhile, inflation rose to 30 percent, causing major increases in local costs. These events forced layoffs of close to 4000 employees at Tungsram, resulting in strained relations with the union. The firm lost $105 million in 1992.

Under communism, Tungsram had concentrated on generating hard currency and paid little attention to cost, productivity, and profit. With the changeover, GE managers from the United States came to help Tungsram managers set up measurement systems based on such critical indicators as shrinkage, costs, quality, and productivity. GE also made numerous investments totaling around $350 million to upgrade technology and equipment as well as fund new-product development.

Another area requiring attention was internal communication, which was almost nonexistent compared with most western companies. Under communism, most of the information had been transmitted to employees by the Communist party or the Young Communist League—even data regarding such issues as production goals and quality control. In the joint venture, consultants helped Tungsram managers set up such basics as company newspapers, bulletin boards, and periodic meetings.

Another concern was Tungsram's lack of a performance appraisal system and a merit pay system. GE's policy is to appraise everyone, even production workers, wherever union rules allow it. At Tungsram, the independent trade union that replaced the former communist-controlled organization agreed to the performance appraisal system, but pay became a source of contention for the union, which has been used to automatic pay raises based on job title and seniority.

Training was another critical ingredient. About 1500 of Tungsram's managerial employees, including first-level supervisors, attended GE or western-style management courses covering such areas as how to be a boss, how to set goals, and how to delegate. For many, the training included trips to GE factories in the United States. About 300 to 400 workers were also sent for training in particular manufacturing techniques. In the process, they, too, gained exposure to other ways of doing things. Many Americans were sent to Tungsram on special projects, furthering the exchange of ideas.

Through such efforts, Tungsram, which exports 90 percent of its production, has helped increase GE's market share in Europe to 18 percent. The company has spent $300 million to build a new major manufacturing complex at Nagykanizsa, Hungary, near the former Yugoslav border. Moreover, GE has been moving some of its European manufacturing capacity from Britain, Austria, and Germany to Hungary. GE has been able to negotiate continued tax breaks from the Hungarian government in return for a pledge to invest at least $78 million over the next 5 years. Still, relations with the government and the union continue to be somewhat fragile. Tungsram plays a key role in GE Lighting's global strategy. Meanwhile the company is under considerable competitive pressure from Osram, owned by Siemens, and Philips. Tungsram will need to help GE Lighting be first or second in its industry—a requirement of the GE parent company—in order to secure its future.[68]

QUESTIONS FOR CONCLUDING CASE 2

1 What external and internal forces for change are impacting Tungsram?

2 To what extent does GE appear to have followed the eight-step model of change management and innovation in attempting to integrate Tungsram into the GE organization?

3 What strategies for overcoming resistance to change are evident in the Tungsram situation? What else could be done?

LEARNING OBJECTIVES

After studying this chapter, you should be able to:

■ Define motivation and outline the motivation process.

■ Compare and contrast the three major need theories of motivation.

■ Describe each of the three major cognitive theories of motivation and explain how they facilitate the motivation process.

■ Explain the reinforcement theory of motivation and discuss how it can be helpful to managers.

■ Discuss the social learning theory of motivation.

GAINING THE EDGE

"ASPIRATIONS" MOTIVATE AT LEVI STRAUSS

Levi Strauss is famous not only for its Levi jeans but also for its longtime commitment to social responsibility and to its employees. The San Francisco–based company was founded in 1850 by the great-great-granduncle of the present chairman and CEO, Robert D. Haas. It is now privately held as a result of a management-led leveraged buyout completed in 1985. In helping to more clearly focus company values after the buyout, Haas oversaw the development of the Levi Strauss Aspirations Statement.

The initial section of the statement sets a theme of shared values that guide management and the work force as they build their own and the company's future:

> We all want a company that our people are proud of and committed to, where all employees have an opportunity to contribute, learn, grow, and advance based on merit, not politics or background. We want our people to feel respected, treated fairly, listened to, and involved. Above all, we want satisfaction from our accomplishments and friendships, balanced personal and professional lives, and to have fun in our endeavors.

The statement goes on to spell out specific areas where action is necessary to make these shared values and aspirations a reality. For example, the statement calls for valuing a diverse work force, recognizing individual and team contributions, and enforcing stated standards of ethical behavior.

Haas says that the company's strategy in the late 1970s and early 1980s emphasized diversification (such as acquiring new companies and creating new brands). "Our people did what they were asked to do, but the problem was they didn't believe in it," notes Haas. Recently, management has been listening more closely to suppliers, customers, and employees. As a result, Haas says, "We have redefined our business strategy to focus on core products, and we have articulated the values that the company stands for—what we call our Aspirations." The new approach has elicited strong support from employees. The reason, says Haas, is "because it's what they *want* to do."

Motivation energizes a work force. These employees at Levi Strauss are empowered to make decisions and exercise initiative on the work floor. An incentive plan rewards every employee if certain company goals are reached. A clear corporate focus and shared values, as expressed in the company's Aspirations Statement, are additional motivating factors.

The Aspirations Statement also emphasizes empowerment, whereby decision making is shifted to the people who are closest to the product and the customer. Haas argues that the traditional, hierarchical command and control approach is no longer effective in today's rapidly changing environment. Such an approach cannot adequately anticipate and respond to shifting customer needs and market changes. Instead, he says, "people have to take responsibility, exercise initiative, be accountable for their own success and for that of the company as a whole." At the same time, the Aspirations Statement gives strong consideration to the needs of the work force in such areas as gaining satisfaction from accomplishments and balancing personal and professional lives. In keeping with the spirit of the Aspirations Statement, Haas recently announced an unusual employee reward program. If privately held Levi Strauss & Co. reaches cumulative cash flow of $7.6 billion for the next 6 years, each of the company's 37,500 employees throughout the world will received a full year's pay as a bonus.[1] ■ ■ ■

By considering the needs of the work force as well as the company, the Aspirations Statement fosters **motivation,** the force that energizes behavior, gives direction to behavior, and underlies the tendency to persist. This definition recognizes that in order to achieve goals, individuals must be sufficiently stimulated and energetic, must have a clear focus on what is to be achieved, and must be willing to commit their energy for a long enough period of time to realize their aim.[2] Since the leading function of management involves influencing others to work toward organizational goals, motivation is an important aspect of that function.

In this chapter, we explore the basic nature of motivation and consider a general model of the motivation process. Next, we examine theories of motivation that are based on individual needs, such as the need for achievement. We also look into motivational approaches that emphasize cognitive aspects, focusing on how individuals think about where to direct their efforts and how to evaluate outcomes. We then analyze reinforcement theory, with its emphasis on the power of rewards. Finally, we review a more contemporary extension called social learning theory.

Motivation The force that energizes behavior, gives direction to behavior, and underlies the tendency to persist

■ THE NATURE OF MOTIVATION

Because motivation is an internal force, we cannot measure the motivation of others directly. Instead, we typically infer whether or not other individuals are motivated by watching their behavior. For example, we might conclude that an engineering friend who works late every evening, goes to the office on weekends, and incessantly reads the latest engineering journals is highly motivated to do well. Conversely, we might suspect that an engineering friend who is usually the first one out the door at quitting time, rarely puts in extra hours, and generally spends little time reading up on new developments in the field is not very motivated to excel.

In the end, how successful these two engineers actually are with their respective projects is likely to depend not only on their motivation, as reflected in effort expended, but also on their ability to handle the engineering subject matter. Furthermore, working conditions can affect their performance. Numerous interruptions, extra assignments, or cramped office space may negatively influence performance. On the other hand, a quiet place to work, the help of assistants, and ample support resources, such as equipment, may have a positive effect on project performance. Thus actual performance is likely to

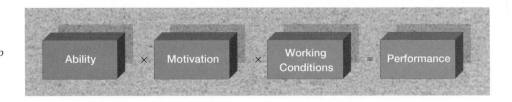

Figure 12-1 *The relationship between performance and ability, motivation, and working conditions.*

be a function of ability, motivation, and working conditions, as shown in Figure 12-1.[3]

As a result, it is important that managers hire individuals who have the ability to do what is required. Then the management challenge is providing working conditions that nurture and support individual motivation to work toward organizational goals.

The main elements in the motivation process are shown in Figure 12-2. As the diagram indicates, our inner needs (such as needs for food, companionship, and growth) and cognitions (such as knowledge and thoughts about efforts we might expend and rewards we might receive) lead to various behaviors. Assuming that the behaviors are appropriate to the situation, they may result in rewards. The rewards then help reinforce our behaviors, fulfill our needs, and influence our cognitions about the linkages between our behaviors and possible future rewards. Conversely, lack of rewards may lead to unfulfilled needs, leave behaviors unreinforced, and influence our thinking about where to expend our efforts in the future. Since motivation is a complex phenomenon, major motivational theories address the various elements in the process

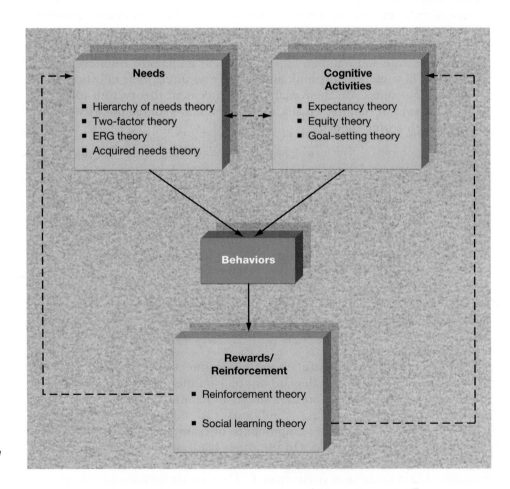

Figure 12-2 *The motivation process.*

(see Figure 12-2). In order to better understand the implications of these elements for managers, we explore the respective theories in subsequent sections of this chapter, beginning with need theories.

■ NEED THEORIES

What makes a person such as Linda Wachner, president of Warnaco, Inc., overcome adolescent spinal surgery that left her in a body cast for over a year, tackle the challenge of successfully turning around the ailing U.S. division of Max Factor & Company, and work 14-hour days to eventually reach her lofty position as head of a Fortune 500 apparel conglomerate?[4] What possessed Kemmons Wilson, founder of the Holiday Inns, to start building another hotel chain at age 75?[5] Need theories argue that we behave the way we do because of internal needs we are attempting to fulfill. These theories are sometimes called *content theories* of motivation because they specify *what* motivates individuals (i.e., the content of needs). In this section, we explore four prominent theories that examine what needs individuals are likely to have and how these needs operate as motivators: hierarchy of needs theory, two-factor theory, ERG theory, and acquired-needs theory.

Hierarchy of Needs Theory

One of the most widely known theories of motivation is the **hierarchy of needs theory,** developed by psychologist Abraham Maslow and popularized during the early 1960s. It argues that individual needs form a five-level hierarchy (shown in Figure 12-3).

According to this hierarchy, our first need is for survival, so we concentrate on basic **physiological needs,** such as food, water, and shelter, until we feel fairly sure that these needs are covered. Next, we concern ourselves with **safety needs,** which pertain to the desire to feel safe, secure, and free from threats to our existence. Once we feel reasonably safe and secure, we turn our attention to relationships with others in order to fulfill our **belongingness needs,** which

Hierarchy of needs theory A theory (developed by Maslow) that argues that individual needs form a five-level hierarchy

Physiological needs Survival needs such as food, water, and shelter

Safety needs Needs that pertain to the desire to feel safe, secure, and free from threats to our existence

Belongingness needs Needs that involve the desire to affiliate with and be accepted by others

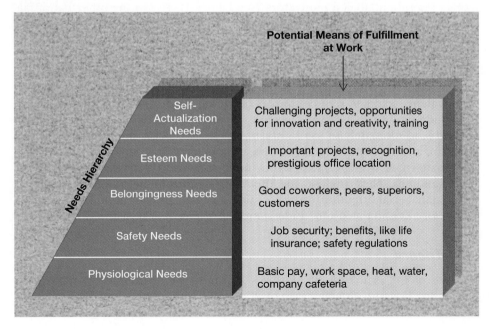

Figure 12-3 *Maslow's hierarchy of needs.*

Esteem needs Needs related to the two-pronged desire to have a positive self-image and to have our contributions valued and appreciated by others

Self-actualization needs Needs that pertain to the requirement of developing our capabilities and reaching our full potential

involve the desire to affiliate with and be accepted by others. With support from loved ones, we focus on **esteem needs,** which are related to the two-pronged desire to have a positive self-image and to have our contributions valued and appreciated by others. Finally, we reach the highest level, **self-actualization needs,** which pertain to the requirement of developing our capabilities and reaching our full potential. We concern ourselves with such matters as testing our creativity, seeing our innovative ideas translated into reality, pursuing new knowledge, and developing our talents in uncharted directions. Needs at this highest level are never completely fulfilled, because as we work to develop our capabilities, both our potential and our needs for self-actualization grow stronger. Some possible work-related means of fulfilling the various needs in the hierarchy are shown in Figure 12-3.

Maslow recognized that a need might not have to be completely fulfilled before we start directing our attention to the next level in the hierarchy. At the same time, he argued that once we have essentially fulfilled a need, that need ceases to be a motivator and we begin to feel tension to fulfill needs at the next level.

While Maslow's hierarchy has stimulated thinking about the various needs that individuals have, it has some serious shortcomings. Research suggests that needs may cluster into two or three categories, rather than five. Also, the hierarchy of needs may not be the same for everyone. Entrepreneurs frequently pursue their dreams for years despite the relative deprivation of lower-level needs. Finally, individuals often seem to work on satisfying several needs at once, even though some needs may be more important than others at a given point in time.[6]

Two-Factor Theory

Building on the work of Maslow, psychologist Frederick Herzberg interviewed accountants and engineers working in the Pittsburgh vicinity.[7] He asked them to relate situations in which they felt particularly good about their jobs and situations in which they felt particularly bad about their jobs. Analysis of the interview data revealed a distinct pattern. Factors that seemed to make individuals feel satisfied with their jobs were associated with the content of the job. These factors were then labeled **motivators** (see Figure 12-4). On the other hand, factors that seemed to make individuals feel dissatisfied were associated with the job context. These were labeled **hygiene factors** (see Figure 12-4).

Motivators Factors that seem to make individuals feel satisfied with their jobs

Hygiene factors Factors that seem to make individuals feel dissatisfied with their jobs

Two-factor theory Herzberg's theory that hygiene factors are necessary to keep workers from feeling dissatisfied, but only motivators can lead workers to feel satisfied and motivated

Herzberg's **two-factor theory** argues that hygiene factors are necessary to keep workers from feeling dissatisfied, but only motivators can lead workers to feel satisfied and motivated. The implications for managers are clear: (1) provide hygiene factors to reduce sources of worker dissatisfaction, and (2) be sure to include motivators because they are the only factors that can motivate workers and lead ultimately to job satisfaction. The two-factor theory has been criticized mainly on the grounds that researchers have been unable to obtain the same pattern of hygiene factors and motivators when they use other types of study methods. Nevertheless, the theory is significant because it has helped focus managerial attention on the critical need to provide motivators and, in doing so, has enhanced our understanding of motivation in the workplace.

ERG theory An alternative (proposed by Alderfer) to Maslow's hierarchy of needs theory which argues that there are three levels of individual needs

ERG Theory

Because of the criticisms of Maslow's hierarchy of needs theory, motivation researcher Clayton Alderfer proposed an alternative known as **ERG theory.**[8] The name stems from combining Maslow's five levels of needs into three lev-

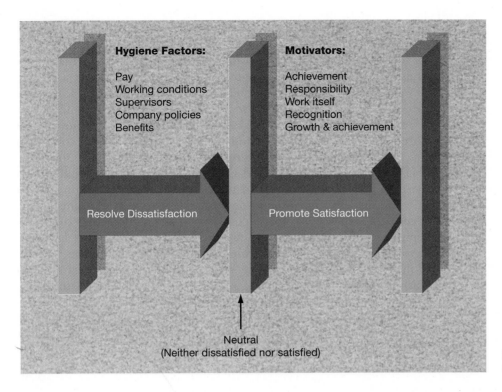

Figure 12-4 *Herzberg's two-factory theory.*

els: existence, relatedness, and growth. **Existence needs** include physiological desires, such as food and water, and work-related material desires, such as pay, fringe benefits, and physical working conditions. **Relatedness needs** address our relationships with significant others, such as families, friendship groups, work groups, and professional groups. They deal with our desire to be accepted by others, achieve mutual understanding on matters that are important to us, and exercise some influence over those with whom we interact on an ongoing basis.[9] **Growth needs** impel creativity and innovation, along with the desire to have a productive impact on our surroundings.

According to ERG theory, we generally tend to concentrate first on our existence requirements. As existence needs are resolved, we have more energy available for concentrating on relatedness needs. Then, as relatedness needs are somewhat fulfilled, we have the energy and support needed to pursue growth needs. Thus ERG theory incorporates a **satisfaction-progression principle** similar to that of Maslow's hierarchy, since satisfaction of one level of need encourages concern with the next level.

Aside from focusing on three need levels instead of five, ERG theory differs from the hierarchy of needs theory in three significant ways. First, although the general notion of a hierarchy is retained, Alderfer's theory argues that we can be concerned with more than one need category at the same time. Needs at lower levels are not necessarily fairly well satisfied before we concern ourselves with other needs. However, satisfaction of lower-level needs can be helpful in allowing us to devote our attention to higher-level needs. For example, even if a worker has skipped lunch and is extremely hungry, she or he may still be primarily concerned with solving a challenging customer problem. At some point the hunger may interfere with the worker's problem-solving efforts. Second, ERG theory is more flexible, since it acknowledges that some individuals' needs may occur in a different order than that posited by the ERG framework. Inventor Godfrey Hounsfield worked so intensely while developing the CAT

Existence needs Needs that include the various forms of material and physiological desires, such as food and water, as well as such work-related forms as pay, fringe benefits, and physical working conditions

Relatedness needs Needs that address our relationships with significant others, such as families, friendship groups, work groups, and professional groups

Growth needs Needs that impel creativity and innovation, along with the desire to have a productive impact on our surroundings

Satisfaction-progression principle A principle that states that satisfaction of one level of need encourages concern with the next level

**Frustration-regression
principle**   A principle that
states that if we are *continually*
frustrated in our attempts to
satisfy a higher-level need, we
may cease to be concerned
about that need

scanner at Britain-based EMI, Ltd., that his boss became worried about his
health and ordered him to take a vacation (see Chapter 5 for further details).[10]
Third, ERG theory incorporates a **frustration-regression principle.** This principle states that if we are *continually* frustrated in our attempts to satisfy a higher-
level need, we may cease to be concerned about that need. Instead, we may
regress to exhibiting greater concern for a lower-level need that is more concrete and seemingly more within our grasp. For example, an employee may
become more concerned with establishing strong relationships with coworkers
if continuing efforts to obtain more interesting work are ignored by the boss.

Both Maslow's hierarchy theory and ERG theory are extremely difficult to
test because they involve measuring and tracking individuals' changing needs
and fulfillment levels over time. So far, the limited research on ERG theory has
generally been supportive.[11] If ERG theory is correct in predicting that individuals attempt to fulfill multiple needs at the same time, motivating individuals is likely to require that a variety of means for need fulfillment be offered.
Because of the frustration-regression aspect of ERG theory, managers need to
be particularly concerned with providing opportunities to satisfy growth needs,
lest employees cease to be interested in them. At Levi Strauss, growth issues figure prominently in the Aspirations Statement as the company shifts to
increased teamwork in the face of growing global competition. A different, but
also challenging, situation exists at Original Copy Centers, Inc. (see the Case
in Point discussion).

CASE IN POINT ORIGINAL WAYS OF MOTIVATING BEHAVIOR

At Original Copy Centers, Inc., a fast-growing corporate and legal copy service
in Cleveland, owners Nancy Vetrone and Robert Bieniek use all the originality
they can muster to motivate their more than 145 employees. The workers perform relatively mundane and repetitive tasks, such as operating copy machines
or picking up and delivering materials. Noting that the average age of their
employees is under 30 and that many are single, Vetrone and Bieniek came up
with an unusual, but well-appreciated, employee amenity: a laundry room at
work where staff members can wash and dry their clothes. Other amenities
include a six-person sauna, locker rooms and showers, a minitheater, a video
library, a game room with a billiards table, an exercise room, company personal
computers for employee use, various arcade games, a kitchen, and free coffee.
Says Bieniek, "We hope that the Original work environment is as nice or better than their private living conditions, so they'll be in a hurry to get here and
they won't be in a hurry to leave."

To afford delivery personnel greater status, these employees are called
"corporate couriers" and wear smart, professional-looking uniforms. They seem
to view themselves as part of the image of a fast-moving company. Since they
are the kingpins in Original's obsessive concern with timely pickups and deliveries, couriers are trained to talk with customers and learn receptionists' names.
They have helped develop detailed maps of the inside of every commercial
building in Cleveland, a factor that speeds up the almost 300 trips per day made
to customer locations. Company employees at all levels (including couriers,
receptionists, and production staff) are invited to assist in attracting new customers by staffing the Original booth at trade shows and dispensing "I'm an
Original" stickers.

Other methods that ensure growth and loyalty within the Original orga-

How do you motivate workers who must perform routine tasks day after day? For one thing, the owners of Original Copy Centers in Cleveland, Ohio, try to make working conditions as pleasant as possible, with such amenities as a laundry room, a sauna, a game room, an exercise room, and a mini-theater. Their delivery personnel, called "corporate couriers," wear smart-looking uniforms (as shown here) and are treated as an important part of the firm. One result of the company's concern with employee morale is extremely low turnover.

nization are having employees train on and use personal computers, trusting employees to complete their own time cards, allowing flexible schedules and up to 20 overtime hours per week, and encouraging staff members to come up with new ideas that involve the successful company slogan, "I'm an Original." These efforts to motivate employees appear to be working. Counter to industry trends, turnover at Original is extremely low. Further, members of the staff are generally willing to work extra hours and postpone weekend plans to help out in emergencies. As a result, the firm has earned a reputation for exceptionally fast copy-service turnaround and has experienced rapid growth.[12]

■■■

Acquired-Needs Theory

While the hierarchy of needs and ERG theories view certain needs as an inherent part of our makeup, psychologist David C. McClelland offers a different perspective, **acquired-needs theory.** McClelland argues that our needs are acquired or learned on the basis of our life experiences. Although these needs tend to be a product of a variety of conditions to which we are exposed, sometimes even a specific event can profoundly influence our desires. For example, Estee Lauder, the billionaire baroness of the beauty-supply industry, was strongly motivated to succeed by a chance incident that occurred during the depression. While selling her uncle's skin cream in a Manhattan beauty salon, she (then Josephine Esther Mentzer) admired the blouse of the owner and asked where the woman had purchased it. The owner curtly replied that it was an irrelevant question because a salesgirl would never be able to afford such a blouse. Those words fanned the young saleswoman's desire for achievement. "I wouldn't have become Estee Lauder if it hadn't been for her," she says.[13]

For more than three decades, McClelland has mainly studied three needs: achievement, affiliation, and power. He measures these needs using the Thematic Apperception Test (TAT), in which test takers write stories about pictures that are purposely ambiguous. The stories are then scored according to the achievement, affiliation, and power themes that they contain. The assumption is that individuals write about themes that are important to them.[14] For most

Acquired-needs theory
A theory (developed by McClelland) stating that our needs are acquired or learned on the basis of our life experiences

Sports participants tend to exhibit high levels of all the acquired needs identified by David McClelland: the need for achievement (playing well), the need for affiliation (teamwork), and the need for institutional power (compiling a winning record in a league).

Need for achievement (nAch)
The desire to accomplish challenging tasks and achieve a standard of excellence in one's work

Need for affiliation (nAff)
The desire to maintain warm, friendly relationships with others

of us, test results would indicate a blending of the achievement, affiliation, and power needs, rather than a high level of just one of these needs and the absence of the others.

McClelland's initial work centered on the **need for achievement (nAch)**, the desire to accomplish challenging tasks and achieve a standard of excellence in one's work. Individuals with a high nAch typically seek competitive situations in which they can achieve results through their own efforts and can receive relatively immediate feedback on how they are doing. They like to pursue moderately difficult goals and take calculated risks. Yet, contrary to what is sometimes believed, high nAchs typically avoid *extremely* difficult goals because of the substantial risk of failure.[15] Since they like problems that require innovative and novel solutions, high-nAch individuals can be a valuable source of creativity and innovative ideas in organizations.[16]

Estimates are that only about 10 percent of the U.S. population has a high nAch. Managers who want to motivate high achievers need to make sure that such individuals have challenging, but reachable, goals that allow relatively immediate feedback about achievement progress. McClelland argues that high-nAch individuals may not be motivated by money per se (because they derive satisfaction mainly from their achievements). Nevertheless, they may still place considerable importance on money as a source of feedback on how they are doing.[17]

To a lesser extent, McClelland's work has also addressed the **need for affiliation (nAff)**, the desire to maintain warm, friendly relationships with others. High-nAff individuals are particularly likely to gravitate toward professions that involve a large amount of interaction with others, such as health care, teaching, sales, and counseling. To motivate high-nAff individuals, managers need to provide them with a cooperative, supportive work environment in which they can meet both performance expectations and their high affiliation needs by working with others. High-nAff individuals can be particular assets in situations that require a high level of cooperation with and support of others, including clients and customers.[18]

As he studied various needs, McClelland gradually came to view the **need for power (nPow),** the desire to influence others and control one's environment, as a particularly important motivator in organizations. Need for power has two forms, personal and institutional. Individuals with a high need for **personal power** want to dominate others for the sake of demonstrating their ability to wield power. They expect followers to be loyal to them personally rather than to the organization, a situation that sometimes causes organizational goals to be thwarted. In contrast, individuals with a high need for **institutional power** focus on working with others to solve problems and further organizational goals. Such individuals like getting things done in an organized fashion. They are also willing to sacrifice some of their own self-interests for the good of the organization.[19] Motivating individuals with a high need for institutional power involves giving them opportunities to hold positions that entail organizing the efforts of others.

McClelland has analyzed various needs in terms of their relationship to managerial effectiveness. He originally thought that individuals with a high need for achievement would make the best managers. His subsequent work suggests that, to the contrary, high-nAch individuals tend to concentrate on their own achievements rather than on the development and achievements of others. As a result, high-nAch individuals often make good entrepreneurs. Individuals with a high need for affiliation may also have a managerial weakness, because they tend to concentrate on maintaining good interpersonal relationships rather than achieving goals. Individuals with a personal-power orientation also tend to run into difficulties as managers because they often attempt to use the efforts of others for their own benefit.[20]

McClelland's work suggests that individuals with a high institutional-power need make the best managers because they are oriented toward coordinating the efforts of others to achieve long-term organizational goals.[21] Thus the need profile of successful managers, at least in competitive environments, appears to include (1) a moderate-to-high need for institutional power, (2) a moderate need for achievement to facilitate individual contributions early in one's career and a desire for the organization to maintain a competitive edge as one moves to higher levels, and (3) at least a minimum need for affiliation to provide sufficient sensitivity for influencing others. McClelland's most recent research indicates that need for achievement may actually be more important than power in running small companies or in large, decentralized companies like Pepsico, when managers are actually running the equivalent of small companies that must improve and grow in cost-efficient ways.[22]

What happens if an individual wants to be a manager but doesn't have the appropriate need profile? McClelland argues that it is possible to develop certain needs in ourselves and others. Through training, McClelland has successfully increased individuals' need for achievement. Subsequently, those who were trained received faster promotions and made more money than those not trained. In this type of training, individuals are exposed to tasks involving the achievement of goals, with the situations becoming more challenging as the individuals increase their ability to handle the tasks. Trainees are also exposed to the behavior of appealing entrepreneurial models. Similar approaches can apparently be used to foster the need for institutional power.[23] Other needs, such as the need for affiliation, may be more difficult to develop through such methods.

Need for power (nPow) The desire to influence others and control one's environment

Personal power A need for power in which individuals want to dominate others for the sake of demonstrating their ability to wield power

Institutional power A need for power in which individuals focus on working with others to solve problems and further organizational goals

Maslow: Hierarchy of Needs Theory	Herzberg: Two-Factor Theory	Alderfer: ERG Theory	McClelland: Acquired Needs Theory
Physiological	Hygiene factors	Existence	
Safety and security			
Belongingness and love		Relatedness	Need for affiliation
Self-esteem	Motivators	Growth	Need for achievement
Self-actualization			Need for power

Figure 12-5 *Comparison of needs in four theories.*

Assessing Need Theories

A comparison of the needs identified by the four theories is shown in Figure 12-5. The theories are generally compatible in pointing to the importance of higher-level needs as a source of motivation. Given the widespread current requirements for innovative ideas, improved quality, and greater capacity to implement needed changes, fostering growth needs is particularly important. For example, Hewlett-Packard generally has an open-stock policy, whereby engineers are free to use electrical and mechanical components from the lab stock area. They are even encouraged to take components home on the assumption that doing so will foster original thinking and innovation. According to one story, when Bill Hewlett, a founder of the company, found the lab stock area locked one Saturday, he got a bolt cutter and removed the padlock. He then left a note saying, "Don't ever lock this door again. Thanks, Bill."[24] The open-stock policy, which fosters employee growth, has helped Hewlett-Packard earn a strong reputation for innovation in the electronics industry.

■ COGNITIVE THEORIES

Cognitive theories Theories that attempt to isolate the thinking patterns that we use in deciding whether or not to behave in a certain way

Need theories try to identify the internal desires that influence our behavior, but they do not go very far in explaining the thought processes that are involved. In contrast, **cognitive theories** attempt to isolate the thinking patterns that we use in deciding whether or not to behave in a certain way. Cognitive theories are not necessarily at odds with need theories; rather, they look at motivation from a different perspective. Because they focus on the thought processes associated with motivation, cognitive theories are sometimes called *process theories*. Three major cognitive theories that address work motivation are the expectancy, equity, and goal-setting theories.

Expectancy Theory

Expectancy theory A theory (originally proposed by Vroom) that argues that we consider three main issues before we expend the effort necessary to perform at a given level

Effort-performance (E→P) expectancy Our assessment of the probability that our efforts will lead to the required performance level

The **expectancy theory** of motivation, originally proposed by Victor H. Vroom, argues that we consider three main issues before we expend the effort necessary to perform at a given level. These issues are shown in the circles of Figure 12-6, which depicts the basic components of expectancy theory.

EFFORT-PERFORMANCE EXPECTANCY When we consider **effort-performance (E→P) expectancy,** we assess the probability that our efforts will lead to the required performance level. Our assessment may include evaluating our own abilities, as well as considering the adequacy of contextual factors such as the availability of resources. To see how effort-performance expectancy works, imagine that your boss has asked you to consider taking on a major special project. The project involves designing and implementing a new computerized tracking system for customer complaints to improve individual customer service and find out more quickly about complaint trends. One of the first things you might think about is the probability of your being able to achieve the high level of performance required, given your abilities and the related environmental factors. If you feel that you don't know very much about developing such systems and/or that the availability of resources is inadequate, you might assess the probability of success as low. That is, your E→P expectancy about this particular assignment might be quite low. On the other hand, if you feel that you are well qualified for the project and that the available resources are adequate, you might assess the probability of your efforts' leading to high performance—the E→P expectancy—as quite high. However, assessment of the effort-performance expectancy is only part of your evaluation of the situation.

PERFORMANCE-OUTCOME EXPECTANCY With **performance-outcome (P→O) expectancy,** we assess the probability that our successful performance will lead to certain outcomes. The major outcomes we consider are potential rewards (such as a bonus, a promotion, or a good feeling of accomplishment), although we are likely also to take into account possible negative results (such as loss of leisure time or family disruption due to putting in extra hours on the job). In your special-project situation, perhaps your boss has a history of giving rewards, such as recognition and bonuses, to individuals who take on special projects. If so, you might assess the P→O expectancy for taking on the project as very high. On the other hand, your past experience with special projects may suggest that the boss sometimes arranges for rewards but other times forgets. If this is the case, you might view the P→O expectancy as medium in strength (perhaps a 50-50 probability of being rewarded). In the worst case, if your boss never rewards extra effort, you might assess the P→O expectancy as virtually zero—at least for rewards available from the boss.

Performance-outcome (P→O) expectancy Our assessment of the probability that our successful performance will lead to certain outcomes

Figure 12-6 *Basic components of expectancy theory.*

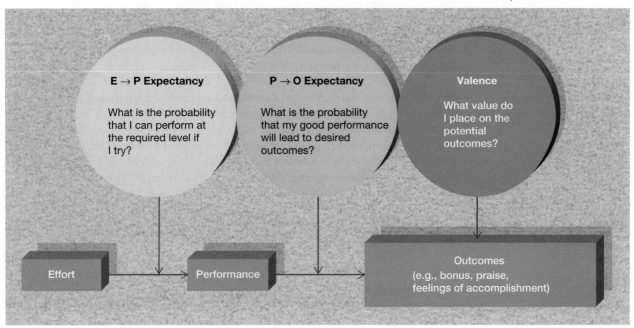

TABLE 12-1 NONMONETARY REWARDS

✔ Weekend trips to resorts	✔ Briefcases
✔ Time off	✔ "Boss of the Day"
✔ Banquets	✔ President's Medallion
✔ Luncheons	✔ Free meals (on-the-spot award)
✔ Tickets to local events	✔ Cookouts
✔ Publicity (company and external)	✔ Attendance at outside seminars or conferences
✔ Certificates of recognition	
✔ "Traveling" awards (monthly)	✔ Photo session with company president
✔ Plaques	✔ Popular company logo items (T-shirts, gym bags, coffee mugs, pen-and-pencil sets, jackets, stadium chairs, ice chests, umbrellas, thermos jugs, paper weights, desk pen sets, leather goods)
✔ Special parking spaces	
✔ Free parking (in large cities)	
✔ Shopping sprees	
✔ Books, tapes, or videos	
✔ Family photo sessions	—K. H. "Skip" Wilson, Senior Training Specialist, Mississippi Power & Light Company
✔ Trophies	
✔ Redeemable "Atta-boys/girls"	

Source: Reprinted from Bob Nelsom, *1001 Ways to Reward Employees,* Workman Publishing, New York, 1994, pp. 44–45.

Extrinsic rewards Rewards that are provided by others, such as bonuses, awards, or promotions

Intrinsic rewards Rewards that are related to our own internal experiences with successful performance, such as feelings of achievement, challenge, and growth

In any given situation, there may be many potential rewards associated with performance. Rewards provided by others, such as bonuses, awards, or promotions, are known as **extrinsic rewards.** In addition to monetary rewards (see Chapter 10 for some innovative approaches to compensation), there are many types of nonmonetary rewards that managers can provide to enhance motivation (for some ideas, see Table 12-1). On the other hand, rewards that are related to our own internal experiences with successful performance, such as feelings of achievement, challenge, and growth, are known as **intrinsic rewards.** Considering various possible outcomes (both positive and negative), we form an assessment of the probability of our performance's leading to desired outcomes. If our assessment of the P→O expectancy is high, the expectancy will contribute to our motivation. If our assessment is low, the expectancy could have a detrimental effect on our willingness to perform at a high level. Still, we have another motivational component to consider—how important the various outcomes are to us.

Valence Our assessment of the anticipated value of various outcomes or rewards

VALENCE With the **valence** component, we assess the anticipated value of various outcomes. If the available rewards interest us, valence will be high. However, the value of possible negative outcomes, such as the loss of leisure time or the disruption of our family, may offset the value of rewards in a given situation. The available rewards will have a motivating effect only when we attach a high overall valence to the situation. In the special-project example, you might view the prospect of a special bonus from the boss in an extremely positive light. On the other hand, if your rich aunt just left you $3 million, the bonus may be much less important. Still, you may attach a high value to the intrinsic rewards that might result if you develop the innovative project.

COMBINING THE ELEMENTS Expectancy theory argues that in deciding whether or not to put forth effort in a particular direction, we will consider all three elements: E→P expectancy, P→O expectancy, and valence. Research suggests that individuals are likely to make global judgments about each of the three elements in a given situation and then combine the elements according to the general overall formula posited by expectancy theory: $(E{\rightarrow}P) \times (P{\rightarrow}O) \times$ valence = motivation.[25] For example, in the special-project situation, suppose that you assess all three elements as relatively high. Chances are that you will be fairly highly motivated to pursue the project: high $E{\rightarrow}P$ expectancy $\times$ high $P{\rightarrow}O$ expectancy $\times$ high valence = high motivation. On the other hand, an assessment of zero for any of the elements will cause the whole equation to equal zero, regardless of the level of the other two elements. This is because you are unlikely to want to pursue the project if you either (1) believe that there is a zero (or an extremely low) probability of being able to perform adequately in the situation, (2) assess a zero (or an extremely low) possibility to the chance that successful performance will lead to certain outcomes, or (3) attach a zero (or an extremely low) valence value to potential outcomes. In more mixed situations, in which none of the elements have extremely low ratings, you will probably compare the situation with alternatives and choose the one that provides the best prospects of leading to outcomes that you value. In the special-project situation, you might try to negotiate with your boss either to improve the prospects of good outcomes or to shift assignments so that you receive a task that offers greater motivational potential.

Expectancy theory has been useful in predicting whether or not individual naval officers would voluntarily decide to retire, foretelling which job a given undergraduate student would choose after graduation, and determining which M.B.A. program a particular college graduate would ultimately select.[26]

IMPLICATIONS FOR MANAGERS Expectancy theory has several major implications for managers. For one thing, managers need to encourage the formation of high $P{\rightarrow}O$ expectancies by being careful to link rewards with high performance. To clarify this idea, consider three possible scenarios involving Alissa, Bob, and Christen. In the first scenario, Alissa performs well, receives a bonus from the boss, and is likely to conclude that high performance has a good chance of leading to a valued outcome (enhanced $P{\rightarrow}O$ expectancy). In the second scenario, though, Bob performs well, but the boss does not even say "good job," much less give him a bonus. As a result, Bob is likely to decide that high performance does not pay, at least in terms of organizational outcomes (reduced $P{\rightarrow}O$ expectancy). In our third scenario, Christen does very little work but still receives a sizable bonus at the end of the year. Christen is likely to surmise that high performance is *not* necessary to receive valued outcomes from the organization (reduced $P{\rightarrow}O$ expectancy). As a result of the manager's actions, Bob and Christen are likely to be less motivated in the future, while Alissa will likely experience increased motivation. In Bob's case, the reduced $P{\rightarrow}O$ expectancy is due to the manager's failure to reward high performance; but in Christen's case, the difficulty stems from the fact that the manager actually rewarded *low* performance.

Aside from the issues relating to the $P{\rightarrow}O$ expectancy, expectancy theory has other major implications for managers. For one thing, managers should foster a high $E{\rightarrow}P$ expectancy in subordinates. They can do this by being very clear about performance expectations; setting challenging, but doable, performance goals; ensuring that employees have the training and resources necessary to reach the required performance levels; and providing encouragement. Managers can also encourage motivation by offering opportunities for rewards (both extrinsic and intrinsic) that have a high valence to employees.[27] Expectancy theory helps explain why Honeywell is making changes in its compensation system to help boost the company's chances of global success (see the Case in Point discussion).

CASE IN POINT

HONEYWELL SEEKS COMPENSATION STRATEGIES FOR GLOBAL SUCCESS

Honeywell is best known as the manufacturer that invented the thermostat. After an ill-fated period during which it made acquisitions in such areas as semiconductors and communication services, the $6 billion company is refocusing on the area it knows best: controls. In the category of home and building controls, Honeywell has thermostats in 60 million U.S. homes, 3 million U.S. office buildings, and 40 million European residences. The company also makes industrial controls used in processing plants in such industries as chemicals, paper, and oil refining. Finally, Honeywell produces space and aviation controls that can be found on board every commercial aircraft produced in the western world.

In total, Honeywell's 55,000 employees use more than 80 languages and serve customers in 95 countries. CEO Michael Bonsignore says the company is entering an era in which the technology underlying its products will not be unique. Successful companies, then, will be those whose employees are able to deploy that technology in ways that will satisfy and delight customers. "The implication here is that more enlightened, more motivated people are the ones who are going to do a better job," Bonsignore says.

To help build and sustain that motivation, Honeywell is placing increased emphasis on pay for performance. Bonsignore wants to be sure that employees are rewarded for their efforts. Because individuals increasingly do some of their work as parts of teams, the company is experimenting with plans that reward team, as well as individual, performance. In one effort aimed at rewarding contributions to overall company success, Honeywell provides employees with extra payments into supplemental retirement plans based on the company's return on investment (ROI) each year. Bonsignore wants Honeywell to get more stock into the hands of employees through an employee stock ownership plan. He believes that stock ownership will help employees consider both the long- and short-run implications of their actions.

Honeywell also emphasizes nonmonetary rewards and recognitions. One is the Chairman's Achievement Award, which involves special thanks from Bonsignore himself for exemplary actions in support of the company's vision and strategies. An award was recently presented to a company chef who, on his own initiative, developed a special Mickey Mouse salad. The salad was served at a luncheon for visiting Disney officials discussing a potential cooperative business venture. The Disney visitors were very impressed with the customer orientation of Honeywell as reflected in the chef's efforts. Honeywell has a number of other awards including the prestigious Lund Award, which is given to leaders in people development who have been recommended by their peers. These and other company awards send important messages about what is important at Honeywell and have helped the company rekindle its success.[28]   ■■■

People across the world rely on Honeywell thermostats. But as other companies break into the controls industry, Honeywell's CEO Michael Bonsignore is turning up the heat on the competition. He believes that the company with the most motivated workers will be the most successful. That is why Honeywell is developing strategies to reward individual efforts, team performance, and companywide achievement. Employee stock ownership and nonmonetary recognition awards are also being used as incentives.

Thus Honeywell has been working on boosting motivation potential not only by offering rewards that are likely to have high valence for employees but also by forging a strong link between performance and outcomes. Although expectancy theory provides useful guidelines, managers still might not obtain the expected results from their motivational efforts unless employees perceive their outcomes as equitable, an issue specifically addressed by equity theory.

Equity Theory

Faced with growing international competition, General Electric's electric motors division imposed an 11 percent pay cut on its hourly workers and required that they give up scheduled raises. GE next closed 2 of 12 plants, but it guaranteed that the remaining 4500 workers could keep their jobs for at least 3 years. The company then spent $200 million to upgrade equipment and product development. Unfortunately, morale plummeted and so did productivity. Although the company saved $25 million in wages with the pay cuts, GE officials now concede that the cuts were a mistake. They say that they should have pursued other means, such as quality programs and worker teams, to increase productivity and fight international competition. Apparently, the work force perceived the pay cuts as inequitable and responded accordingly.[29] To help explain how we identify and react to situations that we perceive as inequitable, J. Stacy Adams developed equity theory while working for the Behavioral Research Service of General Electric.[30]

According to **equity theory,** we prefer situations of balance, or equity, which exists when we perceive the ratio of our inputs and outcomes to be equal to the ratio of inputs and outcomes for a comparison other (or others). The selection of the person or persons with whom we compare ourselves depends on our own view of appropriate comparisons. For example, in considering the equity of a pay raise, a person might compare her or his pay with that of certain coworkers, peers in other units, and/or a friend with similar credentials who works for another company. In making equity judgments, we consider equity in *relative* terms (comparison with another) rather than absolute terms (comparison with a set standard). The inputs we consider in assessing the ratio of our inputs and outcomes relative to the ratios of others may cover a broad range of variables, including educational background, skills, experience, hours worked, and performance results. Outcomes might include such factors as pay, bonuses, praise, parking places, office space, furniture, and work assignments. The inputs and outcomes that we use to assess the equity of a situation are based strictly on our own perceptions of what is relevant.

According to the theory, two types of inequities create tension within us. In the first, *underreward*, we perceive our inputs-outcomes ratio to be *less than* the inputs-outcomes ratio of a comparison other. In the second, *overreward*, we perceive our inputs-outcomes ratio to be *greater than* the inputs-outcomes ratio of a comparison other. Interestingly, research on equity theory suggests that we are usually able to adjust to overreward conditions rather quickly—apparently concluding that our inputs are worth considerably more than we originally thought.[31] Situations of underreward are usually more difficult to rectify.

REDUCING OR ELIMINATING INEQUITY Although the specific actions an individual takes will depend on what appears to be feasible in a given situation of perceived underreward, Adams suggests that maintaining one's self-esteem is an important priority. As a result, an individual will probably first attempt to maximize outcomes and to resist personally costly changes in inputs. Changing perceptions about the inputs and outcomes of others or attempting to alter their side of the equation will usually be more palatable than changing perceptions about or actually altering one's own side of the equation. Leaving the situation will probably be done only in cases of high inequity when the other alternatives are not feasible. Finally, an individual will be highly resistant to

Equity theory A theory that argues that we prefer situations of balance, or equity, which exists when we perceive the ratio of our inputs and outcomes to be equal to the ratio of inputs and outcomes for a comparison other

changing the comparison others, especially if the objects of comparison have stabilized over time.

One particularly interesting study demonstrating the potential impact of inequities traced the performance of 23 major-league baseball players who began the season without contracts. Because of major changes in league contract rules, the researchers speculated that the players would be likely to perceive themselves as underpaid in reference both to others who had signed lucrative contracts and to their own lower compensation as compared with that of the previous year. The prediction that the 23 players would reduce their inputs, one of their few short-term options for reducing the inequity, was confirmed when they logged lower season performance levels for batting average, home runs, and runs batted in.[32]

Adams's equity formulation considered one situation at a given point in time, but recent work indicates that perceptions of inequities may persist over an extended period. The addition of the time dimension helps explain why people sometimes blow up over seemingly small inequities. Residues from previous inequities may pile up until the small incident becomes the "straw that broke the camel's back," and we react strongly.[33]

IMPLICATIONS FOR MANAGERS Equity theory makes several helpful suggestions to supplement the recommendations of expectancy theory. For one thing, managers need to maintain two-way communication with subordinates so that they have some idea of subordinates' equity perceptions. For another, it is important to let subordinates know the "rules" that will govern the allocation of outcomes relative to inputs. Also, since a pattern of inequities over a period of time can build into major difficulties, managers should maintain good communication not only with subordinates but also with superiors, peers, customers, and other individuals associated with the job. The differing views inherent in the growing diversity of the work force have the potential to increase feelings of inequity in organizations. As a result, many companies, such as the Bank of Montreal, have instituted managing diversity programs to increase mutual understanding and help ensure equitable treatment for all employees (see the Managing Diversity box).

Goal-Setting Theory

The many advantages of establishing goals throughout the organization, as well as methods for doing so, are covered extensively in Chapter 6. Here, we briefly summarize the highlights of goal-setting theory as they apply to motivation. While goal setting was originally viewed as a technique, it is developing into a motivational theory as researchers attempt to better understand the cognitive factors that influence its success. Goal-setting experts argue that goal setting works by directing attention and action, mobilizing effort, increasing persistence, and encouraging the development of strategies to achieve the goals. Feedback regarding results is also an essential element.[34]

The success of goal setting in motivating performance depends on establishing goals that have the appropriate attributes, or characteristics. In particular, goals should be specific and measurable, challenging, attainable, relevant to the major work of the organization, and time-limited (i.e., a goal must be accomplished within a defined period of time). At the Intel Corporation, which makes the microprocessor chips that are the "brains" of personal computers, goals have been successfully used to help reduce the time it takes to develop and produce new microprocessors. The company used to develop microprocessors every 4 years. Now Intel uses overlapping cycles. It started develop-

MANAGING DIVERSITY

Bank of Montreal Seeks Workplace Equity and Diversity

The Bank of Montreal, Canada's oldest chartered bank, wanted to increase the diversity of its work force to better reflect the bank's customers. The bank also hoped to gain more innovative solutions to business problems by capitalizing on employees' different knowledge, backgrounds, and experiences. In the process, the bank, with $117 billion in assets, wanted to be sure that its 34,000 employees had equal access to advancement and opportunity. Bank officials reasoned that maximizing each person's potential would be likely to translate into better customer service—thereby creating a competitive advantage over the bank's competitors.

After some initial fact finding, the bank targeted four segments of the work force for particular attention: women, individuals with disabilities, aboriginal people, and "visible" minorities. A task force was created to focus on each area. Priority was given to the Task Force on the Advancement of Women be-

cause women held 91 percent of the bank's nonmanagerial positions, but only 9 percent of executive positions. The task force used the bank's human resource information system to obtain information about employment patterns, conducted interviews, held focus groups, and surveyed employees. A key finding was that women were not being promoted because of stereotypical attitudes, myths, and "conventional wisdom." Ultimately, the task force devised 26 recommendations aimed at breaking down barriers and changing the corporate culture. Recommendations from the Task Force on Employment of People with Disabilities so far have included helping managers make creative accommodation to allow individuals with disabilities to perform a wider spectrum of jobs and providing awareness training to all employees. The other two task forces are also hard at work. Eight divisional advisory councils representing employees from all levels and demographic backgrounds oversee the implementation of various task force recommendations. The bank has received numerous awards for its overall Workplace Equality Program.[35]

The Bank of Montreal is committed to giving its 34,000 employees equal access to advancement and opportunity. Task forces have made recommendations for advancing four segments of the work force: women, individuals with disabilities, aboriginal people, and "visible" minorities. At its Institute of Learning, shown here, 14,000 employees each year are able to participate in programs that promote personal and professional growth through learning and debate.

ment on a new generation chip 2 years before its famous Pentium chip even hit the market.[36]

Goal commitment, one's attachment to or determination to reach a goal, is another important element in the goal-setting process. Goal commitment is affected by the major components of expectancy theory: effort-performance expectancy (can I reach the goal?), performance-outcome expectancy (if I reach it, will I be rewarded?), and valence (do I value the potential rewards?). Individuals are more likely to be committed to attaining goals when they have high expectations of success in reaching the goals, see strong connections between goal accomplishment and rewards, and value the rewards.[37] Hence expectancy theory and goal-setting theory are largely compatible.

The usefulness of goal setting in enhancing performance has strong research support. As a result, managers are likely to find it a very helpful motivational tool.

Assessing Cognitive Theories

Each of the cognitive theories of motivation offers a different perspective, although the three views are somewhat complementary. Expectancy theory advises managers to help employees develop positive assessments of their own effort-performance expectancy through such means as training and encouragement. It also highlights the importance of a clear link between performance and outcomes, as well as the need to offer rewards that have a positive valence for employees (clues about valence come from need theories). Goal setting theory is compatible with expectancy theory in that it can help pinpoint the performance levels associated with both the effort-performance expectancy and performance-outcome expectancy. Finally, equity issues influence how individuals assess the importance of maintaining equity in the motivation process.

■ REINFORCEMENT THEORY

The reinforcement approach to motivation is almost the antithesis of cognitive theories, since it does not concern itself with the thought processes of the individual as an explanation of behavior. The best-known approach to reinforcement theory, sometimes also called *operant conditioning theory* or *behaviorism*, was pioneered by noted psychologist B. F. Skinner. According to **reinforcement theory,** our behavior can be explained by consequences in the environment, and therefore, it is not necessary to look for cognitive explanations.[38] Instead, the theory relies heavily on a concept called the **law of effect,** which states that behaviors having pleasant or positive consequences are more likely to be repeated and behaviors having unpleasant or negative consequences are less likely to be repeated.

In the reinforcement process, a stimulus provides a cue for a response or behavior that is then followed by a consequence. If we find the consequence rewarding, we are more likely to repeat the behavior when the stimulus occurs in the future. If we do not find it rewarding, we are less likely to repeat the behavior. For example, assume that you are the manager of a marketing research unit in a consumer-products company. A product manager from another unit asks you for emergency help with market research data (stimulus). You pull some of your people from other priorities and even stay quite late to produce the needed data (behavior). The product manager makes sure that your unit is recognized for its efforts (pleasant consequence). As a result, you will be likely to put extra effort into helping the product manager in the future. On the other hand, if the product manager complains about a minor error (unpleasant consequence) and says nothing about the rest of the data or the extra effort that went into preparing it (less than pleasant consequence), you will be less likely to put the same effort into helping that manager in the future. The use of techniques associated with reinforcement theory is known as **behavior modification.**

Types of Reinforcement

In behavior modification, four types of reinforcement are available to help managers influence behavior: positive reinforcement, negative reinforcement, extinction, and punishment. Positive reinforcement and negative reinforcement are aimed at increasing a behavior, while extinction and punishment focus on decreasing a behavior (see Figure 12-7). Skinner argued that positive reinforcement and extinction encourage individual growth, whereas negative reinforcement and punishment are likely to foster immaturity in individuals and eventually contaminate the entire organization.

Reinforcement theory A theory that argues that our behavior can be explained by consequences in the environment

Law of effect A concept that states that behaviors having pleasant or positive consequences are more likely to be repeated and that behaviors having unpleasant or negative consequences are less likely to be repeated

Behavior modification The use of techniques associated with reinforcement theory

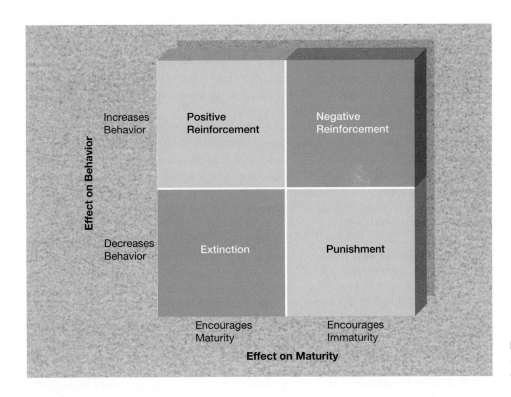

Figure 12-7 *Types of reinforcement situations according to Skinner.*

POSITIVE REINFORCEMENT Aimed at *increasing* a desired behavior, **positive reinforcement** involves providing a pleasant, rewarding consequence to encourage that behavior. The rewarding consequence, such as praise, a raise, or time off, is said to be a positive reinforcer if it leads to repetition of the desired behavior. Since individuals differ in regard to what they find pleasant and rewarding, managers need to monitor the effects of a particular reinforcer to determine whether it is effective in encouraging the desired behavior.

Because individuals frequently do not execute a new behavior exactly as required when they first try it, managers often find it useful to encourage new behaviors through shaping. **Shaping** is the successive rewarding of behaviors that closely approximate the desired response until the actual desired response is made. For example, a manager training a new salesperson may compliment the way that the individual greets customers (if this behavior approximates the desired response). The manager may also suggest questions that the salesperson might ask customers to obtain a better idea of their needs. Then the manager can reward the person's efforts to ask better questions and can make a further suggestion. Through this process the individual's behavior is gradually shaped so that the person becomes a competent salesperson.

NEGATIVE REINFORCEMENT Like positive reinforcement, negative reinforcement focuses on *increasing* a desired behavior, but it operates in a different way. **Negative reinforcement** involves providing noxious (unpleasant) stimuli so that an individual will engage in the desired behavior in order to stop the noxious stimuli. In other words, the desired behavior is reinforced in a negative way because the individual must engage in the behavior in order to get rid of an unpleasant condition. For example, an engineer may work hard to finish a project on time (desired behavior) in order to stop (consequence) the chief engineer's nagging or yelling (noxious stimuli). With negative reinforcement, either the noxious, or unpleasant, stimuli are actually present or the potential is high that

Positive reinforcement A technique, aimed at *increasing* a desired behavior, that involves providing a pleasant, rewarding consequence to encourage that behavior

Shaping The successive rewarding of behaviors that closely approximate the desired response until the actual desired response is made

Negative reinforcement A technique, aimed at *increasing* a desired behavior, that involves providing noxious stimuli so that an individual will engage in the desired behavior in order to stop the noxious stimuli

they will occur unless the individual engages in the desired behavior. For instance, the chief engineer may already be nagging about meeting the project deadline; or the chief engineer may not be yelling or nagging yet, but the engineer may know from past experience that late projects trigger such behavior. In either case, the negative reinforcement increases the likelihood that the engineer will complete the project on time.

Although negative reinforcement may encourage the desired behavior, it may also make the individual feel negatively toward the person providing the reinforcement. If this is the case, the individual may react by doing only what is required, declining to put in extra time when it might be helpful, or even leaving the organization. Negative reinforcement may also foster immature behavior. For example, it may unwittingly encourage the engineer to complete projects on time only when the boss is in the office.

Extinction A technique that involves withholding previously available positive consequences associated with a behavior in order to *decrease* that behavior

EXTINCTION Extinction involves withholding previously available positive consequences associated with a behavior in order to *decrease* that behavior. Suppose that the first few times an employee engages in clowning behavior during a staff meeting, the manager laughs. The laughter might tend to reinforce the clowning to such a point that the behavior becomes disruptive. The employee's clowning behavior would be gradually extinguished if the manager proceeded to refrain from (withhold) laughing in response to it.

Punishment A technique that involves providing negative consequences in order to *decrease* or discourage a behavior

PUNISHMENT Punishment involves providing negative consequences in order to *decrease* or discourage a behavior. Examples are criticizing the unwanted behavior whenever it occurs, suspending an individual without pay, denying training opportunities, or withholding resources such as new equipment. Punishment differs from negative reinforcement in at least two important ways. First, punishment aims to decrease or discourage an undesirable behavior, whereas negative reinforcement attempts to increase or encourage a desirable behavior. Second, punishment is usually applied after the individual has engaged in an undesirable behavior. Conversely, negative reinforcement occurs before the individual engages in a desirable behavior. Both punishment and negative reinforcement constitute negative approaches to affecting behavior, approaches that Skinner maintained have long-run detrimental effects on individuals and organizations.

Arguments against the use of punishment are that it can have undesirable side effects (e.g., negative feelings toward the punisher) and that it may eliminate the undesirable behavior only as long as the threat of punishment remains. Also, it does not provide a model of correct behavior. Still, punishment may be necessary under some circumstances, particularly if the undesirable behavior has a serious impact on the organization or endangers others. In such situations, attempts to use extinction to decrease the undesirable behavior might not be practical because immediate action to stop the behavior is necessary. If punishment must be used, it is likely to be most effective if there are recognized company policies that govern the situation; the punishment is given as soon as possible after the undesirable behavior; the punishment is moderate, rather than severe; and it is applied consistently.[39]

Schedules of Reinforcement

Reinforcement theory emphasizes using positive reinforcement to encourage desired behaviors. In studying positive reinforcement, researchers have discovered that different patterns of rewarding affect the time required to learn a new behavior and the degree to which the behavior persists. These different

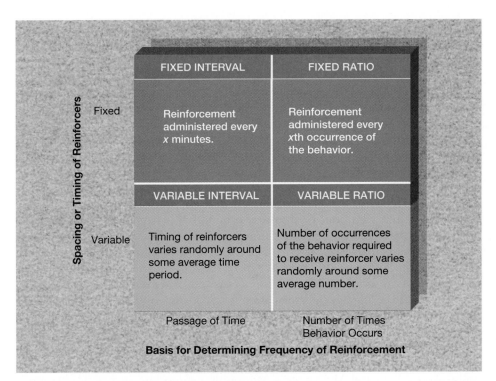

Figure 12-8 *Types of partial reinforcement schedules. (Adapted from Hugh J. Arnold and Daniel C. Feldman,* Organizational Behavior, *McGraw-Hill, New York, 1986, p. 70.)*

patterns, called **schedules of reinforcement,** specify the basis for and timing of positive reinforcement. There are two major types of reinforcement schedules: continuous and partial. With a *continuous* schedule of reinforcement, the desired behavior is rewarded each time it occurs. For example, a manager might praise a worker every time the worker performs a task correctly. This type of reinforcement is very effective during the initial learning process, but it becomes tedious and impractical on an ongoing basis. Further, the desired behavior tends to stop almost immediately (rapid extinction) unless the reinforcement is continued. With a *partial* schedule of reinforcement, the desired behavior is rewarded intermittently rather than each time it occurs. During the initial learning process, the behavior can be rewarded more often to encourage its repetition, and the rewards can become less frequent as time goes on. There are four main types of partial reinforcement schedules: fixed interval, fixed ratio, variable interval, and variable ratio (see Figure 12-8).

Schedules of reinforcement
Patterns of rewarding that specify the basis for and timing of positive reinforcement

FIXED INTERVAL With a **fixed-interval schedule of reinforcement,** a reinforcer is administered on a fixed time schedule, assuming that the desired behavior has continued at an appropriate level. For example, a plant manager might visit a section of the plant every day at approximately the same time and praise efforts being made to increase production quality. A fixed-interval schedule tends to produce an uneven response pattern, with the desired behavior peaking just before the expected reinforcement and then declining somewhat until the next anticipated reinforcement. With this type of schedule, extinction is rapid if the reinforcement is delayed or stopped.

Fixed-interval schedule of reinforcement A pattern in which a reinforcer is administered on a fixed time schedule, assuming that the desired behavior has continued at an appropriate level

FIXED RATIO With a **fixed-ratio schedule of reinforcement,** a reinforcer is provided after a fixed number of occurrences of the desired behavior, rather than according to a fixed time schedule. For example, special awards for innovative ideas might be given to individuals after they have contributed five implemented ideas. Piecework incentive pay systems, in which workers earn an incen-

Fixed-ratio schedule of reinforcement A pattern in which a reinforcer is provided after a fixed number of occurrences of the desired behavior

tive for producing a specified number of units, are another type of fixed-ratio reinforcement. A fixed-ratio schedule tends to elicit a high response rate, but rapid extinction occurs if the reinforcer is discontinued even temporarily.

Variable-interval schedule of reinforcement A pattern in which a reinforcer is administered on a varying, or random, time schedule that *averages* out to a predetermined time frequency

VARIABLE INTERVAL With a **variable-interval schedule of reinforcement,** a reinforcer is administered on a varying, or random, time schedule that *averages* out to a predetermined time frequency. For example, a plant manager might visit a section of the plant to praise good quality an average of five times per week, but at varying times. This type of reinforcement schedule tends to promote a high, steady response rate with slow extinction.

Variable-ratio schedule of reinforcement A pattern in which a reinforcer is provided after a varying, or random, number of occurrences of the desired behavior in such a way that the reinforcement pattern *averages* out to a predetermined ratio of occurrences per reinforcement

VARIABLE RATIO With a **variable-ratio schedule of reinforcement,** a reinforcer is provided after a varying, or random, number of occurrences of the desired behavior (rather than on a varying time schedule) in such a way that the reinforcement pattern *averages* out to a predetermined ratio of occurrences per reinforcement. For example, special awards for innovative ideas might be given to individuals on a ratio average of one award per five innovative ideas (i.e., an award after three ideas one time, after seven ideas another time, etc.). Slot-machine payoff patterns, which provide rewards after a varying number of pulls on the lever, are excellent examples of a variable-ratio schedule. This type of schedule is likely to produce a very high response rate and is the partial reinforcement method with the slowest extinction rate. Variable-ratio reinforcement was used in the McDonald's Monopoly promotion, in which customers were given game pieces that contained stamps corresponding to the properties on a Monopoly game board. Although the odds of winning the top prize of $2 million in one such promotion were very long (1 in 724,214,000), more immediate reinforcement was provided by giving customers the chance to win instant McDonald's food prizes at much better odds (1 in 12), as well as the opportunity to collect stamps for possible bigger prizes. The promotion was so successful that it has been repeated with some modifications several times.

Using Reinforcement Theory

Several guidelines have been proposed to help managers effectively use the reinforcement approach. They advise managers to emphasize positive reinforcement to encourage desired behaviors and to let subordinates know what behaviors will be rewarded. Once desired behaviors have been learned, variable-interval and variable-ratio reinforcement patterns seem to be the most effective approaches to maintaining the behaviors. Finally, if it is necessary to punish, punishment of moderate severity administered quickly and consistently seems to yield the best results.[40] The Union National Bank in Little Rock, Arkansas, has used positive reinforcement principles to increase output in the proof department. Employees there encode machine-readable numbers onto the bottom of checks so that the checks can be credited to the appropriate accounts. As a result of putting up a graph that shows daily production and praising high performers, production increased from 1065 items per hour to 2100 items per hour. With the addition of individual bonuses based on daily output, production rose to 3500 items per hour.[41]

■ SOCIAL LEARNING THEORY

On the basis of his extensive work on reinforcement theory, noted psychologist Albert Bandura became convinced that the apparent success of the approach could not be explained without taking into account the cognitive, or thinking, capacity of individuals. Accordingly, he and others developed **social learning theory,** which argues that learning occurs through the continuous interaction of our behaviors, various personal factors, and environmental forces. Individuals influence their environment, which, in turn, affects the ways that they think and behave. In other words, we learn much of our behavior by observing, imitating, and interacting with our social environment. Although social learning theory combines elements of both the cognitive and the reinforcement approaches, it is discussed at this point because it builds on reinforcement theory.

Social learning theory A theory that argues that learning occurs through the continuous reciprocal interaction of our behaviors, various personal factors, and environmental forces

Major Components

Social learning theory argues that three cognitively related processes are particularly important in explaining our behavior: symbolic processes, vicarious learning, and self-control.[42]

SYMBOLIC PROCESSES According to social learning theory, we rely heavily on **symbolic processes,** the various ways that we use verbal and imagined symbols to process and store experiences in representational forms (words and images) that can serve as guides to future behavior. Through the use of symbols, we can attempt to solve problems without actually trying all the alternative courses of action. We may also be able to visualize an intriguing vacation spot in the South Pacific even if we have never actually been there. Images of desirable futures allow us to set distant goals and fashion actions that will lead to the accomplishment of those goals. Our symbolic processes incorporate a cognitive element called **self-efficacy,** the belief in one's capabilities to perform a specific task. Although somewhat similar to the effort-performance expectancy component of expectancy theory, self-efficacy is more oriented toward our convictions about our own capacities. It may be useful in explaining the levels of goals that we set, as well as task effort and persistence. One study found that faculty members who feel competent at research and writing tend to produce more articles and books, which, in turn, increases their self-confidence and the likelihood of future productivity. Similar findings have emerged from studies of sales performance among life insurance agents.[43]

Symbolic processes The various ways that we use verbal and imagined symbols to process and store experiences in representational forms that can serve as guides to future behavior

Self-efficacy The belief in one's capabilities to perform a specific task

VICARIOUS LEARNING Vicarious learning, or observational learning, is our ability to learn new behaviors and/or assess their probable consequences by observing others. This concept is important because, contrary to the arguments associated with reinforcement theory, we do not actually have to perform a behavior ourselves to learn about the consequences. The process of observing and attempting to imitate the behaviors of others is called **modeling** (see Figure 12-9). If you learned to swim or play tennis by imitating the behaviors of others (perhaps a proficient friend or an instructor), you engaged in modeling. Modeling usually takes place in four stages. In the *attention* stage, we select a model for observation, usually because we perceive the model to be skilled

Vicarious learning Our ability to learn new behaviors and/or assess their probable consequences by observing others

Modeling Actually observing and attempting to imitate the behaviors of others

Figure 12-9 *The modeling process.*

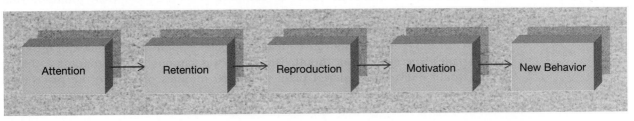

and successful, and we pay attention to the relevant aspects of behavior. In the *retention* stage, we retain information about the behavior through mental images and words. In the *reproduction* stage, we attempt to reproduce the behavior, but we may be only partially successful and need to make further adjustment based on feedback. In the *motivation* stage, we are motivated to adopt the model behavior. For this stage to lead to our actual adoption of the behavior, reinforcement must be present, usually from one of three sources. First, our behavior can be reinforced by the consequences in the environment in a manner similar to that noted by reinforcement theory. Second, reinforcement can occur vicariously through our observations of the consequences that have accrued to others engaging in the particular behavior. Third, we can also engage in self-reinforcement through the process of self-control.

Self-control Our ability to exercise control over our own behavior by setting standards and providing consequences for our own actions

SELF-CONTROL Self-control, or self-regulation, is our ability to exercise control over our own behavior by setting standards and providing consequences (both rewards and punishments) for our own actions. Self-control increases performance when we make our self-rewards conditional on reaching a challenging preset level of performance.[44] For example, we may promise ourselves a 15-minute break if we finish an assignment by a certain time, treat ourselves to something new when we get an A on an exam, or internally congratulate ourselves on a job well done. Since social learning theory recognizes the concept of self-reinforcement, it gives us more credit for control over our own behavior than reinforcement theory.

Using Social Learning Theory

The social learning theory approach has considerable research support, although investigators have only recently begun to explore fully its implications for organizations.[45] The theory has two major managerial implications beyond those offered by other motivational theories. First, providing positive models appears to greatly accelerate the learning of appropriate behaviors, especially if there are opportunities to try the new behaviors in a supportive setting and obtain feedback. Modeling can be particularly useful for training new workers. Second, the notion of vicarious learning indicates that employees are likely to draw conclusions about prospects for rewards and punishments, not only from their own experiences but also from those of others. One company whose operations reflect social learning theory principles, including modeling and various types of reinforcement, is Domino's Pizza, Inc. (see the Case in Point discussion).

CASE IN POINT   **LEARNING THE DOMINO THEORY**

Begun as one small shop in 1960, Domino's Pizza emerged in the late 1980s as the world's largest pizza delivery empire. The company experienced a serious slump in the early 1990s, a couple of years after company founder, Tom Monaghan, had stepped down as CEO to pursue philanthropic interests. Monaghan has since returned as CEO and has the company on a growth path again. Over the years, his innovative ideas have been responsible for much of the company's success. At one point, Domino's was famous for its guarantee that it would deliver an ordered pizza within 30 minutes or reduce the price (this guarantee has now been abandoned because of lawsuits against the company blaming the 30-minute policy whenever a driver would have a car accident).

Every Monday, the owner of the Domino's Pizza franchise in Washington, D.C., takes his store managers for a 6-mile jog. The run is in keeping with the philosophy of Domino's founder and CEO, Tom Monaghan: "Our whole business is built on speed." Monaghan himself religiously runs 6¹/₂ miles a day. By providing good models and comprehensive worker training and by reinforcing employee efforts through contests and other incentives, Domino's motivates its workers.

Monaghan also invented the use of the "hot box," which ensures that the delivered pizza will taste as if it just came out of the oven.

With gross annual sales topping more than $2.5 billion, and over 5000 outlets, the need to train new workers and managers is almost insatiable. To help meet this challenge, the company has developed a variety of videotapes, most of them aimed at the five basic worker positions in an outlet—phone answerer, pizza maker, oven tender, router, and driver. The videos cover such topics as orientation, image, dough management, pizza making, oven tending and maintenance, delivery, and safe driving. They combine detailed instructions with generous sprinklings of humor to hold the attention of new recruits. On the humorous side, for example, one award-winning video on dough management shows a funeral scene featuring uncooked pizza dough that has "died" before its time. Another, on safe driving, shows a hapless driver gradually turning into a werewolf, consumed by the pressure to deliver pizzas within the 30-minute limit. Managers are trained to show the videos; have individuals perform the various tasks in the desired manner, as clearly illustrated on the videos; and give workers appropriate feedback and reinforcement. The videos are supplemented with numerous well-designed posters that provide further models of desired behaviors. For example, just above the counters where the pizzas are actually made, detailed glossy posters show exactly how a pizza should look at various stages in the process.

To make the grade at Domino's, employees must meet challenging time performance standards. Order takers must answer the telephone within three rings and take an order within 45 seconds, pizza makers are expected to have the ordered pizza made and in the oven within 1 minute, and oven tenders are given 5 seconds to load one pizza while unloading another. Management trainees must be able to meet these same standards, as well as others spelled out in detailed behavioral terms in the performance evaluation system.

Reinforcement comes from pay incentives and a heavy dose of competition based on employee contests within stores for the fastest service times and the highest sales figures. A powerful incentive is the prospect that high performers can become store managers and possibly franchisees under very generous terms.[46] ■ ■ ■

Thus social learning theory and the other motivational theories discussed in this chapter can be important assets in attempting to influence various behaviors in organizations. They are a critical factor in effective leadership, a subject to which we turn in the next chapter.

■ CHAPTER SUMMARY

Motivation is the force that energizes behavior, gives direction to behavior, and underlies the tendency to persist. Actual performance is a function of ability and working conditions, as well as motivation. Efforts to understand the motivational process have centered on several major elements: needs, cognitive activities, and reward and reinforcement issues.

Need theories argue that we behave the way we do because we have internal needs we are attempting to fulfill. These theories are sometimes called content theories because they focus on what motivates others. For example, Maslow argues that our needs form a five-level hierarchy, ranging from physiological to self-actualization needs. Herzberg's two-factor theory contends that hygiene factors are necessary to keep workers from feeling dissatisfied, but only motivators can lead workers to feel satisfied and motivated. ERG theory updates Maslow's approach by proposing three need levels and including the frustration-regression principle and the satisfaction-progression explanation of movement among need levels. While the hierarchy of needs and ERG theories view certain needs as inherent, McClelland's acquired-needs theory argues that needs are acquired or learned on the basis of our life experiences. His work has focused particularly on needs for achievement, affiliation, and power, as well as on how these needs affect managerial success.

Cognitive theories, sometimes called process theories, attempt to isolate the thinking patterns we use in deciding whether or not to behave in a certain way. Ex-

pectancy theory posits that in deciding how much effort to expend in a given direction, we consider three issues: effort-performance expectancy (the probability that our efforts will lead to the required performance level), performance-outcome expectancy (the probability that our successful performance will lead to certain outcomes), and valence (the anticipated value of the various outcomes or rewards). Equity theory indicates that we prefer situations of balance, or equity, which occurs when we perceive the ratio of our inputs and outcomes to be equal to the ratio of inputs and outcomes of a comparison other (or others). Goal-setting theory highlights the importance of goal commitment, specific and challenging goals, and feedback. Goal setting works by directing attention and action, mobilizing effort, increasing persistence, and encouraging the development of strategies to achieve the goals.

Reinforcement theory argues that our behavior can be explained by consequences in the environment. The four major types of reinforcement are positive reinforcement, negative reinforcement, extinction, and punishment. Schedules of reinforcement specify the basis for and timing of positive rewards. They include fixed-interval, fixed-ratio, variable-interval, and variable-ratio schedules. Social learning theory argues that learning occurs through the continuous interaction of our behaviors, various personal factors, and environmental forces. Three cognitively related processes are particularly important: symbolic processes, vicarious learning, and self-control.

■ QUESTIONS FOR DISCUSSION AND REVIEW

1   Briefly describe the concept of motivation and explain the motivation process. Describe a situation that illustrates the idea that performance is a function of ability and working conditions, as well as motivation.

2   Explain the hierarchy of needs theory. Assume that you are the manager of a large fast-food outlet. How could this theory help you motivate the various individuals who work for you?

3   Outline the hygiene factors and motivators identified by Herzberg. Why might managers find this theory appealing and useful?

4   Identify the major differences between ERG theory and the hierarchy of needs theory. Suppose you became the new manager of a work unit. How could ERG theory assist you in assessing how to motivate the members of your new unit?

5   Describe the acquired-needs theory of motivation. According to McClelland's work on the need for achievement, what are some of the difficulties in attempting to motivate high-nAch individuals in organizations? How could you encourage the need for achievement in others? How might you encourage the need for institutional power?

6   Outline the expectancy theory of motivation. Suppose you are in charge of a group of engineers who are responsible for the completion of various projects. How would you use expectancy theory to motivate them to perform at a high level?

7   Explain equity theory. In part, equity theory argues that our judgments of equity (or inequity) are based on our own perceptions of situations. What potential difficulties does the perceptual aspect of equity judgments present for managers?

8   Explain the four main types of reinforcement. For each one, identify a situation in which you have seen that type used and assess the outcome.

9   Contrast the four major types of partial reinforcement schedules. Provide an example of each type from your own experience.

10   Explain the social learning theory of motivation. Describe an instance in which you obtained important information through vicarious learning. Also describe a situation in which you learned through modeling. To what extent can you identify the steps in the modeling process in your own situation?

■ DISCUSSION QUESTIONS FOR CHAPTER OPENING CASE

1   How can need theories help provide clues about what is likely to motivate individuals at Levi Strauss?

2   What aspects of expectancy theory are incorporated in the Aspirations Statement? Where are goal-setting theory and equity theory applicable?

3   What evidence exists for the use of various types of reinforcement, vicarious learning, and self-control?

■ EXERCISES FOR MANAGING IN THE TWENTY-FIRST CENTURY

EXERCISE 1
SKILL BUILDING: LEARNING ABOUT REINFORCEMENT SCHEDULES

Positive reinforcement is particularly significant to both a manager and an employee. Understanding the schedules of reinforcement will be helpful in selecting the correct type to use at a particular time. Match the type of partial reinforcement schedule with the examples indicated by placing the first letters of the titles in the blanks.

Fixed Interval   **Fixed Ratio**

Variable Interval   **Variable Ratio**

1 _____ Monthly pay check
2 _____ Jackpot on a slot machine
3 _____ A free trip for two after making sales of $300,000 within a year
4 _____ The company president visits the plant an average of every 2 months to let everyone know their efforts are appreciated
5 _____ State lottery
6 _____ Certificate and pin for 25 years of service
7 _____ Monthly Attendance Award
8 _____ Baseball and football tickets given to employees—usually once or twice a year depending on availability
9 _____ Restaurant waiter/waitress receives an award for serving the chain's 1 millionth customer —a company milestone
10 _____ Refreshment break every morning and afternoon
11 _____ Boss brings in doughnuts an average of every 2 or 3 weeks or so to treat everyone in the work unit
12 _____ $10 each for the first 100, $12 each for the next 30, $15 each for the next 30, and $19 each for all others produced during a work shift

EXERCISE 2

MANAGEMENT EXERCISE: MARKETEER OR ENTREPRENEUR

Lee Brown has been a market planning specialist for the Sweet Tooth Candy Company for the past 2 years. This is her first job following graduation from college, and she is quite pleased with her progress in the organization. She has received three merit raises and expects to be promoted soon to the position of senior market planning specialist. She enjoys her work, and her immediate boss is one of the finest market planners she could ever hope to work with. Her boss gives her autonomy, support, and resources when she needs them. Similarly, he seems to know when she needs help and gives it to her in a way that brings out the best in her. Lee frequently wonders how anyone could be happier than she is with her job and company.

Last week she met Jamie Wilson, one of her former schoolmates, at the local shopping center. Lee recalled that Jamie, an excellent student who majored in human resource management, had accepted a position as a compensation analyst with a local health-care corporation. While catching up on the events of their lives during the previous 2 years, Jamie indicated she had a business proposition that she had been considering for some time but did not believe she could pursue alone. She needed a partner and suggested that Lee be that person.

Her proposition was that child-care centers were desperately needed in their area. The city of approximately 35,000 people had only one small child-care facility, which had a very long waiting list and very high rates. Jamie's research had revealed that three different churches in the area would gladly support additional child-care centers by furnishing their facilities, at little or no cost, provided the centers were managed as separate businesses. Jamie had located a building that could be developed into an excellent child-care center. Jamie reasoned that she and Lee could start the business in one or more of the churches and expand into the building she had found. Financially, the return from operating one child-care center would not quite equal Lee's current total compensation. However, two or more centers would yield a very nice income for both partners. Jamie had determined that appropriate licenses could be obtained in a few weeks and that the financing required to start the business was available at very favorable rates. Other materials and supplies were readily available as well.

Lee was intrigued with this proposition and told Jamie that she wanted a week to think it over. She intends to discuss her interest in this proposition with Jamie tomorrow.

Requirement
Using expectancy theory, indicate the factors that would have an impact on Lee's decision and the strength of her motivation to participate in the proposed business.

CONCLUDING CASE 1

MAKING VISIBLE CHANGES

In an industry characterized by fragmentation, poor management, and mediocre profits, a Houston-based beauty salon chain called Visible Changes is breaking all the records. Average sales at the chain's 20 salons are triple the industry figure. Sales per customer are almost twice the industry average, and sales of retail products as a percentage of revenues typically beat the industry average by a factor of almost four. In addition, turnover is one-third the industry rate.

When they launched their first salon in 1976, John and Maryanne McCormack envisioned a chain of elegant salons, located in shopping malls, that would provide excellent service to both men and women, require no appointments, attract high-volume business, and make large profits. To make their vision a reality, they would need to motivate their hairdressers to provide better service. This was no small challenge, since hairdressers tended to be recent graduates of hairdressing schools who, with salaries of less than $10,000, were trying to find a better way to make a living.

As a solution, the McCormacks came up with an elaborate incentive plan geared to encouraging their hairdressers to provide excellent service. Hairdressers at Visible Changes receive a 35 percent commission on payments from customers who request them by name, as opposed to 25 percent on payments from regular walk-in customers who make no requests. Further, when they are requested more than 75 percent of the time, they can charge a premium price (about

$10 more than the basic fee); for a request rate of 65 percent, there is also an add-on to the basic price. Thus hairdressers who please customers are more likely to be requested and are rewarded for their efforts. Hairdressers can also receive health insurance (an industry rarity) by selling $160 worth of hair-care products per week; for sales beyond that figure, hairdressers receive 15 percent commission. There are also annual bonuses. Once each quarter, each hairdresser is rated on a scale of 1 to 10, with points related to attitude, customer service, and the extent to which individual and salon goals have been met. Individuals who receive all 10 points each quarter are given an additional bonus amounting to 10 percent of their annual commissions. "Super-bonuses" are awarded to the most requested hairdressers and the best achievers in product sales. In addition, there is profit sharing, which was recently 15 percent of gross pay for everyone in the company. For one top hairdresser, these incentives added up to more than $60,000, not counting the trips that employees can win under special promotions. On average, Visible Changes hairdressers earn about $33,000 per year, while the national average is about $12,000.

Advanced training sessions in the latest haircutting techniques must be earned by meeting one's goals. Maryanne also makes videotapes showing the latest cutting techniques so that the hairdressers use standardized terminology and follow the same methods. High performers, who are, by definition, also the high earners, are asked to act as role models and share their

techniques for success. In addition, the hairdressers compete to be chosen for the "artistic team" that travels throughout the United States and abroad developing and demonstrating new haircuts. The McCormacks work hard to make sure that employees understand the incentive system and the rationale behind each element. The hairdressers often contribute ideas for refining the system. John keeps track of these indicators, as well as information about customer traffic and trends, through a computer system that gives him access to data within seconds.

To increase the level of training received by prospective hairdressers, the McCormacks recently opened Visible Changes University. Tuition is $7000 for the 10-month training program, but the McCormacks say that the quality of the training is much higher than average. John also notes that training haircutters will provide a supply of competent personnel needed for Visible Changes expansion. Annual sales at Visible Changes now top $26 million.[47]

QUESTIONS FOR CONCLUDING CASE 1

1 Assess the extent to which hairdressers can meet various needs at Visible Changes.
2 Using the cognitive theories of motivation, evaluate the Visible Changes incentive system.
3 Explain how reinforcement and vicarious learning are used at Visible Changes. What changes would you recommend?

CONCLUDING CASE 2

AVON'S DIRECT-SALES METHOD SUCCEEDS IN CHINA

Avon, a U.S. maker of cosmetics and related items, is experiencing note-worthy success in the city of Guangzhou (Canton), capital of Guangdong Province in the People's Republic of China. This success is largely due to the company's method of doing business. Avon recruits representatives who sell the products directly to customers and are paid a commission based on the volume they sell. In Guangzhou, the uniqueness of this incentive system is attracting a cadre of elite sellers, including doctors, engineers, teachers, and computer scientists. In their regular jobs, these professionals normally work for relatively low wages in a Communist system that gives little weight to performance. Becoming an Avon representative offers these individuals an opportunity to earn extra money on the basis of their selling success.

For example, Liang Yungjuan, a pediatrician, is one of Avon's star salespersons. Dr. Liang earns about $120 per month as a pediatrician, but she makes about 10 times that amount as a part-time Avon representative. "Avon has given me confidence in myself," she says. "I'm thinking of quitting my regular job to sell full-time. My son says I love Avon more than I love him."

Most representatives have full-time jobs, often with government agencies. The work norm, though, tends to follow the old Communist rule: "They pretend to pay us, we pretend to work." As a result, many of the representatives feel justified in spending part of their time at work selling Avon products.

In its representative system, Avon has salaried managers who recruit, train, and manage "fran-chise dealers." The dealers work to build up a clientele and can earn up to a 30 percent commission on their sales. They can also appoint Avon sales representatives. A dealer then earns about one-third of the 30 percent commissions earned by his or her representatives. Each franchise dealer works with an average of four representatives, resulting in about 25,000 local representatives. Dr. Liang is one such franchise dealer. The top dealers can earn between $2400 and $3000 per month (average per capita income in China is $350 to $400 per year). The typical dealer makes between $60 and $80 per month, which is still a sizable amount by local standards.

Unlike their U.S. counterparts, Avon representatives in China do not ring doorbells looking for sales. That type of cold calling would cause suspicion among potential customers. Instead, the representatives make sales to friends, relatives, neighbors, and coworkers. The major sources of sales, however, are offices, factories, and schools. In these settings, franchise dealers are invited by *danwei*, or work units, to make informal presentations on skin care, makeup, and grooming skills.

Before Avon arrived, cosmetics were available mainly in state-owned department stores, where inventories were unreliable and service was poor. Hence, it seems that there is a pent-up demand for cosmetics in the province. The average Avon product sells for $5, which is more expensive than the cosmetics available in the state-owned store but less expensive than most imported products. Unlike American women, who tend to favor makeup, Chinese women have a preference for skin-care products.

Avon's success in China did not come easily. During the mid-1980s, company officials spent 5 years attempting to interest government authorities in Beijing in a venture in northern China. "We didn't get anywhere," reports John Novosad, vice president in charge of Pacific operations for Avon. "They didn't understand the concept of direct selling and didn't know how to deal with it."

Eventually, a representative on Avon's international advisory board suggested that the company explore possibilities in Guangdong Province, where capitalism had begun to flourish despite official communism. After a year of negotiating, Avon was able to develop an agreement with province officials. Under the agreement, Avon owns 60 percent of the joint venture; Guangzhou Cosmetics Factory, a local partner, owns 35 percent; and two Hong Kong business associates hold 5 percent. The Avon cosmetics are bottled and packaged at the Guangzhou factory. Meanwhile, Avon is working on expanding into other cities and other provinces. The company recently opened a new facility in Shanghai to serve as Avon's regional distribution center for central China and has announced that it will build a new $40 million plant in southern China that will triple manufacturing capacity.[48]

QUESTIONS FOR CONCLUDING CASE 2

1 Assess the various motivational needs that underlie the success of Avon in Guangzhou.
2 Use expectancy theory to analyze the likely motivation of Dr. Liang.
3 What role is vicarious learning likely to play in the franchise dealers' success in recruiting and training effective new representatives?

LEARNING OBJECTIVES

After studying this chapter, you should be able to:

■ Outline the major sources of leader power and explain how leaders can use power to encourage subordinate commitment.

■ Describe the current state of efforts to identify leadership traits.

■ Explain the different findings of the Iowa, Michigan, and Ohio State studies of leader behaviors and discuss their implications.

■ Describe the Managerial Grid approach to leadership and assess the extent to which females and males behave differently as leaders.

■ Delineate Fiedler's contingency theory of leadership.

■ Contrast the following situational approaches to leadership: normative leadership model, situational leadership theory, and path-goal theory.

■ Describe transformational leadership and explain its link to innovation.

■ Evaluate the extent to which leaders are necessary in organizations.

GAINING THE EDGE

LEADERSHIP HELPS MATTEL EXCEL

When Jill Elikann Barad first joined Mattel, Inc., the El Segundo, California, toy maker, in 1981, she was made product manager of A Bad Case of Worms, a toy that slithered and slid along walls. The product itself didn't do very well, but she gained notice for her adept handling of a tough situation. Next she worked a stint in the boys' toys division before telling her boss she was ready for more responsibility.

As a result of that conversation, Barad was made a member of the Barbie team, a position in which she had a particular interest. She was soon made marketing director for Barbie, and under her leadership, Barbie doll sales began to mushroom. She is widely credited with seeing the potential of different "play patterns" for Barbie. For example, there is a Gymnast Barbie that can perform gymnastic routines, and a Bicyclin' Barbie that is a biker. "We've created a desire to own more than one Barbie," Barad says, "by allowing each individual Barbie to offer a unique play situation." According to company estimates, the average girl in the United States currently owns eight Barbie dolls. Other accessories, such as clothing and bikes, have boosted sales of the Barbie line to more than $1 billion, compared with $430 million in 1987. Barbie is sold in 144 countries.

On the basis of her spectacular success, Barad was promoted to president and chief operating officer of Mattel in 1992 and was named CEO in 1996. According to *Working Woman* magazine, she is one of the highest paid women in corporate America with recent total annual compensation estimated at $4.67 million.

Barad is known for having an "excellent product sense" and for being a creative thinker. As a leader she outlines visions, sets high goals, and mobilizes teamwork to reach the targets. She actively encourages innovation and is willing to take risks in the face of naysayers. In fact, she says that her pet peeve in a business setting is "hearing why we can't do something. I want to hear what the obstacles are, but I don't want to hear that they're impediments to what we have to do." She is adept at assessing the capabilities of those who work for her and inspiring them to stretch to new levels of achievement.

Barad herself typically wears a golden bumblebee pinned to her left shoulder as a lucky talisman and motivator. She received the bumblebee from her mother, who pointed out that aerodynamicists say bumblebees shouldn't be able to fly, but they do so anyway. The moral: A "can do" attitude is important; never say never. "When I get into a rough situation or when I feel there's something that's going to be particularly difficult, I look at that bumblebee," Barad says.

Overall, including other toy lines, such as Fisher-Price preschool action toys, Disney-licensed characters, Hot Wheels model race cars, and Cabbage Patch Kids, Mattel's annual sales top $3 billion. Barad is currently in the process of linking Barbie with consumer software that will create the world of Barbie on CD-ROM and extend Barbie's life into virtual reality. The plan is to add value to children's playing time through such means as taking journeys with Barbie that will help them explore opportunities open to them.[1] ■■■

As part of the Barbie team at Mattel, Jill Barad promoted the idea of different "play patterns" for Barbie, so that each Barbie model offered a unique play situation. The Barbie shown here can perform gymnastic routines. As a result of this concept, the average girl in the United States owns eight Barbie dolls. Barad's leadership skills moved her up the corporate ladder; she is now president and CEO of the toy company.

Faced with the need to revitalize Mattel's most famous brand name, Barad took firm hold of the reins and provided the leadership the Barbie product area needed. She has played a critical leadership role in creating a new vision for

Mattel and fashioning it into the world's largest toy maker. But what is leadership? **Leadership** is the process of influencing others to achieve organizational goals. It is considered the foundation of the management function known as leading. Being an effective leader is extremely challenging. Recent estimates indicate that as many as 50 to 60 percent of managers in organizations may actually be incompetent leaders.[2]

In this chapter, we explore the means that leaders have for influencing others. We consider the possibility that leaders have common traits, and we review the quest to identify universal leader behaviors that leaders can use in any situation. We then probe recent efforts to develop situational approaches that help leaders decide when certain types of behaviors are applicable. Next, we examine transformational leadership and its linkage to innovation. Finally, we consider the question of whether and under what circumstances leaders are necessary.

■ HOW LEADERS INFLUENCE OTHERS

Why do people accept the influence of a leader? Often, they do so because leaders have power. Yet Katharine Graham, chairperson of the influential Washington Post Company, notes, "Nobody ever has as much power as you think they do."[3] In this section, we examine the major sources of power and the ways that leaders can effectively use the power they potentially have available.

Sources of Leader Power

Power is the capacity to affect the behavior of others.[4] Leaders in organizations typically rely on some or all six major types of power:[5]

Legitimate power stems from a position's placement in the managerial hierarchy and the authority vested in the position. When we accept a job with an organization, we are usually aware that we will be receiving directions related to our work from an immediate boss and others in the hierarchy. Normally, we accept such directions as legitimate because these persons hold positions of authority.

Reward power is based on the capacity to control and provide valued rewards to others. Most organizations offer an array of rewards that may be under a manager's control, including pay raises, bonuses, interesting projects, promotion recommendations, a better office, support for training programs, assignments with high visibility in the organization, recognition, positive feedback, and time off.

Coercive power depends on the ability to punish others when they do not engage in desired behaviors. Forms of coercion or punishment that a manager may be empowered to use include criticisms, reprimands, suspensions, warning letters that go into an individual's personnel file, negative performance appraisals, demotions, withheld pay raises, and terminations.

Expert power is based on the possession of expertise that is valued by others. Managers often have considerable knowledge, technical skills, and experience that can be critical to subordinates' success.

Information power results from access to and control over the distribution of important information about organizational operations and future plans.[6] Managers usually have better access to such information than sub-

Leadership The process of influencing others to achieve organizational goals

Power The capacity to affect the behavior of others

Legitimate power Power that stems from a position's placement in the managerial hierarchy and the authority vested in the position

Reward power Power that is based on the capacity to control and provide valued rewards to others

Coercive power Power that depends on the ability to punish others when they do not engage in desired behaviors

Expert power Power that is based on the possession of expertise that is valued by others

Information power Power that results from access to and control over the distribution of important information about organizational operations and future plans

ordinates and some discretion over how much is disseminated to work-unit members.

Referent power Power that results from being admired, personally identified with, or liked by others

Referent power results from being admired, personally identified with, or liked by others. When we admire people, want to be like them, or feel friendship toward them, we more willingly follow their directions and exhibit loyalty toward them. Some observers argue that former CEO Lee Iacocca's initial success in turning around the Chrysler Corporation was based partially on the fact that he possessed referent power in relation to the work force.

Effective Use of Leader Power

Although all six types of power are potential means of influencing others, in actual usage they may elicit somewhat different levels of subordinate motivation.[7] Subordinates can react to a leader's direction with commitment, compliance, or resistance. With commitment, employees respond enthusiastically and exert a high level of effort toward organizational goals. With compliance, employees exert at least minimal efforts to complete directives but are likely to deliver average, rather than stellar, performance. With resistance, employees may appear to comply but actually do the absolute minimum, possibly even attempting to sabotage the attainment of organizational goals.

The relationship between a leader's use of the different sources of power and likely subordinate reactions is summarized in Table 13-1. As the table illustrates, expert power and referent power are most likely to lead to subordinate commitment, while legitimate power, information power, and reward power tend to result in compliance. The use of coercive power has a strong tendency to provoke resistance in subordinates. For example, when Chicago scrap-metal czar Cyrus Tang bought the ailing McLouth Steel Products Corporation, he relied on legitimate and coercive power to gain worker cooperation. Workers reacted with production slowdowns and a wildcat strike that eventually led to the further deterioration of the company and its sale to employees.[8] Not surprisingly, effective leaders tend to minimize the use of coercive power as much as possible.

Managers usually rely on several different types of power in order to be effective. This approach is evident in the leadership style of Bill Walsh, who coached the San Francisco 49ers to three Super Bowl championships within an 8-year period, and then became head football coach for Stanford University, before returning to assist the 49ers again. Walsh clearly has the legitimate power of his coach's position. However, he relies heavily on expert power by setting a strong standard of competence and exhibiting a thorough working knowledge of the game. For example, Walsh blocks out the whole season's practices minute by minute to ensure that players learn the individual and group skills necessary to be champions. He also uses referent power in the sense of building a reputation for turning his team's disadvantages into advantages. For

	TABLE 13-1 MAJOR SOURCES OF LEADER POWER AND LIKELY SUBORDINATE REACTIONS		
	LIKELY SUBORDINATE REACTION TO POWER SOURCE		
	RESISTANCE	**COMPLIANCE**	**COMMITMENT**
Power source	Coercion	Legitimate Information Reward	Referent Expert

instance, to help overcome the disadvantage of playing on the road, a situation in which the home team often has the advantage, Walsh uses heroic stories from World War II to help his players condition themselves for entering what is essentially enemy territory. He uses informational power to talk with each player and help each one understand his important role in the game. Yet he avoids coercion. According to one of his assistant coaches at Stanford, "One of the primary concerns that Bill passes on to his assistant is that we never demean a player, that we don't even holler. We must coach in a way that is respectful." Instead, he promotes closeness among team members.[9] While power helps explain the inducements behind leader influence, we need to look at additional concepts, such as leadership traits and behaviors, to help explain more fully how leaders exert influence in organizations.

■ SEARCHING FOR LEADERSHIP TRAITS

Although individuals have speculated for centuries on the nature of effective leadership, Army psychologists seeking methods for selecting officers during World War I set the stage for earnest postwar scientific research on the subject.[10] To early researchers, it seemed logical to try to identify significant traits that distinguish effective leaders from nonleaders.[11] **Traits** are distinctive internal qualities or characteristics of an individual, such as physical characteristics (e.g., height, weight, appearance, energy), personality characteristics (e.g., dominance, extroversion, originality), skills and abilities (e.g., intelligence, knowledge, technical competence), and social factors (e.g., interpersonal skills, sociability, and socioeconomic position).

Traits Distinctive internal qualities or characteristics of an individual, such as physical characteristics, personality characteristics, skills and abilities, and social factors

For the most part, early researchers initially measured various traits of individuals and then typically had the individuals work in leaderless groups (without appointed leaders). The idea was to see whether certain traits would predict the individuals who would emerge (be identified by members of the group) as leaders. Research turned away from the trait approach in the 1950s when extensive reviews of various studies suggested there were no traits that consistently distinguished leaders from nonleaders.[12]

More recent efforts, however, suggest the trait approach may have been abandoned prematurely. Sophisticated statistical techniques now allow better assessment of results across studies. Results indicate that several of the traits originally studied are associated with individuals' being identified as leaders by others—namely, intelligence, dominance, aggressiveness, and decisiveness.[13]

It is possible that future research may isolate traits that predict which individuals will be leaders, at least in some situations. For example, one famous study conducted at AT&T found that traits such as oral communication skills, human relations skills, need or motive for advancement, resistance to stress, tolerance of uncertainty, energy, and creativity were predictive of managerial advancement.[14] However, it is still an open question whether a set of traits, if they could be identified, would predict actual performance in leadership positions. Many management experts believe that performance is more closely related to the things leaders actually do than to the traits they possess. As a result, most recent leadership research has focused on leader behaviors.

■ IDENTIFYING LEADER BEHAVIORS

Why was Chairman Raymond L. Hixon able to build the Bonneville Pacific Corporation into a thriving independent power company, while John Kuhns, the Catalyst Energy chief, ran into difficulties leading a similar company?[15] A number of researchers have focused on the intriguing prospect that it may be specific *behaviors* that make some leaders more effective than others. Whereas many inherent traits may be difficult to change, it might be possible for most of us to learn universally effective behaviors—if they could be identified—and become successful leaders. In this section, we review major efforts at identifying important leader behaviors. This research grew largely out of work at the University of Iowa, the University of Michigan, and Ohio State University. We also explore the question of whether females and males exhibit different behaviors in leadership positions.

Iowa and Michigan Studies

Autocratic Behavioral style of leaders who tend to make unilateral decisions, dictate work methods, limit worker knowledge about goals to just the next step to be performed, and sometimes give feedback that is punitive

Democratic Behavioral style of leaders who tend to involve the group in decision making, let the group determine work methods, make overall goals known, and use feedback as an opportunity for helpful coaching

Laissez-faire Behavioral style of leaders who generally give the group complete freedom, provide necessary materials, participate only to answer questions, and avoid giving feedback

University of Iowa researcher Kurt Lewin and his colleagues conducted some of the earliest attempts at scientifically identifying the leader behaviors that are most effective.[16] They concentrated on three leader behaviors, or styles: autocratic, democratic, and laissez-faire. **Autocratic** leaders tend to make unilateral decisions, dictate work methods, limit worker knowledge about goals to just the next step to be performed, and sometimes give punitive feedback. In contrast, **democratic** leaders tend to involve the group in decision making, let the group determine work methods, make overall goals known, and use feedback as an opportunity for helpful coaching. **Laissez-faire** leaders generally give the group complete freedom, provide necessary materials, participate only to answer questions, and avoid giving feedback—in other words, they do almost nothing.

To determine which leadership style is most effective, the Lewin researchers trained different adults to exhibit each of the styles and then placed them in charge of various groups in preadolescent boys' clubs. They quickly found that on every criteria in the study, groups with laissez-faire leaders underperformed in comparison with both the autocratic and democratic groups. On the other hand, while quantity of work was equal in the groups with autocratic and democratic leaders, work quality and group satisfaction were higher in the democratic groups. Thus it appeared that democratic leadership could lead to both good quantity and good quality of work, as well as satisfied workers. Perhaps the key to effective leadership had been found.

Unfortunately, later research produced more mixed results. Democratic leadership sometimes produced higher performance than autocratic leadership but at other times produced performance that was lower than or merely equal to that under the autocratic style. Results related to subordinate satisfaction were more consistent. Satisfaction levels were generally higher with a democratic leadership style than with an autocratic one.[17]

These findings, though, created a dilemma for managers. While a democratic leadership style seemed to make subordinates more satisfied, it did not always lead to higher, or even equal, performance. Furthermore, many managers were not used to operating in a democratic mode. To help managers sort out this dilemma, particularly with regard to making decisions, management scholars Robert Tannenbaum and Warren H. Schmidt developed the continuum of leader behaviors shown in Figure 13-1.[18] The continuum represents various gradations of leadership behavior, ranging from the autocratic (or boss-centered) approach at the extreme left to the democratic (or subordinate-centered) approach at the extreme right. A move away from the autocratic end of the continuum represents a move toward the democratic end and vice versa. In developing the continuum, the researchers softened the meaning of "autocratic" somewhat. In their usage, the term does not necessarily include tendencies to be punitive or keep the ultimate goal of task activities hidden from subordinates. At the autocratic end of the continuum, it does mean that the

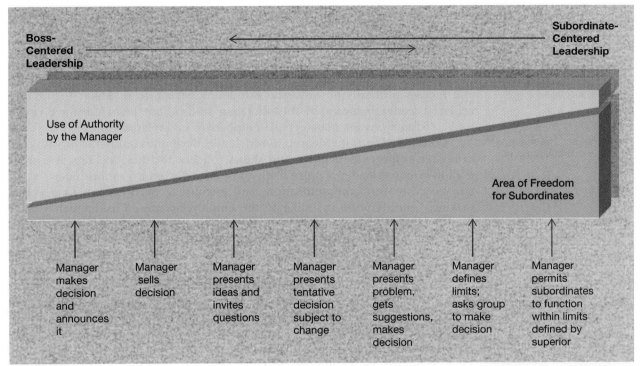

Boss-
Centered
Leadership

Subordinate-
Centered
Leadership

Use of Authority
by the Manager

Area of Freedom
for Subordinates

| Manager makes decision and announces it | Manager sells decision | Manager presents ideas and invites questions | Manager presents tentative decision subject to change | Manager presents problem, gets suggestions, makes decision | Manager defines limits; asks group to make decision | Manager permits subordinates to function within limits defined by superior |

Figure 13-1 *Continuum of leader behaviors. (Robert Tannenbaum and Warren H. Schmidt, "How to Choose a Leadership Pattern,"* Harvard Business Review, *vol. 51, May–June 1973, p. 164.)*

boss makes the decision and lets others know what they are supposed to do, rather than involving them in the decision.

According to Tannenbaum and Schmidt, managers, in deciding which leader behavior pattern to adopt, need to consider forces within themselves (such as comfort level with the various alternatives), within subordinates (such as readiness to assume responsibility), and within the situation (such as time pressures). In the short run managers need to exercise some flexibility in their leader behavior depending on the situation. The researchers advised that in the long run managers should attempt to move toward the subordinate-centered end of the continuum, on the premise that such leader behavior has a higher potential for increasing employee motivation, decision quality, teamwork, morale, and employee development.

Further work on leadership at the University of Michigan seemed to confirm the usefulness of an *employee-centered* approach when compared with a more *job-centered,* or production-centered, approach. With the employee-centered approach, leaders focused on building effective work groups dedicated to high performance goals. With the job-centered approach, leaders divided the work into routine tasks and closely supervised workers to ensure that the prescribed methods were followed and that productivity standards were met. Still, output varied, with the employee-centered approach sometimes resulting in low output and the job-centered approach sometimes resulting in high output.[19] Clearly, further investigation of the leadership question was needed.

Ohio State Studies

A group of researchers at Ohio State University developed another strategy for studying leadership. They began by identifying a number of important leader behaviors. Then they developed a questionnaire that enabled them to measure the behaviors of different leaders and track factors such as group performance and satisfaction to see which behaviors were most effective. Although the researchers isolated a number of different leader behaviors, or styles, two stood out as particularly important: initiating structure and consideration.

Initiating structure is the degree to which a leader defines his or her own role and the roles of subordinates in terms of achieving unit goals. It includes many basic managerial functions, such as planning, organizing, and directing, and focuses primarily on task issues. Initiating structure is similar to the job-centered leader behavior of the Michigan studies, but it includes a broader range of functions for managers. It emphasizes task-related issues.

Consideration is the degree to which a leader builds mutual trust with subordinates, respects their ideas, and shows concern for their feelings. A consideration-oriented leader is more likely to be friendly toward subordinates, maintain good two-way communication, and encourage participation in decision making. Consideration is similar to the employee-centered leader behavior of the Michigan studies. It emphasizes people-related issues.

These two styles are illustrated by managers Ann Fudge and Lynn Shostack, respectively (see the Case in Point discussion).

Initiating structure The degree to which a leader defines his or her own role and the roles of subordinates in terms of achieving unit goals

Consideration The degree to which a leader builds mutual trust with subordinates, respects their ideas, and shows concern for their feelings

---

CASE IN POINT

SUCCESSFUL LEADERS AT MAXWELL HOUSE AND JOYCE

Ann Fudge (top), president of Maxwell House Coffee, exemplifies consideration leadership. Initiating structure is more Lynn Shostack's style as CEO of Joyce International.

Ann Fudge, president of Maxwell House Coffee, runs a $1.4 billion business within Philip Morris Companies' Kraft Foods Division. She is in charge of fighting the stiff competition from specialty coffee makers, such as Starbucks. Fudge is known for finding great ideas to solve business problems and is very willing to listen to the ideas of others. She is known as a team builder who can generate enthusiasm among the people who work for her. To promote new approaches and working together effectively, Fudge holds problem-solving meetings with various employees from secretaries to technical experts. She created a "Blue Sky Room" where her staff can brainstorm and set up an awards program for new ideas. "She is a low-key and confident manager who gets the most out of people who work for her," says one observer. Michael A. Miles, former CEO of Philip Morris, says, "I used to think she ought to lose her temper occasionally and pound the table once in a while."[20] Fudge is a successful manager who relies heavily on the consideration leadership style.

On the other hand, Lynn Shostack, who left a job as head of the Bankers Trust consumer division to take over as CEO of ailing Joyce International, Inc., has a reputation for being "tough, but fair" and for letting employees know what is expected of them. Joyce is an office-furniture company with $350 million in annual sales and more than 4000 employees. Considered a brilliant strategist, Shostack excels at developing plans and organizing others to achieve the necessary goals. She sets high standards and rewards employees who meet them. During her first 21 months at Joyce, Shostack worked hard on innovative cost-cutting measures to stem serious losses. Her efforts produced immediate results: a $5 million pretax profit in her first year.[21] Shostack is a manager who has been successful with a leadership style that emphasizes initiating structure. ■■■

In a major departure from the Iowa and Michigan studies, both of which considered their leadership dimensions to be opposite ends of the same continuum, the Ohio State researchers proposed that initiating structure and con-

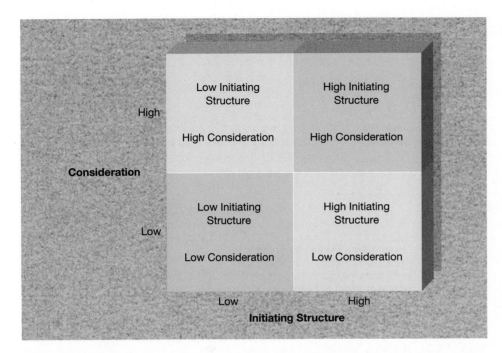

Figure 13-2 *Ohio State two-dimensional model of leader behaviors.*

sideration were two independent behaviors.[22] This meant that the behaviors operated on separate continuums. A leader could be high on both, low on both, or high on one and low on the other, or could display various gradations in between. The Ohio State two-dimensional approach is depicted in Figure 13-2. This configuration made sense, since many leaders seemed to have characteristics of both initiating structure and consideration. For example, Lynn Shostack of Joyce International practices the initiating-structure style but is known for encouraging and supporting good employees. On the other hand, Ann Fudge of Maxwell House Coffee relies on the consideration style, but she instituted a "Shape Up" program to eliminate unnecessary reports and keeps her eye solidly on the bottom line.[23]

The two-dimensional approach led to the interesting possibility that a leader might be able to place high emphasis on task issues and still promote high levels of subordinate satisfaction by simultaneously exhibiting consideration behavior. While initial studies supported the idea that a leader exhibiting both high initiating structure and high consideration would produce the best results, the notion of the great high-high leader was later pronounced a myth.[24] Why did the high-high approach fall from favor? The main reason was that, like the Iowa and Michigan studies, it was too simplistic. As research began to accumulate, it became clear that situational factors, such as the nature of the task and subordinate expectations, also affect the success of leadership behaviors.[25]

The Managerial Grid

One popularized outgrowth of the emphasis on leader behaviors aimed at both task and people issues is the Managerial Grid®, developed by Robert Blake and Jane Srygley Mouton.[26] Rather than focusing directly on the leader behaviors addressed by the Ohio State studies, the grid approach uses parallel leader attitudes—concern for people and concern for production. A recent version of the grid, which has been used as a training device in a large number of organizations, is shown in Figure 13-3. Depending on the degree of concern for

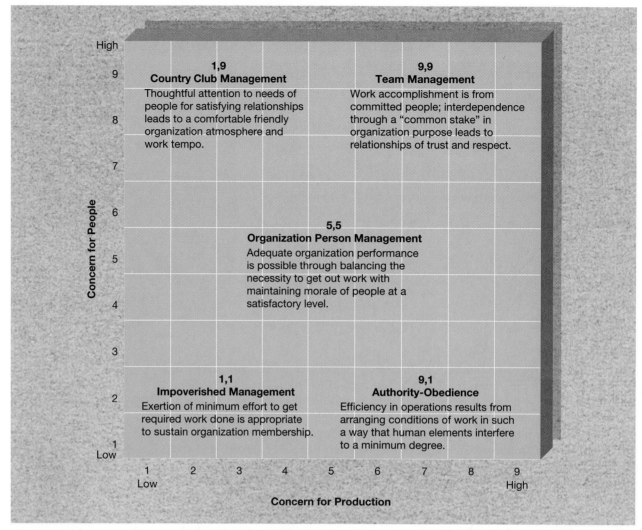

High

9   **1,9**
     Country Club Management
     Thoughtful attention to needs of
8   people for satisfying relationships
     leads to a comfortable friendly
     organization atmosphere and
7   work tempo.

                                          9,9
                                          Team Management
                                          Work accomplishment is from
                                          committed people; interdependence
                                          through a "common stake" in
                                          organization purpose leads to
                                          relationships of trust and respect.

6

                  5,5
                  Organization Person Management
5   Adequate organization performance
                  is possible through balancing the
                  necessity to get out work with
4   maintaining morale of people at a
                  satisfactory level.

3

2   **1,1**
     Impoverished Management
     Exertion of minimum effort to get
     required work done is appropriate
1   to sustain organization membership.

                                          9,1
                                          Authority-Obedience
                                          Efficiency in operations results from
                                          arranging conditions of work in such
                                          a way that human elements interfere
                                          to a minimum degree.

Low

Concern for People

     1   2   3   4   5   6   7   8   9
     Low   High

Concern for Production

Figure 13-3 *The Managerial Grid. (Reprinted from Robert A. Blake and Jane S. Mouton, The Managerial Grid® III, Gulf Publishing, Houston, 1985, p. 12.)*

people and production, a manager can fall anywhere on the grid. Blake and Mouton argue that the most desirable leadership approach is the 9,9 orientation, involving a high concern for both people and production. However, the Ohio State studies suggest that a 9,9 orientation might not always be the best. The grid does allow for some flexibility in actual leader behaviors, depending on a leader's assessment of the people and production issues in a given situation.

Managing Diversity: Female versus Male Leader Behaviors

In the course of studying various leader behaviors, some researchers began to wonder whether female managers exhibit different leader behaviors than male managers. Early survey data indicated that a number of people viewed females as being highly oriented toward interpersonal issues and, therefore, possibly ill-suited for leadership positions. Males were seen as more oriented toward task issues and as better candidates for leadership slots.[27] As it turns out, neither stereotype is correct. Most studies indicate that female and male leaders are similar in the amounts of interpersonal and task behaviors they exhibit or that differences tend to be small. Furthermore, they appear to be equally effective in terms of eliciting subordinate job satisfaction and performance.[28]

Nevertheless, women holding top-level positions in major companies are relatively rare. One recent study indicates that only two CEOs in the Fortune 1000 industrials are female (Linda Wachner of Warnaco, who was profiled in the opening case in Chapter 3, and Marion Sandler, who is co-CEO with her husband, Herbert, of Oakland, California–based Golden West Financial).[29] Since then, Jill Elikann Barad has become CEO of Mattel (see opening case in this chapter). A 1995 federal Glass Ceiling Commission report noted that, although women currently earn about 35 percent of the masters of business administration degrees in the United States, they hold only about 5 percent of senior-level management posts in the Fortune 1000 industrial or Fortune 500 service firms. The federal commission was investigating the "*glass ceiling,*" a term that has been coined to refer to barriers impeding the upward mobility of women to top-level managerial positions in organizations. The commission's recommendations included promotion of work-force diversity programs, expansion of traditional executive recruitment networks, and the establishment of formal mentoring and career development programs to help stop channeling women and minorities into staff positions that lead to diminished prospects for promotion to executive positions.[30]

■ DEVELOPING SITUATIONAL THEORIES

Although they attempted to identify effective leader behaviors that would work in every situation, the various researchers pursuing the behavioral view of leadership eventually found that leader behaviors that worked well in one situation were often not as effective in another situation. As a result, theories of leadership began to emerge that take into consideration important situational factors. Such approaches are called **situational theories** because of their situational emphasis. They are also often called *contingency theories* of leadership because they hold that appropriate leader traits or behaviors are *contingent,* or dependent, on relevant situational characteristics. Since there are potentially many situational factors that could influence the effectiveness of leaders, several different situational approaches have evolved. Among the most prominent are Fiedler's contingency model, the normative leadership model, Hersey and Blanchard's situational theory, and path-goal theory. Each provides useful guidance for managers.

Situational theories Theories of leadership that take into consideration important situational factors

Fiedler's Contingency Model

Arguably the most well known of the situational approaches is **Fiedler's contingency model,** originally developed by leadership researcher Fred Fiedler and his associates.[31] This model posits that leaders differ in the degrees of their orientation toward the task versus toward the people. This difference makes leaders more effective in some types of situations than in others. Fiedler's contingency model identifies the types of situations in which each kind of leader is likely to do best.

Fiedler's contingency model A situational approach (developed by Fiedler and his associates) that posits that leaders differ in the degrees of their orientation toward the task versus toward the people

LPC ORIENTATION A cornerstone of the contingency model, then, is a leader's **LPC (least preferred coworker) orientation,** a personality trait indicating the extent to which an individual places a higher priority or value on task accomplishment than on personal relationships. A leader's LPC orientation can be measured using the LPC scale, which consists of 18 sets of bipolar adjectives. The leader is asked to describe the "person with whom [he or she] can work least well" by rating the person on a range of 1 to 8 points for each set. An example of one of the sets is:

LPC (least preferred coworker) orientation A personality trait indicating the extent to which an individual places a higher priority or value on task accomplishment than on personal relationships

Pleasant ____ : ____ : ____ : ____ : ____ : ____ : ____ : ____ Unpleasant
   8   7   6   5   4   3   2   1

If a leader describes a least preferred coworker in relatively negative terms on the LPC scale, the leader is likely to be task-motivated and inclined to put "business before pleasure." Conversely, if the leader describes the least preferred coworker in relatively positive terms, the leader is likely to be people-motivated and to believe that a close relationship with coworkers is an important variable for team success. The basic idea behind the contingency model, then, is that the leader's LPC orientation should be carefully matched to situational factors that favor that type of leader's prospects for success.

ASSESSING THE SITUATION The contingency model cites three situational factors that affect the degree of favorability or the degree of situational control for a leader:

Leader-member relations is the extent to which a leader has the support of group members. It is the most important situational variable. To assess this factor, a leader considers the issue "Will the group members do what I tell them, are they reliable, and do they support me?"

Task structure is the extent to which a task is clearly specified with regard to goals, methods, and standards of performance. When task assignments are vague, it is difficult to know what should be done and to assess how one is doing. Therefore, low task structure reduces the favorableness, or situational control, of the leader, while high task structure raises it. To analyze this factor, a leader evaluates the question "Do I know what I am supposed to do and how the job is to be done?"

Position power is the amount of power that the organization gives the leader to accomplish necessary tasks. It is strongly related to the ability to reward and punish. To evaluate this factor, a leader considers the issue "Do I have the support and backing of the 'big boss' and the organization in dealing with subordinates?"

MATCHING LEADERSHIP STYLE AND SITUATION The contingency model combines different levels of these three situational factors into eight situations, or octants, that represent different degrees of favorability, or situational control (see Figure 13-4). For example, the combination of good leader-member relations, high task structure, and strong position power—octant 1—is the most favorable situation. The boxes below each octant indicate which type of leader (low LPC or high LPC) matches the situation and thus is likely to be the most effective. According to the contingency model, in situations of either high favorability (octants 1, 2, and 3, on the left) or extremely low favorability (octant 8, on the far right), a low-LPC leader does best; in situations of moderate favorability (octants 4 through 7), a high-LPC leader excels.

The logic behind the contingency model is that when the situation is very unfavorable, the leader must strongly emphasize the need for task accomplishment in order to get the group moving toward its goal. On the other hand, when the situation is very favorable, a task-oriented leader can easily obtain the cooperation of the group in doing whatever is necessary to complete the task, because workers willingly involve themselves. When the situation is only moderately favorable, because of either poor leader-member relations or an unstructured task, a supportive, relationship-oriented leader can emphasize good working relationships among group members or provide support as the group seeks to cope with an unstructured task.[32]

Elements of Situation	Decreasing Situational Favorability/Control							
Leader-Member Relations	Good				Poor			
Task Structure	High		Low		High		Low	
Position Power	Strong	Weak	Strong	Weak	Strong	Weak	Strong	Weak
Octant	1	2	3	4	5	6	7	8
Characteristics of Leader — Relationship-Oriented (High LPC)	Mismatch	Mismatch	Mismatch	Match	Match	Match	Match	Mismatch
Task-Oriented (Low LPC)	Match	Match	Match	Mismatch	Mismatch	Mismatch	Mismatch	Match

Note: Leaders perform best when there exists a match between characteristics of leader and elements of situation.

Figure 13-4 *Fiedler's contingency model of leadership. (Adapted from Arthur G. Jago, "Leadership: Perspectives in Theory and Research,"* Management Science, *vol. 28, 1982, p. 324.)*

Fiedler believes that managers cannot easily change their LPC orientation or management style. As a result, he argues that leaders need to understand their leadership style and analyze the degree of favorability, or situational control. If the match between the two is not good, a leader needs to either make changes (e.g., increase task structure) or find a more compatible leadership situation. Fiedler calls this approach "engineering the job to fit the manager." One task-oriented leader who has been extremely successful is Chung Ju-Yung of Korea's Hyundai Group (see the Case in Point discussion).

COMPANY FOUNDER CHUNG JU-YUNG BUILDS HYUNDAI

CASE IN POINT

Chung Ju-Yung built a small general contracting firm into one of the largest organizations in the world, the Hyundai Group. Chung is famous for his task-oriented approach and the almost military discipline in his workers' ranks.

One manager with a reputation for being extremely task oriented is Chung Ju-Yung, founder and longtime chairman of one of Korea's foremost conglomerates, or *chaebol* (the name often given to large Korean companies operating in many diverse industries). Chung's organization, the Hyundai Group, ranks among the largest organizations in the world.

Chung, who comes from a peasant background and has only a grade-school education, started Hyundai in 1947 as a general contracting firm that built barracks and repaired trucks for the U.S. Army. When the Korean war ended in 1953, Chung turned his company to construction, winning major contracts from the South Korean government to build roads, bridges, office buildings, and other structures. The company also moved into a variety of other businesses, including shipbuilding, automobiles, and electronics. Hyundai became famous in the United States after the company launched its low-priced Excel in 1986, a car that broke automotive import records for first-year sales. Chung has spent millions of advertising dollars to make the Hyundai name familiar to Americans by pointing out that it rhymes with "Sunday."

Because of Chung's strong task orientation, his name has been synonymous with major moves made by the Hyundai Group. Employees at Hyundai have followed his lead willingly because of his "tremendous analytical mind" and his extraordinary record of success. In addition, Chung's two brothers and six sons have held high-level positions in the company, further strengthening the positive leader-member relations. For years, every morning, Chung held a meeting of executives that often included lower-level managers. These meetings were strongly focused on necessary task accomplishments, with Chung clearly specifying what was to be done. At the company's Ulsan complex, where 60,000 of Hyundai's more than 150,000 workers produce ships and automobiles, discipline has been described as almost military in nature. Now in his eighties, Chung remains honorary chairman.[33]　■■■

With his task orientation, Chung has helped Hyundai become a major international success. His leadership behavior contrasts strongly with that of Kim Woo-Choong, chairman of Daewoo, another of Korea's major conglomerates. Kim, who started Daewoo in the mid-1960s, is a graduate of the prestigious Yonsei University and depends on professional managers and task forces. He has traditionally involved himself only in major strategic decisions. Beyond that, he emphasizes positive working relationships among managers and encourages them to be innovative and take risks. Kim has been successful through his relationship-oriented approach because he has built a strong group of very competent employees, whom he encourages to use initiative. Lately, though, Kim has been dissatisfied with the performance of Daewoo, has become more involved in operational decisions, and is now accused of bribing a former South Korean president.[34]

Recent sophisticated analyses of various studies of Fiedler's contingency model support its usefulness for managers. However, these analyses suggest that there are also other factors at work that are not accounted for in the contingency model.[35] Thus managers need to rely on additional situational leadership theories, such as the normative leadership model.

Normative Leadership Model

Normative leadership model
A model that helps leaders assess critical situational factors that affect the extent to which they should involve subordinates in particular decisions

The **normative leadership model** was designed for a fairly narrow, but important, purpose. It helps leaders assess critical situational factors that affect the extent to which they should involve subordinates in particular decisions.[36]

The model includes five types of management decision methods for use with group problems (problems in which the decision can affect more than one subordinate in the work unit). The five methods are shown in Table 13-2. Each method is designated by a letter and a number. "A," "C," and "G" stand for "autocratic," "consultative," and "group," respectively. The autocratic and consultative approaches each have two variations, designated I and II. The decision methods become progressively more participative as one moves from AI (decide yourself) to GII (let the group decide).

To help managers determine which method to use in a given situation, the normative leadership model includes eight basic questions about attributes of the decision problem (see the top of Figure 13-5). For the most part, the questions are self-explanatory. However, two points of clarification may be helpful to you. First, in question QR "technical quality" means the extent to which the solution will facilitate the reaching of external objectives (e.g., better quality, lower cost, more long lasting). Second, the structure aspect of question ST (problem structure) is similar to the structure issue in Fiedler's contingency theory. With structured problems, it is relatively clear where you are, where you want to go, and what you need to do to get there (e.g., deciding when to schedule the manufacturing of extra batches of an existing product). Unstructured problems are more "fuzzy" in regard to understanding the current situation, formulating goals, and determining how to achieve the goals (e.g., deciding which new products to develop).

TABLE 13-2 NORMATIVE LEADERSHIP MODEL DECISION STYLES

SYMBOL	DEFINITION
AI	You solve the problem or make the decision yourself using the information available to you at the present time.
AII	You obtain any necessary information from subordinates, then decide on a solution to the problem yourself. You may or may not tell subordinates the purpose of your questions or give information about the problem or decision on which you are working. The input provided by them is clearly in response to your request for specific information. They do not play a role in the definition of the problem or in generating or evaluating alternative solutions.
CI	You share the problem with the relevant subordinates individually, getting their ideas and suggestions without bringing them together as a group. Then *you* make the decision. This decision may or may not reflect your subordinates' influence.
CII	You share the problem with your subordinates in a group meeting. In this meeting you obtain their ideas and suggestions. Then *you* make the decision, which may or may not reflect your subordinates' influence.
GII	You share the problem with you subordinates as a group. Together you generate and evaluate alternatives and attempt to reach agreement (consensus) on a solution. Your role is much like that of chairperson, coordinating the discussion, keeping it focused on the problem, and making sure that the critical issues are discussed. You can provide the group with information or ideas that you have, but you do not try to "press" them to adopt "your" solution, and you are willing to accept and implement any solution that has the support of the entire group.

Source: Reprinted from Victor H. Vroom and Philip W. Yetton, *Leadership and Decision Making,* University of Pittsburgh Press, Pittsburgh, 1973.

The eight questions are used in conjunction with the two decision trees shown in Figure 13-5. The development-driven decision tree is used when developing subordinates is more important than conserving time in the decision process. The time-driven decision tree is used when minimizing time is more important than developing subordinates.

To see how the decision trees work, let us consider what happened when the Springfield Remanufacturing Corporation of Springfield, Missouri, ran into a crisis. The company had signed a 10-year, $75 million agreement with General Motors to remanufacture automotive diesel engines. The contract helped revive the company, which had previously spent a number of years as a dying division of International Harvester. After spending several hectic years getting production lined up and meeting schedules, Springfield received a sudden call from GM's material scheduling division, which wanted to cut 5000 engines from the annual schedule. Jack Stack, Springfield's CEO, won a 90-day delay in the cuts. During that time he pondered what to do. Analysis showed that the cuts would force him to lay off 100 people, an action Stack had somehow managed to avoid for 19 years. He narrowed down the prospects. If he kept everyone, the workers would need to go out and generate 50,000 person-hours worth of business. But if they weren't successful, there would be no time to recoup. Instead of having to lay off 100, Stack would have to lay off 200. How should he make this decision?

Using the time-driven decision tree (Figure 13-5), the analysis would go like this:

Quality requirement: Low, because both alternatives would allow the company to stay in business.

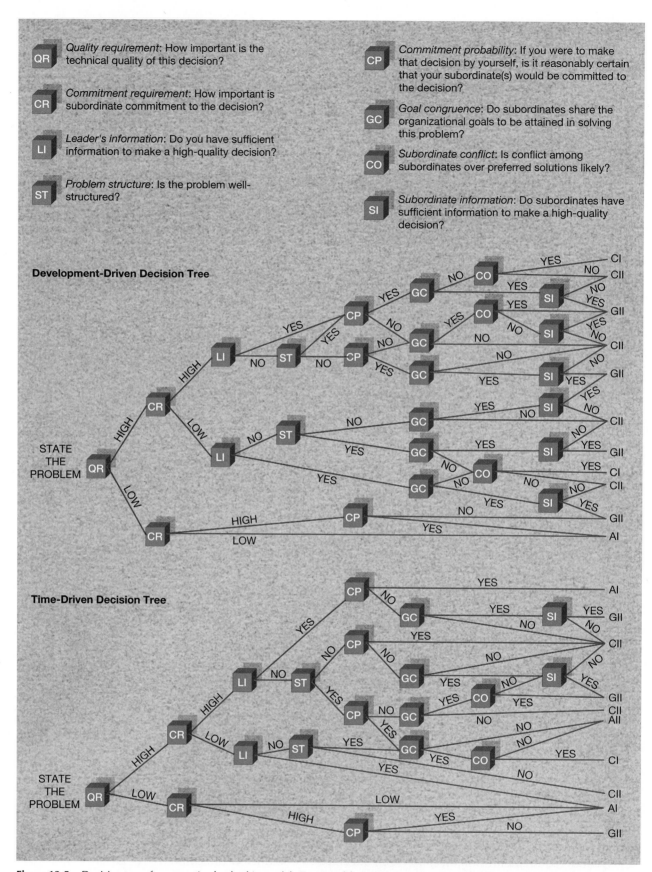

Figure 13-5 *Decision trees for normative leadership model. (Reprinted from Victor H. Vroom and Arthur G. Jago,* The New Leadership: Managing Participation in Organizations, *Prentice-Hall, Englewood Cliffs, N.J., 1988, pp. 184–185.)*

Commitment requirement: High; commitment is needed to make it work.

Commitment probability: No; there might be resentment over the layoffs.

Model's suggested approach: Let the group decide.

Stack called a meeting of all 350 employees, presented the alternatives, and asked them what they wanted to do. Almost unanimously they replied: "Go for it. Let's keep the people." For the next year, they all worked extremely hard, taking any jobs they could get, selling in any kind of market they could get into, and starting product lines with which they had no previous experience. It was brutal, but they did it. The company made $2 million more than in the previous year and even had to add people. "If we had done that layoff," Stack says, "I don't think we ever would have recovered. We'd have lost momentum. As tired as everybody is, they really feel great that they did it."[37]

For this situation it was not necessary to answer all eight decision-tree questions. The decision tree skips over questions that are irrelevant to certain paths. (In this case, use of the development-driven decision tree would yield the same result. Often, however, the results from the two decision trees differ.) Our example considered the normative leadership model as it applies to possible involvement of a group, but there is also a version of the model that can be used for individual decision problems—those involving just one other person.

Situational Leadership Theory

Another widely known contingency theory that can be useful to managers is the **situational leadership theory,** developed by Paul Hersey and Ken Blanchard. It is based on the premise that leaders need to alter their behaviors depending on one major situational factor—the readiness of followers.[38]

The situational theory focuses on two leader behaviors that are similar to the initiating-structure and consideration behaviors pioneered by the Ohio State researchers:

> *Task behavior* refers to the extent to which the leader engages in spelling out the duties and responsibilities of an individual or group. It includes telling people what to do, how to do it, when to do it, where to do it, and who is to do it.

> *Relationship behavior* refers to the extent to which the leader engages in two-way or multiway communication. It includes listening, facilitating, and supportive behaviors.

Since these behaviors, like the Ohio State leader behaviors, are considered to be two independent dimensions, a leader could be high on both, low on both, or high on one and low on the other (see the four quadrants in Figure 13-6).

To determine which combination of leader behaviors to use in a given situation, according to situational leadership theory, a leader must assess an interesting factor: the readiness levels of followers. Follower readiness is the ability and willingness of followers to accomplish a particular task. *Ability* (job readiness) includes the ability, skill, knowledge, and experience that are needed to do a specific task. *Willingness* (psychological readiness) consists of the confidence, commitment, and motivation that are needed to complete a specific task. As can be seen at the bottom of Figure 13-6, the readiness continuum is divided into four levels: low (R1), low to moderate (R2), moderate to high (R3), and high (R4).

Situational leadership theory
A theory (developed by Hersey and Blanchard) based on the premise that leaders need to alter their behaviors depending on one major situational factor—the readiness of followers

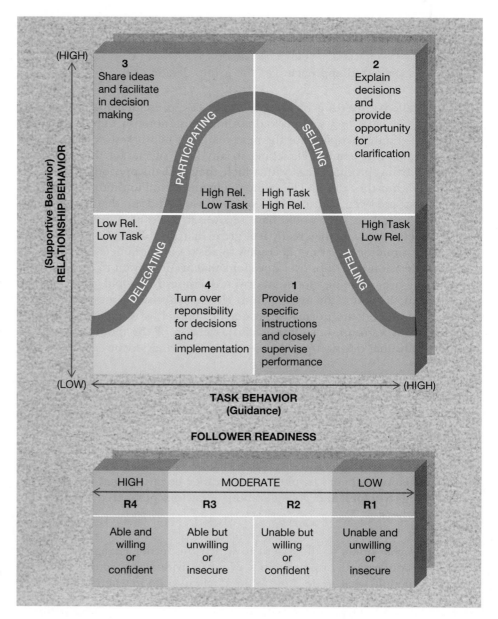

The bell-shaped curve running through the four leadership quadrants prescribes the appropriate leadership style for a given level of readiness:

Telling is used in situations of low readiness, when followers are unable and also unwilling or too insecure to take responsibility for a given task. The telling style involves giving individuals specific directions on what to do and how to do it.

Selling is used for low to moderate readiness, when followers are unable to take responsibility but are willing or feel confident to do so. The selling style is aimed at giving specific directions, but it is also supportive of the individual's willingness and enthusiasm.

Participating is used for moderate to high readiness, when followers are able to take responsibility but are unwilling or too insecure to do so. Since they are able to perform, a supportive, and participating style, in which the leader emphasizes two-way communication and collaboration, is most likely to be effective.

Delegating is used for high readiness, when followers are able and willing or confident enough to take appropriate responsibility. At this point, they need relatively little support or direction; hence the delegating style has the best prospect of success.

To apply the situational theory of leadership, leaders need to determine what task areas they would like to influence, assess the readiness level of the individual, and select the leadership style that corresponds to that level. The theory's underlying notion is that leaders should help increase the task-related readiness of followers as quickly as feasible by appropriately adjusting their own leadership styles to move through the cycle from telling to delegating. Results of one of the most comprehensive tests of the situational theory to date indicate that its best application may be with newly hired employees or employees in new jobs. These are the individuals most likely to benefit from the highly structured leadership behavior of the telling style.[39]

Andrew S. Grove, president of Intel, a company well known for its semiconductor technology, makes extensive use of the situational leadership approach. He assesses a subordinate's task-relevant readiness to help him decide what type of leadership style to use. Grove points out that it is very possible for an individual to have high task-relevant readiness in one job but not in another. He uses as an example a very productive sales manager who was moved from the field to a plant and placed in charge of a factory unit. Although the size and scope of the two jobs were similar, the manager's performance began to deteriorate, and he appeared to be overwhelmed by the assignment. Grove explains that while the individual was extremely capable in his former position, his readiness for the new job was "extremely low, since its environment, content, and task were all new to him." Over time, he gained more experience with the job and his task-relevant readiness began to increase. Simultaneously, his performance began to rise to the outstanding level that the top managers had expected when they promoted him. "What happened here should have been totally predictable," notes Grove, "yet we were surprised."[40]

Path-Goal Theory

The last major situational leadership theory that we consider, the **path-goal theory** of leadership, attempts to explain how leader behavior can positively influence the motivation and job satisfaction of subordinates.[41] It is called path-goal theory because it focuses on how leaders influence the way that subordinates perceive work goals and possible paths to reaching both work goals (performance) and personal goals (intrinsic and extrinsic rewards).

Path-goal theory relies heavily on the expectancy theory of motivation. As discussed more thoroughly in Chapter 12, expectancy theory involves three main elements: effort-performance expectancy (the probability that our efforts will lead to the required performance level), performance-outcome expectancy (the probability that our successful performance will lead to certain outcomes or rewards), and valence (the anticipated value of the outcomes or rewards). Path-goal theory uses expectancy theory for guidance in determining ways that a leader might make the achievement of work goals easier or more attractive.

LEADER BEHAVIORS In order to affect subordinate perceptions of paths and goals, path-goal theory identifies four major leader behaviors that can be used:

> **Directive** leader behavior involves letting subordinates know what is expected of them, providing guidance about work methods, developing

Path-goal theory A theory that attempts to explain how leader behavior can positively influence the motivation and job satisfaction of subordinates

Directive Leader behavior that involves letting subordinates know what is expected of them, providing guidance about work methods, developing work schedules, identifying work evaluation standards, and indicating the basis for outcomes or rewards

How do you make a raft out of 50-gallon drums, two-by-fours, and rope? That's the task top executives at General Foods are asked to perform as part of their leadership training. This group found out that reaching the goal of a workable raft requires a combination of directive, supportive, participative, and achievement-oriented behaviors.

Supportive Leader behavior that entails showing concern for the status, well-being, and needs of subordinates; doing small things to make the work more pleasant; and being friendly and approachable

Participative Leader behavior that is characterized by consulting with subordinates, encouraging their suggestions, and carefully considering their ideas when making decisions

Achievement-oriented Leader behavior that involves setting challenging goals, expecting subordinates to perform at their highest level, and conveying a high degree of confidence in subordinates

work schedules, identifying work evaluation standards, and indicating the basis for outcomes or rewards. It is similar to task orientation.

Supportive leader behavior entails showing concern for the status, well-being, and needs of subordinates; doing small things to make the work more pleasant; and being friendly and approachable. This behavior is similar to relationship-oriented or consideration behavior.

Participative leader behavior is characterized by consulting with subordinates, encouraging their suggestions, and carefully considering their ideas when making decisions.

Achievement-oriented leader behavior involves setting challenging goals, expecting subordinates to perform at their highest level, and conveying a high degree of confidence in subordinates.

SITUATIONAL FACTORS In assessing how the four leader behaviors can be used to enhance the path-goal motivation and job satisfaction of subordinates, leaders need to consider two types of situational factors: subordinate characteristics and context characteristics. *Subordinate characteristics* include the personality traits, skills, abilities, and needs of subordinates. For example, a subordinate with low skills for a particular task is likely to be motivated by directive leadership, while a highly skilled individual is apt to appreciate a participative leader.

Context characteristics fall into three main categories: the task itself, the work group, and the organization's formal authority system (such as levels in the hierarchy, degree of decision centralization, and nature of formal reward system). For example, supportive leadership may foster motivation on a boring task, while achievement orientation may increase motivation on an interesting task.

CHOOSING LEADER BEHAVIORS In using path-goal theory to choose appropriate leader behaviors, leaders need to diagnose various situational factors in terms of their effects on the three expectancy theory elements (the path) and ultimately on the desired end results (the goals). A practical approach to this diagnosis involves three steps. First, think in terms of the expectancy theory elements. Second, diagnose situational factors that could be changed to positively affect the expectancy theory elements (operate to increase motivation). Third, initiate appropriate leader behaviors to change the situational factors. Several examples of how path-goal theory works are shown in Figure 13-7.

Since it is a situational leadership theory, path-goal theory argues that leadership behavior that is effective in one situation is not necessarily effective in another. For example, the use of directive leadership to clarify task demands that are already clear will, at best, have little effect because the behavior is redundant. At worst, it will frustrate employees and reduce the intrinsic valence of work. Notice, however, that unlike Fiedler's contingency approach, path-goal theory assumes that leaders can be flexible in their behaviors and can learn to engage in any of its four leader behaviors as the situation requires.

One manager who has been successful by making sure that employees clearly understand paths to organizational and personal goals is Ursula Burns, an engineer at Xerox who was promoted to general manager of several important product lines. In her role as general manager, Burns uses achievement-oriented behavior by encouraging employees toward high, but reachable, personal and organizational goals. In addition, she is directive by making sure that employees have the skills needed for their jobs and understand the link between performance and reward. She is participative by involving employees in decisions about the fate of the product lines they manage under her direction. Moreover, she is supportive, particularly by backing her employees when

Figure 13-7 *Examples of path-goal theory. (Adapted from Gary A. Yukl,* Leadership in Organizations, *Prentice-Hall, Englewood Cliffs, N.J., 1981, pp. 148, 150.)*

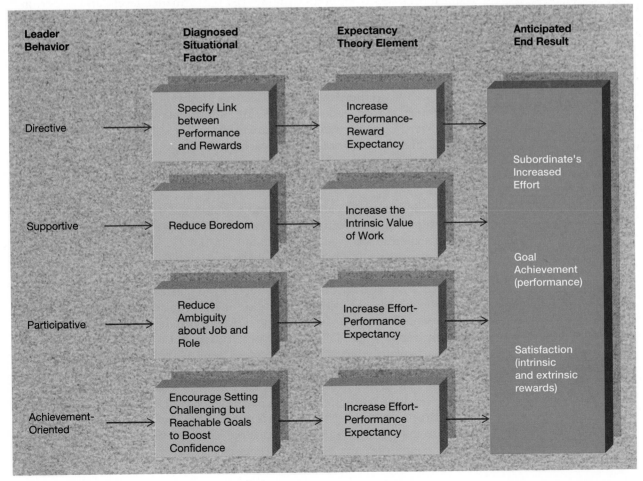

they have made tough decisions. For example, Burns supported her controller in a controversial cost-cutting plan that involved eliminating a project that was favored by Burns' boss. Burns says that "it was not an easy sell," but she finally convinced her boss that the pet project was the one that had to be cut. By effectively using path-goal theory, Burns has been effective in her new job.[42]

Path-goal theory encompasses multiple leader behaviors and a potentially large number of situational variables that operate simultaneously. Its flexibility provides managers with a useful framework for thinking about the likely impacts of their leader behaviors on subordinate motivation, goal attainment, and job satisfaction.[43]

■ PROMOTING INNOVATION: TRANSFORMATIONAL LEADERSHIP

One interesting issue involving leadership is the prospect that managers and leaders are not necessarily one and the same.[44] According to one argument, managers do the same things over and over (do things right), but it takes leaders to innovate (do the right things), bring about major changes, and inspire followers to pursue extraordinary levels of effort.[45] In studying the issue, leadership expert Bernard M. Bass and his colleagues have made a distinction between transactional and transformational leaders.[46]

Transactional leaders motivate subordinates to perform at expected levels. They do this by helping them recognize task responsibilities, identify goals, acquire confidence about meeting desired performance levels, and understand how their needs and the rewards that they desire are linked to goal achievement. As you have probably recognized, transactional leadership is closely allied to the path-goal theory of leadership. The other situational leadership theories discussed in this chapter can also be characterized as transactional leadership approaches.

In contrast, **transformational leaders** motivate individuals to perform beyond normal expectations by inspiring subordinates to focus on broader missions that transcend their own immediate self-interests, to concentrate on intrinsic higher-level goals (such as achievement and self-actualization) rather than extrinsic lower-level goals (such as safety and security), and to have confidence in their abilities to achieve the extraordinary missions articulated by the leader.

Transformational leadership is not a substitute for transactional leadership. It is a supplemental form of leadership with an add-on effect: performance beyond expectations (see Figure 13-8). The logic is that even the most successful transformational leaders need transactional skills as well to manage effectively the day-to-day events that form the basis of the broader mission.

According to Bass, three leader factors are particularly important to transformational leadership: charisma, individualized consideration, and intellectual stimulation. Of these, charisma is the most important. **Charisma** is the leader's ability to inspire pride, faith, and respect; to recognize what is really important; and to articulate effectively a sense of mission, or vision, that inspires followers. Individuals such as Martin Luther King, Mahatma Gandhi, John F. Kennedy, and Franklin D. Roosevelt have been described as charismatic.[47]

Researchers have attempted to identify behavioral components associated with charismatic leaders. Their efforts suggest that such leaders strive to change the status quo, project future goals that are idealized visions very different from current conditions, and behave in somewhat unconventional ways and counter to existing norms. The studies also indicate that charismatic leaders rely heav-

Transactional leaders Leaders who motivate subordinates to perform at expected levels by helping them recognize task responsibilities, identify goals, acquire confidence about meeting desired performance levels, and understand how their needs and the rewards that they desire are linked to goal achievement

Transformational leaders Leaders who motivate individuals to perform beyond normal expectations by inspiring subordinates to focus on broader missions that transcend their own immediate self-interests, to concentrate on intrinsic higher-level goals rather than extrinsic lower-level goals, and to have confidence in their abilities to achieve the extraordinary missions articulated by the leader

Charisma A leadership factor that comprises the leader's ability to inspire pride, faith, and respect; to recognize what is really important; and to articulate effectively a sense of mission, or vision, that inspires followers

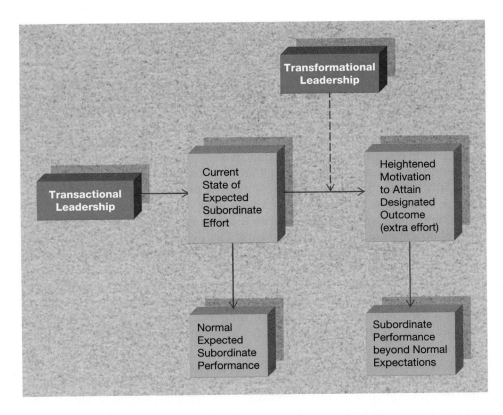

Figure 13-8 *Add-on effect of transformational leadership. (Adapted from Bernard M. Bass,* Leadership and Performance beyond Expectations, *Free Press, New York, 1985, p. 23.)*

ily on referent and expert power and attempt to get others to share a radical vision of changes.[48]

The second factor associated with transformational leadership, **individualized consideration,** involves delegating projects to help develop each follower's capabilities, paying personal attention to each follower's needs, and treating each follower as an individual worthy of respect. The third factor, **intellectual stimulation,** involves offering new ideas to stimulate followers to rethink old ways of doing things, encouraging followers to look at problems from multiple vantage points, and fostering creative breakthroughs in obstacles that had seemed insurmountable.

Not everyone agrees that transformational leaders must have charisma. There does, however, seem to be agreement that such leaders need to provide a vision of a desired future state, mobilize commitment, and bring about changes that enable followers to reach the vision.[49] Norman P. Blake, Jr., engaged in these behaviors when he brought about major changes at an old-line insurance company that had run into trouble (see the Case in Point discussion).

Individualized consideration A leadership factor that involves delegating projects to help develop each follower's capabilities, paying personal attention to each follower's needs, and treating each follower as an individual worthy of respect

Intellectual stimulation A leadership factor that involves offering new ideas to stimulate followers to rethink old ways of doing things, encouraging followers to look at problems from multiple vantage points, and fostering creative breakthroughs in obstacles that had seemed insurmountable

USF&G CEO TRANSFORMS AN AILING INSURER

CASE IN POINT

A few years ago, Baltimore-based USF&G was facing bankruptcy. Although the insurance company had survived for almost 100 years, it suffered a $569 million loss in 1990. Its rating was in danger of being downgraded by services that provide ratings of insurance companies for consumers and investors. Faced with severe declines in the price of its stock, the company hired Norman P. Blake, Jr., as its chief executive officer. Blake came from a Chicago-based industrial

Described as "a nuclear reactor of boundless energy," Norman P. Blake used his dynamic leadership skills to transform an insurance company facing bankruptcy in the early 1990s. Blake mapped out a vision for the future, cut away businesses not related to insurance, and focused on expanding slowly in areas in which the company was doing well.

financing subsidiary of Fuji Bank Ltd. and had a reputation as a turnaround expert.

The crisis facing USF&G enabled Blake to institute massive changes. One of his first actions was to map out a clear strategic vision. The insurer had diversified into a number of noninsurance businesses, such as leasing, real estate development, oil and gas, and travel. Blake sold 13 businesses and refocused the company on its roots as a major insurer, particularly concentrating on its core property/casualty and life insurance operations. He then put the company on a growth track by slowly expanding its very successful reinsurance operations and through the acquisition of Cleveland-based Victoria Financial Corp., a specialty automobile insurer. The company is prepared to expand its growth in these areas, now that profits have rebounded.

Although the situation has improved substantially, USF&G still has one of the highest expense ratios in the industry. The expense ratio refers to the proportion of each premium dollar that an insurance company spends on overhead costs for such items as commissions and marketing. One factor affecting expenses has been the company's antiquated information system. Blake has spent extensively on a new information system, which has increased short-term expenses for the company. But in the long run the new system will be less expensive and greatly enhances USF&G's ability to provide excellent customer service.

In orchestrating these changes, Blake brought in a number of new managers. In his first 3 days on the job, he made an effort to meet and shake hands with every employee in the Baltimore area, which comprises about 2300 employees or 35 percent of the work force. He has introduced a number of programs that highlight employees for their special efforts, such as the "Rave Awards" and special recognitions from the CEO. Many of the awards include cash (up to $10,000) and stock. Every employee's compensation includes a portion that is incentive-based, and all employees are eligible for stock options.

Blake usually arrives at the office by 6 for a morning workout and works in his office until 7 p.m. or later. "He'd never ask you to do anything he wouldn't do," say one senior manager. "It's like working for a nuclear reactor of boundless energy—everyone else is worn out long before he is."[50] ■ ■ ■

■ ARE LEADERS NECESSARY?

Some critics argue that the importance of leadership is greatly overrated and that in many contexts leaders make little or no difference.[51] In this section, we explore the related prospect that there may be substitutes for leadership, and we consider the organizational life-cycle approach to understanding when different leadership styles may be most applicable.

Substitutes for leadership
An approach that attempts to specify some of the main situational factors likely to make leader behaviors unnecessary or to negate their effectiveness

Neutralizers Situational factors that make it *impossible* for a given leader behavior to have an impact on subordinate performance and/or satisfaction

Substitutes for Leadership

An interesting aspect of path-goal theory is the notion that situational factors may sometimes render certain leader behaviors unnecessary and/or ineffective. However, path-goal theory stops short of attempting to specify explicitly the conditions under which leader behavior may be unnecessary because of situational factors. The **substitutes for leadership** approach attempts to specify some of the main situational factors likely to make leader behaviors unnecessary or to negate their effectiveness.[52]

According to this approach, **neutralizers** are situational factors that make it *impossible* for a given leader behavior to have an impact on subordinate performance and/or satisfaction. In other words, they cancel out, or negate, the effects of a leader's behavior. Examples of neutralizers that can negate the impact of both relationship-oriented and task-oriented leader behaviors are high need for subordinate independence, low subordinate valence for available rewards (see Chapter 12), and physical distance between leader and subordinates. Managers need to assess the presence of neutralizers and attempt to alter the situation, if possible, so that appropriate leader behaviors can have the intended effect. (For instance, a manager may develop new reward possibilities, such as training opportunities, if subordinates have a low valence for currently available rewards.)

On the other hand, **substitutes** are situational factors that make leadership impact not only *impossible* but also *unnecessary*. Substitutes for relationship-oriented leader behavior include intrinsically satisfying work and subordinates who have a professional work orientation. Substitutes for task-oriented behavior include able and experienced subordinates and work that is routine, has clearly specified methods, and/or provides clear feedback. The presence of substitutes for leadership can enable a leader to concentrate on other areas in need of her or his attention. For example, Sally Minard, a partner in Lotas Minard Patton McIver, Inc., a New York advertising agency, earned a reputation for giving experienced subordinates latitude. "Sally was one of the best management supervisors I have ever had," says one former subordinate. "She didn't watch over our shoulders. She was aware of what was happening, but she would give us responsibility."[53]

Aside from being concerned about the leadership needs of specific subordinates and work groups, managers also need to consider the broader perspective of the organizational life cycle.

Substitutes Situational factors that make leadership impact not only *impossible* but also *unnecessary*

Leadership and the Organizational Life Cycle

The view of organizations as having life cycles, or predictable stages of development (see Chapter 11), provides some guidance about when either transactional or transformational leadership is likely to be most appropriate (see Table 13-3).[54] When an organization is at its entrepreneurial, or beginning, stage, transformational leadership is particularly instrumental in creating a vision that allows the organization to be born and to take a few first steps. At the collectivity stage, additional workers begin to join the initial core group, and transactional leadership becomes an important aid in handling the accelerating growth. By the formalization and control stage, organizational growth requires even greater emphasis on transactional leadership to maintain direction and control. By the elaboration of structure stage, excessive formalization and control often reduce innovation to a low level, so heavy emphasis on transformational leadership is again needed. Although both transactional and transformational styles of leadership are likely to be utilized at every stage in effective organizations, the amount of emphasis is different in each case. Thus managers

TABLE 13-3 LEADERSHIP AND THE ORGANIZATIONAL LIFE CYCLE

ORGANIZATIONAL LIFE-CYCLE STAGE	MOST IMPORTANT LEADERSHIP EMPHASIS
Entrepreneurial	Transformational
Collectivity	Transactional
Formalization and control	Transactional
Elaboration of structure	Transformational

need to understand both leadership approaches in order to function effectively. Inherent in putting these approaches into practice is the need to be well versed in organizational communication processes, a subject to which we turn in the next chapter.

■ CHAPTER SUMMARY

Leadership is the process of influencing others to achieve organizational goals. Leaders use six major types of power to help affect the behavior of others: legitimate, reward, coercive, expert, information, and referent. Leaders need to use their power carefully in ways that encourage commitment and increase power rather than diminish it.

Researchers have had only limited success in attempting to identify common traits that distinguish leaders from nonleaders. Their efforts suggest that there may be some general distinguishing traits, such as intelligence and dominance, and that some traits may apply only to specific types of situations.

Studying leader behaviors has provided a more promising research direction. The Iowa, Michigan, and Ohio State studies represent prominent initial efforts to identify effective leadership behaviors, or styles. The Ohio State researchers identified two important leadership styles, initiating structure and consideration, which they viewed as independent dimensions rather than opposite ends of a continuum. Unfortunately, leaders exhibiting both high initiating structure and high consideration did not necessarily get the best results. The Managerial Grid popularized a related approach, which emphasized concern for people and concern for production. Studies indicate that female and male managers are similar in the amounts of interpersonal and task behaviors that they exhibit.

Situational leadership theories grew out of the recognition that leader behaviors that work well in one situation are often not as effective in another situation. Fiedler's contingency model holds that the effectiveness of a leader depends on whether the leader's LPC orientation matches the situation as determined by leader-member relations, task structure, and position power.

The normative leadership model helps leaders determine the extent to which they should involve subordinates in particular decisions. The situational leadership theory argues that leaders need to alter their combination of task and relationship behaviors according to the task readiness of their followers. The path-goal theory of leadership relies heavily on the expectancy theory of motivation and attempts to explain how leader behavior influences the motivation and job satisfaction of subordinates.

Transformational leadership can be an important factor in innovation because it motivates individuals to perform beyond normal expectations in pursuit of new visions. It is an add-on to transactional leadership, since both are needed.

There is some evidence that leadership may make little or no difference in certain contexts. One reason why leadership may not be as important as it seems is that there are a number of substitutes for leadership. Also, the organizational life cycle may affect the emphasis that needs to be placed on transactional and transformational leadership.

■ QUESTIONS FOR DISCUSSION AND REVIEW

1 Outline the major types of power available to managers. Think of a situation in which you were a leader. What types of power were available to you? Which ones did you use most? What were the results in terms of follower commitment, compliance, and resistance?

2 Explain the current status of research efforts to identify leader traits. What traits can you identify in an individual whom you consider to be a good leader? Do other leaders with whom you are familiar possess any of the same traits?

3 Describe the continuum of boss-centered (authoritarian) and subordinate-centered (democratic) behaviors. Identify situations in which you have seen a democratic leader in action and situations in which

you have seen an authoritarian one. How did the followers react? Did situational factors make a difference in the followers' reactions?

4 Explain the different findings of the Iowa, Michigan, and Ohio State researchers in investigating leadership. Use these findings to provide advice to managers on how they can lead more effectively.

5 Outline the basic ideas in Fiedler's contingency model of leadership. Analyze a student association or other leadership situation in terms of leader-member relations, task structure, and position power. On the basis of Fiedler's model, what type of leader behavior would the situation require?

6 Describe the normative theory of leadership. Consider a leadership situation that you experienced in

which a decision had to be made. Use the appropriate decision tree to determine the extent to which the group should have been involved. How closely does the recommendation of the decision tree match what was done? What were the results?

7 Explain the basic ideas constituting the path-goal theory of leadership. Use the theory to determine how a leader might improve motivation in a group with which you are familiar.

8 Contrast transactional and transformational leadership. Identify a transactional leader and a transformational leader. To what extent is each one's leadership emphasis appropriate given the life-cycle stage of the organization in which each manages?

9 Differentiate between neutralizers and substitutes for leadership. Give two examples of each in an organization with which you are familiar.

10 Explain how leadership relates to the organizational life cycle. Analyze an organization with which you are familiar in terms of the appropriate use of transactional and transformational leadership.

■ DISCUSSION QUESTIONS FOR CHAPTER OPENING CASE

1 What types of power does Jill Elikann Barad likely have at her disposal as CEO of Mattel? What types of power usage are evident in the opening case?

2 Use the path-goal leadership theory to analyze Barad's use of leader behaviors. What situational factors may have influenced her success?

3 Would you characterize Barad as a transformational leader? Why, or why not?

■ EXERCISES FOR MANAGING IN THE TWENTY-FIRST CENTURY

EXERCISE 1
SELF-ASSESSMENT: DO YOU HAVE CHARISMA?[55]

 Charisma has helped many leaders in accomplishing goals. It may assist you as well in the future. The following questions will help in identifying the amount of your current charisma.

1 I worry most about:
   a. my current competitors
   b. my future competitors
2 I'm most at ease thinking in:
   a. generalities
   b. specifics
3 I tend to focus on:
   a. our missed opportunities
   b. opportunities we've seized
4 I prefer to:
   a. promote traditions that made us great
   b. create new traditions

5 I like to communicate an idea via:
   a. a written report
   b. a one-page chart
6 I tend to ask:
   a. "How can we do this better?"
   b. "Why are we doing this?"
7 I believe:
   a. there's always a way to minimize risk
   b. some risks are too high
8 When I disagree with my boss, I typically:
   a. coax him/her nicely to alter his/her view
   b. bluntly tell him/her, "You're wrong"
9 I tend to sway people by using:
   a. emotions
   b. logic
10 I think this quiz is:
   a. ridiculous
   b. fascinating

EXERCISE 2
MANAGEMENT EXERCISE: THE QUESTION OF SUBORDINATE INVOLVEMENT

Case: Purchasing Decision Problem
You have recently been appointed vice president in charge of purchasing for a large manufacturing company. The company has 20 plants, all located in the midwest. Historically, the company has operated in a highly decentralized fashion with each of the plant managers encouraged to operate with only minimal control and direction from the corporate office. In the area of purchasing, each of the purchasing executives who report to the plant manager does the purchasing for his or her plant. There seems to be little or no coordination among them, and the relationships that do exist are largely competitive.

Your position was created when it began to appear to the president that the company was likely to face increasing difficulty in securing certain essential raw materials.

In order to protect the company against this possibility, the present haphazard decentralized arrangement must be abandoned or at least modified to meet the current problems.

You were chosen for the position because of your extensive background in corporate purchasing with another firm that operated in a much more centralized fashion. Your appointment was announced in the last issue of the company house organ. You are anxious to get started, particularly since the peak buying season is now only 3 weeks away. A procedure must be established that will minimize the likelihood of serious shortages and secondarily achieve the economies associated with the added power of centralized purchasing.[56]

Instructions
Get together with a group designated by your instructor, and use the normative leadership model to determine the degree to which you should involve subordinates in the purchasing decision.

CONCLUDING CASE 1

GE'S CONTROVERSIAL LEADER

In 1981, John W. Welch, Jr., became CEO of General Electric. His appointment ushered in an era of disdain for the elaborate planning and centralized control that had been the hallmark of his predecessor, Reginald Jones. "Jones felt the others would be caretakers," says one former GE vice president. "Welch was the one who would take the company in radical directions if necessary."

Indeed, Welch has proved to be anything but a caretaker. He quickly articulated a plan to change GE from a manufacturing company deriving more than half its revenues from heavy industry to one reaping a larger share of its earnings from technology and services. He also stated that GE would sell those of its businesses that weren't either first or second in their markets.

Since becoming CEO, Welch has sold more than 250 businesses and used $20 billion to purchase more than 300 new ones. Among the acquisitions are the RCA Corporation, the Employers Reinsurance Company, 80 percent of Kidder, Peabody & Company, the medical-equipment business of Thomson SA, the appliance-making Roper Corporation, and the chemical business of the Borg-Warner Corporation. In the process, he has eliminated more than 200,000 jobs through forced retirements, layoffs, resignations, and outright divestitures.

His moves have caused revenues to increase by 50 percent—up to about $70 billion. Admirers say that Welch has vision and is transforming GE from a stodgy bureaucracy to a nimble company much more fit for the challenges ahead. He was named "CEO of the Year" by the American Management Association in 1991. Detractors have dubbed Welch "Neutron Jack," after the bomb that destroys people but leaves buildings intact.

A notorious disliker of bureaucracy and red tape, Welch has cut layers of management, eliminating the group and sector levels that once fell between the heads of the various businesses and the CEO. Having fewer hierarchical levels fit in with his basic philosophy that managers should have the freedom to run their businesses as they see fit and to react to the fast-changing environment.

"The early '80s were a hardware decade, getting the right stuff in the right place," Welch says. "The '90s and late '80s are what we call software. We're working desperately to get everyone participating in the process. To be a winner in the '90s, you've got to have the creativity of everybody in the organization."

To that end, Welch has recently identified four types of leaders. Type One leaders deliver on commitments and share in the values of the company. Such leaders have a promising future at GE, says Welch. Type Two leaders do not deliver on commitments and do not share company values. These leaders will not survive at GE. Type Three leaders miss commitments but share company values, so they will usually be given a second chance. Type Four leaders deliver on commitments, make all the numbers, but do not "share in the values we must have," says Welch. The Type Four leader "is the individual who typically forces performance out of people rather than inspires it: the autocrat, the big shot, the tyrant. Too often all of us have looked the other way," according to Welch. The tendency is to allow Type Four managers to continue to function "because 'they always deliver'—at least in the short run." Now, says Welch, "in an environment where we must have every good idea from every man and woman in the organization, we cannot afford management styles that suppress and intimidate."

In order to further promote creativity and innovation, Welch has been advocating the development of a "boundaryless" company, in which workers at all levels are encouraged to communicate and share ideas with one another. He has also instituted the Best Practices program, in which GE employees study the attitudes and management practices of other admirable companies and adapt the best for use at GE. Another means of fostering change is GE's Work-Out program, in which managers and their subordinates meet in a forum similar to a New England town meeting and seek ways to eliminate unnecessary work and solve problems together.

According to Welch, "Leadership starts with absolute integrity. Leaders need to define and communicate their vision. They must have enormous energy and the ability to energize and excite others. Leaders embrace change—they know it creates opportunities. Leaders are accountable and decisive. They set and meet aggressive targets. They act sooner rather than later on issues." He noted recently, "I don't know what the world's going to be; all I know is it's going to be nothing like it is today. It's going to be faster; information is going to be everywhere." As a result, he says, everyone at GE needs to come to work each day "on the razor's edge of a competitive battle."[57]

QUESTIONS FOR CONCLUDING CASE 1

1 Analyze the sources of power that are likely to be used by the four types of leaders identified by Welch. Note particularly the contrast between Type One and Type Four managers.

2 Use path-goal theory to analyze Welch's leadership approach.

3 Is Welch a transformational leader? Why, or why not? What should Welch do next?

CONCLUDING CASE 2

PROFITS ARE SECONDARY AT BODY SHOP INTERNATIONAL

Body Shop International comprises more than 1300 retail Body Shops in 45 countries offering cosmetics made from natural ingredients. The dynamic growth of this unusual company based in Littlehampton, England, can be traced to founder Anita Roddick. It was Roddick who conceived the idea of selling skin creams, shampoos, and other lotions made from fruit and vegetable oils, rather than animal fats. She opened her first shop in 1976 to support her two children while her husband, Gordon, fulfilled a lifetime dream of riding from Buenos Aires to New York City on horseback. By the time he returned to Great Britain a year later, Roddick was preparing to open her third shop.

Since then, Body Shops have become famous for such exotic-sounding products as Rhassoul Mud Shampoo, White Grape Skin Tone, and Peppermint Foot Lotion. What is more extraordinary is that the company does no advertising. Instead, the shops offer reams of information about Body Shop products. Shelves contain note cards with colorful stories and graphics about the origins and development of various products and their ingredients. Stacks of pamphlets address such issues as "What is natural?" A huge reference book called *The Product Information Manual* provides extensive information on every Body Shop offering. The focus is on educating the customer, rather than on selling. In fact, salespeople are expected to be able to answer questions about the products but are purposely trained not to engage in hard selling.

Roddick spends considerable time each year traveling to different Body Shops, many of which are franchises. She also makes several trips to remote areas of third world countries, where she studies local customs and learns how the native people care for their skin and hair. The ideas she obtains are often incorporated into new products, and the associated information is used to provide background sheets for customers.

Aside from being recognized for its natural cosmetics, Body Shop International is also well known for its support of a variety of environmental and social causes, such as campaigns to save the whales, preserve the rain forests, and support human rights. Information regarding such causes is found in Body Shop stores, usually with a particular cause highlighted at any given time. Customers are given money for each plastic bottle they return for recycling.

Roddick argues that there is too much focus in business on making profits, to the detriment of social responsibility and empowerment of employees. Instead, she says: "I believe quite passionately that there is a better way. I think you can rewrite the book on business. I think you can trade ethically; be committed to social responsibility, global responsibility; empower your employees without being afraid of them. I think you can really rewrite the book. That is the vision and the vision is absolutely clear."[58]

So far she seems to have succeeded in capturing the imagination of a loyal group of employees and franchisees, many of whom say that they cannot imagine going to work for an *ordinary* company after working with the Body Shop. The company's fast growth attests to its popularity with customers, who reportedly are extraordinarily loyal. Some observers credit Roddick with recognizing that customers have become cynical about traditional high-powered marketing techniques, and they argue that her informational approach and emphasis on social responsibility are the wave of the future.

Another reason for the company's success is that Gordon Roddick effectively manages company operations, leaving Anita free to generate new ideas and excitement. Several years ago, the company went public, but Anita and Gordon still own about 25 percent of the stock, which is worth more than $200 million. The company has found it necessary to adopt franchising in order to expand more quickly. In the United States, for example, competitors have been attempting to copy many of the positive features of Body Shops before the company can firmly establish itself throughout the country. One such copier is The Limited's Leslie Wexner, who has started a similar chain called Bath & Body Works. As a result, Body Shops are not doing as well as expected in the United States, although the company has just completed a $1.3 million U.S. headquarters near Raleigh, North Carolina.

Roddick and her husband recently won a libel suit over a British television report accusing the firm of having a false image as a socially conscious company. Anita Roddick and her husband recently investigated taking the company private so that they could give more focus to social concerns without having to worry about pleasing stockholders. However, they have at least temporarily decided against it because of the high debt that would be involved.[59]

QUESTIONS FOR CONCLUDING CASE 2

1 What type or types of power does Anita Roddick appear to rely upon?
2 Would you consider Anita Roddick to be a transformational leader? Why, or why not?
3 How is transactional leadership provided for at Body Shop International?

CHAPTER FOURTEEN

MANAGERIAL COMMUNICATION AND INTERPERSONAL PROCESSES

CHAPTER OUTLINE

The Nature of Managerial Communication
Types of Communication
Managerial Communication Preferences
Basic Components of the Communication Process

Influences on Individual Communication and Interpersonal Processes
Perceptual Processes
Attribution Processes
Semantics
Managing Diversity: Cultural Context
Communication Skills

Group Communication Networks

Organizational Communication Channels
Vertical Communication
Horizontal Communication
Informal Communication: The Grapevine
Using Electronics to Facilitate Communication

LEARNING OBJECTIVES

After studying this chapter, you should be able to:

■ Explain the major types of managerial communication and discuss managerial communication preferences.

■ Outline the basic components of the communication process.

■ Describe how perceptual processes influence individual communication.

■ Explain the role of attribution processes, semantics, cultural context, and communication skills in communication by individuals.

■ Assess the usefulness of centralized and decentralized group communication networks.

■ Distinguish among major organizational communication channels and explain their role in managing effectively.

■ Discuss the growing potential of electronics in regard to organizational communication channels.

GAINING THE EDGE

COMMUNICATION HELPS SOUTHWEST AIRLINES EXCEL

The CEO of Southwest Airlines, Herb Kelleher, is known for his unorthodox management approach that has helped set the standard for productivity in the airline industry. He frequently impersonates Elvis at employee gatherings, has dressed up as a leprechaun to entertain customers on St. Patrick's Day, and sometimes makes appearances as the Easter Bunny. Such antics help set the culture of humor and camaraderie that underlies Southwest Airlines' success.

Southwest, with Kelleher at the helm, has pioneered the concept of a no-frills airline that carries passengers for relatively short distances at low-cost fares. The airline offers no meals, but is known for its friendly service. Following Kelleher's lead, Southwest employees try to make their jobs fun for themselves and their customers. For example, employees have been known to run contests on board to see which customers have the biggest hole in their socks or shoe soles. At the same time, the airline has the best record for on-time performance. Its turnaround time, minutes on the ground before taking off again, has consistently been the best in the industry. The number of passengers carried per employee has been almost double the industry average. These productivity figures are made possible by a heavy emphasis on teamwork, with employees pitching in wherever they are needed. For example, a pilot may help out at the boarding gate or a ticket agent may help with baggage to make sure that the plane leaves on time. Moreover, Southwest has one of the most modern fleets among airlines, flying mainly Boeing 737s to keep everything standardized. The airline has been profitable each year for more than 20 years, a rarity in the volatile airline industry.

Southwest attempts to hire people with a good sense of humor and a bent toward teamwork. Such individuals fit well with the culture that Kelleher works hard to create. According to Kelleher, communication with employees should be a top priority. He remembers being invited to a company to talk about what could be learned from Southwest Airlines' success. While riding in an elevator with the CEO, two employees got on and the CEO did not say a word to them. When Kelleher and the CEO got off the elevator, Kelleher suggested, "You might start by saying hello to your people."

Kelleher notes that a great deal is said about communication, but he believes it must come from the heart and be spontaneous. It often is "Hey Dave, how you doin'? Heard the wife's sick—she okay?" Kelleher likes to spend a great deal of time with Southwest employees. Each year, he helps load baggage on the Wednesday before Thanksgiving, typically the airline's busiest day of the year. He is the type of manager who will stay up talking with mechanics until 4 a.m. to find out their problems and will follow up to make sure the problems are solved. Kelleher's father was general manager of Campbell Soup Co., and he learned great respect for workers during his six summers working on the factory floor.

Kelleher says the people in headquarters are the supply corps, not the heroes. "We supply the heroes, period. The heroes are out there." He argues that before you implement an idea generated at headquarters, you should take it to the field and ask for input. "Pretty soon," he says, "the idea will look like Swiss cheese—full of holes. They know what they're doing and we don't. We may supply the idea, but they know how to implement and execute it." Southwest doesn't use surveys to check how managers are doing. "We are individu-

If you hear the on-board announcements sung you are probably a passenger on a Southwest Airlines flight. The sense of fun that the employees exude comes directly from the CEO, Herb Kelleher, shown here at dinner with fellow workers in Dallas. Kelleher has been known to dress up as the Easter Bunny, Elvis Presley, and other characters. He also is famous for communicating with his employees and getting to know them personally. His contented work force is productive and efficient; as a result, his low-cost, no frills company has been profitable every year.

ally connected enough to each other so we can call and say, 'You've got a problem in your area.'" Southwest faces growing competition as other airlines attempt to emulate its innovative approach.[1]   ■ ■ ■

As the success at Southwest Airlines suggests, good communication and associated interpersonal processes in organizations are important ingredients of organizational effectiveness.[2] Although effective communication is critical to all four major management functions, it is particularly vital to the leading function because it provides a necessary conduit for efforts to interact with and influence others. Kelleher uses communication and interpersonal processes well to nurture Southwest Airlines' unique culture. In this chapter, we closely examine the nature of managerial communication and related interpersonal processes, including the different types of communication that managers use, managerial communication preferences, and the basic components of the communication process. We consider several important factors that can impede or enhance the way that individuals communicate and interact. We also take a brief look at communication networks involving groups. Finally, we consider various communication channels in organizations, investigate how the use of multiple communication channels can help promote innovation, and explore the growing potential of electronics in facilitating organizational communication.

■ THE NATURE OF MANAGERIAL COMMUNICATION

Communication is the exchange of messages between people for the purpose of achieving common meanings.[3] Unless meanings are shared, managers find it extremely difficult to influence others. For example, in looking back on his efforts to revitalize General Motors, former CEO Roger Smith says that he would make the same decisions again regarding the implementation of major changes to move the company toward global leadership in the twenty-first century. But, says Smith:

Communication The exchange of messages between people for the purpose of achieving common meanings

I sure wish I'd done a better job of communicating with GM people. I'd do that differently a second time around and make sure they understood and shared my vision for the company. Then they would have known why I was tearing the place up, taking out whole divisions, changing our whole production structure. If people understand the *why*, they'll work at it. Like I say, I never got all this across. There we were, charging up the hill right on schedule, and I looked behind me and saw that many people were still at the bottom, trying to decide whether to come along. I'm talking about hourly workers, middle management, and even some top management. It seemed like a lot of them had gotten off the train.[4]

As Smith's predicament illustrates, communication is a critical part of every manager's job. Without effective communication, even the most brilliant strategies and best-laid plans may not be successful.[5]

Types of Communication

In their work, managers use two major types of communication: verbal and nonverbal. Each type plays an important part in the effective transmission of messages within organizations.

Verbal communication The written or oral use of words to communicate

VERBAL COMMUNICATION Verbal communication is the written or oral use of words to communicate. Both written and oral communications are pervasive in organizations.

Written communication occurs through a variety of means, such as business letters, office memorandums, reports, résumés, written telephone messages, newsletters, and policy manuals. According to several estimates, the cost of producing a single letter or memo has risen to more than $7, and one estimate places the figure as high as $25 for the average memo.[6] Yet, in one study, more than 80 percent of the managers surveyed judged the quality of the written communications they receive as either fair or poor. They also did not give themselves very high grades, with 55 percent describing their own writing skills as fair or poor.[7]

Despite such shortcomings in writing skills, written communication generally has several advantages over oral communication. It provides a record of the message, can be disseminated widely with a minimum of effort, and allows the sender to think through the intended message carefully. Written communication also has several disadvantages, including the expense of preparation, a relatively impersonal nature, possible misunderstanding by the receiver, and the delay of feedback regarding the effectiveness of the message.[8]

Oral communication, or the spoken word, takes place largely through face-to-face conversation with another individual, meetings with several individuals, and telephone conversations. Oral communication has the advantages of being fast, being generally more personal than written communication, and providing immediate feedback from others involved in the conversation. Among the disadvantages of oral communication are that it can be time-consuming, it can be more difficult to terminate, and additional effort is required to document what is said if a record is necessary.[9]

Given the advantages and disadvantages of written and oral communication, it is not surprising that both types of verbal communication are used by managers. Later in this chapter we give further consideration to managerial preferences for written and oral communication. First, though, we consider another type of communication that is important to managers.

Nonverbal communication Communication by means of elements and behaviors that are not coded into words

NONVERBAL COMMUNICATION Nonverbal communication is communication by means of elements and behaviors that are not coded into words. Studies esti-

Proxemics at work: When Aetna Life reorganized its home office into self-managed teams, it came up with a new office design that allowed the team members to interact and communicate easily with one another. Within small areas called neighborhoods, there is a central work table where teams can meet as needed, while nearby desks provide privacy.

mate that nonverbal aspects account for between 65 and 93 percent of what is communicated.[10] Interestingly, it is quite difficult to engage in verbal communication without some accompanying form of nonverbal communication. Important categories of nonverbal communication include kinesic behavior, proxemics, paralanguage, and object language.

Kinesic behavior (sometimes referred to as "body language") comprises body movements, such as gestures, facial expressions, eye movements, and posture. In assessing people's feelings about an issue, we often draw conclusions not only from their words but also from their nonverbal behavior, such as their facial expressions.

Proxemics is the influence of proximity and space on communication. For example, some managers arrange their offices so that they have an informal area where people can sit without experiencing the spatial distance and formality created by a big desk. Another example of proxemics, which you have probably experienced, is that you are more likely to get to know students whom you happen to sit near in class than students who are sitting in other parts of the room.

Paralanguage consists of vocal aspects of communication that relate to how something is said rather than to what is said. Voice quality, tone of voice, laughing, and yawning are in this category.

Object language is the communicative use of material things, including clothing, cosmetics, furniture, and architecture.[11] If you prepared a job résumé lately, you probably gave some thought to its layout and to the type of paper you wanted it printed on. These are aspects of object language, enabling you to communicate information about yourself beyond that presented by the words on the page. Such nonverbal elements form an important part of the messages that managers communicate.

Evidence suggests that when the verbal and nonverbal elements contradict each other, the receiver is most likely to interpret the nonverbal communication as the true message.[12] This means that managers must pay attention to the nonverbal, as well as the verbal, part of the messages they send. In addition, to gain better insight into the thoughts and feelings of others, managers should scrutinize both the nonverbal and the verbal parts of the messages they receive.

Kinesic behavior Body movements, such as gestures, facial expressions, eye movements, and posture

Proxemics The influence of proximity and space on communication

Paralanguage Vocal aspects of communication that relate to how something is said rather than to what is said

Object language The communicative use of material things, including clothing, cosmetics, furniture, and architecture

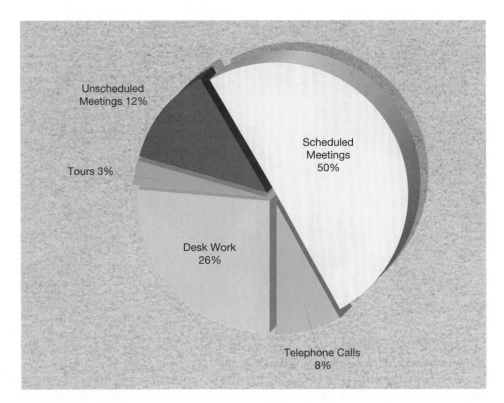

Figure 14-1 *Proportion of time top managers spent on various activities. (Based on Lance B. Kurke and Howard Aldrich, "Mintzberg Was Right!: A Replication and Extension of* The Nature of Managerial Work," *Management Science, vol. 29, 1983, p. 979.)*

Managerial Communication Preferences

Managers spend most of their time communicating in one form or another. Studies show that they tend to prefer oral over written communication, largely because oral communication is usually more informal and timely.[13] One detailed study showed that four top managers in four different types of organizations spent almost 74 percent of their working hours communicating orally with others, through informal and formal meetings, telephone calls, and tours of the organization (see Figure 14-1).[14] The executives spent about 50 percent of that time interacting with subordinates. Most of the remaining contact time was spent with the board of directors, peers, trade organizations, clients, and suppliers. Although the study focused on top-level managers, managers at other levels also lean toward the spoken rather than the written word.[15]

Managers serve as communication centers through several managerial roles that are discussed in Chapter 1 (such as monitor, disseminator, and spokesperson). Managers acting in these roles form the basis for the organization's communication network. If managers and those with whom they interact do not communicate effectively, the repercussions can be serious, not only for a particular manager's work unit but for the rest of the organization as well.

On the other hand, concerted efforts to promote effective communication can be a key ingredient in an organization's success. Recent events at the Scandinavian Airlines System (SAS) help illustrate the importance of both verbal and nonverbal managerial communication in interactions with others (see the Case in Point discussion).

CASE IN POINT

COMMUNICATION HELPS SAS STAGE TURNAROUND

When Jan Carlzon became the president and chief executive officer of SAS, the airline was suffering its second consecutive year of serious losses. Within a year, SAS was posting a profit. The turnaround was based on a clear strategy directed at becoming known as "the best airline in the world for the frequent business traveler." In implementing the strategy, SAS spent heavily to upgrade its facilities so that it could better serve business customers. Yet Carlzon recognized that if the airline was really to be the best at serving these travelers, he had to get the employees behind the shift in strategy. In particular, he needed the help of what he calls SAS's "front line," the ticket agents, flight attendants, baggage handlers, and all the others who interact directly with customers.

To help articulate the change in strategy, all 20,000 employees received a little red book entitled *Let's Get in There and Fight.* The book spelled out in concise terms the company's vision and prime goal. Once they understood the vision, the employees began to support the strategy. During that first year, Carlzon spent half his working hours talking with employees and demonstrating his own enthusiasm and involvement in the strategy. He wanted the staff to understand his notion of "moments of truth," by which he meant the average time of 15 seconds during which the customer has contact with an SAS employee. Arguing that those brief moments form the basis of customers' impressions of SAS, Carlzon emphasized that the front line needs to communicate to business customers that SAS is serious about service. One of his favorite stories is about an SAS ticket agent at the Stockholm airport who sent a limousine to retrieve an American businessman's ticket. The customer had left the ticket in his hotel room, checked out, and traveled to the airport. He would have missed his plane had it not been for the quick-thinking agent.

Carlzon, who is known for his capacity to communicate complicated messages in simple, but meaningful, ways, also understands the importance of nonverbal communication. "Leaders should be aware of how far nonverbal communication can go in illustrating the style that others in the organization should follow," he says. He notes, as an example, that SAS passes out magazines and newspapers for customers to read during their flight, but often there are not enough to go around. As a result, when he flies on SAS, the staff sometimes tries to accommodate him first. "Out of the question," he tells the attendants. "I cannot take any myself until I know that all the passengers have gotten what they want!" Thus Carlzon reinforces both verbally and nonverbally (by example) that he really means what it says in the red book.

Furthermore, top management is willing to support the front line. To celebrate the initial turnaround, Carlzon sent every one of the 20,000 employees a gold wristwatch. Since then, major efforts to communicate with employees have helped SAS earn an international reputation for good service.[16] ■ ■ ■

SAS has built a strong reputation for good service to business travelers by concentrating on "moments of truth." That is the term that the airlines CEO, Jan Carlzon, uses for the average of 15 seconds of communication between SAS employee and customer. Carlzon wants this contact to convey SAS's commitment to service and customer satisfaction. Carlzon is no slouch himself at communication; he distributed to all his employees a book that spells out the company's vision, and he spends half his working time talking with employees.

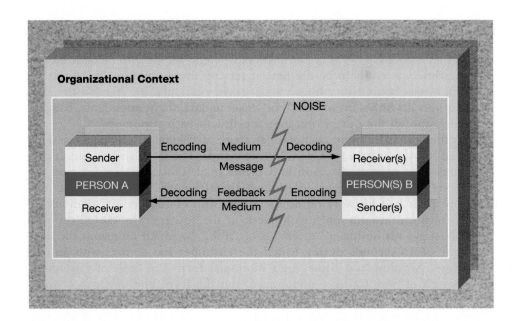

Figure 14-2 *Basic components of the communication process.*

Basic Components of the Communication Process

A look at the basic components of the communication process helps one appreciate the challenge of effective communication in organizations.[17] It also serves to highlight the fact that the only means we have of interacting with others is through the conduit of communication. The communication-process components are shown in Figure 14-2.

Sender The initiator of the message

SENDER The **sender** is the initiator of the message. Messages are usually initiated in response to an outside stimulus, such as a question, a meeting, an interview, a problem, or a report.

Encoding The process of translating the intended message into words and gestures

ENCODING Before the message exchange can take place, however, the sender must engage in **encoding,** the process of translating the intended meaning into words and gestures. The sender's choice of words and gestures will depend upon such factors as sender encoding skills, assessments of the intended receiver's ability to understand various symbols, judgments regarding the appropriateness of certain symbols, past experience in similar situations, job status, education, and emotional state at the time of the communication attempt.

For example, since Americans often do not speak foreign languages, they frequently fail to recognize that the idioms and regional sayings used in English conversation can cause problems for individuals for whom English is a second language. Hence they do not consider such factors in the encoding process. Jarold Kieffer, chairman of Senior Employment Resources, a not-for-profit organization in Annandale, Virginia, that helps individuals find employment, noticed that puzzled looks sometimes appear on the faces of foreign-born clients. Still, he did not recognize the magnitude of the communication problem until he asked one of his counselors who is Vietnamese to help him move a table. "Give me a hand, will ya?" said Kieffer. The bewildered counselor looked at his hands and exclaimed, "But I need them both." Since then, Kieffer has prepared a pocket-size book of common phrases, such as "foot the bill," "dyed-in-the-wool," and "go fly a kite," to help foreign-born job seekers.[18] Of course, similar problems often occur in international business communications, in which one or more participants may be conversing in other than his or her native language.

MESSAGE The outcome of the encoding process is a **message** consisting of the verbal (oral or written) and nonverbal symbols that have been developed to convey meaning to the receiver. The **medium** is the method used to convey the message to the intended receiver. Examples include written words in a memo, spoken words over the telephone, graphics on a slide, and gestures in face-to-face situations. The sender of a message must consider the appropriateness of the medium. For example, a telephone call may be an effective means of resolving a conflict over a minor item, but a face-to-face meeting may be more appropriate for negotiating a major change in a project.

RECEIVER The **receiver** is the person with whom the message is exchanged. If no exchange takes place (i.e., the receiver does not receive the message), there is no communication. There may be one receiver of the message, as in a conversation between two individuals, or many receivers, as in the case of a report sent to various members of the organization.

DECODING When the message is received, the receiver engages in **decoding,** the process of translating the symbols into the interpreted message. When the communication is effective, the sender and the receiver achieve a common meaning. However, the decoding process may result in misunderstandings if the receiver does not decode the message as the sender intended.

NOISE Noise is any factor in the communication process that interferes with exchanging messages and achieving common meaning. Noise includes, for example, interruptions while the sender is encoding, static on telephone lines as a message is being transmitted, and fatigue on the part of the receiver while he or she is decoding.

FEEDBACK Feedback is the receiver's basic response to the interpreted message. This response involves a reversal of the communication process so that the receiver becomes the sender and the sender becomes the receiver. Feedback provides preliminary information to the sender about the success of the communication process.

When the communication process does not allow for feedback, it is called **one-way communication.** Memos, newsletters, and announcements are examples of one-way communication—at least when they do not explicitly request feedback from those to whom the message is directed. When managers do not incorporate means for immediate feedback into the communication process, they run the risk that the intended message will not be understood by the receiver. With one-way communication, they might not find out about miscommunication until it is too late to correct it.

Conversely, when the communication process explicitly includes feedback, as illustrated in Figure 14-2, it is called **two-way communication.** This type of communication has a better chance of resulting in a reasonably accurate exchange of common meaning. Still, effective two-way communication requires that careful attention be paid to the communication process, particularly if several layers of the organization are involved in the message transmission. Such attention is necessary for two reasons. First, each additional link adds to the possibility that the encoding and decoding processes and/or noise will distort the information. Second, subordinates are often reluctant to provide negative information to upper layers of the hierarchy because they fear that they will be criticized.[19] As a result, managers need to expend considerable effort to obtain accurate information even with two-way communication, as top management at Ashland Oil learned when a serious difficulty turned into a crisis (see the Case in Point discussion).

Message The encoding-process outcome, which consists of verbal and nonverbal symbols that have been developed to convey meaning to the receiver

Medium The method used to convey the message to the intended receiver

Receiver The person with whom the message is exchanged

Decoding The process of translating the symbols into the interpreted message

Noise Any factor in the communication process that interferes with exchanging messages and achieving common meaning

Feedback The receiver's basic response to the interpreted message

One-way communication The communication that results when the communication process does not allow for feedback

Two-way communication The communication that results when the communication process explicitly includes feedback

| CASE IN POINT | ASHLAND OIL FACES A MAJOR CRISIS |

When an emergency arose at Ashland Oil, Inc., John R. Hall, the company's CEO, learned firsthand about the perils of information transmission. On a quiet Sunday in January 1988, 1 million gallons of diesel fuel spilled from an Ashland storage tank into the Monongahela River near Pittsburgh. Hall and the company's president spent much of the day in Hall's office (at headquarters in Ashland, Kentucky) talking by speakerphone with colleagues at the accident site and elsewhere. Afterward, Hall believed the situation was under control. He decided against going to the accident scene himself, convinced that his emergency-management team could handle the logistical arrangements. It was still unclear what had caused the leakage.

The next morning, at his regular 3-hour weekly meeting with top executives, Hall devoted only part of the time to discussion of the spill. By mid-morning, however, it was clear that he had not obtained sufficient and accurate information about the situation, which was quickly evolving into a crisis. Reporters had been told by the company spokesperson that the storage tank was new and that a permit had been obtained to build it. Now, new information "from several sources" was indicating that the storage tank involved had been recently reconstructed from steel that was 40 years old, that the construction had been done without a permit, and that less testing than usual had been conducted on the tank.

The degenerating situation turned into a major crisis when the arrangements for containing the spill proved inadequate because of unusually strong river currents. There was no contingency plan in place. As a result, the spill formed a 100-mile oil slick and interrupted water supplies for 750,000 Pennsylvania residents, as well as those of many communities in Ohio and West Virginia. By the following morning, Hall was jetting to Pittsburgh to investigate the situation himself and help subordinates deal with the crisis. In retrospect, Hall "would have wanted more accurate information faster," said his vice president and media chief.[20]   ■ ■ ■

In addition to the usual communication difficulties, such as encoding, decoding, noise, and the reluctance of subordinates to provide negative information, the stress of the situation likely exacerbated the communication breakdown at Ashland Oil. Factors that influence the way in which particular individuals communicate in organizations probably also played a part.

■ INFLUENCES ON INDIVIDUAL COMMUNICATION AND INTERPERSONAL PROCESSES

You may have experienced the frustration of arriving for a meeting only to find that some of the anticipated participants did not seem to know about it. How is it that some individuals receive a particular communication and others do not? While miscommunications are sometimes due to misdirected mail and lost messages, they often arise from individual factors that can impede or enhance the communication process in organizations. Such factors are perceptual issues, attribution processes, semantics, cultural context, and communication skills.

Perceptual Processes

Perception The process that individuals use to acquire and make sense out of information from the environment

Perception is the process that individuals use to acquire and make sense out of information from the environment. The process is complex and involves three main stages. The first stage is *selecting,* the filtering of stimuli that we encounter so that only certain information receives our attention. For example, suppose that a manager taking over a new unit has heard a rumor that a particular individual in the unit has a short temper. If the manager is not careful, this piece of information may cause the manager to pay particular attention to situations in which the person *is* impatient or angry.

The second stage of the perceptual process is *organizing,* the patterning of information from the selection stage. Slowly pronounce each of the following four words:[21]

M-A-C-T-A-V-I-S-H

M-A-C-D-O-N-A-L-D

M-A-C-B-E-T-H

M-A-C-H-I-N-E-R-Y

Like many people, you may have pronounced the last word as "MacHinery." This happens because the previous pattern leads us to expect another word with the same type of pronunciation. This exercise illustrates an interesting characteristic of perception: the tendency to organize information into the patterns that we expect to perceive. In the example of the individual rumored to have a short temper, the manager may begin to organize the selectively perceived behavior into a pattern of incidents in which the individual was angry.

The third stage is *interpreting,* attaching meaning to the information that we have selected and organized. In our example, the manager may, over time, begin to interpret (perhaps unfairly) the organized information as indicating that the person does, indeed, have a short temper.

The perceptions of individuals are affected by a variety of factors such as experiences, needs, personality, culture, and education. As a result, it is very likely that individuals will differ in their perceptions of the very same situations and messages. Several common tendencies to distort perceptions are particularly applicable to managerial communication and interactions. These tendencies are stereotyping, the halo effect, projection, and perceptual defense.[22] Awareness of these perceptual tendencies can help managers avoid the misunderstandings that such distortions often create.

STEREOTYPING Stereotyping is the tendency to attribute characteristics to an individual on the basis of an assessment of the group to which the individual belongs. When a manager engages in stereotyping, two steps occur. First, the manager categorizes the individual as belonging to a group whose members are perceived as sharing certain common characteristics. Second, the manager uses those perceived common characteristics to draw conclusions about the characteristics of the individual, rather than acquiring information about the person's characteristics more directly.

Stereotyping The tendency to attribute characteristics to an individual on the basis of an assessment of the group to which the individual belongs

Stereotyping leads to problems when the generalizations do not apply or do not apply equally to all members of the group or when people try to generalize about less specifically related characteristics. In such situations, managers may communicate inappropriate expectations. For example, at American Medical International, Inc., a publicly owned hospital company based in Beverly Hills, California, the president and chief operating officer, Gene Burleson, ran into communication difficulties because of stereotyping. Burleson was addressing a meeting of several hundred employees when one asked why the company did not have any women directors or top executives. Observers reported that Burleson's response implied that women cannot deal with the stress of the executive suite. His reply offended many members of the audience and caused the incident to be reported in *The Wall Street Journal.* Burleson later "admitted he gave a lame and a stupid answer" to the question.[23]

Halo effect The tendency to use a general impression based on one or a few characteristics of an individual to judge other characteristics of that same individual

HALO EFFECT The **halo effect** is the tendency to use a general impression based on one or a few characteristics of an individual to judge other characteristics of that same individual. For example, a manager may use a general impression based on one thing a worker does, such as compiling a well-done or poorly prepared report, to judge the worker's ability in other areas of work, such as handling customers. To avoid the halo effect, interviewers and managers need to make special efforts to collect enough data to make reasonable judgments in all the specific areas that they are trying to evaluate.

Projection The tendency of an individual to assume that others share his or her thoughts, feelings, and characteristics

PROJECTION Projection is the tendency of an individual to assume that others share his or her thoughts, feelings, and characteristics. Unfortunately, projection can encourage managers to engage in one-way communication because they assume that they know how their employees feel on various issues. Engaging in two-way communication to learn how other individuals really do feel about various issues can help managers avoid the ill effects of projection.

Perceptual defense The tendency to block out or distort information that one finds threatening or that challenges one's beliefs

PERCEPTUAL DEFENSE Perceptual defense is the tendency to block out or distort information that one finds threatening or that challenges one's beliefs.[24] As a result, managers or workers may not be very receptive to certain types of information. This may lead to the "shoot the bearer of bad news" syndrome, in which a person tends to "behead" the bearer of bad news even though the bearer was not the cause of the problem. Thus some managers get angry at employees who provide information about serious problems that cannot be ignored, even though the manager needs to know about them.

Attribution Processes

Attribution theory A theory that attempts to explain how individuals make judgments or attributions about the causes of another's or their own behavior

One aid to understanding how perceptions ultimately influence managerial communication and interpersonal processes is attribution theory. **Attribution theory** attempts to explain how individuals make judgments or attributions about the causes of another's or their own behavior.[25] Such judgments often form the basis for subsequent actions. According to the theory, we make causal judgments that are either *dispositional* (attributed to internal causes, such as personality traits or a person's own efforts) or *situational* (attributed to external causes, such as equipment or luck). For example, if Jane does not complete a work assignment on time, should we attribute it to an internal factor like lack of effort or ability, or should we decide some work context or other external issue is to blame? To make such judgments we consider *consensus* (the degree to which the behavior is similar to the way most people act in a given situation), *consistency* (the degree to which an individual behaves the same way in this or a similar situation at other times), and *distinctiveness* (the degree to which an individual behaves differently in other situations). Thus, if other staff members completed the same assignment on time, Jane has had trouble completing similar assignments on time in the past, and she has missed deadlines on several other types of assignments, we would probably make a dispositional judgment about why the assignment was late. On the other hand, if others also were late in completing the assignment, Jane normally completes such assignments on time, and she usually turns in other types of assignments by the deadline, we are likely to attribute the difficulty to situational factors. The attributions we make are likely to influence how we handle resolving the late assignment.

In making causal judgments, managers need to be particularly aware of the **fundamental attribution error**, the tendency to underestimate the importance of situational influences and to overestimate the importance of dispositional influences in explaining behavior. We are particularly likely to make this error when we are attempting to explain the behavior of *others*. Moreover, when there are successes and failures involved, we are likely to succumb to the self-serving bias. The **self-serving bias** is the tendency to perceive oneself as responsible for successes and others as responsible for failures.[26] This tendency sets the stage for serious communication problems between managers and their subordinates. For instance, a manager may attribute subordinates' successes to her or his own effective leadership but conclude that failures are due to the subordinates' shortcomings. Subordinates, on the other hand, tend to see successes as resulting from their own hard work and ability and to view failures as stemming from bad luck or factors in the work environment, including areas controlled by their supervisor.[27]

Fundamental attribution error The tendency to underestimate the importance of situational influences and to overestimate the importance of dispositional influences in explaining behavior

Self-serving bias The tendency to perceive oneself as responsible for successes and others as responsible for failures

Semantics

Words are symbols; therefore, they do not necessarily have the same meaning for everyone. The study of the meanings and choice of words is called semantics. A **semantic net** is the network of words and word meanings that a given individual has available for recall.[28] Each individual has his or her own semantic net, which overlaps, but does not correspond exactly, with the nets of others. **Semantic blocks** are the blockages or communication difficulties that arise from word choices.[29] Such blocks are commonplace because the various meanings and shades of meanings that individuals attach to words depend on each person's semantic net. Receivers decode words and phrases in conformity with their own semantic networks, which may be very different from those of the senders.[30] The examples presented in Table 14-1 indicate the high potential for semantic blocks between manager and subordinate.

Semantic net The network of words and word meanings that a given individual has available for recall

Semantic blocks The blockages or communication difficulties that arise from word choices

Within organizations, different units can have terminology that has evolved through tradition or is related specifically to the type of work being done. A common cause of semantic blocks is the use of *professional jargon*, language related to a specific profession but unfamiliar to those outside the profession.

TABLE 14-1 EXAMPLES OF SEMANTIC BLOCKS IN COMMUNICATIONS BETWEEN MANAGER AND SUBORDINATE

WHAT THE MANAGER SAID	WHAT THE MANAGER MEANT	WHAT THE SUBORDINATE HEARD
I'll look into hiring another person for your department as soon as I complete my budget review.	We'll start interviewing for that job in about 3 weeks.	I'm tied up with more important things. Let's forget about hiring for the indefinite future.
Your performance was below par last quarter. I really expected more out of you.	You're going to have to try harder, but I know you can do it.	If you screw up one more time, you're out.
I'd like that report as soon as you can get to it.	I need that report within the week.	Drop that rush order you're working on and fill out that report today.

Source: Reprinted from Richard M. Hodgetts and Steven Altman, *Organizational Behavior,* Saunders, Philadelphia, 1979, p. 305.

The medical profession has its own jargon, which is often mystifying to patients and others outside the profession. Such jargon, however, provides short cuts to communication for those in the know.

Such language must be used with care because it can be somewhat bewildering to newcomers, customers, or visitors. Nevertheless, organization-specific language can help build cohesion among employees, reinforce the corporate culture, and, as it does at the Walt Disney Company, support a competitive edge (see the Case in Point discussion).[31]

CASE IN POINT

AT MANY FIRMS, EMPLOYEES SPEAK A LANGUAGE OF THEIR OWN

A hipo, a Wallenda, and an imagineer order drinks at a bar. They do a little work—edit a violin, nonconcur with a wild duck, take care of some bad Mickey—and then ask for the bill. "This is on the mouse," says one of the three. Who picks up the tab?

Organizations often create a language of their own that becomes part of the daily communication among employees. In fact, outsiders may need help translating messages.

For example, a veteran employee at IBM says that a "hipo" (short for "high potential") is an insider designation for an employee who appears to be on the fast track to success. Another IBMer claims that, conversely, an employee perceived as having low potential is known as an "alpo." IBM employees do not disagree with their bosses; instead, they "nonconcur." An individual who nonconcurs fairly frequently, but does so constructively, is known as a "wild duck." The "wild duck" designation was a favorite of the company's former chairman, Thomas Watson, Jr., who borrowed it from Kierkegaard.

Corporate slang can be particularly prevalent in publishing operations, whose employees frequently have a way with words. At *Newsweek,* top editors are often called "Wallendas," after the famous family of aerialists. The designation is an overt recognition of the editors' job vulnerability. Writers at *Newsweek* speak of the weekly's top national story as the "violin."

In an unusual move, the Walt Disney Company has consciously developed its own corporate jargon to directly support its efforts to have employees think of the Disney theme parks as stages. At orientation and training sessions, employees are taught to say that they are "onstage" when working in the theme park itself and "backstage" when they are in the lower environs, where they cannot be seen by the public. They also learn to refer to coworkers as "cast members." An imagineer is a member of Disney's Imagineering division, an innovative group that is mainly responsible for dreaming up new ideas and figuring out how they can be engineered to work.

Jack Herrman, formerly a Walt Disney World publicist, remembers that his coworkers would label anything positive a "good Mickey" and anything negative (like a cigarette butt on the pavement) a "bad Mickey." When employees take someone to lunch on the Walt Disney World expense account, they say that the meal is "on the mouse." "You're immersed in the jargon they impose upon you as a way of life," Herrman says. Through the use of such language, the company continually reminds organization members of their roles in the production being performed at the theme parks. In this way, Disney uses language to support the company's competitive edge.[32] ■ ■ ■

When Disney employees are in the public's eye, they are said to be "on stage." The Walt Disney Company deliberately encourages the use of theater terminology in its theme parks to convey to employees the idea that they are putting on a performance for their customers. (Disney characters © Disney Enterprises, Inc. Used by permission from Disney Enterprises, Inc.)

Managing Diversity: Cultural Context

Communication and interpersonal processes are also influenced by culture. One means of cultural influence is the importance placed on the context within which communication takes place.[33] Context includes such situational factors as the roles of the participants, the nature of the existing relationships, and the nonverbal forms of communication. In **high context cultures** the emphasis in the communication process is on establishing and strengthening relationships in the course of exchanging information. Countries with high context cultures include Mexico, Saudi Arabia, India, and Japan (see Figure 14-3). With individuals from these countries, the surrounding circumstances or context, as well as the nonverbal communication, is likely to be at least as important as what is said. In **low context cultures** the emphasis in the communication process is on exchanging information and is less focused on building relationships. Countries with low context cultures include the United States, Canada, and Germany. Individuals from low context countries are likely to place the main emphasis on the words being spoken and pay less attention to the surrounding circumstances or nonverbal communication. For example, in many Asian cultures, individuals show deference to those high in the social structure by not looking them in the eye; but an individual from a low context country may ignore such subtleties. Thus, individuals from low and high context countries may well experience difficulties in communicating unless they take their differences into consideration.

While knowing an individual's country can provide some clues about cultural context, there can be variances within countries as well. For example, within the United States, there are high and low context cultures. American Indians, and individuals of Asian, Hispanic or African-American heritage, are

High context cultures
Cultures in which the emphasis in the communication process is on establishing and strengthening relationships in the course of exchanging information

Low context cultures
Cultures in which the emphasis in the communication process is on exchanging information and is less focused on building relationships

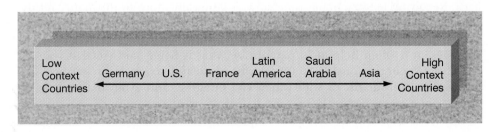

Low Context Countries ← Germany — U.S. — France — Latin America — Saudi Arabia — Asia → High Context Countries

Figure 14-3 *Continuum of low and high context cultures.*

The dissatisfied customer who feels someone is "listening" to his or her complaints is more likely to remain a customer than the person who is not given the opportunity to communicate dissatisfaction. As a result, Bennigan's, the restaurant chain, makes strong efforts to solicit feedback from its customers.

Active listening The process in which a listener actively participates in attempting to grasp the facts and the feelings being expressed by the speaker

more likely to emphasize high context communication. Anglo-American females tend to pay attention to context somewhat more than Anglo-American males, but both are on the medium to low end of the context continuum. One implication is that a low context supervisor who attempts to provide performance feedback to a high context subordinate is likely to experience difficulty if the supervisor concentrates on objective facts concerning the subordinate without focusing some attention on building trust and enhancing the relationship. Strong communication skills can help managers more easily adjust to cultural context issues.

Communication Skills

To be effective communicators in the various settings in which they must function, managers need strong listening skills and feedback skills. These skills are particularly critical because managers spend such a large proportion of their time communicating orally.

LISTENING SKILLS As the earlier discussion of the communication process suggests, receivers need to expend considerable effort to be sure that they have decoded and interpreted the message that the sender intended. Since managers rely heavily on the information inputs that they receive from oral communication, their listening skills are particularly crucial.[34] Experts on listening often differentiate between listening that is relatively passive, in which the listener follows the general gist of the words being spoken, and listening that is active. **Active listening** is the process in which a listener actively participates in attempting to grasp the facts and the feelings being expressed by the speaker. Actively listening for both the content and the feelings is important in understanding the total meaning of the message.[35] Managers leave themselves at a disadvantage when they are not good listeners. For example, Andrew Grove, now president and CEO of Intel, says he initially accepted a job at Intel in 1963 when he was a 27-year-old job candidate because he was impressed with the way in which Intel founder Gordon Moore really listened.[36] For some guidelines on enhancing your listening skills, see the Management Skills for the Twenty-First Century discussion, "How to Listen Actively."

FEEDBACK Other interpersonal communication skills that are particularly important for managers center around the issue of feedback, both giving and receiving. Effective feedback has several main characteristics. It focuses on the relevant behaviors or outcomes, rather than on the individual as a person. It deals with specific, observable behavior, rather than generalities. Perceptions, reactions, and opinions are labeled as such, rather than presented as facts. Finally, feedback spells out what individuals can do to improve themselves.[37] Being skilled in giving feedback makes the task of effectively guiding subordinates considerably easier and increases the prospects for mutual success.

In addition to giving feedback, being able to receive feedback is also important. Typically, most individuals have no difficulty receiving positive feedback. Receiving feedback that is negative is generally more problematic. Yet the way in which managers and others react to feedback is often a factor influencing how much feedback they receive.[38] When you are receiving negative feedback, it is often helpful to paraphrase what is being said (so that you can check your perceptions), ask for clarification and examples regarding any points that are unclear or with which you disagree, and avoid reacting defensively.[39]

Organizations are learning that it pays to obtain feedback from customers,

MANAGEMENT SKILLS FOR THE TWENTY-FIRST CENTURY

How to Listen Actively

The following guidelines will help you be an active listener:

1 Listen patiently to what the other person has to say, even though you may believe it is wrong or irrelevant. Indicate simple acceptance (not necessarily agreement) by nodding or injecting an occasional "um-hm" or "I see."

2 Try to understand the feeling the person is expressing, as well as the intellectual content. Most of us have difficulty talking clearly about our feelings, so careful attention is required.

3 Restate the person's feeling, briefly but accurately. At this stage, simply serve as a mirror and encourage the other person to continue talking. Occasionally make summary responses, such as "You think you're in a dead-end job" or "You feel the manager is playing favorites." In doing so, keep your tone neutral and try not to lead the person to your pet conclusions.

4 Allow time for the discussion to continue without interruption, and try to separate the conversation from more official communication of company plans. That is, do not make the conversation any more "authoritative" than it already is by virtue of your position in the organization.

5 Avoid direct questions and arguments about facts; refrain from saying "That's just not so," "Hold on a minute, let's look at the facts," or "Prove it." You may want to review evidence later, but a review is irrelevant to how a person feels now.

6 When the other person does touch on a point you do want to know more about, simply repeat his or her statement as a question. For instance, if the person remarks, "Nobody can break even on his expense account," you can probe by replying, "You say no one breaks even on expenses?" With this encouragement, he or she will probably expand on the previous statement.

7 Listen for what isn't said—evasions of pertinent points or perhaps too-ready agreement with common clichés. Such omissions may be clues to a bothersome fact the person wishes were not true.

8 If the other person appears to genuinely want your viewpoint, be honest in your reply. But in the listening stage, try to limit the expression of your views, since these may condition or suppress what the other person says.

9 Focus on the content of the message; try not to think about your next statement until the person is finished talking.

10 Avoid making judgments until all information has been conveyed.[40]

particularly dissatisfied ones. For example, Roger Nunley, manager of industry and consumer affairs at Coca-Cola USA, says studies indicate that only 1 dissatisfied consumer in 50 complains; the rest switch brands. Yet when a complaint is redressed, the individual is highly likely to remain a customer. As a result, an increasing number of companies, such as Coca-Cola, American Express, Mattel, Mars, Inc., and Procter & Gamble, maintain 800 telephone numbers to encourage customers to voice their complaints.[41]

■ GROUP COMMUNICATION NETWORKS

When tasks require input from several individuals, managers need to give some thought to the **communication network,** the pattern of information flow among task group members. Considerable research has assessed the impact of different networks on communication and task outcomes. Five major network structures are shown in Figure 14-4.

Three of these networks are fairly centralized, since most messages must flow through a pivotal person in the network. In the *wheel network,* the most centralized, all messages must flow through the individual at the center of the wheel. In the *chain network,* some members can communicate with more than one member of the network, but the individual in the center of the chain tends to emerge as the controller of the messages. In the *Y network,* the member at the fork of the "Y" usually becomes the central person in the network. The last

Communication network
The pattern of information flow among task group members

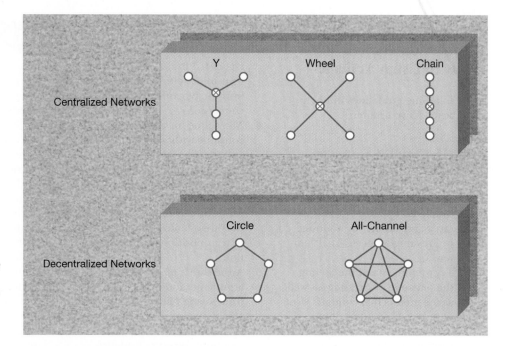

Figure 14-4 *Group communication networks. (Adapted from Otis W. Baskin and Craig E. Aronoff,* Interpersonal Communication in Organizations, *Scott, Foresman and Company, Glenview, Ill., 1980, p. 77.)*

two networks shown in Figure 14-4 are more decentralized, since communication flows more freely among the various members. In the *circle network,* each member can communicate with the individual on either side. Finally, in the *star network,* the most decentralized, each member can communicate with any other member.

For relatively simple, routine tasks, the centralized networks are usually faster and more accurate. This is because in each of the centralized networks, the individual in the central position (marked with an "x" in Figure 14-4) tends to become the coordinator, thereby facilitating the completion of routine tasks. In contrast, for more complex tasks, the decentralized networks most often prove to be faster and more accurate, with the star network showing the best performance. With complex tasks, the free exchange of information provided by the circle and the star facilitates the process and encourages creativity.

An intriguing aspect of the research findings is that group morale in the networks studied was higher in the decentralized ones, regardless of the type of task. These results pose somewhat of a dilemma for managers. Centralized networks appear to be the best for achieving accurate performance on simple tasks, particularly when time is an important factor. However, morale may suffer. For more complex tasks, the decentralized networks achieve both high performance and high morale. From a practical point of view, many organizational tasks are likely to fit into the complex category.[42] If tasks are relatively simple and call for more centralized communication networks, managers may be able to improve morale by providing opportunities for subordinates to work on more complex tasks that allow interactions with others in a more decentralized network.

■ ORGANIZATIONAL COMMUNICATION CHANNELS

An important consideration in assessing organizational communication is the movement of information throughout various parts of the company. When information does not reach the individuals and groups that need it for their work, serious effectiveness and efficiency problems can result. Patterns of organizational communication flow are sometimes referred to as **communication channels** because they represent conduits through which managers and other organization members can send and receive information. In this section, we consider the two major directions of communication flow in organizations: vertical and horizontal. We also examine an informal means of communication flow, the organizational "grapevine." Finally, we consider the implications of communication channel usage for organizational innovation, as well as the growing potential of electronics in facilitating communication in organizations.

Vertical Communication

Vertical communication is communication that involves a message exchange between two or more levels of the organizational hierarchy (see Figure 14-5). Thus vertical communication can involve a manager and a subordinate or can involve several layers of the hierarchy. It can flow in a downward or an upward direction. Studies generally find that managers spend about two-thirds of their communication time engaging in vertical communication.[43]

DOWNWARD COMMUNICATION When vertical communication flows from a higher level to one or more lower levels in the organization, it is known as **downward communication.** This type of communication can take many forms, such as staff meetings, company policy statements, company newsletters, informational memos, and face-to-face contact. Most downward communication involves information in one of five categories: (1) job instructions related to specific tasks, (2) job rationales explaining the relationship between two or more tasks, (3) procedures and practices of the organization, (4) feedback on individual performance, and (5) efforts to encourage a sense of mission and dedication to the organizational goals.[44]

Downward communication across several levels is prone to considerable distortion. A recent survey of middle managers across the United States indicates that the quality of the information they receive is poor.[45] As illustrated by Figure 14-6, as much as 80 percent of top management's message may be lost by the time it reaches five levels below. There are three main reasons for the distortion. First, faulty message transmission may occur because of sender carelessness, poor communication skills, and the difficulty of encoding a message

Communication channels
Patterns of organizational communication flow that represent potential established conduits through which managers and other organization members can send and receive information

Vertical communication
Communication that involves a message exchange between two or more levels of the organizational hierarchy

Downward communication
Vertical communication that flows from a higher level to one or more lower levels in the organization

Figure 14-5 *Vertical and horizontal organizational communication. (Adapted from R. Wayne Pace, Organizational Communication, Prentice-Hall, Englewood Cliffs, N.J., 1983, p. 40.)*

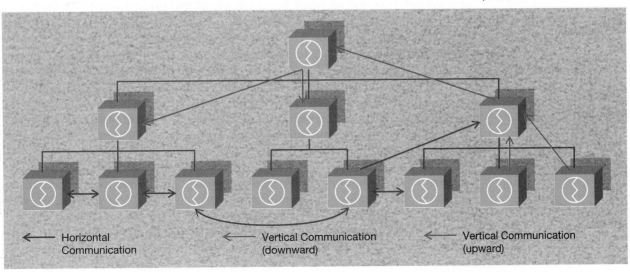

← Horizontal Communication ← Vertical Communication (downward) ← Vertical Communication (upward)

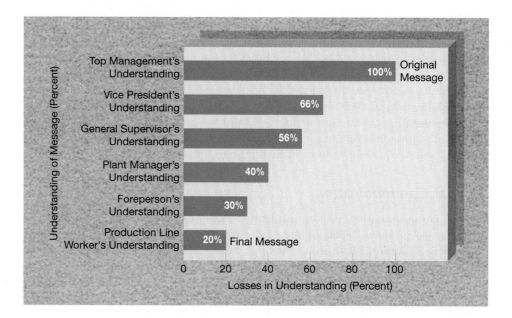

Figure 14-6 *Levels of understanding as information is transmitted down the organization.*

that will be clearly understood by individuals at multiple levels. Second, managers tend to overuse one-way communication, through such means as memos, manuals, and newsletters, leaving little possibility for immediate feedback regarding receiver understanding. Third, some managers may intentionally or unintentionally filter communications by withholding, screening, or manipulating information. Intentional filtering typically occurs when a manager seeks to enhance personal power over subordinates by tightly controlling organizational information.[46]

One way to increase the effectiveness of downward communication is to use multiple channels and repetition. Geneva Steel, located in Provo, Utah, instituted regular meetings for employees and their spouses. It also set up 30-minute cable TV shows, starring Geneva employees, to keep the members of the work force informed about what was happening at the plant and what was expected of them. The change had a positive effect on quality and productivity.[47] Another way to make downward communication more effective is to encourage feedback in the form of upward communication.

UPWARD COMMUNICATION When the vertical flow of communication is from a lower level to one or more higher levels in the organization, it is known as **upward communication.** Forms of upward communication include one-to-one meetings with one's immediate superior, staff meetings with superiors, memos and reports, suggestion systems, grievance procedures, and employee attitude surveys. The information disseminated through upward communication typically pertains to (1) progress of current work projects, (2) serious unsolved problems and situations in which subordinates need help from superiors, (3) new developments arising within or affecting the work unit or organization, (4) suggestions for improvements and innovations, and (5) employee attitudes, morale, and efficiency.[48]

The distortion that characterizes downward communication also plagues upward communication for two main reasons. First, as mentioned previously, information favorable to the sender is very likely to be sent upward, whereas information unfavorable to the sender will probably be blocked, even when it is important to the organization. Subordinates are more likely to filter information when they do not trust their superiors, perceive that their superiors

Upward communication The vertical flow of communication from a lower level to one or more higher levels in the organization

have considerable influence over their careers, and have a strong desire to move up.[49] Second, managers do not expend sufficient effort in encouraging upward communication. In a creative effort to overcome these problems, Robert Darvin, head of Scandinavian Design, Inc., distributes special stationery to every employee at his 21-year-old retail furniture company. The employees include warehouse workers, corporate executives in Natick, Massachusetts, and salespeople in the 70 stores located in the northeastern United States and Hawaii. The stationery is used exclusively for communicating with Darvin, and employees are encouraged to use it to send up bad, as well as good, news.[50] Similarly, Norman P. Blake, CEO of Baltimore-based USF&G (see the related Case in Point in Chapter 13) holds monthly "NB with NB" (which stands for "no bull with Norm Blake") sessions during which employees can ask him any questions that they wish.[51] Encouraging upward communication can be an effective means of fostering quality (see the Valuing Quality box).

Horizontal Communication

Horizontal communication is lateral or diagonal message exchange either within work-unit boundaries, involving peers who report to the same supervisor, or across work-unit boundaries, involving individuals who report to different supervisors (see Figure 14-5). Horizontal communication can take many forms, including meetings, reports, memos, telephone conversations, and face-to-face discussions between individuals. Managers spend about one-third of their communication time in horizontal communication,[52] usually related to one or more of the following areas: (1) task coordination, (2) problem solving, (3) information sharing, (4) conflict resolution, and (5) peer support.[53]

Three major factors tend to impede necessary, work-related horizontal communication. First, rivalry among individuals or work units can lead employees to hide information that is potentially damaging to themselves or that may aid others. Second, specialization may cause individuals to be mainly concerned about the work of their own unit and to have little appreciation for the work and communication needs of others. For example, scientists in an R&D unit that is focused on long-term projects may find it difficult to interrupt their work

Horizontal communication Lateral or diagonal message exchange either within work-unit boundaries, involving peers who report to the same supervisor, or across work-unit boundaries, involving individuals who report to different supervisors

Management by wandering around (MBWA) A practice whereby managers frequently tour areas for which they are responsible, talk to various employees, and encourage upward communication

VALUING QUALITY

Communicating Upward in Turning Detroit Diesel Around

Roger Penske, the former auto racer who is now a transportation tycoon, bought the controlling interest of Detroit Diesel from General Motors in the late 1980s. The firm makes diesel engines used in large trucks, tanks, and similar vehicles. In an address to the employees, he stressed the word "team." He explained that "T" stood for teamwork; "E," for effort; "A," for attitude; and "M," for managing your own business, your job, and your personal life. Penske asked most senior man-

agers to stay and assist him in changing the company culture.

In the new culture, managers seek information from the work force. One technique used at Detroit Diesel that often helps keep managers from becoming isolated is **management by wandering around (MBWA),** a practice whereby managers frequently tour areas for which they are responsible, talk to various employees, and encourage upward communication.[54] Of course, if the "wandering around" is done for the purpose of finding problems so that people can be punished, the practice will probably build mistrust and increase managerial isolation.

Every day, at Detroit Diesel, the general manager tours the plant where the 3000 employees work. Individual workers greet him, and he pauses to hear their concerns. At one stop, Jerry Chouinard takes a break from assembling a massive engine to tell the general manager that his area needs more engineering help. He gets the help immediately. Does this system work? Over a 4-year period, Detroit Diesel increased its share of the market from 3.2 to 28 percent because of the improved quality of the engines produced by its work force—which now speaks out.[55]

to help with current customer problems identified by the sales department. Third, motivation may be lacking when subordinate horizontal communication is not encouraged or rewarded. Committees, task forces, and matrix structures are common means that managers use to help encourage horizontal communication, particularly across work-unit boundaries (see Chapters 8 and 9).[56]

Informal Communication: The Grapevine

Formal communication
Vertical and horizontal communication that follows paths specified by the official hierarchical organization structure and related task requirements

Informal communication
Communication that takes place without regard to hierarchical or task requirements

Grapevine Another term for *informal communication*

The vertical and horizontal communication patterns that we have just discussed are sometimes referred to as **formal communication** patterns, or channels, because the communication follows paths specified by the official hierarchical organization structure and related task requirements. You might think of formal communication as communication relating to one's *position* in the organization. In contrast, **informal communication,** better known as the **grapevine,** is communication that takes place without regard to hierarchical or task requirements. Informal communication can be thought of as relating to *personal* rather than positional issues.[57] For example, personal relationships unrelated to organizational positions might exist among employees who ride to work in the same car pool, attend the same church, or have children in the same school. Grapevine communications stem largely from such relationships, which may overlap, but frequently do not coincide with, communication requirements associated with the hierarchy and the task.

The term "grapevine" can be traced back to the Civil War, when telegraph lines that were strung from tree to tree in grapevinelike patterns often provided intelligence messages that were garbled.[58] Grapevines exist in virtually all organizations, and grapevine communication patterns are likely to include both vertical and horizontal elements. One classic study investigated four possible configurations for grapevine chains (see Figure 14-7). In the *single-strand chain,* communication moves serially from person A to B to C and so on. In the *gossip chain,* person A seeks out and communicates with others. When following the *probability chain,* person A spreads the message randomly, as do individuals F and D. In the *cluster chain,* person A tells the message to three selected individuals, and then one of these tells it to three others. According to the study, the cluster chain is the most predominant type. This finding suggests that individuals who are part of grapevines are likely to be selective about the persons to whom they relay information and that only some of those persons will, in turn, pass the information further.[59]

Overall, grapevines tend to be fast, to carry large amounts of information,

Figure 14-7 *Types of grapevine chains. (Reprinted from Keith Davis, "Management Communication and the Grapevine," in Stewart Ferguson and Sherry Devereaux Ferguson, eds.,* Intercom: Readings in Organizational Communication, *Hayden, Rochelle Park, N.J., 1980, p. 59.)*

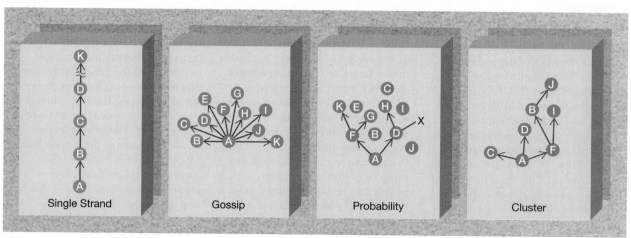

| Single Strand | Gossip | Probability | Cluster |

and to produce data that range in accuracy from 50 to 90 percent.[60] Although grapevine communications are often perceived by organization members as being fairly inaccurate, the problem seems to stem largely from misinterpretation when details are incomplete.[61] At the Digital Equipment Corporation (DEC), for example, insufficient explanations precipitated false rumors that ultimately had serious consequences. At the time, Jack Shields was a senior vice president at DEC and was often mentioned as a possible successor to then president, Kenneth Olson. When Shields did not attend a "state of the company" meeting for top managers, Olson explained the vice president's absence somewhat vaguely. Then a new organization chart of U.S. field operations did not include Shields. As a result, rumors that Shields had been fired started to move through the sales force and soon spread to sources outside the company. The gossip quickly reached Wall Street, raising questions about succession at DEC and causing the company's stock to fall more than a point. Shields, however, had not been fired. At the time of DEC's meeting, he had been attending the annual meeting of a company on whose board of directors he served. His name did not appear on the operations chart because the chart did not extend up to the level of the executive committee, of which he was a member.[62]

Although not officially put in place or even sanctioned, grapevines are a part of every organization and cannot be abolished. They may sometimes create difficulties when they carry gossip and false rumors, but they have many good aspects if managed properly. By dwelling on transgressions, grapevines may be a valuable aid in communicating organizational rules, values, morals, traditions, and history. Grapevines also give employees reaction time to think through impending changes and thus can facilitate employees' contributions to organizational goals.[63] In addition, they may help foster innovation by enhancing communication among various parts of the organization.

Using Electronics to Facilitate Communication

Electronic advances are providing managers with new methods and channels of communication. Four of the most prominent advances are electronic mail systems, voice mail, teleconferencing, and videoconferencing, and there is growing interest in groupware.

An **electronic mail system** is one that allows high-speed exchange of written messages through the use of computerized text-processing and communication networks. Anyone who has access to a computer terminal can develop and send a written message to anyone else who has a computer mailbox on the network. At the Digital Equipment Corporation, managers indicate that they save about 7 hours per week because their electronic mail system has increased the speed of decision making.[64] At Chemical Bank, managers estimate that their system saves them about 3 hours per week, mainly by eliminating unreturned phone calls and reducing other internal correspondence.[65]

There is also evidence that electronic mail leads to information exchanges among managers who previously did not communicate either by mail or by telephone and that managers receive new types of information through the system.[66] Electronic mail systems not only enhance vertical communication but also can facilitate horizontal communication.[67]

One disadvantage of electronic mail is that it eliminates the nonverbal cues (e.g., facial expressions, body movements, tone of voice) that serve as aids in face-to-face communication. (Of course, regular mail also has far fewer nonverbal cues than face-to-face message exchange.) Another disadvantage is that the speed and seemingly temporary nature of e-mail sometimes leads individ-

Electronic mail system A mail system that allows high-speed exchange of written messages through the use of computerized text-processing and communication networks

It helps to be photogenic these days. Many companies now conduct meetings with employees in two or more locations via closed-circuit television—a phenomenon known as videoconferencing.

uals to vent anger (often referred to as "flaming") in an e-mail message that they probably never would have sent had they attempted to commit it to paper. Accordingly, it is probably best to handle significant misunderstandings on a face-to-face basis whenever possible, and to use extreme caution when attempting to resolve difficulties via e-mail. Still another disadvantage is that the ease of sending mail electronically can cause individuals to receive excessive amounts of mail that does not interest them. For example, Andrew Grove, CEO of Intel Corp., pointedly tells subordinates not to copy him on e-mail messages that are not important for him to see.[68]

Voice mail A recording system that provides senders with the opportunity to leave messages for receivers by telephone

An allied form of electronic communication is **voice mail,** a recording system that enables senders to leave messages for receivers by telephone. With voice mail, nonverbal cues such as voice quality and tone of voice are conveyed. Voice mail is particularly useful in imparting short messages that do not require further discussion with the intended receiver.

Teleconferencing The simultaneous communication among a group of individuals by telephone or via computer using specially designed software

Another form of electronic communication, **teleconferencing**, is the simultaneous communication among a group of individuals by telephone or via computer using specially designed software.[69] Such software often is referred to as *groupware* because it facilitates message sharing among group members communicating with one another simultaneously. Groupware is often used to allow the holding of meetings among group members who are not in the same physical location. However, groupware can also be used to facilitate meetings among group members in the same location. In this latter case, group members may each sit in front of a computer. The groupware coordinates the simultaneous electronic messages and displays them on a special screen at the front of the room that all can see. The messages are anonymous, and most of the communicating is done through the computers. Sometimes no one speaks a word. At Boeing, managers say that the time needed to complete a wide variety of team projects has been cut by an average of 91 percent by using groupware to help team members coordinate their views.[70]

Videoconferencing The holding of meetings with individuals in two or more locations by means of closed-circuit television

A related form of electronic communication is **videoconferencing,** the holding of meetings with individuals in two or more locations by means of closed-circuit television. Teleconferencing use is growing in Fortune 500 companies.[71] Top-level managers at Tandem Computers use a form of teleconferencing in monthly television broadcasts over the company's in-house TV station. Employees throughout the world can watch the broadcast and call in with questions and comments.[72] Other companies with their own private television networks include J. C. Penney, Ford, Merrill Lynch, and Xerox.[73]

Since communication frequently involves groups, managers usually find it helpful to have a working knowledge of group dynamics and conflict management. We explore these topics in the next chapter.

■ CHAPTER SUMMARY

Effective communication and interpersonal processes are important in gaining and maintaining the competitive edge in organizations. Communication is the exchange of messages between people for the purpose of achieving common meanings. In their work, managers use two types of communication: verbal (including written and oral) and nonverbal. When the elements contradict each other, the receiver is most likely to interpret the nonverbal communication as the true message. Managers tend to prefer oral over written communication, spending approximately 75 percent of their working hours communicating orally with others.

The communication process has several basic components: sender, encoding, message, receiver, decoding, noise, and feedback. When communication provides for relatively immediate feedback, it is called two-way communication. Without a feedback provision, it is known as one-way communication.

A number of factors affect individual communication. Perception is susceptible to four major types of distortion: stereotyping, the halo effect, projection, and perceptual defense. Attribution theory helps explain how individuals use communicated information to make judgments about the causes of another's or their own behaviors. Semantic blocks sometimes occur because the various meanings and shades of meanings that individuals attach to words depend on each person's semantic net. An individual's cultural orientation to high or low context also can have a major impact on communication and

interpersonal processes. Individual communication is facilitated by the development of skills in such areas as listening, giving feedback, and receiving feedback.

When tasks require input from several individuals, managers need to give some thought to the communication network among task group members. Centralized networks are the wheel, chain, and Y; decentralized networks are the circle and the star. For relatively simple, routine tasks, centralized networks tend to be faster and more accurate. When tasks are more complex, decentralized networks are likely to be faster and more accurate.

Managers need to be concerned with the flow of information among the various parts of the organization. Formal communication in organizations follows channels specified by the official hierarchical organization structure and related task requirements. It flows in two main directions, vertical and horizontal. When vertical communication flows from a higher level to one or more lower levels, it is known as downward communication. When it moves from a lower level to one or more higher levels, it is known as upward communication. Horizontal communication is lateral message exchange. Informal communication, better known as the grapevine, takes place without regard to hierarchical or task requirements or organizational position. Electronic mail systems, voice mail, teleconferencing, and videoconferencing are examples of the communication aids that are being made available to managers through advances in electronics.

■ QUESTIONS FOR DISCUSSION AND REVIEW

1 Explain the major types of communication that managers use, and discuss managerial communication preferences. For an organization with which you are familiar, identify examples of each type. Classify the nonverbal communication examples in terms of kinesic behavior, proxemics, paralanguage, and object language.

2 Outline the basic components of the communication process. Identify these components in a conversation that you witness.

3 Delineate several common tendencies to distort perceptions. Give an example of how each could adversely affect communication.

4 Describe attribution theory, including the fundamental attribution error and the concept of self-serving bias. Identify an example of the fundamental attribution error based on a situation you have witnessed.

5 Explain the notion of semantic blocks. List some words that are used at your university that might cause semantic blocks to outsiders who are unfamiliar with the terminology.

6 Differentiate between high context cultures and low context cultures in terms of the emphasis in the

communication process. How could you use the high/low context concept to help you supervise more effectively?

7 Outline the major types of centralized and decentralized group communication networks. Explain the conditions under which centralized and decentralized networks are likely to result in the best performance. Evaluate how well suited they appear to be for the situations involved.

8 Differentiate between vertical and horizontal communication. Identify the major methods used in your college or university for downward communication from chief administrators to students and for upward communication from students to chief administrators. What mechanisms exist for horizontal communication among students?

9 Assess the organizational implications of the grapevine. What evidence points to the existence of a student grapevine in your department at your college or university?

10 How can managers use electronic mail systems, teleconferencing, and videoconferencing to advantage in communicating? What potential problems exist with each?

■ DISCUSSION QUESTIONS FOR CHAPTER OPENING CASE

1 Identify the vertical communication methods, both downward and upward, used at Southwest Airlines.

2 What methods are used to provide horizontal communication?

3 Would you characterize the management at Southwest Airlines as attempting to foster innovation? What evidence exists for your view?

■ EXERCISES FOR MANAGING IN THE TWENTY-FIRST CENTURY

EXERCISE 1
SELF-ASSESSMENT: LISTENING SELF-INVENTORY[74]

 The purpose of this exercise is to gain insight into how well you listen. Please complete the following 15-item questionnaire twice. The first time check the appropriate response (yes or no) for each question. In checking your response, please think in terms of your behavior in the last few meetings or conversations in which you participated. The second time through the questionnaire, place a plus (+) or a minus (−) in the third column. Mark a plus (+) next to your answer if you are satisfied with that answer, a minus (−) next to the answer if you wish you could have answered that question differently.

	Yes	No	+ or −
1 I frequently attempt to listen to several conversations at the same time.	—	—	—
2 I like people to give me only the facts and then let me make my own interpretations.	—	—	—
3 I sometimes pretend to pay attention to people.	—	—	—
4 I consider myself a good judge of nonverbal communications.	—	—	—
5 I usually know what another person is going to say before he or she says it.	—	—	—

6 I usually end conversations that don't interest me by diverting my attention from the speaker.

7 I frequently nod, frown, or whatever to let the speaker know how I feel about what he or she is saying.	—	—	—
8 I usually respond immediately when someone has finished talking.	—	—	—
9 I evaluate what is being said while it is being said.	—	—	—
10 I usually formulate a response while the other person is still talking.	—	—	—
11. The speaker's delivery style frequently keeps me from listening to content.	—	—	—
12. I usually ask people to clarify what they said rather than guess at the meaning.	—	—	—
13. I make a concerted effort to understand other people's point of view.	—	—	—
14 I frequently hear what I expect to hear rather than what is said.	—	—	—
15 Most people feel that I have understood their point of view when we disagree.	—	—	—

Your instructor will provide instructions for tabulating your answers.

EXERCISE 2
MANAGEMENT EXERCISE: A QUESTION OF INFERENCES

Read the story presented below, and indicate whether you believe the statements that follow the story are true (T), false (F), or unknown(?). Then get together with a group designated by your instructor, and determine as a group whether each statement is true, false, or unknown.

Haney Test of Uncritical Inferences (1979)
The Story[75]

A businessman had just turned off the lights in the store when a man appeared and demanded money. The owner opened a cash register. The contents of the cash register were scooped up, and the man sped away. A member of the police force was notified promptly.

Statements about the Story

1   A man appeared after the owner had turned off his store lights.   T / F / ?
2   The robber was a *man.*   T / F / ?
3   The man who appeared did not demand money.   T / F / ?
4   The man who opened the cash register was the owner.   T / F / ?
5   The store owner scooped up the contents of the cash register and ran away.   T / F / ?
6   Someone opened a cash register.   T / F / ?
7   After the man who demanded the money scooped up the contents of the cash register, he ran away.   T / F / ?
8   While the cash register contained money, the story does *not* state *how much.*   T / F / ?
9   The robber demanded money of the owner.   T / F / ?
10   A businessman had just turned off the lights when a man appeared in the store.   T / F / ?
11   It was broad daylight when the man appeared.   T / F / ?
12   The man who appeared opened the cash register.   T / F / ?
13   No one demanded money.   T / F / ?
14   The story concerns a series of events in which only three persons are referred to: the owner of the store, a man who demanded money, and a member of the police force.   T / F / ?
15   The following events occurred: someone demanded money, a cash register was opened, its contents were scooped up, and a man dashed out of the store.[76]   T / F / ?

CONCLUDING CASE 1

CHAIRMAN'S COST-CUTTING HUMOR AT BEAR, STEARNS

Even before cost cutting replaced scandal dodging as the latest game on Wall Street, one firm kept a sharp eye on its bottom line—thanks mainly to advice from the revered Haimchinkel Malintz Anaynikal, a reclusive philosopher of budgetary restraint.

The fictional Anaynikal resides in the fertile imagination of Alan C. (Ace) Greenberg, chairman of Bear, Stearns & Company, a noted Wall Street investment firm. "I have no further comment about him," Greenberg said when asked to supply details of Anaynikal's biography. "If other firms found out about him, there might be big trouble."

Through a series of memos distributed to employees at Bear, Stearns & Company, Greenberg and Anaynikal have worked overtime to slash costs. For example:

> It may come as a surprise to some of you, but Federal Express is not a wholly owned subsidiary of Bear, Stearns & Co. I mention this because we have been spending $50,000 a month with them and there is no explanation to justify this expenditure unless it was an intercompany transfer.

The company's memos typically contain nuggets of Anaynikal's instructive—and diverting—wisdom. What follows, in chronological order, are excerpts from a few of these memos.

FR: Alan C. Greenberg

June 19

The month of May is history, but it looks like we did get 10 runs in the first inning. I frankly cannot remember any time in the past where we ever broke even in the month of May, much less made money.

Haimchinkel Malintz dropped down, saw the figures and made some suggestions. . . . He pointed out to me that the tendency is to cut expenses when things are tough and how stupid that line of reasoning is. When things are good you should be even more careful of expenses. . . . The partners of this firm must continue to work together and learn to overlook petty differences. We are all expendable and I hope that your Executive Committee does not have to prove that to any of us.

August 9

I was just shown the results for our first quarter. They were excellent. When mortals go through a prosperous period, it seems to be human nature for expenses to balloon. We are going to be the exception. I have just informed the purchasing department that they should no longer purchase paper clips. All of us receive documents every day with paper clips on them. If we save these paper clips, we will not only have enough for our own use, but we will also in a short time be awash in the little critters. Periodically, we will collect excess paper clips and sell them. . . . In addition to the paper clip caper, we also are going to cut down on ordering the blue envelopes used for interoffice mail. These envelopes can be used over and over again. You have probably guessed by now that these thoughts are not original. They came from one of Haimchinkel Molonitz [sic] Anaynikal's earlier works. His thoughts have not exactly steered us wrong so far. Let's stick with his theories till he lets us down.

August 15

Thank you, thank you, thank you! The response to the memo on paper clips and envelopes has been overwhelming. It seems that we already have an excess of paper clips. . . . If we can save paper clips from incoming mail, we can save rubber bands, and my hope is that we can become awash in those little stretchies also. Obviously, if we can handle the rubber band challenge, I have something even bigger in mind.

September 10

We have been supplying everyone with memo pads. These pads have, at the top, our logo and also a person's name and telephone number. This is conceptually wrong. We are in a person-to-person business. It would be much warmer if the sender of a note signed it with his name and telephone number along with some sweet words, such as "I love you" or "I need more business to feed my family." . . . Haimchinkel Malintz Anaynikal just informed me that this superior way of communicating will save us $45,000 a year.

August 29 (the next year)

Because we are rolling along, it is essential that we review the fundamentals of Haimchinkel Malintz Anaynikal. . . . Do not get conceited or cocky. . . . Check on the people that answer telephones. Are they courteous? . . . Return all calls as soon as possible. . . . Watch expenses—like a hawk. Now is the time to cut out fat! The rest of the world cuts expenses when business turns sour. With your help, we will be different, smarter and richer.

August 21 (the following year)

I would like to announce at this time a freeze on expenses and carelessness. We probably throw away millions every year with stupidities and slop. In fact, I have seen more slop in the last three weeks than in the previous six months. Stop it now.

Haimchinkel Malintz Anaynikal is really something. . . . He hates slop even more than I do. In fact, he pointed out to me where our stock could be if we ran a neat, tight shop. I am tired of cleaning up poo-poos. The next associate of mine that does something "un-neat" is going to have a little meeting with me and I will not be the usual charming, sweet, understanding, pleasant, entertaining, affable, yokel from Oklahoma.[77]

Note: Ace Greenberg recently retired from his chairman and CEO position. It is likely that Haimchinkel Malintz Anaynikal will do the same.

QUESTIONS FOR CONCLUDING CASE 1

1 Do the memos effectively communicate the importance of cost cutting?

2 Evaluate the memos in terms of the basic components of the communication process.

3 To what extent do the memos encourage vertical (upward and downward) and horizontal communication?

CONCLUDING CASE 2

CITICORP VIES TO BECOME FIRST TRULY GLOBAL BANK

Ever since John S. Reed took over as chairman and CEO in 1984, Citicorp, one of the largest banks in the United States, has been working to become the world's first truly global bank. To that end, Citicorp has built one of the most sophisticated computerized communication networks in the world. With assets of over $250 billion, Citicorp seeks to become an international star in consumer banking and also wants to have a major presence in global corporate banking.

On the consumer banking side, Citicorp has been extremely successful. Throughout the world, the bank has more than 50 million outstanding charge and credit cards. There are more than 700 Citicorp branches in Europe, and Asian accounts are climbing beyond the 5 million mark. Citicorp is attracting new business because of its 24-hour telephone banking and its ability to offer customers the convenience of using the Citicorp automated teller card from Singapore to New York to Paris.

In researching the requirements to build a global consumer banking presence, Citicorp executives found that consumer banking needs around the world tend to be more similar than different. It also found that consumer attitudes about finance tend to be related more to the way individuals are raised, their education, and their values than to their nationality. As a result, Citibank has concentrated on offering similar services linked throughout the world to achieve global economies of scale.

"To make it work, you need three things," says Reed: "a shared vision and common vocabulary around the world, an organization than can translate global scale into local advantage, and the capacity to transfer local innovations around the world." Citicorp has standardized such services as branch banking, home mortgages, and auto loans, regardless of location. This approach reflects the shared vision of making it easy for consumers to buy things (including stocks and investments).

Reed refers to spreading local innovations around the world as "success transfer." He says that you establish the "demand for sharing ideas with a strong and consistent drive from the top." At first, several top executives helped orchestrate the process by flying around the world and urging people to share successful innovative ideas. Highlighting successes has also encouraged others to adapt and to try new things themselves. Reed says that Citicorp also holds many meetings organized by function or lines of business. For instance, Citicorp might bring all its credit card people together to tell "war stories—what works in Australia, what's working in Germany." In the auto loans area, a global conference might consider issues such as revenues, expenses, and write-offs.

Citicorp has been experiencing much greater difficulty building a truly global presence within the corporate banking sector. Because returns on corporate loans and investments are turning out to be too low, Reed has recently refocused Citicorp's efforts toward loans for midsized companies in developing countries and services for a few huge multinational corporations that can gain advantage from Citicorp's presence in 90 countries. The most important element within Citicorp's global corporate banking sector is its JENA business, a complex organization that handles lending, trading, and high-level deals within the interlinked economies of Japan, Europe, and North America. Whereas Citicorp's consumer bank business can be standardized to a large extent, the JENA operations cannot. There are no common products that can be sold to a wide range of customers, so the business is more customized. Moreover, it is intensely competitive and depends heavily on building unique relationships with various corporations.

To facilitate a global perspective in JENA, Citicorp has developed a structure around approximately 50 units called "activity centers." Centers specialize in such activities as trading on foreign exchanges, serving the financial requirements of specialized sets of customers, handling pension funds, or dealing with mergers and acquisitions. Although the activity centers are carefully defined areas of specialization, they must frequently collaborate with one another in serving customers. As a result, Citicorp is attempting to build the heads of the 50 activity centers into a team. Several levels of hierarchy have been eliminated, and the 50 heads report to the JENA sector executive. Eight coordinators help the sector executive by facilitating the handling of the most complex situations, in which multiple activity centers are involved. Also, the 50 center heads are brought together periodically to help enhance trust and teamwork.[78]

QUESTIONS FOR CONCLUDING CASE 2

1. Using the diagram of the basic components of the communication process (Figure 14-2), analyze likely communication challenges associated with conducting a global consumer banking business.

2. Use the basic components of the communication process to assess the difficulties of building a global corporate banking sector. How do the challenges differ from those in the consumer banking sector?

3. Evaluate Citicorp's use of various communication channels to facilitate communication and promote innovation.

CHAPTER FIFTEEN

MANAGING GROUPS AND TEAMWORK

LEARNING OBJECTIVES

After studying this chapter, you should be able to:

■ Differentiate among different types of groups in the workplace and explain how informal groups develop.

■ Use a systems approach to describe the factors that influence the way that groups operate.

■ Describe the major work group inputs, including group composition, member roles, and group size, and explain how they affect teamwork.

■ Explain the significance of group process factors, such as group norms, group cohesiveness, and group development.

■ Discuss how task forces and teams can be used to promote innovation.

■ Explain the causes of conflict and discuss how to reduce, resolve, and stimulate conflict.

GAINING THE EDGE

TEAMWORK PAYS OFF AT MONSANTO

Managers at the Monsanto chemical and nylon complex just east of Pensacola, Florida, have successfully challenged the traditional belief that an employee's main job is to follow orders. Monsanto employees working in teams are expected to make decisions related to such major issues as hiring, purchasing, job assignments, and production.

The team strategy began by necessity. In the mid-1980s the factory, in which Monsanto had invested $1 billion over the course of three decades, was beginning to lose money. In an attempt to control costs, unprofitable operations were cut, and almost one-third of the jobs were eliminated. More than half of the first-level supervisors took early retirement. Instead of naming new supervisors to fill some of the vacant positions, the remaining managers realized that the situation presented an ideal opportunity for switching to the self-managing team concept. They cut the layers of management from seven to four. Then they organized employees into teams of 10 to 12 persons.

Today, teams perform many of the functions previously executed by managers. For example, teams decide the mix of chemicals going into the production of nylon yarn. They are empowered to—and have—shut down production lines for reasons of quality or safety. For example, on one occasion during a thunderstorm, the appropriate team decided to switch to Monsanto's generators immediately, instead of waiting to see if the electric power would be knocked out by the storm. The move saved hundreds of thousands of dollars by avoiding a shutdown when the local power was subsequently interrupted for several hours. When machines or equipment need repair, teams go directly to the maintenance shop or to suppliers to obtain the necessary assistance. Teams interview prospective employees and rank them in order of qualifications for the job. Managers pay close attention to team hiring recommendations. No one has ever been hired without being recommended by a team.

The team approach has led to a rapid turnaround. Instead of losses, the factory is now achieving its best levels of safety and production ever. As a result, programs are being developed to share profits with teams on the basis of their performance. In addition, the teams are working so well that another layer of management will soon be eliminated.

Despite the successes at the Pensacola plant, there are still areas where team performance can improve. In some cases, teams have not communicated well enough with one another. In other instances, teams have done little to appraise and improve themselves on an ongoing basis. Some jobs have kept employees too busy to confer regularly with fellow team members. In addition, some employees have hesitated to initiate improvements without assurances that team members will be compensated fairly for their achievements. Some team members have also been reluctant to take charge in areas where they are capable of providing leadership.

Still, the results have been so positive that Monsanto is studying the possibility of duplicating the team concept in its plants throughout the world.[1] ■■■

By implementing the team strategy, Monsanto recognizes that individuals working effectively in groups can often be a powerful competitive force. However, to take advantage of the power of teams, managers must have a solid understanding of group behavior—often referred to as group dynamics—because of

This employee involvement team at a Monsanto plant in Springfield, Massachusetts, corrected a defect in one of its products, Saflex, a material used in laminating windshields. Employee teams such as this one have proved effective at resolving problems relating to quality and productivity. Moreover, using decision-making teams has enabled Monsanto to cut out three layers of management.

the ongoing interchanges that characterize groups and teamwork. Managers also need to be aware of their own potential to influence groups and teamwork as part of the leading function.

In this chapter, we examine some basic group characteristics, including types of work groups, the development of informal groups, and the operation of groups. Next, we investigate inputs and processes that affect group outcomes. We also explore how task forces and teams can be used to foster innovation. Finally, we analyze how conflict within and between groups can be managed, addressing possibilities for both reducing and stimulating conflict.

■ FOUNDATIONS OF WORK GROUPS

What Is a Group?

Group Two or more interdependent individuals who interact and influence each other in collective pursuit of a common goal

A **group** is two or more interdependent individuals who interact and influence each other in collective pursuit of a common goal.[2] This definition helps differentiate a group from a mere gathering of individuals. Several strangers who happen to leave by the same door at the theater or who can be found studying in the reference section of a library do not constitute a group. In neither case are those individuals interdependent, nor do they interact and influence one another in collectively attempting to achieve a shared goal. Likewise, groups differ from organizations because the latter involve systematic efforts (through the use of the four major management functions and a formal structure), as well as the production of goods or services. Groups typically do not engage in systematic efforts to the same extent as organizations and may or may not produce goods or services. *Teamwork* occurs when groups are able to work efficiently and effectively together to achieve organizational goals. We discuss the teamwork issue further in a later section focusing on how work groups operate.

Although groups have always been a central part of organizations, they are gaining increasing attention as potentially important organizational assets. Organizations that are making more extensive use of the power of groups and teamwork range from mammoth General Motors to much smaller Castite, a Cleveland firm that employs about 20 people and has sales in the $1 to $1.5

million range. At Castite, when an order for a new part comes in, a team composed of a salesperson, a quality assurance person, and a production worker meet together. They determine exactly what the customer wants, how to get the job done in the best possible way, and how to maximize quality. Castite, which uses an epoxylike resin to fill the tiny holes that are left by gas bubbles in molten metal as it is cast, has customers that include the "Big Three" automakers.[3]

Types of Work Groups

A number of different types of groups exist in the workplace. They can be classified into two main categories: formal and informal. These categories and several subcategories are shown in Figure 15-1.

FORMAL GROUPS A **formal group** is a group officially created by an organization for a specific purpose. There are two major types of formal groups: command and task.

A **command**, or **functional**, **group** is a formal group consisting of a manager and all the subordinates who report to that manager. Each identifiable work unit (manager and subordinates) in an organization is considered to be a command group. For example, if you stay in a large Marriott hotel, your room will be cleaned by one of several housekeepers who report to an area housekeeping supervisor, making up one command group. If you attend a luncheon, the individuals who wait on the tables report to a catering supervisor, forming part of another command group. Each supervisor reports to a respective higher-level manager and belongs to that higher-level command group. In this way, each supervisor forms a linking pin between a lower-level and a higher-level group. A *linking pin* is an individual who provides a means of coordina-

Formal group A group officially created by an organization for a specific purpose

Command, or functional, group A formal group consisting of a manager and all the subordinates who report to that manager

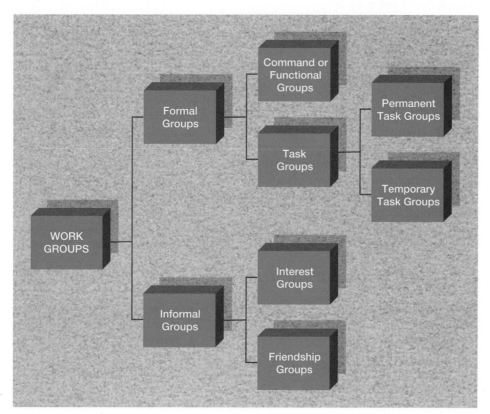

Figure 15-1 *Types of work groups.*

Task group   A formal group that is created for a specific purpose that supplements or replaces work normally done by command groups

Standing committee   A permanent task group charged with handling recurring matters in a narrowly defined subject area over an indefinite, but generally lengthy, period of time

tion between command groups at two different levels by fulfilling a supervisory role in the lower-level group and a subordinate role in the higher-level group. Thus organizations are made up of command, or functional, groups arranged in pyramidal fashion, with linking pins tying them together.

A **task group** is a formal group created for a specific purpose that supplements or replaces work normally done by command groups. Task groups can be either relatively permanent or temporary. A *permanent* task group, often called a **standing committee** or *team*, is charged with handling recurring matters in a narrowly defined subject area over an indefinite, but generally lengthy, period of time. An example is the Quality Improvement Team of Virginia-based COVANCE, a high-level permanent task group charged with facilitating quality improvement efforts across various units of the biotechnology firm. A *temporary* task group is created to deal with a specific issue within a specific time frame. For example, as part of its Profitability Improvement program, Heinz USA frequently organizes temporary teams of managers from different departments to seek out and prioritize projects that can lead to major cost savings.[4] Temporary task groups are often called *ad hoc committees, task forces,* and *project groups* or *teams.*[5] Names vary somewhat across organizations, so it may be necessary to ask about time frames to establish whether a particular task group is relatively permanent or temporary. We discuss task forces and teams in greater detail later in this chapter.

Informal group   A group that is established by employees, rather than by the organization, to serve group members' interests or social needs

INFORMAL GROUPS An **informal group** is a group that is established by employees, rather than by the organization, to serve group members' interests or social needs. Such groups may or may not also further the goals of the organization. Sometimes, an informal group has the same members as a formal group, as when members of a work group begin to have lunch together. Other times, an informal group is made up of only some members of one or more formal groups (see Figure 15-2).

There are two major types of informal groups: interest and friendship.

An *interest group* is an informal group created to facilitate employee pursuits of common concern. The types of interests that spawn informal groups can be wide-ranging, such as a radical new technology that may not be practical for the company to pursue at the time (but which a group of engineers investigate informally), a sport (e.g., volleyball), or a desire to influence the company to alter some policy. A *friendship group* is an informal group that evolves primarily to meet employee social needs. Such groups typically stem from mutual attraction, often based on common characteristics, such as similar work, backgrounds, and/or values. Informal groups can benefit an organization by enhancing the flow of information and reinforcing the willingness of employees to work together cooperatively. They can be detrimental, however, when members place group concerns above important work goals or have a serious falling out. Thus managers need to understand informal groups because of their potential for influencing organizational effectiveness.

How Informal Groups Develop

Work by sociologist George Homans helps explain how informal groups often arise from the dynamics of formal groups.[6] When a formal group is established, certain behaviors and sentiments are required of its members (see Figure 15-3).

Required activities are the behaviors necessary to perform job tasks. *Required interactions* are the dealings with others that are specified as part of the job. *Required sentiments* are the views and attitudes that are necessary to do the job.

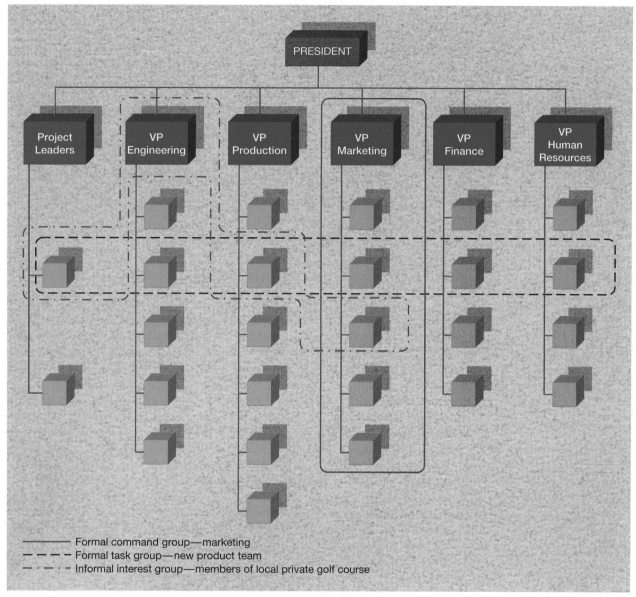

Formal command group—marketing
Formal task group—new product team
Informal interest group—members of local private golf course

Figure 15-2 *Formal and informal groups in an organization.*

Also involved are *given sentiments,* the nonrequired attitudes and values that individuals inevitably bring to their jobs.

For example, when Federal Express was a fledgling company in the early 1970s, there were some basic, but limited, requirements that its employees were expected to meet. Couriers were expected to pick up packages on time, get them to the airport, look clean and professional, and keep their trucks washed (required activities). They were also expected to interact with customers when they picked up and dropped off packages, as well as to cooperate with Federal Express pilots, plane loaders, and other company employees at airports (required interactions). Finally, they were supposed to be courteous and respectful to customers (required sentiments). No doubt, the couriers also held feelings about a variety of issues, such as the way the organization was run, other employees, sports, and politics (given sentiments and values).[7]

During this period, the company was operating on the edge of financial disaster. Skeptics were certain the endeavor would fail. As the couriers in their

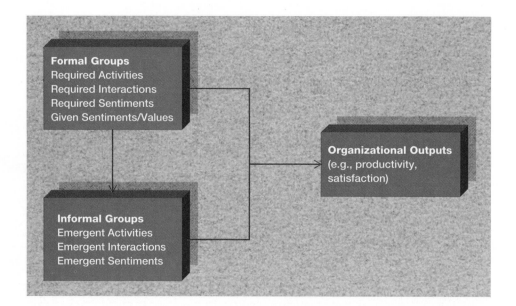

Figure 15-3 *The informal-group emergence process.*

formal groups performed their required behaviors, other behaviors, interactions, and sentiments began to emerge. According to Homans, these emergent activities, interactions, and sentiments are associated with informal groups and can either supplant or supplement required activities, interactions, and sentiments.

In the Federal Express case, the couriers began to form a strong, informal camaraderie with the pilots, plane loaders, and others involved with their packages. Stories abound about couriers who were so dedicated to getting their packages picked up and delivered that they did things like pawning watches to buy gasoline (emergent activities). One observer likened the informal team spirit that arose to that of bomber crews in movies about World War II (emergent sentiments). For Federal Express, the emergence of informal groups was a major factor in the survival of the company.[8]

Most organizations have many formal and informal groups. Because formal groups are created by the organization to fulfill specific purposes, it is particularly important for managers and others in the organization to ensure that they operate effectively. Therefore, most of our discussion in this chapter will focus on formal work groups.

How Work Groups Operate

A number of factors affect teamwork and the ultimate effectiveness of formal work groups. In analyzing these factors, it is useful to think of groups as systems that use inputs, engage in various processes, or transformations, and produce outcomes (see Chapter 2 for a further explanation of the systems approach to analyzing organizations). Figure 15-4 lists several general factors

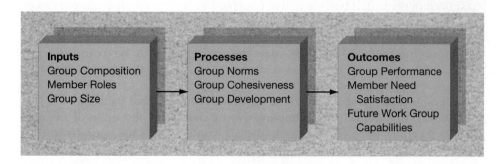

Figure 15-4 *Factors that affect work group behavior.*

that are important in understanding the interactions and outcomes of groups. These factors are organized under the input, process, and outcome categories. Note that important outcomes include not only group performance as measured by such factors as quantity, quality, and costs, but also the satisfaction of group members. Moreover, in well-functioning groups, teamwork increases the capacity of the group to operate effectively and the willingness of team members to work together in the future.

■ WORK GROUP INPUTS

In order for groups to operate, they must have certain basic inputs. Some of the major inputs that affect groups and teamwork are the composition of the group, the roles that members play, and the size of the group.

Managing Diversity: Work Group Composition

The composition of a work group has a strong bearing on a group's ultimate success. Therefore, managers need to consider carefully who they select to be a member of a work group. Two especially important factors to consider in making selections are the characteristics of potential members and the reasons that members are attracted to a particular group.

MEMBER CHARACTERISTICS Managers need to weigh three main types of member characteristics when selecting members for work groups.[9] For one thing, individual group members need to have task-relevant expertise. Another consideration is that group members need to have appropriate interpersonal skills. Finally, for tasks that involve at least some challenge, a moderate degree of diversity (in terms of such differences as personalities, gender, ethnic group, attitudes, background, or experience) in the makeup of a group is useful. If a group is too homogeneous, members may get along well but lack enough differing perspectives to generate new ideas.[10] On the other hand, if a group is too heterogeneous, the advantages of the breadth of talent may be lost because the group may have difficulty coordinating the diverse efforts. Studies show that diversity in groups can lead to greater creativity, superior decision making (see Chapter 5), and increased flexibility in meeting changing requirements.[11]

Like any group that works together, a string quartet needs a dose of diversity to keep from falling into creative complacency. Canadian Peter Oundjian (far left) provided that function when he joined the Tokyo String Quartet. His outsider's perspective and fresh-approach have served to enrich the mix.

At the same time, managers need to recognize that it may take some patience to benefit from diversity in groups. One study of groups that were culturally homogeneous versus culturally diverse (different nationalities and ethnic backgrounds) showed that the culturally diverse groups performed relatively poorly at first, but over time they performed better than the homogeneous groups in analyzing business situations and figuring out what to do.[12] Managers can facilitate gaining benefits from diversity by ensuring that individuals have been trained to function effectively in groups. Many organizations offer diversity training to help members understand, appreciate, and effectively utilize individual differences. For example, General Electric has developed the following vision statement for its diversity program: "To be recognized as one of the world's most competitive companies due to our ability to value and fully utilize the contributions of all employees from all cultural and social backgrounds."[13] Managers can also promote gaining benefits from diversity by monitoring groups to ensure that they develop appropriately (we discuss the stages of group development and efforts at British Petroleum to help an organizational unit develop multicultural teamwork later in this chapter).

ATTRACTION TO THE GROUP Another important factor to consider in composing a group is potential members' attraction to the group. While employees are not always able to choose the groups in which they work, they often have some discretion in the matter, particularly for certain types of task groups, such as task forces and committees.

Why do individuals join or agree to participate in groups?[14] Some may be attracted to or like other members of the group. Others may enjoy the activities of the group—perhaps a committee is exploring new ideas in a technical area of interest. Still others may value the goals or purposes of the group. For example, Michael J. Daly left a $45,000 accounting job with Manufacturers Hanover Bank to join the Peace Corps in the Dominican Republic for $200 per month plus room and board. There, Daly taught peasant-owned financial cooperatives how to operate at a profit and compete with local banks.[15] People also join groups because they help meet individuals' needs for affiliation. According to McClelland's acquired-needs theory of motivation, such needs may be higher in some individuals than in others, but we are all likely to have at least some need for affiliation (see Chapter 12). Finally, individuals may join a group because doing so can be instrumental in achieving a goal outside the group (e.g., joining a committee for the purpose of meeting members of a work unit in which one would like to obtain a job). Individuals may join groups for any or all these reasons.

Member Roles

Role A set of behaviors expected of an individual who occupies a particular position in a group

Why are we likely to expect that the designated chair of a committee will call the meeting to order, a group member from the finance department will provide relevant financial expertise, and the designated secretary will take notes? One reason is that each of these individuals is fulfilling a **role,** a set of behaviors expected of an individual who occupies a particular position in a group. When operating in a work group, individuals typically fulfill several roles. For example, a person may be acting in the role of an expert in a given area, the role of a representative of a particular command group, and the role of a member of the work force interested in the implications of the matter under discussion.

In addition, the fact that an individual is a member of a group brings with it other roles. Common member roles in groups fit into three categories: group task roles, group maintenance roles, and self-oriented roles.[16]

Group task roles help a group develop and accomplish its goals. Among these roles are the following:

Group task roles Roles that help a group develop and accomplish its goals

- **Initiator-contributor:** Proposes goals, suggests ways of approaching tasks, and recommends procedures for approaching a problem or task
- **Information seeker:** Asks for information, viewpoints, and suggestions about the problem or task
- **Information giver:** Offers information, viewpoints, and suggestions about the problem or task
- **Coordinator:** Clarifies and synthesizes various ideas in an effort to tie together the work of the members
- **Orienter:** Summarizes, points to departures from goals, and raises questions about discussion direction
- **Energizer:** Stimulates the group to higher levels of work and better quality

Group maintenance roles do not directly address a task itself but, instead, help foster group unity, positive interpersonal relations among group members, and development of the ability of members to work effectively together. Group maintenance roles include the following:

Group maintenance roles Roles that do not directly address a task itself but, instead, help foster group unity, positive interpersonal relations among group members, and development of the ability of members to work effectively together

- **Encourager.** Expresses warmth and friendliness toward group members, encourages them, and acknowledges their contributions
- **Harmonizer:** Mediates disagreements between other members and attempts to help reconcile differences
- **Gatekeeper:** Tries to keep lines of communication open and promotes the participation of all group members
- **Standard setter:** Suggests standards for the way in which the group will operate and checks whether members are satisfied with the functioning of the group
- **Group observer:** Watches the internal operations of the group and provides feedback about how participants are doing and how they might be able to function better
- **Follower:** Goes along with the group and is friendly but relatively passive

Self-oriented roles are related to the personal needs of group members and often negatively influence the effectiveness of a group. These roles include the following:

Self-oriented roles Roles that are related to the personal needs of group members and often negatively influence the effectiveness of a group

- **Aggressor:** Deflates the contributions of others by attacking their ideas, ridiculing their feelings, and displaying excessive competitiveness
- **Blocker:** Tends to be negative, stubborn, and resistive of new ideas, sometimes in order to force the group to readdress a viewpoint that it has already dealt with
- **Recognition seeker:** Seeks attention, boasts about accomplishments and capabilities, and works to prevent being placed in an inferior position in the group
- **Dominator:** Tries to assert control and manipulates the group or certain group members through such methods as flattering, giving orders, or interrupting others

Group leaders often assume many of the task roles. In addition, the leaders may use some maintenance roles to facilitate group progress. Often, however, it is difficult for a leader to engage in all the necessary task and mainte-nance behaviors without some help from others in the group. In leaderless groups (those with no appointed leader), the individuals most likely to emerge as leaders (be perceived by others as leaders) are active participants who adopt task roles.[17]

Informal leader An individual, other than the formal leader, who emerges from a group, has major influence, and is perceived by group members as a leader

Even when a group has a formally designated leader, one or more infor-mal leaders may develop. An **informal leader** is an individual, other than the formal leader, who emerges from a group, has major influence, and is per-ceived by group members as a leader. Although some group members may attempt to exercise informal leadership regardless of the formal leader's behav-ior, informal leaders are most likely to emerge when the formal leader has dif-ficulty facilitating group progress.[18] In addition to roles, another important group input factor is group size.

Group Size

Research on small groups provides some interesting insights into the effects of group size. One thrust has considered how different numbers of members affect interactions, while another has investigated how group size affects per-formance.[19]

SIZE AND GROUP INTERACTIONS The number of individuals in a group influ-ences how the members interact. With two-person groups, or dyads, the two members tend to be extremely polite and attempt to avoid disagreements or they disagree frequently, causing relations to be somewhat strained. Adding a third person often does not resolve the interaction difficulties because there is a tendency for the group to split into a "two-against-one" situation. Groups with four or six members are susceptible to deadlocks because the groups can eas-ily split into factions of equal size.

On the other hand, midsize groups of five—or possibly seven—members have several advantages. For one thing, deadlocks cannot occur, because of the odd number of members. For another, the groups are large enough to gener-ate many different ideas but small enough to allow various members to partic-ipate fully in the group.

As groups grow beyond seven—and particularly beyond eleven or twelve—it becomes more difficult for all members to participate actively. As a result, the interaction tends to become more centralized, with a few individuals tak-ing more active roles relative to the other members. Disagreements may occur more easily and group satisfaction may decline unless the members put a good deal of effort into group maintenance roles. Moreover, interactions may be lengthy when complex issues are involved.[20] In an effort to be responsive to competitive pressures, at one point Procter & Gamble revamped its highest-ranking group, the administrative committee. Traditionally, the 40-member committee met every Tuesday morning to approve all significant promotions and spending plans. In its place, Procter & Gamble created a 20-member exec-utive committee to meet weekly for a review of only extremely important issues, pushing other decisions down to lower levels in the organization for handling. The change was made because the difficulty of engaging in meaningful dia-logue in such a large group bogged down the whole decision-making process.[21]

SIZE AND PERFORMANCE What impact does size have on group performance? This is not an easy question to answer because the effects of size depend to some degree on the nature of the task. For example, the effects might be dif-

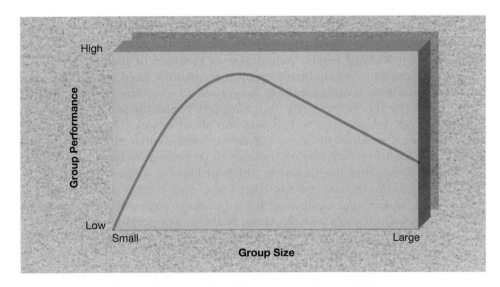

Figure 15-5 *Effects of group size on performance.*

ferent in a group whose members work somewhat independently (such as waiters in a restaurant) and in one whose members must coordinate their efforts closely (such as a rescue team). Generally, though, the impact of size on group performance is shaped like an inverted "U" (see Figure 15-5).[22] Thus, as managers initially add workers to a group, performance goes up; but after a certain point, the added impact of more workers begins to level off performance, and it may even go down.

Why does performance stop rising and even possibly decline as group size increases? One reason is **social loafing,** the tendency of individuals to expend less effort when working in groups than when working alone.[23] The effects can snowball if others in the group detect the social loafing and consequently reduce their own efforts.[24] Individuals who engage in social loafing are often called *free riders* because they benefit from the work of the group without bearing their proportional share of the costs involved.[25] As a result, social loafing is sometimes called *free riding.* There is some evidence that individuals who tend toward individualism are more likely than those who lean toward collectivism to free ride as the group increases in size. **Individualism** is a condition whereby personal interests are afforded greater weight than the needs of the group. Individualists are self-oriented and are likely to ignore group interests if they conflict with their own. **Collectivism** is a condition whereby the demands and interests of the group are given precedence over the desires and needs of individuals. Collectivists will tend to make personal sacrifices for the good of the group.[26]

Managers can take several steps to reduce the likelihood of social loafing.[27] Assigning just enough people to do the work is one prime step. Others are having each group member do different tasks, making each individual's work visible in some way, providing for individual feedback, having individuals work with people they respect, providing a standard against which to measure how the group is doing, and making rewards contingent on individual, as well as group, performance. Finally, since social loafing is less likely to occur when the group is committed to the task, managers should try to design interesting, challenging tasks or select group members who are likely to be committed to particular tasks.[28] Challenging tasks, small work groups, and a committed work force are all factors that have helped boost company success at Brazil's Semco (see the Case in Point discussion).

Social loafing The tendency of individuals to expend less effort when working in groups than when working alone

Individualism A condition whereby personal interests are afforded greater weight than the needs of the group
Collectivism A condition whereby the demands and interests of the group are given precedence over the desires and needs of individuals

CASE IN POINT

GROUPS MAKE A DIFFERENCE AT BRAZIL'S SEMCO

In 1980, when Richard Semler joined Semco, founded by his father 27 years earlier, the company had about 100 employees, manufactured hydraulic pumps for ships, produced about $4 million in revenues, and tottered on the edge of bankruptcy. For the next 2 years, top managers constantly sought bank loans and fought off rumors that the company was about to sink. They also traveled four continents seeking the seven license agreements that enabled the company to reduce its cyclical marine business to 60 percent of total sales.

Today, Semco has five factories, which produce a range of sophisticated products, including marine pumps, digital scanners, commercial dishwashers, truck filters, and mixing equipment for substances ranging from bubble gum to rocket fuel. Customers include Alcoa, Saab, and General Motors. Semco is frequently cited in the press as one of the best companies in Brazil to work for.

The company's survival and ultimate success is due largely to a major change in its management approach. Semco shifted toward an emphasis on three fundamental values—democracy, information, and profit sharing. These values ultimately led to reliance on work groups as a primary mechanism for managing the company.

After some experimentation, Semco found that the optimal number for an effective production unit is about 150 people per factory. In the spirit of democracy and worker involvement, work teams of about 10 employees each were given major responsibility for outcomes associated with their areas. Initially, costs rose because of duplicated effort and lost economies of scale. Within a year, though, sales doubled, inventory dropped from 126 to 46 days, eight new products appeared that had been tied up in R&D for 2 years, and the product rejection rate at inspection dropped from 33 to 1 percent. Increased productivity enabled the company to reduce the work force by 32 percent through attrition and offers of early retirement.

At Semco, once the members of a group agree on a monthly production schedule, they meet it. In one situation, a group determined that it could make 220 meat slicers. As the end of the month approached, everything was completed except for motors that had not yet arrived, despite repeated phone calls

At Semco S/A, a manufacturer of machinery in Brazil, employees are divided into work groups of about ten members each. Each group has access to important company information, undertakes major responsibilities, and is given wide latitude in deciding how to meet goals. The approach is working: Semco's sales and productivity have increased since it was implemented. Moreover, Semco has the reputation of being one of the best companies to work for in Brazil.

to the supplier. Finally, two employees went to the supplier's plant, talked to the supplier, and got delivery on the last day of the month. Then everyone stayed until 4:45 the next morning in order to finish production of the meat slicers on time.

Several factors have contributed to the success of Semco's work teams. One is that the work teams have access to important information. In fact, each Semco employee receives a balance sheet, a profit-and-loss analysis, and a cash-flow statement for his or her division every month. All workers voluntarily attend monthly classes so that they can learn to read and understand the numbers. Another factor is that, although top-level managers are strict about meeting the financial targets, workers have wide latitude in determining the necessary actions and carrying them out. Yet another factor contributing to work team success is the profit sharing plan. Twice a year, employees receive about 25 percent of the after-tax profits for their division. Employees vote on how to disburse the funds, which are usually distributed equally. Semco doesn't bother to advertise job openings because word of mouth brings 300 applications for every open position. A survey of recent college graduates by a major Brazilian magazine found that 25 percent of the men and 13 percent of the women cited Semco as the company they most wanted to work for.[29] ■■■

Selective hiring practices, careful training, efforts to keep work team sizes relatively small, and the sharing of information are just some of the input factors that have made work teams at Semco so productive. The success at Semco is also due to effective interactions among group members, a subject we take up next.

■ WORK GROUP PROCESSES

Why do some groups seem to accomplish very little, while others with similar inputs achieve a great deal? In part, the answer lies in *group processes*, the dynamic, inner workings of groups as they operate over a period of time. As members of a group go about their work, some of their energy must be allocated to developing and operating the group itself. This energy is, in essence, diverted from the task. Therefore, it is sometimes called process loss, since it represents a loss of energy that could have been devoted to the task.[30] Some process loss is inevitable, given the interdependence that is characteristic of groups.

Even with process loss, there are possibilities of tremendous gains from the combined force, or synergy, of group members.[31] **Positive synergy** occurs when the combined gains from group interaction (as opposed to individuals operating alone) are greater than group process losses. When there is positive synergy, the whole (the total effect of the group) is greater than the sum of its parts (the tasks the members could accomplish individually). For instance, Procter & Gamble's premium diaper, Luvs Deluxe, made it to market in half the usual 18 months because of a multidisciplinary team that cut through departmental barriers. **Negative synergy** occurs when group process losses are greater than any gains achieved from combining the forces of group members. If you have ever enlisted the help of a group that proved to be so ineffective that you felt you could have done the job faster yourself, then you have witnessed negative synergy. We next discuss three of the major group process factors that affect group synergy and effectiveness: norms, cohesiveness, and group development.

Positive synergy The force that results when the combined gains from group interaction are greater than group process losses

Negative synergy The force that results when group process losses are greater than any gains achieved from combining the forces of group members

Group Norms

Norms Expected behaviors sanctioned by a group that regulate and foster uniformity in member behaviors

Norms are expected behaviors sanctioned by a group that regulate and foster uniformity in member behaviors.[33] Therefore, for a behavior to fit into the norm category, there must be some recognition among group members that the behavior is generally expected for membership in the group.

Work groups do not try to regulate all behavior through norms. Instead, they attempt to develop and enforce norms that are related to central issues.[34] For example, groups often develop norms concerning production processes. Such norms typically pertain to standards of quality and quantity, as well as how to get the job done. Informal social arrangements are another common issue about which norms are apt to arise. That is, groups often establish norms regarding when and where to have lunch; what type of social function, if any, to have when someone leaves; and how much socializing to do both at and outside of work. Finally, work groups frequently have norms about the allocation of resources, including materials, equipment, the assigned work area (e.g., near a window), and pay.

Norms typically develop through one of the following four mechanisms: explicit statements, critical events, primacy, and carryover behaviors.[35]

EXPLICIT STATEMENTS *Explicit statements* made by supervisors and coworkers can provide important information about the expectations of various group members. Such statements provide a particularly good opportunity for the supervisor to influence the norms of the group. Supervisory statements may be especially important when a new group is formed or when a new person is added to a group. Thomas Tyrrell recognized the potential power of explicit statements when he founded American Steel & Wire in Cuyahoga Heights, Ohio, more than a decade ago. He would have every new employee come to his office for a get-acquainted chat. He also visited each of the company's three plants for 1 day every month to let workers know how business was going and what they could do to cut costs. His efforts paid off and Tyrrell is now vice chairman of Birmingham Steel, which acquired American Steel & Wire in 1993.[36]

CRITICAL EVENTS In any group, there can be *critical events* in the group's history that set precedents for the future. Tyrrell's efforts at American Steel & Wire were aided by the fact that the company's three plants had been acquired from USX after being shut down for 2 years because of a labor dispute. The difficult competitive position of the plants and the past labor dispute encouraged cooperation among employees within the plant.

PRIMACY *Primacy* as a source of norms is the tendency for the first behavior pattern that emerges in a group to establish group expectations from that point on. To get new workers to take responsibility for their actions, Tyrrell insisted that all new hires invest at least $100 cash in company stock on their first day of work, despite the fact that many were steelworkers who had been unemployed for a significant period of time. He wanted the new workers to develop a norm of concern for the welfare of the company right from the start. The plants would shut down for the annual stockholders' meeting so that employees could attend it, and the company also instituted a profit sharing plan.

CARRYOVER BEHAVIORS Many norms are *carryover behaviors* from other groups and perhaps other organizations. When group members share similar past experiences (such as working on similar committees in the company), the establishment of norms progresses quickly. Otherwise, norms may evolve more slowly.[37] Tyrrell wanted to encourage more worker involvement in figuring out ways to cut costs and improve operations, but he found that it was difficult to break down the old norms and taboos that discourage workers from speaking out when they feel that something should be changed. He persisted, though, and now Birmingham Steel has built a new $110 million steel bar mill at the American Steel & Wire division.[38]

Group Cohesiveness

Another factor related to group process is **group cohesiveness,** the degree to which members are attracted to a group, motivated to remain in the group, and influenced by one another. We take a look at some of the consequences of group cohesiveness before exploring more specifically its determinants.[39]

Group cohesiveness The degree to which members are attracted to a group, are motivated to remain in the group, and are mutually influenced by one another

CONSEQUENCES OF GROUP COHESIVENESS The degree of cohesiveness in a group can have important positive consequences for communication and job satisfaction. Members of relatively cohesive groups tend to communicate more frequently and be more sensitive to one another, and they are generally better able to gauge the feelings of other members of the group. Members of highly cohesive groups are apt to feel more satisfied with their jobs and their team members than members of groups that are not very cohesive.[40] This is evident at Cleveland Track Materials, a maker of rail joints used by railroads to lay and repair track. The company has achieved success by training workers in several skills so that work groups can react quickly to the varying product specifications of customers. Welding supervisor Willie Smith says, "This is the best job I've ever had. All the guys—black, white—we're like a family. Everyone is important."[41] Group cohesiveness is also more likely to lead to *organizational citizenship behaviors*, discretionary actions that are not actual job requirements but contribute to reaching organizational goals (such as providing assistance to a coworker who is experiencing difficulties with a task).[42] Although there are some negative possibilities (such as excessive amounts of communication among group members), the enhanced communication and job satisfaction fostered by group cohesiveness are generally positive from an organizational point of view.

Group cohesiveness also tends to influence the degree of hostility and aggression that one group exhibits toward another. Whether the impact is an organizational asset or liability depends largely on where the group's energy is directed. For example, cohesiveness may be helpful when it leads to friendly competition among groups that do the same type of work but do not depend upon each other to get the work done. Aggressiveness as a by-product of group cohesiveness can also energize a group to fight outside competition. On the other hand, among groups that depend on one another to reach organizational goals, hostility or aggression usually leads to a lack of cooperation and related dysfunctional consequences, such as missing deadlines, raising costs, and frustrating customers.

Another area affected by group cohesiveness is performance, since performance levels of group members tend to be more *similar* in highly cohesive groups. This is because members of such groups tend to avoid either letting the group down by underperforming or showing up other group members by performing at a significantly higher level.

The impact of cohesiveness on the actual *level* of performance in a group, however, depends not only on the group's degree of cohesiveness but also on its existing performance norms. This relationship is shown in Figure 15-6. Groups perform at their *highest* level when group cohesion and performance

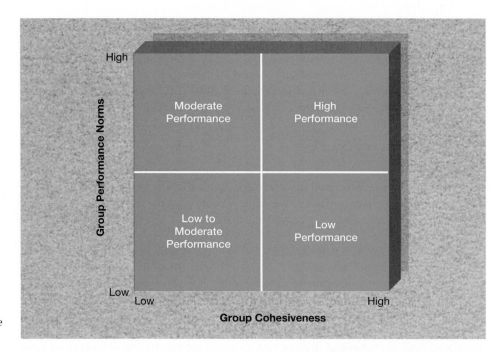

Figure 15-6 *Effects of cohesiveness and performance norms on group performance.*

norms are both high, thus encouraging all group members to perform at the same high level. In contrast, when group cohesion is high but performance norms are low, group performance tends to be at its *lowest* level.[43] Here, the high group cohesion bolsters adherence to the low performance norms. The effects can be seen in an illustration provided by former M.B.A. student Glen Huston, whose summer job experience involved a highly cohesive lawn-care crew with low performance norms. As he was diligently raking grass clippings on his first day of work, members of the crew, and even the crew leader, told him to slow down because they would all get tired if they worked at that pace. Then the crew leader showed him how to use a handkerchief to mop his brow while leaning on his rake so that it would look like he had been working strenuously and just stopped to wipe off the resulting perspiration. The handkerchief routine was for use if one got caught standing around when the supervisor drove up on periodic checks of the various work crews.

Group cohesiveness can also affect a group's willingness to innovate and change. Changes will be more difficult to implement when they are opposed by a highly cohesive group, but they can be greatly facilitated when they have the strong backing of such a group.

DETERMINANTS OF GROUP COHESIVENESS A number of factors have a positive effect on group cohesiveness. For example, similar attitudes and values make it easier for individuals to communicate, find common ground, and develop mutual understandings. External threats, such as fierce outside competition or challenges to survival, can provide a compelling reason for a group to pull together into a cohesive unit. Similarly, outstanding successes often create strong positive feelings about group membership and establish linkages among group members.[44] The difficulty encountered in joining a group can build a common bond based on such factors as high standards (college), sacrifice (the Peace Corps), or difficult training (the Green Berets). Finally, group size can be a factor. Cohesiveness is much easier to attain when groups are relatively small, and it becomes much more difficult to achieve and maintain as groups grow larger. At Patagonia, Inc., a mail-order company well known for its expen-

VALUING DIVERSITY

Multicultural Teamworking at British Petroleum

 British Petroleum (BP) decided to establish the Finance Europe Centre in Brussels to help its associate companies in European countries handle their financial needs. Rob Ruijter, a Hollander who had worked for BP in several countries, was appointed team leader and center manager. Other members of the team were chosen from BP finance centers throughout the world, resulting in a team of 40 professionals representing 13 different nationalities.

From the start, the aim was to consciously implement multicultural teamworking. This meant that the team members had to become aware of each other's different cultural orientations. They also needed to develop into a productive group. Ruijter soon recognized that, given the diversity, some initial support for the group development process would be desirable. Accordingly, the team planned a 2-day event that had several objectives:

■ To make team members aware of the cultural differences and their impact on organizational structure, management style, decision making, and interpersonal behavior
■ To aid team members in recognizing their different roles, preferences, and strengths and understanding how these could complement one another
■ To devise methods of communicating with each other
■ To institute a set of ground rules for maintaining team effectiveness
■ To create a shared vision for the team

In the course of the 2-day discussion, team members exchanged information about cultural differences in how they approach their work. For example, the group learned that a French executive will tend to assume that the authority to make decisions comes as "a right of office and a privilege of rank" and will operate accordingly. In contrast, in the United Kingdom, the Netherlands, and Scandinavia, leaders expect their decisions to be challenged, discussed, or even made by the group. In France, it is customary to shake hands with everyone in your work group each morning as a show of friendliness, whereas U.S. managers regard shaking hands as a formal sign of politeness. German team members normally do not expect to be greeted by their first names, even by people who know them well, and Scandinavians expect to be called by their last name only.

In part of the exercise, the team developed an initial set of norms, or "ground rules." These included "Do not prejudge people, functions, cultures; create a climate where people are not embarrassed to ask; give and ask for feedback; and draw on the strengths of the other person."

A year later the team reviewed its progress. Overall, the team was performing well, further norms were being established, and the operation was meeting the needs of BP.[45]

---

sive, high-performance outdoor clothing, positive norms about quality and innovation, as well as high cohesiveness among employees, have been important factors in the company's success. While the founder spends about half the year traveling the world, employees maintain his vision of producing high-quality, durable clothing that can be worn during such activities as scaling Kilimanjaro or sailing the Atlantic in a one-person boat. Group cohesion is aided by the fact that employees share a common concern for environmental responsibility and have even worked with suppliers to pioneer a new fabric made from recycled plastic bottles. Moreover, organizational members are encouraged to engage in outdoor activities on company time, as long as their work is done.[46]

Group Development

New groups, such as new work units, committees, and task forces, are constantly being formed in organizations. Even existing groups are often in a state of flux as current members leave and new members are added. Such comings and goings affect the inner workings of groups.

A number of researchers argue that groups go through developmental stages that are relatively predictable. Understanding these stages can help managers both participate more effectively in groups and assist groups for which

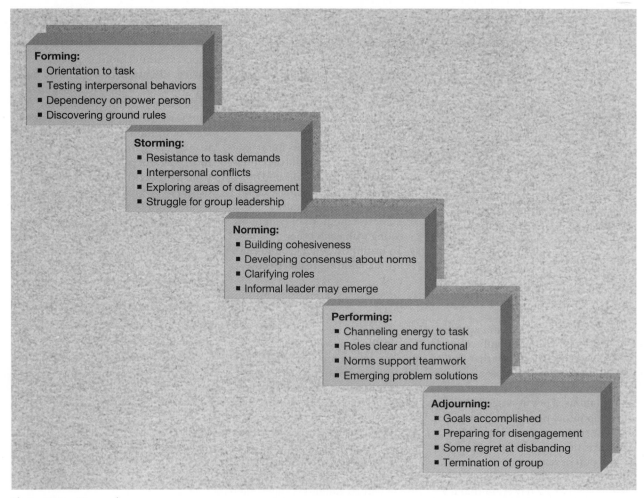

Forming:
- Orientation to task
- Testing interpersonal behaviors
- Dependency on power person
- Discovering ground rules

Storming:
- Resistance to task demands
- Interpersonal conflicts
- Exploring areas of disagreement
- Struggle for group leadership

Norming:
- Building cohesiveness
- Developing consensus about norms
- Clarifying roles
- Informal leader may emerge

Performing:
- Channeling energy to task
- Roles clear and functional
- Norms support teamwork
- Emerging problem solutions

Adjourning:
- Goals accomplished
- Preparing for disengagement
- Some regret at disbanding
- Termination of group

Figure 15-7 *Stages of group development.*

they have managerial responsibility. One of the best-known approaches to analyzing group development holds that there are five major stages: forming, storming, norming, performing, and adjourning (see Figure 15-7).[47]

New groups may progress through these phases, but if there are changes in group membership, the development of the group may regress to an earlier stage—at least temporarily.

Forming A stage in which group members attempt to assess the ground rules that will apply to a task and to group interaction

STAGE 1: FORMING In the **forming** stage of group development, group members attempt to assess the ground rules that will apply to a task and to group interaction. At this point, members seek basic information about the task, make a preliminary evaluation of how the group might interact to accomplish it, and begin to test the extent to which their input will be valued. Some members may try out the acceptability of various interpersonal behaviors, such as engaging in small talk, making jokes, being sarcastic, or leaving the meeting to make telephone calls. Often, because of the uncertainty associated with forming, members may initially depend on a powerful person, if one is present, or on existing norms, if they are commonly known. Because of the need to make sense of the ground rules, groups at the forming stage often require some time to get acquainted with the task and with each other before attempting to proceed in earnest with task responsibilities.

Storming A stage in which group members frequently experience conflict with one another as they locate and attempt to resolve differences of opinion regarding key issues

STAGE 2: STORMING During the **storming** stage, group members frequently experience conflict with one another as they locate and attempt to resolve differences of opinion regarding key issues. The issues in contention might revolve around task requirements and possible resistance to them. Another common area of conflict centers on interpersonal relations—how various group members relate to one another. Often, at this stage, there is a struggle among members for leadership of the group if a leader has not been appointed. Listening and attempting to find mutually acceptable resolutions of major issues are important approaches during this period. Otherwise, the group is not likely to operate effectively; it may not progress beyond this stage, and it may even disband.

STAGE 3: NORMING In the **norming** stage, group members begin to build group cohesion, as well as develop a consensus about norms for performing a task and relating to one another. The idiosyncrasies of individual members are generally accepted, and members start to identify with the group. Member roles also become clearer, and the group shows a greater willingness to engage in mutual problem solving. If there is no appointed leader or the appointed leader is weak, an informal leader may emerge. At this stage, clarifying norms and roles, building cohesiveness, and attempting to use the resources of the group to solve problems are particularly important. In order to help a newly formed multicultural team progress smoothly through the early stages of group development, and particularly through the norming stage, British Petroleum held a special 2-day conference (see the Valuing Diversity box).

> **Norming** A stage in which group members begin to build group cohesion, as well as develop a consensus about norms for performing a task and relating to one another

STAGE 4: PERFORMING The **performing** stage is the period in which energy is channeled toward a task and in which norms support teamwork. Solutions from the problem solving of the previous stage begin to emerge. The roles of group members become clearer and more functional as the group works to achieve positive synergy and group goals. Not all groups reach this stage of development. Those that do are likely to be effective as long as they devote their energies to the task and work to maintain good group relationships.

> **Performing** A stage in which energy is channeled toward a task and in which norms support teamwork

STAGE 5: ADJOURNING During the **adjourning** stage, group members prepare for disengagement as the group nears the successful completion of its goals. While members may be pleased with completing their tasks, they may also feel some regret at the imminent disbanding of the group. The adjourning stage applies more frequently to temporary task groups, such as committees, task forces, or teams of limited duration. With ongoing or permanent formal groups, adjournments apply less frequently. However, reorganizations and related phenomena such as takeovers and mergers can bring about the adjourning stage of a group.

> **Adjourning** A stage in which group members prepare for disengagement as the group nears successful completion of its goals

DO ALL GROUPS HAVE THESE STAGES? The five stages of group development apply mainly to newly formed, relatively unstructured groups. They are less likely to appear in groups with members who work frequently together or in those with fairly well established operating methods or ground rules.[48]

One important forum for group development is meetings. According to one survey, senior executives spend an average of 23 hours per week in meetings, while middle managers attend meetings about 11 hours per week.[49] Many other organization members are likely to be in meetings several hours per week. Meetings are frequently criticized because they are often not run well or do not achieve useful results.[50] One way of facilitating group development in meetings is by giving careful attention to how the meetings are conducted. They are more productive when they are well organized and operate with appropriate ground rules. To learn more about running effective meetings, see the Management Skills for the Twenty-First Century discussion, "How to Lead a Meeting."

 ■ **PROMOTING INNOVATION: USING TASK FORCES AND TEAMS**

Groups are used in many contexts in which organizations can benefit from the experience and ideas of two or more individuals. Increasingly, their efforts are being tapped when creativity and innovation are important to organizational success. In this section, we investigate some current special uses of teams.

Task Forces

Task force A temporary task group usually formed to make recommendations on a specific issue

Ad hoc committee Another term for *task force*

A **task force** is a temporary task group usually formed to make recommendations on a specific issue.[51] It is sometimes called an **ad hoc committee** or a *temporary committee*.[52] Because they deal with issues that typically involve several parts of the organization, task forces are often composed of individuals from the main command groups affected by a given issue. These individuals are usually needed to provide the necessary expertise, to furnish information about the needs of their command groups, and to help develop innovative ideas for solving problems or taking advantage of opportunities. Because task forces promote interaction among individuals from diverse departments, these groups are particularly well suited to fostering creativity and innovation.

Teams

Team A temporary or an ongoing task group whose members are charged with working together to identify problems, form a consensus about what should be done, and implement necessary actions in relation to a particular task or organizational area

A **team** is either a temporary or an ongoing task group whose members are charged with working together to identify problems, form a consensus about what should be done, and implement necessary actions in relation to a particular task or organizational area. Two major characteristics distinguish a team from a task force. First, team members typically identify problems in a given area (rather than deal with them after they have been identified by others). Second, they not only reach a consensus about what should be done but actually implement the decisions as a team (rather than make recommendations that are then implemented by others). Of course, team members (unless they are top-level managers) usually keep their superiors informed, as necessary. Also, they are likely to need their superiors' agreement on decisions that have major implications for others and the organization.

Teams are often, but not always, task groups made up of individuals who cross command groups. Temporary teams handle a specific project to completion, whereas permanent teams have ongoing responsibilities in a given area. Teams sometimes have a fluid membership consisting of individuals who join when their expertise is needed and leave when their work is done.

The use of teams has been highly successful in a wide variety of organizations, including such firms as Monsanto, General Motors, Boeing, Hewlett-Packard, Xerox, and Textron—to name a few. As a result, teams are gaining increasing attention, particularly as means of fostering innovation, increasing quality, and facilitating successful implementation of changes.[53] According to one estimate, 80 percent of organizations with 100 or more employees are using teams in some capacity, and 50 percent of employees in these organizations are part of at least one team.[54] Two types of teams that are of particular current importance are entrepreneurial teams and self-managing teams.

MANAGEMENT SKILLS FOR THE TWENTY-FIRST CENTURY

How to Lead a Meeting

There are three major phases in leading a meeting: preparation, meeting in progress, and follow-up.

PREPARATION

Preparation is a key element in conducting an effective meeting. The following steps are involved:

Make sure the meeting is necessary. According to one estimate, it costs about $100 per hour, including overhead, to have a manager attend a meeting. Therefore, a 2-hour meeting attended by 10 managers can quickly add up to $2000. Colleagues will appreciate not having to attend meetings about routine matters that could be handled with a memo.

Define the meeting's objectives. An objective might be to involve others in a decision, coordinate major activities, or discuss important information. It is helpful to orient attendees by briefly describing each objective either in the memo announcing the meeting or on the agenda. Be specific when stating objectives. For example, "Decide between using sales reps or an in-house sales force" is much more helpful than "Discuss sales."

Identify participants. Try to limit participation to those who are the decision makers, have needed expertise, and/or are affected by the outcome. As noted earlier, a group of five to seven is an ideal number for interaction, but sometimes meetings must be larger to involve all the necessary participants. If the group gets too large, however, the meeting will be more difficult to handle.

Prepare an agenda. When there is time, circulate the agenda early and obtain feedback. The agenda should be a short list of the main topics to be discussed. It helps key participants focus on what preparations they need to make for the meeting and also assists in ensuring that the important topics are covered. Send the final agenda out 2 or 3 days in advance.

Distribute needed background information. Consider what information participants will need to review in advance, and send it out with the final agenda. Avoid sending out huge reports that participants are unlikely to read. A better strategy is to send a summary and note that the full report is available if needed.

MEETING IN PROGRESS

Good preparation helps the meeting progress more smoothly. Actually running the meeting involves these five steps:

Review the agenda. Start on time, and review the agenda and major objectives. The review helps focus participants on why they are there and what outcomes are needed. It often helps to print the agenda on a blackboard or flip chart for easy reference.

Get reports from individuals with preassigned tasks. This should be done as early as feasible, although it may be necessary to wait for a particular agenda item to ask for a report or presentation. Getting reports as early as possible ensures that presenters have adequate time and provides recognition for their premeeting work. It also provides some of the necessary background information for other parts of the agenda.

Encourage participant input. Group effectiveness and member satisfaction are likely to be greater when all the members are able to provide input in their areas of expertise. A meeting leader should ensure that the meeting is not dominated by one faction or a few members. If someone speaks excessively, the leader might say something like "Well, Joan, let me see if I understand what you are saying." Then, after summarizing, the leader might follow with "Perhaps others have views on this issue." If an individual has said little, the leader might say, "Jim, we haven't heard from you yet. What are your views?"

Keep the meeting on track. If the discussion wanders, refer to a point someone made just before the digression to get the discussion back on track. If an issue is raised that cannot be resolved because of insufficient information, ask someone to check into it and report back.

Summarize and review assignments. Summarize what has been agreed upon or accomplished in the meeting. Also, review what each person has agreed to do and make sure that deadlines are set. Review plans for the next meeting if that is appropriate. End the meeting on time.

FOLLOW-UP

The meeting leader should follow up on the meeting:

Send out a memo summarizing the meeting. The memo should summarize the main things that were accomplished, and it should specify the actions that each person agreed to take and the deadlines that were set.

Follow up on assignments where appropriate. This involves checking with the various individuals about their progress, usually in preparation for a subsequent meeting.

Meeting leadership takes practice. It is usually a good idea for individuals to chair small, lower-level meetings early in their careers to gain experience.[55]

Entrepreneurial team A group of individuals with diverse expertise and backgrounds who are brought together to develop and implement innovative ideas aimed at creating new products or services or significantly improving existing ones

ENTREPRENEURIAL TEAMS An **entrepreneurial team** is a group of individuals with diverse expertise and backgrounds who are brought together to develop and implement innovative ideas aimed at creating new products or services or significantly improving existing ones.[56] Entrepreneurial teams focus on new business either by pioneering completely different types of endeavors or by devising novel products and services that are congruent with existing lines of business. For example, an entrepreneurial team at the Ford Motor Company was responsible for the introduction of the very successful Taurus and its companion car, the Mercury Sable (see the Case in Point discussion).

CASE IN POINT

TEAM TAURUS SCORES BIG

During the dark recession days of 1980, Ford Motor Company executives found themselves facing not only a slowed economy but also the toughest foreign-car competition they had ever encountered. "It was painfully obvious that we weren't competitive with the rest of the world in quality," says John A. Manoogian, Ford's chief of quality during that period. Company members decided to fight back. Their basic strategy involved using some of their competitors' methods, such as thoroughly studying the competition, making quality a top priority, and changing the organization of the firm's developmental efforts.

In a major step, Ford departed from the traditional approach to new car development. Normally, the company followed a sequential 5-year process to launch a new automobile. Product planners would start with a basic concept. Next, a design team would develop the look. The designers' work would go to engineering for specifications and then go on to manufacturing and suppliers for process design. Each step in the sequence was done with little ongoing communication with the other parties.

This time, the company put an unprecedented $3 billion behind a new

The 1997 Ford Taurus is a product of team development. Instead of developing a car by the usual means of sequential and separate groups—planning, design, engineering, and manufacturing—Ford created one group that included all these functions. The Taurus became the top-selling car in America in the early 1990s.

group, dubbed Team Taurus. With the team approach, representatives from all the affected units—planning, design, engineering, and manufacturing—worked together. The team had the overall final responsibility of developing the vehicle. With appropriate representatives on the team, issues could be resolved early. For example, manufacturing suggested design changes that made it easier to build in quality during manufacturing.

Some of the investigative work was done by special subteams. For instance, a five-member group had the job of developing comfortable, easy-to-use seats. In the course of their work, the group members took seats from 12 different cars, put them in Crown Victorias, and conducted 100,000 miles of driving tests using a variety of different drivers who indicated what they liked and didn't like.

In a major departure from traditional modes of operation, the team asked assembly-line workers for advice during the design phase and was flooded with helpful ideas. Worker suggestions led to changes such as reducing the parts in a door panel from eight to two for easier handling and ensuring that all the bolts had the same-size head to eliminate the need for different wrenches. "In the past we hired people for their arms and their legs," says Manoogian. "But we weren't smart enough to make use of their brains." In another unusual move, supplier ideas were also tapped during the design stage, and long-term contracts were signed with suppliers so that they had a strong stake in the new car development.

The success of the Taurus, which became the top-selling car in America by the early 1990s, has sold Ford on the team idea for new car development. Team Taurus still faces challenges, though. Wanting to keep the Taurus fresh and appealing, Ford next poured another $3 billion into a major redesign of the automobile, making engineering improvements and also providing a new sleeker look with an oval design repeated in such features as the headlights, taillights, back windows, and door handles. The major improvements also raised the sticker price. It remains to be seen whether the expensive redesign gamble will pay off.[57]   ■■■

SELF-MANAGING TEAMS A **self-managing team** is a work group given responsibility for a task area without day-to-day supervision and with authority to influence and control both group membership and behavior. Another name for a self-managing team is an *autonomous work group*. The Swedish automobile manufacturer A. B. Volvo pioneered such groups at its plant in Kamar, Sweden, during the early 1970s. There, autonomous work teams of about 20 workers each were responsible for putting together entire units of cars, such as the electric system or the engine.[58] An early prominent example of such teams in the United States was the NUMMI project, a joint venture of General Motors and the Toyota Motor Corporation, whose teams build automobiles in Fremont, California.

More recently a growing number of companies in the United States have been experimenting with self-managing teams.[59] For instance, the self-managing team approach is used at Digital Equipment Corporation's Enfield, Connecticut, facility. Compared with DEC's traditional plants, Enfield builds products 40 percent faster, uses fewer workers, maintains lower inventories, has double to triple the quality, and generates lower turnover. Xerox, Corning, and Motorola are just some of the other prominent companies using self-managing teams in at least some of their operations. One recent study indicates that employees in self-managing teams tend to report more favorable work attitudes, such as high job satisfaction and greater organizational commitment, than

Self-managing team A work group given responsibility for a task area without day-to-day supervision and with authority to influence and control both group membership and behavior

When Boots & Coots, an oil-well firefighting company based in Houston, gets a call to put out the flames in an out-of-control oil well, one of these senior hellfighters (as they are called in the business) gathers a team and rushes to the location. Conditions at the site are unpredictable and often dangerous, so the teams have to work quickly and with a great deal of cooperation. Naturally, training is of utmost importance in these self-managed teams.

counterparts in more traditionally designed jobs. However, other studies have obtained mixed results on these outcomes.[60]

One major impediment to the success of self-managing teams is the tendency for some organizations to simply designate a work group as a "self-managing team" without providing the necessary training and support. Four important steps are necessary to increase the prospects of their success.[61] First, before forming a team, there is a need to assess the applicability of using self-managing teams, as well as to determine the tasks and the degree of authority that will be delegated to them. Second, in forming a team, it is critical to give careful consideration to group composition and to allocate necessary material resources. Third, as the group is attempting to move through the stages of group development, training to work effectively on a team and guidance in cultivating appropriate norms are important. Finally, managers need to provide ongoing assistance by removing performance obstacles and helping the group continue to learn. Experts warn that productivity may actually decline initially as new self-managing teams work through the development process. In fact, assuming the appropriate steps are followed, it may take 18 months or longer before there is evidence of increased productivity.[62]

■ MANAGING CONFLICT

Of course, the positive results with task forces and teams typically do not occur without some conflict. In organizations, conflicts within and between groups are common. By **conflict** we mean a process in which one party perceives that its interests are being opposed or adversely affected by one or more other parties.[63]

Conflict A perceived difference between two or more parties that results in mutual opposition

While conflict is often considered to be a negative factor, it can have constructive, as well as destructive, consequences. Some of the destructive prospects are well known. For example, conflict can cause individuals or groups to become hostile, withhold information and resources, and interfere with each other's efforts. It can delay projects, drive up costs, and cause valued employees to leave. On the constructive side, conflict can highlight problems and the need for solutions. It can also promote change as parties work to resolve problems. In addition, conflict can enhance morale and cohesion as group members deal with areas of concern and frustration. Finally, conflict can stimulate interest, creativity, and innovation by encouraging new ideas.[64]

As a result, some conflict in an organization is beneficial, but too much can have a detrimental effect on organizational performance (see Figure 15-8). Conflict levels that are very low may indicate that problems are being hidden and new ideas stifled. For instance, a major factor in the famous failed Edsel project of the Ford Motor Company was the fact that subordinates withheld information because conflict was discouraged and because they felt that managers were already committed to the project.[65] In contrast, too much conflict may indicate that excessive amounts of energy are aimed at dissension and opposition. Accordingly, managers need to understand the causes of conflict and know how to reduce or resolve it when necessary. We discuss these topics next and also consider the question of whether managers should stimulate conflict.

Causes of Conflict

A number of factors contribute to conflict.[66] Several of the most important are discussed below.

TASK INTERDEPENDENCE Two types of task interdependence are particularly prone to conflict. One is *sequential interdependence*, in which one individual or work unit is heavily dependent on another. For example, waiters are generally more reliant on cooks than the reverse because waiters must depend on cooks to furnish good meals in a timely manner. The second form of task interdependence is *reciprocal interdependence*, in which individuals or work units are mutually interdependent. For instance, purchasing agents want engineers to provide detailed generic specifications so that they can negotiate lower costs from suppliers. At the same time, engineers need to obtain materials of the proper quality on a timely basis, so they may find it more convenient to specify a brand name.[67]

SCARCE RESOURCES Possibilities for conflict expand when there are limited resources, such as office space, equipment, training, human resources, operating funds, and pay allocations. For example, if two groups require the same facilities, each may feel that its needs are more important and neither may be willing to compromise.

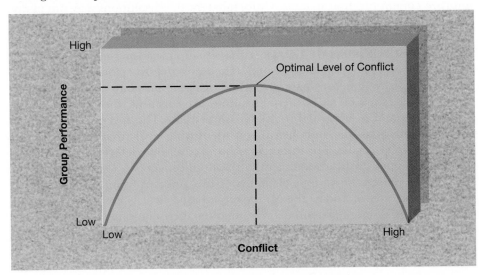

Figure 15-8 *Effects of conflict on group performance.*

GOAL INCOMPATIBILITY Out of necessity, organization members frequently pursue goals that are somewhat different from one another, setting the stage for potential conflicts. For example, sales personnel may find it easier to battle the competition by promising quick deliveries, while people in manufacturing may find that small production runs on short notice interfere with their cost-cutting efforts.

COMMUNICATION FAILURES Breakdowns in communication due to distortions or lack of communication often lead to conflicts. Such breakdowns are more likely to occur when one party dislikes, distrusts, or feels angry toward the other. See Chapter 14 for a more thorough discussion of communication in organizations.

INDIVIDUAL DIFFERENCES Differences in personality, experience, and values make frequent conflicts likely. For example, personality conflicts with Robert A. Schoellhorn, former chairman of Abbott Laboratories, led three potential successors to leave the company, causing concern among board members about who would succeed to the chairperson's position. Critics say Schoellhorn, who was ultimately ousted by the board, was intolerant of dissent and undermined executives who built power of their own.[68]

POORLY DESIGNED REWARD SYSTEMS Reward systems can unwittingly lead to destructive conflict when they reward competition in situations that require cooperation for success.[69] For instance, at Solar Press, Inc., based in Napier, Illinois, a bonus system that rewarded team production also undermined cooperation when sequential dependence was needed among teams. Solar achieved better success by switching to a bonus system tied to company results.[70]

Reducing and Resolving Conflict

Managers can use a number of different approaches to reduce or resolve conflict.[71] Such efforts are typically aimed at minimizing the destructive impact.

CHANGING SITUATIONAL FACTORS One obvious way to reduce conflict is to change the factors in the situation that are causing the problem. For example, a manager might increase the resources available, reorganize to reduce interdependence, redesign reward systems (as Solar Press did), or take steps to improve communication systems. Unfortunately, these solutions may not always be feasible or may be extremely expensive.

Superordinate goals Major common goals that require the support and effort of all parties

APPEAL TO SUPERORDINATE GOALS If the situations causing excessive conflict are difficult to change, managers are sometimes able to refocus the individuals or groups on **superordinate goals,** major common goals that require the support and effort of all parties. Examples are ensuring the survival of the organization and beating highly visible competition. The success of appeals to superordinate goals depends heavily on identifying goals that are sufficiently important to all parties. For instance, word of a serious defect in factory floor sweepers shipped to Japan and Toyota's announcement of a competing product in 1979 united the various elements of the Tennant Company in a lifesaving push for quality. Today, the Minneapolis-based firm is the world's leading manufacturer of nonresidential floor maintenance equipment like sweepers and scrubbers. It has over 50 percent of the global market share in industrial markets, such as manufacturing and warehousing.[72]

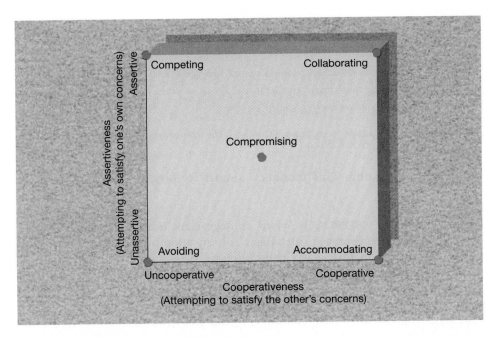

Figure 15-9 *Five major interpersonal conflict-handling modes. (Reprinted from Kenneth W. Thomas, "Conflict and Negotiation Processes in Organizations," in M. D. Dunnette and L. M. Hough, (eds.),* Handbook of Industrial and Organizational Psychology, *2d ed., vol. 3, Consulting Psychologists Press, Palo Alto, Calif., 1992.)*

USE AN INTERPERSONAL CONFLICT-HANDLING MODE Aside from situational changes and appeals to superordinate goals, interpersonal modes are another means of handling conflict. Managers have five major interpersonal modes that they can use to attempt to resolve conflicts in which they themselves are involved (see Figure 15-9):[73]

■ **Avoiding** involves ignoring or suppressing a conflict in the hope that it will either go away or not become too disruptive.
■ **Accommodating** focuses on solving conflicts by allowing the desires of the other party to prevail. Essentially, the manager voluntarily lets the other party have his or her way rather than continue the conflict.
■ **Competing** involves attempting to win a conflict at the other party's expense. In other words, one party wins and the other loses.
■ **Compromising** aims to solve conflict issues by having each party give up some desired outcomes in order to get other desired outcomes. Compromise often involves bargaining by the conflicting parties and generally requires a situation that offers both parties the chance to be in a better position or at least in no worse position after the conflict is resolved. With compromise each person wins some major issues and loses others.
■ **Collaborating** strives to resolve conflicts by devising solutions that allow both parties to achieve their desired outcomes. In other words, the solution is such that both parties win at least their major issues. Collaboration frequently involves considerable creativity in developing solutions that suit the needs of both parties in the conflict.

Although collaboration is often an advantageous way to handle conflict because both sides are likely to be satisfied, evidence suggests that managers often rely on forcing when they are in conflict with subordinates. On the other hand, subordinates are likely to use avoiding accommodating or compromising when in conflict with their boss. In many conflict situations, there is a tendency for one party to reciprocate with the conflict-handling mode initially employed by the other party. For example, forcing by one party often leads to adoption of a forcing approach by the other party. Similarly, accommodating tends to

Avoiding A conflict-handling mode that involves ignoring or suppressing a conflict in the hope that it will either go away or not become too disruptive

Accommodating A conflict-handling mode that focuses on solving conflicts by allowing the desires of the other party to prevail

Competing A conflict-handling mode that involves attempting to win a conflict at the other party's expense

Compromising A conflict-handling mode that aims to solve conflict issues by having each party give up some desired outcomes in order to get other desired outcomes

Collaborating A conflict-handling mode that strives to resolve conflicts by devising solutions that allow both parties to achieve their desired outcomes

TABLE 15-1 STEPS FOR THIRD-PARTY ROLES IN CONFLICTS
1. Establish a positive working relationship with each of the conflicting parties.
2. Encourage a cooperative, problem-solving attitude among the conflicting parties.
3. Acquire substantive knowledge of conflict issues.
4. Facilitate creative joint problem-solving processes.

Source: Based on M. Deutsch, "Sixty Years of Conflict," *The International Journal of Conflict Management,* vol. 1, 1990, pp. 237–263.

beget accommodating. This tendency toward reciprocation does not always occur, however.

USE A THIRD-PARTY APPROACH When managers are not themselves parties to conflicts, they may assume a third-party role in attempting to reach a resolution.[74] Individuals in third-party roles attempt to manage the process of conflict resolution so that the probability of success is enhanced. Usually a manager takes on a third-party role only when the conflicting parties are unable to resolve the conflict themselves and yet resolution is important to the effective functioning of the work unit. Getting involved as a third party does have some potential pitfalls. For one thing, the intervention may disrupt the resolution efforts already being attempted. For another, a manager may be prone to consider his or her own interests in pressing for a resolution, leaving the conflicting parties dissatisfied. Yet another potential pitfall stems from the possibility that the manager may mismanage the process and unwittingly escalate the conflict. In order to avoid missteps, conflict resolution expert M. Deutsch suggests that individuals taking on third-party roles should follow the steps outlined in Table 15-1 in managing the process.

Should Managers Stimulate Conflict?

Since too little conflict can lead to apathy, lethargy, and low performance, should managers stimulate conflict? Although in the past some conflict experts have recommended that managers actually incite conflict, the growing consensus is that such actions are unwise.[75] The benefits to be derived from moderate levels of conflict, such as creativity, problem awareness, and adaptation, can be pursued through alternative means (see, for example, Chapter 5 on decision making and Chapter 11 on innovation and change). On the other hand, the potential negative effects of conflict, such as personal frustration, low job satisfaction, and reduced motivation and performance, can be substantial. Moreover, conflicts are prone to escalation and may spiral out of the manager's control. As we will learn in the next four chapters, which examine the controlling function, managers have many more important things they need to control.

■ CHAPTER SUMMARY

Work groups are becoming an increasingly important competitive factor in organizations. There are two major types of work groups, formal and informal. Formal groups include command, or functional, groups and task groups. Informal groups include interest and friendship groups. Required aspects of formal groups lead to the emergent behaviors, interactions, and sentiments associated with informal groups.

A useful way to analyze groups is to view them as systems that use inputs, engage in various processes or transformations, and produce outcomes. Important group inputs are group composition, particularly member characteristics and reasons for attraction to the group; member roles, including group task roles, group maintenance roles, and self-oriented roles; and group size.

Hopefully, work group processes result in positive synergy. Important factors influencing group processes are group norms, group cohesiveness, and group development. Group norms stem from explicit statements by supervisors and coworkers, critical events in a group's history, primacy, and carryover behaviors. A number of factors contribute to group cohesiveness. Cohesion, in turn, has important consequences for group communication, satisfaction, performance, hostility and aggression toward other groups, and a group's willingness to innovate and change. New groups typically go through five stages of development: forming, storming, norming, performing, and adjourning. Size influences group interactions and may encourage social loafing or free riders. Those who lean toward individualism rather than toward collectivism are more likely to engage in social loafing. Important outcomes to consider in evaluating the effectiveness

of groups are group performance, member need satisfaction, and the degree to which the work group's capabilities to perform effectively together are enhanced.

Some of the major mechanisms that organizations use to tap the creativity and innovative capacity of groups include task forces, or ad hoc committees, and teams, particularly entrepreneurial and self-managing teams.

Managing conflict is also an important managerial skill related to groups. Causes of conflict include task interdependence, scarce resources, goal incompatibility, communication failures, individual differences, and poorly designed reward systems. Methods of reducing or resolving conflict include changing situational factors, appealing to superordinate goals, and using interpersonal conflict-handling modes and taking on a third-party role. Managers should not deliberately stimulate conflict because of potential negative outcomes. Instead, there are alternative means of achieving potential benefits, such as creativity and innovation.

■ QUESTIONS FOR DISCUSSION AND REVIEW

1 Outline the major types of work groups. Identify several work groups at your college or university. Classify them according to work group type.

2 Explain how informal groups develop in organizations. Choose an organization with which you are familiar and identify two informal groups. Trace how the informal groups came about.

3 Explain the basic inputs that groups require to operate. Analyze the inputs of a work group that you think runs effectively. What are the member characteristics that help it operate successfully? What attracts the various members to the group? What roles do members play? How does the number of members affect the group interaction?

4 Explain the significance of norms and cohesiveness in group functioning. Think of a group to which you belong. What are four important norms in the group. How did they develop? Assess the level of group cohesiveness and its consequences.

5 Explain how groups develop. Trace the development of a group in which you have participated.

6 Describe how size influences group performance and interactions. Include an assessment of social loafing and possible effects associated with individualism and collectivism. To what extent have you witnessed these factors at work in groups?

7 Differentiate among task forces and teams. Explain how each can be used to promote innovation. Identify examples of task forces and teams in the business section of your local paper, *The Wall Street Journal,* and/or magazines such as *Business Week* and *Fortune.*

8 Explain why self-managing teams have been so successful. If you were a manager, why would you like or not like to have them in your organization?

9 Explain the causes of conflict in organizations. Describe an organizational conflict situation of which you are aware and trace its causes.

10 Describe several ways to reduce or resolve conflict and to stimulate conflict. Think of a conflict situation that you have witnessed in a group. What approaches could you take to reduce or resolve the conflict?

■ DISCUSSION QUESTIONS FOR CHAPTER OPENING CASE

1 What input factors appear to be helping to make teams successful at Monsanto?

2 How has the group development process worked at Monsanto, and what remains to be done?

3 If you were the local manager, how rapidly would you proceed with implementing the remaining actions? Why?

■ EXERCISES FOR MANAGING IN THE TWENTY-FIRST CENTURY

EXERCISE 1
SKILL BUILDING: ASSESSING GROUP COHESIVENESS

 Cohesiveness can be a very favorable characteristic of a work group. This exercise is designed to assist in evaluating the cohesiveness of a work group of which you currently are a member. This could be a group preparing a paper for a class, a group developing a solution to a case or exercise, a group where you work, or any other group effort. If you are not now involved in a particular work group, please refer to the most recent work group in which you participated.

		Disagree	Agree
1	The individual members of the group are respected by the others.	1 2 3 4 5 6 7 8 9 10	
2	The group goal is enthusiastically supported by the members of the group.	1 2 3 4 5 6 7 8 9 10	
3	The group has quickly established norms that facilitate accomplishing our goal.	1 2 3 4 5 6 7 8 9 10	
4	The group members share similar work values.	1 2 3 4 5 6 7 8 9 10	
5	The group is able to bring out the best performance from each of the members.	1 2 3 4 5 6 7 8 9 10	

		Disagree	Agree
6.	The group members' attitudes toward the ultimate goal are positive.	1 2 3 4 5 6 7 8 9 10	
7	The group members' commitment to the goal increases the longer we work together.	1 2 3 4 5 6 7 8 9 10	
8	Communications within our group improve steadily as we progress.	1 2 3 4 5 6 7 8 9 10	
9	A feeling of "we" versus "I" is evident in our group.	1 2 3 4 5 6 7 8 9 10	
10	The group pulls together, making the task easier.	1 2 3 4 5 6 7 8 9 10	
11	Everyone believes his or her contribution is important.	1 2 3 4 5 6 7 8 9 10	
12	The group seeks input from everyone prior to making decisions.	1 2 3 4 5 6 7 8 9 10	
13	The group interaction seems to bring out the best in each of the members.	1 2 3 4 5 6 7 8 9 10	
14	The size of the group helps promote a feeling of mutual support.	1 2 3 4 5 6 7 8 9 10	
15	If one member of the group needs help, other members are quick to respond.	1 2 3 4 5 6 7 8 9 10	

Your professor will tell you how to interpret your score.

EXERCISE 2
MANAGEMENT EXERCISE: LOST AT SEA

The Situation

 You are adrift on a private yacht in the South Pacific. As a consequence of a fire of unknown origin, much of the yacht and its contents have been destroyed. Your location is unclear because critical navigation equipment was ruined and because you and the crew were distracted trying to bring the fire under control. Your best estimate is that you are approximately 1000 miles south-southwest of the nearest land.

The Problem

The table below lists 15 items that are intact and undamaged after the fire. You have, in addition, a serviceable rubber life raft with oars that is large enough to carry yourself, the crew, and all the items listed. The total contents of all the survivors' pockets are a package of cigarettes, several books of matches, and five $1 bills.

Your task is to rank these items in terms of their importance to your survival. Place "1" by the most important item, "2" by the second most important item, and so on, ending with "15" by the least important. Enter the numbers in the column labeled "Individual Ranking."

Your instructor will tell you the number of individuals in the crew. When you have completed the ranking, your instructor will give you further instructions.[76]

Scoring Sheet

Items	Individual Ranking	Group Ranking	Expert's Ranking	Influence	Individual Accuracy	Group Accuracy
Sextant						
Shaving mirror						
5-gallon can of water						
Mosquito netting						
One case of U.S. Army C-rations						
Maps of Pacific Ocean						
Seat cushion (flotation device approved by Coast Guard)						
2-gallon can of oil-gas mixture						
Small transistor radio						
Shark repellent						
20 square feet of opaque plastic						
1 quart of 160-proof Puerto Rican rum						
15 feet of nylon rope						
Two boxes of chocolate bars						
Fishing kit						

Your accuracy score: Group accuracy score:

CONCLUDING CASE 1

BEN & JERRY'S THRIVES ON COMPANY SPIRIT

Known for its rich ice cream generously laced with tasty tidbits and for its black-and-white cow logo, Ben & Jerry's Homemade, Inc., began simply enough as an ice cream parlor in a renovated gas station. When it opened in 1978 in Burlington, Vermont, it was a social experiment. Cofounders Ben Cohen and Jerry Greenfield wanted to demonstrate that their business could operate differently from many others. They believed that it could be unconventional, share its prosperity with employees, interact responsibly with the community, and still do well from a business standpoint. In fact, they intended to sell the business as soon as it was established and they had proved their point.

But things didn't turn out quite as they planned. Happily, the ice cream was an instant success. Ben and Jerry considered selling the company, but finally decided instead to keep it and use the profits for social change.

As the company continued to grow, Ben and Jerry worked hard to foster fun, charity, goodwill toward coworkers, and the feeling of a small, close-knit group that had helped make the company successful from the start. The company set up various programs to benefit employees. Such programs included hiring the handicapped; providing for free therapy sessions, with drug and alcohol counseling for any worker; and taking employees on all-company trips to see baseball and hockey games. Ben & Jerry's also had a 5-to-1 salary ratio, whereby the highest salaries paid could not equal more than five times the lowest.

Not surprisingly, dedication to the company ran high among the workers. Such dedication was important because the rapid growth of the company and the somewhat informal ways of operating frequently led to crises that required everyone to pitch in. For example, on one such occasion, a new machine to automatically fill pints did not work and production fell behind. Everyone—including Ben and Jerry—worked the production line to fill orders. Some workers made dinner for the rest of the staff, and pizzas were ordered. As always, the group spirit came through.

This spirit that has characterized the company was nurtured by the heavy involvement of the employees in the firm's business affairs. One means was through monthly staff meetings, which all employees were invited to attend. Employees would break into small groups and provide input on solutions to problems.

Gradually, as the company grew bigger, it became more difficult to obtain input from everyone and the meetings became characterized by one-way communication from Ben and other managers. Recognizing the problem, Ben attempted to institute the old format by posing the question: "What are the most pressing problems confronting us?" The approach generated a huge amount of data that was difficult to assimilate. One manager who spent a night helping Ben categorize the responses said, "It was like having this 8-ton dump truck back up and dump its load over you." The overall message to Ben was that the employees were beginning to feel left out.

Growth began to level off at the $150 million range. Consumers were becoming more concerned about eating food high in saturated fat. In reaction, the company developed low-fat and nonfat frozen yogurt products. Heavy competition from Grand Metropolitan's Haagen Dazs brand and cheaper premium ice cream emerged. The company began to experience losses.

Ben was forced to conclude that the company had outgrown his management skills, and he began to search for a CEO who could recharge the organization. The company had to abandon the 5-to-1 salary ratio idea because it was difficult to recruit a new CEO of the necessary caliber given the salary arrangement. After a highly publicized search, Ben & Jerry's hired a new CEO, Robert Holland, Jr., a former McKinsey & Co. consultant. He began by instituting tighter controls. Earnings improved. The company began to expand markets in Europe and launched a very successful fat-free sorbet line to compete with the Haagen Dazs brand. After 19 months on the job, Holland resigned amidst rumors of clashes with the founders over meshing their social agenda with shareholder interests. Publicly, Holland said the company needed a CEO strong in marketing and sales. The company then hired Perry Odak as CEO. Odak has 25 years of experience in consumer products and retailing businesses.

Each year, Ben & Jerry's conducts a self-critical "social performance" audit that is included in its annual report. Part of the audit is based on input from employees, who now number over 700. The employee section of one recent annual report noted that focus groups conducted among employees revealed "a continuing sense of confusion, frustration, and low morale on the part of many staff members."[77]

QUESTIONS FOR CONCLUDING CASE 1

1 What group norms are evident at Ben & Jerry's?
2 What factors have contributed to the development of high cohesiveness among Ben & Jerry's employees?
3 What could Ben and Jerry do to preserve some of the positive aspects of group dynamics?

CONCLUDING CASE 2

PERPETUAL-LEARNING TEAMS OPERATE GE FACTORY IN PUERTO RICO

At the new GE factory in Bayamón, Puerto Rico, the organization structure is extremely flat. There are only three layers: the factory manager, 15 salaried "advisers," and 172 hourly workers. The factory produces arresters, which are surge protectors that guard power stations and transmission lines against lightning strikes.

At Bayamón, every hourly worker is on a team consisting of about 10 employees. Each team "owns" a part of the process, such as assembly, shipping, or receiving. Since the members of each team work in different areas of the plant, they represent operations that provide input to or receive output from the part of the process owned by the team. Team members meet weekly to discuss various issues. A salaried adviser attends the meeting as a resource person, answering questions when queried by members of the team.

What is particularly unique about the Bayamón factory is the institutionalized perpetual learning. Hourly employees change jobs every 6 months, rotating through the four main work areas. In this way, workers learn how their jobs affect every other operation in the plant. To encourage the continual learning, the firm pays workers for their skill, knowledge, and business performance. After each 6-month rotation they receive a 25-cent-an-hour raise. They can then select a "major," such as machine maintenance or quality control, and double their pay. They can receive additional pay by passing courses in English, business practices, and the like. Further, perfect attendance and plantwide performance can result in bonuses of $225 or more each quarter. Promotions and layoffs are decided by ability, not seniority. This is to motivate the employees to achieve higher skill levels.

In the first year and a half of plant operation, the work force was 20 percent more productive than its nearest company equivalent in General Electric. The enhanced learning helps team members contribute to improvement in their own team as well as collaborate across teams. The prediction is that productivity will continue to rise as the teams continue to improve work processes.[78]

QUESTIONS FOR CONCLUDING CASE 2

1 What is the role of groups at the factory in Bayamón, Puerto Rico?
2 Explain how group norms are being established at the factory.
3 When the factory reaches the "performing stage," what changes would you expect? What steps would you take to help new workers assimilate into the organization?

PART FIVE

CONTROLLING

As we learned in the previous parts, the planning function provides the direction, the organizing function arranges the resources, and the leading function adds the action ingredient. Still, how does a manager ensure that an organization performs up to standards and actually achieves its intended goals? The controlling function adds the vital regulatory element, allowing managers to make use of a variety of methods for monitoring performance and taking corrective action when necessary. Controls must be used flexibly, though, because too much control can stifle innovation.

In exploring the controlling function, **Chapter 16** takes a close look at the overall control process. It considers the steps in the process, the major types of controls, various managerial approaches to implementing the controls that are available, and the problems associated with attempting to control innovation.

During the control process, managers use certain major control systems to increase the probability of meeting organizational goals. **Chapter 17** focuses on four of these systems: quality control, financial control, budgetary control, and inventory control.

Another major control system is operations management, which involves overseeing the processes entailed in actually producing a product or service. As **Chapter 18** points out, a key aspect of operations management is productivity. Managers must devise operations strategies, develop operating systems, utilize facilities, and promote innovative technology with productivity in mind.

Finally, as **Chapter 19** shows, information systems are an important means of control. Computer-based systems provide managers with information that helps them make whatever decisions are necessary to adjust performance to meet goals. But information systems do not simply aid in improving an organization's operating efficiency. They also can be used in innovative ways to give an organization a distinctive competitive edge.

CHAPTER SIXTEEN

CONTROLLING THE ORGANIZATION

LEARNING OBJECTIVES

After studying this chapter, you should be able to:

■ Explain the major roles of controls in organizations.

■ Describe how control responsibilities change with the level of management.

■ Outline the general process that can be applied to most control situations.

■ Delineate the principal conditions that managers need to consider in deciding what to control.

■ Explain the major control types based on timing and the use of multiple controls.

■ Differentiate between cybernetic and noncybernetic control.

■ Describe the basic managerial approaches to implementing controls.

■ Outline the potential dysfunctional aspects of control systems and explain the implications of overcontrol and undercontrol.

■ Delineate the major characteristics of effective control systems.

GAINING THE EDGE

CONTROLLING SUCCESS AT McDONALD'S

 The original McDonald's drive-in restaurant in San Bernardino, California, was doing a brisk business in 1955 when Ray Kroc, a milk-shake-mixer salesperson, bought the franchising rights (legal rights that allow people to use the name and methods of a business for a fee). At the time, Kroc did not know the restaurant business and was not wealthy. Nevertheless, he was going into competition against well-established fast-food chains, such as Kentucky Fried Chicken, InstaBurger King (later shortened to Burger King), Dairy Queen, and Big Boy.

While selling milk-shake mixers, Kroc had witnessed many franchised outlets go out of business because of poor management, uneven quality, and financial draining by parent companies. On the basis of his observations, Kroc believed that an organization could run a successful franchising operation if it could control the quality of both the food and the service offered at the franchised outlets. Offering franchisees good financial incentives for adhering to a fair, but closely controlled, system would be another essential element for success.

To develop the kind of controls needed, Kroc designed training programs that were unusual at the time and remain the best in the fast-food industry. He also put together a training manual that has grown to about 600 pages. The manual detailed operating procedures for virtually every aspect of outlet management. Instructions ranged from the cooking time for french fries to expected standards of cleanliness for rest rooms. To help ensure that employees followed the provisions outlined in the manual, Kroc had field inspectors visit outlets and grade their operations against the standards set forth.

Kroc also demanded that suppliers conform to high standards. For example, potato distributors were shocked to learn that McDonald's technicians measured the moisture levels in potatoes by using devices called hydrometers and

A McDonald's customer expects the same kind of food and the same kind of service in every McDonald's restaurant, whether it is in Kansas City or Moscow (shown here). That takes careful control. McDonald's is famous for its employee training programs and its 600-page manual of procedures, specifying everything from the cooking time for french fries to employee uniforms.

rejected batches in which the solids content did not meet requirements. Because cheating on hamburger quality was a common practice in the meat industry at that time, McDonald's inspectors would sometimes show up at a meat-packing plant at 3 a.m., ready to cancel contracts if they found anything amiss. McDonald's still keeps close tabs on suppliers, right down to conducting laboratory tests on the thickness of pickle slices.

Another unique aspect of the McDonald's operation was Kroc's approach to granting franchises. While other chains, such as Dairy Queen and Burger King, usually licensed whole territories in return for sizable front-end payments, Kroc sold franchises one outlet at a time. Only if an operator demonstrated a willingness and an ability to live up to McDonald's standards would that operator be considered for additional outlets. Kroc also made sure that the franchisees would be able to keep a good chunk of the fruits of their labors, giving them ample incentive to work hard.

Because he had the foresight to concentrate on the long run, Kroc began to achieve a vision that would ultimately prove difficult for the competition to duplicate: nationwide standardization. Gradually, customers started to notice that regardless of where they were, they could count on the local McDonald's restaurant to offer reliable food, quick service, and clean rest rooms.

Today, there are more than 20,000 McDonald's outlets located in the United States and in almost 100 other countries, including Japan, Canada, Germany, England, Australia, and France. On average, a new McDonald's outlet opens every 3 hours someplace in the world.[1] ■■■

What explains McDonald's enviable success? One major factor is the extent to which the company maintains strong controls over most aspects of its operations. These controls have helped McDonald's develop a competitive edge in the form of high product and service consistency. A Big Mac is likely to taste pretty much the same whether we are eating it in Boston or Bangkok. As noted economist Robert J. Samuelson reported in praising McDonald's, his Big Mac ordered at an outlet in Tokyo did not "merely taste like an American Big Mac"; it tasted "exactly the same."[2] Still, the company has allowed room for innovation. How are successful companies such as McDonald's able to design and implement effective controls?

To explore this issue, we devote the next four chapters to various aspects of controlling, the fourth major function of management. In this chapter, we consider the significance of control as a management process. We examine the control process itself and discuss how managers decide what to control. We also review the major types of controls and the appropriate times for instituting them. We then describe different approaches that managers can take in implementing controls, including how to do so without unduly hampering innovation. Finally, we analyze how managers can effectively assess the control systems that they use.

■ CONTROL AS A MANAGEMENT FUNCTION

Controlling The process of regulating organizational activities so that actual performance conforms to expected organizational standards and goals

Like their McDonald's counterparts, managers in other organizations also face important issues related to the controlling function. **Controlling** is the process of regulating organizational activities so that actual performance conforms to expected organizational standards and goals.[3] As the definition suggests, controlling means that managers develop appropriate standards, compare ongoing performance against those standards, and take steps to ensure that corrective

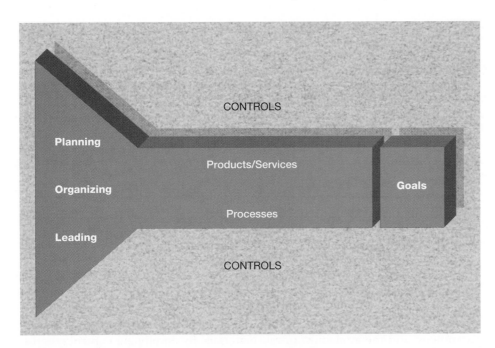

Figure 16-1 *Relationship of controls to the other functions of management.*

actions are taken when necessary. Since most organizational activities ultimately depend on human behavior, controlling is largely geared toward ensuring that employees behave in ways that facilitate the reaching of organizational goals. Thus controls both highlight needed behaviors and discourage unwanted behaviors.[4] For instance, during their 2-year training program, management trainees preparing to become McDonald's franchisees work their way through a thick guide that spells out various aspects of what to do and not do in properly running a McDonald's outlet.[5]

Significance of the Control Process

As you might expect, the controlling function is closely allied to the other three major functions of management: planning, organizing, and leading. It builds most directly on the planning function by providing the means for monitoring and making adjustments in performance so that plans can be realized. Still, controlling also supports the organizing and leading functions by helping ensure that resources are channeled toward organizational objectives (see Figure 16-1). For example, feedback from the control process might signal the need to reorganize, provide more training to workers, clarify communications, increase leadership influence, or take other actions associated with the respective organizing and leading functions.

During the control process, managers set up control systems. A **control system** is a set of mechanisms designed to increase the probability of meeting organizational standards and goals.[6] Control systems can be developed to regulate any area that a manager considers important. They may pertain to such areas as quantity produced, resources expended, profit margins, quality of products or services, client satisfaction, timeliness of deliveries, or specific activities that are performed in producing a product or service. For example, McDonald's has a seven-step procedure that workers must rigidly follow when cooking and bagging french fries to ensure quality. This procedure is one of the operations that corporate evaluation teams check during their unannounced inspections of outlets.[7]

Control system A set of mechanisms designed to increase the probability of meeting organizational standards and goals

Controls can help uncover irregularities. If Japan's Daiwa Bank had instituted standard financial practices in its New York office, a bond trader there would not have been able to amass and hide $1.1 billion in losses over 11 years. Inadequate controls forced Daiwa to cease operations in the United States.

Role of Controls

In evaluating the role of controls, it is useful to consider what can happen when controls are inadequate. Daiwa Bank, Japan's tenth-largest bank, was recently forced to cease operating in the United States when it became public that a bond trader in Daiwa's New York office had amassed a staggering $1.1 billion in losses and managed to hide them over an 11-year period. In one of several letters to Daiwa's top management, Toshihide Iguchi, the bond trader, told of how the New York office had failed to detect a $100 million discrepancy in the books. Iguchi noted that the incident was "indicative of how dysfunctional [controls] were at Daiwa."[8]

Controls can help managers avoid such problems. More specifically, controls play important roles in assisting managers with five particular challenges: coping with uncertainty, detecting irregularities, identifying opportunities, handling complex situations, and decentralizing authority.

COPING WITH UNCERTAINTY Uncertainty arises because organizational goals are set for future events on the basis of the best knowledge at the time, yet things do not always go according to plan. A variety of environmental factors typically operate to bring about changes in such areas as customer demand, technology, and the availability of raw materials. By developing control systems, managers are better able to monitor specific activities and react quickly to significant changes in the environment. For example, by controlling every phase of the manufacturing process, Italy-based Luxottica Group S.p.A. found it could produce high-quality eyeglass frames at a lower price. CEO Leonardo Del Vecchio next began buying out many distributors of eyeglass frames. Thus Luxottica slowly gained control of both the manufacturing and distribution of its products. Recently, Luxottica gained some control over the retailing of its frames as well by purchasing U.S. Shoe, which owns the LensCrafters eyeglass chain.[9]

DETECTING IRREGULARITIES Controls help managers detect undesirable irregularities, such as poor quality, cost overruns, or rising personnel turnover. Early detection of such irregularities can often save a great deal of time and money by preventing minor problems from mushrooming into major ones. Finding aberrations early sometimes also avoids problems that can be difficult to rectify, such as missing important deadlines or selling faulty merchandise to customers. For example, Daiwa Bank might have been able to avoid the international embarrassment and the loss of its U.S. business if it had instituted better controls over its operations. Among other things, Daiwa did not follow the usual financial institution practice of cross-checking daily trades against monthly summaries and balance statements.[10]

IDENTIFYING OPPORTUNITIES Controls also help highlight situations in which things are going better than expected, thereby alerting management to possible future opportunities.[11] At St. Louis–based May Department Stores, division managers prepare special monthly reports that specify the items that are selling well and the amount of money the items are generating. The chain then uses these data to develop successful merchandising strategies for all its stores, including what to buy, which vendors to buy from, and how to display the merchandise.[12]

HANDLING COMPLEX SITUATIONS As organizations grow larger or engage in more complex operations and projects, controls enhance coordination. They help managers keep track of various major elements to be sure that they are well synchronized. For example, operating on an international basis often increases complexity and calls for further consideration of necessary controls as illustrated by the Daiwa situation.

DECENTRALIZING AUTHORITY Another major role of controls is affording managers more latitude to decentralize authority. With controls, managers can foster decision making at lower levels in the organization but still maintain a handle on progress. Alfred Sloan, the noted former chairman of General Motors, implemented controls by setting the standard for the level of return on investment that he expected various GM units to achieve. This approach let him exercise control over major units by monitoring return on investments, yet it allowed him to maintain a philosophy of decentralization.[13] Sloan, of course, was operating at the very top of an organization. As you might expect, control issues tend to vary according to managerial level in the hierarchy.

Levels of Control

Just as planning responsibilities differ by managerial level (see Chapter 6), parallel control responsibilities exist at each level (see Figure 16-2). Strategic, tactical, and operational levels of control increase the probabilities of realizing plans at respective managerial levels.[14]

    Strategic control involves monitoring critical environmental factors to

Strategic control A control type that involves monitoring critical environmental factors that could affect the viability of strategic plans, assessing the effects of organizational strategic actions, and ensuring that strategic plans are implemented as intended

Figure 16-2 *Levels of control. (Adapted in part from Peter Lorange, Michael F. Scott Morton, and Sumantra Ghoshal,* Strategic Control Systems, *West, St. Paul, Minn., 1986, p. 12.)*

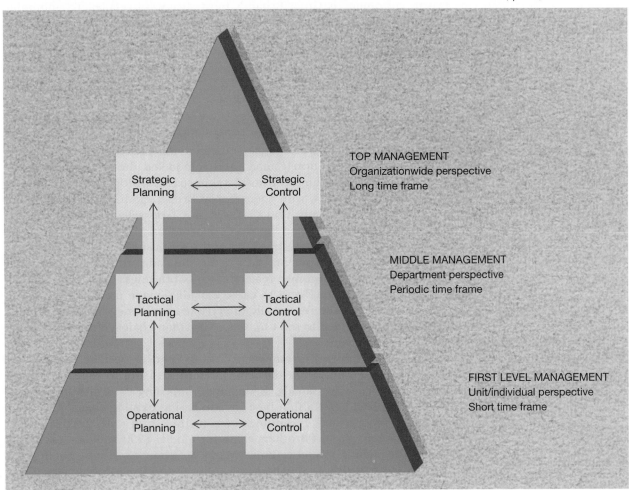

TOP MANAGEMENT
Organizationwide perspective
Long time frame

MIDDLE MANAGEMENT
Department perspective
Periodic time frame

FIRST LEVEL MANAGEMENT
Unit/individual perspective
Short time frame

ensure that strategic plans are implemented as intended, assessing the effects of organizational strategic actions, and adjusting such plans when necessary. Control at the strategic level is mainly the domain of top-level managers, who generally take an organizationwide perspective. Inherent in strategic control is the need for top-level managers to make sure that the organization's core competencies are being developed and maintained in a manner that will ensure the organization's ability to pursue its strategic goals.[15] For strategic control, managers often concentrate on relatively long time frames, such as quarterly, semiannual, and annual reporting cycles, and beyond. If environments are somewhat unstable and/or competition is especially keen, managers may use shorter reporting cycles. At British retailer Marks & Spencer, inadequate strategic controls have led to problems in the company's struggle to become a significant force in North American retailing (see the Case in Point discussion).

CASE IN POINT

MARKS & SPENCER STRUGGLES IN NORTH AMERICA

Marks & Spencer, PLC, is a household name in Britain, where its many conveniently located stores carry well-made, moderately priced clothing and feature food counters with freshly prepared meals bearing the St. Michael label. With more than $10 billion in annual revenues, "Marks & Sparks," as it is often called by British customers, is Great Britain's most successful retailer. Its admirable net profit margins of about 7 percent, which are monitored closely, are approximately double those of comparable U.S. firms. The company, which has 17 percent of Britain's domestic clothing market and 5 percent of food sales, is one of Europe's most respected businesses. It has built a strong reputation by offering a relatively limited range of merchandise, but expending great effort to ensure that quality is high and prices are reasonable.

Because Marks & Spencer began to saturate its home market, the company purchased three Canadian chains in 1973. While retaining the basic thrust of two of the chains, Marks & Spencer changed the name of the third from Walker's to Marks & Spencer Canada and remodeled the stores to resemble smaller versions of their famous British counterparts. Unfortunately, the Marks & Spencer Canada stores, with their sturdy British clothing, relatively plain decor, and imported biscuits and teas, did not fare well compared with the more attractive stores and merchandise of Canadian shopping-mall competitors. Yet Marks & Spencer was slow to sense the seriousness of the problem and take corrective action. Despite low sales levels, the company did not collect sufficient data regarding customer reactions to its offerings. Only gradually did Marks & Spencer Canada begin to carry Canadian-made merchandise and to improve the look of its stores. Finally, after 19 years of losses, Marks & Spencer top management decided to sell two of the Canadian chains, retaining only the D'Allaird grocery chain.

Despite the problems in Canada, Marks & Spencer decided to enter the U.S. market in the late 1980s, but it was determined not to repeat the same mistakes it had made in Canada. Rather than imposing its British formula on acquisitions, it would establish a base by purchasing existing chains with good performance records and expanding them in their own style. To this end, it bought the famous Brooks Brothers chain for a hefty $750 million—two and a half times the chain's annual revenue. Marks & Spencer was subsequently surprised to learn that Brooks Brothers was not as well managed as expected. For example, the former owner had not invested enough in keeping the stores attractive, and inventory controls were grossly inadequate. Marks & Spencer originally planned to boost profits to $75 million in 5 years, but ultimately found the goal was unreachable. The company has faced a significant challenge in attempting to broaden the appeal of Brooks Brothers merchandise by offering new styles without alienating traditional Brooks Brothers customers. Although the U.S. Brooks Brothers operation is still struggling, the British retailer has been very successful at selling copies of the Brooks women's blue blazer and Brooks-styled shirts in Europe.

Top management at Marks & Spencer has recently decided to focus greater attention on expansion into Europe, where there is greater cultural similarity to the company's British home base. It now has stores in France, Spain, Belgium, and Holland, and has recently moved into Germany. Marks & Spencer also has a successful operation in Hong Kong and is making plans for further expansion in the Far East. Because of its problems in North America, the expansion is proceeding slowly so that the company can experiment, gather adequate data to assess progress, and make changes more quickly when strategic plans are not achieving the desired results.[16]   ■■■

Even though they are primarily concerned with strategic issues, top-level managers may also make use of tactical and operational control to ensure that tactical and operational plans are being implemented as intended at the middle and lower management levels.

Tactical control focuses on assessing the implementation of tactical plans at department levels, monitoring associated periodic results, and taking corrective action as necessary. Control at the tactical level mainly involves middle managers, who are concerned with department-level objectives, programs, and budgets. They concentrate on periodic or middle-term time frames and often use weekly and monthly reporting cycles. They also test how the environment reacts to the tactical initiatives of their departments. For example, to fuel growth at Marks & Spencer, food merchandising managers continually work with suppliers to develop new products. When a product looks promising, small batches (e.g., about 10,000 units) are shipped to the chain's busiest stores. If the product sells, it is shipped to other stores for further trials; if not, it is dropped.[17] Although their prime concern is tactical control, middle managers are likely to engage in some strategic control by providing information to upper-level managers on strategic issues. They are also involved in operational control, at least to the extent of checking on some of the more critical aspects of operating plan implementation.

Operational control involves overseeing the implementation of operating plans, monitoring day-to-day results, and taking corrective action when required. Control at the operating level is largely the responsibility of lower-level managers, who are concerned with schedules, budgets, rules, and specific outputs normally associated with particular individuals. For example, managers at individual Mark & Spencer stores closely track such areas as daily sales volume in merchandise and food, cost of reduced merchandise, sales returns, and staff turnover. Operating control provides feedback about what is being done in the very near term to achieve both the short-term and the long-term goals of the organization.

To be effective, the levels of control—strategic, tactical, and operational—must be strongly interrelated in much the same way that planning systems at the different levels are integrated. Such coordination is evident at mall book retailer Waldenbooks, now part of the Borders Group. Top managers keep track of the overall effects of corporate-level strategies. Examples of these strategies

Tactical control A control type that focuses on assessing the implementation of tactical plans at department levels, monitoring associated periodic results, and taking corrective action as necessary

Operational control A control type that involves overseeing the implementation of operating plans, monitoring day-to-day results, and taking corrective action when required

are increasing profit levels by maintaining a better product mix in stores, closing 187 underperforming stores, and publishing the company's own books under the Longmeadow Press label. Middle-level managers monitor the implementation of these strategies throughout the various parts of the bookstore chain and keep tabs on important indicators, such as sales figures in various areas. At the operating level, individual store managers are responsible for ensuring that prominent display areas, such as the front of the store and the main traffic artery (called the "power aisle"), are used for specific materials that support major strategic directions.[18]

■ THE CONTROL PROCESS

Although control systems must be tailored to specific situations, such systems generally follow the same basic process. In this section, we first consider the steps in the control process and then examine more closely the issues related to deciding what to control.

Steps in the Control Process

The basic process used in controlling is shown in Figure 16-3. The process has several major steps.

1 DETERMINE AREAS TO CONTROL Managers must first decide which major areas will be controlled. Choices are necessary because it is expensive and virtually impossible to control every aspect of an organization's activities. In addition, employees typically resent having their every move controlled. Managers usually base their main controls on the organizational goals and objectives developed during the planning process. For example, Briggs & Stratton, the

Figure 16-3 *Steps in the control process.*

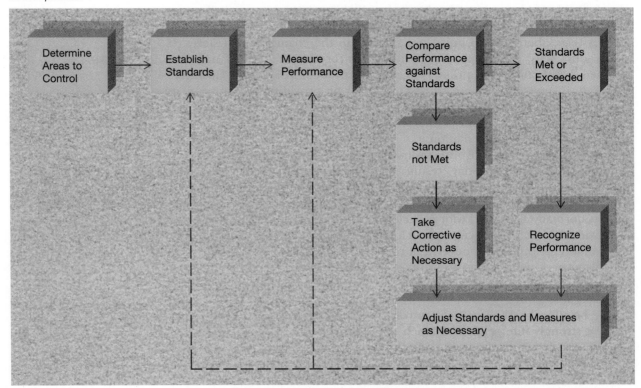

The first step in the control process is to determine what area is in particular need of control. Sea Containers Ltd. of London found that it needed to control debt, especially after maintaining too large a fleet at one point caused it to lose millions of dollars. This Sea Container ship is loading irrigation piping in Houston to be transported to Saudi Arabia.

maker of small engines used on lawn mowers, has been closely monitoring market share ever since the company began to face serious Japanese competition. The company has been raising advertising budgets, increasing research and engineering funding, and lowering production costs in an effort to regain and maintain its former market share of more than 50 percent.[19]

2 ESTABLISH STANDARDS In the control process, standards are essential because they spell out specific criteria for evaluating performance and related employee behaviors. Often such standards are incorporated into the goals when the latter are set in the planning process, so they merely need to be reiterated. Sometimes, though, they need to be developed during the control process. When Chicago-based Marshall Field & Company began its service-improvement program, it discovered that salespeople took an average of 10 minutes to approach a customer. To improve the situation, the company instituted training programs, special incentives for salespeople, and a computerized scheduling program that assigns salespeople to areas where they are most likely to be needed. As a result, Field was able to establish a standard of 2 minutes for salespeople's approach to customers. Field also sets daily sales goals for each salesperson.[20]

Generally, standards serve three major purposes related to employee behavior.[21] For one thing, standards enable employees to understand what is expected and how their work will be evaluated. This helps employees do an effective job. For another, standards provide a basis for detecting job difficulties related to personal limitations of organization members. Such limitations can be based on a lack of ability, training, or experience, or on any other job-related deficiency that prevents an individual from performing properly on the job. Timely identification of deficiencies makes it possible to take corrective action before the difficulties become serious and possibly irresolvable. Finally, standards help reduce the potential negative effects of goal incongruence. **Goal incongruence** is a condition in which there are major incompatibilities between the goals of an organization member and those of the organization. Such

Goal incongruence A condition in which there are major incompatibilities between the goals of an organization member and those of the organization

incompatibilities can occur for a variety of reasons, such as lack of support for organizational objectives (e.g., an employee views the job as temporary and attempts to do the minimum), and often result in behaviors that are incompatible with reaching organizational goals.

One common manifestation of goal incongruence is employee theft, which includes wasting an organization's resources as well as taking equipment, materials, and money.[22] Wasted resources almost led to the demise of Intermedics, Inc., a small pacemaker company located near Houston. A new CEO, who subsequently saved the company from impending bankruptcy, established standards in such areas as working hours and expense account usage. The CEO recalls that upon his arrival he found that "Intermedics was a country club. Most employees were arriving to work late, expense account abuse was rampant, and nobody ever thought we owed the stockholders anything. Values around here were really warped."[23]

3 MEASURE PERFORMANCE Once standards are determined, the next step is measuring performance. For a given standard, a manager must decide both how to measure actual performance and how often to do so. One of the more popular techniques used to help set standards and coordinate the measurement of performance is management by objectives (see Chapter 6).

The means of measuring performance will depend on the standards that have been set. They can include such data as units produced, dollar amount of service rendered, amount of materials used, number of defects found, scrap rate, steps or processes followed, profits, return on investment, quality of output, or stores opened. At American Express, where good service is an important organizational goal, the 12 departments responsible for card operations were asked by top management to develop their own performance standards and measure their own achievements. The departments all seemed to be doing well under this arrangement, but overall service was not improving. Consequently, the company developed a system for measuring the impact of all the departments' activities on customers. The system, called the service tracking report, measures success in processing new applications for cards within 15 days, replacing lost or stolen cards in 1 day, sending out errorless bills, and performing more than 100 other tasks.[24]

Although quantitative measures are often used whenever possible, many important aspects of performance can be difficult to measure quantitatively. Consider the situation at a McDonald's drive-through line. While it may be relatively easy to measure how long it takes to fill an order, it will probably take some managerial judgment to determine how polite employees are to customers. Similarly, areas such as research and development can be difficult to measure quantitatively in the short run because it may take years to determine the final outcomes of research programs. As a result, qualitative judgments by peers are often utilized.[25] Most organizations use combinations of both quantitative and qualitative performance measures in carrying out the control process.

Once they have selected the means of measurement, managers must decide how often they will measure performance for control purposes. In some cases, managers need control data on a daily, hourly, or even more frequent basis (as in the case of supervisors of air traffic controllers). In other cases, weekly, monthly, quarterly, semiannual, or even annual data may be sufficient. The period of measurement generally depends on how important the goal is to the organization, how quickly the situation is likely to change, and how difficult and expensive it would be to rectify a problem if one were to occur. Nuclear power plants, for example, have elaborate systems of controls that continuously provide data on all major aspects of the operation. The extensive controls are important given the potentially serious consequences of a power plant accident.

4 COMPARE PERFORMANCE AGAINST STANDARDS This step consists of comparing the performance measured in step 3 with the standards established in step 2. Managers often base their comparisons on information provided in reports that summarize planned versus actual results. Such reports may be presented orally, forwarded in written form, or generated automatically by computer. Through networks of linked computers, managers can obtain up-to-the-minute status reports on a variety of quantitative performance measures.

Computer systems lend themselves particularly well to applications of **management by exception,** a control principle which suggests that managers should be informed of a situation only if control data show a significant deviation from standards.[26] Use of the management by exception principle, with or without computers, helps save managers time by bringing to their attention only those conditions that appear to need managerial action. While this approach can often be used effectively, managers need to be careful that they do not become so preoccupied with problems that they ignore positive accomplishments of subordinates.

Management by exception
A control principle which suggests that managers should be informed of a situation only if control data show a significant deviation from standards

Managers often make comparisons of performance and standards by walking around work areas and observing conditions, a practice sometimes referred to as management by wandering around (see Chapter 14). For example, executives of the Wal-Mart discount chain are well known for their habitual visits to company stores, where they constantly check merchandise displays, talk with employees, and meet customers.[27] A number of organizations also are establishing *360-degree feedback systems*, an evaluation approach that provides an individual with ratings of performance from a variety of relevant sources, such as superiors, peers, and customers (see Chapter 10).

5A RECOGNIZE POSITIVE PERFORMANCE When performance meets or exceeds the standards set, managers should recognize the positive performance. The recognition given can vary from a spoken "well done" for a routine achievement to more substantial rewards, such as bonuses, training opportunities, or pay raises, for major achievements or consistently good work. This approach is compatible with motivation theories, such as expectancy theory and reinforcement theory, which emphasize the importance of rewarding good performance to sustain it and encourage further improvements (see Chapter 12). For instance, to reinforce Marshall Field's standard of 2 minutes or less for approaching a customer, managers give a silver coin called a "Frangloon" to any salesperson who is observed being extra helpful to a customer. Ten coins earn a box of Field's Frango mint chocolates, while 100 coins can be exchanged for an extra day of paid vacation. When a salesperson meets the day's quota, the computerized cash registers display "Congratulations."[28]

5B TAKE CORRECTIVE ACTION AS NECESSARY When standards are not met, managers must carefully assess the reasons why and take corrective action. During this evaluation, they often personally check the standards and the related performance measures to determine whether these are still realistic. Sometimes, managers may conclude that the standards are, in fact, inappropriate—usually because of changing conditions—and that corrective action to meet standards is therefore not desirable. More often, though, corrective actions are needed to reach standards.

6 ADJUST STANDARDS AND MEASURES AS NECESSARY Control is a dynamic process. As a result, managers need to check standards periodically to ensure that the standards and the associated performance measures are still relevant for the future. For one thing, existing standards and measures can be inappropriate, either because they were not set appropriately to begin with or because circumstances have changed. For another, exceeding a standard may signal unforeseen opportunities, the potential to raise standards, and/or the need for possible major adjustments in organizational plans. Finally, even if standards have simply been met, changing conditions, such as improvements in the skill levels of employees, may make it possible to raise standards for future efforts. Conversely, a manager may feel that achieving a particular standard consumes too many resources and may decide to lower that standard. Thus managers use the control process to keep track of various activities, but they must also review the process itself when necessary to be sure that it meets current needs.

Deciding What to Control: A Closer Look

Well-formulated objectives, strategic plans, and supporting goals provide guidance about what is important to the organization. As a result, they suggest areas for control. While managers need to collect data regarding the extent to which desired ends are being achieved, they may also have to control various elements that lead to those ends.

Resource dependence An approach to controls which argues that managers need to consider controls mainly in areas in which they depend on others for resources necessary to reach organizational goals

One approach that helps managers decide what to control takes a resource dependence point of view.[29] The **resource dependence** approach argues that managers need to consider controls mainly in areas in which they depend on others for resources necessary to reach organizational goals. Resources in this context can be parts, information, service, funding, or any other type of resource that a manager might need in pursuing objectives. Still, just because a manager is dependent upon others does not necessarily mean that an area should be controlled. Four conditions need to be met in making a final determination. Areas that meet all four conditions constitute **strategic control points,** performance areas chosen for control because they are particularly important in meeting organizational goals. The conditions and a related decision tree are shown in Figure 16-4.

Strategic control points Performance areas chosen for control because they are particularly important in meeting organizational goals

FOUR CONDITIONS FOR CONTROL The first two conditions relate to whether or not controls are needed. The second two assess whether controls are feasible and practical.

The first and most basic condition is relatively *high dependence* on the resource. The more important the dependence and the less the resource is available from other sources, the higher the dependence on the resource. If you were running a McDonald's outlet, for example, you would probably find yourself highly dependent on resources such as food, food containers, water, napkins and related items, and equipment that is in good working order. These resources are crucial to operations. On the other hand, if the resource is not very important or a substitute can be obtained easily (e.g., a replacement for a trampled shrub), then the resource is probably not worth elaborate controls.

The second condition for control is a strong likelihood that the *expected resource flow will be unacceptable.* In other words, the manager anticipates that there may be some problems with the resource or at least feels uncertain about it. The anticipated problems can be related to any relevant aspect, but usually they are tied to the quantity of the resource, certain characteristics (such as specifications and quality), and timeliness. The more the manager feels that

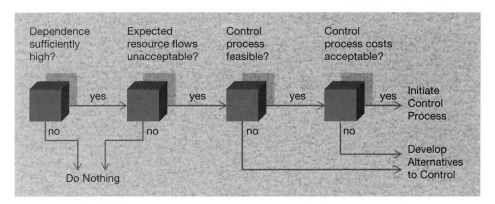

Figure 16-4 *Resource dependence decision tree. (Adapted from Stephen G. Green and M. Ann Welsh, "Cybernetics and Dependence: Reframing the Control Concept," Academy of Management Review, vol. 13, 1988, pp. 287–301.)*

the resource will be a source of problems, the greater the need for controls. For instance, as a manager of a McDonald's outlet, you might find it difficult to stockpile food products (such as lettuce, hamburger buns, and milk) that can spoil. Yet shifting customer patterns can affect usage, making control of food inventory very important. On the other hand, even though water is also an important resource, water supplies (at least in most parts of the United States) are quite reliable, so a formal control system is not generally needed.

The third condition that influences whether to institute controls is *control process feasibility.* Sometimes the basic control process—establishing standards of performance, measuring performance, comparing performance to standards, feeding back information about discrepancies, and allowing for corrective action—is not feasible. Typically, feasibility is an issue when it is difficult to specify standards of performance or when there are problems either with measuring performance or with measuring it in a timely manner. For example, it is difficult for McDonald's to establish rigid standards in the area of price competition overseas. In Japan, at one point McDonald's instituted a 6-week sale, which involved cutting the price of regular hamburgers from $1.75 (about 224 yen) to $.83. The promotion proved to be so successful in the busier stores (particularly in Tokyo) that the chain ran out of buns. McDonald's officials in Japan decided to suspend the promotion at about half of the more than 900 outlets until more buns could be produced. Meanwhile, the company offered medium french fries for $.83 instead of the usual $2.00. In this case, price and promotion issues were controlled locally because it is not feasible for McDonald's to make adequate and timely assessments of such issues from its central headquarters in Oak Brook, Illinois.[30]

Finally, an important condition influencing whether to institute a control process is *cost acceptability.* Managers need to weigh the costs of control against the benefits. Sometimes, a control system can cost more than the organization gains from the controls. Once again, McDonald's provides a good illustration. The company's central headquarters could maintain even better control than it does over outlets by establishing a videoconferencing network, which would include a two-way video-audio connection to every store (see Chapter 14). At this point, though, the cost would be prohibitive given the potential gains.

ALTERNATIVES TO CONTROL What happens if the first two conditions (the questions on the left in Figure 16-4) indicate that controls are needed, but a control process is either infeasible or too costly? Then managers need to develop alternatives to control.

One way to do so is to change the dependence relationship so that control is no longer necessary. For example, a manager might line up several suppliers so that controls are much less important. Because of the scarcity of local suppliers in Saudi Arabia, for example, the Saudi Big Mac includes sesame seeds and onions from Mexico, buns made from Saudi wheat, beef patties and lettuce from Spain, pickles and special sauce from the United States, and cheese from New Zealand.[31] Alternatively, a manager can work with the source of dependence to make it more reliable, thus reducing the need for extensive controls. This approach was used when McDonald's experts helped local farmers in Thailand learn how to cultivate Idaho russet potatoes, a key element in meeting McDonald's standards for french fries at Thai outlets.[32]

Another approach is to change the nature of the dependence to one that is more feasible and/or cost-effective. For instance, redesigning complex jobs so that they involve narrower, simpler tasks reduces dependence on experienced workers. Although there are a number of disadvantages to job simplification (see Chapter 8), the approach may make a situation easier to control in a tight labor market.

Still another approach is to eliminate the dependence. This can be done through vertical integration, in which the organization produces inputs previously provided by suppliers or replaces a customer role by disposing of its own outputs (see Chapter 7). McDonald's used this approach when it ran into continuous problems with suppliers of hamburger buns in Britain and finally put up money, with two partners, to build its own plant.[33] Alternatively, an organization can change its goals and objectives so that it is no longer dependent on the particular source of resources. Changing goals is a fairly drastic step and is not likely to be adopted until other alternatives are ruled out. Still, it may be the best solution in some situations.

■ TYPES OF CONTROLS

In addition to determining the areas that they want to control, managers need to consider the types of controls that they wish to use. In this section, we discuss the major types of controls based on timing, consider the use of multiple controls, and contrast cybernetic and noncybernetic types of controls.

Major Control Types by Timing

Using a systems perspective, one can think of the productive cycle of an organization as encompassing inputs, transformation processes, and outputs that occur at different points in time (see Chapter 2). Accordingly, controls can be classified on the basis of their timing, or stage in the productive cycle, depending on whether they focus on inputs, transformation processes, or outputs (see Figure 16-5). Managers often have options regarding the stage in the transformation cycle at which they will institute controls. The three types of controls based on timing are feedforward, concurrent, and feedback.

Feedforward control The regulation of inputs to ensure that they meet the standards necessary for the transformation process

FEEDFORWARD CONTROL Feedforward control focuses on the regulation of inputs to ensure that they meet the standards necessary for the transformation process (see Figure 16-5). Inputs that can be subject to feedforward control include materials, people, finances, time, and other resources used by an organization. With feedforward control, the emphasis is on prevention to preclude later serious difficulties in the productive process. Feedforward control is also sometimes called *preliminary control, precontrol, preventative control,* or *steering control.*

AutoAlliance International, the joint auto assembly operation of Ford Motor and Mazda Motor Corporation in Flat Rock, Michigan, uses feedforward

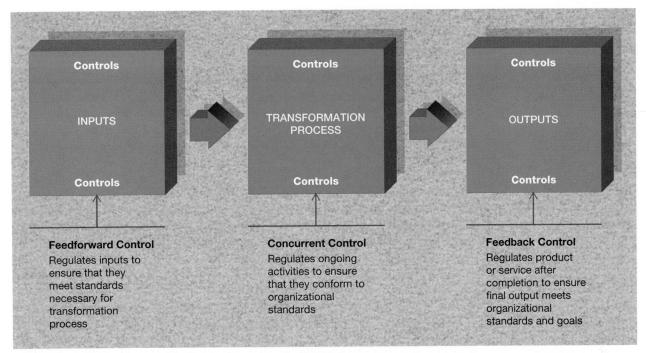

Feedforward Control
Regulates inputs to
ensure that they
meet standards
necessary for
transformation
process

Concurrent Control
Regulates ongoing
activities to ensure
that they conform to
organizational
standards

Feedback Control
Regulates product
or service after
completion to ensure
final output meets
organizational
standards and goals

Figure 16-5 *Major control types by timing.*

control by carefully selecting and training workers. Generally, AutoAlliance's efforts at feedforward control have been successful, since the company has hired relatively competent workers. Still, the $550 million plant ran into some difficulty during its initial year because absenteeism rates were 8 percent, compared with the expected 5 percent, and turnover was 2 percent above the expected 5 percent level. As a result, the plant was forced to reduce training for new workers from 3 weeks to 1 in the struggle to meet annual production quotas.[34] Thus, even though feedforward controls often make a significant contribution to organizational effectiveness, they frequently do not cover every possible contingency. Other types of controls may also be needed.

CONCURRENT CONTROL Concurrent control involves the regulation of ongoing activities that are part of the transformation process to ensure that they conform to organizational standards. The emphasis here is on identifying difficulties in the productive process that could result in faulty output (see Figure 16-5). Concurrent control is sometimes called *screening* or *yes-no control,* because it often entails checkpoints at which determinations are made about whether to continue progress, take corrective action, or stop work altogether on a product or service. Since concurrent control involves regulating ongoing tasks, its use requires clearly specified standards regarding how various activities are to be conducted.[35] At the Ford-Mazda plant, standards cover every aspect of the automobile production line, including how long it takes to move a car through the body shop, the paint shop, and final assembly.[36]

> **Concurrent control** The regulation of ongoing activities that are part of the transformation process to ensure that they conform to organizational standards

FEEDBACK CONTROL Feedback control is regulation exercised after a product or service has been completed to ensure that the final output meets organizational standards and goals (see Figure 16-5). Feedback control, sometimes called *postaction control* or *output control,* fulfills a number of important functions.

For one thing, it is often used when feedforward and concurrent controls are not feasible or are too costly. For example, a sales manager will likely find it difficult to use concurrent control to regulate the daily activities of various

> **Feedback control** Regulation exercised after a product or service has been completed to ensure that the final output meets organizational standards and goals

salespeople who visit customers in the field. Instead, the sales manager will probably emphasize feedforward control by carefully selecting new hires and then use feedback control by periodically comparing sales quotas (standards) with actual sales.

Feedback control is also often used when the exact processes involved in producing a product or service (e.g., performing complex surgery) are difficult to specify in advance. This type of control can also serve as a final means of checking for deviations that were not detected earlier. Recently, many major companies have been making great efforts to improve quality so that either feedback control is unnecessary or there are few deviations to detect and, hence, very little scrap or rework to be done (see Chapter 17). During early operations at the Flat Rock plant, which was initially run by Mazda, 70 percent of the finished cars were parked outside, waiting for repairs of defects identified in final inspections. Still, refusing to ship cars that did not adhere to its high standards, the plant worked instead to reduce the proportion of cars with defects found by feedback control to 15 percent.[37]

Another function of feedback control is providing information that will facilitate the planning process. Such information may include number of units made or sold, cost of various aspects of production, quality measures, return on investment, or clients served. The data can be used in revising existing plans and formulating new ones. Finally, feedback control provides output information that is particularly useful in the process of rewarding employee performance.

Multiple Controls

Multiple control systems
Systems that use two or more of the feedforward, concurrent, and feedback control processes and involve several strategic control points

Organizations typically set up **multiple control systems,** systems that use two or more of the feedforward, concurrent, and feedback control processes and involve several strategic control points. As mentioned earlier, strategic control points are performance areas chosen for control because they are particularly important in meeting organizational goals. Multiple control systems develop because of the need to control various aspects of a productive cycle, including inputs, transformations, and outputs.

Organizations that do not have multiple control systems focusing on strategic control points often experience difficulties that cause managers to reevaluate their control processes. For example, the London-based Filofax Group PLC increased all three types of timing controls as part of an effort to reverse the company's decline and revitalize it. (see the Case in Point discussion).

CASE IN POINT

DEVELOPING BETTER CONTROLS AT FILOFAX

Nicky Lee, who runs a profitable textile firm in Hampstead, London, keeps her busy schedule organized with a Filofax, the well-known, notebooklike personal organizer. Lee purchased her first Filofax in 1984 and has used the system ever since to keep track of a multitude of information, such as deadlines for payments to suppliers, the date her father died, her window cleaner's phone number, her flight schedule to New York, and when she must pick up her daughter.

Filofax Group PLC was almost 60 years old when David and Lesley Collishchon took it over in 1980. Annual sales were just $155,000. By 1988, the pair had built sales to $23 million and taken the company public. Largely by word of mouth, the Filofax became a status symbol for the upwardly mobile, particularly in Great Britain. Then costs began to mount out of control. The average price of a Filofax ballooned to $110, and the company offered an amazing array of covers and fillers. Despite the loyalty of customers like Nicky Lee, by 1990 the company was losing money. As the losses continued, the board installed Robin Field, managing partner of a consulting firm called in to help, as chief executive officer.

One of Field's first moves was to gain control over the swollen product line and inventory. Filofax was offering 1000 different covers including sharkskin. Many of them, like a gold-cornered leather cover retailing for $310, were laying in the warehouse gathering dust. There were also several thousand different fillers, including some geared to audiences as specialized as bird watchers and windsurfers. Top executives were heavily involved in every product development decision even down to what color papers to use.

Field eliminated items that did not generate steady sales, paring the product offerings down to about 100. The reduced product line has led to savings in production, distribution, and administrative costs. Moreover, product design specialists now make more of the product development decisions. Field also learned that the main supplier of printing for Filofax was earning net profit margins on Filofax work that were larger than the gross profit margins of most printing establishments. He renegotiated printing charges and prices charged by other suppliers. Next Field introduced some less expensive Filofax binders that sold in the $50 range in the United States and offered a $20 student version. He also cut the price of a standard Filofax filler from $3.60 to under $2.00. He did so because he realized that there is more money to be made on volume. By reducing prices he makes the various fillers more attractive to purchasers of the basic Filofax system. He and his staff carefully monitor sales to ensure that the product mix continues to include strong-selling items. Field has also taken other cost-saving steps, like hiring subcontractors to handle warehousing. As sales and profits have increased, Filofax has been able to buy some of its distributors, gaining a direct link with its retailers.

Annual sales have grown from 200,000 organizers in the late 1980s to more than 2 million today. Filofax is moving more aggressively into continental Europe where organizers have not been used as extensively as in Britain and the United States.[38] ■■■

Control is at the top of the agenda for Robin Field, CEO of Filofax. When he was named to head the ailing company in the early 1990s, he reduced the bloated product line, renegotiated supplier contracts, and lowered prices to increase sales volume. These multiple controls helped to make the company profitable again. (Filofax is a registered trademark of Filofax Group PLC.)

Multiple controls have helped bring discipline to the burgeoning product line and spiraling costs at Filofax. For example, Field used feedforward control by renegotiating prices charged by suppliers of certain inputs, such as printed fillers. He also exercised concurrent control by acquiring distributors so that Filofax is in a better position to build strong relationships with retailers and provide them with first-class service. Finally, he made use of feedback control by carefully monitoring sales to ensure that the product mix focuses on strong-selling items on which the company can earn. Many of Field's control actions involved considerable human discretion. The degree of human discretion required is another means of distinguishing types of control systems.

Cybernetic and Noncybernetic Control

A basic control process can be either cybernetic or noncybernetic, depending on the degree to which human discretion is part of the system. A **cybernetic control system** is a self-regulating control system that, once put into operation, can automatically monitor the situation and take corrective action when nec-

Cybernetic control system A self-regulating control system that, once it is put into operation, can automatically monitor the situation and take corrective action when necessary

essary. A heating system controlled by a thermostat is a cybernetic control system. Once the thermostat is set, the self-regulating system keeps the temperature at the designated level without requiring human intervention. In some computerized inventory systems, cybernetic control automatically places orders when inventories of certain items reach a designated level. The ordering is done without human discretion, such as managerial approval before an order is placed.

Although the growing use of computers is increasing the possibilities for cybernetic control, most control systems used by organizations are the noncybernetic type. A **noncybernetic control system** is one that relies on human discretion as a basic part of its process. By their very nature, areas that require control in organizations typically go awry in ways that are difficult to predict. Further, they are apt to be complex enough to require human discretion in determining what corrective action is needed. Strictly speaking, even systems that involve relatively little human discretion, such as a computerized inventory system with automatic ordering capacity, generate reports for human perusal. They also typically have built-in monitoring systems designed to alert appropriate organization members if things are not progressing as intended. Still, computers are allowing many controls to be established closer to the cybernetic end of the continuum.

Noncybernetic control system
A control system that relies on human discretion as a basic part of its process

■ MANAGERIAL APPROACHES TO IMPLEMENTING CONTROLS

In addition to considering the types of controls they will employ, managers also have options regarding the mechanisms they will use to implement controls. There are three basic managerial approaches to control: bureaucratic, clan, and market. It is sometimes useful to think of these approaches in terms of how the control is exercised—whether through bureaucratic rules, the clan, or the market. All three approaches are likely to be used to some extent.

Bureaucratic Control

Bureaucratic control A managerial approach that relies on regulation through rules, policies, supervision, budgets, schedules, reward systems, and other administrative mechanisms aimed at ensuring that employees exhibit appropriate behaviors and meet performance standards

Bureaucratic control relies on regulation through rules, policies, supervision, budgets, schedules, reward systems, and other administrative mechanisms aimed at ensuring that employees exhibit appropriate behaviors and meet performance standards. Several characteristics likely to be associated with heavy use of bureaucratic control are shown in Table 16-1. As indicated in the table, the sources of control are mainly external to the individual, the emphasis tends to be on a fixed set of duties that are often narrowly defined, and the focus is on top-down hierarchical control.

With bureaucratic control, rules and policies are typically developed over time to handle a variety of recurring conditions. When unforeseen circumstances or infrequent exceptions occur, supervisors can then decide what corrective action, if any, is necessary. Supervisors are also charged with checking to be sure that individuals follow rules and other administrative mechanisms.

While bureaucratic control is useful for keeping recurring, relatively predictable activities running smoothly, a heavy dosage of it does have some disadvantages. Bureaucratic control is not particularly conducive to innovation, may inhibit needed changes when the environment shifts rapidly, and tends to elicit compliance, rather than commitment, in employees because it emphasizes following regulations developed by others; (see also Chapter 13 on leadership). For these reasons, a number of organizations are attempting to place greater emphasis on clan control.

TABLE 16-1 CHARACTERISTICS ASSOCIATED WITH BUREAUCRATIC AND CLAN CONTROL

CHARACTERISTICS	BUREAUCRATIC CONTROL	CLAN CONTROL
Means of control	Rules, policies, and hierarchy	Shared goals, values, and tradition
Source of control	Mainly external mechanisms	Mainly internal motivation
Job design	Narrow subtasks; doing, rather than thinking	Whole task; doing and thinking
Definition of duties	Fixed	Flexible; contingent on changing conditions
Accountability	Usually individual	Often team
Structure	Tall; top-down controls	Flat; mutual influence
Power usage	Emphasis on legitimate authority	Emphasis on relevant information and expertise
Responsibility	Performing individual job	Upgrading performance of work unit and organization
Reward emphasis	Extrinsic	Intrinsic
Innovation	Less likely	More likely
Likely employee reactions	Compliance	Commitment

Source: Adapted from Richard W. Walton, "From Control to Commitment in the Workplace," *Harvard Business Review,* March–April 1985, p. 81.

Clan Control

Clan control relies on values, beliefs, traditions, corporate culture, shared norms, and informal relationships to regulate employee behaviors and facilitate the reaching of organizational goals. Several characteristics likely to be related to heavy use of clan control are listed in Table 16-1. In contrast to bureaucratic control, clan control places greater emphasis on internal motivation, flexible duties and broad tasks, and influence based on relevant information and expertise rather than on position in the hierarchy.

With clan control, as the name implies, there is greater emphasis on groups, and teams are often the focus of responsibility. This type of control is often used in situations involving professionals, in which professional training and norms, as well as group identification, help substitute for the strong emphasis on rules and regulations characteristic of bureaucratic control.

Clan control enhances prospects for commitment to organizational objectives and generally increases employees' willingness to help bring about improvements in the workplace. Partially for these reasons, a number of organizations with relatively routine types of jobs are also placing greater emphasis on clan control. For example, at Corning, Inc.'s Erwin Ceramics Plant near Corning, New York, eight teams, which vary in size from about 10 to 25 persons, make many of the operational decisions across a broad range of tasks. The teams monitor their own performance against established goals and provide peer appraisals to team members for purposes of feedback and development. The plant also has a skill-based pay plan, whereby most employees receive pay raises for learning new jobs. Since Erwin switched to much greater emphasis on clan control, the plant has registered significant improvement in productivity, defect rates, inventory costs, injury rates, and the length of time required to complete a customer order.[39] Teams are increasingly being used in a variety of businesses, including the insurance, automobile, aerospace, electronics, food-processing, paper, steel, and financial services industries (see also Chapter 15).[40]

Clan control A managerial approach that relies on values, beliefs, traditions, corporate culture, shared norms, and informal relationships to regulate employee behaviors and facilitate the reaching of organizational goals

Market Control

Market control A managerial approach that relies on market mechanisms to regulate prices for certain clearly specified goods and services needed by an organization

Market control relies on market mechanisms to regulate prices for certain clearly specified goods and services needed by an organization, thus relieving managers of the need to establish more elaborate controls over costs. In order to use market control, a reasonable level of competition must exist in the relevant goods or service area and requirements must be specified clearly. For example, purchasing departments frequently develop detailed standards or specifications for goods needed by the organization and then initiate a competitive bidding process. Without the specifications and bidding process (or at least alternative sources for the goods or services that can be compared), purchasing agents might have to determine whether particular price quotes are reasonable on the basis of the productive processes involved. Attempting to control costs in this way can involve considerable time and effort.

Outsourcing The process of employing an outside vendor to perform a function normally carried on within the organization

The use of market control is on the increase because of the trend toward outsourcing. **Outsourcing** is the process of employing an outside vendor to perform a function normally carried on within the organization. For example, General Motors has been pressuring its internal divisions to become more efficient in making parts or face losing the work to outside sources. Until recently, the automaker had been producing about 70 percent of the parts used in its cars. Decisions about who will manufacture certain parts are now being made through market control by comparing the price and quality available through outside suppliers with GM's own internal costs and quality. The resulting outsourcing has caused work stoppages as the United Autoworkers union has sought to stem job losses within GM.[41]

Sometimes market control is used to regulate internal operations by setting up profit centers for service units, such as photocopying operations or computer services, which then charge other parts of the organization for services rendered. Generally, market control does not work well when it is difficult to specify exact requirements because of uncertainty or changing circumstances (e.g., shifting customer requirements) or when there is little or no competition on which to base pricing (e.g., R&D projects).

Promoting Innovation: Controlling While Nurturing Innovation

One major challenge managers face is how to engage in the controlling function without stifling the creativity and innovation necessary for long-term organizational survival. In this section we consider how managers balance four levers of strategic control to foster innovation, while regulating organizational activities. We also review the incrementalist approach to controlling specific projects aimed at innovation.

FOUR LEVERS FOR STRATEGIC CONTROL: A BALANCING ACT Managers actually have four major levers on which they can rely in engaging in effective strategic control.[42] Together the four levers not only encourage accountability but also enable empowerment and allow shifts in strategic direction as necessary. The four levers, shown in Figure 16-6, are closely associated with the planning process (see Chapters 6 and 7) but are used as part of the controlling function to monitor strategic directions and take corrective action as necessary.

1   *Belief systems* are the means through which managers communicate and reinforce the organization's basic mission and values. Mission statements, credos, and slogans can provide inspiration and general direction, guiding organizational efforts and long-term effectiveness. The use of belief systems is strongly associated with clan control.

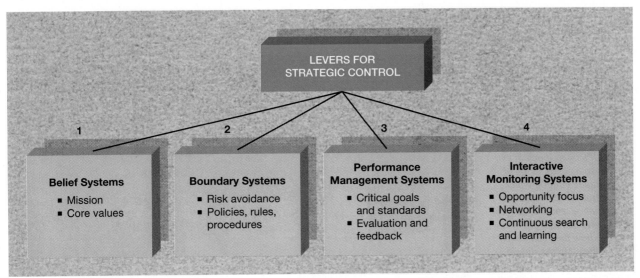

Figure 16-6 *Four levers of strategic control.*

2 *Boundary systems* define the acceptable domain of activities for organizational members. Through such means as policies, rules, and procedures, organizations attempt to reduce the risks that organizational members will dissipate or misuse the resources and energies of the firm by setting boundaries within which they are to operate. Boundary systems are closely allied with bureaucratic control.

3 *Performance management systems* focus on ensuring that specific goals that have been set are achieved. Such systems allow managers to check on progress toward specific targets and facilitate evaluation and feedback relative to achievement of those specific targets. Performance management systems are often associated with bureaucratic control. They can also be used with clan control by specifying the end results needed, but allowing organizational members to determine the best means.

4 *Interactive monitoring* systems encourage continuing search and learning so that the organization can identify and adapt to new opportunities. Without a concerted effort to focus on new opportunities and develop new strategic competencies, organizations may continue to blindly pursue previously established plans that have become obsolete or less than optimal because of changing environmental and competitive circumstances. Such efforts involve continually scanning the environment, gathering internal data on areas that are going better than expected, and encouraging individuals throughout the organization to seize unexpected opportunities and deal with problems. Such systems involve members at all levels of the organization in continuous challenge and debate about data, assumptions, and action plans. One organization that has successfully used the four levels of strategic control is United Parcel Service (see the Case in Point discussion).

UPS RUNS A TIGHT SHIP

CASE IN POINT

A recent company slogan, "We run the tightest ship in the shipping business," sets the theme. Today, United Parcel Service (UPS) is the most profitable package distribution company in the United States, with more than 116,000 vehicles and over 400 aircraft delivering packages around the clock to more than 180 countries and territories. Founded in 1907 in Seattle, Washington, as a mes-

UPS commits itself to running "the tightest ship in the business," whether the packages are delivered in San Francisco, Rome, or Hong Kong (shown here). UPS owes much of its success to a combination of bureaucratic control, which specifies goals and monitors performance, and clan control, which gives employees flexibility in how they carry out their duties. Almost all UPS shares are in the hands of its employees, and they take great pride in the efficiency and egalitarianism of their company.

senger service that would be owned by its managers and managed by its owners, UPS has kept most of its stock in the hands of its 25,000 managers through an annual bonus plan. This closely held ownership allows the company to make long-term strategic decisions without being concerned about reactions of outside investors.

With few exceptions, employees move up only by starting at the bottom and learning firsthand about the company. Because UPS employs about 80,000 college students as part-time package sorters, it has a vast army of workers from which to select full-time employees. For those chosen, the next step is van, or package-car, driver—a job that pays relatively well and is held in high esteem. According to one observer, "The drivers are the real heroes of the company—living, breathing Norman Rockwell portraits. They are 365-day-a-year Santa Clauses bringing the goodies." On average, a middle manager with 10 years of service makes a modest salary but usually also receives profit sharing payments in the form of company stock and a substantial bonus check each year.

Part of the uniqueness of UPS is its corporate culture, described by one former member of the board of directors as half Marine Corps and half Quaker meeting. Teamwork is emphasized over individual glory, and there is a strong norm of egalitarianism. The Atlanta headquarters and the regional centers are extremely Spartan. There are no designated parking places for executives, first names are used for everyone, and no one has a private secretary—not even the chairman of the board. One board member notes, "When we have our meetings, we directors troop downstairs to the cafeteria, stand in line, and pay our $2.17 for a tuna sandwich." As a result of this corporate culture, employees exhibit an enviable commitment to hard work and an unusually strong dedication to the company. It is not uncommon for some 80 percent of the work force to attend voluntary workshops, held after work, on the company's competitive position. Thus clan control and teamwork are strong at UPS.

On the other hand, UPS traditionally has established policies and procedures for every aspect of its operations. Tasks are carefully analyzed to determine appropriate productivity standards. For example, sorters at the massive company hub in Addison (near Chicago), Illinois, are expected to load delivery vans at the rate of 500 to 650 packages per hour and unload them almost twice as fast. All vehicles are rigorously maintained in accordance with computerized schedules. As a result, the vans or package cars used for deliveries remain in service an astounding average of 22 years, and long-haul trucks often run 2 million miles or more.

In the past, pickup and delivery routes have been meticulously timed for each regular stop. Supervisors would determine which packages to deliver first and map out the route; they could usually estimate within 6 minutes just how long each driver's pickups and deliveries would take. Lately, though, the company has been giving drivers more authority to determine what will be delivered and when. For one thing, UPS has learned that customers want more face-to-face interaction with drivers so that they can obtain advice about shipping problems. Schedule flexibility is also increasing productivity as UPS adds new services, such as 3-day guaranteed arrival and overnight express, that complicate the delivery process. The company faces stiff competition from Federal Express and, more recently, from Roadway Package Systems, Inc., which has made major inroads transporting commercial packages between businesses. With drivers making more decisions, fewer supervisors are needed. But the added pressures and increased weight limits for packages are causing strong debate within UPS about whether the current productivity push is exacting too heavy a toll from drivers.

At the same time, UPS is presently attempting the difficult task of developing a worldwide shipping network. For example, it delivers more than 600,000 packages per day in Europe. To bolster efficiencies and make the European business profitable, UPS is investing a whopping $1.1 billion in its European operations. As the company expands internationally and fights increased competition domestically, UPS will need to work hard to preserve its cohesive corporate culture.[43] ■■■

INCREMENTALIST APPROACH When it comes to controlling major innovative efforts, such as R&D projects, innovation expert James Brian Quinn argues that it helps to view the ideal innovation process as "controlled chaos." On the one hand, the process is fairly unpredictable and, hence, somewhat chaotic. On the other hand, the process can be controlled to some degree by combining heavy reliance on clan control with the use of some carefully considered bureaucratic controls. Using an incrementalist approach can provide some control over the process without stifling innovation.[44] The **incrementalist approach** relies heavily on clan control but also involves a phased set of plans and accompanying bureaucratic controls that begin at a very general level and grow more specific as the project progresses. In early stages of the incrementalist approach, managers set general goals, select key individuals for the project, set a few critical limits (such as spending limits), and establish a few major decision points for checking progress.

At the middle stages of the project, when more is known about its technical aspects and/or when market needs become more evident, managers set a few more critical performance goals, limitations, and checkpoints. Still, they allow the members of the technical groups to decide how they will pursue the goals, within the limits and checkpoints, since there are likely to be many questions remaining.

At later stages of the innovation process, when many of the key variables are understood and perhaps demonstrated in laboratory experiments, managers may set more concrete controls to accompany more specific planning. Even at this stage, many factors may be unknown, and several technical options may still be pursued. However, at the specified review points, options that can-

Incrementalist approach An approach to controlling an innovative project that relies heavily on clan control but also involves a phased set of plans and accompanying bureaucratic controls that begin at a very general level and grow more specific as the project progresses

not meet performance targets will be eliminated. The decision to kill a project is a difficult one and will likely involve a managerial judgment call since there are still unknowns. Because of the uncertainty, managers often continue some of the options that appear less promising, but at a lower resource level. It is not uncommon for the smaller-scale options to produce significant break-throughs, while the planned option fails. Sony's famous Walkman, a miniature stereo cassette player with lightweight earphones, grew out of a failed attempt to produce a miniature tape recorder with stereo sound. The idea of combining a miniature player, which was the creation of one engineering group, with the earphones being made by another group came from Honorary Chairman Masaru Ibuka, founder of Sony. Still, the company originally put a minimum amount of money and personnel into the product launch, thinking of the Walkman primarily as a toy for young people.[45]

The incrementalist approach requires that managers strike an appropriate balance among the control approaches in order to encourage innovation. Otherwise, control systems can themselves stifle innovation and inhibit long-term organizational effectiveness.

■ ASSESSING CONTROL SYSTEMS

Whether controls are developed for facilitating innovation or for other purposes, managers need to assess control systems continually to be sure that they are achieving the results intended. In this section, we consider potential dysfunctional aspects of control systems. The presence of any of these aspects indicates that the system needs adjusting. We also examine the issue of overcontrol versus undercontrol, and we conclude by reviewing the characteristics of an effective control system.

Potential Dysfunctional Aspects of Control Systems

As you might imagine, not all effects of control systems are positive. Poorly designed and/or excessive controls may result in one or more major dysfunctional side effects: behavioral displacement, game playing, operating delays, or negative attitudes.[46]

Behavioral displacement A condition in which individuals engage in behaviors that are encouraged by controls and related reward systems even though the behaviors are actually inconsistent with organizational goals

BEHAVIORAL DISPLACEMENT Behavioral displacement is a condition in which individuals engage in behaviors that are encouraged by controls and related reward systems even though the behaviors are actually inconsistent with organizational goals. In one case, a research laboratory decided to use the number of patents filed as an indicator of effectiveness. Unfortunately, there was a major increase in the number of patents filed but a decrease in the number of successful research projects.[47] Displacement can usually be traced to three basic causes: inadequate analysis of the relationship between the controls and the desired outcomes, overemphasis on quantification of control measures when qualitative aspects are also important, and overemphasis on activities, rather than on necessary end results.

GAME PLAYING Game playing with controls occurs when managers attempt to improve their standing on performance measures by manipulating resource usage and/or data rather than by achieving bona fide performance improvements. Manipulating resource usage typically involves negotiating for more resources than necessary to do a job so that objectives can be easily met or exceeded. Some slack in resource levels may be functional, as it provides a buffer against unforeseen contingencies; carried too far, it can undermine the competitive position of the organization through inflated costs. Manipulating data involves either falsifying performance data or influencing performance results during the time period for which the data are reported.

OPERATING DELAYS Operating delays often develop as the result of actions required by feedforward and concurrent controls. To the extent that they are excessive, such controls can seriously cripple, rather than facilitate, efforts to reach organizational goals. They may also provoke actions that undermine the effects of the controls. For example, in one study conducted in a diversified corporation, 74 percent of the general managers reported that they obtained required expenditure approvals *after* the money had in fact been spent.[48]

NEGATIVE ATTITUDES Controls often lead to negative attitudes, especially when they seem excessive or are poorly designed.[49] Professionals, in particular, are likely to resist controls. Most often, they oppose bureaucratic controls that seem to hinder, rather than help, the attainment of organizational goals.

Overcontrol versus Undercontrol

Since excessive amounts of control increase the likelihood of dysfunctional aspects, managers should avoid overcontrol. **Overcontrol** is the limiting of individual job autonomy to such a point that it seriously inhibits effective job performance. At the same time, managers need to avoid going too far in the other direction, producing a situation of undercontrol. **Undercontrol** is the granting of autonomy to an employee to such a point that the organization loses its ability to direct the individual's efforts toward achieving organizational goals. In fact, undercontrol is frequently cited as the reason why organizations do not achieve their goals.[50]

Overcontrol   The limiting of individual job autonomy to such a point that it seriously inhibits effective job performance

Undercontrol   The granting of autonomy to an employee to such a point that the organization loses its ability to direct the individual's efforts toward achieving organizational goals

Characteristics of an Effective Control System

Effective control systems have certain characteristics in common.[51] In assessing control systems, whether they are being designed or are in operation, managers should use these characteristics as a checklist of essential features.

FUTURE-ORIENTED To be effective, control systems need to help regulate future events, rather than fix blame for past ones. A well-designed control system focuses on letting managers know how work is progressing toward unit objectives, pinpointing areas in which future corrective action is needed, and uncovering unforeseen opportunities that might be developed—all aids to future action.

MULTIDIMENSIONAL In most cases, control systems need to be multidimensional to capture the major relevant performance factors. For example, a GM assembly plant would quickly run into difficulty if it focused only on quantity without concern for issues such as quality, scrap rate, and overhead.

COST-EFFECTIVE The cost of controls is an important consideration. One control factor at McDonald's is clean rest rooms. The company manual specifies how often the rest rooms must be cleaned, and there are provisions for both the outlet manager and the company inspection teams to check this factor.[52] Still, McDonald's could control rest-room cleanliness even further by dedicating one person at each outlet to do nothing but ensure cleanliness. The costs of doing so, however, may well be greater than the benefits to be derived from the additional controls, since McDonald's already has one of the best reputations in the industry for cleanliness. Essentially, the benefits of control should outweigh its costs.

ACCURATE Since controls provide the basis for future actions, accuracy is vital. Inaccurate control data may be worse than no controls at all, since managers may make poor decisions on the basis of such data.

REALISTIC Control systems should incorporate realistic expectations about what can be accomplished. Otherwise, employees are likely to view the control system as unreasonable and may ignore or even sabotage it.

TIMELY Control systems are designed to provide data on the state of a given production cycle or process as of a specific time. For example, data may be supplied in a monthly sales report, a weekly update on a project, or a daily production report, or it may come from quality inspections on a production line. In order for managers and employees to respond promptly to irregularities, control systems must provide relevant information soon enough to allow corrective action before there are serious repercussions.

MONITORABLE Control systems should be designed so that they can be monitored to ensure that they are performing as expected. One way of checking a control system is to deliberately insert an imperfection, such as a defective part, and then observe how long it takes the system to detect and report it to the correct individual. Obviously, it is important to keep close tabs on the test to be sure that the imperfection does not cause significant difficulties if the control system fails (as in a test of maintenance quality for airplanes). Other methods of monitoring control systems include conducting audits of various kinds.

ACCEPTABLE TO ORGANIZATION MEMBERS Control systems operate best when they are accepted by the organization members who are affected by them. Otherwise, members may take actions to override and undermine the controls. Employees are apt to accept control systems when the systems focus on important issues that are compatible with organizational goals, when they provide useful data to various levels, when the data collected give a fair and accurate picture of employee performance, and when the emphasis is on using the data for making improvements (as opposed to setting blame).

FLEXIBLE Just as organizations must be flexible to respond rapidly to changing environments, control systems need to be flexible enough to meet new or revised requirements. Accordingly, they should be designed so that they can be changed quickly to measure and report new information and track new endeavors.

While this chapter focuses on basic concepts underlying organizational control systems, the next chapter examines several specific managerial control methods, such as financial control and quality control.

■ CHAPTER SUMMARY

Controlling is the process of regulating organizational activities so that actual performance conforms to expected organizational goals and standards. Controls play impor-

tant roles in helping managers handle five particular challenges: coping with uncertainty, detecting irregularities, identifying opportunities, handling complex situations, and decentralizing authority. Just as planning responsibilities differ by level, parallel control responsibilities exist at the strategic, tactical, and operational levels.

The basic control process entails several major steps: (1) determine areas to control; (2) establish standards; (3) measure performance; (4) compare performance against standards; (5a) if standards are met or exceeded, recognize performance; (5b) if standards are not met, take corrective action as necessary; (6) adjust standards and measures as necessary. The resource dependence approach to controls argues that managers need to consider controls mainly in areas in which they depend on others for resources necessary to reach organizational goals. Four conditions that help delineate when controls should be used are a high dependence on the resource, an expectation that resource flows may be unacceptable without controls, the feasibility of instituting a control process, and acceptable control process costs.

There are several different types of controls. Major control types based on timing are feedforward control, concurrent control, and feedback control. Managers often need to use multiple control systems, which use two or more of the feedforward, concurrent, and feedback control processes and involve several strategic control points. Finally, control systems can be cybernetic or noncybernetic, depending on the degree to which human discretion is part of the system.

Managers also have options regarding the approaches they will use to implement controls. The three basic approaches are bureaucratic, clan, and market. Managers have four levers of strategic control that help them regulate activities while also encouraging motivation: belief systems, boundary systems, performance management systems, and interactive monitoring systems. The incrementalist approach helps to control specific innovation projects. It relies heavily on clan control but also involves a phased set of plans and accompanying bureaucratic controls that begin at a very general level and grow more specific as the project progresses.

Potential dysfunctional aspects of control systems are behavioral displacement, game playing, operating delays, and negative attitudes. To decrease the likelihood of these effects, managers need to avoid engaging in either overcontrol or undercontrol. Effective control systems should be future-oriented, multidimensional, cost-effective, accurate, realistic, timely, monitorable, acceptable to organization members, and flexible.

■ QUESTIONS FOR DISCUSSION AND REVIEW

1 Explain the five major roles of controls. Give three examples from your college or university of controls that fulfill at least one of these roles.

2 Describe the three levels of controls in organizations. For an organization with which you are familiar, identify a control at each level.

3 Outline the general process that can be applied to most control situations. Using this process, explain how you would develop a system to control the home delivery staff of a local pizzeria.

4 Explain the principal factors, or conditions, that managers need to consider in deciding what to control. Use these conditions to assess a control that exists at your college or university.

5 Describe the major types of controls by timing. Suppose that you are managing a small factory that makes specialized microchips for a well-known computer manufacturer. Explain how you would use each control type to help maintain adequate control over the manufacturing process. What strategic control points would you establish?

6 Differentiate between cybernetic and noncybernetic control. Explain how you might use these two types of control in a managerial position.

7 Explain the three basic approaches to implementing controls. For each approach, give an example based on an organization with which you are familiar.

8 Explain the four levers of strategic control. How does the development of Sony's famous Walkman illustrate this approach?

9 Identify the major potential dysfunctional aspects of control systems in organizations. How could overcontrol or undercontrol contribute to these dysfunctional aspects?

10 Delineate the characteristics of effective control systems. Use these characteristics to evaluate controls at United Parcel Service.

■ DISCUSSION QUESTIONS FOR CHAPTER OPENING CASE

1 Assess the extent to which the major roles of controls are evidenced at McDonald's.

2 Explain how McDonald's managers use control types based on timing to increase the prospects for reaching organizational goals.

3 Use the characteristics of effective control systems to assess the effectiveness of controls at McDonald's.

■ EXERCISES FOR MANAGING IN THE TWENTY-FIRST CENTURY

EXERCISE 1
SKILL BUILDING: TIMING THE USE OF CONTROLS

 The timing of the use of controls is particularly important to the achievement of organizational goals. Controls placed at the proper point in the developmental process can yield valuable information concerning quality, quantity, whether expectations are being met or not, and possible solutions or opportunities. Following are examples of controls concerning timing. Indicate whether the type shown is a feedforward (FF), a concurrent (C), or a feedback (FB) control by placing the appropriate letters in the spaces provided.

1 ____ Road testing a new car
2 ____ Daily cash flow report
3 ____ Testing components from vendors prior to assembling a final product
4 ____ Ensuring that employees are properly trained prior to starting a particular function
5 ____ Constantly checking woolen material for irregularities as it is being produced
6 ____ Certification of doctors prior to permitting them to practice
7 ____ A governor (a mechanical device for automatically controlling the speed of an engine by regulating the flow of fuel) that controls the speed of a car or truck
8 ____ A final check of a report before it is sent to a client
9 ____ Individual employees checking their work to ensure it is correct before passing it to someone else
10 ____ Sampling a batch of pills to ensure that the correct amount of proper chemicals is included therein

EXERCISE 2
MANAGEMENT EXERCISE: OPPORTUNITY KNOCKS

 You and a friend have what you believe to be the opportunity of a lifetime. You are both graduating from college this year, and your friend's father has asked whether the two of you would like to buy the air-conditioning and heating business he founded and has operated for the last 30 years. It has been a very lucrative business for him; today he is a millionaire many times over. His firm is the leader in its field in the area, and you and your friend see the possibility of expanding because many new homes are being built in the local three-county region.

Your friend's father will finance the buyout through a loan, which would be paid off over the next 10 years. Both you and your friend have some degree of expertise in the heating and air-conditioning field, as you have both worked for his father during the past four summers and sometimes during the Christmas break from college. His father has agreed to be a consultant to the two of you for a year or so in case his advice is needed.

The firm has almost 60 well-qualified employees, a large inventory, 40 service trucks that are in excellent condition, and a well-established list of clients. At the same time, the return on investment has been lower than average for the past 3 years, labor costs are very high, and the company has attracted only a few new clients during the past 2 years. In addition, there is some indication that the firm is not carrying the most up-to-date heating or air-conditioning equipment, and the four large structures used to house the showrooms and service centers badly need refurbishing.

You and your friend are discussing the possibility of buying the firm. In considering the situation, the two of you are reviewing the forms of control and the control process that should be implemented.

Exercise Requirement
Discuss the types of control you and your friend would use and the control process the two of you would implement as the new owners of the firm.

CONCLUDING CASE 1

LOOSE CONTROLS LEAD TO THE DEMISE OF E. F. HUTTON

Shearson Lehman Brothers, at the time the nation's biggest investment firm, purchased E. F. Hutton, the tenth-largest investment firm, in December 1987. Actually, the demise of the 84-year-old Hutton organization had started several years before.

There were many indicators that the firm was not operating as it should. As one former Hutton officer put it, between 1983 and 1985, Robert Fomon, the chairman and chief executive officer, "lost control of the firm and no one ever regained it."

In 1985, Hutton's plea of guilty to 2000 counts of mail and wire fraud conducted between 1980 and 1982 brought extensive criticism from the press and Congress. The firm had intentionally overdrawn enormous sums from many of its bank accounts for a day or two to gain interest-free cash. Hutton agreed, as part of its guilty plea, to pay a $2 million fine and $750,000 in legal costs to the government and to reimburse $8 million to the banks that had been victimized.

Lack of control was also evident in the way the firm was managed by Robert Fomon, who wielded almost absolute power over the organization for 16 years. Fomon apparently hired and promoted whomever he wanted, including close friends. He personally reviewed the salaries and bonuses of over 1000 employees, disdained organizational budgets and planning, had affairs with a number of Hutton employees, and put his girlfriends on the payroll. To make matters worse, Hutton was hiring women from various escort services to be present at parties

Fomon attended and then was charging the expenses under the category of temporary clerical and secretarial help.

Money was also being squandered in various other areas. One officer charged $900,000 in travel and entertainment expenses in 1986, a year in which the firm was losing money. During the same general period, Hutton spent $30 million sending its best-paid brokers and their wives on all-expenses-paid trips. Perhaps the most flagrant unnecessary expenditure of funds was the huge cost of moving the firm's headquarters from downtown Manhattan to expensive midtown facilities when the firm was not doing well financially.

There were some bright spots in Hutton's otherwise steady decline. Robert Rittereiser, hired as the chief operating officer, was able to set up some legal and financial controls. Unfortunately, the controls were too few and too late to turn the firm around.

Hutton's stock began to drop and fell precipitously from $35 to $15 a share during the October 1987 stock market crash. The decline made Hutton an attractive target for Shearson Lehman Brothers, a rival investment firm largely owned by American Express. Shearson Lehman acquired Hutton for $960 million, absorbed the Hutton assets, changed its name to Shearson Lehman Hutton Holdings, Inc., and set about trying to rein in the out-of-control organization. Unfortunately, successfully combining the two companies into one investment firm was more difficult than anticipated. Internal strife was a problem, and as individual investors shunned the market, Shearson Lehman Hutton had too many stockbrokers and too few customers. By 1990, American

Express was forced to invest roughly $1.35 billion in the firm, which had dropped the Hutton name. In addition, it purchased the remaining 30 percent of the shares owned by the public to protect Shearson Lehman's credit rating and quell rumors of the investment firm's possible collapse. In the face of the firm's chronic losses and continuing insistence on paying lavish bonuses to senior people despite poor performance, in 1993 American Express sold the Shearson brokerage piece to Primerica Corp. Primerica merged Shearson with its own Smith, Barney brokerage firm. The following year, American Express sold the Lehman Brothers investment banking and brokerage piece to Lehman senior management in a leveraged buyout. Delighted with their independence, Lehman Brothers employees are working to pay off their substantial leveraged buyout debt. It remains to be seen whether Lehman can gain control over its high costs and forge a strategy that will allow it to survive independently.[53]

QUESTIONS FOR CONCLUDING CASE 1

1 Discuss the controls employed by Hutton from 1982 to 1987.
2 Evaluate Fomon's actions in terms of goal incongruence and the effects on organizational control.
3 Assume that you accepted the position of controller at Hutton prior to its demise. In an agreement with the firm, you were assured that your recommendations would be implemented. What would you have done to establish a control system? What would you do to establish controls now?

CONCLUDING CASE 2

LEGO BRICKS ARE A LESSON IN CONTROL

Those brightly colored LEGO bricks found in children's toy chests throughout the world are the product of a family-owned business based in Billund, Denmark. The Christiansen family has been making the plastic bricks using the stud-tube clutching principle since 1949.

The bricks form the basis of the "LEGO System of Play," a collection of related offerings that now exceeds 1300 different elements. New products do not replace previous ones but rather enhance them. Thus the earliest LEGO bricks are the basic components used with more recent offerings, such as electric motors, flashing lights, and parts that can be computer-controlled with LEGO software.

As a result, LEGO products can be found in 7 out of 10 homes in the United States and 8 out of 10 homes in northern Europe. According to one estimate, more than 300 million people throughout the world have played with LEGOs, which are sold in more than 120 countries. Two of the eight-stud bricks can be assembled 24 ways, while six bricks assemble into 102,981,500 combinations. One statistician calculates that children worldwide log about 5 billion hours per year playing with LEGOs.

The currently produced LEGO bricks snap on not only to one another but also to bricks bought by customers in previous years. Furthermore, the colors match despite the fact that the bricks and related products are made in five plants located in Denmark, Switzerland, the United States, Brazil, and South Korea.

For the most part, LEGO bricks are made from high-quality, nontoxic ABS plastic. ABS is used because the substance does not wear out and the colors do not fade. Precolored ABS granules are shaped into bricks in injection machines that operate under high temperature and pressure. The process creates bricks with a precision measured to five one-thousandths of a millimeter. Random samplings of materials ensure that the completed bricks will be the proper colors. Samples are also taken to ensure that the bricks fit together properly. The molds used in production are made in Switzerland and Germany to maintain consistency in all five factories. Once the LEGOs are packaged, the boxes are weighed to verify that all the parts have been included.

At the U.S. LEGO plant in Enfield, Connecticut, a recent expansion has made it possible for each of the 60 injection machines to make any of the six colors of bricks. A complex network of vacuum pipes enables an operator to hook into the proper color. This arrangement reduces materials inventory because it is no longer necessary to stack raw materials for each color at each machine. It also minimizes changeover time in switching from making one color to making another. Extreme care has been taken to ensure that the system does not allow different-color ABS granules to enter a pipe. "One wrong pellet can ruin an entire lot," says Mark Chevrier, director of manufacturing engineering. In addition to producing bricks, the Enfield plant also makes a number of specialty items, including the LEGO people that populate the towns and other items constructed with the bricks.

Over the years, LEGO has pursued a strategy of continuously developing a single product idea. The original bricks and subsequent related items all fit the company's standards for the ultimate toy: one that offers unlimited playing possibilities for both girls and boys; incorporates safety and quality; provides stimulation; and is harmonious, imaginative, creative, always topical, and able to be used year-round. One LEGO designer argues that everything that exists in the world can be duplicated with LEGOs, including Betsy Ross, a checkered cab, the U.S. Capitol, and a skateboarding hippo.

More recently, though, the company has been expanding beyond toys, particularly through licensing other companies to manufacture items associated with the LEGO name. For example, there is a line of Kids' Wear made by the Danish clothing maker Kabooki. U.S. and U.K. companies have obtained licenses to publish Duplo Playbooks associated with the LEGO Duplo line of preschool blocks. There are also plans for LEGO theme watches. People come from all over the world to visit the Legoland park located in Billund, Denmark. Now LEGO has a new Legoland theme park down the road from the Queen's castle in Windsor, England, and also is building one near San Diego, California.[54]

QUESTIONS FOR CONCLUDING CASE 2

1. Assess the extent to which LEGO uses the control process to regulate organizational activities.
2. Use the four conditions for control to identify what you believe should be controlled at LEGO.
3. Identify uses of feedforward, concurrent, and feedback control at LEGO.

CHAPTER SEVENTEEN

TQM AND MANAGERIAL CONTROL METHODS

CHAPTER OUTLINE

Major Control Systems
Managerial Level
Timing Emphasis

Total Quality Management
Strategic Implications of Quality
TQM Philosophy
TQM Change Principles
TQM Intervention Techniques
TQM: Does It Work?

Financial Control
Financial Statements
Ratio Analysis
Comparative Financial Analysis

Budgetary Control
Responsibility Centers
Types of Budgets
Impacts of the Budgeting Process

Inventory Control
Significance of Inventory
Costs of Inventory
Economic Order Quantity
Just-in-Time Inventory Control

LEARNING OBJECTIVES

After studying this chapter, you should be able to:

■ Explain how major control systems differ according to managerial level and timing.

■ Explain strategic implications of quality, TQM philosophy, TQM change principles, and TQM intervention techniques.

■ Describe the financial statements, ratio analyses, comparative analyses, and financial audits used in financial control.

■ Distinguish among the different types of responsibility centers and between two major types of budgets.

■ Describe the eight dimensions of quality and discuss their implications for competing on quality.

■ Discuss the significance of inventory and the related costs.

■ Explain the economic order quantity and just-in-time approaches to inventory control.

GAINING THE EDGE

USAA PLACES A PREMIUM ON HIGH-QUALITY SERVICE

When it comes to stellar service, few organizations can equal the United Services Automobile Association (USAA). The San Antonio–based company is the fifth-largest insurer of privately owned automobiles and homes in the United States and is increasingly making inroads in the financial services area. Member-owned USAA has 2.7 million customers, most of whom are active or retired military officers and their dependents. Almost 95 percent of active-duty military officers are USAA members. By law, the company's financial services must be offered to the general public.

USAA was started in 1922 by Army officers who experienced difficulty obtaining auto insurance because they were perceived as poor risks. By the time Robert F. McDermott, a former pilot and retired Air Force brigadier general, took over as CEO in the late 1960s, the company had a good reputation for offering low-cost insurance and paying claims. Service, however, was abysmal—particularly in the promptness category. There was paper everywhere, including files, correspondence, and claims relating to the 650,000 members at the time. In fact, so much paperwork was habitually lost that the company typically had between 200 and 300 college students on the payroll who worked each night searching the desks of the 3000 employees for missing files.

To help improve service, McDermott quickly steered the company toward the use of new technology. A new computer system soon slashed the time required to process a new automobile policy from 13 days to 3. Since then, USAA has pioneered the use of imaging systems that store documents on optical disks. In the property and casualty division, for example, the system scans 40,000 pages of mail per day. As a result, a USAA representative can instantly call up correspondence and other parts of a customer's file on a computer screen. Because the company depends on direct mail and advertising instead of outside agents, almost 90 percent of its business is conducted by telephone. USAA provides an 800 number for customers.

McDermott also broke down barriers between departments and decentralized operations. Policy writing and service, two main divisions that barely communicated with each other, were reorganized into five groups. Each group served one-fifth of the members. Once the groups began to compete with each other in offering the best service, USAA was never the same again.

The company's strategy for high-quality service includes the process of empowering employees. One aspect of this process involves providing employees with increased knowledge. USAA has 75 classrooms, more than 200 full-time instructors, and a training and education budget of $19 million. Service representatives receive at least 16 weeks of training before they begin answering customer telephone calls. That way, they are prepared to answer most questions, even those that involve less common situations. A strong tuition reimbursement program, as well as night college classes offered on the premises, encourages employees to obtain degrees and work toward various certifications in the insurance industry. To encourage computer literacy, USAA has launched a program that subsidizes employees' purchases of home computers. Another aspect of the empowering process entails giving service representatives considerable authority so that they can handle situations without checking with supervisors.

The Family of Measures (FOM) program is used to keep the work force focused on continual improvement of service quality. For example, service rep-

Service representatives are key members of the United States Automobile Association, since almost 90 percent of the insurance company's business is conducted by telephone. The representatives are well-trained in the use of computer technology, and the quality of their phone calls is periodically monitored and scored. At the same time the USAA empowers its representatives by allowing them to handle many situations without consulting their superiors.

resentatives are scored on the quality of phone calls. The scoring is done by auditors who periodically monitor the telephone lines. The representatives are also rated on the number of transactions per hour. "What we're trying to have is a teaching and coaching tool. We're not looking to find fault," says Gerald L. Gass, director of quality measurement and improvement. An FOM for each work unit is developed by a representative group of employees who determine which aspects of the job are most important to track. They ask questions such as "Is the activity under our control? Does it involve some form of data that we can collect? Can we easily analyze the results?" The group then votes on the measures to be used and passes the recommendations to managers, who may make some adjustments before implementing the measures. In addition, an independent team of 14 organizational experts continually evaluates the company, one division at a time, with an eye to areas where innovations and continual improvements can be made.

To help retain its well-trained work force, USAA typically promotes from within. Every year, about 45 percent of employees are promoted and about 50 percent change jobs within the company. The movement broadens employee experience, encourages flexibility, fosters innovation, and enriches jobs. To help employees meet child-care and other personal needs, USAA has an arrangement whereby 70 percent of the work force works a 38-hour, 4-day workweek. The company is located on a 286-acre campus that offers subsidized cafeterias and a health club. The turnover rate of about 7 percent is half the industry average.

USAA has increased the assets that it owns and manages from $200 million when McDermott took over to more than $30 billion when he retired in 1993. USAA profits are among the highest in the insurance industry. But new CEO Robert Herres echoes the McDermott legacy, "service comes first," as USAA expands into home banking.[1]   ■■■

When McDermott became CEO, he quickly recognized that a key element in the future success of USAA would be the ability to offer excellent service. As one part of his effort, he instituted a variety of controls, particularly in the area of quality control, to ensure that excellent service would be achieved. His successor continues that focus on quality service. In the previous chapter, we exam-

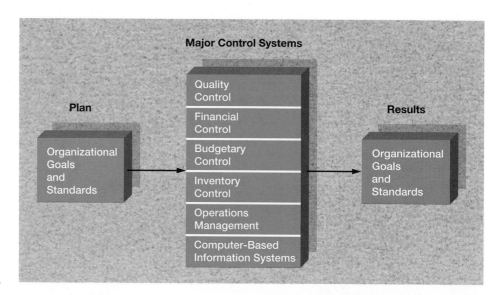

Major Control Systems

Plan

Organizational Goals and Standards

Quality Control

Financial Control

Budgetary Control

Inventory Control

Operations Management

Computer-Based Information Systems

Results

Organizational Goals and Standards

Figure 17-1 *Major organizational control systems.*

ined the basic concepts associated with controls, such as the need for controls, the control process itself, and the types of controls available to managers. In this chapter, we build on those ideas by focusing on specific methods that managers use to maintain control in organizations. Although many control systems must be custom-designed, most organizations share a common need for certain systems. Accordingly, we first describe the general nature of six major control systems that organizations are apt to require to some degree. Throughout the remainder of the chapter, we explore four of these systems in greater depth and will be highlighting one of these, total quality management, because of its critical importance to gaining competitive advantage. Two other major control systems are covered in greater detail in subsequent chapters.

■ MAJOR CONTROL SYSTEMS

If you decided to investigate the major control systems in prominent business organizations such as IBM, Coca-Cola, or American Express, you would likely find the systems shown in Figure 17-1.[2] Since the purpose of control systems is to increase the probability of meeting organizational goals and standards, managers use these systems to boost their prospects for success. For example, total quality management provides a means of increasing the quality of products and services, a critical competitive issue. Financial control systems help managers keep track of important overall money matters, such as whether the organization is making a profit or taking on too much debt. Budgetary control systems assist managers by giving them quantitative tools for monitoring how closely the revenues and costs of various organizational activities match what has been planned. Inventory control systems offer a way to ensure that necessary inputs are available when needed and that the costs involved are kept at a minimum. Operations management involves controlling the processes associated with actually producing a product or service. Finally, computer-based information systems are used to develop sophisticated systems geared toward maintaining better control over information and related functions. We discuss operations management and computer-based information systems in Chapters 18 and 19, respectively. (Management by objectives, which can also be used as a control system, is described in Chapter 6.)

For the remainder of this chapter, we concentrate on quality, financial, budgetary, and inventory control systems. Before considering each one individually, we explore how these systems differ in terms of the level of management to which they are mainly oriented and their timing emphasis.

Managerial Level

Control systems tend to differ somewhat in the degree to which they are used by different managerial levels (see Figure 17-2). For example, total quality management is an important tool used throughout the organization, but because it must be incorporated into the strategic levels of the organization to be effective, we place it at the top level. However, for total quality management to operate properly, all levels of the organization need to be heavily involved. Financial control systems are a primary control mechanism used by top-level management because such systems relate mainly to the overall financial health of the organization. However, middle managers also have an interest in monitoring financial matters as they affect their particular specialized area. On the other hand, middle- and lower-level managers are the main users of budgetary controls, since it is typically their job to run organizational activities so that various budgets are met. Still, top management may monitor overall budget performance, as well as major deviations from what is expected. Finally, inventory control rests largely with lower-level and middle managers, although upper management may use some indexes to evaluate costs.

Timing Emphasis

Major control systems also lean toward different emphases on timing. Timing relates to the degree to which controls take place before (feedforward), during (concurrent), or after (feedback) the transformation process that produces a product or service (see Chapter 16). Financial control systems tend to constitute feedback control because the data are usually evaluated at the end of particular reporting periods. Although it is too late at that point to make changes that will affect the particular data, the information is useful in planning changes that can affect future organizational performance and results. As computer-based information systems are increasingly able to provide ongoing financial data, managers may be able to use information on a more concurrent basis. In contrast to financial control usage, budgetary control often has more of a concurrent focus, since it can be used to regulate ongoing activities so that

Figure 17-2 *Major control systems by managerial level and timing.*

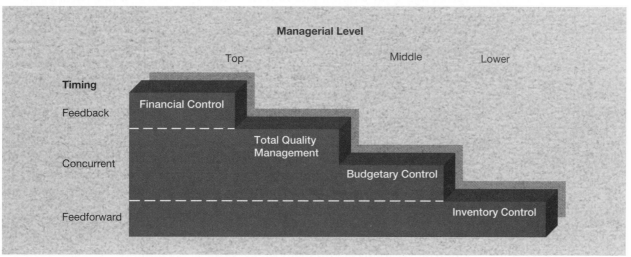

planned budget levels are met. For example, budgets may be checked during expenditure decisions. To the degree that budgets are considered only at the end of particular periods, budgetary control moves closer to being a form of feedback control. Although total quality management applies to all parts of the transformation process, it is heavily used in the mode of concurrent control, since checks are often made during the actual production or service process to be sure that quality standards are being met. If checks are not made until after production, when materials must be scrapped or rejected if they are faulty, quality control fits into the feedback category. Finally, inventory control is mainly oriented toward feedforward control, because it is geared to ensuring that materials and products will be available when needed. In the remaining sections of this chapter, we consider these major control systems in greater detail.

■ TOTAL QUALITY MANAGEMENT

Total quality management (TQM) in some form is increasingly practiced by organizations in the United States and throughout the world.[3] One major impetus toward concern for quality has been fierce global competition from Japan-based companies offering products and services of superior quality, often at relatively low prices. There are many different views of total quality management (and in some cases, names other than TQM are used). For the purposes of our discussion, we define **total quality management (TQM)** as a management system that is an integral part of an organization's strategy and is aimed at continually improving product and service quality so as to achieve high levels of customer satisfaction and build strong customer loyalty.[4]

Although quality itself has been defined in many ways, the American Society for Quality Control offers this standard definition: **Quality** is the totality of features and characteristics of a product or service that bear on its ability to satisfy stated or implied needs.[5] This definition recognizes that quality can involve every aspect of a product or service, that quality affects the ability of a product or service to satisfy needs, and that customer needs for quality may not always be explicitly stated.

The Malcolm Baldrige National Quality award created by Congress is the most prestigious recognition of quality in the United States. The award is given annually to U.S. companies in manufacturing, service, and small-business categories that represent the best in quality management. (For one such company, see the Valuing Quality box.) In examining the issue of quality and the need for quality control, we explore the strategic implications of quality, probe major assumptions underlying the philosophy behind TQM, examine TQM change principles and intervention techniques, and consider some issues related to the actual practice of TQM.

Strategic Implications of Quality

Quality expert David A. Garvin argues that quality can be used in a strategic way to compete effectively.[6] Choosing an appropriate quality strategy, though, depends on thoroughly understanding the important dimensions of quality. Therefore, we explore these dimensions before considering the issue of how to compete through quality.

EIGHT DIMENSIONS From a strategic point of view, there are eight dimensions of quality that are important.

Performance involves a product's primary operating characteristics. For an

Total quality management (TQM) A management system that is an integral part of an organization's strategy and is aimed at continually improving product and service quality so as to achieve high levels of customer satisfaction and build strong customer loyalty

Quality The totality of features and characteristics of a product or service that bear on its ability to satisfy stated or implied needs

VALUING QUALITY

Federal Express Absolutely Positively Controls Quality

When Federal Express won the Malcolm Baldrige National Quality award in 1990, it was the first service company to do so. Since its inception in 1973, FedEx has become the domestic leader in guaranteed overnight delivery, primarily on the basis of its philosophy, "People, Service, and Profit." FedEx continues to expand its vision of quality. Efforts in this direction include refining its measure of customer satisfaction—a critical element in its reputation for excellent service. FedEx's performance is measured each day on 12 service quality indicators, known as SQIs. The SQIs encompass service missteps and are weighted according to their likelihood of resulting in customer dissatisfaction. For example, a late delivery on the right day is given 1 point, while a lost package or a damaged package each receives 10 points.

The SQIs are measured by a variety of information systems and human analysis. The computerized tracking system, COSMOS, which collects package data worldwide on a daily basis, measures the indexes "Right Day Late" and "Wrong Day Late." Such measurement is possible because as packages change hands in the delivery process, each package's bar code is scanned. Couriers have handheld computers, called SuperTrackers, which they use to scan packages and record related information. Even if a package is only a minute late, COSMOS will record a late delivery point. Each day the SQI score is televised to every Federal Express location. The rating helps keep employees focused on the goal of 100 percent customer satisfaction. Quality action teams throughout FedEx work to solve the causes of service problems. They also work to invent innovative ways to improve service still further so that packages "absolutely positively" arrive on time. For example, FedEx has recently launched interNetShip, an innovative interactive Web application that lets customers use the Internet to process and track their FedEx shipments.[7]

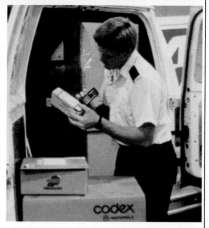

The SuperTracker, a hand-held computer, scans each Federal Express package at the point the package changes hands in the delivery process. This computerized tracking system, called COSMOS, helps Federal Express management control the quality of customer service. Each day the company analyzes service quality data worldwide and relays overall ratings to each Federal Express location.

---

automobile, performance would include acceleration, braking, handling, and fuel usage. In service industries, such as fast-food restaurants, airlines, or hotels, performance is apt to mean prompt service.[8]

Features are supplements to the basic functioning characteristics of the product or service. Examples include complimentary newspapers for hotel guests, extra options on autofocus cameras, or stereo CD players in automobiles.

Reliability addresses the probability of a product's not working properly or breaking down altogether within a specific period. Since a significant amount of usage is typically involved in assessing reliability, this quality dimension does not apply as readily to products and services that are used immediately.

Conformance refers to the degree to which a product's design or operating characteristics conform to preestablished standards. Typically, products and services are developed with some standards or specifications in mind. When the Michigan-based Van Dresser Corporation showed Toyota engineers a prototype part designed for use in the automaker's Kentucky plant, one Toyota engineer got "down on his hands and knees measuring the gap" between the automobile's steel door frame and the interior panel by Dresser. The engineer said, "Look, the gap is a millimeter too wide." Van Dresser retooled the mold that produced the panel.[9]

Durability is a measure of how much use a person gets from a product before it deteriorates or breaks down to such a point that replacement makes more sense than continual repair. For instance, durability for major home appliances varies widely, ranging from 5.8 to 18 years for washing machines and from 6 to 17 years for vacuum cleaners.[10]

Serviceability refers to the promptness, courtesy, proficiency, and ease of repair. For example, General Electric has an 800 number that customers can call when an appliance breaks down. For easy-to-fix items, customers can purchase parts that are mailed with repair directions.

Aesthetics refers to how a product looks, feels, sounds, tastes, or smells—all subjective issues highly dependent on personal judgment and preference.

Perceived quality refers to individuals' subjective assessments of product or service quality. Such assessments may be based on incomplete information, but often it is perceptions that count with customers.

COMPETING ON QUALITY While some dimensions of quality reinforce one another, others do not. For example, adding more features will often reduce reliability, while aesthetics sometimes interferes with durability. As a result, organizations do not usually attempt to compete on the basis of exceptionally high quality on all eight dimensions simultaneously.

In fact, most companies choose a quality niche. Not surprisingly, it is critical to select a quality niche that customers consider important. After deregulation, AT&T assumed that customers equated expensive features with quality in telephones, but durability and reliability proved to be more important.[11] Of course, another crucial issue is actually delivering the intended level of quality, once it has been decided upon.

TQM Philosophy

Although Japanese companies are generally credited with pioneering total quality management, the roots of the concept actually originated in the United States. American quality management expert W. Edwards Deming developed ideas on statistical methods for improving quality, but he took his concepts to Japan in the late 1940s after they were ignored in the United States. He also promoted the concept of involving employees and various units throughout the organization in the quality effort, and he set forth 14 management points that portray his overall philosophy. For Deming's 14 points, see the Management Skills for the Twenty-First Century discussion, "Deming's 14 Points on How to Improve Quality."

Deming's ideas were embraced by Japanese companies, eager to rebuild after World War II. In fact, his contributions were so well appreciated that the Japanese established the Deming prize, a coveted annual award for excellence in quality management. In the 1950s, another American quality expert, J. M. Juran, also helped Japanese companies develop their total quality management efforts. Japanese expert Kaoru Ishikawa also is considered to be one of the primary authorities of the TQM movement.[12]

Deming, Juran, and Ishikawa share a common view that an organization's primary purpose is to remain in business so that it can aid community stability, offer useful products and services that meet customer needs, and foster the work satisfaction and growth of organizational members. Although there are differences on a number of points, examining the writings of these three authorities does provide a reasonable basis for identifying the fundamental assumptions underlying the TQM philosophy.[13]

MANAGEMENT SKILLS FOR THE TWENTY-FIRST CENTURY

Deming's 14 Points on How to Improve Quality

In the course of his work, W. Edwards Deming developed 14 management points that summarize what he believes managers, especially at the upper levels, must do to produce high-quality products:

1 Create constancy of purpose toward improvement of product and service, with the aim to become competitive and to stay in business, and to provide jobs.
2 Adopt the new philosophy. We are in a new economic age. Western management must awaken to the challenge, must learn their responsibilities, and must take on leadership for change.
3 Cease dependence on inspection to achieve quality. Eliminate the need for inspection on a mass basis by building quality into the product in the first place.
4 End the practice of awarding business on the basis of price tag. Instead, minimize total cost. Move toward a single supplier for any one item on a long-term relationship of loyalty and trust.
5 Improve constantly and forever the systems of production and service, to improve quality and productivity, and thus constantly decrease costs.
6 Institute training on the job.
7 Institute leadership. The aim of supervision should be to help people and machines and gadgets to do a better job. Supervision of management is in need of overhaul as well as supervision of production workers.
8 Drive out fear so that everyone may work effectively for the company.
9 Break down barriers between departments. People in research, design, sales, and production must work as a team to foresee problems of production and use that may be encountered with the product or service.
10 Eliminate slogans, exhortations, and targets for the work force asking for zero defects and new levels of productivity. Such exhortations only create adversarial relationships, as the bulk of the causes of low quality and low productivity belong to the system and thus lie beyond the power of the work force.
11 a. Eliminate work standards (quotas) on the factory floor. Substitute leadership.
    b. Eliminate management by objectives. Eliminate management by numbers, numerical goals. Substitute leadership.
12 a. Remove barriers that rob the hourly worker of his right to pride of workmanship. The responsibility of supervisors must be changed from sheer numbers to quality.
    b. Remove barriers that rob people in management and in engineering of their right to pride of workmanship. This means, *inter alia,* abolishment of the annual merit rating and of management by objectives.
13 Institute a vigorous program of education and self-improvement.
14 Put everybody in the company to work to accomplish the transformation. The transformation is everybody's job.[14]

Quality is less costly than poor workmanship: A basic assumption of TQM is that the costs of poor quality (such as inspection, rework, high scrap rates, lost customers, and related factors) greatly exceed the costs of producing high-quality products and services (costs such as training, proper equipment and tools, improving processes, and related factors). According to one estimate, a typical U.S. factory that has not embraced TQM spends between 20 and 25 percent of its operating budget on finding and fixing mistakes.[15]

Employees will naturally try to improve quality as long as they have appropriate support: A second assumption of TQM is that employees will willingly make quality improvements as long as they are given the tools and training necessary to do so. A related prerequisite is that management needs to be willing to listen to the ideas of employees.

Serious quality improvement requires cross-functional efforts: A third assumption of TQM is that most quality problems do not fit neatly within functional areas. For example, to produce high-quality products efficiently, design specialists need to confer closely with manufacturing specialists during the design phase itself.

Quality improvement requires the strong commitment of top management: The reasoning behind this fourth assumption of TQM is that upper-level managers ultimately are responsible for the organizational systems within which products and services are designed and produced. Employees' ability to perform high-quality work, therefore, is a direct function of the quality of the systems that managers create.

TQM Change Principles

According to the work of three major TQM authorities, there are four major TQM change principles that should guide any organizational interventions aimed at quality improvement. These principles are as follows:[16]

1 **Focus on work processes.** The quality of products and services ultimately traces back to the processes that produce them. Therefore, it is necessary not only to specify the need for higher quality, but also to train and coach employees to analyze work processes so that they can make improvements in them.

2 **Analyze and understand variability.** The primary cause of quality problems, in the TQM view, can be traced to variances in processes or outcomes. For example, because of limitations in printing technology, a small amount of variance in photo reproduction in a book, such as this one, is expected (also the quality of the photos being reproduced is a factor). However, when variances are in unacceptable ranges, a search must be made for causes (for example, improperly calibrated printing presses, inadequately trained press operators, or paper problems). Only when the root causes for unwanted variability in products or services have been identified, can employees take steps to make improvements leading to better quality.

3 **Manage by fact.** TQM experts place heavy emphasis on systematically collecting data at every point in the problem-solving cycle. Data are collected to determine the high-priority problems, to trace their causes, and to choose and analyze the impact of solutions. Although the three TQM authorities vary in the exact analytical tools that they emphasize, they all rely on collecting data, using statistics, and experimenting with solutions before fully implementing them.

4 **Emphasize continuous learning and improvement.** The idea here is that it is always possible to improve and such improvements are vital to the long-run health of the organization. A focus on continuous improvement helps to ensure that employees never stop learning and striving to do better.

TQM Intervention Techniques

In putting the change principles into action, various TQM advocates use many different intervention techniques. Some of the most common are as follows:

Cost of quality analysis is used to evaluate the potential cost savings associated with doing the work right the first time. This analysis involves quantifying the costs associated with maintaining quality at the desired level, such as cost of preventing quality problems, against the costs of poor quality. These latter costs include appraisal costs (such as having to conduct constant inspections), internal failure costs (such as scrap and rework costs), and external failure costs (such as costs of customer complaints and returns). Cost of quality analysis helps to earmark areas where improving quality would lead to significant savings.[17]

Quality improvement teams, another widely used TQM intervention technique, are small groups of employees who work on solving specific problems

Quality improvement teams Small groups of employees who work on solving specific problems related to quality and productivity, often with stated targets for improvement

related to quality and productivity, often with stated targets for improvement. Typically, teams consist of individuals who are responsible for the work areas that are the target of quality improvement efforts. Such teams are frequently cross-functional. Problems to be addressed may be identified by management as well as workers, and the groups often set specific improvement goals and compete with one another. A Conference Board survey showed that almost all manufacturing firms involved in TQM and about 90 percent of service firms with TQM use such teams.[18] Quality improvement teams (sometimes other names are used) are proving to be highly successful at tracking down the causes of poor quality and productivity, as well as taking remedial action. For example, Monsanto formed a quality improvement team when Ford Motor reported trouble with Saflex, a Monsanto material used to make laminated windshields. The material's dimensions were changing by the time the Saflex was delivered to Ford. Within 2 months, the quality improvement team traced the trouble to packaging, designed a new prototype, tested it, and implemented a new packaging process that eliminated Ford's complaints.[19]

Training is also an important intervention technique used in implementing TQM. This is not surprising given the philosophy of TQM, which emphasizes the need for workers to have the proper training and tools to produce at high quality levels and make continuous improvements. A Conference Board survey indicates that some 92 percent of manufacturing firms and 75 percent of service companies implementing TQM make training available. Nearly all senior and middle managers receive training. About 80 percent of first-line supervisors and about 50 percent of nonmanagerial employees also are trained.[20] One short survey of Fortune 100 firms found the most common training content (in descending order of use) to be personal interaction skills, team building, running meetings, statistical process control (explained below), supplier qualification training, and benchmarking.[21]

Benchmarking is the process of identifying the best practices and approaches by comparing productivity in specific areas within one's own company with the productivity of other organizations both within and outside the industry.[22] Benchmarking became a commonly used TQM technique only recently as companies with major quality management efforts adopted the approach. Such companies include AT&T, Du Pont, Ford Motor, IBM, Eastman Kodak, Milliken, and Motorola. Xerox is generally credited with the first use of benchmarking by a U.S. company. In 1979, a team of Xerox line managers went to Japan to study the productivity of Japanese photocopy manufacturers. The manufacturers had been selling midsize copiers in the United States for $9600 each, which was substantially less than Xerox's production costs. At first, Xerox management had assumed that the Japanese companies were "dumping"—that is, selling the machines for substantially less than cost to undermine Xerox's market position. However, the benchmark team made the shocking discovery that the Japanese companies could build higher-quality machines for substantially less than Xerox. (Much of the information was provided by Xerox's own joint venture, Fuji-Xerox, which knew the competition well.) The benchmark study marked the beginning of Xerox's recovery and dedication to TQM. Xerox then began to benchmark other companies, even those outside its industry that had expertise which could be of help. For example, a Xerox team studied L. L. Bean, the venerable catalog operation, to learn more about fulfilling orders quickly and accurately. Other companies are now following suit in pursuing benchmarking as a means of enhancing quality and productivity.[23]

Systematic gathering of customer data is another important TQM intervention technique. Since TQM efforts ultimately are focused on satisfying customers and building loyalty, gaining insight into customer needs and satisfaction levels is critical. A variety of approaches can be used ranging from holding dis-

Benchmarking The process of identifying the best practices and approaches by comparing productivity in specific areas within one's own company with the productivity of other organizations both within the outside the industry

Elo TouchSystem's touch-sensitive computer screens are used widely in such products as automatic teller machines. But the company was losing money because of a 25 percent rejection rate in the production line. Tinkering with the production process did not solve the problems, but calling in the statisticians did. Using an experimental method that altered several variables at once, the statisticians discovered that the company had to change many things, not one. The result? A defect rate of less than 1 percent and soaring company profits.

cussions and focus groups to conducting surveys and monitoring complaints.[24] For example, when Massachusetts-based Foxboro Company, a global manufacturer of instrumentation and control systems was losing $20 million per year, the company surveyed customers and learned that they wanted the product quality to be higher and variability to be lower. They also wanted better adherence to promised delivery dates. After solving these problems and discussing customer needs further, Foxboro finally realized that what its customers really want is help from Foxboro to develop products that would enable customers to beat their competitors. Working on that realization has led Foxboro to record profits.[25] A recent Conference Board survey of TQM companies found that 93 percent expected their customers to have higher expectations of them in the next 3 years.[26]

Collaboration with suppliers is also an important intervention of TQM. The potential advantages of developing a partnership with one's suppliers were originally demonstrated by Japanese manufacturers, particularly in the auto industry. One major advantage is improvements in product development. By involving suppliers, it is often possible to design superior products and services. Other major advantages include improved financial results and better productivity based on more reliable supplies. For example, Metropolitan Life Insurance Company (MetLife) has piloted a new supplier partnership program in its personal life insurance division. By designating certain paramedic vendors as partners, MetLife has been able to set up a monitoring system that provides feedback on the vendors' performance. Vendor employees visit MetLife customers who are purchasing life insurance to obtain medical information and materials for further tests. Initial results showed that the vendors have been taking the feedback seriously and are striving to improve.[27]

Statistical process control A statistical technique that uses periodic random samples taken during actual production to determine whether acceptable quality levels are being met or production should be stopped for remedial action

Statistical process control is a statistical technique that uses periodic random samples taken during actual production to determine whether acceptable quality levels are being met or production should be stopped for remedial action. A commonly used TQM intervention technique, it assesses quality during production so that problems can be resolved before materials are completed. Since the emphasis is on prevention of poor-quality output during the actual process, this approach represents concurrent control. Because most production processes produce some variations, statistical process control uses statistical tests to determine when variations fall outside a narrow range around the acceptable quality level. Variations outside the range signal systematic fluctuations attributable to some malfunction in the production process.

TQM: Does It Work?

It is more difficult than might be expected to unequivocally answer the question, "Does TQM work?" A large number of case studies and testimonials suggest that TQM can lead to significant benefits. This has been the case at Dow Chemical USA, which credits its 5-year quality improvement effort with saving $100 million in operating costs.[28] Similarly, total quality efforts have produced a 60 percent reduction in scrap and rework at Harley-Davidson, a 69 percent cutback in customer returns at Westinghouse's semiconductor division, and savings of more than $52 million in 60 days at AT&T (by eliminating errors in service documents).[29] A total quality effort has also paid off handsomely for Spectrum Control, Inc. (see the Case in Point discussion).

UPGRADING QUALITY AT SPECTRUM CONTROL, INC.   CASE IN POINT

When top management at Spectrum Control, Inc., announced with fanfare a new companywide commitment to quality, Ed Leofsky, a process engineer at the company's Fairview, Pennsylvania, electromagnetic division, knew it was time to act. Each week, Leofsky's division solders terminals to about 75,000 tubular ceramic capacitors that are manufactured at Spectrum's material science division in nearby Saegertown. The capacitors are then used in one of the company's primary products, electronic filters.

Unfortunately, for the previous 12 years Leofsky had faced a chronic problem: for unknown reasons, the solder often would not stick. When that happened, all sorts of unusual steps had to be taken, such as inspecting each soldering point with a microscope. Leofsky's efforts to get a vice president at Saegertown interested in solving the problem got nowhere. Just as the quality program was being announced, the soldering problem grew worse. The reject rate jumped from 3 to 32 percent. Leofsky wrote a letter to the vice president at Saegertown, with copies to everyone he could think of who could help.

The letter got people's attention, including concern from top management. The company's leaders had become seriously concerned about quality because of two events: a Japanese company had purchased a major competitor, and Spectrum's principal customers, such as Hewlett-Packard and IBM, had announced that they were adopting a zero-defects approach. In addition, Spectrum's sales and marketing personnel were complaining that the company was not very good at meeting delivery dates. Recognizing that these problems were related to the overall lack of a quality orientation, senior management began reviewing quality programs, attending training sessions, and adapting materials to fit the Spectrum situation. Next, all employees were trained in how to work toward error-free performance.

Leofsky's letter was the first major test of the quality commitment. Laboratory tests subsequently showed that surface contaminants were the problem, but finding the sources was tough. Just as the quality improvement team assigned to the problem would identify one contaminant and eliminate it, another would appear. The problem was ultimately solved, but resolving it required capital, people, and time resources that would have been unthinkable in the past. Soon similar improvements were taking place elsewhere in the company. As a result, overall sales returns and related allowances on Spectrum products plummeted 75 percent, saving more than $767,000 annually. Spectrum's growing reputation for quality recently helped the company gain new Canadian business when several of a competitor's products failed to meet the quality standard set by the Canadian government.[30] ■■■

Many times, though, as TQM is implemented, other changes are made that make it difficult to separate out the effects attributable strictly to TQM. For example, companies that initiate TQM often also move to increase employee involvement, with its emphasis on greater employee participation in decisions and the movement of decisions to the lowest level in the organization.[31] TQM companies frequently make greater use of teams (see Chapter 15) than they did previously, making it difficult to assess the effects attributable to TQM versus the impact of the implementation of teams.

One recent study indicates that some companies have expended considerable time and effort on TQM without major results. In fact, in one notorious example, Texas-based Wallace Co., an oil equipment firm, won the Malcolm Baldrige National Quality Award and 2 years later filed for bankruptcy.[32]

One reason for poor results from TQM programs may be that organizations implementing total quality efforts sometimes attempt to do too much too quickly. According to the study just mentioned, it may be best to concentrate on a few changes that really make a difference and then build on the successes in these areas rather than initiate major changes on many fronts at once. Another reason for difficulties with TQM programs appears to stem from instances where total quality is introduced with fanfare in an organization, but the philosophy, principles, and interventions are not taken seriously and/or implemented properly.[33] Finally, recent evidence suggests that companies sometimes err by making major efforts to improve quality in areas that are relatively unimportant to customers and that may unwittingly compromise quality in areas that are important. For example, Varian Associates, Inc., a Silicon Valley–based maker of vacuum systems for computer clean rooms, introduced a TQM program and succeeded in increasing on-time deliveries from 42 to 92 percent. Unfortunately, the company became so obsessed with maintaining production schedules that it often did not return customer phone calls in a timely manner. The situation led to a loss of market share before Varian refocused its efforts.[34]

As discussed earlier in this chapter, quality is a strategic issue, and it is vital that quality improvement be focused in areas that ultimately translate to improvements in customer satisfaction and loyalty. Overall, it appears that TQM efforts can be highly successful when implemented properly and that TQM is an important managerial tool. Of course, quality is not the only issue: most companies use financial controls as well.

■ FINANCIAL CONTROL

Suppose that you are a top-level manager at a giant organization such as Coca-Cola or a smaller one like Health Management Associates, Inc., which operates hospitals in small cities. What types of financial controls could you use? In this section, we review some of the more common financial control techniques, including the use of financial statements, ratio analysis, and comparative financial analysis. We also consider how managers can avoid some of the major pitfalls associated with financial controls.

Financial Statements

A **financial statement** is a summary of a major aspect of an organization's financial status. The information contained in such statements is essential in maintaining financial control over organizations. Two basic types of financial statements that are typically used by business organizations are the balance sheet and the income statement.[35] Financial statements are typically prepared at the end of reporting periods, such as quarterly and annually, although the widespread availability of computers is facilitating more frequent preparation.

BALANCE SHEET A **balance sheet** is a financial statement that depicts an organization's assets and claims against those assets at a given point in time. A balance sheet for The Coca-Cola Company is shown in Table 17-1. You may find it helpful to think of a balance sheet as a financial "snapshot" that is made up of two main sections. The top half shows current assets, and the bottom half documents existing claims against assets.[36]

Assets, the resources that an organization controls, fall into two categories: current and fixed. *Current assets* consist of cash and other assets that are usually converted to cash or are used within 1 year. (Examples are marketable securities, such as U.S. Treasury bills or money market mutual funds that can be converted to cash within a relatively short period; accounts receivable, which are sales on credit for which payment has not yet been received; and inventory.) *Fixed assets* are assets that have a useful life that exceeds 1 year (such as property, buildings, and equipment). In the case of Coca-Cola, the balance sheet indicates that the company has $5.4 billion in current assets, $4.3 billion in investments and other assets, $4.3 billion in fixed assets (after depreciation), and $944 million in goodwill and other intangible assets, for total assets of $15 billion.

The bottom half of the balance sheet, devoted to claims, includes both liabilities and shareholders' equity. *Liabilities* are claims by nonowners against company assets (in other words, debts owed to nonowners, such as banks). Liabilities also fall into two categories: current and long-term. *Current liabilities* are accounts that are typically paid within 1 year (such as accounts payable—current bills the company must pay—and short-term loans). *Long-term liabilities* are debts usually paid over a period that exceeds 1 year (such as bonds). Coca-Cola has $7.3 billion in current liabilities, $1.1 billion in long-term debt, $966 million in other liabilities, and $194 million associated with deferred income taxes, for a total of $9.6 billion in liabilities.

Shareholders' equity represents claims by owners against the assets. As you might expect, shareholders' equity is equal to the company's assets minus liabilities. Shareholders' equity is, in essence, the organization's net worth. It is represented on the balance sheet by stock and retained earnings (funds accumulated from the profits of the organization). In the case of Coca-Cola, shareholders' equity is equal to $5.4 billion. Since shareholders' equity equals assets minus liabilities, by placing the assets ($15 billion) on the top and the liabilities and shareholders' equity ($9.6 billion plus $5.4 billion, for a total of $15 billion) on the bottom, the balance sheet "balances." By using a comparative balance sheet, which shows figures from one year to the next (as in Table 17-1), it is possible to track trends in the growth of assets, the state of liabilities, and current net worth.

INCOME STATEMENT The balance sheet focuses on the overall financial worth of the organization at a specific point in time. In contrast, an **income statement** is a financial statement that summarizes the financial results of company oper-

Financial statement A summary of a major aspect of an organization's financial status

Balance sheet A financial statement that depicts an organization's assets and claims against those assets at a given point in time

Income statement A financial statement that summarizes the financial results of company operations over a specified time period, such as a quarter or a year

TABLE 17-1 THE COCA-COLA COMPANY AND SUBSIDIARIES

Comparative Balance Sheet
December 31, 1994 and 1995
(in millions of dollars)

	1995	1994
ASSETS		
Current assets:		
Cash and cash equivalents	$ 1,167	$ 1,386
Marketable securities	148	145
Trade accounts receivable	1,695	1,470
Finance subsidiary receivable	55	55
Inventories	1,117	1,047
Paid expenses and other assets	1,268	1,102
Total current assets	5,450	5,205
Investments and other assets	4,311	3,928
Fixed assets:		
Land, buildings, and improvements	2,177	2,035
Machinery, equipment, and containers	4,480	4,122
Total fixed assets	6,657	6,157
Less: Accumulated depreciation	2,321	2,077
Net fixed assets	4,336	4,080
Goodwill and other intangible assets	944	660
Total assets	$15,041	$13,873
LIABILITIES AND SHAREHOLDERS' EQUITY		
Current liabilities:		
Accounts payable and accrued expenses	$ 2,894	$ 2,564
Loans and notes payable	2,371	2,048
Current maturity of long-term debt	552	35
Accrued taxes	1,531	1,530
Total current liabilities	7,348	6,177
Long-term debt	1,141	1,426
Other liabilities	966	855
Deferred income taxes	194	180
Total liabilities	9,649	8,638
Shareholders' equity:		
Common stock, $.25 par value	428	427
Capital surplus	1,291	1,173
Reinvested earnings	12,882	11,006
Unearned compensation related to outstanding restricted stock	(68)	(74)
Foreign currency translation adjustment	(424)	(272)
Unrealized gain on securities available for sale	82	48
	14,191	12,308
Less treasury stock, at cost	8,799	7,073
Total shareholders' equity	5,392	5,235
Total liabilities and shareholders' equity	$15,041	$13,873

Source: The Coca-Cola Company 1995 Annual Report.

ations over a specified time period, such as a quarter or a year. An income statement shows revenues and expenses. *Revenues* are the assets derived from selling goods and services. *Expenses* are the costs incurred in producing the revenue (such as cost of goods sold, operating expenses, interest expense, and taxes). The difference between revenues and expenses represents the profits or losses over a given period of time and is often referred to as the *bottom line*.

As with balance sheets, income statements for different periods of time are frequently compared. A comparative income statement for The Coca-Cola

TABLE 17-2 THE COCA-COLA COMPANY AND SUBSIDIARIES		
Consolidated Statement of Income December 31, 1994 and 1995 (in millions of dollars)		
	1995	**1994**
Net operating revenue	$18,018	$16,181
Cost of goods sold	6,940	6,168
Gross profit	11,078	10,013
Selling, administrative, and general expenses	6,986	6,297
Operating income	4,092	3,716
Interest income	245	181
Interest expense	272	199
Equity income	169	134
Other income (deductions)—net	20	(104)
Gain on issurance of stock by Coca-Cola Amatil	74	——
Income before taxes	4,328	3,728
Income taxes	1,342	1,174
Net income	$ 2,986	$ 2,554

Source: The Coca-Cola Company 1995 Annual Report.

Company is shown in Table 17-2. The statement indicates that net income (revenues minus expenses) is about $3 billion, up from about $2.5 billion the previous year.

Ratio Analysis

In assessing the significance of various financial data, managers often engage in **ratio analysis,** the process of determining and evaluating financial ratios.[37] A *ratio* is an index that measures one variable relative to another, and it is usually expressed as a percentage or a rate. The notion of a ratio will become clearer as we consider specific examples below. Ratios are meaningful only when compared with other information. Since they are often compared with industry data, ratios help managers understand their company's performance relative to that of competitors and are often used to track performance over time. Four types of financial ratios are particularly important to managerial control: liquidity, asset management, debt management, and profitability. Formulas and end-of-the-year data for The Coca-Cola Company for the four types of ratios are shown in Table 17-3.

Ratio analysis The process of determining and evaluating financial ratios

LIQUIDITY RATIOS Liquidity ratios are financial ratios that measure the degree to which an organization's current assets are adequate to pay current liabilities (current debt obligations). A major liquidity ratio is the *current ratio,* which measures a company's ability to meet the claims of short-term creditors by using only current assets. The current ratio shown in Table 17-3 indicates that Coca-Cola has $.74 in current assets for every dollar in current liabilities. Coca-Cola's ratio is somewhat below the industry average of $.90 for large beverage companies, but given the company's long-term success, the ratio may signal a better use of funds to create shareholder value.

Liquidity ratios Financial ratios that measure the degree to which an organization's current assets are adequate to pay current liabilities (current debt obligations)

ASSET MANAGEMENT RATIOS Asset management ratios (sometimes called *activity ratios*) measure how effectively an organization manages its assets. One of the most used asset management ratios is inventory turnover.

Inventory turnover helps measure how well an organization manages its inventory. Low inventory turnover may point to either excess or obsolete inventory. High inventory turnover generally signals effective handling of inventory

Asset management ratios Financial ratios that measure how effectively an organization manages its assets

TABLE 17-3 RATIO ANALYSIS FOR THE COCA-COLA COMPANY AND SUBSIDIARIES

RATIO	FORMULA		CALCULATION		CURRENT YEAR	INDUSTRY AVERAGES
LIQUIDITY RATIOS						
Current ratio	$\dfrac{\text{Current assets}}{\text{Current liabilities}}$	=	$\dfrac{5,450}{7,348}$	=	.74x	.90x
ASSET MANAGEMENT RATIOS						
Inventory turnover	$\dfrac{\text{Cost of goods sold}}{\text{Inventory}}$	=	$\dfrac{6,940}{1,117}$	=	6.2	6.5
DEBT MANAGEMENT RATIOS						
Debt ratio	$\dfrac{\text{Total liabilities}}{\text{Total assets}}$	=	$\dfrac{9,649}{15,041}$	=	64.2%	82.2%
PROFITABILITY RATIOS						
Net profit margin	$\dfrac{\text{Net income}}{\text{Net sales*}}$	=	$\dfrac{2,986}{18,018}$	=	16.6%	7.7%
Return on investment	$\dfrac{\text{Net income}}{\text{Total assets}}$	=	$\dfrac{2,986}{15,041}$	=	19.8%	6.4%

Source: The Coca-Cola Company 1995 Annual Report and Leo Troy, *Almanac of Business & Industrial Financial Ratios,* Englewood Cliffs, Prentice Hall, 1995.

*Coca-Cola refers to net sales as net operating revenue in its financial statements.

relative to selling patterns, because less money is tied up in inventory that is waiting to be sold. It is, of course, possible to have an inventory turnover ratio that is too high. This would be the case if significant sales are lost because items ordered by potential customers are out of stock. With an industry average of 6.5, Coca-Cola's inventory turnover of 6.2 (shown in Table 17-3) is similar.

Debt management ratios Financial ratios that assess the extent to which an organization uses debt to finance investments, as well as the degree to which it is able to meet its long-term obligations

DEBT MANAGEMENT RATIOS Debt management ratios (often called *leverage ratios*) assess the extent to which an organization uses debt to finance investments, as well as the degree to which it is able to meet its long-term obligations. The more an organization uses debt to finance its needs, the more it must commit funds to pay interest and repay principal. As debts increase, so does the risk that the organization may not be able to pay its debts and may end up in bankruptcy. Thus one of the most important ratios is the *debt ratio,* which measures the percentage of total assets financed by debt (including current liabilities). The higher the percentage, the more the organization's assets are furnished by creditors rather than owners. Coca-Cola's debt ratio of 64.2 percent (shown in Table 17-3) indicates that creditors have supplied about 64 cents of every dollar in assets, whereas the industry average is 82.2 percent. Coca-Cola's lower-than-average debt ratio may be helpful if the organization needs to take on additional debt. Future creditors may be more willing to provide loans on favorable terms because of the lowered risk associated with the lower debt ratio.

Profitability ratios Financial ratios that help measure management's ability to control expenses and earn profits through the use of organizational resources

PROFITABILITY RATIOS Profitability ratios help measure management's ability to control expenses and earn profits through the use of organizational resources.[38] Two commonly used profitability ratios are net profit margin and return on investment.

The *net profit margin* indicates the percentage of each sales dollar that is left after deducting all expenses. In the case of The Coca-Cola Company, the net profit margin (shown in Table 17-3) is 16.6 percent. According to this figure, Coke earns about 16½ cents on every dollar of sales, substantially higher than the industry average of 7.7 percent. Comparatively speaking, Coca-Cola appears to be doing a good job in expanding sales or controlling expenses, or both.

The *return on investment,* or ROI (also called *return on assets*), measures the overall effectiveness of management in generating profits from its total investment in assets. The ROI for Coca-Cola (shown in Table 17-3) is 19.8 percent. Given the industry average of 6.4 percent, Coke's ROI is extremely favorable. The ratio suggests that the company is making good investment decisions and is expending considerable effort to ensure that the potential benefits to be derived from those investments are realized.

Top managers in most companies, including a rapidly growing firm, Health Management Associates, make strong use of financial controls (see the Case in Point discussion).

HMA PROSPERS WITH FINANCIAL CONTROLS

CASE IN POINT

Health Management Associates (HMA), Inc., considers itself "the Wal-Mart of the hospital business." Whereas Sam Walton opened Wal-Marts in small towns, Health Management CEO William Schoen buys hospitals in small cities, mainly in the southeastern United States. Usually, the hospitals are struggling financially. Schoen then uses centralized financial controls combined with decentralized operation of the hospitals to effectively manage 8000 employees operating 24 hospitals with a combined total of 2400 beds. HMA runs with a headquarters staff of 40 operating out of Naples, Florida.

HMA's financial results show that the company's average annual operating earnings growth over the past 5 years is 29 percent. Its most recent profit margin based on revenues of $438 million and net income of $47 million is 11 percent, 4 points above the industry average. Schoen developed his strategy of buying hospitals in small cities from his experience running F&M Schaefer Corp., a beer company. He says that small beer companies have to contend with two elephants, Anheuser-Busch and Philip Morris. Using his beer experience, Schoen buys hospitals only in locations where there is one dominant hospital, giving HMA somewhat of a monopoly for the area.

By engaging in careful cost cutting, HMA can usually get a money-losing hospital to break even in 90 to 120 days. Within 3 years, Schoen has the hospital earning HMA's average return on equity of 21 percent. Some of the cost-cutting strategies include saving money through centralized purchasing, computerizing information, and speeding up bill collections. On the other hand, Schoen increases revenues by expanding services into such areas as cardiology, pulmonary medicine, or obstetrics, and purchasing new equipment such as magnetic resonance imagers (body scanners) and lithotripters (ultrasonic kidney stone blasters). Very expensive equipment is shifted among hospitals on a regular schedule to save money. The added services have built up loyalty among local doctors who previously would send patients to hospitals in bigger cities 40 or 50 miles away.[39] ■■■

William Schoen, CEO of Health Management Associates, came up with a way to make hospitals in small cities profitable. His strategy is to buy hospitals in locations where there is no major competition and then increase their profits through centralized financial controls, including centralized purchasing, computerized information, and speedy bill collection. He also increases revenues by expanding services and sharing expensive medical equipment.

Comparative Financial Analysis

Financial statements and ratios are more meaningful when managers can compare the data against some standard. Managers are expected to explain significant variances (positive and negative) so that top-level executives can better understand why the variances are occurring and their implications. The three

TABLE 17-4 SIX POTENTIAL FINANCIAL CONTROL PITFALLS
1. Failing to tailor financial controls to the specific requirements of the organization
2. Neglecting to link financial controls to the strategic planning process
3. Instituting controls that send mixed messages about desired behaviors
4. Allowing financial controls to stifle innovation and creativity
5. Forcing the same financial controls on various subunits that have different control requirements
6. Implementing financial controls that are too sophisticated for organizational needs

major standards that managers most often use to compare data are management goals, historical standards, and industry standards.

Management financial goals are frequently set during the planning process. Then they become standards against which actual achievements are compared during the control process. In the case of The Coca-Cola Company, top management has consistently set goals that exceed the industry averages on most of the major ratios shown in Table 17-3, and for the reporting period indicated, the company has substantially exceeded industry averages on most of the measures.[40]

In contrast to management goals, which project future standards, *historical financial standards* are financial data from past years' statements or ratios that are used as a basis for comparing the current year's financial performance. The balance sheet and income statement for The Coca-Cola Company illustrate uses of historical standards since they include data from the previous year for comparison.

Another method of comparison is the use of *industry financial standards*, financial data based on averages for the industry. Financial ratios for a variety of industries are published by several sources, including Robert Morris Associates and Dun & Bradstreet.[41] Our discussion of The Coca-Cola Company's financial ratios and the data in Table 17-3 reflect the use of industry standards.

While financial controls can be extremely helpful to top management, there are six primary pitfalls that can short-circuit their usefulness. These pitfalls are summarized in Table 17-4.[42] Thus managers need to give careful consideration to how they institute and use financial controls in order to derive the potential benefits.

■ BUDGETARY CONTROL

Budgeting The process of stating in quantitative terms, usually dollars, planned organizational activities for a given period of time

While financial controls are a major tool of top management, budgetary controls are a mainstay for middle managers. Lower-level managers also use budgets to help track progress in their own units. **Budgeting** is the process of stating in quantitative terms, usually dollars, planned organizational activities for a given period of time. Budgets, the quantitative statements prepared through the budgeting process, may include such figures as projected income, expenditures, and profits. Budgets are useful because they provide a means of translating diverse activities and outcomes into a common measure, such as dollars.

Budgets are typically prepared for the organization as a whole, as well as for various subunits (such as divisions and departments). For budgetary purposes, organizations define subunits as responsibility centers.

Responsibility Centers

Responsibility center A subunit headed by a manager who is responsible for achieving one or more goals

A **responsibility center** is a subunit headed by a manager who is responsible for achieving one or more goals.[43] In fact, organizations can be thought of as forming a hierarchy of responsibility centers, ranging from small subunits at the bottom to large ones at the top. For example, the local AT&T phone store and the marketing division of AT&T are responsibility centers at different levels of the organization. There are five main types of responsibility centers: standard cost centers, discretionary expense centers, revenue centers, profit centers, and investment centers. The particular designation that a unit receives for budgetary purposes depends on how much control the unit has over the major elements, such as revenues and expenses, that contribute to profits and return on investment.

STANDARD COST CENTERS A **standard cost center** is a responsibility center whose budgetary performance depends on achieving its goals by operating within standard cost constraints. Because standard costs are often determined by using engineering methods, this type of center is also called an *engineered expense center*. With a standard cost center, managers face the challenge of controlling input costs (e.g., labor, raw materials) so that they do not exceed predetermined standards. For example, at the Nabisco Biscuit Company, the bakery operations have standard costs for cracker production that are based on such factors as ingredients, expected breakage rates, and a "giveaway" rate (the overweight amount in an average package of Nabisco crackers).[44] Therefore, one measure of the efficiency of baking operations is the unit's ability to turn out the required number of boxes of crackers at a given level of quality within specified cost constraints. A standard cost center is appropriate only if (1) standards for costs involved in producing a product or service can be estimated with reasonable accuracy and (2) the unit cannot be held directly responsible for profit levels because it does not have significant control over other expenses and/or revenues.

Standard cost center A responsibility center whose budgetary performance depends on achieving its goals by operating within standard cost constraints

DISCRETIONARY EXPENSE CENTERS A **discretionary expense center** is a responsibility center whose budgetary performance is based on achieving its goals by operating within predetermined expense constraints set through managerial judgment or discretion. Discretionary expense centers are commonly departments such as research and development, public relations, human resources, and legal units, in which it is difficult to determine standard costs or to measure the direct profit impact of the unit's efforts.

Discretionary expense center A responsibility center whose budgetary performance is based on achieving its goals by operating within predetermined expense constraints set through managerial judgment or discretion

REVENUE CENTERS A **revenue center** is a responsibility center whose budgetary performance is measured primarily by its ability to generate a specified level of revenue. Prime examples of revenue centers are sales and marketing divisions, which are typically evaluated on the sales (and thus revenues) that they generate in relation to the level of resources that they are allocated. For example, Nabisco's cookies are delivered directly to supermarkets and other outlets by combination driver-salespersons, who are part of revenue centers. They can influence revenues but have little control over the costs of the products they handle.[45] Revenue centers are used when the unit in question is responsible for revenues but does not have control over all the costs associated with a product or service, which makes it difficult to hold the unit responsible for profit levels.

Revenue center A responsibility center whose budgetary performance is measured primarily by its ability to generate a specified level of revenue

PROFIT CENTERS A **profit center** is a responsibility center whose budgetary performance is measured by the difference between revenues and costs—in other words, profits. Profit centers are appropriate only when the organizational unit in question has significant control over both costs and revenues, since these are the elements that ultimately affect profit levels. At troubled Cunard, the luxury cruise shipping line, the company is trying to encourage more concern

Profit center A responsibility center whose budgetary performance is measured by the difference between revenues and costs—in other words, profits

with the bottom line by designating each ship a profit center.[46] Organizations as a whole are also considered to be profit centers.

Investment center A responsibility center whose budgetary performance is based on return on investment

INVESTMENT CENTERS An **investment center** is a responsibility center whose budgetary performance is based on return on investment. The ROI ratio, discussed earlier in this chapter, entails not only revenues and costs but also the assets involved in producing a profit. Thus investment centers motivate managers to concern themselves with making good decisions about investments in facilities and other assets. Of course, this type of center works best if the unit has at least some control over investment decisions, as well as over both revenues and expenses. For example, at General Electric, businesses such as its aircraft engine, broadcasting (NBC), and major appliance divisions are operated as investment centers.[47]

USES OF RESPONSIBILITY CENTERS The uses of responsibility centers depend to a great extent on the type of organization structure involved (see Chapter 9). Standard cost centers, discretionary expense centers, and revenue centers are more often used with functional organization designs and with the functional units in a matrix design. Thus manufacturing or production units are likely to be treated as standard cost centers, while accounting, finance, and human resources are usually designated as discretionary expense centers. Sales or marketing units are normally considered to be revenue centers.

In contrast, with a divisional organization design, it is possible to use profit centers because the large divisions in such a structure usually have control over both the expenses and the revenues associated with profits. Of course, within divisions, various departments may operate as other types of responsibility centers. Major companies that operate their divisions as separate and autonomous businesses often use investment centers for budgetary purposes. For years, Hanson PLC, a British-based conglomerate, ran businesses as investment centers, but put major emphasis on generating cash and required managers of operating units to obtain permission from superiors for all significant capital investments. The strategy worked well for more than 20 years, but ran into trouble during the 1990s as businesses began to suffer from low levels of investment (see the Case in Point discussion).

CASE IN POINT

BUDGET-DRIVEN HANSON PLC BREAKS UP

For years Hanson managers from all over the world would go to Iselin, New Jersey, or London at budget time to present their cost and revenue projections for the forthcoming year to the senior management of Hanson PLC. The sprawling transatlantic conglomerate had products ranging from Jacuzzi whirlpool baths and Smith Corona typewriters to bricks and cement. The conglomerate had grown to be Britain's seventh-largest business empire by following a simple formula: Buy undervalued companies with poor management in mature industries, and then improve the management practices. In the process, Hanson typically sold off some businesses of the acquired companies and kept others, particularly low-technology businesses that did not require continual major capital expenditures. For more than 20 years, Hanson posted record profits, with earnings per share as high as 38 percent annually. But by the 1990s, the picture began to change.

Hanson Trust specialized in buying low-technology companies that don't require huge infusions of capital, such as London Brick, which owns enough clay to make bricks well into the next century. But Hanson's close attention to budget control may have backfired: investors soured on the conglomerate when it appeared that many businesses were undercapitalized. Hanson recently broke itself up into four specialty companies, each run by a high-level executive who plans to infuse more capital into the operations.

Hanson had a reputation for granting a great deal of autonomy to local managers, yet maintaining tight control through budgets. At Hanson, budgets were considered sacred. For each business, "it's a promise from the operating CEO to us," noted one senior vice president. In the United States alone, some 150 Hanson investment centers filed monthly and quarterly reports to their Iselin headquarters. The reports, a little more than a yard high when stacked up, were generally considered to be the company bible. Several group vice presidents and their controllers would review the reports, which showed how pretax profits and other financial data compared with budget projections. One expectation was that Hanson managers would produce a pretax payback on investment in 3 years. The emphasis was on generating large amounts of cash to buy more businesses and pay high dividends to investors. For meeting their return on investment targets, the managers were rewarded well with bonuses that could be as much as 60 percent of base pay.

At Hanson, capital expenditures were very closely controlled. Every capital investment of $1000 or more had be approved by headquarters. If a manager argued that an investment in more efficient machinery would reduce labor costs, the manager had to furnish the names of employees who would be cut from the payroll as a result. Critics argued that such tight control would discourage managers from requesting capital investments that may be important for future earnings. Eventually, the critics appeared to be correct as Hanson's stock price began to languish. Because the conglomerate was composed of so many different businesses, investors found it difficult to assess the company's future prospects. Moreover, some businesses were viewed as suffering from a lack of investment. In a bold move, Hanson recently decided to break itself up into four specialty companies—chemicals, tobacco, energy, and building materials. Each company is run by a high-level Hanson executive, but there are plans to do more investing within the four companies. So far, the reaction of investors to the breakup has been mixed. No doubt, though, budgets will still be sacred.[48] ■■■

Types of Budgets

To maintain budgetary control, organizations usually have a master budget that includes a number of other budgets which together summarize the planned activities of the organization. Two major types of budgets that are typically included in the master budget are operating budgets and capital expenditures budgets.[49]

Operating budget A statement that presents the financial plan for each responsibility center during the budget period and reflects operating activities involving revenues and expenses

OPERATING BUDGETS An **operating budget** is a statement that presents the financial plan for each responsibility center during the budget period and reflects operating activities involving revenues and expenses.[50] The overall operating budget allows management to assess the resulting profit levels after taking into consideration the anticipated revenues and expenses across the responsibility centers. If profits are too small, managers can plan actions that will raise revenues (such as conducting marketing promotions to increase sales) and/or reduce expenses (such as cutting proposed expenditures for travel or delaying the purchase of nonessential equipment).

Capital expenditures budget A plan for the acquisition or divestiture of major fixed assets, such as land, buildings, or equipment

CAPITAL EXPENDITURES BUDGETS A **capital expenditures budget** is a plan for the acquisition or divestiture of major fixed assets, such as land, buildings, or equipment. Acquisitions of such assets are often referred to as *capital investments*. Since capital investments must be paid for over a long period of time and companies often borrow to cover the investments, they represent important organizational decisions. As a result, top-level managers are usually heavily involved, and the decision process often includes the board of directors.

Impacts of the Budgeting Process

Depending on how they are used, budgets can have either positive or negative effects on managerial behavior in organizations. On the positive side, budgets can help keep managers informed about organizational activities, enhance coordination across various units, and ensure appropriate investments in the future. They can also provide standards against which managers' efforts will be evaluated, and they can offer a means of making adjustments when corrective action is needed. Yet budgets can also have negative effects, particularly if they are used in a rigid manner and managers have concerns about fair treatment. Poorly run budgetary processes sometimes produce negative managerial behaviors. These include politicking to increase budget allocations, overstating needs so that allocations will be increased, and abandoning potential innovations because the fight for resources is too formidable.[51]

■ INVENTORY CONTROL

Inventory A stock of materials that are used to facilitate production or to satisfy customer demand

Another major type of control system found in most organizations is inventory control. **Inventory** is a stock of materials that are used to facilitate production or to satisfy customer demand. There are three major types of inventory: raw materials, work in process, and finished goods.[52]

Raw materials inventory The stock of parts, ingredients, and other basic inputs to a production or service process

Raw materials inventory is the stock of parts, ingredients, and other basic inputs to a production or service process. For example, McDonald's raw materials inventory includes hamburgers, cheese slices, buns, potatoes, and soft-drink syrup. The raw materials inventory at a bicycle factory includes such items as chains, sprockets, handlebars, and seats.

Work-in-process inventory The stock of items currently being transformed into a final product or service

Work-in-process inventory is the stock of items currently being transformed into a final product or service. For McDonald's, work-in-process inventory includes the hamburgers being assembled, the salads being made, and the syrup and soda water being mixed to make a soft drink. A bicycle frame with only the handlebars and seat attached would be work in process at a bicycle factory.

Finished-goods inventory is the stock of items that have been produced and are awaiting sale or transit to a customer. At McDonald's, finished-goods inventory includes the hamburgers waiting on the warmer and the salads in the refrigerated case. Bicycles constitute the finished-goods inventory at a bicycle factory. Organizations that provide mainly services, rather than products, such as hospitals, beauty salons, or accounting firms, do not have finished-goods inventory, since they are not able to stockpile finished goods (e.g., kidney operations, haircuts, and audits).

Finished-goods inventory
The stock of items that have been produced and are awaiting sale or transit to a customer

Significance of Inventory

Inventory serves several major purposes in organizations.[53] For one thing, it helps deal with uncertainties in supply and demand. For example, having extra raw materials inventory may preclude shortages that hold up a production process. Having extra finished-goods inventory makes it possible to serve customers better. Inventory also facilitates more economic purchases, since materials are sometimes less expensive when purchased in large amounts at one time. Finally, inventory may be a useful means of dealing with anticipated changes in demand or supply, such as seasonal fluctuations or an expected shortage. However, caution must be exercised in predicting changes. During the 1995 Christmas season, Apple Computer, Inc., misread the market and produced large numbers of low-end computers and too few high-end computers. The company was left with $80 million in unsold inventory, while competitors like IBM, Compaq Computer, and Hewlett-Packard had made huge profits.[54]

Costs of Inventory

Inventory is important to organizations because it represents considerable costs. For one thing, there is **item cost**, the price of an inventory item itself (the cost of the handlebars or seats). Then there is the **ordering cost**, the expenses involved in placing an order (such as paperwork, postage, and time). There is also the **carrying**, or **holding, cost**, the expenses associated with keeping an item on hand (such as storage, insurance, pilferage, breakage). Finally, there is **stockout cost**, the economic consequences of running out of stock. Stockout costs include the loss of customer goodwill and possibly sales because an item requested by customers is not available. During the first three quarters of 1995, Apple Computer was not able to keep up with the demand for its hardware, and by September it had $1 billion worth of backorders. When Apple could not fill the orders in a timely fashion, many customers chose other brands.[55] Inventory control aims to minimize the costs of inventory (including considerations of stockout costs). One approach to minimizing such costs is the use of an inventory method called the economic order quantity.

Item cost The price of an inventory item itself

Ordering cost The expenses involved in placing an order (such as paperwork, postage, and time)

Carrying, or **holding, cost** The expenses associated with keeping an item on hand (such as storage, insurance, pilferage, breakage)

Stockout cost The economic consequences of running out of stock (such as loss of customer goodwill and possibly sales)

Economic Order Quantity

The **economic order quantity (EOQ)** is an inventory control method developed to minimize ordering plus holding costs, while avoiding stockout costs. The method involves an equation that includes annual demand (D), ordering costs (O), and holding costs (H). Assume that a bicycle manufacturer estimates a

Economic order quantity (EOQ) An inventory control method developed to minimize ordering plus holding costs, while avoiding stockout costs

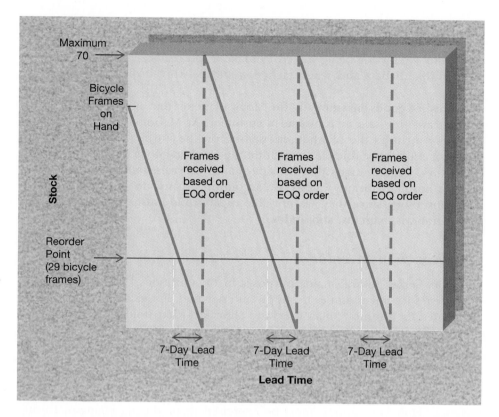

Figure 17-3 *EOQ inventory control system.*

total annual demand of 1470 bicycle frames for use in the manufacturing process, ordering costs of $10 per order, and holding costs of $6 per unit per year. Substituting these estimates into the equation indicates that the economic order quantity is 70 bicycle frames:

$$\text{EOQ} = 2DO/H \text{ (square root)} = [2(1470)(10)]/6 = 70$$

Reorder point (ROP) The inventory level at which a new order should be placed

The EOQ equation helps managers decide how much to order, but they also need to know the **reorder point (ROP),** the inventory level at which a new order should be placed. To determine the reorder point, managers estimate *lead time (L),* the time between placing an order and receiving it. In the case of the bicycle manufacturer, the lead time for obtaining frames from a nearby producer is 7 days. In the equation for ROP, lead time is multiplied by average daily demand (annual demand ÷ 365 days). Conceptually, the bicycle frames should be ordered when there are just enough frames to keep making bicycles until the new frames come in. Substituting the data for the bicycle manufacturer into the ROP equation indicates that an order should be placed when the stock of bicycle frames reaches 29:

$$\text{ROP} = (L)(D/365) = (7)(1470/365) = 28.19, \text{ or } 29 \text{ (rounded)}$$

The EOQ inventory control system, which requires continuous monitoring of inventories, is depicted in Figure 17-3. Although the approach assumes that demand and unit costs are constant, in many cases demand may vary substantially and suppliers may offer quantity discounts and special promotions. Still, the EOQ often gives a useful approximation. (We consider more sophisticated approaches to inventory issues in Chapter 18.) In using the EOQ, an organization will often add some slack to the system in the form of *fluctuation,* or *safety, stock.* This is extra inventory kept on hand in case of unforeseen contingencies such as quality problems or reorder delays.[56] On the other hand, a number of U.S. companies are taking a completely different approach to inventory control by emulating the "just-in-time" method pioneered in Japan.

Just-in-Time Inventory Control

Just-in-time (JIT) inventory control is an approach to inventory control that emphasizes having materials arrive just as they are needed in the production process.[57] The JIT approach to inventory is actually part of the broader JIT philosophy of manufacturing. According to this philosophy, organizations should attempt to eliminate all sources of waste, including any activities that do not add value, by focusing on having the right part at the right place at exactly the right time. Thus applying the JIT concept to inventory means having materials arrive only as required, rather than holding backup parts in inventory for a period of time. This approach enables an organization to minimize holding costs and to save space that is usually taken up by inventory waiting in the production area.

The JIT philosophy was popularized by the Toyota Motor Company in Japan during the mid-1970s and was transferred to the United States at Kawasaki's Lincoln, Nebraska, plant around 1980. At that point, one report indicated that a Japanese plant designed to produce 1000 cars per day required 1 million square feet and a just-in-time inventory of $150 per car. In contrast, a U.S. car manufacturer producing the same number of cars per day but not using a just-in-time system required 2 million square feet and a conventional inventory of $775 per car.[58] With such potential savings, it is not surprising that the JIT inventory approach has been adopted to some degree by most of the Fortune 1000 largest industrial companies.[59] In its focus on eliminating waste, the JIT philosophy also calls for utilizing the full capabilities of workers, giving them greater responsibilities for the production process, and involving them in continual efforts at improving the production process.

For handling inventory, the JIT approach uses a subsystem called **Kanban** (Japanese for "card" or "signal"), a simple parts-movement system that depends on cards and containers to pull parts from one work center to another. With the Kanban system, workstations along the production process produce only enough to fill the containers that they are given. They begin producing again only when they receive a card and an empty container from the next workstation, indicating that more parts will be needed shortly. If the process stops because of machine breakdowns or quality problems, all the workstations involved in the process produce only until their containers are full and then they stop.

With a JIT system, high quality is a vital necessity. Since materials are either delivered by suppliers or made in various internal work centers just before they will be used, the items must be perfect. Otherwise, not only is there waste, but the production process itself must be halted because there is no significant amount of inventory to cover mistakes. Because of the high need for coordination and control, JIT inventory systems often help forge close relationships between suppliers and customers. In the case of Polycom Hunstman, Inc., and GM's Harrison radiator division in Lockport, New York, the relationship is exceptionally close—just 1500 feet, to be exact. After GM invited suppliers to move closer to its Harrison plant, Polycom built a new plant right next door so that a pneumatic conveying system could connect the two plants, thereby eliminating shipping costs. Now, when the GM plant begins to run low on the plastic compounds that Polycom supplies, a computer-based control system automatically begins sending materials from Polycom's facility to the Harrison

Rebecca Matthia is founder and president of Mothers Work Inc., a retail chain selling upscale maternity clothing. Matthia found that a just-in-time inventory system suited her type of retailing. Her small stores must have a wide selection of items for mothers-to-be who make many purchases at once. So she stocks only one of each size for all but the best-selling items. A software program tracks store sales by item and sends replacements via UPS. A nearby network of contractors can swiftly manufacture items that sell out. As a result, Mothers Work is never caught with a great deal of excess inventory.

Just-in-time (JIT) inventory control An approach to inventory control that emphasizes having materials arrive just as they are needed in the production process

Kanban A simple parts-movement system that depends on cards and containers to pull parts from one work center to another

plant.[60] Of course, it takes time to install a JIT system, and the system is dependent on near-perfect coordination. For example, a recent walkout at GM's brake-parts plant in Dayton, Ohio, eventually led to the idling of 175,800 workers at a number of other GM plants in the United States, Mexico, and Canada that depended on the just-in-time parts fabricated at Dayton. By the time the strike was settled 17 days later, GM had lost an estimated $900 million in production. Fortunately, GM was able to subsequently make up for a large part of the loss by scheduling maximum overtime for several months at some assembly plants.[61] We discuss other inventory and production-related concepts in conjunction with operations management, the subject of the next chapter.

■ CHAPTER SUMMARY

Among the major control systems used in organizations are financial control, budgetary control, quality control, and inventory control. These systems vary in the degree to which they are used at different managerial levels, ranging from financial controls, which are used more at the top, to inventory controls, which are used more at the lower levels. Timing also varies, with financial control representing mainly feedback control, quality and budgetary control being more concurrent, and inventory control often matching feedforward timing.

Total quality management (TQM) is a management system that is an integral part of an organization's strategy and is aimed at continually improving product and service quality so as to achieve high levels of customer satisfaction and build strong customer loyalty. From a strategic point of view, eight dimensions of quality are important: performance, features, reliability, conformance, durability, serviceability, aesthetics, and perceived quality. TQM philosophy includes several important concepts: quality is less costly than poor workmanship, employees will naturally try to improve quality as long as they have appropriate support, serious quality improvement requires cross-functional efforts, and quality improvement requires the strong commitment of top management. There also are four major change principles: focus on work processes, analyze and understand variability, manage by fact, and emphasize continuous learning and improvement. Some of the most common intervention techniques used in TQM include cost of quality analysis,

quality improvement teams, training, benchmarking, customer data gathering, collaboration with suppliers, and statistical process control.

Financial controls consist mainly of financial statements, ratio analysis, and comparative financial analysis. The primary financial statements are the balance sheet and the income statement. The major types of ratios used in financial control are liquidity, asset management, debt management, and profitability ratios. Financial statements and ratios can be assessed through the use of comparative financial analysis based on management financial goals, historical financial standards, or industry financial standards. Managers need to guard against major pitfalls associated with financial controls.

Budgetary control requires that various organizational units be designated as responsibility centers, such as standard cost centers, discretionary expense centers, revenue centers, profit centers, and investment centers. The specific designation depends mainly on the type of organization structure involved. Two major types of budgets are operating budgets and capital expenditures budgets. Depending on how they are used, budgets can have either positive or negative effects on managerial behavior in organizations.

Inventory control serves a number of important purposes in organizations and involves several significant costs. Two major inventory control methods are the economic order quantity and just-in-time inventory control.

■ QUESTIONS FOR DISCUSSION AND REVIEW

1 How do major control systems differ in their emphasis on timing control? In what ways might the timing of these control systems be altered?

2 Explain the total quality management approach. Identify an organization with which you do business that shows some evidence of using TQM. What is the evidence?

3 Describe the eight dimensions of quality. Choose an item that you recently purchased, and rate your purchase on each of the dimensions. What dimension

was most important in your decision to purchase the item?

4 Outline the four TQM change principles. Describe a situation you are familiar with in which an improvement in quality is needed. How could you use these four change principles in that situation?

5 Delineate the seven commonly used TQM intervention techniques. From the point of view of a consumer, how would you like to see these quality control aids used by the companies whose products you buy?

6 Identify and briefly explain the main types of financial statements and financial ratios used by organizations. Suppose that your friend asks you to help rescue a motorcycle factory that is losing money. How would you use the various financial analyses to help assess the situation?

7 There are a number of potential pitfalls associated with financial controls. Do any of these pitfalls appear to apply at Hanson PLC (see the Case in Point)?

8 Explain each type of responsibility center, and show the connection with organization structure. Identify the type of responsibility center in which you or a friend works. Give reasons for your classification of the center's type.

9 Contrast operating budgets and capital expenditures budgets. How can budgets be used so that they have positive, rather than negative, effects on managerial behavior?

10 Compare and contrast the economic order quantity and just-in-time approaches to inventory control. Why do you think that so many companies are attempting to make greater use of the JIT approach?

■ DISCUSSION QUESTIONS FOR CHAPTER OPENING CASE

1 In what ways does USAA probably use financial and budgetary control techniques to help meet its service and profit goals?

2 Although it is a service, in what ways does USAA use the dimensions of quality to compete? To what extent is benchmarking in evidence at the company?

3 Assess the quality improvement efforts at USAA in terms of Deming's 14 points on how to improve quality. If you were called in as a consultant, what advice would you give USAA?

■ EXERCISES FOR MANAGING IN THE TWENTY-FIRST CENTURY

EXERCISE 1
SKILL BUILDING: IDENTIFYING CRITICAL
QUALITY DIMENSIONS

 Eight dimensions of quality have been identified as being important. Managers should know these and understand how they are implemented in the workplace. Examples of how these could be used are indicated below. Place the letters representing the quality dimension being implemented in the blank preceding the example.

Performance   Features   Reliability
Conformance   Durability   Aesthetics
Perceived Quality   Serviceability

1 _____ Providing plug-in components that can be rapidly replaced when equipment breaks down

2 _____ Ensuring that a microchip meets the design specifications

3 _____ A lightbulb guaranteed for "life" (100 years; normal use)

4 _____ A TV set that can display several programs simultaneously

5 _____ A watch that will lose less than 1 minute over 30 years

6 _____ A 200,000-mile guarantee on a particular car engine

7 _____ Producing a particularly attractive line of clothing

8 _____ Being rated number one in the annual J. D. Power survey of satisfaction with a particular car

9 _____ An access panel that permits quick repairs

10 _____ A type of roofing material guaranteed for 30 years

11 _____ A telephone with caller identification, call forwarding, voice mail, visual display, and an answering device

12 _____ Ensuring that a study follows the parameters established for it when conceived

13 _____ The most attractive design for a 4 × 4 vehicle

14 _____ A power lawn mower guaranteed to start on the first pull

15 _____ A fighter-bomber that can outmaneuver and fly faster than any other airplane

16 _____ Preferring one brand of soup over another

17 _____ Immediately responding to a customer's request for assistance

18 _____ Shoes that last longer than average

19 _____ A battery for an automobile that has a 99 percent chance of producing maximum voltage for 4 years without failure

20 _____ A pen that has a light in the head for writing in the dark

EXERCISE 2
MANAGEMENT EXERCISE: MEETING WATER BED DEMAND

 A recent announcement from your state health department has proclaimed that water beds are very good for people with minor back pains. This has resulted in an extremely high demand for the water beds your firm produces. Although this is very good news, as the operating manager of the firm, you are concerned that your company's ability to produce may be impeded by several considerations. You review these:

Market share: The firm currently has about 12 percent of the local market. You recognize that you will need to increase productivity 5 percent just to maintain the current market position. However, to reach your goal of a 5 percent increase in market share, you must further step up productivity.

Capacity: You believe that you have the plant capacity to expand productivity to 6500 water beds annually. The firm now produces and sells 5000 water beds each year. The increase in market share, for both maintaining the current position and achieving your stated goal, will require 5500 water beds per year.

Inventory: You have storage capacity for raw materials for 450 water beds per month, and your work-in-process inventory is normally 470 beds per month. The finished-goods inventory is usually 8 percent of monthly production.

Quality: Inspections conducted after the water beds are made typically result in about 10 percent of them being rejected because of quality problems. Only about 50 percent of these can be repaired; the others must be scrapped.

Human resources: You have the skilled employees required to support increased production but will need additional unskilled workers. There are many potential employees in the local labor market.

Tomorrow you must tell the president of the firm whether or not you can meet the projected production schedule. If you need to make some modifications in your procedures to meet the projected schedule, these changes should be included in your discussion with the president. What are you going to tell the president tomorrow morning?

CONCLUDING CASE 1

POOR QUALITY LEADS TO FINANCIAL PROBLEMS FOR REGINA

In late 1988 the Regina Company, the fourth-largest maker of vacuum cleaners in North America, began having return rates as high as 30 to 50 percent on some of its House-keeper and Housekeeper Plus models. These lines were sold primarily through discount stores. Further, Regina's Stutz vacuum cleaner, an upgraded version sold in specialty stores, was introduced that same year with many quality problems.

As a result of these problems, the Dayton Hudson Corporation dropped one line. Target Stores discontinued Regina's Housekeeper Plus 500 line after reporting that "at least half of those sold were returned." At K mart, which accounted for about a quarter of the Housekeeper 1000 sales, 1 out of every 5 machines sold was returned. To help service customer complaints, Regina set up an 800 telephone number for customers to contact the firm directly.

It should be noted that the Hoover Company and the Eureka Corporation, both leaders in the vacuum cleaner industry, reported return rates for their machines of less than 1 percent. They further indicated that they would have cause for alarm if the return rate reached 3 percent.

The many returns caused Regina's shareholders to question the 1988 fiscal earnings report. Furthermore, both inventories and accounts receivable doubled during that year. At the end of 1988, Regina's chairman and 40 percent stockholder resigned. His resignation was closely followed by a company announcement stating that the financial results reported for the 1988 fiscal year were materially incorrect and had been withdrawn. This announcement brought a suit from shareholders who had bought

Regina stock on the basis of the 1988 earnings report. Regina filed for bankruptcy protection under Chapter 11 of the Federal Bankruptcy Code in 1989. A few months later, it agreed to be acquired by a unit of Electrolux, a vacuum cleaner and water-purification company based in Marietta, Georgia.

Under Electrolux, Regina shut down production while engineers worked to solve the problems inherent in the Housekeeper and Housekeeper Plus vacuums. In September 1990, Electrolux and Regina decided to separate the two companies, but Regina was left with little capital to invest in new products or to use for expansion. Nevertheless, Regina began regaining market share with its Housekeeper Upright line. The vacuums were popular because they carry on-board tools and offer the capability of cleaning above the floor. Unfortunately, competitors began copying the on-board tools concept. After struggling for 3 years, Regina began to seek a purchaser who could provide working capital. The company was acquired by Israel-based Pass-Port Ltd. A year later, Pass-Port Ltd. had pumped $7.5 million into Regina but was unable to solve the company's cash-flow problem caused largely by high costs and fierce competition. Faced with the need to invest still more, Pass-Port decided to allow Regina to again file for bankruptcy under Chapter 11 in 1995. The situation was so dire that Regina stopped manufacturing and was filling orders from existing inventory.

Within a few months the assets of bankrupt Regina were acquired by Philips Electronics N.V. of the Netherlands. Philips immediately brought in a team of experts from its Hoogeveen, Netherlands, facility, which meets international quality standards. The Regina plant layout in Long Beach, Mississippi, was changed to make it more efficient,

and there were major investments in equipment. Philips instituted quality controls, set standards, and put up signs stressing teamwork. Philips discontinued the Housekeeper II vacuum cleaner line because the quality problems were extensive, but it has helped the Regina unit solve the noise problem with its Electrik-Broom line. Philips also set a new policy called the "rip cord system" whereby any plant worker can stop the entire line if there is a problem with quality. The line is not to resume until the problem is resolved.

Within 30 days under Philips, the new Regina consumer products division had resumed manufacturing, developed a new strategy, improved quality, and shipped its first order. Philips wants to restore Regina to its former position as a leading supplier of vacuum cleaners. For now Regina will concentrate on the low and middle end of the market, where it has been most successful in the past. Over time, however, Philips plans to move toward the high end with more features and better performance. Regina will need to resume the innovations for which it was known in the past in order to regain market share against its major competitors—Hoover, Eureka, and Royal. Philips is a leading vacuum cleaner manufacturer in Europe and has plans to become a global force in floor care.[62]

QUESTIONS FOR CONCLUDING CASE 1

1. If you were sent by Philips to help solve the quality problems at Regina, what actions would you take?
2. How can Philips use financial and budgetary controls to help avoid a repeat of Regina's past problems?
3. What considerations would you give to instituting improved inventory control?

CONCLUDING CASE 2

SAMSONITE CANADA TAKES CONTROL

During the late 1980s, Samsonite Canada, Inc., began to question its prospects for survival. The market for Canadian luggage was maturing, and the 17 percent tariff on imported luggage was to be phased out by the end of the 1990s. Moreover, Samsonite Canada, based in Stratford, Ontario, had recently lost a contract for making plastic parts for a European toy company. (The parts were made with the same injection-molding equipment used in the manufacture of hard luggage.) Until this point, the company's balance sheet had always shown a reasonable profit. Profits in the future looked less certain.

Although management had always suspected that its luggage manufacturing costs were high relative to those of its Denver-based U.S. parent, an investigation showed the situation to be worse than anticipated. Comparative indicators pointed to costs that were 50 to 70 percent higher than those in Denver. Company officials concluded that if the firm was to remain in operation, they would need to both cut costs and find ways to expand business.

As a result, Samsonite Canada initiated a rejuvenation program in 1991. The company received both financial and expert assistance from a Canadian federal agency, Employment and Immigration of Canada. The agency helped establish and chair a steering committee with equal representation from employees and management. The steering committee manages the ongoing process of change. Because of the focus on teams, as well as employee empowerment, continuous improvement, and training, the new program was called SPIRIT (Samsonite's Purpose Is Resulting In Teamwork). In regard to financial help, the agency provided half of the

$392,000 cost for the first 2 years of the program. The company also received support from its Denver parent.

During the first year of the program, the company met its goal of cutting costs by half a million dollars. The cost cutting has continued at a brisk pace as employees have been offering many cost-saving ideas.

Many of the ideas have come from teams created to focus on continuous improvement. The teams, which meet on a weekly or biweekly basis, look for cost-cutting ideas in their work areas. They also consider ways to improve products and enhance service.

One initial problem was that the employees were accustomed to taking orders rather than taking the initiative to solve problems. To help employees learn appropriate skills and adapt to the required new culture, the company brought in a training program developed by the Canadian Manufacturers' Association with the help of the Canadian federal government. During a 6-month period, every employee, including management, received some or all components of the training program. The training focused on leadership and continuous improvement.

One result was the reorganization of the production area into work cells, where teams of workers collaborated with engineering to determine the best ways to lay out their work areas for manufacture and assembly of products. Because of these efforts, production runs more smoothly, a JIT inventory approach has been adopted, and materials are handled more efficiently. Quality control has also improved. The new work cell arrangements are 60 to 70 percent on their way to eliminating the need for quality inspectors. Instead, the workers themselves will take responsibility for maintaining quality at a

sufficient level. Moreover, profit margins are up, and the streamlined work cells have freed up space that the company is now leasing to other businesses.

The push for higher quality has had another benefit. Samsonite Canada decided to pursue further business with FAG Bearings Limited, a major supplier for the Ford Motor Company. Samsonite had done a small amount of business with FAG Bearings in the past, but now it wanted to become the firm's single source for molding automotive strut bearings. FAG Bearings required the entire Samsonite Canada company to submit to a quality audit, not just the molding department. Samsonite Canada has also been working to shift some of its luggage expertise toward making other types of specialty containers. To that end, it has established its own research and development department. Already, specialty products account for 25 percent of gross sales.

The continuous improvements, even many minor ones, have made a big difference at Samsonite Canada. Samsonite recently signed an agreement with the Tracker Corporation for a 1-year exclusive use of Tracker's WorldWide Recovery Service in luggage within Canada. Tracker will provide digitally coded labels that can identify the owner of lost luggage and arrange for its return via an international courier network.[63]

QUESTIONS FOR CONCLUDING CASE 2

1   What role did financial controls play in helping Samsonite identify the need for change?
2   To what extent does Samsonite Canada appear to have initiated total quality management?
3   Explain how quality improvement teams operated in the Samsonite environment. What evidence exists that benchmarking was done?

CHAPTER EIGHTEEN

OPERATIONS AND SERVICE MANAGEMENT

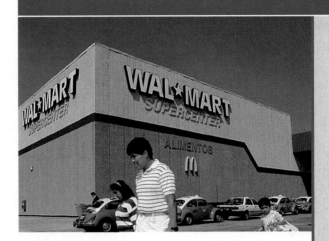

LEARNING OBJECTIVES

After studying this chapter, you should be able to:

■ Explain productivity and its linkage to the operations management process.

■ Contrast manufacturing and service organizations.

■ Identify four strategic role stages that govern the role of operations management in strategy development.

■ Explain each of the major systems used in operations management and discuss their interrelationships.

■ Describe the matrix of service characteristics.

■ Outline the steps involved in making expansion and contraction decisions regarding facilities.

■ Identify the four categories of facility location problems and the three main types of facility layouts.

■ Explain the role of process technology in promoting innovation through reengineering, computer-integrated manufacturing, and related means.

■ Discuss the five steps involved in improving productivity.

GAINING THE EDGE

FANUC LEADS THE WORLD IN ELECTRONIC FACTORY HELP

 If you had an opportunity to visit some of the world's most highly automated factories, chances are that you would quickly run into the name "Fanuc" (an acronym for Fuji Automatic Numerical Control). Japan-based Fanuc (pronounced "fa-NUKE") is the world's top supplier of devices that control the machines in automated factories. The company is also the foremost producer of industrial robots.

Fanuc constantly beats the competition by being the lowest-cost producer of high-quality automation components. In fact, its devices are considered to be the highest-quality components available anywhere in the world. The 650 robots at the Mount Fuji complex outnumber the 400 production workers. The other 1600 workers are research engineers, administrators, and salespersons. In one plant, which cost about one-tenth the price of a conventional facility, 70 workers and 130 robots turn out 18,000 electric motors per month. To make a factory of this type possible, Fanuc had to redesign the motors, greatly reducing the number of parts needed for each one.

A large part of Fanuc's success can be attributed to Dr. Seiuemon Inaba, a directive leader who is uncompromising in his emphasis on product quality and reliability. Subordinates generally do not speak in meetings unless he addresses them. Yet Inaba has been able to provide a vision for the company that has inspired employees to put forth their best efforts.

Dr. Inaba rewards employees exceptionally well. The earnings of managers at Fanuc are generally about 50 percent more than the usual salaries at other Japanese companies, and engineers earn about 30 percent more than their counterparts in other organizations. The company also takes care of employees in other significant ways. For example, within the factory grounds there is family housing, as well as dorms for single men, single women, and married people living away from their families. Workers may stay in these living facilities even past retirement—until death if they wish. In the Fanuc cultural center, employees and their families can pursue leisure interests by studying such subjects as flower arranging or the tea ceremony.

Fanuc Robotics North America, Inc., headquartered in Auburn Hills, Michigan, is North America's industry leader with nearly 20,000 units in service. Fanuc has been attempting to expand further in Asia, but is facing stiff competition. Dr. Inaba says it makes the most sense to manufacture numerical control equipment in Japan because the overall volume is not high. While he concedes that it may be possible to have some of the parts that are manufactured in Japan assembled in other countries, the cost-effectiveness of such an approach is still being studied. In the meantime, some of Fanuc's competitors are making inroads in particular countries, like China, by establishing production facilities there. Fanuc has recently built a programmable-controller factory in Singapore that has state-of-the art robotics. Only three employees monitor the 30,000-unit-capacity plant.

General Electric has a joint venture with Fanuc. The venture, the GE Fanuc Automation Corporation, specializes in devices that control automated machines, particularly computerized numerical controls. The controls are the electronic boxes that form the "brains" and "nervous systems" of automated versions of such tools as lathes and milling machines. GE Fanuc has won two pres-

Fanuc, nestled at the foot of Japan's Mount Fuji, produces high-quality automation products. In order to lower costs and compete effectively in the world market, Fanuc makes extensive use of robotic automation at its own plants. Fanuc's production methods are among the best in the world, a reflection of efficient operations management.

tigious awards: the Electronics Factory Automation award and the Manufacturing Excellence award.[1]   ■ ■ ■

Few leaders are as directive as Dr. Inaba. Yet, within the broad parameters and major directions that he outlines, workers have considerable latitude in pursuing the innovations that have made Fanuc a world-class supplier of factory automation devices. Thus much of its success can be attributed to the emphasis on innovation within its own factory operations. In addition, Fanuc has been able to achieve high-quality outputs, yet, compared with the competition, it uses relatively fewer inputs. What accounts for such enviable productivity? In large part, it stems from the company's excellence in operations management, the functional area responsible for producing the goods and services that Fanuc has to offer.

Operations management is considered part of the controlling function because much of the emphasis is on regulating the productive processes that are critical to reaching organizational goals. In considering operations management, we first explore its basic nature, as well as examine its linkage to productivity issues. We next investigate how operations management can be tied to an organization's overall strategy. We then consider several other major aspects of operations management, including operating systems, facilities, and the use of reengineering and other forms of process technology in promoting innovation. Finally, we take a closer look at the major steps involved in improving productivity within operations management.

■ DEFINING OPERATIONS MANAGEMENT

Operations management is the management of the productive processes that convert inputs into goods and services.[2] Because of its close association with manufacturing, operations management is sometimes called *production-operations management*. Recently, though, the term "production" is increasingly being dropped in favor of simply "operations management," a term that has less of a manufacturing connotation. The operations management function is carried out by the part of the organization directly involved in producing the primary goods and services.

Operations management The management of the productive processes that convert inputs into goods and services

In the case of a manufacturing organization such as Fanuc, the operations management function would include plant managers and all the other managers who work in the factories (e.g., production managers, inventory control managers, quality assurance managers, and line supervisors). When an organization's structure has a corporate level, operations would also encompass any manufacturing or operations vice presidents at that level, as well as related corporate operations staff (such as those primarily concerned with production, inventory, quality, facilities, and equipment).

In a service industry such as the hotel business, the operations management function would include hotel managers and the various managers who work in the hotels (e.g., housekeeping managers, food and beverage managers, and conventional managers). Again, if there is a corporate level, operations would also comprise the managers and staff at that level who are directly involved in actually running the hotels (as opposed to managers who are involved in other related functions, such as marketing and finance). Regardless of whether an organization produces a service, a product, or both, operations managers need to be acutely concerned about productivity.

The Productivity–Operations Management Linkage

Productivity The efficiency concept that gauges the ratio of outputs relative to inputs into a production process

Productivity is an efficiency concept that gauges the ratio of outputs relative to inputs into a productive process.[3] In Chapter 1, we discuss the concepts of organizational *effectiveness* and *efficiency* in performance. Effectiveness relates to the extent to which performance reaches organizational goals. In contrast, efficiency addresses the resource usage (inputs) involved in achieving outcomes (outputs). Productivity is aimed at assessing the efficiency aspect of organizational performance—the ratio of outputs relative to inputs. As such, productivity can be a useful tool for managers because it helps them track progress toward the more efficient use of resources in producing goods and services.

Organizational productivity is often measured by using this equation:

$$\text{Productivity} = \frac{\text{goods and services produced (outputs)}}{\text{labor} + \text{capital} + \text{energy} + \text{technology} + \text{materials (inputs)}}$$

Total-factor productivity A productivity approach that considers all the inputs involved in producing outputs

Partial-factor productivity A productivity approach that considers the total output relative to a specific input, such as labor

An approach, like this one, that considers all the inputs involved in producing outputs is sometimes referred to as **total-factor productivity.** Managers also use **partial-factor productivity,** a productivity approach that considers the total output relative to a specific input, such as labor. For example:

$$\text{Productivity} = \frac{\text{goods and services produced (outputs)}}{\text{labor hours (labor input)}}$$

In addition, managers often develop specific ratios that gauge productivity for particular outputs and inputs. Examples include sales per square foot of floor space, profit per sales dollar, return on investment, claims processed per employee, and lab tests completed per dollar of labor cost.

To understand the implications of productivity differences in organizations, consider this comparison: Wal-Mart's recent expenses have been running at about 15.8 percent of sales, while at Bradlees Inc. and Caldor Corp., expenses have been totaling 29.4 percent and 24.4 percent of sales, respectively. These latter two discounters ultimately found it necessary to file for Chapter 11 bankruptcy.[4] While expenses per sales constitutes only one gauge of productivity, the figures indicate why managers must concern themselves with productivity issues. If competitors can produce a given level of output (dollars of sales) with fewer inputs (expenses), they will be more profitable and have greater resources to expend on strengthening their competitive position. There are also differences between manufacturing and service organizations that influence productivity prospects.

Manufacturing versus Service Organizations

Manufacturing and service organizations differ in several important respects.[5] *Manufacturing organizations* transform inputs into identifiable, tangible goods, such as soft drinks, cars, or videocassette recorders. Typically, the tangible goods they produce can be stored (at least to some degree), and the ultimate customer does not usually need to be present while the transformation process is taking place. As a result, manufacturing can often be done at centralized locations, and the products can be shipped to customers. In addition, a manufacturing concern can often avoid wasting capacity during slack periods by using available capacity to produce inventory in anticipation of future sales. Thus manufacturing organizations typically have considerable control over when and how their operations will run, and they can attempt to organize their activities to maximize productivity.

In contrast, *service organizations* transform inputs into intangible outcomes, such as education, health care, transportation services, and personal services. Such outcomes are produced and consumed more or less simultaneously, cannot be stored, and involve the customer. For example, you are involved with a service organization when you attend a class, see a doctor, visit a bank, catch an airplane flight, or obtain a haircut. All these are activities in which you must participate to receive the service, and all are activities that cannot be stored. Unlike their manufacturing counterparts, service organizations cannot use idle capacity to produce stored inventory, and they must often operate in geographically dispersed locations to be near their customers, since their services cannot be stored and shipped. Compared with manufacturing organizations, service organizations often have somewhat less control over when and exactly how their operations take place, as their activities may depend on customer volume and customer needs that are difficult to determine fully in advance. A clas-

Zack, a golden retriever, has been trained to serve as the arms and legs of his companion, a 10-year-old boy stricken with cerebral palsy. Zack can even take items off the shelf of a store and place them in the boy's lap. East Coast Assistance Dogs is the service organization that trains dogs like Zack for the disabled.

sic example of a service organization that has continually strived to increase productivity is ServiceMaster (see the Case in Point discussion).

CASE IN POINT　　　**SERVICEMASTER CLEANS, REPAIRS, AND MAINTAINS**

ServiceMaster, an organization with about $3 billion in annual revenues, provides its clients with a wide range of services. These include pest control, plumbing, lawn care, maid service, and appliance maintenance. It serves commercial, residential, educational, and health care customers through its own organization and its subsidiaries, which include Terminix, TruGreen Chemlawn, Merry Maids, and American Home Shield. ServiceMaster has more than 6 million customers in the United States and in 30 countries around the world.

The company was founded in 1958 by Marion Wade, a devout Christian who established four commandments for the organization. The first, "To honor God in all we do," is the basis for the firm's name ("ServiceMaster" is short for "Service to the Master"). The second commandment is "To help people develop." The third is "To pursue excellence," and the last is "To grow profitably." Their success, says Chairman William Pollard, is built on the philosophy that it is important to honor and realize the potential of every worker in the organization.

The company, headquartered in Downers Grove, near Chicago, earned its stellar reputation by furnishing cleaning services for hospitals and factories. Today it has over 4900 franchisees located throughout the United States. The franchisees are allowed to provide ServiceMaster services in specific areas. In return, they pay ServiceMaster various fees and/or royalties, as well as agree to follow the company's standard operating procedures.

To facilitate efficient and effective service, the company has produced a 3-inch-thick manual that provides detailed instructions for franchisees and their workers. For example, the task of polishing floors is broken down into a series of specific 5-minute steps. Other services are similarly explained, with very precise directions for their completion. In addition to standardizing tasks in its manual, ServiceMaster makes its own chemicals and designs its own equipment. For instance, for polishing floors, ServiceMaster produces a special floor-finish product with a prescribed drying time. Likewise, the company has designed a battery-operated vacuum cleaner so that the operator does not have to waste time moving an electric cord.

One of the environmental forces behind the company's success is the growth of two-income families that find little time for cleaning the house or mowing the lawn. Also the aging population of the United States has created a demand for various types of assistance, including health care.[6]　■■■

In reality, many organizations provide both goods and services. As illustrated in the continuum shown in Figure 18-1, some organizations (such as factories, farms, and mines) produce mainly goods. Others (such as consulting firms, hospitals, government agencies, and ServiceMaster) produce mainly services. Still others produce a combination of goods and services. For example, in addition to the cars that they sell, Ford and General Motors provide many services, such as financing, insurance, and repairs. Similarly, when you visit your local Burger King outlet, you receive services in the form of order taking, order filling, and availability of tables for eating, yet you also receive a product in the form of, perhaps, a newly produced cheeseburger.

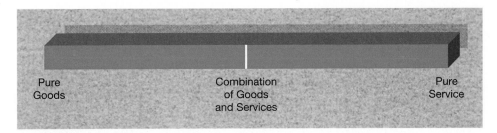

Figure 18-1 *Continuum of goods and services.*

One way to classify organizations according to the degree of service they provide is to measure the percentage of production process time that is spent in direct contact with the customer.[7] A pure producer of goods would have zero contact with the ultimate customer, while a pure producer of services would have 100 percent contact. High customer contact often reduces organizational efficiency and productivity, since customers' arrival patterns may vary and they may make particular demands that require customized service. For example, you may have noticed that lines move slower at Burger King when individuals order nonstandard items, such as a Whopper burger without pickles.

The Operations Management Process

In the process of transforming inputs into goods and services, operations management involves several major elements (see Figure 18-2).[8] For one thing, there is *operations strategy,* the role played by operations management in both formulating and implementing strategies to achieve organizational goals (see Chapter 7). For another, operations management includes various *operating systems,* major methods used to achieve efficiency and effectiveness in manufacturing and service operations. Yet another major element is *facilities,* the land, buildings, equipment, and other major physical assets that directly affect an organization's capacity to deliver goods and services. Finally, *process technology,* the technology used in transforming inputs into goods and services, is also an important ingredient in operations management. We consider each of these elements in the next several sections of this chapter.

■ FORMULATING OPERATIONS STRATEGY

Boston-based Fidelity Investments, the largest mutual fund company in the world, has opened a $100 million, state-of-the-art mail processing facility in Cov-

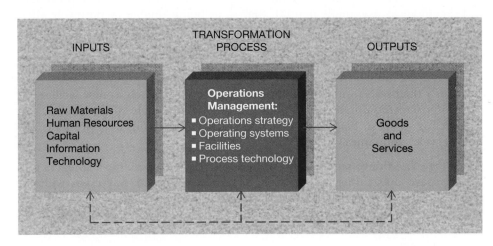

Figure 18-2 *Operations management process.*

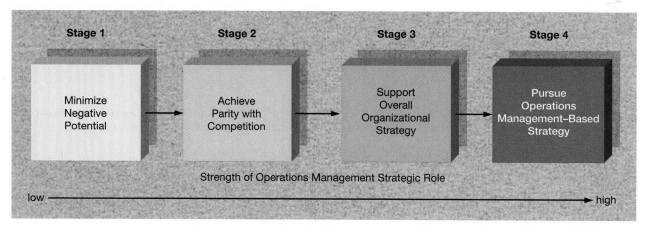

Stage 1	Stage 2	Stage 3	Stage 4
Minimize Negative Potential	Achieve Parity with Competition	Support Overall Organizational Strategy	Pursue Operations Management–Based Strategy

Strength of Operations Management Strategic Role

low ⟶ high

Figure 18-3 *Stages in operations management strategic role. (Based on Steven C. Wheelwright and Robert H. Hayes, "Competing through Manufacturing," Harvard Business Review, January–February 1985, pp. 99–109.)*

ington, Kentucky. Operating 7 days a week and 24 hours per day, the facility generates more than 140 million pieces of mail annually. To do so, robots and conveyor belts run by Fidelity-developed software help retrieve prospectuses and other materials that are part of as many as 3000 different "kits" Fidelity mails to customers. To keep the ink from smearing or edges from curling on customer statements, the paper is dried out for 24 hours in climate-controlled rooms kept at 70 degrees Fahrenheit and within a humidity range of 45 to 55 percent. Fidelity promises customers that the company will mail requested material the next day. Customer requests are downloaded to the facility at 2 a.m. EST the next morning. The facility has already assembled much of the most requested materials. Machines "ink-jet" names and addresses on materials, apply metered postage, spray on a Postal Service bar code, and sort the letters. About 90 percent of the mail goes to Postal Service trucks for movement directly to airports and never enters a post office. Fidelity considers its mail system a key part of its effort to build and maintain competitive advantage.[9] Such strategic use of operations management is becoming more commonplace in the face of increasing domestic and global competition in virtually every industry.

Operations management plays different roles in determining strategy, depending on an organization's strategic role stage.[10] The four stages are shown in Figure 18-3.

Stage 1: Minimize negative potential: During this stage, top managers attempt to neutralize any negative impact that internal operations may have on the organization. They do so because they regard operations management as essentially neutral, that is, as being unable to positively affect the organization's competitive success. Thus they typically use detailed measures and controls to ensure that the operations function does not veer too far off track before corrective action is taken. Generally, top managers minimize their involvement with operations areas. However, they do concern themselves with major investment decisions (such as new facilities or important equipment purchases) through the vehicle of the capital budgeting process. Stage 1 is characteristic of many consumer-products and service companies.

Stage 2: Achieve parity with competition: In this stage, top managers seek to have operations management maintain parity, or stay even, with the competition. Organizations at this stage typically attempt to maintain such equality by adopting industry practices related to work-force matters (such as labor negotiations), equipment purchases, and upgrades of capacity.

Typically, they view capital investments in new equipment and facilities as the best means of gaining a temporary jump on the competition, and they consider economies of scale (producing in large amounts) as the best source of efficiency. Traditional manufacturing-intensive industries, such as steel, autos, and heavy equipment, are among the organizations often found in this stage.

Stage 3: Support overall organizational strategy: In this stage, top managers expect the operations management function to actively support and strengthen the organization's overall strategy. The role of operations managers, then, is to gain a thorough understanding of the organizational strategy formulated by top management and to consider innovations that will help implement that strategy effectively. In contrast to those at stage 2, organizations at stage 3 see technological progress as a viable option that can enhance an organization's competitive position. Nonetheless, at this stage, operations managers are involved in implementing and supporting strategy but not in formulating it. The beer industry includes many stage 3 organizations. After building a number of new, large-scale facilities in the 1970s and streamlining their existing operations, they began to drift back into a "business as usual" attitude (i.e., stages 1 and 2) toward the manufacturing function.

Stage 4: Pursue operations management–based strategy: During this stage, top managers view operations management as a strong strategic resource that can be used as a basis for strategy development. Therefore, they include operations managers in the strategy development process and formulate a strategy that depends to a significant degree on operations capabilities. Operations managers try to anticipate potential technological advances that could affect operations, and they attempt to gain the necessary internal expertise well before the implications are obvious. At this stage, organizations attempt to use innovation as a means of making incremental strategic jumps ahead of the competition. Stage 4 is characteristic of all companies that have reached the status of world-class manufacturers or service providers. These companies typically place a great deal of emphasis on ongoing innovations developed within the organization, particularly on improving the processes used to produce goods and services. For example, Motorola has reached stage 4 through its "Operation Bandit" robotic production line (see the Case in Point discussion).

MOTOROLA'S BANDIT LINE MAKES 29 MILLION VARIATIONS   CASE IN POINT

A dominant force in the U.S. market for pocket pagers, Motorola watched as Japanese producers forced out half a dozen other domestic pager makers. Determined to stay competitive, Motorola's paging division developed a $9 million state-of-the-art manufacturing assembly line that operates along one wall of Motorola's Boynton Beach plant in southern Florida. The production line is dubbed "Operation Bandit" because it borrows heavily from the best legally available manufacturing methods, including those used by Seiko and Honda.

The Bandit line produces one type of pager, the "Bravo," which is marketed under several different brand names. Because the pagers work by a unique combination of access codes and radio frequencies, the Bandit line is able to produce pagers in an astronomical 29 million variations.

On the Bandit line, robots dominate. They receive production orders by computer and then perform a large part of the assembling, adjusting, and checking. They carry out these functions within one-hundredth of the time and with half the defect rate of conventional manufacturing methods. Originally, the Bandit robots were aided by about a dozen human employees who monitored the system and loaded it with sufficient parts to operate for an 8-hour stretch. Recently more humans have been added to the line to add to the line's flexibility. When a unique pager component must be placed on the circuit board, humans are able to quickly make the adjustment to place the component properly. In the same situation, robots sometimes do not place the part with the desired accuracy.

It took Motorola 18 months to design and install the Bandit system. In the process, the design team reconfigured the insides of the Bravo pager to facilitate its assembly by robots. In making decisions whether to add humans in place of robots, Motorola's director of manufacturing for the plant considers velocity and productivity. Velocity is the time a unit spends on the assembly line. Productivity is considered in terms of units of direct labor hours. For some applications, humans are faster and, in some cases, produce better quality.[11]   ■■■

■ DEVELOPING AND IMPLEMENTING OPERATING SYSTEMS

Successfully carrying out an operations strategy requires the design and implementation of well-conceived operating systems, the major methods used to achieve efficiency and effectiveness in manufacturing and service operations. The primary operating systems used in operations management are forecasting, capacity planning, aggregate production planning, scheduling, materials requirements planning, and purchasing (see Figure 18-4). In this section, we also consider some important aspects of service delivery systems. Quality control, another important system in operations management, is discussed extensively in Chapter 17.

Forecasting

Forecasting is the process of making predictions about changing conditions and future events that may significantly affect the business of an organization. Major forecasting methods are explained in the Supplement to Chapter 5.

For operations management purposes, forecasting efforts are aimed mainly at predicting goods or services *demand*. Forecasts of demand can range from short- to long-term and typically depend on quantitative and judgmental forecasting methods. Forecasting short-term demand (up to 1 year, but often ranging from less than a month to 3 months) is important because demand predictions affect relatively short-run conditions, such as scheduling production and having sufficient materials on hand to meet the schedule. For example, in Rubbermaid's home-products division, quantitative methods are used each month to make 30-day, 60-day, 90-day, and annual forecasts of demand for 600 item packs (because products are often marketed in several different packaging schemes). The product managers then add their judgment to the statistical data to achieve the final forecasts.[12] Forecasting intermediate-term (1 to 5 years) or long-term (5 years or more) demand has a major impact on expansion decisions, such as acquiring important equipment and new facilities.

After preparing demand forecasts, managers use the information in two main ways. As indicated in Figure 18-4, forecasts of demand influence capacity

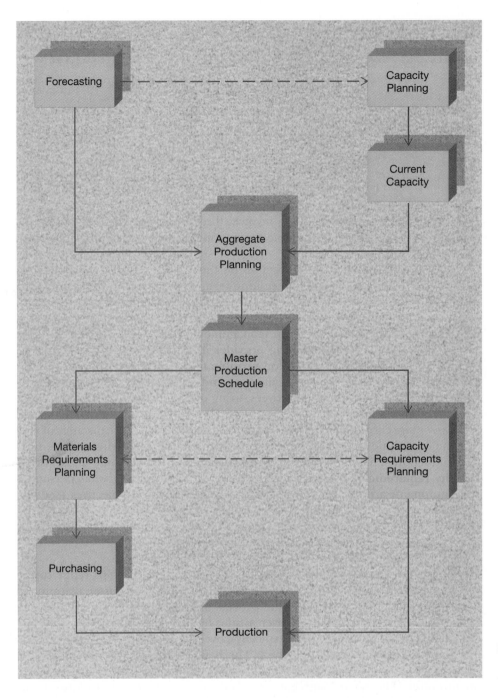

Figure 18-4 *Major systems used in operations management.*

planning and aggregate production planning. We consider capacity planning first.

Capacity Planning

Capacity planning is the process of determining the people, machines, and major physical resources, such as buildings, that will be necessary to meet the production objectives of the organization.[13] *Capacity* is the maximum output capability of a productive unit within a given period of time. For example, a car wash can handle only so many cars within an hour because of the physical constraints of the facility. Some common measures of capacity according to organization type are shown in Table 18-1.

Capacity planning The process of determining the people, machines, and major physical resources, such as buildings, that will be necessary to meet the production objectives of the organization

TABLE 18-1 MEASURES OF CAPACITY BY TYPE OF ORGANIZATION	
TYPES OF ORGANIZATION	**CAPACITY MEASURE**
Airline	Available seat-miles
Brewery	Kegs of beer
University	Class sections/seats
Restaurant	Seats and tables
Power company	Megawatts of electricity
Cannery	Tons of food
Retail store	Square feet of selling space
Auto repair shop	Service bays

TIME HORIZONS Capacity planning involves three different time horizons: long-, medium-, and short-range. Each time horizon involves somewhat different capacity-related issues.[14]

Long-range capacity planning focuses on the human, physical, and financial resources that are needed to meet long-term organizational goals. Because adding significantly to long-term capacity usually requires major capital expenditures for facilities and has considerable implications for employment, such decisions are typically made by top management.

Medium-range capacity planning provides information on the capacities of current major facilities, as well as on possible means of making limited adjustments in capacity during the intermediate and short terms. Such adjustments include hiring and laying off employees, using overtime, and building up inventory.

Short-range capacity planning is aimed at ensuring that the capacities of current major facilities are being utilized effectively within the context of the master production schedule. Planning within this time horizon may make use of **capacity requirements planning,** a technique for determining what personnel and equipment are needed to meet short-term production objectives (see Figure 18-4).

> **Capacity requirements planning** A technique for determining what personnel and equipment are needed to meet short-term production objectives

Aggregate Production Planning

Short-term forecasts of demand, as well as intermediate- and short-range capacity planning, are particularly important in aggregate production planning.[15] **Aggregate production planning** is the process of planning how to match supply with product or service demand over a time horizon of about 1 year (see Figure 18-4). Although the process typically covers 1 year, the aggregate plan is updated periodically (often monthly). The basic idea in aggregate planning is to achieve a rough balance between market demand and the capacity of the organization. The term "aggregate" is used because production plans at this point are stated in global units of output, such as number of automobiles, tons of steel, or seat-miles, rather than individual car models, specific steel products, or particular airline flights.

> **Aggregate production planning** The process of planning how to match supply with product or service demand over a time horizon of about 1 year

Aggregate planning relies on two assumptions. First, the maximum capacity of major facilities, such as plants, retail outlets, or extensive equipment, cannot be altered within the time frame. Second, short- and intermediate-term demands are subject to fluctuations because of uncertainties, seasonal influences, or other market-related factors. As a result, operations managers need to plan how to meet the fluctuating demand given the fixed capacities of their facilities.

Operations managers can use several major approaches to meet short-term and intermediate-term fluctuating demand. These approaches are summarized in Table 18-2.

Scheduling

Aggregate planning lays the rough groundwork for the next step, creating the master production schedule (see Figure 18-4). The **master production schedule (MPS)** translates the aggregate plan into a formalized production plan encompassing specific products to be produced or services to be offered and specific capacity requirements over a designated time period. Master scheduling involves some trial-and-error work and typically begins with a tentative schedule that is refined through several revisions.

TIME HORIZON The time horizon covered by a master schedule may be a few weeks or a year or more, depending on product or service characteristics and the lead times necessary for obtaining materials. Within the master schedule, the various activities are often broken down on a weekly basis. Some organizations use weekly intervals for 13 weeks (one quarter) and monthly intervals beyond the quarter.

MPS ADVANTAGES Using a master production schedule has several advantages. For one thing, master scheduling helps managers evaluate alternative schedules. Many computerized production and inventory control systems enable managers to simulate the effects of a proposed production schedule. By means of the simulation, planners can determine what lead times for materials and what delivery dates to customers would result from alternative schedules. Another advantage of the master scheduling process is that it helps determine the materials required. It does so by providing specific information about what products or services are to be produced. This ensures that materials are purchased and delivered in time to meet scheduled production. Still another advantage is that an MPS provides specific information about immediate capacity requirements (such as labor and equipment resources) for use in capacity requirements planning (see Figure 18-4). If the requirements exceed the available capacity, schedule adjustments, such as delaying the production of some items or services, may be required. On the other hand, underutilization of capacity may call for producing some items ahead of schedule, if feasible, or possibly generating greater demand (perhaps through a special promotion).

Master production schedule (MPS) A schedule that translates the aggregate plan into a formalized production plan encompassing specific products to be produced or services to be offered and specific capacity requirements over a designated time period

TABLE 18-2 MAJOR APPROACHES TO COPING WITH FLUCTUATING DEMAND

MAJOR APPROACH	RELATED ISSUES
Pay overtime	Expensive, but possibly less expensive than hiring extra workers who are idle part of the time
Hire temporary workers	Helpful for predictable demand increases of some duration; may be difficult to obtain the necessary skills
Hire part-time workers	May be more helpful to address demand peaks in service than in manufacturing
Develop multiskilled staff	May involve considerable time and expense, but allows workers to help out where needed
Build inventory	May be good utilization for slow periods; runs risk that inventory will become obsolete; increases holding costs; usually not appropriate for service
Take back orders; have customer returns policy	Customers may be dissatisfied and/or go to a competitor; may be effective if time frame is reasonable
Subcontract work to vendors	Expensive; less control over quality
Offer premiums/discounts for customer flexibility	Provide discounts for orders/service during slow periods or charge less for service flexibility (e.g., third-class mail)

Finally, the master schedule facilitates sharing relevant information about marketing (such as customer deliveries), inventory, and personnel matters (such as personnel needs).

Materials Requirements Planning

While developing a master schedule is important, scheduled production cannot occur unless the appropriate materials are in place at the right time to do the job. One effective means of handling materials issues is the use of materials requirements planning, which must be closely coordinated with the master production schedule (see Figure 18-4). **Materials requirements planning (MRP)** is a computer-based inventory system that projects materials requirements for the goods and services specified in the master schedule and initiates the actions necessary to acquire the materials when needed.

MRP systems can handle various types of inventory, but they are particularly adept at dealing with **dependent demand inventory,** the raw materials, components, and subassemblies that are used in the production of an end product or service. For example, if a company makes wheelbarrows, components such as tires, wheels, and axles are considered to be dependent demand inventory items because they are used to create end products (wheelbarrows), rather than being end products in themselves. In other words, the inventory *demand* for these items is *dependent* on the need for the end products. In contrast, **independent demand inventory** consists of end products, parts used for repairs, and other items whose demand is tied more directly to market issues. While MRP systems are common in manufacturing, the approach is only beginning to be applied to service organizations, but it offers tremendous possibilities for productivity improvements in operations such as restaurants, hotels, legal offices, and health care.

INPUTS TO MRP SYSTEMS In manufacturing, MRP systems use three major inputs: the master production schedule, bill-of-materials information, and inventory status information. The MRP system obtains specific information about products to be produced from the master production schedule.

The system then consults the bill of materials for each product and model to determine the exact materials required. A **bill of materials (BOM)** is a listing of all components, including partially assembled pieces and basic parts, that make up an end product. The bill of materials usually includes the part numbers and quantities required per unit of end product. It is often organized in a hierarchy so that it is possible to determine the most basic ingredients as well as the subassemblies. For example, Figure 18-5 shows a product structure tree indicating the BOM levels for a wheelbarrow. As the figure indicates, the bars and grips at level 2 are assembled to make up the handle assembly in level 1. Similarly, the tire at level 3 (the most basic level) and the axle, bearings, and wheel at level 2 make up the wheel assembly in level 1. The top level (0) shows the end product. Bill-of-materials information is kept in computer files for ready access by the MRP system so that exact materials requirements for a proposed master schedule can be determined rapidly. The larger the number of levels in the BOM, the more likely that an MRP system is needed to help manage materials in the production process.[16] The MRP system also makes use of computerized inventory status information to determine quantities of needed materials on hand, scheduled receipts of already ordered materials, and orders about to be released.

For service applications, the bill of materials might be replaced by a bill of activities. Combined with the master production schedule and inventory sta-

Materials requirements planning (MRP) A computer-based inventory system that develops materials requirements for the goods and services specified in the master schedule and initiates the actions necessary to acquire the materials when needed

Dependent demand inventory A type of inventory consisting of the raw materials, components, and subassemblies that are used in the production of an end product or service

Independent demand inventory A type of inventory consisting of end products, parts used for repairs, and other items whose demand is tied more directly to market issues than that for dependent demand inventory items

Bill of materials (BOM) A listing of all components, including partially assembled pieces and basic parts, that make up an end product

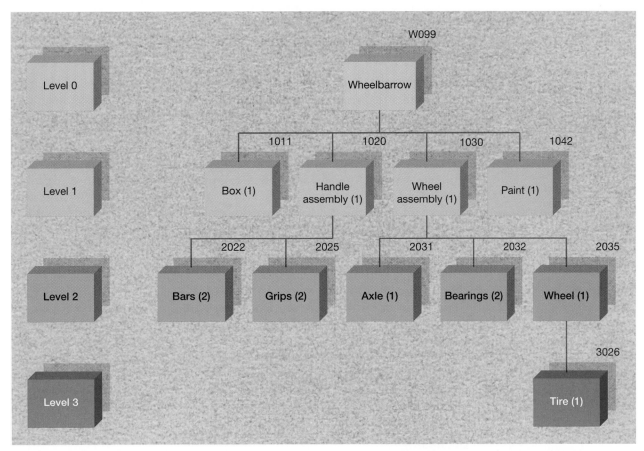

Figure 18-5 *Bill-of-materials levels for a wheelbarrow. (Reprinted from Joseph G. Monks,* Operations Management, *McGraw-Hill, New York, 1987, p. 444.)*

tus information, the bill of activities might be used as a basis for determining all the activities and personnel required to produce a particular combination of services. If materials are an important part of the service to be delivered, a bill of materials may also be needed. In one application of the MRP system at a utility, new customer requests for electric service are entered into a computer system that prepares a detailed estimate of the labor, materials, and work activities required. Estimates for various service requests are then combined to determine whether sufficient capacity is available. Ultimately, utility work crews are given work orders from the system. The crews report back to the system as work is completed.[17]

BENEFITS FROM MRP SYSTEMS Four major types of outputs come from MRP systems. First, the system triggers orders for materials. The orders go to purchasing for handling or to internal departments that will supply the necessary components. Second, the system supplies information to master production schedulers, indicating any materials procurement difficulties that will interfere with the proposed master schedule. Third, the MRP system gives information to individuals in charge of capacity planning. These individuals can then make short-run changes such as shifting equipment and adding people (through capacity requirements planning) or can consider longer-run changes based on trends. Fourth, the system can provide management with valuable information in such areas as costs, quality, and supplier activities.

MRP systems operate very differently from the just-in-time (JIT) inventory approach described in Chapter 17. Like the JIT approach, MRP is aimed at reducing inventory costs and keeping the production line supplied with the materials it needs to run smoothly. However, MRP systems do so by planning extensively and using lead times to order exactly what is needed on the basis of the master production schedule (plus perhaps a small amount of safety stock to allow for some schedule changes).

MANUFACTURING RESOURCE PLANNING On the basis of the success of materials requirements planning systems, a number of organizations have instituted an expanded version of MRP. **Manufacturing resource planning (MRP II)** is a computer-based information system that integrates the production planning and control activities of basic MRP systems with related financial, accounting, personnel, engineering, and marketing information. MRP II systems tie operations management information into a common system with other organizational functions.[18] For example, when an organization with an MRP II system produces an item, the system analyzes the labor and materials costs, captures the cash-flow implications, and notifies marketing that the product is in stock. These and other activities enable the operations management function to coordinate its efforts with the rest of the organization.

> **Manufacturing resource planning (MRP II)** A computer-based information system that integrates the production planning and control activities of basic MRP systems with related financial, accounting, personnel, engineering, and marketing information

Although MRP II systems can be expensive and time-consuming to implement successfully, results have been impressive. For example, at Tektronix, a manufacturer of oscilloscopes, computer workstations, and related products, an MRP II system led to a 61 percent cut in inventory and a 47 percent reduction in needed warehouse space.[19] Pharmaceutical firms, aerospace and defense contractors, and automotive and parts manufacturers are among the biggest users of MRP II systems.[20] Again, such systems are potentially applicable to service organizations, but they are only beginning to be implemented in that sector.

Purchasing

> **Purchasing** The process of acquiring necessary goods or services in exchange for funds or other remuneration

In order to conduct their business, most organizations need materials and services that they obtain through **purchasing,** the process of acquiring necessary goods or services in exchange for funds or other remuneration.[21] Purchasing needs are identified through materials requirements planning (see Figure 18-4). Then the purchasing process takes place. This involves such actions as investigating vendors to determine whether they are qualified to provide supplies, seeking alternative sources of supplies, and negotiating low, favorable purchasing prices.

Traditionally, the purchasing function has been viewed as almost a clerical task, aimed at buying commodities that meet specifications, rather than as a technical or managerial task. More recently, though, this view has been changing because of environmental and competitive developments.[22] Four factors, in particular, have contributed to the growing importance of purchasing. One is rising costs. Materials and supplies can amount to significant expenditures, and small savings on purchases can make a considerable difference to a company's bottom line.

Another factor is advancing technology. Many of today's products are highly complex and difficult to evaluate. As a result, greater technical expertise is required to make good purchasing decisions. Companies such as Eli Lilly and Motorola have begun to hire M.B.A.s with technical backgrounds to take charge of purchasing in crucial technical areas. Yet another factor is the rising importance of obtaining high-quality materials and services from suppliers. Without high-quality input, organizations have much greater difficulty producing the high-quality outputs that are necessary for competing effectively in the marketplace.

Finally, the increasing rate of technological change has led to more new product and service introductions with shorter lead times. Organizations can shorten development time and reduce expenses by obtaining more materials from outside vendors and involving the vendors in the actual product or service design phase. For example, General Electric's jet engine division has used 16 design teams to work on various aspects of its new commercial engine. Each of the teams included members from the purchasing staff who could help involve vendors in the design process. GE expects that the involvement of purchasing and vendors will ultimately reduce product development costs by as much as 20 percent.

The Service Delivery System

As pointed out earlier in the chapter, service delivery differs from manufacturing in a number of important ways. In addition, there are considerable differences among services. The prime purpose of a service delivery system is to maximize the perceived benefits to the customer relative to the costs involved in providing the service. We first examine these service differences through the mechanism of the matrix of service characteristics. We then consider ways in which organizations attempt to manage customer contact so that customer service is both effective and efficient.[23]

MATRIX OF SERVICE CHARACTERISTICS The matrix of service characteristics divides services into four groups depending on the complexity of service and the degree of customization required (see Figure 18-6). Complexity is related to the extent of knowledge and skill or capital investment involved. The customer often can perform many of the services on the right side of the matrix, but would likely require some practice and considerable time. Thus, consumers purchase these services mainly to save time and money. Services on the left side require more knowledge or equipment than can usually be readily obtained by

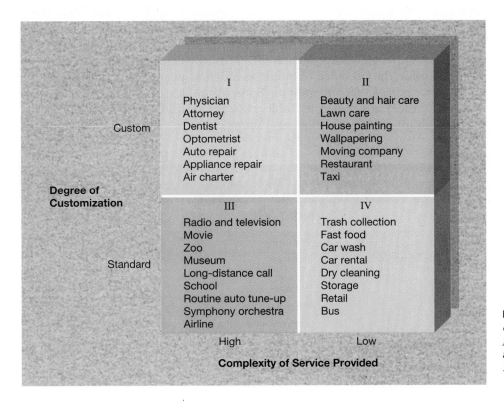

Figure 18-6 *Matrix of service characteristics. (Reprinted from James B. Dilworth,* Production and Operations Management, *5th ed., McGraw-Hill, New York, 1993, p. 371.)*

the average consumer. Customization refers to the extent to which the service is tailored to the needs of a specific customer. Services in the top half of the matrix require considerable customization, while those in the bottom half are relatively standardized.

Since services in all the quadrants typically involve some customer contact, businesses in all the quadrants are likely to attempt to hire workers who have good interpersonal skills in terms of interacting with customers. For many of the services in quadrants II and IV, businesses can train workers to provide the necessary levels of service, but workers in quadrant II will need to be more flexible in tailoring services to customer needs. The services associated with quadrant I, though, require workers with professional training that usually must be obtained outside the business. Significant investments in facilities and equipment are often required to offer services in quadrant III. Costs associated with the special training required for the service workers in this quadrant often are high, but economies of scale help lower the price charged to individual consumers. To be successful, businesses in quadrant III must offer a mix of services that will attract large numbers of customers.

MANAGING CUSTOMER CONTACT Experts argue that the degree to which a service can be efficient is directly related to the extent of customer contact. The more the customer contact, the greater the prospects for unusual requests, changes in customer instructions, the desire of the customer to chat, and other customer behaviors that tend to reduce service delivery efficiency. By their nature, some services, such as mail service or shopping from mail-order catalogs, tend to involve relatively low levels of customer contact. Others, though, such as restaurants and hotels, involve moderate levels of contact. Still others, such as physician's care or counseling, normally necessitate a high level of customer contact.

A common strategy to aid service delivery efficiency is to separate from customer contact those parts of the operation that do not require customer interaction. In hotels, for example, some functions, such as registration clerk, bell captain, and cashier, are oriented to heavy customer contact and strong efforts to establish a friendly, responsive atmosphere. These are called *front office* operations. Other functions, such as the cleaning of customers' rooms, are conducted outside the presence of guests as much as possible. Such functions are referred to as *back office* operations. Some examples of operations with front and back offices are shown in Table 18-3. Besides limiting customer contact, another advantage of back office operations is that they can often be conducted

TABLE 18-3 EXAMPLES OF SERVICE OPERATIONS WITH FRONT AND BACK OFFICES		
OPERATION	**FRONT OFFICE**	**BACK OFFICE**
Bank	Tellers, loan officers	Posting clerks, encoders
Stock brokerage office	Brokers	Transaction clerks, keypunch operators
Restaurant	Hostesses, waiters	Chefs, cooks, dishwashers
Library	Reference desk	Purchasing, reshelving
Auto shop	Service writers	Mechanics
Laundry	Pickup counter	Pressers, folders

Source: Reprinted from James B. Dilworth, *Production and Operations Management,* 5th ed., McGraw-Hill, New York, 1993, p. 375.

in less expensive locations and can be centralized for economies of scale. For example, Taco Bell greatly reduced costs and at the same time increased customer perceptions of service when the chain shifted most of the food preparation (such as chopping taco ingredients) to a central location and delivered the prepared materials to the restaurants for final assembly. This enabled the restaurant personnel to spend more time interacting with the customers to establish a warm, friendly, service-oriented atmosphere.

■ DESIGNING AND UTILIZING FACILITIES

Facilities is an area closely related to the issue of capacity planning. **Facilities** are the land, buildings, equipment, and other major physical inputs that substantially determine productive capacity, require time to alter, and involve significant capital investments. Facilities issues confronting managers focus mainly on expansion and contraction decisions, facilities location, and facilities layout.

Facilities The land, buildings, equipment, and other major physical inputs that substantially determine productivity capacity, require time to alter, and involve significant capital investments

Expansion and Contraction Decisions

Making decisions about expanding or contracting available facilities is directly related to long-range capacity planning. Typically, the facilities decision process involves four steps.[24] First, managers use forecasts to determine the probable future demand for products or services. Since it often takes 2 or more years to build facilities and put them into operation, relevant forecasts must extend over several years, adding to the uncertainty involved.

Second, managers compare current capacity with projected future demand. *Current capacity* is the maximum output rate possible from current operations. By comparing it with future demand, managers can determine whether current capacity is insufficient, about right, or excessive.

Third, when there is either insufficient or excess capacity, managers need to generate and then evaluate alternatives. In many cases, the number of alternatives available for making changes in facilities is large. In others, it may be difficult to develop even one feasible alternative. Alternatives typically involve location considerations, an issue we discuss below.

Fourth, managers carefully consider the risks and decide on a plan that includes the timing of capacity expansion or contraction, if any. Facilities decisions usually involve considerable risk because additional facilities raise fixed costs that must be paid even if the expected demand does not materialize. On the other hand, insufficient capacity may provide competitors with opportunities to attract customers that would otherwise have been yours. Because of such considerations, Ford Motor's top executives have faced difficult decisions. They foresaw a worldwide capacity glut in the automobile industry for the 1990s, so they were reluctant to add to capacity by building new plants. Yet at various points Ford automobiles, such as the Taurus and the Explorer, have sold so well that the company could not meet the demand, even with extensive overtime.[25]

Facilities Location

The location of plants, warehouses, and service facilities is an important aspect of facilities decisions. In fact, for the most part, decisions about additional facilities are closely connected to location considerations. Most facilities location problems fall into one of four categories: single facility, multiple factories and warehouses, competitive retail outlets, and emergency services. Each of these categories entails somewhat different criteria for deciding on facilities locations.

Wal-Mart carefully locates a number of retail facilities within a 400-mile radius of a warehouse. This allows the company to cut costs by pooling the overhead for advertising and distribution.

A *single-facility* location involves a facility that does not need to interact with any other facilities that the organization might have. A single factory or warehouse or a single retail store would fit into this category. Location decisions for a single facility typically revolve around multiple criteria, such as labor costs, labor supply, raw materials, transportation availability, community services, taxes, and other relevant issues.

Locations for *multiple factories and warehouses* usually involve strong consideration of the costs associated with distributing products to customers. For complex problems involving multiple facilities, operations research methods may be used to help determine locations that will minimize distribution costs. Much of Wal-Mart's phenomenal success comes from its policy of carefully locating warehouses and then opening multiple stores within a 400-mile radius to pool distribution and advertising overhead.[26] Recently, efforts to adapt just-in-time inventory methods are causing manufacturing organizations to consider facility sites closer to major customers.

Locations for *competitive retail outlets* must be oriented toward consideration of the revenue that can be obtained from various locations. For example, the location of a bank, shopping center, or movie theater relative to both customers and competitors usually has a strong bearing on how much revenue the facility generates. A number of commercially available computer programs use census and other data to help major retailers, such as Woolworth, choose new locations for retail outlets.[27]

The location of *emergency services* is often connected to response time. For example, police and fire departments must be located where they can provide an acceptable level of service, which includes a speedy response in emergencies.

Facilities Layout

Another important aspect of facilities is the layout, the configuration of processing components (departments, workstations, and equipment) that make up the production sequence. There are three main types of layouts for facilities: process, product, and fixed position.[28]

Process layout A production configuration in which the processing components are grouped according to the type of function that they perform

PROCESS LAYOUT A **process layout** is a production configuration in which the processing components are grouped according to the type of function that they perform. The product being made or the client receiving service moves from function to function depending on the particular needs for that product or client. As a result, the demand for any particular function is somewhat intermittent, since some products or clients may not require the use of a given function. With intermittent demand, a function can be idle at some times and backed up with waiting work at other times. A process layout makes sense when a variety of products and services are produced or when many variations of a particular product or service require different functions for production. See Figure 18-7 for examples of process layouts for a product (machine shop) and a service (medical clinic).

Product layout A production configuration in which the processing components are arranged in a specialized line along which the product or client passes during the production process

PRODUCT LAYOUT A **product layout** is a production configuration in which the processing components are arranged in a specialized line along which the product or client passes during the production process. With this arrangement, a product or service is produced through a somewhat standardized production sequence geared specifically to the particular characteristics of the product or service. Examples of product layouts for a product (a separate, specialized assembly line for each of three products) and a service (a driver's license pro-

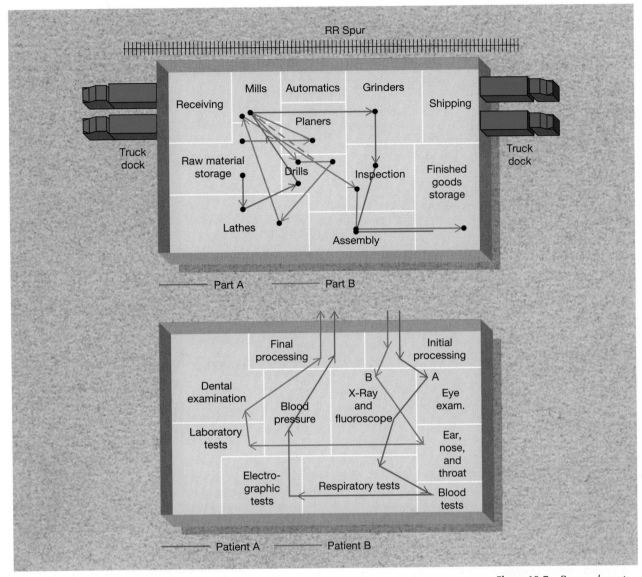

Figure 18-7 *Process layouts for (top) a machine shop and (bottom) a medical clinic. (Reprinted from Elwood S. Buffa,* Modern Production/Operations Management, *Wiley, New York, 1983, p. 32.)*

cessing center set up to render one type of specialized service) are shown in Figure 18-8. Other common examples of product layouts are the configurations at automatic car washes, cafeteria lines, and mass medical examinations for military recruits.

Product layouts are used mainly when one standardized product or service is produced, usually in large volume. Each item or service being produced requires essentially the same or a similar production process, with perhaps a limited number of variations. The problems at Winnebago Industries, Inc., illustrate the difficulties that can ensue when too many product variations are attempted with a product layout (see the Case in Point discussion).

WINNEBAGO'S PRODUCTION LINES GO AWRY
CASE IN POINT

When Gerald Gilbert took the job of chief executive officer of Winnebago Industries, Inc., he assessed conditions in the Forest City, Iowa, factory as "still in the Dark Ages." He found excess inventory, outdated design methods, and

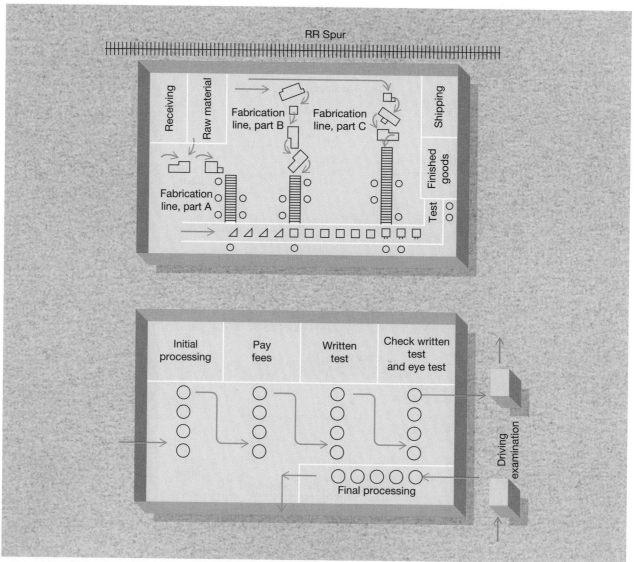

Figure 18-8 *Product layouts for (top) a three-product plant and (bottom) a driver's license processing center. (Reprinted from Elwood S. Buffa,* Modern Production/Operations Management, *Wiley, New York, 1983, p. 33.)*

few standardized parts. "There were something like 800 different cabinet doors, some an eighth of an inch apart" in measurement, according to Gilbert. To solve these problems, he quickly hired Richard Berreth, his friend and a manufacturing expert, as executive vice president. Berreth, like Gilbert, had been a vice president at Control Data and had managed factories making key components and employing between 2000 and 7200 people.

Berreth tackled inventory costs by having workers unload heavily used components from trucks and take them directly to the assembly line. He created employee teams that were responsible for the quality of particular parts of the assembly process. His various efforts soon halved the time it took to make a motor home.

Unfortunately, a steep stock market decline caused the motor-home recreation vehicles to slow to a crawl. Berreth took the opportunity created by the slower sales to institute an even bigger change: merging three assembly lines into two. The move ushered in a new approach to assembly, one in which appliances and cabinets were attached to the walls before the walls were hoisted onto the vehicle on the assembly line. Previously, workers had first assembled the walls on the vehicle and then loaded the appliances and cabinets through windows or the side door, a process that often led to dents and scratches.

The merged lines progressed well at first. Sales began to pick up significantly just as another big change was being implemented. This move involved switching from batch production, in which 50 to 100 vehicles of the same model were made at one time, to mixed production, in which any of 58 models could come down the line. With the batch system, the workers had quickly adjusted to a change in the model and soon picked up their production rhythm again. With the new system, every vehicle was a different model from the previous one, and the workers began to get confused and frustrated.

Going to two lines also meant that the workers were crowded together. As production accelerated in response to the growing number of orders, the assembly lines began to get jammed. Soon overtime, including Saturdays, became mandatory. Meanwhile, new models were being rushed into production. A sign over one of the production lines read, "Quality is chief on this reservation." In actuality, the lines were producing anything but quality. Holes in parts wouldn't line up, fasteners couldn't be inserted, and parts weren't available when they were needed. The parking lot began to fill up with motor homes needing further work before they could be shipped.

As if conditions were not bleak enough, a summer heat wave arrived that sent temperatures in the factory, which had no air-conditioning, soaring to almost 100 degrees. Tempers flared out of control. Workers punched holes in carpeting and scrawled epithets on plant walls. Some quit. The chaos caused Winnebago to lose an estimated 1000 motor home sales because orders could not be filled. Finally, after checking with the board of directors, founder and chairman of the board John K. Hanson fired both Gilbert and Berreth. Soon after, Winnebago switched back to three production lines, instead of two, and once again began filling its orders as it worked to regain market share.[29]

■■■

FIXED-POSITION LAYOUT A **fixed-position layout** is a production configuration in which the product or client remains in one location and the tools, equipment, and expertise are brought to it, as necessary, to complete the productive process. This arrangement is typically used when it is not feasible to move the product—because of size, shape, or any other characteristic—or when it makes more sense to take the service to the client. For example, the fixed-position

Fixed-position layout A production configuration in which the product or client remains in one location and the tools, equipment, and expertise are brought to it, as necessary, to complete the productive process

Aircraft manufacturing companies, such as this General Dynamics plant in Fort Worth, use the fixed-position layout. It's easier for workers to bring tools, parts, and expertise to the aircraft under production than to move it down an assembly line.

layout is often used in building ships, locomotives, and aircraft. It can also be used for services, such as furnace repair (in which the equipment, supplies, and repairing expertise are brought to the home or building) or a mobile CAT scanner (in which the unit is brought to various hospitals because it is more economical to share a scanner). Having appropriate facilities in which to work, of course, is critical to another major aspect of operations management, process technology.

■ PROMOTING INNOVATION: PROCESS TECHNOLOGY

Process technology is the technology used in transforming inputs into goods and services. It includes the tools, methods, procedures, equipment, and various steps involved in the production process.[30] Increasingly, process technology is an important factor in competitive success. One reason is the recent interest in reengineering, an approach aimed at developing innovative ways to perform the transformation process. Another is the increased possibility of using sophisticated technology in producing goods and services because of accelerating advances in computer software, computer-controlled machines, and robots such as those made by Fanuc. In this section, we explore the reengineering concept, examine recent innovations in computer-integrated manufacturing, and consider the application of advanced technology to service organizations.

Reengineering

Reengineering The thorough analysis and radical redesign of existing business processes to achieve breakthrough improvements by focusing on critical performance criteria, such as cost, quality, service, and speed

A number of organizations have been using reengineering to achieve competitive advantage in operations and other areas within the firm. **Reengineering** (sometimes called *business process redesign or BPR*) is the thorough analysis and radical redesign of existing business processes to achieve breakthrough improvements by focusing on critical performance criteria, such as cost, quality, service, and speed.[31] The original popularization of reengineering envisioned that such efforts would rely heavily on information technology as the vehicle for radical change. While information technology has been an important element, one study of 23 reengineering projects suggested that a key driving force behind reengineering efforts seems to be a major change in goal, such as a new emphasis on reducing costs or reducing cycle time. Such goals are typically set by senior management, whose support of reengineering efforts is usually critical to subsequent success. The researchers also found that reengineering efforts typically involved cross-functional teams who work together to make recommendations and help implement the newly designed processes.[32]

For example, Baxter International has used reengineering to make major cost cuts in its distribution unit, which delivers more than 200,000 different medical supplies to hospitals and other health care providers. One team was charged with reducing the number of different products held in the 68 warehouses located close to customers. After analyzing and reanalyzing inventory and sales data, the team was surprised to discover that 57 percent of the products on warehouse shelves accounted for just 2 percent of sales. One result was a radical shift to a three-tiered inventory system. Under the new system, products that hospitals order frequently, such as popular styles of gloves, caps, needles, and sutures, are still stocked in the warehouses located near customers. Supplies that hospitals order somewhat less frequently, such as odd sizes of gloves or special types of sutures, are now shipped nationwide from a Baxter Midwest distribution center in Waukegan, Illinois. Slow-moving items are ordered from the manufacturer and shipped directly to the customer.[33]

Computer-Integrated Manufacturing

Computer-integrated manufacturing (CIM) is the computerized integration of all major functions associated with the production of a product. Such functions typically include designing and engineering products, instructing machines, handling materials, controlling inventories, and directing the production process. Operations that use CIM are sometimes referred to as "factories of the future" because they use the latest technology to create world-class production facilities. CIM systems typically make extensive use of sophisticated materials requirements planning (MRP) systems. They usually rely on several other types of computerized systems as well, such as computer-aided design, computer-aided manufacturing, and flexible manufacturing systems.

COMPUTER-AIDED DESIGN **Computer-aided design (CAD)** is a system that uses computers to geometrically prepare, review, and evaluate product designs. With CAD, engineers and designers can alter and evaluate initial designs easily. Thus the system involves considerably less time and expense than conventional methods such as making physical mock-ups of various designs. Because the design is in a computer data base, it can be accessed later for further work and additional tests. CAD systems also allow designers to test such factors as stress tolerance and reliability by computer.

COMPUTER-AIDED MANUFACTURING **Computer-aided manufacturing (CAM)** is a system that uses computers to design and control production processes. To put products into production, CAM systems access the computer-stored information on product designs developed through CAD. With CAM, it is usually possible to change machine setups automatically by computer, as well as to move materials and work in progress from one machine to the other automatically. For example, Westt, Inc., of Menlo, California, makes parts for Silicon Valley's Watkins-Johnson, a manufacturer of chipmaking equipment and electronics products. Watkins-Johnson develops the specifications by CAD and sends them to Westt via the Internet. Westt converts the CAD specs to CAM instructions that it downloads to its manufacturing machines. For simple parts, the whole process from transmission of the CAD materials to manufacture can take place within one half hour.[34]

FLEXIBLE MANUFACTURING SYSTEMS Computer-integrated manufacturing often incorporates another computer-related manufacturing concept, flexible manufacturing systems. A **flexible manufacturing system (FMS)** is a system that uses computers to control machines and the production process automatically so that different types of parts or product configurations can be handled on the same production line. Flexible manufacturing typically makes use of **group technology,** the classification of parts into families (groups of parts or products that have some similarities in the way they are manufactured) so that members of the same family can be manufactured on the same production line. By grouping similar products together for manufacture, an FMS can be programmed for rapidly setting up machines to handle both very small and very large quantities of particular parts through the same production process. This flexibility can make it cost-effective to manufacture products in lots as small as one and enables manufacturers to be more responsive to customers.[35] The benefits of flexible manufacturing can be seen at Allen-Bradley, a subsidiary of Rockwell International. The company took 3 years to install computer-integrated manufacturing in its Milwaukee, Wisconsin, plant, which produces contactors (devices that turn motors on and off). The plant now turns out 600 units per hour in more than 777 varieties in lot sizes as small as one or two.[36]

Computer-integrated manufacturing (CIM) The computerized integration of all major functions associated with the production of a product

Computer-aided design (CAD) A system that uses computers to geometrically prepare, review, and evaluate product designs

Computer-aided manufacturing (CAM) A system that uses computers to design and control production processes

Flexible manufacturing system (FMS) A manufacturing system that uses computers to control machines and the production process automatically so that different types of parts or product configurations can be handled on the same production line

Group technology The classification of parts into families (groups of parts or products that have some similarities in the way they are manufactured) so that members of the same family can be manufactured on the same production line

Service Applications

Advanced technology is also providing possibilities for innovation in service industries, although the vast potential is only beginning to be tapped.[37] For example, automated teller machines (ATMs) enabled the Wells Fargo Bank to eliminate 700 employees from its work force and close 30 bank branches within 2 years of the machines' installation.

Super Valu, a grocery wholesaler that mainly serves independently owned supermarkets, offers a program called SLASH (Site Location Analysis Strategy Heuristic) that helps its retailer customers select advantageous store locations. The program incorporates a CAD system that enables architects to assess more than 100 store plans on a computer screen. Similarly, Fidelity Investments has enhanced its customer service by means of an advanced telephone system that can handle 864 calls simultaneously through automated, toll-free lines. A master computer console at headquarters in Boston routes calls to the 1000 available operators in telephone centers throughout the United States. The representative can then obtain instant computer access to the caller's Fidelity accounts, trading history over the last 12 months, and age—information that helps the representative serve the caller more effectively.[38] Effective use of advanced technology in service organizations requires careful identification of the areas in which the technology can make a major difference in services offered and productivity.

■ IMPROVING PRODUCTIVITY

As the clock struck noon in Appleton, Wisconsin, the entire 500-member insurance staff of the Aid Association for Lutherans (AAL), a fraternal society that operates as a large insurance business, piled their personal belongings on chairs and rolled the chairs to other parts of headquarters. Corridors were jammed as "organized chaos" brought a reorganization of insurance operations into reality. Within 2 hours, the move transformed the functionally organized bureaucracy into self-managing teams (see Chapter 15) that would eventually operate without several layers of supervisors. Under the new arrangement, all the policies related to a particular customer would be handled by a single team, rather than being routed to separate departments. Within a year of the move, productivity rose 20 percent—a significant amount, particularly for a service organization.[39]

The results at AAL are only one example of what can be accomplished when productivity improvements in operations are given high priority. Within organizations, attempts to improve productivity—that is, to generate more outputs from the same or fewer inputs—depend on the five-step process described below:

1 **Establish a base point against which to assess future improvements.** Measures that managers could use as a base point include the number of claims processed daily, dollar income per square foot of selling space, amount produced per day, percentage of output passing inspection, percentage of repaired items that had to be returned for further repairs, or customers served per hour. The important thing is to choose measures that focus on important aspects of productivity for the particular organization or work unit. The continuous improvement principle associated with total quality management (see Chapter 17) also can be a helpful tool for encouraging productivity enhancement.

2 **Set goals to establish the desired productivity level.** A number of studies in

Only two workers are needed to look after 50 knitting machines in the automated mills of Milliken & Co., the South Carolina textile company. Yet the cost of turning cloth into clothing is still higher in the United States than abroad, making it difficult for American manufacturers to compete with cheaper imports. Milliken has found a way to compete by speedily responding to customer needs. Its workers can turn out additional cloth on very short notice, so that garment makers can quickly make copies of best-selling items.

a wide variety of jobs and industries support the usefulness of goal setting as a means of raising productivity levels.

3 **Review methods for increasing productivity.** Managers have a number of options for increasing productivity. Useful methods include improving employee selection techniques, placing people in jobs that are well matched to their qualifications, training workers in job-related skills, redesigning jobs to give workers more control over their own productivity, providing financial incentives that are carefully tied to productivity issues, and using feedback and performance appraisals to let workers know how they are doing.[40] Other approaches aimed at improving productivity involve many of the operations management techniques discussed in this chapter.

   One productivity expert argues that managers sometimes overemphasize cost cutting related to current processes, seeing it as the principal means of increasing productivity, and fail to adopt major new process technologies that would lead to significant breakthroughs in productivity and competitiveness.[41] Often, rethinking the work process itself, as suggested by the reengineering concept discussed earlier in this chapter, can result in breakthroughs. The new Sleep Inn hotel chain introduced by Manor Care has been developed with labor productivity in mind. For example, the hotels have a sophisticated washer and dryer installed behind the desk so that the night-shift desk operator can also do the laundry by pushing a few buttons. Concrete and shrubs eliminate grass cutting. Shower stalls are round so that they are easier to keep clean. Because of such labor-saving changes, a typical 100-bed Sleep Inn employs only 12 full-time employees, 13 percent fewer than the average for a no-frills hotel.

4 **Select a method and implement.** Managers should choose the method that appears to have the best chance of success in the particular situation. Implementation is likely to involve some considerations about the best way to bring about change (see Chapter 11).

5 **Measure results and modify as necessary.** Further modifications are necessary only if productivity is not improving as planned. Met goals, of course, lead to new goals, since increasing productivity is a continual challenge for successful organizations.

   One way to meet the productivity challenge is through judicious use of information technology, the subject of the next chapter.

■ CHAPTER SUMMARY

Operations management is the management of the productive processes that convert inputs into goods and services. The concept applies to both manufacturing and service industries, even though their characteristics differ to some degree. Major aspects of operations management include operations strategy, operating systems, facilities, and process technology.

Productivity is an efficiency concept that gauges the ratio of outputs relative to inputs into a productive process. Operations management plays different roles in determining strategy, depending on the strategic role stage into which an organization falls: stage 1, minimize negative potential; stage 2, achieve parity with competition; stage 3, support overall organizational strategy; and stage 4, pursue operations management–based strategy.

A number of systems are particularly important for effective operations management. Forecasting helps predict the demand for goods and services. Capacity planning is the process of determining the people, machines, and major physical resources, such as buildings, that will be needed to meet the production objectives of the organization. Capacity planning involves three different time horizons: long-, medium-, and short-term. Aggregate production planning helps match supply with product or service demand over a time horizon of about 1 year. The master production schedule translates the aggregate plan into a formalized production plan encompassing specific products to be produced and specific capacity requirements over a designated period. Materials requirements planning is a computer-based inventory system that develops materials requirements for the goods and services

specified in the master schedule and initiates the actions necessary to acquire the materials when needed. Manufacturing resource planning expands MRP systems to include related financial, accounting, personnel, engineering, and marketing information. Purchasing is the process of acquiring necessary goods and services in exchange for funds or other remuneration. The matrix of service characteristics classifies services according to complexity and degree of customization. Managing customer contact may involve separating service components into front office and back office operations.

Facilities issues focus mainly on expansion and contraction decisions, facilities location, and facilities layout. Most facilities location options fall into one of four categories: single facility, multiple factories and warehouses, competitive retail outlets, and emergency services. There are three major types of facilities layouts: process, product, and fixed position.

Recent innovations in process technology include reengineering and computer-integrated manufacturing. Major aspects of CIM include computer-aided design, computer-aided manufacturing, and flexible manufacturing systems. Process technology advances are also increasingly applicable to organizations in service industries.

Improving productivity involves five main steps: establish a base point, establish a desired productivity level, review methods for increasing productivity, select a method and implement, and measure results and modify as necessary.

■ QUESTIONS FOR DISCUSSION AND REVIEW

1 Explain the concept of productivity, including its linkage to operations management. Why is the operations management process a focal point for productivity improvements in organizations?

2 Describe the major ways in which producing manufactured goods differs from producing a service. Use two services that you have received recently to illustrate the characteristics of a service. Classify these services using the matrix of service characteristics.

3 Describe each of the four strategic role stages that influence the role operations management plays in an organization's strategy development. What information would you need to determine the strategic role stage of a particular organization?

4 Explain how each of the following systems is used in operations management: forecasting, capacity planning, aggregate planning, scheduling, materials requirements planning, and purchasing.

5 If you were in charge of aggregate planning for an organization, how might you cope with short- and intermediate-term fluctuations in demand?

6 Explain the steps involved in making expansion and contraction decisions about facilities. Identify an organization that has made an expansion and contraction decision recently and evaluate the apparent effectiveness of the decision.

7 Contrast the criteria used in locating facilities for each of the following types of organizations: single facility, multiple factories and warehouses, competitive retail outlets, and emergency services. Think of a retail outlet that has gone out of business. To what extent do you think location affected its demise?

8 Give an example of each of the three main types of facilities layouts.

9 Explain the process technology concept of reengineering. Identify an existing process that might benefit from reengineering and explain how you think it might be radically improved.

10 Explain the main steps involved in productivity improvement. For a job with which you are familiar, identify five ways to increase productivity.

■ DISCUSSION QUESTIONS FOR CHAPTER OPENING CASE

1 In relation to operations management, in which strategic role stage would you place Fanuc? What is your evidence?

2 What process technologies are in use at Fanuc? How does Dr. Inaba attempt to overcome potential barriers to computer-integrated manufacturing and related technologies?

3 What evidence exists of attempts to increase productivity at Fanuc? How are these efforts tied to Fanuc's operations strategy?

■ EXERCISES FOR MANAGING IN THE TWENTY-FIRST CENTURY

EXERCISE 1
SKILL BUILDING: IDENTIFYING ELEMENTS OF THE OPERATIONS MANAGEMENT PROCESS

 There are four major elements in the operations management process. These include developing an operations strategy, implementing operating systems, selecting proper facilities, and using available technologies. Examples of these elements are indicated below. Specify the element of the operations process discussed in the example by placing the appropriate letters on the line preceding the example.

Operations **S**trategy   **O**perating **S**ystems
Facilities   **P**rocess **T**echnology

1 ____ A hospital normally uses a process layout

2 ____ Planning the capacity of a part of the organization

3 ____ Installation of an FMS

4 ____ The organization keeps up with the competition

5 ____ Reviewing a proposed design using CAD

6 ____ Aggregate production planning is conducted annually and updated monthly

7 ____ Operations managers are creative in finding ways to implement a chosen strategy

8 ____ A television set is assembled using a product layout

9 ____ The master production schedule is monitored hourly in many situations

10 ____ Managers participate in planning operations, focusing on innovations and any other means to gain the competitive edge

EXERCISE 2
MANAGEMENT EXERCISE: OPERATION LANDSCAPING

 You have a successful landscaping company that has been growing in sales at the rate of about 20 percent annually. In addition to designing landscapes and selling, planting, pruning, and caring for plants, shrubs, and trees, your organization also provides complete lawn-care service. The company has a reputation for high-quality work, a reputation of which you are quite proud.

A local developer has just asked you to do the landscaping and lawn-care work for the general-use areas of a very large local community he is going to develop. The job is massive and will last at least 5 years. A quick estimate of its size and duration indicates that you may have to double the size of your work force, buy additional equipment, and construct a building (the developer will give you the land) in the area for your operations.

You recognize that there are many issues to be considered before you can decide whether to accept the job. Among them are several related to operations management, including forecasting, capacity planning, aggregate production planning, scheduling, MRP, facilities layout, and type of process technology that could be used.

Explain the major issues to be addressed in each category of operations management.

CONCLUDING CASE 1

CATERPILLAR USES OPERATIONS MANAGEMENT TO BECOME COMPETITIVE AGAIN

"Caterpillar" is a name known for quality. Since the 1920s, the company has been the world pacesetter in earth-moving equipment. More than half its business is conducted overseas. Caterpillar had experienced 50 straight years of profits until 1982, when it lost $180 million. During the next 2 years, it lost approximately $770 million more. The company knew that it had to change. By 1985, Caterpillar had turned around, and it has been making a profit ever since.

Caterpillar's return to profitability was the result of very deliberate actions. The company began to concentrate on driving costs down and improving its enviable reputation for quality. Cat slashed its work force by one-third, or 30,000 jobs. It also closed seven factories and canceled construction of its partially completed 1.8-million-square-foot parts distribution center in its headquarters town of Peoria, Illinois. Productivity rose by 30 percent.

An important part of the company's new direction was the decision to completely redesign and outfit its remaining 30 factories, a $1.8 billion modernization effort called Plant With A Future. In making this massive investment, Cat reworked its traditional manufacturing process. In the past, components or products were worked on in specialized areas, such as grinding or heat treating. Under the new system, activities are grouped by "cells," a form of flexible manufacturing whereby machines and workers operate in groups, with each group performing a variety of operations on products. With the new machines in the cells, setup time for working on new tasks is seconds (compared with 4 hours to 2 days with older machines). Furthermore,

the need for adjustments is minimal because the computer monitors the machine settings, so there is little scrap. The various cells are linked by computer and also tied into the materials supply system. The revamped factories use computerized machine tools, laser-read bar codes, and automated carrier systems for materials, but they stop short of computerized integration of everything from engineering to finance. Caterpillar has reduced the time necessary to make a machine from 24 to 6 days. It now takes 3.8 people to build a piece of equipment, compared with the 6 who were necessary before.

Another advantage of Caterpillar's new manufacturing flexibility is that the company can ship parts for both new equipment and equipment that is 20 years old or more within 24 hours. Caterpillar services about 480,000 items (different part numbers). The company stocks 320,000 of them, but makes the remaining 160,000 on demand. Caterpillar ships 84,000 parts per day, or about 1 per second every day of the year. The approach has given Caterpillar one of the fastest and most comprehensive parts-delivery systems in the world. Caterpillar guarantees delivery of any part anywhere within 48 hours.

To stimulate more worker involvement in the operations and improvement efforts, the company has its machinists take part in certifying suppliers. Since 1982, Caterpillar has certified more than 800 of its major suppliers. Certification means that the suppliers get preferential treatment as long as they agree to furnish parts that are close to perfect. The reject rate from certified suppliers runs .6 percent, compared with 2.8 percent from noncertified suppliers. In 1992, a 5½-month strike (by workers represented by the United Auto Workers union) ended when Cat threatened to hire permanent replacements for the striking workers. However, the lin-

gering bitter feelings jeopardized worker involvement efforts aimed at higher productivity and led to a second strike in 1995. After almost a year, UAW members rejected the company's proposed contract but quit their strike, with most returning to work. During the strike various company employees, as well as temporary workers from Mississippi and other states, managed to carry on production, and Caterpillar expanded its worldwide market share.

The company has also been vigorously developing new products. Since 1984, it has more than doubled its original product line of 150 models. Recognizing the trend toward smaller construction projects and fewer new superhighways, Cat has shifted its emphasis to smaller equipment. A new sprocket design is now used in all its tractors, an innovation that makes the machines last longer. In addition, Caterpillar is making light construction equipment with Mitsubishi Heavy Industries, Ltd., a company with which Cat has had several joint ventures over the past 25 years. The current joint venture manufactures products for sale both in the United States and in Pacific Rim countries.[42]

QUESTIONS FOR CONCLUDING CASE 1

1. In what strategy role stage would you place Caterpillar during the early 1980s? Where would you place the company now? Why?
2. What approach did Caterpillar take to adjust to the suddenly shifting demand for its products that took place in the early 1980s? What approaches could the company use now?
3. What operations management systems and new process technologies are in evidence as Caterpillar changes its manufacturing methods?

CONCLUDING CASE 2

CP GROUP REACHES FOR WORLD RECOGNITION

Charoen Pokphand Group (CP Group), headquartered in Bangkok, specializes in preparing and distributing processed chicken, shrimp, and animal feed. Its products, with sales in excess of $6.5 billion, are grown, processed, and sold in many countries. It is one of Asia's largest and most successful business empires and consists of more than 250 companies. One of CP's goals is to become the largest chicken, prawn, and feedstuff producer in the world. CP Group is concentrating on markets in the Far East, Europe, and the United States.

As personal incomes rise in Asia, diets are beginning to include more poultry and fish. For example, Thailand's per capita consumption of poultry has risen tenfold since the early 1970s. Chinese consumption has more than doubled since 1987. Elsewhere the demand for chicken and fish is also growing. CP's primary markets for these products are Thailand (60 million people), Indonesia (180 million), and China (1.2 billion).

The company began when a young man named Chia Ek Chor left southern China and moved to Bangkok. He had with him seeds from his family's farm for growing cabbages, parsnips, radishes, turnips, and cauliflower—all vegetables that were scarce throughout Southeast Asia. He began a seed company with supplies from his brother, who remained in China. In 1953, Mr. Chia's eldest son set up a feed mill for chickens and registered the business under the name Charoen Pokphand.

Mr. Chia's youngest son is Dhanin Chearavanont, the current chairman of CP Group, who acquired chickens from a supplier in the United States in 1973. He next hired nutritionists overseas to formulate a special feed that would fatten the chickens into 4-pound broilers in less than the normally required 3 to 4 months. The newly developed feed and day-old chicks were supplied to Thai farmers, who raised the chickens. CP then bought the chickens back at a guaranteed price, under a process called contract farming. With the newly developed feed, the chickens were ready for market in 6 to 7 weeks, and only half the previously required feed was necessary to get them to the desired 4-pound weight.

CP has applied this type of efficient production to several other aspects of its chicken business, such as processing. In one of its streamlined plants in Thailand, some 5000 workers cut up and debone 1 million broilers a week. In one room, 800 workers string chunks of chicken on skewers for freezing and export to Japan. In the next room, 600 workers cut breast meat into filets, which are later sold in Japanese supermarkets. The protein-rich chicken feathers are recycled into chicken feed, and the innards are used to make feed for the fish farms. The carcasses are fed to crocodiles, which are raised for their meat and hides. In addition, CP has developed a line of TV dinners, including microwave-ready prefried chicken, cabbage rolls stuffed with chicken, and Chinese dumplings. These products are destined for Japanese, Chinese, and European markets.

In 1986, CP Group diversified into shrimp farming. As with chickens, it contract-farms its shrimp, supplying farmers with larvae and feed. The feed is specially developed, sells for four times the price of chicken feed, and earns double the margins. CP buys the farmers' grown shrimp, processes them, and exports the frozen shrimp to Japan, the United States, and Europe.

Although CP Group began contract farming both chickens and shrimp in Thailand, it has now expanded the program to other countries in Asia and Europe. CP has made major in-roads into China, where CP's agribusiness group operates more than 80 companies, including feed mills, chicken farms, processing factories, and chicken fast-food shops. CP companies produce more than 300 million chickens annually in China, a number that is expected to increase rapidly. According to one estimate, CP Group may have more investments in China than any other multinational company in the world. In the United States, CP Group owns chicken farm operations in Maine, Kentucky, and Texas.

CP Group also has numerous other business ventures. In Thailand, it has the 7-Eleven franchise for the entire country, its own chain of Chester's sit-down grilled-chicken restaurants, and a network of 300 company-operated 5-Star Brand carry-out chicken booths. CP is also involved in a $320 million joint venture with Belgium's Solvay in petrochemicals, a $3 billion joint venture with NYNEX (of New York) and Siemens of Germany building a 2-million-line telephone concession in Bangkok, and a licensing arrangement with the Honda Motor Company to make 200,000 motorcycles in Shanghai annually. Recently, the company has begun importing wine into Thailand and expects this market to expand by about 35 percent annually.[43]

QUESTIONS FOR CONCLUDING CASE 2

1   Explain how the operations process works in CP Group core operations.

2   Assume that you are in charge of production planning for chicken in China. How would you match supply and demand for the next 2 years?

3   As CP Group moves into operating more restaurants and fast-food outlets, what additional operations management challenges is the company likely to face?

CHAPTER OUTLINE

LEARNING OBJECTIVES

After studying this chapter, you should be able to:

■ Distinguish between data and information, as well as describe how the systems view helps managers understand information processing.

■ Explain the computer components of information systems.

■ Indicate how information needs differ by managerial level and specialized area.

■ Compare and contrast the major types of information systems.

■ Explain how considering competitive strategies and strategic linkages can help managers use information systems to competitive advantage.

■ Delineate the systems development life cycle and identify the major alternative means of systems development.

■ Evaluate the impact of information technology on organizations in the areas of organization structure, individual jobs, communication patterns, and organizational risk.

GAINING THE EDGE

MICROSOFT MAPS THE INFORMATION ROAD AHEAD

Starting out with the vision "A computer on every desk and in every home," Microsoft has made itself into an indispensable element of the dream becoming a reality. More than 60 million computers are now sold annually throughout the world, and a Microsoft product constitutes the operating system in 4 out of every 5 of them.

According to company lore, Microsoft Chairman Bill Gates dropped out of Harvard University to start the software company with his high school friend, Paul Allen, after the pair saw a picture of the first personal computer, the Altair, on the January 1975 cover of *Popular Electronics.* The two developed a Disk Operating System (DOS), which was licensed by IBM for its new personal computers in 1981. Microsoft, now the world's largest software company, went on to develop the famous rival operating system, Windows, which has become the platform of choice in most personal computers. Since then the company has created a wide variety of well-known, office-related software packages, including Word for word processing and Excel for spreadsheets. These Microsoft packages are used in more than 50 countries and are available in more than 30 languages. Microsoft's 17,000-plus employees work in 48 countries.

In the process of leading Microsoft, Gates has amassed a personal fortune estimated at $18 billion. He is widely credited with not only technological expertise but also visionary leadership. In a recent poll of CEOs by *Industry Week* magazine, Gates was voted the "most respected CEO" in America.

Not surprisingly, computer-based information systems are an integral part of Microsoft's own internal operations. The nerve center is e-mail, which is used extensively by Gates and everyone else in the company. Anyone at Microsoft is free to e-mail Gates, who tries to respond within 1 day. Even major strategic issues are usually the subject of several rounds of e-mail among top-level managers before someone decides to call a meeting. Computers are used in a wide variety of other capacities as well. For example, there are computer-based systems to log and search the 12,000 applicant résumés the company receives each month, to track deadlines for the multiple project teams working on Microsoft's growing arsenal of software products, to help programmers write code more easily, to help customers evaluate alternative means of migrating from one type of operating platform to another, and to monitor inventory levels.

At Microsoft, though, the challenge extends beyond internal use to the creation of computer-based products customers will find useful. Since information technology changes rapidly, it falls to Gates to try to envision the future and keep the company steered in the right direction. In his vision, the power of computing will be an integral part of our everyday lives and will connect us globally with the digital transfer of voice, text, and video data.

To that end, Gates has been buying the rights to a vast library of digital images, some of which he displays in the new house he and his wife have been building on the shores of Lake Washington, near the Redmond, Washington, headquarters of Microsoft. The house helps to test part of Gates's view of the future. For example, instead of pictures on the wall, the house has video monitors that can display an endless variety of images. Visitors receive a pin to wear. It allows the information system to detect the individual's presence so that lights automatically go on as the person enters a room. Similarly, music suited to the individual's preferences begins playing and video displays change to show

"Every day we have to renew ourselves," says CEO Bill Gates of Microsoft, the multibillion-dollar software company he founded. The challenge is to stay at the cutting edge of technology so that the company is able to provide customers with the most up-to-date software and other computer-related products. Microsoft does not just provide these products for others, but uses them within the organization to communicate ideas, coordinate research, monitor inventories, keep track of job resumes, and so on.

images of interest. These and other features may well become commonplace in many homes of the future.

Meanwhile, Microsoft is expanding into many new areas related to computer-based information. Microsoft Network offers 24-hour communication connections to commercial services and the Internet. The company is a participant in a growing number of joint ventures, including a Dream-Works interactive venture to create CD-ROMs, video games, and on-line and interactive TV services. Microsoft also has forged a strategic alliance with NBC to integrate interactive products with cable and broadcast television.

Gates recently noted that few companies make a successful transition from one era to another because they do not recognize their environment is changing until it is too late. Gates is trying to avoid that trap. He says that the company has been focused on making excellent products for personal computers, but the Internet poses a huge challenge. "The Internet phenomenon is the single-most-important development to come along since the IBM PC was introduced in 1981," he says. "What we try to do is to invest heavily in the long term and hire smart people, because every day we have to renew ourselves."[1] ■■■

Microsoft's software has helped make possible the mushrooming use of information technology not only at Microsoft itself but literally all over the globe. Yet Microsoft, like many organizations, must continually monitor technological advances so that it is positioned to utilize the growing power of information for competitive advantage. For Microsoft, this need constitutes a dual challenge, because it must not only continually seek ways to use computers to improve its own operations but also create the software that can ultimately be used to competitive advantage by a wide variety of other organizations. We discuss the vast potential of computer-based information systems and related technology in this part of the text because many of the applications of computer technology are particularly relevant to the controlling function.

Often with the help of Microsoft products, companies are increasingly finding creative ways to use computers to regulate organizational activities so that actual performance conforms to expected organizational standards and goals. For example, Joel C. Turner, CEO of Undercover Book Service, closed his bookstore chain in the Cleveland area and took to cyberspace and fax machines to provide top-notch service, particularly to corporate clients. He maintains computer links to publishers and distributors so that he can locate difficult-to-find books and have them quickly dispatched to his customers.[2] United Technologies' Pratt & Whitney division was able to trim a whole year from the development time required on its giant jet engine for the Boeing 777 by using special software that helps coordinate product development.[3]

In exploring the many ways computer-based information systems can be useful to management processes, we first investigate the basic nature of such systems, including various information needs of managers. We next analyze six major types of information systems and examine the growing importance of using these systems innovatively to enhance organizational strategies. We then explore several ways to develop effective information systems. Finally, we look at major influences of information technology on organizations.

■ COMPUTER-BASED INFORMATION SYSTEMS: AN OVERVIEW

We are in the midst of an information technology revolution that is fundamentally changing many of the ways organizations conduct business. Most experts seem to agree that information technology is causing vast changes in the way that information is handled and used in organizations. For one thing, the number of personal computers in offices has been increasing exponentially. This proliferation offers increasing opportunities for managers to have more and better information at their fingertips. To make use of such opportunities, managers need to have a solid understanding of computer-based information systems and their various characteristics.

The Nature of Information Systems

Despite the sophisticated technology, the basic concepts involved in information systems are fairly straightforward and somewhat familiar. To understand such systems, it helps to differentiate between data and information, as well as to use a systems view to examine the nature of information processing.

DATA VERSUS INFORMATION Although we might frequently use "data" and "information" interchangeably, professionals in the computer field make important distinctions between the two terms. **Data** are unanalyzed facts and figures. For example, when you buy a quart of milk in a major supermarket, the cash register hooked to a central computer records that a quart of milk has been sold. However, this piece of data has little direct relevance to management.

To be useful in managing the supermarket, such data need to be transformed into **information,** data that have been analyzed or processed into a form that is meaningful for decision makers. For instance, the data on the purchased quart of milk may be processed with other related data to produce current inventory figures for milk in the store. This information would be useful to individuals in charge of purchasing, delivery, and stocking. The milk data may also be processed to develop figures on store sales—perhaps broken down by shift for the store manager, by day for the district manager, and by week for upper management. Thus the milk-purchase data may become an analyzed element in these and many other informational reports.

Data Unanalyzed facts and figures

Information Data that have been analyzed or processed into a form that is meaningful for decision makers

The difference between data and information is important for managers. Consider the situation at Bethlehem Steel. Faced with stiff foreign competition and the need to operate with a smaller work force, the company began to explore information technology as an aid to remaining competitive. A special internal management team, working with 14 handpicked experts from IBM, carefully studied the information needs of the $4.3 billion steelmaker. After interviews with 239 workers from all levels of the organization, one issue stood out. "There was too much data and too little information," said George T. Fugere, vice president of information services at Bethlehem Steel. As a result, the company built better systems that transform data into the information that organization members need to be more productive.[4] To be useful, information needs to be *relevant* to the decisions managers make, *accurate, timely* in the sense of being available when needed, *complete* in covering the areas required for the particular decision, and *concise* in presenting information summarized to the level that is meaningful to the decision maker.[5] With computers, it is all too easy to generate wasteful reports that do not meet the needs of managers and actually have a detrimental impact on productivity.

INFORMATION PROCESSING: A SYSTEMS VIEW To obtain the information needed for various purposes, organizations develop information systems. The notion of an information system is closely akin to the systems approach to understanding organizations (see Chapter 2). An information system can be thought of as involving inputs, transformations, and outputs. The basic elements of an information-processing system are shown in Figure 19-1.

In an information system, data captured from within the organization or from the environment are the *inputs*. The data then undergo transformation, or processing. *Processing* involves the various forms of data manipulation and analyses (such as classifying, sorting, calculating, and summarizing) that transform data into information. Information-processing systems typically make use of *data storage,* a system of storing data for use at a later point. The *outputs* are the reports, documents, and other system outcomes that supply needed information to decision makers. *Feedback* represents safeguards used to ensure that the outputs are appropriate and serve their intended purposes. Such safeguards can be checks within the system to verify the accuracy (to the extent possible) of the data and processing, as well as to determine the usefulness of the outputs to users.

Given its nature, then, an **information system** can be defined as a set of

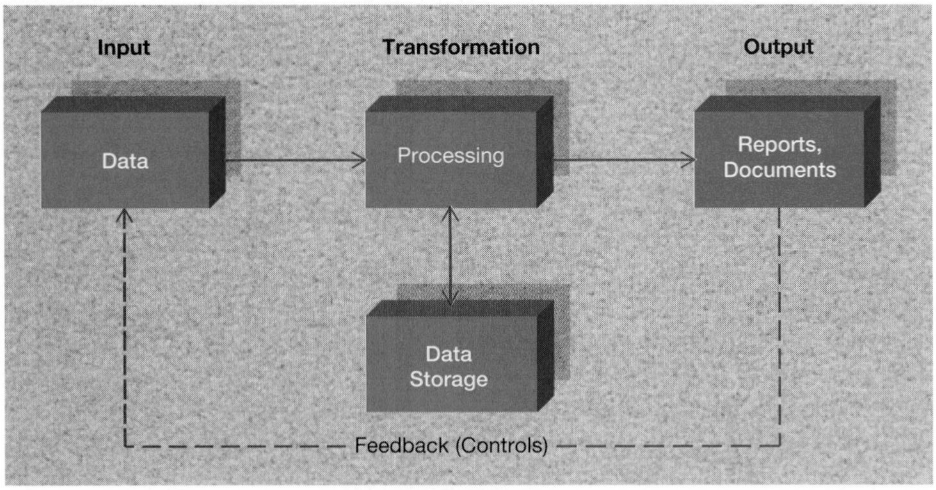

Information system A set of procedures designed to collect (or retrieve), process, store, and disseminate information to support planning, decision making, coordination, and control

Figure 19-1 *Basic components of an information system.*

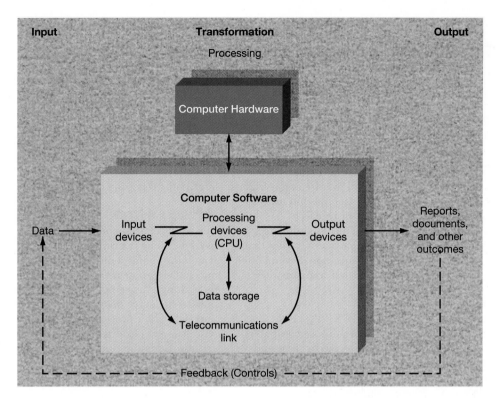

Figure 19-2 *Basic components of a computer-based information system.*

procedures designed to collect (or retrieve), process, store, and disseminate information to support planning, decision making, coordination, and control.[6] Information systems are not necessarily computerized. For example, one could develop a spreadsheet by hand instead of using a computerized one like Microsoft's Excel (although doing so would be more difficult without the computer). Our focus here, however, is on **computer-based information systems (CBISs).** Therefore, when we speak of information systems during the remainder of this chapter, we mean those that use computer technology.

Computer-based information systems (CBISs) Information systems that involve the use of computer technology

Computer-Based Information System Technology

The technology associated with computer-based information systems falls into three main categories: hardware, software, and telecommunications technology (see Figure 19-2).

HARDWARE The **computer hardware** is the physical equipment used for input, processing, and output within a computer-based information system. It includes input devices (such as keyboards and optical scanners), the computer central processing unit (the main memory and processing section of a computer), storage devices (such as magnetic tape and optical disks), output devices (such as printers and on-line display terminals), and the physical media used to connect these various devices. For a guide to the major types of computers used for information systems, see the Management Skills for the Twenty-First Century discussion, "A Guide to Major Types of Computers."

Computer hardware Physical computer equipment, including the computer itself and related devices

Originally, most electronic information processing in organizations was done on mainframe computers operated by a central data-processing department. The emergence of microcomputers during the 1980s, as well as the decreasing cost and increasing capacity of workstations and minicomputers, has

MANAGEMENT SKILLS FOR THE TWENTY-FIRST CENTURY

A Guide to the Major Types of Computers

Several different types of computers are available for use in organizations. The major types are described and illustrated below.

MICROCOMPUTERS
General-purpose desktop computers, also called personal computers, that use 16- or 32-bit microprocessors (the more bits, the faster a computer works).

WORKSTATIONS
High-performance computers used by engineers, scientists, and technical professionals who need superior graphics or upgraded mathematical capabilities. Workstations are commonly used in computer-aided design and typically have very high

resolution screens. The station often sits on or beside a desk and connects to other workstations in a network.

MINICOMPUTERS
Midsize computers that handle complex computations for engineers, scientists, and researchers. They are about the size of a refrigerator and are often used in universities, factories, or research laboratories. They sometimes serve needs of a department, rather than an entire organization. Several often connect to form a companywide network.

MAINFRAME COMPUTERS
Large, general-purpose computers that serve hundreds or thousands of users, all tied to a corporate data-processing center. A typical mainframe is slightly smaller than a

Volkswagen Beetle and requires an atmospherically controlled room. Mainframes generally handle the major data-processing needs of large corporations, such as the weekly payroll. Despite encroachments by networks of super-minicomputers, mainframes remain the staple of large data-processing centers.

SUPERCOMPUTERS
The world's fastest computers, used in science, engineering, and research for the most difficult processing challenges, such as weather forecasting. An average supercomputer is no larger than a mainframe but packs faster processors that are more closely connected, providing greater computing speed. Several organizations often share time on one supercomputer to offset the high cost.[7]

greatly expanded organizational information-processing options. Microcomputers have become so powerful that it is now possible to operate them effectively as part of organizational networks, linked to other microcomputers, telecommunication devices, or larger computers. Supercomputers, with their great processing speed, have made it possible to tackle problems that involve highly complex and time-consuming calculations, such as weather predictions. Overall, the trend toward greater computer hardware power for less cost is gradually reducing the differences among types of computers.

Computer software   The set of programs, documents, procedures, and routines associated with the operation of a computer system that makes the hardware capable of its various activities

SOFTWARE The **computer software** is the set of programs, including associated documentation, that control and coordinate the various hardware elements in a computer system. Most computers are general-purpose machines that can perform a variety of tasks, such as computing the appropriate amount of pay for an individual, keeping track of a customer's charges, or assessing current inventory levels. The software provides the instructions that enable the computer to perform various tasks.

Data base   A set of data organized efficiently in a central location so that it can serve a number of information system applications

Data-base management system The software that allows an organization to build, manage, and provide access to its stored data

There are many software packages that can be purchased. Among the most well known are packages for word processing (e.g., WordPerfect and Word) and spreadsheets (e.g., Excel and Quattro Pro). Almost as familiar are packages for data-base management (e.g., Access and Paradox). A **data base** is a set of data organized efficiently in a central location so that it can serve a number of information system applications. A **data-base management system** is the software that allows an organization to build, manage, and provide access to its stored data.[8] Increasingly, organizations are using data bases for competitive advantage. For example, major catalog companies, such as Lands' End, depend heavily on a data base of customer-related information (names, addresses, ordering history, status of current orders, etc.). The data-base management system that facilitates building the data base also allows access to the data for such activities as pro-

Computer stores display a wide array of software, the encoded instructions that enable computers to perform various tasks, ranging from word processing and data management to formatting screenplays and organizing schedules.

ducing mailing labels for catalogs and special marketing promotions, processing orders that come in by telephone and mail, printing shipping labels and invoices, providing various reports to management, and providing quick, efficient service to customers.

In addition to the packages already available for use, software is often developed by an organization's own computer specialists for unique applications. Although such custom-designed software is often expensive to create, it can be developed to suit a particular organization's needs and may be more difficult for competitors to duplicate. We discuss examples of such software in a later section on strategic implications of information systems.

TELECOMMUNICATIONS TECHNOLOGY Telecommunications is the electronic communication of information over a distance. *Telecommunications technology* comprises the physical devices and the software necessary to connect various pieces of computer hardware and enable the transfer of information from one location to another.[9] Telecommunications has vastly increased the potential for sharing information within and across organizations. For example, Visa International has developed a private information network, called VisaInfo, which links the credit-card giant's 2500 employees. The network contains large amounts of need-to-know information, such as a list of Visa's 19,000 member banks. Visa also is linking the member banks via a network of their own. The goal is to greatly reduce the 2 million pages of paper documents that the banks send to Visa daily.[10]

The availability of various types of hardware, software, and telecommunications technology provides numerous options for configuring the use of information technology in organizations. Therefore, organizations need to develop an **information architecture,** a long-range plan for investing in and organizing information technology so as to facilitate reaching organizational goals.[11] The process of designing an organization's information architecture helps determine the extent to which data and processing will be centralized versus distributing the functions to various locations in the organization. It also addresses such questions as whether microcomputers and workstations will be largely controlled by a centralized main frame or minicomputer or whether minicomputers and workstations will be the main focus of processing and control.

Telecommunications The electronic communication of information over a distance

Information architecture A long-range plan for investing in and organizing information technology so as to facilitate reaching organizational goals

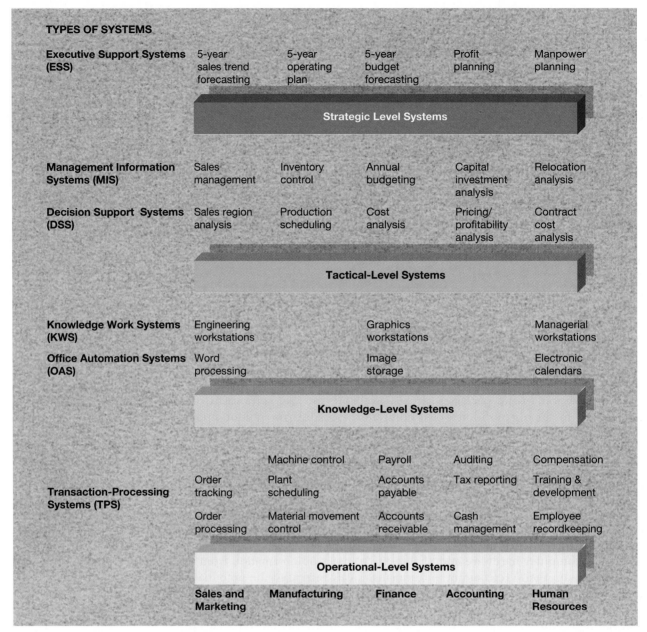

TYPES OF SYSTEMS

Executive Support Systems (ESS)	5-year sales trend forecasting	5-year operating plan	5-year budget forecasting	Profit planning	Manpower planning

Strategic Level Systems

Management Information Systems (MIS)	Sales management	Inventory control	Annual budgeting	Capital investment analysis	Relocation analysis
Decision Support Systems (DSS)	Sales region analysis	Production scheduling	Cost analysis	Pricing/ profitability analysis	Contract cost analysis

Tactical-Level Systems

Knowledge Work Systems (KWS)	Engineering workstations		Graphics workstations		Managerial workstations
Office Automation Systems (OAS)	Word processing		Image storage		Electronic calendars

Knowledge-Level Systems

		Machine control	Payroll	Auditing	Compensation
Transaction-Processing Systems (TPS)	Order tracking	Plant scheduling	Accounts payable	Tax reporting	Training & development
	Order processing	Material movement control	Accounts receivable	Cash management	Employee recordkeeping

Operational-Level Systems

Sales and Marketing	Manufacturing	Finance	Accounting	Human Resources

Figure 19-3 *Examples of information systems for various functional areas by management level. (Reprinted from Kenneth C. Laudon and Jane Price Laudon,* Management Information Systems: A Contemporary Perspective, *3d ed., Macmillan, New York, 1994, p. 36.)*

Knowledge workers
Specialists, such as engineers, architects, or scientists, who design products, services, or processes and create new knowledge for organizations

Information Needs by Organizational Level

In designing information systems that effectively enhance organizational information use, it is important to consider that information needs differ by level. This is not surprising, since managerial responsibilities in such areas as planning and organizing differ according to level.[12] For purposes of discussing information systems, it is useful to think in terms of the four general organizational levels shown in Figure 19-3. *Strategic-level systems* serve the needs of senior managers largely in the areas of long-range planning and control. *Tactical-level systems* help middle managers with planning, decision making, and monitoring at the tactical level. *Knowledge-level systems* assist technical specialists known as knowledge workers in creating and integrating new knowledge in the organization. **Knowledge workers** are specialists, such as engineers, architects, or scientists, who design products, services, or processes and create new knowledge for the organization. They are usually highly educated members of recognized professions. Their efforts are supported by **data workers,** individuals who mainly process and disseminate documents, messages, and related information. They include secretaries, filing clerks, or managers who focus primarily on processing and distributing information created by others. *Operational-level systems* support activities of operating personnel in the organization and monitor activities at the operating level.

Information Needs by Specialized Area

In most companies, information needs also vary by specialized area, such as manufacturing, finance, and human resources. During the late 1960s and early 1970s, when computers began to be used extensively in organizations, computer specialists often envisioned a future in which the information needs of all the specialized areas would be met through one giant information system. More recently, they have increasingly been recognizing that it is difficult for a single system to simultaneously meet all the information needs of an organization, particularly large ones like American Express or General Electric. In addition, the information requirements of various organizational parts are dynamic and can change rapidly, making one major system all the more difficult to design and implement.

A contemporary view is that information system efforts are likely to be more productive if they are aimed at developing specialized systems to meet the needs of specific areas, such as manufacturing and accounting (see Figure 19-3). The data used and the information produced are, however, increasingly shared by other systems for various purposes.

To facilitate the sharing of such information, many organizations are installing **local area networks (LANs),** interconnections (usually by cable) that allow communications among computers within a single building or in close proximity. Many companies are also establishing **wide area networks (WANs),** which provide communications among computers over long distances, usually through the facilities and services of public communications companies (in most countries) or private companies (in the United States), such as AT&T, MCI, and Sprint. For example, Ford Motor Company has an international network, called its "electronic roof." The network links its European, Asian, and North American design operations through the use of satellite links, land lines, and cable lines.[13] More recently, many of these companies are further developing their networks into intranets. An *intranet* is an internal organizational network that relies on Internet technologies to allow employees to easily browse and share information. In essence, an intranet is a private version of the Internet's World Wide Web and is made accessible only to individuals within the organization or others with whom the organization wishes to share information, such as customers and suppliers.

■ TYPES OF INFORMATION SYSTEMS

To serve the needs of different organizational levels, there are six major types of information systems: transaction processing, office automation, knowledge work, management information, decision support, and executive support.[14] These types of systems, the organizational level to which each is primarily geared, and some examples of each type of system for different functional areas are shown in Figure 19-4. Of course, these different information systems often are used at multiple levels, even though they may be developed mainly for certain types of needs.

Data workers Individuals who mainly process and disseminate documents, messages, and related information

Local area networks (LANs) Interconnections (usually by cable) that allow communications among computers within a single building or in close proximity

Wide area networks (WANs) Networks that provide communications among computers over long distances, usually through the facilities and services of public or private communications companies

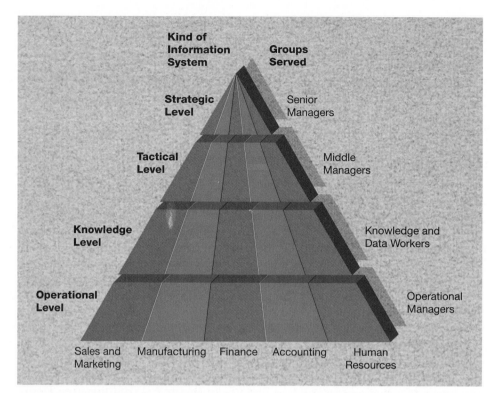

Figure 19-4 *Types of information systems by level and organization members served. (Adapted from Kenneth C. Laudon and Jane Price Laudon,* Management Information Systems: A Contemporary Perspective, *3d ed., Macmillan, New York, 1994, p. 13.)*

Transaction-Processing Systems

Transaction-processing system (TPS) A computer-based information system that executes and records the routine day-to-day transactions required to conduct an organization's business

A **transaction-processing system (TPS)** is a computer-based information system that executes and records the routine day-to-day transactions required to conduct an organization's business. For example, each time you charge gas at a major service station, register to take a college or university class, renew your driver's license, or make a withdrawal from a bank account, a computerized transaction-processing system is at work. Transaction systems are used in highly structured and repetitive situations in which the tasks to be done and the criteria involved are clear. The situations' structured nature makes it possible to write detailed and unequivocal instructions that enable the computer to handle and record the transactions properly. A TPS provides direct assistance to the operational level of an organization. TPSs are a main source of data used by other types of computer-based information systems within an organization.

Office Automation Systems

Office automation system (OAS) A computer-based information system aimed at facilitating communication and increasing the productivity of managers and office workers through document and message processing

An **office automation system (OAS)** is a computer-based information system aimed at facilitating communication and increasing the productivity of data workers and other users through document and message processing. The earliest, most widely used, and best-known OASs are *word-processing* systems, which allow text to be created, edited, and printed quickly and easily. More recent, increasingly popular OASs are *electronic mail (e-mail)* systems, which allow the high-speed exchange of written messages by means of computer text processing and communications networks (see Chapter 14). Other important OASs include the following applications:[15]

> **Voice mail:** A means of recording a telephone message and storing it in a computer's secondary storage for later retrieval by the intended receiver.

> **Electronic calendaring:** A method of maintaining an appointments schedule electronically.

Teleconferencing: The simultaneous communication among a group of individuals by telephone or via computer using specially designed software.

Document retrieval: The use of one or more electronic devices to store documents as digitized images or some other medium and to facilitate the later location and copying of the stored images.

Facsimile (FAX) transmission: A means of sending documents over telephone linkages that arrive in printed form at the receiving location.

Groupware: Software designed to support collaborative efforts among group members, such as scheduling meetings, holding meetings, collaborating on projects, and sharing documents.

Graphics: A means of creating charts and diagrams.

Knowledge Work Systems

A **knowledge work system (KWS)** is a computer-based information system that assists knowledge workers in the creation of new knowledge for the organization. Knowledge workers often use office automation systems, but knowledge work systems provide them with important additional tools for designing new products, services, and processes and developing other useful organizational knowledge. Knowledge workers frequently use workstations that have capabilities for advanced graphics, complex mathematical calculations, and large database access. Workstations are used in specialized areas such as medical diagnosis, legal document searches for court case preparation, scientific analysis, and computer-aided design. For example, engineers at Square D, an electrical component manufacturer, use a knowledge work system. The system does the design work for giant units of electrical equipment, which generally share the same basic elements but vary in required size, specifications, and features. An engineer then checks the drawing that the computer produces before putting the equipment into production.[16]

> **Knowledge work system (KWS)** A computer-based information system that assists knowledge workers in the creation of new knowledge for the organization

Management Information Systems

A **management information system (MIS)** is a computer-based information system that produces routine reports and often allows on-line access to current and historical information needed by managers mainly at the middle level but also at first-line levels. MISs are oriented principally to tactical and operational issues and are particularly important in planning, decision making, and controlling. Typically, they summarize information from transaction-processing systems to produce routine and exception reports for managers and supervisors. For example, materials requirements planning systems used in operations management (see Chapter 18) supply information to master schedulers concerning any potential difficulties with materials procurement that will affect the schedule. They also provide information to capacity planners about necessary short- or long-run needs for capacity changes. In addition, they produce reports for first- and middle-level managers in such areas as costs, quality, and supplier activities.

> **Management information system (MIS)** A computer-based information system that produces routine reports and often allows on-line access to current and historical information needed by managers mainly at the middle and first-line levels

Some computer specialists use the term "management information systems" in a broad sense to describe all computer-related systems relevant to management, including the six major types of systems under discussion here. The term is also often used to designate the field of management that focuses on designing and implementing computer-based information systems for use by management. In this chapter we use "computer-based information systems" or "information systems" as the overall term denoting all such systems related to the various levels of management. We reserve the term "management information systems" for the more narrow meaning just described above.

Decision Support Systems

Decision support system (DSS)
A computer-based information system that supports the process of managerial decision making in situations that are not well structured

A **decision support system (DSS)** is a computer-based information system that supports the process of managerial decision making in situations that are not well structured. Such systems generally do not actually provide "answers" or point to optimal decisions for managers. Rather, they attempt to improve the decision-making *process* by providing tools that help managers and professionals analyze situations more clearly.

There are several differences between a DSS and an MIS. For one thing, compared with an MIS, a typical DSS provides more advanced analysis and greater access to various models that managers can use to examine a situation more thoroughly. For another, a DSS often relies on information from external sources, as well as from the internal sources that are largely the domain of the TPS and MIS. Finally, a DSS tends to be more highly interactive than an MIS. It enables managers to communicate directly (often back and forth) with computer programs that control the system and to obtain the results of various analyses almost immediately (see the Case in Point discussion).

CASE IN POINT

DECISION SUPPORT AT IBERDROLA

Iberdrola is one of the largest electric utilities in Spain, with about 40 percent of the market. The company owns a major interest in several large nuclear generating facilities, and it runs numerous thermal plants that use coal and oil for fuel. Managing the generation of hydroelectric energy effectively is particularly important to the company. This is because the greater the amount of hydro-generated energy, the less the company is required to use more expensive fuels, such as coal and oil, to meet the energy demands of its customers. Yet maximizing the use of hydro-generated energy is a challenging task.

Within Iberdrola, the Departamento de Operación del Sistemas (DOS) makes the decisions about hydro releases, the discharge of water from various reservoirs within its purview. The DOS concerns itself particularly with generating hydro power on a major river and reservoir system southwest of Madrid. Rainfall in the area varies drastically from one year to the next, with most of the rain falling between November and May. When precipitation does occur, it tends to fall within a relatively short time period. As a result, the water levels in the reservoirs may become very high, making it necessary to release water without generating energy. Doing so precludes using the water to generate energy at a future date. Furthermore, such releases can be dangerous, since they may be adding water to the river system at a time of considerable precipitation. Yet failure to release water may cause spilling (reservoir overflow), a situation that can result in considerable damage. On the other hand, keeping the reservoirs too low can prevent the company from generating hydro power when necessary if expected additional rainfall does not materialize. Decisions made on a given day about the generation of hydroelectric power and water release depend on such factors as electricity demand, expected rainfall, current and anticipated reservoir levels, and availability of the hydro turbines that generate electricity at the reservoirs. In dealing with the situation in the past, managers tended to focus on the immediate situation, using general and sometimes inconsistent notions about the implications of their decisions for future time periods of up to a year or so.

To help managers make better assessments of the yearlong implications of their actions, Iberdrola developed a decision support system. The system is based on mathematical models and incorporates forecasts for both energy demand and likely precipitation that are based on historical data, current indicators, and estimates by managers. Managers can vary their estimates of future conditions and then evaluate the computer-generated implications before making their final decisions about water release and hydro-generation of energy. At first, DOS managers had difficulty accepting the decision support system because it made recommendations about water release that ran counter to their intuition. Since then, they have made many suggestions that have helped refine the support system, which is now used extensively to help guide water release and hydro-generation decisions. Use of the system has led to estimated annual savings ranging from $1 to $3 million (depending on rainfall levels) and decreased the risk of reservoir overflows.[17]   ■■■

One relatively new specialized type of DSS is a **group decision-support system (GDSS),** a computer-based information system that supports decision makers working together to solve problems that are not well structured. A GDSS focuses specifically on solving a problem or making a decision, while groupware is generally considered to be more broadly concerned with facilitating communication.

Another specialized type of DSS that is coming into increased use is the expert system.[18] **Expert systems** are computer-based systems that apply the substantial knowledge of an expert to help solve specialized problems. In fact, in developing such systems, designers typically work with experts to determine the information and heuristics, or decision rules, that the experts use when confronted with particular types of problems. One well-known example is XCON (for "eXpert CONfigurer"), developed by the Digital Equipment Corporation. The system uses more than 10,000 decision rules and more than 5000 product descriptions to analyze sales orders and design layouts to be sure that the equipment will work when it reaches DEC's customers. XCON catches most configuration errors, and it eliminates the need for completely assembling a computer system to check it and then breaking it down again for shipment to the customer. Expert systems are extremely difficult and costly to develop. A moderate-size system, comprising about 300 decision rules, generally costs about $250,000 to $500,000 to design. The Digital Equipment Corporation spends more than $2 million per year just to update its XCON system.[19]

Expert systems are one outgrowth of **artificial intelligence,** a field of information technology aimed at developing computers that have humanlike capabilities, such as seeing, hearing, and thinking.[20] Artificial intelligence is an area of scientific inquiry, rather than an end product such as an expert system. One new area of development is experimentation with *fuzzy logic,* a rule-based approach that involves pattern recognition and allows inferences from data that is incomplete or somewhat inaccurate. For example, Ford Motor Co. is experimenting with a fuzzy logic system that backs a simulated truck into a parking place based on a few rules such as "IF the truck is near jackknifing, THEN reduce the steering angle." Computers today are still far from being able to conceptualize or reason.[21] Nevertheless, efforts in the area of artificial intelligence have laid the groundwork for significant developments, such as expert systems.

Group decision-support system (GDSS) A computer-based information system that supports decision makers working together to solve problems that are not well structured

Expert systems Computer-based systems that apply the substantial knowledge of an expert to help solve specialized problems

Artificial intelligence A field of information technology aimed at developing computers that have humanlike capabilities, such as seeing, hearing, and thinking

Executive Support Systems

Executive support system (ESS)
A computer-based information system that supports decision making and effective functioning at the top levels of an organization

An **executive support system (ESS)** is a computer-based information system that supports decision making and effective functioning at the top levels of an organization. Such systems, which are a relatively recent development, are sometimes called *executive information systems* (EISs).[22]

Unlike a DSS, which tends to be more narrowly focused, an ESS involves more general computing capabilities, telecommunications, and display options (such as graphs and charts) that are applicable to many different problems. An ESS tends to make less use of analytical models than a DSS, delivers information from a variety of sources on demand, and allows more general queries in a highly interactive way. For instance, at the Phillips 66 Company, a division of the Phillips Petroleum Company, top-level managers have an ESS that helps them watch important indicators, such as oil-pricing trends, refinery operating results, and chemical-plant product statistics. The system has been credited with greatly increasing the stability and profitability of the firm.[23]

In essence, ESSs are information systems that are tailor-made to fit the needs of executives working in particular situations and are often geared to the individual work habits of those managers. The general characteristics of executive support systems, as well as of the other major types of systems, are summarized in Table 19-1.

■ PROMOTING INNOVATION: STRATEGIC IMPLICATIONS OF INFORMATION SYSTEMS

During the 1980s, a number of strategic planning experts began to highlight the innovative possibilities and strategic implications of the emerging informa-

TABLE 19-1 CHARACTERISTICS OF INFORMATION-PROCESSING SYSTEMS

TYPE OF SYSTEM	INFORMATION INPUTS	PROCESSING	INFORMATION OUTPUTS	USERS
ESS	Aggregate data; external, internal	Graphics; simulations; interactive	Projections; responses to queries	Senior managers
DSS	Low-volume data; analytic models	Interactive; simulations; analysis	Special reports; decision analyses; responses to queries	Professionals; staff managers
MIS	Summary transaction data; high-volume data; simple models	Routine reports; simple models; low-level analysis	Summary and exception reports	Middle managers
KWS	Design specifications; knowledge base	Modeling; simulations	Models; graphics	Professionals; technical staff
OAS	Documents; schedules	Document; management; scheduling; communication	Documents; schedules; mail	Clerical workers
TPS	Transactions; events	Sorting; listing; merging; updating	Detailed reports; lists; summaries	Operations personnel; supervisors

Source: Reprinted from Kenneth C. Laudon and Jane Price Laudon, *Management Information Systems: A Contemporary Perspective,* Macmillan, New York, 1994, p. 40.

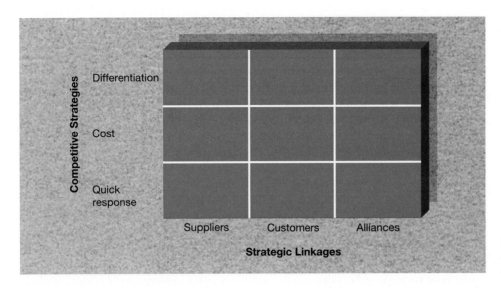

Figure 19-5 *Matrix of strategic options related to information technology.*

tion technology.[24] Before then, top-level managers had generally viewed computers as a means of streamlining internal processes in order to operate more efficiently. Today there is broad recognition that information technology can be a valuable means of gaining competitive advantage. In fact, many large organizations appoint a *chief information officer (CIO)*, a high-level executive who is responsible for recommending and overseeing the implementation of information systems designed to enhance an organization's competitive position.

In thinking about how to use information technology to develop specific strategies for competitive advantage, managers may find it helpful to use the matrix of strategic options shown in Figure 19-5. The matrix is related to Michael Porter's work on competitive strategy (see Chapter 7). The matrix considers two main dimensions: competitive strategies and strategic linkages (see Figure 19-5).[25]

Competitive Strategies

According to the matrix, organizations may be able to combine information technology with three major competitive strategies to gain competitive advantage. The competitive strategies are differentiation, cost leadership, and quick response (see Chapter 7).

DIFFERENTIATION The goal of the differentiation approach is either to increase the differentiation advantages of an organization in relation to those of relevant others (e.g., suppliers, customers, or competitors) or to decrease the differentiation advantages of others relative to those of the organization. One of the most famous examples of the differentiation approach is the SABRE reservation system owned by AMR, the parent of American Airlines (see the Case in Point discussion).

THE SABRE SYSTEM IS BEING RATTLED   CASE IN POINT

This sophisticated transaction-processing system, known as SABRE, was originally developed in the 1970s as a proprietary computerized reservation system (CRS) for American Airlines. At that time it cost more than $300 million to establish. It was created, in part, to preclude travel agencies from joining together to develop their own system. SABRE serves travel agents in more than 60 countries. The agents typically have rented the terminals from American or have hooked microcomputers to the system. Other airlines pay a service fee whenever the terminals are used to make reservations on one of their flights. American has expanded the system to cover reservations for hotels, cars, and other services. The system has about 75,000 travel agent terminals and micro-computers tied to its network. It handles 150 million transactions per day, encompassing about 30 percent of all CRS airline reservations and travel spending, valued at about $40 billion. SABRE itself has an annual revenue of over $1.5 billion.

With technology changing, the SABRE system faces new competitive threats, and American Airlines is spending $100 million to aggressively respond. A variety of new competitors, some of them current SABRE customers, are planning to offer travel reservation possibilities via the Internet. Such systems could bypass the SABRE network. Because of these expanding alternatives, some of SABRE's major customers, such as Delta Airlines, have been pressuring for lower fees to have their customers use the SABRE system. As a result, SABRE is trying to lower costs. The system also is attempting to enhance service, in terms of both upgrading the technology to be faster and offering an increasing array of travel services. SABRE itself offers the most popular on-line reservation software package, called easySABRE, which makes it possible for individuals to make travel reservations via on-line services. At this point, it generates only about 1 million reservations per year, a very small part of SABRE's volume. To help upgrade the technology and explore new possibilities, SABRE has recently added 1000 specialists to its team of 7000 working on the SABRE system. There has also been some discussion of spinning off the SABRE subsidiary to provide AMR with cash for new acquisitions and free the system from its long-terms ties to American Airlines. Some argue that such a move would make it easier for SABRE to form better alliances with other airlines and keep them in the SABRE fold.[26] ■■■

COST LEADERSHIP A cost approach is oriented toward reducing an organization's costs in relation to the costs of others (suppliers, customers, or competitors), helping suppliers or customers reduce their costs so that they want to do business with the organization, or increasing competitors' costs. General Motors and the Ford Motor Company, for example, have indicated that they will make purchases only from suppliers that have telecommunications equipment for sending and receiving messages electronically. The automakers want to use telecommunications to facilitate moving toward just-in-time inventory methods, which would reduce inventory costs. They also want to use the system to reduce the cost of paying supplier bills. For instance, GM has been working on eliminating the 300,000 monthly paper checks that it sends out to almost 6000 suppliers.[27]

QUICK RESPONSE The quick response approach is focused on recognizing, adapting to, and meeting changing customer needs with greater speed than competitors.[28] This strategy is associated with how quickly an organization can make improvements in products or services or possibly even a decision that affects a customer.[29] For example, at Tampa-based Anchor Glass, telephone order takers can check on-line production schedules and promise delivery dates during the initial telephone call placing the order. When an order is accepted, the information system actually reserves production capacity, taking into account any changes in materials, capacity, and equipment downtime. The $1.1

billion company makes glass bottles for Coke, Pepsi, Anheuser-Busch, Coors, Smuckers, and others. Before the new system was implemented, it would sometimes take a few days or a week to provide a delivery date to a customer.[30]

Strategic Linkages

The matrix (see Figure 19-5) also suggests three major areas in which strategic information systems linkages can be formed for competitive advantage. The targets for such linkages are suppliers, customers, and alliances.

SUPPLIER LINKAGES Suppliers include providers of raw materials, capital, labor, or services. In one system aimed at suppliers, Equitable Life Assurance, one of the nation's largest insurance companies, installed a telecommunications network that links its field offices with regional offices, four warehouses, and its New York headquarters. The company also installed a new inventory and purchasing system. Before its installation, warehouse purchasing agents had experienced difficulty assessing vendor prices and choosing the best deals. With the new system, corporate headquarters makes major purchases of needed items from a New York distributor and offers them to the warehouses at somewhat higher prices. The warehouses can buy supplies from headquarters or shop elsewhere if they can get better prices. The system enables them to compare prices and check the terms of recent contracts for similar purchases made by the company. Thus the system puts the purchasing agents and the company in a better bargaining position relative to suppliers.[31]

CUSTOMER LINKAGES Customers include organizations that retail, wholesale, warehouse, distribute, or use a company's products or services. American President Companies (APC), an organization that has been successful in the fiercely competitive shipping industry, has made strategic use of information technology aimed at customers. APC's subsidiary, American President Lines, ships containerized freight for customers throughout North America and Asia. Faced with heavy competition from foreign carriers, APC managers felt the company could charge premium prices for better service on urgently needed or high-value items, such as materials for just-in-time production systems or parts for computers. APC's strategy involved making huge investments in information technology so that the company could offer expanded services. As a result of this effort, APC provides coordinated shipping over both land and water, computerized aid for cargo clearance by U.S. Customs, and customer access to computerized information that lets clients track their shipments 24 hours per day.[32]

ALLIANCE LINKAGES *Strategic alliances* are arrangements whereby independent organizations form a cooperative partnership to gain some mutual strategic advantage (see Chapter 3).[33] They can be formed within the same industry or by firms in different industries. In the context of information technology, organizations in strategic alliances usually exchange information electronically, trade information technology expertise, or share information technology resources. One example is the agreement between Citibank and American Airlines that combines a credit card with a frequent flier program, an alliance that depends on information technology and has been profitable for both organizations.[34] Another is the Brussels-based Society for Worldwide Interbank Financial Telecommunications (SWIFT), an international organization owned by 2795 banks from 130 countries. The alliance of banks was created to standardize, develop, and control a network for electronically transferring funds across borders. The SWIFT network transmits 2.7 million messages and over $2

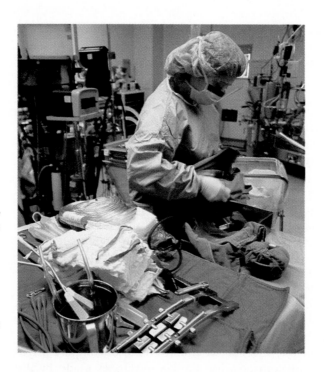

At Duke University's Medical Center, the supplies for a bypass surgery arrive as a package, arranged in the precise order that they will be used in the four-hour operation. Computer technology enables the distribution unit of Baxter International, a hospital supply company, to store and deliver the requisite supplies on a just-in-time basis. This computerized service saves hospitals the costs of storing supplies and maintaining inventory, and it gives Baxter a competitive advantage in the hospital supply industry.

trillion in funds daily on behalf of member banks and 2300 other nonowner customers that are primarily securities firms.[35]

Sustaining Competitive Advantage

A major issue in pursuing competitive advantage through information technology is sustainability.[36] A competitive advantage is considered sustainable when it can be maintained over the long term regardless of competitor action or industry environmental factors. In practice, few competitive advantages are sustainable over a long period of time without further improvements. One survey suggests that strategic information systems provide competitive advantage for only about 12 to 18 months.[37] The potential advantage with information technology appears to come from three factors. The first factor is making a *preemptive strike*—that is, being the first with a strategic information system. For example, American Hospital Supply Corporation (now part of Baxter International) was first in its industry to develop a computerized system that greatly streamlined the ordering, tracking, and management of supplies by hospital customers. The system, called ASAP (analytic systems automated purchasing), enabled hospitals to cut administrative costs and reduce inventories. The second factor is continually improving the strategic information system in important ways. American Hospital Supply continued to improve its system by customizing it to meet the specialized needs of its various hospital customers, thereby entrenching itself and making it difficult for competitors to develop a comparable system. The third factor is using strategic information systems to complement and support other sustainable competitive advantages. For example, American Hospital Supply already had the advantage of a relatively large market share in comparison to fragmented, regional competitors when it launched its ASAP system. Moreover, it had a centralized order entry system. This became important when American Hospital Supply merged with Baxter International, which also had hospital supply operations. The merger made the new unit, operating under the Baxter name, a major threat to Johnson & Johnson. J&J had divisions that were highly decentralized, making it difficult for that company to develop a comparable system.[38]

■ DEVELOPING COMPUTER-BASED INFORMATION SYSTEMS

Developing computer-based information systems like the one at American Hospital Supply can be difficult and expensive, particularly when the applications are large and complex. In fact, time and cost overruns are common. According to one study, only 9 percent of large companies' software projects come in on time and on budget.[39]

Furthermore, the resulting systems sometimes spew out errors that cause serious business problems. During the late 1980s when the Bank of America attempted a conversion to a new information system called MasterNet, the system failed. It was intended to better manage $34 billion in institutional trust accounts and to attract new business. Unfortunately, after the system was implemented, the bank could not provide customers with adequate statements about their accounts for months, and large pension funds withdrew at least $1.5 billion. Finally, the bank scrapped MasterNet, wrote off its $20 million investment in the system, set up a $60 million fund to correct the problems with customer accounts, and contracted the work out to other banks.[40] Because of the disastrous dimensions of such problems, as well as the potential strategic value of information technology, managers must have at least a general knowledge of what is involved in information systems development.

The Systems Development Life Cycle

Traditionally, the development of new information systems has followed a process known as the systems development life cycle (see Figure 19-6). The **systems development life cycle** is a series of stages that are used in the development of most medium- and large-size information systems. The approach is often used more informally in developing small-scale systems. Typically, systems development is carried out by a project team consisting of managers, users, systems analysts, programmers, and other technical personnel needed for the success of the project.

Systems development life cycle A series of stages that are used in the development of most medium- and large-size information systems

THREE STAGES The *definition stage* is aimed at evaluating the proposed idea and defining system parameters. This stage is extremely important because, according to one estimate, mistakes and omissions that are not detected until later can cost from 10 to 100 times more to fix than oversights detected during the definition stage.[41]

The *physical design stage* carries the project from concept to reality. This

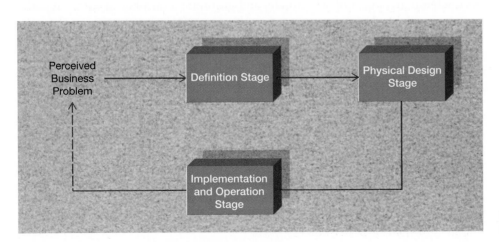

Figure 19-6 *The systems development life cycle.*

stage includes developing a detailed systems design, carrying out the necessary programming and debugging, and planning the implementation.

The *implementation and operation stage* includes implementing the system, evaluating its effectiveness, and maintaining its effective operation. A typical medium-size development project requires about 2 years to reach the implementation stage and is likely to have an expected life span of 5 to 8 years from that point. During this time, ongoing maintenance will need to be conducted and operating costs will be incurred.[42]

ASSESSING THE LIFE-CYCLE APPROACH The life-cycle approach has several advantages. For one thing, it provides a series of stages and phases as guidelines for major systems development efforts. For another, it focuses considerable effort on early definition of both the necessary functions and the outputs of the system. Finally, the approach allows for the involvement of potential users, particularly at the definition stage.

Unfortunately, the life-cycle approach also has some disadvantages. One drawback is that the cycle is very costly. Another disadvantage is that the intended users often have difficulty specifying all the functions and outputs of the system early in the life cycle, as required. Yet another disadvantage is that the life-cycle approach tends to discourage changes in the system definition once the definition stage is over. Finally, there may be a long backlog of projects waiting to enter the cycle.

Overall, the life-cycle approach appears to be the best alternative when projects are very large and/or complex and when the applications are fairly well structured so that parameters can be reasonably well defined early in the project. Evidence suggests that systems development efforts that run into difficulty usually have not adequately followed the steps involved in the life cycle.[43]

Alternative Means of Systems Development

Given the potential problems associated with information systems developed through the traditional life cycle and the potentially long time frame for design and implementation, other alternatives are emerging. Among the most prominent are applications software packages, prototyping, end-user development, and outsourcing.[44]

Applications software packages Software programs available for sale or lease from commercial sources

APPLICATIONS SOFTWARE PACKAGES Applications software packages are software programs available for sale or lease from commercial sources. The packages are typically geared to handle specialized areas that are required by a large number of organizations. For applications such as payroll, inventory control, work scheduling, accounts receivable, and graphics, a number of software packages are available from various vendors. Commercial vendors take on the considerable expense of developing such packages because they are able to make a profit by selling the same programs to many organizations. As a result, organizations can often obtain commercial packages at substantially less cost than that of in-house, custom-developed software.

There are, however, disadvantages to using commercial packages. The main one stems from the fact that the packages are somewhat generic in orientation. Although they usually offer considerable options, they sometimes cannot accommodate extraordinary circumstances or uncommon procedures. On the other hand, if the savings are substantial, it may sometimes be feasible to change the organization's operations to make them compatible with the parameters of the software package. Another disadvantage is that using commercial packages in attempts to exploit information technology ahead of competitors may make it easy for competitors to follow suit quickly. Finally, applications software packages can have major errors that cause serious malfunctions.

PROTOTYPING **Prototyping** is the process of building a rough, working model of all or parts of a proposed information system for purposes of preliminary evaluation and further refinement. Unlike the traditional approach, which involves attempting to specify clearly all user needs in the early development stages, the prototype approach is based on the idea of providing a quick response to loosely defined user specifications. The prototype system may then go through a number of modifications and enhancements before it finally meets evolving user requirements. Companies that are using prototyping report that it can cost 25 percent less than the traditional development approach, usable results are typically produced faster, and the systems generally earn better acceptance from users because they meet user needs.[45]

USER-DEVELOPED SYSTEMS In the world of information systems, a **user** is an individual, other than an information system professional, who is engaged in the development and/or management of computer-based information systems. (A user is often called an **end user.**) **End-user computing,** the development and/or management of information systems by users, is a growing trend in organizations. For example, during the early 1980s over 40 percent of the computer resources at Xerox were devoted to supporting end-user computing, a figure that rose to about 75 percent by the early 1990s.[46]

User-developed systems, then, are created with little or no help from information system professionals. The trend toward increasing end-user computing stems from several sources. First, the rise of microcomputers, or personal computers, has enabled users to gain basic computer experience. Second, the availability of applications software packages and other user-friendly tools makes it more feasible for individuals who are not computer professionals to tackle information system development. Third, the long line of projects waiting to be developed by information system departments has caused users to take matters into their own hands. Finally, end users may be in a better position to recognize innovative ideas for information systems that can lead to competitive advantage.[47]

Still, end-user development may not be best in all circumstances. Some types of systems may be too complex for nonprofessionals to tackle. Also, if systems are poorly designed, they may make errors that are not detected until considerable damage has been done. In addition, the systems may not tie in well to other systems in the organization. Finally, if such systems are developed by individuals who keep poor notes or documentation about how the systems work, others may not be able to work with a system should the key person leave.

OUTSOURCING *Outsourcing* is the process of employing an outside vendor to perform a function normally carried on within the organization (see Chapter 16). In the context of information systems, outsourcing is most frequently done in areas such as computer center operations, telecommunications networks, or applications development. As an applications development option, outsourcing can offer advantages in terms of providing specialized expertise, lower costs, and flexibility (because additional help can be obtained on an as-needed basis rather than hiring additional in-house staff). One major disadvantage is that it is more difficult to build competitive advantage when an outside vendor is the system developer. This is because the outside vendor can then use the expertise gained to develop similar systems for others or can offer similar information processing services to others. Therefore, outsourcing of systems develop-

Prototyping The process of building a rough, working model of all or parts of a proposed information system for purposes of preliminary evaluation and further refinement

User An individual, other than an information system professional, who is engaged in the development and/or management of computer-based information systems

End user The same as a *user*

End-user computing The development and/or management of information systems by users

ment is probably best reserved for systems that have low potential for building competitive advantage, do not involve the handling of important proprietary information, and do not relinquish control over systems that are central to organizational operations.[48]

Selecting a Development Approach

Three project criteria are useful in determining the appropriate development approach.[49] The first is *commonality,* the degree to which there is likely to be a common need for the type of system in other organizations. When commonality is high, commercial software packages probably exist that are at least worth investigating as a possible alternative to custom development. It also may be possible to outsource the function. For example, an increasing number of organizations are outsourcing payroll processing, a relatively routine function. The second criterion is *impact,* the degree to which the system will affect the organization in terms of the number of individuals affected, importance to organizational operations, or potential for competitive advantage. The greater the impact, the more important it is to have the heavy involvement of in-house information system professionals in the development effort. The third criterion is *structure,* the degree to which the problem and its probable solution are understood. When structure is low, prototyping begins to look more attractive, particularly if the system rates high on impact.

■ INFLUENCE OF INFORMATION TECHNOLOGY ON ORGANIZATIONS

As computers grow more pervasive, information technology is having a considerable influence on many aspects of organizations. Major areas of influence include organization structure, individual jobs, communication patterns, and organizational risk.[50]

Organization Structure

Aside from the issue of how to organize the information system function itself, CBISs are gradually influencing the overall structures of organizations. Early researchers and observers anticipated that computers would eventually reduce the need for middle managers, cause top management to assume more of the responsibility for innovating and planning, and lead large organizations to recentralize decision making.[51] Indeed, there does appear to be a recent trend toward eliminating some layers of middle management in organizations. This has been made possible, to some extent, by the increased ability of top-level managers to obtain needed information through computers. At the same time, early researchers and observers did not foresee the onslaught of microcomputers, a technological breakthrough that allows information to be shared and decision making to be decentralized. In terms of overall impact on organization structure, computers appear to increase the structural options available to managers. They do so by potentially facilitating decentralized decision making while allowing higher-level managers to retain control by keeping informed through computer networks.[52]

Individual Jobs

Computers can influence individual jobs in a number of ways. Three of the most significant effects are alterations in the design of jobs, the job-related stress and health consequences of computers, and increasing options regarding the location of work.

NATURE OF JOBS The relatively recent invasion of personal computers in the workplace has made it difficult to gauge the total impact of computers on work. For clerical jobs, the trends so far suggest that computers can lead either to jobs that are extremely simple and require little skill or to jobs that involve considerable creativity and skill.[53] At the professional level, computers seem to be reducing the number of routine tasks while increasing the ability of professionals to communicate with others and use some of the same decision-making tools being developed for managers. At the managerial level, computers offer managers new aids to help with decision making, communication, and control.

STRESS AND HEALTH CONSEQUENCES Stress and health issues related to computers center largely on their impact on lower-level white-collar jobs. One controversial topic is the effects of **electronic monitoring,** the practice of using computers to continually assess employee performance. For example, computers are used by a number of airlines to monitor both telephone and computer use. At Pacific Southwest Airlines, spokesman William Hastings says, "Our customer complaints have gone down since we've instituted monitoring. Our productivity numbers have improved markedly." Still, critics argue that monitoring reduces customer service and increases stress.[54] One study concluded that monitoring has the effect of degrading the quality of customer service and of the work environment itself. Yet, the study found that some workers were able to internalize the standards of the system, used the data for feedback on how they were doing, and were not bothered by the monitoring. Thus using computers to give employees direct, regular feedback, but providing feedback to supervisors less frequently, may be a more effective approach to monitoring.[55]

> **Electronic monitoring**   The practice of using computers to continually assess employee performance

Working at a computer for long hours has caused a number of health-related complaints. The most prevalent are concerns about *repetitive stress injury (RSI),* which occurs when muscle groups are put through the same motions repeatedly. One of the most common forms of RSI is *carpal stress injury (CSI),* which affects the muscles in the wrists. The number of RSI-related cases reported each year is 332,000 and growing. According to one estimate, annual workers' compensation payments related to RSI now surpass $2 billion. Experts recommend proper posture, frequent stretching, and ergonomic office furniture to help avoid such injuries.[56]

LOCATION OF WORK Advances in information technology are increasing the options related to the location of work. One outgrowth is **telecommuting,** a form of working at home that is made possible by using computer technology to remain in touch with the office. Yet telecommuting may not be satisfactory for many individuals because of their need for social interaction with coworkers and the inherent difficulties in separating work and home roles. One study found that if respondents were given a choice between telecommuting or working at the office, 56 percent would prefer to work at the office, 36 percent would like to split their time between home and office, and just 7 percent would want to work only at home.[57]

> **Telecommuting**   A form of working at home that is made possible by using computer technology to remain in touch with the office

Another possibility that derives from advanced technology is the **logical office,** the concept that portable microcomputers allow an individual's office to be anywhere the individual is, rather than being restricted to one specific location. Portable microcomputers, which run on batteries and usually plug into modular phone jacks for transmission, are often referred to as *laptop computers.* By using laptops, Ruth L. Otte, president of the Discovery Channel, oper-

> **Logical office**   The concept that portable microcomputers allow an individual's office to be anywhere the individual is, rather than being restricted to

Two satellite dishes, 14 lines for phone, fax, and modems, and 11 personal computers allow stock trader Salem Abraham to operate a logical office out of the tiny town of Canadian, Texas (pop. 2500). Smith Barney gave Abraham a $130 million portfolio to handle after one of its managers visited Abraham and saw him conduct a trade of 1.5 billion Japanese yen from the cellular phone in his pickup during a campfire dinner.

ates with 40 percent fewer people than a major competitor. Based in Landover, Maryland, the Discovery Channel acquires, promotes, and transmits some 200 television programs per month to more than 30 million U.S. homes. Otte uses a sophisticated communications system to keep in touch with her 105-member staff and receives an average of 100 memos per day wherever she is. "I feel like I'm never out of the office," she says. Nonetheless, managers who use laptops as they travel often have to cope with such inconveniences as extra scrutiny by airport security, batteries that lose power, and inadequate phone-jack facilities in hotel rooms (a condition that is improving rapidly).[58]

Communication Patterns

The advent of various computer-related communications tools, such as e-mail, teleconferencing, groupware, and group decision support systems, has greatly expanded the channels and methods of communication available (see also Chapter 14).[59] They have also altered the flow of information exchange both within the organization and between organizations. Telecommunications technology allows for the increasingly easy exchange of information not only locally but literally across the globe. Such technology also permits *electronic data interchange (EDI)*, the direct exchange of standard business transaction documents between the computers of two different organizations.[60] EDI has made possible new electronic partnerships among suppliers, producers, distributors, and retailers.

Roger Milliken, chairman of Milliken & Company, a major textile firm, headed an effort by 220 top retail and clothing executives to establish technical standards for electronic data interchange. With EDI, specially formatted documents, such as purchase orders and shipping invoices, can be sent directly from the computer of one company to the computer of another. Likewise, an EDI system at the Seminole Manufacturing Company has increased the speed of ordering and reduced prospects for human error. As a result, the company has halved the time required to resupply its major customer, Wal-Mart Stores, with men's slacks.[61] Some experts argue that information technology is likely to radically alter the hierarchical nature of organizations by greatly enhancing possibilities for cooperation and collaboration among employees at varying levels within organizations.

Organizational Risk

Despite all the potential benefits, information technology does pose some considerable risks to organizations. Among the most significant are possible errors, physical calamities, theft, sabotage and security breaches, invasion of privacy, and resistance to major systems.

ERRORS With complex software, it is almost impossible to test for every possible error and contingency. As a result, errors and problems do sometimes occur. For instance, in 1990, a software problem caused the AT&T long-distance phone network to malfunction. The error shut off service to tens of millions of customers throughout the United States for several hours and disrupted many businesses that depend heavily on telephone communications, such as airline reservation systems.[62]

PHYSICAL CALAMITIES Physical damage caused by fires, floods, power failures, earthquakes, and similar factors can severely disrupt an organization's information flows. Recognizing the seriousness of having its computers damaged, American Airlines has spent $34 million to create an underground facility in Tulsa, Oklahoma, where its SABRE system operates. The facility has foot-thick concrete walls, a 42-inch steel-reinforced concrete ceiling covered with 7½ feet of earth, and a barbed-wire fence. It is made to withstand earthquakes, floods, and winds of up to 350 miles per hour.[63] Visa USA has a duplicate data center in McLean, Virginia, which handles half of the credit-card-related transactions and serves as a backup system for the primary center in San Mateo, California.

THEFT According to one estimate, theft committed by means of computers amounts to $3 to $5 billion per year in the United States alone. Computer theft is often internal in origin. In one incident, a group of employees wired $54 million from the London office of the Union Bank of Switzerland to another Swiss bank by using all the proper authorization codes. They were caught only because the second bank's computer malfunctioned, bringing the attention of the auditors to the transaction. While the typical bank robber usually steals about $5000, electronic thefts average about $500,000 per incident.[64]

SABOTAGE AND SECURITY BREACHES Both sabotage and security breaches are becoming major problems related to information technology. Computer sabotage is the deliberate disruption of computer-related activities and/or the destruction of computer equipment, software, or data. Computer security breaches include gaining unauthorized entry to computers or computer-related networks, as well as gaining access to stored data.

Acts of sabotage may be pranks perpetrated by employees or hackers. **Hackers** are individuals who are knowledgeable about computers and who gain unauthorized entry to, and sometimes tamper with, computer networks and files of organizations with which they have no affiliation. One famous incident occurred in December 1987. A West German law student used an academic research network to gain access to IBM's 145-country electronic mail network, where he planted a seemingly innocuous picture of a Christmas tree and a holiday message. To get rid of the greeting, individuals were instructed to type "Christmas." However, when they did so, they unwittingly triggered a program that caused the greeting to be reproduced and sent to others in chain-letter fashion. Before long, the entire system was forced to shut down.[65] The tool of the prank was a **computer virus,** a small program, usually hidden inside another

Hackers Individuals who are knowledgeable about computers and who gain unauthorized entry to, and sometimes tamper with, computer networks and files of organizations with which they have no affiliation

Computer virus A small program, usually hidden inside another program, that replicates itself and surfaces at a predetermined time to cause disruption and possibly destruction

AT&T's electronic display at its operations center in New Jersey tracked one of the worst computer breakdowns in the history of the telephone system in 1990. It started with a computer in New York City that erroneously thought it was overloaded and began to reject calls. Computers across the country took up the slack but then developed the same difficulty. Malfunctioning is one of the risks that organizations must accept when they make use of complex information systems.

program, that replicates itself and surfaces at a predetermined time to cause disruption and possibly destruction. After heavy press coverage about a virus called "Michelangelo," which is programmed to destroy data on March 6 each year (the Italian Renaissance artist's birthday), a large number of companies have installed programs that can detect many types of viruses. According to one estimate, there are now as many as 7500 known viruses, quadruple the number existing in 1990. According to the National Computer Security Association, damage from viruses cost U.S. companies $996 million in 1995 alone.[66] Still, there is always the possibility that an inventive hacker would be able to thwart such antivirus programs.

Data security is also subject to threats. Crucial corporate data bases and proprietary software can be compromised. For example, Rockwell International, Inc., has been experiencing constant problems with hackers on the Internet attempting to break into its research and development data bases, which contain important proprietary and defense-related information. Government agencies have informed Rockwell that some of the hackers are from foreign countries. Roy Alzua, Rockwell's program manager for telecommunications security, says, "But it's everything from industrial espionage to disgruntled ex-employees to hackers." According to one survey of 1290 information systems executives, one in five of the companies had experienced actual or attempted computer break-ins. The actual number is likely much higher since only half of the executives expressed confidence that such attempts would be detected.[67]

As a result of such sabotage and security breaches, many companies are tightening their computer security. They are using such means as increasingly sophisticated password systems, dial-back systems that check to be sure that an incoming call is from an authorized phone number, and encryption hardware that disguises data by converting it to a code that is difficult for outsiders to decipher.

PRIVACY ISSUES The widespread use of information technology has given rise to a number of privacy issues. For one thing, the data security issues mentioned above threaten the privacy of sensitive personal data, such as personnel, medical, and credit records. For another, the ease of building data bases can allow organizations to collect massive amounts of data about individuals. For example, Equifax, Inc., the nation's largest consumer credit vendor, has information on approximately 190 million individuals. One service being tested allows retailers to clear checks within 10 seconds. Another lets bank employees know whether to offer a credit card to a new customer opening an account; at least 30 major banks use this service. Equifax can also provide speedy information about driving records to employers that hire delivery truck drivers.[68]

A related issue is the privacy of e-mail and voice mail communications within companies. Courts have generally upheld the right of employers to monitor or retrieve voice and e-mail communications sent by or to employees as long as they have an appropriate published policy. Such policies should include clarification that the voice, e-mail, and related systems (such as facilities for Internet access) are company assets, that all entries are company property, and that such communications should not be considered private. Such a policy is prudent because there have been instances of gross misuse of company communication facilities for such purposes as hacking and sexual harassment. (Indeed, employees should be made aware that even though they may have erased an e-mail message, backup facilities necessary to run e-mail typically can continue to retain copies of such messages for a significant period.) However, a major purpose of such a policy is to inform employees of guidelines for appropriate uses of communications facilities so that such problems are avoided.[69] In another area of misuse, some employers have complained that employees waste many hours playing computer games or surfing on the Internet in pursuit of non-business-related activities. To help curb such problems, Texaco, Inc.'s Internet usage policy specifies that computer activity logs are being monitored.[70]

RESISTANCE Another risk is that significant resources might be allocated to developing systems that managers and their subordinates will resist using. For example, one group of division heads at AT&T was reluctant to provide data to a system that could be used by top-level executives in assessing the progress of various operations at any point in time. The division heads apparently feared that top-level managers would be able to check on and interfere with their activities more directly with the new system. Innovative new uses of information technology are critical to the future efficiency and effectiveness of most organizations, particularly those going global—a subject to which we turn in the next chapter.

■ CHAPTER SUMMARY

An information system is a set of procedures designed to collect (or retrieve), process, store, and disseminate information to support planning, decision making, coordination, and control. Information systems can be thought of as involving inputs, transformations, and outputs. Such systems transform data into information that has meaning for decision makers. Information systems that make use of computers are often referred to as computer-based information systems. The computer components of a CBIS fall into three categories: hardware, software, and telecommunications technology. Managerial needs for information tend to differ for top, middle, and first-line levels and to vary by specialized area.

To serve the needs of different organizational levels, there are six major types of information systems: transac-

tion processing, office automation, knowledge work, management information, decision support, and executive support. Decision support systems and related expert systems represent outgrowths of a specialized information technology field called artificial intelligence.

In thinking about how to use information technology to achieve competitive advantage, one managerial aid is the matrix of strategic options for such technology. The matrix consists of two main dimensions: competitive strategies (differentiation, cost leadership, and quick response) and strategic linkages (suppliers, customers, and alliances).

Traditionally, the development of new information systems has followed a process known as the systems development life cycle, which includes three stages: definition, physical design, and implementation and operation. Among the most prominent alternative means of systems development are software packages, prototyping, end-user development, and outsourcing.

As computers grow more pervasive, information technology is having a considerable impact on many aspects of organizations. Major areas of influence include organization structure, individual jobs, communication patterns, and organizational risk.

■ QUESTIONS FOR DISCUSSION AND REVIEW

1 Differentiate between data and information, and use the systems view to explain the general process by which information is created. Give an example from your own experience of data versus information.

2 Identify the major components of computer-based information systems. Describe the types of computers that you have used or seen used. For what major purposes were they being used?

3 Discuss how information needs differ by managerial level. How are information needs likely to vary among levels of administration at your college or university?

4 Explain the concept of a transaction-processing system. List five activities in which you engage that involve interacting with a TPS in some way.

5 Distinguish among the other five major types of information systems (besides TPS). On the basis of what you have seen or read about, explain a recent change in the features offered by these systems or in the way they are used.

6 Describe how considering competitive strategies and strategic linkages can facilitate the development of information systems that provide a competitive advantage. Identify a system that you believe provides a competitive advantage in some way. Where would it fit on the matrix of strategic options for information technology?

7 Describe the systems development life cycle. Research suggests that systems development efforts that run into difficulty have often deviated from the life cycle. Why are such deviations likely to create problems?

8 Identify four alternative means of systems development, and explain the advantages of each. Which means would probably be appropriate for developing an information system to record routine employee information and produce basic reports? Which means would you consider for developing a unique new application involving better servicing of client needs, some of which are unclear and evolving? Give your reasoning.

9 Describe the major impacts of CBISs on organization structure, individual jobs, and communication patterns. Give an example from your own experience and observations that illustrates how computers and information technology have influenced jobs.

10 Explain the major risks associated with information technology in organizations. To what extent do you expect such risks to increase or decrease in the future? Explain the reasons for your view.

■ DISCUSSION QUESTIONS FOR CHAPTER OPENING CASE

1 What types of information systems are in evidence at Microsoft? What other information systems would you expect to be used in this type of setting?

2 Use the strategic options matrix to analyze how Microsoft has used information technology to achieve a competitive advantage. What other steps could be taken?

3 Microsoft faces new competitive threats because of the Internet. What adjustments should Bill Gates make in the company's direction?

4 If Bill Gates is correct about his view of the future, what impact would you expect information technology to have on organizations in such areas as organization structure, individual jobs, communication patterns, and organizational risk over the next decade?

■ EXERCISES FOR MANAGING IN THE TWENTY-FIRST CENTURY

EXERCISE 1
SKILL BUILDING: IDENTIFYING TYPES OF INFORMATION SYSTEMS

 There are six major types of information systems currently being used. They are executive support system, decision support system, management information system, knowledge work system, office automation system, and transaction-processing system. Examples of each follow. Use the letters in boldface to indicate the type of system that would include the example.

Executive **S**upport **S**ystem

Decision **S**upport **S**ystem

Management **I**nformation **S**ystem

Knowledge **W**ork **S**ystem

Office **A**utomation **S**ystem

Transaction-**P**rocessing **S**ystem

1 _____ When queried, a system that displays market share of major organizations, and those factors affecting market share, for a particular industry

2 _____ Sending a significant message to several members of an office by electronic mail

3 _____ A daily report of finished-goods inventory

4 _____ A system that allows managers to substitute numerous types of raw materials (providing costs, availability, durability, and other data) in deciding which products to produce

5 _____ A system that supports preparation of detailed, multilevel graphics

6 _____ Use of ATM to obtain cash from checking account

7 _____ Routine report of aircraft that are deadlined

8 _____ A word-processing system for a large group of administrative employees

9 _____ A system that provides alternatives that can be used to help decide the number and type of hospitals required in a specific geographic area

10 _____ A system used for estimating the future need for heavy construction equipment (used to build large structures, bridges, airports, and other facilities in the infrastructure) in a specific geographic region, such as North or South America, for strategic planning purposes

11 _____ Conducting a search of legal precedents

12 _____ Paying for a meal with a credit card

EXERCISE 2
MANAGEMENT EXERCISE: SOXSPORT, INC.

 You have just landed a job with a relatively new and growing company by the name of Soxsport. The company makes different types of socks for different sports, such as running, tennis, golf, and skiing. The products are designed to give the best foot comfort (through padding, materials, weave, etc.) when the wearer is engaged in the sport for which his or her socks were made. Recently, the company has begun to move into sports clothing that coordinates with the fashionable colors of the socks and meets the needs of individuals who engage heavily in sports. The company's products have proved to be extremely popular, particularly with sporting-goods stores, and sales have been rising steadily.

One major difficulty confronting management is that it takes about 16 people to process an order from the initial customer contact to shipping. One person takes the order, another checks the customer's credit rating, another checks inventory to be sure the items are in stock, another prepares the invoice, another pulls the items from inventory, another boxes the items, and so on. Furthermore, it takes almost a week to fill a customer's order. So far, the delay is not much of a problem with individual orders that come through the company's small catalog operation. However, it is somewhat of an annoyance to the growing list of sporting-goods stores and specialty shops that are the main source of business.

A related problem involves telephone orders. It isn't possible to check whether the items are in inventory while the customer is on the telephone. As a result, if the items are not available, a member of the staff must call the customer back to ask if a partial shipment is acceptable. During the call, it is difficult to talk about substituting other items, since a substitute order would entail another inventory check. Some of the customers have been grumbling lately that they get better service from other vendors, and Soxsport's president, Jerry Clark, is beginning to get concerned.

Clark is also having some difficulty determining which items are most profitable. Clark has someone plow through stacks of order forms periodically to tally what is selling and what is not. Unfortunately, the information is somewhat dated by the time it is available for Clark, the designers, and the production group.

When Clark is away, his work falls behind. Clark would like to find ways of keeping things moving while on trips.

Clark is interested in hearing your suggestions about types of information systems that could help Soxsport operate more efficiently internally. Clark also wants your ideas on how Soxsport could use information technology to ensure its advantage over potential competitors. What will you tell him?

CONCLUDING CASE 1

DU PONT'S EDGE IN MANAGING INFORMATION TECHNOLOGY

E. I. Du Pont de Nemours and Co., the chemical and energy giant, has earned a reputation for being at the forefront of managing information technology. The company spends about $700 million per year on computers, software, and related salaries. This budget figure represents a reduction of $540 million in annual spending. The cost savings were orchestrated by Cinda Hallman, Du Pont's chief information officer, and represented nearly 20 percent of cost reductions recently made at the company to improve its competitive cost structure.

Hallman was recently named *InformationWeek*'s Technology Chief of the Year for her success in patiently building successful information technology relationships with management and the business units. In one action, she formed the Business Information Board to help spearhead information technology projects and was able to persuade John Krol, who is now CEO (but was vice chairman when he joined the board) to become a board member. At the same time, she has been very successful in leading the information technology function so that there are significant bottom-line results that can be attributed to new information systems. She has orchestrated the delivery of new collaborative information tools, such as Lotus Notes, the creation of internal and external Internet Web sites, the installation of desktop teleconferencing technology, and the development of specialized software for various Du Pont units. Hallman oversees four global information technology units (for data and applications, architecture and planning, telecommunication, and processing and delivery of integrated information), six regional units, and the information systems groups for application development and planning purposes, located within the 20 strategic business units.

Hallman says she is seeking more "step changes." She describes a step change as "a very noticeable change, not continuous improvement . . . like the change we made over the last three or four years, where we improved our productivity by 45 percent." In the area of future development, Hallman says, "China is one of our biggest challenges." In addition to the telephone, fax, and e-mail, she envisions increased use of videoconferencing over the Internet to help overcome shortages of local experts and managers and for discussing product development.

Du Pont is teaming up with Andersen Consulting in a 3-year agreement called the Global Applications Alliance, which calls for Andersen to bring information technology tools and consulting services to the chemical giant. The purpose is to achieve a 25 percent improvement in the maintenance, development, and implementation of strategic applications. Du Pont wants to upgrade its business requirements planning and enhance its electronic business capabilities—particularly its linkages to customers and suppliers. Du Pont decided to form a strategic alliance with Andersen, rather than outsource applications development, because it did not want to cede management of very strategic systems. Instead, Du Pont will be reinvesting in its own information systems personnel and building on existing strengths, while also gaining expertise through the Andersen alliance.

Du Pont already has a number of strategic systems in place. In one competitive environment, the company was involved in a fairly long distribution chain (e.g., wholesalers, distributors, retailers) between the manufacturing of the product and its distribution to the ultimate consumer. Because of the multiple links in the chain, Du Pont had difficulty obtaining sound market knowledge about the consumers, yet such information was critical to an effective marketing effort. In assessing the problem, marketing managers recognized that using computer-based information systems could help change the situation. Accordingly, a team of marketing and information specialists was formed. They conceived of an information system that could be used to alter the role of a major part of the distribution chain and, in the process, provide access to previously unavailable market information. Within 1 year of implementation, the new system had helped Du Pont significantly increase its market share.

Du Pont also makes use of expert systems and other types of decision support systems, says Ed G. Mahler, manager of decision support and artificial intelligence. For example, one of its expert systems helps manufacturers design items such as squeezable ketchup bottles or microwave containers, very complex engineering design problems. Du Pont sells the system to outside manufacturers as a means of expanding the market for one of its products—resin—a substance used in making the various bottles and containers that can be designed with the expert system.[71]

QUESTIONS FOR CONCLUDING CASE 1

1. Use the matrix of strategic options to analyze Du Pont's use of strategic information systems. Give reasons for your assessments.

2. Identify the types of computer-based information systems that are in evidence in the case. What other types might be appropriate for the chemical giant?

3. Criticize or defend Du Pont's decision not to outsource the development of strategic information systems.

CONCLUDING CASE 2

TEXAS INSTRUMENTS INNOVATES OVER A GLOBAL NETWORK

Texas Instruments (TI), the Dallas-based electronics firm, has long used its resources worldwide to design new products—but how things have changed. Days used to be lost when designers and engineers around the world worked together. Drawings they needed to see before they could talk might take 2 weeks to arrive. Faxing helped only a little, since blurry faxes of blueprints cut into letter-size pieces and taped back together at the other end often proved to be indecipherable.

Now, detailed designs are sent instantly over the computer network, enabling TI employees to work on them simultaneously, regardless of location. As a result, development time has dwindled. The time needed to develop a calculator, for instance, shrank 20 percent as soon as TI began sending drawings electronically in 1989. It has shrunk another 17 percent since.

Far-flung units of TI routinely work simultaneously—and speedily—on separate parts of a project, keeping everything coordinated over the computer network. Across the globe from Texas, a memory chip design project progresses at TI's engineering facility in Bangalore, India. The location offers the advantages of a growing Asian market and a large, lower-cost pool of talented engineers. The facility itself is connected to the TI system by an earth station that TI had to haul in by oxcart. Engineers in Dallas and in Hiho, Japan, provide elements of the design, sent by satellite. When the computer-aided design is done, Bangalore will forward it to Dallas, where the chip will be fabricated before being sent back to India for debugging. Says TI group vice president Wayne Spence, "Problems that used to take 3 years now take a year."

Time is compressed in another way: departments scattered across the globe can work on a project 24 hours a day. For example, when a U.S. financial exchange asked TI to come up with a quote to make a handheld bidding device for traders, designers on three continents worked around the clock. The company's design department began working on the problem in Dallas. At quitting time, they electronically sent what they had done to designers in Tokyo. When their workday ended, they passed the work on to designers in Nice, France. By the next day in Dallas, TI not only had a pretty accurate quote but also could show the customer a computer-generated photo of what the product would look like.

Distance also disappears. Through the network, a process engineer in Dallas can look at the data from TI's assembly and test plant in Kuala Lumpur and spot any disturbing trends that the Malaysian staff must examine. As a result, the Malaysian plant, staffed by relatively low-cost labor, needs few high-priced engineers. Even more global is a TI unit called Tiris (Texas Instruments Registration and Identification System), which makes tiny communication devices used for security and identification purposes. Tiris is managed out of England, develops products in the Netherlands and Germany, and manufactures and assembles products in those two places plus Japan and Malaysia. All these centers send text, diagrams, and mock-up drawings to each other over the computer network. They are also tied in to the nine centers that design the various applications for Tiris's products around the world. The computer network allowed Tiris to create a new business quickly and cheaply by making use of existing TI facilities. Says Tiris North American general manager David Slinger: "We're probably 18 to 24 months ahead of the competition, partly as a result of this communications expertise."[72]

QUESTIONS FOR CONCLUDING CASE 2

1 What types of information systems are in evidence at TI? Explain your conclusions.
2 Use the matrix of strategic options for information technology to categorize TI's efforts to use information systems in a strategic manner.
3 Assess the impact of TI's wide area network on its structure and the nature of individual jobs. What future changes might be anticipated?

Previous parts of this book introduce management and examine its four major functions: planning, organizing, leading, and controlling. Now, in Part Six, we see how these various functions apply in two particularly significant management situations: conducting business in the international arena and engaging in entrepreneurship and small-business management. Fostering innovation is especially important within these realms because global businesses must keep pace with rapidly changing world conditions, new technology, and increasing competition, while new ventures and small businesses often must maintain a competitive edge just to stay alive.

Since managers in many organizations increasingly must take a worldwide perspective, **Chapter 20** pinpoints the strategic issues and the structural alternatives associated with conducting business across national boundaries. An essential aspect of being an international manager is learning how to adapt to cultural differences and how to deal with the special social and ethical concerns that can arise in the international domain.

At the same time, most businesses in the United States are relatively small, and even large businesses typically start small. Thus it is important to understand the phenomenon of entrepreneurship, which involves the creation of new businesses or ventures, and the particular issues related to managing a small business. **Chapter 21** examines the role of the entrepreneur and explores major considerations that managers of small businesses must address.

CHAPTER TWENTY

INTERNATIONAL MANAGEMENT

CHAPTER OUTLINE

LEARNING OBJECTIVES

After studying this chapter, you should be able to:

■ Explain the concept of a multinational corporation and describe four major orientations toward
international management.

■ Delineate several elements that are important in
assessing the international environment.

■ Explain the concept of the competitive advantage
of nations and its linkage to innovation.

■ Outline the major methods of entry into the international business arena.

■ Contrast four major strategies for multinational
corporations.

■ Enumerate the main structural alternatives for
conducting international business.

■ Explain the principal issues related to assignment
policies and the recruitment, selection, training,
and repatriation of managerial personnel.

■ Describe the adjustments in leadership style that
may be necessary because of cultural differences.

■ Delineate the major social responsibility and
ethics issues related to international management.

GAINING THE EDGE

UNILEVER: ONE OF THE WORLD'S LARGEST MULTINATIONAL CORPORATIONS

It is said that the sun never sets on Unilever. The company's more than 300,000 employees operate 500 businesses in 70 countries. Although its corporate name, Unilever, may not be readily recognized, its products are household names. They include such famous labels in the United States as Lipton, Dove, Lever 2000, Caress, Wisk, Pepsodent, Ragu spaghetti sauces, Pond's face creams, and Calvin Klein cosmetics, to name only a few. With more than $55 billion in annual revenues, Unilever is one of the world's largest consumer-goods companies, with 1 percent of the total world food market and 10 percent of the personal-products market.

A unique aspect of Unilever is its dual structure: it is actually two companies with two sets of shareholders and two headquarters. Unilever PLC (for Public Limited Company) is based in London, while Unilever NV (for Naamloze Vennootschap, meaning "limited-liability company") is based in Rotterdam. The dual structure can be traced back to a merger of two companies (British Lever Brothers, Ltd., and Dutch Margarine Unie) in 1930. However, the shareholders of each company participate in the prosperity of the entire Unilever organization by receiving dividends that are equalized across both companies.

For most of the past three decades, Unilever was run by a triumvirate modestly called the "Special Committee." The Special Committee was made up of the chairman of PLC, the chairman of NV, and a third senior director. All top-level strategic and operational decisions were made by this group. Various product coordinators from each subsidiary helped develop and implement product strategies worldwide. More recently, Unilever has reorganized to make the company more nimble, particularly with regard to one of its most aggressive competitors, Procter & Gamble. Under the new structure, Unilever will be led by a seven-member executive committee headed jointly by the chairman of PLC and the chairman of NV. The committee will concentrate on strategic issues and leave operating decisions to 14 newly defined business groups.

The company has traditionally followed a form of polycentric orientation, which it calls "-ization," or nationalization of management, whereby efforts were made to develop local managers in various countries. The policy was based on the belief that such managers understand local needs better than managers who were raised elsewhere. Under the new structure, the company has shifted to a somewhat greater emphasis on regions. Eleven of the fourteen business groups encompass some regional emphasis, such as Food & Beverage Europe; the others are specialized product groups.

Part of the impetus for the change in structure seemed to stem from an embarrassing situation in which Unilever heavily advertised a new stain-fighting Power line of detergents in Europe. Procter & Gamble subsequently publicized laundry test results showing that the Power detergents faded dark colors and weakened the fibers of clothing. Unilever was forced to withdraw the new brand from the market. The fiasco seriously damaged consumer confidence in Unilever and led to a market-share drop for its existing detergents.

Whenever possible, Unilever likes to sell the same product throughout the world. Lux soap is perhaps the classic example. It's in every country, and it's largely the same in every country. Other products, such as a shampoo called Sunsilk and a body spray called Impulse, also appear in many countries, although the formulation may change somewhat. Food, however, is unlikely to

Soap operas, Indian-style. One way that Hindustan Lever, a subsidiary of Unilever, sells its soap and detergent products is by sending video vans (with appropriate advertising messages) into the villages of India. Unilever's many subsidiaries make it one of the world's largest multinational companies.

be the same everywhere. One of the best-known Unilever divisions operating in the United States is Lever Brothers, which mainly markets soap and laundry products. Recently Unilever purchased Helene Curtis Industries, acquiring brands like Suave, Finesse, and Salon Selectives. As a result, Unilever is number one in the U.S. conditioners market and number two in shampoos.[1] ■ ■ ■

Unilever is just one of many international companies that touch our lives. We can easily name others that are even more visible, such as Fiat, Honda, Volvo, Michelin, Nestlé, Sony, NEC, Toyota, and Volkswagen. Many observers argue that organizations increasingly need to adopt a global perspective in planning and carrying out their various activities. By viewing the entire world as their operating area, managers can tap vast worldwide markets and conduct business activities wherever conditions appear to be most conducive to meeting organizational goals. In fact, one expert argues that a worldwide outlook is already a necessity for competing effectively in a number of industries, such as automobiles, banking, consumer electronics, entertainment, pharmaceuticals, publishing, travel services, and washing machines.[2]

Not only are managers increasingly likely to be engaging in international business themselves, but they are also highly likely to face competition from international organizations or to deal with them in other capacities (e.g., as suppliers or customers). Such developments make it imperative that managers have a solid understanding of international management issues. Accordingly, in this chapter, we explore the basic nature of international management, building further on the coverage of international management issues provided throughout this text. We also probe various environmental factors that are likely to affect managerial success in the international arena, and we consider the notion of the competitive advantage of nations and its relationship to innovation. We then examine a number of strategic issues associated with international management and consider structural alternatives that aid in conducting international business. We next investigate several means of adapting to cultural differences. Finally, we turn to ethical questions that may arise when organizations are conducting business throughout the world.

■ THE NATURE OF INTERNATIONAL MANAGEMENT

If you took an inventory of the items in your living quarters, you would probably find many that reflect the increasing volume of business conducted on an international basis. For example, you might have shoes from Italy or Brazil, a television and VCR from Japan, and a shirt made in Korea. Even items that bear the brand name of a U.S.-based company may have been produced in a far-off land in the course of international business. **International business** refers to profit-related activities conducted across national boundaries. Such activities encompass importing supplies from other countries, selling products or services to customers abroad, and providing for the transfer of funds to subsidiaries in other countries. **International management** is the process of planning, organizing, leading, and controlling in organizations engaged in international business.

As is pointed out in earlier chapters, the United States is facing increasing competition in world markets. According to some accounts, the United States enjoyed an abnormal advantage for several decades after World War II because the productive facilities of other large industrial powers had been severely damaged by wartime activities.[3] Now countries such as Japan and Germany have become formidable competitors; and developing nations such as Brazil, India, and South Korea are emerging as potential major players. Despite the increased competition, though, international markets are growing rapidly, providing expanded opportunities for many U.S.-based businesses.

International business Profit-related activities conducted across national boundaries

International management The process of planning, organizing, leading, and controlling in organizations engaged in international business

Organizations Engaging in International Management

Organizations that engage in international management vary considerably in size and in the extent to which their business activities cross national boundaries. One special type of organization involved in international management is the multinational corporation. Although definitions differ somewhat, the term **multinational corporation (MNC)** is typically reserved for an organization that engages in production or service activities through its own affiliates in several countries, maintains control over the policies of those affiliates, and manages from a global perspective.[4] With a global perspective, top managers allocate resources and coordinate activities to take the best possible advantage of favorable business conditions throughout the world.

Multinational corporations are not always easy to identify, since it may be difficult to determine from the outside how much control management maintains over the policies of affiliates or whether management actually uses a global perspective. As a result, for purposes of gathering statistics, an arbitrary percentage (such as 25 percent of sales from foreign sources) is sometimes used to distinguish multinational corporations from other types of international businesses. However, there is no single universally accepted percentage of foreign sales that clearly separates multinational corporations from others.[5] The 25 largest multinational corporations in the world are listed in Table 20-1.

Although multinational companies tend to be rather large and to engage in a substantial amount of business transactions across borders, an increasing number of midsize and small companies also conduct international business. According to one estimate approximately 10 percent of U.S. companies employing 100 or fewer employees export.[6] Regardless of their size, managers need to think through their basic orientation toward international management.

Multinational corporation (MNC) An organization that engages in production or service activities through its own affiliates in several countries, maintains control over the policies of those affiliates, and manages from a global perspective

The face of international business is rapidly changing. Western and Japanese partners are providing their local employees in less developed countries with the expertise to do more sophisticated work than assembling parts. These Malaysian engineers employed by Intel are designing state-of-the-art computer chip packages. Spreading high-tech expertise can make America more competitive now but may create future trade rivals.

Orientations toward International Management

Top-level managers in companies that are expanding internationally (particularly those in multinational corporations) tend to subscribe to one of four basic orientations, or philosophies, regarding the degree to which methods of oper-

TABLE 20-1 THE WORLD'S 25 LARGEST MULTINATIONAL CORPORATIONS				
RANK				
1995	**1994**	**COMPANY**	**HEADQUARTERS**	**INDUSTRY**
1.	1.	Mitsubishi	Japan	Trading
2.	2.	Mitsui	Japan	Trading
3.	3.	Itochu	Japan	Trading
4.	5.	General Motors	U.S.	Motor vehicles
5.	4.	Sumitomo	Japan	Trading
6.	6.	Marubeni	Japan	Trading
7.	7.	Ford Motor	U.S.	Motor vehicles
8.	11.	Toyota Motor	Japan	Motor vehicles
9.	8.	Exxon	U.S.	Petroleum refining
10.	10.	Royal Dutch/Shell Group	Britain/Netherlands	Petroleum refining
11.	9.	Nissho Wai	Japan	Trading
12.	12.	Wal-Mart Stores	U.S.	General merchandisers
13.	13.	Hitachi	Japan	Electronics
14.	14.	Nippon Life Insurance	Japan	Electronics
15.	16.	Nippon Telegraph & Telephone	Japan	Telecommunications
16.	15.	AT&T	U.S.	Telecommunications
17.	20.	Daimler-Benz	Germany	Motor vehicles
18.	21.	International Business Machines	U.S.	Computers
19.	17.	Matsushita Electric Industrial	Japan	Electronics
20.	19.	General Electric	U.S.	Electronics
21.	18.	Tomen	Japan	Trading
22.	22.	Mobil	U.S.	Petroleum refining
23.	23.	Nissan Motor	Japan	Motor vehicles
24.	34.	Volkswagen	Germany	Motor vehicles
25.	30.	Siemens	Germany	Electronics

Source: Adapted from "Fortune's Global; The World's Largest Corporations," *Fortune,* Aug. 5, 1996, p. F-1.

ating are influenced by headquarters or by company members in other parts of the world. These orientations are ethnocentric (home-country oriented), polycentric (host-country oriented), regiocentric (region oriented), and geocentric (world oriented).[7] A *home country* is the country in which an organization's headquarters is located, whereas a *host country* is a foreign country in which an organization is conducting business.

An **ethnocentric** (or home-country) **orientation** is an approach to international management whereby executives assume, albeit sometimes mistakenly, that practices that work in the headquarters or home country must necessarily work elsewhere. During the period 1973 to 1986, Procter & Gamble lost an estimated quarter of a billion dollars of business in Japan partially because of an ethnocentric orientation. As one former Japanese employee stated, "They did not listen to anybody." One of the most serious blunders was a commercial for Camay soap that was used in the late 1970s. The commercial showed a Japanese man meeting a Japanese woman for the first time and immediately comparing her skin to that of a fine porcelain doll. Although this commercial had worked well in the Philippines, South America, and Europe, it was a disaster in Japan. A Japanese advertising specialist who worked on the commercial had warned Procter & Gamble that only an unsophisticated or rude man would say something like that to a Japanese woman, but company representatives would not listen. As the vice-chairman of Procter & Gamble later noted, "We learned a lesson here [in Japan] about tailoring your products and marketing to the market." Today, Procter & Gamble is doing considerably better in Japan.[8] Although an ethnocentric orientation is often a phase that organizations go through when they enter the international arena, it can prove extremely difficult to eradicate.

A **polycentric** (or host-country) **orientation** is an approach to international management whereby executives believe that the parts of the organization located in a given host country should be staffed by local individuals to the fullest extent possible. Locals—or nationals, as they are sometimes called—are thought to know their own culture, mores, work ethics, and markets best. As a result, subsidiaries in various countries operate almost independently under the direction of local individuals and are tied to the parent company mainly through financial controls. The parent company may maintain a very low public profile relative to the subsidiary, as was the case until recently with Unilever and its major U.S. subsidiary, Lever Brothers. It is very possible that you only discovered that Lever Brothers was owned by a foreign company when you read this chapter's introductory case.

A **regiocentric** (or regional) **orientation** is an approach to international management whereby executives believe that geographic regions have commonalities that make a regional focus advantageous and that company problems related to that region are generally best solved by individuals from the region. Typically, regional headquarters coordinate collaborative efforts among the local subsidiaries within the region, while world headquarters handles overall issues, such as global strategy, basic research and development, and long-term financing.[9] For example, the continuing process of forming a more unified multination European Union by "harmonizing" various national rules (e.g., adopting common standards for electric plugs) is opening new opportunities for a regional focus. Previously, many manufacturers in Europe established plants in host countries that served the specific needs of the host country and perhaps small neighboring nations. The plant would produce the full range of products to be sold in the particular host country. With the more unified European Union, it has become feasible in many cases to achieve economies of scale by having different products made in different factories located somewhere in

Ethnocentric orientation
An approach to international management whereby executives assume that practices that work in the headquarters or home country must necessarily work elsewhere

Polycentric orientation
An approach to international management whereby executives believe that the parts of the organization located in a given host country should be staffed by local individuals to the fullest extent possible

Regiocentric orientation
An approach to international management whereby executives believe that geographic regions have commonalities that make a regional focus advantageous and that company problems related to that region are generally best solved by individuals from the region

the region. Products are then shipped over a broad geographical area to customers. For example, Warner Lambert Co., which operates in Europe through its Parke-Davis subsidiary, had a number of manufacturing operations that made many products and concentrated on meeting local needs. Recently, Warner Lambert closed about half of these facilities and had the remaining factories each specialize in a smaller number of products for the entire European market.[10] The region created by the North American Free Trade Association (NAFTA) agreement that encompasses Canada, the United States, and Mexico is attracting increasing attention.[11]

Geocentric orientation   An approach to international management whereby executives believe that a global view is needed in both the headquarters of the parent company and its various subsidiaries and that the best individuals, regardless of host- or home-country origin, should be utilized to solve company problems anywhere in the world

The **geocentric** (or world) **orientation** is an approach to international management whereby executives believe that a global view is needed in both the headquarters of the parent company and its various subsidiaries and that the best individuals, regardless of home- or host-country origin, should be utilized to solve company problems anywhere in the world. Major issues are viewed globally at both headquarters and subsidiaries, which consider questions such as "Where in the world shall we raise money, build our plant, conduct R&D, and develop and launch new ideas to serve our present and future customers?"[12] The geocentric approach is the most difficult to achieve because it requires that managers acquire both local and global knowledge.

A geocentric approach helped Boeing save its 737 airplane. When sales began to slow down in the early 1970s, a group of Boeing engineers began to recognize that they had not given enough attention to a major potential market, the developing regions of the world. Through visits abroad, the engineers found that runways in developing countries were generally too short for the 737 and were mainly asphalt, a softer material than concrete. Consequently, they redesigned the wings to allow shorter landings on soft pavement and changed the engine so that takeoffs would be quicker. They also developed a new landing gear and installed low-pressure tires. Boeing soon began to get small orders for the 737 from a number of developing countries, which later bought larger Boeing planes because of their satisfaction with the 737. The 737 ultimately became the best-selling commercial jet in aviation history and is still selling well.[13] The Boeing situation helps illustrate the importance of understanding the international environment within which one is attempting to conduct business.

■ ASSESSING THE INTERNATIONAL ENVIRONMENT

While international management opens up vast opportunities, it also presents the challenge of attempting to understand a much broader set of environmental factors than those typically encountered in managing a strictly domestic business. In this section, we explore the effects of various elements of the international environment and also consider a broader concept, the competitive advantage of nations.

Environmental Elements

The notion of the general environment, or mega-environment, can be helpful in exploring the nature of international management. The general environment is the segment of the external environment that reflects broad conditions and trends in the societies within which an organization operates (see Chapter 3). Major elements of the general environment, such as economic, legal-political, sociocultural, and technological factors, can be used to explore the international realm more thoroughly.

As a country's industrial development grows, so does its middle class. Gillette finds receptive customers in China's increasingly consumer-oriented society.

THE ECONOMIC ELEMENT Different economic systems of various countries are discussed in Chapter 3. Additional economic factors that influence the ability of organizations to conduct international business successfully are the levels of economic development in countries, the presence of adequate infrastructures, a country's balance of payments, and monetary exchange rates.

Countries, other than those that are Communist, fall into two major classifications based on the economic or industrial level of development. The first group, known as **developed countries,** is characterized by a high level of economic or industrial development and includes the United States, western Europe, Canada, Australia, New Zealand, and Japan. The second group, known as **less developed countries (LDCs)** or *developing countries* (often called the "third world"), consists primarily of relatively poor nations characterized by low per capita income, little industry, and high birthrates. Within the LDCs, countries that are emerging as major exporters of manufactured goods are often referred to as **newly industrialized countries (NICs),** a designation that covers such nations as Hong Kong, Taiwan, and South Korea.

We may often think of multinational corporations as operating extensively throughout the world. Actually, about 95 percent of such companies are based in developed countries and about 75 percent of foreign investment has been channeled to developed countries. Nevertheless, the rising prosperity of many less developed countries (particularly those in the NIC group) provides the potential for tremendous expansion of current world markets.[14]

The decision to conduct business in a given area will also depend heavily on the availability of an adequate infrastructure. **Infrastructure** is a broad term that refers to the highways, railways, airports, sewage facilities, housing, educational institutions, communications networks, recreation facilities, and other economic and social amenities that signal the extent of economic development in an area. Because of the increasing importance of information technology, the presence of communications and information infrastructures in various countries is becoming more critical. According to one recent estimate by the Asian Development Bank, countries within its region will need to spend $150 billion over the next 5 to 10 years on upgrading their telecommunications infra-

Developed countries A group of countries that is characterized by a high level of economic or industrial development and that includes the United States, western Europe, Canada, Australia, New Zealand, and Japan

Less developed countries (LDCs) A group of noncommunist countries, often called the "third world," that consists primarily of relatively poor nations characterized by low per capita income, little industry, and high birthrates

Newly industrialized countries (NICs) Countries within the LDCs that are emerging as major exporters of manufactured goods, including such nations as Hong Kong, Taiwan, and South Korea

Infrastructure The highways, railways, airports, sewage facilities, housing, educational institutions, recreation facilities, and other economic and social amenities that signal the extent of economic development in an area

Balance of payments An account of goods and services, capital loans, gold, and other items entering and leaving a country

Balance of trade The difference between a country's exports and imports

Exchange rate The rate at which one country's currency can be exchanged for another country's currency

structure. Another $300 billion will need to be invested in the transportation, power, and water systems of the region. Hence, building necessary infrastructures to support economic development is a very expensive proposition.[15]

Another significant economic variable is a country's **balance of payments,** an account of goods and services, capital loans, gold, and other items entering and leaving a country. The **balance of trade,** the difference between a country's exports and imports, is generally the most critical determinant of a country's balance of payments. Constant trade deficits result in the exportation of a country's wealth, whereas surpluses enhance a country's ability to expand and conduct even more international trade. Recently, the United States has been suffering from an imbalance in trade resulting from more imports than exports.[16]

A related issue is the **exchange rate,** the rate at which one country's currency can be exchanged for another country's currency. Since exchange rates affect the relative prices of goods from various countries, changes in the rates can have a profound impact on a firm's ability to engage in international business. For example, the declining value of the dollar in recent years has made imported Japanese automobiles more expensive in the United States. This is because Japanese companies need to charge more dollars to earn the same amount of profit in their own currency. As one means around this problem, a number of Japanese automobile companies, like Toyota and Honda, have established automobile manufacturing operations in the United States. On the other hand, the declining dollar has made U.S. goods cheaper on world markets. This situation helps companies such as Caterpillar, a U.S. maker of tractors and other earth-moving machinery, which has been locked in ferocious competition with foreign companies, particularly Komatsu, Ltd., of Japan.[17]

THE LEGAL-POLITICAL ELEMENT Both legal and political conditions affect the ability of organizations to conduct business in foreign countries. Major considerations include the level of political risk associated with doing business in a particular country and the degree to which trade barriers are erected by various governments.

Political risk The probability of the occurrence of political actions that will result in either loss of enterprise ownership or significant benefits from conducting business

Expropriation The seizure of a foreign company's assets by a host-country government

Corporations must closely assess the political risk involved in establishing themselves in a given country.[18] **Political risk** is the probability of the occurrence of political actions that will result in either loss of enterprise ownership or significant benefits from conducting business. The seizure of a foreign company's assets by a host-country government is called **expropriation.** In the past, such countries as Cuba, Zambia, and Iran have expropriated assets of foreign-owned corporations located within their borders. Iran seized the assets of many American companies, including the Iranian operations of Xerox, R. J. Reynolds, and United Technologies, which were valued at an estimated $5 billion when the Ayatollah Khomeini took over the Iranian government in 1979. Since 1960 more than 1535 companies have been expropriated by 76 nations.[19] A related major risk is associated with the presence of **indigenization laws**, which require that citizens of the host country hold a majority interest in all firms operating within the country's borders. Other political risks are less severe but may make it more difficult or expensive to conduct business in a host country.

Indigenization laws Laws which require that citizens of the host country hold a majority interest in all firms operating within the country's borders

Tariff A type of trade barrier in the form of a customs duty, or tax, levied mainly on imports

Another aspect of the legal-political environment is trade control, the creation of barriers or limitations on goods entering or leaving a country.[20] Such barriers are often erected so that domestically produced goods will have a competitive price advantage over the goods of foreign competitors. The most common type of barrier is the **tariff,** a customs duty, or tax, levied mainly on imports. For example, Ford Motor Company's recent efforts to increase sales in Russia are hampered by high import tariffs. A combination of tariffs, excise taxes, and value-added taxes increases the sticker price on Ford cars by an average of 100 percent.[21] Another type of barrier is an **import quota,** a limit on the amount of a product that may be imported over a given period of time. Import quotas can protect a domestic market by restricting the availability of foreign competitors' products.[22]

Because tariffs and quotas tend to provoke direct reprisals from countries whose products are affected, a country may use the more subtle approach of **administrative protections.** These are various rules and regulations that make it more difficult for foreign firms to conduct business in a particular country. In one well-known situation, Japanese video recorders were required to pass through French customs at a small facility at Poitiers, where they were inspected one by one. The procedure created tremendous delays, and actual importation of the recorders slowed to a dribble. As a result, the Japanese manufacturers eventually agreed to a "voluntary export quota," limiting the number of recorders that they shipped to France.[23]

THE SOCIOCULTURAL ELEMENT The sociocultural element of the environment includes the attitudes, values, norms, beliefs, behaviors, and associated demographic trends that are characteristic of a given geographic area. When comparing individuals in different nations, people commonly speak in terms of cultural differences.

Dutch social scientist Geert Hofstede has developed a framework for studying the effects of societal culture on individuals.[24] In the course of his work, he researched the values and beliefs of more than 100,000 IBM employees in 40 countries throughout the world. Hofstede's approach involves four cultural dimensions that can be used to analyze societies: power distance, uncertainty avoidance, individualism-collectivism, and masculinity-femininity. Each dimension represents a continuum from high to low.

Power distance is the degree to which individuals in a society accept differences in the distribution of power as reasonable and normal. In low-power-distance societies, such as those of Sweden, Denmark, and Israel, people from different backgrounds interact more frequently with one another, and members of lower-status groups can move more easily to higher-status positions. In contrast, in societies with high power distance, such as those of Mexico, the Philippines, and India, individuals of high status have very limited interaction with lower-status individuals, and it is difficult to raise one's status. Such differences affect the degree of collaboration between subordinates and their bosses. With high power distance, managers are more likely to tell subordinates what to do rather than consult with them. On the other hand, greater collaboration between managers and subordinates is likely in a low-power-distance society.

The second dimension in Hofstede's framework, **uncertainty avoidance,** is the extent to which members of a society feel uncomfortable with and try to avoid situations that they perceive as unstructured, unclear, or unpredictable. For example, in low-uncertainty-avoidance countries, such as Sweden, Great Britain, and the United States, organizations tend to have fewer written rules and regulations. Such an approach facilitates the development of generalists (who know about many different areas) as opposed to specialists (who know a great deal about a narrow area) and encourages risk taking among managers. Organizations operate in opposite ways in countries with high uncertainty avoidance, such as Japan, Peru, and France.

Individualism-collectivism, the third dimension, refers to the degree to which individuals concern themselves with their own interests and those of

Import quota A type of trade barrier in the form of a limit on the amount of a product that may be imported over a given period of time

Administrative protections A type of trade barrier in the form of various rules and regulations that make it more difficult for foreign firms to conduct business in a particular country

Power distance A cultural dimension that involves the degree to which individuals in a society accept differences in the distribution of power as reasonable and normal

Uncertainty avoidance A cultural dimension that involves the extent to which members of a society feel uncomfortable with and try to avoid situations that they perceive as unstructured, unclear, or unpredictable

Individualism-collectivism A cultural dimension that involves the degree to which individuals concern themselves with their own interests and those of their immediate families as opposed to the interests of a larger group

Oulu, a small town in Finland, boasts one of the world's most impressive technology parks. More than 100 companies in telecommunications and electronics industries produce more than $1 billion in sales each year. Finland's emphasis on female values can be seen in its companies' clean and secure working conditions, internal spirit of cooperation, and affinity for intuitive decision-making. In fact, most important management decisions are made in the sauna, not on the golf course.

Masculinity-femininity
A cultural dimension that involves the extent to which a society emphasizes traditional male values, such as assertiveness, competitiveness, and material success, rather than traditional female values, such as passivity, cooperation, and feelings

their immediate families as opposed to the interests of a larger group. In cultures that place a high value on individualism, managers are more likely to switch companies when opportunities arise, feel less responsible for the general welfare of employees, and rely more on individual than on group decision making. High-individualism countries include the United States, Great Britain, and Canada. In contrast, in cultures that value collectivism, managers tend to focus on team achievements rather than individual ones, emphasize employee welfare, and view the organization as if it were a family. Countries that are high on collectivism include Venezuela, Taiwan, and Mexico.

The fourth dimension, **masculinity-femininity,** involves the extent to which a society emphasizes traditional male values, such as assertiveness, competitiveness, and material success, rather than traditional female values, such as passivity, cooperation, and feelings. In relatively masculine societies, such as those of Japan, Italy, and Mexico, employees tend to believe that jobs should be vehicles for recognition, growth, and challenge. In more feminine societies, such as those of Sweden and Finland, greater emphasis is placed on good working conditions, security, feelings, and intuition in decision making. Masculine societies tend to define very different roles for men and women. As a result, opportunities for women in organizations tend to be limited to some degree. Of course, Hofstede's labels reflect common stereotypes about male and female values, which may not apply to particular individuals.

In the course of his work, Hofstede developed clusters, or groups, of countries that have similarities on the four value dimensions. The United States falls in a cluster that is characterized by lower-than-average power-distance and uncertainty-avoidance values, higher-than-average masculinity values, and high individualism. Hofstede's study showed that people in the United States placed a higher value on individualism than people in any other country in the study. Other researchers suggest that individualism in the United States is reflected in the fact that successful individuals like the late Sam Walton of Wal-Mart Stores are widely considered to be heroes.[25]

Still, there are many differences among countries and within countries that must be taken into account. Even within the United States, we recognize significant regional differences. For example, PepsiCo divides its U.S. operations into four regions to take into consideration the variations in regional markets. McDonald's works with more than 74 different advertising agencies serving various parts of its U.S. market.[26]

THE TECHNOLOGICAL ELEMENT The technological element is a significant aspect of the international environment because the levels of technology in various countries affect the nature of markets and the ability of companies to conduct business. In fact, considerable technological transfer typically takes place in the course of international business. **Technological transfer** is the transmission of technology from those who possess it to those who do not. The technology can be tangible goods or processes, such as component parts or machinery, or it can be intangible know-how, such as advanced knowledge of road-building techniques. For example, after purchasing the Tungsram Company, a state-owned lightbulb maker based in Budapest, Hungary, to boost its own position in Europe, General Electric undertook major technological overhauls of Tungsram's factories and computer systems.[27]

Technological transfer The transmission of technology from those who possess it to those who do not

Promoting Innovation: The Competitive Advantage of Nations

In considering the impact of environmental factors on organizations, strategy expert Michael E. Porter has developed the notion of the competitive advantage of nations.[28] The **competitive advantage of nations** is a concept which holds that environmental elements within a nation can foster innovation in certain industries, thereby increasing the prospects for the success of home-based companies operating internationally within those industries. The competitive success of such companies has positive implications for national prosperity as well.

Porter's views are based on the argument that companies achieve competitive advantage through innovations. Such innovations may be radical breakthroughs or small incremental improvements (see Chapter 11), as long as organizations continually upgrade their innovative efforts to stay ahead of the competition. The likelihood of innovation among companies in given industries, though, is influenced by the characteristics of the nations within which the companies are based.

Competitive advantage of nations The concept that environmental elements within a nation can foster innovation in certain industries, thereby increasing the prospects for the success of home-based companies operating internationally within those industries

THE DIAMOND OF NATIONAL ADVANTAGE In explaining why certain companies are able to innovate on a consistent basis, Porter identifies four national attributes that individually and as a system establish the diamond of national advantage (see Figure 20-1).

Factor conditions are components of production, such as skilled labor or infrastructure, that are needed to compete effectively in a particular industry. Factors have the most impact on competitive success when they are highly specialized, require continual heavy investment, and are directly related to an industry's needs. For example, Holland's leading research institutes in the cultivating and shipping of flowers continually build the expertise that has made the country the world's principal flower exporter.

Demand conditions are the characteristics of the domestic demand for the products and services of an industry. When domestic buyers are sophisticated and exacting, companies are pressured to innovate and meet high standards. For example, strong environmental concerns in Denmark have prodded companies in that country to develop world-class expertise in water-pollution control equipment and windmills.

The attribute of *related and supporting industries* refers to the availability

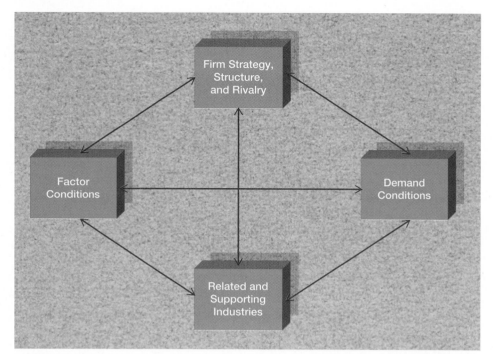

Figure 20-1 Determinants of national competitive advantage. *(Reprinted by permission of* Harvard Business Review. *An exhibit from "The Competitive Advantage of Nations," by Michael E. Porter, March–April 1990. Copyright © 1990 by the President and Fellows of Harvard College; all rights reserved.)*

within the nation of supplier and other related industries that compete effectively on an international basis. Such industries can provide cost-effective inputs and the latest developments rather quickly to home-based companies. Moreover, companies can become testing sites for potential supplier breakthroughs, thus hastening the tempo of innovation. For example, the presence of many automobile parts suppliers in the Michigan area and directly south has helped make the United States a principal manufacturer of automobiles.

Firm strategy, structure, and rivalry constitute the major conditions in a nation that affect the way in which organizations are created, organized, and managed, as well as the character of domestic rivalry. For example, successful international firms in Italy tend to be small- or medium-size companies that are privately owned and function almost as extended families. This profile is well suited to the industries in which Italian firms tend to excel, such as lighting, furniture, footwear, and woolen fabrics—all of which require strategies that include customized products, fast change, and ample flexibility. On the other hand, companies in Germany are likely to be fairly hierarchical in orientation and to have top managers with strong technical backgrounds. The German approach has been particularly successful in industries that rely on strong technical and engineering expertise, such as optics, chemicals, and complicated machinery. Porter believes that domestic rivalry is a vital factor because it pressures all the local members of an industry to innovate and upgrade their efforts. For example, the rivalry between the major Swiss drug firms (Hoffman-La Roche and Novartis) serves to enhance their leading global positions.

IMPLICATIONS FOR ORGANIZATIONS AND THEIR MANAGERS According to Porter, companies must take action on the basis of the factors contained in the diamond of national advantage and particularly must recognize the "central role" played by innovation in achieving a competitive advantage. A company should also expand its international business dealings on a selective basis that enables it to tap other nations' advantages, such as sophisticated buyers or important research. For example, the Electro Rent Corporation, which rents and leases electronic equipment, entered the Japanese market to facilitate staying abreast of technological developments in both the United States and Japan.[29] The issues raised by Porter further highlight the importance of long-range planning and strategic management in the realm of international business.

■ GAUGING INTERNATIONAL STRATEGIC ISSUES

Many companies involved in international business, particularly multinational corporations, engage in long-range planning. The planning period normally incorporates a 3-, 5-, or 7-year horizon. Studies of U.S., German, and Japanese multinationals indicate that much of the planning is done at the headquarters level, with some involvement by subsidiaries.[30]

Although most companies conducting international business appear to engage in long-range planning, their initial efforts to do business in other countries are likely to focus on more narrow goals than becoming a full-fledged multinational corporation. Accordingly, we consider the major methods of international entry before examining several strategic approaches for multinational corporations.

Methods of International Entry

There are four main entry methods that organizations can use to expand into different countries: exporting, licensing, establishing strategic alliances, and operating wholly owned subsidiaries.[31]

EXPORTING For organizations that manufacture products, **exporting,** the process of making a product in the home country and sending it overseas, is a common means of entering international markets. Exporting has the advantage of requiring very little in the way of additional capital if the product does not need modifications for sale abroad. It also involves relatively low risk, especially if the company ships products only after payment has been guaranteed.

Exporting The process of making a product in the home country and sending it overseas

Exporting does have some serious potential disadvantages. For one thing, various tariffs and taxes, as well as transportation costs, are typically involved. In addition, the exporter may have difficulty promoting products adequately in other countries. If the product is successful, local competition may emerge. To minimize the disadvantages of exporting, many companies engage *foreign sales representatives,* local individuals who have a good understanding of product and market needs and whose activities may also help to deter the emergence of competition.

LICENSING Licensing is an agreement in which one organization gives limited rights to another to use certain of its assets, such as expertise, patents, copyrights, or equipment, for an agreed upon fee or royalty. Typically, a license allows the licensee to use the assets within a certain territory and for a specified length of time. A main advantage of licensing is that an organization can make profits without having to lay out the large sums required to conduct business directly. Also, since the licensee is usually from the particular country involved, the licensee is familiar with the culture and the methods of doing business there.

Licensing An agreement in which one organization gives limited rights to another to use certain of its assets, such as expertise, patents, copyrights, or equipment, for an agreed-upon fee or royalty

Licensing has several major potential disadvantages, however. Perhaps the most important is that it usually precludes the licenser from conducting business involving the licensed product or service in a given territory for 5, 10, or even 20 years. If the product or service is very successful, the licenser will have

What's cooking? In this case, a joint venture between this Wedel Chocolate factory in Warsaw, Poland, and Culinar, a Canadian company. International joint ventures allow companies to combine expertise with capital and to share risks, but they are also susceptible to partner disagreements that may prove stubborn to resolve.

given up the much greater profits associated with doing business directly. Another major disadvantage is that the licenser may be establishing a potential competitor, since licensees often have the right to produce an equivalent product or service after the license has expired. Also, the licensee may not perform at a desired level, affecting licensing revenues and long-term business potential. For example, Anheuser-Busch Company, the St. Louis–based brewer, had attempted to enter the beer market in Japan through a licensing agreement with Suntory, Ltd., the weakest of Japan's four major brewers. After 12 years, Anheuser-Busch's Budweiser brand accounted for only a little more than 1 percent of the Japanese beer market.

STRATEGIC ALLIANCES A *strategic alliance* is an arrangement whereby two or more independent organizations form a cooperative partnership to gain some mutual strategic advantage. Under such arrangement none of the organizations is owned by another member of the strategic alliance. Often strategic alliances involve a joint venture. A *joint venture* is an agreement involving two or more organizations that arrange to produce a product or service through a jointly owned enterprise (see Chapter 3).[32] Because of poor results, Anheuser-Busch canceled the licensing agreement with Suntory and, instead, has formed a joint venture with Kirin Brewery Co., which commands about half of the Japanese beer market. The new venture, called Budweiser Japan Co., will market and distribute Bud through Kirin's channels, but the venture can also establish its own channels and also use Kirin's production facilities. International joint ventures typically represent a **direct investment,** the establishment of operating facilities in a foreign country. However, with a joint venture the direct investment is limited to the degree of ownership that a company has in the venture. For its 10 percent investment, Kirin gains access to Anheuser-Busch's knowledge of the worldwide beer market.[33] According to one estimate, approximately 20 percent of direct investments are in joint ventures.[34] Many companies seek to have a majority interest in joint ventures, where possible, so that they can maintain control over operations.

Direct investment The establishment of operating facilities in a foreign country

One advantage of strategic alliances is that they can provide a means of gaining access to countries where full equity is not permitted. Other advantages include possibilities for lowering the risk of introducing new products, for staying abreast of new technology, and for combining the technical expertise and capital available from the home-country partner with the local knowledge held by the host-country partner. Potential disadvantages include losses if the venture is not successful, expropriation, and disagreements among partners that may be difficult and time-consuming to resolve.

WHOLLY OWNED SUBSIDIARIES A **wholly owned subsidiary** is an operation on foreign soil that is totally owned and controlled by a company with headquarters outside the host country. Like joint ventures, wholly owned subsidiaries represent direct investments. However, in this case, the productive facilities are totally owned by one company. Wholly owned subsidiaries can be established either through acquisitions (buying an existing company in a foreign country) or through start-ups (developing a company from scratch).

Wholly owned subsidiaries offer several major advantages. For one thing, the parent company has sole management authority to operate the subsidiary within the existing laws of the foreign country where it is located. Likewise, technology and expertise remain under the control of the parent company. In addition, profits do not need to be shared with partners. Moreover, the subsidiary may enhance the ability of the parent company to service worldwide customers. The most important disadvantage, aside from the substantial costs involved, is that the facilities and considerable expertise—representing a substantial investment and completely located within foreign borders—may be subject to expropriation if there is a major shift in the political environment. A company that has used both licensing and wholly owned subsidiaries to expand worldwide is Italy's Benetton Group (see the Case in Point discussion).

Wholly owned subsidiary An operation on foreign soil that is totally owned and controlled by a company with headquarters outside the host country

---

BENETTON MAKES UNIQUE IDEAS WORK WORLDWIDE

CASE IN POINT

Sometimes called "the McDonald's of fashion," Italy's Benetton Group now has about 7000 sportswear shops, featuring brightly colored knit clothing, in over 120 countries. The development of Benetton is a rags-to-riches story about four siblings, one sister and three brothers. Together, they built a $2 billion empire after the sister, Giulianna, began designing attractive knitwear in the early sixties.

The basic idea behind the company's success is to make clothing that not only is fashionable but also can be produced on a major scale so that prices are affordable. To boost affordability, the Benettons have eliminated the wholesaler and all the intermediaries. They rely mainly on independent licensees who sell Benetton merchandise directly to customers in specially designed stores with the now-famous Kelly-green fronts. Benetton's licensees pay no fees or royalties. Instead, they commit to selling only Benetton-made goods. Although it can cost more than $100,000 for a licensee to set up a Benetton store in the United States, profits can be sizable if the sales volume is high. The profits come from the markup on the clothing purchased from the Benetton Group.

Benetton goods are manufactured mainly in Italy, where the company has several factories as well as subcontracting arrangements with many small Italian firms. In addition, the company has wholly owned manufacturing facilities in other countries, such as France, Spain, the United Kingdom, and the United States. A U.S. facility in North Carolina helps meet domestic demand for cotton and denim goods, shortens ordering time, and shelters U.S. licensees from

Luciano Benetton, chief of Benetton Group, is one of four siblings who founded the sports clothing empire that now boasts 7000 shops worldwide. Benetton's global strategies call for mass manufacturing in several locations around the world, the elimination of wholesalers, and computerized inventory and warehouse systems.

the impact of the falling dollar, which on occasion has pushed up the prices of Italian-made Benetton goods.

Part of the company's success is attributable to a special technique for making sweaters in undyed wool and dyeing them a short time before shipping. This approach has enabled the company to react rapidly to fashion trends and fill orders from licensees quickly. To make the system work, Benetton has invested in a computerized inventory system and a huge $20 million computer-controlled warehouse that is bigger than a domed sports arena. The warehouse has 16 robots and a complex conveyor system to help handle the massive volume.

At one point, licensees in the United States complained that Benetton was licensing too many stores in close proximity. Since that time Benetton has reduced the number of stores by almost two-thirds to about 200, but many of them are double the square footage to enable better displays and a wide selection of offerings. The company has also been branching into other areas, such as children's wear under the Benetton 012 label and trendier sportswear under the Sisley name. Their recent attempts to launch fragrance and cosmetic lines were not successful, and Benetton has licensed the lines to a joint venture between Jacques Bogart SA and Fragrance Marketing Group.[35] ■ ■ ■

Multinational Corporation Strategies

As companies such as Benetton expand their international business dealings, they need to develop appropriate international strategies. Multinational corporations, and to a lesser extent other organizations conducting business in the international arena, must weigh two important factors: the need to make optimum economic decisions on a global basis and the requirement to be responsive to significant host-country differences. Accordingly, multinationals have four major strategy options: worldwide integration, national responsiveness, regional responsiveness, and multifocal emphasis.

Worldwide integration strategy, or **globalization**
A strategy aimed at developing relatively standardized products with global appeal, as well as rationalizing operations throughout the world

Rationalization The strategy of assigning activities to those parts of the organization, regardless of their location, that are best suited to produce the desired results and then selling the finished products where they are likely to yield the best profits

National responsiveness strategy A strategy of allowing subsidiaries to have substantial latitude in adapting products and services to suit the particular needs and political realities of the countries in which they operate

WORLDWIDE INTEGRATION A **worldwide integration strategy,** sometimes called **globalization** (or globalism), is aimed at developing relatively standardized products with global appeal, as well as rationalizing operations throughout the world. Rationalizing operations, or **rationalization,** involves assigning activities to those parts of the organization, regardless of their location, that are best suited to produce the desired results and then selling the finished products where they are likely to yield the best profits. Thus a multinational might consider such factors as costs, expertise, raw materials, and availability of capacity in deciding where particular work is to be done. Rationalization facilitates taking advantage of economies of scale and making the best use of worldwide organizational resources.

Globalization is based on the notion that there are a number of products that can be used around the globe with little alteration of specifications. Coca-Cola, which is sold in more than 160 countries, is a classic example of a global product requiring only limited alterations of formula. Not all products and situations lend themselves to globalization.

NATIONAL RESPONSIVENESS A **national responsiveness strategy** allows subsidiaries to have substantial latitude in adapting products and services to suit the particular needs and political realities of the countries in which they operate. Hence, this strategy sacrifices many of the potential advantages of worldwide integration. Subsidiaries operate almost as if they were national companies, although they retain many of the substantial benefits of being affiliated with a multinational company, such as shared financial risks and access to global R&D resources. A national responsiveness strategy may be a successful approach in situations in which globalization is not feasible because of the need to cater to national differences.

Parker Pen, Ltd., was doing well with a national responsiveness strategy that involved about 500 styles of pens produced in 18 plants. Local offices in about 150 countries created their own packaging and advertising geared to local tastes. Then, at one point, company officials read a *Harvard Business Review* article highlighting the advantages of globalization. The article contended that technology has created immense global markets for standardized consumer products and that "different cultural preferences, national tastes and standards, and business institutions are vestiges of the past."[36]

Taking the globalization argument to heart, Parker officials consolidated pen styles down to about 100 choices manufactured in 8 plants. They also developed one international advertising campaign that was translated into a number of local languages. Profits plunged when local managers resisted the singular advertising approach, which ultimately failed. After a $12 million loss in fiscal 1985, Parker was sold to a group of its British managers the following year. Profits rebounded when the company switched back to a national responsiveness strategy. The firm was recently acquired by Gillette.[37] Thus, in developing an international strategy, managers need to evaluate their situations carefully, testing for a global market before making massive moves in that direction.

Teams from a number of different countries participate each year in Land Rover's Camel Trophy competition, which involves driving a Land Rover through punishing conditions in some inhospitable region of the world. This team of U.S. drivers placed second in the first ever east-west vehicle crossing of the Indonesian province of Kalimantan on the island of Borneo. Land Rover uses the results of such treks to improve the global capabilities of its vehicles, as part of a worldwide integration strategy.

REGIONAL RESPONSIVENESS A **regional responsiveness strategy** allows regional offices to have substantial latitude in coordinating the activities of local subsidiaries and adapting products and services to suit the particular needs and political realities of the regions in which they operate. This strategy sacrifices some of the potential advantages of worldwide integration but retains others because the regions typically cover large areas, such as Europe, Africa, or the Asia-Pacific region. Regional offices are able to obtain some economies of scale and make adjustments to suit regional tastes, yet still retain many of the substantial benefits of being affiliated with a multinational company, such as shared financial risks and access to global R&D resources. For example, France-based Thomson Consumer Electronics, Inc., a major international manufacturer of television sets, recently switched from national responsiveness to a regional responsiveness strategy. In doing so, Thomson established four factories in Europe that assemble specific types of television sets for the European market. For instance, the factory in Germany produces high-feature large television sets for the entire European region, while the factory in Spain concentrates on low-cost, small-screen sets for the region.[38]

Regional responsiveness strategy A strategy of allowing regional offices to have substantial latitude in coordinating the activities of local subsidiaries and adapting products and services to suit the particular needs and political realities of the regions in which they operate

MULTIFOCAL EMPHASIS A **multifocal strategy** is aimed at achieving the advantages of worldwide integration whenever possible, while still attempting to be responsive to important national needs. Thus the strategy encompasses both worldwide integration and national responsiveness. Organizations with multifocal strategies are typically more difficult to manage because they need to be concerned with two dimensions simultaneously. An organization that is implementing a multifocal strategy is Texas Instruments, a longtime leader in microchips (see the Case in Point discussion).

Multifocal strategy A strategy aimed at achieving the advantages of worldwide integration whenever possible, while still attempting to be responsive to important national needs

CASE IN POINT

TEXAS INSTRUMENTS STRIVES FOR A MULTIFOCAL PERSPECTIVE

Although Texas Instruments (TI) had been operating throughout the world, including Asia, for more than two decades, the company was deriving only some of the potential benefits of a multinational corporation. For the most part, the subsidiaries in various countries operated as separate fiefdoms, with little regard for the overall needs of the company or other subsidiaries. By operating independently, the subsidiaries contributed to a huge buildup of excess capacity. This excess caused the company serious problems when the international semiconductor market took a severe downturn in 1985. TI has since been working to take better advantage of its global position.

TI wants its managers to consider the capabilities and needs of the company as a whole, as well as the requirements of their own particular subsidiaries when making decisions. As a result, the company is taking steps to bring about the desired multifocal perspective. For example, the executive in charge of TI operations in Japan has been given responsibility for TI's global memory-chip business. Because Japan is such a heavy user of memory chips, it is tempting to add to local production capacity. But since the operations manager in Japan is responsible for the global business as well, this individual must weigh carefully any further investments in Japanese plants when chip capacity is available in other parts of TI. As a result, the manager placed a large order with a TI plant in the United States for chips slated for export to Japan. In making the deal, the manager in Japan exacted a commitment from the U.S. plant that the order would receive first priority even if chip demand increased in the United States.

Another part of TI's campaign for a multifocal view is the company's requirement that managers with global responsibilities meet once each quarter to set worldwide strategy. The executives work in small groups to resolve the various conflicts that arise from attempts to coordinate their individual investment and product development plans. They ultimately produce a detailed agreement that spells out how much money will be spent on each program and where. To signal commitment to the plan, each manager must individually stand up and write his or her name on a blackboard, while the group leader makes a permanent record of the event with a Polaroid picture. TI managers and their staffs keep in touch through the company's worldwide private communications network, involving 40,000 terminals in 50 countries.

TI is trying to create an organization that can learn to utilize global economies of scale effectively to make a profit in the viciously competitive memory-chip business. At the same time, the company wants to gain and maintain the competitive edge that comes from producing customized chips. With these chips, customers design their own products around state-of-the-art electronics produced by companies such as TI. The worldwide strategy meetings help managers pinpoint various customers' needs so that investments can be geared to satisfying the largest number of buyers regardless of their global location. Helped by a worldwide increase in the demand for chips, TI's new multifocal approach appears to be working.[39]   ■■■

■ ORGANIZING INTERNATIONAL BUSINESS

In addition to considering strategic issues, managers involved in international business need to choose the most appropriate organization structure, given the nature of the company's global pursuits. Most of the research on appropriate organization designs has centered on multinational corporations. Such corporations tend to adopt one of five types of organization structures: worldwide functional divisions, worldwide product divisions, international division, geographic regions, and global matrix.[40]

Worldwide Functional Divisions

With worldwide functional divisions, top-level functional executives at the parent company have worldwide responsibility for the separate functions, such as manufacturing, marketing, and finance (see Figure 20-2). Thus the various functional units within a foreign subsidiary report directly to the respective functional units of the parent company. The strength of this structure is that it provides strong functional expertise to foreign subsidiaries in areas such as manufacturing and engineering. However, because actions must be coordinated across various functional units, the structure can hamper quick reactions to changing circumstances in various countries and to competition if there are a number of diverse products. Generally, this structure works best when a few related products are sold in a relatively uniform market worldwide and there are few foreign subsidiaries.

Worldwide Product Divisions

With worldwide product divisions, top-level executives are responsible for particular product areas worldwide (see Figure 20-3). With this type of structure, the parent company tends to put particular emphasis on coordination of product-related decisions but to allow the foreign subsidiaries to run other aspects of their businesses. Because of its product focus, this structure is likely to be most effective in organizations whose products are technologically complex, highly diverse, or subject to rapid change. It is highly compatible with a worldwide integration strategy when there are a number of diverse products to consider.

Figure 20-2 *Worldwide functional divisions structure.*

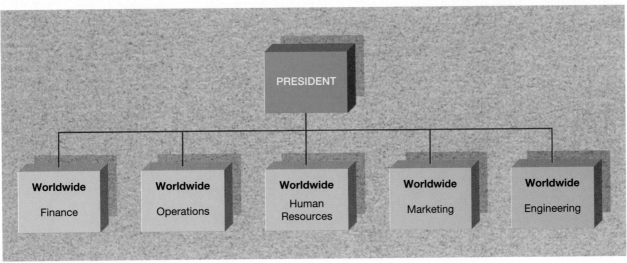

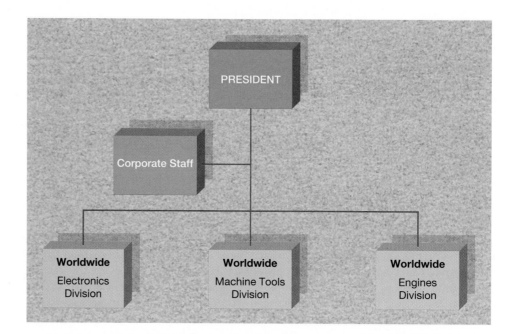

Figure 20-3 *Worldwide product divisions structure.*

Figure 20-4 *International division structure.*

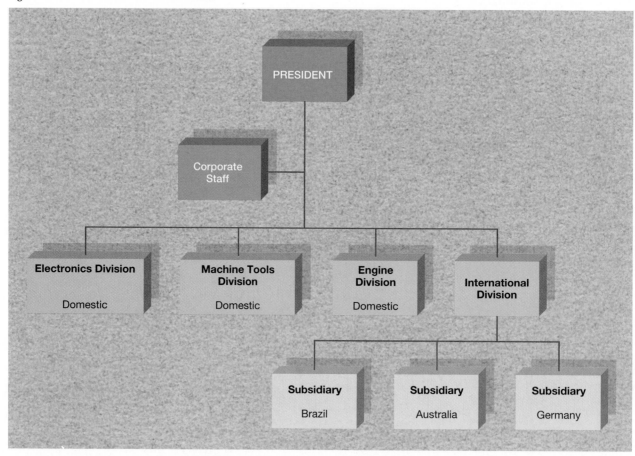

International Division

With an international division structure, a separate division is created to which all foreign subsidiaries report. Figure 20-4 shows a multinational company with domestic product divisions and an international division. (An international division could also be added to a functional structure, but the form is less prevalent.)[41] The international division structure enables geographic interests and product interests to be represented at the same level. However, the arrangement makes it more difficult to coordinate information between domestic product divisions and the international division. One study of 37 large U.S. multinationals showed that the international division was the most prevalent structure.[42]

Geographic Regions

In this organization design, the world is divided into regional divisions, with subsidiaries reporting to the appropriate one according to location (see Figure 20-5). This type of structure facilitates the flow of information within regions but inhibits information exchange across regions. As a result, it is particularly well suited to catering to regional and national differences and provides strong support for a regional or national responsiveness strategy. The geographic regions structure is used much more widely by European than by U.S. multinational firms.[43]

Global Matrix

In the global matrix structure, equal authority and responsibility are assigned along at least two dimensions, with one dimension being region and the second usually being either product or function. A global matrix, with region and product as the two dimensions, is shown in Figure 20-6. With this structure, middle-level executives report to two bosses who share authority over decisions

Figure 20-5 *Geographic regions structure.*

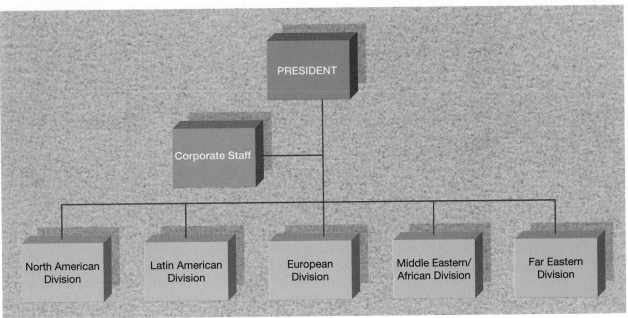

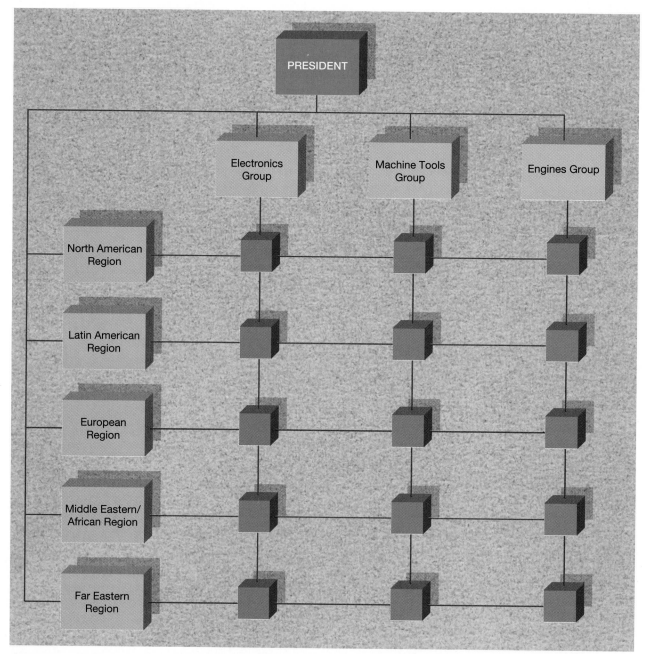

Figure 20-6 *Global matrix structure.*

affecting a particular region and particular product area of business. Some authors have argued that a global matrix structure, usually with two dimensions (region and product), is necessary when an organization is pursuing a multifocal strategy.[44] Yet a survey of 93 U.S. multinationals found that only one had this structure. Several executives reported that they prefer to use other mechanisms to address multifocal issues, such as task forces and liaison positions (see Chapter 8).[45] Zurich-based ABB (Asea Brown Boveri) is one non-U.S. multinational that has successfully used a global matrix structure in conjunction with a multifocal strategy (see Concluding Case 2, Chapter 9). The increasing development of a global information infrastructure provided by telecommunications and computer companies is likely to make the global matrix a more feasible option for many multinational companies in the future.

Networked Structure

The *networked structure* is a form of organizing in which many functions are contracted out to other independent firms and coordinated through the use of information technology networks to operate as if they were within a single corporation. This type of structure often is called the *virtual corporation* because it performs as if it were virtually one corporation (see Chapter 9). Given the rapidly expanding availability of sophisticated telecommunications capabilities, such a structure may be feasible for companies wishing to engage in international business that require a great deal of flexibility and are able to contract out certain functions while still maintaining control over the core competencies associated with their competitive advantage. Benetton is a well-known example of a company that uses a networked structure (see the Case in Point discussion).

■ MANAGING DIVERSITY: ADAPTING TO CULTURAL DIFFERENCES

While structural considerations are important, another major aspect of effective international management is adapting to cultural differences. Critical issues include managing international human resources and adjusting leadership styles.

Managing International Human Resources

According to one prominent researcher on international management, U.S. companies operating overseas need to place greater emphasis on the strategic management of human resources to gain a competitive edge in international markets.[46] Multinationals, in particular, require a carefully developed cadre of managerial talent to function effectively. Areas of particular concern are assignment policies, recruitment approaches, and the selection and training of managerial personnel.

ASSIGNMENT POLICIES An international organization basically has four major policy options regarding staffing sources for key managerial slots in overseas operations: local nationals, parent company personnel, international personnel, or mixed sources. With the *local option,* key positions for each subsidiary are filled with nationals from the country where the subsidiary is located.

With the *parent company option,* the parent has a representative in each subsidiary who is well versed in the policies and procedures of the overall multinational company. This individual may be more knowledgeable than local employees about the latest technological developments of the parent and probably has good lines of communication back to parent headquarters. In addition to normal salaries and benefits, expenses related to the position may include allowances for such items as a car, education for children, housing, cost-of-living adjustments, international medical coverage, and moving costs. Recently companies have been trying to cut down on expenses by emphasizing frugality and providing less generous allowances for luxuries while out of the country.[47]

With the *regional option,* important positions are generally filled by highly qualified individuals from a geographical region. The premise behind this assignment policy is that both commonalities within regions and major differences across regions make individuals with experience in a particular region the best candidates for important assignments within that region. On the other hand, with the *international option,* multinationals attempt to assign the best person to do the job, regardless of the person's nationality or the location of the job. Such a policy helps a multinational foster a geocentric approach to global management and develop multinational managers capable of implementing a worldwide integration strategy. Currently, most multinationals follow a mixed option, generally assigning mostly local nationals to foreign subsidiaries, home-country nationals to headquarters, and developing a cadre of managers with regional and/or global experience to staff higher level positions requiring a broader perspective.[48]

RECRUITMENT Regardless of the assignment policy followed, ample evidence suggests that companies engaged in international business need to expend greater effort in recruiting competent individuals for key overseas positions. U.S.-educated foreign students are a potential, but underutilized, source of national management talent for foreign subsidiaries.[49]

Expatriates Individuals who are not citizens of the countries in which they are assigned to work

Women are another inadequately utilized source of managerial talent. One study conducted during the 1980s found that women constituted only 3 percent of expatriate managers in a sample of 686 U.S. and Canadian companies engaged in international business. **Expatriates** are individuals who are not citizens of the countries in which they are assigned to work. According to a follow-up study involving 60 of the previously studied multinationals, the firms' international personnel managers felt that women face major barriers in overseas assignments that do not exist in domestic ones.[50] For example, the managers cited foreigners' prejudice, as well as the reluctance of company managers to select women for foreign assignments. Nevertheless, when the same researcher subsequently interviewed 52 female expatriate managers, almost all of them reported success on the job. Interestingly, nearly half of these women reported that being female was advantageous in their assignments, largely because it made them more visible.[51] The situation has been reversing rapidly, however. According to one estimate, women will constitute 20 percent of expatriates by the year 2000.

Because more than 80 percent of marriages in the United States now involve dual-career couples, the issue of sending employees abroad is becoming more complex. Individuals often turn down foreign assignments because of concern about the potential negative impact on a spouse's career. To obtain high-caliber individuals for foreign assignments, organizations will increasingly need to aid the job-seeking efforts of "trailing" spouses. Without such assistance, there is a high likelihood that the trailing spouse will exhibit depression, develop health problems, demonstrate limited involvement in the new community, and require a great deal of emotional support from the expatriate working spouse.[52]

SELECTION AND TRAINING The failure rate of expatriates assigned to various countries is substantial, ranging between 25 and 40 percent. Such failures are expensive in terms of the direct costs of bringing an expatriate home early and providing a replacement. Indirect costs, such as the executives' loss of self-esteem and the resultant business difficulties in the subsidiary, add to the total.[53] At least part of the high failure rate among expatriates stems from serious shortcomings in expatriate selection and training.

Most multinational corporations tend to use technical skills as the major criterion for selecting individuals for overseas assignments. While technical skills are extremely important for expatriate success, considerable evidence indicates that organizations should also consider *relational skills,* the ability of the expatriate to relate and communicate effectively with host nationals. The necessary communication skills typically involve a willingness to use the host nationals' language; confidence in carrying on communication with others; the ability to engage in local small talk, such as anecdotes, jokes, and comments on movies and sports events; and the desire to understand and relate well with host nationals.[54] Indicative of the flexibility required, Australian Ben Lochtenberg, who at one point was chairman of the American subsidiary of Great Britain's Imperial Chemical Industries (ICI) and now heads ICI's Australian subsidiary, has found it necessary to adjust his communication style even in countries with a common language. For example, when he worked in England, his direct Australian manner created difficulties, so he learned the more indirect British approach. Thus he would say "Perhaps you ought to think about this a little more" to convey "You must be mad—forget it." In the United States, though, when Lochtenberg said "Perhaps you ought to think about this a little more" the subordinate interpreted his words literally and forged ahead with the project.[55]

Unfortunately, sufficient training of expatriates for assignments is often lacking. Inadequate training seems to stem from feelings among human resource administrators that training is ineffective, dissatisfaction of expatriate trainees with the training, insufficient time for training before departure, or views that the assignments are too short to warrant expensive training.[56] Yet insufficient training can lead to serious difficulties, as one American manager discovered. Shortly after his arrival in France, he rented a luxurious apartment and invited all the personnel in his office to a large party. Unfortunately, he did not realize that it is unusual for French employees to be invited to their superior's home. Furthermore, the party involved people from all levels of the organization, as well as employees' spouses, individuals who normally did not mix socially. This extremely awkward situation got things off to a bad start, from which the manager was never able to recover.[57]

REPATRIATION Another important area requiring effective human resource management is **repatriation**, the process of returning to one's home country after an assignment in a host country.[58] For U.S. expatriates, foreign assignments typically last 2 to 3 years. The major reasons why expatriates return home are (1) the agreed upon period of the foreign assignment has ended, (2) expatriates want their children to be further educated in home-country schools, (3) they are unhappy in the foreign assignment, and (4) they are ineffective in the foreign assignment.

Repatriation The process of returning to one's home country after an assignment in a host country

Readjustment problems during repatriation are common, because many find it difficult to adjust when they return home. For one thing, their authority and status may be lower back at the home office than it had been in the foreign assignment. Moreover, they may perceive that their foreign experience is not valued sufficiently at the home office. They also may find that their previous job has changed dramatically and/or their technical expertise may have become somewhat obsolete.

It can take several months, and possibly even up to a year, for a returning manager to regain effectiveness. One helpful strategy to ease the repatriation process and reduce anxiety is to develop a *repatriation agreement* that promises a position in the home country at least equal in level to the position the individual left to accept the foreign assignment. Other useful steps include renting or maintaining the individual's home while the person is on foreign assignment, appointing a senior executive mentor to help keep the individual's career on track during the foreign assignment and repatriation, and maintaining communication with expatriates so that they do not become isolated from home office activities. At KMPG Peat Marwick, a global accounting and management consulting organization, international employees working in the United States are assigned two mentors, a personal one to help with the adjustment to uniquely American traditions, such as Thanksgiving and the Super Bowl, and a professional one to provide assignment and career guidance. The arrangement helps ease the transition to the foreign assignment and facilitate later successful repatriation.[59]

Adjusting Leadership Styles

Although some researchers argue that behavior in organizations is becoming more similar across nations, overseas managers may still find it necessary to adjust their leadership styles because of cultural factors.[60] In studying leadership issues, management researchers have found it difficult to isolate the effects of culture from those of other variables such as differences in economic development and resources in various countries. As a result, there is still a great deal to be learned about effective leadership in different nations and cultures.

On the basis of his major study of a large American multinational (discussed earlier in this chapter), Hofstede believes that managers should give particular consideration to the power-distance index in determining appropriate leadership styles in different countries. In high-power-distance countries (such as Mexico, the Philippines, and India), individuals tend to accept large differences in the distribution of power in institutions and organizations. Subordinates are likely to expect superiors to act fairly autocratically, be somewhat paternalistic, be subject to different rules than subordinates, and enjoy privileges not available to subordinates. In medium-power-distance countries (such as the United States, Japan, and Italy), subordinates are likely to expect to be consulted but will accept some autocratic behavior. They also expect laws and rules to apply to all, but they will accept some degree of privileges and status symbols for superiors that are not available to subordinates. In low-power-distance countries (such as Sweden, Denmark, and Israel), subordinates expect to be consulted on most issues, prefer a participative democratic style of leadership, and may rebel or strike if superiors appear to be stepping outside their authority. Typically, laws and rules are seen as applying to all employees, and privileges and status symbols for superiors are viewed as unacceptable.[61] Research such as Hofstede's provides a basic framework for thinking about leadership issues in different cultures, such as the need to adjust leadership styles. Organizational social responsibility and managerial ethics are other important areas that require special consideration when companies are operating in the international realm.

■ HANDLING SOCIAL RESPONSIBILITY AND ETHICAL ISSUES

Issues of organizational social responsibility and managerial ethics were addressed extensively in Chapter 4. In this section, we examine several major concerns that relate particularly to international management.

International Social Responsibility

Many of the issues relating to social responsibility are compounded when an organization engages in a substantial amount of international business. This is largely due to the great increase in the number of social stakeholders involved (customers in various countries, communities in various countries, etc.; see Chapter 4), particularly when business is conducted through subsidiaries in multiple countries. During the early 1970s, large multinational corporations came under particularly severe criticism for their potentially harmful effects in developing nations. Concerns focused on such matters as exhausting natural resources, diverting wealth to developed nations, and attempting to manipulate LDC governments. Currently, the severity of the criticisms has dissipated, for a number of reasons. These include stronger LDC governments, the rise of multinationals based in developed countries besides the United States, the emergence of LDC multinationals, the growing number of smaller multinationals, greater adaptability of multinationals to local conditions, and increased concern for the environment.[62] Still, controversies continue to arise, such as the recent concern about "sweatshops" that emerged when the executive director of the National Labor Committee Education Fund in Support of Worker and Human Rights in Central America testified before Congress that Wal-Mart's Kathie Lee clothing line was being made by 13- and 14-year-olds working 20-hour days in factories in Honduras.[63] Thus, the debate continues regarding the benefits of versus the harm wrought by the world's large, powerful corporations, particularly in LDCs.[64]

Questionable-Payments Issue

One of the most pervasive international ethical issues involves **questionable payments,** business payments that raise significant ethical questions of right or wrong either in the host country or in other nations.[65] Difficulties arise because of differences in the customs, ethics, and laws of various countries regarding different types of payments. The most common forms of questionable payments are

Questionable payments
Business payments that raise significant ethical questions of right or wrong either in the host country or in other nations

> **Political payments:** Usually funds to support a political party or candidate
>
> **Bribes:** Money or valuables given to a powerful person to influence decisions in favor of the giver
>
> **Extortion:** Payments made to protect a business against some threatened action, such as cancellation of a franchise
>
> **Sales commissions:** Payments of a percentage of a sale, which become questionable if paid to a government official or political figure or if unusually large
>
> **Expediting payments** Normally, money given to lower-level government officials to ensure cooperation and prompt handling of routine transactions

Many of these types of payments are considered to be legal and acceptable in many parts of the world, but they are generally viewed as unethical and/or illegal in the United States.

The U.S. Foreign Corrupt Practices Act, passed in 1977 and recently amended, prohibits most of the questionable payments listed above when they are made by U.S. companies doing business in other nations. (Making expediting payments to low-level government officials is generally permitted.) Supporters argue that the law will ensure ethical conduct, encourage other nations to discontinue questionable payments, help discourage corruption in the governments of other nations, and increase accurate reporting to shareholders. Detractors contend that the law represents an ethnocentric attempt to impose

U.S. ethical standards on the rest of the world regardless of other nations' laws and customs. They also say that the law places U.S. companies at a disadvantage when they are competing with businesses from countries where such payments are allowed. In a *Business Week* survey of 1200 senior U.S. executives, 78 percent agreed that the law makes it difficult to do business in countries where bribery is an accepted way of life, and they felt that the law hurts U.S. exports. About 20 percent said that they had actually lost business because of the act.[66] IBM has recently been under investigation by the Justice Department regarding allegations that the computer giant paid bribes to Argentine government officials to obtain a $250 million contract to modernize the nation's largest bank, the state-owned Banco de la Nacion Argentina. The scandal has cost the jobs of three IBM Argentine executives and led several government officials to resign.[67]

With its complex issues and intriguing prospects, the international realm offers a rich source of opportunities for new ventures and small businesses, subjects that we explore further in the next chapter.

■ CHAPTER SUMMARY

International management is the process of planning, organizing, leading, and controlling in organizations engaged in international business. A considerable amount of international business is conducted by multinational corporations. These are organizations that engage in production or service activities through their own affiliates in several countries, maintain control over the policies of those affiliates, and manage from a global perspective. Multinationals and other organizations engaged in international business typically subscribe to one of four basic orientations, or philosophies, toward international management: ethnocentric, polycentric, regiocentric, and geocentric.

Various elements of the international environment affect organizations' ability to engage in business beyond national borders. The economic element includes the levels of economic development in countries, the presence of adequate infrastructures, a country's balance of payments, and monetary exchange rates. Major issues related to the legal-political element are the degree of political risk associated with a particular country and the degree to which trade barriers are erected by governments. Within the sociocultural element, Hofstede has identified four major dimensions related to cultural values: power distance, uncertainty avoidance, individualism-collectivism, and masculinity-femininity. The technological element includes various methods of technological transfer, an important aspect of international business. The concept of the competitive advantage of nations holds that elements within a nation can foster innovation in

certain industries, thereby increasing the prospects for the success of home-based companies operating internationally within those industries. The elements make up the diamond of national advantage and include factor conditions, demand conditions, related and supporting industries, and firm strategy, structure, and rivalry.

Organizations have four main entry methods that they can use to expand into different countries: exporting, licensing, establishing strategic alliances, and operating wholly owned subsidiaries. Major strategies used by multinational corporations include worldwide integration, national responsiveness, regional responsiveness, and multifocal emphasis. The main organization structures for multinational corporations are worldwide functional divisions, worldwide product divisions, international division, geographic regions, and global matrix.

Adapting to cultural differences requires careful consideration of managing international human resources, including assignment policies, recruitment approaches, the selection and training of personnel, and repatriation. Although some scholars argue that leadership issues are becoming more similar across nations, there still appear to be differences in the leadership styles that are likely to be effective in various cultures.

Conducting international business raises complex issues regarding social responsibility, international value conflicts, and questionable payments. The U.S. Foreign Corrupt Practices Act prohibits most questionable payments when they are made by U.S. companies doing business in other nations.

■ QUESTIONS FOR DISCUSSION AND REVIEW

1 Explain the concept of a multinational corporation. Identify several major companies that are probably multinationals. Give reasons for your selections.

2 Describe four major orientations toward international management. Find a newspaper or magazine article that discusses a company engaged in international business. Which orientation appears to best depict the company's approach to international management?

3 Outline several elements that are useful in assessing the international environment. How could you use these elements to help provide advice to a foreign company interested in doing business in the United States?

4 Explain the concept of the competitive advantage of nations. Use the concept to assess the ability of conditions in the United States to foster innovation among home-based companies in an industry of your choice. What suggestions do you have to improve conditions?

5 Enumerate the principal methods of entry into international business. Explain the advantages and disadvantages of each. Which would you be likely to use if you were running a small company with few resources but had a product with potentially broad international appeal? Would you use a different approach if you were running a large company that had considerable funds available? Give your reasons.

6 Explain the four major strategic alternatives for con-ducting international business. For each alternative, recommend a type of business that would likely be successful if it adopted that strategy.

7 Describe the five main organization structures used by international businesses. Identify a type of business that you would like to manage on an international basis, and explain the organization structure that you believe would be most appropriate. Explain your reasoning.

8 Discuss the principal issues related to assignment policies and the recruitment, selection, training, and repatriation of managerial personnel for international assignments. What recommendations would you make to companies that are just beginning their international expansions?

9 Assess the types of adjustments in leadership style that managers may need to make because of cultural differences. What advice might you give to members of a local company who are going to set up a wholly owned subsidiary in the Philippines? How would your advice differ if the subsidiary was to be in Denmark?

10 Explain the social responsibility and ethical issues that international managers are likely to confront. What steps would you, as a manager, take to prevent subordinates from making questionable payments while they are engaging in international business on behalf of your company?

■ DISCUSSION QUESTIONS FOR CHAPTER OPENING CASE

1 Unilever prefers to have local managers for its subsidiaries, yet in the past it has had mainly British and Dutch employees on its board of directors and Special Committee. Is this approach viable or not? Would you insist that other nationalities be represented on the board of directors and the Special Committee? Why, or why not?

2 To what extent does Unilever appear to be shifting its strategy for conducting international business? Is its approach appropriate given the current international environment?

3 Assess Unilever's use of organization structure to support its international management orientation.

■ EXERCISES FOR MANAGING IN THE TWENTY-FIRST CENTURY

EXERCISE 1
SKILL BUILDING: IDENTIFYING INTERNATIONAL MANAGEMENT ORIENTATIONS

 Senior managers normally adopt an ethnocentric, polycentric, regiocentric, or geocentric orientation or philosophy in dealing with the overseas parts of their organizations. Examples of these orientations follow. Indicate the orientation being exhibited in the example.

Ethnocentric	**P**olycentric
Regiocentric	**G**eocentric

1. _____ The best people are selected from all parts of the organization throughout the world.
2. _____ Basic market decisions are made by local employees.
3. _____ The system used at the multinational headquarters is always best.
4. _____ This firm attempts to develop managers who excel in a particular part of the world.
5. _____ The firm is run by host-country nationals.
6. _____ The corporate goal is to produce a product that will be used in many countries globally.
7. _____ The organization is focused on the western European approach to managing.
8. _____ Managers from the home country are given the best jobs and promoted ahead of their peers, regardless of their performance.
9. _____ The subsidiary is highly visible to the local population, whereas the multinational headquarters is relatively invisible.
10. _____ The multinational considers the world as the base for money, resources, suppliers, and customers.

EXERCISE 2
MANAGEMENT EXERCISE: GOING INTERNATIONAL

 You have spent many years working on a revolutionary combination automatic washer and dryer, which went into production for the first time last year. It has been an astounding success in the United States, and you are considering going international with your new product. You have had numerous inquiries and offers from businesses around the world but believe that you will concentrate on business in Canada, Great Britain, western Europe, Australia, and New Zealand for the near future. You are going to meet with your director of marketing tomorrow to discuss expanding your business into Canada. You recognize that there are several options available to you, including exporting, licensing, strategic alliances, and wholly owned subsidiaries. In addition, you must consider your philosophy of international management, select a strategy, decide on a structure, determine how you will select and train your managers, and determine the appropriate leadership style to use.

Consider the issues indicated above. Then, with two other classmates, discuss how you would proceed with the possibility of conducting business in Canada. You want to expand into the international marketplace and believe that this is the place to start. Explain your rationale for the decisions you make, pointing out the advantages and disadvantages of each of your choices.

CONCLUDING CASE 1

LOCTITE CREATES INTERNATIONAL COHESION

The Loctite Corporation is hardly a household word, but one of its products, Super-Glue, is widely known. Headquartered in Newington, Connecticut, Loctite is a multinational firm, with about 60 percent of its more than $785 million in annual sales coming from business conducted in 80 countries. Most of that business is in anaerobic adhesives, which form a tight bond when air is removed. The adhesives work well with bolts and other types of airtight applications.

Loctite began pursuing international business when it was a very small company, with only $1 million in annual sales. Because its adhesives are useful for joining the components of the flat motors that run videocassette recorders and compact disc players, it has developed considerable business in Japan. Nevertheless, building its business in Japan involved a series of small steps. At first, Loctite had a licensing arrangement and then a joint venture before it was able to develop a wholly owned subsidiary—its preferred approach.

A key to its success is its large team of Japanese engineers, who work with designers of videocassette recorders and compact disc players to show them how Loctite adhesives can be used. As a result, Loctite dominates the industrial market in Japan and is able to sell its adhesives at higher prices than most domestic competitors. The process has also helped Loctite improve its products, since Japanese customers demand high quality. Loctite received an additional bonus from its work in Japan when Nissan and Honda built plants in Mexico and the United States and incorporated Loctite products into their manufacturing processes.

Being able to operate effectively abroad is important for Loctite personnel, because they must work closely with customers to develop applications for their products. For example, the head of Loctite's international division took a special team to a government-run factory in China to help with a serious leakage problem. The team spent 2000 hours in testing and field trials to find a way to assemble engines through the use of adhesives that form gaskets and hold bolts in place. Five years of further negotiations finally allowed Loctite to form a 50-50 joint venture with the Chinese to build a Loctite plant in Shandong Province.

Meanwhile, Loctite trained Baosheng Xu, a Chinese native who earned an M.B.A. in Boston, to manage the plant. Baosheng exemplifies the Loctite approach to managing in foreign markets: recruit a local national. "I have the language, and—most important—I know where to get things done," says Baosheng. He currently is overseeing expansion of the Shandong plant so that it can supply products for the entire Asia-Pacific region. Loctite has a history of making great efforts to hire local nationals for managerial positions.

The company also has factories in Ireland and Brazil and is expanding into Latin America and other parts of Asia. In addition, it operates in Europe and is currently attempting to develop markets in Russia. At this point, Loctite does not have a unified global structure. Its major divisions—industrial, vehicle, and consumer— are managed on a regional basis in Europe. In the rest of the world, the three groups are managed together on a country basis. For example, Loctite has recently set up a regional hub in Singapore to help with its rapid growth in Asia. Still, the managing director says that the emerging status of the region (Vietnam, the Philippines, Australia, New Zealand, Indonesia, Malaysia, and Thailand) makes it most feasible to use country-based management.

Loctite is continually attempting to innovate and make its products more valuable to customers. Recently, the company has had success in developing new ultraviolet-cured silicones, which have a variety of applications in electronics, such as sealing switches in automobiles. The newer products set in seconds rather than hours and can help expedite assembly processes for manufacturers. The company also has launched Quicktite, a new consumer-oriented instant adhesive sold in an innovative, clog-free dispenser.

Loctite officials argue that American companies pursuing foreign business are too impatient and are not willing to expend enough effort to ensure success. As one manager has said, "Americans cannot go to China, Japan, or Korea one time and walk away with an agreement. It takes a tremendous amount of work."[68] Loctite recently was acquired by Hankel KGaA, a German consumer goods and chemical conglomerate.

QUESTIONS FOR CONCLUDING CASE 1

1 What strengths have made Loctite a successful multinational?
2 Characterize Loctite's basic philosophy of international management and its strategy. How appropriate are its approaches for a company in this type of business?
3 Considering Loctite's success overseas, what advice would you give regarding its current expansion into the Far East, Latin America, and Russia?

CONCLUDING CASE 2

THE KING OF CORK

If you ever opened a bottle of wine or replaced a head gasket on an automobile, you probably noticed that the stopper and the head gasket are made of cork. This soft liquid-resistant material comes from the bark of the cork oak tree, which is native to Portugal, Spain, and Italy. Thus the source of supply for this highly desired raw material is limited. Américo Ferreira de Amorim runs Corticeira Amorim, headquartered in Oporto, Portugal, which controls 35 percent of the world's cork market. The demand for cork products is growing at a rate of 7 to 8 percent annually. The market for champagne stoppers, alone, is growing at 4 percent annually.

Amorim obtained a head start in the cork industry when his grandfather opened a factory in 1870 that made cork stoppers for port wine bottles. At age 18, Amorim joined the family business. Convinced that there might be a demand for cork products outside Portugal, he began touring Germany, the United Kingdom, and France. He expanded his travels to central and eastern Europe, north Africa, and Latin America, obtaining orders and signing up additional suppliers as the business grew. Ahead of his time in setting up business in eastern Europe, Amorim established a small sales office in Vienna in 1967. Today the company exports almost 25 percent of its products to countries that were formerly part of the eastern bloc.

While visiting western Europe, Amorim conceived the idea of making cork composite board from the waste left from producing stoppers. As a result, the orientation of the business changed somewhat, and now the stoppers and cork composite products both contribute to the estimated $405 million annual revenues of Corticeira Amorim.

Over the years, Amorim has acquired extensive cork plantation property in central Portugal. In addition, he purchased land in southern Portugal that he has been developing for tourism, luxury housing, and offices. He holds a 25 percent interest in Banco Comercial de Portugues, a major Portuguese commercial bank that he helped found. He recently took the cork business public, but retains a 55 percent interest.

Cork is taken from the bark of the tree every 9 years. The material is being used in an expanded range of products including wall covering and the thermal shield that protects the nose of American space shuttles. Researchers at Corticeira Amorim are investigating the possibility of using powdered cork to combat oil slicks. The material could be dropped by airplane to absorb surface oil, which could then be recovered from the cork. Although various efforts have been made to develop a substitute, for years cork has remained the only material that can regain its original form after being compressed. Recently, a Norwegian company, Corex, claimed to have developed a substitute made from ethyl vinyl acetate that is superior to cork. Corex hopes to be able to make 200 million of these "ecorks" annually by the year 2000. Assuming that the "ecorks" are functional, that would still constitute a small portion of the 25 billion corks that are sold throughout the world each year.

Besides the potential threat of substitutes, another possible risk is that cork is not sheltered from the effects of nature. The Portuguese press regularly reports on any potential diseases that could adversely affect the cork oak forests, which cover about 7 percent of the country and account for about 30 percent of the world's supply. The Lisbon Forestry Institute says there are no major diseases on the horizon, although the trees are subject to "a general degradation of eco-systems" affecting many areas of the earth. The institute says there is "no cause for alarm."

During the early 1990s, earnings declined partly because of slow sales in the automobile industry, which uses the cork gaskets. Amorim reacted by saying that he knows "how the world markets are progressing" and claimed that "there's no reason to worry." Recently the situation has improved. Corticeira Amorim is actively expanding markets internationally and is in the process of setting up a joint venture in the People's Republic of China. For the past few years, Amorim has been buying up cork distributors in almost 30 countries and lately has begun to distribute for some of the smaller Portuguese cork producers. These moves may give Corticeira Amorim some power over cork prices, which the company has generally not been able to appreciably influence in the past.[69]

QUESTIONS FOR CONCLUDING CASE 2

1   How have various aspects of the environment affected the building of Corticeira Amorim? Assume that you are Américo Amorim and are traveling throughout the world looking for new cork markets. What would you look for?

2   What would you consider as possibilities for strategic alliances, licensing, or wholly owned subsidiaries in foreign countries if you were Amorim?

3   What type of international strategy does Amorim appear to be following? What advice would you offer about future strategies? How does the diamond of national advantage apply to this situation?

ENTREPRENEURSHIP AND SMALL BUSINESS

LEARNING OBJECTIVES

After studying this chapter, you should be able to:

■ Define entrepreneurship and explain the role that innovation plays in creating entrepreneurial opportunities.

■ Outline the major economic and social contributions made by entrepreneurship and the small businesses that it spawns.

■ Explain the factors that influence the decision to engage in entrepreneurship.

■ Explain the main development approaches that one might consider pursuing in establishing a small business.

■ Enumerate the major purposes of developing a business plan.

■ Describe what is involved in obtaining resources and selecting an appropriate business site.

■ Trace the major stages in new venture growth.

■ Explain several special issues and problems associated with entrepreneurship and small-business ownership.

GAINING THE EDGE

COLBY CARE NURSES MAKE A DIFFERENCE

Colby Care Nurses, Inc., founded by Carolyn Colby in 1988, serves a special niche. The firm provides home health-care services to individuals in Los Angeles County's predominantly black and Hispanic communities. "Because we're a black-owned company," says its founder, "we can cover areas that other companies cannot and will not cover."

Colby's firm addresses an important community need while also earning a profit. Much of the Culver, California–based company's business comes from state agencies that serve neighborhoods like South Central Los Angeles. Colby Care's revenues are now about $4 million. Many of the more than 250 nurses who work for Colby Care live near the areas where they work. About three-fourths of the nurses are black or Hispanic.

Colby views her diverse staff as one of the company's major strengths. One reason is that the nurses often are in a better position to understand the needs of its diverse customer base. In many cases, nurses must be sensitive to a variety of household customs. For example, they must sometimes remove their shoes at the door or find a way to provide treatment without disrupting religious rituals.

Because Colby Care specializes in serving minority patients, the firm frequently receives subcontracts from larger home-care companies. Despite the rapid growth of home health-care agencies in the United States, studies show that black and Hispanic communities tend to be underserved. The growth of minority-owned firms like Colby Care is increasing the availability and quality of home health care in areas with insufficient coverage.

Colby Care also works extensively with special needs children. For example, one Colby Care nurse provides daily care for a severely disabled 10-year-old. The nurse spends 12 hours each day in the apartment where the child lives with her family exercising the girl's limbs and monitoring the child's breathing. The nurse also helps the girl's mother, who speaks limited English, to complete the required paperwork for federal and state aid.

Colby never planned to own her own company. She previously worked for Kimberly Nurses, a temporary-help agency for whom she opened branch offices and brought in new business. She had risen to the rank of vice president when she left Kimberly after it was sold to a larger company that she felt was overly impersonal in managing the business. "Then it occurred to me that if I could run a business for Kimberly, I could probably do it for myself," she says.

She notes that starting Colby Care proved to be more difficult than she had anticipated. One major problem was that she had great difficulty securing a loan and had to initially obtain financing through a loan company that charged 36 percent annual interest. She was a registered nurse at the time, but went back to school and earned a degree in health administration and an M.B.A.—all while she was building her company.

Colby Care faces several challenges. Cost-containment pressures and possibilities of state and federal funding cuts could stifle growth or cause profit declines. At the same time, the home-health industry tends to be dominated by large corporations that can negotiate regional and national contracts with insurance companies. As a result, Colby and six other California women in the industry have formed the National Independent Nursing Network. The network makes bulk purchases and negotiates contracts to cover various parts of the state.

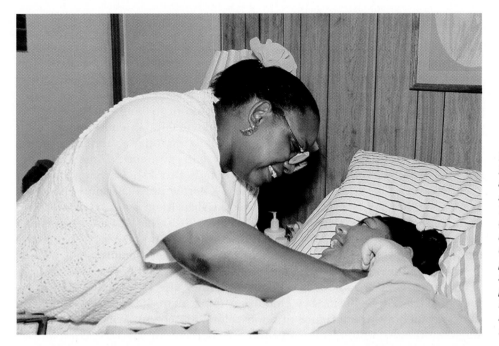

Nurse Iris Long comes to the home of this 13-year-old disabled girl a couple of times a week to help care for her. This nurse works for Colby Care Nurses, a home health-care service started by Carolyn Colby to care for minority patients in the Los Angeles area. Not only does Colby provide a needed service with her business; she also has been able to earn a profit with revenues of $4 million.

Regardless of the challenges, Colby intends to keep the company focused on its mission of serving minority patients. "If I can make enough money to pay the expenses of the company and still take care of these people, why not do it?" she says.[1] ■ ■ ■

If there are heroes and heroines in American business in recent years, they are entrepreneurs like Carolyn Colby. Entrepreneurs create new organizations, provide innovative services and products, pique our imagination, and stimulate the economy. The insights into Carolyn Colby's world help us better understand entrepreneurs and the phenomenon called entrepreneurship. An understanding of entrepreneurship is particularly important for aspiring managers because 99 percent of the businesses in the United States are small, and most of them have been created by entrepreneurs. Most likely, many of you who read this book will become entrepreneurs or operate one of the small companies that result from entrepreneurial activities. Some businesses created by entrepreneurs quickly become large. Most, though, spend a significant period of time as relatively small businesses, assuming that they survive beyond the initial start-up period. In this chapter, we explore the nature of entrepreneurship, including the role of innovation in entrepreneurial endeavors. We investigate the factors that influence the entrepreneurship phenomenon. We also analyze the development approaches that entrepreneurs and small-business owners can pursue, and we discuss the main preparations necessary to operate a small business. Finally, we consider some of the principal issues involved in the ongoing management of small companies.

■ THE NATURE OF ENTREPRENEURSHIP

What is entrepreneurship? In this section, we explore the meaning of the term, consider the importance of innovation in assessments of entrepreneurial opportunities, and examine some of the major economic and social contributions of entrepreneurship.

Defining Entrepreneurship

Entrepreneurship The creation of new enterprise

Entrepreneurship is the creation of new enterprise.[2] Although one could conceivably engage in entrepreneurship geared toward establishing a new not-for-profit organization (such as an association or a cultural center), most entrepreneurship activities involve profit-oriented businesses. Accordingly, this chapter focuses on entrepreneurship aimed at profit making.

Entrepreneur An individual who creates a new enterprise

On the basis of our definition of entrepreneurship, an **entrepreneur** is an individual who creates a new enterprise. Many of today's familiar product names were born in enterprises created by entrepreneurs. Some examples include Brooks Brothers apparel (Henry Sands Brooks), Gerber baby food (Dan Gerber), Gucci loafers (Guccio Gucci), Barbie dolls (Barbara Handler), Wurlitzer instruments (Rudolph Wurlitzer), Calvin Klein jeans (Calvin Klein), Hummel figurines (Berta Hummel), Post cereals (Charles W. Post), and Heinz ketchup (Henry J. Heinz).[3] When an enterprise is in the process of being created by an entrepreneur, it is often referred to as a **new venture.**

New venture An enterprise that is in the process of being created by an entrepreneur

New ventures typically fall into the category of "small businesses," a classification that is itself somewhat difficult to define. The U.S. Chamber of Commerce suggests that businesses employing fewer than 500 persons are small. Others sometimes use a figure of fewer than 100 persons. With either figure, small businesses would still constitute 99 percent of all U.S. companies.[4] Another criterion that is often used to identify a small business is independent ownership. In other words, it is not a subsidiary of a larger organization. Accordingly, we consider a *small business* to be an independently owned company that employs fewer than 500 persons. For the most part, we use the terms "entrepreneurship" and "entrepreneur" in conjunction with creating new ventures. We use "small business" or "small-business owner" when the discussion applies more generally. In some cases, we may refer to both small businesses and new ventures (or owners and entrepreneurs) to make clear that the discussion applies to both. So far, researchers have experienced difficulty determining precisely when the creation phase attributable to entrepreneurship ends.

Promoting Innovation: Assessing Entrepreneurial Opportunities

In his book *Innovation and Entrepreneurship,* noted management consultant and writer Peter Drucker observes, "Innovation is the specific tool of entrepreneurs, the means by which they exploit change as an opportunity for a different business or a different service."[5] Essentially, it is difficult to be an entrepreneur without engaging in at least some innovation, since merely duplicating what is already being done will usually attract insufficient customers.[6] The innovation dilemma related to entrepreneurship is illustrated in Table 21-1.

As shown in the table, opportunity conditions vary according to the degree of innovation. The probable conditions associated with a particular innovation level can be assessed in terms of risk, evaluation, and profit potential. *Risk* is the probability of the venture's failing. *Evaluation* is the ease of estimating the significance and feasibility of a new venture idea. *Profit potential* is the likely level of return or compensation to the entrepreneur for taking on the risk of developing an idea into an actual business venture. As the table indicates, if a new venture is very much like the competition (a copycat), its significance and feasibility are easy to evaluate (since others are already doing it). Unfortunately, such a venture involves high risk because there is little to attract customers, and thus its profit potential is low. As new venture ideas become somewhat more innovative, the risk goes down because there is something new to offer the customer. As ideas become more innovative, though, the significance and

TABLE 21-1 OPPORTUNITY CONDITIONS ASSOCIATED WITH NEW VENTURE INNOVATION					
			LEVELS OF INNOVATION		
OPPORTUNITY CONDITIONS	NEW INVENTION	HIGHLY INNOVATIVE	MODERATELY INNOVATIVE	SLIGHTLY INNOVATIVE	COPYCAT
Risks	Very high	High	Moderate	Moderate to low	Very high
Evaluation	Very difficult	Difficult	Somewhat difficult	Easy	Easy
Profit potential	Very high	High	High to moderate	Moderate to low	Low to nil

Source: Reprinted from John G. Burch, *Entrepreneurship,* Wiley, New York, 1986, p. 72.

feasibility become more difficult to evaluate and the risk begins to reach high levels again. Gordon Moore and his partner Robert Noyce faced this dilemma when they founded Intel Corp. some 30 years ago. The company was going to make some of the first integrated circuits that combined several functions on one chip. They had three choices of technology: an easy one that could quickly be copied by competitors, a very difficult one that might lead to bankruptcy before they could complete it, or a moderately complicated chip. They chose the middle alternative. "The key was the right degree of difficulty," says Moore, who is now a billionaire and continues to serve as Intel's chairman.[7]

Economic and Social Contributions of Entrepreneurship

Entrepreneurship has been receiving increasing attention from both scholars and the popular press. This focus reflects the growing recognition of the substantial economic and social contributions of entrepreneurship and the small businesses it spawns. In this section, we consider major contributions associated with entrepreneurship in the areas of economic growth, innovation, employment opportunities, career alternatives for women and minorities, and home-based businesses.

ECONOMIC GROWTH Entrepreneurship leads to the creation of many new businesses that help fuel economic growth. Since there is no central source of data on new company formations, accurate numbers are impossible to obtain. However, according to one report, more than 2,694,859 new companies were formed between 1987 and 1990.[8] Of course, many of these new ventures failed. While statistics vary, as many as 50 to 70 percent of new businesses fail or merge with other organizations within their first 5 years.[9] Nevertheless, there is little doubt that new ventures make a significant contribution to economic expansion.[10]

INNOVATION As might be anticipated given the innovation requirements for successful entrepreneurship that were just discussed, entrepreneurs have introduced many new products and services that have changed the way we live. Henry Ford's automobile, Joyce Hall's Hallmark greeting cards, Isaac Singer's sewing machine, and King Gillette's razors are just a few examples.[11] Evidence suggests that compared with larger, more established firms, new ventures produce a disproportionately large share of product and process innovations.[12]

EMPLOYMENT OPPORTUNITIES New ventures and small businesses help create new job opportunities in the United States.[13] A debate continues to rage over whether small companies account for most of the new job creation or play a relatively minor role. One reason why their impact is difficult to assess is that while small businesses do create jobs, they also tend to account for significant

Julie Nguyen Brown, a Vietnamese refugee, was a product-design engineer for Ford Motor Company when she saw an opportunity to go into business on her own. With the aid of a minority development loan, she bought two parts-making companies that were in financial trouble and turned them around. Today her company, Plastech Engineered Products Inc., is worth $25 million.

"job destruction" through business failures.[14] Also it is difficult to accurately count new and small businesses. The economic impact of small-business job growth is likely to be the greatest during times of economic slowdown, when larger companies are cutting back.[15] During such reductions, many individuals whose jobs are eliminated find employment with small businesses. According to one estimate, as many as 20 percent of the managers who have lost their jobs as a result of downsizing in recent years have become entrepreneurs.[16] The number of new small businesses grew by 26 percent during the period 1987–1992.[17]

OPPORTUNITIES FOR WOMEN AND MINORITIES Entrepreneurship offers an alternative avenue into business for women and minorities. One major attraction is the possibility of avoiding patterns of discrimination. In established organizations, women and minorities may often be channeled to relatively lower-level and poorly paid positions. Another attraction is the prospect of material independence and the ability to control the outcomes of one's own efforts.[18] Finally, some government agencies, at the federal, state, and local levels, have been encouraging businesses owned by minorities and women. They have established programs whereby such businesses are favored in the awarding of some government contracts.

In the 5 years through 1992, the number of woman-owned sole proprietorships, partnerships, and similar businesses, as determined by "business" filed tax returns, soared 43 percent.[19] One recent study of successful corporate women managers and entrepreneurs suggests that the managers view corporate environments as safe and supportive, whereas the entrepreneurs viewed them as confining.[20] Women are estimated to now own close to 6 million companies, or about one-third of all U.S. businesses. However, men are still twice as likely as women to attempt to start a new business.[21] Moreover, businesses owned by women accounted for only about 11 percent of U.S. business revenue in 1992. One reason may be that 80 percent of women-owned businesses are concentrated in the retailing and service sectors. As women move into alternative industries, such as manufacturing, construction, and consulting, revenues are likely to rise.[22]

Minorities are starting more new businesses. For instance, even though African Americans (who constitute 11.6 percent of the labor force) presently own only about 3 percent of U.S. companies, the number of African American–owned businesses is on the rise.[23] One example of the new entrepreneurs is Lillian Lincoln, the daughter of a Virginia subsistence farmer. She attended segregated schools before managing to earn a Harvard M.B.A. Since then, she has founded Centennial One, a successful company based in Crofton, Maryland, that provides cleaning and pest-control services to major corporations, such as IBM and Westinghouse. As she notes, "Where I have to go can't be as rough climbing as where I've been."[24] According to recent Census Bureau data, the number of black-owned businesses increased by 46 percent between 1987 and 1992. During the same 5-year period, the number of businesses owned by Hispanics, Asians and Pacific Islanders, and American Indians and Alaskan Natives rose 76, 56, and 93 percent, respectively. The growth rate for the total number of U.S. businesses was 26 percent for the same time period.[25]

HOME-BASED BUSINESSES No one knows how many entrepreneurs operate home-based businesses, but the numbers are reputedly in the multimillions.[26] Changes in technology, such as computers, fax machines, separate telephone lines, and relatively inexpensive copy machines, have made home-based busi-

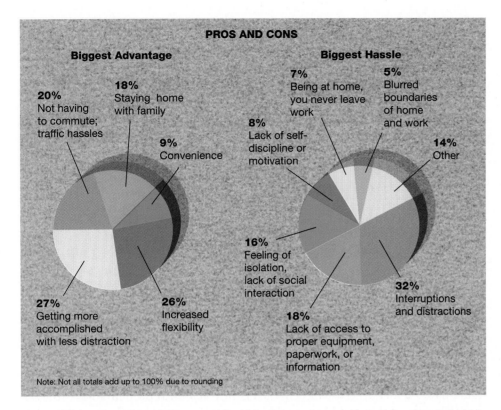

Figure 21-1 *Pros and cons of home-based businesses. (Reprinted from Gallup Organization survey results,* Detroit Free Press, *Mar. 25, 1996, p. 6F.)*

nesses more feasible. Ameritech commissioned the Gallup Organization to learn about the attitudes and behaviors of people who work at home. The survey was conducted among a sample of 300 people running home-based businesses in the Detroit area. Ninety-three percent said they would become self-employed and operate a home-based business if they could make the decision all over again.[27] The biggest advantage and the biggest hassle associated with running a home-based business, as identified by each of the survey respondents, are summarized in Figure 21-1. Experts point out that entrepreneurs running home-based businesses must possess a significant amount of self-discipline, enabling them to stay focused on the business matters in the face of many potential distractions at home. Still, the low overhead associated with running a home-based business and the new possibilities for setting up an office at home for a reasonable cost make the prospects potentially attractive.

■ FACTORS INFLUENCING ENTREPRENEURSHIP

What makes someone like Lillian Lincoln create a successful new business? To find the answer, researchers have explored several different avenues. They have focused on characteristics of the entrepreneur, theorizing that there may be some special traits involved. They have also begun to examine more closely the life-path circumstances of individuals that might influence them to become entrepreneurs. In addition, researchers have considered the possibility that certain environmental factors might encourage entrepreneurship. Finally, they have examined perceptions of the desirability and feasibility of becoming an entrepreneur, which also appear to affect the decision to engage in entrepreneurship.[28] These factors are shown in Figure 21-2 and are discussed in detail below.

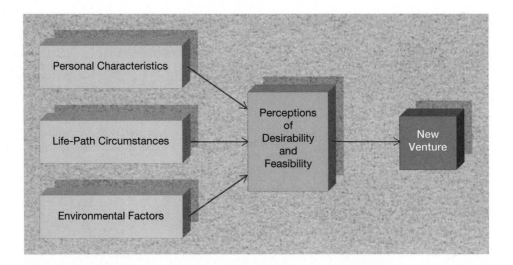

Figure 21-2 *Factors influencing entrepreneurship.*

Personal Characteristics

One fascinating question surrounding entrepreneurship is whether entrepreneurs have personality traits and background experiences that set them apart from others. A number of studies have addressed this issue.[29]

PERSONALITY CHARACTERISTICS Given the variety of businesses that entrepreneurs have created, identifying characteristics that entrepreneurs have in common is a formidable task. So far, the search for personality characteristics has yielded only a few results that may be helpful in separating potential entrepreneurs from the general population, but the traits that have surfaced are also often indicative of managers.

Psychologist David C. McClelland, who is the chief architect of acquired-needs theory (see Chapter 12), has argued that entrepreneurs tend to have a *high need for achievement* (nAch). Such individuals gravitate toward situations in which they can achieve results through their own efforts, pursue moderately difficult goals, and receive relatively immediate feedback on how they are doing.[30]

While evidence suggests that entrepreneurs do have a relatively high need for achievement, it also indicates that high nAch, by itself, does not single out entrepreneurs. High nAch can be found among salespeople, professionals, and managers as well. Most likely, high nAch is an important ingredient in entrepreneurial success, just as it is a useful trait in other occupations that involve taking personal responsibility in order to reach significant achievements.

Another characteristic that has been found in entrepreneurs is an *internal locus of control.* Individuals with an internal locus of control tend to feel that they control their fate largely through their own efforts. (In contrast, individuals with an external locus of control view their fate as mainly determined by outside forces and luck.) Again, though, an internal locus of control often characterizes managers as well as entrepreneurs.

One characteristic that does seem to separate entrepreneurs from managers is a *high tolerance for ambiguity,* an ability to continue to function effectively and persist even when situations are highly uncertain. Since entrepreneurship involves starting new organizations, a great deal of uncertainty is frequently involved. Managers often have fairly high levels of tolerance for ambiguity, but not as high as those of entrepreneurs.[31]

BACKGROUND CHARACTERISTICS A variety of studies have attempted to isolate important background characteristics of entrepreneurs. Much of the focus has been on the areas of childhood family environment, education, age, and work history.[32]

Inquiries into the *childhood family environment* of entrepreneurs have considered issues such as birth order and occupations of parents. One recurring question is whether entrepreneurs tend to be the firstborn or only children in the family. The basic idea is that such children are likely to gain a greater share of their parents' time, leading to an increased self-confidence that may fuel entrepreneurship. Although some studies have found a firstborn or only-child effect, others have not, leaving the theory in doubt.[33]

On the other hand, there is considerable evidence that entrepreneurs tend to have self-employed fathers. They often also have self-employed mothers or parents who jointly own (or owned) a business.[34] Apparently, having one or both parents as business owners provides a salient role model for potential entrepreneurs.

Another focus of inquiry has been the level of entrepreneurs' *education*. Usually, entrepreneurs tend to be better-educated than the general population, although they may be less well educated than individuals who pursue managerial careers, particularly in large organizations. Within the entrepreneurial ranks there is wide variation in educational attainment, with some entrepreneurs lacking high school diplomas and others having graduate degrees.[35] Female entrepreneurs are particularly likely to have college degrees.[36]

Age has been another variable of interest in explaining entrepreneurial activity. Although individuals are more likely to become entrepreneurs between the ages of 25 and 40, some do so across a wider age span—more like 22 to 55. Individuals can become entrepreneurs before age 22, but such endeavors are less likely because they do not have the education, experience, and financial resources needed to create new ventures. According to one recent study, as many as 10 percent of individuals between the ages of 25 and 34 are attempting to start their own businesses.[37] By the mid-50s, however, they often have pursued other career paths and may be unwilling to risk their financial standing at this stage in their lives. Nevertheless, there are certainly a number of

After fifteen years as a bank executive, Sally Narodick got the "entrepreneurial itch." After forming a consulting practice she found her way to the CEO position at Edmark Corp., which she transformed from a small firm specializing in special education materials into a player in the multimedia children's software market. Her son Philip, shown with her here, helps to test the software. Narodick's confidence and willingness to take risks are evidence of an internal locus of control, a characteristic of entrepreneurs.

entrepreneurs at the higher end of the age span and beyond. For example, the late Ray Kroc founded McDonald's when he was over 50.[38]

Not surprisingly, there is evidence that *work history* and related experience is an important factor in initiating a new enterprise. Several studies indicate that in new ventures at least one of the company founders had previously worked in the same industry as the new business. Moreover, creating new ventures seems to become easier after the first one, giving rise to the corridor principle. The **corridor principle** states that the process of beginning a new venture helps entrepreneurs visualize other opportunities that they could not envision or take advantage of until they started the initial venture.[39] For example, Phil Romano developed ideas for several other businesses after he created Fuddruckers (see the Case in Point discussion).

Corridor principle A principle which states that the process of beginning a new venture helps entrepreneurs visualize other opportunities that they could not envision or take advantage of until they started the initial venture

---

CASE IN POINT

PHIL ROMANO KEEPS SCORING ENTREPRENEURIAL SUCCESSES

Phil Romano is perhaps best known for one of his most intriguing creations, Fuddruckers, the upscale hamburger chain that he founded in 1979. When developing a new venture, Romano typically starts with a "concept," a basic idea about what he wants to do. He then thinks about it, talks with others, and puts the concept on paper. Next, he is likely to get help from other experts, such as architects and market researchers. If conditions look favorable, he usually puts together a business plan that includes a detailed description of the concept and related business issues. The business plan is particularly helpful during the process of lining up financing for the new venture, although lately Romano is doing most of his work with Brinker International, owner of Chili's and a number of other restaurant chains.

In creating Fuddruckers, Romano built his concept around freshness and quality. By the time the business had gone public and developed into a $25 million company with restaurants in 19 states and Canada, Romano had already trained his successor as CEO. After selling a large part of his interest in Fuddruckers, Romano left the business in January 1985 to create more new ventures.

Actually, Fuddruckers was the twelfth new venture that Romano had started. Within a year of leaving, he started two new businesses, a restaurant named Stix and a fashionable men's clothing store named Baroni. Both subsequently failed, costing Romano almost $1.5 million. Undaunted, in 1988 he opened Romano's Macaroni Grill, which quickly won the Silver Spoon award as the best restaurant in San Antonio. It specializes in fresh vegetables, grilled meats, gourmet pizzas, and other northern Italian fare. In December 1989, Phil Romano sold the popular restaurant and concept to Brinker International for a reported $4.5 million. Brinker has been expanding the chain to such cities as Dallas, Chicago, Houston, Kansas City, Tulsa, Orlando, and Miami. As part of the deal, Phil Romano was retained as a consultant.

Since then, Romano has worked with Brinker International on several restaurant ventures. One of the latest is Eatzi's in Dallas. It's a cross between a restaurant and a corner market. There is very little seating. It features prepared meals and also the raw materials (e.g., asparagus, uncooked salmon, and stuffed uncooked chicken breasts) to make one's dinner at home. "We want people to get out of their car, shop and be back in their car within 15 minutes or less," Romano explains. He say he wants Eatzi's "to be everybody's refrigerator, kitchen and pantry." A whole team of cooks, all dressed in chef's garb, do the

For Phil Romano, the developer of a successful upscale hamburger chain called Fuddruckers, one venture leads to another. He subsequently created Romano's Macaroni Grill, specializing in northern Italian fare, and Eatzi's, where one can purchase a prepared meal to take home or the ingredients to create a meal. This photo shows a birthday party at Cozymel's, one of his most recent ventures in Dallas.

food preparation in an open kitchen. Music, sometimes operatic, is piped out into the parking lot. As many as 70 freshly made items are offered at a time. So far, Eatzi's has proved to be even more popular than expected with customers and is attracting national attention within both the restaurant and the supermarket industry.

Romano's advice to potential entrepreneurs is straightforward. Find an industry you really like, search out the problems, and create solutions.[40] ■ ■ ■

Of course, individuals who begin their entrepreneurship at the lower end of the age scale may be better able to exploit the corridor principle because of their potentially longer careers.

All in all, there do appear to be a few characteristics that separate entrepreneurs from the general population and even, in some cases, from managers. Yet personal characteristics are relatively weak predictors of entrepreneurship. What distinguishes those who make the decision to become entrepreneurs from those who do not? Some further clues come from recent efforts to study the life-path circumstances of entrepreneurs.

Life-Path Circumstances

Several types of life-path, or individual, circumstances seem to increase the probability that an individual will become an entrepreneur. The four major types of circumstances are unsatisfactory work environment, negative displacement, career transition points, and the presence of positive-pull influencers.[41]

UNSATISFACTORY WORK ENVIRONMENT An unsatisfactory work environment is a job situation characterized by circumstances that impel the worker to think about leaving and starting a new venture. One common factor is strong dissatisfaction with either the work itself or some other aspect of the work environment, such as supervision. Another is an employer's refusal to recognize the value of an innovative idea.[42] For example, H. Ross Perot tried to get IBM to adopt his idea of selling customers computer software services along with

A Korean immigrant blossoms in America. When Whee Kim and his wife arrived in this country penniless, they started a business on borrowed money. At first they had to live in the back of their minimarket and take cold-water showers with the garden hose. Their hard work paid off: today they still own the store as well as several houses in New York City.

the company's hardware. When IBM refused to support his idea, he quit and started Electronic Data Services. The company netted him close to a billion dollars when he sold his final holdings in 1984, 22 years after founding it.[43]

NEGATIVE DISPLACEMENT Negative displacement, or disruption, occurs when circumstances in a person's life situation cause the person to make major changes in lifestyle. Factors in this category include being fired or downsized, getting a divorce, becoming widowed, reaching middle age, or emigrating from another country. For instance, negative displacement precipitated a very different lifestyle for brother and sister Marty and Helen Shih when they came to Los Angeles from Taiwan in 1979. At the time, they had $500 between them to start a new business. The pair opened a flower shop because they felt that their English language skills were not sufficient to land good corporate jobs. Within a few years there were 15 Shih's Flower shops (the downtown store alone grossed $1 million per year). The Shihs began telemarketing flowers to Asian-American customers and then extended their service to other companies that wanted to reach the Asian-American market. Their new $25 million company, Asian Business Co-op, currently has more than 400 operators, covering six languages—Mandarin, Cantonese, Japanese, Korean, Vietnamese, and Tagalog (spoken in the Philippines). Telemarketing has proved more lucrative and less capital-intensive, so they have sold their flower shop chain.[44]

CAREER TRANSITIONS Career transition points are circumstances in which an individual is moving between one type of career-related activity and another. Such points are completing studies or a degree, being discharged from military service, finishing a major project, or having children leave home. For example, Nancy Barocci was at a transition point when she returned to Wilmette, Illinois, with her husband and children after several years in Europe. She had been studying Italian food and wines and wanted to put her learning to good use. So, in 1980, she opened an Italian restaurant, called Canvito Italiano, that was an immediate hit. Since then she has opened several other successful restaurants in the Chicago area, including Betise, a Mediterranean bistro.[45]

POSITIVE-PULL INFLUENCERS Positive-pull influencers are individuals, such as mentors, investors, customers, or potential partners, who urge an individual to start a business. For instance, Scott McNealy, cofounder and chief executive of Sun Microsystems, Inc., got involved in starting the company when his former Stanford roommate, Vinod Khosia, approached him with the idea. The pair teamed up with two other Stanford M.B.A.s in 1982 and have built the company into a multi-billion-dollar player in the field of engineering workstations.[46] The pull notion is unlike the other life-path changes discussed above, since they involve circumstances that push individuals toward the entrepreneurial life. Individuals in push situations must either take action or suffer negative consequences. While life-path circumstances can be an impetus for entrepreneurship, real and perceived environmental conditions favoring new businesses are also an ingredient.

Favorable Environmental Conditions

A number of environmental conditions appear to influence entrepreneurs. Generally, they deal with the basic prerequisites of running a business, such as adequate financing, a technically skilled labor force, accessibility of suppliers, accessibility of customers or new markets, availability of land or facilities, accessibility of transportation, and availability of supporting services.

Other, more indirect, conditions provide support as well, such as the presence of incubator organizations, government influences, experienced entrepreneurs, support networks, proximity of universities, attitude of the area's population, and living conditions. An **incubator** is an organization whose purpose is to nurture new ventures in their very early stages by providing space (usually at a site housing other new ventures as well), stimulation, support, and a variety of basic services, often at reduced fees. The idea is to help the new ventures during their first 2 or 3 years or so, until they have grown enough to "hatch" and join the normal business world.[47] Although there were only about 50 incubators in the United States in 1984, the number had grown to more than 600 by 1992, according to figures from the National Business Incubation Association.[48]

Two different support networks are typically important to entrepreneurs.[49] A *moral-support network* is a set of family members and/or friends who provide encouragement, understanding, and even assistance. The assistance may be in

Incubator An organization whose purpose is to nurture new ventures in their very early stages by providing space (usually at a site housing other new ventures as well), stimulation, support, and a variety of basic services, often at reduced fees

The Mexican-born Acevedo brothers, Benjamin and Victor, located their wood-products company in a suburb of San Diego, just across the Mexican border. As trade has opened up with Mexico in the last few years, the Acevedos have taken advantage of environmental conditions and their bicultural heritage. Now they ship all over Mexico and find their export business booming.

the form of aiding with home and family matters so that the entrepreneur has more time to devote to the business or helping in the business itself. A *professional-support network* is a set of cooperative relationships with experts who can provide advice and counsel that help an entrepreneur function effectively. This type of network can be developed through linkages with business associates, professional associations, and other personal affiliations, such as hobbies, civic groups, and school alumni groups.

Perceptions of Desirability and Feasibility

When personal characteristics and life-path circumstances either push or pull individuals toward entrepreneurship, such individuals are likely to increasingly perceive entrepreneurship as desirable. However, even with perceived desirability, would-be entrepreneurs must also make an assessment of the feasibility of creating a new enterprise.[50] While personal characteristics and life-path circumstances play a part in this judgment, environmental conditions are a critical aspect of feasibility assessments. Thus perceptions of feasibility are influenced by seeing oneself as having the necessary background, the presence of successful role models, the availability of advice from knowledgeable others, and the availability of financial support and other resources. For example, after graduating from college and moving to Hong Kong, Katha Diddel began to perceive that she, too, could start her own business (see the Case in Point discussion).

CASE IN POINT

KATHA DIDDEL LAUNCHES HER HOME COLLECTION

When Katha Diddel graduated from college in 1979, she went directly to mainland China seeking a job in which she could use her 6 years of intensive language training in Mandarin Chinese. After a few short-term jobs as an interpreter, she landed a position in the China trade division of the Associated Merchandising Corporation (AMC) in Hong Kong. She worked as a merchandiser and market guide for American retailers who wanted to meet Chinese suppliers on the mainland. This position enabled her to build a network of business contacts at a time when China was beginning to show interest in exporting products to U.S. markets. In the process, she slowly put together a business plan to fulfill her dream of having a business of her own—a company that would market exquisite Chinese embroidery in the United States.

Diddel traveled around the country visiting dozens of tiny villages and remote islands before finally finding what she was looking for in an old factory in a mountain community. There she located workers doing lovely embroidery in patterns that earlier generations had learned from European missionaries. Unfortunately, the workers were using "garish" colors and cheap polyester fabric. She proposed that the workers embroider fine linens, and her plan was accepted by the plant managers. Afterward, she stayed to supervise the learning process by, for example, picking out the thread colors and showing the artisans where to put the designs on the fabric.

Having developed the products, Diddel now needed to find interested importers in the United States. In New York, she made numerous calls to importers listed in the telephone book, went to trade shows and collected names of potential customers, advertised in trade journals, and sent out over 1000 letters to prospects. "The process took a very long time," she says. "It was not the most pleasant period of my life." Nevertheless, she was ultimately successful. To finance her operation, she obtained a $5000 loan from a Hong Kong bank. She also worked out an arrangement with her importers that guaranteed immediate payment for products received.

With the pieces in place, Diddel launched Twin Panda, Inc., just when the U.S. home-furnishings market was expanding rapidly. For the next 5 years, sales boomed. Then, suddenly, she began to notice signs of trouble. Diddel says that competitors, taking note of her success, went to her sources and set up rival contracts for imitations using cheaper materials that allowed them to undercut her prices. Since copyright laws in China are weak, Diddel decided to fight the low-cost approach of her competitors by means of a differentiation strategy. She focused on top-of-the-line, hand-worked products and a greater variety of designs. As part of the implementation process, Diddel went to China and renegotiated contracts for higher volumes in return for guaranteed protection of her designs. She has also renamed her product line the Katha Diddel Home Collection, to denote that the products are created by a designer. Recently she has been emphasizing very high quality needlepoint decorative pillows and accent rugs. She focuses mainly on the "highest level of the decorator/designer market."[51] ■■■

Because of the current interest in entrepreneurs like Katha Diddel, our emphasis here has been on factors that influence individuals to create new ventures. Of course, creating a new organization is not the only way to engage in small-business ownership. There are alternative approaches.

■ DECIDING ON A DEVELOPMENT APPROACH

One major aspect of both entrepreneurship and small-business ownership is determining which development path to pursue.[52] There are three general approaches: starting a new firm, buying an existing business, or purchasing a franchise.

Starting a New Firm

A new firm started from scratch by an entrepreneur is often referred to as a **start-up.** A study of 106 entrepreneurs offers clues about the types of new firms, or start-ups, that one might create.[53] On the basis of interviews with a reasonably representative sample of entrepreneurs, the researchers identified the following reasons why these individuals started new firms:

Start-up A type of new firm or venture started from scratch by an entrepreneur

> **Escaping to something new:** In starting a new firm, the entrepreneur in this category is attempting to escape from his or her previous type of job, which the individual feels did not offer prospects for sufficient rewards in terms of salary, challenging work, promotion opportunities, or other factors.

> **Putting the deal together:** The individual in this category aims to bundle the different aspects of the business (such as suppliers, wholesale and retail channels, and customers) into a "deal," from which each participant will gain.

> **Rolling over skills and contacts:** Before establishing the new firm, the individual in this category worked in a position that involved technical skills

and expertise closely related to those needed in the new enterprise. The venture offers goods and services that rely on the owner's professional expertise and are most often generic in nature (e.g., auditing or advertising).

Leveraging expertise: The individual is one of the top people in his or her technical field. The entrepreneur brings in partners to help start the firm. The venture enters an established market and competes through flexibility in adapting to customer needs, which is based on the entrepreneur's keen awareness of environmental changes.

Forming an aggressive service: The entrepreneur creates an aggressive service-oriented firm, usually a consulting firm in a highly specialized area.

Pursuing the unique idea: The venture develops because of an idea for a product or service that is not being offered. The product or service is not technically sophisticated or difficult to produce.

Organizing methodically: The entrepreneur in this category uses extensive planning both to acquire the skills and to perform the tasks required in the new venture. The products or services are similar to those of competitors, but the firm provides a new twist, usually either a slightly different way to produce the product or service or a slightly different customer to sell to.

Buying an Existing Business

The second major approach to developing a new venture is purchasing an existing business. This can also apply to acquiring and managing a small business. Entrepreneurs typically acquire an existing business when they believe that they can quickly change its direction in a fairly substantial way so that it will grow in major new areas. Often the organization may be faltering. For example, in the late 1980s, a group of entrepreneurs purchased Cuisinarts, Inc., the company that pioneered the food processor, after it failed to capitalize on its name in developing new products. Unfortunately, the entrepreneurs were not experienced in the small-kitchen-appliance business and 1 year later were forced to file for bankruptcy protection themselves.[54] In contrast, prospective small-business owners tend to purchase an existing business with the idea of retaining the business in basically the same form, although it may possibly need to be managed more effectively (especially if it was doing poorly). In the long run, of course, small-business owners may make substantial changes.

Several of the major considerations that go into purchasing an existing business are shown in Figure 21-3. It is usually imperative to obtain professional help, particularly from a lawyer (to review such matters as current contracts with suppliers and to set up an acquisition agreement) and an accountant (to audit the financial records and to help determine a purchase price).[55]

Purchasing a Franchise

Franchise A continuing arrangement between a franchiser and a franchisee in which the franchiser's knowledge, image, manufacturing or service expertise, and marketing techniques are made available to the franchisee in return for the payment of various fees or royalties and conformity to standard operating procedures

The third major approach to developing a small business is purchasing a franchise. (The study of entrepreneurs discussed earlier did not cover franchises.) A **franchise** is a continuing arrangement between a franchiser and a franchisee in which the franchiser's knowledge, image, manufacturing or service expertise, and marketing techniques are made available to the franchisee in return for the payment of various fees or royalties and conformity to standard oper-

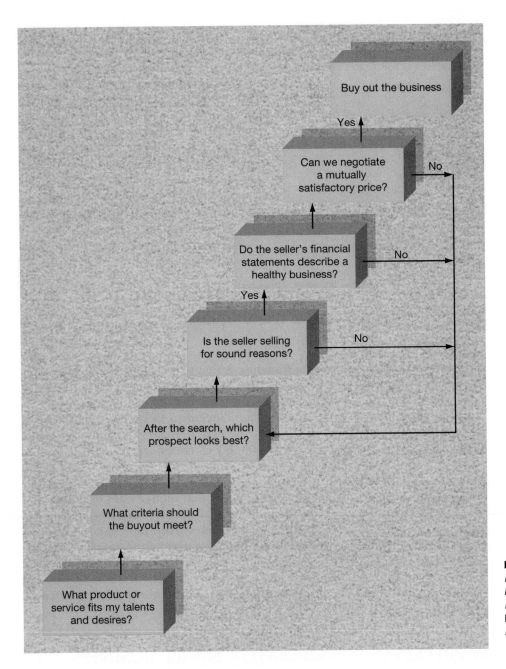

Figure 21-3 *Considerations in purchasing an existing business. (Adapted from Nicholas C. Siropolis,* Small Business Management, *5th ed., Houghton Mifflin, Boston, 1994, p. 112.)*

ating procedures.[56] A **franchiser** is usually a manufacturer or sole distributor of a trademarked product or service who typically has considerable experience in the line of business being franchised. Recent evidence indicates that emphasizing franchising as an expansion strategy is likely to have a positive effect on the franchiser's growth and survival.[57] A **franchisee** is an individual who purchases a franchise and, in the process, is given an opportunity to enter a new business, hopefully with an enhanced chance of success.[58] When one mentions franchises, fast-food operations, such as McDonald's, often come to mind.

Franchises are normally considered to be small businesses but not new ventures, since the creation process is largely controlled by the franchiser, rather than the franchisee. In fact, some writers do not include most franchise arrangements in the small-business category. Instead, they view franchises as appendages of larger organizations.[59]

Franchiser A manufacturer or sole distributor of a trademarked product or service who typically has considerable experience in the line of business being franchised

Franchisee An individual who purchases a franchise and, in the process, is given the opportunity to enter a new business, hopefully with an enhanced chance of success

RANKING	FRANCHISE FEE*	START-UP COSTS†
TABLE 21-2 *ENTREPRENEUR* MAGAZINE'S TOP 10 FRANCHISES		
1. Subway	$10,000	$55,720–$140,700
2. 7-Eleven	Varies	$12,500+
3. Burger King	$40,000	$247,000–$1,320,000
4. McDonald's	$60,000	$363,000–$591,000
5. Dunkin' Donuts	$40,000	$181,600–$255,100
6. Dairy Queen	$30,000	$370,000–$715,000
7. Snap-On Inc. hardware	$4,000	$104,300–$186,750
8. Mail Boxes Etc.	$24,950	$68,500–$112,400
9. Baskin-Robbins	to $15,000	$42,000–$370,000
10. KFC (Kentucky Fried Chicken)	$25,000	$125,000

*The amount of cash you must put up.
†Can usually include cash and financing. This figure is affected by real estate and construction costs (if applicable), inventory location, type of business, and many other variables. Some franchisers charge annual royalties and marketing and advertising fees.
Source: List is compiled from *Entrepreneur,* January 1996, pp. 211–305.

The primary advantage of a franchise is that the franchisee gains access to the proven business methods, established reputation, training, and assistance of the franchiser, so the new venture risk is minimized. On the other hand, there are a number of disadvantages. These include a lack of independence in regard to making major modifications, the considerable difficulty involved in canceling franchise contracts, the likelihood of continual monitoring by the franchiser, and the substantial expense that may be involved in establishing a franchise with a well-known company.[60] One recent study of small-business formations during the period 1984–1987 suggests that higher rates of failure and lower rates of profitability are associated with franchise start-ups when compared with independent start-ups.[61] Nevertheless, for individuals who lack expertise in a viable business specialty, a franchise may be the answer. Table 21-2 provides a recent list of the top 10 franchises as assessed by *Entrepreneur* magazine. The magazine says it considers factors such as years of business, number of franchises, start-up costs, financing available, and the parent company's financial strength in choosing its top 10.

■ PREPARING TO OPERATE A SMALL BUSINESS

Regardless of which development path an individual decides to pursue, there are major preparations involved in starting a small business. Important steps include developing a business plan, obtaining the necessary resources, and selecting an appropriate site for the business.

Developing a Business Plan

Business plan A document written by the prospective owner or entrepreneur that details the nature of the business, the product or service, the customers, the competition, the production and marketing methods, the management, the financing, and other significant aspects of the proposed business venture

Most small-business and entrepreneurship experts strongly recommend the development of a business plan. A **business plan** is a document written by the prospective owner or entrepreneur that details the nature of the business, the product or service, the customers, the competition, the production and marketing methods, the management, the financing, and other significant aspects of the proposed business venture.[62]

MANAGEMENT SKILLS FOR THE TWENTY-FIRST CENTURY

Steps in Developing a Business Plan

The steps below will give you a good idea of what is involved in putting together a business plan. The timetable for developing the plan will depend on the complexity of the situation and your own time schedule.

1 Make the commitment to go into business for yourself.
2 Analyze your strengths and weaknesses, paying special attention to your business experience, business education, and desires. Then answer this question: Why should I be in business for myself?
3 Choose the product or service that best fits your strengths and desires. Then answer these questions: What need will my product or service fill? What is unique about my product or service? How do I know it is unique? What will my product or service do for customers? What will it not do? What should it do later that it does not do now?
4 Research the market for your product or service to find answers to such questions as these: Who are my customers? Where are they? What is their average income? How do they buy? At what price? In what quantities? When do they buy? When will they use my product or service? Where will they use it? Why will they buy it? Who are my com-

petitors? Where are they? How strong are they? What is the total market potential? Is it growing?
5 Forecast your share of market, if possible. Then forecast your sales revenues over a 3-year period, broken down as follows: first year, monthly; second year, quarterly; third year, yearly. Next, answer this question: Why do I believe my sales revenue forecast is realistic?
6 Choose a site for your business. Then answer this question: Why do I prefer this site to other possible sites?
7 *This step applies only to entrepreneurs who plan to go into manufacturing.* Develop your production plan, answering these questions: How big should my plant be? How should my production process be laid out? What equipment will I need? In what size? How will I control the waste, quality, and inventory of my product?
8 Develop your marketing plan, answering such questions as these: How am I going to create customers? At what price? By what kinds of advertising and sales promotion? Through personal selling? How?
9 Develop your organizational plan, answering this question: What kinds of skills and talents will I need to make my business grow? Draw up an organization chart that spells out who does what, who has what authority, and who reports to whom.

10 Develop your legal plan, focusing on whether to form a sole proprietorship, a partnership, or a corporation, and then explain your choice.
11 Develop your accounting plan, explaining the kinds of records and reports you need and how you will use them.
12 Develop your insurance plan, answering this question: What kinds of insurance will I need to protect my venture against possible loss from unforeseen events?
13 Develop a computer plan, spelling out the ways that computer services may help you plan and control your business.
14 Develop your financial plan by preparing a 3-year cash budget. Show how much cash you will need before opening for business and how much cash you expect will flow in and out of your business, broken down as follows: first year, monthly; second year, quarterly; third year, yearly. In addition, prepare an income statement for the first year only, balance sheets for the beginning and end of the first year, and a profit graph (break-even chart), showing when you will begin to make a profit. Then determine how you will finance your business and where you expect to raise money.
15 Write a cover letter summarizing your business plan, stressing its purpose and its promise.[63]

A well-prepared business plan can take 200 to 400 hours or even more to complete, depending on the complexity of the business contemplated, the strength of the competition, the number of different parties involved, and the number of other factors that must be considered.[64] For an outline of the major steps involved in developing a business plan, see the Management Skills for the Twenty-First Century discussion, "Steps in Developing a Business Plan."

A business plan serves several important purposes.[65] First, it helps prospective owners and entrepreneurs carefully think through every aspect of their proposed endeavor. Since the plan requires writing down information about such aspects as the risks involved, financing requirements, and intended markets, prospective owners and entrepreneurs are forced to think concretely about such matters.

Second, a business plan helps prospective owners and entrepreneurs obtain financing. For example, the U.S. Small Business Administration (SBA) requires that a business plan accompany applications for the agency's small-business loan program. Most private investors will not even consider financing a venture without seeing a well-thought-out plan. For example, Phil Romano uses business plans to help obtain outside funding for his various ventures. Obtaining significant funding from banks will also involve submitting a business plan. Even short-run loans may be easier to negotiate when an entrepreneur can demonstrate that a new business venture is progressing according to plan.

Third, a business plan provides a basis for measuring plan progress. Some experts argue that planning is particularly important for new ventures because of their inherent instability. A business plan can help establish milestones for periodic reviews, during which assumptions and accomplishments can be compared. Careful monitoring increases the likelihood of identifying significant deviations from the plan and making modifications before the frail new venture is forced out of business.

Fourth, business plans often help prospective owners and entrepreneurs establish credibility with others. For example, potential employees may need to be convinced that they are joining an organization with a strong chance of success. Suppliers may be more willing to extend a line of credit when the business plan appears sound. Major customers may be more inclined to place orders when there are convincing arguments that the new venture or small business will be able to deliver the necessary products or services.

Obtaining Resources

Two of the most important resources typically needed in starting a new firm or acquiring an existing small business are financing and human resources. Each plays a crucial role.

FINANCING New ventures, even small ones, require funds to operate. Moreover, most of their revenues in the early years must be plowed back into the business to fuel growth. There are many sources of financing for entrepreneurs and prospective small-business owners. The most common are personal savings and loans from family and friends, as well as loans from banks. For example, Katha Diddel started her business with a $5000 loan from a Hong Kong bank. Phil Romano has initiated several businesses with loans from banks, money borrowed from friends, loans from the U.S. Small Business Administration, and funds from stock sold to private investors, as well as with his own funds. Potential sources of funding for entrepreneurs and prospective small-business owners are shown in Table 21-3.

One of the major issues associated with securing funding is the amount of equity (or ownership of the firm) and potential control an entrepreneur or prospective small-business owner must relinquish to obtain the necessary financing. There are two major types of funding available.[66] The first is **debt capital,** financing that involves a loan to be repaid, usually with interest. Typically, part of the loan arrangement involves putting up some asset (such as a car, a house, or machinery) as collateral in case the firm is not able to repay the debt. Banks are the major source of debt capital to new ventures and small businesses, although some debt capital is available through other sources, such as the Small Business Administration.

Debt capital A type of financing that involves a loan to be repaid, usually with interest

TABLE 21-3 POTENTIAL SOURCES OF FUNDING NEW VENTURES AND SMALL BUSINESSES

Wealthy individuals: Go to these individuals either directly or through a third party. These people normally prefer common stock and secured loans, expect a substantial ownership stake in the company, and like to keep tabs on their investment.

Venture capitalists: These institutional risk takers are normally located through CPAs, attorneys, and bankers. They usually have formulas for evaluating a business, tend to specialize in certain types of businesses, and prefer strong minority positions. They often structure deals with both equity and debt characteristics.

Small Business Administration: The SBA has a variety of loan programs for small businesses that cannot borrow from conventional vendors on reasonable terms. There are normally limits on the amount of money available, but the interest rates are slightly lower than those on regular commercial loans.

Commercial banks: Banks generally require security and guarantees before making start-up loans and sometimes impose other restrictions on the borrower. A borrower can expect to pay the prime rate plus 1 to 4 points.

Business development corporations: BDCs are privately owned corporations charted by about half the states to make loans to small businesses. They can develop creative financing packages, and their loans are generally guaranteed by the SBA.

State venture-capital funds: About half the states have programs that provide venture-capital funds. Most make loans, and some provide equity capital. Information about these sources of funding can normally be obtained from the local state economic or industrial development office.

Shares sold by the entrepreneur or small-business owner: To attract outside investors, some entrepreneurs and small-business owners sell shares at private or public offerings. Such offerings are very technical and require expert legal help to conform to the federal securities laws and appropriate state laws.

Source: Adapted from *Changing Times,* September 1985, pp. 38–43. [Also reprinted in "How to Bankroll Your Future," in Clifford M. Baumback and Joseph Mancuso (eds.), *Entrepreneurship and Venture Management,* Prentice-Hall, Englewood Cliffs, N.J., 1987, pp. 188–189.]

The second major type of funding is **equity capital,** financing which usually requires that the investor be given some form of ownership in the venture. The investor shares in the profits and in any proceeds from the sale of assets in proportion to the equity held. For example, Phil Romano gave up 48 percent of his equity in Fuddruckers to obtain the $150,000 that he needed to start the business. When he later sold the company, the investors were entitled to 48 percent of the proceeds. Because of the success of the venture, a $15,000 investment in Fuddruckers was worth about $3.5 million 3 years later. One study of entrepreneurs showed that the overall equity relinquished by their firms in order to obtain capital during the early stages averaged 45.1 percent.[67]

New venture capital has recently been playing a major role in the creation of start-up companies in eastern Europe. In one such case, Jan Bednarek, the general manager of Wistom, a synthetic fibers company in Poland, has used some of the profits from the company to furnish seed money for 18 start-up companies. His goal is to create enough jobs and pump enough profits into the local economy of Tomaszow Mazowiecki (a town of 70,000 people, located 60 miles southwest of Warsaw) to enable him to close his antiquated synthetic fibers plant. Wistom invests in new ventures for an agreed-upon amount of stock. In one case, a new venture began by designing and producing improved lighting fixtures for the Wistom factory. Another start-up, which specializes in factory automation and industrial processing equipment, is housed in the Wistom facility. It is currently making $20,000 per month in profits, and Bednarek is looking forward to the time when its employees can buy out Wistom's stake in the company.[68]

In the United States, new ventures typically use a combination of debt and

Equity capital A type of financing which usually requires that the investor be given some form of ownership in the venture

equity capital. Debt capital tends to be used for short-time financing (funds needed for a year or less) to pay for such things as monthly expenses, advertising, special sales from suppliers, and unforeseen emergencies. For the longer range, both long-term debt capital (funds for 1 to 5 years or more) and equity capital are often used to finance basic start-up costs, the purchase or replacement of equipment, expansions, and other major expenditures. Small businesses that are aiming for relatively moderate growth frequently use mainly debt capital, with the owners retaining most or all of the equity.

Venture team A group of two or more individuals who band together for the purpose of creating a new venture

HUMAN RESOURCES Although many new ventures are initiated by entrepreneurs, others have multiple founders who are often referred to as a venture team. A **venture team** is a group of two or more individuals who band together for the purpose of creating a new venture. Ideally, venture-team members complement one another's skills, thus strengthening the prospects of the new venture. Mutual trust and strong commitment to the start-up are also essential ingredients. Potential venture-team members need to explore their mutual expectations carefully, since a breakup of the team early in the venture can have a serious detrimental effect on the success of the endeavor.[69]

Of course, new ventures and small businesses typically require the help of others besides entrepreneurs or owners. In fact, a poll of small-business owners showed that their most difficult problem is finding competent workers and then motivating them to perform.[70] Since each employee in a small business represents a large percentage of the workforce, a given individual's contribution can be particularly significant to the success of the organization. Thus entrepreneurs and small-business owners need to use good selection processes to find individuals who will be strong assets as the organization grows. (Selection issues are discussed in Chapter 10.) For example, one reason why Steve Bernard, founder of Cape Cod Potato Chips Company, bought the company back from Anheuser-Busch when the opportunity arose recently was to save the jobs of the 100 people who worked in the Hyannis, Massachusetts, plant. Bernard had hired many of the workers before he sold the company to Anheuser-Busch a decade ago. With the help of these "dedicated, hard-working people," Bernard believes he can grow the company as an independent entity now that Anheuser-Busch has decided to exit its snack operations.[71]

Selecting an Appropriate Site

Choosing a location for a business is typically an important decision. For instance, a fast-food restaurant depends in large part on having potential customers pass by. On the other hand, a general contracting operation that relies heavily on advertising to reach customers will not be as directly affected by its location. In selecting an appropriate business site, entrepreneurs and small-business owners usually take into consideration major factors such as the community, the trade area, lease or buy trade-offs, zoning or licensing requirements, and cost per square foot.[72]

COMMUNITY The community in which an entrepreneur or small-business owner chooses to operate is often a matter of personal choice. Some may prefer a specific geographic location, such as the northwest; others may wish to operate in a small town; while still others will opt for a large metropolitan area. Some local governments offer benefits and incentives to businesses willing to locate in their areas.

TRADE AREA Usually, location decisions also involve identifying a *trade area*, the geographic area that contains the firm's prospective customers. Determining a trade area includes deciding who the customers will be and learning about their buying habits. For example, a study of food-store purchases in a major city found that close to 70 percent of the customers shopped at stores within one to five blocks of their homes. For suburban locations, the majority of customers lived within 3 miles of the stores, although some traveled as far as 5 miles. In rural locations, most of the customers lived a 10-minute drive away, with the trade area extending as far as a 20-minute drive.

LEASE OR BUY New businesses typically lease facilities, sometimes with an option to buy. This is partly because financing sources are normally reluctant to provide funds for the purchase of physical facilities when a firm has no established track record. As the business develops, small-business owners tend to purchase facilities.

ZONING AND LICENSING Zoning laws can sometimes have a bearing on the location of new ventures and small businesses. For example, many types of businesses, such as light manufacturing or automobile sales, are usually not permitted in residential areas. Moreover, licenses are frequently required in many jurisdictions in order to operate certain types of businesses, such as restaurants, dry cleaners, gas stations, liquor stores, and bars. For these reasons, a thorough investigation into zoning and licensing requirements is usually conducted early in the site selection process.

COST PER SQUARE FOOT Rental or lease costs will vary and can be substantial for a new venture or other small business. Commercial property is usually rented or leased on a cost-per-square-foot basis. These costs are normally determined by location, condition of property, services furnished, and availability of parking for both employees and customers. Sometimes, starting a business in an incubator or an industrial park can greatly reduce such costs, although the location may not be suitable in many cases. One expert suggests that if your business is one where you visit your clients rather than have them visit you, operating an office in your home is worth investigating.[73]

■ MANAGING A SMALL BUSINESS

As new ventures begin to take shape and other small businesses engage in commerce, they must be managed. In this section we consider the growth stages of small businesses as they emerge and develop, the transition from entrepreneurship to intrapreneurship, and some special issues and problems associated with entrepreneurship and small-business management.

Stages of Small-Business Growth

While some researchers have examined the growth stages of organizations (see Chapter 11), others have explored the stages of small-business growth in order to better understand the very early life of organizations.[74] According to one analysis, small-business growth consists of five major stages, as shown in Figure 21-4.

STAGE I: EXISTENCE In the existence stage, the small business is just getting started. The main problems it faces are attracting customers and delivering the products and services required. Critical questions are whether or not sufficient

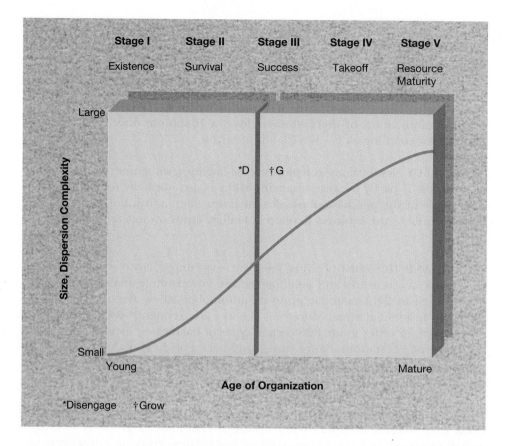

Figure 21-4 *Stages of new venture growth. (Reprinted by permission of* Harvard Business Review. *An exhibit from "The Five Stages of Business Growth," by Neil C. Churchill and Virginia L. Lewis, May–June 1983. Copyright © 1983 by the President and Fellows of Harvard College; all rights reserved.)*

customers can be lined up, whether the production process can actually fulfill the needs of customers, and whether there are sufficient funds to cover the emerging start-up costs. Companies at this stage are struggling for their existence. Many times, customers or adequate production capabilities do not materialize before funds run out. When this happens, the new venture collapses or perhaps is sold for asset value.

STAGE II: SURVIVAL In the survival stage, the problem changes from concern for mere existence to concern for revenues relative to expenses. Two issues are critical at this point: Can the company break even and make enough profit to repair and replace assets, and can it generate enough funds to finance the growth necessary for eventually earning a good return on assets and labor? The main concern at this stage is survival, and the owner still makes most of the important decisions concerning the organization. New businesses often dissipate their resources at this stage serving the wrong customers. Some organizations may remain at this level for a long time, barely making ends meet, until the owner gives up or retires. Others may grow in size and begin to earn a reasonable profit, thereby moving to the next stage.

STAGE III: SUCCESS At the success stage, the owner faces a major decision. Should the owner stabilize at a profitable level that can be used to support his or her other interests (success-disengagement substage) or build on the accomplishments so far and go for further growth (success-growth substage)?

In *substage III-D* (disengagement), the company has good economic health and earns average or above-average profits. If it does not adapt to environmental changes, the organization may go under or revert to the survival stage.

In *substage III-G* (growth), the owner pulls together the cash and borrowing power of the company to invest in significant further growth. Important tasks are managing the business so that it continues to be profitable and developing managers to handle the expansion. Strategic planning becomes critical, and the owner is involved in all phases of the business. If successful, the company moves to the next stage. If not, it may be able to shift to III-D. Otherwise, it may slide back to the survival stage or be sold.

STAGE IV: TAKEOFF In the takeoff stage, the key problems are how rapidly to grow and how to finance the growth. One critical issue is whether the owner is willing to delegate responsibilities to others in order to handle the growing enterprise. Another is whether the cash flow will be sufficient. Both operational planning and strategic planning are extremely important. Entrepreneurs, and some small-business owners, often do not have the breadth of managerial skills and experience that is needed to handle a company at this stage. In some cases, entrepreneurs recognize their shortcomings and move aside so that professional managers can steer the company.

One company in which entrepreneurs successfully turned the operation of an organization over to professional managers is BDM International, headquartered in McLean, Virginia. The high-technology consulting firm was founded in 1959 by three physicists. It was awarded its first major contract by the U.S. Army in 1960. A president was promoted from within in 1972. The founders remained major shareholders and advisers to the organization. The company had $8.1 million in contract awards and 434 employees in 1972. By 1995 it had $1.7 billion and employed 7900 people.[75]

If efforts at this stage are unsuccessful, a company may fold or revert to one of its former stages. One company that ran into difficulty attempting to move from substage III-G (success-growth) to stage IV (takeoff) is J. Bildner & Sons (see the Case in Point discussion).

J. Bruce Llewellyn is an entrepreneur who can get businesses to take off and knows how to manage them. He started out by developing a small supermarket chain in New York City. He went on to manage a Coca-Cola bottling company, and buy and manage a network-affiliated TV station.

JAMES BILDNER'S SPECTACULAR RISE AND FALL   CASE IN POINT

When James Bildner opened his first upscale grocery store in 1984, it was greeted with rave reviews. Bildner and his company, J. Bildner & Sons, Inc., were even featured in a *Newsweek* cover story on yuppies. Within 3 years, the company had 21 stores, more than 2000 employees, and sales approaching $50 million. Yet 1 year later, the company was in proceedings under Chapter 11 of the Federal Bankruptcy Code, with debts exceeding assets by about $30 million. The number of stores had shrunk to six, and the work force had been cut to 250 members. How could a business that started up so well turn so sour?

The first J. Bildner & Sons was located in an ornate Boston building dating back to 1865. It stayed open long hours, took phone orders, allowed credit cards, and offered free delivery. In fact, delivery people would even pick up a customer's dry cleaning on the way and shop at other stores for items that Bildner's didn't have. Bildner's itself was well stocked with an enticing array of selections, including such delights as hot red-pepper fettucine and salmon spinach, prepared in Bildner's own kitchens.

The store was extremely popular from the day it opened. Since its success relied on a concept, rather than a patentable product, Bildner was concerned that competitors would attempt to establish similar stores. Accordingly, he opened five more stores in the Boston area in 1985. The following year, he opened eight more, including locations in Atlanta and in Birmingham.

In September 1986, the company sold stock to the public at $13 per share in order to raise $15 million for further expansion. Shortly thereafter, Bildner's had a store in New York City, as well as leases for seven additional stores in New York. Leases were also signed for nine other stores in such cities as Philadelphia, Chicago, and Fairfax, Virginia. The expansion had reached a feverish pace.

By the following summer, though, trouble signs were appearing. That's when the company closed its Birmingham store and its first two New York stores. By July 1988, Bildner's had filed for bankruptcy protection.

In sorting out what went wrong, some observers say that the company's executives didn't do enough planning before expanding. For example, the company expected costs in New York to be about 10 percent higher than in Boston, but they were actually 40 percent more. Construction problems and an attempt to unionize the New York stores delayed openings and drove up costs. In addition, company executives underestimated the competition in New York, where Bildner's offerings were not as unique as those in Boston. Furthermore, the expansion into some other cities involved locating outlets in department stores, a concept far different from the original Bildner's site.

The company's management also found it difficult to make the transition from a small number of stores with a local orientation to a larger company in multiple cities. Top managers became so absorbed in the expansion that they soon began to lose touch with what was going on in individual stores. Financial controls were fairly loose, so the company's good cash position faded quickly.

Still, the struggling company has managed to emerge from bankruptcy. Since then, Bildner has worked hard with the remaining Boston-area stores to bring them back into line with his original concept. His scaled-down chain appears to be prospering again.[76] ■■■

Unfortunately, James Bildner was not able to effectively navigate his company from the success-growth stage to takeoff. He is again attempting to position his company in the takeoff, and if he is successful, J. Bildner & Sons will eventually move on to the next stage, resource maturity.

STAGE V: RESOURCE MATURITY At this stage, the company needs to consolidate and control the financial gains resulting from rapid growth, but it must also attempt to retain the spirit that brought it this far. However, growing size may cause **ossification,** a condition characterized by lack of innovation and avoidance of risk (which may be in marked contrast to the company's orientation in its early days). Eventually, depending on how quickly the environment changes, ossification can lead to decline, perhaps even back to the survival stage or to the end of the business. At this stage, the company must begin aggressive steps to encourage innovation. Here the emphasis shifts from entrepreneurship to intrapreneurship.

Ossification A condition that is characterized by lack of innovation and avoidance of risk

Entrepreneurship versus Intrapreneurship

We have discussed many means of fostering innovation in the Promoting Innovation sections throughout this book. When a company reaches the resource maturity stage, its need for the initial momentum of entrepreneurship is replaced by a strong need for intrapreneurship. *Intrapreneurship* is the practice of innovating by developing new products, processes, or services while one is part of an organization (see Chapters 1 and 11). Entrepreneurship, as we have

TABLE 21-4 THE RISKIEST AND SAFEST INDUSTRIES	
INDUSTRY	**FAILURE RATE PER 10,000 (1990)**
Amusement and recreation services	578
Oil and gas extraction	166
Lumber and wood manufacturing	106
General building contractors	101
Furniture and home-furnishings stores	99
Personal services	39
Insurance agents and brokers	28
Legal services	25
Health services	21
Educational services (private education)	13

Source: Bruce Phillips, Small Business Administration, Office of Economic Research at the Office of Advocacy, Washington, D.C. Reprinted from *INC. The State of Small Business, 1995,* p. 20.

seen, also involves innovating, but the innovations are carried out by creating a new organization.

Major Issues and Problems

New ventures and small businesses can bring considerable satisfaction in terms of both accomplishments and financial remuneration. On the other hand, such endeavors involve several relatively unique issues and problems.

BANKRUPTCY AND FAILURE PROSPECTS As we saw with J. Bildner & Sons, small businesses do not always progress smoothly. In fact, the odds of failure are quite high. When things do go wrong and a company fails, what are the major reasons? According to one study of 570 businesses that went bankrupt, owners tend to blame such factors as the economy, insufficient capital, and strong competition. On the other hand, the creditors most often cited insufficient management as the reason for the business failures. Hence, the study's data cast some doubt on the explanations frequently given by small-business owners and managers to the effect that the blame necessarily lies mainly with outside factors.[77] A study by the Small Business Administration's Office of Economic Research of failures in small-business dominated industries during 1990 found vast differences in the failure rates by industry. For example, 578 per 10,000 companies in the amusement and recreation services industry went out of business, while only 13 per 10,000 companies in the educational services industry failed (see Table 21-4). These results suggest that industry conditions may be an important factor in small business and new venture failures.

ETHICAL ISSUES Some experts believe that small businesses are particularly vulnerable to unethical practices. Reasons include the weak financial condition of many small firms, the temptation to offer bribes in order to lure business away from larger competitors, and the relatively small number of checks and balances usually in place in small firms. Other experts argue that small businesses have an advantage in regard to maintaining ethical standards, since their small size enables the owner to detect unethical practices within the firm.[78] Moreover, entrepreneurs who are particularly successful financially can often spearhead ethical actions. For example, Sung Hak Baik, founder of South Korea's Young An Hat Company, contributes 10 to 30 percent of his company's profits each year to charity. The firm is the world's largest manufacturer of hats, many of them licensed sports team caps. Baik became separated from his family during the Korean war and was befriended by a G.I. Among other things, he has purchased the 50-acre site of the G.I. camp where he spent the Korean war and turned it into a complex that includes an orphanage, medical clinic, church, vocational school, and homes for the handicapped and elderly, as well as two hat factories.[79]

FAMILY-LIFE STRESSES Both small-business owners and entrepreneurs often work grueling hours, frequently neglecting their families in the process. One survey found that entrepreneurs commonly work 60 to 70 hours per week and sometimes more during the early years of establishing their businesses. Although some managers, particularly top-level executives of large corporations, also work long hours, small-business owners face added pressure because of the high odds of failure associated with young small ventures. In one case, business pressures led entrepreneur Carl R. Zwerner and his wife of 19 years to obtain a divorce. Zwerner, who runs Glass, Inc., a glass-importing firm in Miami, later donated $500,000 to Georgia State University for a professorship in family-run businesses, with strong emphasis on the conflict between family and business.[80]

DARK SIDE OF ENTREPRENEURSHIP One researcher writes of the "dark side of entrepreneurship," alluding to the creative energy of entrepreneurs that can, at the same time, be a destructive force in building a company. For example, their bias toward action sometimes causes entrepreneurs to act without thinking. Moreover, they often find it very difficult to take directions from others, and they frequently have high needs for control that make it hard for them to delegate responsibility.[81]

NEED FOR OUTSIDE ASSISTANCE Entrepreneurs and small-business owners often do not recognize the need to seek outside assistance from local agencies, such as a state-sponsored small-business development center, or from other advisers. Yet small firms that receive such assistance tend to perform better than those that do not. The best results are usually achieved when the assistance also addresses strategic management issues, which are likely to be somewhat neglected by small businesses.[82]

■ CHAPTER SUMMARY

Entrepreneurship is the creation of new enterprise, and it involves innovation. Three criteria that can be used to evaluate the entrepreneurial opportunity conditions associated with different degrees of innovation are risk, evaluation, and profit potential. Entrepreneurship has been the subject of increasing research and public interest because of important contributions made by new ventures and related small businesses in the areas of economic growth, innovation, employment opportunities, alternatives for women and minorities, and home-based businesses.

A number of factors influence the decision of whether to engage in entrepreneurship. Entrepreneurs tend to have a few personality, background, and other characteristics in common, but these same characteristics are often also associated with managers and individuals in other occupations. Certain life-path circumstances seem to increase the probability that an individual will become an entrepreneur: unsatisfactory work environment,

negative displacement, career transition points, and the presence of positive-pull influencers. Favorable environmental conditions and positive perceptions of desirability and feasibility can also influence individuals to become entrepreneurs.

In considering which development path to pursue, entrepreneurs and prospective small-business owners have three main choices. Entrepreneurs most often start a new firm, although they may sometimes acquire an existing firm and quickly make major changes in its direction. Other small-business owners may acquire existing businesses and retain their basic direction. Alternatively, they may purchase a franchise.

Most experts on small business and entrepreneurship strongly recommend that individuals preparing to start a business develop a business plan. Two of the most important resources needed in starting a new firm are adequate financing and human resources. A number of major factors must be considered when selecting an appropriate site for a business, including the community, the trade area, lease or buy trade-offs, zoning or licensing requirements, and cost per square foot.

The process of managing and developing new ventures and small businesses comprises five major stages of growth: existence, survival, success (including disengagement or growth substages), takeoff, and resource maturity. As businesses reach the resource maturity stage, the emphasis needs to shift from entrepreneurship to intrapreneurship. Entrepreneurs and owners face several particularly important issues and problems in managing their small businesses. These include high bankruptcy and failure prospects, ethical issues, family-life stresses, behaviors of entrepreneurs that can undermine a growing organization, and the need for outside help.

■ QUESTIONS FOR DISCUSSION AND REVIEW

1 Define entrepreneurship. What difficulties might you have in attempting to use this definition to separate entrepreneurship from managing a small business?
2 Outline three criteria that can be used to assess the probable opportunity conditions associated with different degrees of new venture innovation. Use the criteria to evaluate the opportunity conditions inherent in two recent new ventures in your geographic area.
3 Explain the major economic and social contributions of new ventures and other small businesses. Identify specific situations in your geographic area in which entrepreneurship and small-business ownership have made such contributions.
4 What personality traits and other personal characteristics would you use to identify potential entrepreneurs? What advantages and disadvantages exist in using this approach to determine who should receive a loan for a new venture?
5 Explain other important factors that can influence an individual to become an entrepreneur. To what extent could these factors be used to encourage entrepreneurship among one's friends and associates?
6 What major options exist in deciding on a development approach for a new venture? If you were considering a new venture, which would you prefer and why? What are some advantages and disadvantages of purchasing an existing small business or a franchise?
7 Explain the main purposes of a business plan. Why is a well-constructed business plan an important factor in obtaining outside financing and other resources for a new venture?
8 Enumerate several major considerations involved in selecting an appropriate site for a new business. Use these considerations to evaluate the sites of two small businesses in your geographic area.
9 Outline the principal stages in new venture growth. Explain how the J. Bildner & Sons new venture (see the Case in Point) got off track.
10 Identify three common pitfalls associated with entrepreneurship. What could be done to minimize these pitfalls?

■ DISCUSSION QUESTIONS FOR CHAPTER OPENING CASE

1 What factors probably influenced Carolyn Colby to start her new venture?
2 What types of resource problems has Carolyn Colby faced? What resource challenges do you think she will face in the future?
3 From what you know, in which stage of small-business growth would you place Colby Care Nurses, Inc.? On the basis of your analysis, what issues is Carolyn Colby likely to face in the relatively near future?

■ EXERCISES FOR MANAGING IN THE TWENTY-FIRST CENTURY

EXERCISE 1
SELF-ASSESSMENT: LOCUS OF CONTROL ORIENTATION[83]

 The purpose of this exercise is to determine whether you are inclined toward internal or external control. From the pair indicated, select the statement with which you most nearly agree.

1. ____ A. Promotions are earned through hard work and persistence.

   ____ B. Making a lot of money is largely a matter of getting the right breaks.

2. ____ A. In my experience I have noticed that there is usually a direct connection between how hard I study and the grades I get.

   ____ B. Many times the reactions of teachers seem haphazard to me.

3. ____ A. The number of divorces indicates that more and more people are not trying to make their marriages work.

   ____ B. Marriage is largely a gamble.

4. ____ A. When I am right, I can convince others.

   ____ B. It is silly to think that one can really change another person's basic attitudes.

5. ____ A. In our society a person's future earning power is dependent on his or her ability.

   ____ B. Getting promoted is really a matter of being a little luckier than the next guy.

6. ____ A. If one knows how to deal with people, they are really quite easily led.

   ____ B. I have little influence over the way other people believe.

7. ____ A. In my case the grades I make are the results of my own efforts; luck has little or nothing to do with it.

   ____ B. Sometimes I feel that I have little to do with the grades I get.

8. ____ A. People like me can change the course of world affairs if we make ourselves heard.

   ____ B. It is only wishful thinking to believe that one can really influence what happens in society at large.

9. ____ A. I am the master of my life.

   ____ B. A great deal that happens to me is probably a matter of chance.

10. ____ A. Getting along with people is a skill that must be practiced.

    ____ B. It is impossible to figure out how to please some people.

EXERCISE 2
MANAGEMENT EXERCISE: AN ENTREPRENEURIAL OPPORTUNITY

 You have been working as an appliance salesperson at a local store for 3 years. This is your first job after graduating from college, and you took it for several reasons: You wanted to see how a small business is organized and operates, and you wanted some practical, hands-on small-business experience. You were also looking for a niche in which you could eventually set up your own business. Finally, the business is located in an area where you thought you might want to set up a business in the future. You believe your experience in this job has been very valuable.

Yesterday, while you were talking to the owner, he confided that he had long dreamed of setting up a kitchen design and appliance shop in an affluent area on the other side of town. The population of the area is expanding and is expected to continue to do so for the next two decades. The shop would be oriented toward dual-career couples who share some cooking chores, and it would focus on kitchen atmosphere, as well as utility. The owner said that he would be willing to finance such a start-up but could not actually take charge of setting it up himself because of family obligations. He wondered if you knew anyone who would be interested in developing such a project for a large chunk of equity.

You are surprised to learn of his interest in the kitchen design and appliance shop and are definitely interested in the opportunity yourself. The next day, you indicate your interest to the owner, who tells you how much financing he could make available and what equity he would expect in return. His proposal seems fair to you, and you talk it over with several people whom you trust. You are convinced that you could be successful in this type of business, but must study it further.

You recognize that you will need much more information before deciding whether or not to take on this entrepreneurial endeavor. Describe the information you will need and the decisions you should make before involving yourself in this start-up.

CONCLUDING CASE 1

BARBARA GROGAN BEATS OUT BIG-NAME COMPETITION

At 35, Barbara Grogan was out of work and ending a 12-year marriage. For the first time in her life, she faced the problem of how to pay the mortgage and feed her two children. In figuring out what to do, Grogan chose a relatively unusual niche in the construction industry—millwrighting. Her company, Denver-based Western Industrial Contractors, Inc. (WIC), moves and installs mammoth industrial equipment. Millwrighting involves projects such as hanging a four-story theater screen, installing a freestanding stack of storage cubicles eight stories high where the maximum vertical variance cannot exceed an eighth of an inch, and guiding a 100-ton cooling system into a plant with a crane that comes within one-sixteenth of an inch of the building's main support.

Grogan had heard of millwrighting during a 9-month period when she served as general manager of her former husband's crane- and truck-rental company, but she didn't know much about the business. Millwrighting requires huge equipment, such as cranes up to 20 stories high, trucks that are as big as railroad cars, and intricate machinery that must be synchronized perfectly to get the job done.

To compete with the other 4600 millwrighting contractors nationwide, Grogan works hard to get customers and then tries to keep them through outstanding service. "Once I get the clients, I service their socks off," says Grogan. "The client has to win for us to win." For example, Grogan recently received a call at 6 a.m. from a client at a cement factory where a kiln had been knocked out of service by an explosion. The client was losing thousands of dollars every hour that the kiln was out of commission. Grogan had a staff of 12 at the site by 9 a.m.

and had shifts work around the clock for 4 days to repair the kiln. Nevertheless, Grogan charged only her usual fees. She says that she does not like to take advantage of clients when they have troubles. She prefers establishing long-term relationships, which is one reason for her company's success. Recent annual sales exceeded $5 million.

When she began in 1982, Grogan had $50,000 in capital and a limited knowledge of cranes. She went into partnership with a man who had 15 years' experience as a millwright. At the time, the Denver economy was experiencing the beginnings of an economic decline linked to problems in the energy industry. As a result, many construction companies were abandoning union contracting. In a contrary move, Grogan allied herself with the millwright's union. "My business is so specialized," she says. "When you are installing a Mylar press and it can have a vertical variance of only one ten-thousandth of an inch every 80 feet, you need people who know what they are doing." By being a union contractor, Grogan can get the skilled help she needs.

Start-up was difficult. Her initial business plan was sketchy, and people were skeptical. However, when Grogan began interviewing insurance companies to determine insurance needs, she found two people who were receptive and helped her make connections with bankers and a CPA. At this point, she was ready for customers and began making calls. Most of her contact attempts were rebuffed, but she managed to talk with an engineer who had worked in her grandfather's firm. He introduced her to others, and she finally got a contract to install equipment in a bakery.

Her major breakthrough came after she was in business for 8 months and was running out of money. She bid on a contract from the Manville Corporation to disassemble a pipe-manufacturing plant

in Florida, ship it to Malaysia, and reassemble it. Although her own experience was meager, she highlighted the credentials of her employees and won the bid for the 5-month job. Successful completion of this project gave her credibility.

One of her efforts led to a small contract with United Airlines to modify an odd-size conveyor belt at Denver's airport. United was impressed with WIC's service orientation. A series of other contracts with United finally led to a major contract to install an underground baggage-sorting system at Chicago's O'Hare International Airport. The project involved 3 miles of conveyor belts and took 1 year to complete. WIC also does millwrighting for other large firms, including AT&T, Ralston Purina, Nabisco Brands, IBM, and ITT.

Grogan has been able to finance growth from sales, leaving the company in a sound financial position with very little debt. She now employs more than 80 people, has moved her firm into its own new 7000-square-foot building, and recently served as the chair of the Greater Denver Chamber of Commerce. She also has teamed up with a Phoenix relocation expert, Nelson Strickland, to form a new corporate relocation company called Grogan & Strickland, with offices in Denver and Phoenix.[84]

QUESTIONS FOR CONCLUDING CASE 1

1 Why did Grogan decide to become an entrepreneur?

2 Assess the process Grogan followed in setting up business.

3 At what stage of the small-business growth cycle would you place WIC? What factors led to Grogan's success, and how did she enhance her company's success? What dilemmas does she now face in terms of the small-business growth cycle?

CONCLUDING CASE 2

AN ENTREPRENEUR'S GLOBAL STRATEGY

Li Ka-shing is the richest man in Hong Kong, a billionaire many times over. He came from very humble beginnings. After the premature death of his father, the 14-year-old Li began working 16 hours each day, selling plastic belts and watchbands to dealers so that he could support his mother and two younger siblings. At 20, he became general manager of a small company, but 2 years later he started his own business, which made plastic combs and soap boxes. He added plastic flowers to his inventory during the 1950s, when they were popular, and made a fortune exporting them to Europe and America.

Li next launched into real estate development, made a fortune in Hong Kong, and has been expanding his holdings to other parts of the globe. His method of attracting investors in his real estate ventures is unique. He begins by shopping for undervalued assets. For example, in 1988, he acquired 204 acres of waterfront land in Vancouver for the equivalent of $637,000 an acre. (Recently, he sold a 14-acre slice of that property for $2.38 million an acre.) He then sells the investors parts of the to-be-finished product, such as a block of apartments, before he starts construction. Thus the investors cover the construction costs of his projects.

Among Li's many businesses are public firms such as Hutchison Telecom, a mobile phone company that operates in Asia and Europe; drugstores and supermarkets in Hong Kong, China, and Singapore; container ports in Hong Kong and in Felixstowe, England; and 49 percent of Husky Oil. He also has joint ventures with Lockheed (for aircraft maintenance in Guangzhou, China) and Procter & Gamble (for the manufacture of shampoo and face lotion in south China). His personal investments include 49 percent of a building at 60 Broad Street, New York City; 49 percent of Husky Oil; and 9 percent of the Canadian Imperial Bank of Commerce. He recently sold his 50 percent interest in STAR TV, which broadcasts via satellite to Asia and the Middle East, to Rupert Murdoch's New Corp. for $525 million in cash and stock (the sale also included another 14 percent owned through Hutchison).

Li is expanding internationally in several areas. He is now negotiating with Chinese officials to develop a container port in Shanghai. He recently sold 400 condos, in just 3 days, in the first two high-rise apartment buildings in the Vancouver area. He is also negotiating to sell AT&T up to 40 percent of Hutchison Telecom (for a sum reported to be in excess of $500 million).

Li Ka-shing has given his two sons some advice that might be helpful to all who wish to be successful entrepreneurs:

- Be honorable and treat partners right.
- If a 10 percent share is reasonable and you can get 11 percent, take 9 percent because a hundred more deals will come to you.
- Use the expertise of others, whether it's your staff, your partner, or the government.
- Keep your reputation good, work hard, be nice to people, keep your promises. This will always make your business much easier.[85]

QUESTIONS FOR CONCLUDING CASE 2

1 How would you describe Li Ka-shing's personal characteristics?
2 What life-path circumstances could have influenced Li to become an entrepreneur?
3 Explain how Li moved through the stages of starting a small business, enlarging, and finally establishing a global empire.

GLOSSARY

acceptance theory of authority A theory that argues that authority does not depend as much on "persons of authority" who *give* orders as on the willingness to comply of those who *receive* the orders

accommodating A conflict-handling mode that focuses on solving conflicts by allowing the desires of the other party to prevail

accountability The requirement to provide satisfactory reasons for significant deviations from duties or expected results

achievement-oriented Leader behavior that involves setting challenging goals, expecting subordinates to perform at their highest level, and conveying a high degree of confidence in subordinates

acquired-needs theory A theory (developed by McClelland) stating that our needs are acquired or learned on the basis of our life experiences

acquisition The purchase of all or part of one organization by another

active listening The process in which a listener actively participates in attempting to grasp the facts and the feelings being expressed by the speaker

activity A work component to be accomplished

ad hoc committee Another term for *task force*

adjourning A stage in which group members prepare for disengagement as the group nears successful completion of its goals

administrative management An approach that focuses on principles that can be used by managers to coordinate the internal activities of organizations

administrative protections A type of trade barrier in the form of various rules and regulations that make it more difficult for foreign firms to conduct business in a particular country

adverse impact The effect produced when a job selection rate for a protected group is less than 80 percent of the rate for the majority group

affirmative action Any special activity undertaken by employers to increase equal employment opportunities for groups protected by federal equal employment opportunity laws and related regulations

affirmative action plan A written, systematic plan that specifies goals and timetables for hiring, training, promoting, and retaining groups protected by federal equal employment laws and related regulations

aggregate production planning The process of planning how to match supply with product or service demand over a time horizon of about 1 year

alternative work schedules Schedules based on adjustments in the normal work schedule rather than in the job content or activities

amoral management An approach that is neither immoral nor moral but, rather, ignores or is oblivious to ethical considerations

anchoring and adjustment The tendency to be influenced by an initial figure, even when the information is largely irrelevant

antifreeloader argument An argument that holds that since businesses benefit from a better society, they should bear part of the costs by actively working to bring about solutions to social problems

application blank A form containing a series of inquiries about such issues as an applicant's educational background, previous job experience, physical health, and other information that may be useful in assessing an individual's ability to perform a job

applications software packages Software programs available for sale or lease from commercial sources

artificial intelligence A field of information technology aimed at developing computers that have humanlike capabilities, such as seeing, hearing, and thinking

assessment center A controlled environment used to predict the probable managerial success of individuals mainly on the basis of evaluations of their behaviors in a variety of simulated situations

asset management ratios Financial ratios that measure how effectively an organization manages its assets

attribution theory A theory that attempts to explain how individuals make judgments or attributions about the causes of another's or their own behavior

authority The right to make decisions, carry out actions, and direct others in matters related to the duties and goals of a person

autocratic Behavioral style of leaders who tend to make unilateral decisions, dictate work methods, limit worker knowledge about goals to just the next step to be performed, and sometimes give feedback that is punitive

autonomy The amount of discretion allowed in determining schedules and work methods for achieving the required output

availability The tendency to judge the likelihood of an occurrence on the basis of the extent to which other like instances or occurrences can easily be recalled

avoiding A conflict-handling mode that involves ignoring or suppressing a conflict in the hope that it will either go away or not become too disruptive

balance of payments An account of goods and services, capital loans, gold, and other items entering and leaving a country

balance of trade The difference between a country's exports and imports

balance sheet A financial statement that depicts an organization's assets and claims against those assets at a given point in time

bankruptcy A strategy in which an organization that is unable to pay its debts can seek court protection from creditors and from certain contract obligations while it attempts to regain financial stability

BCG growth-share matrix A four-cell matrix (developed by the Boston Consulting Group) that compares various businesses in an organization's portfolio on the basis of relative market share and market growth rate

behavior modification The use of techniques associated with reinforcement theory

behavioral displacement A condition in which individuals engage in behaviors that are encouraged by controls and related reward systems even though the behaviors are actually inconsistent with organizational goals

behavioral science An approach that emphasizes *scientific research* as the basis for developing theories about human behavior in organizations that can be used to establish practical guidelines for managers

behavioral viewpoint A perspective on management that emphasizes the importance of attempting to understand the various factors that affect human behavior in organizations

behaviorally anchored rating scales (BARS) Scales that contain sets of specific behaviors that represent gradations of performance used as common reference points (or anchors) for rating employees on various job dimensions

belongingness needs Needs that involve the desire to affiliate with and be accepted by others

benchmarking The process of identifying the best practices and approaches by comparing productivity in specific areas within one's own company with the productivity of other organizations both within and outside the industry

benefits Forms of compensation beyond wages for time worked, including various protection plans, services, pay for time not worked, and income supplements

bill of materials (BOM) A listing of all components, including partially assembled pieces and basic parts, that make up an end product

bona fide occupational qualification (BFOQ) A legitimate job qualification that necessitates an employer's selecting an individual in a certain sex, religion, national-origin, or age group

boundary spanning Creating roles within the organization that interface with important elements in the environment

bounded rationality A concept that suggests that the ability of managers to be perfectly rational in making decisions is limited by such factors as cognitive capacity and time constraints

brainstorming A technique that encourages group members to generate as many novel ideas as possible on a given topic without evaluating them

break-even analysis A graphic model that helps decision makers understand the relationships among sales volume, costs, and revenues in an organization

broadbanding A compensation approach whereby as many as four or five traditional grades are collapsed into a single grade or band, thus providing managers with more flexibility in setting salaries

budgeting The process of stating in quantitative terms, usually dollars, planned organizational activities for a given period of time

buffering Stockpiling either inputs into or outputs from a production or service process in order to cope with environmental fluctuations

bureaucratic control A managerial approach that relies on regulation through rules, policies, supervision, budgets, schedules, reward systems, and other administrative mechanisms aimed at ensuring that employees exhibit appropriate behaviors and meet performance standards

bureaucratic management An approach that emphasizes the need for organizations to operate in a rational manner rather than relying on the arbitrary whims of owners and managers

business plan A document written by the prospective owner or entrepreneur that details the nature of the business, the product or service, the customers, the competition, the production and marketing methods, the management, the financing, and other significant aspects of the proposed business venture

business-level strategy A type of strategy that concentrates on the best means of competing within a particular business while also supporting the corporate-level strategy

capacity argument An argument that states that the private sector, because of its considerable economic and human resources, must make up for recent government cutbacks in social programs

capacity planning The process of determining the people, machines, and major physical resources, such as buildings, that will be necessary to meet the production objectives of the organization

capacity requirements planning A technique for determining what personnel and equipment are needed to meet short-term production objectives

capital expenditures budget A plan for the acquisition or divestiture of major fixed assets, such as land, buildings, or equipment

capitalist economy An economy in which economic activity is governed by market forces and the means of production are privately owned by individuals

carrying, or **holding, cost** The expenses associated with keeping an item on hand (such as storage, insurance, pilferage, breakage)

centralization The extent to which power and authority are retained at the top organizational levels

ceremonial A system of rites performed in conjunction with a single occasion or event

chain of command The unbroken line of authority that ultimately links each individual with the top organizational position through a managerial position at each successive layer in between

change Any alteration of the status quo

change agent An individual with a fresh perspective and a knowledge of the behavioral sciences who acts as a catalyst in helping the organization approach old problems in new or innovative ways

charisma A leadership factor that comprises the leader's ability to inspire pride, faith, and respect; to recognize what is really important; and to articulate effectively a sense of mission, or vision, that inspires followers

clan control A managerial approach that relies on values, beliefs, traditions, corporate culture, shared norms, and informal relationships to regulate employee behaviors and facilitate the reaching of organizational goals

classical viewpoint A perspective on management that emphasizes finding ways to manage work and organizations more efficiently

closed system A system that does little or no interacting with its environment and receives little feedback

code of ethics A document prepared for the purpose of guiding organization members when they encounter an ethical dilemma

coercive power Power that depends on the ability to punish others when they do not engage in desired behaviors

cognitive theories Theories that attempt to isolate the thinking patterns that we use in deciding whether or not to behave in a certain way

collaborating A conflict-handling mode that strives to resolve conflicts by devising solutions that allow both parties to achieve their desired outcomes

collectivism A condition whereby the demands and interests of the group are given precedence over the desires and needs of individuals

command, or **functional, group** A formal group consisting of a manager and all the subordinates who report to that manager

communication The exchange of messages between people for the purpose of achieving common meanings

communication channels Patterns of organizational communication flow that represent potential established conduits through which managers and other organization members can send and receive information

communication network The pattern of information flow among task group members

compensation Wages paid directly for time worked, as well as more indirect benefits that employees receive as part of their employment relationship with an organization

competing A conflict-handling mode that involves attempting to win a conflict at the other party's expense

competitive advantage A significant edge over the competition in dealing with competitive forces

competitive advantage of nations The concept that environmental elements within a nation can foster innovation in certain industries, thereby increasing the prospects for the success of home-based companies operating internationally within those industries

competitors Other organizations that either offer or have a high potential of offering rival products or services

complacency A condition in which individuals either do not see the signs of danger or opportunity or ignore them

compressed workweek A work schedule whereby employees work four 10-hour days or some similar combination, rather than the usual five 8-hour days

compromising A conflict-handling mode that aims to solve conflict issues by having each party give up some desired outcomes in order to get other desired outcomes

computer hardware Physical computer equipment, including the computer itself and related devices

computer software The set of programs, documents, procedures, and routines associated with the operation of a computer system that makes the hardware capable of its various activities

computer virus A small program, usually hidden inside another program, that replicates itself and surfaces at a predetermined time to cause disruption and possibly destruction

computer-aided design (CAD) A system that uses computers to geometrically prepare, review, and evaluate product designs

computer-aided manufacturing (CAM) A system that uses computers to design and control production processes

computer-based information systems (CBISs) Information systems that involve the use of computer technology

computer-integrated manufacturing (CIM) The computerized integration of all major functions associated with the production of a product

concentration An approach that focuses on effecting the growth of a single product or service or a small number of closely related products or services

conceptual skills Skills related to the ability to visualize the organization as a whole, discern interrelationships among organizational parts, and understand how the organization fits into the wider context of the industry, community, and world

concurrent control The regulation of ongoing activities that are part of the transformation process to ensure that they conform to organizational standards

conflict A perceived difference between two or more parties that results in mutual opposition

consideration The degree to which a leader builds mutual trust with subordinates, respects their ideas, and shows concern for their feelings

contingency planning The development of alternative plans for use in the event that environmental conditions evolve differently than anticipated, rendering original plans unwise or unfeasible

contingency theory A viewpoint that argues that appropriate managerial action depends on the particular parameters of the situation

contingent workers Those workers hired on a temporary or sporadic basis to handle areas of fluctuating demand or changing needs that cannot be met by the organization's traditional, full-time workers

continuous-process production A type of technology in which products are liquids, solids, or gases that are made through a continuous process

control system A set of mechanisms designed to increase the probability of meeting organizational standards and goals

controlling The process of regulating organizational activities so that actual performance conforms to expected organizational standards and goals

convergent thinking The effort to solve problems by beginning with a problem and attempting to move logically to a solution

co-opting Absorbing key members of important environmental elements into the leadership or policy-making structure of an organization

corporate culture The term sometimes used for *organizational culture*

corporate philanthropy Corporate contributions for charitable and social responsibility purposes

corporate social responsibility A term often used in reference to the concept of organizational social responsibility as applied to business organizations

corporate social responsiveness A term used in reference to the concept of organizational social responsiveness as applied to business organizations

corporate-level strategy A type of strategy that addresses what businesses the organization will operate, how the strategies of those businesses will be coordinated to strengthen the organization's competitive position, and how resources will be allocated among the businesses

corridor principle A principle which states that the process of beginning a new venture helps entrepreneurs visualize other opportunities that they could not envision or take advantage of until they started the initial venture

cost leadership strategy A strategy outlined by Porter that involves emphasizing organizational efficiency so that the overall costs of providing products and services are lower than those of competitors

creativity The cognitive process of developing an idea, concept, commodity, or discovery viewed as novel by its creator or a target audience

crisis problem A serious difficulty requiring immediate action

critical path The path in the network that will take the longest to complete

customer divisions Divisions set up to service particular types of clients or customers

customers and clients Those individuals and organizations that purchase an organization's products and/or services

cybernetic control system A self-regulating control system that, once it is put into operation, can automatically monitor the situation and take corrective action when necessary

data Unanalyzed facts and figures

data base A set of data organized efficiently in a central location so that it can serve a number of information system applications

data workers Individuals who mainly process and disseminate documents, messages, and related information

data-base management system The software that allows an organization to build, manage, and provide access to its stored data

debt capital A type of financing that involves a loan to be repaid, usually with interest

debt management ratios Financial ratios that assess the extent to which an organization uses debt to finance investments, as well as the degree to which it is able to meet its long-term obligations

decentralization The extent to which power and authority are delegated to lower levels

deciding to decide A response in which decision makers accept the challenge of deciding what to do about a problem and follow an effective decision-making process

decision making The process through which managers identify organizational problems and attempt to resolve them

decision support system (DSS) A computer-based information system that supports the process of managerial decision making in situations that are not well structured

decision tree A graphic model that displays the structure of a sequence of alternative courses of action and usually shows the payoffs associated with various paths and the probabilities associated with potential future conditions

decoding The process of translating the symbols into the interpreted message

defensive avoidance A condition in which individuals either deny the importance of a danger or an opportunity or deny any responsibility for taking action

defensive strategies Strategies that focus on the desire or need to reduce organizational operations, usually through cost and/or asset reductions

delegation The assignment of part of a manager's work to others, along with both the responsibility and the authority necessary to achieve expected results

delphi method A structured approach to gaining the judgments of a number of experts on a specific issue relating to the future

democratic Behavioral style of leaders who tend to involve the group in decision making, let the group determine work methods, make overall goals known, and use feedback as an opportunity for helpful coaching

departmentalization The clustering of individuals into units and of units into departments and larger units in order to facilitate achieving organizational goals

dependent demand inventory A type of inventory consisting of the raw materials, components, and subassemblies that are used in the production of an end product or service.

descriptive decision-making models Models of decision making that attempt to document how managers actually *do* make decisions

developed countries A group of countries that is characterized by a high level of economic or industrial development and that includes the United States, western Europe, Canada, Australia, New Zealand, and Japan

devil's advocates Individuals who are assigned the role of making sure that the negative aspects of any attractive decision alternatives are considered

dialectical inquiry A procedure in which a decision situation is approached from two opposite points of view

differentiation The extent to which organizational units differ from one another in terms of the behaviors and orientations of their members and their formal structures

differentiation paradox The idea that although separating efforts to innovate from the rest of the organization increases the likelihood of developing radical ideas, such differentiation also decreases the likelihood that the radical ideas will ever be implemented

differentiation strategy A strategy outlined by Porter that involves attempting to develop products and services that are viewed as unique in the industry

direct contact Communication between two or more persons at similar levels in different work units for purposes of coordinating work and solving problems

direct investment The establishment of operating facilities in a foreign country

directive Leader behavior that involves letting subordinates know what is expected of them, providing guidance about work methods, developing work schedules, identifying work evaluation standards, and indicating the basis for outcomes or rewards

discretionary expense center A responsibility center whose budgetary performance is based on achieving its goals by operating within predetermined expense constraints set

through managerial judgment or discretion

distinctive competence A strength that is unique and that competitors cannot easily match or imitate

divergent thinking The effort to solve problems by generating new ways of viewing a problem and seeking novel alternatives

diversification An approach that entails effecting growth through the development of new areas that are clearly distinct from current businesses

divestiture A strategy that involves an organization's selling or divesting of a business or part of a business

divisional structure A structure in which positions are grouped according to similarity of products, services, or markets

domain shifts Changes in the mix of products and services offered so that an organization will interface with more favorable environmental elements

downsizing The process of significantly reducing the layers of middle management, increasing the spans of control, and shrinking the size of the work force

downward communication Vertical communication that flows from a higher level to one or more lower levels in the organization

driving forces Factors that pressure *for* a particular change

econometric models Systems of simultaneous multiple regression equations involving several predictor variables that are used to identify and measure relationships or interrelationships that exist in the economy

economic element The systems of producing, distributing, and consuming wealth

economic order quantity (EOQ) An inventory control method developed to minimize ordering plus holding costs, while avoiding stockout costs

effectiveness The ability to choose appropriate goals and achieve them

efficiency The ability to make the best use of available resources in the process of achieving goals

effort-performance (E→P) expectancy Our assessment of the probability that our efforts will lead to the required performance level

electronic mail system A mail system that allows high-speed exchange of written messages through the use of computerized text-processing and communication networks

electronic monitoring The practice of using computers to continually assess employee performance

employee assistance program (EAP) A program through which employers help employees overcome personal problems that are adversely affecting their job performance

employment test A means of assessing a job applicant's characteristics through paper-and-pencil responses or simulated exercises

encoding The process of translating the intended message into words and gestures

end user The same as a *user*

end-user computing The development and/or management of information systems by users

enlightened self-interest argument An argument that holds that businesses exist at society's pleasure and that, for their own legitimacy and survival, businesses should meet the expectations of the public regarding social responsibility

entrepreneur An individual who creates a new enterprise

entrepreneurial team A group of individuals with diverse expertise and backgrounds who are brought together to develop and implement innovative ideas aimed at creating new products or services or significantly improving existing ones

entrepreneurship The creation of new enterprise

environmental complexity The number of elements in an organization's environment and their degree of similarity

environmental dynamism The rate and predictability of change in the elements of an organization's environment

environmental munificence The extent to which the environment can support sustained growth and stability

environmental uncertainty A condition in which future environmental circumstances affecting an organization cannot be accurately assessed and predicted

equity capital A type of financing which usually requires that the investor be given some form of ownership in the venture

equity theory A theory that argues that we prefer situations of balance, or equity, which exists when we perceive the ratio of our inputs and outcomes to be equal to the ratio of inputs and outcomes for a comparison other

ERG theory An alternative (proposed by Alderfer) to Maslow's hierarchy of needs theory which argues that there are three levels of individual needs

escalation situations Situations that signal the strong possibility of escalating commitment and accelerating losses

esteem needs Needs related to the two-pronged desire to have a positive self-image and to have our contributions valued and appreciated by others

ethics audits Systematic efforts to assess conformance to organizational ethical policies, aid understanding of those policies, and identify serious breaches requiring remedial action

ethics committee A group charged with helping to establish policies and resolve major questions involving ethical issues confronting organization members in the course of their work

ethics hot line A special telephone line established to enable employees to bypass the normal chain of command in reporting grievances and serious ethical problems

ethnocentric orientation An approach to international management whereby executives assume that practices that work in the headquarters or home country must necessarily work elsewhere

exchange rate The rate at which one country's currency can be exchanged for another country's currency

executive support system (ESS) A computer-based information system that supports decision making and effective functioning at the top levels of an organization

existence needs Needs that include the various forms of material and physiological desires, such as food and water, as well as such work-related forms as pay, fringe benefits, and physical working conditions

expatriates Individuals who are not citizens of the countries in which they are assigned to work

expectancy theory A theory (originally proposed by Vroom) that argues that we consider three main issues before we expend the effort necessary to perform at a given level

expected value The sum of the payoffs times the respective probabilities for a given alternative

expert power Power that is based on the possession of expertise that is valued by others

expert systems Computer-based systems that apply the substantial knowledge of an expert to help solve specialized problems

explanatory, or **causal, models** Models that attempt to identify the major variables that are related to or have caused particular past conditions and then use current measures of those variables (predictors) to predict future conditions

exporting The process of making a product in the home country and sending it overseas

expropriation The seizure of a foreign company's assets by a host-country government

external environment The major forces outside the organization that have the potential to significantly influence the likely success of products or services

extinction A technique that involves withholding previously available positive consequences associated with a behavior in order to *decrease* that behavior

extrinsic rewards Rewards that are provided by others, such as bonuses, awards, or promotions

facilities The land, buildings, equipment, and other major physical inputs that substantially determine productivity capacity, require time to alter, and involve significant capital investments

feedback Information about results and organizational status relative to the environment; the degree to which the job provides for clear, timely information about performance results; the receiver's basic response to the interpreted message

feedback control Regulation exercised after a product or service has been completed to ensure that the final output meets organizational standards and goals

feedforward control The regulation of inputs to ensure that they meet the standards necessary for the transformation process

Fiedler's contingency model A situational approach (developed by Fiedler and his associates) that posits that leaders differ in the degrees of their orientation toward the task versus toward the people

financial statement A summary of a major aspect of an organization's financial status

finished-goods inventory The stock of items that have been produced and are awaiting sale or transit to a customer

first-line managers/supervisors Managers at the lowest level of the hierarchy who are directly responsible for the work of operating (nonmanagerial) employees

five competitive forces model Porter's approach to analyzing the nature and intensity of competition in a given industry in terms of five major forces

fixed-interval schedule of reinforcement A pattern in which a reinforcer is administered on a fixed time schedule, assuming that the desired behavior has continued at an appropriate level

fixed-position layout A production configuration in which the product or client remains in one location and the tools, equipment, and expertise are brought to it, as necessary, to complete the productive process

fixed-ratio schedule of reinforcement A pattern in which a reinforcer is provided after a fixed number of occurrences of the desired behavior

flat structure A structure that has few hierarchical levels and wide spans of control

flexible manufacturing system (FMS) A manufacturing system that uses computers to control machines and the production process automatically so that different types of parts or product configurations can be handled on the same production line

flextime A work schedule that specifies certain core hours when individuals are expected to be on the job and then allows flexibility in starting and quitting times as long as individuals work the total number of required hours per day

focus strategy A strategy outlined by Porter that entails specializing by establishing a position of overall cost leadership, differentiation, or both, but only within a particular portion, or segment, of an entire market

force-field analysis A method that involves analyzing the two types of forces, driving forces and restraining forces, that influence any proposed change and then assessing how best to overcome resistance

forecasting The process of making predictions about changing conditions and future events that may significantly affect the business of an organization

formal communication Vertical and horizontal communication that follows paths specified by the official hierarchical organization structure and related task requirements

formal group A group officially created by an organization for a specific purpose

formalization The degree to which written policies, rules, procedures, job descriptions, and other documents specify what actions are (or are not) to be taken under a given set of circumstances

forming A stage in which group members attempt to assess the ground rules that will apply to a task and to group interaction

framing The tendency to make different decisions depending on how a problem is presented

franchise A continuing arrangement between a franchiser and a franchisee in which the franchiser's knowledge, image, manufacturing or service expertise, and marketing techniques are made available to the franchisee in return for the payment of various fees or royalties and conformity to standard operating procedures

franchisee An individual who purchases a franchise and, in the process, is given the opportunity to enter a new business, hopefully with an enhanced chance of success

franchiser A manufacturer or sole distributor of a trademarked product or service who typically has considerable experience in the line of business being franchised

frustration-regression principle A principle that states that if we are *continually* frustrated in our attempts to satisfy a higher-level need, we may cease to be concerned about that need

functional authority The authority of staff departments over others in the organization in matters related directly to their respective functions

functional managers Managers who have responsibility for a specific, specialized area of the organization and supervise mainly individuals with expertise and training in that area

functional structure A structure in which positions are grouped according to their main functional (or specialized) area

functional-level strategy A type of strategy that focuses on action plans for managing a particular functional area within a business in a way that supports the business-level strategy

fundamental attribution error The tendency to underestimate the importance of situational influences and to overestimate the importance of dispositional influences in explaining behavior

futurists Individuals who track significant trends in the environment and attempt to predict their impact on the organization

gainsharing A compensation system in which employees throughout an organization are encouraged to become involved in solving problems and are then given bonuses tied to organizationwide performance improvements

Gantt chart A specialized bar chart developed by Henry L. Gantt that shows the current progress on each major project activity relative to necessary completion dates

garbage-can model A model stating that managers behave in virtually a random pattern in making nonprogrammed decisions

general managers Managers who have responsibility for a whole organization or a substantial subunit that includes most of the common specialized areas

geocentric orientation An approach to international management whereby executives believe that a global view is needed in both the headquarters of the parent company and its various subsidiaries and that the best individuals, regardless of host- or home-country origin, should be utilized to solve company problems anywhere in the world

geographic divisions Divisions designed to serve different geographic areas

goal A future target or end result that an organization wishes to achieve

goal commitment One's attachment to, or determination to reach, a goal

goal incongruence A condition in which there are major incompatibilities between the goals of an organization member and those of the organization

government agencies Agencies that provide services and monitor compliance with laws and regulations at local, state or regional, and national levels

grand strategy A master strategy that provides the basic strategic direction at the corporate level

grapevine Another term for *informal communication*

graphic rating scales Scales that list a number of factors, including general behaviors and characteristics, on which an employee is rated by the supervisor

group Two or more interdependent individuals who interact and influence each other in collective pursuit of a common goal

group cohesiveness The degree to which members are attracted to a group, are motivated to remain in the group, and are mutually influenced by one another

group decision-support system (GDSS) A computer-based information system that supports decision makers working together to solve problems that are not well structured

group maintenance roles Roles that do not directly address a task itself but, instead, help foster group unity, positive interpersonal relations among group members, and development of the ability of members to work together effectively

group task roles Roles that help a group develop and accomplish its goals

group technology The classification of parts into families (groups of parts or products that have some similarities in the way they are manufactured) so that members of the same family can be manufactured on the same production line

groupthink The tendency in cohesive groups to seek agreement about an issue at the expense of realistically appraising the situation

groupware Software designed to support collaborative efforts among group members, such as scheduling meetings, holding meetings, collaborating on projects, and sharing documents

growth needs Needs that impel creativity and innovation, along with the desire to have a productive impact on our surroundings

growth strategies Grand strategies that involve organizational expansion along some major dimension

growth-need strength The degree to which an individual needs personal growth and development on the job

hackers Individuals who are knowledgeable about computers and who gain unauthorized entry to, and sometimes tamper with, computer networks and files of organizations with which they have no affiliation

halo effect The tendency to use a general impression based on one or a few characteristics of an individual to judge other characteristics of that same individual

hand of government A view that argues that the interests of society are best served by having the regulatory hands of the law and the political process, rather than the invisible

hand, guide the results of corporations' endeavors

hand of management A view that states that corporations and their managers are expected to act in ways that protect and improve the welfare of society as a whole as well as advance corporate economic interests

harvest A strategy that entails minimizing investments while attempting to maximize short-run profits and cash flow, with the long-run intention of exiting the market

Hawthorne effect The possibility that individuals singled out for a study may improve their performance simply because of the added attention they receive from the researchers, rather than because of any specific factors being tested

Hawthorne studies A group of studies conducted at the Hawthorne plant of the Western Electric Company during the late 1920s and early 1930s whose results ultimately led to the human relations view of management

hierarchy of needs theory A theory (developed by Maslow) that argues that individual needs form a five-level hierarchy

high context cultures Cultures in which the emphasis in the communication process is on establishing and strengthening relationships in the course of exchanging information

horizontal communication Lateral or diagonal message exchange either within work-unit boundaries, involving peers who report to the same supervisor, or across work-unit boundaries, involving individuals who report to different supervisors

horizontal coordination The linking of activities across departments at similar levels

human resource management (HRM) The management of various activities designed to enhance the effectiveness of an organization's work force in achieving organizational goals

human resource planning The process of determining future human resource needs relative to an organization's strategic plan and devising the steps necessary to meet those needs

human skills Skills associated with a manager's ability to work well with

others, both as a member of a group and as a leader who gets things done through others

hybrid structure A structure that adopts parts of both functional and divisional structures at the same level of management

hygiene factors Factors that seem to make individuals feel dissatisfied with their jobs

hypercompetition A state of rapidly escalating competition in which competitors make frequent, daring, and aggressive moves that have the cumulative effect of creating conditions of continual disequilibrium and change in the industry

idea champion An individual who generates a new idea or believes in the value of a new idea and supports it in the face of numerous potential obstacles

immoral management An approach that not only lacks ethical principles but is actively opposed to ethical behavior

import quota A type of trade barrier in the form of a limit on the amount of a product that may be imported over a given period of time

income statement A financial statement that summarizes the financial results of company operations over a specified time period, such as a quarter or a year

incremental model A model stating that managers make the smallest response possible that will reduce the problem to at least a tolerable level

incrementalist approach An approach to controlling an innovative project that relies heavily on clan control but also involves a phased set of plans and accompanying bureaucratic controls that begin at a very general level and grow more specific as the project progresses

incubator An organization whose purpose is to nurture new ventures in their very early stages by providing space (usually at a site housing other new ventures as well), stimulation, support, and a variety of basic services, often at reduced fees

independent demand inventory A type of inventory consisting of end products, parts used for repairs, and other items whose demand is tied more directly to market issues than that for dependent demand inventory items

indigenization laws Laws which require that citizens of the host country hold a majority interest in all firms operating within the country's borders

individualism A condition whereby personal interests are afforded greater weight than the needs of the group

individualism-collectivism A cultural dimension that involves the degree to which individuals concern themselves with their own interests and those of their immediate families as opposed to the interests of a larger group

individualized consideration A leadership factor that involves delegating projects to help develop each follower's capabilities, paying personal attention to each follower's needs, and treating each follower as an individual worthy of respect

informal communication Communication that takes place without regard to hierarchical or task requirements

informal group A group that is established by employees, rather than by the organization, to serve group members' interests or social needs

informal leader An individual, other than the formal leader, who emerges from a group, has major influence, and is perceived by group members as a leader

information Data that have been analyzed or processed into a form that is meaningful for decision makers

information architecture A long-range plan for investing in and organizing information technology so as to facilitate reaching organizational goals

information power Power that results from access to and control over the distribution of important information about organizational operations and future plans

information system A set of procedures designed to collect (or retrieve), process, store, and disseminate information to support planning, decision making, coordination, and control

infrastructure The highways, rail-

ways, airports, sewage facilities, housing, educational institutions, recreation facilities, and other economic and social amenities that signal the extent of economic development in an area

initiating structure The degree to which a leader defines his or her own role and the roles of subordinates in terms of achieving unit goals

innovation A new idea applied to initiating or improving a process, product, or service

inputs The various human, material, financial, equipment, and informational resources required to produce goods and services

institutional power A need for power in which individuals focus on working with others to solve problems and further organizational goals

integration The extent to which there is collaboration among departments that need to coordinate their efforts

intellectual stimulation A leadership factor that involves offering new ideas to stimulate followers to rethink old ways of doing things, encouraging followers to look at problems from multiple vantage points, and fostering creative breakthroughs in obstacles that had seemed insurmountable

internal environment The general conditions that exist within an organization

international business Profit-related activities conducted across national boundaries

international element The developments in countries outside an organization's home country that have the potential to influence the organization

international management The process of planning, organizing, leading, and controlling in organizations engaged in international business

intrapreneurs Individuals who engage in entrepreneurial roles inside organizations

intrapreneurship The process of innovating within an existing organization

intrinsic rewards Rewards that are related to our own internal experiences with successful performance,

such as feelings of achievement, challenge, and growth

inventory A stock of materials that are used to facilitate production or to satisfy customer demand

investment center A responsibility center whose budgetary performance is based on return on investment

invisible hand A view that holds that the entire social responsibility of a corporation can be summed up as "make profits and obey the law"

iron law of responsibility A law that states that "in the long run, those who do not use power in a manner that society considers responsible will tend to lose it"

issues management The process of identifying a relatively small number of emerging social issues of particular relevance to the organization, analyzing their potential impact, and preparing an effective response

item cost The price of an inventory item itself

Japanese management An approach that focuses on aspects of management in Japan that may be appropriate for adoption in the United States

job analysis The systematic collection and recording of information concerning the purpose of a job, its major duties, the conditions under which it is performed, the contacts with others that job performance requires, and the knowledge, skills, and abilities needed to perform the job effectively

job characteristics model A model developed to guide job enrichment efforts that include consideration of core job characteristics, critical psychological states, and outcomes

job depth The degree to which individuals can plan and control the work involved in their jobs

job description A statement of the duties, working conditions, and other significant requirements associated with a particular job

job design The specification of task activities associated with a particular job

job enlargement The allocation of a wider variety of similar tasks to a job in order to make it more challenging

job enrichment The process of upgrading the job-task mix in order to increase significantly the potential for growth, achievement, responsibility, and recognition

job evaluation A systematic process of establishing the relative worth of jobs within a single organization in order to determine equitable pay differentials among jobs

job posting A practice whereby information about job vacancies is placed in conspicuous places in an organization, such as on bulletin boards or in organizational newsletters

job rotation The practice of periodically shifting workers through a set of jobs in a planned sequence

job scope The number of different tasks an employee performs in a particular job

job sharing A work practice in which two or more people share a single full-time job

job simplification The process of configuring jobs so that jobholders have only a small number of narrow activities to perform

job specification A statement of the skills, abilities, education, and previous work experience that are required to perform a particular job

joint venture An agreement involving two or more organizations that arrange to produce a product or service jointly

judgmental forecasting A type of forecasting that relies mainly on individual judgments or committee agreements regarding future conditions

jury of executive opinion A means of forecasting in which organization executives hold a meeting and estimate, as a group, a forecast for a particular item

just-in-time (JIT) inventory control An approach to inventory control that emphasizes having materials arrive just as they are needed in the production process

Kanban A simple parts-movement system that depends on cards and containers to pull parts from one work center to another

kinesic behavior Body movements, such as gestures, facial expressions, eye movements, and posture

knowledge work system (KWS) A computer-based information system that assists knowledge workers in the creation of new knowledge for the organization

knowledge workers Specialists, such as engineers, architects, or scientists, who design products, services, or processes and create new knowledge for organizations

labor supply Those individuals who are potentially employable by an organization

labor-management relations The process through which employers and unions negotiate pay, hours of work, and other conditions of employment; sign a contract governing such conditions for a specific period of time; and share responsibilities for administering the resulting contract

laissez-faire Behavioral style of leaders who generally give the group complete freedom, provide necessary materials, participate only to answer questions, and avoid giving feedback

large-batch and mass production A type of technology in which products are manufactured in large quantities, frequently on an assembly line

lateral relations The coordination of efforts through communicating and problem solving with peers in other departments or units, rather than referring most issues up the hierarchy for resolution

law of effect A concept that states that behaviors having pleasant or positive consequences are more likely to be repeated and that behaviors having unpleasant or negative consequences are less likely to be repeated

leadership The process of influencing others to achieve organizational goals

leading The process of influencing others to engage in the work behaviors necessary to reach organizational goals

leading indicators Variables that tend to be correlated with the phenomenon of major interest but also tend to occur in advance of that phenomenon

legal-political element The legal and governmental systems within which an organization must function

legitimate power Power that stems from a position's placement in the managerial hierarchy and the authority vested in the position

less developed countries (LDCs) A group of noncommunist countries, often called the "third world," that consists primarily of relatively poor nations characterized by low per capita income, little industry, and high birthrates

liaison role A role to which a specific individual is appointed to facilitate communication and resolution of issues between two or more departments

licensing An agreement in which one organization gives limited rights to another to use certain of its assets, such as expertise, patents, copyrights, or equipment, for an agreed-upon fee or royalty

life cycles Predictable stages of development that organizations typically follow

line authority The authority that follows the chain of command established by the formal hierarchy

line position A position that has authority and responsibility for achieving the major goals of the organization

linear programming (LP) A quantitative tool for planning how to allocate limited or scarce resources so that a single criterion or goal (often profits) is optimized

liquidation A strategy that entails selling or dissolving an entire organization

liquidity ratios Financial ratios that measure the degree to which an organization's current assets are adequate to pay current liabilities (current debt obligations)

local area networks (LANs) Interconnections (usually by cable) that allow communications among computers within a single building or in close proximity

logical office The concept that portable microcomputers allow an individual's office to be anywhere the individual is, rather than being restricted to one specific location

low context cultures Cultures in which the emphasis in the communication process is on exchanging information and is less focused on building relationships

LPC (least preferred coworker) orientation A personality trait indicating the extent to which an individual places a higher priority or value on task accomplishment than on personal relationships

management The process of achieving organizational goals by engaging in the four major functions of planning, organizing, leading, and controlling

management by exception A control principle which suggests that managers should be informed of a situation only if control data show a significant deviation from standards

management by objectives (MBO) A process through which specific goals are set collaboratively for the organization as a whole and every unit and individual within it; the goals are then used as a basis for planning, managing organizational activities, and assessing and rewarding contributions

management by wandering around (MBWA) A practice whereby managers frequently tour areas for which they are responsible, talk to various employees, and encourage upward communication

management information system (MIS) A computer-based information system that produces routine reports and often allows on-line access to current and historical information needed by managers mainly at the middle and first-line levels

management information systems The field of management that focuses on designing and implementing computer-based information systems for use by management

management science An approach aimed at increasing decision effectiveness through the use of sophisticated mathematical models and statistical methods

managerial ethics Standards of conduct and moral judgment used by managers of organizations in carrying out their business

managerial integrator A separate manager who is given the task of coordinating related work that involves several functional departments

managing diversity The planning and implementing of organizational systems and practices that maximize the potential of employees to contribute to organizational goals and develop their capabilities unhindered by group identities such as race, gender, age, or ethnic group

manufacturing resource planning (MRP II) A computer-based information system that integrates the production planning and control activities of basic MRP systems with related financial, accounting, personnel, engineering, and marketing information

market control A managerial approach that relies on market mechanisms to regulate prices for certain clearly specified goods and services needed by an organization

masculinity-femininity A cultural dimension that involves the extent to which a society emphasizes traditional male values, such as assertiveness, competitiveness, and material success, rather than traditional female values, such as passivity, cooperation, and feelings

master production schedule (MPS) A schedule that translates the aggregate plan into a formalized production plan encompassing specific products to be produced or services to be offered and specific capacity requirements over a designated time period

materials requirements planning (MRP) A computer-based inventory system that develops materials requirements for the goods and services specified in the master schedule and initiates the actions necessary to acquire the materials when needed

matrix structure A structure that superimposes a horizontal set of divisional reporting relationships onto a hierarchical functional structure

mechanistic characteristics Characteristics such as highly centralized decision making, many rules and regulations, and mainly hierarchical communication channels

medium The method used to convey the message to the intended receiver

mega-environment The broad conditions and trends in the societies in which an organization operates

merger The combining of two or more companies into one organization

message The encoding-process outcome, which consists of verbal and nonverbal symbols that have been developed to convey meaning to the receiver

middle managers Managers beneath the top levels of the hierarchy who are directly responsible for the work of managers at lower levels

mission The organization's purpose or fundamental reason for existence

mission statement A broad declaration of the basic, unique purpose and scope of operations that distinguish the organization from others of its type

modeling Actually observing and attempting to imitate the behaviors of others

moral management An approach that strives to follow ethical principles and precepts

motivation The force that energizes behavior, gives direction to behavior, and underlies the tendency to persist

motivators Factors that seem to make individuals feel satisfied with their jobs

multifocal strategy A strategy aimed at achieving the advantages of worldwide integration whenever possible, while still attempting to be responsive to important national needs

multinational corporation (MNC) An organization that engages in production or service activities through its own affiliates in several countries, maintains control over the policies of those affiliates, and manages from a global perspective

multiple control systems Systems that use two or more of the feedforward, concurrent, and feedback control processes and involve several strategic control points

national responsiveness strategy A strategy of allowing subsidiaries to have substantial latitude in adapting products and services to suit the particular needs and political realities of the countries in which they operate

natural selection model A term sometimes used for the *population ecology model*

need for achievement (nAch) The desire to accomplish challenging tasks and achieve a standard of excellence in one's work

need for affiliation (nAff) The desire to maintain warm, friendly relationships with others

need for power (nPow) The desire to influence others and control one's environment

needs analysis An assessment of an organization's training needs that is developed by considering overall organizational requirements, tasks associated with jobs for which training is needed, and the degree to which individuals are able to perform those tasks effectively

negative entropy The ability of open systems to bring in new energy, in the form of inputs and feedback from the environment, in order to delay or arrest entropy

negative reinforcement A technique, aimed at *increasing* a desired behavior, that involves providing noxious stimuli so that an individual will engage in the desired behavior in order to stop the noxious stimuli

negative synergy The force that results when group process losses are greater than any gains achieved from combining the forces of group members

network A set of cooperative relationships with individuals whose help is needed in order for a manager to function effectively

network diagram A graphic depiction of the interrelationships among activities

networked structure A form of organizing in which many functions are contracted out to other independent firms and coordinated through the use of information technology networks to operate as if they were within a single corporation

neutralizers Situational factors that make it *impossible* for a given leader behavior to have an impact on subor-dinate performance and/or satisfaction

new venture An enterprise that is in the process of being created by an entrepreneur

new venture teams Temporary task forces or teams made up of individuals who have been relieved of their normal duties in order to develop a new process, product, or program

new venture units Either separate divisions or specially incorporated companies created for the specific purpose of developing new products or business ideas and initiatives

newly industrialized countries (NICs) Countries within the LDCs that are emerging as major exporters of manufactured goods, including such nations as Hong Kong, Taiwan, and South Korea

node, or event An indication of the beginning and/or ending of activities in the network

noise Any factor in the communication process that interferes with exchanging messages and achieving common meaning

nominal group technique (NGT) A technique that integrates both individual work and group interaction within certain ground rules

noncrisis problem An issue that requires resolution but does not simultaneously have the importance and immediacy characteristics of a crisis

noncybernetic control system A control system that relies on human discretion as a basic part of its process

nonprogrammed decisions Decisions for which predetermined decision rules are impractical because the situations are novel and/or ill-structured

nonrational escalation The tendency to increase commitment to a previously selected course of action beyond the level that would be expected if the manager followed an effective decision-making process; also called *escalation phenomenon*

nonrational models Models that suggest that information-gathering and processing limitations make it difficult for managers to make optimal decisions

nonverbal communication Com-munication by means of elements and behaviors that are not coded into words

normative decision-making models Models of decision making that attempt to prescribe how managers *should* make decisions

normative leadership model A model that helps leaders assess critical situational factors that affect the extent to which they should involve subordinates in particular decisions

norming A stage in which group members begin to build group cohesion, as well as develop a consensus about norms for performing a task and relating to one another

norms Expected behaviors sanctioned by a group that regulate and foster uniformity in member behaviors

not-for-profit organization An organization whose main purposes center on issues other than making profits

object language The communicative use of material things, including clothing, cosmetics, furniture, and architecture

office automation system (OAS) A computer-based information system aimed at facilitating communication and increasing the productivity of managers and office workers through document and message processing

one-way communication The communication that results when the communication process does not allow for feedback

open system A system that operates in continual interaction with its environment

operating budget A statement that presents the financial plan for each responsibility center during the budget period and reflects operating activities involving revenues and expenses

operational control A control type that involves overseeing the implementation of operating plans, monitoring day-to-day results, and taking corrective action when required

operational goals Targets or future end results set by lower management that address specific measurable outcomes required from the lower levels

operational plans The means devised to support implementation of tactical plans and achievement of operational goals

operations management The function, or field of expertise, that is primarily responsible for managing the production and delivery of an organization's products and services; the management of the productive processes that convert inputs into goods and services

operations research Another name commonly used for management science

opportunity problem A situation that offers a strong potential for significant organizational gain if appropriate actions are taken

orchestrator A high-level manager who articulates the need for innovation, provides funding for innovating activities, creates incentives for middle managers to sponsor new ideas, and protects idea people

ordering cost The expenses involved in placing an order (such as paperwork, postage, and time)

organic characteristics Characteristics such as decentralized decision making, few rules and regulations, and both hierarchical and lateral communication channels

organization Two or more persons engaged in a systematic effort to produce goods or services

organization chart A line diagram that depicts the broad outlines of an organization's structure

organization design The process of developing an organization structure

organization structure The formal pattern of interactions and coordination designed by management to link the tasks of individuals and groups in achieving organizational goals

organizational culture A system of shared values, assumptions, beliefs, and norms that unite the members of an organization

organizational development (OD) A change effort that is planned, focused on an entire organization or a large subsystem, managed from the top, aimed at enhancing organizational health and effectiveness, and based on planned interventions

organizational problems Discrepancies between a current state or condition and what is desired

organizational social responsibility The obligation of an organization to seek actions that protect and improve the welfare of society along with its own interests

organizational social responsiveness A term that refers to the development of organizational decision processes whereby managers anticipate, respond to, and manage areas of social responsibility

organizational termination The process of ceasing to exist as an identifiable organization

organizing The process of allocating and arranging human and nonhuman resources so that plans can be carried out successfully

ossification A condition that is characterized by lack of innovation and avoidance of risk

outputs The products, services, and other outcomes produced by the organization

outsourcing The process of employing an outside vendor to perform a function normally carried on within the organization

overconfidence The tendency to be more certain of judgments regarding the likelihood of a future event than one's actual predictive accuracy warrants

overcontrol The limiting of individual job autonomy to such a point that it seriously inhibits effective job performance

panic A reaction in which individuals become so upset that they frantically seek a way to solve a problem

paralanguage Vocal aspects of communication that relate to how something is said rather than to what is said

partial-factor productivity A productivity approach that considers the total output relative to a specific input, such as labor

participative Leader behavior that is characterized by consulting with subordinates, encouraging their suggestions, and carefully considering their ideas when making decisions

path-goal theory A theory that attempts to explain how leader behavior can positively influence the motivation and job satisfaction of subordinates

pay survey A survey of the labor market to determine the current rates of pay for benchmark, or key, jobs

payoff The amount of decision-maker value associated with a particular decision alternative and future condition

payoff table or **decision matrix** A two-dimensional matrix that allows a decision maker to compare how different future conditions are likely to affect the respective outcomes of two or more decision alternatives

perception The process that individuals use to acquire and make sense out of information from the environment

perceptual defense The tendency to block out or distort information that one finds threatening or that challenges one's beliefs

performance appraisal The process of defining expectations for employee performance; measuring, evaluating, and recording employee performance relative to those expectations, and providing feedback to the employee

performance-outcome (P→O) expectancy Our assessment of the probability that our successful performance will lead to certain outcomes

performing A stage in which energy is channeled toward a task and in which norms support teamwork

personal power A need for power in which individuals want to dominate others for the sake of demonstrating their ability to wield power

physiological needs Survival needs such as food, water, and shelter

plan The means devised for attempting to reach a goal

planned change Change that involves actions based on a carefully thought-out process that anticipates future difficulties, threats, and opportunities

planning The process of setting goals and deciding how best to achieve them

planning staff A small group of individuals who assist top-level managers in developing the various components of the planning process

point factor method A job evaluation approach in which points are assigned to jobs on the basis of the degree to which the jobs contain selected compensable factors

policy A general guide that specifies the broad parameters within which organization members are expected to operate in pursuit of organizational goals

political risk The probability of the occurrence of political actions that will result in either loss of enterprise ownership or significant benefits from conducting business

polycentric orientation An approach to international management whereby executives believe that the parts of the organization located in a given host country should be staffed by local individuals to the fullest extent possible

pooled interdependence A relationship in which units operate independently but their individual efforts are important to the success of the organization as a whole

population ecology model A model that focuses on populations or groups of organizations and argues that environmental factors cause organizations with appropriate characteristics to survive and others to fail

portfolio strategy approach A method of analyzing an organization's mix of businesses in terms of both individual and collective contributions to strategic goals

positive reinforcement A technique, aimed at *increasing* a desired behavior, that involves providing a pleasant, rewarding consequence to encourage that behavior

positive synergy The force that results when the combined gains from group interaction are greater than group process losses

power The capacity to affect the behavior of others

power distance A cultural dimension that involves the degree to which individuals in a society accept differences in the distribution of power as reasonable and normal

procedure A prescribed series of related steps to be taken under certain recurring circumstances

process consultation A technique concerned with the interpersonal relations and dynamics operating in work groups

process layout A production configuration in which the processing components are grouped according to the type of function that they perform

process structure A type of departmentalization in which positions are grouped according to a complete flow of work

product divisions Divisions created to concentrate on a single product or service or at least a relatively homogeneous set of products or services

product layout A production configuration in which the processing components are arranged in a specialized line along which the product or client passes during the production process

product/market evolution matrix A 15-cell matrix (developed by Hofer) in which businesses are plotted according to the business unit's business strength, or competitive position, and the industry's stage in the evolutionary product/market life cycle

productivity The efficiency concept that gauges the ratio of outputs relative to inputs into a production process

profit center A responsibility center whose budgetary performance is measured by the difference between revenues and costs—in other words, profits

profitability ratios Financial ratios that help measure management's ability to control expenses and earn profits through the use of organizational resources

program A comprehensive plan that coordinates a complex set of activities related to a major nonrecurring goal

Program Evaluation and Review Technique (PERT) A network planning method for managing large projects

Programmed decisions Decisions made in routine, repetitive, well-structured situations through the use of predetermined decision rules

project A plan that coordinates a set of limited-scope activities that do not need to be divided into several

major projects in order to reach a major nonrecurring goal

project managers Managers who have responsibility for coordinating efforts involving individuals in several different organizational units who are all working on a particular project

projection The tendency of an individual to assume that others share his or her thoughts, feelings, and characteristics

prospect theory A theory positing that decision makers find the prospect of an actual loss more painful than giving up the possibility of a gain

prototyping The process of building a rough, working model of all or parts of a proposed information system for purposes of preliminary evaluation and further refinement

proxemics The influence of proximity and space on communication

public affairs department A permanent department that coordinates various ongoing social responsibilities and identifies and recommends policies for new social issues

punishment A technique that involves providing negative consequences in order to *decrease* or discourage a behavior

purchasing The process of acquiring necessary goods or services in exchange for funds or other remuneration

quality The totality of features and characteristics of a product or service that bear on its ability to satisfy stated or implied needs

quality improvement teams Small groups of employees who work on solving specific problems related to quality and productivity, often with stated targets for improvement

quantitative forecasting A type of forecasting that relies on numerical data and mathematical models to predict future conditions

questionable payments Business payments that raise significant ethical questions of right or wrong either in the host nation or in other nations

queuing, or **waiting-line, models** Mathematical models that describe the operating characteristics of queuing situations, in which service is provided to persons or units waiting in line

ratio analysis The process of determining and evaluating financial ratios

rational model A model that suggests that managers engage in completely rational decision processes, ultimately make optimal decisions, and possess and understand all information relevant to their decisions at the time they make them

rationalization The strategy of assigning activities to those parts of the organization, regardless of their location, that are best suited to produce the desired results and then selling the finished products where they are likely to yield the best profits

rationing Providing limited access to a product or service that is in high demand

raw materials inventory The stock of parts, ingredients, and other basic inputs to a production or service process

reactive change Change that occurs when one takes action in response to perceived problems, threats, or opportunities

realistic job preview A technique used during the recruiting process in which the job candidate is presented with a balanced view of both the positive and the negative aspects of the job and the organization

receiver The person with whom the message is exchanged

reciprocal interdependence A relationship in which one unit's outputs become inputs to the other unit and vice versa

recruitment The process of finding and attempting to attract job candidates who are capable of effectively filling job vacancies

reengineering The thorough analysis and radical redesign of existing business processes to achieve breakthrough improvements by focusing on critical performance criteria, such as cost, quality, service, and speed

reference checks Attempts to obtain job-related information about job applicants from individuals who are knowledgeable about the applicant's qualifications

referent power Power that results from being admired, personally identified with, or liked by others

regiocentric orientation An approach to international management whereby executives believe that geographic regions have commonalities that make a regional focus advantageous and that company problems related to that region are generally best solved by individuals from the region

regional responsiveness strategy A strategy of allowing regional offices to have substantial latitude in coordinating the activities of local subsidiaries and adapting products and services to suit the particular needs and political realities of the regions in which they operate

regression models Equations that express the fluctuations in the variable being forecasted in terms of fluctuations in one or more other variables (predictors)

reinforcement theory A theory that argues that our behavior can be explained by consequences in the environment

relatedness needs Needs that address our relationships with significant others, such as families, friendship groups, work groups, and professional groups

reorder point (ROP) The inventory level at which a new order should be placed

repatriation The process of returning to one's home country after an assignment in a host country

replacement chart A partial organization chart showing the major managerial positions in an organization, current incumbents, potential replacements for each position, and the age of each person on the chart

representativeness The tendency to be overly influenced by stereotypes in making judgments about the likelihood of occurrences

reservations Organizational units that devote full time to the generation of innovative ideas for future business

resource dependence An approach to controls which argues that managers need to consider controls mainly in areas in which they depend

on others for resources necessary to reach organizational goals

resource dependence model A model that highlights organizational dependence on the environment for resources and argues that organizations attempt to manipulate the environment to reduce that dependence

responsibility The obligation to carry out duties and achieve goals related to a position

responsibility center A subunit headed by a manager who is responsible for achieving one or more goals

restraining forces Factors that pressure *against* a change

restructuring The process of making a major change in organization structure that often involves reducing management levels and possibly changing components of the organization through divestiture and/or acquisition, as well as shrinking the size of the work force

revenue center A responsibility center whose budgetary performance is measured primarily by its ability to generate a specified level of revenue

revitalization The renewal of the innovative vigor of organizations

reward power Power that is based on the capacity to control and provide valued rewards to others

risk The possibility that a chosen action could lead to losses rather than the intended results

rite A relatively elaborate, dramatic, planned set of activities intended to convey cultural values to participants and, usually, an audience

role A set of behaviors expected of an individual who occupies a particular position in a group; an organized set of behaviors associated with a particular office or position

routing, or **distribution, models** Quantitative models that can assist managers in planning the most effective and economical approaches to distribution problems

rule A statement that spells out specific actions to be taken or not taken in a given situation

safety needs Needs that pertain to the desire to feel safe, secure, and free from threats to our existence

sales-force composite A means of forecasting that is used mainly to predict future sales and typically involves obtaining the views of various salespeople, sales managers, and/or distributors regarding the sales outlook

satisfaction-progression principle A principle that states that satisfaction of one level of need encourages concern with the next level

satisficing model A model stating that managers seek alternatives only until they find one that looks *satisfactory*, rather than seeking the optimal decision

scenario analysis An approach that addresses a variety of possible futures by evaluating major environmental variables, assessing the likely strategies of other significant actors, devising possible counterstrategies, developing ranked hypotheses about the variables, and formulating alternative scenarios

schedules of reinforcement Patterns of rewarding that specify the basis for and timing of positive reinforcement

scientific management An approach that emphasizes the scientific study of work methods in order to improve worker efficiency

selection The process of determining which job candidates best suit organizational needs

selection interview A relatively formal, in-depth conversation conducted for the purpose of assessing a candidate's knowledge, skills, and abilities, as well as providing information to the candidate about the organization and potential jobs

self-actualization needs Needs that pertain to the requirement of developing our capabilities and reaching our full potential

self-control Our ability to exercise control over our own behavior by setting standards and providing consequences for our own actions

self-efficacy The belief in one's capabilities to perform a specific task

self-managing team A work group given responsibility for a task area without day-to-day supervision and with authority to influence and control both group membership and behavior

self-oriented roles Roles that are related to the personal needs of group members and often negatively influence the effectiveness of a group

self-serving bias The tendency to perceive oneself as responsible for successes and others as responsible for failures

semantic blocks The blockages or communication difficulties that arise from word choices

semantic net The network of words and word meanings that a given individual has available for recall

sender The initiator of the message

sequential interdependence A relationship in which one unit must complete its work before the next unit in the sequence can begin work

shaping The successive rewarding of behaviors that closely approximate the desired response until the actual desired response is made

simulation A mathematical imitation of reality

single-use plans Plans aimed at achieving a specific goal that, once reached, will most likely not recur in the future

situational leadership theory A theory (developed by Hersey and Blanchard) based on the premise that leaders need to alter their behaviors depending on one major situational factor—the readiness of followers

situational theories Theories of leadership that take into consideration important situational factors

skill variety The extent to which the job entails a number of activities that require different skills

skill-based pay A compensation system in which employees' rates of pay are based on the number of predetermined skills the employees have mastered

skills inventory A data bank (usually computerized) containing basic information about each employee that can be used to assess the likely availability of individuals for meeting current and future human resource needs

slack Latitude about when various activities on the noncritical paths can be started without endangering the completion date of the entire project

slack resources A cushion of resources that facilitates adaptation to internal and external pressures, as well as initiation of changes

smoothing Taking actions aimed at reducing the impact of fluctuations, given the market

social audit A systematic study and evaluation of the social, rather than the economic, performance of an organization

social forecasting The systematic process of identifying social trends, evaluating the organizational importance of those trends, and integrating these assessments into the organization's forecasting program

social learning theory A theory that argues that learning occurs through the continuous reciprocal interaction of our behaviors, various personal factors, and environmental forces

social loafing The tendency of individuals to expend less effort when working in groups than when working alone

social scanning The general surveillance of various elements in the task environment to detect evidence of impending changes that will affect the organization's social responsibilities

socialist economy An economy in which the means of production are owned by the state and economic activity is coordinated by plan

sociocultural element The attitudes, values, norms, beliefs, behaviors, and associated demographic trends that are characteristic of a given geographic area

soldiering Deliberately working at less than full capacity

span of management or **span of control** The number of subordinates who report directly to a specific manager

sponsor A middle manager who recognizes the organizational significance of an idea, helps obtain the necessary funding for development of the innovation, and facilitates its actual implementation

stability strategy A strategy that involves maintaining the status quo or growing in a methodical, but slow, manner

staff position A position whose primary purpose is providing specialized expertise and assistance to line positions

staffing The set of activities aimed at attracting and selecting individuals for positions in a way that will facilitate the achievement of organizational goals

standard cost center A responsibility center whose budgetary performance depends on achieving its goals by operating within standard cost constraints

standing committee A permanent task group charged with handling recurring matters in a narrowly defined subject area over an indefinite, but generally lengthy, period of time

standing plans Plans that provide ongoing guidance for performing recurring activities

start-up A type of new firm or venture started from scratch by an entrepreneur

statistical process control A statistical technique that uses periodic random samples taken during actual production to determine whether acceptable quality levels are being met or production should be stopped for remedial action

stereotyping The tendency to attribute characteristics to an individual on the basis of an assessment of the group to which the individual belongs

stockout cost The economic consequences of running out of stock (such as loss of customer goodwill and possibly sales)

storming A stage in which group members frequently experience conflict with one another as they locate and attempt to resolve differences of opinion regarding key issues

story A narrative based on true events, which sometimes may be embellished to highlight the intended value

strategic alliance An arrangement whereby two or more independent organizations form a cooperative partnership to gain some mutual strategic advantage

strategic business unit (SBU) A distinct business, with its own set of competitors, that can be managed relatively independently of other businesses within the organization

strategic control A control type that involves monitoring critical environmental factors that could affect the viability of strategic plans, assessing the effects of organizational strategic actions, and ensuring that strategic plans are implemented as intended

strategic control points Performance areas chosen for control because they are particularly important in meeting organizational goals

strategic goals Broadly defined targets or future end results set by top management

strategic management A process through which managers formulate and implement strategies geared toward optimizing strategic goal achievement, given available environmental and internal conditions

strategic plans Detailed action steps mapped out to reach strategic goals

strategies Large-scale action plans for interacting with the environment in order to achieve long-term goals

strategy formulation The process of identifying the mission and strategic goals, conducting competitive analysis, and developing specific strategies

strategy implementation The process of carrying out strategic plans and maintaining control over how those plans are carried out

substitutes Situational factors that make leadership impact not only *impossible* but also *unnecessary*

substitutes for leadership An approach that attempts to specify some of the main situational factors likely to make leader behaviors unnecessary or to negate their effectiveness

sunk costs Costs that, once incurred, are not recoverable and should not enter into considerations of future courses of action

superordinate goals Major common goals that require the support and effort of all parties

suppliers Those organizations and individuals that supply the resources an organization needs to conduct its operations

supportive Leader behavior that entails showing concern for the status, well-being, and needs of subordinates; doing small things to make the work more pleasant; and being friendly and approachable

SWOT analysis A method of analyzing an organization's competitive situation that involves assessing organizational strengths (S) and weaknesses (W), as well as environmental opportunities (O) and threats (T)

symbol An object, act, event, or quality that serves as a vehicle for conveying meaning

symbolic processes The various ways that we use verbal and imagined symbols to process and store experiences in representational forms that can serve as guides to future behavior

synergy The ability of the whole to equal more than the sum of its parts

system A set of interrelated parts that operate as a whole in pursuit of common goals

systems development life cycle A series of stages that are used in the development of most medium- and large-size information systems

systems theory An approach based on the notion that organizations can be visualized as systems

tactical control A control type that focuses on assessing the implementation of tactical plans at department levels, monitoring associated periodic results, and taking corrective action as necessary

tactical goals Targets or future end results usually set by middle management for specific departments or units

tactical plans The means charted to support implementation of the strategic plan and achievement of tactical goals

tall structure A structure that has many hierarchical levels and narrow spans of control

tariff A type of trade barrier in the form of a customs duty, or tax, levied mainly on imports

task environment The specific outside elements with which an organization interfaces in the course of conducting its business

task force A temporary task group usually formed to make recommendations on a specific issue

task group A formal group that is created for a specific purpose that supplements or replaces work normally done by command groups

task identity The degree to which the job allows the completion of a major identifiable piece of work, rather than just a fragment

task significance The extent to which the worker sees the job output as having an important impact on others

team A temporary or an ongoing task group whose members are charged with working together to identify problems, form a consensus about what should be done, and implement necessary actions in relation to a particular task or organizational area

team building A technique aimed at helping work groups become effective at task accomplishment

technical skills Skills that reflect both an understanding of and a proficiency in a specialized field

technological element The current state of knowledge regarding the production of products and services

technological interdependence The degree to which different parts of the organization must exchange information and materials in order to perform the required activities

technological transfer The transmission of technology from those who possess it to those who do not

technological, or **qualitative, forecasting** A type of forecasting aimed primarily at predicting long-term trends in technology and other important aspects of the environment

technology The knowledge, tools, equipment, and work techniques used by an organization in delivering its product or service

technostructural activities Activities intended to improve work technology and/or organization structure

telecommunications The communication of information over a distance electronically

telecommuting A form of working at home that is made possible by using computer technology to remain in touch with the office

teleconferencing The simultaneous communication among a group of individuals by telephone or via computer using specially designed software

Theory Z A concept that combines positive aspects of American and Japanese management into a modified approach aimed at increasing U.S. managerial effectiveness while remaining compatible with the norms and values of American society and culture

third-party intervention A technique concerned with helping individuals, groups, or departments resolve serious conflicts that may relate to specific work issues or may be caused by suboptimal interpersonal relations

time-series methods Methods that use historical data to develop forecasts of the future

top managers Managers at the very top levels of the hierarchy who are ultimately responsible for the entire organization

total quality management (TQM) A management system that is an integral part of an organization's strategy and is aimed at continually improving product and service quality so as to achieve high levels of customer satisfaction and build strong customer loyalty

total-factor productivity A productivity approach that considers all the inputs involved in producing outputs

trade associations Organizations composed of individuals or firms with common business concerns

training and development A planned effort to facilitate employee learning of job-related behaviors in order to improve employee performance

traits Distinctive internal qualities or characteristics of an individual, such as physical characteristics, personality characteristics, skills and abilities, and social factors

transaction-processing system (TPS) A computer-based information system that executes and records the routine day-to-day transactions required to conduct an organization's business

transactional leaders Leaders who motivate subordinates to perform at expected levels by helping them recognize task responsibilities, identify goals, acquire confidence about meeting desired performance levels, and understand how their needs and the rewards that they desire are linked to goal achievement

transformation processes The organization's managerial and technological abilities that are applied to convert inputs into outputs

transformational leaders Leaders who motivate individuals to perform beyond normal expectations by inspiring subordinates to focus on broader missions that transcend their own immediate self-interests, to concentrate on intrinsic higher-level goals rather than extrinsic lower-level goals, and to have confidence in their abilities to achieve the extraordinary missions articulated by the leader

turnaround A strategy designed to reverse a negative trend and restore the organization to appropriate levels of profitability

two-factor theory Herzberg's theory that hygiene factors are necessary to keep workers from feeling dissatisfied, but only motivators can lead workers to feel satisfied and motivated

two-way communication The communication that results when the communication process explicitly includes feedback

uncertainty A condition in which the decision maker must choose a course of action without complete knowledge of the consequences that will follow implementation

uncertainty avoidance A cultural dimension that involves the extent to which members of a society feel uncomfortable with and try to avoid situations that they perceive as unstructured, unclear, or unpredictable

undercontrol The granting of autonomy to an employee to such a point that the organization loses its ability to direct the individual's efforts toward achieving organizational goals

unions Employee groups formed for the purpose of negotiating with management about conditions relating to their work

unit and small-batch production A type of technology in which products are custom-produced to meet custom specifications or they are made in small quantities primarily by craft specialists

upward communication The vertical flow of communication from a lower level to one or more higher levels in the organization

user An individual, other than an information system professional, who is engaged in the development and/or management of computer-based information systems

valence Our assessment of the anticipated value of various outcomes or rewards

validity The degree to which a measure actually assesses the attribute that it is designed to measure

variable-interval schedule of reinforcement A pattern in which a reinforcer is administered on a varying, or random, time schedule that *averages* out to a predetermined time frequency

variable-ratio schedule of reinforcement A pattern in which a reinforcer is provided after a varying, or random, number of occurrences of the desired behavior in such a way that the reinforcement pattern *averages* out to a predetermined ratio of occurrences per reinforcement

venture team A group of two or more individuals who band together for the purpose of creating a new venture

verbal communication The written or oral use of words to communicate; communication that involves a message exchange between two or more levels of the organizational hierarchy

vertical coordination The linking of activities at the top of the organization with those at the middle and lower levels in order to achieve organizational goals

vertical integration An approach that involves effecting growth through the production of inputs previously provided by suppliers or through the replacement of a customer role by disposing of one's own outputs

vicarious learning Our ability to learn new behaviors and/or assess their probable consequences by observing others

videoconferencing The holding of meetings with individuals in two or more locations by means of closed-circuit television

voice mail A recording system that provides senders with the opportunity to leave messages for receivers by telephone

whistle-blower An employee who reports a real or perceived wrongdoing under the control of his or her employer to those who may be able to take appropriate action

wholly owned subsidiary An operation on foreign soil that is totally owned and controlled by a company with headquarters outside the host country

wide area networks (WANs) Networks that provide communications among computers over long distances, usually through the facilities and services of public or private communications companies

work agenda A loosely connected set of tentative goals and tasks that a manager is attempting to accomplish

work specialization The degree to which the work necessary to achieve organizational goals is broken down into various jobs

work-in-process inventory Items in stock that are currently being transformed into a final product or service

worldwide integration strategy, or **globalization** A strategy aimed at developing relatively standardized products with global appeal, as well as rationalizing operations throughout the world

REFERENCES

CHAPTER 1

1. Based on Ken Yamada, "Hewlett-Packard Names Lewis E. Platt President and Chief, Succeeding Young," *The Wall Street Journal,* July 7, 1992, p. B2; Peter Barrows, "The Printer King Invades Home PCs," *Business Week,* Aug. 21, 1995, pp. 74–75; Dana Wechsler Linden and Bruce Upbin, "Top Performance of 1995. Boy Scouts on a Rampage," *Forbes,* Jan. 1, 1996, pp. 66–70; Michelle Slatalla, "The Cutting Edge: H-P Team an Anomaly in Engineering," *Los Angeles Times,* May 6, 1996, p. D1; "Future Printing: HP Unveils Its Long-Term Vision for Commercial Hardcopy Business," *Edge: Work-Group Computing Report,* May 20, 1996, p. 1; "Corporate Responsibility: Nonprofit Group, Lawmakers, Honor Corporate Citizens for Effort," *Daily Labor Report,* June 6, 1996, p. d11.

2. *Hewlett-Packard in Brief,* Hewlett-Packard, March 1995.

3. Regina Fazio Maruca, "The Right Way to Go Global: An Interview with Whirlpool CEO David Whitwam," *Harvard Business Review,* March–April 1994, pp. 135–145.

4. Patrick Oster and John Rossant, "Call It Worldpool," *Business Week,* Nov. 28, 1994; Todd Mason, "The Downfall of a CEO," *Business Week,* Feb. 16, 1987, pp. 76–84; "Diamond Shamrock Pursues Margin-Resistant Projects to Increase Value," *Petroleum Finance Week,* Oct. 30, 1995, p. 1.

5. See Stephen J. Carroll and Dennis J. Gillen, "Are the Classical Management Functions Useful in Describing Managerial Work?" *Academy of Management Review,* vol. 12, 1987, pp. 38–51, for a review of the continuing importance of the functions of management as a framework for studying management.

6. Regina Fazio Maruca, "The Right Way to Go Global: An Interview with Whirlpool CEO David Whitman," *Harvard Business Review,* March–April 1994, pp. 135–145; Patrick Oster and John Rossant, "Call It Worldpool," *Business Week,* Nov. 28, 1994.

7. Todd Mason, "The Downfall of a CEO," *Business Week,* Feb. 16, 1987, pp. 76–84.

8. Regina Fazio Maruca, "The Right Way to Go Global: An Interview with Whirlpool CEO David Whitwam," *Harvard Business Review,* March–April 1994, pp. 135–145.

9. Todd Mason, "The Downfall of a CEO," *Business Week,* Feb. 16, 1987, pp. 76–84.

10. Regina Fazio Maruca, "The Right Way to Go Global: An Interview with Whirlpool CEO David Whitwam," *Harvard Business Review,* March–April 1994, pp. 135–145.

11. Todd Mason, "The Downfall of a CEO," *Business Week,* Feb. 16, 1987, pp. 76–84.

12. William H. Newman, *Constructive Control,* Prentice-Hall, Englewood Cliffs, N.J., 1975.

13. Regina Fazio Maruca, "The Right Way to Go Global: An Interview with Whirlpool CEO David Whitwam," *Harvard Business Review,* March–April 1994, pp. 135–145; Bill Vlasic and Zachary Schiller, "Did Whirlpool Spin Too Far Too Fast?" *Business Week,* June 24, 1996, pp. 135–136.

14. Todd Mason, "The Downfall of a CEO," *Business Week,* Feb. 16, 1987, pp. 76–84.

15. Steven J. Carroll and Dennis J. Gillen, "Are the Classical Management Functions Useful in Describing Managerial Work?" *Academy of Management Review,* vol. 12, 1987, pp. 38–51.

16. Ran Lachman, "Public and Private Sector Differences: CEOs' Perceptions of Their Role Environments," *Academy of Management Journal,* September 1985, pp. 671–680.

17. Henry Mintzberg, *The Nature of Managerial Work,* Prentice-Hall, Englewood Cliffs, N.J., 1980.

18. Ford S. Worthy, "How CEOs Manage Their Time," *Fortune,* Jan. 18, 1988, pp. 88–97.

19. Alan Deutschman, "The CEO's Secret of Managing Time," *Fortune,* June 1, 1992, pp. 135–146.

20. Lance B. Kurke and Howard E. Aldrich, "Mintzberg Was Right!: A Replication and Extension of *The Nature of Managerial Work,*" *Management Science,* vol. 29, 1983, pp. 975–984; Barrie Gibbs, "The Effect of Environment and Technology on Managerial Roles," *Journal of Management,* vol. 20, 1994, pp. 581–604.

21. Robert H. Guest, "Of Time and the Foreman," *Personnel,* vol. 32, 1955–1956, pp. 478–486.

22. Fred Luthans, "Successful vs. Effective Real Managers," *Academy of Management Executive,* vol. 2, no. 2, 1988, pp. 127–132.

23. Based on Allan R. Cohen and David L. Bradford, "Influence without Authority: The Use of Alliances, Reciprocity, and Exchange to Accomplish Work," *Organizational Dynamics,* Winter 1989, pp. 5–17; see also Wayne E. Baker, *Networking Smart,* McGraw-Hill, New York, 1994 for further ideas about networking effectively.

24. Henry Mintzberg, *The Nature of Managerial Work,* Prentice-Hall, Englewood Cliffs, N.J., 1980.

25. Stephen J. Carroll and Dennis J. Gillen, "Are the Classical Management Functions Useful in Describing Managerial Work?" *Academy of Management Review,* vol. 12, 1987, pp. 38–51.

26. John P. Kotter, *The General Managers,* Free Press, New York, 1982.

27. Adapted (with minor changes) from John P. Kotter, "What Effective General Managers Really Do," *Harvard Business Review,* November–December 1982, pp. 156–167.

28. Ford S. Worthy, "How CEOs Manage Their Time," *Fortune,* Jan. 18, 1988, pp. 88–97.

29. Rosemary Stewart, "A Model for Understanding Managerial Jobs and Behavior," *Academy of Management Review,* vol. 7, 1982, pp. 7–13.

30. John P. Kotter, *The General Managers,* Free Press, New York, 1982.

31. Richard E. Boyatzis, *The Competent Manager: A Model for Effective Performance,* Wiley, New York, 1982.

32. Lucy Kraus, "Tough, with a Velvet Glove," *American Way,* Fall 1988, pp. 48–51; Barbara Jepson, "Wonder Woman of Carnegie Hall," *Connoisseur,* September 1990, pp. 106–153; information from Carnegie Hall, February 1996.

33. Peter F. Drucker, *The Effective Executive,* Harper & Row, New York, 1967.

34. Kenneth Labich, "Is Herb Kelleher America's Best CEO?" *Fortune,* May 2, 1995, pp. 44–49.

35. Ibid.; John Lippert, "Wings of Desire," *Detroit Free Press, Business Monday,* Aug. 15, 1994, pp. 8F–9F.

36. Peter F. Drucker, "Tomorrow's Restless Managers," *Industry Week,* Apr. 18, 1988, pp. 25–27; "Presidents on the Record: GM on the Mend; Recovery Fraught with Challenges," *Automotive News,* May 19, 1995, p. 23.

37. John J. Keller, "AT&T's Robert Allen Gets Sharp Criticism over Layoffs, Losses," *The Wall Street Journal,* Feb. 22, 1996, pp. A1, A8.

38. Ron Zemke, "Putting the SQUEEZE on Middle Managers," *Training,* December 1988, pp. 41–46; Anne B. Fisher, "Welcome to the Age of Overwork," *Fortune,* Nov. 30, 1992, pp. 64–71.

39. Robert J. Grossman, "Damaged, Downsized Souls," *HR Magazine,* May 1996, pp. 54–62.

40. Rosabeth Moss Kanter, "The New Managerial Work," *Harvard Business Review,* November–December 1989, pp. 85–92.

41. David J. Rachman, Michael H. Mescon, Courtland L. Bovee, and John V. Thill, *Business Today,* 7th ed., McGraw-Hill, New York, 1993; John A. Pearce II and Shaker A. Zahra, "The Relative Power of CEOs and Boards of Directors: Associations with Corporate Performance," *Strategic Management Journal,* vol. 12, 1991, pp. 135–153.

42. Paula L. Rechner and Dan R. Dalton, "CEO Duality and Organizational Performance: A Longitudinal Analysis," *Strategic Management Journal,* vol. 12, 1991, pp. 155–160.

43. Approximations of importance are based on Thomas A. Mahoney, Thomas H. Jerdee, and Stephen J. Carroll, "The Job(s) of Management," *Industrial Relations,* February 1965, pp. 97–110; and Luis R. Gomez-Mejia, Joseph E. McCann, and Ronald C. Page, "The Structure of Managerial Behaviors and Rewards," *Industrial Relations*, Winter 1985, pp. 147–154.

44. Robert L. Katz, "Skills of an Effective Administrator," *Harvard Business Review*, September–October 1974, pp. 90–102.

45. Regina Fazio Maruca, "The Right Way to Go Global: An Interview with Whirlpool CEO David Whitwam," *Harvard Business Review*, March–April 1994, pp. 135–145.

46. Derek Torrington and Jane Weightman, "Middle Management Work," *Journal of General Management*, vol. 13, 1987, pp. 74–89.

47. Cynthia M. Pavett and Alan W. Lau, "Managerial Work: The Influence of Hierarchical Level and Functional Specialty," *Academy of Management Journal*, vol. 26, 1983, pp. 170–177.

48. Ellen Van Velsor and Jean Brittain Leslie, "Why Executives Derail: Perspectives across Time and Cultures," *Academy of Management Executive*, vol. 9, 1995, pp. 62–72.

49. Henry Mintzberg, *The Nature of Managerial Work*, Prentice-Hall, Englewood Cliffs, N.J., 1980.

50. Cynthia M. Pavett and Alan W. Lau, "Managerial Work: The Influence of Hierarchical Level and Functional Specialty," *Academy of Management Journal*, vol. 26, 1983, pp. 170–177.

51. Ibid.

52. Rosabeth Moss Kanter, "The Middle Manager as Innovator," *Harvard Business Review*, July–August 1982, pp. 95–105; Andrall E. Pearson, "Tough-Minded Ways to Get Innovative," *Harvard Business Review*, May–June 1988, pp. 99–106.

53. For a similar definition, see Rosabeth Moss Kanter, *The Change Masters*, Simon and Schuster, New York, 1983, p. 20.

54. Jay R. Galbraith, "Designing the Innovating Organization," *Organizational Dynamics*, Winter 1982, pp. 5–25; Andrall E. Pearson, "Tough-Minded Ways to Get Innovative," *Harvard Business Review*, May–June 1988, pp. 99–106.

55. Based on "JVC and VCR Miracle: You Should Be Very Polite and Gentle," in P. Ranganath Nayak and John M. Ketteringham, *Break-Throughs*, Rawson Associates, New York, 1986, pp. 23–49.

56. John P. Kotter, *The General Managers*, Free Press, New York, 1982; see also Andrall E. Pearson, "Six Basics for General Managers," *Harvard Business Review*, July–August 1989, pp. 94–101.

57. Stanley M. Davis and Paul R. Lawrence, *Matrix*, Addison-Wesley, Reading, Mass., 1977.

58. Louis E. Boone, David L. Kurtz, and C. Patrick Fleenor, "CEOs: Early Signs of a Business Career," *Business Horizons*, September–October 1988, pp. 20–24.

59. Harold Stieglitz, *Chief Executives View Their Jobs: Today and Tomorrow*, Conference Board, New York, 1985.

60. Louis E. Boone, David L. Kurtz, and C. Patrick Fleenor, "CEOs: Early Signs of a Business Career," *Business Horizons*, September–October 1988, 20–24.

61. Harold Stieglitz, *Chief Executives View Their Jobs: Today and Tomorrow*, Conference Board, New York, 1985.

62. Cynthia A. Lengnick-Hall, "Innovation and Competitive Advantage: What We Know and What We Need to Learn," *Journal of Management*, vol. 18, 1992, pp. 399–429; Joseph L. Bower and Clayton M. Christensen, "Disrup-

tive Technologies: Catching the Wave," *Harvard Business Review*, January–February 1995, pp. 43–53.

63. Jay Mathews, "Utensil Strength: Rubbermaid's Relentless Innovation Gains Success, Respect," *The Washington Post*, Apr. 2, 1995, p. 1H; Raju Narisetti, "Can Rubbermaid Crack Foreign Markets," June 20, 1996, pp. B1, B4.

64. W. B. Johnston and A. E. Packer, *Workforce 2000: Creative Affirmative Action Strategies for a Changing Workforce*, Hudson Institute, Indianapolis, Ind., 1987.

65. Taylor Cox, Jr., *Cultural Diversity in Organizations: Theory, Research & Practice*, Berrett-Koehler Publishers, San Francisco, 1994.

66. "Survey Shows Many Companies Have Diversity Programs, Changes in Affirmative Action Perspectives," *Mosaics*, March 1995, Society for Human Resource Management, Alexandria, Va., p. 1.

67. Linda Thornburg, "Journey toward a More Inclusive Culture," *HR Magazine*, February 1994, pp. 79–86.

68. Mary J. Winterle, *Work Force Diversity: Corporate Challenges, Corporate Responses*, Report Number 1013, The Conference Board, New York, 1992; Susan E. Jackson and Eden B. Alvarez, "Working through Diversity as a Strategic Imperative," in Susan E. Jackson and Associates, *Diversity in the Workplace: Human Resources Initiatives*, Guilford Press, New York, 1992.

69. Brian Dumaine, "What the Leaders of Tomorrow See," *Fortune*, July 3, 1989, pp. 48–62.

70. Hewlett-Packard in Brief, Hewlett-Packard, March 1995.

71. "What Today's Leading CEOs, Management Gurus, and Futurists See Coming for Your Company, Your Job, and Your Life between 1995 and 2020," *Industry Week*, Aug. 21, 1995, p. 40.

72. Robert L. Rose, "For Whirlpool, Asia Is the New Frontier," *The Wall Street Journal*, Apr. 25, 1996, p. 1B.

73. Greg Bounds, Lyle Yorks, Mel Adams, and Gipsie Ramney, *Beyond Total Quality Management: Toward the Emerging Paradigm*, McGraw-Hill, New York, 1994; Frederick F. Riechheld, "Learning from Customer Defections," *Harvard Business Review*, March–April 1996, pp. 56–69.

74. Based on David Garfinkel, "What I Do on the Job: Bank Manager," *Business Week Careers*, February 1987, pp. 50–56.

75. Peter Nulty, "Kodak Grabs for Growth Again," *Fortune*, May 16, 1994, pp. 76–78; Wendy Bounds, "Kodak under Fisher: Upheaval in Slow Motion," *The Wall Street Journal*, Dec. 12, 1994, p. B1; Mark Maremount, "Kodak's New Focus," *Fortune*, Jan. 30, 1995, pp. 62–68; Peter Nulty, "Digital Imaging Had Better Boom before Kodak Film Busts," *Fortune*, May 1, 1995, 80–83; Wendy Bounds, "George Fisher Pushes Kodak into Digital Era," *The Wall Street Journal*, June 9, 1995, p. B1; Wendy Bounds, "Kodak Rebuilds Photofinishing Empire, Quietly Buying Labs, Wooing Retailers," *The Wall Street Journal*, June 4, 1996, p. B1; Linda Grant, "The Bears Back Off Kodak," *Fortune*, June 24, 1996, pp. 24–25.

CHAPTER 2

1. Based on Peter F. Drucker, *Management*, Harper & Row, New York, 1973, p. 53; Robert Lacey, *Ford—The Men and the Machine*, Little, Brown, Boston, 1986; and Peter Collier and David Horowitz, *The Fords*, Summit, New York, 1987.

2. Daniel A. Wren, *The Evolution of Management Thought*, 2d ed., Wiley, New York, 1979; W. Jack Duncan, *Great Ideas in Management*, Jossey-Bass, San Francisco, 1989.

3. W. Jack Duncan, *Great Ideas in Management*, Jossey-Bass, San Francisco, 1989; Maurice V. Wilkes, "Charles Babbage—The Great Uncle of Computing?" *Communications of the ACM*, March 1992.

4. Charles Babbage, *On the Economy of Machinery and Manufactures*, Charles Knight, London, 1832, reprinted by Augustus Kelly, New York, 1963.

5. Henry R. Towne, "The Engineer as an Economist," *Transactions of the American Society of Mechanical Engineers*, vol. 7, 1886, pp. 428–432; David F. Noble, *America by Design: Science, Technology and the Rise of Corporate Capitalism*, Knopf, New York, 1977; Daniel A. Wren, "Years of Good Beginnings: 1886 and 1936," in Daniel A. Wren and John A. Pearce II (eds.), *Papers Dedicated to the Development of Modern Management*, Academy of Management, 1986, pp. 1–4; W. Jack Duncan, *Great Ideas in Management*, Jossey-Bass, San Francisco, 1989.

6. Hannah Sampson, "The Army's Clausewitz of the Meeting Room," *Army*, January 1988, pp. 49–50.

7. For a fascinating series of reviews of the works of major contributors to the classical viewpoint, see Allen C. Bluedorn (ed.), "Special Book Review Section on the Classics of Management," *Academy of Management Review*, vol. 11, 1986, pp. 442–464.

8. W. Jack Duncan, *Great Ideas in Management*, Jossey-Bass, San Francisco, 1989.

9. Frederick Winslow Taylor, *The Principles of Scientific Management*, Hive, Easton, Pa., 1985.

10. Edwin A. Locke, "The Ideas of Frederick W. Taylor: An Evaluation," *Academy of Management Review*, vol. 7, 1982, pp. 14–24.

11. Ibid.

12. Daniel A. Wren, *The Evolution of Management Thought*, 2d ed., Wiley, New York, 1979.

13. John Breeze, "Paul Devinat's Scientific Management in Europe—A Historical Perspective," in Daniel A. Wren and John A. Pearce II (eds.), *Papers Dedicated to the Development of Modern Management*, Academy of Management, 1986, pp. 58–63. Critics argue that Taylor failed to acknowledge some previous work by others on the issue of shoveling. On the other hand, supporters state that the issues raised by critics are misguided or involve minor issues. See Charles D. Wrege and Amedeo G. Perroni, "Taylor's Pig Tale: A Historical Analysis of Frederick W. Taylor's Pig Iron Experiment," *Academy of Management Journal*, vol. 17, 1974, pp. 6–27; Charles Wrege and Anne Marie Stotka, "Cooke Creates a Classic: The Story behind F. W. Taylor's Principles of Scientific Management," *Academy of Management Review*, vol. 3, 1978, pp. 736–749; Louis W. Fry, "The Maligned F. W. Taylor: A Reply to Many of His Critics," *Academy of Management Review*, vol. 1, 1976, pp. 124–129; and Edwin A. Locke, "The Ideas of Frederick W. Taylor: An Evaluation," *Academy of Management Review*, vol. 7, 1982, pp. 14–24.

14. Daniel A. Wren, *The Evolution of Management Thought*, 2d ed., Wiley, New York, 1979.

15. Ibid.

16. L. M. Gilbreth, *The Psychology of Management*, Sturgis and Walton, 1914, reissued by Macmillan, New York, 1921.

17. Daniel A. Wren, *The Evolution of Management Thought*, 2d ed., Wiley, New York, 1979.

18. Ibid.

19. This section is based on Daniel A. Wren,

The Evolution of Management Thought, 2d ed., Wiley, New York, 1979; W. Jack Duncan, *Great Ideas in Management*, Jossey-Bass, San Francisco, 1989.

20. This section is based mainly on Daniel A. Wren, *The Evolution of Management Thought*, 2d ed., Wiley, New York, 1979; W. Jack Duncan, *Great Ideas in Management*, Jossey-Bass, San Francisco, 1989; see also Arnold Eisen, "The Meanings and Confusions of Weberian 'Rationality,'" *British Journal of Sociology*, March 1978, pp. 57–70.

21. Richard M. Weiss, "Weber on Bureaucracy: Management Consultant or Political Theorist?" *Academy of Management Review*, vol. 8, 1983, pp. 242–248; Robert N. Stern and Stephen R. Barley, "Organizations and Social Systems: Organization Theory's Neglected Mandate," *Administrative Science Quarterly*, vol. 41, 1996, pp. 146–162; W. Richard Scott, "The Mandate Is Still Being Honored: In Defense of Weber's Disciples," *Administrative Science Quarterly*, vol. 41, 1996, pp. 163–171.

22. Jeffrey M. Laderman, "The Family That Hauls Together Brawls Together," *Business Week*, Aug. 29, 1988, pp. 64–68; Robert Tomsho, "U-Haul Patriarch Now Battles Offspring in Bitterest of Feuds," *The Wall Street Journal*, July 16, 1990, pp. A1–A6; "Verdicts," *The National Law Journal*, Feb. 6, 1995, Supplement, C2.

23. This section is based mainly on Daniel A. Wren, *The Evolution of Management Thought*, 2d ed., Wiley, New York, 1979; and W. Jack Duncan, *Great Ideas in Management*, Jossey-Bass, San Francisco, 1989.

24. This section is based mainly on W. Jack Duncan, *Great Ideas in Management*, Jossey-Bass, San Francisco, 1989.

25. Correspondence to Daniel A. Wren from William B. Wolf, cited in Daniel A. Wren, *The Evolution of Management Thought*, 2d ed., Wiley, New York, 1979, p. 250; thirtieth-anniversary edition of Chester I. Barnard, *The Functions of the Executive*, Harvard, Cambridge, Mass., 1968.

26. Claude S. George, Jr., *The History of Management Thought*, Prentice-Hall, Englewood Cliffs, N.J., 1972; Frank J. Landy, "Hugo Münsterberg: Victim or Visionary," *Journal of Applied Psychology*, vol. 77, pp. 787–802.

27. Joe Sherman, *In the Rings of Saturn*, New York, Oxford University Press, 1994.

28. Kenneth R. Andrews, in the introduction to the thirtieth-anniversary edition of Chester I. Barnard, *The Function of the Executive*, Harvard, Cambridge, Mass., 1968; W. Jack Duncan, *Great Ideas in Management*, Jossey-Bass, San Francisco, 1989.

29. Henry C. Metcalf and Lyndall Urwick (eds.), *Dynamic Administration: The Collected Papers of Mary Parker Follett*, Harper & Row, New York, 1940, pp. 32–33.

30. Daniel A. Wren, *The Evolution of Management Thought*, 2d ed., Wiley, New York, 1979; L. D. Parker, "Control in Organizational Life: The Contribution of Mary Parker Follett," *Academy of Management Review*, vol. 9, 1984, pp. 736–745; Dana Wechsler Linden, "The Mother of Them All," *Forbes*, Jan. 16, 1995, pp. 75–76.

31. L. D. Parker, "Control in Organizational Life: The Contribution of Mary Parker Follett," *Academy of Management Review*, vol. 9, 1984, pp. 736–745.

32. *Mary Parker Follett–Prophet of Management: A Celebration of Writings from the 1920s*, Boston, Harvard Business School Press, 1995.

33. Ronald G. Greenwood and Charles D. Wrege, "The Hawthorne Studies," in Daniel A. Wren and John A. Pearce II (eds.), *Papers Dedicated to the Development of Modern Management*, Academy of Management, 1986, pp. 24–35.

34. Ronald G. Greenwood and Charles D. Wrege, "The Hawthorne Studies," in Daniel A. Wren and John A. Pearce II (eds.), *Papers Dedicated to the Development of Modern Management*, Academy of Management, 1986, pp. 24–35.

35. John G. Adair, "The Hawthorne Effect: A Reconsideration of the Methodological Artifact," *Journal of Applied Psychology*, vol. 69, 1984, pp. 334–345.

36. Ronald G. Greenwood and Charles D. Wrege, "The Hawthorne Studies," in Daniel A. Wren and John A. Pearce II (eds.), *Papers Dedicated to the Development of Modern Management*, Academy of Management, 1986, pp. 24–35.

37. Berkeley Rice, "The Hawthorne Defect: Persistence of a Flawed Theory," *Psychology Today*, February 1982, pp. 70–74.

38. John G. Adair, "The Hawthorne Effect: A Reconsideration of the Methodological Artifact," *Journal of Applied Psychology*, vol. 69, 1984, pp. 334–345.

39. Daniel A. Wren, *The Evolution of Management Thought*, 2d ed., Wiley, New York, 1979; Dana Bramel and Ronald Friend, "Hawthorne, the Myth of the Docile Worker, and Class Bias in Psychology," *American Psychologist*, August 1981, pp. 867–878.

40. John G. Adair, "The Hawthorne Effect: A Reconsideration of the Methodological Artifact," *Journal of Applied Psychology*, vol. 69, 1984, pp. 334. The Hawthorne studies have been severely criticized mainly because they often had major flaws (such as changing several factors at the same time) and because important data were sometimes ignored in drawing conclusions (especially in discounting the potential importance of pay). In their defense, the studies were conducted at a time when knowledge about how to conduct such studies was fairly embryonic. For criticisms and clarifications, see, for example, Alex Carey, "The Hawthorne Studies: A Radical Criticism," *American Sociological Review*, June 1967, pp. 403–416; John M. Shepard, "On Alex Carey's Radical Criticisms of the Hawthorne Studies," *Academy of Management Journal*, March 1971, pp. 23–32; Dana Bramel and Ronald Friend, "Hawthorne, the Myth of the Docile Worker, and Class Bias in Psychology," *American Psychologist*, August 1981, pp. 867–878; Ronald G. Greenwood, Alfred A. Bolton, and Regina A. Greenwood, "Hawthorne a Half Century Later: Relay Assembly Participants Remember," *Journal of Management*, vol. 9, 1983, pp. 217–231; and Jeffrey A. Sonnenfeld, "Shedding Light on the Hawthorne Studies," *Journal of Occupational Behavior*, vol. 6, 1985, pp. 111–130.

41. W. Jack Duncan, *Great Ideas in Management*, Jossey-Bass, San Francisco, 1989.

42. A. H. Maslow, "A Theory of Human Motivation," *Psychological Review*, vol. 50, 1943, pp. 370–396, and *Motivation and Personality*, Harper & Row, New York, 1954.

43. Douglas McGregor, *The Human Side of Enterprise*, McGraw-Hill, New York, 1960.

44. Edwin A. Locke, Karyll N. Shaw, Lise M. Saari, and Gary P. Latham, "Goal Setting and Task Performance: 1969–1980," *Psychological Bulletin*, vol. 90, 1982, pp. 125–152; Robert D. Pritchard, Steven D. Jones, Philip L. Roth, Karla K. Stuebing, and Steven E. Ekeberg, "Effects of Group Feedback, Goal Setting, and Incentives on Organizational Productiv-

ity," *Journal of Applied Psychology*, vol. 73, 1988, pp. 337–358.

45. Norman Gaither, "Historical Development of Operations Research," in Daniel A. Wren and John A. Pearce II (eds.), *Papers Dedicated to the Development of Modern Management*, Academy of Management, 1986, pp. 71–77.

46. James R. Miller and Howard Feldman, "Management Science—Theory, Relevance, and Practice in the 1980s," *Interfaces*, October 1983, pp. 56–60.

47. Hicks Waldon, "Putting a New Face on Avon," *Planning Review*, July 1985, pp. 18–25; John Thackray, "Planning an Avon Turnaround," *Planning Review*, January 1985, pp. 6–11.

48. William J. Sawaya, Jr., and William C. Giauque, *Production and Operations Management*, Harcourt Brace Jovanovich, San Diego, 1986.

49. Edward O. Welles, "The Company Money Almost Killed," *INC.*, November 1988, pp. 46–60.

50. Fremont E. Kast and James E. Rosenzweig, "General Systems Theory: Applications for Organization and Management," *Academy of Management Journal*, vol. 15, pp. 447–465.

51. Ludwig von Bertalanffy, "General Systems Theory: A New Approach to the Unity of Science," *Human Biology*, December 1951, pp. 302–361, and "General Systems Theory—A Critical Review," *General Systems*, vol. 7, 1962, pp. 1–20; Daniel Katz and Robert L. Kahn, *The Social Psychology of Organizations*, Wiley, New York, 1978; see also Kenneth E. Boulding, "General Systems Theory—The Skeleton of Science," *Management Science*, vol. 2, 1956, pp. 197–208.

52. Arkalgud Ramaprasad, "On the Definition of Feedback," *Behavioral Science*, January 1983, pp. 4–13.

53. Donde P. Ashmos and George P. Huber, "The Systems Paradigm in Organization Theory: Correcting the Record and Suggesting the Future," *Academy of Management Review*, vol. 12, 1987, pp. 607–621.

54. J. Miller, *Living Systems*, McGraw-Hill, New York, 1978.

55. Fremont E. Kast and James E. Rosenzweig, *Organization and Management: A Systems Approach*, 2d ed., McGraw-Hill, 1974.

56. Fremond E. Kast and James E. Rosenzweig, "General Systems Theory: Applications for Organization and Management," *Academy of Management Journal*, vol. 15, 1972, pp. 447–465; Daniel Katz and Robert L. Kahn, *The Social Psychology of Organizations*, Wiley, New York, 1978.

57. Fred Luthans, "The Contingency Theory of Management," *Business Horizons*, June 1973, pp. 67–72; Sang M. Lee, Fred Luthans, and David L. Olson, "A Management Science Approach to Contingency Models of Organizational Structure," *Academy of Management Journal*, vol. 25, 1982, pp. 553–566.

58. Jay W. Lorsch, "Making Behavioral Science More Useful," *Harvard Business Review*, March–April 1979, pp. 171–180; Henry L. Tosi, Jr., and John W. Slocum, Jr., "Contingency Theory: Some Suggested Directions," *Journal of Management*, vol. 10, 1984, pp. 9–26.

59. See J. Bernard Keys, Luther Trey Denton, and Thomas R. Miller, "The Japanese Management Theory Jungle—Revisited," *Journal of Management*, vol. 20, pp. 373–402.

60. Greg Bounds, Lyle Yorks, Mel Adams, and Gipsie Ranney, *Beyond Total Quality Management: Toward the Emerging Paradigm*, McGraw-Hill, New York, 1994; Frederick F. Reichheld,

"Learning from Customer Defections," *Harvard Business Review*, March–April 1996, pp. 56–69.

61. Based on Anne B. Fisher, "Ford Is Back on the Track," *Fortune*, Dec. 23, 1985, pp. 18–22; Steve Kichen and Jerry Flint, "Supercharged," *Forbes*, Sept. 5, 1988, pp. 74–78; "How to Go Global—And Why," *Fortune*, Aug. 28, 1989, pp. 73–74; Mary Connelly, "Trotman Passes the Word: Becoming No. 1 Is Job 1," *Automotive News*, Nov. 7, 1994, pp. 1, 48; "Trotman's Task: Keep Ford's Focus on Goals," *Automotive News*, Nov. 7, 1994, p. 28; Jerry Flint, "You Know What's in My Heart," *Forbes*, Feb. 13, 1995, pp. 42–104; Alex Taylor III, "Ford's Really Big Leap at the Future: It's Risky, It's Worth It, and It May Not Work," *Fortune*, Sept. 18, 1995, pp. 134–143; Keith Bradsher, "Ford Tests the Price Barrier," *New York Times*, Jan. 24, 1996, p. D1; Keith Bradsher, "Ford Reverses Field and Starts Cutting Costs," *New York Times*, Mar. 5, 1996, p. D1; Keith Naughton, "Trotman's Trials," *Business Week*, Apr. 8, 1996, pp. 30–31; "Ford Auto President Fine-Tunes Overhaul," *Automotive News*, May 27, 1996, p. 20.

62. Based on Gail E. Schares, "The New Generation at Siemens," *Business Week*, Mar. 9, 1992, pp. 46–48; Karen Lowry Miller, "Siemens Shapes Up," *Business Week*, International Edition, May 1, 1995, p. 46; David Crossland, "Siemens Cuts 2,000 German Jobs, Hires Abroad," *The Reuter European Business Report*, Feb. 22, 1996, p. 1; "Siemens Chief Grants More Autonomy," *The Reuter European Business Report*, May 12, 1996, p. 1.

CHAPTER 3

1. Susan Caminiti, "America's Most Successful Businesswoman," *Fortune*, June 15, 1992, pp. 102–107; "Leaders of Corporate Change," *Fortune*, Dec. 14, 1992, pp. 104–114; Ellen Neuborne, "Lingerie Firm's CEO Steers a Turnaround," *USA Today*, Aug. 4, 1994, pp. 1B–2B; "Wachner Takes on the World," *Working Woman*, February 1995, p. 11.

2. Linda Smircich, "Concepts of Culture and Organizational Analysis," *Administrative Science Quarterly*, vol. 28, 1983, pp. 339–358; Ralph H. Kilmann, Mary J. Saxton, and Roy Serpa, "Issues in Understanding and Changing Culture," *California Management Review*, vol. 28, 1986, pp. 87–94.

3. Eric Morgenthaler, "A 19th-Century Firm Shifts, Reinvents Itself and Survives 100 Years," *The Wall Street Journal*, May 9, 1989, pp. A1, A16.

4. Fred R. David, *Concepts of Strategic Management*, Merrill, Columbus, Ohio, 1987, pp. 104–121; Richard H. Hall, *Organizations: Structures, Processes, and Outcomes*, 4th ed., Prentice-Hall, Englewood Cliffs, N.J., 1987, pp. 219–225.

5. Michael L. Tushman and Philip Anderson, "Technological Discontinuities and Organization Environments," *Administrative Science Quarterly*, vol. 31, 1986, pp. 439–465; William P. Barnett, "The Organizational Ecology of a Technological System," *Administrative Science Quarterly*, vol. 35, 1990, pp. 31–60.

6. Edwin A. Finn, Jr., "Megatort Mania," *Forbes*, June 1, 1987, pp. 114–120; Cindy Skrzycki, "Just Who's in Charge Here, Anyway?" *The Washington Post*, Jan. 29, 1989, pp. H1, H8; Idalene F. Kesner and Roy B. Johnson, "An Investigation of the Relationship between Board Composition and Stockholder Suits," *Strategic Management Journal*, vol. 11, 1990, pp. 327–336.

7. Kathleen Deveny, "McWorld?" *Business Week*, Oct. 13, 1986, pp. 80–81.

8. Daniel Bell, "The World and the United States in 2013," *Daedalus*, Summer 1987, pp. 1–31; Carl Davies, "Growing Elderly Population Prompts Rise in Businesses Catering to Seniors," *Warfield's*, July 14, 1995, pp. 9, 13.

9. Based on Eugene Carlson, "How a Major Swedish Retailer Chose a Beachhead in the U.S.," *The Wall Street Journal*, Apr. 7, 1987, p. 37; Barbara Solomon, "A Swedish Company Corners the Business: Worldwide," *Management Review*, April 1991, pp. 10–13; Jack Burton, "Rearranging the Furniture," *International Management*, September 1991, pp. 58–61; and information from an IKEA representative, May 29, 1992; Lissa Wyman, "Rugs Roll at IKEA; Latest Theme at Manhattan Store," *HFN The Weekly Newspaper for the Home Furnishing Network*, Apr. 8, 1996, p. 11.

10. "Little IKEA in Manhattan," *The New York Times*, Sept. 7, 1995, p. 5C; June Carolyn Erlick, "IKEA Bites the Big Apple," *HFN The Weekly Newspaper for the Home Furnishing Network*, Sept. 18, 1995, p. 6; Lissa Wyman, "Rugs Roll at IKEA; Latest Theme at Manhattan Store," *HFN The Weekly Newspaper for the Home Furnishing Network*, Apr. 8, 1996, p. 11.

11. Mary Kuntz, "Reinventing the Store," *Business Week*, Nov. 27, 1995, pp. 84–96.

12. Maggie McComas, "Cutting Costs without Killing the Business," *Fortune*, Oct. 13, 1986, p. 71.

13. John A. Byrne, "Culture Shock at Xerox," *Business Week*, June 22, 1987, pp. 106–110.

14. Rudolph A. Pyatt, Jr., "AAA's Lesson for Fairfax," *The Washington Post*, Oct. 3, 1986, pp. F1–F2.

15. Based on Leonard M. Fuld, "How to Get the Scoop on Your Competition," *Working Woman*, January 1989, pp. 39–42; and Leonard M. Fuld, *Monitoring the Competition*, Wiley, New York, 1988.

16. William B. Johnston, "Global Work Force 2000: The New World Labor Market," *Harvard Business Review*, March–April 1991, pp. 115–127.

17. Joan E. Rigdon, "PepsiCo's KFC Scouts for Blacks and Women for Its Top Echelons," *The Wall Street Journal*, Nov. 13, 1991, p. A1.

18. This section relies heavily on Richard H. Hall, *Organizations*, 4th ed., Prentice-Hall, Englewood Cliffs, N.J., 1987; and David Ulrich and Jay B. Barney, "Perspectives in Organizations: Resource Dependence, Efficiency, and Population," *Academy of Management Review*, vol. 9, 1984, pp. 471–481.

19. Michael T. Hannan and John Freeman, "The Population Ecology of Organizations," *American Journal of Sociology*, vol. 82, 1977, pp. 929–964; John Betton and Gregory G. Dess, "The Application of Population Ecology Models to the Study of Organizations," *Academy of Management Review*, vol. 10, 1985, pp. 750–757.

20. "It's Tough Up There," *Forbes*, July 13, 1987, pp. 145–160.

21. Jeffrey Pfeffer and Gerald Salancik, *The External Control of Organizations*, Harper & Row, New York, 1978; David Ulrich and Jay B. Barney, "Perspectives in Organizations: Resource Dependence, Efficiency, and Population," *Academy of Management Review*, vol. 9, 1984, pp. 471–481.

22. G. Pascal Zachary, "Software Makers Get a Chill from Microsoft's Windows," *The Wall Street Journal*, Oct., 10, 1989, pp. B1, B8; John Burgess, "IBM Finishes One Race, Starts Another," *The Washington Post*, Mar. 31, 1992, p. C1.

23. Jeffrey Pfeffer and Gerald Salancik, *The External Control of Organizations*, Harper & Row, New York, 1978.

24. Karl E. Weick, *Sensemaking in Organizations*, Sage Publications, Thousand Oaks, Calif., 1995.

25. Brian K. Boyd, Gregory G. Dess, and Abdul M. A. Rasheed, "Divergence between Archival and Perceptual Measures of the Environment: Causes and Consequences," *Academy of Management Review*, vol. 18, 1993, pp. 204–226.

26. Jeffrey Pfeffer and Gerald Salancik, *The External Control of Organizations*, Harper & Row, New York, 1978, p. 67.

27. Gregory G. Dess and Donald W. Beard, "Dimensions of Organizational Task Environments," *Administrative Science Quarterly*, vol. 29, 1984, pp. 52–73.

28. Howard E. Aldrich, *Organizations and Environments*, Prentice-Hall, Englewood Cliffs, N.J., 1979, pp. 63–66; Gregory G. Dess and Donald W. Beard, "Dimensions of Organizational Task Environments," *Administrative Science Quarterly*, vol. 29, 1984, pp. 52–73.

29. Gary J. Castrogiovanni, "Environmental Munificence: A Theoretical Assessment," *Academy of Management Review*, vol. 16, 1991, pp. 542–565.

30. Based on Barry Stavro, "Loser and Still Champion," *Forbes*, Nov. 17, 1986, p. 176; Stephen Phillips, "Champion Is Starting to Show a Little Spark," *Business Week*, Mar. 21, 1988, p. 87; Jacob M. Schlesinger, "Champion Spark to Be Acquired for $800 Million," *The Wall Street Journal*, Feb. 22, 1989, p. A4; William P. Barrett, "I Get a Kick Out of Seeing Something Being Made," *Forbes*, Feb. 5, 1990, pp. 96–98; B. McMenamin, "Waste Not, Earn a Lot," *Forbes*, Jan. 6, 1992, p. 103; David J. Collis and Cynthia A. Montgomery, "Competing on Resources: Strategy in the 1990s," *Harvard Business Review*, July–August 1995, pp. 118–128.

31. Cathy Booth, "Against the Time," *Time*, Feb. 17, 1992, pp. 54–56.

32. James D. Thompson, *Organizations in Action*, McGraw-Hill, New York, 1967, pp. 20–37; John P. Kotter, "Managing External Dependence," *Academy of Management Review*, vol. 4, 1979, pp. 87–92.

33. James D. Thompson, *Organizations in Action*, McGraw-Hill, New York, 1967, pp. 20–23.

34. Peter Fuhrman, "The Workers' Friend," *Forbes*, Mar. 21, 1988, pp. 124–128.

35. John P. Kotter, "Managing External Dependence," *Academy of Management Review*, vol. 4, 1979, pp. 87–92.

36. Howard Aldrich and Diane Herker, "Boundary Spanning Roles and Organization Structure," *Academy of Management Review*, vol. 2, 1977, pp. 217–230; Michael L. Tushman and Thomas J. Scanlan, "Boundary Spanning Individuals: Their Role in Information Transfer and Their Antecedents," *Academy of Management Journal*, vol. 24, 1981, pp. 289–305.

37. Mark S. Mizruchi, "Who Controls Whom? An Examination of the Relation between Management and Boards of Directors in Large American Corporations," *Academy of Management Review*, vol. 8, 1983, pp. 426–435; Elizabeth Lesly, "Are These 10 Stretched Too Thin?" *Business Week*, Nov. 13, 1995, p. 78.

38. Alex Miller and Gregory G. Dess, *Strategic Management*, McGraw-Hill, 1996; Michael Y. Yoshino and U. Srinivasa Rangan, *Strategic Alliance: An Entrepreneurial Approach to Globalization*, Harvard Business School, Boston, 1995.

39. Erin Anderson, "Two Firms, One Frontier: On Assessing Joint Venture Performance," *Sloan Management Review,* Winter 1990, pp. 19–26.

40. Mark Potts, "Toys 'R' US and McDonald's Take on Japanese Toy Market," *The Washington Post,* Sept. 27, 1989, p. B1; "Expansion Abroad Outpaces Domestic Growth. The Power Retailers: Toys 'R' Us," *Discount Store News,* Feb. 5, 1996, p. 52.

41. Jonathan B. Levine and John A. Byrne, "Corporate Odd Couples," *Business Week,* July 21, 1986, pp. 100–105.

42. "Washington, D.C.: Home of the Association Business," *The Washington Times,* Jan. 29, 1986, p. 3E.

43. Caroline E. Mayer, "Minn. Passes Bill to Aid Dayton Hudson," *The Washington Post,* June 26, 1987, p. F1.

44. Burr Leonard, "Life after Death," *Forbes,* May 4, 1987, pp. 132–133.

45. Michael Oneal, "Harley-Davidson: Ready to Hit the Road Again," *Business Week,* July 21, 1986, p. 70; Peter C. Reid, "How Harley Beat Back the Japanese," *Fortune,* Sept. 25, 1989, pp. 155–164; Lore Crogham, "Customers for Life: How to Hang On to Your Core Market the Harley-Davidson Way," *Financial World,* Sept. 26, 1995, pp. 26–31; Diane Trommer, "Suppliers Key to New Harley," *Electronic Buyers' News,* May 13, 1996, p. 54.

46. Peter C. Reid, "How Harley Beat Back the Japanese," *Fortune,* Sept. 25, 1989, pp. 155–164.

47. Linda Smircich, "Concepts of Culture and Organizational Analysis," *Administrative Science Quarterly,* vol. 28, 1983, pp. 339–358; Ralph H. Kilmann, Mary J. Saxton, and Roy Serpa, "Issues in Understanding and Changing Culture," *California Management Review,* vol. 28, 1986, pp. 87–94.

48. Ralph H. Kilmann, "Five Steps for Closing Culture-Gaps," in Ralph H. Kilmann, Mary J. Saxton, Roy Serpa, and associates, *Gaining Control of the Corporate Culture,* Jossey-Bass, San Francisco, 1985, pp. 351–369.

49. Ralph H. Kilmann, Mary J. Saxton, and Roy Serpa, "Issues in Understanding and Changing Culture," *California Management Review,* vol. 28, 1986, pp. 87–94; Joanne Martin, *Cultures in Organizations: Three Perspectives,* Oxford University Press, New York, 1992; Edgar H. Schein, *Organizational Culture and Leadership,* 2d ed., Jossey-Bass, San Francisco, 1992.

50. Jay B. Barney, "Organizational Culture: Can It Be a Source of Sustained Competitive Advantage?" *Academy of Management Review,* vol. 11, 1986, pp. 656–665.

51. Linda Smircich, "Concepts of Culture and Organizational Analysis," *Administrative Science Quarterly,* vol. 28, 1983, pp. 339–358. This section relies heavily on Harrison M. Trice and Janice M. Beyer, *The Cultures of Work Organizations,* Prentice-Hall, Englewood Cliffs, N.J., 1993.

52. Jagannath Dubashi, "Through a Glass Lightly," *Financial World,* May 19, 1987, pp. 20–29.

53. Terrence E. Deal and Allan A. Kennedy, *Corporate Cultures: The Rites and Rituals of Corporate Life,* Addison-Wesley, Reading, Mass., 1982.

54. Ibid.

55. This section is based on Howard H. Stevenson and David E. Gumpert, "The Heart of Entrepreneurship," *Harvard Business Review,* March–April 1985, pp. 85–94; see also John P. Kotter and James L. Heskett, *Corporate Culture and Performance,* Free Press, New York, 1992.

56. Robert D. Hof, "From Dinosaur to Gazelle," *Business Week/Reinventing America 1992,* Oct. 23, 1992, p. 65.

57. This section is based on Eric Abrahamson and Charles J. Fombrun, "Macrocultures: Determinants and Consequences," *Academy of Management Review,* vol. 19, 1994, pp. 728–755; see also Jennifer A. Chatman and Karen A. Jehn, "Assessing the Relationship between Industry Characteristics and Organizational Culture: How Different Can You Be?" *Academy of Management Journal,* vol. 37, 1994, pp. 522–553.

58. Jay W. Lorsch, "Managing Culture: The Invisible Barrier to Strategic Change," *California Management Review,* Winter 1986, pp. 95–109.

59. Ralph H. Kilmann, "Five Steps for Closing Culture-Gaps," in Ralph H. Kilmann, Mary J. Saxton, Roy Serpa, and associates, *Gaining Control of the Corporate Culture,* Jossey-Bass, San Francisco, 1985, pp. 351–369.

60. This section is based on John P. Kotter and James L. Heskett, *Corporate Culture and Performance,* Free Press, New York, 1992.

61. Gary Jacobson and John Hillrirk, *Xerox, American Samurai,* Macmillan, New York, 1986; John A. Byrne, "Culture Shock at Xerox," *Business Week,* June 22, 1987, pp. 106–110; John Holusha, "Stress on Quality Lifts Xerox's Market Share," *The New York Times,* Nov. 9, 1989, pp. D1–D11; James R. Norman, "Xerox on the Move," *Forbes,* June 10, 1991, pp. 70–71; John Holusha, "Japan Is Tough, but Xerox Prevails," *The New York Times,* Sept. 3, 1992, pp. D1, D16; Sandra Sugawara, "A Wrenching Reinvention," *The Washington Post,* Sept. 25, 1994, pp. H7–H8; Surata N. Chakravarty, "Back in Focus," *Forbes,* June 6, 1994, pp. 72–76; Phillip Fiorini, "Xerox's Back-to-Basics Plan Working," *USA Today,* Feb. 3, 1995, p. 3B; Richard J. Lee, "Xerox 2000: From Survival to Opportunity," *Quality Progress,* March 1996, pp. 65–71.

62. Sandra Sugawara and Kara Swisher, "Corporate Culture Tug of War," *The Washington Post,* Sept. 28, 1992, Washington Business sec., pp. 1, 22ff.; Gail E. Schares, "Capitalism That Would Make Karl Marx Proud," *Business Week,* Nov. 16, 1992, pp. 82–83; and Sandra Sugawara, "Software AG's Chief Executive Quits Abruptly," *The Washington Post,* Nov. 24, 1992, pp. D1, D12; Scott Leibs, "Only the Strong Survive: Top 50 Software Vendors," *Information Week,* May 22, 1995, p. 44.

CHAPTER 4

1. Frederick G. Harmon and Garry Jacobs, "Company Personality: The Heart of the Matter," *Management Review,* October 1985, pp. 36–37; Thaddeus F. Tuleja, *Beyond the Bottom Line: How Business Leaders Are Turning Principles into Profits,* Facts on File, New York, 1985, pp. 78–80; Sana Siwolop and Christopher Eklund, "The Capsule Controversy: How Far Should the FDA Go?" *Business Week,* Mar. 3, 1986, p. 37.

2. Edward C. Baig, "America's Most Admired Corporations," *Fortune,* Jan. 19, 1987, pp. 18–23; Kate Ballen, "America's Most Admired Corporations," *Fortune,* Feb. 10, 1992, pp. 40–46; "J&J Is on a Roll," *Fortune,* Dec. 26, 1994, pp. 178–192; Kate Walter, "Values Statements That Augment Corporate Success," *HR Magazine,* October 1995, p. 87.

3. Laura L. Nash, *Good Intentions Aside: A Manager's Guide to Resolving Ethical Problems,* Harvard Business School Press, Boston, 1990; James O'Toole, "Do Good, Do Well: The Business Enterprise Trust Awards," *California Management Review,* Spring 1991, pp. 9–22.

4. James O'Toole, *Vanguard Management: Redesigning the Corporate Future,* Doubleday, Garden City, N.Y., 1985, pp. 235–236.

5. Charles E. Shepard, "United Way Report Criticizes Ex-Leader's 'Lavish' Lifestyle," *The Washington Post,* Apr. 4, 1992, pp. A1, A9; Charles W. Hall, "Ex-United Way Chief Sentenced to 7 Years," *The Washington Post,* June 23, 1995, p. 1A.

6. Milton R. Moskowitz, "Company Performance Roundup," *Business and Society Review,* Winter 1994, p. 64.

7. William M. Carley, "Artificial Heart Valves That Fail Are Linked to Falsified Records," *The Wall Street Journal,* Nov. 11, 1991, pp. A1, A6.

8. Daniel Pearl, "How 2 Florida Firms Fooled Stockholders, Auditors and the SEC," *The Wall Street Journal,* July 8, 1992, pp. A1, A5.

9. Laura Johannes, "Astra Suspends Two Officials in Probe of Alleged Harassment, Fiscal Misdeeds," *The Wall Street Journal,* May 6, 1996, p. A4.

10. Stephen H. Wildstrom, "A Risky Tack for Democrats," *Business Week,* July 20, 1987, p. 71.

11. James E. Post, William C. Frederick, Anne T. Lawrence, and James Weber, *Business and Society,* 8th ed., McGraw-Hill, New York, 1996.

12. Archie Carroll, *Business and Society: Ethics and Stakeholder Management,* South-Western, Cincinnati, 1989.

13. The framework is based on Kenneth E. Goodpaster and John B. Matthews, Jr., "Can a Corporation Have a Conscience?" *Harvard Business Review,* January–February 1982, pp. 134–141.

14. Milton Friedman, *Capitalism and Freedom,* University of Chicago, 1962, pp. 133–136.

15. One proponent of this view is John Kenneth Galbraith, *The New Industrial State,* University of Chicago, 1962, and *The Age of Uncertainty,* Houghton-Mifflin, Boston, 1975.

16. James E. Post, William C. Frederick, Anne T. Lawrence, and James Weber, *Business and Society,* 8th ed., McGraw-Hill, New York, 1996.

17. Thaddeus F. Tulejo, *Beyond the Bottom Line: How Business Leaders Are Turning Principles into Profits,* Facts on File, New York, 1985.

18. James E. Post, William C. Frederick, Anne T. Lawrence, and James Weber, *Business and Society,* 8th ed., McGraw-Hill, New York, 1996.

19. Cited in Thaddeus F. Tuleja, *Beyond the Bottom Line: How Business Leaders Are Turning Principles into Profits,* Facts on File, New York, 1985, p. 118.

20. Archie B. Carroll, "A Three-Dimensional Conceptual Model of Corporate Performance," *Academy of Management Review,* vol. 4, 1979, pp. 499–500; Robert D. Gatewood and Archie B. Carroll, "Assessment of Ethical Performance of Organization Members: A Conceptual Framework," *Academy of Management Review,* vol. 16, 1991, pp. 667–690.

21. James E. Post, William C. Frederick, Anne T. Lawrence, and James Weber, *Business and Society,* 8th ed., McGraw-Hill, New York, 1996.

22. "Public Service," *Business Week,* Jan. 11, 1988, p. 156.

23. Thaddeus F. Tuleja, *Beyond the Bottom Line: How Business Leaders Are Turning Principles into Profits,* Facts on File, New York, 1985, pp. 41–131; Thomas Donaldson and Lee E. Preston, "The Stakeholder Theory of the Corporation: Concepts, Evidence, and Implications," *Academy of Management Review,* vol. 20, 1995, pp. 65–91.

24. This section relies heavily on James E.

Post, William C. Frederick, Anne T. Lawrence, and James Weber, *Business and Society*, 8th ed., McGraw-Hill, New York, 1996.

25. John A. Byrne, "Gross Compensation?" *Business Week*, Mar. 18, 1996, pp. 32–33.

26. Cathy Trost, "Bhopal Disaster Spurs Debate over Usefulness of Criminal Sanctions in Industrial Accidents, *The Wall Street Journal*, Jan. 7, 1985, p. 18.

27. Joseph Weber, "Meet Du Pont's 'In-House Conscience,'" *Business Week*, June 24, 1991, pp. 62–65.

28. Taylor Cox, Jr., *Cultural Diversity in Organizations: Theory, Research & Practice*, Berrett-Koehler Publishers, San Francisco, 1994.

29. Mark Potts, "Bic Stock Dives after Report about Lighters," *The Washington Post*, Apr. 11, 1987, p. D10.

30. Susan Caminiti, "The Payoff from a Good Reputation," *Fortune*, Feb. 10, 1992, pp. 74–77.

31. Warren Brown, "Perrier's Market Share Fizzles in the Aftermath of Its Recall," *The Washington Post*, Jan. 4, 1991, p. F3; E. S. Browning, "Nestlé Appears to Win Battle to Acquire Source Perrier," *The Wall Street Journal*, Mar. 24, 1992, p. A13; E. S. Browning, "Perrier Tries to Rejuvenate Stodgy Image," *The Wall Street Journal*, Sept. 2, 1993, p. B1.

32. James E. Post, William C. Frederick, Anne T. Lawrence, and James Weber, *Business and Society*, 8th ed., McGraw-Hill, New York, 1996.

33. Lisa Atkinson and Joseph Galaskiewicz, "Stock Ownership and Company Contributions to Charity," *Administrative Science Quarterly*, vol. 33, 1988, pp. 82–100.

34. Milton R. Moskowitz, "Company Performance Roundup," *Business and Society Review*, Winter 1989, pp. 72–78.

35. Troy Segal, "Saving Our Schools," *Business Week*, Sept. 14, 1992, pp. 70–78; Aaron Bernstein, "Teaching Business How to Train," *Business Week/Reinventing America 1992*, Oct. 23, 1992. pp. 82–90.

36. Edward Cornish, "A Short List of Global Concerns," *The Futurist*, January–February 1990, pp. 29–36.

37. Susan Caminiti, "The Payoff from a Good Reputation," *Fortune*, Feb. 10, 1992, pp. 74–77.

38. Peter Arlow and Martin J. Gannon, "Social Responsiveness, Corporate Structure, and Economic Performance," *Academy of Management Review*, vol. 7, 1982, pp. 235–241; Kenneth E. Aupperle, Archie B. Carroll, and John D. Hatfield, "An Empirical Examination of the Relationship between Corporate Social Responsibility and Profitability," *Academy of Management Journal*, vol. 28, 1985, pp. 446–463.

39. Jean B. McGuire, Alison Sundgren, and Thomas Schneeweis, "Corporate Social Responsibility and Firm Financial Performance," *Academy of Management Journal*, vol. 31, 1988, pp. 854–872.

40. Wallace N. Davison III and Dan I. Worrell, "The Impact of Announcements of Corporate Illegalities on Shareholder Returns," *Academy of Management Journal*, vol. 31, 1988, pp. 195–200.

41. Richard E. Wokutch and Barbara A. Spencer, "Corporate Saints and Sinners: The Effects of Philanthropic and Illegal Activity on Organizational Performance," *California Management Review*, vol. 29, 1987, pp. 62–77.

42. Nelson Schwartz, "Giving—And Getting Something Back," *Business Week*, Aug. 28, 1995, p. 81; Craig Smith, "The New Corporate Philanthropy," *Harvard Business Review*, May–June 1994, pp. 105–116.

43. James O'Toole, *Vanguard Management: Redesigning the Corporate Future*, Doubleday, Garden City, N.Y., 1985.

44. "Low Grade Government," *USA Today*, Sept. 3, 1992, p. A1.

45. James E. Post, William C. Frederick, Anne T. Lawrence and James Weber, *Business and Society*, 8th ed., McGraw-Hill, New York, 1996.

46. Ben & Jerry's Homemade, Inc., *Annual Report*, 1995.

47. John E. Fleming, "Public Issues Scanning," in Lee Preston (ed.), *Research in Corporate Social Performance and Policy*, vol. 3, JAI, Greenwich, Conn., 1981, pp. 154–174; Steven L. Wartick and Philip L. Cochran, "The Evolution of the Corporate Social Performance Model," *Academy of Management Review*, vol. 10, 1985, pp. 758–769.

48. Stephen E. Littlejohn, "Competition and Cooperation: New Trends in Corporate Public Issues Identification and Resolution," *California Management Review*, vol. 29, Fall 1986, pp. 109–123.

49. Richard L. Daft, Juhani Sormunen, and Don Parks, "Chief Executive Scanning, Environmental Characteristics, and Company Performance: An Empirical Study," *Strategic Management Journal*, vol. 9, 1988, pp. 123–139.

50. Sadahei Kusumoto, "We're Not in Honshu Anymore," *Across the Board*, June 1989, pp. 49–50; Michael Schroeder, "Charity Doesn't Begin at Home Anymore," *Business Week*, Feb. 25, 1991, p. 91.

51. Rich Strand, "A Systems Paradigm of Organizational Adaptations to the Social Environment," *Academy of Management Review*, vol. 8, 1987, pp. 93–94.

52. This section is based mainly on Sandra L. Holmes, "Adapting Corporate Structure for Social Responsiveness," *Business Horizons*, Fall 1978, pp. 47–54; see also, James E. Post, William C. Frederick, Anne T. Lawrence, and James Weber, *Business and Society: Corporate Strategy, Public Policy, Ethics*, McGraw-Hill, New York, 1996.

53. Michael L. Lovdal, Raymond A. Bauer, and Nancy H. Treverton, "Public Responsibility Committees on the Board," *Harvard Business Review*, May–June 1977, pp. 41–64.

54. James E. Post, Edwin A. Murray, Jr., Robert B. Dickie, and John F. Mahon, "Managing Public Affairs: The Public Affairs Function," *California Management Review*, Fall 1983, pp. 135–136; James E. Post and the Foundation for Public Affairs, "The State of Corporate Public Affairs in the United States," *Research in Corporate Social Performance and Policy*, vol. 14, 1993, pp. 81–91.

55. Arvind Bhambri and Jeffrey Sonnenfeld, "Organization Structure and Corporate Social Performance: A Field Study in Two Contrasting Industries," *Academy of Management Journal*, vol. 31, 1988, pp. 642–662.

56. Adapted (with minor changes) from Rod Willis, "The Levi Strauss Credo: Fashion and Philanthropy," *Management Review*, July 1986, pp. 51–54.

57. Arthur P. Brief, Janet M. Dukerich, Paul R. Brown, and Joan F. Brett, "What's Wrong with the Treadway Commission Report?" *Journal of Business Ethics*, February 1996, pp. 183–198.

58. "How You Play the Game Says Whether You Win," *The Wall Street Journal*, Apr. 18, 1989, p. B1; Randy N. Myers, "At Martin Marietta, This Board Game Is Lesson in Ethics," *The Wall Street Journal*, Sept. 25, 1992, p. B7A.

59. *Webster's New World Dictionary*, 2d College Edition, New York, Simon & Schuster, 1984.

60. Stephen Koepp, "Having It All, Then Throwing It All Away," *Time*, May 25, 1987, pp. 22–23; Ezra Bowen, "Looking to Its Roots," *Time*, May 25, 1987, pp. 26–29; Bryan Burrough, "Broken Barrier: More Women Join Ranks of White-Collar Criminals," *The Wall Street Journal*, May 29, 1987, p. 29.

61. James E. Post, William C. Frederick, Anne T. Lawrence, and James Weber, *Business and Society*, 8th ed., McGraw-Hill, New York, 1996.

62. This section, including the examples, is based on Archie B. Carroll, "In Search of the Moral Manager," *Business Horizons*, March–April 1987, pp. 7–15.

63. "Can You Afford to Be Ethical?" *INC.*, December 1992, p. 16.

64. Thaddeus F. Tuleja, *Beyond the Bottom Line: How Business Leaders Are Turning Principles into Profits*, Facts on File, New York, 1985.

65. These guidelines are offered by James O'Toole, *Vanguard Management: Redesigning the Corporate Future*, Doubleday, Garden City, N.Y., 1985, p. 349.

66. "Former Head of Charity Charged with Embezzling," *The Wall Street Journal*, Oct. 31, 1995, p. B11; David Stipp, "I Stole to Get Even: Yet Another Charity Scam," *Fortune*, Oct. 30, 1995, p. 24.

67. Milton R. Moskowitz, "Company Performance Roundup," *Business and Society Review*, Winter 1987, pp. 69–70.

68. Richard W. Stevenson, "Catering to Consumers' Ethnic Needs," *The New York Times*, Jan. 23, 1992, pp. D1, D8.

69. Thaddeus F. Tuleja, *Beyond the Bottom Line: How Business Leaders Are Turning Principles into Profits*, Facts on File, New York, 1985, p. 25.

70. Milton R. Moskowitz, "Company Performance Roundup," *Business and Society Review*, Winter 1987, p. 69.

71. Ibid., pp. 70–71.

72. Reprinted from Laura L. Nash, "Ethics without the Sermon," *Harvard Business Review*, November–December 1981, p. 81.

73. This section is based on Arvind Bhambri and Jeffrey Sonnenfeld, "The Man Who Stands Alone," *New Management*, Spring 1987, pp. 29–33.

74. Abridged (with minor changes) from Martha Brannigan, "Auditor's Downfall Shows a Man Caught in Trap of His Own Making," *The Wall Street Journal*, Mar. 4, 1987, p. 32.

75. "Aftermath of Huge Fraud Prompts Claims of Regret," *The Wall Street Journal*, Mar. 4, 1987, p. 32; Alison Leigh Cowan, "Big Law and Auditing Firms to Pay Millions in S. & L. Suit," *The New York Times*, Mar. 31, 1992, p. A1.

76. This section relies heavily on Henry C. Finney and Henry R. Lesieur, "A Contingency Theory of Organizational Crime," *Research in the Sociology of Organizations*, vol. 1, 1982, pp. 255–299; and Melissa S. Baucus and Janet P. Near, "Can Illegal Corporate Behavior Be Predicted? An Event History Analysis," *Academy of Management Journal*, vol. 34, 1991, pp. 9–36.

77. Chris Welles, "What Led Beech-Nut Down the Road to Disgrace," *Business Week*, Feb. 22, 1988, pp. 124–128; Joe Queenan, "Juice Men," *Barrons*, June 20, 1988, pp. 37–38.

78. Joseph Pereeira and Joseph Rebello, "Production Problems at Generic-Drug Firm Lead to Serious Claims," *The Wall Street Journal*, Feb. 2, 1995, p. A1.

79. Bruce Ingersoll, "Generic-Drug Scandal at the FDA Is Linked to Deregulation Drive," *The Wall Street Journal*, Sept. 13, 1989, pp. A1, A14.

80. Kurt Eichenwald, "Two Sued by S.E.C. in Bidding Scandal at Salomon Bros.," *The New York Times*, Dec 3, 1992, p. A1.

81. Diana T. Kurylko, "Opel Says Empowerment Was Factor in Wrongdoing," *Automotive News*, July 17, 1995, pp. 1, 36.

82. Barry Z. Posner and Warren H. Schmidt, "Values and the American Manager: An Update," *California Management Review*, vol. 26, 1984, pp. 202–216.

83. This section relies heavily on James E. Post, William C. Frederick, Anne T. Lawrence, and James Weber, *Business and Society*, 8th ed., McGraw-Hill, New York, 1996.

84. Alan L. Otten, "Ethics on the Job: Companies Alert Employees to Potential Dilemmas," *The Wall Street Journal*, July 14, 1986, p. 21.

85. Catherine C. Langlois and Bodo B. Schlegelmilch, "Do Corporate Codes of Ethics Reflect National Character? Evidence from Europe and the United States," *Journal of International Business Studies*, vol. 21, 1990, pp. 519–539.

86. John A. Byrne, "The Best-Laid Ethics Programs . . . ," *Business Week*, Mar. 9, 1992, pp. 67–69; Thomas M. Burton, "Jury in Breast-Implant Case Finds Dow Chemical Co. Solely Liable," *The Wall Street Journal*, Oct. 30, 1995, p. B5; Thomas M. Burton, "Breast-Implant Study Is Fresh Fuel for Debate," *The Wall Street Journal*, Feb. 28, 1996, p. B1; Richard B. Schmitt, "U.S. Judge in Silicon-Gel Implant Case May Appoint National Panel of Experts," *The Wall Street Journal*, May 22, 1996, p. 4A.

87. Janelle Brinker Dozier and Marcia P. Miceli, "Potential Predictors of Whistle-Blowing: A Prosocial Behavior Perspective," *Academy of Management Review*, vol. 10, 1985, pp. 823–836; Janet P. Near and Marcia P. Miceli, "Effective Whistle-Blowing," *Academy of Management Review*, vol. 20, 1995, 679–708.

88. Terence R. Mitchell, Denise Daniels, Heidi Hopper, Jane George-Falvy, and George R. Ferris, "Perceived Correlates of Illegal Behavior in Organizations," *Journal of Business Ethics*, April 1996, pp. 439–455.

89. From Lockheed Martin's "Gray Matters: The Ethics Game Manual," 1992, pp. 9, 25, and 29.

90. Adapted (with minor changes) from "A Question of Ethics," *National Business Employment Weekly*, Special Edition, Managing Your Career, Spring 1987, p. 4.

91. Abridged (with minor changes) from Arvind Bhambri and Jeffrey Sonnenfeld, "The Man Who Stands Alone," *New Management*, Spring 1987, pp. 30–31.

92. Copyright 1992 by Brad Brown and Susan Perry. Reprinted by permission.

CHAPTER 5

1. Based on Thomas Moore, "He Put the Kick Back into Coke," *Fortune*, Oct. 26, 1987; also Jaclyn Fierman, "How Coke Decided a New Taste Was It," *Fortune*, May 27, 1985, p. 80; Scott Scredon and Marc Frons, "Coke's Man on the Spot," *Business Week*, July 29, 1985, pp. 56–61; "Some Things Don't Go Better with Coke," *Forbes*, Mar. 21, 1988, pp. 34–35; "New Coke," *Chief Executive*, May–June 1988, pp. 36–40; Michael J. McCarthy, "As a Global Marketer, Coke Excels by Being Tough and Consistent," *The Wall Street Journal*, Dec. 19, 1989, pp. A1, A6; Patricia Winters, "Coke II Enters Market without Splashy Fanfare," *Advertising Age*, Aug. 24, 1992, p. 2; John Huey, "The World's Best Brand," *Fortune*, May 31,

1993, pp. 44–62; Glenn Collins, "Ten Years Later, Coca-Cola Laughs at 'New Coke,'" *The New York Times*, Apr. 11, 1995, p. C4; Robert Frank, "Coca-Cola Is Shedding Its Once-Stodgy Image with Swift Expansion," *The Wall Street Journal*, Aug. 22, 1995, pp. A1, A5; *The Coca-Cola Company 1995 Annual Report;* Chris Roush, "The Georgia 100," *The Atlanta Journal and Constitution*, May 19, 1996, p. 1; Roderick Oram, "European Marketing Strategy in a Bottle," *Financial Times*, June 5, 1996, p. 37.

2. Lois Therrien, "The Rival Japan Respects," *Business Week*, Nov. 13, 1989, pp. 108–118.

3. See Alvin Elbing, *Behavioral Decisions in Organizations*, Scott, Foresman, Glenview, Ill., 1978.

4. George P. Huber, *Managerial Decision Making*, Scott, Foresman, Glenview, Ill., 1980.

5. Henry Mintzberg, Duru Raisignhani, and Andre Theoret, "The Structure of 'Unstructured' Decision Processes," *Administrative Science Quarterly*, vol. 21, 1976, pp. 246–275; Paul C. Nutt, "Types of Organizational Decision Processes," *Administrative Science Quarterly*, vol. 29, 1984, pp. 414–450.

6. Glenn Collins, "Ten Years Later, Coca-Cola Laughs at 'New Coke,'" *The New York Times*, Apr. 11, 1995, p. C4.

7. Betsy Morris, "Shaking Things Up at Coca-Cola Foods," *The Wall Street Journal*, Apr. 3, 1987, p. 36.

8. Robert Frank, "Coca-Cola Is Shedding Its Once-Stodgy Image with Swift Expansion," *The Wall Street Journal*, Aug. 22, 1995, pp. A1, A5.

9. Paul C. Nutt, "Types of Organizational Decision Processes," *Administrative Science Quarterly*, vol. 29, 1984, pp. 414–450.

10. Arthur M. Louis, "America's New Economy: How to Manage in It," *Fortune*, June 23, 1986, pp. 21–25.

11. See, for example, Max H. Bazerman, *Judgment in Managerial Decision Making*, Wiley, New York, 1986.

12. Ronald N. Taylor, *Behavioral Decision Making*, Scott, Foresman, Glenview, Ill., 1984.

13. Katherine Weisman, "Safe Harbor," *Forbes*, Sept. 4, 1989, pp. 58–62.

14. Bernard M. Bass, *Organizational Decision Making*, Irwin, Homewood, Ill., 1983; Gidean Keren, "Perspectives of Behavioral Decision Making: Some Critical Notes," *Organizational Behavior and Human Decision Processes*, vol. 65, 1996, pp. 169–178.

15. See, for example, Herbert A. Simon, "A Behavioral Model of Rational Choice," *Quarterly Journal of Economics*, vol. 69, 1955, pp. 99–118, and "Rational Choice and the Structure of the Environment," *Psychological Review*, vol. 63, 1956, pp. 129–138.

16. Max H. Bazerman, *Judgment in Managerial Decision Making*, Wiley, New York, 1986.

17. George P. Huber, *Managerial Decision Making*, Scott, Foresman, Glenview, Ill., 1980.

18. Pranay Gupte, "Merge in Haste, Repent in Leisure," *Forbes*, Aug. 22, 1988, p. 85.

19. Bernard M. Bass, *Organizational Decision Making*, Irwin, Homewood, Ill., 1983.

20. George P. Huber, *Managerial Decision Making*, Scott, Foresman, Glenview, Ill., 1980.

21. Michael D. Cohen, James G. March, and Johan P. Olsen, "A Garbage Can Model of Organizational Choice," *Administrative Science Quarterly*, vol. 17, 1972, pp. 1–25; Anna Grandori, "A Prescriptive Contingency View of Organizational Decision Making," *Administrative Science Quarterly*, vol. 29, 1984, pp. 192–209.

22. Steve Weiner, "Taking the Pledge," *Forbes*,

June 29, 1987, pp. 41–42; Stephen Kindel, "The 10 Worst Managed Companies in America," *Financial World*, July 26, 1988, pp. 28–39; Michael Oneal, "Gould Is So Thin You Can Hardly See It," *Business Week*, Aug. 29, 1988, p. 74; "Japan Makes a Bid for the Merger Business," *The Economist*, Sept. 17, 1988, pp. 85–86.

23. Daniel D. Wheeler and Irving L. Janis, *A Practical Guide for Making Decisions*, Free Press, New York, 1980.

24. This section is based on David A. Cowan, "Developing a Process Model of Problem Recognition," *Academy of Management Review*, vol. 11, 1986, pp. 763–776.

25. The Swiss watchmaker example is based mainly on Margaret Studer, "SMH Leads a Revival of Swiss Watchmaker Industry," *The Wall Street Journal*, Jan. 20, 1992, p. B4; and Peter Fuhrman, "Jewelry for the Wrist," *Forbes*, Nov. 23, 1992, pp. 173–178.

26. Ronald N. Taylor, *Behavioral Decision Making*, Scott, Foresman, Glenview, Ill., 1984.

27. A. F. Osborn, *Applied Imagination*, Scribner, New York, 1963.

28. Norman R. F. Maier, *Problem-Solving Discussions and Conferences: Leadership Methods and Skills*, McGraw-Hill, New York, 1963.

29. Harvey Gittler, "Decisions Are Only as Good as Those Who Can Change Them," *The Wall Street Journal*, Oct. 7, 1985, p. 22.

30. "Swatch Out!" *Forbes*, June 5, 1995, pp. 150–152.

31. Laura Sessions Stepp, "In Search of Ethics: Alcoa Pursues a Corporate Conscience through Emphasis on 'Core Values,'" *The Washington Post*, Mar. 31, 1991, pp. H1, H4, and "New Test of Values," *The Washington Post*, Aug. 4, 1991, pp. H1, H4.

32. Robert L. Desatnick, "Service: A CEO's Perspective," *Management Review*, October 1987, pp. 41–45.

33. Daniel D. Wheeler and Irving L. Janis, *A Practical Guide for Making Decisions*, Free Press, New York, 1980.

34. Fred Barbash, "Barings Executives Blamed for Fall," *The Washington Post*, July 19, 1995, p. F3; "Leeson Sentenced to 6½ Years for Causing Barings Collapse," *The Washington Post*, Dec. 2, 1995, p. 1F.

35. Giora Keinan, "Decision Making under Stress: Scanning of Alternatives under Controllable and Uncontrollable Threats," *Journal of Personality and Social Psychology*, vol. 52, 1987, pp. 639–644.

36. Paul C. Nutt, "Types of Organizational Decision Processes," *Administrative Science Quarterly*, vol. 29, 1984, pp. 414–450.

37. This section, including the problems, is based on Kevin McKean, "Decisions," *Discover*, June 1985, pp. 22–31.

38. For recent research on prospect theory and the framing effect, see Kenneth J. Dunegan, "Framing, Cognitive Modes, and Image Theory: Toward an Understanding of a Glass Half Full," *Journal of Applied Psychology*, vol. 78, 1993, pp. 491–503; Paul Slovic, "The Construction of Preference," *American Psychologist*, vol. 50, 1995, pp. 364–371.

39. Daniel Southerland, "They Want the Card-Carrying Customer," *The Washington Post*, Oct. 19, 1994, p. G1.

40. S. Lichtenstein, P. Slovic, B. Fischhoff, M. Layman, and B. Combs, "Judged Frequency of Lethal Events," *Journal of Experimental Psychology: Human Learning and Memory*, vol. 4, 1978, pp. 551–578.

41. Adapted from Max H. Bazerman, *Judgment in Managerial Decision Making*, Wiley, New York, 1986.

42. Ronald N. Taylor, *Behavioral Decision Making*, Scott, Foresman, Glenview, Ill., 1984.

43. Max H. Bazerman, *Judgment in Managerial Decision Making*, Wiley, New York, 1986.

44. Eric Schine, "The Fall of a Timber Baron," *Business Week*, Oct. 2, 1995, pp. 85–92.

45. A. Koriat, S. Lichtenstein, and B. Fischoff, "Reasons for Confidence," *Journal of Experimental Psychology: Human Learning and Memory*, vol. 6, 1980, pp. 107–118.

46. Gideon Keren, "Perspectives of Behavioral Decision Making: Some Critical Notes," *Organizational Behavior and Human Decision Processes*, vol. 65, 1996, 169–178.

47. This example and section rely heavily on work by Max H. Bazerman, *Judgment in Managerial Decision Making*, Wiley, New York, 1986.

48. Jerry Ross and Barry M. Staw, "Organizational Escalation and Exit: Lessons from the Shoreham Nuclear Power Plant," *Academy of Management Journal*, vol. 36, 1993, pp. 701–732.

49. Max H. Bazerman, *Judgment in Managerial Decision Making*, Wiley, New York, 1986.

50. J. Z. Rubin, "Experimental Research on Third Party Intervention in Conflict: Toward Some Generalizations," *Psychological Bulletin*, vol. 87, 1980, pp. 379–391; Joel Brockner, "The Escalation of Commitment to a Failing Course of Action: Toward Theoretical Progress," *Academy of Management Review*, vol. 17, 1992, pp. 39–61.

51. Sarah Lubman, "Hubris and Ambition in Orange County: Robert Citron's Story," *The Wall Street Journal*, Jan. 18, 1995, pp. A1, A8.

52. Elizabeth M. Fowler, "Management Participation by Workers," *The New York Times*, Dec. 27, 1988, p. D6.

53. This section is based largely on George P. Huber, *Managerial Decision Making*, Scott, Foresman, Glenview, Ill., 1980; and Norman R. F. Maier, "Assets and Liabilities in Group Problem Solving: The Need for an Integrative Function," in Michael T. Matteson and John M. Ivancevich (eds.), *Management and Organizational Behavior Classics*, 4th ed., BPI/Irwin, Homewood, Ill., 1989.

54. Larry K. Michaelsen, Warren E. Watson, and Robert H. Black, "A Realistic Test of Individual versus Group Consensus Decision Making," *Journal of Applied Psychology*, vol. 74, 1989, pp. 834–839.

55. Irving L. Janis, *Groupthink*, 2d ed., Houghton Mifflin, Boston, 1982.

56. Arie W. Kruglanski, "Freeze-think and the Challenger," *Psychology Today*, August 1986, pp. 48–49.

57. Carrie R. Leana, "A Partial Test of Janis' Groupthink Model: Effects of Group Cohesiveness and Leader Behavior on Defective Decision Making," *Journal of Management*, vol. 11, 1985, pp. 5–17. For alternative explanations of groupthink, see Glen Whyte, "Groupthink Reconsidered," *Academy of Management Review*, vol. 14, 1989, pp. 40–56.

58. Ramon J. Aldag and Sally Riggs Fuller, "Beyond Fiasco: A Reappraisal of the Groupthink Phenomenon and a New Model of Group Decision Processes," *Psychological Bulletin*, vol. 113, pp. 533–552; Brian Mullen, Tara Anthony, Eduardo Salas, James E. Driskell, "Group Cohesiveness and Quality of Decision Making: An Integration of Tests of the Groupthink Hypothesis," *Small Group Research*, vol. 25, 1994, pp. 189–204.

59. Warren E. Watson, Kamalesh Kumar, and Larry K. Michaelsen, "Cultural Diversity's Impact on Interaction Process and Performance: Comparing Homogeneous and Diverse Task Groups," *Academy of Management Journal*, vol. 36, 1993, 590–602.

60. Deborah Gladstein Ancona and David F. Caldwell, "Demography and Design: Predictors of New Product Team Performance," *Organization Science*, vol. 3, 1992, pp. 321–341; Susan E. Jackson and Associates, *Diversity in the Workplace: Human Resources Initiatives*, Guilford Press, New York, 1992; Srilata Zaheer, "Overcoming the Liability of Foreignness," *Academy of Management Journal*, vol. 38, 1995, pp. 341–363.

61. Daniel D. Wheeler and Irving L. Janis, *A Practical Guide for Making Decisions*, Free Press, New York, 1980; Charles R. Schwenk, "Effects of Devil's Advocacy and Dialectical Inquiry on Decision Making: A Meta-Analysis," *Organizational Behavior and Human Decision Processes*, vol. 47, 1990, pp. 161–176; Charles Schwenk and Joseph S. Valacich, "Effects of Devil's Advocacy and Dialectical Inquiry on Individuals versus Groups," *Organizational Behavior and Human Decision Processes*, vol. 59, pp. 210–222.

62. Kenneth C. Laudon and Jane Price Laudon, *Management Information Systems*, 3d ed., Macmillan, New York, 1994.

63. This section is based largely on A. B. Hollingshead and J. E. McGrath, "Computer-Assisted Groups: A Critical Review of the Empirical Research," in Richard A. Guzzo and Eduardo Salas, *Team Effectiveness in Organizations*, Jossey-Bass, San Francisco, 1995, pp. 46–78; Richard A. Guzzo and Marcus W. Dickson, "Teams in Organizations: Recent Research on Performance and Effectiveness," *Annual Review of Psychology*, 1996, pp. 307–38.

64. P. L. McLeod, "An Assessment of the Experimental Literature on Electronic Support of Group Work: Results of a Meta-Analysis," *Human-Computer Interaction*, vol. 7(3), 257–280.

65. Max H. Bazerman, *Judgment in Managerial Decision Making*, Wiley, New York, 1986.

66. Teresa M. Amabile, *The Social Psychology of Creativity*, Springer-Verlag, New York, 1983.

67. Quoted in Alfie Kohn, "Art for Art's Sake," *Psychology Today*, September 1987, p. 54.

68. Gene Bylinsky, "Trying to Transcend Copycat Science," *Fortune*, Mar. 30, 1987, pp. 42–46.

69. This analogy is based on Edward de Bono, *New Think*, Basic Books, New York, 1968.

70. Teresa M. Amabile, *The Social Psychology of Creativity*, Springer-Verlag, New York, 1983.

71. Reprinted from Diane E. Papalia and Sally Wendkos Olds, *Psychology*, 2d ed., McGraw-Hill, New York, 1988, p. 293.

72. J. W. Haefele, *Creativity and Innovation*, Reinhold, New York, 1962; Max H. Bazerman, *Judgment in Managerial Decision Making*, Wiley, New York, 1986, pp. 89–91.

73. Based on "Problems! We've Got to Have Problems!" in P. Ranganath Nayak and John M. Ketteringham, *Breakthroughs*, Rawson Associates, New York, 1986, pp. 151–178.

74. R. Brent Gallupe, William H. Cooper, Mary-Liz Grisé, and Lana M. Bastianutti, "Blocking Electronic Brainstorms," *Journal of Applied Psychology*, vol. 79, 1994, pp. 77–86.

75. Andre L. Delbecq, Andrew H. Van de Ven, and D. H. Gustafson, *Group Techniques for Program Planning*, Scott, Foresman, Glenview, Ill., 1975; see also George P. Huber, *Managerial Decision Making*, Scott, Foresman, Glenview, Ill., 1980.

76. See A. H. Van de Ven and A. L. Delbecq, "The Effectiveness of Nominal, Delphi, and Interacting Group Processes," *Academy of Management Journal*, vol. 17, 1974, pp. 605–621; Alan R. Dennis and Joseph S. Valacich, "Group, Sub-Group, and Nominal Group Idea Generation: New Rules for a New Media?" *Journal of Management*, vol. 20, 1994, 723–736.

77. Adapted from Laurie Hays, "Book Maps *USA Today's* Costly Road," *The Wall Street Journal*, July 14, 1987, p. 6.

78. Paul Farhi, "*USA Today:* Looking Ahead to Tomorrow," *The Washington Post*, Aug. 29, 1988, Washington Business section, pp. 1, 22; Joshua Hammer, "The McPaper Route," *Newsweek*, Apr. 27, 1992, p. 58; Paul D. Colford, "*USA Today* Looks To Tomorrow," *Newsday*, Dec. 22, 1994, p. B02; Joseph Cosco, "Loyal to the Core," *Journal of Business Strategy*, March–April, 1996, p. 42.

79. Based mainly on Christopher Knowlton, "Shell Gets Rich by Beating Risk," *Fortune*, Aug. 26, 1991, pp. 79–82; also on James R. Norman, "The Opportunities Are Enormous," *Forbes*, Nov. 9, 1992, pp. 92–94; James R. Norman, "Slow Payoff," *Forbes*, Feb. 27, 1995, pp. 62–64; Paula Dwyer, "The Passing of 'The Shell Man,'" *Business Week*, April 24, 1995: 134P; Simon Caulkin, "Shell Needs to Get Cracking," *The Observer*, Oct. 8, 1995, p. 3; Patrick Harverson, "Shell Shares Jump on Payout Hopes After First-Term Record," *Financial Times*, May 10, 1996, p. 23; David Lascelles, "Shell Searches Its Soul During Troubled Times," *Financial Times*, May 10, 1996, p. 24; Patrick Harverson, "UK: Protestors Attack Shell Over Nigeria," *Financial Times*, May 16, 1996, p. 27.

SUPPLEMENT TO CHAPTER 5

1. Based on Thomas J. Holloran and Judson E. Burn, "United Airlines Station Manpower Planning System," *Interfaces*, January–February 1986, pp. 39–50; Kenneth Labich, "Winners in the Air Wars," *Fortune*, May 11, 1987, pp. 68–79; "Product News," *World Airlines News*, Jan. 9, 1995, p. 1.

2. J. T. Mentzer and J. E. Cox, "Familiarity, Application and Performance of Sales Forecasting Techniques," *Journal of Forecasting*, vol. 3, 1984, pp. 27–36.

3. This section relies heavily on Steven C. Wheelwright and Spyros Makridakis, *Forecasting Methods for Management*, Wiley, New York, 1989.

4. Jay Mathews, "Increasingly, Coffee Isn't Our Cup of Tea," *The Washington Post*, Nov. 4, 1994, p. C3.

5. Charles A. Gallagher and Hugh J. Watson, *Quantitative Methods for Business Decisions*, McGraw-Hill, New York, 1980.

6. John Merwin, "A Billion in Blunders," *Forbes*, Dec. 1, 1986, p. 104.

7. Peter Finch and Marc Frons, "Gurus Who Called the Crash—Or Fell on Their Faces," *Business Week*, Nov. 30, 1985, pp. 124–125; Susan Antilla, "The Hottest Woman on Wall Street," *Working Woman*, August 1991, pp. 49–51; Anne Kates Smith, "Five Investors' Biggest Goofs," *U.S. News & World Report*, Dec. 11, 1995, p. 121.

8. Lawrence M. Fisher, "Chip Index Dips for 6th Month in Row," *The New York Times*, May 10, 1996, p. D3.

9. "PLYGEM Posts Encouraging First Quarter Results," *Canada NewsWire*, May 9, 1996.

10. George P. Huger, *Managerial Decision Making*, Scott, Foresman, Glenview, Ill., 1980.

11. John F. Preble, "The Selection of Delphi

Panels for Strategic Planning Purposes," *Strategic Management Journal,* vol. 5, 1984, pp. 157–170; W. F. Wolff, "Japan Study Team Probes Management of R&D," *Research-Technology Management* March–April 1996, pp. 4–5.

12. Ted G. Eschenbach and George A. Geistauts, "A Delphi Forecast for Alaska," *Interfaces,* November–December 1985, pp. 100–109.

13. Other examples can be found in George P. Huber, *Managerial Decision Making,* Scott, Foresman, Glenview, Ill., 1980; and Steven C. Wheelwright and Spyros Makridakis, *Forecasting Methods for Management,* Wiley, New York, 1989.

14. V. D. Garde and R. R. Patel, "Technological Forecasting for Power Generation—A Study Using the Delphi Technique," *Long Range Planning,* August 1985, pp. 73–79.

15. Paul J. H. Schoemaker, "Scenario Planning: A Tool for Strategic Thinking," *Sloan Management Review,* Winter 1995, pp. 25–40; Eric K. Clemons, "Using Scenario Analysis to Manage the Strategic Risks of Reengineering," *Sloan Management Review,* Summer 1995, pp. 61–71.

16. Paul J. H. Schoemaker, "Scenario Planning: A Tool for Strategic Thinking," *Sloan Management Review,* Winter 1995, pp. 25–40.

17. Steven C. Wheelwright and Spyros Makridakis, *Forecasting Methods for Management,* Wiley, New York, 1989.

18. See, for example, Mike Hack, "Harvard Project Manager Serves Pros, Casual Users," *InfoWorld,* Jan. 30, 1989, pp. 54–55.

19. James B. Dilworth, *Production and Operations Management,* McGraw-Hill, New York, 1993.

20. These steps and the following material on PERT are based heavily on Everett E. Adam, Jr., and Ronald J. Ebert, *Production and Operations Management,* 5th ed., Prentice-Hall, Englewood Cliffs, N.J., 1992.

21. K. Roscoe Davis and Patrick G. McKeown, *Quantitative Models for Management,* 2d ed., Kent, Boston, 1984.

22. William E. Pinney and Donald B. McWilliams, *Management Science: An Introduction to Quantitative Analysis for Management,* Harper & Row, New York, 1982.

23. Bruce L. Golden and Edward A. Wasil, "Computerized Vehicle Routing in the Soft Drink Industry," *Operations Research,* vol. 35, 1987, pp. 6–17.

24. William E. Pinney and Donald B. McWilliams, *Management Science: An Introduction to Quantitative Analysis for Management,* Harper & Row, New York, 1982.

25. Adapted from Norma Welch and James Gussow, "Expansion of Canadian National Railway's Line Capacity," *Interfaces,* January–February 1986, pp. 51–64; see also John F. Burns, "Trains to Be Cut in Canada," *The New York Times,* Oct. 5, 1989, pp. D1, D2.

26. George P. Huber, *Managerial Decision Making,* Scott, Foresman, Glenview, Ill., 1980.

27. The example is based on E. Frank Harrison, *The Managerial Decision-Making Process,* 2d ed., Houghton Mifflin, Boston, 1981.

28. E. Frank Harrison, *The Managerial Decision-Making Process,* 2d ed., Houghton Mifflin, Boston, 1981.

29. George P. Huber, *Managerial Decision Making,* Scott, Foresman, Glenview, Ill., 1980; Dennis H. Ferguson and Thomas I. Selling, "Probability Analysis: A System for Making Better Decisions," *The Cornell H.R.A. Quarterly,* August 1985, pp. 35–42.

30. F. Hutton Barron, "Payoff Matrices Pay Off at Hallmark," *Interfaces,* July–August 1985, pp. 20–25.

31. Jacob W. Ulvila, "Postal Automation (ZIP + 4) Technology: A Decision Analysis," *Interfaces,* March–April 1987, pp. 1–12.

32. Everett E. Adam, Jr., and Ronald J. Ebert, *Production and Operations Management,* 5th ed., Prentice-Hall, Englewood Cliffs, N.J., 1992.

33. See Richard A. Brealey and Stewart C. Myers, *Principles of Corporate Finance,* 4th ed., McGraw-Hill, 1991, for a mathematical treatment of break-even analysis.

34. Michael Mecham, "Instant Success Fuels Korean Air Expansion," *Air Transport,* vol. 143, 1995, p. 28.

35. "Bill Gates and Paul Allen Talk," *Fortune,* Oct. 2, 1995, pp. 68–86.

CHAPTER 6

1. Steve Kaufman, "Turbo MBOs Spell Success for Chip Maker," *San Jose Mercury News,* June 1, 1987, p. 2D; Allan E. Alter, "Compact Competitors," *CIO,* July 1989, pp. 40–44; Steven B. Kaufman, "The Goal System That Drives Cypress," *Business Month,* July 1987, pp. 30–32; interview with Dr. T. J. Rodgers, Aug. 21, 1989; Stan Baker, "Rodgers' Revolution," *Electronic Engineering Times,* July 17, 1989, pp. 1, 67–68; 1990 Annual Report, Cypress Semiconductor; Brian Dumaine, "Bureaucracy Busters," *Fortune,* June 17, 1991; Don Clark, "Cypress Aims to Rise Above Other Midsize Chip Makers," *The Wall Street Journal,* Aug. 18, 1994, p. B4; Crista Hardie, "CEO Sees End to 'Cowboy' Chip Purchasing," *Electronic Business Buyer,* July 1995, p. 12; Jerry Mahoney, "Industry's 'Contrarian' Tough, Bold, Fast-Moving," *Austin American-Statesman,* Feb. 22, 1996, p. C1.

2. "Thriving on Order," *INC.,* December 1989, pp. 47–62.

3. Leslie W. Rue and Phyllis G. Holland, *Strategic Management: Concepts and Experiences,* 2d ed., McGraw-Hill, New York, 1989.

4. John A. Pearce II and Richard B. Robinson, Jr., *Strategic Management,* Irwin, Homewood, Ill., 1988.

5. Laura Nash, "Mission Statements—Mirrors and Windows," *Harvard Business Review,* March–April 1988, pp. 155–156.

6. Jerome H. Want, "Corporate Mission: The Intangible Contributor to Performance," *Management Review,* August 1986, pp. 46–50; George L. Morrisey, "Who Needs a Mission Statement? You Do," *Training and Development Journal,* March 1988, pp. 50–52.

7. John A. Pearce II and Fred David, "Corporate Mission Statements: The Bottom Line," *Academy of Management Executive,* vol. 1, 1987, pp. 109–116.

8. Fred R. David, "How Companies Define Their Mission," *Long Range Planning,* vol. 22, 1989, pp. 90–97.

9. Laura Nash, "Mission Statements—Mirrors and Windows," *Harvard Business Review,* March–April 1988, pp. 155–156.

10. Edwin A. Locke and Gary P. Latham, *Goal Setting: A Motivational Technique That Works!* Prentice-Hall, Englewood Cliffs, N.J., 1984; Max D. Richards, *Setting Strategic Goals and Objectives,* 2d ed., West, St. Paul, Minn., 1986.

11. Robert D. Pritchard, Philip L. Roth, Steven D. Jones, Patricia J. Galgay, and Margaret D. Watson, "Designing a Goal-Setting System to Enhance Performance: A Practical Guide," *Organizational Dynamics,* Summer 1988, pp. 69–78.

12. Charles Siler, "The Goal Is 0%," *Forbes,* Oct. 30, 1989, pp. 95–98; information from a company official, March 1990; discussion with a company official, May 1992.

13. Gary P. Latham and Edwin A. Locke, "Goal Setting—A Motivational Technique That Works," *Organizational Dynamics,* Autumn 1979, pp. 68–80.

14. Thomas W. Lee, Edwin A. Locke, and Gary P. Latham, "Goal Setting Theory and Job Performance," in Lawrence A. Pervin (ed.), *Goal Concepts in Personality and Social Psychology,* Erlbaum, Hillsdale, N.J., 1989.

15. Charles Perrow, "The Analysis of Goals in Complex Organizations," *American Sociological Review,* vol. 26, 1961, pp. 854–866; Max S. Richards, *Setting Strategic Goals and Objectives,* 2d ed., West, St. Paul, Minn., 1986.

16. 1988 Annual Report, Cypress Semiconductor.

17. See also George L. Morrisey, *A Guide to Long-Range Planning,* Jossey-Bass, San Francisco, 1996.

18. 1988 Annual Report, Cypress Semiconductor.

19. Lynne Duke, "Employer Puts Pluralism First," *The Washington Post,* Aug. 4, 1991, p. A1; Michael Tarsala, "After Affirmative Action: Focus on Diversity," *The Arizona Republic/The Phoenix Gazette,* Apr. 3, 1995, p. JF14; "Hispanic Association on Corporate Responsibility to Honor US West Communications President and CEO Sol Trujillo," *PR Newswire,* Oct. 27, 1995, p. 1.

20. Correspondence from John W. Hamburger, marketing communications manager, Cypress Semiconductor, Aug. 24, 1989.

21. Laura Jereski, "I'm a Bad Manager," *Forbes,* Feb. 8, 1988, pp. 134–135.

22. Edwin A. Locke and Gary P. Latham, *Goal Setting: A Motivational Technique That Works!* Prentice-Hall, Englewood Cliffs, N.J., 1984.

23. Shawn Tully, "Why to Go for Stretch Targets," *Fortune,* Nov. 14, 1994, pp. 145–156.

24. Patrick M. Wright and K. Michele Kacmar, "Goal Specificity as a Determinant of Goal Commitment and Goal Change," *Organizational Behavior and Human Decision Processes,* vol. 29, 1994, pp. 242–260; Jay Mathews, "Utensile Strength: Rubbermaid's Relentless Innovation Gains Success, Respect," *The Washington Post,* Apr. 2, 1995, p. 1H.

25. Gary P. Latham and Kenneth N. Wexley, *Increasing Productivity through Performance Appraisal,* Addison-Wesley, Reading, Mass., 1981.

26. "Being the Boss," *INC.,* October 1989, pp. 49–65.

27. Edwin A. Locke, Gary P. Latham, and Miriam Erez, "The Determinants of Goal Commitment," *Academy of Management Review,* vol. 13, 1988, pp. 23–39.

28. Edwin A. Locke and Gary P. Latham, *Goal Setting: A Motivational Technique That Works!* Prentice-Hall, Englewood Cliffs, N.J., 1984.

29. Francine Schwadel, "Nordstrom's Push East Will Test Its Renown for the Best in Service," *The Wall Street Journal,* Aug. 1, 1989, pp. A1, A4.

30. Ibid.

31. Edwin A. Locke, Gary P. Latham, and Miriam Erez, "The Determinants of Goal Commitment," *Academy of Management Review,* vol. 14, 1988, pp. 23–39.

32. Lisa Banian, "Natuzzi's Huge Selection of Leather Furniture Pays Off," *The Wall Street Journal,* Nov. 17, 1994, p. B4; Pablo Balarza, "Cushy Seat," *Investor's Business Daily,* May 10, 1995, p. A4; Scott Andro, "Upholstery Maker Is Spreading Out," *News & Record* (Greensboro, N.C.), Apr. 17, 1996, p. M3.

33. Robert E. Wood, A. J. Mento, and Edwin A. Locke, "Task Complexity as a Moderator of

Goal Effects: A Meta Analysis," *Journal of Applied Psychology*, vol. 72, 1987, pp. 416–425.

34. Edwin A. Locke, Karyl N. Shaw, Lisa M. Saari, and Gary P. Latham, "Goal Setting and Task Performance," *Psychological Bulletin*, vol. 90, 1981, pp. 125–152.

35. Edwin A. Locke and Gary P. Latham, *Goal Setting: A Motivational Technique That Works!* Prentice-Hall, Englewood Cliffs, N.J., 1984, and *A Theory of Goal Setting & Task Performance*, Prentice-Hall, Englewood Cliffs, N.J., 1990.

36. Edwin A. Locke and Gary P. Latham, *Goal Setting: A Motivational Technique That Works!* Prentice-Hall, Englewood Cliffs, N.J., 1984.

37. Arthur A. Thompson, Jr., and A. J. Strickland III, *Strategic Management: Concepts and Cases*, 4th ed., Business Publications, Plano, Tex., 1987.

38. William H. Newman and James P. Logan, *Strategy, Policy, and Central Management*, 8th ed., South-Western, Cincinnati, 1981.

39. Robert T. Grieves, "Hold the Phone," *Forbes*, June 13, 1988, p. 52; William C. Symonds, "People Aren't Laughing at U.S. Sprint Anymore," *Business Week*, July 31, 1989, pp. 82–86.

40. William C. Symonds, "People Aren't Laughing at U.S. Sprint Anymore," *Business Week*, July 31, 1989, pp. 82–86.

41. This section relies heavily on Leslie W. Rue and Phyllis G. Holland, *Strategic Management: Concepts and Experiences*, 2d ed., McGraw-Hill, New York, 1989.

42. Patricia Sellers, "How to Handle Customers' Gripes," *Fortune*, Oct. 24, 1988, pp. 88–100.

43. This section is based mainly on Teresa M. Amabile, "A Model of Creativity and Innovation in Organizations," *Research in Organizational Behavior*, vol. 10, 1988, pp. 123–167.

44. 1988 Annual Report, Cypress Semiconductor.

45. Shawn Tully "Why to Go for Stretch Targets," *Fortune*, Nov. 14, 1994, pp. 145–158; "The Mass Production of Ideas, and Other Impossibilities," *The Economist*, Mar. 18, 1995, p. 72; Tim Stevens, "Tool Kit for Innovators," *Industry Week*, June 5, 1995, p. 28; "How Can Big Companies Keep the Entrepreneurial Spirit Alive?" *Harvard Business Review*, November–December 1995, pp. 183–192; Terry Fiedler, "Despite 3M's Big Changes, All Is Quiet at Meeting," *Star Tribune*, May 15, 1996, p. 1D.

46. "Thriving on Order," *INC.*, December 1989, pp. 47–62.

47. Henry Mintzberg, *The Nature of Managerial Work*, Prentice-Hall, Englewood Cliffs, N.J., 1980.

48. Daniel H. Gray, "Uses and Misuses of Strategic Planning," *Harvard Business Review*, January–February 1986, pp. 89–97.

49. Leslie W. Rue and Phyllis G. Holland, *Strategic Management: Concepts and Experiences*, 2d ed., McGraw-Hill, New York, 1989.

50. "The New Breed of Strategic Planner," *Business Week*, Sept. 17, 1984, pp. 62–68.

51. Peter F. Drucker, *The Practice of Management*, Harper, New York, 1954; Roland G. Greenwood, "Management by Objectives: As Developed by Peter Drucker, Assisted by Harold Smiddy," *Academy of Management Review*, vol. 6, 1981, pp. 225–230.

52. Anthony P. Raia, *Managing by Objectives*, Scott, Foresman, Glenview, Ill., 1974; Max D. Richards, *Setting Strategic Goals and Objectives*, 2d ed., West, St. Paul, Minn., 1986.

53. Anthony P. Raia, *Managing by Objectives*, Scott, Foresman, Glenview, Ill., 1974; Max D. Richards, *Setting Strategic Goals and Objectives*, 2d ed., West, St. Paul, Minn., 1986.

54. Steven J. Carroll and Henry L. Tosi, *Management by Objectives: Applications and Research*, Macmillan, New York, 1973; Anthony P. Raia, *Managing by Objectives*, Scott, Foresman, Glenview, Ill., 1974; Joseph W. Leonard, "Why MBO Fails So Often," *Training and Development Journal*, June 1986, pp. 38–39; Max D. Richards, *Setting Strategic Goals and Objectives*, 2d ed., West, St. Paul, Minn., 1986.

55. Andy Zipser, "How Pressure to Raise Sales Led MiniScribe to Falsify Number," *The Wall Street Journal*, Sept. 11, 1989, pp. A1, A8; Lee Berton, "How MiniScribe Got Its Auditor's Blessing on Questionable Sales," *The Wall Street Journal*, May 14, 1992, pp. A1, A6.

56. Susan C. Faludi, "At Nordstrom Stores, Service Comes First—But at a Big Price," *The Wall Street Journal*, Feb. 20, 1990, pp. A1, A16.

57. Jan P. Muczyk, "Dynamics and Hazards of MBO Application," *Personnel Administrator*, May 1979, pp. 51–61.

58. Robert Rodgers and John E. Hunter, "Impact of Management by Objectives on Organizational Productivity," *Journal of Applied Psychology*, vol. 76, no. 2, 1991, pp. 322–336.

59. John Huet, "WAL-MART Will It Take Over the World?" *Fortune*, Jan. 30, 1989, pp. 52–59; "Fact Sheet about Wal-Mart Stores Inc.," Wal-Mart Stores, Inc., Corporate Public Relations Office, Bentonville, Ark.; Arthur A. Thompson, Jr., and A. J. Strickland III, *Strategic Management: Concepts and Cases*, 4th ed., Business Publications, Plano, Tex., 1987, pp. 936–954; discussion between Brenda Lockhart, corporate coordinator of public relations, and David C. Martin, November 1989; Kevin Helliker, "Sam Walton, the Man Who Made Wal-Mart No. 1 Retailer, Dies," *The Wall Street Journal*, Apr. 6, 1992, p. A1; Wal-Mart Annual Report, 1994; "Wal-Mart to Expand in the U.S. and Abroad," *Food Institute Report*, Oct. 16, 1995, p. 1; Louise Lee and Kevin Helliker, "Humbled Wal-Mart Plans More Stores," *The Wall Street Journal*, Jan. 13, 1996, p. B1; Mark Tosh, "Wal-Mart Aims to Get Back on Growth Track by Cutting Costs, Prices," *WWD*, Apr. 10, 1996, p. 22; Patricia Sellers, "Can Wal-Mart Get Back the Magic?" *Fortune*, Apr. 29, 1996, pp. 130–136.

60. Toshio Nakahara and Yutaka Isono, "Strategic Planning for Canon; The Crises and the New Vision," *Long Range Planning*, vol. 25, 1992, pp. 63–72.

CHAPTER 7

1. Based on Stephen J. Sansweet, "Disney's 'Imagineers' Build Space Attraction Using High-Tech Gear," *The Wall Street Journal*, Jan. 6, 1987, pp. 1, 24; Ronald Grover, "Disney's Magic," *Business Week*, Mar. 9, 1987, pp. 62–69; Stephen Koepp, "Do You Believe in Magic?" *Time*, Apr. 25, 1988, pp. 66–73; Richard Turner and Peter Gumbel, "As Euro Disney Braces for Its Grand Opening, the French Go Goofy," *The Wall Street Journal*, Apr. 10, 1992, p. A1; *The Walt Disney Company 1994 Annual Report*; "Disney's Kingdom," *Business Week*, Aug. 14, 1995, pp. 30–34; Ronald Grover, "Out of the Inkless Well," *Business Week*, Oct. 30, 1995, p. 46; Frank Rose, "Can Disney Tame 42nd Street?" *Fortune*, June 24, 1996, pp. 94–104.

2. Lawrence R. Jauch and William F. Glueck, *Business Policy and Strategic Management*, 5th ed., McGraw-Hill, New York, 1988; John A. Pearce II and Richard B. Robinson, Jr., *Strategic Management: Strategy Formulation and Implementation*, 3d ed., Irwin, Homewood, Ill., 1988.

3. Arthur A. Thompson, Jr., and A. J. Strickland III, *Strategic Management: Concepts and Cases*, 6th ed., BPI/Irwin, Homewood, Ill., 1992.

4. Ibid.; Leslie W. Rue and Phyllis G. Holland, *Strategic Management: Concepts and Experiences*, 2d ed., McGraw-Hill, New York, 1989.

5. Arthur A. Thompson, Jr., and A. J. Strickland III, *Strategic Management: Concepts and Cases*, 6th ed., BPI/Irwin, Homewood, Ill., 1992.

6. Ibid.

7. Michael E. Porter, *Competitive Advantage: Creating and Sustaining Superior Performance*, Free Press, New York, 1985.

8. Steve Weiner, "Electrifying," *Forbes*, Nov. 30, 1987, pp. 196–198; "Roaming the Hardware Show for High-Margin Items," *Discount Store News*, Sept. 18, 1995, p. 112.

9. Warren Keith Schilit, "An Examination of the Influence of Middle-Level Managers in Formulating and Implementing Strategic Decisions," *Journal of Management Studies*, May 1987, pp. 271–293.

10. Arthur A. Thompson, Jr., and A. J. Strickland III, *Strategic Management: Concepts and Cases*, 6th ed., BPI/Irwin, Homewood, Ill., 1992. Thompson and Strickland also include an operating strategy level that addresses strategy for managers within functional areas.

11. Robert Mueller, "Criteria for the Appraisal of Directors," *Harvard Business Review*, vol. 57, 1979, pp. 48–56.

12. Leslie W. Rue and Phyllis G. Holland, *Strategic Management: Concepts and Experiences*, 2d ed., McGraw-Hill, New York, 1989.

13. Arthur A. Thompson, Jr., and A. J. Strickland III, *Strategic Management: Concepts and Cases*, 6th ed., BPI/Irwin, Homewood, Ill., 1992.

14. Caroline E. Mayer, "There's a Price War Inside the Box!" *The Washington Post*, July 11, 1996, pp. D1, D2.

15. Norm Alster, "Unlevel Playing Field," *Forbes*, June 26, 1989, pp. 53–57; Alex Taylor III, "The Auto Industry Meets the New Economy," *Fortune*, Sept. 5, 1994, pp. 52–60.

16. Stewart Toy, "Waiter, a Magnum of Your Best Portland Champagne," *Business Week*, Dec. 11, 1989, pp. 92–94.

17. Julia Flynn Siler, "A Warning Shot from the King of Beers," *Business Week*, Dec. 18, 1989, p. 124.

18. Jay Mathews, "Increasingly, Coffee Isn't Our Cup of Tea," *The Washington Post*, Nov. 4, 1994, p. 1.

19. Richard A. D'Aveni, *Hypercompetitive Rivalries*, The Free Press, New York, 1995.

20. Jeffery Young, "Digital Octopus," *Forbes*, June 17, 1996, pp. 102–106.

21. Danny Miller and Jamal Shamsie, "The Resource-Based View of the Firm in Two Environments: The Hollywood Film Studios from 1936 to 1965," *Academy of Management Journal*, vol. 39, pp. 519–543. This section is based mainly on Jay B. Barney, "Look Inside for Competitive Advantage," *Academy of Management Executive*, vol. 9, no. 4, 1995, pp. 49–61.

22. Steven V. Brull and Neil Gross, "Sony's New World," *Business Week*, May 27, 1996, pp. 100–108.

23. John A. Pearce II and Richard B. Robinson, Jr., *Strategic Management: Strategy Formulation and Implementation*, 3d ed., Irwin, Homewood, Ill., 1988.

24. This section relies heavily on Leslie W. Rue and Phyllis G. Holland, *Strategic Management: Concepts and Experiences*, 2d ed., McGraw-Hill, New York, 1989.

25. E. S. Browning, "Long-Term Thinking

and Paternalistic Ways Carry Michelin to Top," *The Wall Street Journal,* Jan. 5, 1990, pp. A1, A8.

26. Ted Kumpecb and Piet T. Bolwijn, "Manufacturing: The New Case for Vertical Integration," *Harvard Business Review,* March–April 1988, pp. 75–81.

27. Richard Behar, "Spreading the Wealth," *Forbes,* Aug. 10, 1987, pp. 74–81; Leonard Shapiro, "To Beaman, It's a Flat-Out Tour de Force," *The Washington Post,* Jan. 9, 1992, p. B3.

28. Christie Brown, "The Body-Bending Business," *Forbes,* Sept. 11, 1995, pp. 196–204; Laura Bird and Laura Jereski, "Warnaco May Buy Authentic Fitness Corp.," *The Wall Street Journal,* June 7, 1996, p. A2.

29. Kathryn Rudie Harrigan, "Vertical Integration and Corporate Strategy," *Academy of Management Journal,* vol. 28, 1985, pp. 397–425.

30. Raphael Amit and Joshua Livnat, "A Concept of Conglomerate Diversification," *Journal of Management,* vol. 14, 1988, pp. 593–604.

31. Seth Lubove, "New-Tech, Old-Tech," *Forbes,* July 17, 1995, pp. 58–60.

32. Based on Brian O'Reilly, "Leslie Wexner Knows What Women Want," *Fortune,* Aug. 19, 1985, pp. 154–160; Steven B. Weiner, "The Unlimited?" *Forbes,* Apr. 6, 1987, pp. 76–80; "The Limited's Approach," *Chain Store Age Executive,* December 1988, pp. 28–36; Laura Zinn, "Maybe the Limited Has Limits after All," *Business Week,* Mar. 18, 1991; Dyan Machan, "Knowing Your Limits," *Forbes,* June 5, 1995, pp. 128–132; Dyan Machan, "Sharing Victoria's Secrets," *Forbes,* June 5, 1995, pp. 132–133; David Moin, "Henri Bendel Outlines an Ambitous Vision: 50 Units in Five Years," *Women's Wear Daily,* Oct. 16, 1995, p. 1; David Moin, "Bath & Body Works Slated for UK in 97," *WWD,* Apr. 4, 1996, p. 10; Debbie Gebolys, "Limited Focuses on Strength of Intimate Brands," *The Columbus Dispatch,* May 21, 1996, p. 1D; Laura Bird, "Limited's Intimate Brands Will Test Toiletries Sales at Sears, Disney Stores," *The Wall Street Journal,* May 21, 1996, p. B9.

33. John A. Pearce and James W. Harvey, "Concentrated Growth Strategies," *Academy of Management Executive,* vol. 4, no. 1, 1990, pp. 61–68.

34. David J. Jefferson, "Dream to Nightmare: When Growth Gets Out of Hand," *The Wall Street Journal,* Jan. 23, 1990, p. B2.

35. John A. Pearce II and Richard B. Robinson, Jr., *Strategic Management: Strategy Formulation and Implementation,* 3d ed., Irwin, Homewood, Ill., 1988.

36. Arthur A. Thompson, Jr., and A. J. Strickland III, *Strategic Management: Concepts and Cases,* 6th ed., BPI/Irwin, Homewood, Ill., 1992.

37. Jack Willoughby, "The Last Iceman," *Forbes,* July 13, 1987, pp. 183–204.

38. Cynthia A. Montgomery, Ann R. Thomas, and Rajan Kamath, "Divestiture, Market Valuation, and Strategy," *Academy of Management Journal,* vol. 27, 1984, pp. 830–840.

39. "Bankruptcy Petition Brings Fresh Risks for Allied, Federated," *The Wall Street Journal,* Jan. 16, 1990, pp. A1, A10; Todd Mason, "It'll Be a Hard Sell," *Business Week,* Jan. 29, 1990, pp. 30–31; Carl T. Hall, "Retail Deal Is Done; Federated Finishes Broadway Takeover," *The San Francisco Chronicle,* Oct. 12, 1995, p. B1.

40. Sometimes other criteria, such as a 10 percent growth rate, are used to gauge high and low market growth; see Leslie W. Rue and Phyllis G. Holland, *Strategic Management: Con-*

cepts and Experiences, 2d ed., McGraw-Hill, New York, 1989.

41. Janet Guyon, "GE to Acquire Borg-Warner's Chemical Lines," *The Wall Street Journal,* June 17, 1988, p. 3.

42. Richard Phalon, "Roto-Rooter's New Drill," *Forbes,* Dec. 11, 1989, pp. 176–178; "Roto-Rooter Continues Growth as Residential Service Giant," *Contractor,* April 1995, p. 8.

43. Ibid.

44. Laura Landro and Douglas R. Sease, "General Electric to Sell Consumer Electronics Lines to Thomson S.A. for Its Medical Gear Business, Cash," *The Wall Street Journal,* July 23, 1987, p. 3; Janet Guyon, "GE Chairman Welch, Though Much Praised, Starts to Draw Critics," *The Wall Street Journal,* Aug. 4, 1988, pp. 1, 8.

45. Donald C. Hambrick, Ian C. MacMillan, and Diana L. Day, "Strategic Attributes and Performance in the BCG Matrix: A PIMS-Based Analysis of Industrial Product Businesses," *Academy of Management Journal,* vol. 25, 1982, pp. 510–531.

46. Ibid.

47. Graham Turner, "Inside Europe's Giant Companies: Daimler-Benz Goes Top of the League," *Long Range Planning,* vol. 19, 1986, pp. 12–17.

48. Bill Saporito, "The Tough Cookie at RJR Nabisco," *Fortune,* July 18, 1988, pp. 32–46; Peter Waldman, "New RJR Chief Faces a Daunting Challenge at Debt-Heavy Firm," *The Wall Street Journal,* Mar. 14, 1989, pp. A1, A19; Pan Demetrakes, "Food Plants: Apt to Adapt," *Food Processing,* March 1995, p. 52.

49. Anil K. Gupta and V. Govindarajan, "Build, Hold, Harvest: Converting Strategic Intentions into Reality," *Journal of Business Strategy,* March 1984, pp. 34–47.

50. Donald C. Hambrick, Ian C. Macmillan, and Diana L. Day, "Strategic Attributes and Performance in the BCG Matrix: a PIMS-Based Analysis of Industrial Product Businesses," *Academy of Management Journal,* vol. 25, 1982, pp. 510–531.

51. Charles W. Hofer and Dan Schendel, *Strategy Formulation: Analytical Concepts,* West, St. Paul, Minn., 1978.

52. Arthur A. Thompson, Jr., and A. J. Strickland III, *Strategic Management: Concepts and Cases,* 6th ed., BPI/Irwin, Homewood, Ill., 1992.

53. Charles W. L. Hill and Gareth R. Jones, *Strategic Management: An Integrated Approach,* Houghton Mifflin, Boston, 1989.

54. Malcolm Schofield and David Arnold, "Strategies for Mature Businesses," *Long Range Planning,* vol. 21, 1988, pp. 69–76.

55. Steve Glain, "Samsung Is Spending Billions to Diversify," *The Wall Street Journal,* Feb. 10, 1995, p. B6.

56. This section is based mainly on Michael E. Porter, *Competitive Strategy: Techniques for Analyzing Industries and Competitors,* Free Press, New York, 1980.

57. James Cook, "We're the Low-Cost Producer," *Forbes,* Dec. 25, 1989, pp. 65–66; Tim Smart, "A Lot of the Weaknesses Carbide Had Are Behind It," *Business Week,* Jan. 23, 1995, pp. 83–84.

58. Gregory L. Miles, "Heinz Ain't Broke, but It's Doing a Lot of Fixing," *Business Week,* Dec. 11, 1989, pp. 84–88.

59. Based on Richard C. Morais, "Cock-a-Leekie," *Forbes,* Sept. 7, 1987, pp. 68–69; "UK: Baxters Welcomes an Outside Influence," *Grocer,* Oct. 15, 1994, p. 1; "UK: Focus on Scotland—Family Values," *Grocer,* Sept. 2, 1995, p. 1.

60. Kerry Hannon, "Shifting Gears," *Forbes,* Dec. 11, 1989, pp. 124–130; Anthony Todd Carlisle, "Airport Region: Massive Complex Mirrors Growth of Booming RPS," *Pittsburgh Business Times & Journal,* Sept. 18, 1995, p. 10.

61. Gregory G. Dess, Anil Gupta, Jean-Francois Hennart, and Charles W. L. Hill, "Conducting and Integrating Strategy Research at the International, Corporate, and Business Levels: Issues and Directions," *Journal of Management,* vol. 21, 1995, pp. 357–393.

62. Anita Lienert, "A Dinosaur of a Different Color," *Management Review,* February 1995, pp. 24–29.

63. Jay R. Galbraith and Robert K. Kazanjian, *Strategy Implementation: Structure, Systems and Process,* 2d ed., West, St. Paul, Minn., 1986.

64. Marc Beauchamp, "Food for Thought," *Forbes,* Apr. 17, 1989, p. 73.

65. Ruth E. Thaler-Carter, "MetLife Tests 'Focus Circle' Approach to Enhancing Diversity," *Mosaics,* a publication of the Society for Human Resource Management, May–June, 1995, pp. 1, 5.

66. Based on Tom Alexander, "Cray's Way of Staying Super-Duper," *Fortune,* Mar. 18, 1985, pp. 56–76; Richard Gibson, "Cray Plans to Spin Off Founder's Efforts on New Computer; Cites Research Costs," *The Wall Street Journal,* May 16, 1989, p. A3; Russell Mitchell, "Now Cray Faces Life without Cray," *Business Week,* May 29, 1989, p. 31; Russell Mitchell, "The Numbers Aren't Crunching Cray Research," *Business Week,* June 1, 1992, p. 35; William M. Bulkley, "Cray Research to Unveil Supercomputer Likely to Tighten Its Hold on Market," *The Wall Street Journal,* Feb. 22, 1995, p. 4B; John W. Verity, "How the Numbers Crunched Cray Computer," *Business Week,* Apr. 10, 1995, p. 42; William M. Bulkeley, "Cray Research Names Samper Chairman, CEO," *The Wall Street Journal,* May 18, 1995, p. B2; Drew DeSilver, "Cray May Attract Shareholder Heat," *Minneapolis–St. Paul City Business,* Oct. 6, 1995, p. 14; Joan E. Rigdon and William M. Bulkeley, "Silicon Graphics Inc. Agrees to Acquire Cray Research in $739.2 Million Deal," *The Wall Street Journal,* Feb. 27, 1996, p. A3; Steve Lohr, "Silicon Graphics Reported Ready to Rescue Cray," *The New York Times,* Feb. 26, 1996, p. D1; "Silicon Graphics Jurassic Pact," *The Economist,* Mar. 2, 1996, pp. 58–59; "Life on the Visual Edge," *Computer Business Review,* Apr. 1, 1996, p. 4.

67. Andrew Tanzer, "The Asian Village," *Forbes,* Nov. 11, 1991, pp. 58–60; Laurence Zuckerman, "Satellite TV Makes Broadcasting Waves," *International Herald Tribune,* Dec. 10, 1992, p. 1; James W. Michaels, "There Are More Patels Out There Than Smiths," *Forbes,* Mar. 14, 1995, pp. 84–88; Pete Engardio, "Murdoch in Asia: Think Globally, Broadcast Locally," *Business Week,* June 6, 1994, p. 29; Kevin Maney, "Media Firms Shift to Gain Product Control," *USA Today,* Sept. 14, 1995, p. B1; Simon Holberton, "News Corp. Raises Stakes in Star Television Gamble," *Financial Times,* Oct. 11, 1995, p. 29; Jason Szep, "Murdoch Says STAR Still Bleeding, But Growth Ahead," *Reuters World Service,* Oct. 10, 1995, p. 1; Janian Stein, "Twelve to Watch in 1996; Star TV's Gary Davey," *Electronic Media,* Jan. 22, 1996, p. 114; Nichole Dickenson, "The Explosion of Asian Satellite TV," *Campaign,* June 7, 1996.

CHAPTER 8

1. "Flower Power: A Talk with Jim McCann," *Management Review,* March 1995, pp. 9–12;

Michael Warshaw, "Flower Superpower," *Success*, February 1996, pp. 33–34; "Managing with Lou Dobbs," *CNN*, Sept. 23, 1995, Transcript #211.

2. "Flower Power: A Talk with Jim McCann," *Management Review*, March 1995, pp. 9–12.

3. John Child, *Organization: A Guide to Problems and Practice*, Harper & Row, New York, 1977.

4. W. Jack Duncan, *Great Ideas in Management*, Jossey-Bass, San Francisco, 1989.

5. George T. Milkovich and William F. Glueck, *Personnel/Human Resource Management: A Diagnostic Approach*, 4th ed., Business Publications, Plano, Tex., 1985.

6. Adam Smith, *The Wealth of Nations*, Dent, London, 1910.

7. J. Richard Hackman and Greg R. Oldham, *Work Redesign*, Addison-Wesley, Reading, Mass., 1980; J. R. Galbraith, *Designing Organizations*, Jossey-Bass, San Francisco, 1995.

8. Robert H. Waterman, Jr., "The Power of Teamwork," *Best of Business Quarterly*, Spring 1988, pp. 17–25.

9. Michael A. Campion, Lisa Cheraskin, and Michael J. Stevens, "Career-Related Antecedents and Outcomes of Job Rotation," *Academy of Management Journal*, vol. 37, 1994, pp. 1518–1542.

10. M. D. Kilbridge, "Reduced Costs through Job Enrichment: A Case," *Journal of Business*, vol. 33, 1960, pp. 357–362.

11. Michael A. Campion and Carol L. McClelland, "Follow-Up and Extension of the Interdisciplinary Costs and Benefits of Enlarged Jobs," *Journal of Applied Psychology*, vol. 78, 1993, pp. 339–351.

12. Frederick Herzberg, *Work and the Nature of Man*, World Publishing, Cleveland, Ohio, 1966.

13. J. Richard Hackman and Greg R. Oldham, *Work Redesign*, Addison-Wesley, Reading, Mass., 1980.

14. Considerable research support exists for the importance of the job characteristics model, particularly as it relates to the job satisfaction of workers. See, for example, Brian T. Lohner, Raymond A. Noe, Nancy L. Moeller, and Michael P. Fitzgerald, "A Meta-Analysis of the Relation of Job Characteristics to Job Satisfaction," *Journal of Applied Psychology*, vol. 70, 1985, pp. 280–289; Ricky W. Griffin, "Effects of Work Redesign on Employee Perceptions, Attitudes, and Behaviors: A Long-Term Investigation," *Academy of Management Journal*, vol. 34, 1991, pp. 425–435.

15. F. K. Plous, Jr., "Focus on Innovation: Chicago Bank Eliminates Paperwork Assembly Line," *World of Work Report*, November 1986, pp. 1–2.

16. R. T. Golembiewski and C. W. Proehl, "A Survey of the Empirical Literature on Flexible Workhours: Character and Consequences of a Major Innovation," *Academy of Management Review*, vol. 3, 1978, pp. 837–853; Simcha Ronen and Sophia B. Primps, "The Compressed Work Week as Organizational Change: Behavioral and Attitudinal Outcomes," *Academy of Management Review*, vol. 6, 1981, pp. 61–74; Dan R. Dalton and Debra J. Mesch, "The Impact of Flexible Scheduling on Employee Attendance and Turnover," *Administrative Science Quarterly*, vol. 35, 1990, pp. 370–387; Cathy Trost, "To Cut Costs and Keep the Best People, More Concerns Offer Flexible Work Plans," *The Wall Street Journal*, Feb. 2, 1992, p. B1.

17. "Why a Big Steelmaker Is Mimicking the Minimills," *Business Week*, Mar. 27, 1989, p. 92.

18. J. M. Ivancevich and H. L. Lyon, "The Shortened Workweek: A Field Experiment," *Journal of Applied Psychology*, vol. 62, 1977, pp. 34–37.

19. Lisa Genasci, "That Was the Workweek That Was," *The Washington Post*, Oct. 15, 1995, p. H4.

20. Edward G. Thomas, "Flextime Doubles in a Decade," *Management World*, April–May 1987, pp. 18–19; D'Vera Cohn, "Workers Double Up to Get a Job Done," *The Washington Post*, Jan. 23, 1995, p. D5.

21. This section is based largely on Robert Duncan, "What Is the Right Organization Structure? Decision Tree Analysis Provides the Answer," *Organizational Dynamics*, Winter 1979, pp. 59–80; and Daniel Robey, *Designing Organizations*, Irwin, Homewood, Ill., 1986, pp. 210–213.

22. Richard L. Daft, *Organization Theory and Design*, 3d ed., West, St. Paul, Minn., 1989; John Child, *Organization: A Guide to Problems and Practice*, Harper & Row, London, 1984.

23. Richard H. Hall, *Structures, Processes, and Outcomes*, Prentice-Hall, Englewood Cliffs, N.J., 1987; John Child, *Organization: A Guide to Problems and Practice*, Harper & Row, London, 1984.

24. Alfred A. Marcus, "Responses to Externally Induced Innovation: Their Effects on Organizational Performance," *Strategic Management Journal*, vol. 9, 1988, pp. 387–402.

25. Buck Brown, "James Bildner's Spectacular Rise and Fall," *The Wall Street Journal*, Oct. 24, 1988, p. B1.

26. Eric Morgenthaler, "Herb Tea's Pioneer: From Hippie Origins to $16 Million a Year," *The Wall Street Journal*, May 6, 1981, p. 1; Nora Gallagher, "We're More Aggressive Than Our Tea," *Across the Board*, July–August 1983, pp. 45–50; "Kraft Is Celestial Seasonings' Cup of Tea," *Business Week*, July 28, 1986, p. 73; Susan D. Atchison, "Putting the Red Zinger Back into Celestial," *Business Week*, Nov. 4, 1991, pp. 74–78; Lisa Finnegan, "Boulder County's Public Companies: Top 10 Profit Growth—Celestial Boosts Bottom Line, Remains on Acquisition Path," *Boulder County Business Report*, June 1995, p. 8; Jane McCabe, "Herbal Tea Pioneer: Celestial Seasonings," *Tea & Coffee Trade Journal*, July 1995, p. 38; "Celestial Seasonings Names Dailey & Associates to Manage $6 Million Ad Account," *PR Newswire*, May 31, 1996, p. 1.

27. John Child, *Organization: A Guide to Problems and Practice*, Harper & Row, London, 1984.

28. Robert D. Dewar and Donald P. Simet, "A Level Specific Prediction of Spans of Control Examining the Effects of Size, Technology, and Specialization," *Academy of Management Journal*, vol. 24, 1981, pp. 5–24; David D. Van Fleet, "Span of Management Research and Issues," *Academy of Management Journal*, vol. 26, 1983, pp. 546–552; C. W. Barkdull, "Span of Control: A Method of Evaluation," *Michigan Business Review*, vol. 15, 1963, pp. 25–32; John Child, *Organization: A Guide to Problems and Practice*, Harper & Row, London, 1984, pp. 58–59.

29. This example is based on Stephen P. Robbins, *Organization Theory, Structure, Design, and Applications*, 3rd ed., Prentice-Hall, Englewood Cliffs, N.J., 1990.

30. W. Norman Smallwood and Eliot Jacobsen, "Is There Life after Downsizing?" *Personnel*, December 1987, pp. 42–46; George Bailey and Julia Szerdy, "Is There Life after Downsizing?" *The Journal of Business Strategy*, January–February 1988, pp. 8–11; Sarah J. Freeman and Kim S. Cameron, "Organizational Downsizing: A Convergence and Reorientation Framework," *Organization Science*, February 1993, pp. 10–29.

31. Norman R. Horton, "Restructurings and Dismemberments," *Management Review*, March 1988, pp. 5–6; George Bailey and David Sherman, "Downsizing: The Alternatives May Be Cheaper," *Management Review*, April 1988, pp. 54–55.

32. Phil Nienstedt and Richard Wintermantel, "Motorola Restructures to Improve Productivity," *Management Review*, January 1987, p. 47 (reprinted from *Personnel*, August 1985).

33. Joseph B. White, "Toyota Wants More Managers Out on the Line," *The Wall Street Journal*, Aug. 2, 1989, p. A10; Yumiko Ono and Marcus W. Brauchli, "Japan Cuts the Middle-Management Fat," *The Wall Street Journal*, Aug. 8, 1989, p. B1; Valerie Reitman, "Toyota Names a Chief Likely to Shake Up Global Auto Business," *The Wall Street Journal*, Aug. 11, 1995, pp. A1, A4; Neil Winberg, "Shaking Up an Old Giant," *Forbes*, May 20, 1996, pp. 68–80.

34. Sandra Sugawara, "Japan Inc. Finds a Way to Keep the Lid on Layoffs," *The Washington Post*, Mar. 12, 1996, p. D11.

35. Philip R. Nienstedt, "Effectively Downsizing Management Structures," *Human Resource Planning*, vol. 12, 1989, pp. 155–156; Andrea Knox, "The Downside and Dangers of Downsizing," *The Washington Post*, Mar. 15, 1992, p. H2; John A. Burne, "The Pain of Downsizing," *Business Week*, May 9, 1994, p. 61.

36. Bernard Wysocki, Jr., "Some Companies Cut Costs Too Far, Suffer 'Corporate Anorexia,'" *The Wall Street Journal*, July 5, 1995, p. A1.

37. Jay R. Galbraith, *Designing Organizations*, Jossey-Bass, San Francisco, 1995.

38. Howard M. Carlisle, "A Contingency Approach to Decentralization," *Advanced Management Journal*, July 1974, pp. 9–18.

39. Ibid.

40. John Child, *Organization: A Guide to Problems and Practice*, Harper & Row, London, 1984.

41. Michael Schroeder, "The Recasting of Alcoa," *Business Week*, Sept. 9, 1991, pp. 62–64; Dana Milbank, "Changes at Alcoa Point Up Challenges and Benefits of Decentralized Authority," *The Wall Street Journal*, Nov. 7, 1991, pp. B1–B2.

42. W. Jack Duncan, *Great Ideas in Management*, Jossey-Bass, San Francisco, 1989.

43. Carrie R. Leana, "Predictors and Consequences of Delegation," *Academy of Management Journal*, vol. 29, 1986, pp. 754–774.

44. Adapted from Laurie Baum, "Delegating Your Way to Job Survival," *Business Week*, Nov. 2, 1987, p. 206.

45. "Flower Power: A Talk with Jim McCann," *Management Review*, March 1995, pp. 9–12.

46. Morgan W. McCall, Jr., and Michael M. Lombardo, "What Makes a Top Executive?" *Psychology Today*, February 1983, pp. 26–31.

47. Vivian Nossiter, "A New Approach toward Resolving the Line and Staff Dilemma," *Academy of Management Review*, vol. 4, 1979, pp. 103–106.

48. "The Shrinking of Middle Management," *Business Week*, Apr. 25, 1983, pp. 53–54.

49. Thomas Moore, "Goodbye, Corporate Staff," *Fortune*, Dec. 21, 1987, pp. 65–76.

50. Jay R. Galbraith, *Organization Design*, Addison-Wesley, Reading, Mass., 1977.

51. Lucien Rodes, "At the Crossroads," *INC.*, February 1988, pp. 66–76.

52. Michael Tushman and David Nadler, "Organizing for Innovation," *California Management Review*, vol. 28, 1986, pp. 74–92; Rosabeth Moss Kanter, "When a Thousand Flowers Bloom: Structural, Collective, and Social Conditions for Innovation in Organizations," *Research in Organizational Behavior*, vol. 10, 1988, pp. 169–211.

53. This section relies heavily on Jay R. Galbraith, *Organization Design*, Addison-Wesley, Reading, Mass., 1977.

54. L. J. Bourgeois, "On the Measurement of Organizational Slack," *Academy of Management Review*, vol. 6, 1981, pp. 29–39.

55. Ibid.

56. Henry C. Mishkoff, "The Network Nation Emerges," *Management Review*, August 1986, pp. 29–31.

57. The material in this section is based largely on Jay R. Galbraith, *Organization Design*, Addison-Wesley, Reading, Mass., 1977.

58. Elizabeth V. Reynolds and J. David Johnson, "Liaison Emergence: Relating Theoretical Perspectives," *Academy of Management Review*, vol. 7, 1982, pp. 551–559.

59. Jerry Flint with William Heuslein, "An Urge to Service," *Forbes*, Sept. 18, 1989, pp. 172–176.

60. Ibid.

61. Charles Child, "Olds Hires New Brand Manager from Cereal Maker," *Automotive News*, Dec. 25, 1995, p. 5.

62. John R. Adams and Nicki S. Kirchof, "The Practice of Matrix Management," in David I. Cleland (ed.), *Matrix Management Systems Handbook*, Van Nostrand Reinhold, New York, 1984, p. 21; Bill Vlasic and Kathleen Kerwin, "GM's Man in Merging Traffic," *Business Week*, Mar. 4, 1996, p. 38.

63. Tom Nicholson, James C. Jones, and Erik Ipsen, "GM Plans a Great Divide," *Newsweek*, Jan. 9, 1984, pp. 68–69; Urban C. Lehner and Robert L. Simpson, "GM Unveils Plan for Realigning Auto Making," *The Wall Street Journal*, Jan. 11, 1984, p. 3; Michael Brody, "Can GM Manage It All?" *Fortune*, July 8, 1985, pp. 22–28; David E. Whiteside, "Roger Smith's Campaign to Change the GM Culture," *Business Week*, Apr. 7, 1986, pp. 84–85; Warren Brown, "If You Were at the Helm of GM," *The Washington Post*, Jan. 14, 1990, pp. H1, H4; Alex Taylor III, "The Road Ahead at General Motors," *Fortune*, May 4, 1992, pp. 94–95; Frank Swoboda and Warren Brown, "GM Cutting Headquarters Staff by 74%" *The Washington Post*, July 15, 1992, pp. D1, D4; Jerry Flint, "Darkness before Dawn," *Forbes*, Nov. 23, 1992, pp. 42–43; "Rx for the General," *Automotive News*, May 8, 1993, p. 30; Keith Naughton and Kathleen Kerwin, "At GM, Two Heads May Be Worse Than One," *Business Week*, Aug. 14, 1995, p. 46.

64. Based on Bernard Avishai, "A European Platform for Global Competition: An Interview with VW's Carl Hahn," *Harvard Business Review*, July–August 1991, pp. 104–113; and John Templeman, "VW's New Boss Has the Beetle in His Blood," *Business Week*, Apr. 13, 1992, p. 56; Jonathan Steele, "On the Wagon," *The Guardian*, Sept. 21, 1995, p. T2; "VW Group Looks for 'Markedly Better Profit' This Year," *Agence France Presse*, Nov. 30, 1995, p. 1; David Woodruff, "VW Is Back—But for How Long?" *Business Week*, Mar. 4, 1996, pp. 86–87.

CHAPTER 9

1. Based on materials in P. Ranganath Nayak and John M. Ketteringham, *Break-Throughs*, Rawson Associates, New York, 1986; Alicia Johnson, "3M Organized to Innovate," *Management Review*, July 1986, pp. 38–39; Christopher Knowlton, "Keeping the Fires Lit under the Innovators," *Fortune*, Mar. 28, 1988, p. 45; Russell Mitchell, "Mining the Work Force for Ideas," *Business Week*, Innovation 1989 issue, June 16, 1989, p. 121; L. D. Simóne, "How Can Big Companies Keep the Entrepreneurial Spirit Alive?" *Harvard Business Review*,

November–December 1995, pp. 183–185; and Thomas A. Stewart, "3M Fights Back," *Fortune*, Feb. 5, 1996, pp. 94–99.

2. Alfred D. Chandler, *Strategy and Structure*, M.I.T., Cambridge, Mass., 1962.

3. James W. Frederickson, "The Strategic Decision Process and Organizational Structure," *Academy of Management Review*, vol. 11, 1986, pp. 280–297.

4. Alex Taylor III, "The U.S. Gets Back in Fighting Shape," *Fortune*, Apr. 24, 1989, pp. 42–48.

5. David Nadler and Michael Tushman, *Strategic Organization Design*, Scott, Foresman, Glenview, Ill., 1988.

6. This section is based largely on Robert Duncan, "What Is the Right Organization Structure? Decision Tree Analysis Provides the Answer," *Organizational Dynamics*, Winter 1979, pp. 59–80; and Daniel Robey, *Designing Organizations*, Irwin, Homewood, Ill., 1986, pp. 210–213.

7. Daniel Robey, *Designing Organizations*, Irwin, Homewood, Ill., 1986.

8. John Child, *Organization: A Guide to Problems and Practice*, Harper & Row, London, 1984.

9. Andrew Albert, "Citicorp Shuffles Units to Emphasize Management of Institutional Assets," *American Banker*, July 5, 1985, p. 1.

10. Robert Duncan, "What Is the Right Organization Structure? Decision Tree Analysis Provides the Answer," *Organizational Dynamics*, Winter 1979, pp. 59–80; Daniel Robey, *Designing Organizations*, Irwin, Homewood, Ill., 1986, pp. 219–222.

11. This section relies heavily on Richard L. Daft, *Organization Theory and Design*, 3d ed., West, St. Paul, Minn., 1989; and Daniel Robey, *Designing Organizations*, Irwin, Homewood, Ill., 1986, pp. 219–222.

12. This discussion relies heavily on Stanley M. Davis and Paul R. Lawrence, *Matrix*, Addison-Wesley, Reading, Mass., 1977.

13. William Jerkovsky, "Functional Management in Matrix Organizations," *IEEE Transactions on Engineering Management*, May 1983, pp. 89–97.

14. Jay R. Galbraith and Robert K. Kazanjian, *Strategy Implementation*, 2d ed., West, St. Paul, Minn., 1986.

15. William C. Goggins, "How the Multidimensional Structure Works at Dow Corning," *Harvard Business Review*, January–February 1974.

16. The following sections rely on Stanley M. Davis and Paul R. Lawrence, *Matrix*, Addison-Wesley, Reading, Mass., 1977, pp. 129–154; John R. Adams and Nicki S. Kirchof, "The Practice of Matrix Management," in David I. Cleland (ed.), *Matrix Management Systems Handbook*, Van Nostrand Reinhold, New York, 1984, pp. 13–30; and Robert C. Ford and W. Alan Randolph, "Cross-Functional Structures: A Review and Integration of Matrix Organization and Project Management," *Journal of Management*, vol. 18, 1992, pp. 267–294.

17. Ann M. Morrison, "The General Mills Brand of Managers," *Fortune*, Jan. 12, 1981, pp. 99–107; Julie B. Solomon and John Bussey, "Pressed by Its Rivals, Procter & Gamble Co. Is Altering Its Ways," *The Wall Street Journal*, May 20, 1985, pp. 1, 22; John Smale, "Behind the Brands at P&G," *Harvard Business Review*, November–December 1985, pp. 79–89; Zachary Schiller, "No More Mr. Nice Guy at P&G—Not by a Long Shot," *Business Week*, Feb. 3, 1992, pp. 54–56; Weld F. Royal, "Marketing Strategies of Procter & Gamble,"

Sales & Marketing Management, November 1995, p. 62.

18. Shelly Katz, "An About-Face in TI's Culture," *Business Week*, July 5, 1982, p. 77.

19. Stanley M. Davis and Paul R. Lawrence, *Matrix*, Addison-Wesley, Reading, Mass., 1977, pp. 11–20.

20. William F. Joyce, "Matrix Organization: A Social Experiment," *Academy of Management Journal*, vol. 29, 1986, pp. 536–561.

21. Harvey F. Kolodny, "Evolution to a Matrix Organization," *Academy of Management Review*, vol. 4, 1979, pp. 543–553, and "Managing in a Matrix," *Business Horizons*, March–April 1981, pp. 17–24.

22. This section is based on Jay R. Galbraith, *Designing Organizations*, Jossey-Bass, San Francisco, 1995.

23. Charles Child, "GMAC Reorganizes Field Staff for Better Service," *Automotive News*, Dec. 25, 1995, p. 8.

24. Henry W. Chesbrough and David J. Teece, "Organizing for Innovation," *Harvard Business Review*, January–February 1996, pp. 65–73.

25. Louis W. Fry, "Technological-Structure Research: Three Critical Issues," *Academy of Management Journal*, vol. 25, 1982, pp. 532–552.

26. Joan Woodward, *Management and Technology*, Her Majesty's Stationery Office, London, 1958, and *Industrial Organizations: Theory and Practice*, Oxford University, London, 1965.

27. Joan Woodward, *Industrial Organizations: Theory and Practice*, Oxford University, London, 1965. Also see Paul D. Collins and Frank Hull, "Technology and Span of Control: Woodward Revisited," *Journal of Management Studies*, March 1986, pp. 143–164.

28. Louis W. Fry, "Technological-Structure Research: Three Critical Issues," *Academy of Management Journal*, vol. 25, 1982, pp. 532–552; Frank M. Hull and Paul D. Collins, "High-Technology Batch Production Systems: Woodward's Missing Type," *Academy of Management Journal*, vol. 30, 1987, pp. 786–797.

29. Louis W. Fry, "Technological-Structure Research: Three Critical Issues," *Academy of Management Journal*, vol. 25, 1982, pp. 532–552.

30. James D. Thompson, *Organizations in Action*, McGraw-Hill, New York, 1967, pp. 54–55.

31. W. Graham Astley, "Organizational Size and Bureaucracy," *Organization Studies*, vol. 6, 1985, pp. 201–228; John B. Cullen, Kenneth S. Anderson, and Douglas D. Baker, "Blau's Theory of Structural Differentiation Revisited: A Theory of Structural Change or Scale?" *Academy of Management Journal*, vol. 29, 1986, pp. 203–229.

32. John B. Cullen, Kenneth S. Anderson, and Douglas D. Baker, "Blau's Theory of Structural Differentiation Revisited: A Theory of Structural Change or Scale?" *Academy of Management Journal*, vol. 29, 1986, pp. 203–229.

33. Richard Z. Goodling and John A. Wagner III, "A Meta-Analytic Review of the Relationship between Size and Performance: The Productivity and Efficiency of Organizations and Their Subunits," *Administrative Science Quarterly*, vol. 30, 1985, pp. 462–481.

34. Stephen P. Robbins, *Organization Theory: The Structure and Design of Organizations*, 3d ed., Prentice-Hall, Englewood Cliffs, N.J., 1990.

35. S. C. Gwynne, "The Right Stuff," *Time*, Oct. 29, 1990, pp. 74–84; David Woodruff, "Saturn," *Business Week*, Aug. 17, 1992, pp.

86–91; David A. Aaker, "Building a Brand: The Saturn Story," *California Management Review*, Winter 1994, pp. 114–133; Chad Rubel, "Partnerships Steer Saturn to New Marketing Mix," *Marketing News TM*, Jan. 29, 1995, p. 5.
36. Brian Dumaine, "Is Big Still Good?" *Fortune*, Apr. 20, 1992, pp. 50–60.
37. Tom Burns and G. M. Stalker, *The Management of Innovation*, Tavistock, London, 1961.
38. Jay W. Lorsch, "Contingency Theory and Organization Design: A Personal Odyssey," in Ralph H. Kilmann, Louis R. Pondy, and Dennis P. Slevin (eds.), *The Management of Organization Design: Strategies and Implementation*, vol. 1, North-Holland, New York, 1976, p. 143.
39. Paul R. Lawrence and Jay W. Lorsch, *Organization and Environment*, Irwin, Homewood, Ill., 1969, pp. 20–45.
40. Danny Miller, "Configurations of Strategy and Structure: Toward a Synthesis," *Strategic Management Journal*, vol. 7, 1986, pp. 233–249, and "Relating Porter's Business Strategies to Environment and Structure: Analysis and Performance Implications," *Academy of Management Journal*, vol. 31, 1988, pp. 280–308.
41. This section is based heavily on Jay R. Galbraith, "Designing the Innovating Organization," *Organizational Dynamics*, vol. 10, 1982, pp. 12–13.
42. Modesto A. Maidique, "Enterpreneurs, Champions, and Technological Innovation," *Sloan Management Review*, Winter 1980, pp. 59–76.
43. Robert A. Burgelman, "Managing the New Venture Division: Research Findings and Implications for Strategic Management," *Strategic Management Journal*, vol. 6, 1985, pp. 39–54; Christopher K. Bart, "New Venture Units: Use Them Wisely to Manage Innovation," *Sloan Management Review*, Summer 1988, pp. 35–43.
44. Subrata N. Chakravarty, "Back in Focus," *Forbes*, June 6, 1994, pp. 72–76.
45. Michael Schrage, "Bell Labs Is Long on Genius but Short in the Marketplace," *The Washington Post*, Mar. 1, 1987, pp. H1, H4.
46. Based on Jules Arbose, "How Perstorp Persuades Its Managers to Innovate," *International Management*, June 1987, pp. 41–47; Stuart Nathan, "Eyeing Expansion in America," *Chemistry and Industry*, July 3, 1995, p. 489; and "China: Perstorp Moves into Chinese Market with Floor Coatings Joint," *Chemical Business News Base*, Mar. 8, 1996, p. 1.
47. Based on Linda S. Ackerman, "Transition Management: An In-Depth Look at Managing Complex Change," *Organizational Dynamics*, Summer 1982, pp. 46–66.
48. Deborah Wise and Catherine Harris, "Apple's New Crusade," *Business Week*, Nov. 26, 1984, pp. 146–156; Bro Uttal, "Behind the Fall of Steve Jobs," *Fortune*, Aug. 5, 1985, pp. 20–24; Katherine M. Hafner and Geoff Lewis, "Apple's Comeback," *Business Week*, Jan. 19, 1987, pp. 84–89; Jim Bartimo, "Rapid Growth at Apple Triggers Troubles," *The Washington Post*, Feb. 4, 1989, p. C1; Barbara Buell, "Apple: New Team, New Strategy," *Business Week*, Oct. 15, 1990, pp. 86–96; Kathy Rebello, "Apple's Daring Leap into the All-Digital Future," *Business Week*, May 25, 1992, pp. 120–122; Jim Carlton, "What's Eating Apple? Computer Maker Hits Some Serious Snags," *The Wall Street Journal*, Sept. 21, 1995, pp. A1, A16; Julie Schmit and James Kim, "Apple CEO on the Hot Seat," *USA Today*, Oct. 9, 1995, p. 2B; "Looking Up At Apple," *Business Week*, Nov.

27, 1995, p. 49; Elizabeth Corcoran, "Spindler Is Out at Apple," *The Washington Post*, Feb. 3, 1996, pp. H1, H2.
49. Reprinted from William Taylor, "The Organizing Logic of ABB," *Harvard Business Review*, March–April 1991, p. 93; figures updated from John A. McClenahen, "Percy Barnevik . . . and the ABBs of Competition," *Industry Week*, June 6, 1994, pp. 20–22, and "ABB Asea Brown Boveri Group Results 1995 Record Growth in Earnings," *Business Wire*, Feb. 28, 1996, p. 1.

CHAPTER 10
1. Amanda Bennett, "CARE Makes a Comeback after Drive to Revamp Its Management Practices," *The Wall Street Journal*, Feb. 9, 1987, p. B1; Gwen Kinhead, "America's Best-Run Charities," *Fortune*, Nov. 9, 1987, pp. 145–150; additional information obtained from telephone interviews with company representative, January 1996.
2. Herbert G. Heneman III, Donald P. Schwab, John A. Fossum, and Lee D. Dyer, *Personnel/Human Resource Management*, 4th ed., Irwin, Homewood, Ill., 1989; William B. Werther, Jr., and Keith Davis, *Personnel Management and Human Resources*, 5th ed., McGraw-Hill, New York, 1996.
3. Cynthia A. Lengnick-Hall and Mark L. Lengnick-Hall, "Strategic Human Resources Management: A Review of the Literature and a Proposed Typology," *Academy of Management Review*, vol. 13, 1988, pp. 454–470; "Strategic HR: Trends Shaping HR," *Human Resources Management News*, Jan. 2, 1995, p. 2.
4. Wayne F. Cascio, *Managing Human Resources*, 4th ed., McGraw-Hill, New York, 1995.
5. "HR Helps The Mirage Thrive in Crowded Vegas," *Personnel Journal*, January 1995, p. 72.
6. James W. Walker, *Human Resource Planning*, McGraw-Hill, New York, 1980; Cynthia A. Lengnick-Hall and Mark L. Lengnick-Hall, "Strategic Human Resources Management: A Review of the Literature and a Proposed Typology," *Academy of Management Review*, vol. 13, 1988, pp. 454–470.
7. Edward L. Levine, *Everything You Always Wanted to Know about Job Analysis*, Mariner, Tampa, Fla., 1983; George T. Milkovich and John W. Boudreau, *Personnel/Human Resource Management*, 5th ed., Business Publications, Plano, Tex., 1988.
8. Patrick M. Wright and Kenneth N. Wexley, "How to Choose the Kind of Job Analysis You Really Need," *Personnel*, May 1985, pp. 51–55.
9. *Survey on Downsizing*, American Management Association, New York, 1993; Dwight L. Gertz and João P. A. Baptista, *Grow to Be Great*, The Free Press, New York, 1995.
10. This section is based on Douglas T. Hall and James G. Goodale, *Human Resource Management: Strategy, Design, and Implementation*, Scott, Foresman, Glenview, Ill., 1986; and Randall S. Schuler and Vandra L. Huber, *Personnel and Human Resource Management*, 4th ed., West, St. Paul, Minn., 1990.
11. Bartley A. Brennan and Nancy Kubasek, *The Legal Environment of Business*, Macmillan, New York, 1988; David P. Twomey, *Equal Employment Opportunity Law*, South-Western, Cincinnati, Ohio, 1990.
12. William B. Werther, Jr., and Keith Davis, *Personnel Management and Human Resources*, 5th ed., McGraw-Hill, New York, 1996.
13. Randall S. Schuler and Vandra L. Huber, *Personnel and Human Resource Management*, 5th ed., West, St. Paul, Minn., 1993; Susan Meisinger, "Affirmative Action Comes Under

Review by States, Nation—An Analysis of the Issue," *Mosaics, SHRM Focuses on Work Place Diversity*, April 1995, pp. 1, 8.
14. Wayne F. Cascio, *Managing Human Resources*, 4th ed., McGraw-Hill, New York, 1995.
15. See *Adarand Contractors v. Pena*; Paul M. Barrett, "Supreme Court Ruling Imperils U.S. Programs of Racial Preference," *The Wall Street Journal*, June 13, 1995, pp. A1, A10.
16. Taylor Cox, Jr., *Cultural Diversity in Organizations: Theory, Research & Practice*, Berrett-Koehler Publishers, San Francisco, 1994.
17. Joel Dreyfuss, "Get Ready for the New Work Force," *Fortune*, Apr. 23, 1990, pp. 165–181.
18. Daniel C. Feldman, "Reconceptualizing the Nature and Consequences of Part-Time Work," *Academy of Management Review*, vol. 15, 1990, pp. 103–112; Jolie Solomon and Gilbert Fuchsberg, "Great Number of Older Americans Seen Ready to Work," *The Wall Street Journal*, Jan. 26, 1990, p. B1.
19. Jeffery Pfeffer, *Competitive Advantage through People*, Harvard Business School Press, Boston, 1994.
20. William B. Werther, Jr., and Keith Davis, *Personnel Management and Human Resources*, 5th ed., McGraw-Hill, New York, 1996; Randall S. Schuler and Vandra L. Huber, *Personnel and Human Resource Management*, 4th ed., West, St. Paul, Minn., 1990.
21. Benjamin Schneider and Neal Schmitt, *Staffing Organizations*, 2d ed., Scott, Foresman, Glenview, Ill., 1986.
22. Ibid.
23. Philip G. Swaroff, Lizabeth A. Barclay, and Alan R. Bass, "Recruiting Sources: Another Look," *Journal of Applied Psychology*, vol. 70, 1985, pp. 720–728; Benjamin Schneider and Neal Schmitt, *Staffing Organizations*, 2d ed., Scott, Foresman, Glenview, Ill., 1986.
24. Bruce M. Meglino, Angelo S. DeNisi, Stuart A. Youngblood, and Kevin J. Williams, "Effects of Realistic Job Previews: A Comparison Using an Enhancement and a Reduction Preview," *Journal of Applied Psychology*, vol. 73, 1988, pp. 259–266.
25. Steven L. Premack and John P. Wanous, "A Meta-Analysis of Realistic Job Preview Experiments," *Journal of Applied Psychology*, vol. 70, 1985, pp. 706–719; Alan M. Saks, Willi H. Wiesner, and Russel J. Summers, "Effects of Job Previews on Self-Selection and Job Choice," *Journal of Vocational Behavior*, vol. 44, 1994, pp. 297–316.
26. Vida Gulbinas Scarpello and James Ledvinka, *Personnel/Human Resource Management*, PWS-Kent, Boston, 1988; Randall S. Schuler and Vandra L. Huber, *Personnel and Human Resource Management*, 4th ed., West, St. Paul, Minn., 1990.
27. Robert D. Gatewood and Hubert S. Feild, *Human Resource Selection*, 2d ed., Dryden, Chicago, 1990.
28. Vida Gulbinas Scarpello and James Ledvinka, *Personnel/Human Resource Management*, PWS-Kent, Boston, 1988.
29. Randall S. Schuler and Vandra L. Huber, *Personnel and Human Resource Management*, 4th ed., West, St. Paul, Minn., 1990.
30. Robert D. Gatewood and Hubert S. Feild, *Human Resource Selection*, 2d ed., Dryden, Chicago, 1990; Barbara K. Brown and Michael A. Campion, "Biodata Phenomenology: Recruiters' Perceptions and Use of Biographical Information in Resume Screening," *Journal of Applied Psychology*, vol. 79, 1994, pp. 897–908.
31. William B. Werther, Jr., and Keith Davis, *Personnel Management and Human Resources*, 5th

ed., McGraw-Hill, New York, 1996; Robert D. Gatewood and Hubert S. Feild, *Human Resource Selection*, 2d ed., Dryden, Chicago, 1990.

32. *Personnel Policies Forum*, Survey No. 114, Selection Procedures and Personnel Records, Bureau of National Affairs, Washington, D.C., September 1976; Milton Hakel, "Employment Interview," in K. Rowland and G. Ferris (eds.), *Personnel Management: New Perspectives*, Allyn and Bacon, Boston, 1982.

33. The material on the types of interviews is based heavily on William B. Werther, Jr., and Keith Davis, *Personnel Management and Human Resources*, 5th ed., McGraw-Hill, New York, 1996.

34. Michael A. McDaniel, Deborah L. Whetzel, Frank L. Schmidt, and Steven D. Maurer, "The Validity of Employment Interviews: A Comprehensive Review and Meta-Analysis," *Journal of Applied Psychology*, vol. 79, 1994, pp. 599–616; Allen I. Huffcutt and Winfred Arthur, Jr., "Hunter and Hunter (1984) Revisited: Interview Validity for Entry-Level Jobs," *Journal of Applied Psychology*, vol. 79, 1994, pp. 184–190.

35. Based on Tom Janz, Lowell Hellervik, and David C. Gilmore, *Behavior Description Interviewing*, Allyn and Bacon, Boston, 1986; James M. Jenks and Brian L. P. Zevnik, "ABCs of Job Interviewing," *Harvard Business Review*, July–August 1989, pp. 38–42; Robert D. Gatewood and Hubert S. Feild, *Human Resource Selection*, 2d ed., Dryden, Chicago, 1990; Stephan J. Motowidlo, Gary W. Carter, Marvin D. Dunnette, Nancy Tippins, Steve Werner, Jennifer R. Burnett, and Mary Jo Vaughan, "Studies of the Structured Behavioral Interview," *Journal of Applied Psychology*, vol. 77, 1992, pp. 571–587.

36. Laura M. Graves and Ronald J. Karren, "The Employee Selection Interview: A Fresh Look at an Old Problem," *Human Resource Management*, Summer 1996, pp. 163–180.

37. This section is based on Robert D. Gatewood and Hubert S. Feild, *Human Resource Selection*, 2d ed., Dryden, Chicago, 1990.

38. Vida Gulbinas Scarpello and James Ledvinka, *Personnel/Human Resource Management*, PWS-Kent, Boston, 1988.

39. Glenn M. McEvoy and Richard W. Beatty, "Assessment Centers and Subordinate Appraisals of Managers: A Seven-Year Examination of Predictive Validity," *Personnel Psychology*, vol. 42, 1989, pp. 37–52.

40. R. L. LoPresto, D. E. Mitcham, and D. E. Ripley, *Reference Checking Handbook*, American Society for Personnel Administration, Alexandria, Va., 1986.

41. Kenneth N. Wexley and Gary P. Latham, *Developing and Training Human Resources in Organizations*, Scott, Foresman, Glenview, Ill., 1981; Douglas T. Hall and James G. Goodale, *Human Resource Management*, Scott, Foresman, Glenview, Ill., 1986.

42. Randall S. Schuler and Vandra L. Huber, *Personnel and Human Resource Management*, 4th ed., West, St. Paul, Minn., 1990.

43. E. B. Fiske, "Booming Corporate Education Efforts Rival College Programs, Study Says," *The New York Times*, Jan. 28, 1985, p. A10.

44. Wayne F. Cascio, *Managing Human Resources*, 4th ed., McGraw-Hill, New York, 1995.

45. Kenneth N. Wexley and Gary P. Latham, *Developing and Training Human Resources in Organizations*, Scott, Foresman, Glenview, Ill., 1981.

46. Vida Gulbinas Scarpello and James Ledvinka, *Personnel/Human Resource Management*, PWS-Kent, Boston, 1988.

47. Arnold H. Wensky and Robin J. Legendre, "Incentive Training at First Service Bank," *Personnel Journal*, April 1989, pp. 102–110.

48. Allan M. Mohrman, Jr., Susan M. Resnick-West, and Edward E. Lawler III, *Designing Performance Appraisal Systems*, Jossey-Bass, San Francisco, 1989.

49. C. A. Peck, *Pay and Performance: The Interaction of Compensation and Performance Appraisal*, Research Bulletin No. 155, Conference Board, New York, 1984.

50. Wayne F. Cascio, *Managing Human Resources*, 4th ed., McGraw-Hill, New York, 1995.

51. H. John Bernardin and Richard W. Beatty, *Performance Appraisal: Assessing Human Behavior at Work*, Kent, Boston, 1984.

52. Frank J. Landy, James L. Farr, Frank E. Saal, and Walter R. Freytag, "Behaviorally Anchored Scales for Rating the Performance of Police Officers," *Journal of Applied Psychology*, vol. 61, 1976, pp. 750–758.

53. Robert Giles and Christine Landauer, "Setting Specific Standards for Appraising Creative Staffs," *Personnel Administrator*, March 1984, pp. 35–47.

54. H. John Bernardin and Richard W. Beatty, *Performance Appraisal: Assessing Human Behavior at Work*, Kent, Boston, 1984; Stephen J. Carroll, Jr., and Craig Eric Schneier, *Performance Appraisal and Review Systems*, Scott, Foresman, Glenview, Ill., 1982.

55. David E. Smith, "Training Programs for Performance Appraisal: A Review," *Academy of Management Review*, vol. 11, 1986, pp. 22–40; David C. Martin and Kathryn M. Bartol, "Training the Raters: A Key to Effective Performance Appraisal," *Public Personnel Management*, vol. 15, 1986, pp. 101–110.

56. H. H. Meyer, "Self-Appraisal of Job Performance," *Personnel Psychology*, vol. 33, 1980, pp. 291–296.

57. David C. Martin, "Performance Appraisal: Improving the Rater's Effectiveness," *Personnel*, August 1986, pp. 28–33.

58. Clinton O. Longenecker, Dennis A. Gioia, and Henry P. Sims, Jr., "Behind the Mask: The Politics of Employee Appraisal," *Academy of Management Executive*, August 1987, pp. 183–193.

59. David C. Martin, Kathryn M. Bartol, and Marvin J. Levine, "The Legal Ramifications of Performance Appraisal," *Employee Relations Law Journal*, Winter 1986–1987, pp. 370–396; David C. Martin and Kathryn M. Bartol, "The Legal Ramifications of Performance Appraisal: An Update," *Employee Relations Law Journal*, Autumn 1991, pp. 257–286.

60. Robert Hoffman, "Ten Reasons You Should Be Using 360-Degree Feedback," *HRMagazine*, April 1995, pp. 82–85; Robert E. Kaplan and Charles J. Palus, *Enhancing 360-Degree Feedback for Senior Executives*, Center for Creative Leadership, Greensboro, N.C., 1994.

61. This section is based largely on Robert M. McCaffery, *Employee Benefit Programs*, PWS-Kent, Boston, 1988; Charles H. Fay, *Glossary of Compensation & Benefits Terms*, 2d ed., American Compensation Association, Scottsdale, Ariz., 1989; and George T. Milkovich and Jerry M. Newman, *Compensation*, 3d ed., BPI/Irwin, Homewood, Ill., 1990.

62. Marc J. Wallace, Jr., and Charles H. Fay, *Compensation Theory and Practice*, 2d ed., PWS-Kent, Boston, 1988.

63. George T. Milkovich and Jerry W. Newman, *Compensation*, 5th ed., Irwin, Chicago, 1986.

64. Richard L. Bunning, "Skill-Based Pay," *Personnel Administrator*, June 1989, pp. 65–68.

65. Roy Merrills, "How Northern Telecom Competes on Time," *Harvard Business Review*, July–August 1989, pp. 108–114.

66. Theresa M. Welbourne and Luis R. Gomez Mejia, "Gainsharing: A Critical Review and a Future Research Agenda," *Journal of Management*, vol. 21, 1995, pp. 559–609.

67. U.S. Chamber of Commerce, *Employee Benefits, 1994*, Washington, D.C., 1995.

68. Discussion between Martin Leskowitz, U.S. Chamber of Commerce, and David C. Martin, Aug. 3, 1992.

69. Walter Roessing, "High Marks for Hallmark," *Compass Readings*, March 1990, pp. 32–39.

70. Vida Gulbinas Scarpello and James Ledvinka, *Personnel/Human Resource Management*, PWS-Kent, Boston, 1988.

71. Jeanne M. Brett, "Why Employees Want Unions," *Organizational Dynamics*, Spring 1980, pp. 47–59; George T. Milkovich and John W. Boudreau, *Personnel/Human Resource Management*, 5th ed., Business Publications, Plano, Tex., 1988.

72. The basis for the number of employees belonging to unions changed in 1979 from annual dues-paying members to union members who are employed wage and salary workers; based on information from the U.S. Bureau of Labor Statistics, Industrial Relations Research Division, Washington, D.C., August 1992, and Bureau of Labor Statistics, Union Membership Survey: Union Members in 1995, Press Release, February 1996.

73. Vida Gulbinas Scarpello and James Ledvinka, *Personnel/Human Resource Management*, PWS-Kent, Boston, 1988.

74. This section is based largely on Wayne F. Cascio, *Managing Human Resources*, 4th ed., McGraw-Hill, New York, 1995.

75. Information obtained from the National Labor Relations Board Research Department, August 1992.

76. David M. Noer, *Healing the Wounds*, Jossey-Bass, San Francisco, 1993; Douglas L. Heerema and R. Thomas Lenz, "Managerial Loyalty: Beyond the Towering Ziggurats of the Old Industrial System," *Business Horizons*, March–April 1996, pp. 85–92.

77. Douglas L. Heerema and R. Thomas Lenz, "Managerial Loyalty: Beyond the Towering Ziggurats of the Old Industrial System," *Business Horizons*, March–April 1996, pp. 85–92.

78. Robert J. Grossman, "Damaged, Downsized Souls," *HRMagazine*, May 1996, pp. 54–62; Elizabeth Kolbert and Adam Clymer, "The Politics of Layoffs: In Search of a Message," *The New York Times*, Apr. 8, 1996, pp. A1, A22.

79. Denise M. Rousseau and Kimberly A. Wade-Benzoni, "Changing Individual-Organizational Attachments: A Two Way Street," in Ann Howard (ed.), *The Changing Nature of Work*, Jossey-Bass, San Francisco, 1995, pp. 290–322.

80. Study conducted for *The Washington Post* and reported in Kirstin Downey Grimsley, "Co-Workers Cited in Most Sexual Harassment Cases," *The Washington Post*, June 14, 1996, p. D1.

81. Rochelle Sharpe, "EEOC Sues Mitsubishi Unit for Harassment," *The Wall Street Journal*, Apr. 10, 1996, p. B1.

82. Randall S. Schuler and Vandra L. Huber, *Personnel and Human Resource Management*, 5th ed., West, St. Paul, Minn., 1993; Allen I. Fagin and Myron D. Rumeld, "Employer Liability for Sexual Harassment," *Society for Human Resource Management Legal Report*, Fall 1991, pp. 1–4.

83. *Public Health Report*, U.S. Department of Health and Human Services, June 1991, pp. 280–292.

84. H. W. French, "Helping the Addicted Worker," *The New York Times*, Mar. 26, 1987, pp. 29, 34.

85. "Labor Letter," *The Wall Street Journal*, Dec. 2, 1986, p. 1.

86. Judy D. Olian, "Genetic Screening for Employment Purposes," *Personnel Psychology*, vol. 37, 1984, pp. 423–438.

87. Cindy Skrzycki, "Family-Issues Experts See Rising Demand," *The Washington Post*, Jan. 7, 1990, p. H3.

88. George Gendron, "Steel Man: Ken Iverson," *INC.*, April 1986, pp. 41–48; John Ortman, "Nucor's Ken Iverson on Productivity and Pay," *Personnel Administrator*, October 1986, pp. 46–108; Ruth Simon, "Nucor's Boldest Gamble," *Forbes*, Apr. 3, 1989, pp. 122–124; Stephenie Overman, "No-Frills HR at Nucor," *HRMagazine*, June 1994, pp. 56–60; Stephen Baker, "Testing Nucor's Mettle," *Business Week*, June 5, 1995, pp. 58–60; Joseph L. McCarthy, "Passing the Torch at Big Steel; John Correnti Succeeds F. Kenneth Iverson as Nucor CEO," *Chief Executive (U.S.)*, March 1996, p. 22.

89. Speech by Arne Olsson and Richard P. Randazzo, Institute for International Human Resources annual conference, Toronto, Canada, Mar. 30, 1992; Carol Kennedy, "ABB: Model Merger for the New Europe," *Long Range Planning*, vol. 25, 1992, pp. 10–17; John S. McClenahan, "Percy Barnevik . . . and the ABBs of Competition," *Industry Week*, June 6, 1994, pp. 20–22; James Bredin, Peter Fletcher, Jack Gee, and John S. McClenahen, "Europe's Best Practices," *Industry Week*, Oct. 2, 1995, pp. 66; Sumanta Ghoshal and Christopher A. Bartlett, "Rebuilding Behavioral Context: A Blueprint for Corporate Renewal," *Sloan Management Review*, January 1996, p. 23.

CHAPTER 11

1. Based on Stuart Gannes, "Merck Has Made Biotech Work," *Fortune*, Jan. 19, 1987, pp. 58–64; John A. Byrne, "The Miracle Company," *Business Week*, Oct. 19, 1987, pp. 84–90; Joseph Weber, "Merck Needs More Gold from the White Coats," *Business Week*, Mar. 18, 1991, pp. 102–104; Brian O'Reilly, "Why Merck Married the Enemy," *Fortune*, Sept. 20, 1993, pp. 60–64; Nancy A. Nichols, "Scientific Management at Merck," *Harvard Business Review*, January–February 1994, pp. 89–99; Joseph Weber, "Merck Finally Gets Its Man," *Business Week*, June 27, 1994, pp. 22–25; and Shawn Tully, "Super CFOs: They Can't Jump . . . ," *Fortune*, Nov. 13, 1995, pp. 160–172.

2. Peter F. Drucker, "A Prescription for Entrepreneurial Management," *Industry Week*, Apr. 29, 1985, pp. 33–38.

3. "The New Breed of Strategic Planner," *Business Week*, Sept. 17, 1984, pp. 62–68.

4. Boyce Rensberger, "Lessons of the VCR Revolution: How U.S. Industry Failed to Make American Ingenuity Pay Off," *The Washington Post*, Apr. 13, 1987, pp. 1, 10.

5. For a similar definition, see Rosabeth Moss Kanter, *The Change Masters*, Simon and Schuster, New York, 1983, p. 20.

6. Gerald Zaltman, Robert Duncan, and Jonny Holbek, *Innovations and Organizations*, Wiley, New York, 1973; Andrew H. Van de Ven, "Central Problems in the Management of Innovation," *Management Science*, vol. 32, 1986, pp. 590–607.

7. Connie J. G. Gersick, "Revolutionary Change Theories: A Multilevel Exploration of the Punctuated Equilibrium Paradigm," *Academy of Management Review*, vol. 16, 1991, pp. 10–36.

8. Neil Gross, "A Wave of Ideas, Drop by Drop," *Business Week*, Innovation 1989 issue, June 16, 1989, pp. 22–30.

9. Deborah Funk, "Insurance Industry on Rebound After Recent Wave of Consolidations," *Warfield's Business Record*, June 3, 1996, pp. 9, 12.

10. Heather A. Haveman, "Between a Rock and a Hard Place: Organizational Change and Performance under Conditions of Fundamental Environmental Transformation," *Administrative Science Quarterly*, vol. 37, 1992, pp. 48–75.

11. Dyan Machan, "Eager Pupils," *Forbes*, Sept. 16, 1991, p. 118.

12. Adapted from Julian Flynn Siler and Sandra Atchison, "The Rx at Work in Utah," *Business Week/Quality 1991*, Oct. 25, 1991, p. 113.

13. The material on organizational life cycles is based primarily on Robert E. Quinn and Kim Cameron, "Organizational Life Cycles and Shifting Criteria of Effectiveness: Some Preliminary Evidence," *Management Science*, vol. 29, 1983, pp. 33–51; and Larry Greiner, "Evolution and Revolution as Organizations Grow," *Harvard Business Review*, July–August 1972, pp. 37–46.

14. James Brian Quinn, "Technological Innovation, Entrepreneurship, and Strategy," *Sloan Management Review*, Spring 1979, p. 20.

15. Bro Uttal, "Behind the Fall of Steve Jobs," *Fortune*, Aug. 5, 1985, pp. 20–24.

16. "The Shrinking of Middle Management," *Business Week*, Apr. 25, 1983, p. 56.

17. Jay R. Galbraith, "Designing the Innovating Organization," *Organizational Dynamics*, Winter 1982, p. 5.

18. Barbara Gray and Sonny S. Ariss, "Politics and Strategic Change across Organizational Life Cycles," *Academy of Management Review*, vol. 10, 1985, pp. 707–723.

19. Kim S. Cameron, David A. Whetten, and Myung U. Kim, "Organizational Dysfunctions of Decline," *Academy of Management Journal*, vol. 30, 1987, pp. 126–138.

20. Arthur M. Louis, "Doctor Wang's Toughest Case," *Fortune*, Feb. 3, 1986, pp. 106–109; Garry McWilliams, "Pulling It All Together: A Troubled Wang Labs Tries to Put Itself Back on Track," *Datamation*, Mar. 1, 1987, pp. 24–30; John R. Wilke, "Wang Founder Apparently Forces His Son to Step Down as President," *The Wall Street Journal*, Aug. 9, 1989, pp. A3, A4; "Wang Labs Names Computer Novice President and Chief Operating Officer," *The Wall Street Journal*, Aug. 24, 1989, p. B6; Joseph Nocera, "What Went Wrong at Wang," *The Wall Street Journal*, Feb. 26, 1992, p. A10; William M. Bulkeley and John R. Wilke, "Filing in Chapter 11, Wang Sends Warning to High-Tech Circles," *The Wall Street Journal*, Aug. 19, 1992, p. A1; Laura B. Smith, "In a Word: Service," *PC Week*, June 3, 1996, p. A8.

21. "After Its Recovery, New Headaches for Tylenol," *Business Week*, May 14, 1984, p. 137.

22. Sana Siwolop and Christopher Eklund, "The Capsule Controversery: How Far Should the FDA Go?" *Business Week*, Mar. 3, 1986, p. 37.

23. This section is based mainly on John P. Kotter, "Leading Change: Why Transformation Efforts Fail," *Harvard Business Review*, March–April 1995, pp. 59–67, and also on Gerald Zaltman, Robert Duncan, and Jonny Holbek, *Innovations and Organizations*, Wiley, New York, 1973; Modesto A. Maidique, "Entrepreneurs, Champions, and Technological Innovation," *Sloan Management Review*, Winter 1980, pp. 59–76.

24. The material on Lexmark in this section is based on Patrick Flanagan, "IBM One Day, Lexmark the Next," *Management Review*, January 1994, pp. 38–44.

25. "Conversation with Roberto Goizueta and Jack Welch," *Fortune*, Dec. 11, 1995, pp. 96–102.

26. Peter F. Drucker, "A Prescription for Entrepreneurial Management," *Industry Week*, Apr. 29, 1985, pp. 33–34.

27. Barbara Ettorre, "GE Brings a New Washer to Life," *Management Review*, September 1995, pp. 33–38.

28. Anne B. Fisher, "Making Change Stick," *Fortune*, Apr. 17, 1995, pp. 121–128.

29. Barbara Ettorre, "GE Brings a New Washer to Life," *Management Review*, September 1995, pp. 33–38.

30. Richard Beckhard, *Organizational Development: Strategies and Models*, Addison-Wesley, Reading, Mass., 1969; Michael Beer, *Organization Change and Development: A Systems View*, Goodyear, Santa Monica, Calif., 1980.

31. Wendell L. French and Cecil H. Bell, Jr., *Organization Development: Behavioral Interventions for Organizational Improvement*, Prentice-Hall, Englewood Cliffs, N.J., 1978; Edgar F. Huse and Thomas G. Cummings, *Organization Development and Change*, 3d ed., West, St. Paul, Minn., 1985; Allan M. Mohrman, Jr., Susan Albers Mohrman, Gerald E. Ledford, Jr., Thomas G. Cummings, Edward E. Lawler III, and associates, *Large-Scale Organizational Change*, Jossey-Bass, San Francisco, 1989.

32. Larry Reibstein, "A Finger on the Pulse: Companies Expand Use of Employee Surveys," *The Wall Street Journal*, Oct. 27, 1986, p. A31.

33. Wendell L. French and Cecil H. Bell, Jr., *Organizational Development: Behavior Science Interventions for Organizational Improvement*, 2d ed., Prentice-Hall, Englewood Cliffs, N.J., 1978; Edgar F. Huse and Thomas G. Cummings, *Organization Development and Change*, 3d ed., West, St. Paul, Minn., 1985.

34. John P. Kotter and Leonard A. Schlesinger, "Choosing Strategies for Change," *Harvard Business Review*, March–April 1979, pp. 106–114.

35. "Citicorp Loses Top Investment Talent Abroad," *Dun's Business Month*, November 1986, p. 21.

36. Bill Saporito, "The Revolt against 'Working Smarter,'" *Fortune*, July 21, 1986, pp. 58–65.

37. Kurt Lewin, "Frontiers in Group Dynamics: Concept, Method, and Reality in Social Science," *Human Relations*, vol. 1, 1947, pp. 5–41; Edgar F. Huse and Thomas G. Cummings, *Organization Development and Change*, 3d ed., West, St. Paul, Minn., 1985.

38. John P. Kotter and Leonard A. Schlesinger, "Choosing Strategies for Change," *Harvard Business Review*, March–April 1979, pp. 106–114.

39. Ibid.

40. Maggie McComas, "Cutting Costs without Killing the Business," *Fortune*, Oct. 13, 1986, pp. 70–78.

41. Paul C. Nutt, "Tactics of Implementation," *Academy of Management Journal*, vol. 29, 1986, pp. 230–261.

42. Jacob M. Schlesinger, "Plant-Level Talks Rise Quickly in Importance; Big Issue: Work Rules," *The Wall Street Journal*, Mar. 16, 1987, p. A16.

43. David Kirkpatrick, "What Givebacks Can Get You," *Fortune*, Nov. 24, 1986, p. 61.

44. Paul C. Nutt, "Tactics of Implementation," *Academy of Management Journal*, vol. 29, 1986, pp. 230–261.

45. Alison Leigh Cowan, "Getting Rich on Other People's Pay Checks," *Business Week*, Nov. 17, 1986, pp. 148–149; Fleming Meeks, "Tom Golisano and the Red Tape Factory," *Forbes*, May 15, 1989, pp. 80–82; Robyn Taylor

Parets, "Payout," *Investor's Business Daily,* Aug. 23, 1995, p. A6.

46. Kurt Lewin, *Field Theory in Social Science: Selected Theoretical Papers,* Harper, New York, 1951; Paul Strebel, "Choosing the Right Change Path," *California Management Review,* vol. 36, 1994, pp. 29–51.

47. David Kirkpatrick, "What Givebacks Can Get You," *Fortune,* Nov. 24, 1986, pp. 60–72.

48. Cynthia A. Lengnick-Hall, "Innovation and Competitive Advantage: What We Know and What We Need to Learn," *Journal of Management,* vol. 18, 1992, pp. 399–429.

49. Seth Lubove, "Salad in a Bag," *Forbes,* Oct. 23, 1995, pp. 201–203.

50. Rhonda L. Rundle, "Avery Dennison Dusts Itself Off After Rough Merger," *The Wall Street Journal,* Mar. 11, 1992, p. B4; Damon Darlin, "Thank You, 3M," *Forbes,* Sept. 25, 1995, pp. 86–88; Norton Paley, "A Sticky Situation: How Avery Dennison Rebounded from a Marketing Flop with New Products," *Sales & Marketing Management,* May 1996, p. 40.

51. Gifford Pinchot III, *Intrapreneuring,* Harper & Row, New York, 1985.

52. Ibid.

53. Ibid.

54. Harold J. Leavitt, "Applied Organization Change in Industry: Structural, Technical, and Human Approaches," in W. W. Cooper, H. J. Leavitt, and M. W. Shelly II (eds.), *New Perspectives in Organization Research,* Wiley, New York, 1964, pp. 55–71; Edgar F. Huse and Thomas G. Cummings, *Organization Development and Change,* 3d ed., West, St. Paul, Minn., 1985.

55. John Child, *Organization: A Guide to Problems and Practice,* Harper & Row, New York, 1977.

56. George Russell, "Rebuilding to Survive," *Time,* Feb. 16, 1987, p. 44.

57. Danny Miller and Peter H. Friesen, "Structural Change and Performance: Quantum versus Piecemeal-Incremental Approaches," *Academy of Management Journal,* vol. 25, 1982, pp. 867–892; Elaine Romanelli and Michael L. Tushman, "Organizational Transformation as Punctuated Equilibrium: An Empirical Test," *Academy of Management Journal,* vol. 37, 1994, pp. 1141–1166.

58. Andrew Tanzer, "Create or Die," *Forbes,* Apr. 6, 1987, p. 57.

59. Ibid. (adapted from pp. 124–125).

60. Marilyn Chase, "Robot Apprentices," *The Wall Street Journal,* Nov. 16, 1986, p. D16.

61. Debra Eller, "Motorola Trains VPs to Become Growth Leaders," *HRMagazine,* June 1995, pp. 82–87.

62. V. Sathe, "Implications of Corporate Culture: A Manager's Guide to Acting," *Organizational Dynamics,* Autumn 1983, pp. 5–23; Linda Smircich, "Concepts of Culture and Organizational Analysis," *Administrative Science Quarterly,* vol. 28, 1983, pp. 339–358; Ralph H. Kilmann, Mary J. Saxton, and Roy Serpa, "Issues in Understanding and Changing Culture," *California Management Review,* vol. 28, 1986, pp. 87–94.

63. Edgar F. Huse and Thomas G. Cummings, *Organization Development and Change,* 3d ed., West, St. Paul, Minn., 1985, p. 350; Charles Goldsmith, "British Airways' New CEO Envisions a Marriage of Travel and Amusement," *The Wall Street Journal,* Nov. 6, 1995, p. B11.

64. John P. Kotter and James L. Heskett, *Corporate Culture and Performance,* Free Press, New York, 1992; Paula Dwyer, "Air Raid: British Air's Bold Global Push," *Business Week,* Aug. 24, 1992, pp. 54–61.

65. Based on Graham Turner, "Inside Europe's Giant Companies: Cultural Revolution at Philips," *Long Range Planning,* vol. 19, 1986, pp. 12–17; Jonathan Kapstein, "Enough with the Theory—Where's the Thingamajig?" *Business Week,* Mar. 21, 1988, pp. 155–158; Jonathan Kapstein, "A Chilling New Era for Philips—and Europe," *Business Week,* Nov. 12, 1990, pp. 58–59; Jonathan B. Levine, "Philips' Big Gamble," *Business Week,* Aug. 5, 1991, pp. 34–36; Gail Edmondson, "Philips May Be Putting Too Many Chips on Chips," *Business Week,* Aug. 14, 1995, p. 55; and Martin Du Bois, "Chip Slowdown, Other Woes Still Press Philips Electronics, Despite Cost-Cutting," *The Wall Street Journal,* Apr. 24, 1996, p. A11.

66. Based on Kurt Lewin, *Field Theory in Social Science: Selected Theoretical Papers,* Harper, New York, 1951.

67. Based on James L. Rowe, Jr., "Armacost to Resign as BankAmerica Chief," *The Washington Post,* Oct. 11, 1986, pp. C1–C2; Robert N. Beck, "Visions, Values, and Strategies: Changing Attitudes and Culture," *Academy of Management Executive,* February 1987, pp. 33–39; Charles McCoy, "A Slashing Pursuit of Retail Trade Brings BankAmerica Back," *The Wall Street Journal,* Oct. 2, 1989, pp. A1, A8; Julia Leung and Stephen Duthie, "BankAmerica Sorts Its Options in Asia," *The Wall Street Journal,* Jan. 31, 1992, p. B4; Ralph T. King, Jr., "New Bank Behemoth Has Big Burdens, Rich Potential," *The Wall Street Journal,* Apr. 23, 1992, p. B4; David Mutch, "BankAmerica Relishes Its Restored Prosperity," *The Christian Science Monitor,* Aug. 31, 1995, p. 9; Sam Zuckerman, "The Redemption of Richard Rosenberg," *U.S. Banker,* September 1995, p. 31; Barton Crockett, "B of A Hits Its Stride As Low-Profile Exec Prepares for Top Job," *The American Banker,* Dec. 21, 1995, p. 6; and Sam Zuckerman, "New Man Atop the Pyramid," *Business Week,* Jan. 22, 1996, pp. 76–77.

68. John S. McClenahen, "Light in the East," *Industry Week,* Mar. 2, 1992, p. 14; "G.E.–Tungsram Venture in Hungary Hits Snags," *The New York Times,* Mar. 28, 1992, p. A37; Richard Bruner, "Tungsram's Leading Light," *International Management,* December 1992, pp. 42–45; Michel Syrett and Klari Kingston, "GE's Hungarian Light Switch," *Management Today,* April 1995, p. 52; "GE Tungsram Names Its New President," *MTI (Hungarian News Agency) Econews,* Apr. 10, 1996, p. 1.

CHAPTER 12

1. Based on Robert Howard, "Values Make the Company: An Interview with Robert Haas," *Harvard Business Review,* September–October 1990, pp. 133–144; Levi Strauss Aspiration Statement obtained January 1996; and Joan O'C. Hamilton, "Levi's Pot O' Gold," *Business Week,* June 24, 1996, p. 44.

2. Richard M. Steers and Lyman W. Porter (eds.), *Motivation and Work Behavior,* 5th ed., McGraw-Hill, New York, 1991, pp. 5–6.

3. John P. Campbell and Richard D. Prichard, "Motivation Theory in Industrial and Organizational Psychology," in Marvin D. Dunnette (ed.), *Handbook of Industrial and Organizational Psychology,* Rand McNally, Chicago, 1976, pp. 62–130.

4. Reva B. Tooley, "Turning Trials into Triumph," *Working Woman,* January 1987, pp. 66–70; Susan Caminiti, "America's Most Successful Businesswoman," *Fortune,* June 15, 1992, pp. 102–107.

5. Dean Foust, "Innkeepers, Beware: Kemmons Wilson Is Checking In Again," *Business Week,* Feb. 1, 1988, pp. 70–80.

6. Mahmoud A. Wahba and Lawrence G. Bridwell, "Maslow Reconsidered: A Review of Research on the Need Hierarchy Theory," *Organizational Behavior and Human Performance,* vol. 16, 1976, pp. 212–240; Vance F. Mitchell and Pravin Moudgill, "Measurement of Maslow's Need Hierarchy," *Organizational Behavior and Human Performance,* vol. 16, 1976, pp. 334–349.

7. This section is based heavily on Richard M. Steers, Lyman W. Porter, and Gregory A. Bigley, *Motivation and Leadership at Work,* McGraw-Hill, New York, 1996.

8. Clayton P. Alderfer, *Existence, Relatedness, and Growth: Human Needs in Organizational Settings,* Free Press, New York, 1972.

9. See Roy F. Baumeister and Mark R. Leary, "The Need to Belong: Desire for Interpersonal Attachments as a Fundamental Human Motivation," *Journal of Applied Psychology,* vol. 117, 1995, pp. 497–529, for recent evidence regarding the importance of this need.

10. P. Ranganath Nayak and John M. Ketteringham, *Break-Throughs,* Rawson Associates, New York, 1986.

11. Richard M. Steers, Lyman W. Porter, Gregory A. Bigley (eds.), *Motivation and Leadership at Work,* 6th ed., McGraw-Hill, New York, 1996.

12. Robert A. Mamis, "Details, Details," *INC.,* March 1988, pp. 96–98.

13. Jaclyn Fierman, "The Entrepreneurs: The Best of Their Class," *Fortune,* Oct. 12, 1987, p. 144.

14. William D. Spangler, "Validity of Questionnaire and TAT Measures of Need for Achievement: Two Meta-Analyses," *Psychological Bulletin,* vol. 112, 1992, pp. 140–154.

15. David C. McClelland, *Human Motivation,* Scott, Foresman, Glenview, Ill., 1985.

16. Richard M. Steers, "Murray's Manifest Needs Theory," in Richard M. Steers and Lyman W. Porter (eds.), *Motivation and Work Behavior,* 4th ed., McGraw-Hill, New York, 1987, pp. 59–67.

17. David C. McClelland, "Power Is the Great Motivator," *Harvard Business Review,* March–April 1976, pp. 100–110, and *Human Motivation,* Scott, Foresman, Glenview, Ill., 1985.

18. Richard M. Steers, "Murray's Manifest Needs Theory," in Richard M. Steers and Lyman W. Porter (eds.), *Motivation and Work Behavior,* 4th ed., McGraw-Hill, New York, 1987, pp. 59–67.

19. David C. McClelland, "Power Is the Great Motivator," *Harvard Business Review,* March–April 1976, pp. 100–110, and *Human Motivation,* Scott, Foresman, Glenview, Ill., 1985.

20. David C. McClelland, *Human Motivation,* Scott, Foresman, Glenview, Ill., 1985.

21. J. D. W. Andrews, "The Achievement Motive and Advancement in Two Types of Organizations," *Journal of Personality and Social Psychology,* vol. 6, 1967, pp. 163–168; David C. McClelland and Richard E. Boyatzis, "Leadership Motive Pattern and Long-Term Success in Management," *Journal of Applied Psychology,* vol. 67, 1982, pp. 737–743.

22. David C. McClelland, "Retrospective Commentary," *Harvard Business Review,* January–February 1995, pp. 138–139.

23. David C. McClelland, "Achievement Motivation Can Be Developed," *Harvard Business Review,* November–December 1965, pp. 6–25; David C. McClelland and David H. Burnham, "Power Is the Great Motivator," *Harvard Business Review,* March–April 1976, pp. 100–110; David C. McClelland, *Human*

Motivation, Scott, Foresman, Glenview, Ill., 1985, pp. 547–586.

24. Thomas J. Peters and Robert H. Waterman, *In Search of Excellence,* Harper & Row, New York, 1982.

25. Barry M. Staw, "Organizational Behavior: A Review and Reformulation of the Field's Outcome Variables," *Annual Review of Psychology,* vol. 35, 1984, pp. 627–666.

26. D. F. Parker and L. Dyer, "Expectancy Theory as a Within Person Behavioral Choice Model: An Empirical Test of Some Conceptual and Methodological Refinements," *Organizational Behavior and Human Performance,* vol. 17, 1976, pp. 97–117; H. J. Arnold, "A Test of the Validity of the Multiplicative Hypothesis of Expectancy-Valence Theories of Work Motivation," *Academy of Management Journal,* vol. 24, 1981, pp. 128–141; John P. Wanous, Thomas L. Keon, and Janina C. Latack, "Expectancy Theory and Occupational/Organizational Choices: A Review and Test," *Organizational Behavior and Human Performance,* vol. 32, 1983, pp. 66–86; Richard M. Steers and Lyman W. Porter, *Work and Motivation,* 5th ed., McGraw-Hill, New York, 1991.

27. David A. Nadler and Edward E. Lawler III, "Motivation: A Diagnostic Approach," in J. Richard Hackman, Edward E. Lawler III, and Lyman W. Porter (eds.), *Perspectives on Behavior in Organizations,* McGraw-Hill, New York, 1983, pp. 67–78.

28. Marcia Berss, "Under Control," *Forbes,* Jan. 31, 1994, pp. 50–52; Edward E. Lawler III, "Compensation Strategies for the Global Organization: An Exclusive Interview with Honeywell CEO Michael R. Bonsígnore," *ACA Journal,* Spring 1994, pp. 6–17; and Steve Alexander, "Improved Honeywell Earnings Meet or Exceed Analysts' Expectations," *Star Tribune,* Jan. 17, 1996, p. 1D.

29. Aaron Bernstein, "GE's Hard Lesson: Pay Cuts Can Backfire," *Business Week,* Aug. 10, 1992, p. 53.

30. J. Stacy Adams, "Inequity in Social Exchange," in L. Berkowitz (ed.), *Advances in Experimental Social Psychology,* vol. 2, Academic, New York, 1965, pp. 267–299.

31. Edwin A. Locke, "The Nature and Causes of Job Satisfaction," in M. Dunnette (ed.), *Hand book of Industrial and Organizational Psychology,* Rand McNally, Chicago, 1976, pp. 1297–1349; Richard T. Mowday, "Equity Theory Predictions of Behavior in Organizations," in Richard M. Steers and Lyman W. Porter (eds.), *Motivation and Work Behavior,* 5th ed., McGraw-Hill, New York, 1991, pp. 111–131.

32. Robert G. Lord and Jeffrey A. Hohenfeld, "Longitudinal Field Assessment of Equity Effects on the Performance of Major League Baseball Players," *Journal of Applied Psychology,* vol. 64, 1979, pp. 19–26. For a related study, see Robert D. Bretz, Jr., and Steven L. Thomas, "Perceived Equity, Motivation, and Final-Offer Arbitration in Major League Baseball," *Journal of Applied Psychology,* vol. 77, 1992, pp. 280–287.

33. Richard A. Cosier and Dan R. Dalton, "Equity Theory and Time: A Reformulation," *Academy of Management Review,* vol. 8, 1983, pp. 311–319.

34. Edwin A. Locke and Gary P. Latham, *Goal Setting: A Motivational Technique That Works!* Prentice-Hall, Englewood Cliffs, N.J., 1984; Edwin A. Locke and Gary P. Latham, *A Theory of Goal Setting & Task Performance,* Prentice-Hall, Englewood Cliffs, N.J., 1990.

35. Michelle Neely Martinez, "Equality Effort Sharpens Bank's Edge," *HRMagazine,* January 1995, pp. 38–43.

36. Robert D. Hof, "Intel: Far Beyond the Pentium," *Business Week,* Feb. 20, 1995, pp. 88–90.

37. Edwin A. Locke, Gary P. Latham, and Miriam Erez, "The Determinants of Goal Commitment," *Academy of Management Review,* vol. 31, 1988, pp. 23–39.

38. Fred Luthans and Robert Kreitner, *Organizational Behavior Modification,* Scott, Foresman, Glenview, Ill., 1975.

39. Richard D. Arvey and John M. Ivancevich, "Punishment in Organizations: A Review, Propositions, and Research Suggestions," *Academy of Management Review,* vol. 5, 1980, pp. 123–132; Janice M. Beyer and Harrison M. Trice, "A Field Study of the Use and Perceived Effects of Discipline in Controlling Work Performance," *Academy of Management Journal,* vol. 27, 1984, pp. 743–764.

40. Janice M. Beyer and Harrison M. Trice, "A Field Study of the Use and Perceived Effects of Discipline in Controlling Work Performance," *Academy of Management Journal,* vol. 27, 1984, pp. 743–764; W. Clay Hamner, "Reinforcement Theory and Contingency Management in Organizational Settings," in Richard M. Steers and Lyman W. Porter (eds.), *Motivation and Work Behavior,* 5th ed., McGraw-Hill, New York, 1991, pp. 61–87.

41. Wayne Dierks and Kathleen McNally, "Incentives You Can Bank On," *Personnel Administrator,* March 1987, pp. 60–65.

42. Albert Bandura, *Social Learning Theory,* Prentice-Hall, Englewood Cliffs, N.J., 1977, and *Social Foundations of Thought and Action: A Social Cognitive Theory,* Prentice-Hall, Englewood Cliffs, N.J., 1986; Robert Krietner and Fred Luthans, "A Social Learning Approach to Behavioral Management: Radical Behaviorists 'Mellowing Out,'" in Richard M. Steers and Lyman W. Porter (eds.), *Motivation and Work Behavior,* 5th ed., McGraw-Hill, New York, 1991, pp. 164–179.

43. J. Barling and R. Beattie, "Self-Efficacy Beliefs and Sales Performance," *Journal of Organizational Behavior Management,* vol. 5, 1983, pp. 41–51; M. Susan Taylor, Edwin A. Locke, Cynthia Lee, and Marilyn Gist, "Type A Behavior and Faculty Research Productivity: What Are the Mechanisms?" *Organizational Behavior and Human Performance,* vol. 34, 1984, pp. 402–418.

44. Albert Bandura, *Social Learning Theory,* Prentice-Hall, Englewood Cliffs, N.J., 1977, pp. 128–131.

45. Tim R. V. Davis and Fred Luthans, "A Social Learning Approach to Organizational Behavior," *Academy of Management Review,* vol. 5, 1980, pp. 281–290; Martin G. Evans, "Organizational Behavior: The Central Role of Motivation," *Journal of Management,* vol. 12, 1986, pp. 203–222.

46. Based on Aimee Stern, "Domino's: A Unique Concept Pays Off," *Dun's Business Month,* May 1986, pp. 50–51; Dale Feuer, "Training for Fast Times," *Training,* July 1987, pp. 25–30; John Duggleby, "The Domino's Recipe for Making Dough," *Business Week Careers,* February 1988, p. 81; Gregory A. Patterson, "Domino's Founder Monaghan Regains Control by Ousting Four Top Managers," *The Wall Street Journal,* Dec. 9, 1991, p. B6; and Michael Oneal "God, Family, and Domino's—That's It," *Business Week,* Jan. 30, 1995, p. 57–60.

47. Based on Bruce G. Posner and Bo Burlingham, "The Hottest Entrepreneur in America," *INC.,* January 1988, pp. 44–58; Pat Rosen, "John McCormack: Haircut King and School Headmaster," *Houston Business Journal,* May 21, 1990, pp. 1, 15–16; and Darrin Schlegel, "New Class of Entrepreneurs Created on College Campus," *Houston Business Journal,* Feb. 7, 1994, p. 16.

48. Based on Andrew Tanzer, "Ding-Dong, Capitalism Calling," *Forbes,* Oct. 14, 1991, pp. 184–186; Avon 1995 Annual Report; "Scents and Sensibility," *The Economist,* July 13, 1996, p. 57.

CHAPTER 13

1. Eric Schine, "Barbie Is Her Best Friend," *Business Week,* June 8, 1992, p. 80; Blair S. Walker, "Mattel President Makes Beeline to Top," *USA Today,* Aug. 10, 1992, p. 4b; Marilyn Much, "What Makes Barbie a Girl's Favorite Doll?" *Investor's Business Daily,* Apr. 12, 1995, p. A4; Katherine and Richard Greene, "The 20 Top-Paid Women in Corporate America," *Working Woman,* February 1996, pp. 40–44; John S. Jones, "Mattel Rolls On with Top Toys Despite Retailers' Slump," *Investor's Business Daily,* Jan. 17, 1996, p. B12; Martha Groves, "Special Report: Executive Pay in California," *Los Angeles Times,* May 26, 1996, p. D1; Lisa Bannon, "Mattel Names Jill Barad Chief Executive," *The Wall Street Journal,* Aug. 23, 1996, p. B2.

2. Robert Hogan, Gordon J. Curphy, and Joyce Hogan, "What We Know about Leaders," *American Psychologist,* June 1994, pp. 493–504.

3. "The Top 25," *Forbes,* June 15, 1987, p. 151.

4. Henry Mintzberg, *Power in and around Organizations,* Prentice-Hall, Englewood Cliffs, N.J., 1983, pp. 4–5; Jeffrey Pfeffer, *Power in Organizations,* Pitman, Boston, 1981, pp. 2–4.

5. J. R. P. French and B. Raven, "The Bases of Social Power," in D. Cartwright (ed.), *Studies in Social Power,* Institute for Social Research, Ann Arbor, Mich., 1959; Bertram H. Raven, "The Bases of Power: Origins and Recent Developments," *Journal of Social Issues,* vol. 49, 1993, pp. 227–251.

6. Information power was added in later work on important power bases; see B. H. Raven and A. W. Kruglanski, "Conflict and Power," in P. Swingle (ed.), *The Structure of Conflict,* Academic, New York, 1970.

7. This section based on Gary Yukl, *Leadership in Organizations,* 3d ed., Prentice-Hall, Englewood Cliffs, N.J., 1994. See also Paula Phillips Carson, Kerry D. Carson, and C. William Roe, "Social Power Bases: A Meta-Analytic Examination of Interrelationships and Outcomes," *Journal of Applied Social Psychology,* vol. 23, 1993, pp. 1150–1169.

8. James R. Norman, "A Hardheaded Takeover by McLouth's Hardhats," *Business Week,* June 6, 1988, pp. 90–91; Luther Jackson, "Steel Zeal," *Detroit Free Press,* Mar. 12, 1990, pp. 1E, 5E.

9. Richard Rapaport, "To Build a Winning Team: An Interview with Head Coach Bill Walsh," *Harvard Business Review,* January–February 1993, pp. 111–120.

10. Ralph M. Stogdill, *Handbook of Leadership,* Free Press, New York, 1974, p. 72.

11. This section is based heavily on Arthur G. Jago, "Leadership: Perspectives in Theory and Research," *Management Science,* vol. 28, 1982, pp. 315–336.

12. Ralph M. Stogdill, "Personal Factors Associated with Leadership: A Survey of the Literature," *Journal of Psychology,* vol. 25, 1948, pp. 35–71; R. D. Mann, "A Review of the Relationships between Personality and Performance in Small Groups," *Psychological Bulletin,* vol. 56, 1959, pp. 241–270.

13. Robert G. Lord, Christy L. De Vader, and

George M. Alliger, "A Meta-Analysis of the Relation between Personality Traits and Leadership Perceptions: An Application of Validity Generalization Procedures," *Journal of Applied Psychology*, vol. 71, 1986, pp. 402–410.

14. D. W. Bray, R. J. Campbell, and D. L. Grant, *Formative Years in Business: A Long Term AT&T Study of Managerial Lives*, Wiley, New York, 1974.

15. Tom Richman, "In the Black," *INC.*, May 1988, pp. 116–120.

16. See, for example, K. Lewin and R. Lippitt, "An Experimental Approach to the Study of Autocracy and Democracy: A Preliminary Note," *Sociometry*, vol. 1, 1938, pp. 292–300.

17. Bernard M. Bass, *Stogdill's Handbook of Leadership*, Free Press, New York, 1981, pp. 289–299.

18. Robert Tannenbaum and Warren H. Schmidt, "How to Choose a Leadership Pattern," *Harvard Business Review*, May–June 1973, pp. 162–180.

19. Bernard M. Bass, *Stogdill's Handbook of Leadership*, Free Press, New York, 1981; Rensis Likert, *New Patterns of Management*, McGraw-Hill, New York, 1961, and "From Production- and Employee-Centeredness to Systems 1–4," *Journal of Management*, vol. 5, 1979, pp. 147–156.

20. Judith H. Dobrzynski, "Way Beyond the Glass Ceiling," *The New York Times*, May 11, 1995, pp. D1, D6.

21. Mary Rowland, "Creating a Plan to Reshape a Business," *Working Woman*, August 1988, pp. 70–74; "Lynn Shostack Receives AMA Services Award," *Marketing News TM*, Jan. 2, 1995, p. 22.

22. Chester A. Schriesheim and Barbara J. Bird, "Contributions of the Ohio State Studies to the Field of Leadership," *Journal of Management*, vol. 5, 1979, pp. 135–145.

23. Mary Rowland, "Creating a Plan to Reshape a Business," *Working Woman*, August 1988, pp. 70–74; Judith H. Dobrzynski, "Way Beyond the Glass Ceiling," *The New York Times*, Mar. 11, 1995, pp. D1, D6.

24. L. L. Larson, J. G. Hunt, and R. N. Osborn, "The Great Hi-Hi Leader Behavior Myth: A Lesson from Occam's Razor," *Academy of Management Journal*, vol. 19, 1976, pp. 628–641.

25. Steven Kerr, Chester A. Schriesheim, Charles J. Murphy, and Ralph Stogdill, "Toward a Contingency Theory of Leadership Based on the Consideration and Initiating Structure Literature," *Organizational Behavior and Human Performance*, May 1975, pp. 62–82; Charles N. Greene, "Questions of Causation in the Path-Goal Theory of Leadership," *Academy of Management Journal*, vol. 22, 1979, pp. 22–41.

26. Robert R. Blake and Jane S. Mouton, *The Managerial Grid® III*, Gulf Publishing, Houston, 1985.

27. B. M. Bass, J. Krusell, and R. A. Alexander, "Male Managers' Attitudes toward Working Women," *American Behavioral Scientist*, vol. 15, 1971, pp. 221–236; B. Rosen and T. H. Jerdee, "Perceived Sex Differences in Managerially Relevant Characteristics," *Sex Roles*, vol. 4, 1978, pp. 837–843.

28. Kathryn M. Bartol and David C. Martin, "Women and Men in Task Groups," in R. D. Ashmore and F. K. Del Boca (eds.), *The Social Psychology of Female-Male Relations*, Academic, Orlando, Fla., 1986, pp. 259–310; Gregory H. Dobbins and Stephanie J. Platz, "Sex Differences in Leadership: How Real Are They?" *Academy of Management Review*, vol. 11, 1986, pp. 118–127; Gary N. Powell, *Women and Men in Management*, 2d ed., Sage, Newbury Park, Calif., 1993.

29. Tom Dunkel, "The Front Runners," *Working Woman*, April 1996, pp. 30–35.

30. Renee Redwood, "Giving Credit Where Credit Is Due: The Work of the Federal Glass Ceiling Commission," *Credit World*, May–June 1996, pp. 34–36.

31. Fred E. Fiedler, *A Theory of Leadership Effectiveness*, McGraw-Hill, New York, 1967. Much of our description of the contingency model is based on information in Fred E. Fiedler and Joseph E. Garcia, *New Approaches to Effective Leadership: Cognitive Resources and Organizational Performance*, Wiley, New York, 1987. This source also outlines a revision and extension called cognitive resource theory.

32. See Fred E. Fiedler and Martin M. Chemers, *Improving Leadership Effectiveness: The Leader Match Concepts*, rev. ed., Wiley, New York, 1976, pp. 134–137.

33. Based on "Hyundai's Chung Ju-Yung: From Rags to Richest Man in Town," *Business Week*, Dec. 23, 1985, p. 48; Laxmi Nakarmi, "Daewoo vs. Hyundai: Battle of the Korean Giants," *Business Week*, Dec. 15, 1986, pp. 72–73; Michael Kublin, "Hyundai's Success and Mark Twain's Obituary," *Industrial Management*, November–December 1987, pp. 12–18; Philip Glouchevitch, "Chung Ju-Yung and Family," *Forbes*, July 24, 1989, p. 206; Laxmi Nakarmi, "A *Chaebol* Plays Hardball with Roh Tae Woo," *Business Week*, Feb. 24, 1992, p. 50, and "Korea: Hyundai's Chung May Play Kingmaker," *Business Week*, Aug. 3, 1991, p. 39; "Hyundai Chief Steps Aside," *Automotive News*, Jan. 1, 1996, p. 6; and Ed Paisley, "Can the *Chaebol* Change?" *Institutional Investor*, March 1996, p. 60.

34. Laxmi Nakarmi, "Daewoo vs. Hyundai: Battle of the Korean Giants," *Business Week*, Dec. 15, 1986, pp. 72–73; Andrew Tanzer, "Samsung: South Korea Marches to Its Own Drummer," *Forbes*, May 16, 1988, pp. 84–89; Laxmi Nakarmi, "At Daewoo, a 'Revolution' at the Top," *Business Week*, Feb. 18, 1991, pp. 68–69; Ed Paisley, "Can the *Chaebol* Change?" *Institutional Investor*, March 1996, p. 60.

35. M. Strube and J. Garcia, "A Meta-Analysis Investigation of Fiedler's Contingency Model of Leadership Effectiveness," *Psychological Bulletin*, vol. 90, 1981, pp. 307–321; Lawrence H. Peters, Darrell D. Hartke, and John T. Pohlmann, "Fiedler's Contingency Theory of Leadership: An Application of the Meta-Analysis Procedures of Schmidt and Hunter," *Psychological Bulletin*, vol. 97, 1985, pp. 274–285.

36. This discussion is based on the revised model by Victor H. Vroom and Arthur G. Jago, *The New Leadership: Managing Participation in Organizations*, Prentice-Hall, Englewood Cliffs, N.J., 1988.

37. Jack Stack, "Crisis Management by Committee," *INC.*, May 1988, p. 26, and "The Great Game of Business," *INC.*, June 1992, pp. 53–62.

38. The discussion of situational leadership theory is based on Paul Hersey and Kenneth H. Blanchard, *Management of Organizational Behavior: Utilizing Human Resources*, 5th ed., Prentice-Hall, Englewood Cliffs, N.J., 1988. Some of the variable names and/or definitions have changed somewhat from previous delineations.

39. Robert P. Vecchio, "Situational Leadership Theory: An Examination of a Prescriptive Theory," *Journal of Applied Psychology*, vol. 72, 1987, pp. 444–451. For other criticisms of the theory, see Claude L. Graeff, "The Situational Leadership Theory: A Critical View," *Academy of Management Review*, vol. 8, 1983, pp. 285–291; and Warren Blank, John R. Weitzel, and Stephen G. Green, "A Test of the Situational Leadership Theory," *Personnel Psychology*, vol. 43, 1990, pp. 579–597.

40. Andrew S. Grove, *High Output Management*, Random House, New York, 1983, pp. 172–177.

41. Although other individuals had a hand in its early development, path-goal theory is associated mainly with leadership researcher Robert J. House and his colleagues. The basic foundations of the theory are contained in Robert J. House and Terence R. Mitchell, "Path-Goal Theory of Leadership," *Journal of Contemporary Business*, vol. 3, 1974, pp. 81–97.

42. Andrea Gabor, "The Making of a New-Age Manager," *Working Woman*, December 1994, pp. 18–22.

43. Gary Yukl, *Leadership in Organizations*, 3d ed., Prentice-Hall, Englewood Cliffs, N.J., 1994.

44. Abraham Zaleznik, "The Leadership Gap," *Academy of Management Executive*, vol. 4, 1990, pp. 7–22.

45. Charles R. Holloman, "Leadership and Head: There Is a Difference," *Personnel Administration*, July–August 1968, pp. 38–44; Abraham Zaleznik, "Managers and Leaders: Are They Different?" *Harvard Business Review*, May–June 1977, pp. 47–60.

46. This distinction was first made by James McGregor Burns, *Leadership*, Harper & Row, New York, 1978. See also Bernard M. Bass, *Leadership and Performance beyond Expectations*, Free Press, New York, 1985; and John J. Hater and Bernard M. Bass, "Superiors' Evaluations and Subordinates' Perceptions of Transformational and Transactional Leadership," *Journal of Applied Psychology*, vol. 73, 1988, pp. 695–702.

47. Robert J. House and Jetendra V. Singh, "Organizational Behavior: Some New Directions for I/O Psychology," *Annual Review of Psychology*, vol. 38, 1987, pp. 669–718.

48. Jay A. Conger and Rabindra N. Kanungo, "Toward a Behavioral Theory of Charismatic Leadership in Organizational Settings," *Academy of Management Review*, vol. 12, 1987, pp. 637–647.

49. Jane M. Howell and Peter J. Frost, "A Laboratory Study of Charismatic Leadership," *Organizational Behavior and Human Decision Processes*, vol. 43, 1989, pp. 243–269; Noel M. Tichy and David O. Ulrich, "The Leadership Challenge—A Call for the Transformational Leader," *Sloan Management Review*, Fall 1984, pp. 59–68.

50. Molly Baker, "USF&G Chief Executive Transforms an Ailing Insurer," *The Wall Street Journal*, Mar. 24, 1995, p. 4B; Bill Atkinson, "USF&G Turning 100," *The Sun (Baltimore)*, Mar. 24, 1996, p. 1E.

51. Gary Yukl, "Managerial Leadership: A Review of Theory and Research," *Journal of Management*, vol. 15, 1989, pp. 251–289.

52. This section is based on Steven Kerr and John M. Jermier, "Substitutes for Leadership: Their Meaning and Measurement," *Organizational Behavior and Human Performance*, vol. 22, 1978, pp. 375–403. See also Philip M. Podsakoff, Brian P. Niehoff, Scott B. MacKenzie, and Margaret L. Williams, "Do Substitutes for Leadership Really Substitute for Leadership? An Empirical Examination of Kerr and Jermier's Situational Leadership Model," *Organizational Behavior and Human Decision Processes*, vol. 54, 1993, pp. 1–44.

53. Kathleen Brady, "The Power of Positive Stress," *Working Woman*, July 1987, pp. 74–77.

54. See B. R. Baliga and James G. Hunt, "An Organizational Life Cycle Approach to Leadership," in James Gerald Hunt, B. Rajaram Baliga, H. Peter Dachler, and Chester A. Schriesheim (eds.), *Emerging Leadership Vistas*, Heath, Boston, 1987, pp. 129–149.

55. From *Fortune*, Jan. 15, 1996, p. 74, developed with assistance of Dr. Jay Conger, Uni-

versity of Southern California Business School.
56. Reprinted from Victor H. Vroom and Arthur G. Jago, *The New Leadership: Managing Participation in Organizations,* Prentice-Hall, Englewood Cliffs, N.J., 1988, pp. 163, 166–167.
57. Aaron Bernstein and Zachary Schiller, "Jack Welch: How Good a Manager?" *Business Week,* Dec. 14, 1987, pp. 92–103; Mark Potts, "GE's Management Mission," *The Washington Post,* May 22, 1988, pp. H1, H4; Janet Guyon, "GE Chairman Welch, Though Much Praised, Starts to Draw Critics," *The Wall Street Journal,* Aug. 4, 1988, pp. 1, 8; Stratford P. Sherman, "The Mind of Jack Welch," *Fortune,* Mar. 27, 1989, pp. 39–50; Thomas A. Stewart, "GE Keeps Those Ideas Coming," *Fortune,* Aug. 12, 1991, pp. 41–49; James C. Hyatt, "GE Is No Place for Autocrats, Welch Decrees," *The Wall Street Journal,* Mar. 3, 1992, pp. B1–B10; Mark Potts, "A New Vision for Leadership from GE's Visionary," *The Washington Post,* Mar. 8, 1992, p. H2; Frank Swoboda, "Up Against the Walls," *The Washington Post,* Feb. 27, 1994, pp. H1, H6–H7; Polly LaBarre, "The Light's Still On at This 'Family Grocery,'" *Industry Week,* Nov. 20, 1995, p. 17; "A Conversation with Roberto Goizueta and Jack Welch," *Fortune,* Dec. 11, 1995, pp. 96–102; Tim Smart, "GE's Welch: 'Fighting Like Hell to Be No. 1,'" *Business Week,* July 8, 1996, p. 48.
58. Bo Burlingham, "This Woman Has Changed Business Forever," *INC.,* June 1990, p. 46.
59. Jeffrey Ferry, "Looking Good," *Continental Profiles,* September 1988, pp. 29, 52–58; Bo Burlingham, "This Woman Has Changed Business Forever," *INC.,* June 1990, pp. 34–48; Laura Zinn, "Whales, Human Rights, Rain Forests—And the Heady Smell of Profits," *Business Week,* July 15, 1991, pp. 114–115; Jean Sherman Chatzky, "Changing the World," *Forbes,* Mar. 2, 1992, pp. 83–84; Jennifer Conlin, "Survival of the Fittest," *Working Woman,* February 1994, pp. 29–31, 68–73; Tara Parker-Pope, "Body Shop Shares Jump on Reports It Will Go Private," *The Wall Street Journal,* Nov. 1, 1995, p. B11; "I Didn't Get Where I Am Today Without . . ." *Daily Mail,* Apr. 25, 1996, p. 62.

CHAPTER 14

1. Kenneth Labich, "Is Herb Kelleher America's Best CEO?" *Fortune,* May 2, 1994, pp. 44–49; John Lippert, "Wings of Desire," *Business Monday/Detroit Free Press,* Aug. 15, 1994, pp. 8F–9F; "Southwest Airlines' Herb Kelleher: Unorthodoxy at Work," *Management Review,* January 1995, pp. 9–12; Karen West, "Unique CEO Makes Airline Fly," *Seattle Post-Intelligence*®, June 1, 1995, p. 5; Cheryl Hall, "Still Crazy after 25 Years," *The Dallas Morning News,* June 9, 1996, p. 1H.
2. Gerald M. Goldhaber, *Organizational Communication,* 4th ed., Brown, Dubuque, Iowa, 1986, pp. 4–33.
3. O. W. Baskin and Craig E. Aronoff, *Interpersonal Communication in Organizations,* Scott, Foresman, Santa Monica, Calif., 1980, p. 4.
4. Roger Smith, "The U.S. Must Do as GM Has Done," *Fortune,* Feb. 13, 1989, pp. 70–73.
5. J. Thomas and P. Sireno, "Assessing Management Competency Needs," *Training and Development Journal,* vol. 34, 1980, pp. 47–51; H. W. Hildebrant, F. A. Bon, E. L. Miller, and A. W. Swinyard, "An Executive Appraisal of Courses Which Best Prepare One for General Management," *The Journal of Business Communication,* Winter 1982, pp. 5–15.
6. Robert R. Max, "Wording It Correctly," *Training and Development Journal,* March 1985, pp. 50–51; Joy Van Skiver, quoted in Neil

Chesanow, "Quick, Take This Memo," *The Washington Post,* Sept. 7, 1987, p. C5.
7. Walter Kiechel III, "The Big Presentation," *Fortune,* July 26, 1982, pp. 98–100.
8. Phillip V. Lewis, *Organizational Communication: The Essence of Effective Management,* 2d ed., Prentice-Hall, Englewood Cliffs, N.J., 1980, p. 11.
9. Ibid.
10. R. Birdwhistell, *Kenesics and Context,* University of Pennsylvania, Philadelphia, 1970; A. Mehrabian, *Silent Messages,* Wadsworth, Belmont, Calif., 1972.
11. Otis W. Baskin and Craig E. Aronoff, *Interpersonal Communication in Organizations,* Scott, Foresman, Santa Monica, Calif., 1980.
12. M. A. Hayes, "Nonverbal Communication: Expression without Word," in R. C. Huseman, C. M. Logue, and D. L. Freshley (eds.), *Readings in Interpersonal and Organizational Communication,* Holbrook, Boston, 1973; Otis W. Baskin and Craig E. Aronoff, *Interpersonal Communication in Organizations,* Goodyear, Santa Monica, Calif., 1980.
13. Henry Mintzberg, *The Nature of Managerial Work,* Prentice-Hall, Englewood Cliffs, N.J., 1973; Lance B. Kurke and Howard E. Alrich, "Mintzberg Was Right! A Replication and Extension of the Nature of Managerial Work," *Management Science,* vol. 29, 1983, pp. 975–984.
14. Larry L. Smeltzer and Gail L. Fann, "Comparison of Managerial Communication Patterns in Small, Entrepreneurial Organizations and Large, Mature Organizations," *Group and Organization Studies,* vol. 14, 1989, pp. 198–215. Also see Henry Mintzberg, *The Nature of Managerial Work,* Prentice-Hall, Englewood Cliffs, N.J., 1975.
15. Phillip V. Lewis, *Organizational Communication: The Essence of Effective Management,* 2d ed., Prentice-Hall, Englewood Cliffs, N.J., 1980; Larry R. Smeltzer and Gail L. Fann, "Comparison of Managerial Communication Patterns in Small, Entrepreneurial Organizations and Large, Mature Organizations," *Group and Organization Studies,* vol. 14, 1989, pp. 198–215.
16. Jan Carlzon, *Moments of Truth,* Ballinger, Cambridge, Mass., 1987; Amanda Bennett, "SAS's 'Nice Guy' Aiming to Finish First," *The Wall Street Journal,* Mar. 2, 1989, p. B12; Jonathan Kapstein, "Can SAS Keep Flying with the Big Birds?" *Business Week,* Nov. 27, 1989, pp. 142–146.
17. For a discussion of different theoretical perspectives on communication, see Kathleen J. Krone, Fredric M. Jablin, and Linda L. Putnam, "Communication Theory and Organizational Communication: Multiple Perspectives," in Fredric M. Jablin, Linda L. Putnam, Karlene H. Roberts, and Lyman W. Porter (eds.), *Handbook of Organizational Communication: An Interdisciplinary Perspective,* Sage, Newbury Park, Calif., 1987, pp. 18–40.
18. Don Oldenburg, "What Do You Say?" *The Washington Post,* Aug. 23, 1989, p. C5.
19. Charles A. O'Reilly III and Karlene H. Roberts, "Information Filtration in Organizations: Three Experiments," *Organizational Behavior and Human Performance,* vol. 11, 1974, pp. 253–265; Robert E. Kaplan, Wilfred H. Drath, and Joan R. Kofodimos, "Power and Getting Criticism," *Center for Creative Leadership Issues and Observations,* August 1984, pp. 1–6.
20. Based on Clare Ansberry, "Oil Spill in the Midwest Provides Case Study in Crisis Management," *The Wall Street Journal,* Jan. 8, 1988, p. 21.

21. Fred Luthans, *Organizational Behavior,* 7th ed., McGraw-Hill, New York, 1995.
22. Judith R. Gordon, *Organizational Behavior: A Diagnostic Approach,* 5th ed., Prentice-Hall, Allyn and Bacon, Boston, 1996; Fred Luthans, *Organizational Behavior,* 7th ed., McGraw-Hill, New York, 1995.
23. William Mathewson, "Shop Talk," *The Wall Street Journal,* Sept. 30, 1988, p. 29.
24. Fred Luthans, *Organizational Behavior,* 7th ed., McGraw-Hill, New York, 1995.
25. This section is based largely on Fred Luthans, *Organizational Behavior,* 7th ed., McGraw-Hill, New York, 1995; H. H. Kelley, "Attribution Theory in Social Psychology," *Nebraska Symposium on Motivation,* vol. 15, 1967, pp. 192–238.
26. Henry L. Tosi, John R. Rizzo, and Stephen J. Carroll, *Managing Organizational Behavior,* Pitman, Marshfield, Mass., 1986; Gary Johns, *Organizational Behavior,* 2d ed., Scott, Foresman, Glenview, Ill., 1987.
27. C. S. Carver, E. DeGregoria, and R. Gillis, "Field-Study Evidence of an Attribution among Two Categories of Observers," *Personality and Social Psychology Bulletin,* vol. 6, 1980, pp. 44–50; D. G. Myers, *Social Psychology,* McGraw-Hill, New York, 1983.
28. Phillip V. Lewis, *Organizational Communication: The Essence of Effective Management,* 2d ed., Prentice-Hall, Englewood Cliffs, N.J., 1980, p. 54.
29. Mary Munter, *Business Communication: Strategy and Skill,* Prentice-Hall, Englewood Cliffs, N.J., 1987, p. 15.
30. Stephen R. Axley, "Managerial and Organizational Communication in Terms of the Conduit Metaphor," *Academy of Management Review,* vol. 9, 1984, pp. 428–437.
31. Ernest G. Bormann, "Symbolic Convergence: Organizational Communication and Culture," in Linda Putnam and Michael E. Pacanowsky (eds.), *Communication and Organizations: An Interpretive Approach,* Sage, Beverly Hills, Calif., 1983, p. 99–122.
32. Based on Michael W. Miller, "At Many Firms, Employees Speak a Language That's All Their Own," *The Wall Street Journal,* Dec. 29, 1987, p. 17.
33. This section is based on Edward T. Hall, *The Silent Language,* Doubleday, New York, 1959; Edward T. Hall, *Beyond Culture,* Anchor Press/Double Day, Garden City, N.Y., 1976; Jim Kennedy and Anna Everest, "Put Diversity in Context," *Personnel Journal,* September 1991, pp. 50–54.
34. Marilyn H. Lewis and N. L. Reinsch, Jr., "Listening in Organizational Environments," *Journal of Business Communication,* Summer 1988, pp. 49–67.
35. Judith Gordon, "Learn How to Listen," *Fortune,* Aug. 17, 1987, pp. 107–108.
36. Robert Lenzner, "The Reluctant Entrepreneur," *Forbes,* Sept. 11, 1995, pp. 162–167.
37. Robert E. Kaplan, Wilfred H. Drath, and Joan R. Kofodimos, "Power and Getting Criticism," *Center for Creative Leadership Issues and Observations,* August 1984, pp. 1–8.
38. Ibid.
39. "Essentials of Feedback," *A Seven-Day Leadership Development Course,* Center for Creative Leadership, Greensboro, N.C., 1976, pp. 77–78, as cited in Phillip V. Lewis, *Organizational Communication: The Essence of Effective Management,* 2d ed., Prentice-Hall, Englewood Cliffs, N.J., 1980, pp. 157–158.
40. Reprinted from Judith R. Gordon, *A Diagnostic Approach to Organizational Behavior,* 2d ed., Allyn and Bacon, Boston, 1987, p. 230.

41. Patricia Sellers, "How to Handle Customers' Gripes," *Fortune,* Oct. 24, 1988, pp. 88–100; Carl Quintanilla and Richard Gibson, "'Do Call Us': More Companies Install 1-800 Phone Lines," *The Wall Street Journal,* Apr. 20, 1994, p. B1.

42. Marvin E. Shaw, *Group Dynamics: The Psychology of Small Group Behavior,* McGraw-Hill, New York, 1981, pp. 150–157.

43. Lyman W. Porter and Karlene Roberts, "Communication in Organizations," in Marvin D. Dunnette (ed.), *Handbook of Industrial and Organization Psychology,* Rand McNally, Chicago, 1976, pp. 1553–1589.

44. David Katz and Robert Kahn, *The Social Psychology of Organizations,* Wiley, New York, 1966.

45. Jules Harcourt, Virginia Richerson, and Mark Wattier, "A National Study of Middle Managers' Assessment of Organizational Communication Quality," *Journal of Business Communication,* vol. 28, 1991, pp. 348–365.

46. Otis W. Baskin and Craig E. Aronoff, *Interpersonal Communication in Organizations,* Scott, Foresman, Santa Monica, Calif., 1980, pp. 92–93; Phillip V. Lewis, *Organizational Communication: The Essence of Effective Management,* 2d ed., Prentice-Hall, Englewood Cliffs, N.J., 1980, pp. 62–63.

47. Clare Ansberry, "Utah's Geneva Steel, Once Called Hopeless, Is Racking Up Profits," *The Wall Street Journal,* Nov. 20, 1991, p. A1.

48. Earl Planty and William Machaver, "Upward Communications: A Project in Executive Development," *Personnel,* vol. 28, 1952, pp. 304–318; J. R. Cranwell, "How to Have a Well-Informed Boss," *Supervisory Management,* May 1969, pp. 5–6; Gerald M. Goldhaber, *Organizational Communication,* 4th ed., Brown, Dubuque, Iowa, 1986, pp. 170–173.

49. Charles A. O'Reilly III and Karlene H. Roberts, "Information Filtration in Organizations: Three Experiments," *Organizational Behavior and Human Performance,* vol. 11, 1974, pp. 253–265.

50. Nelson W. Aldrich, Jr., "Lines of Communication," *INC.,* June 1986, pp. 140–144.

51. Bill Atkinson, "USF&G Turning 100, a Gleam in Its Eye," *The Sun (Baltimore),* Mar. 24, 1996, p. 1E.

52. Lyman W. Porter and Karlene Roberts, "Communication in Organizations," in Marvin D. Dunnette (ed.), *Handbook of Industrial and Organization Psychology,* Rand McNally, Chicago, 1976, pp. 1553–1589.

53. R. Wayne Pace, *Organizational Communication: Foundations for Human Resource Development,* Prentice-Hall, Englewood Cliffs, N.J., 1983, pp. 53–54.

54. T. J. Peters and R. H. Waterman, *In Search of Excellence: Lessons from America's Best-Run Companies,* Harper & Row, New York, 1982; Peter R. Monge, Lynda White Rothman, Eric M. Eisenberg, Katherine I. Miller, and Kenneth K. Kirste, "The Dynamics of Organizational Proximity," *Managment Science,* vol. 31, 1985, pp. 1129–1141.

55. Joseph B. White, "How Detroit Diesel, Out from under GM, Turned Around Fast," *The Wall Street Journal,* Aug. 16, 1991, p. A1.

56. Gerald M. Goldhaber, *Organizational Communication,* 4th ed., Brown, Dubuque, Iowa, 1986, pp. 174–175.

57. R. Wayne Pace, *Organizational Communication: Foundations for Human Resource Development,* Prentice-Hall, Englewood Cliffs, N.J., 1983, pp. 56–57.

58. Keith Davis, *Human Behavior at Work,* McGraw-Hill, New York, 1972.

59. Keith Davis, "Management Communication and the Grapevine," in Stewart Ferguson and Sherry Devereaux Ferguson (eds.), *Intercom: Readings in Organizational Communication,* Hayden, Rochelle Park, N.J., 1980, pp. 55–66.

60. S. Friedman, "Where Employees Go for Information: Some Surprises," *Administrative Management,* vol. 42, 1981, pp. 72–73; Gerald M. Goldhaber, *Organizational Communication,* 4th ed., Brown, Dubuque, Iowa, 1986, pp. 176–177; Alan Zaremba, "Working with the Organizational Grapevine," *Personnel Journal,* July 1988, pp. 38–42.

61. R. Wayne Pace, *Organizational Communication: Foundations for Human Resource Development,* Prentice-Hall, Englewood Cliffs, N.J., 1983, pp. 57–58.

62. "Out of Sight, Not Out of Mind," *The Wall Street Journal,* June 20, 1989, p. B1.

63. J. G. March and G. Sevon, "Gossip, Information, and Decision Making," in L. S. Sproull and P. D. Larkey (eds.), *Advances in Information Processing in Organizations,* vol. 1, JAI, Greenwich, Conn., 1984, pp. 95–107; Karl E. Weick and Larry D. Browning, "Argument and Narration in Organizational Communication," *Journal of Management,* vol. 12, 1986, pp. 243–259; Jitendra Mishra, "Managing the Grapevine," *Public Personnel Management,* Summer 1990, pp. 213–228.

64. Albert B. Crawford, "Corporate Electronic Mail—A Communication-Intensive Application of Information Technology," *MIS Quarterly,* vol. 6, 1982, pp. 1–14.

65. Edward H. Nyce and Richard Groppa, "Electronic Mail at MHT," *Management Technology,* May 1983, pp. 65–72.

66. R. E. Rice and D. Case, "Electronic Message Systems in the University: A Description of Use and Utility," *Journal of Communication,* vol. 33, 1983, pp. 131–152; Lee Sproull and Sara Kiesler, "Reducing Social Context Cues: Electronic Mail in Organizational Communication," *Management Science,* vol. 32, 1986, 1492–1512.

67. Richard C. Huseman and Edward W. Miles, "Organizational Communication in the Information Age: Implications of Computer-Based Systems," *Journal of Management,* vol. 14, 1988, pp. 181–204.

68. G. Pascal Zachary, "It's a Mail Thing: Electronic Messaging Gets a Rating—Ex," *The Wall Street Journal,* June 22, 1994, p. A1.

69. Kenneth C. Laudon and Jane Price Laudon, *Management Information Systems,* Macmillan, New York, 1994.

70. David Kirkpatrick, "Here Comes the Payoff from PCs," *Fortune,* Mar. 23, 1992, pp. 93–102; Jim Bartino, "At These Shouting Matches, No One Says a Word," *Business Week,* June 11, 1992, p. 78.

71. Susan Hellweg, Kevin Freiberg, and Anthony Smith, "The Pervasiveness and Impact of Electronic Communication Technologies in Organizations: A Survey of Major American Corporations," paper presented at a meeting of the Speech Communication Association, Chicago, 1984.

72. Nelson W. Aldrich, Jr., "Lines of Communication," *INC.,* June 1986, p. 140.

73. Fleming Meeks, "Live from Dallas," *Forbes,* Dec. 26, 1988, pp. 112–113.

74. Adapted from Ethel C. Glenn and Elliot A. Pood, "Listening Self-Inventory," *Supervisory Management,* January 1989, pp. 12–15.

75. The story and statements are a portion of the Uncritical Inference Test, copyrighted 1955, 1964, 1979 by William V. Haney. The full-length test is available for educational purposes from the International Society for General Semantics, P.O. Box 2469, San Francisco, California 94126.

76. The Haney Test of Uncritical Inferences is reprinted with permission from William V. Haney (ed.), *Communication and Interpersonal Relations,* 5th ed., Irwin, Homewood, Ill., 1986, pp. 214–222.

77. Steve Coll and David A. Vise, "Chairman's Cost-Cutting Humor," *The Washington Post,* Oct. 18, 1987, pp. H1, H20; Alan C. Greenberg, *Memos from the Chairman,* Workman Publishing, New York, 1996.

78. Noel Tichy and Ram Charan, "Citicorp Faces the World: An Interview with John Reed," *Harvard Business Review,* November–December 1990, pp. 1135–1144; Pete Engardio, "For Citibank, There's No Place Like Asia," *Business Week,* Mar. 30, 1992, pp. 66–69; Saul Hansell, "Citicorp Announces High-Level Personnel Shifts," *The New York Times,* July 1, 1995, p. 35; Pei-yuan Chia, "Citibanking the World," *The Magazine of Bank Management,* July 1995, p. 30; Carol J. Loomis and Tim Carvell, "Citicorp: John Reed's Second Act" *Fortune,* Apr. 29, 1996, p. 88.

CHAPTER 15

1. Barnaby J. Feder, "At Monsanto, Teamwork Works," *The New York Times,* June 25, 1991, p. D1; Raymond C. Cole and H. Lee Hales, "How Monsanto Justified Automation," *Management Accounting,* January 1992, p. 39; Paul M. Villane, "A Behavior-Based Safety Process Gets Results," *Chemical Engineering,* August 1995, p. 119; "Managing for Change," *St. Louis Commerce,* January 1996, Sec. 1, p. 8.

2. Based on Marvin E. Shaw, *Group Dynamics: The Psychology of Small Group Behavior,* 3d ed., McGraw-Hill, New York, 1981; and Clayton P. Alderfer, "An Intergroup Perspective on Group Dynamics," in Jay W. Lorsch (ed.), *Handbook of Organizational Behavior,* Prentice-Hall, Englewood Cliffs, N.J., 1987.

3. Myron Magnet, "The Resurrection of the Rust Belt," *Fortune,* Aug. 15, 1988, pp. 40–48; Becky Yerak, "Castite Owner Lets Dream Have Its Way," *The Plain Dealer,* June 1, 1994, p. 1C.

4. Bill Saporito, "Heinz Pushes to Be the Low Cost Producer," *Fortune,* June 24, 1985, pp. 44–54.

5. Ernest Stech and Sharon A. Ratliffe, *Effective Group Communication: How to Get Action by Working in Groups,* National Textbook, Lincolnwood, Ill., 1985.

6. George Homans, *The Human Group,* Harcourt, Brace, New York, 1950.

7. P. Ranganath Nayak and John M. Ketteringham, *Break-Throughs,* Rawson Associates, New York, 1986.

8. Ibid.; see also Robert A. Sigafoos, *Absolutely Positively Overnight!* St. Luke's Press, Memphis, Tenn., 1988.

9. J. Richard Hackman, "The Design of Work Teams," in Jay W. Lorsch (ed.), *Handbook of Organizational Behavior,* Prentice-Hall, Englewood Cliffs, N.J., 1987, pp. 315–342.

10. Susan E. Jackson, K. E. May, and K. Whitney, "Understanding the Dynamics of Diversity in Decision-Making Teams," in Richard A. Guzzo and E. Salas (eds.), *Team Effectiveness and Decision Making in Organizations,* Jossey-Bass, San Francisco, 1995.

11. Paul S. Goodman, Elizabeth C. Ravlin, and Linda Argote, "Current Thinking about Groups: Setting the Stage for New Ideas," in Paul S. Goodman and associates (eds.), *Designing Effective Work Groups,* Jossey-Bass, San Francisco, 1986, pp. 1–33; Taylor H. Cox and Stacy Blacke, "Managing Cultural Diversity: Implications for Organizational Competitiveness," *The Academy of Management Executive,* August 1991, pp. 45–56.

12. Warren E. Watson, Kamalesh Kumar, and Larry K. Michaelsen, "Cultural Diversity's Impact on Interaction Process and Performance: Comparing Homogeneous and Diverse Task Groups," *Academy of Management Journal,* vol. 36, 1993, pp. 590–602.

13. Genevieve Capowski, "Managing Diversity," *Management Review,* June 1996, pp. 13–19.

14. Marvin E. Shaw, *Group Dynamics: The Psychology of Small Group Behavior,* 3d ed., McGraw-Hill, New York, 1981.

15. Pete Engardio, "The Peace Corps' New Frontier," *Business Week,* Aug. 22, 1988, pp. 62–63.

16. This section is based largely on Kenneth Benne and P. H. Sheats, "Functional Roles of Group Members," *Journal of Social Issues,* vol. 4, 1948, pp. 41–49; and Seth Allcorn, "What Makes Groups Tick," *Personnel,* September 1985, pp. 52–58.

17. Bernard M. Bass, *Stogdill's Handbook of Leadership,* Free Press, New York, 1981.

18. William B. Eddy, *The Manager and the Working Group,* Praeger, New York, 1985.

19. This section is based on Fremont A. Shull, Jr., Andre L. Delbecq, and L. L. Cummings, *Organizational Decision Making,* McGraw-Hill, New York, 1970; and Marvin E. Shaw, *Group Dynamics: The Psychology of Small Group Behavior,* 3d ed., McGraw-Hill, New York, 1981.

20. William J. Altier, "SMR Forum: Task Forces—An Effective Management Tool," *Sloan Management Review,* Spring 1986, pp. 69–76.

21. Zachary Schiller, "The Marketing Revolution at Procter & Gamble," *Business Week,* July 25, 1988, pp. 72–76.

22. L. L. Cummings, George P. Huber, and Eugene Arendt, "Effects of Size and Spatial Arrangements on Group Decision Making," *Academy of Management Journal,* vol. 17, 1974, pp. 460–475; Paul S. Goodman, Elizabeth C. Ravlin, and Linda Argote, "Current Thinking about Groups: Setting the Stage for New Ideas," in Paul S. Goodman and associates (eds.), *Designing Effective Work Groups,* Jossey-Bass, San Francisco, 1986, pp. 1–33.

23. Richard Z. Gooding and John A. Wagner III, "A Meta-Analytic Review of the Relationship between Size and Performance: The Productivity and Efficiency of Organizations and Their Subunits," *Administrative Science Quarterly,* vol. 30, 1985, pp. 462–481; Steven J. Karau and Kipling D. Williams, "Social Loafing: Research Findings, Implications, and Future Directions," *Current Directions in Psychological Science,* vol. 4, October 1995, pp. 134–140.

24. Roland E. Kidwell, Jr., and Nathan Bennett, "Employee Propensity to Withhold Effort: A Conceptual Model to Intersect Three Avenues of Research," *Academy of Management Review,* vol. 18, 1993, pp. 429–456.

25. Robert Alabanese and David D. Van Fleet, "Rational Behavior in Groups: The Free-Riding Tendency," *Academy of Management Review,* vol. 10, 1985, pp. 244–255.

26. John A. Wagner III, "Studies of Individualism-Collectivism Effects on Cooperation in Groups," *Academy of Management Journal,* vol. 28, 1995, pp. 152–172.

27. Steven J. Karau and Kipling D. Williams, "Social Loafing: Research Findings, Implications, and Future Directions," *Current Directions in Psychological Science,* vol. 4, October 1995, pp. 134–140.

28. Ibid.; Jeffrey M. Jackson and Stephen G. Harkins, "Equity in Effort: An Explanation of the Social Loafing Effect," *Journal of Personality and Social Psychology,* vol. 49, 1985, pp. 1199–1206; Stephen J. Zaccaro, "Social Loafing: The Role of Task Attractiveness," *Personality and Social Psychology Bulletin,* vol. 10, 1984, pp. 99–106.

29. Based on Ricardo Semler, "Managing without Managers," *Harvard Business Review,* September–October 1989, pp. 76–84; Ricardo Semler, "Who Needs Bosses?" *Across the Board,* February 1994, p. 23.

30. James A. Shepperd, "Productivity Loss in Performance Groups: A Motivational Analysis," *Psychological Bulletin,* vol. 113, 1993, pp. 67–81.

31. The discussion of synergy is based on J. Richard Hackman, "The Design of Work Teams," in Jay W. Lorsch (ed.), *Handbook of Organizational Behavior,* Prentice-Hall, Englewood Cliffs, N.J., 1987.

32. Bill Saparito, "Luv That Market," *Fortune,* Aug. 3, 1987, p. 56.

33. Paul S. Goodman, Elizabeth Ravlin, and Marshall Schminke, "Understanding Groups in Organizations," *Research in Organizational Behavior,* vol. 9, 1987, pp. 121–173.

34. Ibid.

35. Daniel C. Feldman, "The Development and Enforcement of Group Norms," *Academy of Management Review,* vol. 9, 1984, pp. 47–53.

36. The information regarding American Steel & Wire in this section is from Myron Magnet, "The Resurrection of the Rust Belt," *Fortune,* Aug. 15, 1988, pp. 40–48; "Birmingham Steel Will Build New Bar and Rod Mill in Ohio," *New Steel,* November 1994, p. 12.

37. Kenneth Bettenhausen and J. Keith Murnighan, "The Emergence of Norms in Competitive Decision-Making Groups," *Administrative Science Quarterly,* vol. 30, 1985, pp. 350–372.

38. David Prinzinsky, "New Bar Mill Guaranteed Fast Start," *Crain's Cleveland Business,* Feb. 5, 1996, p. 3.

39. This section relies heavily on Fred Luthans, *Organizational Behavior,* 7th ed., McGraw-Hill, New York, 1995; Hugh J. Arnold and Daniel C. Feldman, *Organizational Behavior,* McGraw-Hill, New York, 1986.

40. Gregory H. Dobbins and Stephen J. Zaccaro, "The Effects of Group Cohesion and Leader Behavior on Subordinate Satisfaction," *Group and Organizational Studies,* vol. 11, 1986, pp. 203–219.

41. Myron Magnet, "The Resurrection of the Rust Belt," *Fortune,* Aug. 15, 1988, pp. 40–48.

42. Dennis W. Organ and Katherine Ryan, "A Meta-Analytic Review of Attitudinal and Dispositional Predictors of Organizational Citizenship Behavior," *Personnel Psychology,* vol. 48, 1995, pp. 775–802.

43. Stanley Seashore, *Group Cohesiveness in the Industrial Work Group,* Institute for Social Research, Ann Arbor, Mich., 1954; Ralph M. Stogdill, "Group Productivity, Drive, and Cohesiveness," *Organizational Behavior and Human Performance,* vol. 8, 1972, pp. 26–43.

44. Brian Mullen and Carolyn Copper, "The Relation between Group Cohesiveness and Performance: An Integration," *Psychological Bulletin,* vol. 115, 1994, pp. 210–227.

45. Rosemary Neale and Richard Mindel, "Rigging Up Multicultural Teamworking," *Personnel Management,* January 1992, pp. 36–39.

46. Paul B. Brown, "The Anti-Marketers," *INC.,* March 1988, pp. 62–72; Fleming Meeks, "The Man Is the Message," *Forbes,* Apr. 17, 1989, pp. 148–152; Polly Labarre, "Patagonia Comes of Age," *Industry Week,* Apr. 3, 1995, p. 42.

47. Bruce W. Tuckman, "Developmental Sequence in Small Groups," *Psychological Bulletin,* vol. 63, 1965, pp. 384–399; Bruce W. Tuckman and Mary Ann C. Jensen, "Stages of Small-Group Development Revisited," *Group and Organization Studies,* vol. 2, 1977, pp. 419–427.

48. John A. Seeger, "No Innate Phases in Group Problem Solving," *Academy of Management Review,* vol. 8, 1983, pp. 683–689.

49. Study by Wharton Center for Applied Research, cited in Carol Hymowitz, "A Survival Guide to the Office Meeting," *The Wall Street Journal,* June 21, 1988, p. 41.

50. Helen B. Schwartzman, "The Meeting as a Neglected Social Form in Organizational Studies," *Research in Organizational Behavior,* vol. 8, 1986, pp. 233–258.

51. William J. Altier, "SMR Forum: Task Forces—An Effective Management Tool," *Sloan Management Review,* Spring 1986, pp. 69–75; Richard A. Guzzo and Marcus W. Dickson, "Teams in Organizations: Recent Research on Performance and Effectiveness," *Annual Review of Psychology,* vol. 47, 1996, 307–338.

52. Ernest Stech and Sharon A. Ratliffe, *Effective Group Communication: How to Get Action by Working in Groups,* National Textbook, Lincolnwood, Ill., 1985; Walter Kiechel III, "The Art of the Corporate Task Force," *Fortune,* Jan. 29, 1991, pp. 104–105.

53. Robert B. Reich, "Entrepreneurship Reconsidered: The Team as Hero," *Harvard Business Review,* May–June 1987, pp. 77–83.

54. J. Gordon, "Work Teams—How Far Have They Come?" *Training,* vol. 29, 1992, pp. 59–65.

55. Based on Anthony Jay, "How to Run a Meeting," *Harvard Business Review,* March–April 1976, pp. 120–134; George Huber, *Managerial Decision Making,* Scott, Foresman, Glenview, Ill., 1980; David A. Whetten and Kim S. Cameron, *Developing Management Skills,* Scott, Foresman, Glenview, Ill., 1984; Julie Bailey, "The Fine Art of Leading a Meeting," *Working Woman,* August 1987, pp. 68–70, 103; Catherine Dressler, "We've Got to Stop Meeting Like This," *The Washington Post,* Dec. 31, 1995, p. H2.

56. Jerome M. Rosow, *World of Work Report,* cited in Jeffrey P. Davidson, "A Way to Work in Concert," *Management World,* March 1986, pp. 9–12.

57. Russell Mitchell, "How Ford Hit the Bull's-Eye with Taurus," *Business Week,* June 30, 1986, pp. 69–70; Warren Brown, "Ford Tinkers with Success," *The Washington Post,* Jan. 15, 1995, p. H5; Warren Brown, "Inauspicious Signs?" *The Washington Post,* Feb. 7, 1996, pp. F1, F10.

58. Steve Lohr, "Manufacturing Cars the Volvo Way," *The New York Times,* June 23, 1987, pp. D1, D5.

59. Brian Dumaine, "Who Needs a Boss?" *Fortune,* May 7, 1990, pp. 52–60; Dean Tjosvold, *Teamwork for Customers,* Jossey-Bass, San Francisco, 1993.

60. John L. Cordery, Walter S. Mueller, and Leigh M. Smith, "Attitudinal and Behavioral Effects of Autonomous Group Working: A Longitudinal Field Study," *Academy of Management Journal,* vol. 34, 1991, pp. 464–476; Richard A. Guzzo and Marcus W. Dickson, "Teams in Organizations: Recent Research on Performance and Effectiveness," *Annual Review of Psychology,* vol. 47, 1996, pp. 307–338.

61. J. Richard Hackman, "The Design of Work Teams," in Jay W. Lorsch (ed.), *Handbook of Organizational Behavior,* Prentice-Hall, Englewood Cliffs, N.J., 1987.

62. Henry P. Sims, Jr., "Challenges to Implementing Self-Managing Teams—Part 2," *Journal for Quality & Participation*, March 1995, pp. 24–31.

63. James A. Wall, Jr., and Ronda Roberts Callister, "Conflict and Its Management," *Journal of Management*, vol. 21, 1995, pp. 515–558.

64. Dean Tjosvold, "Making Conflict Productive," *Personnel Administrator*, June 1984, pp. 121–130.

65. Ibid.

66. This section is based largely on Richard E. Walton and John M. Dutton, "The Management of Interdepartmental Conflict: A Model and Review," *Administrative Science Quarterly*, March 1969, pp. 73–84; Stephen P. Robbins, *Organizational Theory: The Structure and Design of Organizations*, Prentice-Hall, Englewood Cliffs, N.J., 1983; and James A. Wall, Jr., and Ronda Roberts Callister, "Conflict and Its Management," *Journal of Management*, vol. 21, 1995, pp. 515–558.

67. George Strauss, "Work Flow Frictions, Interfunctional Rivalry, and Professionalism: A Case Study of Purchasing Agents," *Human Organization*, vol. 23, 1964, pp. 137–149.

68. Julia Flynn Siler, "The Slippery Ladder at Abbott Labs," *Business Week*, Oct. 30, 1989, pp. 136–137; Jeff Bailey, "Ousted Chairman of Abbott Accuses Company in Filing," *The Wall Street Journal*, June 6, 1990, p. A6.

69. Alfie Kohn, *No Contest: The Case against Competition*, Houghton Mifflin, Boston, 1986; Alfie Kohn, "It's Hard to Get Left Out of a Pair," *Psychology Today*, October 1987, pp. 53–57.

70. Bruce G. Posner, "If at First You Don't Succeed," *INC.*, May 1989, pp. 132–134.

71. This section is based on Stephen P. Robbins, *Organizational Theory: The Structure and Design of Organizations*, Prentice-Hall, Englewood Cliffs, N.J., 1983; and James A. Wall, Jr., and Ronda Roberts Callister, "Conflict and Its Management," *Journal of Management*, vol. 21, 1995, pp. 515–558.

72. Christopher Knowlton, "Making It Right the First Time," *Fortune*, Mar. 28, 1988, p. 48; "Tennant Reveals Fourth Quarter Results," *PR Newswire*, Feb. 8, 1995.

73. Kenneth W. Thomas, "Toward Multi-Dimensional Values in Teaching: The Example of Conflict Behaviors," *Academy of Management Review*, vol. 2, 1977, pp. 484–490; H. Joseph Reitz, *Behavior in Organizations*, 3d ed., Irwin, Homewood, Ill., 1987; M. Afzalur Rahim and Nace R. Magner, "Confirmatory Factor Analysis of the Styles of Handling Interpersonal Conflict: First-Order Factor Model and Its Invariance across Groups," *Journal of Applied Psychology*, vol. 80, 1995, pp. 122–132.

74. James A. Wall, Jr., and Rhonda Roberts Callister, "Conflict and Its Management," *Journal of Management*, vol. 21, 1995, pp. 515–558.

75. This section is based largely on James A. Wall, Jr., and Rhonda Roberts Callister, "Conflict and Its Management," *Journal of Management*, vol. 21, 1995, pp. 515–558.

76. Adapted from John E. Jones and J. William Pfeiffer, *The 1975 Annual Handbook for Group Facilitators*, University Associates, La Jolla, Calif., 1975, pp. 28–34.

77. Based on Erik Larson, "Forever Young," *INC.*, July 1988, pp. 50–62; N. R. Kleinfield, "Wanted: C.F.O. with 'Flair for Funk,'" *The New York Times*, Mar. 26, 1989, p. D5; Joe Queenan, "Purveying Yuppie Porn," *Forbes*, Nov. 13, 1989, pp. 60–64; Maxine Lipner, "Ben & Jerry's: Sweet Ethics Evince Social Awareness," *COMPASS Readings*, July 1991, pp. 22–30; Fleming Meeks, "We All Scream for Rice and Beans,"

Forbes, Mar. 30, 1992, p. 20; Joseph Pereira and Joann S. Lublin, "A New CEO for Cherry Garcia's Creators," *The Wall Street Journal*, Feb. 2, 1995, p. 1B; Daniel Kadlec, "Here's the Scoop on Ben & Jerry's," *USA Today*, Jan. 31, 1996, p. 4B; *Ben & Jerry's 1995 Annual Report*; Paul C. Judge, "Is It Rainforest Crunch Time?" *Business Week*, July 15, 1996, pp. 70–71; Earle Eldridge, "Ben & Jerry's Gears up for CEO Search, *USA Today*, Sept. 30, 1996, p. 58.

78. Rahul Jacob, "The Search for the Organization of Tomorrow," *Fortune*, May 18, 1992, pp. 93–94; Joan Kremer Bennett, "The 12 Building Blocks of the Learning Organization," *Training*, June 1994, p. 41.

CHAPTER 16

1. Kathleen Deveny, "McWorld?" *Business Week*, Oct. 13, 1986, pp. 79–86; Stephen Koepp, "Big Mac Strikes Back," *Time*, Apr. 13, 1987, p. 58; John Case, "Hamburger Heaven," *INC.*, September 1987, pp. 26, 28; Penny Moser, "The McDonald's Mystique," *Fortune*, July 4, 1988, pp. 112–116; Richard Phalon, "Japan's Great Burger War," *Forbes*, Oct. 17, 1988, pp. 64–65; Richard Gibson, "McDonald's Makes a Fast Pitch to Pizza Buffs Who Hate to Wait," *The Wall Street Journal*, Aug. 28, 1989, p. B5; Brian Bremner, "McDonald's Stoops to Conquer," *Business Week*, Oct. 30, 1989, pp. 120–124; Robert J. Samuelson, "In Praise of McDonald's," *The Washington Post*, Nov. 1, 1989, p. A25; *Welcome to McDonald's*, McDonald's Corporation, 1996.

2. Robert J. Samuelson, "In Praise of McDonald's," *The Washington Post*, Nov. 1, 1989, p. A25.

3. William H. Newman, *Constructive Control*, Prentice-Hall, Englewood Cliffs, N.J., 1975; David C. Brand and Gerald Scanlan, "Strategic Control through Core Competencies," *Long Range Planning*, vol. 28, no. 2, 1995, pp. 102–114.

4. Kenneth A. Merchant, *Control in Business Organizations*, Pitman, Boston, 1985, p. 4; Eric G. Flamholtz, *Effective Management Control: Theory and Practice*, Kluwer Academic Publishers, Boston, 1996.

5. Barbara Marsh, "Going for the Golden Arches," *The Wall Street Journal*, May 1, 1989, p. B1; McDonald's Corporation materials, 1995.

6. Eric Flamholtz, "Behavioral Aspects of Accounting/Control Systems," in Steven Kerr (ed.), *Organizational Behavior*, Grid Publishing, Columbus, Ohio, 1979, p. 290.

7. Kathleen Deveny, "Bag Those Fries, Squirt That Ketchup, Fry That Fish," *Business Week*, Oct. 13, 1986, p. 86; information from Colesville, Maryland McDonald's, March 1996.

8. Norihiro Shirouzu, "Daiwa Bank's Oversight Is Called Lax in Letter by Trader Who Hid Losses," *The Wall Street Journal*, Dec. 12, 1995, p. A16.

9. Sharen Kindel, "Eye-Opening Management: Luxottica Group S.p.A.," *Hemisphere Magazine*, August 1995, pp. 31–34.

10. Norihiro Shirouzu, "Daiwa Bank's Oversight Is Called Lax in Letter by Trader Who Hid Losses," *The Wall Street Journal*, Dec. 12, 1995, p. A16.

11. Peter F. Drucker, "A Prescription for Entrepreneurial Management," *Industry Week*, Apr. 29, 1985, pp. 33–34.

12. Amy Dunkin and Michael O'Neal, "Power Retailers," *Business Week*, Dec. 21, 1987, pp. 86–92.

13. Alfred P. Sloan, Jr., *My Years with General Motors*, Doubleday, New York, 1964.

14. This section relies heavily on Peter Lorange, Michael F. Scott Morton, and Sumantra Ghoshal, *Strategic Control Systems*, West, St. Paul, Minn., 1986; and George Schreyoff and Horst Steinmann, "Strategic Control: A New Perspective," *Academy of Management Review*, vol. 12, 1987, pp. 91–103. See also Robert Simons, *Levers of Control: How Managers Use Innovative Control Systems to Drive Strategic Renewal*, Harvard Business School Press, Boston, 1995.

15. Ibid.

16. Steve Weiner, "Low Marks, Few Sparks," *Forbes*, Sept. 18, 1989, pp. 146–147; John Marcom, Jr., "Blue Blazers and Guacamole," *Forbes*, Nov. 25, 1991, pp. 64–68; Adam Spielmal, "Marks & Spencer Seeks to Drape Europe," *The Wall Street Journal*, Jan. 6, 1992, p. B5; Jordan D. Lewis, *The Connected Corporation*, Free Press, New York, 1995; "Company Vitae: Marks & Spencer," *The Guardian*, Feb. 3, 1996, p. 3; Ann Simpson, "Clara Freeman Is the First Woman to Become an Executive Director at Marks & Spencer," *The Herald* (Glasgow), Feb. 5, 1996, p. 14.

17. John Marcom, Jr., "Blue Blazers and Guacamole," *Forbes*, Nov. 25, 1991, pp. 64–68.

18. Cynthia Crossen, "Waldenbooks Peddles Books a Bit Like Soap, Transforming Market," *The Wall Street Journal*, Oct. 10, 1988, pp. A1, A6; Meg Cox, "Waldenbooks' Big-Buyer Lure May Mean War," *The Wall Street Journal*, Feb. 27, 1990, pp. B1, B7; Jim Milliot, "Expansion Slated for Longmeadow Press," *Publishers Weekly*, Mar. 27, 1995, p. 13; Jim Milliot, "Walden's Relocation to Michigan Is Hitting Some Bumps," *Publishers Weekly*, Mar. 27, 1995, p. 13.

19. James Cook, "We Are the Market," *Forbes*, Apr. 7, 1986, pp. 54–55; Lore Croghan, "Why It's Time for Local 7232 to Make Peace with Briggs & Stratton," *Financial World*, Jan. 30, 1996, p. 30.

20. Joan O'C. Hamilton, "Why Rivals Are Quaking as Nordstroms Heads East," *Business Week*, June 15, 1987, pp. 99–100; Paul Galloway, "Counterattack," *Chicago Tribune*, Dec. 19, 1990, p. C1; Ruth Richman, "Christmas: Science of the Sell," *Chicago Sun Times*, Dec. 5, 1993, p. 14.

21. Kenneth A. Merchant, *Control in Business Organizations*, Pitman, Boston, 1985, pp. 5–8.

22. Richard D. Hollinger and John P. Clark, *Theft by Employees*, Lexington Books, Lexington, Mass., 1983.

23. Richard Behar, "How the Rich Get Richer," *Forbes*, Oct. 31, 1988, p. 70.

24. Bro Uttal, "Companies That Serve You Best," *Fortune*, Dec. 7, 1987, pp. 98–116. For a discussion of the service tracking system in the Traveler's Cheque Group, see James F. Welch, "Service Quality Measurement at American Express Traveler's Cheque Group," *National Productivity Review*, Sept. 22, 1992, p. 463.

25. Ibid.

26. William H. Newman, *Constructive Control*, Prentice-Hall, Englewood Cliffs, N.J., 1975.

27. Bill Saporito, "A Week Aboard the Wal-Mart Express," *Fortune*, Aug. 24, 1992, pp. 77–84.

28. Joan O'C. Hamilton, "Why Rivals Are Quaking as Nordstroms Heads East," *Business Week*, June 15, 1987, pp. 99–100; Paul Galloway, "Counterattack," *Chicago Tribune*, Dec. 19, 1990, p. C1.

29. Stephen G. Green and M. Ann Welsh, "Cybernetics and Dependence: Reframing the Control Concept," *Academy of Management Review*, vol. 13, 1988, pp. 287–301.

30. "Buns Run Out at McDonald's," *The New York Times,* Oct. 10, 1992, p. 39.
31. McDonald's Corporatoin 1994 Annual Report.
32. Kathleen Deveny, "McWorld?" *Business Week,* Oct. 13, 1986, pp. 79–86.
33. Ibid.
34. John Lippert and Nunzio Lupo, "A Not-So-Happy Birthday," *Detroit Free Press,* Aug. 28, 1988, pp. F1, F2; "Ford-Mazda to Cut White-Collar Jobs," *The Detroit News,* May 23, 1995, p. B1.
35. W. G. Ouchi and M. A. Maguire, "Organizational Control: Two Functions," *Administrative Science Quarterly,* vol. 20, 1975, pp. 559–569.
36. John Lippert and Nunzio Lupo, "A Not-So-Happy Birthday," *Detroit Free Press,* Aug. 28, 1988, pp. F1, F2.
37. Ibid.
38. Richard C. Morais, "The Filofax Fiasco," *Forbes,* Nov. 20, 1995, pp. 70–71; Richard W. Stevenson, "Filofax, 80's Talisman, Thrives in Too-Busy 90's," *The New York Times,* Dec. 29, 1995, p. D1.
39. S. Jay Liebowitz and Kevin T. Holden, "Are Self-Managing Teams Worthwhile? A Tale of Two Companies," *SAM Advanced Management Journal,* Mar. 22, 1995, p. 11.
40. John Hoerr, "Work Teams Can Rev Up Paper-Pushers, Too," *Business Week,* Nov. 28, 1988, pp. 64–72, and "The Payoff from Teamwork," *Business Week,* July 10, 1989, pp. 56–62; Thomas Li-Ping Tang and Amy Beth Crofford, "Self-Managing Work Teams," *Employment Relations Today,* Winter 1995–1996, pp. 29–39.
41. David Sedwick, "Competitive Brake Market at Strike's Root," *Automotive News,* Mar. 18, 1996, pp. 1, 50; Bill Vlasic, "Can the UAW Put a Brake on Outsourcing?" *Business Week,* June 17, 1996, pp. 66, 70.
42. This section is based largely on Robert Simons, *Levers of Control: How Managers Use Innovative Control Systems to Drive Strategic Renewal,* Harvard Business School Press, Boston, 1995.
43. Larry Reibstein, "Federal Express Faces Challenges to Its Grip on Overnight Delivery," *The Wall Street Journal,* Jan. 6, 1988, p. A1; Kenneth Labich, "Big Changes at Big Brown," *Fortune,* Jan. 18, 1988, pp. 56–64; Todd Vogel, "Can UPS Deliver the Goods in a New World?" *Business Week,* June 4, 1990, pp. 80–82; Chuck Hawkins, "After a U-Turn, UPS Really Delivers," *Business Week,* May 31, 1993, pp. 92–93; Robert Frank, "Efficient UPS Tries to Increase Efficiency," *The Wall Street Journal,* May 24, 1995, p. B1; Emory Thomas, Jr., "UPS Plans to Make $1.1 Billion Outlay on Europe Market," *The Wall Street Journal,* June 1, 1995, p. B3; Christopher Drew, "In the Productivity Push, How Much Is Too Much?" *The New York Times,* Dec. 17, 1995, pp. F1, 12; Carey Gillam, "Delivering the Dream," *Sales & Marketing Management,* June 1996, p. 74.
44. This section is based on James Brian Quinn, "Technological Innovation, Entrepreneurship, and Strategy," *Sloan Management Review,* Spring 1979, pp. 19–30, and "Managing Innovation: Controlled Chaos," *Harvard Business Review,* May–June 1985, pp. 73–84.
45. P. Ranganath Nayak and John M. Ketteringham, *Break-Throughs,* Rawson Associates, New York, 1986.
46. This section is based on Kenneth A. Merchant, *Control in Business Organizations,* Pitman, Boston, 1985.
47. John P. Kotter, Leonard A. Schlesinger, and Vijay Sathe, *Organization: Text, Cases, and Readings on the Management of Organizational Design and Change,* Irwin, Homewood, Ill., 1979.
48. Kenneth A. Merchant, "The Effects of Organizational Controls," working paper, Harvard University, Graduate School of Business Administration, 1984, cited in Kenneth A. Merchant, *Control in Business Organizations,* Pitman, Boston, 1985, p. 82.
49. David B. Greenberger and Stephen Strasser, "Development and Application of a Model of Personal Control in Organizations," *Academy of Management Review,* vol. 11, 1986, pp. 164–177.
50. Bernard J. Jaworski, Vlasis Stathakopoulos, and H. Shanker Krishnan, "Control Combinations in Marketing: Conceptual Framework and Empirical Evidence," *Journal of Marketing,* vol. 57, 1993, pp. 57–69; Kenneth A. Merchant, "The Control Function of Management," *Sloan Management Review,* Summer 1982, pp. 43–55.
51. Kenneth A. Merchant, *Control in Business Organizations,* Pitman, Boston, 1985, pp. 10–11; James A. F. Stoner and Charles Wankel, *Management,* 3d ed., Prentice-Hall, Englewood Cliffs, N.J., 1986, pp. 586–587.
52. Penny Moser, "The McDonald's Mystique," *Fortune,* July 4, 1988, pp. 112–116.
53. Based on Roy Rowan, "E. F. Hutton's New Man on the Hot Seat," *Fortune,* Nov. 11, 1985, pp. 130–136; Brett Duvall Fromson, "The Slow Death of E. F. Hutton," *Fortune,* Feb. 29, 1988, pp. 82–88; Matthew Winkler, "American Express Plans Huge Shearson Recapitalization," *The Wall Street Journal,* Dec. 7, 1989, p. C1; William Power, "Shearson Gets Cash Infusion," *The Wall Street Journal,* Feb. 27, 1990, p. C1; Leah Nathans Spiro, "Lehman Brothers: Free At Last," *Business Week,* May 22, 1995, pp. 112–113; Shawn Tully, "Can Lehman Survive?" *Fortune,* Dec. 11, 1995, pp. 154–160.
54. Hesh Kestin, "Nothing Like a Dane," *Forbes,* Nov. 3, 1986, pp. 145–148; "LEGO Finds Success Easy to Assemble," *COMPASS Readings,* February 1991, pp. 36–42; Jack K. Rogers and Keith R. Kreisher, "Special Report, Materials Handling," *Modern Plastics,* February 1992, p. 46; Calilie Rohwedder, "Lego Interlocks Toy Bricks, Theme Parks," *The Wall Street Journal,* Dec. 27, 1994, p. B2; "Lego Looks Beyond Its Blocks," *Chicago Tribune,* Jan. 14, 1996, Business, p. 9; Peter Marsh, "Celebration of Plastic Bricks," *Financial Times,* Apr. 13, 1996, p. 13.

CHAPTER 17
1. Wendy Zellner, "USAA: Premium Treatment," *Business Week,* Oct. 25, 1991, p. 124; Thomas Teal, "Service Comes First: An Interview with USAA's Robert F. McDermott," *Harvard Business Review,* September–October 1991, pp. 117–127; David A. Garvin, "Leveraging Processes for Strategic Advantage: A Roundtable with Zerox's Allaire, USAA's Herres, SmithKline Beechan's Leschly, and Pepsi's Weatherup," *Harvard Business Review,* September–October 1995, pp. 77–90; G. R., "USAA: Conquering a Paper Mountain," *Forbes ASAP,* Oct. 9, 1995, p. 56.
2. Eric G. Flamholtz, Effective Management Control: Theory and Practice, Kluwer Academic Publishers, Boston, 1996; Robert N. Anthony, John Dearden, and Norton M. Bedford, *Management Control Systems,* 5th ed., Irwin, Homewood, Ill., 1984.
3. Conference Board, *Linking Quality to Business Results,* New York, 1994.
4. Greg Bounds, Lyle Yorks, Mel Adams, and Gipsie Ranney, *Beyond Total Quality Management: Toward the Emerging Paradigm,* McGraw-Hill, New York, 1994; Frederick F. Reichheld, "Learning from Customer Defections," *Harvard Business Review,* March–April 1996, pp. 56–69.
5. "Quality Glossary," *Quality Progress,* February 1992, p. 26, and memo on quality to management textbook authors, American Society for Quality Control, 1987. For an analysis of alternative definitions, see Carol A. Reeves and David A. Bednar, "Defining Quality: Alternatives and Implications," *Academy of Management Review,* vol. 19, 1994, pp. 419–445.
6. David A. Garvin, "Competing on the Eight Dimensions of Quality," *Harvard Business Review,* November–December 1987, pp. 101–109.
7. Based on Patricia A. Galagan, "Training Delivers Results to Federal Express," *Training & Development,* December 1991, pp. 27–33; Patricia L. Panchak, "How to Implement a Quality Management Initiative," *Modern Office Technology,* February 1992, pp. 27–31; "Federal Express Launches Internet Shipping," *Business Wire,* Feb. 29, 1996.
8. G. M. Hostage, "Quality Control in a Service Business," *Harvard Business Review,* July–August 1975, pp. 98–106; William A. Sherden, "Gaining the Service Quality Advantage," *Journal of Business Strategy,* March–April 1988, pp. 45–48.
9. Joseph B. White, "U.S. Car-Parts Firms Form Japanese Ties," *The Wall Street Journal,* Apr. 12, 1988, p. 6.
10. Roger B. Yepsen, Jr. (ed.), *The Durability Factor,* Rodale, Emmaus, Pa., 1982, cited in David A. Garvin, "Competing on the Eight Dimensions of Quality," *Harvard Business Review,* November–December 1987, pp. 101–109.
11. Ibid.
12. James R. Evans and William M. Lindsay, *The Management and Control of Quality,* 3d ed., West, Minneapolis/St. Paul, 1996. See also J. M. Juran, *Juran on Planning for Quality,* Free Press, New York, 1988.
13. This section is based heavily on J. Richard Hackman and Ruth Wagemen, "Total Quality Management: Empirical, Conceptual, and Practical Issues," *Administrative Science Quarterly,* vol. 40, 1995, pp. 309–342.
14. Adapted from W. Edwards Deming, *Out of the Crisis,* M.I.T., Center for Advanced Engineering Study, Cambridge, Mass., 1986.
15. Otis Port, "The Push for Quality," *Business Week,* June 8, 1987, pp. 130–136.
16. This section is based heavily on J. Richard Hackman and Ruth Wagemen, "Total Quality Management: Empirical, Conceptual, and Practical Issues," *Administrative Science Quarterly,* vol. 40, 1995, pp. 309–342.
17. James R. Evans and William M. Lindsay, *The Management and Control of Quality,* West, Minneapolis/St. Paul, 1996.
18. Beverly Geber, "Quality Circles: The Second Generation," *Training,* December 1986, pp. 54–61; Conference Board, *Employee Buy-in to Total Quality,* New York, 1991.
19. Ellen Goldbaum, "How Quality Programs Win Respect—And Get Results," *Chemical Week,* Oct. 5, 1988, pp. 30–33.
20. Conference Board, *Employee Buy-in to Total Quality,* New York, 1991.
21. Judy D. Olian and Sara L. Rynes, "Making Total Quality Work: Aligning Organizational Processes, Performance Measures, and Stakeholders," *Human Resource Management,* Fall 1991, pp. 303–333.

22. Jonathan D. Weatherly, "Dare to Compare for Better Productivity," *HR Magazine,* September 1992, pp. 42–46.

23. Jeremy Main, "How to Steal the Best Ideas Around," *Fortune,* Oct. 19, 1992, pp. 102–106.

24. Tom Hinton and Wini Schaeffer, *Customer-Focused Quality: What to Do on Monday Morning,* Prentice-Hall, Englewood Cliffs, N.J., 1994.

25. John Rabbitt, "A Global Market Challenge: Developing Teams That Excel," in *Linking Quality to Business Results,* Conference Board, New York, 1994, pp. 14–15.

26. Conference Board, *Quality Outlook,* New York, 1994.

27. Conference Board, *TQM and Supplier Relationships,* New York, 1994.

28. Ellen Goldbaum, "How Quality Programs Win Respect and Get Results," *Chemical Week,* Oct. 5, 1988, pp. 30–33.

29. James Houghton, "For Better Quality, Listen to the Workers," *The New York Times,* Forum, Oct. 18, 1987, section 3, p. 3.

30. Based on Craig R. Waters, "Quality Begins at Home," *INC.,* August 1985, pp. 68–71; and Daniel Bates, "Spectrum Gets a Break, Moves to Capture Greater Market Share," *Pittsburgh Business Times & Journal,* Sept. 2, 1991, p. 11.

31. Edward E. Lawler III, "Total Quality Management and Employee Involvement: Are They Compatible?" *Academy of Management Executive,* vol. 8, no. 1, 1994, pp. 68–76; J. Richard Hackman and Ruth Wagemen, "Total Quality Management: Empirical, Conceptual, and Practical Issues," *Administrative Science Quarterly,* vol. 40, 1995, pp. 309–342.

32. Gilbert Fuchsberg, "Total Quality Is Termed Only Partial Success," *The Wall Street Journal,* Oct. 1, 1992, pp. B1, B9; Michael S. Leibman, "Getting Results from TQM," *HR Magazine,* September 1992, pp. 34–38.

33. Mark Graham Brown, Darcy E. Hitchcock, and Marsha L. Willard, *Why TQM Fails and What to Do about It,* Irwin, Burr Ridge, Ill., 1994.

34. David Greising, "Quality: How to Make It Pay," *Business Week,* Aug. 8, 1994, pp. 54–58.

35. Robert F. Meigs and Walter B. Meigs, *Accounting: The Basis for Business Decisions,* 9th ed., McGraw-Hill, New York, 1993.

36. The definitions of financial control measures are based on information from H. Kent Baker, *Financial Management,* Harcourt Brace Jovanovich, San Diego, Calif., 1987, pp. 88–122.

37. Robert F. Meigs and Walter B. Meigs, *Accounting: The Basis for Business Decisions,* 9th ed., McGraw-Hill, New York, 1993.

38. Ibid.

39. Jerry Flint, "Legal Monopolies," *Forbes,* Aug. 28, 1995, pp. 90–92.

40. See "A Conversation with Roberto Goizueta and Jack Welch," *Fortune,* Dec. 11, 1995, pp. 96–102.

41. The major sources are *Annual Statement Studies,* Robert Morris Associates, Philadelphia; *Key Business Ratios,* Dun & Bradstreet, New York; *Almanac of Business and Industrial Financial Ratios,* Prentice-Hall, Englewood Cliffs, N.J.; *Quarterly Financial Report for Manufacturing Corporations,* Federal Trade Commission and Securities and Exchange Commission, Washington, D.C.; and data from various trade associations.

42. Scott S. Cowen and J. Kendall Middaugh II, "Designing an Effective Financial Planning and Control System," *Long Range Planning,* vol. 21, 1988, pp. 83–92.

43. This section is based heavily on Joseph A. Maciariello, *Management Control Systems,* Prentice-Hall, Englewood Cliffs, N.J., 1984.

44. Peter Waldman, "New RJR Chief Faces a Daunting Challenge at Debt-Heavy Firm," *The Wall Street Journal,* Mar. 14, 1989, pp. A1, A19; Roger E. Bohn, "Measuring and Managing Technological Knowledge," *Sloan Management Review,* Sept. 22, 1994, p. 61.

45. Bill Saporito, "The Tough Cookie at RJR Nabisco," *Fortune,* July 18, 1988, pp. 32–46.

46. Rufus Olins and John Waples, "Cunard Sails into Unknown Waters," *The Times (London),* Mar. 10, 1996, Business, p. 1.

47. Stratford P. Sherman, "Inside the Mind of Jack Welch," *Fortune,* Mar. 27, 1989, pp. 39–50.

48. Based on John A. Burne, "Hanson: The Dangers of Living by Takeover Alone," *Business Week,* Aug. 15, 1988, pp. 62–64; Richard W. Stevenson, "Hanson P.L.C. to Be Broken Up into 4 Companies," *The New York Times,* Jan. 31, 1996, p. D1; Sara Calian and Janet Guyon, "Hanson's Four-Way Split Panned by Many Analysts," *The Wall Street Journal,* Feb. 1, 1996, p. A12; Paula Dwyer, "The Urge to Demerge Hits Hanson," *Business Wire,* Feb. 12, 1996, p. 1.

49. Walter B. Meigs and Robert F. Meigs, *Accounting: The Basis for Business Decisions,* 9th ed., McGraw-Hill, New York, 1993.

50. Joseph A. Maciariello, *Management Control Systems,* Prentice-Hall, Englewood Cliffs, N.J., 1984; H. Kent Baker, *Financial Management,* Harcourt Brace Jovanovich, San Diego, Calif., 1987.

51. V. Bruce Irvine, "Budgeting: Functional Analysis and Behavioral Implications," *Cost and Management,* March–April 1970, pp. 6–16; Henry L. Tosi, Jr., "The Human Effects of Budgeting Systems on Management," *MSU Business Topics,* Autumn 1974, pp. 53–63.

52. This discussion is based largely on Roger G. Schroeder, *Operations Management,* 3d ed., McGraw-Hill, New York, 1989; and James B. Dilworth, *Production and Operations Management,* 5th ed., McGraw-Hill, New York, 1993.

53. Ibid.

54. Kathy Rebello and Peter Burrows, "The Fall of an American Icon," *Business Week,* Feb. 5, 1996, pp. 34–42.

55. Ibid.

56. Dennis W. McLeavey and Seetharama L. Narasimhan, *Production Planning and Inventory Control,* Allyn and Bacon, Boston, 1985.

57. This discussion is based largely on Roger G. Schroeder, *Operations Management,* 3d ed., McGraw-Hill, New York, 1989.

58. Charles G. Burck, "Can Detroit Catch Up?" *Fortune,* Feb. 8, 1982, pp. 34–39.

59. Richard J. Schonberger, "An Assessment of Just-in-Time Implementation," in *Readings in Zero Inventory* (APICS 27th Annual International Conference proceedings, Las Vegas, Oct. 9–12, 1984), p. 57.

60. Martha E. Mangelsdorf, "Beyond Just-in-Time," *INC.,* February 1989, p. 21.

61. Andrea Puchalsky, "GM Recouping Ground Lost in Strike," *The Wall Street Journal,* June 24, 1996, p. B2.

62. Andrea Rothman, "High Return Rate for Regina Vacuums May Have Added to Financial Problems," *The Wall Street Journal,* Sept. 29, 1988, p. 4, and "Judge's Opinion Says Regina Had Product Problems," *The Wall Street Journal,* Oct. 5, 1988, p. 5; Terry Troy, "From Sweeping to Suction," *The Weekly Home Furnishings Newspaper,* Nov. 25, 1991, p. 1, and "Carpet Bombing the Mass Market," *The Weekly Home Furnishings Newspaper,* Aug. 3, 1992, p. 48; Sandra Frinton, "New Rule at Regina," *HFN The Weekly Newspaper for the Home Furnishing Network,* June 26, 1995, p. 29; Bill McLoughlin, "Regina's Full-Line Revamp," *HFN The Weekly Newspaper for the Home Furnishing Network,* Jan. 29, 1996, p. 39.

63. Ken Maver, "Taking Up the Gauntlet," *London Business Monthly Magazine,* September 1992, p. 7; "Samsonite Canada Inc. and The Tracker Corporation Jointly Announce a Strategic Alliance," *Canada NewsWire,* Mar. 8, 1996.

CHAPTER 18

1. "The Big Chill," *Fortune,* Jan. 7, 1985, pp. 56–65; Gene Bylinsky, "Japan's Robot King Wins Again," *Fortune,* May 25, 1987, pp. 53–58; James F. Manji, "Manufacturing Excellence Awards," *Controls and Systems,* January 1992, p. 28; Peter Burrows, "GE Fanuc Rethinks the Factory of the Future; Earns the 1991 Factory Automation Award," *Electronic Business,* February 1992, p. 50; Yoshikazu Miura, "Fanuc's Factories Fan Out across Asia," *The Nikkei Weekly,* Oct. 2, 1995, p. 18; Kazuo Mori, "Machine-Tool Maven Expects Imperative of Cost-Cutting to Sharpen Fanuc's Future," *The Nikkei Weekly,* Jan. 22, 1996, p. 12.

2. Richard B. Chase and Nicholas J. Aquilano, *Production & Operations Management,* 6th ed., Irwin, Homewood, Ill., 1992.

3. Thomas A. Mahoney, "Productivity Defined: The Relativity of Efficiency, Effectiveness, and Change," in John P. Campbell, Richard J. Campbell, and associates, *Productivity in Organizations,* Jossey-Bass, San Francisco, 1988, pp. 13–39.

4. Mary Kuntz, "Reinventing the Store," *Business Week,* Nov. 27, 1995, pp. 84–96.

5. This section is based heavily on Roger G. Schroeder, *Operations Management,* 4th ed., McGraw-Hill, New York, 1993.

6. Michael Oneal, "ServiceMaster: Looking for New Worlds to Clean," *Business Week,* Jan. 19, 1987, pp. 60–61; Charles Siler, "Cleanliness, Godliness, and Business," *Business Week,* Nov. 28, 1988, pp. 219–220; discussion between Al Sutherland of ServiceMaster and David C. Martin, Oct. 30, 1992; Casey Bukro, "Bow to God No Hindrance to Profits; But ServiceMaster Stock Could Use Assistance," *Chicago Tribune,* June 12, 1995, p. 1.

7. Richard B. Chase, "Where Does the Customer Fit in a Service Operation?" *Harvard Business Review,* November–December 1978, pp. 137–142; Richard B. Chase and Nicholas J. Aquilano, *Production & Operations Management,* 6th ed., Irwin, Homewood, Ill., 1992.

8. Ibid.

9. James S. Hirsch, "A High-Tech System for Sending Mail Unfolds at Fidelity," *The Wall Street Journal,* March 20, 1996, pp. A1; A5.

10. Stephen C. Wheelwright and Robert H. Hayes, "Competing through Manufacturing," *Harvard Business Review,* January–February 1985, pp. 99–109.

11. Based on William J. Hampton, "What Is Motorola Making at This Factory? History," *Business Week,* Dec. 5, 1988, pp. 168D–168H; Ronald Henkoff, "What Motorola Learns from Japan," *Fortune,* Apr. 24, 1989, pp. 157–168; Matt Krantz, "Is Automation Going Too Far at Some Plants?" *Investor's Business Daily,* Dec. 12, 1995, p. A8.

12. Richard B. Barrett and David J. Kistka, "Forecasting System at Rubbermaid," *Journal of Business Forecasting,* Spring 1987, pp. 7–9.

13. Roger G. Schroeder, *Operations Management,* 4th ed., McGraw-Hill, New York, 1993.

14. Joseph G. Monks, *Operations Management,* 3d ed., McGraw-Hill, New York, 1987; Roger G. Schroeder, *Operations Management,* 4th ed., McGraw-Hill, New York, 1993.

15. This section is based mainly on Joseph G. Monks, *Operations Management*, 3d ed., McGraw-Hill, New York, 1987, and James B. Dilworth, *Production and Operations Management*, 5th ed., McGraw-Hill, New York, 1993.

16. Byron J. Finch and James F. Cox, "Process-Oriented Production Planning and Control: Factors That Influence System Design," *Academy of Management Journal*, vol. 31, 1988, pp. 123–153.

17. Roger G. Schroeder, *Operations Management*, 4th ed., McGraw-Hill, New York, 1993.

18. V. Chopra, "Productivity Improvement through Closed Loop MRP (Part One)," *Production and Inventory Management Review and APCIS News*, March 1982, pp. 18–21, and "Productivity Improvement through Closed Loop MRP (Part Two)," *Production and Inventory Management Review and APCIS News*, April 1982, pp. 49–51; James B. Dilworth, *Production and Operations Management*, 5th ed., McGraw-Hill, New York, 1993.

19. Bryan Cockel, "Textronix," *Distribution*, August 1986, p. 54.

20. Mary Jo Foley, "Post-MRPII: What Comes Next?" *Datamation*, Dec. 1, 1988, pp. 24–36; James B. Dilworth, *Production and Operations Management*, 5th ed., McGraw-Hill, New York, 1993.

21. Joseph G. Monks, *Operations Management*, 3d ed., McGraw-Hill, New York, 1987; James B. Dilworth, *Production and Operations Management*, 5th ed., McGraw-Hill, New York, 1993.

22. This section relies heavily on David N. Burt and William R. Soukup, "Purchasing's Role in New Product Development," *Harvard Business Review*, September–October 1985, pp. 90–97; Shawn Tully, "Purchasing's New Muscle," *Fortune*, Feb. 20, 1995, pp. 75–83.

23. This section relies heavily on James B. Dilworth, *Production and Operations Management*, 5th ed., McGraw-Hill, New York, 1993; see also James A. Fitzsimmons and Mona J. Fitzsimmons, *Service Management for Competitive Advantage*, McGraw-Hill, New York, 1994, and Benjamin Schneider and David E. Bowen, *Winning the Service Game*, Harvard Business School Press, Boston, 1995.

24. This section is based partially on Elwood S. Buffa, *Modern Production/Operations Management*, 7th ed., Wiley, New York, 1983.

25. Paul Ingrassia and Bradley A. Stertz, "Ford's Strong Sales Raise Agonizing Issue of Additional Plants," *The Wall Street Journal*, Oct. 26, 1988, pp. A1, A10; Alex Taylor III, "U.S. Cars Come Back," *Fortune*, Nov. 16, 1992, pp. 52–85.

26. Howard Rudnitsky, "How Sam Walton Does It," *Forbes*, Aug. 16, 1982, pp. 42–44, and "Play It Again, Sam," *Forbes*, Aug. 10, 1987, p. 48.

27. Donald Dawson, "Place for a Store," *Marketing*, Apr. 7, 1988, pp. 35–36; James B. Dilworth, *Production and Operations Management*, 5th ed., McGraw-Hill, New York, 1993.

28. This section is based on Everett E. Adam, Jr., and Ronald J. Ebert, *Production and Operations Management*, 5th ed., Prentice-Hall, Englewood Cliffs, N.J., 1992; and Elwood S. Buffa, *Modern Production/Operations Management*, 7th ed., Wiley, New York, 1983.

29. Jeff Bailey and Robert L. Rose, "Maybe Winnebago Just Wasn't Ready for Big-City Bosses," *The Wall Street Journal*, Oct. 17, 1988, pp. A1, A12; Rick Reiff, "Bad News, Good Prospects," *Forbes*, Oct. 31, 1988, p. 39; Robert L. Rose, "Winnebago Dismisses Conner as Chief, as Founder Again Is Tough to Please," *The Wall Street Journal*, Apr. 13, 1990, p. A3;

William Ryberg, "Winnebago Hits the Road to Lure Workers, Keep Up with Growth," *Gannett News Service*, Apr. 29, 1996, p. S12.

30. Roger G. Schroeder, *Operations Management*, 4th ed., McGraw-Hill, New York, 1993.

31. J. Robb Dixon, Peter Arnold, Janelle Heineke, Jay S. Kim, Paul Mulligan, "Business Process Reengineering: Improving in New Strategic Directions," *California Management Review*, vol. 36, Spring 1994, pp. 9–31; James T. C. Teng, Varun Grover, and Kirk D. Fiedler, "Business Process Reengineering: Charting a Strategic Path for the Information Age," *California Management Review*, vol. 36, Summer 1994, pp. 93–108.

32. J. Robb Dixon, Peter Arnold, Janelle Heineke, Jay S. Kim, Paul Mulligan, "Business Process Reengineering: Improving in New Strategic Directions," *California Management Review*, vol. 36, Spring 1994, pp. 9–31.

33. Mary Connors, "Baxter's Big Makeover in Logistics," *Fortune*, July 8, 1996, pp. 106C–106N.

34. Gene Bylinsky, "To Create Products, Go into a Cave," *Fortune*, Feb. 5, 1996, pp. 80A–80D.

35. Patricia Nemetz and Louis W. Fry, "Flexible Manufacturing Organizations: Implications for Strategy Formulation and Organizational Design," *Academy of Management Review*, vol. 13, 1988, pp. 627–638.

36. Bernard Avishai, "A CEO's Common Sense of CIM: An Interview with J. Tracy O'Rourke," *Harvard Business Review*, January–February 1989, pp. 110–117; "Rockwell Marks 10-Year Anniversary of Allen-Bradley Purchase," *PR Newswire*. Feb. 20, 1995, pp. 1–3.

37. This section is based largely on James L. Heskett, *Managing in the Service Economy*, Harvard Business School, Boston, 1986.

38. Jaclyn Fierman, "Fidelity's Secret: Faithful Service," *Fortune*, May 7, 1990, pp. 86–92; Suein Hwang, "Getting Personal," *The Wall Street Journal*, Apr. 6, 1992, p. R19; James S. Hirsch, "A High-Tech System for Sending the Mail Unfolds at Fidelity," *The Wall Street Journal*, Mar. 20, 1996, pp. A1, A5.

39. John Hoerr, "Work Teams Can Rev Up Paper-Pushers, Too," *Business Week*, Nov. 28, 1988, pp. 64–72.

40. Richard A. Guzzo, "Productivity Research: Reviewing Psychological and Economic Perspectives," in John P. Campbell, Richard J. Campbell, and associates, *Productivity in Organizations*, Jossey-Bass, San Francisco, 1988; Daniel R. Ilgen and Howard J. Klein, "Individual Motivation and Performance: Cognitive Influences on Effort and Choice," in ibid.

41. Wickham Skinner, "The Productivity Paradox," *Harvard Business Review*, July–August 1986, pp. 55–59.

42. "No Trend Lasts Forever," *Forbes*, Dec. 1, 1986, pp. 108–109; Ronald Henkoff, "The Cat Is Acting Like a Tiger," *Fortune*, Dec. 19, 1988, pp. 69–76; Kathleen Deveny, "For Caterpillar, the Metamorphosis Isn't Over," *Business Week*, Aug. 31, 1987, pp. 72–74; Kathleen Deveny, Corie Brown, William J. Hampton, and James B. Treece, "Going for the Lion's Share," *Business Week*, July 18, 1988, pp. 70–72; Jeremy Main, "Manufacturing the Right Way," *Fortune*, May 21, 1990, pp. 54–64; Kevin Kelly, "Caterpillar's Don Fites: Why He Didn't Blink," *Business Week*, Aug. 10, 1992, pp. 56–57; Robert L. Rose and Alex Kotlowitz, "Strife between UAW and Caterpillar Blights Promising Labor Idea," *The Wall Street Journal*, Nov. 23, 1992, pp. A1, A8; Robert L. Rose, "Caterpillar Continues to Stand Tough

as Strikers Return," *The Wall Street Journal*, Dec. 8, 1995, p. 1B; Robert L. Rose, "Caterpillar's Profit Is Surprisingly Strong," *The Wall Street Journal*, Jan. 19, 1996, p. B4; Bob Bouyea, "Plant with a Future Arrives at Caterpillar," *Peoria Journal Star*, Jan. 10, 1995, p. 1; Donald V. Fites, "Make Your Dealers Your Partners," *Harvard Business Review*, March–April 1996, p. 84.

43. Andrew Tanzer, "The Birdman of Bangkok," *Forbes*, Apr. 13, 1992, pp. 86–89; Edward A. Gargan, "When Family Empires Shape Asian Expansion," *International Herald Tribune*, Nov. 16, 1995, p. 1; Peter Janssen, "Chicken Breeder Leads in Thailand's Multinational Race," *Deutsche Presse-Agentur*, Nov. 19, 1995, p. 1; Phusadee Arunmart, "CP Group Division Bullish on Exports," *Bangkok Post*, Feb. 8, 1996, p. 1; Ted Bardacke, "Thai Group May Float Store Unit," *Financial Times*, Mar. 7, 1996, p. 29.

CHAPTER 19

1. Brenton Schlender, "How Bill Gates Keeps the Magic Going," *Fortune*, June 18, 1990, pp. 82–89; Kathy Rebello, "After Win95, What Do You Do for an Encore?" *Business Week*, Oct. 16, 1995, pp. 68–72; George Taninecz, "Gates Wins Respect," *Industry Week*, Nov. 20, 1995, p. 12; Elizabeth Corcoran, "Microsoft's Man: A Regular Guy Who's a Legend," *The Washington Post*, Dec. 3, 1995, pp. A1, A8; Bill Gates, "Excerpted from *The Road Ahead*," *Working Women*, January 1996, pp. 34–41; "Wired for Hiring: Microsoft's Slick Recruiting Machine," *Fortune*, Feb. 5, 1996, pp. 123–124.

2. Gary McWilliams, "Small Fry Go Online," *Business Week*, Nov. 20, 1995, pp. 158–164.

3. Gene Bylinsky, "Fast-Selling Software That Hurries Products to Market," *Fortune*, Apr. 29, 1996, p. 150C–150L.

4. Ralph Emmett Carlyle, "Managing IS at Multinations," *Datamation*, Mar. 1, 1988, pp. 54–66.

5. Lee L. Gremillion and Philip J. Pyburn, *Computers and Information Systems in Business: An Introduction*, McGraw-Hill, New York, 1988.

6. Kenneth C. Laudon and Jane Price Laudon, *Management Information Systems*, 3d ed., Macmillan, New York, 1994.

7. Michael R. Leibowitz, "Clash of the High Speed Titans," *High Technology Business*, July 1988, pp. 50–51; Kenneth C. Laudon and Jane P. Laudon, *Essentials of Management Information Systems*, Prentice-Hall, Englewood Cliffs, N.J., 1995.

8. The definitions related to data bases are based on Kenneth C. Laudon and Jane Price Laudon, *Management Information Systems*, 3d ed., Macmillan, New York, 1994; and Donald H. Sanders, *Computer Concepts and Applications*, McGraw-Hill, New York, 1987.

9. Kenneth C. Laudon and Jane Price Laudon, *Management Information Systems*, 3d ed., Macmillan, New York, 1994.

10. Mary E. Thyfault, "The Intranet Rolls In," *Information Week*, Jan. 29, 1996, pp. 15, 76–78.

11. Stephen R. Gordon and Judith R. Gordon, *Information Systems: A Management Approach*, Dryden Press, 1996.

12. Ibid.

13. Sue Barnes and Leonore M. Greller, "Computer-Mediated Communication in Organizations," *Communication Education*, vol. 43, 1994, pp. 129–142.

14. This section is largely based on Kenneth C. Laudon and Jane Price Laudon, *Management Information Systems*, 3d ed., Macmillan, New York, 1994.

15. Raymond McLeod, Jr., *Management Information Systems*, Science Research Associates, Chicago, 1986; Kenneth C. Laudon and Jane Price Laudon, *Management Information Systems*, 3d ed., Macmillan, New York, 1994.

16. Myron Magnet, "Who's Winning the Information Revolution," *Fortune*, Nov. 30, 1992, pp. 110–117.

17. Ron S. Dembo, Angel Chiarri, Jesus Gomez Martin, and Luis Paradinas, "Managing Hidroeléctrica Española's Hydroelectric Power System," *Interfaces*, January–February 1990, pp. 115–135; Hidroeléctrica Española's recently merged with the Iberduero electric company to form Iberdrola, see "Spain: Fewer Operators in Spain's Restructured Electricity Sector," *Reuter Textline El Pais*, June 8, 1993, p. 1.

18. Efraim Turban and Paul R. Watkins, "Integrating Expert Systems and Decision Support Systems," *MIS Quarterly*, June 1986, pp. 121–138; Paul Finlay, *Introducing Decision Support Systems*, NCC Blackwell, Manchester, 1994.

19. Ruth Simon, "The Morning After," *Forbes*, Oct. 19, 1987, pp. 164–168.

20. Dorothy Leonard-Barton and John J. Sviokla, "Putting Expert Systems to Work," *Harvard Business Review*, March–April 1988, pp. 91–98.

21. Kenneth C. Laudon and Jane Price Laudon, *Management Information Systems*, 3d ed., Macmillan, New York, 1994.

22. Hugh J. Watson, R. Kelly Rainer, Jr., and Chang E. Koh, "Executive Information Systems: A Framework for Development and a Survey of Current Practices," *MIS Quarterly*, March 1991, pp. 13–30.

23. Susan M. Gelfond, "The Computer Age Dawns in the Corner Office," *Business Week*, June 27, 1988, pp. 84–86; Mary E. Boone, "Computers Reshape Phillips 66," *Industry Week*, July 1, 1991, p. 12.

24. For example, Robert I. Benjamin, John F. Rockart, Michael S. Scott Morton, and John Wyman, "Information Technology: A Strategic Opportunity," *Sloan Management Review*, Spring 1984, pp. 3–10; Michael E. Porter and Victor E. Millar, "How Information Gives You Competitive Advantage," *Harvard Business Review*, July–August 1985, pp. 149–160.

25. This section is based on Seev Neumann, *Strategic Information Systems*, Macmillan, New York, 1994; Alex Miller and Gregory G. Dess, *Strategic Management*, McGraw-Hill, New York, 1996; Charles Wiseman and Ian C. MacMillan, "Creating Competitive Weapons from Information Systems," *Journal of Business Strategy*, Fall 1984, pp. 42–49; Michael E. Porter, *Competitive Strategy*, Free Press, New York, 1980.

26. "SABRE Gives the Edge to American Airlines," *Information Week*, May 26, 1986, p. 28; "American's Crandall Proves DP Profit Potential," *Computerworld*, June 9, 1986, p. 54; Kenneth Labich, "Bob Crandall Soars by Flying Solo," *Fortune*, Sept. 29, 1986, pp. 118–124; "American Airlines: Managing the Future," *The Economist*, Dec. 19, 1992, p. 68; Julie Schmidt, "AMR Spins Off Non-Airline Works," *USA Today*, Apr. 7, 1993, p. 2B; Jeff Moad, "Sabre Rattled," *PC Week*, Jan. 29, 1996, p. E1; "Sabre Group Ready to Go It Alone," *The Dallas Morning News*, July 3, 1996, p. 10D.

27. David Wessel, "Computer Finds a Role in Buying and Selling, Reshaping Business," *The Wall Street Journal*, Mar. 8, 1987, pp. 1, 10; Warren Brown, "Electronic Pulses Replacing Paper in Workplace," *The Washington Post*, Sept. 2, 1988, pp. F1, F2.

28. Alex Miller and Gregory G. Dess, *Strategic Management*, McGraw-Hill, New York, 1996.

29. Ibid.

30. Doug Bartholomew, "Boost to Response Time," *Information Week*, Feb. 19, 1996, p. 73.

31. Charles Wiseman and Ian C. MacMillan, "Creating Competitive Weapons from Information Systems," *Journal of Business Strategy*, Fall 1984, pp. 42–49.

32. "Ocean Freighters Turn to High Tech on the High Seas," *Datamation*, Mar. 1, 1988, pp. 25–26.

33. Alex Miller and Gregory G. Dess, *Strategic Management*, McGraw-Hill, New York, 1996; Michael Y. Yoshino and U. Srinivasa Ranga, *Strategic Alliance: An Entrepreneurial Approach to Globalization*, Harvard Business School, Boston, 1995.

34. Megan Santosus, "Tactical Maneuvers," *CIO*, Apr. 1, 1996, pp. 54–56.

35. Richard Pastore, "Great Expectations," *CIO*, Jan. 15, 1996, pp. 46–50.

36. This section is based on Seev Neumann, *Strategic Information Systems*, Macmillan, New York, 1994.

37. M. L. Sullivan-Trainor and J. Maglitta, "Competitive Advantage Fleeting," *Computerworld*, Oct. 8, 1990, p. 1.

38. Seev Neumann, *Strategic Information Systems*, Macmillan, New York, 1994.

39. Peter Fabris, "Ground Control," *CIO*, Apr. 1, 1996, pp. 40–45.

40. Otis Port, "The Software Trap: Automate—Or Else," *Business Week*, May 9, 1988, pp. 142–154.

41. Donald H. Sanders, *Computer Concepts and Applications*, McGraw-Hill, New York, 1987.

42. Kenneth C. Laudon and Jane Price Laudon, *Management Information Systems*, 3d ed., Macmillan, New York, 1994.

43. Paul S. Licker, *The Art of Managing Software Development People*, Wiley, New York, 1985; Peter Tait and Iris Vessey, "The Effect of User Involvement on System Success: A Contingency Approach," *MIS Quarterly*, March 1988, pp. 91–108.

44. Kenneth C. Laudon and Jane Price Laudon, *Essentials of Management Information Systems*, Prentice-Hall, Englewood Cliffs, N.J., 1995; Lee L. Gremillion and Philip J. Pyburn, *Computers and Information Systems in Business: An Introduction*, McGraw-Hill, New York, 1988.

45. Lee L. Gremillion and Philip J. Pyburn, *Computers and Information Systems in Business: An Introduction*, McGraw-Hill, New York, 1988. See also Lowell Jay Arthur, "Quick and Dirty," *Computerworld*, Dec. 14, 1992, p. 4.

46. R. I. Benjamin, "Information Technology in the 1990s: A Long-Range Planning Scenario," *MIS Quarterly*, June 1982, pp. 11–31.

47. Thomas P. Gerrity and John F. Rockart, "End-User Computing: Are You a Leader or a Laggard?" *Sloan Management Review*, Summer 1986, pp. 25–34.

48. Steven R. Gordon and Judith R. Gordon, *Information Systems: A Managerial Approach*, Dryden, Fort Worth, Tex., 1996.

49. Lee L. Gremillion and Philip J. Pyburn, *Computers and Information Systems in Business: An Introduction*, McGraw-Hill, New York, 1988.

50. This sectin is based in part on Gordon B. Davis and Margreth H. Olson, *Management Information Systems: Conceptual Foundations, Structure, and Development*, 2d ed., McGraw-Hill, New York, 1985.

51. Harold J. Leavitt and Thomas L. Whisler, "Management in the 1980s," *Harvard Business Review*, November–December 1958, pp. 41–48.

52. Lynda M. Applegate, James I. Cash, Jr., and D. Quinn Mills, "Information Technology and Tomorrow's Manager," *Harvard Business Review*, November–December 1988, pp. 128–136; M. Malone and W. Davidow, "Virtual

Corporation," *Forbes ASAP*, Dec. 7, 1992, pp. 103–107.

53. P. Attewell and J. Rule, "Computing and Organizations: What We Know and What We Don't Know," *Communications of the ACM*, December 1984, pp. 1184–1192.

54. Ross Gelbspan, "Keeping a Close Watch on Electronic Work Monitoring," *The Washington Post*, Dec. 13, 1987, p. H4.

55. Rebecca A. Grant, Christopher A. Higgins, and Richard H. Irving, "Computerized Performance Monitors: Are They Costing You Customers?" *Sloan Management Review*, Spring 1988, pp. 39–45.

56. Richard Adhikari, "Do Vendors Feel Your Pain?" *Informatin Week*, Mar. 4, 1996, pp. 44–47.

57. Alex Kotlowitz, "Working at Home While Caring for a Child Sounds Fine—In Theory," *The Wall Street Journal*, Mar. 30, 1987, p. 21.

58. William M. Bulkeley, "When Laptop Computers Go on the Road, the Hassles Can Cancel Out the Benefits," *The Wall Street Journal*, May 16, 1990, pp. B1, B4.

59. This section relies heavily on Sue Barnes and Leonore M. Greller, "Computer-Mediated Communication in the Organization," *Communication Education*, vol. 43, 1994, pp. 129–142.

60. Kenneth C. Laudon and Jane Price Laudon, *Management Information Systems*, 3d ed., Macmillan, New York, 1994.

61. Catherine L. Harris and Dean Foust, "An Electronic Pipeline That's Changing the Way America Does Business," *Business Week*, Aug. 3, 1987, pp. 80–82.

62. John J. Keller, "Software Glitch at AT&T Cuts Off Phone Service for Millions," *The Wall Street Journal*, Jan. 16, 1990, pp. B1, B4.

63. Ibid.; John Burgess, "Searching for a Better Computer Shield," *The Washington Post*, Nov. 13, 1988, p. H1.

64. Katherine M. Hafner, "Is Your Computer Secure?" *Business Week*, Aug. 1, 1988, pp. 64–72.

65. John Burgess, "Prankster's Christmas Greeting Generates Few Ho-Ho-Hos at IBM," *The Washington Post*, Dec. 18, 1987, pp. F1, F10; Katherine M. Hafner, "Is Your Computer Secure?" *Business Week*, Aug. 1, 1988, pp. 64–72.

66. Stephanie Stahl and Bob Violino, "Viruses Still Pose a Threat," *Information Week*, Mar. 4, 1996, p. 30.

67. Bob Violino, "Internet Insecurity: Your Worst Nightmare," *Information Week*, Feb. 19, 1996, pp. 34–36.

68. Janet Novack, "Lender's Best Friend," *Forbes*, Dec. 18, 1995, pp. 198–199.

69. Attorneys at the law firm of Backer & Daniels, "Whose Mail Is It Anyway?" *Indiana Employment Law Letter*, June 1995, and "Defensive Driving on the Information Superhighway," *Indiana Employment Law Letter*, July 1995; both reprinted in *1996 Executive File: Hot Employment Issues*, M. Lee Smith Publishers, Nashville, 1996.

70. Elizabeth Weiss, "Employees: Stop Goofing Off on Net," *Warfield's Business Record*, Mar. 11, 1996, p. 18.

71. Based on David Wessel, "First, Ask the Right Questions," *The Wall Street Journal*, June 12, 1987, pp. D11–D13; discussions with Thomas Holmes and Ed Mahler of Du Pont on June 6, 1990; "No Glass Ceiling for This CEO: Information Week Names Du Pont's Hallman Technology Chief of the Year," *PR Newsline*, Dec. 14, 1995; Elizabeth Heichler, "Du Pont Picks Andersen to Overhaul Applications," *Computerworld*, Aug. 14, 1995, p. 63; Bruce

Caldwell, "IW's 1995 Chief of the Year," *InformationWeek*, Dec. 23, 1995, p. 26.
72. Adapted from Myron Magnet, "Who's Winning the Information Revolution," *Fortune*, Nov. 30, 1992, pp. 110–117; "Texas Instruments: A Case of Permanent Revolution," *Software Futures*, Oct. 1, 1995, pp. 1–4.

CHAPTER 20

1. Based on "How a Binational Troika Manages the World's Most Multinational Group," *International Management*, March 1985, pp. 38–42; "How Unilever Moves the Earth," *Across the Board*, September 1985, pp. 38–48; Karen Hoggan, "Eyes on the Global Prize: Through Careful Planning of Its Marketing Strategies, Unilever Hopes to Expand into Every Corner of the Globe," *Marketing*, Dec. 6, 1990, pp. 25–30; "Unilever Moves from Global to Regional Structure," *Euromarketing*, Mar. 19, 1996; Pat Sloan, "Unilever Raises Stature in Haircare," *Advertising Age*, Feb. 19, 1996, p. 3; Pat Sloan, "Unilever Sharpens Regional Focus," *Advertising Age*, Mar. 18, 1996, p. 6.
2. Jeremy Main, "How to Go Global—And Why," *Fortune*, Aug. 28, 1989, pp. 70–76.
3. Stuart Auerback, "America, the 'Diminished Giant,'" *The Washington Post*, Apr. 15, 1987, pp. A1, A18.
4. Franklin R. Root, *International Trade & Investment*, 5th ed., South-Western, Cincinnati, 1984; Alan M. Rugman and Richard M. Hodgetts, *International Business: A Strategic Management Approach*, McGraw-Hill, New York, 1995.
5. Alan M. Rugman and Richard M. Hodgetts, *International Business: A Strategic Management Approach*, McGraw-Hill, New York, 1995.
6. James Aley, "New Lift for the U.S. Export Boom," *Fortune*, Nov. 13, 1995, pp. 73–78.
7. This section relies heavily on Howard V. Perlmutter, "The Tortuous Evolution of the Multinational Corporation," *Columbia Journal of World Business*, January–February 1969, pp. 9–18, and Balagi S. Chakravarthy and Howard V. Perlmutter, "Strategic Planning for a Global Business," *Columbia Journal of World Business*, Summer 1985, pp. 5–6; Allen J. Morrison, David A. Ricks, Kendall Roth, "Globalization versus Regionalization: Which Way for the Multinational?" *Organizational Dynamics*, Winter 1991, pp. 17–29.
8. Jeffrey A. Trachtenberg, "They Didn't Listen to Anybody," *Forbes*, Dec. 15, 1986, pp. 168–169; "Lessons from Doing Business in Japan," *Financial Times*, Apr. 12, 1996, p. 10.
9. Robert T. Moran, Philip R. Harris, and William G. Stripp, *Developing the Global Organization*, Gulf, Houston, 1993.
10. Allen J. Morrison, David A. Ricks, and Kendall Roth, "Globalization versus Regionalization: Which Way for the Multinational?" *Organizational Dynamics*, Winter 1991, pp. 17–29.
11. Robert Collins and Roger Schmenner, "Pan-Regional Manufacturing: The Lessons from Europe," *Financial Times*, Feb. 2, 1996, p. 8.
12. Howard V. Perlmutter, "The Tortuous Evolution of the Multinational Corporation," *Columbia Journal of World Business*, January–February 1969, p. 13.
13. Andrew Kupfer, "How to Be a Global Manager," *Fortune*, Mar. 14, 1988, pp. 52–58; Stanley Holmes, "Politics Key to Boeing Sales in China?" *The Seattle Times*, Apr. 10, 1995, p. A1; Jeff Cole, "Boeing Will Offer a Luxury

737 as Entry to Business-Jet Market," *The Wall Street Journal*, July 2, 1996, p. B4.
14. Mark Mendenhall, Betty Jane Punnett, and David Ricks, *Global Management*, Blackwell, Cambridge, Mass., 1995.
15. Donald Marchand, "The Information Infrastructure—Promises and Realities," *Financial Times*, Jan. 5, 1996, p. 8.
16. Christopher Knowlton, "The New Export Entrepreneurs," *Fortune*, June 6, 1988, pp. 89–102; Alan M. Rugman and Richard M. Hodgetts, *International Business: A Strategic Management Approach*, McGraw-Hill, New York, 1995.
17. George Melloan, "Caterpillar Rides the Economic Policy Bumps," *The Wall Street Journal*, Apr. 5, 1988, p. 37; Paul Magnusson, "Grabbing New World Orders," *Business Week*, Reinventing America 1992, Oct. 23, 1992, pp. 110–118; Robert L. Rose, "Caterpillar's Profit Is Surprisingly Strong," *The Wall Street Journal*, Jan. 19, 1996.
18. Joseph V. Micallef, "Political Risk Assessment," *Columbia Journal of World Business*, Summer 1981, pp. 47–52.
19. David A. Jodice, "Sources of Change in Third World Regimes for Direct Investment," *International Organization*, Spring 1980, pp. 177–206.
20. Alan M. Rugman and Richard M. Hodgetts, *International Business: A Strategic Management Approach*, McGraw-Hill, New York, 1995.
21. Peter Serenyi, "Ford Opens Office to Boost Sales," *The Moscow Times*, Mar. 29, 1996, p. 1.
22. John D. Daniels and Lee H. Radebaugh, *International Business*, Addison-Wesley, Reading, Mass., 1989.
23. "Japan to Curb VCR Exports," *The New York Times*, Nov. 21, 1983, p. D5.
24. This section is based heavily on the interpretation of Hofstede's work contained in Ellen F. Jackofsky, John W. Slocum, Jr., and Sara J. McQuaid, "Cultural Values and the CEO: Alluring Companions?" *Academy of Management Executive*, vol. 11, 1988, pp. 39–49. See also Geert Hofstede, "Motivation, Leadership, and Organization: Do American Theories Apply Abroad?" *Organizational Dynamics*, Summer 1980, pp. 42–63, and "The Cultural Relativity of the Quality of Life Concept," *Academy of Management Review*, vol. 9, 1984, pp. 389–398.
25. Ellen F. Jackofsky, John W. Slocum, Jr., and Sara J. McQuaid, "Cultural Values and the CEO: Alluring Companions?" *Academy of Management Executive*, vol. 11, 1988, pp. 39–49.
26. Joanne Lipman, "Marketers Turn Sour on Global Sales Pitch Harvard Guru Makes," *The Wall Street Journal*, May 12, 1988, pp. 1, 13.
27. Jonathan B. Levine, "GE Carves Out a Road East," *Business Week*, July 30, 1990, pp. 32–33; Michel Syrett and Klari Kingston, "GE's Hungarian Light Switch," *Management Today*, April 1995, p. 52.
28. Michael E. Porter, "The Competitive Advantage of Nations," *Harvard Business Review*, March–April 1990, pp. 73–93, and *The Competitive Advantage of Nations*, Free Press, New York, 1990.
29. Cindy Skrzycki, "How Some Firms Become Foreign Success Stories," *The Washington Post*, Nov. 15, 1987, p. H1.
30. George Steiner and Warren M. Cannon, *Multinational Corporate Planning*, Macmillan, New York, 1966, pp. 295–314; Anant R. Negandhi and Martin K. Welge, *Beyond Theory Z*, JAI, Greenwich, Conn., 1984, pp. 47–53.

31. Martin C. Schnitzer, Marilyn L. Liebrenz, and Konrad W. Kubin, *International Business*, South-Western, Cincinnati, 1985, pp. 55–73; Alan M. Rugman and Richard M. Hodgetts, *International Business: A Strategic Management Approach*, McGraw-Hill, New York, 1995.
32. Alex Miller and Gregory G. Dess, *Strategic Management*, 2d ed., McGraw-Hill, New York, 1996; Michael Y. Yoshino and U. Srinivasa Rangan, *Strategic Alliance: An Entrepreneurial Approach to Globalization*, Harvard Business School, Boston, 1995; see also Andrew Inkpen, *The Management of International Joint Ventures*, Routledge, London, 1995.
33. Yuminko Ono, "'King of Beers' Wants to Rule More in Japan," *The Wall Street Journal*, Oct. 28, 1993, p. B1.
34. Dorothy B. Christelow, "International Joint Ventures: How Important Are They?" *Columbia Journal of World Business*, Summer 1987, pp. 7–13.
35. Based on Rose Brady, "McSweater, the Benettoning of America," *Working Woman*, May 1986, pp. 114–117; William C. Symonds and Amy Dunkin, "Benetton Is Betting on More of Everything," *Business Week*, Mar. 23, 1987, p. 93; Amy Dunkin, "Why Some Benetton Shopkeepers Are Losing Their Shirts," *Business Week*, Mar. 14, 1988, pp. 78–79; John Rossant, "Benetton Strips Back Down to Sportswear," *Business Week*, Mar. 5, 1990, p. 42; Ruth Sullivan, "Dropping the Shock for the New," *Marketing*, Apr. 20, 1995, p. 12; Sara Gay Forden, "Luciano Benetton Sees a Rosy Future Despite Cloudy Days," *Women's Wear Daily*, Apr. 20, 1995, p. 1.
36. Theodore Levitt, "The Globalization of Markets," *Harvard Business Review*, May–June 1983, p. 96.
37. Joanne Lipman, "Marketers Turn Sour on Global Sales Pitch Harvard Guru Makes," *The Wall Street Journal*, May 12, 1988, pp. 1, 13; Rita Koselka, "It's My Favorite Statistic," *Forbes*, Sept. 12, 1994, pp. 162–176.
38. Allen J. Morrison, David A. Ricks, and Kendall Roth, "Globalization versus Regionalization: Which Way for the Multinational?" *Organizational Dynamics*, Winter 1991, pp. 17–29.
39. Based on Andrew Kupfer, "The Long Arm of Jerry Junkins," *Fortune*, Mar. 14, 1988, p. 48; Alison Rogers, "It's the Execution That Counts," *Fortune*, Nov. 30, 1992, pp. 80–83; Peter Burrows, "Texas Instruments' Global Chip Payoff," *Business Week*, Aug. 7, 1995, p. 64.
40. Stefan H. Robock and Kenneth Simmonds, *International Business and Multinational Enterprises*, 4th ed., Irwin, Homewood, Ill., 1989.
41. John D. Daniels, Robert A. Pitts, and Marietta J. Tretter, "Organizing for Dual Strategies of Product Diversity and International Expansion," *Strategic Management Journal*, vol. 6, 1985, p. 301.
42. Stefan H. Robock and Kenneth Simmonds, *International Business and Multinational Enterprises*, 4th ed., Irwin, Homewood, Ill., 1989.
43. Ibid.
44. C. K. Prahalad and Yves L. Dox, *The Multinational Mission: Balancing Local Demands and Global Vision*, Free Press, New York, 1987.
45. Robert A. Pitts and John D. Daniels, "Aftermath of the Matrix Mania," *Columbia Journal of World Business*, Summer 1984, pp. 48–54.
46. Rosalie L. Tung, "Strategic Management of Human Resources in the Multinational Enterprise," *Human Resource Management*, vol. 23, 1984, pp. 129–143; see also Peter J. Dowl-

ing, Randall S. Schuler, and Denice E. Welch, *Human Resource Management,* 2d ed., Wadsworth, Belmont, Calif., 1995.

47. Deborah Lohse, "For Foreign Postings, the Accent Is on Frugality," *The Wall Street Journal,* June 23, 1995, p. 1C.

48. Richard M. Hodgetts and Fred Luthans, *International Management,* McGraw-Hill, 1991; Allen J. Morrison, David A. Ricks, and Kendall Roth, "Globalization versus Regionalization: Which Way for the Multinational?" *Organizational Dynamics,* Winter 1991, pp. 17–29; Peter J. Dowling, Randall S. Schuler, and Denice E. Welch, *Human Resource Management,* 2d ed., Wadsworth, Belmont, Calif., 1995.

49. Rosalie L. Tung, "Strategic Management of Human Resources in the Multinational Enterprise," *Human Resource Management,* vol. 23, 1984, pp. 129–143.

50. Nancy J. Adler, "Expecting International Success: Female Managers Overseas," *Columbia Journal of World Business,* Fall 1984, pp. 79–85.

51. Mariann Jelinek and Nancy J. Adler, "Women: World-Class Managers for Global Competition," *Academy of Management Executive,* vol. 11, 1988, pp. 11–19.

52. Michael G. Harvey, "The Impact of Dual-Career Families on International Relocations," *Human Resource Management Review,* vol. 3, 1995, pp. 223–244.

53. Mark Mendenhall and Gary Oddou, "The Dimensions of Expatriate Acculturation: A Review," *Academy of Management Review,* vol. 10, 1985, pp. 39–47.

54. Ibid.

55. Jeremy Main, "How to Go Global—And Why," *Fortune,* Aug. 28, 1989, pp. 70–76; Lisa Kearns, "Australia: Imperial Chairman," *The Age* (Melbourne), Jan. 28, 1995, p. C1.

56. Mark Mendenhall and Gary Oddou, "The Dimensions of Expatriate Acculturation: A Review," *Academy of Management Review,* vol. 10, 1985, pp. 39–47.

57. Lennie Copeland and Lewis Griggs, "Getting the Best from Foreign Employees," *Management Review,* June 1986, pp. 19–26.

58. This section is based heavily on Alan M. Rugman and Richard M. Hodgetts, *International Business: A Strategic Management Approach,* McGraw-Hill, New York, 1995; Nancy J. Adler, *International Dimensions of Organizational Behavior,* 2d ed., Wadsworth, Belmont, Calif., 1991.

59. Martha I. Finney, "Global Success Rides on Keeping Top Talent," *HR Magazine,* April 1996, pp. 69–72.

60. Nancy J. Adler, Robert Dokter, and S. Gordon Redding, "From the Atlantic to the Pacific Century: Cross-Cultural Management Reviewed," *Journal of Management,* vol. 12, 1986, pp. 295–318; Lane Kelley, Arthur Whatley, and Reginald Worthley, "Assessing the Effects of Culture on Managerial Attitudes: A Three-Culture Test," *Journal of International Business Studies,* Summer 1987, pp. 17–31.

61. Geert Hofstede, "Motivation, Leadership, and Organization: Do American Theories Apply Abroad?" *Organizational Dynamics,* Summer 1980, pp. 42–63.

62. Alan M. Rugman and Richard M. Hodgetts, *International Business: A Strategic Management Approach,* McGraw-Hill, New York, 1995.

63. Stephanie Strom, "A Sweetheart Becomes Suspect; Looking behind Those Kathie Lee Labels," *The New York Times,* June 27, 1996, p. D1.

64. Karen Paul and Robert Barbato, "The Multinational Corporation in the Less Developed Country: The Economic Development Model versus the North-South Model," *Academy of Management Review,* vol. 10, 1985, pp. 8–14; Georges Haour, "Environmental Concerns: Are They a Threat or an Opportunity?" *Financial Times,* Mar. 15, 1996, p. 4.

65. William C. Frederick, Keith Davis, and James E. Post, *Business and Society: Corporate Strategy, Public Policy, Ethics,* 7th ed., McGraw-Hill, New York, 1992; Jack Mahoney, "Gifts, Grease and Graft—Business Ethics," *Financial Times,* Dec. 8, 1995.

66. "The Antibribery Act Splits Executives," *Business Week,* Sept. 19, 1983, p. 16; Ford S. Worthy, "When Somebody Wants a Payoff," *Fortune,* Pacific Rim issue, Fall 1989, pp. 117–122.

67. Jonathan Friedland, "Did IBM Unit Bribe Officials in Argentina to Land a Contract?" *The Wall Street Journal,* Dec. 11, 1995, pp. A1, A5.

68. Andrew Kupfer, "How to Be a Global Manager," *Fortune,* Mar. 14, 1988, pp. 52–58; Resa A. King, "You Don't Have to Be a Giant to Score Big Overseas," *Business Week,* Apr. 13, 1987, p. 63; Cindy Skrzycki, "How Some Firms Become Foreign Success Stories," *The Washington Post,* Nov. 15, 1987, pp. H1, H6; Tim Smart, "Why Ignore 95% of the World's Market?" *Business Week,* Reinventing America 1992, Oct. 23, 1992, p. 64; Kevin Sullivan, "Glue Maker Sees Asian Growth," *Business Times,* Nov. 6, 1995, p. 2; William H. Miller, "Managing in China," *Industry Week,* July 17, 1995, p. 20; Barbara A. Nagy, "State Companies Lured by China's Vast Market," *The Hartford Courant,* July 8, 1996, p. 1.

69. M. Kripalani, "The King of Cork," *Forbes,* Oct. 26, 1992, p. 1; "Portuguese Industry Seeking to Corner World Market," *Agri-Industry Europe,* July 27, 1995, p. 1; Armand Chauvel, "Portuguese Corks Are Tops," *Agence France Presse,* July 21, 1995, p. 1; "It Grows on Trees," *The Economist,* May 4, 1996, p. 64.

CHAPTER 21

1. Stephanie N. Mehta, "Home-Care Concern Caters to Minorities," *The Wall Street Journal,* Oct. 19, 1995, p. 1B.

2. Murray B. Low and Ian C. MacMillan, "Entrepreneurship: Past Research and Future Challenges," *Journal of Management,* vol. 14, 1988, pp. 139–161. The meaning of this term is somewhat controversial; see Max S. Wortman, Jr., "Entrepreneurship: An Integrating Typology and Evaluation of the Empirical Research in the Field," *Journal of Management,* vol. 13, 1987, pp. 259–279; William B. Gartner, "'Who Is an Entrepreneur?' Is the Wrong Question," *American Journal of Small Business,* Spring 1988, pp. 11–39.

3. Joseph J. Fucini and Suzy Fucini, *Entrepreneurs,* Hall, Boston, 1985.

4. *The State of Small Business—1985: A Report to the President,* GPO, Washington, D.C., 1985; Charles R. Kuehl and Peggy A. Lambing, *Small Business,* 2d ed., Dryden, Chicago, 1990.

5. Peter F. Drucker, *Innovation and Entrepreneurship,* Harper & Row, New York, 1985, p. 19.

6. John G. Burch, *Entrepreneurship,* Wiley, New York, 1986.

7. Robert Lenzner, "The Reluctant Entrepreneur," *Forbes,* Sept. 11, 1995, pp. 162–166.

8. *The State of Small Business—1990: A Report to the President,* GPO, Washington, D.C., 1990, p. 22.

9. For a compilation of some recent statistics relating to failure rates, see Barbara J. Bird, *Entrepreneurial Behavior,* Scott, Foresman, Glenview, Ill., 1989.

10. John Case, "The Disciples of David Birch," *INC.,* January 1989, pp. 39–45.

11. Joseph F. Fucini and Suzy Fucini, *Entrepreneurs,* Hall, Boston, 1985, p. 240.

12. Howard Aldrich and Ellen R. Auster, "Even Dwarfs Started Small: Liabilities of Age and Size and Their Strategic Implications," *Research in Organizational Behavior,* vol. 8, 1986, pp. 165–198.

13. David L. Birch, *The Job Generation Process,* M.I.T. Program on Neighborhood and Regional Change, Cambridge, Mass., 1979.

14. "Small Is Beautiful! Big Is Best!" *INC., The State of Small Business* (Special Issue), 1995, pp. 39–49.

15. John Case, "The Disciples of David Birch," *INC.,* January 1989, pp. 39–45; Gene Koretz, "Small Businesses Tend to Stay Pint-Size," *Business Week,* July 31, 1989, p. 20.

16. Thomas W. Zimmerer and Norman M. Scarborough, *Entrepreneurship and New Venture Formation,* Prentice-Hall, Upper Saddle River, N.J., 1996.

17. Stephanie N. Mehta, "Number of Woman-Owned Businesses Surged 43% in 5 Years through 1992," *The Wall Street Journal,* Jan. 29, 1996, p. B2.

18. Lois A. Stevenson, "Against All Odds: The Entrepreneurship of Women," *Journal of Small Business Management,* October 1986, pp. 30–36.

19. Stephanie N. Mehta, "Number of Woman-Owned Businesses Surged 43% in 5 Years through 1992," *The Wall Street Journal,* Jan. 29, 1996, p. B2.

20. Marcia A. Brodsky, "Successful Female Corporate Managers and Entrepreneurs: Similarities and Differences," *Group & Organization Management,* vol. 18, 1993, pp. 366–378.

21. Paul Reynolds, "What We Don't Know May Hurt Us," *INC.,* September 1994, pp. 25–26.

22. Stephanie N. Mehta, "Number of Woman-Owned Businesses Surged 43% in 5 Years through 1992," *The Wall Street Journal,* Jan. 29, 1996, p. B2.

23. Robert D. Hisrich and Candida Bruch, "Characteristics of the Minority Entrepreneur," *Journal of Small Business Management,* October 1986, pp. 1–8; U.S. Department of Commerce, *Statistical Abstract of the United States,* GPO, Washington, D.C., 1989.

24. Janice Castro, "She Calls All the Shots," *Time,* July 4, 1988, pp. 54–57.

25. Michael Selz, "Asian, Pacific Islander Firms Grow in U.S.," *The Wall Street Journal,* Aug. 2, 1996, p. A11A.

26. Thomas W. Zimmerer and Norman M. Scarborough, *Entrepreneurship and New Venture Formation,* Prentice-Hall, Upper Saddle River, N.J., 1996.

27. Maureen McDonald, "Home Is Where the Work Is," *Detroit Free Press,* Mar. 25, 1995, pp. 6F–8F.

28. Andrew H. Van de Ven, Roger Hudson, and Dean M. Schroeder, "Designing New Business Startups: Entrepreneurial, Organizational, and Ecological Considerations," *Journal of Management,* vol. 10, 1984, pp. 87–107; William B. Gartner, "A Conceptual Framework for Describing the Phenomenon of New Venture Creation," *Academy of Management Review,* vol. 10, 1985, pp. 696–706; Albert Shapero and Lisa Sokol, "The Social Dimensions of Entrepreneurship," in Calvin A.

Kent, Donald L. Sexton, and Karl H. Vesper (eds.), *Encyclopedia of Entrepreneurship*, Prentice-Hall, Englewood Cliffs, N.J., 1982, pp. 72–90; Robert D. Hisrich and Michael P. Peters, *Entrepreneurship*, 3d ed., Irwin, Chicago, 1995.

29. This section relies extensively on Murray B. Low and Ian C. MacMillan, "Entrepreneurship: Past Research and Future Challenges," *Journal of Management*, vol. 14, 1988, pp. 139–161; Robert H. Brockhaus, Sr., and Pamela S. Horwitz, "The Psychology of the Entrepreneur," in Donald L. Sexton and Raymond W. Smilor, *The Art and Science of Entrepreneurship*, Ballinger, Cambridge, Mass., 1986, pp. 25–48; Robert H. Brockhaus, Sr., "The Psychology of the Entrepreneur," in Calvin A. Kent, Donald L. Sexton, and Karl H. Vesper (eds.), *Encyclopedia of Entrepreneurship*, Prentice-Hall, Englewood Cliffs, N.J., 1982; Yvon Gasse, "Elaboration on the Psychology of the Entrepreneur," in ibid.; G. T. Lumpkin and Gregory G. Dess, "Clarifying the Entrepreneurial Orientation Construct and Linking It to Performance," *Academy of Management Review*, vol. 21, 1996, pp. 135–172.

30. David C. McClelland, *Human Motivation*, Scott, Foresman, Glenview, Ill., 1985.

31. Bernard M. Bass, *Stogdill's Handbook of Leadership*, Free Press, New York, 1981; D. L. Sexton and N. Bowman, "The Entrepreneur: A Capable Executive and More," *Journal of Business Venturing*, vol. 1, 1985, pp. 129–140.

32. This section relies heavily on Yvon Gasse, "Elaboration on the Psychology of the Entrepreneur," in Calvin A. Kent, Donald L. Sexton, and Karl H. Vesper (eds.), Encyclopedia of Entrepreneurship, Prentice-Hall, Englewood Cliffs, N.J., 1982; and Robert D. Hisrich and Michael P. Peters, *Entrepreneurship*, 3d ed., Irwin, Chicago, 1995.

33. Robert D. Hisrich and Candida G. Bruch, "The Woman Entrepreneur: Management Skills and Business Problems," *Journal of Small Business Management*, vol. 22, 1984, pp. 30–37.

34. A. C. Cooper and W. C. Dunkelberg, "Entrepreneurial Research: Old Questions, New Answers, and Methodological Issues," *American Journal of Small Business*, Winter 1987, pp. 1–20.

35. Ibid.

36. Donald D. Bowen and Robert D. Hisrich, "The Female Entrepreneur: A Career Development Perspective," *Academy of Management Review*, vol. 11, 1986, pp. 393–407.

37. Study by Paul Reynolds of Babson College cited in Stephanie N. Mehta, "Young Entrepreneurs Turn Age to Adventure," *The Wall Street Journal*, Sept. 1, 1995, p. B1.

38. Jeffry A. Timmons, Leonard E. Smollen, and Alexander L. M. Dingee, Jr., *New Venture Creation*, 2d ed., Irwin, Homewood, Ill., 1985.

39. Robert Ronstadt, "The Corridor Principle," *Journal of Business Venturing*, vol. 3, 1988, pp. 31–40.

40. Sherrie Brammall, "Romano Unveils His Macaroni Masterpiece," *San Antonio Business Journal*, June 13–19, 1988, pp. 1, 16–17; "Fuddruckers: A New Generation of Fast Food," *Restaurant Hospitality*, December 1984, pp. 45–50; Chuck McCollough, "Starting Anew Ends Boredom," *San Antonio Sunday Express-News*, Feb. 9, 1986, pp. 1K, 10K; interview with David C. Martin, Mar. 18, 1989; Ron Ruggless, "Eatzi's Is Turning Segment into One Super Market," *Nation's Restaurant News*, Mar. 18, 1996, p. 11; Martin Zimmerman, "Brinker Exec to Focus on Eatzi's," *The Dallas Morning News*, June 7, 1996, p. 1D.

41. Albert Shapero and Lisa Sokol, "The Social Dimensions of Entrepreneurship," in Calvin A. Kent, Donald L. Sexton, and Karl H. Vesper (eds.), *Encyclopedia of Entrepreneurship*, Prentice-Hall, Englewood Cliffs, N.J., 1982, pp. 72–90. This section also relies heavily on Robert D. Hisrich and Michael P. Peters, *Entrepreneurship*, 3d ed., Irwin, Chicago, 1995.

42. Robert H. Brockhaus, Sr., "The Psychology of the Entrepreneur," in Calvin A. Kent, Donald L. Sexton, and Karl H. Vesper (eds.), *Encyclopedia of Entrepreneurship*, Prentice-Hall, Englewood Cliffs, N.J., 1982.

43. Bo Burlingham and Curtis Hartman, "Cowboy Capitalist," *INC.*, January 1989, pp. 54–69.

44. David J. Jefferson, "Land of Opportunity," *The Wall Street Journal*, June 10, 1988, p. R29; Damon Darlin, "Flower Power," *Forbes*, Apr. 22, 1996, pp. 102–103.

45. Denie S. Weil, "Doing Business in the Burbs," *Working Woman*, August 1989, pp. 58–66; Ann Taubeneck, "The Art of Dining," *Chicago Sun-Times*, June 7, 1995, p. 1N.

46. Mark Lewyn, "Scott McNealy," *USA Today*, Jan. 19, 1988, p. 7B; James Kim, "Sun CEO Takes Shine to Challenge," *USA Today*, Jan. 29, 1996, p. 4B.

47. Barbara J. Bird, *Entrepreneurial Behavior*, Scott, Foresman, Glenview, Ill., 1989.

48. Martha T. Moore, "Fledgling Firms Learn to Fly in Incubators," *USA Today*, May 8, 1989, p. 3E; National Business Incubation Association.

49. Robert D. Hisrich and Michael P. Peters, *Entrepreneurship*, 3d ed., Irwin, Chicago, 1995.

50. Albert Shapero and Lisa Sokol, "The Social Dimensions of Entrepreneurship," in Calvin A. Kent, Donald L. Sexton, and Karl H. Vesper (eds.), *Encyclopedia of Entrepreneurship*, Prentice-Hall, Englewood Cliffs, N.J., 1982, pp. 72–90; Robert Hisrich and Michael P. Peters, *Entrepreneurship*, 3d ed., Irwin, Chicago, 1995.

51. Based on Elizabeth A. Conlin and Louise Washer, "They Tried to Steal My Business. . . ." *Working Woman*, October 1988, pp. 43–46; Kimberly Pfaff, "Luxury Orientation," *Weekly Home Furnishings Newspaper*, Dec. 23, 1991, p. 33; "Textiles Express," *Weekly Newspaper for the Home Furnishings Network*, Apr. 17, 1995, p. 26.

52. Robert D. Hisrich and Michael P. Peters, *Entrepreneurship*, 3d ed., Irwin, Chicago, 1995.

53. William B. Gartner, Terrence R. Mitchell, and Karl H. Vespers, "A Taxonomy of New Business Ventures," *Journal of Business Venturing*, vol. 4, 1989, pp. 169–186.

54. Lena H. Sun, "Cuisinart's Finances Dicey; It Seeks Bankruptcy Protection," *The Washington Post*, Aug. 4, 1989, p. D1.

55. Nicholas C. Siropolis, *Small Business Management*, 5th ed., Houghton Mifflin, Boston, 1994.

56. Ibid.; D. D. Seltz, *The Complete Handbook of Franchising*, Addison-Wesley, Reading, Mass., 1982.

57. Schott A. Shane, "Hybrid Organizational Arrangement and Their Implications for Firm Growth and Survival: A Study of New Franchisors," *Academy of Management Journal*, vol. 39, 1995, pp. 216–234.

58. Robert D. Hisrich and Michael P. Peters, *Entrepreneurship*, 3d ed., Irwin, Chicago, 1995.

59. Nicholas C. Siropolis, *Small Business Management*, 5th ed., Houghton Mifflin, Boston, 1994.

60. Derek T. Dingle, "Franchising's Fast Track to Freedom," *Money Extra*, 1990, p. 40;

Michelle Singletary, "Franchisees Fight Back," *The Washington Post*, Washington Business Section, Sept. 27, 1993, pp. 1, 14–15.

61. Timothy Bates, "Analysis of Survival Rates among Franchise and Independent Small Business Startups," *Journal of Small Business Management*, April 1995, pp. 26–36.

62. John G. Burch, *Entrepreneurship*, Wiley, New York, 1986.

63. Adapted from Nicholas C. Siropolis, *Small Business Management*, 5th ed., Houghton Mifflin, Boston, 1994, pp. 74–75.

64. Carson R. Kennedy, "Thinking of Opening Your Own Business? Be Prepared," *Business Horizons*, September–October 1985, pp. 38–42.

65. Jeffry A. Timmons, Leonard E. Smollen, and Alexander L. M. Dingee, Jr., *New Venture Creation*, 2d ed., Irwin, Homewood, Ill., 1985; John G. Burch, *Entrepreneurship*, Wiley, New York, 1986.

66. This section relies heavily on Jeffry A. Timmons, Leonard E. Smollen, and Alexander L. M. Dingee, Jr., *New Venture Creation*, 2d ed., Irwin, Homewood, Ill., 1985; and Robert D. Hisrich and Michael P. Peters, *Entrepreneurship*, 3d ed., Irwin, Chicago, 1995.

67. Albert V. Bruno and Tyzoon T. Tyebjee, "The Entrepreneur's Search for Capital," *Journal of Business Venturing*, vol. 1, 1985, pp. 61–74.

68. Steven Greenhouse, "In Poland, a Small Capitalist Miracle," *The New York Times*, Dec. 19, 1989, pp. D1, D13.

69. Jeffry A. Timmons, Leonard E. Smollen, and Alexander L. M. Dingee, Jr., *New Venture Creation*, 2d ed., Irwin, Homewood, Ill., 1985.

70. Robert D. Gatewood and Hubert S. Field, "A Personnel Selection Program for Small Business," *Journal of Small Business Management*, October 1987, pp. 16–25.

71. "Statement from Steve Bernard, Founder of Cape Cod Potato Chips Regarding the Possible Sale of Cape Cod Potato Chips by Anheuser-Busch," *PR Newswire*, Feb. 9, 1996, p. 1.

72. This section is based on Charles R. Kuehl and Peggy A. Lambing, *Small Business*, 2d ed., Dryden, Chicago, 1990.

73. James W. Halloran, *Entrepreneurship*, McGraw-Hill, 1994.

74. Neil C. Churchill and Virginia L. Lewis, "The Five Stages of Small Business Growth," *Harvard Business Review*, May–June 1983, pp. 30–50.

75. Information obtained from the Government Relations Office, BDM International, McLean, Va., Jan. 2, 1990; BDM 1991 Annual Report; "Top 100 Public Companies in the Washington Area," *The Washington Post*, *Washington Business*, Apr. 22, 1996, p. 8.

76. Buck Brown, "James Bildner's Spectacular Rise and Fall," *The Wall Street Journal*, Oct. 24, 1988, p. B1; Thomas Vannah, "Rebuilding a Business," *New England Business*, June 1990, p. 21; John Robinson, "Bildner's Back in the Swim," *The Boston Globe*, Apr. 30, 1994, p. 21.

77. Clifford M. Baumback, *How to Organize and Operate a Small Business*, 8th ed., Prentice-Hall, Englewood Cliffs, N.J., 1988, p. 17.

78. Charles R. Kuehl and Peggy A. Lambing, *Small Business*, 2d ed., Dryden, Chicago, 1990. See also Justin G. Longnecker, Joseph A. McKinney, and Carlos W. Moore, "Ethics in Small Business," *Journal of Small Business Management*, January 1989, pp. 27–31.

79. Andrew Tanzer, "The 60 Million Hats of Sung Hak Baik," *Forbes*, Oct. 14, 1991, pp. 72–74.

80. Mark Robichaux, "Business First, Family

Second," *The Wall Street Journal,* May 12, 1989, p. B1.

81. Manfred F. R. Kets de Vries, "The Dark Side of Entrepreneurship," *Harvard Business Review,* November–December 1985, pp. 160–167.

82. Richard B. Robinson, Jr., "The Importance of Outsiders in Small Firm Planning and Performance," *Academy of Management Journal,* vol. 25, 1982, pp. 80–93; James J. Chrisman and John Leslie, "Strategic, Admin-istrative, and Operating Problems: The Impact of Outsiders on Small Firm Performance," *Entrepreneurship Theory and Practice,* Spring 1989, pp. 37–51.

83. Julian B. Rotter, "External Control and Internal Control," *Psychology Today,* June 1971, p. 42.

84. Based on Barbara Wright, "How to Beat Out Big-Name Competition," *Working Woman,* May 1988, pp. 55–57; Sharon Nelton, "When Failure Is Not an Option; Making a New Company Work," *Nation's Business,* May 1992, p. 20; Paula Moore, "Grogan, Partner Open Relocation Firm in Phoenix," *Denver Business Journal,* Sept. 9, 1994, p. 3; "Apogee Enterprises Elects Two New Board Members," *PR Newswire,* June 18, 1996, p. 1.

85. Louis Kraar, "A Billionaire's Global Strategy," *Fortune,* July 13, 1992, pp. 106–109; "Hong Kong: Li Ka-Shing Still Holds Tight Reins on Cheung Kong," *Lloyds List (Reuter Textline),* June 3, 1996, p. 1.

ACKNOWLEDGMENTS

CHAPTER 1

Quotations in Text
Pages 12–13: Reprinted by permission of *Harvard Business Review.* "What Effective General Managers Really Do," by John Kotter, November/December 1982, pp. 156–167. Copyright © 1982 by the President and Fellows of Harvard College; all rights reserved.

Tables
Table 1-1: Henry Mintzberg, *The Nature of Managerial Work.* Copyright © 1980 by Addison-Wesley Educational Publishers, Inc. Reprinted by permission of publisher.
Table 1-2: Ellen Van Velsor and Jean Brittain Leslie, "Why Executives Derail: Perspectives Across Time and Cultures," *Academy of Management Executive,* vol. 9, 1995, p. 64. Copyright © 1995 by Academy of Management. Adapted with permission.
Table 1-3: *Forbes,* July 17, 1995, pp. 274–275. Reprinted with permission of publisher.

Figures
Figure 1-2: Stephen J. Carroll and Dennis J. Gillen, "Are the Classical Management Functions Useful in Describing Managerial Work?" *Academy of Management Review,* vol. 12, 1987, pp. 38–51. Copyright © 1987 by the Academy of Management. Adapted with permission of publisher and authors.
Figure 1-6: Mary J. Winterle, *Work Force Diversity: Corporate Challenges,*

Corporate Responses, Report No. 1013, 1992. Copyright © 1992 by The Conference Board, Inc. Reprinted with permission.

CHAPTER 2

Tables
Table 2-4: Henri Fayol, *General and Industrial Management,* Pittman & Sons, 1949, pp. 19–42. Translator: Constance Storrs. Used with permission from Center for Effective Performance.

Figures
Figure 2-5: William G. Ouchi and Alfred M. Jaeger, "Theory Z Organizations: Stability in the Midst of Mobility," *Academy of Management Review,* vol. 3, 1978, pp. 308, 311. Copyright © 1978 by the Academy of Management. Adapted by permission of publisher and authors.

CHAPTER 3

Tables
Table 3-3: Reprinted by permission of *Harvard Business Review.* "The Heart of Entrepreneurship," adapted from Howard H. Stevenson and David E. Gumpert, March–April 1985, p. 89. Copyright © 1985 by the President and fellows of Harvard College. All rights reserved.

Figures
Figure 3-4: Robert Duncan, "What Is the Right Organizational Structure? Decision Tree Analysis Provides the

Answer," *Organizational Dynamics,* Winter 1979, p. 63. Copyright © 1979, American Management Association, New York. Reprinted by permission of publisher. All rights reserved.

CHAPTER 4

Tables
Table 4-1: *Business Week,* March 11, 1996, p. 65. Copyright © 1996 by the McGraw-Hill Companies, Inc. Used with permission.
Table 4-3: *Wall Street Journal,* June 5, 1996, p. B1. Copyright © 1996 by Dow Jones & Company. All rights reserved.

Figures
Figure 4-1: Archie B. Carroll, "A Three-Dimensional Conceptual Model of Corporate Performance," *Academy of Management Review,* vol. 4, 1979, p. 499. Copyright © 1979 by Academy of Management and the authors. Adapted with permission.
Figure 4-3: Marc J. Epstein, *Measuring Corporate Environmental Performance: Best Practices for Costing and Managing an Effective Environmental Strategy,* 1st edition, p. 37. Copyright © 1996 by Richard D. Irwin. Used with permission.
Figure 4-4: Archie B. Carroll, "In Search of the Moral Manager," *Business Horizons,* March–April, 1987, p. 8. Copyright © 1987 by JAI Press. Reprinted with permission.
Figure 4-5: Copyright © Johnson & Johnson.

CHAPTER 5

Tables
Table 5-3: Daniel D. Wheeler and Irving L. Janis, *A Practical Guide for Making Decisions.* Copyright © 1980 by The Free Press, a division of Simon & Schuster. Adapted with permission.

Figures
Figure 5-1: George P. Huber, *Managerial Decision Making*, p. 8. Copyright © 1980 by Scott, Foresman & Company, Glenview, Ill. Reprinted with permission of publisher and author.

Figure 5-3: E. Frank Harrison, *The Managerial Decision-Making Process*, 3d edition. Copyright © 1987 by Houghton Mifflin Company. Used by permission of publisher.

Figure 5-5: James L. Adams, *Conceptual Blockbusting: A Guide to Better Ideas*, Addison-Wesley Longman, pp. 25, 29–31. Copyright © 1986 by James L. Adams. Reprinted by permission of author and Addison-Wesley Longman, Inc.

CHAPTER 5 SUPPLEMENT

Tables
Table 5S (Supplement) 1: Paul C. Nystrom et al. (eds.), *Handbook of Organizational Design*, p. 132. Copyright © 1981 by Oxford University Press, Inc. Used with permission.

Table 5S (Supplement) 2: Everett E. Adam, Jr., and Ronald E. Ebert, *Production and Operations Management*, 5th ed., p. 342. Copyright © 1992, Prentice-Hall. Reprinted with permission.

Table 5S (Supplement) 3: E. Frank Harrison, *The Managerial Decision-Making Process*, 3d edition. Copyright © 1987 by Houghton Mifflin Company. Reprinted with permission.

Figures
Figure 5S-1: Charles A. Gallagher and Hugh J. Watson, *Quantitative Methods for Business Decisions*, p. 116. Copyright © 1980 by McGraw-Hill. Reprinted with permission.

Figure 5s-5: Everett E. Adam, Jr., and Ronald J. Ebert, *Production and Oper-* *ations Management*, 5th ed., p. 343. Copyright © 1992 by Prentice-Hall. Reprinted with permission.

CHAPTER 6

Tables
Table 6-1: Fred David, "How Companies Define Their Mission," *Long Range Planning*, February 1989, pp. 92–93. Copyright © 1989 with kind permission from Elsevier Science Ltd., The Boulevard, Langford Lane, Kidlington OX 5, 1GB, UK.

Table 6-2: Peter F. Drucker, *Management, Tasks, Responsibilities*, pp. 103–117. Copyright © 1974 by Harper & Row. Reprinted with permission of publisher.

Table 6-3: Edwin A. Locke and Gary P. Latham, *Goal Setting: A Motivational Technique That Works*, pp. 171–172. Copyright © 1984 by Prentice-Hall, Inc. Reprinted with permission of authors.

Figures
Figure 6-4: Thomas W. Lee, Edwin A. Locke, & Gary P. Latham, "Goal Setting Theory and Job Performance," in Lawrence A. Pervin (ed.), *Goal Concepts in Personality and Social Psychology*, Copyright © 1989 by Lawrence Erlbaum Associates. Adapted with permission of the publisher and authors.

CHAPTER 7

Tables
Tables 7-1 and 7-3: Michael E. Porter, *Competitive Strategy: Techniques for Analyzing Industries and Competitors.* Copyright © 1980 by the Free Press, a division of Simon & Schuster. Adapted with permission.

Table 7-2: Jay B. Barney, "Looking Inside for Competitive Advantage," *Academy of Management Executive*, vol. 9, no. 4, 1995, pp. 49–61. Copyright © 1995 by Academy of Management. Reprinted with permission.

Figures
Figure 7-2: John A. Pearce and Richard Robinson, *Strategic Management: Strategy Formulation and Imple-* *mentation*, 3d edition, p. 9. Copyright © 1988 by Irwin/McGraw-Hill. Adapted with permission of the publisher.

CHAPTER 8

Quotations in Text
Page 253: Jenny C. McCune, "Flower Power: A Talk with Jim McCann," *Management Review*, March 1995, pp. 9–12. Copyright © 1995 by American Management Association, New York. All rights reserved.

Tables
Table 8-1: *Human Resources Magazine*, May 1996, p. 56. Copyright © 1996 by Challenger, Gray & Christmas, Inc. Adapted with permission.

Figures
Figure 8-1: Adapted from "Flower Power: A Talk with Jim McCann," *Management Review*, March 1995, p. 10. Copyright © 1995 by 1-800-Flowers. Reprinted with permission.

Figure 8-4: J.R. Hackman and G. R. Oldham, *Work Design*, p. 90. Copyright © 1980 by Addison-Wesley Publishing Co., Inc. Reprinted by permission of the publisher.

CHAPTER 9

Tables
Table 9-5: Joan Woodward, *Industrial Organization, Theory and Practice*, pp. 52–62. Copyright © 1965, Oxford University Press, London. Used with permission of publisher.

Table 9-6: T. Burns and G. M. Stalker, *The Management of Innovation*, Tavistock, 1961, pp. 119–122. Reprinted with permission of publisher.

CHAPTER 10

Tables
Table 10-2: David J. Rachman, Michael H. Mescon, Courtland L. Bovee, and John V. Thill, *Business Today*, 6th edition, McGraw-Hill, 1990, p. 244. Reprinted with permission of publisher.

Table 10-4: Marc J. Wallace and Charles H. Fay, *Compensation Theory* *and Practice*, 2d ed., p. 214. Copyright © 1988, PWS-KENT Publishing Company, Boston, a division of Wadsworth, Inc. Adapted by permission.

Figures

Figure 10-3: Wayne F. Cascio, *Managing Human Resources*, 4th edition, McGraw-Hill, 1995, p. 287. Reprinted with permission of publisher and author.

Figure 10-4: Adapted from R. Harvey, "Job Analysis," in M. P. Dunnette and L. M. Hough (eds.), *Handbook of Industrial and Organizational Psychology*, 2d ed., vol. 2, 1991, p. 138. Copyright 1991 by CPP. All rights reserved. Modified and reproduced with special permission of the publisher, Consulting Psychologists Press, Inc., Palo Alto, California 94303. Further reproduction is prohibited without the publisher's written conent.

CHAPTER 11

Tables

Table 11-1: Robert E. Quinn and Kim Cameron, "Organizational Life Cycles and Shifting Criteria of Effectiveness: Some Preliminary Evidence," *Management Science*, vol. 29, no. 8, 1983, pp. 35–37. Copyright © 1983 by The Institute of Management Science (currently INFORMS). Reprinted by permission.

Table 11-2: Kim S. Cameron, David A. Whetton, and Myung U. Kim, "Organizational Dysfunctions of Decline," *Academy of Management Journal*, vol. 30, 1987. Copyright © 1987 by Academy of Management. Reprinted with publisher's permission.

Table 11-4: Reprinted by permission of *Harvard Business Review*. "Choosing Strategies for Change," by John P. Kotter and Leonard A. Schlesinger, March–April 1979, p. 111. Copyright © 1979 by the President and Fellows of Harvard College. All rights reserved.

CHAPTER 12

Quotations in Text

Page 382: Levi Strauss Aspirations Statement, reprinted with permission of Levi Strauss & Co.

Pages 382–383: Reprinted by permission of *Harvard Business Review*. "Values Make the Company: Interview with Robert Haas," by Robert Howard, September/October 1990, pp. 133–144. Copyright © 1990 by the President and Fellows of Harvard College; all rights reserved.

Tables

Table 12-1: Bob Nelson, *1001 Ways to Reward Employees*, pp. 44–45. Copyright © 1994 by permission of Workman Publishing, New York. Used with permission.

Figures

Figure 12-8: Hugh J. Arnold and Daniel J. Feldman, *Organizational Behavior*, McGraw-Hill Company. Copyright © 1986 McGraw-Hill, Inc. Adapted by permission of publisher.

CHAPTER 13

Quotations in Text

Page 439: Jay Conger, "Have You Got It?" *Fortune*, January 15, 1996, p. 74. Reprinted by permission of the authors.

Page 442: Bo Burlingham, "This Woman Has Changed Forever," *Inc. Magazine*, June 1990, p. 47. Copyright 1990 © by the Goldhirsch Group, Inc. Used with permission.

Tables

Table 13-2: Victor H. Vroom and Philip W. Yetton, *Leadership and Decision Making*. Copyright © 1973 by University of Pittsburgh Press. Reprinted by permission.

Figures

Figure 13-1: Reprinted by permission of *Harvard Business Review*. "How to Choose a Leadership Pattern," by Robert Tannenbaum and Warren H. Schmidt, vol. 51, May–June 1973, p. 164. Copyright © 1973 by the President and Fellows of Harvard College, all rights reserved. Copyright © 1973 by the President and Fellows of Harvard College. All rights reserved.

Figure 13-3: Robert A. Blake and Jane S. Mouton, *The Managerial Grid III R: The Key to Leadership*. Copyright © 1985 by Gulf Publishing, Houston, Texas. Used with permission. All rights reserved.

Figure 13-4: Arthur G. Jago, "Leadership: Perspectives in Theory and Research," *Management Science*, vol. 28, no. 3, 1982, p. 324. Copyright © 1982 by The Institute of Management Science (currently INFORMS). Reprinted by permission.

Figure 13-5: Victor H. Vroom and Arthur G. Jago, *The New Leadership: Managing Participation in Organizations*, 1988, Prentice-Hall, Englewood Cliffs, N.J. Copyright © by V.H. Vroom and A.G. Jago. Reprinted by permission of authors.

Figure 13-6: Kenneth H. Blanchard and Paul Hersey, *Management of Organizational Behavior: Utilizing Human Resources*, 6th edition. Copyright © 1993 by the Center for Leadership Studies. Reprinted with permission. Situational Leadership® is a registered trademark of the Center for Leadership Studies, Escondido, California. All rights reserved.

Figure 13-7: Gary A. Yukl, *Leadership in Organizations*, 3d edition. Copyright © 1989 by Prentice-Hall, Inc., Upper Saddle River, NJ. Adapted with permission.

Figure 13-8: Bernard M. Bass, *Leadership and Performance Beyond Expectations*. Copyright © 1985 by the Free Press, a division of Simon & Schuster. Adapted with permission.

CHAPTER 14

Quotations in Text

Page 446: Roger Smith, "The U.S. Must Do as GM Has Done," *Fortune*, February 13, 1989, pp. 70–73. Copyright © 1989 by Time, Inc. All rights reserved.

Page 468: Ethel C. Gunn and Elliot A. Pood, "Listening Self-Assessment," *Supervisory Management*, January 1989, pp. 12–15. Copyright © 1989 by American Management Association, New York. All rights reserved.

Page 469: William V. Haney, *Communication and Interpersonal Relations*,

5th edition, Richard D. Irwin, Inc., 1986, pp. 214–222. Reprinted by permission of publisher and author.
Page 470: Alan C. Greenberg, *Memos from The Chairman*, Workman Publishing, Inc., 1996. Copyright © 1996 by Alan C. Greenberg. Used with permission.

Tables
Table 14-1: Richard M. Hodgetts and Steven Altman, *Organizational Behavior,* W. B. Saunders, 1979, p. 305. Reprinted by permission.

Figures
Figure 14-1: Lance B. Kurke and Howard Aldrich, "Mintzberg Was Right! A Replication and Extension of The Nature of Managerial Work," *Management Science*, vol. 29, no. 8, 1983, p. 979. Copyright © 1983 by The Institute of Management Science (currently INFORMS). Reprinted by permission of publisher.
Figure 14-4: Otis W. Baskin and Craig E. Aronoff, *Interpersonal Communication in Organizations*, p. 77. Copyright © 1980 by Scott, Foresman & Company. Adapted by permission of publisher and authors.
Figure 14-5: R. Wayne Pace and D. F. Faules, *Organizational Communication*, p. 40. Copyright © 1983 by Allyn and Bacon. Adapted by permission of publisher.
Figure 14-7: Keith Davis and John W. Newstrom, *Human Behavior at Work: Organizational Behavior*, 8th ed., McGraw-Hill Book Company, 1989, p. 373. Reprinted by permission.

CHAPTER 15

Quotations in Text
Pages 502–503: J.E. Jones and J.W. Pfeiffer (eds), *The Annual Handbook for Group Facilitators*, San Francisco, CA: Pfeiffer, an imprint of Jossey-Bass Inc., 1975. Used with permission.

Tables
Table 15-1: M. Deutsch, "Sixty Years of Conflict," *The International Journal of Conflict Management*, vol. 1, 1990, pp. 237–263. Copyright © 1990 by the Center for Advanced Studies

in Management. Used with permission.

CHAPTER 16

Figures
Figure 16-1: Richard E. Walton, "From Control to Commitment in the Workplace," *Harvard Business Review*, March–April, 1985, p. 81. Copyright © 1985 by the President and Fellows of Harvard College. All rights reserved. Reprinted by permission of *Harvard Business Review*.
Figure 16-2: Peter Lorange, Michael F. Scott Morton, and Sumanatra Ghostal, *Strategic Control Systems*, 1986, p. 12. Copyright © 1986 by West Publishing Company. Reprinted by permission of publisher and authors. All rights reserved.
Figure 16-4: Stephen G. Green and M. Ann Welsh, "Cynerics and Dependence: Reframing the Control Concept," *Academy of Management Review*, vol. 13, 1988, pp. 287–301. Copyright © 1988 by Academy of Management. Adapted by permission of the Academy of Management and the authors.

CHAPTER 17

Quotations in Text
Page 547: W. Edwards Deming, *Out of Crisis*, published by MIT, Center for Advanced Educational Services, Cambridge, MA 02139. Copyright © 1986 by The W. Edwards Deming Institute. Used with permission.

Tables
Table 17-1 and Table 17-2: Coca-Cola Company and subsidiaries information from 1995 Annual Report. Copyright © by Coca-Cola Company, 1995. Reprinted with permission.
Table 17-3: Leo Troy, *Almanac of Business and Industrial Financial Ratios*. Copyright © 1995 by Prentice Hall/Career & Personal Development. Used by permission.

CHAPTER 18

Tables
Table 18-3: James B. Dilworth, *Pro-*

duction and Operations Management, 5th ed., p. 375. Copyright © 1993 by McGraw-Hill. Reprinted by permission of publisher.

Figures
Figure 18-3: Steven C. Wheelwright and Robert H. Hayes, "Completing Through Manufacturing," *Harvard Business Review*, January–February, 1985, pp. 99–109. Copyright © 1985 by the President and Fellows of Harvard College, all rights reserved. Reprinted by permission of *Harvard Business Review*.
Figure 18-5: Joseph G. Monks, *Operations Management*, 1987, p. 444. Copyright © 1987 by McGraw-Hill. Reprinted by permission of publisher.
Figure 18-6: James B. Dilworth, *Production and Operations Management,* 5th ed., p. 371. Copyright © by McGraw-Hill. Reprinted by permission of publisher.
Figure 18-7: Elwood S. Buffa, *Modern Production Operations Management*, p. 32. Copyright © 1983 by John Wiley & Sons, Inc. Reprinted by permission of the publisher.
Figure 18-8: Elwood S. Buffa, *Modern Production Operations Management*, p. 33. Copyright © 1983, John Wiley & Sons, Inc. Reprinted by permission of the publisher.

CHAPTER 19

Tables
Table 19-1: Kenneth C. Laudon and Jane Price Laudon, *Management Information Systems: A Contemporary Approach*, 4th edition. Copyright © 1996 by permission of Prentice-Hall Inc., Upper Saddle River, NJ. Reprinted by permission.

Figures
Figure 19-3: Kenneth C. Laudon and Jane Price Laudon, *Management Information Systems: A Contemporary Approach*, 4th edition. Copyright © 1996 by Prentice-Hall Inc., Upper Saddle River, NJ. Reprinted by permission.
Figure 19-4: Kenneth C. Laudon and Jane Price Laudon, *Management Information Systems: A Contemporary Approach*, 4th edition Copyright ©

1996 by Prentice-Hall, Inc., Upper Saddle River, NJ. Reprinted by permission.

CHAPTER 20

Tables
Table 20-1: "Fortune's Global; the World's Largest Corporations," *Fortune*, August 5, 1996, p. F-1. Copyright © by Time Inc. Adapted with permission. All rights reserved.

Figures
Figure 20-1: Reprinted by permission of *Harvard Business Review*. Michael E. Porter, "The Competitive Advantage of Nations," by Michael E. Porter, March–April, 1990. Copyright © 1990 by the President and Fellows of Harvard College, all rights reserved.

CHAPTER 21

Quotations in Text
Pages 670–671: Stephanie N. Mehta, "Home-Care Concern Caters to Minorities," *Wall Street Journal*, October 19, 1995, p. 1B. Copyright © 1995, Dow Jones & Company, Inc. All rights reserved worldwide.
Page 698: Julian B. Rotter, "External Control and Internal Control," *Psychology Today*, June 1971, p. 42. Copyright © 1971 by *Psychology Today*. Used with permission.

Tables
Table 21-1: John H. Burch, *Entrepreneurship*, John Wiley & Sons, Inc. Copyright © 1986 by John H. Burch. Reprinted by permission of author.
Table 21-2: Compiled from *Entrepreneur Magazine*, January, 1996, pp. 211–305. Reprinted with permission of publisher.
Table 21-3: Reprinted by permission from the September 1985 issue of *Changing Times Magazine*. Copyright © 1985 by The Kiplinger Washington Editors, Inc.
Table 21-4: Bruce Phillips, "The State of Small Business" issue of *Inc.*, 1995, p. 20. Copyright © 1995 by Goldhirsch Group, Inc. Used with permission.

Figures
Figure 21-1: Graphic by Rick Nease, Gallup survey material in Maureen McDonald, "Home Is Where the Work Is," *Detroit Free Press*, March 25, 1996, p. 6F. Reprinted by permission of the *Detroit Free Press*.
Figure 21-3: Nicholas C. Siropolis, *Small Business Management*, 5th edition, p. 112. Copyright © 1994 by Houghton Mifflin Company. Adapted with permission.
Figure 21-4: Neil C. Churchill and Virginia L. Lewis, "The Five Stages of Small Business Growth," *Harvard Business Review*, May/June 1983, p. 31. Copyright © 1983 by the President and Fellows of Harvard College, all rights reserved. Reprinted by permission of *Harvard Business Review*.

PHOTO CREDITS

CHAPTER 14
Page 445, Louis Psihoyos/Matrix; **p. 447,** Ovak Arslanian; **p. 449,** Frank Micelotta; **p. 456,** Peter Saloutos/The Stock Market; **p. 457,** Akhtar Hussein/Woodfin Camp & Assoc. Disney characters © Disney Enterprises, Inc. Used by permission from Disney Enterprises, Inc.; **p. 458,** Tony Freeman/PhotoEdit; **p. 466,** Jon Feingersh/The Stock Market.

CHAPTER 15
Page 474, Neil Selkirk, courtesy of Monsanto; **p. 479,** Louis Psihoyos/Matrix; **p. 484,** Wagner Avancini/Angular Fotojornalismo, Sao Paulo, Brazil; **p. 494,** Courtesy of Ford Motor Company; **p. 496,** Louis Psihoyos/Matrix.

CHAPTER 16
Page 509, Robert Wallis/SABA; **p. 512,** J. L. Bulcao/Gamma-Liaison; **p. 517,** Courtesy of Sea Containers Services Ltd.; **p. 525,** Courtesy of Filofax Limited; **p. 530,** Courtesy of United Parcel Service.

CHAPTER 17
Page 541, Courtesy of USAA; **p. 545,** © Federal Express; **p. 550,** Manuello Paganelli; **p. 557,** David Carter; **p. 561,** Graham Finlayson; **p. 565,** David Fields.

CHAPTER 18
Page 573, Courtesy of Fanuc; **p. 575,** Codlewski/Gamma-Liaison; **p. 589,** Keith Dannemiller/SABA; **p. 593,** Peter Poulides; **p. 597,** Charles Gupton.

CHAPTER 19
Page 604, Francis Apesteguy/Gamma-Liaison; **p. 609,** Mike Kagan/Monkmeyer; **p. 620,** Ron Haviv/SABA; **p. 626,** Doug Milner; **p. 628,** Allan Tannenbaum/Sygma.

CHAPTER 20
Page 638, Raghu Rai/Magnum; **p. 640,** R. Ian Lloyd; **p. 643,** Bradshaw/SABA; **p. 646,** Juha Sarkkine; **p. 650,** Attal-REA/SABA; **p. 652,** J. Donoso/Sygma; **p. 653,** Courtesy of Land Rover North America.

CHAPTER 21
Page 671, Cindy Darby; **p. 674,** Peter Yates/SABA; **p. 677,** Rex Rystedt; **p. 679,** Courtesy of Brinker International; **p. 680,** Randy Duchaine; **p. 681,** Robert Burroughs; **p. 693,** Nick Kelsh

NAME INDEX

SUBJECT INDEX

ORGANIZATIONS INDEX

INTERNATIONAL ORGANIZATIONS INDEX